Lecture Notes in Computer Science 13093

More information about this subseries at https://link.springer.com/bookseries/7410

Mehdi Tibouchi · Huaxiong Wang (Eds.)

Advances in Cryptology – ASIACRYPT 2021

27th International Conference on the Theory
and Application of Cryptology and Information Security
Singapore, December 6–10, 2021
Proceedings, Part IV

Springer

Editors
Mehdi Tibouchi
NTT Corporation
Tokyo, Japan

Huaxiong Wang
Nanyang Technological University
Singapore, Singapore

ISSN 0302-9743 ISSN 1611-3349 (electronic)
Lecture Notes in Computer Science
ISBN 978-3-030-92067-8 ISBN 978-3-030-92068-5 (eBook)
https://doi.org/10.1007/978-3-030-92068-5

LNCS Sublibrary: SL4 – Security and Cryptology

This Springer imprint is published by the registered company Springer Nature Switzerland AG
The registered company address is: Gewerbestrasse 11, 6330 Cham, Switzerland

Preface

Asiacrypt 2021, the 27th Annual International Conference on Theory and Application of Cryptology and Information Security, was originally planned to be held in Singapore during December 6–10, 2021. Due to the COVID-19 pandemic, it was shifted to an online-only virtual conference.

The conference covered all technical aspects of cryptology, and was sponsored by the International Association for Cryptologic Research (IACR).

We received a total of 341 submissions from all over the world, and the Program Committee (PC) selected 95 papers for publication in the proceedings of the conference. The two program chairs were supported by a PC consisting of 74 leading experts in aspects of cryptology. Each submission was reviewed by at least three PC members (or their sub-reviewers) and five PC members were assigned to submissions co-authored by PC members. The strong conflict of interest rules imposed by IACR ensure that papers are not handled by PC members with a close working relationship with the authors. The two program chairs were not allowed to submit a paper, and PC members were limited to two submissions each. There were approximately 363 external reviewers, whose input was critical to the selection of papers.

The review process was conducted using double-blind peer review. The conference operated a two-round review system with a rebuttal phase. After the reviews and first-round discussions the PC selected 233 submissions to proceed to the second round and the authors were then invited to provide a short rebuttal in response to the referee reports. The second round involved extensive discussions by the PC members.

Alongside the presentations of the accepted papers, the program of Asiacrypt 2021 featured an IACR distinguished lecture by Andrew Chi-Chih Yao and two invited talks by Kazue Sako and Yu Yu. The conference also featured a rump session which contained short presentations on the latest research results of the field.

The four volumes of the conference proceedings contain the revised versions of the 95 papers that were selected, together with the abstracts of the IACR distinguished lecture and the two invited talks. The final revised versions of papers were not reviewed again and the authors are responsible for their contents.

Via a voting-based process that took into account conflicts of interest, the PC selected the three top papers of the conference: “On the Hardness of the NTRU problem” by Alice Pellet-Mary and Damien Stehlé (which received the best paper award); “A Geometric Approach to Linear Cryptanalysis” by Tim Beyne (which received the best student paper award); and “Lattice Enumeration for Tower NFS: a 521-bit Discrete Logarithm Computation” by Gabrielle De Micheli, Pierrick Gaudry, and Cécile Pierrot. The authors of all three papers were invited to submit extended versions of their manuscripts to the Journal of Cryptology.

Many people have contributed to the success of Asiacrypt 2021. We would like to thank the authors for submitting their research results to the conference. We are very grateful to the PC members and external reviewers for contributing their knowledge and expertise, and for the tremendous amount of work that was done with reading papers and contributing to the discussions. We are greatly indebted to Jian Guo, the General Chair, for his efforts and overall organization. We thank San Ling and Josef Pieprzyk, the advisors of Asiacrypt 2021, for their valuable suggestions. We thank Michel Abdalla, Kevin McCurley, Kay McKelly, and members of IACR's emergency pandemic team for their work in designing and running the virtual format. We thank Chitchanok Chuengsatiansup and Khoa Nguyen for expertly organizing and chairing the rump session. We are extremely grateful to Zhenzhen Bao for checking all the LaTeX files and for assembling the files for submission to Springer. We also thank Alfred Hofmann, Anna Kramer, and their colleagues at Springer for handling the publication of these conference proceedings.

December 2021

Mehdi Tibouchi
Huaxiong Wang

Organization

General Chair

Jian Guo	Nanyang Technological University, Singapore

Program Committee Co-chairs

Mehdi Tibouchi	NTT Corporation, Japan
Huaxiong Wang	Nanyang Technological University, Singapore

Steering Committee

Masayuki Abe
Lynn Batten
Jung Hee Cheon
Steven Galbraith
D. J. Guan
Jian Guo
Khalid Habib
Lucas Hui
Nassar Ikram
Kwangjo Kim
Xuejia Lai
Dong Hoon Lee
Satya Lokam
Mitsuru Matsui (Chair)
Tsutomu Matsumoto
Phong Nguyen
Dingyi Pei
Duong Hieu Phan
Raphael Phan
Josef Pieprzyk (Vice Chair)
C. Pandu Rangan
Bimal Roy
Leonie Simpson
Huaxiong Wang
Henry B. Wolfe
Duncan Wong
Tzong-Chen Wu
Bo-Yin Yang
Siu-Ming Yiu
Yu Yu
Jianying Zhou

Program Committee

Shweta Agrawal	IIT Madras, India
Martin R. Albrecht	Royal Holloway, University of London, UK
Zhenzhen Bao	Nanyang Technological University, Singapore
Manuel Barbosa	University of Porto (FCUP) and INESC TEC, Portugal
Lejla Batina	Radboud University, The Netherlands
Sonia Belaïd	CryptoExperts, France
Fabrice Benhamouda	Algorand Foundation, USA
Begül Bilgin	Rambus - Cryptography Research, The Netherlands
Xavier Bonnetain	University of Waterloo, Canada
Joppe W. Bos	NXP Semiconductors, Belgium

Wouter Castryck	KU Leuven, Belgium
Rongmao Chen	National University of Defense Technology, China
Jung Hee Cheon	Seoul National University, South Korea
Chitchanok Chuengsatiansup	The University of Adelaide, Australia
Kai-Min Chung	Academia Sinica, Taiwan
Dana Dachman-Soled	University of Maryland, USA
Bernardo David	IT University of Copenhagen, Denmark
Benjamin Fuller	University of Connecticut, USA
Steven Galbraith	The University of Auckland, New Zealand
María Isabel González Vasco	Universidad Rey Juan Carlos, Spain
Robert Granger	University of Surrey, UK
Alex B. Grilo	CNRS, LIP6, Sorbonne Université, France
Aurore Guillevic	Inria, France
Swee-Huay Heng	Multimedia University, Malaysia
Akinori Hosoyamada	NTT Corporation and Nagoya University, Japan
Xinyi Huang	Fujian Normal University, China
Andreas Hülsing	Eindhoven University of Technology, The Netherlands
Tetsu Iwata	Nagoya University, Japan
David Jao	University of Waterloo and evolutionQ, Inc., Canada
Jérémy Jean	ANSSI, France
Shuichi Katsumata	AIST, Japan
Elena Kirshanova	I. Kant Baltic Federal University, Russia
Hyung Tae Lee	Chung-Ang University, South Korea
Dongdai Lin	Institute of Information Engineering, Chinese Academy of Sciences, China
Rongxing Lu	University of New Brunswick, Canada
Xianhui Lu	Institute of Information Engineering, Chinese Academy of Sciences, China
Mary Maller	Ethereum Foundation, UK
Giorgia Azzurra Marson	NEC Labs Europe, Germany
Keith M. Martin	Royal Holloway, University of London, UK
Daniel Masny	Visa Research, USA
Takahiro Matsuda	AIST, Japan
Krystian Matusiewicz	Intel Corporation, Poland
Florian Mendel	Infineon Technologies, Germany
Nele Mentens	Leiden University, The Netherlands, and KU Leuven, Belgium
Atsuko Miyaji	Osaka University, Japan
Michael Naehrig	Microsoft Research, USA
Khoa Nguyen	Nanyang Technological University, Singapore
Miyako Ohkubo	NICT, Japan
Emmanuela Orsini	KU Leuven, Belgium
Jiaxin Pan	NTNU, Norway
Panos Papadimitratos	KTH Royal Institute of Technology, Sweden

Alice Pellet–Mary	CNRS and University of Bordeaux, France
Duong Hieu Phan	Télécom Paris, Institut Polytechnique de Paris, France
Francisco Rodríguez-Henríquez	CINVESTAV, Mexico
Olivier Sanders	Orange Labs, France
Jae Hong Seo	Hanyang University, South Korea
Haya Shulman	Fraunhofer SIT, Germany
Daniel Slamanig	AIT Austrian Institute of Technology, Austria
Ron Steinfeld	Monash University, Australia
Willy Susilo	University of Wollongong, Australia
Katsuyuki Takashima	Waseda University, Japan
Qiang Tang	The University of Sydney, Australia
Serge Vaudenay	EPFL, Switzerland
Damien Vergnaud	Sorbonne Université and Institut Universitaire de France, France
Meiqin Wang	Shandong University, China
Xiaoyun Wang	Tsinghua University, China
Yongge Wang	UNC Charlotte, USA
Wenling Wu	Institute of Software, Chinese Academy of Sciences, China
Chaoping Xing	Shanghai Jiao Tong University, China
Sophia Yakoubov	Aarhus University, Denmark
Takashi Yamakawa	NTT Corporation, Japan
Bo-Yin Yang	Academia Sinica, Taiwan
Yu Yu	Shanghai Jiao Tong University, China
Hong-Sheng Zhou	Virginia Commonwealth University, USA

Additional Reviewers

Behzad Abdolmaleki
Gorjan Alagic
Orestis Alpos
Miguel Ambrona
Diego Aranha
Victor Arribas
Nuttapong Attrapadung
Benedikt Auerbach
Zeta Avarikioti
Melissa Azouaoui
Saikrishna Badrinarayanan
Joonsang Baek
Karim Baghery
Shi Bai
Gustavo Banegas
Subhadeep Banik
James Bartusek
Balthazar Bauer
Rouzbeh Behnia
Yanis Belkheyar
Josh Benaloh
Ward Beullens
Tim Beyne
Sarani Bhattacharya
Rishiraj Bhattacharyya
Nina Bindel
Adam Blatchley Hansen
Olivier Blazy
Charlotte Bonte
Katharina Boudgoust
Ioana Boureanu
Markus Brandt

Anne Broadbent
Ileana Buhan
Andrea Caforio
Eleonora Cagli
Sébastien Canard
Ignacio Cascudo
Gaëtan Cassiers
André Chailloux
Tzu-Hsien Chang
Yilei Chen
Jie Chen
Yanlin Chen
Albert Cheu
Jesús-Javier Chi-Domíguez
Nai-Hui Chia
Ilaria Chillotti
Ji-Jian Chin
Jérémy Chotard
Sherman S. M. Chow
Heewon Chung
Jorge Chávez-Saab
Michele Ciampi
Carlos Cid
Valerio Cini
Tristan Claverie
Benoît Cogliati
Alexandru Cojocaru
Daniel Collins
Kelong Cong
Craig Costello
Geoffroy Couteau
Daniele Cozzo
Jan Czajkowski
Tianxiang Dai
Wei Dai
Sourav Das
Pratish Datta
Alex Davidson
Lauren De Meyer
Elke De Mulder
Claire Delaplace
Cyprien Delpech de Saint Guilhem
Patrick Derbez
Siemen Dhooghe
Daniel Dinu
Christoph Dobraunig
Samuel Dobson
Luis J. Dominguez Perez
Jelle Don
Benjamin Dowling
Maria Eichlseder
Jesse Elliott
Keita Emura
Muhammed F. Esgin
Hulya Evkan
Lei Fan
Antonio Faonio
Hanwen Feng
Dario Fiore
Antonio Florez-Gutierrez
Georg Fuchsbauer
Chaya Ganesh
Daniel Gardham
Rachit Garg
Pierrick Gaudry
Romain Gay
Nicholas Genise
Adela Georgescu
David Gerault
Satrajit Ghosh
Valerie Gilchrist
Aron Gohr
Junqing Gong
Marc Gourjon
Lorenzo Grassi
Milos Grujic
Aldo Gunsing
Kaiwen Guo
Chun Guo
Qian Guo
Mike Hamburg
Ben Hamlin
Shuai Han
Yonglin Hao
Keisuke Hara
Patrick Harasser
Jingnan He
David Heath
Chloé Hébant
Julia Hesse
Ryo Hiromasa
Shiqi Hou

Lin Hou
Yao-Ching Hsieh
Kexin Hu
Jingwei Hu
Zhenyu Huang
Loïs Huguenin-Dumittan
Arnie Hung
Shih-Han Hung
Kathrin Hövelmanns
Ilia Iliashenko
Aayush Jain
Yanxue Jia
Dingding Jia
Yao Jiang
Floyd Johnson
Luke Johnson
Chanyang Ju
Charanjit S. Jutla
John Kelsey
Taechan Kim
Myungsun Kim
Jinsu Kim
Minkyu Kim
Young-Sik Kim
Sungwook Kim
Jiseung Kim
Kwangjo Kim
Seungki Kim
Sunpill Kim
Fuyuki Kitagawa
Susumu Kiyoshima
Michael Klooß
Dimitris Kolonelos
Venkata Koppula
Liliya Kraleva
Mukul Kulkarni
Po-Chun Kuo
Hilder Vitor Lima Pereira
Russell W. F. Lai
Jianchang Lai
Yi-Fu Lai
Virginie Lallemand
Jason LeGrow
Joohee Lee
Jooyoung Lee
Changmin Lee
Hyeonbum Lee
Moon Sung Lee
Keewoo Lee
Dominik Leichtle
Alexander Lemmens
Gaëtan Leurent
Yannan Li
Shuaishuai Li
Baiyu Li
Zhe Li
Shun Li
Liang Li
Jianwei Li
Trey Li
Xiao Liang
Chi-Chang Lin
Chengjun Lin
Chao Lin
Yao-Ting Lin
Eik List
Feng-Hao Liu
Qipeng Liu
Guozhen Liu
Yunwen Liu
Patrick Longa
Sebastien Lord
George Lu
Yuan Lu
Yibiao Lu
Xiaojuan Lu
Ji Luo
Yiyuan Luo
Mohammad Mahzoun
Monosij Maitra
Christian Majenz
Ekaterina Malygina
Mark Manulis
Varun Maram
Luca Mariot
Loïc Masure
Bart Mennink
Simon-Philipp Merz
Peihan Miao
Kazuhiko Minematsu
Donika Mirdita
Pratyush Mishra

Tomoyuki Morimae
Pratyay Mukherjee
Alex Munch-Hansen
Yusuke Naito
Ngoc Khanh Nguyen
Jianting Ning
Ryo Nishimaki
Anca Nitulescu
Kazuma Ohara
Cristina Onete
Jean-Baptiste Orfila
Michele Orrù
Jong Hwan Park
Jeongeun Park
Robi Pedersen
Angel L. Perez del Pozo
Léo Perrin
Thomas Peters
Albrecht Petzoldt
Stjepan Picek
Rafael del Pino
Geong Sen Poh
David Pointcheval
Bernardo Portela
Raluca Posteuca
Thomas Prest
Robert Primas
Chen Qian
Willy Quach
Md Masoom Rabbani
Rahul Rachuri
Srinivasan Raghuraman
Sebastian Ramacher
Matthieu Rambaud
Shahram Rasoolzadeh
Krijn Reijnders
Joost Renes
Elena Reshetova
Mélissa Rossi
Mike Rosulek
Yann Rotella
Joe Rowell
Arnab Roy
Partha Sarathi Roy
Alexander Russell
Carla Ráfols
Paul Rösler
Yusuke Sakai
Amin Sakzad
Yu Sasaki
Or Sattath
John M. Schanck
Lars Schlieper
Martin Schläfer
Carsten Schmidt
André Schrottenloher
Jacob Schuldt
Jean-Pierre Seifert
Yannick Seurin
Yaobin Shen
Yixin Shen
Yu-Ching Shen
Danping Shi
Omri Shmueli
Kris Shrishak
Hervais Simo Fhom
Luisa Siniscalchi
Daniel Smith-Tone
Fang Song
Pratik Soni
Claudio Soriente
Akshayaram Srinivasan
Douglas Stebila
Damien Stehlé
Bruno Sterner
Christoph Striecks
Patrick Struck
Adriana Suarez Corona
Ling Sun
Shi-Feng Sun
Koutarou Suzuki
Aishwarya T
Erkan Tairi
Akira Takahashi
Atsushi Takayasu
Abdul Rahman Taleb
Younes Talibi Alaoui
Benjamin Hong Meng Tan
Syh-Yuan Tan
Titouan Tanguy
Alexander Tereshchenko
Adrian Thillard

Emmanuel Thomé
Tyge Tiessen
Radu Titiu
Ivan Tjuawinata
Yosuke Todo
Junichi Tomida
Bénédikt Tran
Jacques Traoré
Ni Trieu
Ida Tucker
Michael Tunstall
Dominique Unruh
Thomas Unterluggauer
Thomas van Himbeeck
Daniele Venturi
Jorge Villar
Mikhail Volkhov
Christine van Vredendaal
Benedikt Wagner
Riad Wahby
Hendrik Waldner
Alexandre Wallet
Junwei Wang
Qingju Wang
Yuyu Wang
Lei Wang
Senpeng Wang
Peng Wang
Weijia Wang
Yi Wang
Han Wang
Xuzi Wang
Yohei Watanabe
Florian Weber
Weiqiang Wen
Nils Wisiol
Mathias Wolf
Harry H. W. Wong
Keita Xagawa
Zejun Xiang
Jiayu Xu
Luyao Xu
Yaqi Xu
Shota Yamada
Hailun Yan
Wenjie Yang
Shaojun Yang
Masaya Yasuda
Wei-Chuen Yau
Kazuki Yoneyama
Weijing You
Chen Yuan
Tsz Hon Yuen
Runzhi Zeng
Cong Zhang
Zhifang Zhang
Bingsheng Zhang
Zhelei Zhou
Paul Zimmermann
Lukas Zobernig

Contents – Part IV

Lattice Cryptanalysis

NTRU Fatigue: How Stretched is Overstretched? 3
Léo Ducas and Wessel van Woerden

Faster Dual Lattice Attacks for Solving LWE with Applications to CRYSTALS 33
Qian Guo and Thomas Johansson

Lattice Sieving via Quantum Random Walks 63
André Chailloux and Johanna Loyer

A Systematic Approach and Analysis of Key Mismatch Attacks on Lattice-Based NIST Candidate KEMs 92
Yue Qin, Chi Cheng, Xiaohan Zhang, Yanbin Pan, Lei Hu, and Jintai Ding

Post-Quantum Cryptography

Gladius: LWR Based Efficient Hybrid Public Key Encryption with Distributed Decryption 125
Kelong Cong, Daniele Cozzo, Varun Maram, and Nigel P. Smart

Lattice-Based Group Encryption with Full Dynamicity and Message Filtering Policy 156
Jing Pan, Xiaofeng Chen, Fangguo Zhang, and Willy Susilo

A New Variant of Unbalanced Oil and Vinegar Using Quotient Ring: QR-UOV 187
Hiroki Furue, Yasuhiko Ikematsu, Yutaro Kiyomura, and Tsuyoshi Takagi

Shorter Lattice-Based Group Signatures via "Almost Free" Encryption and Other Optimizations 218
Vadim Lyubashevsky, Ngoc Khanh Nguyen, Maxime Plancon, and Gregor Seiler

Séta: Supersingular Encryption from Torsion Attacks 249
Luca De Feo, Cyprien Delpech de Saint Guilhem, Tako Boris Fouotsa, Péter Kutas, Antonin Leroux, Christophe Petit, Javier Silva, and Benjamin Wesolowski

SHealS and HealS: Isogeny-Based PKEs from a Key Validation Method for SIDH 279
Tako Boris Fouotsa and Christophe Petit

Advanced Encryption and Signatures

Adaptive Security via Deletion in Attribute-Based Encryption: Solutions from Search Assumptions in Bilinear Groups 311
Rishab Goyal, Jiahui Liu, and Brent Waters

Public Key Encryption with Flexible Pattern Matching 342
Élie Bouscatié, Guilhem Castagnos, and Olivier Sanders

Bounded Collusion ABE for TMs from IBE 371
Rishab Goyal, Ridwan Syed, and Brent Waters

Digital Signatures with Memory-Tight Security in the Multi-challenge Setting 403
Denis Diemert, Kai Gellert, Tibor Jager, and Lin Lyu

(Compact) Adaptively Secure FE for Attribute-Weighted Sums from k-Lin 434
Pratish Datta and Tapas Pal

Boosting the Security of Blind Signature Schemes 468
Jonathan Katz, Julian Loss, and Michael Rosenberg

Zero-Knowledge Proofs, Threshold and Multi-Signatures

PrORAM: Fast $O(\log n)$ Authenticated Shares ZK ORAM 495
David Heath and Vladimir Kolesnikov

Compressed Σ-Protocols for Bilinear Group Arithmetic Circuits and Application to Logarithmic Transparent Threshold Signatures 526
Thomas Attema, Ronald Cramer, and Matthieu Rambaud

Promise Σ-Protocol: How to Construct Efficient Threshold ECDSA from Encryptions Based on Class Groups 557
Yi Deng, Shunli Ma, Xinxuan Zhang, Hailong Wang, Xuyang Song, and Xiang Xie

The One-More Discrete Logarithm Assumption in the Generic Group Model 587
Balthazar Bauer, Georg Fuchsbauer, and Antoine Plouviez

Verifiably-Extractable OWFs and Their Applications to Subversion Zero-Knowledge 618
Prastudy Fauzi, Helger Lipmaa, Janno Siim, Michał Zając, and Arne Tobias Ødegaard

Chain Reductions for Multi-signatures and the HBMS Scheme 650
Mihir Bellare and Wei Dai

Authenticated Key Exchange

Symmetric Key Exchange with Full Forward Security and Robust Synchronization 681
Colin Boyd, Gareth T. Davies, Bor de Kock, Kai Gellert, Tibor Jager, and Lise Millerjord

Security Analysis of CPace 711
Michel Abdalla, Björn Haase, and Julia Hesse

Modular Design of Role-Symmetric Authenticated Key Exchange Protocols 742
Yuting Xiao, Rui Zhang, and Hui Ma

Author Index 773

Lattice Cryptanalysis

NTRU Fatigue: How Stretched is Overstretched?

Léo Ducas(✉) and Wessel van Woerden(✉)

Cryptology Group, CWI, Amsterdam, The Netherlands
{leo.ducas,wvw}@cwi.nl

Abstract. Until recently lattice reduction attacks on NTRU lattices were thought to behave similar as on (ring-)LWE lattices with the same parameters. However several works (Albrecht-Bai-Ducas 2016, Kirchner-Fouque 2017) showed a significant gap for large moduli q, the so-called overstretched regime of NTRU.

With the NTRU scheme being a finalist to the NIST PQC competition it is important to understand —both asymptotically and concretely— where the fatigue point lies exactly, *i.e.* at which q the overstretched regime begins. Unfortunately the analysis by Kirchner and Fouque is based on an impossibility argument, which only results in an asymptotic upper bound on the fatigue point. It also does not really *explain* how lattice reduction actually recovers secret-key information.

We propose a new analysis that asymptotically improves on that of Kirchner and Fouque, narrowing down the fatigue point for ternary NTRU from $q \leqslant n^{2.783+o(1)}$ to $q = n^{2.484+o(1)}$, and finally explaining the mechanism behind this phenomenon. We push this analysis further to a concrete one, settling the fatigue point at $q \approx 0.004 \cdot n^{2.484}$, and allowing precise hardness predictions in the overstretched regime. These predictions are backed by extensive experiments.

1 Introduction

1.1 Context

One should certainly recognize that in the field of lattice-based cryptography the NTRU cryptosystem of Hoffstein, Pipher and Silverman [HPS98,CDH+20] was particularly ahead of its time. After two decades spent basing cryptography [Ajt99,Reg05,SSTX09] on the worst-case hardness of lattice problems and concretising this theory into practical cryptosystems for standardisation [PAA+19,SAB+20,DKR+20], it is quite remarkable to see these constructions landing not so far away from the original design of NTRU (q-ary lattices, module structure over similar polynomial rings). In fact, it was even discovered a posteriori, that, up to the choice of parameters, the NTRU scheme itself can also be supported by worst-case hardness [SS11].

Regarding cryptanalysis, it was only recently discovered that the security of NTRU is in fact more subtle than the problem of finding a single unusually

M. Tibouchi and H. Wang (Eds.): ASIACRYPT 2021, LNCS 13093, pp. 3–32, 2021.
https://doi.org/10.1007/978-3-030-92068-5_1

short vector in a lattice. The first dent in this status quo came in 2016, from two concurrent works work of Albrecht et al., and Cheon et al. [ABD16,CJL16], which exploits the specific algebraic structure of the NTRU lattice to improve upon pure lattice reduction attacks[1]. This approach was shown to be applicable when the modulus q is large enough (say, super-polynomial), a regime coined "overstretched".

Shortly thereafter Kirchner and Fouque [KF17] showed that this improved complexity does *not* require any algebraic structure, and is instead rooted in the purely geometrical fact that the NTRU lattice contains an unusually dense sublattice of large dimension, *i.e.* a sublattice of small determinant.[2] They also go further in their analysis, and conclude that moduli q as small as $n^{2.783+o(1)}$ already belong to the overstretched regime —for random ternary secrets. In particular, for q larger than this bound, the security of NTRU is significantly less than that of Learning With Errors [Reg04] and of its Ring variant [SSTX09, LPR13] using similar parameters.[3]

However, it is not so clear from the analysis of Kirchner and Fouque whether this asymptotic quantity $n^{2.783+o(1)}$ is an estimate or merely an upper bound on the *fatigue point*, that is the value of q separating the standard regime from the overstretched regime. Their analysis is based on a lemma of Pataki and Tural [PT08], that constraints the shape of lattice basis in terms of the volume of their sublattices. While it allows to conclude that the dense sublattice must be discovered after reducing the lattice basis beyond these constraints, it does not really explain *how* lattice reduction ends up discovering the dense sublattice, nor does it exclude that the discovery could happen earlier.

So far, it has been generally considered that only advanced schemes —requiring very large q— such as NTRU-based Homomorphic Encryption [BLLN13] or candidate cryptographic multi-linear maps [GGH13] could be affected by this overstretched regime. Yet, because the analysis of Kirchner and Fouque is only asymptotic, and because it may only provide an upper bound on the fatigue point, there is at the moment little documented evidence that the overstretched regime may not in fact extend further down, maybe down to the NTRU encryption scheme itself [HPS98,CDH+20]! Admittedly, this seems like a far fetched concern: asymptotically this scheme chooses $q = O(n)$, with a hidden constant between 4 and 5 in practice. However, this scheme being now a finalist of the NIST standardisation process for post-quantum cryptography, it appears rather imperious to refine our understanding of the phenomenon, and to finally close this pending question.

We found further motivation to go down this rabbit hole by measuring the concrete value of fatigue point experimentally. Until now, all documented

[1] Though the idea had been inconclusively considered already in 2002 by Gentry, Jonsson, Nguyen Stern and Szydlo as reported in [GS02, Sect. 6].

[2] Note that one may associate a short vector to a dense sublattice of dimension 1.

[3] In fact, the presence of n rotations of the secret key already implies a minor security degradation compared to (Ring)-LWE already in the standard regime [MS01, DDGR20].

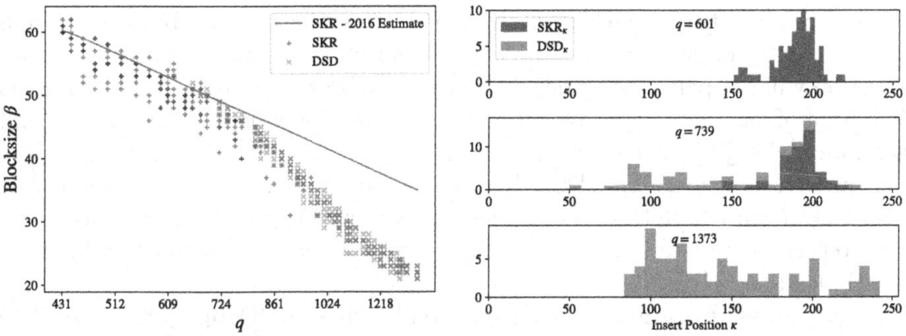

Fig. 1. Progressive BKZ with 8 tours per blocksize on matrix NTRU instances with parameters $n = 127, \sigma^2 = \frac{2}{3}$ for several moduli q. **Left:** the first blocksize β at which Progressive BKZ detects the Secret Key Recovery (SKR_κ) or Dense Sublattice Discovery (DSD_κ) event. We did 10 runs per modulus q. For the 2016-estimates, we use the geometric series assumption (GSA) for the shape of the basis and a probabilistic model for the discovery of the secret vector (see Sect. 2.4). **Right:** the positions κ at which a secret key or dense sublattice vector are detected over 80 runs per modulus.

experiments on the overstretched regime [ABD16, KF17, LW20] have focused on rather large values of q, and only used weak lattice reduction (LLL [LLL82], BKZ with blocksize 20): their goal was to demonstrate the claimed general behaviour when parameters are far in the overstretched regime. On the contrary, we focus our attention to the fatigue point for this preliminary experiment. That is, we ran strong reduction (progressive-BKZ [Sch87, AWHT16] up to blocksize 60) until a vector related to the secret key appeared for a range of moduli q. We distinguished the standard regime from the overstretched regime by classifying according to which event occurs first

- Secret Key Recovery (SKR_κ): a vector as short as a secret key vector is inserted in the basis at any given position κ.
- Dense Sublattice Discovery (DSD_κ): a vector strictly longer than the secret key but belonging to the dense sublattice generated by the secret key is inserted in the basis at any given position κ.

The result (Fig. 1) is rather striking: for $n = 127$, we start seeing a deviation from the standard regime for q as small as 700, while a naive interpretation of the prediction by Kirchner and Fouque [KF17] would suggest a fatigue point at $q \approx n^{2.783} \approx 700\,000$. We can conclude either that the asymptotic bound is not tight, or that the hidden asymptotic term (the $o(1)$ in $n^{2.783+o(1)}$) is significantly negative in practice. In any case, the bound of Kirchner and Fouque does not seem to provide accurate concrete predictions.

Remark. At this point, we should clarify why the DSD event should essentially be considered a successful attack. First, for q not too much larger than the fatigue point, an SKR event typically quickly follows after the DSD event; what happens is that DSD events cascade, until the full dense sublattice has been extracted: the first half of the reduced basis precisely generates the dense sublattice. Lattice reduction will happen independently on each half of the basis, meaning that the dimension of the search space for the secret key has effectively been halved, and therefore making the problem much easier.

However, as q increases, DSD becomes easier and easier, to the point that it becomes even easier than secret key recovery within the dense sublattice. In other terms, there is a *superstretched* regime for larger q, where DSD does not directly lead to SKR.

Nevertheless, we argue —essentially rephrasing [ABD16]— that the DSD event is typically sufficient for an attack. First, the dense sublattice vector discovered is of length significantly lower than q; in an FHE scheme such as [BLLN13] it is sufficient to decrypt fresh ciphertexts.[4] Secondly, in the case of cyclotomic or circulant NTRU, it is possible to recover the secret key from the dense sublattice by other means than pure lattice reduction; in particular the recent line of work on the principal ideal-SVP [EHKS14,CDPR16,BEF+17] showed that this can be done classically in sub-exponential time $\exp(\tilde{O}(\sqrt{n}))$ and quantumly in polynomial time.

1.2 Our Work

Having identified precisely what event distinguishes the standard regime of NTRU from its overstretched regime, we may now proceed to a refined analysis, and determine precisely both the fatigue point and the precise cost[5] of attacks in the overstretched regime. Our refined analysis diverges from the one of Kirchner and Fouque [KF17] on the following points:

1. we exploit the fact that BKZ runs SVP on large blocks ($\beta \geqslant 2$) not only to deduce the shape of the basis, but also to actually discover dense sublattice vectors,
2. we do not solely focus on the behaviour at position $\kappa = n - \beta + 1$ out of $d = 2n$ dimensions, but instead predict the most relevant position,
3. we propose an average-case analysis of volumes of the relevant lattices and sublattices, leading to a concrete prediction rather than a worst-case bound,
4. we also validate our intermediate and final predictions quantitatively with extensive experiments.

We note that contributions 1 and 2 alone already give us an important asymptotic result: the fatigue point of NTRU is indeed lower than predicted by Kirchner and Fouque, namely, it should happen at $q = n^{2.484+o(1)}$ instead of $n^{2.783+o(1)}$.

[4] The secret key being shorter is only required to deal with ciphertexts obtained by homomorphic computation.

[5] In this work, we only measure cost of lattice reduction in terms of the required BKZ blocksize; the computational cost of BKZ is essentially an orthogonal question.

Furthermore, our concrete average case analysis also differentiates the *circulant* version of NTRU [HPS98] from its *matrix* version [CG05, GGH+19]. We note minor deviations in the concrete analysis of volumes of relevant sublattices, that on average slightly favours the attacker in the matrix case, but also shows a larger variance in the concrete hardness of the circulant case.

In summary: we achieve an explicative and predictive model for the fatigue of NTRU, with concrete predictions confirmed in practice. In particular, the fatigue point is estimated to be at $q \approx 0.004 \cdot n^{2.484}$ for $n > 100$. All our artefacts for experiments and predictions are open-source and can be accessed at https://github.com/WvanWoerden/NTRUFatigue. These are based on the FPLLL and FPyLLL libraries [dt21a, dt21b].

Impact. We wish to clarify that this work *does not* contradict the concrete security of the NTRU candidate to the NIST competition [CDH+20]; on the contrary, we close a pending question regarding a potential vulnerability.

Limitation: the Lucky-Lifts. During our experiments, we also noted rare occurrence of DSD events that qualitatively differ from what we expected. Namely, the vector from the dense sublattice was found at positions κ quite larger than what was predicted by our model. More remarkable, these vectors were extremely unbalanced: their $2n - \kappa$ last (Gram-Schmidt) coordinates were much smaller than the κ first coordinates We call these DSD events lucky-lifts (DSD-LL), while the one we model and mostly observe are called after the Pataki-Tural Lemma (DSD-PT). Despite those two phenomena being very distinct, they nevertheless occured for the same BKZ blocksizes β, at least in the range of parameters we could experiment with.

It could very well be that these rare DSD-LL events are just artefacts of the modest parameters of our experiments and that these events vanish as the dimension grows. Yet, as they seem of a very different nature, a definitive conclusion would require a dedicated study.

1.3 Organisation

We introduce some preliminaries, the NTRU lattice, and the state-of-the-art estimates in Sect. 2. In Sect. 3 we introduce our new DSD-PT estimate and give an asymptotic analysis. In Sect. 4 we give an average-case analysis to construct a concrete estimator. In the final Sect. 5 we compare our estimate with experiments.

2 Preliminaries

2.1 Notation and Distributions

All vectors and matrices are denoted by bold lower and upper case letters respectively. All vectors are column-vectors and we write $\boldsymbol{B} = [\mathbf{b}_0, \ldots, \mathbf{b}_{n-1}]$ for a matrix where the i-th column vector is $\mathbf{b}_i$. If a matrix $\boldsymbol{B} \in \mathbb{R}^{d \times n}$ has full rank n we denote by $\mathcal{L}(\boldsymbol{B}) := \{\boldsymbol{B}\mathbf{x} : \mathbf{x} \in \mathbb{Z}^n\}$ the lattice spanned by the columns of $\boldsymbol{B}$. We call a lattice vector $\mathbf{v} \in \mathcal{L}$ primitive if it is not a strict integer multiple of another lattice vector. For a basis $\boldsymbol{B}$ and $i \in \{0, \ldots, d-1\}$ we define π_i as the orthogonal projection away from $\mathbf{b}_0, \ldots, \mathbf{b}_{i-1}$, and the Gram-Schmidt vectors as $\mathbf{b}_0^*, \ldots, \mathbf{b}_{d-1}^*$ where $\mathbf{b}_i^* := \pi_i(\mathbf{b}_i)$. We write $\boldsymbol{B}_{[l:r)}$ for the matrix $[\pi_l(\mathbf{b}_l), \ldots, \pi_l(\mathbf{b}_{r-1})]$, and denote the projected[6] sublattice $\mathcal{L}(\boldsymbol{B}_{[l:r)})$ as $\mathcal{L}_{[l:r)}$ when the basis is clear from the context. We denote the Euclidean norm of a vector $\mathbf{v}$ by $\|\mathbf{v}\|$ and the volume of a lattice by $\mathrm{vol}(\mathcal{L}(\boldsymbol{B})) := \prod_{i=0}^{n-1} \|\mathbf{b}_i^*\|$. We write $\lambda_1(\mathcal{L}) := \min_{\mathbf{v} \in \mathcal{L} \setminus \{0\}} \|\mathbf{v}\|$ for the first minimum of a lattice $\mathcal{L}$. For a lattice $\mathcal{L}$ we denote the dual lattice as $\mathcal{L}^* := \{\mathbf{w} \in \mathrm{span}(\mathcal{L}) : \langle \mathbf{w}, \mathbf{v} \rangle \in \mathbb{Z} \text{ for all } \mathbf{v} \in \mathcal{L}\}$. We use 'claim' to refer to an informal statement based on heuristics.

We denote the continuous centered Gaussian (normal) distribution with variance σ^2 by χ_{σ^2}. We denote the unit sphere over k coordinates as $\mathcal{S}^{k-1}$ and call the uniform distribution over $\mathcal{S}^{k-1}$ the spherical distribution. We write $\mathcal{B}_1^d$ for the d-dimensional unit ball. We write the chi-square distribution with k degrees of freedom as $\chi^2_{k,\sigma^2} := \sum_{i=1}^k X_i^2$, where $X_1, \ldots, X_k$ are independently distributed as χ_{σ^2}. The chi-square distribution has expectation $k\sigma^2$, but for our concrete estimates we consider the log-expectation.

Lemma 2.1. *Let X be distributed as χ^2_{k,σ^2}, then*

$$\mathbb{E}[\ln(X)] = \ln(2\sigma^2) + \psi(k/2),$$

where $\psi(x) := \Gamma'(x)/\Gamma(x)$ is the digamma function.

2.2 NTRU and Lattice Attacks

We start with the historical definition of NTRU.

Definition 2.2 (NTRU). *Let n be prime, q a positive integer and let $\boldsymbol{f}, \boldsymbol{g} \in (\mathbb{Z}/q\mathbb{Z})[X]$ be polynomials of degree n with small coefficients sampled from some distribution χ under the condition that $\boldsymbol{f}$ is invertible in $\mathcal{R}_q := (\mathbb{Z}/q\mathbb{Z})[X]/(X^n - 1)$. The pair $(\boldsymbol{f}, \boldsymbol{g})$ forms the secret key, and the public key is defined as $\boldsymbol{h} := \boldsymbol{g}/\boldsymbol{f} \bmod \mathcal{R}_q$. The* NTRU problem *is to recover any rotation $(X^i\boldsymbol{f}, X^i\boldsymbol{g})$ of the secret key from $\boldsymbol{h}$.*

For *NTRUencrypt* [HPS98, CDH+20] $\boldsymbol{f}$ and $\boldsymbol{g}$ have ternary coefficients, with a fixed number of about $n/3$ of each value in $\{-1, 0, 1\}$. For our analysis we

[6] When $l = 0$, no projection is applied, and $\mathcal{L}_{[0:r)}$ is simply a sublattice of $\mathcal{L}$.

consider the case where each coefficient is sampled from a discrete Gaussian over $\mathbb{Z}$ with some variance $\sigma^2 > 0$. For simplicity the ternary case is treated as a discrete Gaussian with variance $\sigma^2 = \frac{2}{3}$.

More generally we consider a matrix description of NTRU where the polynomials are replaced by matrices $\boldsymbol{F}, \boldsymbol{G}, \boldsymbol{H} \in \mathbb{Z}^{n \times n}$ such that $\boldsymbol{H} := \boldsymbol{G} \cdot \boldsymbol{F}^{-1} \bmod q$ [CG05, GGH+19]. Variants of NTRU, e.g. based on different algebraic rings [BBC+20], can be encoded in the structure of the matrices. For example, the original problem can be encoded by setting $\boldsymbol{F}_{i,j} := f_{(i+j \bmod n)}$ where $\boldsymbol{f} = \sum_{i=0}^{n-1} f_i X^i$, for each polynomial respectively. We call the original variant *circulant NTRU*, based on the resulting shape of the matrices $\boldsymbol{F}, \boldsymbol{G}$, and we treat $\boldsymbol{f}, \boldsymbol{g}$ as n-dimensional vectors. We also consider the variant, called *matrix NTRU*, where the matrices $\boldsymbol{F}, \boldsymbol{G}$ have no extra structure and the coefficients are independently sampled from a discrete Gaussian.

To reduce the NTRU problem to a lattice problem we define the *NTRU lattice*, which contains a particularly *dense* sublattice generated by the secret key.

Definition 2.3. *Let $(n, q, \boldsymbol{F}, \boldsymbol{G}, \boldsymbol{H})$ be an NTRU instance. We define the NTRU lattice as*

$$\mathcal{L}^{\boldsymbol{H},q} := \begin{pmatrix} q\boldsymbol{I}_n & \boldsymbol{H} \\ \boldsymbol{0} & \boldsymbol{I}_n \end{pmatrix} \cdot \mathbb{Z}^{2n},$$

and its (secret) dense sublattice of rank n by:

$$\mathcal{L}^{\boldsymbol{GF}} := \boldsymbol{B}^{\boldsymbol{GF}} \cdot \mathbb{Z}^n \subset \mathcal{L}^{\boldsymbol{H},q}, \text{ where } \boldsymbol{B}^{\boldsymbol{GF}} := \begin{pmatrix} \boldsymbol{G} \\ \boldsymbol{F} \end{pmatrix}.$$

Solving the NTRU problem is equivalent to recovering the dense sublattice basis $\boldsymbol{B}^{\boldsymbol{GF}} = [\boldsymbol{G}; \boldsymbol{F}]$ up to some permutation of the columns. For uniformity of notation we will denote such a column by $(\boldsymbol{g}|\boldsymbol{f})$. These column vectors have a length of about $\|(\boldsymbol{g}|\boldsymbol{f})\| \approx \sqrt{2n\sigma^2}$, which for common parameters is much shorter than the expected minimal length $\lambda_1(\mathcal{L}^{\boldsymbol{H},q}) \approx \sqrt{nq/(\pi e)}$ of the full lattice $\mathcal{L}^{\boldsymbol{H},q}$ for a truly uniform random $\boldsymbol{H} \in (\mathbb{Z}/q\mathbb{Z})^{n \times n}$. To recover the secret key we thus have to find these exceptionally short vectors in the full lattice $\mathcal{L}^{\boldsymbol{H},q}$.

In [CS97] Coppersmith and Shamir showed that we can slightly relax the problem as any small vector from the dense sublattice $\mathcal{L}^{\boldsymbol{GF}}$ is enough to decode a message. We therefore focus our analysis on the recovery of elements from $\mathcal{L}^{\boldsymbol{GF}}$, and not (directly) on the full secret basis $\boldsymbol{B}^{\boldsymbol{GF}}$. To recover short vectors we resort to lattice reduction.

2.3 Lattice Reduction

Any lattice $\mathcal{L} = \mathcal{L}(\boldsymbol{B})$ with basis $\boldsymbol{B} \in \mathbb{R}^{d \times d}$ has (for $d > 1$) an infinite number of other bases $\boldsymbol{B} \cdot \boldsymbol{U}$ with $\boldsymbol{U} \in \mathrm{GL}_d(\mathbb{Z})$. The goal of lattice reduction is to find a *good* basis: the basis vectors are preferably short and somewhat orthogonal. Looking at the Gram-Schmidt vectors $\mathbf{b}_0^*, \ldots, \mathbf{b}_{d-1}^*$ we have the invariant $\prod_{i=0}^{d-1} \|\mathbf{b}_i^*\| =$

$\det(\boldsymbol{B}) = \mathrm{vol}(\mathcal{L})$ which is independent of the basis. Therefore decreasing the length of the first basis vector $\mathbf{b}_0 = \mathbf{b}_0^*$ forces some of the other Gram-Schmidt vectors to increase in length. We call these lengths $(\|\mathbf{b}_i^*\|)_{i=0,\dots,d-1}$ the *profile* of a basis $\boldsymbol{B}$. A good basis has a well balanced profile; in particular one that does not decrease too fast.

The most famous lattice reduction algorithm is the polynomial time LLL algorithm, which gives some guarantees on the slope of an LLL-reduced basis. We consider a generalisation, namely the BKZ algorithm, that gives a flatter slope, but at a higher cost. A basis is BKZ reduced with blocksize β if $\mathbf{b}_\kappa^*$ is a shortest vector of the projected sublattice $\mathcal{L}_{[\kappa:\min(\kappa+\beta,d))}$ at each position κ. LLL-reduction corresponds to the case that $\beta = 2$.

Definition 2.4 (BKZ). *A basis $\boldsymbol{B} = [\mathbf{b}_0, \dots, \mathbf{b}_{d-1}]$ is called BKZ-β reduced if*

$$\|\mathbf{b}_\kappa^*\| = \lambda_1(\mathcal{L}_{[\kappa:\min(\kappa+\beta,d))}) \text{ for all } \kappa = 0, \dots, d-1.$$

A BKZ-reduced basis has several provable bounds on the slope of the profile. In the context of cryptanalysis we are more interested in the average-case behaviour and thus we fall back on heuristics to describe the shape of a BKZ-reduced profile. The most commonly used heuristic for lattices is the Gaussian Heuristic, that states that for a measurable volume $\mathcal{V}$ the number of lattice points $|\mathcal{L} \cap \mathcal{V}|$ approximately equals $\mathrm{vol}(\mathcal{V})/\mathrm{vol}(\mathcal{L})$. Applying this to a ball allows to estimate the first minimum of a lattice.

Heuristic 2.5. *Let $\mathcal{L}$ be a d-dimensional lattice with volume $\mathrm{vol}(\mathcal{L})$. The expectation of the first minimum $\lambda_1(\mathcal{L})$ under the Gaussian Heuristic is given by*

$$\mathrm{gh}(\mathcal{L}) := \frac{\mathrm{vol}(\mathcal{L})^{1/d}}{\mathrm{vol}(\mathcal{B}_1)^{1/d}} \approx \sqrt{d/(2\pi e)} \cdot \mathrm{vol}(\mathcal{L})^{1/d}.$$

We also denote $\mathrm{gh}(d) \approx \sqrt{d/(2\pi e)}$ for the expected first minimum of a d-dimensional lattice with volume 1.

Applying the above heuristic to the value of $\|\mathbf{b}_\kappa^*\| = \lambda_1(\mathcal{L}_{[\kappa:\min(\kappa+\beta,d))})$ at each position κ gives us relations between the Gram-Schmidt lengths $\|\mathbf{b}_0^*\|, \dots, \|\mathbf{b}_{d-1}^*\|$. Solving these relations for $\beta \ll d$ shows that $\|\mathbf{b}_\kappa^*\| / \|\mathbf{b}_{\kappa+1}^*\| \approx \alpha_\beta$ for some constant α_β only depending on β. So heuristically the profile forms a geometric series. This is made more precise by the Geometric Series Assumption.

Heuristic 2.6 (Geometric Series Assumption (GSA)). *Let $\boldsymbol{B}$ be a BKZ-β reduced basis, then the profile satisfies*

$$\ln(\|\mathbf{b}_i^*\|) = \frac{d-1-2i}{2} \cdot \ln(\alpha_\beta) + \frac{\ln(\det(\boldsymbol{B}))}{d},$$

where $\alpha_\beta = \mathrm{gh}(\beta)^{2/(\beta-1)}$.

The GSA is reasonably precise for say $\beta \geqslant 50$ and a not too large blocksize $\beta \ll d$ compared to the lattice dimension.

The BKZ algorithm (see Algorithm 1) computes a BKZ-reduced basis from any other basis. The algorithm greedily attempts to satisfy the BKZ condition at each position by computing a shortest vector in each *block* $\boldsymbol{B}_{[\kappa:\min(\kappa+\beta,d))}$, and replacing the basis vector $\mathbf{b}_\kappa$ accordingly. This makes the basis BKZ-β reduced at position κ, but might invalidate the condition at other positions. Applying this once to all positions $\kappa = 0,\ldots,d-2$ is called a *tour*. The BKZ algorithms repeats such tours until the basis remains unchanged and is thus BKZ-reduced.

Algorithm 1: The BKZ algorithm.

Data: A lattice basis $\boldsymbol{B}$, blocksize β.
while $\boldsymbol{B}$ *is not BKZ-β reduced* **do**
  for $\kappa = 0,\ldots,d-2$ **do** `// A single BKZ-β tour`
    $\mathbf{w} \leftarrow$ a shortest vector in $\mathcal{L}\left(\boldsymbol{B}_{[\kappa:\min(\kappa+\beta,d))}\right)$;
    Lift $\mathbf{w}$ to a full vector $\mathbf{v} \in \mathcal{L}\left(\boldsymbol{B}_{[0:\min(\kappa+\beta,d))}\right)$ s.t. $\pi_\kappa(\mathbf{v}) = \mathbf{w}$;
    Insert $\mathbf{v}$ in $\boldsymbol{B}$ at position κ and use LLL to resolve linear dependencies;

The number of tours is polynomially bounded, and in practice not much improvement is attained after say a few dozen tours. The cost of BKZ is thus mainly dominated by the exponential (in β) cost of finding a shortest vector in a β-dimensional lattice. *Progressive* BKZ reduces this cost in practice, where instead of running many tours of BKZ-β, one runs only a few tours for increasing $\beta' = 2,3,\ldots,\beta$.

For our experiments we also added a hook to BKZ, using secret key information, to detect if a vector $\mathbf{v}$ is part of the dense sublattice $\mathcal{L}^{\boldsymbol{GF}}$ and to abort early if this is the case.

While the Geometric Series Assumption gives a good first order estimate of the basis profile after BKZ-reduction, it is known to be inaccurate in small dimensions or when the dimension is only a small multiple of the blocksize. Additionally it does not account for the slower convergence when running progressive BKZ with only a few tours. To resolve this problem [CN11] introduced a BKZ simulator based on the Gaussian Heuristic, that was later refined in [YD17, BSW18]. These allow for accurate and efficient predictions of the profile shape for *random* lattices, even for progressive BKZ with a limited number of tours.

Behaviour on q-ary lattices. While by now the behaviour of BKZ on random lattices is reasonably understood, this is less the case for q-ary lattices (for certain parameters) such as the NTRU lattice $\mathcal{L}^{\boldsymbol{H},q}$.

Definition 2.7 (q-ary lattices). *A lattice $\mathcal{L}$ of dimension d is said to be q-ary if for some $q > 0$ we have*

$$q\mathbb{Z}^d \subset \mathcal{L} \subset \mathbb{Z}^d.$$

Note that the first n basis vectors of $\mathcal{L}^{H,q}$ are orthogonal q-vectors $(q, 0, \ldots, 0)$, $(0, q, 0, \ldots, 0), \ldots$, and so the initial basis profile starts with $\|\mathbf{b}_0^*\| = \cdots = \|\mathbf{b}_{n-1}^*\| = q$. Additionally after projecting away from these q-vectors, the remaining basis vectors are again orthogonal with length 1, and thus we have $\|\mathbf{b}_n^*\| = \cdots = \|\mathbf{b}_{d-1}^*\| = 1$. Note that in the BKZ algorithm the length of $\mathbf{b}_0$ can not increase, and is thus always at most q. Also $\mathbf{b}_1$ can not increase in length if $\mathbf{b}_0$ remains unchanged, and so on. For dual-BKZ or the self-dual LLL the profile lengths can not drop below 1 anywhere by the same reasoning. Still LLL and BKZ guarantee that the profile slope in the middle is not too steep. So after LLL reduction the profile must be flat at the start and end, and have a sloped part in the middle, we call this a Z-shape [AD21]. Because BKZ is not self-dual we do not have any guarantee that the last profile elements do not drop below 1, however we could for example run BKZ only on an appropriate middle context $\mathcal{L}_{[n-m:n+m)}$ to force this behaviour. With this description one would expect the middle part to follow the GSA, leading to an alternative heuristic for q-ary lattices.

Heuristic 2.8 (ZGSA). *Let $\boldsymbol{B}$ be a basis of a $2n$-dimensional q-ary lattice $\mathcal{L}$ with n q-vectors. After BKZ-β reduction the profile has the following shape:*

$$\|\mathbf{b}_i^*\| = \begin{cases} q & \text{if } i \leqslant n-m, \\ \sqrt{q} \cdot \alpha_\beta^{\frac{2n-1-2i}{2}}, & \text{if } n-m < i < n+m-1, \\ 1, & \text{if } i \geqslant n+m-1, \end{cases}$$

where $\alpha_\beta = \mathrm{gh}(\beta)^{2/(\beta-1)}$, and $m = \frac{1}{2} + \frac{\ln(q)}{2\ln(\alpha_\beta)}$.

Again this gives us a good first order estimate. Asymptotically setting $\beta = \mathcal{B} \cdot n$ and $q = n^{\mathcal{Q}}$, we obtain $\ln(\alpha_\beta) = \frac{\ln(n)}{\mathcal{B} \cdot n} + O\left(n^{-1}\right)$, and $m = \frac{1}{2}\mathcal{Q}\mathcal{B} \cdot n + O\left(\frac{n}{\ln(n)}\right)$.

2.4 Estimates

The main question of our work is to better understand how BKZ recovers the dense sublattice $\mathcal{L}^{GF}$ from an NTRU lattice $\mathcal{L}^{H,q}$. Several works exist that give estimates on the blocksize β for which BKZ successfully recovers the secret key $(\boldsymbol{g}, \boldsymbol{f})$, or more generally a vector from the dense sublattice. We discuss the state-of-the-art estimates, one known as the *2016 Estimate* [ADPS16] with further refinements [DDGR20, PV21], and one by Kirchner and Fouque [KF17].

While the 2016 Estimate already gives a clear explanation *how* BKZ recovers a suitable vector, the Kirchner and Fouque estimate is only based on an impossibility result. To be more precise about what we mean with recovery we define the following two events.

Definition 2.9 (BKZ Events). *For a BKZ run on an NTRU lattice $\mathcal{L}$ with dense sublattice $\mathcal{L}^{GF}$ we define two events:*

1. ***Secret Key Recovery** (SKR): The first time one the secret keys $(\boldsymbol{g}|\boldsymbol{f})$ is inserted.*

2. ***Dense Sublattice Discovery** (DSD): The first time a dense lattice vector $\mathbf{v} \in \mathcal{L}^{GF}$ strictly longer than the secret key(s) is inserted.*

We further specify SKR_κ and DSD_κ when the insertion takes place at position κ in the basis.

2016 Estimate [ADPS16] **for SKR.** The 2016 Estimate is aimed at the more general problem of detecting an unusually short vector in a lattice. To obtain an estimate for the NTRU problem, and more specifically the SKR event, we apply it to the unusually short vector $(\boldsymbol{g}|\boldsymbol{f}) \in \mathcal{L}^{\boldsymbol{H},q}$.

Claim 2.10 (SKR – 2016 Estimate). *Let $\mathcal{L}$ be a lattice of dimension d and let $\mathbf{v} \in \mathcal{L}$ be a unusually short vector $\|\mathbf{v}\| \ll \mathrm{gh}(\mathcal{L})$. Then under the Geometric Series Assumption BKZ recovers $\mathbf{v}$ if*

$$\sqrt{\beta/d} \cdot \|\mathbf{v}\| < \sqrt{\alpha_\beta}^{2\beta-d-1} \cdot \mathrm{vol}(\mathcal{L})^{1/d},$$

where $\alpha_\beta = \mathrm{gh}(\beta)^{2/(\beta-1)}$.

The left hand side of the inequality is an estimate for $\|\pi_{d-\beta}(\mathbf{v})\|$, while the right hand size is the expected norm of $\mathbf{b}^*_{d-\beta}$ under the GSA. When the inequality is satisfied we expect that the shortest vector in $\mathcal{L}_{[d-\beta:d)}$ is in fact (a projection of) the unusually short vector, and thus it is inserted by BKZ at position $d-\beta$.

For q-ary lattices we can easily change the estimate to make use of the ZGSA instead, although for successful blocksizes $\mathbf{b}^*_{d-\beta}$ will not lie on the flat tail-part, and thus this will not change anything. Additionally for q-ary lattices it can be beneficial to apply the estimate not to the full lattice but on some projected sublattice $\mathcal{L}_{[i:d)}$ for $i \leqslant n$; the left hand side of the equation is expected to remain unchanged, while the right hand side might decrease as $\mathrm{vol}(\mathcal{L})$ loses a factor q^i. Note that we do not necessarily have to explicitly let BKZ act on this projected sublattice, as BKZ already does this naturally.

Asymptotics. Consider the NTRU lattice $\mathcal{L}^{\boldsymbol{H},q}$ and suppose that $q = \Theta(n^{\mathcal{Q}})$, $\|\mathbf{v}\| = \|(\boldsymbol{g}, \boldsymbol{f})\| = \Theta(n^{\mathcal{S}})$ and $\beta = (\mathcal{B} + o(1))n$. Applying the 2016 Estimate the right hand side of the inequality is minimised when only keeping $k = \min\left((\sqrt{2\mathcal{B}\mathcal{Q}} - 1)n, n\right)$ of the q-vectors, so by applying the estimate to the projected sublattice $\mathcal{L}^{\boldsymbol{H},q}_{[n-k:2n)}$. For $\mathcal{S} \geqslant 1$ we have $k = n$, and solving the equation gives $\mathcal{B} = \frac{2}{\mathcal{Q}+2-2\mathcal{S}}$. For $\mathcal{S} < 1$ we have $k = (\sqrt{2\mathcal{B}\mathcal{Q}} - 1)n$, and solving gives $\mathcal{B} = \frac{2\mathcal{Q}}{(\mathcal{Q}+1-\mathcal{S})^2}$. Note in particular that in terms of q we require a blocksize of $\beta = \tilde{\Theta}\left(n/\ln(q)\right)$.

Refinements. The 2016 Estimate gives a clear explanation on how and where the secret vector is recovered. This also allows to further refine the estimate and give concrete predictions. For example by using a BKZ-simulator instead of the GSA, and by accounting for the probability that after the projection $\|\pi_{d-\beta}(\mathbf{v})\|$ has been found, it is successfully lifted to the full vector $\mathbf{v}$. Also instead of working with the expected length of the projection, we can directly model the probability distribution under the assumption that $\mathbf{v}$ is distributed as a Gaussian vector. Such refinements were applied in [DDGR20,PV21], and the resulting concrete predictions match with experiments to recover an unusually short vector. In this work, we use the (Z)GSA for the basis shape, but adjusting the slope to account for the speed of convergence using experimentally determined values. However, we do use the advanced probabilistic model for the detection and lifting of the short vector.

For NTRU there is not just a single unusually short vector, but there are $n = d/2$ of them, which makes it more likely that at least one of them is recovered. Because the refined concrete estimator already works with a probability distribution, we can easily take multiple vectors into account. The resulting predictions for the SKR event match the experiments reasonably well for smallish q as can be seen in Fig. 1. For large q, the so-called *overstretched* regime, the estimate is however too pessimistic.

Kirchner–Fouque Estimate [KF17] **for DSD.** In 2016 Albrecht, Bai and Ducas [ABD16] showed that for very large values of q one can mount an algebraic *subfield attack* on the cyclotomic NTRU problem with sub-exponential or even polynomial complexity. This allowed them to break several homomorphic encryption schemes that relied on NTRU in the overstretched regime.

However soon after, Kirchner–Fouque [KF17] showed that this elaborate algebraic attack was unnecessary: (dual-)BKZ already behaves much better in this regime than the 2016 Estimate predicts, leading to the same asymptotic improvements. The key idea behind their analysis is that in the overstretched regime the NTRU lattice $\mathcal{L}^{\boldsymbol{H},q}$ contains an exceptionally dense sublattice $\mathcal{L}^{\boldsymbol{G}\boldsymbol{F}}$ of low volume. This gives a constraint on the basis profile via the following lemma by Pataki and Tural.

Lemma 2.11 (Pataki and Tural [PT08]**).** *Let $\mathcal{L}$ be a d-dimensional lattice with basis $\mathbf{b}_0, \ldots, \mathbf{b}_{d-1}$. For any k-dimensional sublattice $\mathcal{L}' \subset \mathcal{L}$ we have*

$$\mathrm{vol}(\mathcal{L}') \geqslant \min_J \prod_{j \in J} \|\mathbf{b}_j^*\|,$$

where J ranges over the k-size subsets of $\{0, \ldots, d-1\}$.

Applying Lemma 2.11 to the n-dimensional sublattice $\mathcal{L}^{\boldsymbol{G}\boldsymbol{F}} \subset \mathcal{L}^{\boldsymbol{H},q}$, and assuming a non-increasing profile, we obtain an upper bound on the volume of $\mathcal{L}^{\boldsymbol{H},q}_{[n:2n)}$. Assuming the ZGSA the latter volume increases when running BKZ-β for increasing blocksizes, eventually contradicting the upper bound. This allows us to detect if a q-ary lattice is in fact an NTRU lattice, but additionally Kirchner–Fouque argue that BKZ must *somehow* have detected the dense sublattice after this point. Based on this impossibility argument they introduced the following estimate.

Claim 2.12 (DSD – Kirchner–Fouque Estimate). *Let $\mathcal{L}^{\boldsymbol{H},q}$ be an NTRU lattice of dimension $2n$, with dense sublattice $\mathcal{L}^{\boldsymbol{G}\boldsymbol{F}} \subset \mathcal{L}^{\boldsymbol{H},q}$. Under the Z-shape*

Geometric Series Assumption BKZ-β triggers the DSD event if

$$\mathrm{vol}(\mathcal{L}^{GF}) < q^{\frac{m-1}{2}} \cdot \alpha_\beta^{-\frac{1}{2}(m-1)^2},$$

where $\alpha_\beta = \mathrm{gh}(\beta)^{2/(\beta-1)}$, *and* $m = \frac{1}{2} + \frac{\ln(q)}{2\ln(\alpha_\beta)}$.

To apply this estimate we can bound $\mathrm{vol}(\mathcal{L}^{GF})$ using the Hadamard inequality by $\|(\boldsymbol{g}|\boldsymbol{f})\|^n$. As a first approximation this is reasonably tight because the secret basis $\boldsymbol{B}^{GF}$ is close to orthogonal.

Asymptotics. Consider the NTRU lattice $\mathcal{L}^{\boldsymbol{H},q}$ and suppose that $q = \Theta(n^{\mathcal{Q}})$, $\|(\boldsymbol{g},\boldsymbol{f})\| = \Theta(n^{\mathcal{S}})$ and $\beta = (\mathcal{B}+o(1))n$. We apply the Kirchner–Fouque Estimate using that $m \approx \frac{\mathcal{B}\mathcal{Q}}{2}n$ and $\alpha_\beta \approx (\mathcal{B}n)^{1/(\mathcal{B}n)}$. The left hand side of the inequality is bounded by $n^{n\mathcal{S}+o(n)}$ and the right hand side equals $n^{\frac{\mathcal{B}\mathcal{Q}^2}{8}n+o(n)}$; solving gives $\mathcal{B} \geqslant \frac{8\mathcal{S}}{\mathcal{Q}^2}$. Note that in terms of q we require a blocksize of $\beta = \tilde{\Theta}\left(n/\ln^2(q)\right)$, improving upon the 2016 Estimate by a factor $\ln(q)$. So for large enough q the Kirchner–Fouque Estimate predicts a lower successful blocksize than the 2016 Estimate. We call the value of q for which BKZ starts to behave better than predicted by the 2016 Estimate the *fatigue point.* For the common situation that $\mathcal{S} = \frac{1}{2}$, e.g. when each secret coefficient has standard deviation $\sigma = \Theta(1)$, the Kirchner–Fouque Estimate predicts that the fatigue point lies at some $q \leqslant n^{2.783+o(1)}$.

3 A New Estimate

3.1 Preliminary Experiments

Both the 2016 Estimate and the Kirchner–Fouque Estimate analyse an event that leads to successful recovery of a vector of the dense NTRU sublattice. This only gives an upper bound on the hardness; a different event leading to the recovery might happen at a lower blocksize. Additionally the Kirchner–Fouque Estimate is only based on an impossibility result and gives no explanation as to how BKZ actually recovers a vector from the dense sublattice. In order to derive a tight estimate we first run experiments to track down at which point a dense sublattice vector is actually found during the BKZ tours, i.e. when the DSD_κ event is triggered and at what position. Then we model this event in order to hopefully derive a tight estimate.

We run progressive BKZ on NTRU lattices $\mathcal{L}^{\boldsymbol{H},q}$ for fixed parameters $n = 127, \sigma^2 = \frac{2}{3}$, and several moduli q. For each BKZ insertion at position κ we check if the inserted vector belongs to the dense sublattice $\mathcal{L}^{GF}$, and thereby if the SKR_κ or DSD_κ event takes place, after which we stop.

The results are shown in Fig. 1. We take a closer look at the observed SKR_κ and DSD_κ events and where they are triggered. We can group our observations in three typical circumstances.

- **SKR-2016**. The SKR_κ event is mostly triggered for small values of q, and this mostly happens at the position $\kappa = 2n - \beta$, so in the last block $[2n - \beta : 2n)$, or slightly earlier. This coincides exactly with the $\mathrm{SKR}_{2n-\beta}$ event as predicted by the 2016 Estimate [ADPS16, AGVW17].
- **DSD-PT**. The DSD_κ event is mostly triggered at positions $\kappa = n + k - \beta$ for $0 < k \ll n$. The inserted dense vector $\mathbf{v}$ is often significantly longer than the secret key but still shorter than the q-vectors. On closer inspection the projected length $\|\pi_{n+k-\beta}(\mathbf{v})\|$ is close to the expected length $\sqrt{\frac{\beta}{n+k}}\,\|\mathbf{v}\|$ for all instances, more specifically the length of $\mathbf{v}$ is well balanced over the Gram-Schmidt directions $\mathbf{b}_0^*, \ldots, \mathbf{b}_{n+k-1}^*$. We name these events after the Pataki–Tural Lemma (DSD-PT).
- **DSD-LL**. For a few instances the DSD_κ event is triggered at large positions κ, up to $2n - \beta$. The inserted dense vector $\mathbf{v}$ is again significantly longer than the secret key, but it has an unexpectedly short projection $\pi_\kappa(\mathbf{v})$ on the BKZ block $[\kappa : \kappa + \beta)$. We call these events lucky-lifts (DSD-LL).

The DSD-LL event could potentially be explained by the relatively large amount of shortish vectors in the close to orthogonal dense sublattice $\mathcal{L}^{GF}$ compared to what one would expect based on the Gaussian Heuristic. These many vectors might compensate for the low probability event that: (1) such a long vector has such a short projection, and (2) the projected vector is correctly lifted by Babai's nearest plane algorithm (thus a *lucky lift*). The DSD-LL event remains rare for all parameters we used in our experiments, and the successful blocksizes do not seem to deviate from the DSD-PT events. Although we think this circumstance deserves further analysis we therefore base our estimate on the more common DSD-PT event.

For the DSD-PT event the projected length $\|\pi_{n+k-\beta}(\mathbf{v})\|$ is close to $\sqrt{\frac{\beta}{n+k}}\,\|\mathbf{v}\|$, and thus the inserted dense vector $\mathbf{v}$ must in fact be (close to) a shortest vector of the intersected sublattice $\mathcal{L}^{\boldsymbol{H},q}_{[0:n+k)} \cap \mathcal{L}^{GF}$. If not, the shortest vector would typically have an even smaller projection and would thus be inserted instead. For ease of analysis we therefore assume that $\mathbf{v}$ is a shortest vector of $\mathcal{L}^{\boldsymbol{H},q}_{[0:n+k)} \cap \mathcal{L}^{GF}$. In short our new estimate can be described as follows.

Claim 3.1 (DSD-PT estimate). *A tour of BKZ-β triggers the DSD event if*

$$\pi_{n+k-\beta}(\mathbf{v}) < \left\|\mathbf{b}^*_{n+k-\beta}\right\|,$$

where $\mathbf{v}$ is a shortest vector of $\mathcal{L}^{\boldsymbol{H},q}_{[0:)} \cap \mathcal{L}^{GF}$ for some $0 < k \leqslant n$.

3.2 Asymptotic Analysis

We denote the intersected sublattice by $\mathcal{L}^{GF}_{\cap[0:r)} := \mathcal{L}^{\boldsymbol{H},q}_{[0:r)} \cap \mathcal{L}^{GF}$. To directly apply Claim 3.1 we are interested in the length of $\mathbf{v}$, and thus the value of $\lambda_1(\mathcal{L}^{GF}_{\cap[0:n+k)})$. We break down the analysis into several steps. In order to obtain a bound on the first minimum we first compute a bound on the volume of the intersection $\mathcal{L}^{GF}_{\cap[0:n+k)}$ in terms of the basis profile and the volume of $\mathcal{L}^{GF}$. Together with the GSA and a simple bound for $\mathrm{vol}(\mathcal{L}^{GF})$ we can then apply Minkowski's bound on the first minimum. By optimising $\kappa = n + k - \beta$ we obtain our new asymptotic estimate.

Intersection. To understand the behaviour of the volume of the intersected lattice we first need a small technical Lemma.

Lemma 3.2 ([DDGR20]). *Given a lattice $\mathcal{L}$ with volume $\mathrm{vol}(\mathcal{L})$, and a primitive vector $\mathbf{v}$ with respect to $\mathcal{L}^*$. Let $\mathbf{v}^\perp$ denote the subspace orthogonal to $\mathbf{v}$. Then $\mathcal{L} \cap \mathbf{v}^\perp$ is a lattice with volume $\mathrm{vol}(\mathcal{L} \cap \mathbf{v}^\perp) = \|\mathbf{v}\| \cdot \mathrm{vol}(\mathcal{L})$.*

The following Lemma generalises the Pataki–Tural Lemma on which the estimate of Kirchner–Fouque is based. More specifically the Pataki–Tural Lemma only considers the case where the intersection is always trivial ($s = 0$).

Lemma 3.3 (Generalisation of [PT08]). *Let $\mathcal{L}$ be a d-dimensional lattice with basis $\mathbf{b}_0, \ldots, \mathbf{b}_{d-1}$, and consider the sublattice $\mathcal{L}_{[0:s)}$. For any n-dimensional sublattice $\mathcal{L}' \subset \mathcal{L}$ we have*

$$\mathrm{vol}(\mathcal{L}_{[0:s)} \cap \mathcal{L}') \leqslant \mathrm{vol}(\mathcal{L}') \cdot \left(\min_J \prod_{j \in J} \|\mathbf{b}_j^*\| \right)^{-1},$$

where $k := \dim(\mathcal{L}_{[0:s)} \cap \mathcal{L}')$ and J ranges over the $(n-k)$-size subsets of $\{s, \ldots, d-1\}$.

Proof. We write $\mathcal{L}'_{\cap[0:r)} := \mathcal{L}_{[0:r)} \cap \mathcal{L}'$. For $j = k, \ldots, n$ we define $s_j \in \{s, \ldots, d\}$ as the maximal index such that $\dim\left(\mathcal{L}'_{\cap[0:s_j)}\right) = j$, i.e. we obtain the following strict chain of sublattices:

$$\mathcal{L}'_{\cap[0:s)} = \mathcal{L}'_{\cap[0:s_k)} \subsetneq \mathcal{L}'_{\cap[0:s_{k+1})} \subsetneq \cdots \subsetneq \mathcal{L}'_{\cap[0:s_n)} = \mathcal{L}'.$$

Fix $j \in \{k, \ldots, n-1\}$. Because the basis vectors $\mathbf{b}_0, \ldots, \mathbf{b}_{d-1}$ are linearly independent we have that $\mathcal{L}'_{\cap[0:s_{(j+1)})} = \mathcal{L}'_{\cap[0:s_j+1)}$. This allows us to focus on the volume decrease from index $s_j + 1$ to s_j, for which we know that

$$\mathcal{L}'_{\cap[0:s_j)} = \mathcal{L}'_{\cap[0:s_j+1)} \cap (\mathbf{b}^*_{s_j})^\perp,$$

where $(\mathbf{b}^*_{s_j})^\perp$ denotes the subspace orthogonal to $\mathbf{b}^*_{s_j}$. The corresponding dual basis of $\mathbf{b}_0, \ldots, \mathbf{b}_{s_j}$ contains a dual vector $\mathbf{d} \in \mathcal{L}^*_{[0:s_j+1)}$ of length $\left\|\mathbf{b}^*_{s_j}\right\|^{-1}$ with $\mathrm{span}(\mathbf{d}) = \mathrm{span}(\mathbf{b}^*_{s_j})$. Let π be the orthogonal projection onto $\mathrm{span}\big(\mathcal{L}'_{\cap[0:s_j+1)}\big)$, then $\pi(\mathbf{d}) \in \big(\mathcal{L}'_{\cap[0:s_j+1)}\big)^*$. Let $m \in \mathbb{Z}_{\geqslant 1}$ be such that $\pi(\mathbf{d})/m$ is primitive w.r.t. $\big(\mathcal{L}'_{\cap[0:s_j+1)}\big)^*$, then by Lemma 3.2 we obtain:

$$\mathrm{vol}\left(\mathcal{L}'_{\cap[0:s_j)}\right) = \mathrm{vol}\left(\mathcal{L}'_{\cap[0:s_j+1)}\right) \cdot \|\pi(\mathbf{d})/m\| \leqslant \mathrm{vol}\left(\mathcal{L}'_{\cap[0:s_{j+1})}\right) \cdot \left\|\mathbf{b}^*_{s_j}\right\|^{-1}.$$

We conclude the proof by chaining the above inequality for $j = k, \ldots, n-1$. □

Before recovering a dense lattice vector we heuristically assume that there is no special relation between the current lattice basis and the dense sublattice. More specific we can consider that the span of $\mathbf{b}_0, \ldots, \mathbf{b}_{n-1}$ and that of $\mathcal{L}^{GF}$ behave like random n-dimensional subspaces, and thus they have a trivial intersection with high probability in the $2n$-dimensional space. As a direct result we have that $\dim\left(\mathcal{L}^{GF}_{\cap[0:n+k)}\right) = k$ for $k = 0, \ldots, n$. Applying this to Lemma 3.3 we obtain the following corollary.

Corollary 3.4. *Let $\mathcal{L}^{H,q}$ be an NTRU lattice with dense sublattice $\mathcal{L}^{GF}$ of dimension n, if $\dim\left(\mathcal{L}^{GF}_{\cap[0:n+k)}\right) = k$ for some $k \geqslant 0$, then*

$$\mathrm{vol}\left(\mathcal{L}^{GF}_{\cap[0:n+k)}\right) \leqslant \mathrm{vol}\left(\mathcal{L}^{GF}\right) \cdot \left(\prod_{j=n+k}^{d-1} \|\mathbf{b}_j^*\|\right)^{-1}.$$

Note that Corollary 3.4 already shows that the new estimate can not be worse than the Kirchner–Fouque Estimate. Namely if the Kirchner–Fouque Estimate is triggered, then for intersection dimension $k = 1$ the right hand side is smaller than $\|\mathbf{b}_n^*\|$. Assuming a non-decreasing profile we then have $\lambda_1\left(\mathcal{L}^{GF}_{\cap[0:n+1)}\right) = \mathrm{vol}\left(\mathcal{L}^{GF}_{\cap[0:n+1)}\right) \leqslant \|\mathbf{b}_n^*\| \leqslant \left\|\mathbf{b}_{n+1-\beta}^*\right\|$, which implies that BKZ-β would find a dense sublattice vector in this block (or earlier).

Volume Dense Sublattice. To use Corollary 3.4 we also need to bound the volume of the dense sublattice $\mathcal{L}^{GF}$. Because the secret basis is close to orthogonal the Hadamard Inequality $\mathrm{vol}(\mathcal{L}^{GF}) \leqslant \|(\boldsymbol{g}|\boldsymbol{f})\|^n$ is sufficient as a first order approximation.

Conclusion. To obtain a heuristic asymptotic estimate we will assume that before finding a dense lattice vector the basis follows the ZGSA shape.

Claim 3.5. *The BKZ algorithm with blocksize $\beta = \mathcal{B}n$ applied to an NTRU instance with parameters $q = \Theta(n^{\mathcal{Q}}), \|(\boldsymbol{g}|\boldsymbol{f})\| = O(n^{\mathcal{S}})$ triggers the DSD event if*

$$\mathcal{B} = \frac{8\mathcal{S}}{\mathcal{Q}^2 + 1} + o(1).$$

Justification. By the Hadamard Inequality we have $\ln(\mathrm{vol}(\mathcal{L}^{GF})) \leqslant \mathcal{S} n \ln(n) + O(n)$. Let $k := \mathcal{K}n > 0$. Heuristically we expect that $\dim(\mathcal{L}^{H,q}_{[0:n+k)} \cap \mathcal{L}^{GF}) = k$, and thus by Corollary 3.4 and by assuming the ZGSA we obtain a bound on the volume of the intersected sublattice:

$$\begin{aligned}\ln(\mathrm{vol}(\mathcal{L}^{H,q}_{[0:n+k)} \cap \mathcal{L}^{GF})) &\leqslant \mathcal{S} n \ln(n) - \frac{1}{2} \sum_{i=n+k}^{n+m-1} \left(\mathcal{Q} + \frac{2n-1-2i}{\mathcal{B}n}\right) \ln(n) + O(n) \\ &= \mathcal{S} n \ln(n) - \frac{(\mathcal{B}\mathcal{Q} - 2\mathcal{K})^2}{8\mathcal{B}} n \ln(n) + O(n)\end{aligned}$$

By Minkowski's bound we bound the first minimum using the above volume

$$\ln(\lambda_1(\mathcal{L}^{\boldsymbol{H},q}_{[0:n+k)} \cap \mathcal{L}^{GF})) \leqslant \frac{1}{2}\ln(\mathcal{K}n) + \frac{\ln(\mathrm{vol}(\mathcal{L}^{\boldsymbol{H},q}_{[0:n+k)} \cap \mathcal{L}^{GF}))}{\mathcal{K}n} + O(1)$$
$$\leqslant \left(-\frac{(\mathcal{B}\mathcal{Q}-2\mathcal{K})^2}{8\mathcal{B}\mathcal{K}} + \frac{\mathcal{S}}{\mathcal{K}} + \frac{1}{2}\right)\ln(n) + O(1).$$

After projecting onto the block $[n+k-\beta : n+k)$ the above short vector does not increase in length.[7] BKZ detects the projected dense lattice vector in this block if the length is less than $\|\mathbf{b}^*_{n+k-\beta}\| = \left(\frac{1}{2}\mathcal{Q} + \frac{\mathcal{B}-\mathcal{K}}{\mathcal{B}}\right)\ln(n) + O(1)$. Solving for $\mathcal{B}$ shows that this is the case when

$$\mathcal{B} \geqslant \frac{2\sqrt{(2\mathcal{S}-\mathcal{K})^2 + \mathcal{K}^2\mathcal{Q}^2} + 2(2\mathcal{S}-\mathcal{K})}{\mathcal{Q}^2}.$$

When $\mathcal{K} = \frac{4\mathcal{S}}{\mathcal{Q}^2+1}$ the right hand side is minimised and we obtain that BKZ detects the projected dense lattice vector when $\mathcal{B} \geqslant \frac{8\mathcal{S}}{\mathcal{Q}^2+1}$, which concludes the claim. This routine computation can be verified symbolically via our sage notebook `claim3_5.ipynb`. △

Our new estimate gives an asymptotic improvement over the Kirchner–Fouque Estimate ($\frac{8\mathcal{S}}{\mathcal{Q}^2}$). Asymptotically the optimal position is at $\kappa = n+k-\beta \approx n - \frac{1}{2}\beta$. Interestingly, if we do not optimize k and only consider $k = O(1)$ we obtain the same asymptotic estimate as Kirchner–Fouque, which again emphasizes that we generalised their analysis.

For the fatigue point we compare the relative blocksize of $\frac{8\mathcal{S}}{\mathcal{Q}^2+1}$ to that of the 2016 Estimate given by $\frac{2\mathcal{Q}}{(\mathcal{Q}+1-\mathcal{S})^2}$ for $\mathcal{S} < 1$ and by $\frac{2}{\mathcal{Q}+2-2\mathcal{S}}$ for $\mathcal{S} \geqslant 1$. For ternary secrets ($\mathcal{S} = \frac{1}{2}$) this narrows down the fatigue point from $q \leqslant n^{2.783+o(1)}$ to $q = n^{2.484+o(1)}$ compared to the Kirchner–Fouque Estimate. This is still far above the (sub)linear parameters used for NTRU encryption schemes, and thus asymptotically we can close the pending question if these parameters fall in the weaker overstretched regime or not. In practice however we do observe fatigue points that are significantly lower than the naive value of $q = n^{2.484}$, which motivates a concrete analysis with concrete predictions (Fig. 2).

4 Concrete Analysis

In this section we consider a concrete analysis of our new DSD-PT estimate, based on simple heuristics, to better predict the behaviour in practice, and to show that our analysis matches experiments and is thus likely to be tight. The first order asymptotics shown in Sect. 3.2 will remain unchanged, but the differences are significant for practical parameters. Again we split the analysis

[7] One may also be concerned that the short vector would collapse to $\mathbf{0}$ after projection onto the block $[n+k-\beta : n+k)$, but this becomes increasingly unlikely as the dimension β of the block grows.

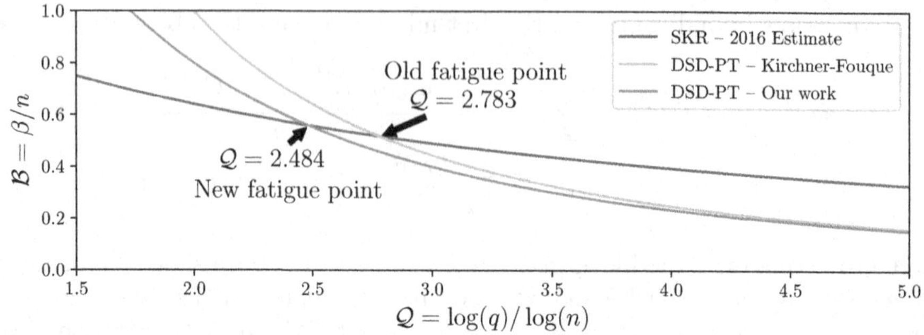

Fig. 2. Comparison of asymptotic estimates and new fatigue point for $n \to \infty$ when the secret key coefficients have standard deviation $\sigma = \Theta(1)$.

into several steps, but now derive heuristic expectations instead of loose upper bounds.

We assume that lattice vectors we encounter follow the Gaussian heuristic, and thus in particular that vectors are spherically distributed after normalisation. When projecting such vectors to a lower dimension they become shorter. The following Lemma shows how much shorter we expect them to become.

Lemma 4.1. *Let $\mathbf{x} \in \mathcal{S}^{d-1}$ follow a spherical distribution, and let $\pi_V : \mathbb{R}^d \to V$ be a projection to some k-dimensional subspace $V \subset \mathbb{R}^d$, then*

$$\mathbb{E}[\ln(\|\pi_V(\mathbf{x})\|)] = \frac{1}{2}(\psi(k/2) - \psi(d/2)).$$

Proof. Let $X_0, \ldots, X_{d-1}$ be standard normal random variables, then the vector $\mathbf{x} = (x_0, \ldots, x_{d-1})$, with $x_j = X_j / \sqrt{\sum_{i=0}^{d-1} X_i^2}$, is spherically distributed. Without loss of generality we can assume that π_V projects onto the first k-coordinates. Then we conclude by Lemma 2.1 that

$$\begin{aligned}\mathbb{E}[\ln(\|\pi_V(\mathbf{x})\|)] &= \frac{1}{2}\mathbb{E}\left[\ln\left(\frac{\sum_{i=0}^{k-1} X_i^2}{\sum_{i=0}^{d-1} X_i^2}\right)\right] \\ &= \frac{1}{2}\mathbb{E}\left[\ln\left(\sum_{i=0}^{k-1} X_i^2\right)\right] - \frac{1}{2}\mathbb{E}\left[\ln\left(\sum_{i=0}^{d-1} X_i^2\right)\right] \\ &= \frac{1}{2}(\psi(k/2) - \psi(d/2)).\end{aligned}$$

□

4.1 Intersection

We start by giving a concrete average-case estimate for the intersection volumes. Assuming that projections behave as random we obtain the following concrete estimate.

Claim 4.2. *Let $\mathcal{L}$ be a $2n$-dimensional NTRU lattice with dense sublattice $\mathcal{L}^{GF}$, before the DSD event is triggered we have for $k = 1, \ldots, n$ that* $\dim\left(\mathcal{L}^{GF}_{\cap[0:n+k)}\right) = k$, *and*

$$\mathbb{E}[\ln \operatorname{vol}(\mathcal{L}^{GF}_{\cap[0:n+k)})] = \ln \operatorname{vol}(\mathcal{L}^{GF}) - \left(\sum_{j=n+k}^{2n-1} \ln \left\|\mathbf{b}_j^*\right\|\right) + \sum_{l=k+1}^{n} \psi\left(\frac{l}{2}\right) - \psi\left(\frac{n+l}{2}\right) + \frac{\zeta'(l)}{\zeta(l)},$$

where $\zeta(l) := \sum_{m=1}^{\infty} \frac{1}{m^l}$ is the Riemann zeta function and $\zeta'(l) := \sum_{m=1}^{\infty} \frac{\ln(m)}{m^l}$ its derivative.

Justification. We follow the proof of Lemma 3.3. It is tight except for the length decrease from $\|\mathbf{d}\|$ to the projected and primitive vector $\|\pi(\mathbf{d})\|/m$. Note that when obtaining $\ln \operatorname{vol}\left(\mathcal{L}^{GF}_{\cap[0:n+l-1)}\right)$ from $\ln \operatorname{vol}\left(\mathcal{L}^{GF}_{\cap[0:n+l)}\right)$ for some $l = k+1, \ldots, n$, the dual vector $\mathbf{d}$ lives in a $(n+l)$-dimensional space and is projected to an l-dimensional space. Heuristically we assume that the normalisation of $\mathbf{d}$ is spherically distributed (or that π projects to a random l-dimensional subspace). By Lemma 4.1 the log-expected decrease in length from this projection then equals

$$\mathbb{E}\left[\ln(\pi(\|\mathbf{d}\|)) - \ln(\|\mathbf{d}\|)\right] = \psi\left(\frac{l}{2}\right) - \psi\left(\frac{n+l}{2}\right).$$

To conclude we also have to include the primitivity of $\pi(\mathbf{d})$ and thus the log-expectation of $m \geqslant 1$ such that $\pi(\mathbf{d})/m$ is primitive. For any basis $\mathbf{d}_0, \ldots, \mathbf{d}_{l-1}$ and $\pi(\mathbf{d}) = \sum_{i=0}^{l-1} x_i \mathbf{d}_i$, we have $m = \gcd(x_0, \ldots, x_{l-1})$. Heuristically we assume that the absolute coefficients $|x_0|, \ldots, |x_{l-1}|$ are random integers in the interval $\{1, \ldots, B\}$ and we let $B \to \infty$. For $l \geqslant 2$ we have (see e.g. [DE+04])

$$\mathbb{P}_{\mathbf{x} \in \{1,\ldots,B\}^l}\left[\gcd(x_0, \ldots, x_{l-1}) = m\right] = \frac{1}{\zeta(l)} \cdot \frac{1}{m^l} + O(\ln(B)/(Bm^{l-1})),$$

where the Riemann zeta function $\zeta(l) = \sum_{m=1}^{\infty} \frac{1}{m^l}$ is just the normalisation factor. From this we conclude that

$$\begin{aligned}\lim_{B\to\infty} \mathbb{E}_{\mathbf{x} \in \{1,\ldots,B\}^l}[\ln \gcd(x_0, \ldots, x_{l-1})] &= \lim_{B\to\infty} \frac{1}{\zeta(l)} \sum_{m=1}^{B} \left[\frac{\ln(m)}{m^l} + O\left(\frac{\ln(m)\ln(B)}{Bm^{l-1}}\right)\right] \\ &= -\frac{\zeta'(l)}{\zeta(l)}\end{aligned}$$

for $l \geqslant k+1 \geqslant 2$. △

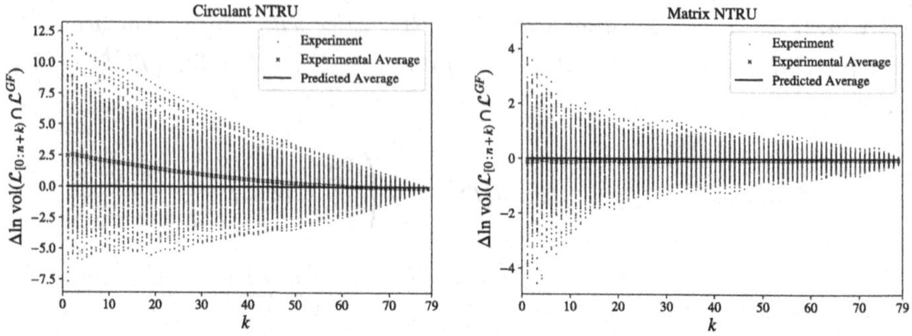

Fig. 3. Experimental values of $\ln \mathrm{vol}\left(\mathcal{L}^{GF}_{\cap[0:n+k)}\right)$ versus Claim 4.2 for circulant and matrix NTRU respectively. For each variant we used 256 LLL reduced NTRU lattices with parameters $q = 257, n = 79, \sigma^2 = \frac{2}{3}$ and computed the intersection for each k.

Validation. To validate Claim 4.2 we computed the actual intersection volumes $\mathrm{vol}\left(\mathcal{L}^{GF}_{\cap[0:n+k)}\right)$ for LLL reduced NTRU instances. We observed here, and also in further experiments, that the dimension assumption $\dim\left(\mathcal{L}^{GF}_{\cap[0:n+k)}\right) = k$ holds before we get close to triggering the DSD event. Figure 3 shows that our prediction perfectly matches the experiments for matrix NTRU. For circulant NTRU we see both that the expectation is slightly off and that the variance is much higher. The higher variance can be explained from the fact that the projections are very much dependent due to the circulant structure; in fact a closer inspection shows that for k close to n the differences with the prediction are highly correlated. We were not able to explain the error in the predicted expectation, but it seems to be caused by the circulant structure in combination with the Z-shape: the error decreased and eventually disappeared for large values of q and σ, for which the Z-shape disappeared (and before the DSD event was triggered). A maximal log-error of 2.5 is reached at $k = 1$. Note that a log-error of ϵ on $\mathrm{vol}\left(\mathcal{L}^{GF}_{\cap[0:n+k)}\right)$ translate into a factor of $e^{\epsilon/k}$ on the predicted length for the shortest vector. Except for very small k, this error appears benign.

4.2 Dense Sublattice

In this section we give a concrete estimate for the expected volume of the dense NTRU sublatice $\mathcal{L}^{GF}$. Directly from the construction we obtain a basis $[\boldsymbol{G}|\boldsymbol{F}]$ of $\mathcal{L}^{GF}$, with $\boldsymbol{F}$ invertible. We consider two cases, that of regular NTRU where $\boldsymbol{F}$ and $\boldsymbol{G}$ are circulant matrices, and that of matrix NTRU, where all entries are independently sampled. For both constructions the entries are sampled from independent discrete Gaussians over $\mathbb{Z}$, with some standard deviation $\sigma > 0$. As the only heuristic we assume that the individual entries in fact follow a *continuous* Gaussian instead of the discrete one.

Matrix NTRU. We start with matrix NTRU, where we heuristically assume that all $2n \times n$ coefficients of the basis $[\boldsymbol{G}|\boldsymbol{F}]$ are sampled according to independent continuous Gaussians with standard deviation σ. Under this heuristic we can derive an exact expression for the expected log-volume of the dense sublattice.

Lemma 4.3. *Let $[\boldsymbol{G}|\boldsymbol{F}]$ be a basis of the lattice $\mathcal{L}^{\boldsymbol{GF}}$ where all sampled entries are i.i.d. continuous Gaussians with standard deviation $\sigma > 0$, then*

$$\mathbb{E}[\ln(\mathrm{vol}(\mathcal{L}^{\boldsymbol{GF}}))] = \frac{1}{2}n\left(\ln(2\sigma^2) + \psi(n)\right) + \sum_{i=0}^{n-1}\left[\psi\left(\frac{2n-i}{2}\right) - \psi(n)\right].$$

Proof. By Lemma 2.1 the log-expectation of the norm of each basis element equals $(\ln(2\sigma^2)+\psi(n))/2$. Note that the i-th Gram-Schmidt vector $\mathbf{b}_i^*$ is obtained after projecting the i-th basis vector orthogonally away from an i-dimensional subspace, and thus onto a $2n-i$ dimensional subspace. However after normalisation the basis vectors follow a spherical distribution and thus by Lemma 4.1 we have

$$\mathbb{E}[\ln \|\mathbf{b}_i^*\|] = (\ln(2\sigma^2) + \psi(n))/2 + \psi\left(\frac{2n-i}{2}\right) - \psi(n).$$

We conclude by noting that $\mathbb{E}[\ln(\mathrm{vol}(\mathcal{L}^{\boldsymbol{GF}}))] = \sum_{i=0}^{n-1}\mathbb{E}[\ln \|\mathbf{b}_i^*\|]$. $\square$

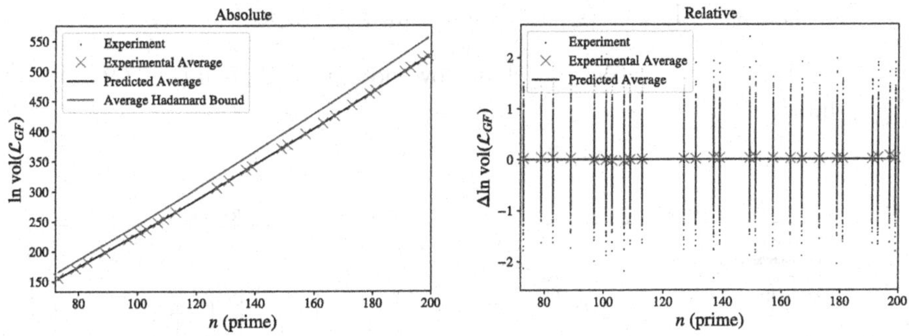

Fig. 4. Experimental values of $\ln(\mathrm{vol}(\mathcal{L}^{\boldsymbol{GF}}))$ versus Lemma 4.3 for matrix NTRU with discrete Gaussians and variance $\sigma^2 = \frac{2}{3}$. For each parameter n we generated 512 instances.

Circulant NTRU. For circulant NTRU both $\boldsymbol{G}$ and $\boldsymbol{F}$ in the basis $[\boldsymbol{G}|\boldsymbol{F}]$ are circulant matrices. Again we replace discrete with continuous Gaussians. The eigenvalues and eigenvectors of a circulant matrix are well known and we use this to obtain an exact expression for the expected volume of the dense sublattice.

Lemma 4.4. *Let $[\boldsymbol{G}|\boldsymbol{F}]$ be a basis of the lattice $\mathcal{L}^{GF}$ where $\boldsymbol{G}, \boldsymbol{F}$ are circulant and all sampled entries are i.i.d. continuous Gaussians with standard deviation $\sigma > 0$, then*

$$\mathbb{E}[\ln(\text{vol}(\mathcal{L}^{GF}))] = \frac{1}{2}n\left(\ln(2n\sigma^2) + \psi(1)\right) + \frac{1}{2}(n-1)(1-\ln(2)).$$

Proof. For $n \times n$ circulant matrices $\boldsymbol{G}, \boldsymbol{F}$ the eigenvectors are identical and given by $\mathbf{v}_j := (1, \omega^j, \omega^{2j}, \omega^{(n-1)j})$ for $j = 0, \ldots, n-1$, where $\omega := e^{2\pi i/n} \in \mathbb{C}$ is a primitive n-th root of unity. Suppose that the circulant matrix $\boldsymbol{G}$ is generated by the vector $\mathbf{c} = (c_0, \ldots, c_{n-1})$, then the corresponding eigenvalues are given by the DFT coefficients of $\mathbf{c}$, namely $\lambda_j := c_0 + c_{n-1}\omega^j + \ldots + c_1\omega^{(n-1)j}$. We have that $\lambda_0 = \sum_{j=0}^{n-1} c_j$, and thus λ_0 follows a Gaussian distribution with variance $n\sigma^2$, and in particular $\lambda_0^2 \sim \chi^2_{1,n\sigma^2}$. Additionally for $j = 1, \ldots, n-1$ we can write $\lambda_j = X + i \cdot Y \in \mathbb{C}$ where $X, Y \in \mathbb{R}$ are both linear combinations of the c_i's and thus (X, Y) follows a jointly Gaussion distribution. A simple computation shows that X and Y both have variance $n\sigma^2/2$ and that they are uncorrelated, which for Gaussians implies that they are independent [PS89, p. 212]. So $|\lambda_j|^2 = X^2 + Y^2 \sim \chi^2_{2,n\sigma^2/2}$. Note that all circulant matrices have the same eigenvectors and thus the squared singular values of the concatenation of two circulant matrices are the sum of the squared absolute eigenvalues. So $[\boldsymbol{G}|\boldsymbol{F}]$ has one squared singular value s_0^2 distributed as $\chi^2_{1,n\sigma^2} + \chi^2_{1,n\sigma^2} = \chi^2_{2,n\sigma^2}$, and $n-1$ squared singular values $s_1^2, \ldots, s_{n-1}^2$ distributed as $\chi^2_{2,n\sigma^2/2} + \chi^2_{2,n\sigma^2/2} = \chi^2_{4,n\sigma^2/2}$. By Lemma 2.1 they have a log-expectation of

$$\mathbb{E}[\ln s_0^2] = \ln(2n\sigma^2) + \psi(1), \text{ and } \mathbb{E}[\ln s_j^2] = \ln(n\sigma^2) + \psi(2)$$

for $j = 1, \ldots, n-1$. We conclude by noting that $\mathbb{E}[\ln(\text{vol}(\mathcal{L}^{GF}))] = \frac{1}{2}\sum_{i=0}^{n-1} \ln(s_i^2)$. □

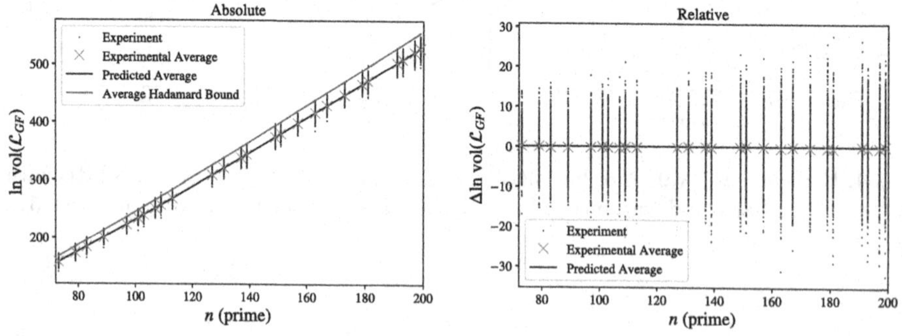

Fig. 5. Experimental values of $\ln(\text{vol}(\mathcal{L}^{GF}))$ versus Lemma 4.4 for circulant NTRU with discrete Gaussians and variance $\sigma^2 = \frac{2}{3}$. For each parameter n we generated 512 instances.

Validation. To validate our concrete estimate for $\mathrm{vol}(\mathcal{L}^{GF})$ we generated the NTRU sublattice for several dimensions and computed its volume. We sample the secret coefficients following a discrete Gaussian with variance $\sigma^2 = \frac{2}{3}$ and ran experiments for both matrix NTRU and circulant NTRU. In Figs. 4 and 5 we see that the predictions from Lemmas 4.3 and 4.4 perfectly fit the observed volumes in all dimensions. We do note that the variance is quite significant for the circulant case, but it can be fully explained by the computed eigenvalue distributions in the proof of Lemma 4.4.

4.3 Further Refinements

We discuss some further refinements, some of which were already successfully applied to the 2016 Estimate [AGVW17, DDGR20, PV21].

Gaussian Heuristic. For our asymptotic analysis we used Minkowski's bound to estimate the length $\lambda_1\left(\mathcal{L}^{GF}_{\cap[0:n+k)}\right)$ in terms of the volume $\mathrm{vol}\left(\mathcal{L}^{GF}_{\cap[0:n+k)}\right)$. A natural way to obtain a concrete estimate for the expected minimal length is by assuming that the intersection $\mathcal{L}^{GF}_{\cap[0:n+k)}$ follows the Gaussian Heuristic and thus for our prediction we assume that

$$\lambda_1\left(\mathcal{L}^{GF}_{\cap[0:n+k)}\right) = \mathrm{gh}(\mathcal{L}^{GF}_{\cap[0:n+k)}) \approx \sqrt{k/(2\pi e)} \cdot \mathrm{vol}\left(\mathcal{L}^{GF}_{\cap[0:n+k)}\right)^{1/k}.$$

We should however be careful with this assumption, as in fact it is false for $k = n$. E.g. the above predicts that $\lambda_1(\mathcal{L}^{GF}) \approx \sqrt{n/(2\pi e)} \cdot \sqrt{2n\sigma^2}$, while we know that $\lambda_1(\mathcal{L}^{GF}) = \|(\boldsymbol{g}, \boldsymbol{f})\| \approx \sqrt{2n\sigma^2}$, a factor $\Theta(\sqrt{n})$ shorter than predicted. The reason for this is that the dense sublattice is up to rotation and scaling very similar to the orthogonal lattice $\mathbb{Z}^n$, precisely the lattice for which it is well known that the Gaussian Heuristic is false. For small $k \ll n$ we do observe that the intersected lattice $\mathcal{L}^{GF}_{\cap[0:s)}$ follows the Gaussian Heuristic; the orthogonal structure seems to be broken by the intersection. However we do not have a clear idea how large k can become before the orthogonal structure returns and the minimal length stops following the prediction from the Gaussian Heuristic. We think this behaviour deserves some further investigation, e.g. if the transition is very sudden or not, and we leave it as an open problem. This near-orthogonality of $\mathcal{L}^{GF}_{\cap[0:s)}$ may be critical to model the DSD-LL events.

Probabilities. So far we have only considered expectations of volumes and projections. While this is enough to give a rough concrete estimate we want to be more precise. Success probabilities can accumulate up over multiple BKZ blocks and (progressive) tours, possibly leading to success at much lower blocksizes than the rough estimate. We continue using the expected values for the volume of the dense sublattice and the intersection volumes to obtain the expected length $\lambda_1(\mathcal{L}^{GF}_{\cap[0:s)})$ of the dense sublattice vector via the Gaussian Heuristic. However we then model the short dense sublattice vector $\mathbf{v} \in \mathcal{L}^{GF}_{\cap[0:s)}$ as an s-dimensional Gaussian vector with the same expected length; allowing us to compute the exact probability that $\|\pi_{s-\beta}(\mathbf{v})\| \leqslant \|\mathbf{b}^*_{s-\beta}\|$ using the CDF of the chi-square distribution with β degrees of freedom.

Up to now we have ignored the probability that after $\pi_{s-\beta}(\mathbf{v})$ is inserted, it is also correctly lifted to the full vector $\mathbf{v}$ by later BKZ tours. While this almost always happens for higher blocksizes, it is not so likely for lower blocksizes, and ignoring this leads to overly optimistic predictions. For BKZ-β to successfully lift or *eventually* pull the vector $\mathbf{v}$ to the front it should also satisfy $\|\pi_i(\mathbf{v})\| \leqslant \|\mathbf{b}^*_i\|$ for all $i = s - 2\beta + 1, s - 3\beta + 2, \ldots$. These conditions are not independent which makes them hard to compute exactly. We simplify the computation by only considering the dependence for consecutive positions $i, i - \beta + 1$ as done in [DDGR20]. We iteratively run our estimator for progressive $\beta = 2, 3, \ldots$ and take account of all probabilities assuming that all tours behave completely independently. Our new concrete estimate will be the expected successful blocksize. Additionally this allows us to combine both the (probabilistic) SKR 2016 Estimate and our new DSD-PT estimate in a single estimator. With some more administration we can also predict the distribution of the successful location κ, and predict the probability that the SKR event happens before the DSD event.

BKZ Shape for Low Blocksizes. While the formulas for the (Z)GSA slope α_β and the expected first minimum $\mathrm{gh}(\beta)$ convert to the experimental values for large blocksizes of say $\beta \geqslant 50$, they are not as accurate for small β. As expected the convergence is worse for progressive BKZ when we only use a few tours of each blocksize. We ran some experiment on random low dimensional q-ary lattices to obtain practical estimates for $\mathrm{gh}(\beta)$ with $\beta \leqslant 50$. Earlier works about the 2016 Estimate resorted to BKZ simulators to predict the BKZ shape, which account for the number of tours and also the special shape of the head and tail that do not perfectly follow the GSA shape. Together with the earlier mentioned refinements this resulted in very precise predictions [DDGR20,PV21]. However how BKZ acts on a Z-shaped basis is much less understood [AD21] and as of yet there are no accurate BKZ simulators. Understanding the behaviour and creating an accurate simulator would be very interesting, but is out of the scope of this work. We continue using the ZGSA, but we resort to experimental values for α_β obtained by running BKZ on random q-ary lattices for large q. To remain consistent we also do not use a simulator for the GSA shape, and accept the small discrepancy between the predictions and practical experiments.

5 Experimental Verification

In this section we experamentally confirm our predicitions. Further detailed experimental data and discussion is given in the eprint version[8].

5.1 Successful Blocksize

We start with comparing our concrete predictions to the preliminary experiment from Sect. 3.1. We ran progressive BKZ with 8 tours on matrix NTRU instances

[8] Section 5.2 in https://eprint.iacr.org/2021/999.

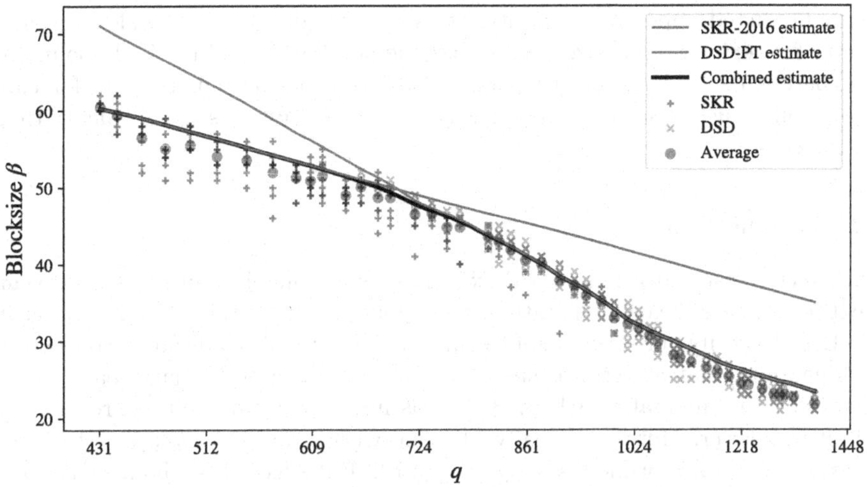

Fig. 6. Experiment versus prediction for progressive BKZ with 8 tours on matrix NTRU instances with parameters $n = 127, \sigma^2 = \frac{2}{3}$ for several moduli q. We did 10 runs per modulus q.

with parameters $n = 127, \sigma^2 = \frac{2}{3}$ for several moduli q. In Fig. 6 we show the blocksizes at which the SKR or DSD event is first detected, and compare them to our concrete estimator. We ran the estimator three times for each modulus q: only accounting for SKR, only accounting for DSD-PT, and accounting for both. Note that the combined estimate can be strictly lower than both the first two because the probabilities to succeed accumulate over both events. We calibrated the values of α_β by running the same BKZ routine on $(2 \cdot 127)$-dimensional q-ary lattices with $q \approx 2^{20}$.

We observe that the experiments match the estimates reasonably well, with an average blocksize error of less than 2 for the DSD events and less than 3 for the SKR events. We shortly discuss potential sources of the small errors error.

- We do not actually run the classical BKZ algorithm, but the BKZ 2.0 algorithm as it is more feasible to run for large blocksizes. One part of the latter algorithm is that in each BKZ block $[\kappa : \kappa + \beta)$ the last $\beta - 1$ vectors are randomised before finding a short projected vector. This temporarily breaks the GSA shape and results a small 'bump' in the profile that is pushed to the right during a tour. On average we measured at the SKR events a log-increase of 0.048 on the value of $\|\mathbf{b}_\kappa^*\|$ compared to the GSA (while the rest of the basis matches very closely). Although anecdotal, adjusting our estimator with this offset of 0.048 resulted in very close predictions for the SKR events.
- For small blocksizes $\beta \leqslant 30$ we see that our DSD-PT estimate is slightly pessimistic compared to the experiments. However the successful profile slope α_β (computed from the profile at the moment of detection) does closely match

the predicted slope $\alpha_{\beta_{pred}}$, pointing to a wrong calibration of the slope parameter for very low blocksizes. Note that the non-flat part of the Z-shape in our experiments has size less than the $2 \cdot 127$ dimensional lattice used for calibration, which plausibly explain why the slope converges more quickly than expected.

5.2 Fatigue Point

Our concrete estimator follows the experiments reasonably well and thus we can use it to estimate the concrete fatigue point for dimensions that are not feasible in practice. To verify our estimate of the fatigue point we also did some experiments in dimensions that are still feasible. For this we ran a *soft* binary search, only decreasing the interval length by 3/4 so as not view a probabilistic result as a definitive answer. More specifically, starting with a range of $[q_{\min}, q_{\max}]$ we ran an experiment for a prime $q \approx (q_{\min} + q_{\max})/2$. If it succeeds with an SKR event we update $q_{\min}$ to $(q_{\min} + q)/2 + 1$, if it succeeds with a DSD event we update $q_{\max}$ to $(q_{\max} + q)/2 - 1$. We repeat this until the interval does not contain any prime and we return $(q_{\min} + q_{\max})/2$ as a rough estimate of the fatigue point. We averaged this over 20 experiments for each parameter n. We chose for matrix NTRU because of the lower variance in the hardness of these instances.

We compared this to our prediction. Because the estimator accounts for probabilities of events, we can predict for which value of q about 50% of the instances succeeds with a DSD event. Because it would be unreasonable to calibrate the

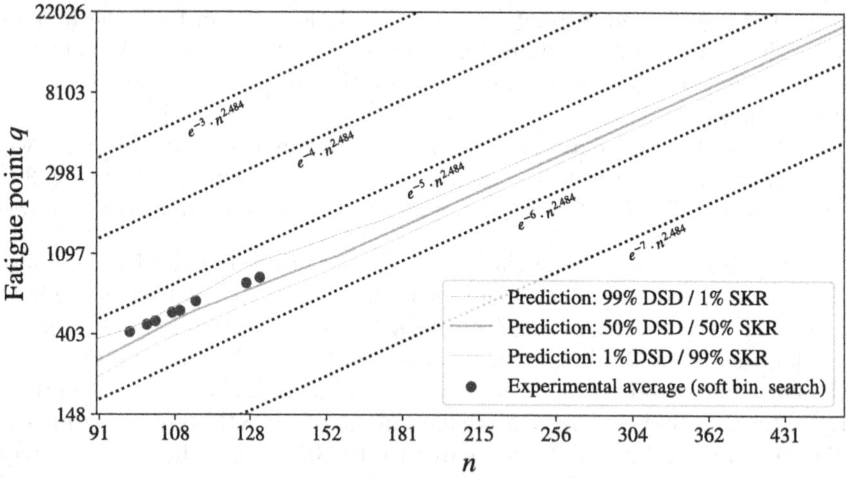

Fig. 7. Concrete fatigue point versus asymptotics using progressive BKZ with 8 tours on matrix NTRU instances with variance $\sigma^2 = \frac{2}{3}$. The 0.5 percentile line shows for which q we estimate that the DSD event is triggered before the SKR event for about 50% of the instances.

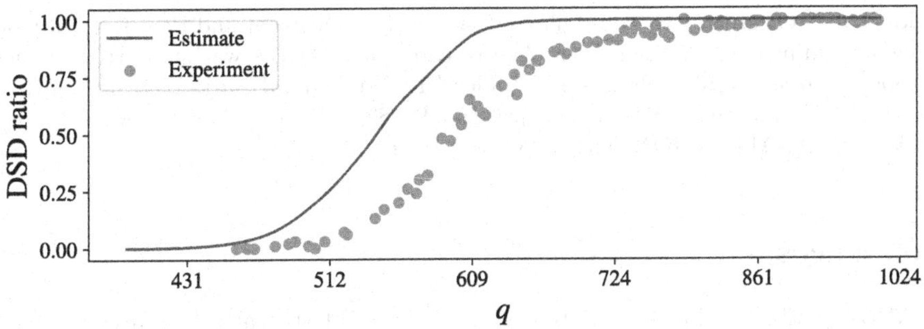

Fig. 8. Experiment versus prediction for progressive BKZ with 8 tours on matrix NTRU instances with parameters $n = 113, \sigma^2 = \frac{2}{3}$ for several moduli q. We did 100 runs per modulus q and the plot shows the ratio of these runs succeeding with a DSD event (before an SKR event).

low blocksize slope values α_β for each dimension we reused those of the $2 \cdot 127$ dimensional q-ary lattice from an earlier experiment. This might make the estimates a bit less precise for $n \ll 127$, and $n \gg 127$ if the successful blocksize is small around the fatigue point.

The results are shown in Fig. 7 and plotted against $Cn^{2.484}$ for several constants C. Remarkably the experiments and concrete predictions closely follow the asymptotics already for reasonably small values of n. A loglog-linear regression of the 50% DSD-PT estimate over all primes $199, \ldots, 499$ gives $0.0034 \cdot n^{2.506}$. Restricting the exponent to 2.484 gives $0.0038 \cdot n^{2.484}$ with a log-standard deviation of only 0.006.

The experimental average appears slightly higher than the estimator prediction for 50% DSD - 50% SKR. The main reason for this seems to be that the estimator is slightly pessimistic for detecting the SKR event, as already observed and explained in Sect. 5.1. Another small detail is that the binary search is slightly biased to higher values of q because at each iteration we pick the *next* prime after $(q_{\min} + q_{\max})/2$.

5.3 Zoom on the Fatigue Point: A Smooth Probabilistic Transition

We take a closer look at the transition from the non-overstretched to the overstretched regime. For this we ran several experiments on matrix NTRU instances with parameters $n = 113, \sigma^2 = \frac{2}{3}$ for several moduli q, with 100 runs each. We compare the DSD success ratio with our probabilistic concrete estimate. The results are shown in Fig. 8. Just as in Fig. 7 we see a shift between the experiment and prediction, which can again be explained by our SKR estimator being too pessimistic. Note however that while the discrepancy looks significant in this zoomed plot, it only emphasises a small error of about 2 block sizes between the experiments and our predictions. Ignoring this shift the shape of the predicted transition matches the experiments very well.

Acknowledgements. We would like to thank Martin Albrecht and Paul Kirchner for valuable comments and discussions. The research of L. Ducas was supported by the European Union's H2020 Programme under PROMETHEUS project (grant 780701) and the ERC-StG-ARTICULATE project (no. 947821). W. van Woerden is funded by the ERC-ADG-ALGSTRONGCRYPTO project (no. 740972).

References

[ABD16] Albrecht, M., Bai, S., Ducas, L.: A subfield lattice attack on overstretched NTRU assumptions. In: Robshaw, M., Katz, J. (eds.) CRYPTO 2016. LNCS, vol. 9814, pp. 153–178. Springer, Heidelberg (2016). https://doi.org/10.1007/978-3-662-53018-4_6

[AD21] Albrecht, M., Ducas, L.: Lattice attacks on NTRU and LWE: a history of refinements. Cryptology ePrint Archive, Report 2021/799 (2021). https://eprint.iacr.org/2021/799

[ADPS16] Alkim, E., Ducas, L., Pöppelmann, T., Schwabe, P.: Post-quantum key exchange - a new hope. In: USENIX Security 2016, pp. 327–343. USENIX Association (2016)

[AGVW17] Albrecht, M.R., Göpfert, F., Virdia, F., Wunderer, T.: Revisiting the expected cost of solving uSVP and applications to LWE. In: Takagi, T., Peyrin, T. (eds.) ASIACRYPT 2017. LNCS, vol. 10624, pp. 297–322. Springer, Cham (2017). https://doi.org/10.1007/978-3-319-70694-8_11

[Ajt99] Ajtai, M.: Generating hard instances of the short basis problem. In: Wiedermann, J., van Emde Boas, P., Nielsen, M. (eds.) ICALP 1999. LNCS, vol. 1644, pp. 1–9. Springer, Heidelberg (1999). https://doi.org/10.1007/3-540-48523-6_1

[AWHT16] Aono, Y., Wang, Y., Hayashi, T., Takagi, T.: Improved progressive BKZ algorithms and their precise cost estimation by sharp simulator. In: Fischlin, M., Coron, J.-S. (eds.) EUROCRYPT 2016. LNCS, vol. 9665, pp. 789–819. Springer, Heidelberg (2016). https://doi.org/10.1007/978-3-662-49890-3_30

[BBC+20] Bernstein, D.J., et al.: NTRU Prime. Technical report, National Institute of Standards and Technology (2020)

[BEF+17] Biasse, J.-F., Espitau, T., Fouque, P.-A., Gélin, A., Kirchner, P.: Computing generator in cyclotomic integer rings. In: Coron, J.-S., Nielsen, J.B. (eds.) EUROCRYPT 2017. LNCS, vol. 10210, pp. 60–88. Springer, Cham (2017). https://doi.org/10.1007/978-3-319-56620-7_3

[BLLN13] Bos, J.W., Lauter, K., Loftus, J., Naehrig, M.: Improved security for a ring-based fully homomorphic encryption scheme. In: Stam, M. (ed.) IMACC 2013. LNCS, vol. 8308, pp. 45–64. Springer, Heidelberg (2013). https://doi.org/10.1007/978-3-642-45239-0_4

[BSW18] Bai, S., Stehlé, D., Wen, W.: Measuring, simulating and exploiting the head concavity phenomenon in BKZ. In: Peyrin, T., Galbraith, S. (eds.) ASIACRYPT 2018. LNCS, vol. 11272, pp. 369–404. Springer, Cham (2018). https://doi.org/10.1007/978-3-030-03326-2_13

[CDH+20] Chen, C., et al.: NTRU. Technical report, National Institute of Standards and Technology (2020)

[CDPR16] Cramer, R., Ducas, L., Peikert, C., Regev, O.: Recovering short generators of principal ideals in cyclotomic rings. In: Fischlin, M., Coron, J.-S. (eds.) EUROCRYPT 2016. LNCS, vol. 9666, pp. 559–585. Springer, Heidelberg (2016). https://doi.org/10.1007/978-3-662-49896-5_20

[CG05] Coglianese, M., Goi, B.-M.: MaTRU: a new NTRU-based cryptosystem. In: Maitra, S., Veni Madhavan, C.E., Venkatesan, R. (eds.) INDOCRYPT 2005. LNCS, vol. 3797, pp. 232–243. Springer, Heidelberg (2005). https://doi.org/10.1007/11596219_19

[CJL16] Cheon, J.H., Jeong, J., Lee, C.: An algorithm for NTRU problems and cryptanalysis of the ggh multilinear map without a low-level encoding of zero. LMS J. Comput. Math. 19(A), 255–266 (2016)

[CN11] Chen, Y., Nguyen, P.Q.: BKZ 2.0: better lattice security estimates. In: Lee, D.H., Wang, X. (eds.) ASIACRYPT 2011. LNCS, vol. 7073, pp. 1–20. Springer, Heidelberg (2011). https://doi.org/10.1007/978-3-642-25385-0_1

[CS97] Coppersmith, D., Shamir, A.: Lattice attacks on NTRU. In: Fumy, W. (ed.) EUROCRYPT 1997. LNCS, vol. 1233, pp. 52–61. Springer, Heidelberg (1997). https://doi.org/10.1007/3-540-69053-0_5

[DDGR20] Dachman-Soled, D., Ducas, L., Gong, H., Rossi, M.: LWE with side information: attacks and concrete security estimation. In: Micciancio, D., Ristenpart, T. (eds.) CRYPTO 2020. LNCS, vol. 12171, pp. 329–358. Springer, Cham (2020). https://doi.org/10.1007/978-3-030-56880-1_12

[DE+04] Diaconis, P., Erdös, P., et al.: On the distribution of the greatest common divisor. In: A festschrift for Herman Rubin, pp. 56–61. Institute of Mathematical Statistics (2004)

[DKR+20] D'Anvers, J.: SABER. Technical report, National Institute of Standards and Technology (2020)

[dt21a] The FPLLL development team. FPLLL, a lattice reduction library, Version: 5.4.1 (2021). https://github.com/fplll/fplll

[dt21b] The FPLLL development team. fpylll, a Python wraper for the fplll lattice reduction library, Version: 0.5.6 (2021). https://github.com/fplll/fpylll

[EHKS14] Eisenträger, K., Hallgren, S., Kitaev, A., Song, F.: A quantum algorithm for computing the unit group of an arbitrary degree number field. In: 46th ACM STOC, pp. 293–302. ACM Press (2014)

[GGH13] Garg, S., Gentry, C., Halevi, S.: Candidate multilinear maps from ideal lattices. In: Johansson, T., Nguyen, P.Q. (eds.) EUROCRYPT 2013. LNCS, vol. 7881, pp. 1–17. Springer, Heidelberg (2013). https://doi.org/10.1007/978-3-642-38348-9_1

[GGH+19] Genise, N., Gentry, C., Halevi, S., Li, B., Micciancio, D.: Homomorphic encryption for finite automata. In: Galbraith, S.D., Moriai, S. (eds.) ASIACRYPT 2019. LNCS, vol. 11922, pp. 473–502. Springer, Cham (2019). https://doi.org/10.1007/978-3-030-34621-8_17

[GS02] Gentry, C., Szydlo, M.: Cryptanalysis of the revised NTRU signature scheme. In: Knudsen, L.R. (ed.) EUROCRYPT 2002. LNCS, vol. 2332, pp. 299–320. Springer, Heidelberg (2002). https://doi.org/10.1007/3-540-46035-7_20

[HPS98] Hoffstein, J., Pipher, J., Silverman, J.H.: NTRU: a ring-based public key cryptosystem. In: Buhler, J.P. (ed.) ANTS 1998. LNCS, vol. 1423, pp. 267–288. Springer, Heidelberg (1998). https://doi.org/10.1007/BFb0054868

[KF17] Kirchner, P., Fouque, P.-A.: Revisiting lattice attacks on overstretched NTRU parameters. In: Coron, J.-S., Nielsen, J.B. (eds.) EUROCRYPT 2017. LNCS, vol. 10210, pp. 3–26. Springer, Cham (2017). https://doi.org/10.1007/978-3-319-56620-7_1

[LLL82] Lenstra, A.K., Lenstra, H.W., Jr., Lovász, L.: Factoring polynomials with rational coefficients. Mathematische Annalen **261**(4), 515–534 (1982)

[LPR13] Lyubashevsky, V., Peikert, C., Regev, O.: On ideal lattices and learning with errors over rings. J. ACM **60**(6), 43:1–43:35 (2013). Preliminary version in Eurocrypt 2010

[LW20] Lee, C., Wallet, A.: Lattice analysis on MiNTRU problem. Cryptology ePrint Archive, Report 2020/230 (2020). https://eprint.iacr.org/2020/230

[MS01] May, A., Silverman, J.H.: Dimension reduction methods for convolution modular lattices. In: Silverman, J.H. (ed.) CaLC 2001. LNCS, vol. 2146, pp. 110–125. Springer, Heidelberg (2001). https://doi.org/10.1007/3-540-44670-2_10

[PAA+19] Poppelmann, T., et al.: NewHope. Technical report, National Institute of Standards and Technology (2019)

[PS89] Papoulis, A., Saunders, H.: Probability, random variables and stochastic processes (1989)

[PT08] Pataki, G., Tural, M.: On sublattice determinants in reduced bases. arXiv preprint arXiv:0804.4014 (2008)

[PV21] Postlethwaite, E.W., Virdia, F.: On the success probability of solving unique SVP via BKZ. In: Garay, J.A. (ed.) PKC 2021. LNCS, vol. 12710, pp. 68–98. Springer, Cham (2021). https://doi.org/10.1007/978-3-030-75245-3_4

[Reg04] Regev, O.: Quantum computation and lattice problems. SIAM J. Comput. **33**(3), 738–760 (2004). Preliminary version in FOCS 2002

[Reg05] Regev, O., et al.: On lattices, learning with errors, random linear codes, and cryptography. In: 37th ACM STOC, pp. 84–93. ACM Press (2005)

[SAB+20] Schwabe, P., et al.: CRYSTALS-KYBER. Technical report, National Institute of Standards and Technology (2020)

[Sch87] Schnorr, C.-P.: A hierarchy of polynomial time lattice basis reduction algorithms. Theor. Comput. Sci. **53**, 201–224 (1987)

[SS11] Stehlé, D., Steinfeld, R.: Making NTRU as secure as worst-case problems over ideal lattices. In: Paterson, K.G. (ed.) EUROCRYPT 2011. LNCS, vol. 6632, pp. 27–47. Springer, Heidelberg (2011). https://doi.org/10.1007/978-3-642-20465-4_4

[SSTX09] Stehlé, D., Steinfeld, R., Tanaka, K., Xagawa, K.: Efficient public key encryption based on ideal lattices. In: Matsui, M. (ed.) ASIACRYPT 2009. LNCS, vol. 5912, pp. 617–635. Springer, Heidelberg (2009). https://doi.org/10.1007/978-3-642-10366-7_36

[YD17] Yu, Y., Ducas, L.: Second order statistical behavior of LLL and BKZ. In: Adams, C., Camenisch, J. (eds.) SAC 2017. LNCS, vol. 10719, pp. 3–22. Springer, Cham (2018). https://doi.org/10.1007/978-3-319-72565-9_1

Faster Dual Lattice Attacks for Solving LWE with Applications to CRYSTALS

Qian Guo(✉) and Thomas Johansson(✉)

Department of Electrical and Information Technology, Lund University, P.O. Box 118, 221 00 Lund, Sweden
{qian.guo,thomas.johansson}@eit.lth.se

Abstract. Cryptosystems based on the learning with errors (LWE) problem are assigned a security level that relates to the cost of generic algorithms for solving the LWE problem. This includes at least the so-called primal and dual lattice attacks. In this paper, we present an improvement of the dual lattice attack using an idea that can be traced back to work by Bleichenbacher. We present an improved distinguisher that in combination with a guessing step shows a reduction in the overall complexity for the dual attack on all schemes. Our second contribution is a new two-step lattice reduction strategy that allows the new dual lattice attack to exploit two recent techniques in lattice reduction algorithms, i.e., the "dimensions for free" trick and the trick of producing many short vectors in one sieving. Since the incompatibility of these two tricks was believed to be the main reason that dual attacks are less interesting, our new reduction strategy allows more efficient dual approaches than primal attacks, for important cryptographic parameter sets.

We apply the proposed attacks on CRYSTALS-Kyber and CRYSTALS-Dilithium, two of the finalists in the NIST post-quantum cryptography project and present new lower complexity numbers, both classically and quantumly in the core-SVP model. Most importantly, for the proposed security parameters, our new dual attack with refined lattice reduction strategy greatly improves the state-of-the-art primal attack in the classical gate-count metric, i.e., the classical Random Access Machine (RAM) model, indicating that some parameters are really on the edge for their claimed security level. Specifically, the improvement factor can be as large as 15 bits for Kyber1024 with an extrapolation model (Albrecht et al. at Eurocrypt 2019). Also, we show that Kyber768 could be solved with classical gate complexity below its claimed security level. Last, we apply the new attack to the proposed parameters in a draft version of Homomorphic Encryption Standard (see https://homomorphicencryption.org) and obtain significant gains. For instance, we could solve a parameter set aiming for 192-bit security in $2^{187.0}$ operations in the classical RAM model. Note that these parameters are deployed in well-known Fully Homomorphic Encryption libraries.

Keywords: Lattice-based cryptography · NIST post-quantum cryptography standardization · Dual attacks · CRYSTALS · Learning with errors · Fast fourier transform · Fully homomorphic encryption

M. Tibouchi and H. Wang (Eds.): ASIACRYPT 2021, LNCS 13093, pp. 33–62, 2021.
https://doi.org/10.1007/978-3-030-92068-5_2

1 Introduction

The LWE problem was introduced by Regev [51] and has quickly become one of the main problems in cryptography. One reason is the fear of future quantum computers being able to solve the factoring and discrete log problems efficiently. In the search for new future cryptographic schemes not based on the previous standard problems factoring and discrete log, the LWE problem has received a central role. One advantage for LWE is that this problem is claimed to be as hard as worst-case approximation problems in lattices, such as the shortest vector problem (SVP) [25,49]. Another reason for the importance of LWE is its usefulness in a variety of cryptographic constructions and primitives. This, in particular, includes Fully Homomorphic Encryption (FHE), which is a very important primitive that allows operations on encrypted data without decrypting it. The most efficient FHE schemes today are constructed using LWE or some version of the problem as the underlying difficult problem. Examples of such FHE schemes can be found in [2,4,26,27,36].

Returning to the post-quantum scenario, the need for new cryptographic primitives has been identified and in 2015 NIST started the project which we refer to as the NIST PQC standardization process [5]. The goal was to accept candidates for public-key encryption schemes (PKE), key encapsulation mechanisms (KEM), and digital signature schemes, and then to evaluate their security under the assumption that quantum computations can be done. In the end, a few proposals will be selected for possible standardization. The project has now entered the third round, where in the move to each round the number of candidates has been reduced. Many of the candidates in the project as a whole as well as among the remaining round 3 candidates, are based on some LWE-related problem. The round 3 candidates are split in two groups, being the main and the alternate ones.

Proposals are giving parameters in relation to target security categories. Among the 5 defined security categories, category 1, 3 and 5 correspond to the complexity of exhaustive key search on AES with key size 128, 192, and 256, respectively. A proposal with parameters given for category 1 thus has to meet the requirement that any attack on the scheme requires a complexity larger than or comparable to the complexity of exhaustive key search on AES with key size 128.

Any cryptosystem based on the learning with errors (LWE) problem can be assigned a security level that corresponds to the lowest cost among any possible attack, which includes generic algorithms for solving the LWE problem. Possible algorithms include at least the so-called primal and dual lattice attacks. These attacks make use of the BKZ lattice reduction algorithm [31], which in turn uses as a subroutine a solver for SVP in projected sublattices (also referred to as blocks). Connected to both the primal and dual lattice attacks is the *cost* of performing them, which relates to the cost of running the BKZ algorithm. Due to the somewhat complicated nature of the BKZ algorithm, there has been several different cost models used in previous literature [11]. The cost model can either be an expression for the asymptotic behaviour of the cost of running BKZ, or it can be an attempt to express the actual complexity in number of operations of some kind. As we are interested in the actual complexity, we use cost models for this latter case. Another distinguishing factor is the choice of the subroutine for solving SVP in projected sublattices inside BKZ, which can be either enumeration or lattice sieving [44,45]. Sieving gives the better performance but requires more memory. Established cost models for BKZ are used by designers to evaluate the cost of different attacks on their design which in turn gives an indication of the expected security level.

Briefly, we may describe LWE as the problem of recovering a secret vector $\mathbf{s} \in \mathbb{Z}_q^n$ after receiving $(\mathbf{A}, \mathbf{b})$ for which $\mathbf{b} = \mathbf{A}\mathbf{s} + \mathbf{e}$, where $\mathbf{A}$ is an $m \times n$ matrix with entries in $\mathbb{Z}_q$ and $\mathbf{e} \in \mathbb{Z}_q^m$. It is also assumed that both the noise vector $\mathbf{e}$ as well as the secret $\mathbf{s} \in \mathbb{Z}_q^n$ itself are *small*. It means that the entries are small in relation to $\mathbb{Z}_q = \{\frac{-(q-1)}{2}, \dots, \frac{(q-1)}{2}\}$ (for q odd prime). In the dual attack, the idea is to find short vectors in the dual lattice defined as $\Lambda' = \{(\mathbf{x}, \mathbf{y}) \in \mathbb{Z}^m \times \mathbb{Z}^n : \mathbf{A}^T\mathbf{x} = \mathbf{y} \mod q\}$. For each short vector, denote it $(\mathbf{w}, \mathbf{v})$, we can observe that $\mathbf{w}^T \cdot \mathbf{b} = \mathbf{v}^T \cdot \mathbf{s} + \mathbf{w}^T \cdot \mathbf{e}$ is somewhat small. So with enough short vectors from Λ' we get a distinguisher that can separate whether $\mathbf{b}$ is from the LWE distribution or whether $\mathbf{b}$ is from a uniform distribution. The distinguisher is used in combination with a guessing step where a few entries of the secret $\mathbf{s}$ are guessed and corresponding positions are excluded from $\mathbf{A}$. If the guess is correct, $\mathbf{b}$ will come from the LWE distribution but if the guess is wrong then $\mathbf{b}$ will be from a uniform distribution (or close to). In this way the distinguisher will recover the guessed entries of $\mathbf{s}$ and eventually the full secret is recovered.

1.1 Contributions

In this paper, we present an improvement of the dual lattice attack using an idea that can be traced back to work by Bleichenbacher [22,23] on attacking on ECDSA. We present an improved distinguisher that in combination with a guessing step shows a reduction in the overall complexity for the dual attack on all schemes. This results in a strictly better dual attack than previous ones.

The main idea is to reduce the FFT distinguisher over a very large alphabetic size q to another distinguisher with a very small alphabetic size, say of only size 2 (or 3 for certain proposals where q is not a prime but a power of 2). We design a new mapping technique to map the secret points close to one point in a set of points equally dividing the cycle. Then one can apply the new FFT techniques to accelerate the guessing procedure in a combination of guessing some entries only modulo 2. From an implementation point of view, the transform step can be more efficiently implemented through a Fast Walsh-Hadamard transform (FWHT) instead of the standard FFT approach.

The complexity reduction depends on the attacked scheme. In particular, we apply the proposed dual attack on CRYSTALS-Kyber and CRYSTALS-Dilithium in the NIST post-quantum cryptography project and present new lower complexity numbers measured in the core-SVP model (see the second and the third columns in Table 1).

Table 1. The complexity comparison on the security parameter sets of the round-3 CRYSTALS. Cost is given in $\log_2$ of operations.

	Classical core-SVP		Refined classical attacks (gates)		
	Claim [52]	New	Claim [52]	New	NIST [6]
Kyber512	118	115	151	147	143
Kyber768	182	174	215	**205**	207
Kyber1024	256	243	287	272	272
	Claim [46]	New	Claim [46]	New	NIST [6]
Dilithium-II	123	122	159	154	146
Dilithium-III	182	179	217	210	207
Dilithium-V	252	246	285	274	272

We also investigate the complexity of the new attack in the classic gate-count metric, i.e., the Random Access Machine (RAM) model. This model is more interesting in the NIST Post-Quantum Cryptography Standardization Project because it is difficult to determine if the classical complexity of 2^{174} in the core-SVP model meets the security requirement for NIST-3 defined as 2^{205} classic gates. The official documents of round-3 Kyber and Dilithium set their security parameters by counting the classical gates of primal attacks. One main obstacle is to measure the classic cost in the RAM model of the Nearest Neighbor Search used in lattice sieving, which is addressed by Albrecht et al. in [14]. The designers of Kyber and Dilithium dismiss the dual attack because "..First, most of those vectors are larger by a factor $\sqrt{4/3}$, secondly the trick of exploiting all those vectors is not compatible with the 'dimension for free' trick.." (cited from [46]).

We show in this paper that dual attacks could be more efficient in the classical gate-count metric even if most of short vectors obtained are larger by a factor $\sqrt{4/3}$. Our novel idea is a new two-step lattice reduction strategy that could exploit both the "dimension for free" (d4f) trick and the "exploiting many short vectors in one sieving" (msv) trick. Furthermore, since BKZ typically includes calling an SVP oracle for many times, we can sieve in the second step with a larger dimension to balance the costs of the two steps. From this perspective, we exploit the d4f trick twice and also produce an exponential number of short vectors. Similar to the official documents of CRYSTALS [46,52], we employ the analysis from [14] to evaluate the sieving cost in the classical RAM model.

The classical complexity comparisons in the gate-count metric for CRYSTALS-Kyber and CRYSTALS-Dilithium are shown in the last columns of Table 1. The gain is generally significant and could be as large as 15 bits for Kyber1024; some parameters, therefore, are really on the edge for their claimed security level. Last, we show that Kyber768 could be solved with complexity below its claimed security level in the gate-count metric.

Lastly, we show that the new dual attack with refined lattice reduction strategy could solve certain parameter sets in a draft version of the Homomorphic Encryption Standard [7] faster than the claimed security levels under the classical RAM model.

Remarks. This algorithmic improvement has very wide applications in lattice-based cryptography—lattice-based proposals need to recheck their security parameter sets for the dual attack. It could lead to a security problem if the original security margin is small. On the other hand, the reported complexity numbers in the classical RAM model assume that the cost of one RAM query is constant. These complexity numbers will increase if a more realistic memory access cost model is taken into consideration. Further research on this is beyond the scope of the paper.

1.2 Related Works

There are a few different classes of algorithms for solving LWE problems, see e.g. [16]. The algebraic method of Arora-Ge [18] and its extension using Gröbner basis techniques [8] is a powerful method when applicable. The combinatorial approach called BKW [24] and its many extensions [10,38,41] is another approach that for some parameter choices can be the most efficient solver for LWE. However, in general both these methods require a larger number of samples than what is available in the cryptanalysis of LWE-based constructions of KEMs, signatures, or FHEs. So the security of such constructions is almost always derived by analyzing the cost of attacks based on lattice reduction. These attacks are either the primal attacks, where one finds the solution by solving a decoding problem in the lattice, or reduce it to solving unique SVP [13,44,45].

The second type of lattice attack is the dual lattice attacks [47]. The basic form of the attack builds a distinguisher from many short vectors in the dual lattice. However, by simply guessing a part of the secret this is turned into a recovery of the secret vector. An efficient guessing procedure can be achieved by use of the Fast Fourier Transform [33]. Various improvements can be achieved if the secret is small and sparse [9,28,32], which is often the case in constructions, in particular for FHE constructions.

To the best of our knowledge, Albrecht [9] firstly studied the problem of efficiently producing many short vectors in the dual lattice attacks. He proposed an amortization approach using re-randomization and lattice reductions with a smaller dimension, but his approach is more heuristic and has worse performance compared with our new two-step lattice reduction approach with sieving.

Independently of this work, the paper [35] was recently posted on eprint. This work also considers the dual attack but in our understanding it uses an idea of generating LWE instances with bigger noise that correspond to a fraction of the secret vector, a different approach to the ideas suggested in this paper. Our approach of reducing the FFT distinguisher over a very large alphabetic size q to another distinguisher with a very small alphabetic size have some similarity to work by Bleichenbacher [22] on attacking on ECDSA. In [29] a similar but different reduction was used in connection with implementing the BKW algorithm.

Finally, these attacks can sometimes be used in the form of hybrid lattice reduction attacks as introduced in [40]. Such attacks combine a meet-in-the-middle approach and/or guessing with lattice reduction and this can sometimes be the best attack [28,42,53].

Notes. We found another independent work [21] on eprint (posted on Feb 12, 2021) studying dual attacks on round-3 lattice-based primitives in the core-SVP model. Also focusing on the core-SVP model, a first version of our paper was submitted to Eurocrypt 2021 (with deadline on Oct 8th, 2020). Similar to [35], the work [21] studies exhaustive guessing in the dual lattice attacks. We additionally propose a novel FFT distinuisher to further reduce the solving complexity. Our second main contribution, i.e., a new two-step lattice reduction algorithm allowing us to exploit the recent advances in lattice algorithms, and the corresponding complexity results in the classical RAM model are not discussed in [21,35].

1.3 Organization

The remaining of the paper is organized as follows. We first introduce some preliminaries in Sect. 2, and present the newly proposed FFT distinguisher in Sect. 3. We then apply this new distinguisher to improve the general dual lattice-reduction approach in Sect. 4, which is followed by its applications to CRYSTALS in the core-SVP model in Sect. 5. We then present the new two-step reduction idea and the refined classic attacks beyond the core-SVP estimation in Sect. 6.

Its application to FHE parameters is shown in Sect. 7. The theory is validated by experimental verification in Sect. 8. We lastly conclude the paper in Sect. 9.

2 Preliminaries

We denote vectors in lower-case bold, e.g. $\mathbf{a}$, and matrices in upper-case bold, e.g. $\mathbf{A}$. All vectors are column vectors by default. We denote $\mathbf{a}^T$ (or $\mathbf{A}^T$) its transpose for a vector $\mathbf{a}$ (or matrix $\mathbf{A}$). The matrix $\mathbf{I}_n$ is an identity matrix with dimension $n \times n$. The inner product of two vectors $\mathbf{a}$ and $\mathbf{b}$ with the same dimension is denoted by $\langle \mathbf{a}, \mathbf{b} \rangle$. For a vector $\mathbf{a}$ with dimension n, we denote its i-th entry as a_i, for $0 \leq i \leq n-1$, and define its norm as

$$\|a\| = \sqrt{\sum_{i=0}^{n-1} a_i^2}.$$

For a complex number $x \in \mathbb{C}$, we denote $\mathfrak{Re}(x)$ its real part. Let θ_q be the q-th root of unity, i.e., the complex number $\exp(2\pi i_0/q)$, where $i_0^2 = -1$. We also write it as θ if there is no ambiguity.

2.1 LWE

The Learning with Errors problem is defined as follows.

Definition 1 ([51]). *Let n be a positive integer, q a prime, and let $\mathcal{X}$ be an error distribution. Fix $\mathbf{s}$ to be a secret vector in $\mathbb{Z}_q^n$, chosen according to a uniform distribution. Denote by $L_{\mathbf{s},\mathcal{X}}$ the probability distribution on $\mathbb{Z}_q^n \times \mathbb{Z}_q$ obtained by choosing $\mathbf{a} \in \mathbb{Z}_q^n$ uniformly at random, choosing an error $e \in \mathbb{Z}_q$ according to $\mathcal{X}$ and returning*

$$(\mathbf{a}, z) = (\mathbf{a}, \langle \mathbf{a}, \mathbf{s} \rangle + e)$$

in $\mathbb{Z}_q^n \times \mathbb{Z}_q$. The (search) LWE *problem is to find the secret vector $\mathbf{s}$ given a fixed number of samples from $L_{\mathbf{s},\mathcal{X}}$.*

The definition above gives the *search* LWE problem, and one could similarly define the *decision* LWE problem to distinguish between samples drawn from $L_{\mathbf{s},\mathcal{X}}$ and a uniform distribution on $\mathbb{Z}_q^n \times \mathbb{Z}_q$.

The error distribution $\mathcal{X}$ is usually selected as the discrete Gaussian distribution on $\mathbb{Z}_q$ with mean 0 and variance σ^2, obtained by assigning a probability proportional to $\exp(\frac{-x^2}{2\sigma^2})$ to each $x \in \mathbb{Z}$ and then accumulating the probability mass function over all integers in each residue class modulo q. The error distribution is also denoted as $\mathcal{X}_\sigma$. One useful heuristic assumption is that the sum of two independent random variables X_1 and X_2 drawn from $\mathcal{X}_{\sigma_1}$ and $\mathcal{X}_{\sigma_2}$ respectively is drawn form $\mathcal{X}_{\sqrt{\sigma_1^2+\sigma_2^2}}$.

It is proven in [25] that LWE with small secrets remains hard, so many cryptosystems base their security on these variants such as LWE with *binary* or *ternary* secrets.

2.2 Dual Lattice Attacks

A *lattice* $\mathcal{L}$ is a discrete subgroup of $\mathbb{R}^d$. Let the columns $\mathbf{b}_0, \ldots, \mathbf{b}_{d-1}$ be linearly independent, and then it is a basis of the lattice $\{\sum v_i \mathbf{b}_i | v_i \in \mathbb{Z}\}$. In lattices, a central hard problem is to find a non-zero shortest vector in this lattice, which is called the shortest vector problem (SVP).

In the dual attack, the aim is to find a short vector $(\mathbf{w}, \mathbf{v})$ in the dual lattice $\mathcal{L}' = \{(\mathbf{x}, \mathbf{y}) \in \mathbb{Z}^m \times \mathbb{Z}^n : \mathbf{A}^T\mathbf{x} = \mathbf{y} \mod q\}$. Thus, given a sequence of LWE instances $(\mathbf{A}, \mathbf{b})$ s.t., $\mathbf{b} = \mathbf{A}\mathbf{s} + \mathbf{e}$, we have that

$$\mathbf{w}^T \cdot \mathbf{b} = \mathbf{w}^T \cdot (\mathbf{A}\ \mathbf{I}) \begin{pmatrix} \mathbf{s} \\ \mathbf{e} \end{pmatrix} = (\mathbf{v}^T\ \mathbf{w}^T) \begin{pmatrix} \mathbf{s} \\ \mathbf{e} \end{pmatrix},$$

which is small and can be distinguished from the uniform. Therefore, the problem is transformed to finding a short column vector in the lattice

$$\mathbf{B} = \begin{pmatrix} \mathbf{I}_m & 0 \\ \mathbf{A}^T & q\mathbf{I}_n \end{pmatrix}$$

The efficiency of the dual lattice attacks highly depends on how short the found vectors are. We have the following lemma to measure the advantage of the distinguishing problem.

Lemma 1 ([44]). *Given an LWE instance characterized by* n, q, σ *and a vector* $\mathbf{h}$ *with length* l *such that* $\mathbf{h}^T\mathbf{A} = 0 \pmod q$, *the advantage of distinguishing* $\langle \mathbf{h}, \mathbf{e} \rangle$ *from random is close to*

$$\epsilon = \exp\left(-2\pi^2\tau^2\right),$$

where $\tau = \frac{l\sigma}{q}$.

It is also known from statistical theory that if $\mathcal{O}\left(1/\epsilon^2\right)$ independent such samples are available, the success probability for the distinguisher is close to 1.

2.3 Cost Model for BKZ

To achieve high-quality short vectors, we normally use a class of lattice reduction algorithms called BKZ, an iterative, block-wise algorithm for basis reduction. This algorithm solves an SVP problem with a small dimension β and is denoted $\text{BKZ}_{\beta,d}$, where d is the dimension of the lattice. The time complexity of $\text{BKZ}_{\beta,d}$ is denote $T(\text{BKZ}_{\beta,d})$.

For a lattice $\mathcal{L}$, $\text{BKZ}_{\beta,d}$ produces vectors with length

$$\|v\| = \delta_0^d \cdot vol(\mathcal{L})^{\frac{1}{d}}, \tag{1}$$

where $\delta_0 \approx \left(\frac{\beta}{2\pi e}(\pi\beta)^{\frac{1}{\beta}}\right)^{\frac{1}{2(\beta-1)}}$ (see [30] for details), and $vol(\mathcal{L})$ is defined as the volume of the lattice $\mathcal{L}$.

There are several models to estimate the time complexity of $\text{BKZ}_{\beta,d}$, which are generally classified into two categories depending on the method to implement the SVP solver in the BKZ reduction. Here we mainly focus on the sieving approach, the most relevant one for choosing security parameters ([12,34]).

The first model we discuss is the core-SVP model, which was proposed in [17] and is then used in many candidates in the NIST Post-Quantum Cryptography Standardization Project, such as NewHope [50], CRYSTALS-Kyber [52], and CRYSTALS-Dilithium [46]. In the core-SVP model, the classic complexity of BKZ reduction $T(\text{BKZ}_{\beta,d})$ can be estimated as $2^{0.292\beta}$ and the quantum complexity is $2^{0.265\beta}$. This simplified model is definitely useful and allows us to compare the security strength of different lattice-based candidates. However, this model is far from being accurate when considering the security requirement from NIST, which is defined by the gate complexity.

Another model is the gate-count metric, i.e., the cost in the Random Access Machine (RAM) model, which has been studied for the primal lattice attack in the round-3 versions of CRYSTALS-Kyber [52] and CRYSTALS-Dilithium [46]. They use the results from [14] as a black-box to estimate how many gates are required in one operation called 'AllPairSearch'. The overall sieving cost can then be estimated according to the current understanding on sieving algorithms [12,34].

2.4 The Classic FFT Distinguisher

We now assume for an LWE problem with reduced dimension t, i.e., we have a list of m LWE samples $(\mathbf{a}_j, b_j)$, where

$$b_j = \sum_{i=0}^{t-1} a_{i,j} s_i + e_j \mod q,$$

for $j = 1..m$.

The normal approach to use the FFT is to classify the samples by $\mathbf{a}_j$ and compute

$$f(\mathbf{a}_j) = \sum_{j_0 \in I(\mathbf{a}_j)} \theta^{b_{j_0}}, \tag{2}$$

where $I(\mathbf{a}_j)$ is the index set such that $\mathbf{a}_{j_0} = \mathbf{a}_j$ for $j_0 \in I(\mathbf{a}_j)$.

Then we compute

$$F(\tilde{\mathbf{s}}) = \sum_{\mathbf{a}_j} f(\mathbf{a}_j)\theta^{-\sum_{i=0}^{t-1} \mathbf{a}_{i,j}\tilde{s}_i}, \tag{3}$$

for all possible $\tilde{\mathbf{s}}$ by using the Fast Fourier Transformation (FFT), and return the guessed secret to be $\mathbf{s_0}$ s.t.,

$$\mathbf{s_0} = \operatorname*{argmax}_{\tilde{\mathbf{s}}} \mathfrak{Re}(F(\tilde{\mathbf{s}})), \tag{4}$$

where $\mathfrak{Re}(F(\tilde{\mathbf{s}}))$ is the real part of $F(\tilde{\mathbf{s}})$.

For the right guess, the computed $F(\mathbf{s})$ is exactly

$$\sum_{j=1}^{m} \theta^{e_j},$$

having a large real part since e_j is sampled from a discrete gaussian distribution.

For a wrong guess, the value

$$\mathfrak{Re}(\sum_{j=1}^{m} \theta^{e'_j}) \to 0,$$

since e'_j is uniformly distributed over $\mathbb{Z}_q$.

Note that the FFT distinguisher has performance close to the optimal distinguisher (see [39]). With the distinguishing advantage ϵ defined in Lemma 1, we could bound the required number of samples by

$$\mathcal{O}\left(\frac{\ln(q^t)}{\epsilon^2}\right),$$

since we need to statistically determine the secret from q^t hypotheses. Similar formulas without the asymptotic notation can be obtained via Hoeffding's bound in [33].

The complexity for the Fast Fourier Transform with size t is $\mathcal{O}(q^t \cdot t \cdot \log_2(q))$. This complexity quickly becomes prohibitively high since in lattice-based schemes when increasing the FFT size, as the parameter q is typically chosen as a large integer. Thus, the length of the partial secret vector that can be guessed via the FFT is rather small, highly limiting the gain of applying the FFT technique.

3 A New FFT Distinguisher

In this section, we describe a new distinguisher with the FFT technique, where the underlying idea is similar to that of Bleichenbacher's attacks on ECDSA [23]. We pick an integer γ much smaller than q and attempt to recover one secret entry ($s_i \mod \gamma$) rather than the exact value of s_i. Thus, the complexity of the FFT with dimension t is reduced from $\mathcal{O}(q^t \cdot t \cdot \log_2(q))$ to $\mathcal{O}(\gamma^t \cdot t \cdot \log_2(\gamma))$, thereby allowing us to reach a much larger dimension when a certain computational resource is assumed.

If γ is chosen to be 2, then the employed Fast Fourier Transform is actually a Fast Walsh-Hadamard Transform over the complex field. For simplicity, we use the term Fast Fourier Transform (FFT) throughout the paper.

3.1 New Transformation Technique

Let γ be a small element in the ring $\mathbb{Z}_q$ such that $\gamma \cdot \rho = \pm 1 \mod q$, for some element ρ. So γ^{-1} is well-defined, i.e., being ρ or $-\rho$. To be more specific, the field size q is typically chosen as a prime or a power-of-two integer. When q is a prime, we could pick $\gamma = 2$; for the latter case we pick $\gamma = 3$. Now we take the q prime case as an instance to show how this distinguisher works.

We can rewrite the LWE samples as $(\hat{\mathbf{a}}_j, b_j)$ such that,

$$b_j = \sum_{i=0}^{t-1} \hat{a}_{i,j}\hat{s}_i + e_j \mod q,$$

where $\hat{\mathbf{s}} = \gamma^{-1}\mathbf{s} \mod q$ and $\hat{\mathbf{a}}_j = \gamma \mathbf{a}_j \mod q$. Note that we assume $\gamma = 2$.

We then write the equations in the real set $\mathbb{R}$, i.e.,

$$b_j = \sum_{i=0}^{t-1} \hat{a}_{i,j}\hat{s}_i + e_j + l_j \cdot q,$$

for each LWE sample. We could then apply some reduction techniques such as lattice reduction algorithms to make $\hat{a}_{i,j}$ small. We have that

$$\begin{aligned} b_j &= \sum_{i=0}^{t-1} \hat{a}_{i,j}(q+1)/2 \cdot s_i + e_j + l_j \cdot q \\ &= \sum_{i=0}^{t-1} \hat{a}_{i,j} \cdot q/2 \cdot s_i + \sum_{i=0}^{t-1} \hat{a}_{i,j}/2 \cdot s_i + e_j + l_j \cdot q. \end{aligned} \tag{5}$$

Let us compute

$$F(\mathbf{s} \mod 2) = \sum_{j=0}^{m-1} \theta^{b_j - \sum_{i=0}^{t-1} \hat{a}_{i,j} \cdot q/2 \cdot s_i} = \sum_{j=0}^{m-1} \theta^{b_j} \cdot \exp(-\sum_{i=0}^{t-1} \hat{a}_{i,j} \cdot s_i \cdot 2\pi i_0/2).$$

Here we use the notation $F(\mathbf{s} \mod 2)$ to define the above computation, so the function $F(\cdot)$ is different from the one used in Sect. 2.4.

For the right guess, from Eq. (5), the computed value is

$$\sum_{j=0}^{m-1} \theta^{\sum_{i=0}^{t-1} \hat{a}_{i,j}/2 \cdot s_i + e_j} = \sum_{j=0}^{m-1} \exp\left(2\pi i_0/q \cdot (\frac{1}{2} \cdot \sum_{i=0}^{t-1} \hat{a}_{i,j} \cdot s_i + e_j)\right), \quad (6)$$

which is biased if $\hat{a}_{i,j}$ is small. The reason is that the standard deviations of the random variables s_i and e_j are small. Otherwise, the computed value is close to 0 (see Fig. 1 for a graphical illustration). Note that the noise for the t positions (for $0 \le i \le t-1$) involved in the Fast Fourier Transform, i.e. $\sum_{i=0}^{t-1} \hat{a}_{i,j} \cdot s_i$ is reduced (see Eq. (6)).

We next show a smart approach to perform the computation for all possible guesses using the FFT technique. Since $(-1)^2 = 1$, we could further classify θ^{b_j} into 2^t groups according to the vector $\mathbf{c} = (\hat{\mathbf{a}}_j \pmod 2)$ and define

$$f(\mathbf{c}) = \sum_{j_0 \in I(\mathbf{c})} \theta^{b_{j_0}}.$$

Here $I(\mathbf{c})$ is the index set such that $\hat{\mathbf{a}}_{j_0} \pmod 2$ is equal to $\mathbf{c}$ for $j_0 \in I(\mathbf{c})$.

We then have the following equation

$$F(\mathbf{s} \mod 2) = \sum_{\mathbf{c}} f(\mathbf{c})(-1)^{-\langle \mathbf{c}, \mathbf{s} \rangle}. \quad (7)$$

We exhaustively guess all the binary vector $\tilde{\mathbf{s}} \in \mathbb{Z}_2^t$ and compute the corresponding $F(\tilde{\mathbf{s}})$. This procedure can be done in $O(m + t \cdot 2^t)$ via using the Fast Fourier Transform. The guessed vector is a binary vector $\mathbf{s_0} \in \mathbb{Z}_2^t$ s.t.,

$$\mathbf{s_0} = \operatorname*{argmax}_{\tilde{\mathbf{s}} \in \mathbb{Z}_2^t} \mathfrak{Re}(F(\tilde{\mathbf{s}})), \quad (8)$$

where $\mathfrak{Re}(F(\tilde{\mathbf{s}}))$ is the real part of $F(\tilde{\mathbf{s}})$. With sufficient samples, the guessed vector should be $(\mathbf{s} \mod 2)$.

Up to this point, the attacker has recovered t bits of the secret information, which is the most difficult part. If we write $\mathbf{s} = 2 \cdot \mathbf{s}' + \mathbf{s_0}$ and recover the value of $\mathbf{s_0}$, then the norm of $\mathbf{s}'$ is smaller by a factor of almost 2 compared to $\mathbf{s}$. Let $b_j = \langle \mathbf{a}_j, \mathbf{s} \rangle + e_j \mod q$, and we rewrite it as

$$b_j - \langle \mathbf{a}_j, \mathbf{s_0} \rangle = \langle 2\mathbf{a}_j, \mathbf{s}' \rangle + e_j \mod q.$$

Thus, we have a new LWE problem with secret $\mathbf{s}'$. Since $\|\mathbf{s}'\|$ is much smaller if we recover a sufficient number of bits, which is true for the parameters discussed later, the cost of recovering the remaining secret by iteratively calling the dual approach is negligible.

The Gain. We present a simple example to discuss the pros and cons when comparing the new FFT distinguisher with the classic FFT distinguisher. Let q be a prime of size about 2^{12} and assume that the complexity constraint only allows to perform the classic FFT distinguisher with dimension 2. Thus, two positions are zeroed-out by this distinguisher. Applying the new FFT distinguisher with $\gamma = 2$, we could instead reduce 24 positions, but a certain amount of noise remains in each reduced position.

Another small (or practical) gain is that the new FFT distinguisher allows more flexible parameter selections to meet the time complexity constraint. For the classical FFT distinguisher, the complexity increases by a factor of about q if the FFT size is increased by one, which is much larger than the factor, i.e., γ, increased for the new FFT distinguisher.

3.2 The Distinguishing Property

We show the visual explanation of the distinguishing property in Fig. 1. The FFT distinguisher computes the value

$$\mathfrak{Re}(\sum_{j=1}^{m} \theta_{2q}^{X_j}),$$

where $X_j = Y_j + E_j$ and E_j is drawn from a discrete Gaussian $\mathcal{X}_{2\sigma}$ over $\mathbb{Z}_{2q}$. The random variable $Y_j = \lambda \cdot q$ is 0 for the right guess. For the wrong guess, the variable λ is uniformly distributed over $\mathbb{Z}_2$ and the FFT distinguisher computes $\mathfrak{Re}(\sum_{j=1}^{m} \theta_{2q}^{X_j}) \to 0$, due to the symmetry. We verified numerically that this is true for the relevant parameters in this paper since $\hat{a}_{i,j}$ drawn from a reasonably small discrete Gaussian still ensures that $\hat{a}_{i,j} \pmod 2$ is very close to the uniform.

Both the new distinguisher and the classic FFT distinguisher are estimating $\frac{1}{m}\sum_{j=1}^{m} \cos(\theta^{X_j})$, with $\mathbb{E}[\cos(\theta^{X_j})]$ having the same value away from 0 for the right guess and $\mathbb{E}[\cos(\theta^{X_j})] = 0$ for the wrong guess. Hoeffding's bound could then be applied, implying that the data complexity of the new distinguisher can be estimated in a similar manner to the classic FFT distinguisher.

4 Improving the Dual Lattice-Reduction Approach

The new distinguisher is now put into a framework of a dual attack to present a full LWE solving algorithm. The general steps of the new algorithm are described in Algorithm 1.

(a) The right guess case. (b) The wrong guess case.

Fig. 1. Graphical representation of the new distinguishing property ($\gamma = 2$).

Algorithm 1. New dual algorithm for solving LWE.

Input: The m LWE samples.

Output: A partial secret vector.

1: Map the entries in the matrix $\mathbf{A}$ as described in Eq. (9).
2: Find sufficiently many short vectors in the lattice $\mathcal{L}$ via lattice reductions, where $\mathcal{L}$ is the lattice formed in Eq. (10).
3: Guess the last t_1 positions of $\mathbf{s}$ exhaustively.
4: Use the new FFT procedure to guess the last t unknown entries in $\mathbf{s} \mod \gamma$.

Assume that the secret variables are distributed as a discrete gaussian distribution with standard deviation σ and the noise variables is distributed as a discrete gaussian distribution with standard deviation $c \cdot \sigma$. The general idea is that we assume for $t_a = t + t_1$ positions to be determined partially or fully in one run of the algorithm. Once the secret is partially determined, the problem of recovering the remaining positions of the secret is of much lower complexity and hence this part is discarded in the analysis[1].

We exhaustively guess the last t_1 positions in the secret. This may become beneficial if e.g. the secret variables take values in a very small alphabet. We write

$$\mathbf{A} = \left(\mathbf{A}_0 \ \hat{\mathbf{A}}_1 \ \mathbf{A}_2\right),$$

where $\hat{\mathbf{A}}_1$ is an $m \times t$ matrix, and $\mathbf{A}_2$ an $m \times t_1$ matrix, respectively. Here $\mathbf{A}_0$ is the matrix that corresponds to the remaining positions that are not directly affected by our procedure.

We perform the transformation and obtain

$$\mathbf{A}_1 = \gamma \hat{\mathbf{A}}_1 \mod q, \tag{9}$$

[1] For all parameter choices used in this paper (where t_1 and t are somewhat large), the statement is true as knowledge of t_1 entries and t bits then reduces the difficulty of the remaining problem considerably. For example, considering the parameters for solving Kyber768 in the classical RAM model (see Table 5), the cost of solving the remaining problem can be bounded by 2^{188}, which is negligible compared to the main cost of 2^{205}.

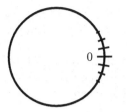

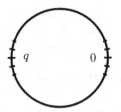

so we have a new matrix of $(\mathbf{A}_0\ \mathbf{A}_1\ \mathbf{A}_2)$. The contribution from the t_1 positions that are exhaustively guessed, corresponding to the $\mathbf{A}_2$, is just computed and subtracted from $\mathbf{b}$ and can thus be removed.

According to the analysis in the previous section, if we use the FFT to guess the t values that are secret $s_i \pmod{\gamma}$, then the noise from these t positions are reduced by a factor of γ. We can thus search for a short vector $(\mathbf{w}, \mathbf{v}_0, \mathbf{v}_1)$ in the lattice $\mathcal{L}$ constructed as

$$\{(c\mathbf{x}, \mathbf{y}_0, \mathbf{y}_1/\gamma) \in c\mathbb{Z}^m \times \mathbb{Z}^{n-t_a} \times \frac{1}{\gamma}\mathbb{Z}^t : (\mathbf{A}_0\ \mathbf{A}_1)^T\mathbf{x} = \begin{pmatrix}\mathbf{y}_0\\ \mathbf{y}_1\end{pmatrix} \mod q\} \quad (10)$$

to balance the noise from each position. The lattice has dimension $d = m+n-t_1$ and volume $c^m \cdot \frac{q^{n-t_1}}{\gamma^t}$ with high probability. This scaling trick is similar to [19].

If we compute $(\mathbf{w}/c)^T \cdot \mathbf{b}$, then the final noise after partial guessing and FFT is formed as

$$e = (\mathbf{w}/c)^T(\mathbf{A}_0\ \mathbf{A}_1)\begin{pmatrix}\mathbf{s}_0\\ \frac{1}{\gamma}\mathbf{s}_1\end{pmatrix} + \langle \mathbf{w}/c, \mathbf{e}\rangle = \langle \mathbf{w}/c, \mathbf{e}\rangle + \langle \mathbf{v}_0, \mathbf{s}_0\rangle + \langle \gamma \cdot \mathbf{v}_1, \mathbf{s}_1\rangle \cdot \frac{1}{\gamma}.$$

Assume that the norm of the short vector $(\mathbf{w}, \mathbf{v}_0, \mathbf{v}_1)$ is l. The noise size is estimated as $\sigma \cdot l$, since the standard deviation of each entry in $\mathbf{e}$ ($\mathbf{s}$) is $c\sigma$ (σ).

For a BKZ reduction $\text{BKZ}_{\beta,d}$, the shortest vector produced is expected to be of size $l = \delta_0^d \cdot (\frac{c^m \cdot q^{n-t_1}}{\gamma^t})^{\frac{1}{d}}$, where $\delta_0 \approx \left(\frac{\beta}{2\pi e}(\pi\beta)^{\frac{1}{\beta}}\right)^{\frac{1}{2(\beta-1)}}$. For the decision-LWE problem, the advantage is estimated as

$$\epsilon = \exp(-2\pi^2\tau^2),$$

where $\tau = \frac{\sigma \cdot l}{q}$.

Note that this is a general setting and for the schemes studied in this paper, i.e. CRYSTALS-Kyber and CRYSTALS-Dilithium, the constant c is always set to be 1.

4.1 Complexity Analysis

We present the complexity analysis of the new algorithm.

Bounded Secret Distribution. In many lattice-based primitives, the secret vector entries are chosen from an bounded alphabet of size B. For instance, the value B is 3 if the secret is ternary. We also assume that a lattice reduction algorithm could produce many (say $N(\beta)$) short vectors simultaneously with length $l = c_s \cdot \delta_0^d \cdot (\frac{c^m \cdot q^{n-t_1}}{\gamma^t})^{\frac{1}{d}}$, where c_s is a small constant. If $c_s = 1$, we assume that all the short vectors are as short as the shortest vector obtained from a BKZ reduction, which is definitely optimistic. Let the required number of samples for successful distinguishing be

$$N \geq \frac{c_0 \cdot \ln(\gamma^t \cdot B^{t_1})}{\epsilon^2}, \quad (11)$$

where c_0 is a constant factor[2] chosen as 4 and the factor $\ln(\gamma^t \cdot B^{t_1})$ comes from the fact that the FFT distinguisher finds the secret among $\gamma^t \cdot B^{t_1}$ hypotheses. To count the overall complexity of the new algorithm, we accumulate the complexity of different steps.

- The first step is a mapping for a small matrix with negligible cost.
- The second step involves $\max(1, \frac{N}{N(\mathsf{RED})})$ lattice reduction steps to produce sufficiently many short vectors, where $N(\mathsf{RED})$ denotes the number of short vectors produced via one lattice reduction. Thus, the complexity is $T(\mathsf{RED}) \cdot \max(1, \frac{N}{N(\mathsf{RED})})$, where $T(\mathsf{RED})$ denotes the complexity for one reduction procedure.
- We then guess t_1 positions with B^{t_1} possibilities in total. For each guess, the inner product of the guessed partial secret key and the corresponding coefficient vector needs to be subtracted for N samples outputted from the previous lattice reduction procedure and a large FFT transform with size t needs to be performed. For each FFT transform, the complexity is $t \cdot \gamma^t \cdot \log_2 \gamma$.

The exhaustive guessing approach could be done using a trick of storing intermediate values in memory. Now assuming that we need to compute $b - \langle \mathbf{a}, \mathbf{s} \rangle$, where $\mathbf{s}$ run through all the vectors of length t_1 and each entry in $\mathbf{s}$ has B choices. Notice that this computation needs to be done for N times since we have N short vectors from the previous lattice reductions.

We first build a table by computing $B \cdot t_1$ vectors of length N with entry $a_i s_i$ for $0 \leq i \leq t_1 - 1$ and s_i runs through all B choices. The cost $B \cdot t_1 \cdot N$ is much smaller than $B^{t_1} \cdot N$ for our targeted parameters; we, therefore, omit this cost in the complexity formula.

We could then enumerate all the possible $\mathbf{s}$ and build an enumeration tree of depth t_1. The starting point is an all-zero vector and the computation is trivial. The output $\mathbf{b}$ of the all-zero guess of $\mathbf{s}$ is placed in a leaf node and all the nodes in the path from the root to this all-zero leaf store the same vector $\mathbf{b}$ of length N. Afterwards, the computation of a new guess is only to add the vector stored in the parent node and a vector from a look-up table, which costs roughly N operations. Note that it is unnecessary to store all the enumeration tree, since only the vector in its parent node is needed to compute the vector in the new node. The memory cost of this enumeration is at most $O(t_1 \cdot N)$.

This technique is a general method used in different scenarios such as Information Set Decoding. As the complexity of the exhaustive guessing procedure can be bounded by the size of the guessing tree, the overall complexity is then estimated as

$$C = T(\mathsf{RED}) \cdot \max(1, \frac{N}{N(\mathsf{RED})}) + B^{t_1} \cdot (N + t \cdot \gamma^t \cdot \log_2 \gamma). \qquad (12)$$

[2] For solving the Learning Parity with Noise (LPN) problem, this constant is chosen to be 4, which is verified in [37]. We adopt this setting and verify it via experiments in Sect. 8. Theoretical results [33,35] from Hoeffding's inequality bounds this value by roughly 8 multiplying some other terms related to the success probability.

Another Optimization Trick. One general optimization trick is to guess a fixed number of most probable choices in the alphabet and take into account the probability P_0 that the partial secret is one of the guessed vectors. Thus, in such an approach the overall complexity can be estimated as $\frac{C}{P_0}$.

In lattice research, we usually pick the secret pattern with bounded Euclidean distance. Now assuming the number of guessed patterns is $N(\mathsf{guess})$, we have the following theorem to bound the complexity of the new algorithm.

Theorem 1. *Let n, q, σ, c be the parameters for the LWE problem and m be the number of LWE samples used. Let t_1 be the guessing positions and t be the FFT size. Let the constants c_0, c_s and γ be as defined before. Assume that the lattice reduction algorithms include BKZ reductions $\mathrm{BKZ}_{\beta,d}$ to produce a reduced basis with good quality and one reduction procedure can produce $N(\mathsf{RED})$ short vectors with norm $l = c_s \cdot \delta_0^d \cdot (\frac{c^m \cdot q^{n-t_1}}{\gamma^t})^{\frac{1}{d}}$, $d = m+n-t_1$ and $\delta_0 \approx \left(\frac{\beta}{2\pi e}(\pi\beta)^{\frac{1}{\beta}}\right)^{\frac{1}{2(\beta-1)}}$. Let $T(\mathsf{RED})$ denote the complexity for one reduction procedure and N the required number of short vectors for the distinguisher. Let $N(\mathsf{guess})$ be the number of guessed patterns in the exhaustively guessing step.*

The time complexity of the new algorithm can be estimated as $\frac{C}{P_0}$, where P_0 is the probability that the partial secret is one of the guessed vector and,

$$C = T(\mathsf{RED}) \cdot \max(1, \frac{N}{N(\mathsf{RED})}) + N(\mathsf{guess}) \cdot (N + t \cdot \gamma^t \cdot \log_2 \gamma), \tag{13}$$

supposing that

$$N \geq \frac{c_0 \cdot \ln(\gamma^t \cdot N(\mathsf{guess}))}{\epsilon^2},$$

where $\epsilon = \exp(-2\pi^2\tau^2)$ and $\tau = \frac{\sigma \cdot l}{q}$.

Remarks. We describe a general formula for estimating the complexity of the new dual attack in Theorem 1. We mainly discuss two types of cost models in this paper, i.e., the core-SVP model and the classical RAM model (also called the gate-count model in the official documents of CRYSTALS). In different models, many functions, such as $T(\mathsf{RED})$, $N(\mathsf{RED})$, and l, need to be specified. For instance, a typical assumption in the core-SVP model is that a BKZ procedure $\mathrm{BKZ}_{\beta,d}$ could produce $2^{0.2075\beta}$ short vectors that are as short as the shortest one. In the RAM model, we use more realistic settings where $T(\mathsf{RED})$ and $N(\mathsf{RED})$ are studied in [14], and the produced short vectors are larger by a factor of $\sqrt{4/3}$ than the shortest one. Note that the latter assumption is suggested by theoretical analysis in [48], and is extensively verified in recent works [12,15,34].

5 Application to CRYSTALS

In this section we discuss the application of the algorithm to two of the seven finalists, i.e., CRYSTALS-Kyber [52] and CRYSTALS-Dilithium [46], in the

NIST Post-Quantum Cryptography Standardization Project, under the core-SVP estimation model. In the core-SVP model, the lattice reduction procedure is one BKZ reduction, denoted $\mathrm{BKZ}_{\beta,d}$, with time complexity $2^{0.292\beta}$ for a classic computer and $2^{0.265\beta}$ for a quantum computer. Such a reduction step is supposed to output $2^{0.2075\beta}$ short vectors with size as short as the shortest one. Thus, in this model $T(\mathsf{RED})$ is $2^{0.292\beta}$ for a classic computer and is $2^{0.265\beta}$ for a quantum computer, $N(\mathsf{RED}) = 2^{0.2075\beta}$, and $l = c_s \cdot \delta_0^d \cdot (\frac{c^m \cdot q^{n-t_1}}{\gamma^t})^{\frac{1}{d}}$ with $c_s = 1$.

These two cryptosystems are both from the "Cryptographic Suite for Algebraic Lattices" (CRYSTALS) [1], thus sharing similar designs. We fix γ to be 2 since in CRYSTALS the parameter q is always selected as an odd prime. We also know $c = 1$ since the secret distributions are the same as the noise ones.

The security of Kyber and Dilithium is related to solving LWE problems with different parameters. We numerically investigate the concrete complexity for solving the transformed LWE problems in the core-SVP model and show the estimation in Tables 2 and 4.

Table 2. The complexity estimation on the security parameters of CRYSTALS-Kyber in the core-SVP model. Here n is the dimension when transforming the key-recovery problem to an LWE problem and q is the alphabetic size. Cost is given in $\log_2$ of operations. Here $\gamma = 2$.

	Kyber512	Kyber768	Kyber1024
Claimed security level	NIST-1	NIST-3	NIST-5
n	512	768	1024
q	3329	3329	3329
η	3	2	2
Classical core-SVP			
Claim [52]	118	182	256
Sect. 5	115	174	243
BKZ block-size β	394	595	829
Guessing size t_1	10	23	32
FFT size t	75	113	163
Quantum core-SVP			
Claim [52]	107	165	232
Sect. 5	105	160	223
BKZ block-size β	397	602	840
Guessing size t_1	7	15	21
FFT size t	72	117	163

Kyber. CRYSTALS-Kyber [52] is an IND-CCA2-secure KEM in the finalists of the NIST Post-Quantum Cryptography Standardization Project. We describe the detailed parameter sets of Kyber in Table 2. The scheme fixes the alphabetic size to 3329. In the round-3 specification, each secret/noise entry is sampled from a centered binomial distribution B_η, where B_η is implemented as

1. Sample $(a_1, \dots, a_\eta, b_1, \dots, b_\eta) \leftarrow_\$ \{0,1\}^{2\eta}$;
2. Output $\sum_{i=1}^{\eta}(a_i - b_i)$.

For Kyber768 and Kyber1024, the secret and noise distributions are set to be B_2, while the distributions are B_3 for Kyber512. The distribution of B_2 is shown in Table 3.

Table 3. The distribution of B_2.

	0	±1	±2
Probabilities	$\frac{3}{8}$	$\frac{1}{4}$	$\frac{1}{16}$

We could have an efficient approach to guess a vector of dimension t_1 with entries sampled from B_2 for Kyber768 and Kyber1024. For such a vector, we numerically compute the distribution of the norm of the vector. We pick a bound R to ensure that the probability that the norm of the vector is smaller than R is larger than P_0. In our estimation, we fix P_0 to be 0.9 to reduce the cost of searching for the optimal parameter. We could then count $N(\mathsf{guess})$, the number of patterns that the norm is no larger than R. This optimization trick could offer a small gain of less than 1 bit for the targeted parameter sets.

We see from Table 2 that our new attack could have a gain in the core-SVP model as large as 13 bits classically and 9 bits with quantum computers, for Kyber1024. The gain is also significant for Kyber768.

Dilithium. CRYSTALS-Dilithium [46] is an EUF-CMA-secure digital signature algorithm in the finalists of the NIST Post-Quantum Cryptography Standardization Project. It has a large alphabetic size $q = 8380417$ and a larger dimension (than Kyber) for the same security level. For Dilithium-2 and Dilithium-5, the secret/noise distributions are set to be S_2, while they are S_4 for Dilithium-3. Here S_η is the uniform distribution over integers in $[-\eta, \eta]$. Under the core-SVP model, we describe in detail the attack complexity on parameter settings of Dilithium in Table 4. This table shows that we could improve the state-of-the-art attacks for all the three parameter sets, though the gain is smaller than that for Kyber.

6 Beyond Core-SVP Estimation

In the previous section, we have shown the improvement from the new dual attacks in the core-SVP model. However, it is unclear to compare these numbers

Table 4. The complexity of the new attack on the security parameters of CRYSTALS-Dilithium in the core-SVP model. The value n is the dimension of the transformed LWE problem, q the alphabetic size and η the parameter in the noise generation of S_η. Cost is given in $\log_2$ of operations. Here $\gamma = 2$.

	Dilithium-2	Dilithium-3	Dilithium-5
Claimed security level	NIST-2	NIST-3	NIST-5
n	1024	1280	1792
q	8380417	8380417	8380417
η	2	4	2
Classical core-SVP			
Claim [46]	123	182	252
Sect. 5	122	179	246
BKZ block-size β	417	613	842
Guessing size t_1	13	15	29
FFT size t	75	116	163
Quantum core-SVP			
Claim [46]	112	165	229
Sect. 5	111	163	225
BKZ block-size β	419	616	848
Guessing size t_1	9	10	19
FFT size t	76	116	164

with the security requirements from NIST. In the official documents of round-3 Kyber and Dilithium, the designers also presented security numbers in the gate-count metric. They, however, excluded the analysis against dual attacks since "..First, most of those vectors are larger by a factor $\sqrt{4/3}$, secondly the trick of exploiting all those vectors is not compatible with the 'dimension for free' trick of [34].." (cited from [46]).

We in this section investigate the complexity of our new dual attacks in the gate-count metric and show that dual attacks could be more efficient even if most of short vectors obtained are larger by a factor $\sqrt{4/3}$. The novel idea is rather simple – we propose a new two-step lattice reduction algorithm where the first and second steps exploit the "dimension for free" (d4f) gain and the "many short vectors" (msv) gain, respectively. Also, a BKZ procedure typically includes calling an SVP oracle for many times. Thus, in the second step we could perform a sieving algorithm with a larger dimension to balance the costs of the two steps. From this perspective, we exploit the d4f trick twice and also produce an exponential number of short vectors.

6.1 A New Lattice Reduction Strategy

We describe the new two-step lattice reduction algorithm. The framework is shown in Algorithm 2. The first step is just a BKZ reduction where the d4f

Algorithm 2. Two-step Lattice Reduction

Input: A lattice.
Output: A list of short vectors.

1: Do BKZ reductions with size β. Then we obtain a reduced basis with a short vector $\mathbf{b}_0$ as the first vector in the basis.
2: For the lattice $\mathcal{L}'$ generated by the first β_0 vectors in the reduced basis, we perform a sieving step and get a list of $N(\beta_0)$ short vectors with size no larger than $\sqrt{4/3} \cdot \lambda_1(\mathcal{L}')$, where $\lambda_1(\mathcal{L}')$ is the shortest vector in the lattice $\mathcal{L}'$.

gain could be exploited, meaning that for a BKZ reduction $\text{BKZ}_{\beta,d}$, the actual costs correspond to a smaller β'. We use this step to improve the quality of the reduced basis.

Exploiting the d4f Gain. It is observed in [34] that the SVP in dimension β could be solved using a sieve in dimension $\beta' = \beta - d_{4f}$, where $d_{4f} = \Theta(\beta/\log\beta)$. Actually, this d4f gain comes from the fact that one sieving procedure could produce many short vectors. In [34], an "optimistic" estimation for d_{4f} is given as

$$d_{4f} = \frac{\beta \log(4/3)}{\log(\beta/(2\pi e))}. \tag{14}$$

This estimation is asymptotic and denoted by the *Asymptotic Model*. However, it is shown in [12] that the G6K sieve framework can achieve a larger dimension for free via a technique called "on the fly" lifting. By extrapolating from experimental data, they set d_{4f} as

$$d_{4f} = 11.46 + 0.0757 \cdot \beta. \tag{15}$$

We denote the latter extrapolated estimation the *G6K Model.*

Exploiting the msv Gain. The second step is just one sieving procedure on the lattice $\mathcal{L}'$ generated by the first β_0 vectors in the reduced basis outputted by the previous step. We could then get a list of $N(\beta_0)$ short vectors with size no larger than $\sqrt{4/3} \cdot \lambda_1(\mathcal{L}')$, where $\lambda_1(\mathcal{L}')$ is the shortest vector in the lattice $\mathcal{L}'$. One important problem is thus to estimate the value of $\lambda_1(\mathcal{L}')$.

As we already know a short vector $\mathbf{b}_0$ in the lattice $\mathcal{L}'$, we could use $\|\mathbf{b}_0\|$ to upper-bound the value of $\lambda_1(\mathcal{L}')$. One could also use Gaussian Heuristics to estimate the value of $\lambda_1(\mathcal{L}')$. Note that the two approaches lead to quite close complexity numbers (see Sect. 6.3 for details). The number of short vectors produced is denoted $N(\beta_0)$, where $N(\beta_0) = 1/\mathsf{Caps}(\beta_0, \pi/3)$ and $\mathsf{Caps}(\beta_0, \pi/3)$ is the probability that a vector randomly drawn from the unit sphere of dimension $(\beta_0 - 1)$ has angle at most $\pi/3$ with some fixed vector. The number $N(\beta_0)$ can be concretely estimated from the source code in the appendix of [14].

6.2 Complexity Analysis

We analyze the complexity of the algorithm in the gate-metric count model. Let the lattice dimension be $d = m + n - t_1$. Theorem 1 could also apply since the structure of the dual algorithm is unchanged, but the terms $T(\mathsf{RED})$ and $N(\mathsf{RED})$ and the length of the short vectors need to be updated.

We use a similar approach to that in round-3 Kyber [52] and Dilithium [46] for analyzing the cost of sieving and BKZ in the gate-metric count. To be more specific, we employ the analysis in [14] of the gate count of a 'AllPairSearch' operation for different sieving dimensions. We build a table with table entry $GT(\beta)$ storing this cost in gate count metric for dimension β.

Also, similar to [52], we assume that the 'AllPairSearch' operation needs to be called only once using progressive sieving [34,43], and define the *progressivity overhead* $c_{\mathsf{po}} = 1/(1 - 2^{-0.292}) = 5.46$, i.e., the limit of ratio between $\sum_{i \le b} 2^{0.292i+o(i)}$ and $2^{0.292b+o(b)}$ as b grows. We estimate $T(\mathsf{RED})$ as follows.

- For the first BKZ size β, we compute the sieving dimension $\beta' = \beta - d_{4f}$ and could check the GT table to have the complexity $GT(\beta')$. Similar to the analysis in [52], the complexity for BKZ is $(d - \beta)c_{\mathsf{po}}^2 GT(\beta')$.
- For the second step of the reduction, as the basis has been well-reduced by the first BKZ reduction and the d4f gain is no longer achieved, we do progressive sieving and the sieving complexity is estimated as $c_{\mathsf{po}} \cdot GT(\beta_0)$ for a sieving dimension β_0. So we set $(d-\beta)c_{\mathsf{po}} \cdot GT(\beta') \approx GT(\beta_0)$ to balance the cost, and produce $N(\beta_0)$ short vectors. We could achieve a slightly larger dimension of β_0 than β'. Also, the term $N(\mathsf{RED})$ is equal to $N(\beta_0)$, estimated with the concrete analysis from [14].

Thus, one new two-step reduction algorithm will cost

$$T(\mathsf{RED}) = (d - \beta)c_{\mathsf{po}}^2 \cdot GT(\beta') + c_{\mathsf{po}} \cdot GT(\beta_0).$$

The short vectors are as short as $\sqrt{4/3} \cdot \lambda_1(\mathcal{L}')$, where $\lambda_1(\mathcal{L}')$ can be estimated using the Gaussian Heuristic or be upper-bounded by

$$\|\mathbf{b}_0\| = \delta_0^d \cdot (\frac{c^m \cdot q^{n-t_1}}{\gamma^t})^{\frac{1}{d}}.$$

We have $\delta_0 \approx \left(\frac{\beta}{2\pi e}(\pi\beta)^{\frac{1}{\beta}}\right)^{\frac{1}{2(\beta-1)}}$. For Kyber and Dilithium, the constant c is always 1 and γ is 2 since the secret and noise distributions are the same and q is a prime.

When analyzing the primal attacks in the official documents of CRYSTALS, the designers use BKZ simulators to replace the simple geometric-series assumption, mainly due to its inaccuracy caused by the "tail" phenomenon. The situation is different in our dual lattice attack where the "head" phenomenon of BKZ reduction is the most important. Bai et al. in [20] stated that "Our simulator, which accurately predicts the head phenomenon, suggests that the head phenomenon vanishes when the block-size becomes large.. Quantitatively, the phenomenon has almost fully disappeared for $\beta \approx 200$".

The focus of the paper is to assess the strength of the security parameters proposed in various cryptographic primitives with the BKZ block-size $\beta \gg 200$. Thus, the geometric-series assumption is accurate, and we stick with it mainly due to its simplicity. It could be more accurate to instead use BKZ simulators when discussing the complexity of solving smaller LWE instances (with the BKZ block-size $\beta \ll 200$).

Table 5. The gate complexity comparison on the security parameters of CRYSTALS-Kyber. Here n is the dimension when transforming the key-recovery problem to an LWE problem and q is the alphabetic size. Cost is given in $\log_2$ of operations. Here $\gamma = 2$.

	Kyber512	Kyber768	Kyber1024
Claimed security level	NIST-1	NIST-3	NIST-5
n	512	768	1024
q	3329	3329	3329
η	3	2	2
Claim [52]	151.5	215.1	287.3
Sect. 6			
Asymptotic Model	148.3	207.3	275.4
BKZ block-size β	398	604	848
BKZ sieving dimension $\beta' = \beta - d_{4f}$	361	555	785
Second sieving dimension β_0	400	596	827
Guessing size t_1	20	36	45
FFT size t	78	118	166
G6K Model [12]	147.1	**205.2**	272.3
BKZ block-size β	399	606	850
BKZ sieving dimension $\beta' = \beta - d_{4f}$	357	548	774
Second sieving dimension β_0	396	589	816
Guessing size t_1	20	36	45
FFT size t	77	116	164
Required by NIST	143	207	272

6.3 Results

We show in Tables 5 and 6 the estimated complexity in the classical RAM model (also called gate-count metric in the official documents of CRYSTALS) for the security parameter sets of round-3 Kyber and Dilithium. The gain compared with the primal lattice attack is generally significant, ranging from 4 bits to 15

Table 6. The gate complexity of the new attack on the security parameters of round-3 CRYSTALS-Dilithium. The value n is the dimension of the transformed LWE problem, q the alphabetic size and η the parameter in the noise generation of S_η. Cost is given in $\log_2$ of operations. Here $\gamma = 2$.

	Dilithium-2	Dilithium-3	Dilithium-5
Claimed security level	NIST-2	NIST-3	NIST-5
n	1024	1280	1792
q	8380417	8380417	8380417
η	2	4	2
Claim [46]	158.6	216.7	285.4
Sect. 6			
Asymptotic Model	155.4	212.9	278.1
BKZ block-size β	418	620	853
BKZ sieving dimension $\beta' = \beta - d_{4f}$	380	570	790
Second sieving dimension β_0	424	616	837
Guessing size t_1	25	24	41
FFT size t	81	126	167
G6K Model [12]	153.8	210.4	274.4
BKZ block-size β	418	621	854
BKZ sieving dimension $\beta' = \beta - d_{4f}$	374	562	774
Second sieving dimension β_0	418	608	824
Guessing size t_1	26	24	41
FFT size t	80	120	165
Required by NIST	146	207	272

bits in the G6K Model (and from 3 bits to 12 bits in the Asymptotic Model), and the gain in the gate-count metric is larger than that in the core-SVP model, since in the prior model we could have a larger guessing size and also a larger FFT size.

These two tables show that some parameter sets such as Kyber512, Dilithium-2 and Dilithium-3 have a rather limited security margin, some such as Kyber1024 and Dilithium-5 are really on the edge, and the parameter set Kyber768 fails[3] to achieve the security requirement from NIST. In these tables, we use $\|\mathbf{b}_0\|$ to upper-bound the value of $\lambda_1(\mathcal{L}')$. We also employ the Gaussian Heuristics to estimate $\lambda_1(\mathcal{L}')$ and obtain similar complexity numbers. For instance, the complexity of solving Kyber768 increases from 205 bits to 206 bits, but is still below its claimed security level.

[3] One may argue that the extrapolated G6K Model could be optimistic when the dimension is large. As the $\log_2$ of the gate count in the Asymptotic Model is so close to the NIST requirement (207.3 v.s. 207) for Kyber768, however, a small number of extra dimensions for free could make the scheme insufficient for its claimed security level.

Table 7. The complexity comparison for the security parameters in the Homomorphic Encryption Standardization draft aiming for classic security. Here n is the dimension when transforming the key-recovery problem to an LWE problem and q is the alphabetic size. Cost is given in $\log_2$ of operations. The secret distribution is a uniform distribution from $\{-1, 0, 1\}$. The columns of uSVP, dec, and dual represent the complexity of the methods of uSVP, decoding, and dual, respectively, stated in the official documents of the Homomorphic Encryption Standard [7]. Here we pick $\gamma = 3$.

Security Level	n	$\log_2(q)$	uSVP	dec (from [7])	dual	New Dual (RAM model)
128	1024	27	131.6	160.2	138.7	131.6
192	1024	19	193.0	259.5	207.7	187.0
256	1024	14	265.6	406.4	293.8	251.1

This new method can be partially understood as a time-memory trade-off trick since we use a sieving procedure with larger dimension (i.e., β_0) to produce more short vectors. We also have some other memory costs such as the cost for the FFT procedure. However, these costs are negligible compared with the cost of the main sieving step.

7 Application to the Homomorphic Encryption Standard

The Homomorphic Encryption Standard [7] was initiated by several famous researchers/research groups in this area during the Homomorphic Encryption Standardization Workshop [3], hosted at Microsoft Research in Redmond. It suggests security parameters at security level of 128, 192, and 256, respectively.

In the suggested parameter settings, the standard deviation of the noise variable is chosen to be 3.2. The secret distribution could be uniform, the same as noise, or the bounded size in $\{-1, 0, 1\}$. We focus on the bounded secret case since it is the main parameter choice of many important implementations (e.g., the default parameters in the Microsoft SEAL [4]) that could lead to preferable performance.

We set $\gamma = 3$, and the complexity comparison for the security parameters aiming for classic security is shown in Table 7. We only consider the classic gate complexity, i.e., the cost in the Random Access Machine (RAM) model and we fix n to be 1024. The improvement factors vary for different parameter sets. For a parameter set designed for 256-bit security, the new dual approach with the refined lattice reduction strategy could lead to a security loss of about 5 bits.

8 Experimental Verification

In this section we experimentally verify the theoretical complexity estimation. The assumptions in lattice reduction algorithms, such as the d4f gain and the msv gain, have been verified in previous research [12,15,34]. Thus, we mainly perform experimental validation of the success rate of the new FFT distinguisher.

We have generated the samples in $\mathbb{Z}_q$ s.t.,

$$b_j = \sum_{i=0}^{t-1} \hat{a}_{i,j} \cdot \frac{q+1}{2} \cdot s_i, +e_j,$$

in the simulation, where each $\hat{a}_{i,j}$ was generated from a discrete Gaussian distribution $\mathcal{X}_{\sigma_1}$ and e_j was from another discrete Gaussian distribution $\mathcal{X}_{\sigma_2}$. We then implemented the new distinguisher to recover the secret vector of length t. These experiments simulate the processing steps after receiving many short vectors from the BKZ reduction algorithms. The alphabetic size q is set to be 3329, the same value as that in CRYSTALS-Kyber. For simplicity, we generated s_i from a uniform distribution in $\mathbb{Z}_2$. Note that, for parameter sets in public key encryption primitives, the secret s_i is usually set to be small and the variables $\hat{a}_{i,j}$ and e_j are (a sum of) entries from reduction algorithms, thus being wide.

We aim to verify in the experiments that

1. the sample complexity estimation in Eq. (11) is correct;
2. and it is sufficient to choose c_0 to be 4 to ensure a high success probability.

For the first purpose, we designed two types of experiments with different values of σ_1 and σ_2, since different noise parts contribute to the final noise with different weights (scales) according to our theoretical analysis. For the second purpose, we ran experiments with sample complexity computed by Eq. (11) where c_0 is set to $1, 2$ and 4, respectively.

In each experiment, we chose a typical key with length t and weight $\frac{t}{2}$ and ran the simulation test for 1000 times. The success probabilities in simulation are shown in Table 8. The experimental data match the theoretical prediction from Eq. (11) very well. To be more specific, the success probabilities are always 100% in our experiments when the value c_0 is set to 4. We already ensure a high success probability (of 95%) when setting $c_0 = 2$.

In addition, we have simulated the success probability when generating a new key in each run of the test. The secret entry s_i, as before, was generated from a uniform distribution in $\mathbb{Z}_2$, but the weight of the secret vector was not controlled. Thus, the error probability could be slightly higher if the weight of the secret is high. We have only run **Type-II experiments** with the FFT dimension 8 and 16, respectively, and performed 10000 tests in each setting. The coefficient c_0 is set to 4, the value in the theoretical prediction. We succeeded 9979 times for $t = 8$ and 9975 times for $t = 16$, strongly supporting our theoretical estimation.

Table 8. Experimental success probabilities with the novel FFT distinguisher. Here $\gamma = 2$ and the prime field size q is 3329. The value t is the FFT dimension and c_0 is the coefficient in Eq. (11). The rows with $c_0 = 4$ correspond to the experiments with number of samples predicted by our theory.

t	c_0	#(samples) $\log_2(\cdot)$	#(success)	#(test)	success rate
Type-I experiments ($\sigma_1 = 700, \sigma_2 = 1350$)					
8	4	16.36	1000	1000	100%
	2	15.36	976	1000	97.6%
	1	14.36	701	1000	70.1%
12	4	18.20	1000	1000	100%
	2	17.20	990	1000	99.0%
	1	16.20	741	1000	74.1%
16	4	19.87	1000	1000	100%
	2	18.87	999	1000	99.9%
	1	17.87	770	1000	77.0%
Type-II experiments ($\sigma_1 = 500, \sigma_2 = 1500$)					
8	4	17.32	1000	1000	100%
	2	16.32	956	1000	95.6%
	1	15.32	677	1000	67.7%
12	4	18.55	1000	1000	100%
	2	17.55	979	1000	97.9%
	1	16.55	686	1000	68.6%
16	4	19.60	1000	1000	100%
	2	18.60	991	1000	99.1%
	1	17.60	651	1000	65.1%

9 Concluding Remarks

We have presented a novel fast dual-type lattice attack for solving the LWE problem, based on two main contributions. Firstly, we have proposed a new efficient distinguisher using the FFT technique with a small alphabetic size. Secondly, we have described a new two-step reduction strategy that first uses a BKZ reduction for a high-quality lattice basis and then employs a progressive sieving step to produce many short vectors. This new reduction framework allows us to take into account the recent advances in lattice algorithms, such as the "dimensions for free" trick and more precise gate estimations on nearest neighbor search. The proposed new algorithm improves the complexity of solving the security parameter sets in the round-3 submissions of CRYSTALS-Kyber and CRYSTALS-Dilithium in both the core-SVP model and the gate-count metric. This new algorithm could recover the secret key of Kyber768 with classical gate complexity below its claimed security level under a model in [12] extrapolated from experimental data. Also, this new algorithm could improve the best-known attacks on certain FHE parameters. This new dual attack has rather wide applications and could affect many lattice-based primitives.

Acknowledgements. The authors would like to thank the anonymous reviewers for their helpful comments. This work was supported in part by the Swedish Research Council (Grant No. 2019-04166), by the Swedish Foundation for Strategic Research (Grant No. RIT17-0005), and by the Wallenberg Autonomous Systems and Software Program (WASP). The computations/simulations were enabled by resources provided by LUNARC.

References

1. Cryptographic suite for algebraic lattices. https://pq-crystals.org/index.shtml. Accessed 31 Aug 2020
2. HElib. https://github.com/homenc/HElib. Accessed 31 Aug 2020
3. Homomorphic encryption standardization workshop. https://www.microsoft.com/en-us/research/event/homomorphic-encryption-standardization-workshop/. Accessed 07 Oct 2020
4. Microsoft SEAL. https://www.microsoft.com/en-us/research/project/microsoft-seal. Accessed 31 Aug 2020
5. NIST post-quantum cryptography standardization. https://csrc.nist.gov/Projects/Post-Quantum-Cryptography/Post-Quantum-Cryptography-Standardization. Accessed 24 Sept 2018
6. Submission requirements and evaluation criteria for the post-quantum cryptography standardization process. https://csrc.nist.gov/CSRC/media/Projects/Post-Quantum-Cryptography/documents/call-for-proposals-final-dec-2016.pdf. Accessed 18 Feb 2021
7. Albrecht, M., et al.: Homomorphic encryption security standard. Technical report. HomomorphicEncryption.org, Toronto, Canada (2018)
8. Albrecht, M., Cid, C., Faugere, J.C., Fitzpatrick, R., Perret, L.: Algebraic algorithms for LWE problems (2014)
9. Albrecht, M.R.: On dual lattice attacks against small-secret LWE and parameter choices in HElib and SEAL. In: Coron, J.-S., Nielsen, J.B. (eds.) EUROCRYPT 2017. LNCS, vol. 10211, pp. 103–129. Springer, Cham (2017). https://doi.org/10.1007/978-3-319-56614-6_4
10. Albrecht, M.R., Cid, C., Faugere, J.C., Fitzpatrick, R., Perret, L.: On the complexity of the BKW algorithm on LWE. Des. Codes Crypt. **74**(2), 325–354 (2015)
11. Albrecht, M.R., et al.: Estimate all the LWE, NTRU schemes! In: Catalano, D., De Prisco, R. (eds.) SCN 2018. LNCS, vol. 11035, pp. 351–367. Springer, Cham (2018). https://doi.org/10.1007/978-3-319-98113-0_19
12. Albrecht, M.R., Ducas, L., Herold, G., Kirshanova, E., Postlethwaite, E.W., Stevens, M.: The general Sieve Kernel and new records in lattice reduction. In: Ishai, Y., Rijmen, V. (eds.) EUROCRYPT 2019. LNCS, vol. 11477, pp. 717–746. Springer, Cham (2019). https://doi.org/10.1007/978-3-030-17656-3_25
13. Albrecht, M.R., Fitzpatrick, R., Göpfert, F.: On the efficacy of solving LWE by reduction to unique-SVP. In: Lee, H.-S., Han, D.-G. (eds.) ICISC 2013. LNCS, vol. 8565, pp. 293–310. Springer, Cham (2014). https://doi.org/10.1007/978-3-319-12160-4_18

14. Albrecht, M.R., Gheorghiu, V., Postlethwaite, E.W., Schanck, J.M.: Estimating quantum speedups for lattice sieves. In: Moriai, S., Wang, H. (eds.) ASIACRYPT 2020. LNCS, vol. 12492, pp. 583–613. Springer, Cham (2020). https://doi.org/10.1007/978-3-030-64834-3_20
15. Albrecht, M.R., Heninger, N.: On bounded distance decoding with predicate: breaking the "lattice barrier" for the hidden number problem. IACR Cryptol. ePrint Arch. 2020, 1540 (2020). https://eprint.iacr.org/2020/1540
16. Albrecht, M.R., Player, R., Scott, S.: On the concrete hardness of learning with errors. J. M. Cryptol. **9**(3), 169–203 (2015)
17. Alkim, E., Ducas, L., Pöppelmann, T., Schwabe, P.: Post-quantum key exchange - a new hope. In: Holz, T., Savage, S. (eds.) USENIX Security 2016: 25th USENIX Security Symposium, 10–12 August 2016, pp. 327–343. USENIX Association, Austin, TX, USA (2016)
18. Arora, S., Ge, R.: New algorithms for learning in presence of errors. In: Aceto, L., Henzinger, M., Sgall, J. (eds.) ICALP 2011. LNCS, vol. 6755, pp. 403–415. Springer, Heidelberg (2011). https://doi.org/10.1007/978-3-642-22006-7_34
19. Bai, S., Galbraith, S.D.: Lattice decoding attacks on binary LWE. In: Susilo, W., Mu, Y. (eds.) ACISP 2014. LNCS, vol. 8544, pp. 322–337. Springer, Cham (2014). https://doi.org/10.1007/978-3-319-08344-5_21
20. Bai, S., Stehlé, D., Wen, W.: Measuring, simulating and exploiting the head concavity phenomenon in BKZ. In: Peyrin, T., Galbraith, S. (eds.) ASIACRYPT 2018. LNCS, vol. 11272, pp. 369–404. Springer, Cham (2018). https://doi.org/10.1007/978-3-030-03326-2_13
21. Bi, L., Lu, X., Luo, J., Wang, K., Zhang, Z.: Hybrid dual attack on LWE with arbitrary secrets. Cryptology ePrint Archive, Report 2021/152 (2021). https://eprint.iacr.org/2021/152
22. Bleichenbacher, D.: On the generation of DSA one-time keys. Presentation at cryptography research, Inc., San Francisco, CA (2007)
23. Bleichenbacher, D.: On the generation of one-time keys in DL signature schemes. Presentation at IEEE P1363 Working Group Meeting (2000)
24. Blum, A., Kalai, A., Wasserman, H.: Noise-tolerant learning, the parity problem, and the statistical query model. J. ACM (JACM) **50**(4), 506–519 (2003)
25. Brakerski, Z., Langlois, A., Peikert, C., Regev, O., Stehlé, D.: Classical hardness of learning with errors. In: Boneh, D., Roughgarden, T., Feigenbaum, J. (eds.) 45th Annual ACM Symposium on Theory of Computing, 1–4 June 2013, pp. 575–584. ACM Press, Palo Alto, CA, USA (2013)
26. Brakerski, Z., Vaikuntanathan, V.: Efficient fully homomorphic encryption from (standard) LWE. In: Ostrovsky, R. (ed.) 52nd Annual Symposium on Foundations of Computer Science, 22–25 October 2011, pp. 97–106. IEEE Computer Society Press, Palm Springs, CA, USA (2011)
27. Brakerski, Z., Vaikuntanathan, V.: Fully homomorphic encryption from ring-LWE and security for key dependent messages. In: Rogaway, P. (ed.) CRYPTO 2011. LNCS, vol. 6841, pp. 505–524. Springer, Heidelberg (2011). https://doi.org/10.1007/978-3-642-22792-9_29
28. Buchmann, J., Göpfert, F., Player, R., Wunderer, T.: On the hardness of LWE with binary error: revisiting the hybrid lattice-reduction and meet-in-the-middle attack. In: Pointcheval, D., Nitaj, A., Rachidi, T. (eds.) AFRICACRYPT 2016. LNCS, vol. 9646, pp. 24–43. Springer, Cham (2016). https://doi.org/10.1007/978-3-319-31517-1_2

29. Budroni, A., Guo, Q., Johansson, T., Mårtensson, E., Wagner, P.S.: Making the BKW algorithm practical for LWE. In: Bhargavan, K., Oswald, E., Prabhakaran, M. (eds.) INDOCRYPT 2020. LNCS, vol. 12578, pp. 417–439. Springer, Cham (2020). https://doi.org/10.1007/978-3-030-65277-7_19
30. Chen, Y.: Réduction de réseau et sécurité concrète du chiffrement complètement homomorphe. Ph.D. thesis, Paris 7 (2013)
31. Chen, Y., Nguyen, P.Q.: BKZ 2.0: better lattice security estimates. In: Lee, D.H., Wang, X. (eds.) ASIACRYPT 2011. LNCS, vol. 7073, pp. 1–20. Springer, Heidelberg (2011). https://doi.org/10.1007/978-3-642-25385-0_1
32. Cheon, J.H., Hhan, M., Hong, S., Son, Y.: A hybrid of dual and meet-in-the-middle attack on sparse and ternary secret LWE. IEEE Access **7**, 89497–89506 (2019)
33. Duc, A., Tramèr, F., Vaudenay, S.: Better algorithms for LWE and LWR. In: Oswald, E., Fischlin, M. (eds.) EUROCRYPT 2015. LNCS, vol. 9056, pp. 173–202. Springer, Heidelberg (2015). https://doi.org/10.1007/978-3-662-46800-5_8
34. Ducas, L.: Shortest vector from lattice sieving: a few dimensions for free. In: Nielsen, J.B., Rijmen, V. (eds.) EUROCRYPT 2018. LNCS, vol. 10820, pp. 125–145. Springer, Cham (2018). https://doi.org/10.1007/978-3-319-78381-9_5
35. Espitau, T., Joux, A., Kharchenko, N.: On a hybrid approach to solve small secret LWE. Cryptology ePrint Archive, Report 2020/515 (2020). https://eprint.iacr.org/2020/515
36. Gentry, C., Sahai, A., Waters, B.: Homomorphic encryption from learning with errors: conceptually-simpler, asymptotically-faster, attribute-based. In: Canetti, R., Garay, J.A. (eds.) CRYPTO 2013. LNCS, vol. 8042, pp. 75–92. Springer, Heidelberg (2013). https://doi.org/10.1007/978-3-642-40041-4_5
37. Guo, Q., Johansson, T., Löndahl, C.: Solving LPN using covering codes. J. Cryptol. **33**(1), 1–33 (2020)
38. Guo, Q., Johansson, T., Stankovski, P.: Coded-BKW: solving LWE using lattice codes. In: Gennaro, R., Robshaw, M. (eds.) CRYPTO 2015. LNCS, vol. 9215, pp. 23–42. Springer, Heidelberg (2015). https://doi.org/10.1007/978-3-662-47989-6_2
39. Guo, Q., Mårtensson, E., Wagner, P.S.: On the sample complexity of solving LWE using BKW-style algorithms. In: IEEE International Symposium on Information Theory, ISIT 2021, Melbourne, Australia, 12–20 July 2021, pp. 2405–2410. IEEE (2021). https://doi.org/10.1109/ISIT45174.2021.9518190
40. Howgrave-Graham, N.: A hybrid lattice-reduction and meet-in-the-middle attack against NTRU. In: Menezes, A. (ed.) CRYPTO 2007. LNCS, vol. 4622, pp. 150–169. Springer, Heidelberg (2007). https://doi.org/10.1007/978-3-540-74143-5_9
41. Kirchner, P., Fouque, P.-A.: An improved BKW algorithm for LWE with applications to cryptography and lattices. In: Gennaro, R., Robshaw, M. (eds.) CRYPTO 2015. LNCS, vol. 9215, pp. 43–62. Springer, Heidelberg (2015). https://doi.org/10.1007/978-3-662-47989-6_3
42. Kirchner, P., Fouque, P.-A.: Revisiting lattice attacks on overstretched NTRU parameters. In: Coron, J.-S., Nielsen, J.B. (eds.) EUROCRYPT 2017. LNCS, vol. 10210, pp. 3–26. Springer, Cham (2017). https://doi.org/10.1007/978-3-319-56620-7_1
43. Laarhoven, T., Mariano, A.: Progressive lattice sieving. In: Lange, T., Steinwandt, R. (eds.) PQCrypto 2018. LNCS, vol. 10786, pp. 292–311. Springer, Cham (2018). https://doi.org/10.1007/978-3-319-79063-3_14
44. Lindner, R., Peikert, C.: Better key sizes (and attacks) for LWE-based encryption. In: Kiayias, A. (ed.) CT-RSA 2011. LNCS, vol. 6558, pp. 319–339. Springer, Heidelberg (2011). https://doi.org/10.1007/978-3-642-19074-2_21

45. Liu, M., Nguyen, P.Q.: Solving BDD by enumeration: an update. In: Dawson, E. (ed.) CT-RSA 2013. LNCS, vol. 7779, pp. 293–309. Springer, Heidelberg (2013). https://doi.org/10.1007/978-3-642-36095-4_19
46. Lyubashevsky, V., et al.: CRYSTALS-DILITHIUM. Technical report. National Institute of Standards and Technology (2020). https://csrc.nist.gov/projects/post-quantum-cryptography/round-3-submissions
47. Micciancio, D., Regev, O.: Lattice-based cryptography. In: Bernstein, D.J., Buchmann, J., Dahmen, E. (eds.) Post-quantum Cryptography, pp. 147–191. Springer, Heidelberg (2009). https://doi.org/10.1007/978-3-540-88702-7_5
48. Nguyen, P.Q., Vidick, T.: Sieve algorithms for the shortest vector problem are practical. J. Math. Cryptol. **2**(2), 181–207 (2008). https://doi.org/10.1515/JMC.2008.009
49. Peikert, C.: Public-key cryptosystems from the worst-case shortest vector problem: extended abstract. In: Mitzenmacher, M. (ed.) 41st Annual ACM Symposium on Theory of Computing, 31 May–2 Jun 2009, pp. 333–342. ACM Press, Bethesda, MD, USA (2009)
50. Poppelmann, T., et al.: NewHope. Technical report. National Institute of Standards and Technology (2019). https://csrc.nist.gov/projects/post-quantum-cryptography/round-2-submissions
51. Regev, O.: On lattices, learning with errors, random linear codes, and cryptography. In: Gabow, H.N., Fagin, R. (eds.) 37th Annual ACM Symposium on Theory of Computing, 22–24 May 2005, pp. 84–93. ACM Press, Baltimore, MA, USA (2005)
52. Schwabe, P., et al.: CRYSTALS-KYBER. Technical report. National Institute of Standards and Technology (2020). https://csrc.nist.gov/projects/post-quantum-cryptography/round-3-submissions
53. Son, Y., Cheon, J.H.: Revisiting the hybrid attack on sparse and ternary secret LWE. IACR Cryptol. ePrint Arch. 2019, 1019 (2019)

Lattice Sieving via Quantum Random Walks

André Chailloux(✉) and Johanna Loyer(✉)

Inria de Paris, EPI COSMIQ, Paris, France
{andre.chailloux,johanna.loyer}@inria.fr

Abstract. Lattice-based cryptography is one of the leading proposals for post-quantum cryptography. The Shortest Vector Problem (SVP) is arguably the most important problem for the cryptanalysis of lattice-based cryptography, and many lattice-based schemes have security claims based on its hardness. The best quantum algorithm for the SVP is due to Laarhoven [Laa16] and runs in (heuristic) time $2^{0.2653d+o(d)}$. In this article, we present an improvement over Laarhoven's result and present an algorithm that has a (heuristic) running time of $2^{0.2570d+o(d)}$ where d is the lattice dimension. We also present time-memory trade-offs where we quantify the amount of quantum memory and quantum random access memory of our algorithm. The core idea is to replace Grover's algorithm used in [Laa16] in a key part of the sieving algorithm by a quantum random walk in which we add a layer of local sensitive filtering.

1 Introduction

Lattice-based cryptography is one of the most appealing modern public-key cryptography. It has worst case to average case reductions [Ajt96], efficient schemes and allows more advanced primitives such as fully homomorphic encryption [Gen09]. Another important aspect is that lattice based problems are believed to be hard even for quantum computers. Lattice-based cryptography is therefore at the forefront of post-quantum cryptography, especially in the NIST post-quantum standardization process. It is therefore very important to put a large effort on quantum cryptanalysis and to understand the quantum hardness of lattice problems in order to increase our trust in these post-quantum solutions.

For a given lattice $\mathcal{L}$, the Shortest Vector Problem (SVP) asks to find a short vector of this lattice. Solving the SVP is arguably the most important problem for the cryptanalysis of lattice-based cryptography. Additionally to its own importance, it is used as a subroutine in the BKZ algorithm, which is often the best attack on lattice-based schemes. There are two main families of algorithms for SVP: enumeration algorithms [FP85,Kan83,Poh81] which are asymptotically slow but have small memory requirements, and sieving algorithm which have the best asymptotic complexities but have large memory requirements. For finding very small vectors, which is required by the BKZ algorithm, sieving algorithms are currently the most efficient algorithms despite their large memory requirements. Indeed, in the SVP challenge, the 10 top performances are done by sieving

M. Tibouchi and H. Wang (Eds.): ASIACRYPT 2021, LNCS 13093, pp. 63–91, 2021.
https://doi.org/10.1007/978-3-030-92068-5_3

algorithms and the current record (since February 2021) solves SVP for $d = 180$[1]. However, for large approximation factors, enumeration algorithms are more efficient and these 2 methods are both of wide interest.

For a lattice $\mathcal{L}$ of dimension d, sieving algorithms solve SVP classically in time $2^{0.292d+o(d)}$ (with a heuristic analysis) using the local filtering technique introduced in [BDGL16]. Laarhoven presented a quantum equivalent of this algorithm that runs in time $2^{0.265d+o(d)}$ while using as much space as in the classical setting, namely $2^{0.208d+o(d)}$. The BKZ algorithm is the most efficient known attack against all lattice-based schemes which were chosen at the third round of NIST standardization process[2]. These two exponents are used for determining the number of bits of security in all these schemes hence improving the time exponent for SVP has direct implications on the security claims of these schemes.

Related Work. Heuristic sieving algorithms were first introduced by Nguyen and Vidick [NV08] that presented an algorithm running in time $2^{0.415d+o(d)}$ and using $2^{0.2075d}$ memory. A more efficient sieve in practice but with the same asymptotic running time was presented in [MV10]. Then, there has been improvements by considering k-sieve algorithms [WLTB11, ZPH14, Laa16]. Also, several works showed how to use nearest neighbor search to improve sieving algorithms [LdW15, Laa15, BL16]. The best algorithm [BDGL16] runs in time $2^{0.292d+o(d)}$ and uses locality-sensitive filtering.

In the quantum setting, quantum analogues of the main algorithms for sieving were studied [LMvdP15, Laa16]. The best algorithm runs in time $2^{0.265d+o(d)}$ and is the quantum analogue of [BDGL16]. There has been two more recent works on quantum sieving algorithms. First, quantum variants of the k-sieve were studied in [KMPM19], giving interesting time-space trade-off and a recent article [AGPS20] studied more practical speedups of these quantum algorithms, *i.e.* when do these gains in the exponent actually translate to quantum speedups.

Contributions. In this article, we study and improve the asymptotic complexity of quantum sieving algorithm for SVP. This is the first improvement on the asymptotic running time[3] of quantum sieving algorithms since the work of Laarhoven [Laa16].

It is not *a priori* clear how to use quantum random walks to adapt the algorithm from [BDGL16]. This algorithm is divided into a pre-processing phase and a query phase. In this query phase, we have several points that are in a filter F, which means here that there are close to a specific point. We are then given a new point $\vec{v}$ and we want to know whether there exists a point $\vec{w} \in F$ such

[1] The SVP challenge can be accessed here https://www.latticechallenge.org/svp-challenge.

[2] At this stage, there are 3 encryption schemes/key encapsulation mechanisms: KYBER, NTRU and SABER as well as two signature schemes: DILITHIUM and FALCON.

[3] We are talking here only about the asymptotic running time, there are other metrics of interest that have been covered in [KMPM19, AGPS20] where there were some improvements.

that $\|\vec{v} \pm \vec{w}\|$ is smaller than $\min\{\|\vec{v}\|, \|\vec{w}\|\}$[4]. Then we do not know how to do better here than Grover's algorithm, which takes time $\sqrt{|F|}$. On the other hand, if instead of this query framework, we start from a filter F and we want to find all the pairs $\vec{v}, \vec{w}$, then we can apply a quantum random walk.

Even within this framework, there are many ways of constructing quantum random walks and most of them do not give speedups over [Laa16]. What we show is that by adding proper additional information in the vertices of the random walk, in particular by adding another layer of filters within the vertices of the graph on which we perform the quantum walk, we can actually get some improvement over Grover's algorithm and achieve our speedups.

Presentation of Our Contributions. Our main theorem is an improvement of the best asymptotic quantum heuristic running time for the SVP bringing down the asymptotic running time from $2^{0.2653d+o(d)}$ (Laarhoven's algorithm [Laa16]) to $2^{0.2570d+o(d)}$.

Theorem 1. *Our algorithm using quantum random walks solves the SVP on dimension d which heuristically solves SVP on dimension d in time* $2^{0.2570d+o(d)}$*, uses QRAM of maximum size* $2^{0.0767d}$*, a quantum memory of size* $2^{0.0495d}$ *and a classical memory of size* $\mathsf{poly}(d) \cdot 2^{0.2075d}$.

Our results are in the QRAM model where QRAM operations can be done efficiently. Notice that Laarhoven's result is in this model so our results are directly comparable to his. We can see that additionally to improving the best asymptotic running time, this algorithm uses much less quantum resources (both quantum memory and quantum RAM) than its running time which makes it fairly practical. This theorem can also be helpful if we want to optimize other performance measures. For example, it has been argued that having efficient QRAM operations is too strong and that performing a QRAM operation should require time at least $r^{1/3}$ where r is the number of QRAM registers. In this model, the best running time was $2^{0.2849d+o(d)}$ (this is still using Laarhoven's algorithm but the result has been explicitly stated in [AGPS20]). As a consequence of Theorem 1, we have the following

Corollary 1. *In the model where quantum random access to a memory of size* r *can be done in time* $r^{1/3}$*, our quantum algorithm solves SVP on dimension d in time* $2^{0.2826d+o(d)}$.

Proof. This is a direct consequence of Theorem 1 where in this model, the running time is $2^{0.2570d+o(d)} \cdot \left(2^{0.0767d}\right)^{1/3} = 2^{0.2826d+o(d)}$. □

We also present two trade-offs: a quantum memory-time trade-off and a QRAM-time trade-off. For a fixed amount of quantum memory, our algorithm performs as follows.

[4] We remain a bit imprecise and informal here as we haven't properly described sieving algorithms yet.

Theorem 2 (Trade-off for fixed quantum memory). *Our algorithm using quantum random walks solves the SVP on dimension d which, for a parameter $M \in [0, 0.0495]$, heuristically runs in time $2^{\tau_M d + o(d)}$, uses QRAM of maximum size $2^{\gamma_M d}$ and quantum memory of size $2^{\mu_M d}$ and a classical memory of size* $\mathsf{poly}(d) \cdot 2^{0.2075d}$ *where*

$$\tau_M \in 0.2653 - 0.1670M + [-2{\cdot}10^{-5}; 4{\cdot}10^{-5}]$$

$$\gamma_M \in 0.0578 + 0.3829M - [0; 2{\cdot}10^{-4}] \quad ; \quad \mu_M = M.$$

With this theorem, we obtain for $M = 0$ the quantum running time of Laarhoven's quantum algorithm and, for $M = 0.0495$, the result of Theorem 1. We now present our second trade-off theorem where we fix the amount of QRAM.

Theorem 3 (Trade-off for fixed QRAM). *Our quantum algorithm using quantum random walks solves SVP on dimension d which for a parameter $M' \in [0, 0.0767]$ heuristically runs in time $2^{\tau_{M'} d + o(d)}$, uses QRAM of maximum size $2^{\gamma_{M'} d}$, a quantum memory of size $2^{\mu_{M'} d}$ and uses a classical memory of size* $\mathsf{poly}(d) \cdot 2^{0.2075d}$ *where*

$$\tau_{M'} \in 0.2925 - 0.4647M' - [0; 6{\cdot}10^{-4}] \quad ; \quad \gamma_{M'} = M'$$

$$\mu_{M'} \in \max\{2.6356(M' - 0.0579), 0\} + [0; 9{\cdot}10^{-4}].$$

With this theorem, we obtain for $M' = 0$, the best classical exponent of [BDGL16] (we can actually show the algorithm uses no quantum resources in this case). For $M' = 0.0577$, we retrieve Laarhoven's quantum exponent and for $M' = 0.0767$, we get Theorem 1.

Organisation of the Paper. In Sect. 2, we present preliminaries on Quantum computing. In Sect. 3, we then present sieving algorithm, as well as useful statements on lattices. In Sect. 4, we present the general framework we use for sieving algorithm. Next, we use and perform a first study of its complexity in Sect. 5, whose Sect. 6 improves. In Sect. 7, we present the space-time trade-offs. We perform a final discussion in Sect. 8 and talk about parallelization of our algorithm as well as possible improvements.

2 Quantum Computing Preliminaries

2.1 Quantum Circuits

We consider here quantum circuits consisting of 1 and 2 qubit gate, without any locality constraint, meaning that we can apply a 2 qubit gate from a universal set of gates to any pair of qubits in time[5] 1. We use the textbook gate model

[5] We are only interested in asymptotic running time here so we are not interested in the choice of this universal gate set, as they are all essentially equivalent from the Solovay-Kitaev theorem (see [NC00], Appendix 3).

where the running time of a quantum circuit is just the number of gates used. The width of a circuit is the number of qubits it operates on, including the ancilla qubits. This quantity is important as it represents the number of qubits that have to be manipulated simultaneously and coherently. We will also call this quantity quantum memory.

When we will know much more precisely how quantum architectures look like, it will be possible to make these models more precise and replace the gate model with something more adequate. The gate model is still the most widely used in the scientific community and is very practical to compare different algorithms. We will use the gate model as our main model for computing quantum times but we will also include other interesting quantum figures of merit, such as quantum memory or Quantum Random Access Memory usage.

2.2 Quantum Random Access Memory

Quantum Random Access Memory (denoted hereafter QRAM) is a type of quantum operation which is not captured by the circuit model. Consider N registers $x_1, \ldots, x_N \in \{0,1\}^d$ stored in memory. A QRAM operation consists of applying the following unitary

$$U_{\mathrm{QRAM}} : |i\rangle|y\rangle \rightarrow |i\rangle|x_i \oplus y\rangle.$$

We say that we are in the QRAM model if the above unitary can be constructed efficiently, typically in time $O(d + \log(N))$.

QRAM operations are theoretically allowed by the laws of quantum mechanics and there are some proposals for building efficiently QRAM operations, such as [GLM08], even though its robustness has been challenged in [AGJO+15]. The truth is that it very premature to know whether QRAM operations will be efficiently available in quantum computers. This would definitely require a major hardware breakthrough but as does quantum computing in general.

While our results are mainly in the QRAM model, we also discuss other metrics where the cost of a QRAM operation is not logarithmic in N but has a cost of N^x for a constant x.

2.3 Grover Algorithm

One formulation of Grover's search problem [Gro96] is the following. We are given a list of data $x_1, \ldots, x_r$, with $x_i \in E$. Given a function $f : E \rightarrow \{0,1\}$, the goal is to find an i such that $f(x_i) = 1$, and to output "no solution" if there are no such i. Let $\mathrm{Sol} = \{i \in [r] : f(x_i) = 1\}$.

Classically, we cannot solve this problem with a better average complexity than $\Theta(\frac{r}{|\mathrm{Sol}|})$ queries, which is done by examining random x_i one by one until we find one whose image is 1 through f. Quantum computing allows a better complexity. Grover's algorithm solves this search problem in $O\left(\sqrt{\frac{r}{|\mathrm{Sol}|}}\right)$ queries to f. Applying Grover's algorithm this way requires efficient QRAM access to the data $x_1, \ldots, x_r$.

2.4 Quantum Random Walks

We present here briefly quantum random walks (QRW). There are several variants of QRW and we will use the MNRS framework, first presented in [MNRS11].

We start from a graph $G = (V, E)$ where V is the set of vertices and $E \subseteq V \times V$ is the set of edges. We do not allow self loops which means that $\forall x \in V, (x, x) \notin E$ and the graph will be undirected so $(x, y) \in E \Rightarrow (y, x) \in E$. Let also $N(x) = \{y : (x, y) \in E\}$ be the set of neighbors of x. We have a set $M \subseteq V$ of marked elements and the goal of a QRW is to find $v \in M$.

Let $\varepsilon = \frac{|M|}{|V|}$ be the fraction of marked vertices and let δ be the spectral gap of G[6]. For any vertex x, we define $|p_x\rangle = \sum_{y \in N(x)} \frac{1}{\sqrt{|N(x)|}} |y\rangle$. We also define $|U\rangle = \frac{1}{\sqrt{|V|}} \sum_{x \in V} |x\rangle |p_x\rangle$. We now define the following quantities:

- SETUP cost $\mathcal{S}$: the SETUP cost $\mathcal{S}$ is the cost of constructing $|U\rangle$.
- UPDATE cost $\mathcal{U}$: here, it is the cost of constructing the unitary

$$U_{\text{UPDATE}} : |x\rangle|0\rangle \to |x\rangle|p_x\rangle.$$

- CHECK cost $\mathcal{C}$: it is the cost of computing the function $f_{\text{CHECK}} : V \to \{0, 1\}$ where $f_{\text{CHECK}}(v) = 1 \Leftrightarrow v \in M$.

Proposition 1 [MNRS11]. *There exists a quantum random walk algorithm that finds a marked element $v \in M$ in time*

$$\mathcal{S} + \frac{1}{\sqrt{\varepsilon}} \left(\frac{1}{\sqrt{\delta}} \mathcal{U} + \mathcal{C} \right).$$

Quantum Random Walks on the Johnson Graph. A very standard graph on which we can perform QRW is the Johnson graph $J(n, r)$. Each vertex v consists of r different (unordered) points $x_1, \ldots, x_r \in [n]$ as well as some additional data $D(v)$ that depends on the QRW we want to perform.

$v = (x_1, \ldots, x_r, D(v))$ and $v' = (x'_1, \ldots, x'_r, D(v'))$ form an edge in $J(n, r)$ iff. we can go from $(x_1, \ldots, x_r)$ to $(x'_1, \ldots, x'_r)$ by removing exactly one value and then adding one value. The Johnson graph $J(n, r)$ has spectral gap $\delta = \frac{n}{r(n-r)} \approx \frac{1}{r}$ when $r \ll n$ [dW19].

The additional data $D(v)$ here is used to reduce the checking time $\mathcal{C}$ with the drawback that it will increase the update time $\mathcal{U}$. Johnson graphs were often used, for example when trying to solve the element distinctness problem [Amb07], but also for the subset-sum problem [BJLM13, HM18, BBSS20] or for code-based problems [KT17].

[6] For a regular graph, if $\lambda_1 > \cdots > \lambda_{|V|}$ are the eigenvalues of the normalized adjacency matrix of G, then $\delta = \lambda_1 - \max_{i=2\ldots n} |\lambda_i|$.

Quantum Data Structures. A time analysis of quantum random walks on the Johnson graph was done in [Amb07] when studying the element distinctness problem. There, Ambainis presented a quantum data structure that uses efficient QRAM that allows in particular insertion and deletion in $O(\log(n))$ time where n is the database size while maintaining this database in quantum superposition. Another paper on quantum algorithm for the subset problem using quantum random walks [BJLM13] also presents a detailed analysis of a quantum data structure based on radix trees to perform efficient insertion and deletion in quantum superposition. All of these data structures require as much QRAM registers as the number of registers to store the whole database and this running time holds only in the QRAM model. In our work, we will use such a quantum data structure and refer to the above two papers for explicit details on how to construct them.

3 Lattice and Geometric Preliminaries

Notations. Let d be a positive integer. The norm $\|\cdot\|$ we use throughout this paper is the Euclidian norm, so for a vector $\vec{v} = (v_1, \ldots, v_d) \in \mathbb{R}^d$, $\|\vec{v}\| = \sqrt{\sum_{i=1}^{d} v_i^2}$. The inner product of $\vec{v} = (v_1, \ldots, v_d)$ and $\vec{w} = (w_1, \ldots, w_d)$ is $\langle \vec{v}, \vec{w} \rangle := \sum_{i=1}^{d} v_i w_i$. The non-oriented angle between $\vec{v}$ and $\vec{w}$ is denoted $\theta(\vec{v}, \vec{w}) := \arccos\left(\frac{\langle \vec{v}, \vec{w} \rangle}{\|\vec{v}\|\|\vec{w}\|}\right)$. We denote the d-dimensional sphere of radius R by $\mathcal{S}_R^{d-1} := \{\vec{v} \in \mathbb{R}^d : \|\vec{v}\| = R\}$, and $\mathcal{S}^{d-1} := \mathcal{S}_1^{d-1}$. Throughout the paper, for a known integer d, we will write $N := (\sqrt{4/3})^d$. The meaning of this number N is detailed in Sect. 3.1.

Lattices and SVP. The d-dimensional lattice $\mathcal{L} \subset \mathbb{R}^m$ generated by the basis $B = (b_1, ..., b_n)$ with $\forall i, b_i \in \mathbb{R}^m$ is the set of all integer linear combinations of its basis vectors: $\mathcal{L}(B) = \left\{ \sum_{i=1}^{d} \lambda_i\, b_i,\ \lambda_i \in \mathbb{Z} \right\}$. Given a basis of a lattice $\mathcal{L}$, the Shortest Vector Problem (SVP) asks to find a non-zero vector in $\mathcal{L}$ of minimal norm. SVP is known to be NP-hard [Ajt98]. This problem and its derivatives (SIS, LWE) have been used in several public-key cryptosystems, specifically as candidate for quantum-resistant cryptography [DKL+19, FHK+19, CDH+19]. Thereby, one of the most important ways to know their security and choose parameters is to estimate the computational hardness of the best SVP-solving algorithms.

3.1 An Overview of Sieving Algorithms for SVP

The algorithm LLL [LLL82] returns a reduced basis of a lattice in a polynomial time. However it is not sufficient to solve SVP. All the fastest known algorithms to solve SVP run in exponential time. A first method is enumeration [Kan83], that solves deterministically SVP using low space but in super-exponential time in the lattice dimension d.

Another method, which will interest us in this article, is lattice sieving [NV08, MV10]. They are heuristic algorithms that probably solve SVP in time and space $2^{\Omega(d)}$. To this day, the best complexity for sieving in the QRAM model is obtained by quantum hypercone LSF [Laa16] in $2^{0.2653d+o(d)}$ time and $2^{0.2075d+o(d)}$ space. Another algorithm [KMPM19] uses k-lists to solve SVP in $2^{0.2989d+o(d)}$ time and $2^{0.1395d+o(d)}$ space.

The NV-sieve. The NV-sieve [NV08] is a heuristic algorithm. It starts with a list of lattice vectors, that we can consider of norm at most 1 by normalization. Given this list and a constant $\gamma < 1$, the NV-sieve returns a list of lattice vectors of norm at most γ. It iteratively builds lists of shorter lattice vectors by applying a sieve. This sieve step consists in computing all the sums (plus and minus) of two list vectors, and fills the output list with those which have norm at most γ. For γ tending to 1, two vectors form a reducing pair - *i.e.* their sum is of norm at most γ - iff. they are of angle at most $\pi/3$. The first list of lattice vectors can be sampled with Klein's algorithm [Kle00] for example. A list size of $N^{1+o(1)} = (\sqrt{4/3})^{d+o(d)}$ suffices to have about one reducing vector in the list for each list vector, as stated in [NV08]. Because of the norms of the list vectors reduces with a factor by $\gamma < 1$ at each application of the algorithm, the output list will hopefully contain a non-zero shortest lattice vector after a polynomial number of application of the NV-sieve.

NNS and Application to Lattice Sieving. A logic improvement of this algorithm is to use Neighbor Nearest Search (NNS) [IM98] techniques. The NNS problem is: given a list L of vectors, preprocess L such that one can efficiently find the nearest vector in L to a target vector given later. Used in the NV-sieve, the preprocessing partitions the input list in several buckets of lattice points, each bucket being associated with a hash function. The algorithm will only sum vectors from a same bucket, which are near to each other, instead of trying all pairs of vectors.

Locality-Sensitive Hashing (LSH). A method to solve NNS is locality-sensitive hashing (LSH) [IM98]. An LSH function is a hash-function that have high probability to collide for two elements if they are close, and a low one if they are far. Several categories of LSH functions exists: hyperplane LSH [Cha02], hypercone or spherical LSH [AINR14, AR15] and cross-polytope LSH [TT07].

Locality-Sensitive Filtering (LSF). More recently, [BDGL16] improved NNS solving by introducing locality-sensitive filtering (LSF). LSF functions, called filters, map a vector $\vec{v}$ to a boolean value: 1 if $\vec{v}$ survives the filter, and 0 otherwise. These filters are instantiated by hypercone filters, which correspond to spherical caps centered around points which form an efficiently decodable code on the sphere (the efficient decodability part ensures that we can efficiently determine whether a point is in a filter or not). We present now geometrical preliminaries that will allow us to describe more formally these algorithms.

3.2 Geometrical Preliminaries

Spherical Caps/Hypercone Filters. We define the spherical cap of center $\vec{v}$ and angle α as follows:

$$\mathcal{H}_{\vec{v},\alpha} := \{\vec{x} \in \mathcal{S}^{d-1} \mid \theta(\vec{x},\vec{v}) \leqslant \alpha\}.$$

We will use spherical caps to filter points that are close to a center $\vec{v}$ and we will sometimes use the term filter or hypercone filter to descibe a spherical cap.

Proposition 2 [MV10]. *For an angle $\alpha \in [0,\pi/2]$ and $\vec{v} \in \mathcal{S}^{d-1}$, the ratio of the volume of a spherical cap $\mathcal{H}_{\vec{v},\alpha}$ to the volume of the sphere $\mathcal{S}^{d-1}$ is*

$$\mathcal{V}_d(\alpha) := \mathsf{poly}(d) \cdot \sin^d(\alpha).$$

Proposition 3 [BDGL16]. *For an angle $\alpha \in [0,\pi/2]$ and two vectors $\vec{v},\vec{w} \in \mathcal{S}^{d-1}$ such that $\theta(\vec{v},\vec{w}) = \theta$, the ratio of the volume of a wedge $\mathcal{H}_{\vec{v},\alpha} \cap \mathcal{H}_{\vec{w},\alpha}$ to the volume of the sphere $\mathcal{S}^{d-1}$ is*

$$\mathcal{W}_d(\alpha,\theta) := \mathsf{poly}(d) \cdot \left(1 - \frac{2\cos^2(\alpha)}{1+\cos(\theta)}\right)^{d/2}.$$

If we consider any vector $\vec{w} \in \mathcal{S}^{d-1}$ and N^{ρ_0} random points $\vec{s}_1,\ldots,\vec{s}_{N^{\rho_0}}$ in $\mathcal{H}_{\vec{v},\alpha}$ for $\rho_0 := \frac{\mathcal{V}_d(\alpha)}{\mathcal{W}_d(\alpha,\theta)}$; then this proposition implies that there exists, with constant probability, an $i \in [N^{\rho_0}]$ such that $\vec{s}_i \in \mathcal{H}_{\vec{w},\alpha}$.

Reducing Vectors at the Border of a Spherical Cap. The idea a first putting vectors in a spherical cap is that 2 vectors $\vec{x}_0,\vec{x}_1 \in \mathcal{H}_{\vec{s},\alpha}$ have a larger probability of being reducible (*i.e.* $\theta(\vec{x}_0,\vec{x}_1) \leq \pi/3$) than random vectors. We quantify this now. We first define the border of a filter

$$\mathcal{B}_{\vec{s},\alpha} := \{\vec{x} \in \mathcal{S}^{d-1} \mid \theta(\vec{x},\vec{s}) = \alpha\}.$$

Working with points on the border makes the calculations easier. We argue later that random points in a spherical cap $\mathcal{H}_{\vec{v},\alpha}$ are actually very close to the border, so this result will approximately be also true for random points in a spherical cap.

Proposition 4. *Let $\vec{x}_0,\vec{x}_1 \in \mathcal{B}_{\vec{s},\alpha}$. This means we can write*

$$\vec{x}_0 = \cos(\alpha)\vec{s} + \sin(\alpha)\vec{y}_0 \tag{1}$$
$$\vec{x}_1 = \cos(\alpha)\vec{s} + \sin(\alpha)\vec{y}_1 \tag{2}$$

with $\vec{y}_0,\vec{y}_1$ of norm 1 and orthogonal to $\vec{s}$. We have for $\alpha \in (0,\pi/2]$

$$\theta(\vec{y}_0,\vec{y}_1) \leqslant 2\arcsin\left(\frac{1}{2\sin(\alpha)}\right) \iff \theta(\vec{x}_0,\vec{x}_1) \leqslant \frac{\pi}{3}.$$

Proof. We denote for simplicity $\theta_y := \theta(\vec{y}_0, \vec{y}_1)$. By subtracting Eqs. 2 from 1 and then by squaring, we have

$$\begin{aligned}
\|\vec{x}_0 - \vec{x}_1\|^2 \leqslant 1 &\Leftrightarrow \sin^2(\alpha)\|\vec{y}_0 - \vec{y}_1\|^2 \leqslant 1\\
&\Leftrightarrow \sin^2(\alpha)(2 - 2\cos(\theta_y)) \leqslant 1\\
&\Leftrightarrow \cos(\theta_y) \geqslant 1 - \frac{1}{2\sin^2(\alpha)}\\
&\Leftrightarrow \theta_y \leqslant \arccos\left(1 - \frac{1}{2\sin^2(\alpha)}\right) = 2\arcsin\left(\frac{1}{2\sin(\alpha)}\right), \text{ true for } \alpha \in (0, \pi/2].
\end{aligned}$$

□

These $\vec{y}_0, \vec{y}_1$ will be called residual vectors. If $\vec{x}_0, \vec{x}_1$ are random points in the border then the $\vec{y}_0, \vec{y}_1$ are called the residual points and are random points of $\mathcal{S}_{d-1}$ (the sphere of dimension $d-1$ of points orthogonal to $\vec{s}$). From there, we have

Corollary 2. *Let $\alpha \in (0, \pi/2]$ and a random pair of vectors $\vec{x}_0, \vec{x}_1 \in \mathcal{B}_{\vec{s},\alpha}$. The probability that the pair is reducing is equal to $\mathcal{V}_{d-1}(\theta^*_\alpha)$, with*

$$\theta^*_\alpha := 2\arcsin\left(\frac{1}{2\sin(\alpha)}\right).$$

Notice that we have $\mathcal{V}_{d-1}$ because we work with residual vectors (orthogonal to $\vec{s}$) but since $\mathcal{V}_d$ and $\mathcal{V}_{d-1}$ are asymptotically equivalent, we will keep writing $\mathcal{V}_d(\theta^*_\alpha)$ everywhere for simplicity.

Probabilistic Arguments. We first recall the multiplicative Chernoff bound.

Proposition 5 (Multiplicative Chernoff bound, see for example [TKM+13]). *Suppose $X_1, ..., X_M$ are independent random variables taking values in $\{0, 1\}$, $Y = \sum_{i=1}^{M}$ and $\delta > 0$. We have*

$$\Pr[Y \geq (1+\delta)\mathbb{E}[Y]] \leq e^{-\frac{\delta^2\mathbb{E}[Y]}{3}}.$$

We now present a direct application of this bound which we will use in our analysis. Consider a set $S = \vec{s}_1, \ldots, \vec{s}_M$ points taken from the uniform distribution on the sphere S^{d-1} and $\vec{v}$ another point randomly chosen on the sphere. Fix also an angle $\alpha \in (0, \pi/2)$. We have the following statements:

Proposition 6. $\forall i \in [M]$, $\Pr[\vec{v} \in \mathcal{H}_{\vec{s}_i,\alpha}] = \Pr[\vec{s}_i \in \mathcal{H}_{\vec{v},\alpha}] = \mathcal{V}_d(\alpha)$.

Proof. Immediate by definition of $\mathcal{V}_d(\alpha)$ considering that both $\vec{v}$ and $\vec{s}_i$ are uniform random points on the sphere. □

From the above proposition, we immediately have that $\mathbb{E}[|S \cap \mathcal{H}_{\vec{v},\alpha}|] = M\mathcal{V}_d(\alpha)$. We now present a standard concentration bound for this quantity.

Proposition 7. *Assume we have $MV_d(\alpha) = N^x$ with $x > 0$ an absolute constant. Then*

$$\Pr[|S \cap \mathcal{H}_{\vec{v},\alpha}| \geq 2N^x] \leq e^{-\frac{N^x}{3}}.$$

Proof. Let X_i be the random variable which is equal to 1 if $\vec{s}_i \in \mathcal{H}_{\vec{v},\alpha}$ and is equal to 0 otherwise. Let $Y = \sum_{i=1}^{M} X_i$ so $\mathbb{E}[Y] = N^x$. Y is equal to the quantity $|S \cap \mathcal{H}_{\vec{v},\alpha}|$. A direct application of the multiplicative Chernoff bound gives

$$\Pr[Y \geq 2N^x] \leq e^{-\frac{N^x}{3}}$$

which is the desired result. □

Random Product Codes (RPC). We assume $d = m \cdot b$, for $m = O(\mathsf{polylog}(d))$ and a block size b. The vectors in $\mathbb{R}^d$ will be identified with tuples of m vectors in $\mathbb{R}^b$. A random product code C of parameters $[d, m, B]$ on subsets of $\mathbb{R}^d$ and of size B^m is defined as a code of the form $C = Q \cdot (C_1 \times C_2 \times \cdots C_m)$, where Q is a uniformly random rotation over $\mathbb{R}^d$ and the subcodes $C_1, ..., C_m$ are sets of B vectors, sampled uniformly and independently random over the sphere $\sqrt{1/m} \cdot \mathcal{S}^{b-1}$, so that codewords are points of the sphere $\mathcal{S}^{d-1}$. We can have a full description of C by storing mB points corresponding to the codewords of $C_1, \ldots, C_m$ and by storing the rotation Q. When the context is clear, C will correspond to the description of the code or to the set of codewords. Random product codes can be easily decoded in some parameter range:

Proposition 8 ([BDGL16]). *Let C be a random product code of parameters $[d, m, B]$ with $m = \log(d)$ and $B^m = N^{O(1)}$. For any $\vec{v} \in \mathcal{S}^{d-1}$ and $\alpha \in [0, \pi/2]$, one can compute $\mathcal{H}_{\vec{v},\alpha} \cap C$ in time $N^{o(1)} \cdot |\mathcal{H}_{\vec{v},\alpha} \cap C|$.*

4 General Framework for Sieving Algorithms Using LSF

We present here a general framework for sieving algorithms using LSF. We present here one sieving step where we start from a list L of $N' = N^{1+o(1)}$ lattice vectors of norm 1 and output N' lattice vectors of norm $\gamma < 1$. Sieving algorithms for SVP then consists of applying this subroutine $\mathsf{poly}(d)$ times (where we renormalize the vectors at each step) to find at the end a small vector. We can actually take γ very close to 1 at each iteration, and we refer for example to [NV08] for more details. This framework will encompass the best classical and quantum sieving algorithms.

Algorithm 1. Sieving algorithms using LSF with parameter c

Input: a list L of $N' = N^{1+o(1)}$ lattice vectors of norm 1, a constant $\gamma < 1$ and parameter $c \in (0,1)$.
Output: a list L' of N' lattice vectors of norm at most γ.
Algorithm:
$L' := \{\}$ (empty list)
while $|L'| \leq N'$ **do**
Sample a random product code C of parameter $[d, \log(d), N^{\frac{1-c}{\log(d)}}]$. Let $\vec{s}_1, \dots, \vec{s}_{N^{1-c}}$ be the code points of C and let $\alpha \in [\pi/3, \pi/2]$ st. $\mathcal{V}_d(\alpha) = \frac{1}{N^{1-c}}$.
for $\vec{v}$ in L **do**
Add $\vec{v}$ to its α-filter's buckets $f_\alpha(\vec{s}_i)$
for each $i \in [N^{1-c}]$ **do**
$S \leftarrow$ **FindAllSolutions**$(f_\alpha(\vec{s}_i), \gamma)$
$L' := L' \cup S$
return L'

The **FindAllSolutions**$(f_\alpha(\vec{s}_i), \gamma)$ subroutine starts from a list of vectors $\vec{x}_1, \dots, \vec{x}_{N^c} \in f_\alpha(\vec{s}_i)$ and outputs all vectors of the form $\vec{x}_i \pm \vec{x}_j$ (with $i \neq j$) of norm less than γ. We want to find asymptotically all the solutions and not strictly all of them. Let's say here we want to output half of them. Sometimes, there are no solutions so the algorithm outputs an empty list.

4.1 Analysis of the Above Algorithm

Heuristics and Simplifying Assumptions. We first present the heuristic arguments and simplifying assumptions we use for our analysis.

1. The input lattice points behave like random points on the sphere $\mathcal{S}^{d-1}$. Also, at each step of the sieving process, the points of the list L behave like random points on the sphere. The relevance of this heuristic has been studied and confirmed in a few papers starting from the initial NV-sieve [NV08].
2. The code points of C behave like random points of the sphere $\mathcal{S}^{d-1}$. This was argued in [BDGL16], see for instance Lemma 5.1 and Appendix C therein.
3. We assume that a random point in $f_\alpha(\vec{s}_i)$ is on the border of the filter, *i.e.* that it can be written $\vec{x} = \cos(\alpha)\vec{s}_i + \sin(\alpha)\vec{y}$ with $\vec{y} \perp \vec{s}_i$ and of norm 1. As we argue below, this will be approximately true with very high probability.

In order to argue point 3, notice that for any angle $\alpha \in (\pi/4, \pi/2)$ and $\varepsilon > 0$, we have $\mathcal{V}_d(\alpha) \gg \mathcal{V}_d(\alpha - \epsilon)$. Indeed, for an angle $\epsilon > 0$, $\mathcal{V}_d(\alpha - \epsilon) = \sin^d(\alpha - \epsilon) = \mathcal{V}_d(\alpha) \cdot (\epsilon')^d$ with $\epsilon' = \cos\epsilon - \frac{\sin\epsilon\cos\alpha}{\sin\alpha} < 1$ for $\alpha > \epsilon$. So the probability for a point to be at angle α with the center of the cap is exponentially higher than to be at angle $\alpha - \epsilon$. That justifies that with very high probability, points in $f_\alpha(\vec{s}_i)$ lie very close to the border of the cap and hence justifies point 3.

Completion. We start from a list L of N' points. The heuristic states that each point in L is modeled as a random point on the sphere S^{d-1} so each pair of points $\vec{x}, \vec{x}' \in L$ reduces with probability $\mathcal{V}_d(\pi/3) = \frac{1}{N}$. Since there are $\frac{N'(N'-1)}{2}$ pairs of points in L, we have on average $\frac{N'(N'-1)}{2N}$ pairs in L that are reducible. We can take for example $N' = 6N$ to ensure that there are on average $\approx 3N'$ pairs. Therefore, each time we find a random reducible pair, with probability at least $\frac{3N'-|L'|}{3N'} \geq 2/3$, it wasn't already in the list L'.

Time Analysis. From Corollary 2, we have that for an α-filter that has N^c points randomly distributed in this filter, the expected number of reducing pairs is $N^{2c} \cdot \mathcal{V}_{d-1}(\theta^*_\alpha)$. We now present the full time analysis of the above algorithm.

Proposition 9. *Consider Algorithm 1 with parameter $c \in [0,1]$ and associated angle $\alpha \in [\pi/3, \pi/2]$ satisfying $\mathcal{V}_d(\alpha) = N^{-(1-c)}$. Let ζ such that $N^\zeta = N^{2c} \cdot \mathcal{V}_{d-1}(\theta^*_\alpha)$. The above algorithm runs in time $T = \mathrm{NB_{REP}} \cdot (\mathrm{INIT} + \mathrm{FAS})$ where*

$$\mathrm{NB_{REP}} = \max\{1, N^{c-\zeta+o(1)}\} \quad ; \quad \mathrm{INIT} = N^{1+o(1)} \quad ; \quad \mathrm{FAS} = N^{1-c}\mathrm{FAS}_1$$

where FAS_1 *the running time of a single call to the* **FindAllSolutions** *subroutine.*

Proof. We first analyze the two **for** loops. INIT is the running time of the first loop. For each point $\vec{v} \in L$, we need to compute $\mathcal{H}_{\vec{v},\alpha} \cap C$ and update the corresponding buckets $f_\alpha(\vec{s}_i)$. We have $|C| = N^{1-c}$ and we chose α such that $\mathcal{V}_d(\alpha) = N^{-(1-c)}$, so the expected value of $|\mathcal{H}_{\vec{v},\alpha} \cap C|$ is 1. For each point $\vec{v}$, we can compute $\mathcal{H}_{\vec{v},\alpha} \cap C$ in time $N^{o(1)}|\mathcal{H}_{\vec{v},\alpha}|$ using Proposition 8. From there, we can conclude that we compute the filter for the N' points in time $\mathrm{INIT} = N^{1+o(1)}$.

The second loop runs in time $\mathrm{FAS} = N^{1-c}\mathrm{FAS}_1$ by definition. After this loop, the average number of solutions found is N^ζ for each call to **FindAllSolutions** so $N^{1-c+\zeta}$ in total (notice that we can have $\zeta < 0$, which means that we can find on average much less that one solution for each call of **FindAllSolutions**). We run the **while** loop until we find N' solutions so we must repeat this process $\mathrm{NB_{REP}} = \max\{1, N^{1-(1-c+\zeta)+o(1)}\} = \max\{1, N^{c-\zeta+o(1)}\}$ times. □

This formulation of sieving algorithms is easy to analyze. Notice that the above running time depends only on c (since α can be derived from c and ζ can be derived from c, α) and on the **FindAllSolutions** subroutine. We now retrieve the best known classical and quantum sieving algorithm in this framework.

Best Classical Algorithm. In order to retrieve the time exponent of [BDGL16], we take $c \to 0$, which implies $\alpha \to \pi/3$. We can compute $\theta^*_{\pi/3} \approx 1.23\text{rad} \approx 70.53°$ and $\zeta = -0.4094$. In this case, we have $\mathrm{FAS}_1 = O(1)$. From the above proposition, we get a total running time of $T = N^{1.4094+o(1)} = 2^{0.2925d+o(d)}$.

Best Quantum Algorithm. In order to retrieve the time exponent of [Laa16], we take $c = 0.2782$. This value actually corresponds to the case where $\zeta = 0$, so we have on average one solution per α-filter. For the **FindAllSolutions** subroutine, we can apply Grover's algorithm on pairs of vectors in the filter to find this solution in time $\sqrt{N^{2c}} = N^c$ (there are N^{2c} pairs) so $\mathrm{FAS}_1 = N^c$. Putting this together, we obtain $T = N^{1+c+o(1)} = N^{1.2782+o(1)} = 2^{0.2653d+o(d)}$.

In the next section, we show how to improve the above quantum algorithm. Our main idea is to replace Grover's algorithm used in the **FindAllSolutions** subroutine with a quantum random walk. In the next section, we present the most natural quantum walk which is done over a Johnson graph and where a vertex is marked if the points of a vertex contain a reducible pair, in a similar way than for element distinctness. We then show in a later section how this random walk can be improved by relaxing the condition on marked vertices.

5 Quantum Random Walk for the FindAllSolutions Subroutine: A First Attempt

5.1 Constructing the Graph

We start from an unordered list $\vec{x}_1, \dots, \vec{x}_{N^c}$ of distinct points in a filter $f_\alpha(\vec{s})$ with α satisfying $\mathcal{V}_d(\alpha) = \frac{1}{N^{1-c}}$. Let L_x be this list of $\vec{x}_i$. For each $i \in [N^c]$, we write $\vec{x}_i = \cos(\alpha)\vec{s} + \sin(\alpha)\vec{y}_i$ where each $\vec{y}_i$ is of norm 1 and orthogonal to $\vec{s}$. Recall from Proposition 4 that a pair $(\vec{x}_i, \vec{x}_j)$ is reducible iff. $\theta(\vec{y}_i, \vec{y}_j) = \theta^*_\alpha = 2\arcsin(\frac{1}{2\sin(\alpha)})$. We will work only on the residual vectors $\vec{y}_i$ and present the quantum random walk that finds pairs $\vec{y}_i, \vec{y}_j$ such that $\theta(\vec{y}_i, \vec{y}_j) = \theta^*_\alpha$ more efficiently than with Grover's algorithm. Let $L_y = \vec{y}_1, \dots, \vec{y}_{N^c}$ be the list of all residual vectors.

The quantum walk has two extra parameters $c_1 \in [0, c]$ and $c_2 \in [0, c_1]$. From these two parameters, let $\beta \in [\pi/3, \pi/2]$ st. $\mathcal{V}_d(\beta) = N^{c_2 - c_1}$ and ρ_0 st. $N^{\rho_0} = \frac{\mathcal{V}_d(\beta)}{\mathcal{W}_d(\beta, \theta^*_\alpha)}$. We start by sampling a random product code $\mathcal{C}_2$ with parameters $[(d-1), \log(d-1), N^{\frac{\rho_0 + c_1 - c_2}{\log(d-1)}}]$ which has therefore $N^{\rho_0 + c_1 - c_2} = \frac{1}{\mathcal{W}_d(\beta, \theta^*_\alpha)}$ points denoted $\vec{t}_1, \dots, \vec{t}_{N^{\rho_0 + c_1 - c_2}}$. We perform our quantum random walk on a graph $G = (V, E)$ where each vertex $v \in V$ contains:

- An unordered list $L^v_y = \vec{y}_1, \dots, \vec{y}_{N^{c_1}}$ of distinct points taken from L_y.
- For each $\vec{t}_i \in \mathcal{C}_2$, we store the list of elements of $J^v(\vec{t}_i) := f_\beta(\vec{t}_i) \cap L^v_y$. For each $\vec{t}_i$, we do this using a quantum data structure that stores $J^v(\vec{t}_i)$ where we can add and delete efficiently in quantum superposition. This can be done with QRAM. Notice that we have on average

$$|J^v(\vec{t}_i)| = N^{c_1} \cdot \mathcal{V}_d(\beta) = N^{c_2},$$

  and we need to store in total $|\mathcal{C}_2| \cdot N^{c_2} = N^{c_1 + \rho_0}$ such elements in total for each vertex.
- A bit that says whether the vertex is marked (we detail the marked condition below).

The vertices of G consists of the above vertices for all possible lists L_y^v. We have $(v, w) \in E$ if we can go from L_y^v to L_y^w by changing exactly one value. In order words

$$(v, w) \in E \Leftrightarrow \exists \vec{y}_{old} \in L_y^v \text{ and } \vec{y}_{new} \in L_y \backslash L_y^v \text{ st. } L_y^w = \left(L_y^v \backslash \{\vec{y}_{old}\}\right) \cup \{\vec{y}_{new}\}.$$

This means the graph G is exactly a Johnson graph $J(N^c, N^{c_1})$ where each vertex also has some additional information as we described above. Once we find a marked vertex, it contains a pair $(\vec{y}_i, \vec{y}_j)$ such that $\theta(\vec{y}_i, \vec{y}_j) \leq \theta_\alpha^*$ from which we directly get a reducible pair $(\vec{x}_i, \vec{x}_j)$.

Condition for a Vertex to be Marked. We define the following subsets of vertices. We first define the set M_0 vertices for which there exists a pair of points which is reducible.

$$M_0 := \{v \in V : \exists \vec{y}_i, \vec{y}_j \neq \vec{y}_i \in L_y^v, \theta(\vec{y}_i, \vec{y}_j) \leq \theta_\alpha^*\}.$$

Ideally, we would want to mark each vertex in M_0, however this would induce a too large update cost when updating the bit that specifies whether the vertex is marked or not. Instead, we will consider as marked vertices subsets of M_0 but for which the update can be done more efficiently, but losing only a small fraction of the marked vertices. For each $J^v(\vec{t}_i)$, we define $\widetilde{J^v}(\vec{t}_i)$ which consists of the first $2N^{c_2}$ elements of $J^v(\vec{t}_i)$[7] and if $|J^v(\vec{t}_i)| \leq 2N^{c_2}$, we have $\widetilde{J^v}(\vec{t}_i) = J^v(\vec{t}_i)$. We define the set of marked elements M as follows:

$$M := \{v \in V : \exists \vec{t} \in \mathcal{C}_2, \exists \vec{y}_i, \vec{y}_j \neq \vec{y}_i \in \widetilde{J^v}(\vec{t}), \text{ st. } \theta(\vec{y}_i, \vec{y}_j) \leq \theta_\alpha^*\}.$$

The reason for using such a condition for marked vertices is that when we will perform an update, hence removing a point $\vec{y}_{old}$ from a vertex and adding a point $\vec{y}_{new}$, we will just need to look at the points in $\widetilde{J^v}(\vec{t})$ for $\vec{t} \in f_\beta(\vec{y}_{new}) \cap \mathcal{C}_2$ which can be done faster than by looking at all the points of the vertex. If we used $J^v(\vec{t})$ instead of $\widetilde{J^v}(\vec{t})$ then the argument would be simpler but we would only be able to argue about the average running time of the update but the quantum walk framework require to bound the update for any pair of adjacent vertices[8]. Also notice that each vertex still contain the sets $J^v(\vec{t}_i)$ (from which one can easily compute $\widetilde{J^v}(\vec{t}_i)$).

---

[7] We consider an global ordering of elements of L_y, for example with respect to their index, and $J^v(\vec{t}_i)$ consists of the $2N^{c_2}$ elements of $J^v(\vec{t}_i)$ which are the smallest with respect to this ordering.

[8] This problem arises in several quantum random walk algorithms, for example for quantum subset-sum algorithms. One solution is to use a heuristic that essentially claims that we can use the average running time of the update cost instead of the worst case. In our case, we don't need this heuristic as we manage to bound the update cost in the worst case. We refer to [BBSS20] for an interesting discussion on the topic.

5.2 Time Analysis of the Quantum Random Walk on This Graph

We are now ready to analyze our quantum random walk, and compute its different parameters. Throughout our analysis, we define $K(\vec{y_i}) := f_\beta(\vec{y_i}) \cap \mathcal{C}_2$ and we have on average

$$|K(\vec{y_i})| = N^{\rho_0+c_1-c_2} \cdot \mathcal{V}_d(\beta) = N^{\rho_0}.$$

Using Proposition 7, we have for each i,

$$\Pr[|K(\vec{y_i})|] > 2N^{\rho}] \le e^{-\frac{N^{\rho_0}}{3}} \tag{3}$$

and using a union bound, we have for any absolute constant $\rho_0 > 0$:

$$\Pr[\forall i \in [N^c],\ |K(\vec{y_i})| \le 2N^{\rho}] \ge 1 - N^c e^{-\frac{N^{\rho_0}}{3}} = 1 - o(1). \tag{4}$$

So for a fixed α-filter, we have with high probability that each $|K(\vec{y_i})|$ is bounded by $2N^{\rho_0}$ and we assume we are in this case. The sets $K(\vec{y_i})$ can hence be constructed in time $N^{\rho_0+o(1)}$ using the decoding procedure (Proposition 8) for $\mathcal{C}_2$.

Setup Cost. In order to construct a full vertex v from a list $L_y^v = \vec{y}_1, \ldots, \vec{y}_{N^{c_1}}$, the main cost is to construct the lists $J^v(\vec{t_i}) = f_\beta(\vec{t_i}) \cap L_y^v$. To do this, we start from empty lists $J^v(\vec{t_i})$. For each $\vec{y_i} \in L_y^v$, we construct the list $K(\vec{y_i}) = f_\beta(\vec{y_i}) \cap \mathcal{C}_2$ and for each codeword $\vec{t_j} \in K(\vec{y_i})$, we add $\vec{y_i}$ in $J^v(\vec{t_i})$.

This takes time $N^{c_1} \cdot N^{\rho_0+o(1)}$. We can perform a uniform superposition of the vertices by performing the above procedure in quantum superposition. This can also be done in $N^{c_1} \cdot N^{\rho_0+o(1)}$ since we use a quantum data structure that performs these insertions in $J^v(\vec{t_i})$ efficiently. So in conclusion,

$$\mathcal{S} = N^{c_1+\rho_0+o(1)}.$$

Update Cost. We show here how to go from a vertex v with associated list L_y^v to a vertex w with $L_y^w = \left(L_y^v \backslash \{\vec{y}_{old}\}\right) \cup \{\vec{y}_{new}\}$. We start from a vertex v so we also have the lists $J^v(\vec{t_i}) = f_\beta(\vec{t_i}) \cap L_y^v$.

In order to construct the lists $J^w(\vec{t_i})$, we first construct $K(\vec{y}_{old}) = f_\beta(\vec{y}_{old}) \cap \mathcal{C}_2$ and for each $\vec{t_i}$ in this set, we remove $\vec{y}_{old}$ from $J^v(\vec{t_i})$. Then, we construct $K(\vec{y}_{new})$ and for each $\vec{t_i}$ in this set, we add $\vec{y}_{new}$ to $J^v(\vec{t_i})$, thus obtaining all the $J^w(\vec{t_i})$. Constructing the two lists takes time on average $N^{\rho_0+o(1)}$ and we then perform at most $2N^{\rho_0}$ deletion and insertion operations which are done efficiently. These operations take $N^{\rho_0+o(1)}$ deletions and insertions, which can be done efficiently.

If v was marked and $\vec{y}_{old}$ is not part of the reducible pair then we do not change the last registers for L_y^w. If v was not marked, then we have to ensure that adding $\vec{y}_{new}$ doesn't make it marked. So we need to check whether there exists $\vec{y'} \neq \vec{y}_{new}$ such that

$$\exists \vec{t} \in \mathcal{C}_2, \vec{y}_{new}, \vec{y_0} \in J^w(\vec{t}) \text{ and } (\vec{y}_{new}, \vec{y_0}) \text{ are reducible.}$$

If such a point $\vec{y}_0$ exists, it necessarily lies in the set $\cup_{\vec{t} \in K(\vec{y}_{new})} \widetilde{J^v}(\vec{t})$ which is of size at most $2N^{\rho} \cdot 2N^{c_2} = 4N^{\rho_0 + c_2}$. We perform a Grover search on this set to determine whether there exists a $\vec{y}_0 \in \cup_{\vec{t} \in \mathcal{C}_2} \widetilde{J^v}(\vec{t})$ that reduces with $\vec{y}_{new}$, and this takes time $N^{\frac{\rho_0 + c_1 + o(1)}{2}}$. In conclusion, we have that the average update time is

$$\mathcal{U} = N^{\rho_0 + o(1)} + N^{\frac{\rho_0 + c_2 + o(1)}{2}} \leq N^{\max\{\rho_0, \frac{\rho_0 + c_2}{2}\} + o(1)}.$$

Checking Cost. Each vertex has a bit that says whether it is marked or not so we have

$$\mathcal{C} = 1.$$

Computing the Fraction of Marked Vertices Epsilon. We prove here the following proposition

Proposition 10. $\varepsilon \geq \Theta\left(\min\left\{N^{2c_1} \mathcal{V}_d(\beta), 1\right\}\right)$.

Proof. We consider a random vertex in the graph and lower bound the probability that it is marked. A sufficient condition for a vertex v to be marked is if it satisfies the following 2 events :

- $E_1 : \exists \vec{t} \in \mathcal{C}_2, \exists \vec{y}_i, \vec{y}_j \neq \vec{y}_i \in J^v(\vec{t}),$ st. $\theta(\vec{y}_i, \vec{y}_j) \leq \theta^*_\alpha$.
- $E_2 : \forall \vec{t} \in \mathcal{C}_2, |J^v(\vec{t})| \leq 2N^{c_2}$.

The second property implies that $\forall \vec{t} \in \mathcal{C}_2,\ J^v(\vec{t}) = \widetilde{J^v}(\vec{t})$ and in that case, the first property implies that v is marked. We now bound the probability of each event

Lemma 1. $\Pr[E_1] \geq \Theta\left(\min\left\{N^{2c_1} \mathcal{V}_d(\beta), 1\right\}\right)$.

Proof. For a fixed pair $\vec{y}_i, \vec{y}_j \neq \vec{y}_i \in L^v_y$, we have $\Pr[\theta(\vec{y}_i, \vec{y}_j) \leq \theta^*_\alpha] = \mathcal{V}_d(\theta^*_\alpha)$. Since there are $\Theta(N^{2c_1})$ such pairs, if we define the event E_0 as: $\exists \vec{y}_i, \vec{y}_j \neq \vec{y}_i \in L^v_y$, st. $\theta(\vec{y}_i, \vec{y}_j) \leq \theta^*_\alpha$, we have

$$\Pr[E_0] \geq \Theta\left(\min\left\{N^{2c_1} \mathcal{V}_d(\beta), 1\right\}\right).$$

Now we assume E_0 holds and we try to compute the probability that E_1 is true conditioned on E_0. So we assume E_0 and let $\vec{y}_i, \vec{y}_j \neq \vec{y}_i \in L^v_y$, st. $\theta(\vec{y}_i, \vec{y}_j) \leq \theta^*_\alpha$. For each code point $\vec{t} \in \mathcal{C}_2$, we have

$$\Pr[\vec{y}_i, \vec{y}_j \in J^v(\vec{t})] = \Pr[\vec{t} \in \mathcal{H}_{\vec{y}_i,\beta} \cap \mathcal{H}_{\vec{y}_j,\beta}] = \mathcal{W}_d(\beta, \theta^*_\alpha).$$

Therefore, we have

$$\Pr[\exists \vec{t} \in \mathcal{C}_2,\ \vec{y}_i, \vec{y}_j \in J^v(\vec{t})] = 1 - (1 - \mathcal{W}_d(\beta, \theta^*_\alpha))^{|\mathcal{C}_2|}. \tag{5}$$

Since $|\mathcal{C}_2| = \frac{1}{\mathcal{W}_d(\beta, \theta^*_\alpha)}$, we can conclude

$$\Pr[E_1|E_0] \geq \Pr[\exists \vec{t} \in \mathcal{C}_2,\ \vec{y}_i, \vec{y}_j \in J^v(\vec{t})] = 1 - (1 - \mathcal{W}_d(\beta, \theta^*_\alpha))^{|\mathcal{C}_2|} \geq \Theta(1),$$

which implies $\Pr[E_1] \geq \Pr[E_1|E_0] \cdot \Pr[E_0] \geq \Theta\left(\max\left\{N^{2c_1} \mathcal{V}_d(\beta), 1\right\}\right)$. □

Lemma 2. $\Pr[E_2] \geq 1 - |C_2|e^{-\frac{N^{c_2}}{3}}$.

Proof. For each $\vec{t} \in \mathcal{C}_2$, we have using Proposition 7 that $\Pr[|J^v(\vec{t})| \leq 2N^{c_2}] \geq 1 - e^{-\frac{N^{c_2}}{3}}$. Using a union bound, we have

$$\Pr[\forall \vec{t} \in \mathcal{C}_2, |J^v(\vec{t})| \leq 2N^{c_2}] \geq 1 - |C_2|e^{-\frac{N^{c_2}}{3}}.$$

□

We can now finish the proof of our Proposition. We have

$$\begin{aligned}\varepsilon \geq \Pr[E_1 \wedge E_2] &\geq \Pr[E_1] + \Pr[E_2] - 1 \\ &\geq \Theta\left(\max\left\{N^{2c_1}\mathcal{V}_d(\beta), 1\right\}\right) - |C_2|e^{-\frac{N^{c_2}}{3}} \\ &\geq \Theta\left(\max\left\{N^{2c_1}\mathcal{V}_d(\beta), 1\right\}\right)\end{aligned}$$

The last inequality comes from the fact that $|C_2|e^{-\frac{N^{c_2}}{3}}$ is vanishing doubly exponentially in d (N is exponential in d) so it is negligible compared to the first term and is absorbed by the $\Theta(\cdot)$. □

Computing the Spectral Gap Delta. We are in a $J(N^c, N^{c_1})$ Johnson graph so we have

$$\delta \approx N^{-c_1}.$$

Running Time of the Quantum Walk. The running time T_1 of the quantum walk is (omitting the $o(1)$ terms and the $O(\cdot)$ notations)

$$\begin{aligned}T_1 &= \mathcal{S} + \frac{1}{\sqrt{\varepsilon}}\left(\frac{1}{\sqrt{\delta}}\,\mathcal{U} + \mathcal{C}\right) \\ &= N^{c_1+\rho_0} + \frac{1}{\max\{1, N^{c_1}\sqrt{\mathcal{V}_d(\theta^*_\alpha)}\}}\left(N^{\max\{\rho_0, \frac{\rho_0+c_2}{2}\}+\frac{c_1}{2}}\right)\end{aligned}$$

In this running time, we can find one marked vertex with high probability if it exists. We repeat this quantum random walk until we find $\max\{\frac{N^\zeta}{2}, 1\}$ solutions.

Algorithm for the FindAllSolutions procedure

Pick a random product code $\mathcal{C}_2$.
while the number of solutions found is $< \frac{N^\zeta}{2}$:
  Run our QRW to find a solution and add it to the list of solutions if it hasn't been found.

For $\zeta > 0$, there are N^ζ different solutions that can be found in each α-filter. Each time we find a solution, since the list of solutions found is $< \frac{N^\zeta}{2}$. Therefore, the probability that each solutions found by the QRW is new is at least $\frac{1}{2}$. We have therefore

$$\mathrm{FAS}_1 = \max\{N^{\zeta}, 1\} \cdot T_1.$$

If $\zeta > 0$, our algorithm finds $\Theta(N^{\zeta})$ solutions in time $N^{\zeta}T_1$ and if $\zeta \leq 0$, our algorithm finds 1 solution in time T_1 with probability $\Theta(N^{-\zeta})$.

5.3 Memory Analysis

Classical Space. We have to store at the same time in classic memory the N list vectors of size d, and the buckets of the α-filters. Each vector is in $N^{o(1)}$ α-filter, so our algorithm takes classical space $N^{1+o(1)}$.

Memory Requirements of the Quantum Random Walk. Each vertex v of the graph stores all the $J^v(\vec{t_i})$ which together take space $N^{c_1+\rho_0}$. We need to store a superposition of vertices so we need $N^{c_1+\rho_0}$ quantum registers and we need that same amount of QRAM because we perform insertions and deletions in the database in quantum superposition. All the operations require QRAM access to the whole list L_y which is classically stored and is of size N^c. Therefore, we also require N^c QRAM.

5.4 Optimal Parameters for This Quantum Random Walk

Our algorithm takes in argument three parameters: $c \in [0, 1]$, $c_1 \leq c$ and $c_2 \leq c_1$ from which we can express all the other variables we use: α, θ^*_α, β, ρ_0 and ζ. We recall these expressions as they are scattered throughout the previous sections:

- α: angle in $[\pi/3, \pi/2]$ that satisfies $\mathcal{V}_d(\alpha) = \frac{1}{N^{1-c}}$.
- $\theta^*_\alpha = 2\arcsin(\frac{1}{2\sin(\alpha)})$.
- β: angle in $[\pi/3, \pi/2]$ that satisfies $\mathcal{V}_d(\beta) = \frac{1}{N^{c_1-c_2}}$.
- ρ_0: non-negative real number such that $N^{\rho_0} = \frac{\mathcal{V}_d(\beta)}{\mathcal{W}_d(\beta,\theta^*_\alpha)}$.
- ζ: real number such that $N^{\zeta} = N^{2c}\mathcal{V}_d(\theta^*_\alpha)$.

Plugging the value of FAS_1 from the end of Sect. 5.2 in Proposition 9, we find that the total running time of our quantum sieving algorithm with parameters c, c_1, c_2 is

$$T = N^{c-\zeta}\left(N + N^{1-c}\max\{N^{\zeta}, 1\}\left(N^{c_1+\rho_0} + \frac{1}{\max\{1, N^{c_1}\sqrt{\mathcal{V}_d(\theta^*_\alpha)}\}}\left(N^{\max\{\rho_0, \frac{\rho_0+c_2}{2}\}+\frac{c_1}{2}}\right)\right)\right).$$

We ran a numerical optimization over c, c_1, c_2 to get our optimal running time, summed up in the following theorem.

Proposition 11. *Our algorithm with parameters*

$$c \approx 0.3300 \quad ; \quad c_1 \approx 0.1952 \quad ; \quad c_2 \approx 0.0603$$

heuristically solves SVP on dimension d in time $T = N^{1.2555+o(1)} = 2^{0.2605d+o(d)}$, *uses QRAMM of maximum size* $N^{0.3300+o(1)} = 2^{0.0685d+o(d)}$, *a quantum memory of size* $N^{0.2555+o(1)} = 2^{0.0530d+o(d)}$ *and uses a classical memory of size* $N^{1+o(1)} = 2^{0.2075d+o(d)}$.

With these parameters, we obtain the values of the other parameters:

$$\alpha \approx 1.1388\text{rad} \approx 65.25°; \quad \theta^*_\alpha \approx 1.1661\text{rad} \approx 66.46°; \quad \beta \approx 1.3745\text{rad} \approx 78.75°$$

$$\rho_0 \approx 0.0603; \quad \zeta \approx 0.0745.$$

As well as the quantum walk parameters:

$$\mathcal{S} = N^{c_1+\rho_0} = N^{0.2555}; \quad \mathcal{U} = N^{\rho_0} = N^{0.0603}; \quad \mathcal{C} = 0; \quad \varepsilon = \delta = N^{-c_1} = N^{-0.1952}.$$

The equality $\rho_0 = c_2$ allows to balance the time of the two operations during the update step. With these parameters we also obtain $\mathcal{S} = \mathcal{U}/\sqrt{\epsilon\ \delta} = N^{c_1+\rho_0} = N^{0.2555d}$, which balances the overall time complexity.

Notice that with these parameters, we can rewrite T as

$$T = N^{c-\zeta}\left(N + N^{1-c+\zeta+c_1+\rho_0}\right) = N^{1+c-\zeta} + N^{1+c_1+\rho_0}.$$

Also, we have $c_1 + \rho_0 = c - \zeta$, which equalizes the random walk step with the initialization step. From our previous analysis, the amount of required QRAM is N^c and the amount of quantum memory needed is $N^{c_1+\rho_0}$.

6 Quantum Random Walk for the FindAllSolutions Subroutine: An Improved Quantum Random Walk

We now add a variable $\rho \in (0, \rho_0]$ that will replace the choice of ρ_0 above. ρ_0 was chosen in order to make sure that if a pair $\vec{y}_i, \vec{y}_j$ exists in a vertex v, then it will appear on one of the $J^v(\vec{t})$ for $\vec{t} \in \mathcal{C}_2$. However, we can relax this and only mark a small fraction of these vertices. This will reduce the fraction of marked vertices, which makes it harder to find a solution, but having a smaller ρ will reduce the running time of our quantum random walk.

The construction is exactly the same as in the previous section just that we replace ρ_0 with ρ. This implies that $|C_2| = N^{\rho+c_1-c_2}$. We can perform the same analysis as above

Time Analysis of this QRW in the Regime $\zeta + \rho - \rho_0 > 0$. We consider the regime where $\zeta + \rho - \rho_0 > 0$ and $\rho \in (0, \rho_0]$ (in particular $\zeta > 0$, since $\rho_0 > 0$). This regime ensures that even when if we have less marked vertices, then there on average more than one marked vertex, so our algorithm at least finds one solution with a constant probability.

The analysis walk is exactly the same than in Sect. 5.2, each repetition of the quantum random walk takes time T_1 with

$$T_1 = \mathcal{S} + \frac{1}{\sqrt{\varepsilon}}\left(\frac{1}{\sqrt{\delta}}\mathcal{U} + \mathcal{C}\right)$$

with

$$\mathcal{S} = N^{c_1+\rho}, \quad \mathcal{U} = N^{\max\{\rho, \frac{\rho+c_2}{2}\}+o(1)}, \quad \mathcal{C} = 1,$$
$$\varepsilon = N^{2c_1} N^{\rho-\rho_0} \mathcal{V}_d(\theta^*_\alpha), \quad \delta = N^{-c1}.$$

The only thing maybe to develop is the computation of ε. We perform the same analysis as above but with $|C_2| = N^{\rho+c_1-c_2}$. This means that Eq. 5 of Lemma 1 becomes

$$\begin{aligned}\Pr[\exists \vec{t} \in \mathcal{C}_2,\ \vec{y}_i, \vec{y}_j \in J^v(\vec{t})] &= 1 - (1 - \mathcal{W}_d(\beta, \theta^*_\alpha))^{|C_2|} \\ &\geq |C_2| \mathcal{W}_d(\beta, \theta^*_\alpha) = N^{\rho-\rho_0}.\end{aligned}$$

which gives the extra term $N^{\rho-\rho_0}$ in ε. Another issue is that now, we can only extract $N^{\zeta+\rho-\rho_0}$ solutions each time we construct the graph, we have therefore to repeat this procedure to find $\frac{N^{\zeta+\rho-\rho_0}}{2}$ solutions with this graph and then repeat the procedure with a new code $\mathcal{C}_2$. The algorithm becomes

Algorithm from Sect. 6 with parameter ρ

while the total number of solutions found is $< \frac{N^\zeta}{2}$:
  Pick a random product code $\mathcal{C}_2$.
  while the number of solutions found is $< \frac{N^{\zeta+\rho-\rho_0}}{2}$ with this $\mathcal{C}_2$:
    Run our QRW with ρ to find a new solution.

With this procedure, we also find $\Theta(N^\zeta)$ solutions in time $N^\zeta T_1$ and $\mathrm{FAS}_1 = N^\zeta T_1$ (Recall that we are in the case $\zeta \geq \zeta + \rho - \rho_0 > 0$). Actually, optimal parameters will be when $c_2 = 0$ and $\rho \to 0$.

6.1 Analysis of the Above Algorithm

This change implies that some reducing pairs are missed. For the quantum random walk complexity, this only change the probability, denoted ϵ, so that a vertex is marked. Indeed, it is equal to the one so that there happens a collision between two vectors through a filter, which is no longer equal to the existence of a reducing pair within the vertex. Indeed, to have a collision, there is the supplementary condition of both vectors of a reducing pair are inserted in the same filter, which is of probability $N^{\rho_0-\rho}$. So we get a higher value of $\epsilon = N^{2c_1} \mathcal{V}_d(\theta^*_\alpha) \cdot N^{\rho_0-\rho}$.

However, this increasing is compensated by the reducing of the costs of the setup ($N^{c_1+\rho+o(1)}$) and the update ($2N^{\max\{\rho, \frac{\rho+c_2}{2}\}+o(1)}$).

A numerical optimisation over ρ, c, c_1 and c_2 leads to the following theorem.

Theorem 4 (Theorem 1 restated). *Our algorithm with a free ρ with parameters*

$$\rho \to 0 \quad ; \quad c \approx 0.3696 \quad ; \quad c_1 \approx 0.2384 \quad ; \quad c_2 = 0$$

heuristically solves SVP on dimension d in time $T = N^{1.2384+o(1)} = 2^{0.2570d+o(d)}$, uses QRAM of maximum size $N^{0.3696} = 2^{0.0767d}$, a quantum memory of size $N^{0.2384} = 2^{0.0495d}$ and uses a classical memory of size $N^{1+o(1)} = 2^{0.2075d+o(d)}$.

With these parameters, we obtain the values of the other parameters:

$$\alpha \approx 1.1514 \text{ rad}; \quad \theta^*_\alpha \approx 1.1586 \text{ rad}; \quad \beta \approx 1.1112 \text{ rad}; \quad \zeta \approx 0.1313.$$

As well as the quantum walk parameters:

$$\mathcal{S} = N^{c_1+\rho} = N^{0.2384}; \quad \mathcal{U} = N^{\rho} = N^{o(1)}; \quad \mathcal{C} = 0; \quad \varepsilon = \delta = N^{-c_1} = N^{-0.2384}.$$

With these parameters, we also have $\rho_0 = 0.107$ so we are in the regime where $\zeta + \rho - \rho_0 > 0$. As in the previous time complexity stated in Theorem 11, we reach the equality $S = U/\sqrt{\epsilon\delta}$, which allows to balance the time of the two steps of the quantum random walk: the setup and the search itself.

Notice that with these parameters, we can rewrite T as

$$T = N^{c-\zeta}\left(N + N^{1-c+\zeta+c_1+\rho}\right) = N^{1+c-\zeta} + N^{1+c_1+\rho}.$$

With our optimal parameters, we have $\rho = 0$ and $c - \zeta = c_1$, which equalizes the random walk step with the initialization step. From our previous analysis, the amount of required QRAM is N^c and the amount of quantum memory needed is N^{c_1}.

7 Space-Time Trade-Offs

By varying the values c, c_1, c_2 and ρ, we can obtain trade-offs between QRAM and time, and between quantum memory and time. All the following results come from numerical observations.

7.1 Trade-Off for Fixed Quantum Memory

We computed the minimized time if we add the constraint that the quantum memory must not exceed 2^{Md}. For a chosen fixed M, the quantum memory is denoted is $2^{\mu_M d} = 2^{Md}$ and the corresponding minimal time by $2^{\tau_M d}$. The variation of M also impacts the required QRAM to run the algorithm, that we denote by $2^{\gamma_M d}$.

So we get a trade-off between time and quantum memory in Fig. 1, and the evolution of QRAM in function of M for a minimal time is in Fig. 2.

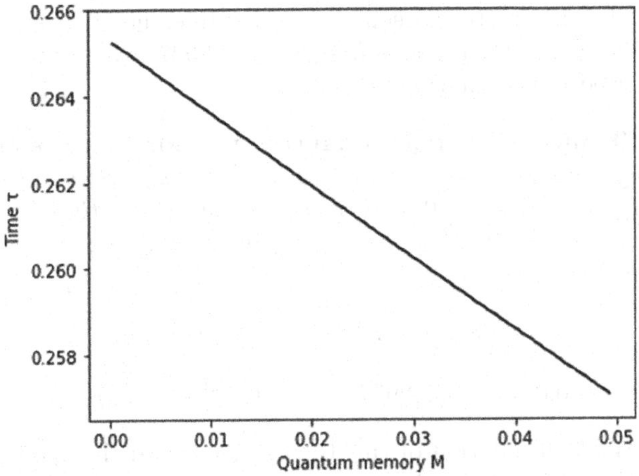

Fig. 1. Quantum memory-time trade-off.

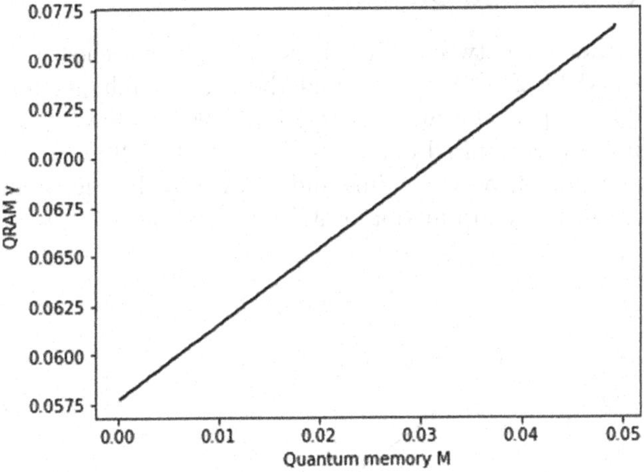

Fig. 2. QRAM in function of available quantum memory for minimized time.

For more than $2^{0.0495d}$ quantum memory, increasing it does not improve the time complexity anymore. An important fact is that for a fixed M the corresponding value τ_M from Fig. 1 and γ_M from Fig. 2 can be achieved simultaneously with the same algorithm.

We observe that from $M = 0$ to 0.0495 these curves are very close to affine. Indeed, the function that passes through the two extremities points is of expression $0.2653 - 0.1670M$. The difference between τ_M and its affine approximation does not exceed $4 \cdot 10^{-5}$. By the same way, the difference between γ_M and its affine average function of expression $0.0578 + 0.3829M$ is inferior to $2 \cdot 10^{-4}$. All this is summarized in the following theorem.

Theorem 5 (Trade-off for fixed quantum memory). *There exists a quantum algorithm using quantum random walks that solves SVP on dimension d which for a parameter $M \in [0, 0.0495]$ heuristically runs in time $2^{\tau_M d + o(d)}$, uses QRAM of maximum size $2^{\gamma_M d}$, a quantum memory of size $2^{\mu_M d}$ and a classical memory of size $2^{0.2075d}$ where*

$$\tau_M \in 0.2653 - 0.1670M + [-2 \cdot 10^{-5}; 4 \cdot 10^{-5}]$$

$$\gamma_M \in 0.0578 + 0.3829M - [0; 2 \cdot 10^{-4}] \quad ; \quad \mu_M = M.$$

In the informal formulation of this theorem, we used the symbols $\lessapprox$ and $\gtrapprox$ that refers to these hidden small values.

7.2 Trade-Off for Fixed QRAM

We also get a trade-off between QRAM and time. For a chosen fixed M', the QRAM is denoted by $2^{\gamma_{M'} d} = 2^{M'd}$, and the corresponding minimal time by $2^{\tau_{M'} d}$. The required quantum memory is denoted $2^{\mu_{M'} d}$. Note that $2^{\mu_{M'} d}$ is the also the amount of the required quantum QRAM called "QRAQM".

This gives a trade-off between time and QRAM in the Fig. 3, and the evolution of quantum memory in function of M' is in the Fig. 4.

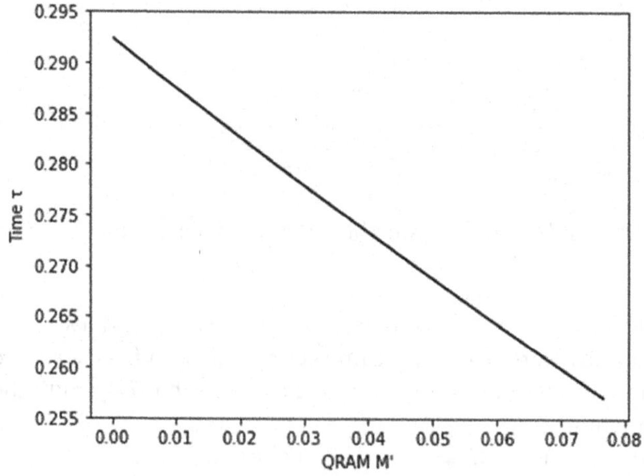

Fig. 3. QRAM-time trade-off.

For more than $2^{0.0767d}$ QRAM, increasing it does not improve the time complexity.

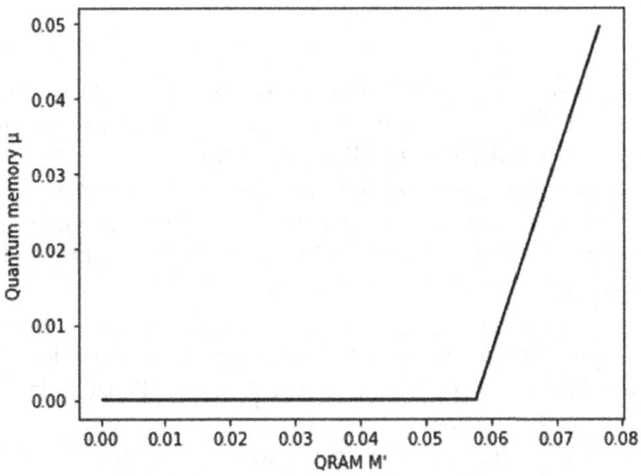

Fig. 4. Quantum memory in function of available QRAM for minimized time.

The difference between the function $\tau_{M'}$ and its average affine function of expression $0.2926 - 0.4647 \cdot M'$ does not exceed $6 \cdot 10^{-4}$. This affine function is a upper bound of $\tau_{M'}$.

From $M' = 0$ to 0.0579 the function $\gamma_{M'}$ is at 0. Then, it is close to the affine function of expression $2.6356(M' - 0.0579)$. So $\gamma_{M'}$ can be approximated by $\max\{2.6356(M' - 0.0579), 0\}$, and the difference between $\gamma_{M'}$ and this approximation does not exceed $9 \cdot 10^{-4}$. All this is summarized in the following theorem.

Theorem 6 (Trade-off for fixed QRAM). *There exists a quantum algorithm using quantum random walks that solves SVP on dimension d which for a parameter* $M' \in [0, 0.0767]$ *heuristically runs in time* $2^{\tau_{M'} d + o(d)}$, *uses QRAM of maximum size* $\mathsf{poly}(d) \cdot 2^{\gamma_{M'} d}$, *a quantum memory of size* $\mathsf{poly}(d) \cdot 2^{\mu_{M'} d}$ *and uses a classical memory of size* $\mathsf{poly}(d) \cdot 2^{0.2075d}$ *where*

$$\tau_{M'} \in 0.2927 - 0.4647M' - [0; 6 \cdot 10^{-4}] \quad ; \quad \gamma_{M'} = M'$$

$$\mu_{M'} \in \max\{2.6356(M' - 0.0579), 0\} + [0; 9 \cdot 10^{-4}].$$

Finally, we present a table with a few values that presents some of the above trade-offs (Fig. 5).

Time $\tau_{M'}$	**0.2925**	0.2827	0.2733	**0.2653**	0.2621	0.2598	**0.2570**
QRAM $\gamma_{M'}$	**0**	0.02	0.04	**0.0578**	0.065	0.070	**0.0767**
Q. memory $\mu_{M'}$	0	0	0	**0**	0.0190	0.0324	**0.0495**
Comment	[BDGL16] alg.			[Laa16] alg.			Thm 1.

Fig. 5. Time, QRAM and quantum memory values for our algorithm.

8 Discussion

Impact on Lattice-Based Cryptography. Going from a running time of $2^{0.2653d+o(d)}$ to $2^{0.2570d+o(d)}$ slightly reduces the security claims based on the analysis of the SVP (usually via the BKZ algorithm). For example, if one claims 128 bits of security using the above exponent then one must reduce this claim to 124 bits of quantum security. This of course can usually be fixed with a slight increase of the parameters but cannot be ignored if one wants to have the same security claims as before.

Parallelization. On thing we haven't talked about in this article is whether our algorithm paralellizes well. Algorithm 1 seems to parallelize very well, and we argue that it is indeed the case.

For this algorithm, the best classical algorithm takes $c \to 0$. In this case, placing each $\vec{v} \in L$ in its corresponding α-filters can be done in parallel and with N processors (or N width) it can be done in time $\mathsf{poly}(d)$. Then, there are N separate instances of **FindAllSolutions** which can be also perfectly parallelized and each one also takes time $\mathsf{poly}(d)$ when $c \to 0$. The **while** loop is repeated $N^{-\zeta} = N^{0.409d}$ times so the total running time (here depth) is $N^{0.409d+o(d)}$ with a classical circuit of width N. Such a result already surpasses the result from [BDGL16] that achieves depth $N^{1/2}$ with a quantum circuit of width N using parallel Grover search.

In the quantum setting, our algorithm parallelizes also quite well. If we consider our optimal parameters ($c = 0.3696$) with a similar reasoning, our algorithm will parallelize perfectly with N^{1-c} processors (so that there is exactly one for each call to **FindAllSolutions** *i.e.* for the quantum random walk). Unfortunately, after that, we do not know how to parallelize well within the quantum walk. When we consider circuits of width N, our optimizations didn't achieve better than a depth of $N^{0.409+o(d)}$ which is the classical parallelization. This is also the case if we use Grover's algorithm as in [Laa16] for the **FindAllSolutions** and we use parallel Grover search as in [BDGL16] so best known (classical or quantum) algorithm with lowest depth that uses a circuit of width N is the classical parallel algorithm described above.

Acknowledgments and Paths for Improvements. The authors want to thank Simon Apers for helpful discussions about quantum random walks, in particular about the fact that there are no better generic algorithms for finding k different marked than to run the whole random walk (including the setup) $O(k)$ times. There could however be a smarter way to do this in our setting which would improve the overall complexity of our algorithm. Another possible improvement would be to embed the local sensitivity property in the graph on which we perform the random walk instead of working on the Johnson graph.

References

[AGJO+15] Arunachalam, S., Gheorghiu, V., Jochym-O'Connor, T., Mosca, M., Srinivasan, P.V.: On the robustness of bucket brigade quantum RAM. New J. Phys. **17**(12), 123010 (2015)

[AGPS20] Albrecht, M.R., Gheorghiu, V., Postlethwaite, E.W., Schanck, J.M.: Estimating quantum speedups for lattice sieves. In: Moriai, S., Wang, H. (eds.) ASIACRYPT 2020. LNCS, vol. 12492, pp. 583–613. Springer, Cham (2020). https://doi.org/10.1007/978-3-030-64834-3_20

[AINR14] Andoni, A., Indyk, P., Nguyên, H.L., Razenshteyn, I.: Beyond locality-sensitive hashing. In: SODA, pp. 1018–1028 (2014)

[Ajt96] Ajtai, M.: Generating hard instances of lattice problems (extended abstract). In: Proceedings of the Twenty-Eighth Annual ACM Symposium on Theory of Computing, STOC'96, pp. 99–108. Association for Computing Machinery, New York, NY, USA (1996)

[Ajt98] Ajtai, M.: The shortest vector problem in L2 is NP-hard for randomized reductions (extended abstract). In: 30th Annual ACM Symposium on Theory of Computing Proceedings, pp. 10–19 (1998)

[Amb07] Ambainis, A.: Quantum walk algorithm for element distinctness. SIAM J. Comput. **37**(1), 210–239 (2007)

[AR15] Andoni, A., Razenshteyn, I.: Optimal data-dependent hashing for approximate near neighbors. In: STOC, pp. 793–801 (2015)

[BBSS20] Bonnetain, X., Bricout, R., Schrottenloher, A., Shen, Y.: Improved classical and quantum algorithms for subset-sum. In: Moriai, S., Wang, H. (eds.) ASIACRYPT 2020. LNCS, vol. 12492, pp. 633–666. Springer, Cham (2020). https://doi.org/10.1007/978-3-030-64834-3_22

[BDGL16] Becker, A., Ducas, L., Gama, N., Laarhoven, T.: New directions in nearest neighbor searching with applications to lattice sieving. In: Proceedings of the 2016 Annual ACM-SIAM Symposium on Discrete Algorithms (2016)

[BJLM13] Bernstein, D.J., Jeffery, S., Lange, T., Meurer, A.: Quantum algorithms for the subset-sum problem. In: Gaborit, P. (ed.) PQCrypto 2013. LNCS, vol. 7932, pp. 16–33. Springer, Heidelberg (2013). https://doi.org/10.1007/978-3-642-38616-9_2

[BL16] Becker, A., Laarhoven, T.: Efficient (ideal) lattice sieving using cross-polytope LSH. In: Pointcheval, D., Nitaj, A., Rachidi, T. (eds.) AFRICACRYPT 2016. LNCS, vol. 9646, pp. 3–23. Springer, Cham (2016). https://doi.org/10.1007/978-3-319-31517-1_1

[CDH+19] Chen, C., et al.: NTRU. Round-3 submission to the NIST PQC project (2019)

[Cha02] Charikar, M.S.: Similarity estimation techniques from rounding algorithms. In: STOC, pp. 380–388 (2002)

[DKL+19] Ducas, L., et al.: Crystals-dilithium, algorithm specifications and supporting documentation. Round-3 submission to the NIST PQC project (2019)

[dW19] de Wolf, R.: Quantum computing: Lecture notes (2019)

[FHK+19] Fouque, P.-A., et al.: Falcon: fast-fourier lattice-based compact signatures over NTRU. Round-3 submission to the NIST PQC project (2019)

[FP85] Fincke, U., Pohst, M.: Improved methods for calculating vectors of short length in a lattice. Math. Comput. **44**(170), 463–471 (1985)

[Gen09] Gentry, C.: Fully homomorphic encryption using ideal lattices. In: Proceedings of the Forty-First Annual ACM Symposium on Theory of Computing, STOC '09, pp. 169–178. Association for Computing Machinery, New York, NY, USA (2009)

[GLM08] Giovannetti, V., Lloyd, S., Maccone, L.: Quantum random access memory. Phys. Rev. Lett. **100**, 160501 (2008)

[Gro96] Grover, L.: A fast quantum mechanical algorithm for database search. In: Proceedings 28th Annual ACM Symposium on the Theory of Computing STOC, pp. 212–219 (1996)

[HM18] Helm, A., May, A.: Subset sum quantumly in 1.17^n. In: Jeffery, S., (ed.), 13th Conference on the Theory of Quantum Computation, Communication and Cryptography, TQC 2018, 16–18 July 2018, Sydney, Australia, volume 111 of LIPIcs, pp. 5:1–5:15. Schloss Dagstuhl - Leibniz-Zentrum für Informatik (2018)

[IM98] Indyk, P., Motwani, R.: Approximate nearest neighbors: towards removing the curse of dimensionality. In: STOC, pp. 604–613 (1998)

[Kan83] Kannan, R.: Improved algorithms for integer programming and related lattice problems. In: Proceedings of the 15th Symposium on the Theory of Computing (STOC), pp. 99–108. ACM Press (1983)

[Kle00] Klein, P.: Finding the closest lattice vector when it's unusually close. In: SODA, pp. 937–941 (2000)

[KMPM19] Kirshanova, E., Martensson, E., Postlethwaite, E.W., Moulik, S.R.: Quantum algorithms for the approximate k-list problem and their application to lattice sieving. In: Galbraith, S.D., Moriai, S. (eds.) ASIACRYPT 2019. LNCS, vol. 11921, pp. 521–551. Springer, Cham (2019). https://doi.org/10.1007/978-3-030-34578-5_19

[KT17] Kachigar, G., Tillich, J.-P.: Quantum information set decoding algorithms. In: Lange, T., Takagi, T. (eds.) PQCrypto 2017. LNCS, vol. 10346, pp. 69–89. Springer, Cham (2017). https://doi.org/10.1007/978-3-319-59879-6_5

[Laa15] Laarhoven, T.: Sieving for shortest vectors in lattices using angular locality-sensitive hashing. In: Gennaro, R., Robshaw, M. (eds.) CRYPTO 2015. LNCS, vol. 9215, pp. 3–22. Springer, Heidelberg (2015). https://doi.org/10.1007/978-3-662-47989-6_1

[Laa16] Laarhoven, T.: Search problems in cryptography, from fingerprinting to lattice sieving. Ph.D. thesis, Eindhoven University of Technology (2016)

[LdW15] Laarhoven, T., de Weger, B.: Faster sieving for shortest lattice vectors using spherical locality-sensitive hashing. In: Lauter, K., Rodríguez-Henríquez, F. (eds.) LATINCRYPT 2015. LNCS, vol. 9230, pp. 101–118. Springer, Cham (2015). https://doi.org/10.1007/978-3-319-22174-8_6

[LLL82] Lenstra, A.K., Lenstra, H.W., Lovasz, L.: Factoring polynomials with rational coefficients. Math. Ann. **261**, 513–534 (1982)

[LMvdP15] Laarhoven, T., Mosca, M., van de Pol, J.: Finding shortest lattice vectors faster using quantum search. Des. Codes Cryptogr. **77**(2–3), 375–400 (2015)

[MNRS11] Magniez, F., Nayak, A., Roland, J., Santha, M.: Search via quantum walk. SIAM J. Comput. **40**(1), 142–164 (2011)

[MV10] Micciancio, D., Voulgaris, P.: Faster exponential time algorithms for the shortest vector problem. In: SODA, pp. 1468–1480 (2010)

[NC00] Nielsen, M.A., Chuang, I.L.: Quantum Computation and Quantum Information. Cambridge University Press, New York, NY, USA (2000)

[NV08] Nguyen, P.Q., Vidick, T.: Sieve algorithms for the shortest vector problem are practical. J. Math. Crypt. **2**, 181–207 (2008)

[Poh81] Pohst, M.E.: On the computation of lattice vectors of minimal length, successive minima and reduced bases with applications. ACM SIGSAM Bull. **15**(1), 37–44 (1981)

[TKM+13] Tulsiani, M., Kundu, S.K., Mitzenmacher, M., Upfal, E., Spencer, J.H.: Probability and Computing: Randomized Algorithms and Probabilistic Analysis. Cambridge University Press, Cambridge (2013)

[TT07] Terasawa, K., Tanaka, Y.: Spherical LSH for approximate nearest neighbor search on unit hypersphere. In: Dehne, F., Sack, J.-R., Zeh, N. (eds.) WADS 2007. LNCS, vol. 4619, pp. 27–38. Springer, Heidelberg (2007). https://doi.org/10.1007/978-3-540-73951-7_4

[WLTB11] Wang, X., Liu, M., Tian, C., Bi, J.: Improved Nguyen-Vidick heuristic sieve algorithm for shortest vector problem. In: Proceedings of the 6th ACM Symposium on Information, Computer and Communications Security, ASIACCS '11, pp. 1–9. Association for Computing Machinery, New York, NY, USA (2011)

[ZPH14] Zhang, F., Pan, Y., Hu, G.: A three-level sieve algorithm for the shortest vector problem. In: Lange, T., Lauter, K., Lisoněk, P. (eds.) SAC 2013. LNCS, vol. 8282, pp. 29–47. Springer, Heidelberg (2014). https://doi.org/10.1007/978-3-662-43414-7_2

A Systematic Approach and Analysis of Key Mismatch Attacks on Lattice-Based NIST Candidate KEMs

Yue Qin[1,2,6], Chi Cheng[1,2,3(✉)], Xiaohan Zhang[1], Yanbin Pan[4], Lei Hu[5], and Jintai Ding[6,7]

[1] China University of Geosciences, Wuhan 430074, China
{qy52hz,chengchi}@cug.edu.cn
[2] State Key Laboratory of Cryptology, P.O. Box 5159, Beijing 100878, China
[3] Guangxi Key Laboratory of Trusted Software, Guilin University of Electronic Technology, Guilin 541004, China
[4] Key Laboratory of Mathematics Mechanization, Academy of Mathematics and Systems Science, Chinese Academy of Sciences, Beijing, China
panyanbin@amss.ac.cn
[5] State Key Lab of Information Security, Institute of Information Engineering, Chinese Academy of Sciences, Beijing, China
hulei@iie.ac.cn
[6] Ding Lab, Yanqi Lake Beijing Institute of Mathematical Sciences and Applications, Beijing, China
[7] Yau Mathematical Sciences Center, Tsinghua University, Beijing, China

Abstract. Research on key mismatch attacks against lattice-based KEMs is an important part of the cryptographic assessment of the ongoing NIST standardization of post-quantum cryptography. There have been a number of these attacks to date. However, a unified method to evaluate these KEMs' resilience under key mismatch attacks is still missing. Since the key index of efficiency is the number of queries needed to successfully mount such an attack, in this paper, we propose and develop a systematic approach to find lower bounds on the minimum average number of queries needed for such attacks. Our basic idea is to transform the problem of finding the lower bound of queries into finding an optimal binary recovery tree (BRT), where the computations of the lower bounds become essentially the computations of a certain Shannon entropy. The optimal BRT approach also enables us to understand why, for some lattice-based NIST candidate KEMs, there is a big gap between the theoretical bounds and bounds observed in practical attacks, in terms of the number of queries needed. This further leads us to propose a generic improvement method for these existing attacks, which are confirmed by our experiments. Moreover, our proposed method could be directly used to improve the side-channel attacks against CCA-secure NIST candidate KEMs.

1 Introduction

The Diffie-Hellman (DH) key exchange [24] and its Elliptic Curve counterpart have played a fundamental role in many standards, such as Transport Layer Security (TLS) and IP security (IPSec), securing communications over the Internet.

M. Tibouchi and H. Wang (Eds.): ASIACRYPT 2021, LNCS 13093, pp. 92–121, 2021.
https://doi.org/10.1007/978-3-030-92068-5_4

However, these public key primitives based on number theoretic problems would be broken if quantum computers become practical. Due to the rapid progresses in quantum technology [32], the transition from the currently used public key cryptographic blocks to their post-quantum counterparts has become urgent.

Since February 2016, NIST has begun the call for post-quantum cryptographic algorithms from all over the world [44]. The goal of post-quantum cryptography standardization is to establish cryptographic systems that are secure against both quantum and classical computers, integrating with existing communication protocols and networks [19]. There are 17 public key encryption (PKE) or key encapsulation mechanism (KEM) candidates in the second round [2], among which 9 are based on lattices [1]. On the third-round list, there are still 3 lattice-based KEMs out of the 4 finalists [45].

Most of these candidates follow a similar structure: First a chosen-plaintext attack (CPA) secure construction is proposed, and then it is converted into a chosen-ciphertext attack (CCA) secure one using some transformation such as the Fujisaki-Okamoto (FO) transformation [29]. We have to point out that there is no security guarantee on the CPA secure ones when the public key is reused. However, first, it is an important part of the cryptographic assessment of these candidates to understand their key-reuse resilience in even misuse situations. Secondly, all LWE-based KEMs in Rounds 2 and 3 of the NIST standardization use an FO transform to achieve IND-CCA security. By doing so, the private key security is provided for only one party, while the other party is required that his secret key should be fully disclosed. What's more, the full re-encryption in the FO transform is typically the main cost during decapsulation, which makes it less efficient than the IND-CPA version. To improve the efficiency, there have been many efforts in designing various authenticated key exchanges using the CPA version without FO transform. In these cases, key reuse is no doubt essential. Therefore, analysis of the key reuse resilience of these CPA-secure schemes makes sense. Finally, as shown in [23,50], side-channel information can be employed to successfully mount similar chosen-ciphertext attacks against the CCA-secure ones in an efficient way. Therefore, the line of research focusing on the key reuse attacks against the CPA secure ones is important and has been actively studied.

Research on the security of IND-CPA secure public-key cryptosystem in the case of key reuse can be dated back to 1998, when Bleichenbacher considered the security of the RSA PKCS#1 [15]. After that, similar attacks have been proposed against several public key cryptosystems including the Diffie-Hellman key exchange [33,43]. There are two kinds of key reuse attacks against lattice-based key exchange. One is the signal leakage attack, which employs the additional signal information in the shared key reconciliation between two parties. The other key reuse attack is called key mismatch attack, which launches the attack by simply knowing whether the shared two keys match or not. In [25], Ding, Alsayigh and Saraswathy first launched signal leakage attacks to the key exchange protocol in [28] by using the leaked information about the secret key from the signal messages. Then, a signal leakage attack is proposed in [39] against the reconciliation-based NewHope-Usenix protocol [6]. Just recently in [14], Bindel, Stebila and

Veitch proposed an improved signal leakage attack and further showed how to apply their method to an authenticated scheme in [26].

The idea of key mismatch attack on lattice-based key exchange is first proposed by Ding, Fluhrer and Saraswathy [27] against the one-pass case of the protocol in [28]. In a key mismatch attack, a participant's public key is reused and its private key is recovered by comparing whether the shared keys between two participants match or not. In [10], Bauer et al. proposed a key mismatch attack against NewHope KEM [3], which is further analyzed and improved by Qin, Cheng, and Ding [48]. In [46], Okada, Wang, and Takagi improved the method in [48] to further reduce the number of queries. The work of [49] gave a similar key mismatch attack on Kyber. In [31] a key mismatch attack was proposed against LAC, requiring up to 8 queries for each coefficient. Recently, Zhang et al. proposed an efficient method to launch key mismatch attacks on NTRU-HRSS [55], which can recover the complete secret key with a probability of 93.6%.

Although there have been a number of key reuse attacks on the lattice-based key exchange schemes, a fundamental problem is still open: Can we find a unified method to evaluate the key reuse resilience of NIST candidates against key mismatch attacks? Since the key index of the efficiency of these attacks is the number of queries (matches and mismatches) needed to successfully mount such attacks, a unified method to find bounds with fewest queries for all the candidates is appealing. In Eurocrypt 2019, Băetu et al. tried to answer this problem, but most of their result is related to a limited number of the first-round candidates which did not enter into the second round [9]. In a recent work of Huguenin-Dumittan and Vaudenay [37], they proposed similar key mismatch attacks on only some of the lattice-based second-round candidates, Kyber-512, LAC-128, LightSaber, Round5 (HILA5 [11]) and Frodo640. But no unified theoretical bound is given in their work. Therefore, a big picture about the evaluation of key reuse resilience of these candidates is still missing.

Contributions. In this paper, we propose and develop a systematic approach to find the lower bounds on the minimum average number of queries needed for mounting key mismatch attacks, which further motivates us to propose a generic improvement method that is not only suitable for CPA-secure KEMs, but also for side-channel attacks against CCA-secure KEMs. The main contributions of this paper include:

- We propose a unified method to find lower bounds for all the lattice-based NIST candidate KEMs. Our basic idea is to convert the problem into finding an optimal binary recovery tree (BRT). By using the technique of Huffman coding, we successfully build the optimal BRT and get the bounds. Further analysis shows that the calculation of these bounds becomes essentially the computation of a certain Shannon entropy, which means that on average one cannot find a better attack with fewer queries than our bound in the full key recovery.
- According to our proposed bound, in terms of number of needed queries, there is still a huge gap between the bound and practical attacks against some candidates such as NewHope, FrodoKEM, and Saber [37,46,48]. The

introduction of the optimal BRT approach enables us to understand causes of these gaps, guiding us to select proper parameters to improve the practical attacks. Compared to the existing results in [37] and [46], we have improved attacks against Frodo640 and LightSaber with 71.99% and 27.93% reduced number of queries respectively, which is also confirmed by our experiments.

- Our improved method could be directly used to further optimize the efficiency of side-channel attacks against CCA-secure NIST candidate KEMs. For example, we can reduce the needed number of queries (or traces) from 2560 to 1183 for Kyber512.
- From the analysis of our proposed attacks, we find that the ranges of the coefficients in the secret key and the corresponding occurrence probabilities, as well as the employment of Encode/Decode functions are the three most important factors in evaluating their key reuse resilience. More specifically, larger ranges of the coefficients increase the needed number of queries. On the other side, encoding/decoding several coefficients at one time reduces the number of queries needed.

2 Preliminaries

2.1 Lattice-Based Key Encapsulation Mechanisms

In [21], Cramer and Shoup introduced the notion of KEM. Generally, a KEM consists of three algorithms: a probabilistic polynomial-time (PPT) key generation algorithm KEM.Gen, a PPT encryption algorithm KEM.Enc, and a deterministic polynomial-time decryption algorithm KEM.Dec.

The main difficulty in constructing a lattice-based DH-like key exchange protocol is how to effectively reconcile errors to negotiate a consistent shared key. In [28], Ding, Xie, and Lin first proposed a "robust extractor" to reconcile the errors, in which one of the participants needs to send an additional signal message to the other party, so that the two participants can agree on a shared key. Ding, Xie, and Lin's schemes base their security on the Learning with Errors (LWE) problem and Ring LWE problem. The latter can be seen as the polynomial version of the former. In [47] Peikert proposed a KEM using a similar error correction mechanism, and then in [17] the reformulated key exchange proposed by Bos et al. has been integrated into TLS. More and more lattice-based KEMs have been proposed since then. For example, in NIST's second-round list, there are FrodoKEM [4], NewHope [3,5], LAC [40], Kyber [7,16], Threebears [34], Round5 [8], Saber [22], NTRU [18] and NTRU Prime [13]. Recently, NIST [45] has announced the third-round finalists, among which the lattice-based KEMs include Kyber, NTRU and Saber. NIST also announced two alternate lattice-based candidates: FrodoKEM and NTRU Prime.

We can roughly divide the existing lattice-based KEMs into two categories. The first category is in line with the work of Regev [51], Lyubashevsky-Peikert-Regev [41], and lattice-based key exchange scheme proposed by Ding, Xie and Lin [28]. The other is NTRU [35] and NTRU Prime [12].

In Fig. 1 we present the meta structure of the CPA-secure KEMs in the first category of the NIST second-round candidates, in which

Alice		**Bob**
1. ▷KEM.Gen()		
1.1 Gen $\mathbf{a} \xleftarrow{\$} \mathcal{R}$		
1.2 $\mathbf{s}_A, \mathbf{e}_A \xleftarrow{\$} \chi$		2. $\mathbf{m} \xleftarrow{\$} \{0,1\}^\lambda$
1.3 $P_A \leftarrow \mathbf{a} \circ \mathbf{s}_A + \mathbf{e}_A$		3. KEM. Enc$(P_A, \mathbf{m})$
1.4 Output: $(P_A, \mathbf{s}_A)$	$\xrightarrow{P_A}$	3.1 Gen $\mathbf{a} \xleftarrow{\$} \mathcal{R}$
		3.2 $\mathbf{s}_B, \mathbf{e}_B, \mathbf{e}'_B \xleftarrow{\$} \chi$
		3.3 $P_B \leftarrow \mathbf{s}_B \circ \mathbf{a} + \mathbf{e}_B$
5. KEM.Dec$(P_B, \bar{\mathbf{c}}, \mathbf{s}_A)$		3.4 $\mathbf{k} \leftarrow$Encode$(\mathbf{m})$
5.1 $\mathbf{c}' \leftarrow$ Decompress$(\bar{\mathbf{c}})$		3.5 $\mathbf{c} \leftarrow \mathbf{s}_B \circ P_A + \mathbf{e}'_B + \mathbf{k}$
5.2 $\mathbf{k}' = \mathbf{c}' - P_B \circ \mathbf{s}_A$	$\xleftarrow{(P_B, \bar{\mathbf{c}})}$	3.6 $\bar{\mathbf{c}} \leftarrow$ Compress$(\mathbf{c})$
5.3 $\mathbf{m} \leftarrow$ Decode$(\mathbf{k}')$		3.7 Output: $(P_B, \bar{\mathbf{c}})$
5.4 Output: $\mathbf{m}'$		4. $K_B \leftarrow \mathbf{H}(\mathbf{m} \| (P_B, \bar{\mathbf{c}}))$
6.$K_A \leftarrow \mathbf{H}(\mathbf{m}' \| (P_B, \bar{\mathbf{c}}))$		

Fig. 1. The structure of CPA-secure LWE-based KEM

- $\mathcal{R}$ be some ring equipped with the multiplication $\circ$.
- $\mathbf{a}$ is generated by a public seed and pseudorandom function.
- The distribution χ is chosen to be the discrete Gaussian distribution or the central binomial distribution $\mathbf{B}_\eta$ whose sample is generated by $\sum_{i=1}^{\eta}(a_i - b_i)$, where a_i and b_i are independently uniformly randomly sampled from $\{0, 1\}$. When we say a sample is chosen according to χ, we mean every component is chosen randomly according to χ.
- The Encode and Decode process is not necessary but usually employed. A typical code is $D-v$ lattice code with $v = 2$ or 4 that encodes every coefficient into v coefficients. We list the Encode and Decode functions in Algorithm 1.
- The Compress/Decompress function is usually used to decrease the communication cost. A typical compress function transforms a coefficient from module q to module p by

$$\mathrm{Compress_q}(\mathbf{c}[\mathrm{i}], \mathrm{p}) = \lceil \mathbf{c}[\mathrm{i}] \cdot \mathrm{p}/\mathrm{q} \rfloor \pmod{\mathrm{p}},$$

and the decompress function operates in an opposite way:

$$\mathrm{Decompress_q}(\bar{\mathbf{c}}[\mathrm{i}], \mathrm{p}) = \lceil \bar{\mathbf{c}}[\mathrm{i}] \cdot \mathrm{q}/\mathrm{p} \rfloor.$$

Next, we describe the MLWE-based Kyber in details.

Algorithm 1 The Encode and Decode functions for the D-v lattice code

⋄ **Encode**$(\mathbf{m}, v)$

Input: $\mathbf{m} \leftarrow \{0,1\}^{\lambda}, v$

Output: $\mathbf{k}$

1: **for** $i = 0$ to $\lambda - 1$ **do**
2:      **for** $j = 0$ to $v - 1$ **do**
3:          $\mathbf{k}[i \cdot v + j] = \mathbf{m}[i] \cdot \frac{q-1}{2}$
4:      **end for**
5: **end for**
6: **Return k**

⋄ **Decode**$(\mathbf{k}, v)$

Input: $\mathbf{k} \leftarrow \{0, \frac{q-1}{2}\}^{v\lambda}, v$

Output: $\mathbf{m}'$

7: **for** $i = 0$ to $\lambda - 1$ **do**
8:      **if** $\sum_{j=0}^{v-1} |\mathbf{k}[i \cdot v + j] - \frac{q-1}{2}| < \frac{v \cdot q}{4}$ **then**
9:          $\mathbf{m}'[i] = 1$
10:      **else**
11:          $\mathbf{m}'[i] = 0$
12:      **end if**
13: **end for**
14: **Return m′**

Kyber. Kyber is on the third-round list of the NIST competition, and regarded as one of the most promising ones for the final standard. In Kyber the authors have warned about the harm of key reuse, but in practice there may still be some users who ignore the warnings and try to create one. So it is reasonable to assume that Kyber has a CPA-secure version to evaluate its key reuse resilience.

Alice	Bob
1. ▷ Kyber. CPAPKE. KeyGen()	
1.1 Generate matrix $\mathbf{a} \in \mathcal{R}_q^{k \times k}$	
1.2 Sample $\mathbf{s}_A, \mathbf{e}_A \in \mathbf{B}_{\eta}^k$	2. $\mathbf{m} \xleftarrow{\$} \{0,1\}^{256}$
1.3 $\mathbf{P}_A \leftarrow \mathbf{a} \circ \mathbf{s}_A + \mathbf{e}_A$	3. ▷ Kyber. CPAPKE. Enc$(\mathbf{P}_A, \mathbf{m})$
1.4 Output: $(\mathbf{s}_A, \mathbf{P}_A)$ $\xrightarrow{\;\mathbf{P}_A\;}$	3.1 Generate matrix $\mathbf{a} \in \mathcal{R}_q^{k \times k}$
	3.2 Sample $\mathbf{s}_B, \mathbf{e}_B \in \mathbf{B}_{\eta}^k$, $\mathbf{e}'_B \in \mathbf{B}_{\eta}$
	3.3 $\mathbf{P}_B \leftarrow \mathbf{a}^T \circ \mathbf{s}_B + \mathbf{e}_B$
5. ▷ Kyber. CPAPKE. Dec$(\mathbf{s}_A, \mathbf{P}_B, \mathbf{c}_1, \mathbf{c}_2)$	3.4 $\mathbf{v}_B \leftarrow \mathbf{P}_A^T \circ \mathbf{s}_B + \mathbf{e}'_B + \mathbf{Decompress}_q(\mathbf{m}, 2)$
5.1 $\mathbf{u}_A \leftarrow \mathbf{Decompress}_q(\mathbf{c}_1, 2^{d_{\mathbf{P}_B}})$	3.5 $\mathbf{c}_1 \leftarrow \mathbf{Compress}_q(\mathbf{P}_B, 2^{d_{\mathbf{P}_B}})$
5.2 $\mathbf{v}_A \leftarrow \mathbf{Decompress}_q(\mathbf{c}_2, 2^{d_{\mathbf{v}_B}})$ $\xleftarrow{(\mathbf{P}_B, \mathbf{c}_1, \mathbf{c}_2)}$	3.6 $\mathbf{c}_2 \leftarrow \mathbf{Compress}_q(\mathbf{v}_B, 2^{d_{\mathbf{v}_B}})$
5.3 $\mathbf{m}' \leftarrow \mathbf{Compress}_q(\mathbf{v}_A - \mathbf{s}_A^T \circ \mathbf{u}_A, 2)$	3.7 Output: $(\mathbf{c}_1, \mathbf{c}_2)$
5.4 Output: $\mathbf{m}'$	4. $K_B \leftarrow \mathbf{H}(\mathbf{m} \| (\mathbf{P}_B, (\mathbf{c}_1, \mathbf{c}_2)))$
6. $K_A \leftarrow \mathbf{H}(\mathbf{m}' \| (\mathbf{P}_B, (\mathbf{c}_1, \mathbf{c}_2)))$	

Fig. 2. The CPA version of Kyber

Figure 2 shows pseudo-code for a possible instantiation of the CPA-secure Kyber, which directly invokes the three functions of Kyber.CPAPKE in [7]: Kyber.CPAPKE.KeyGen(), Kyber.CPAPKE.Enc() and Kyber.CPAPKE.Dec().

In Kyber.CPAPKE.KeyGen(), Alice first generates a matrix $\mathbf{a} \in R_q^{k\times k}$. Here R_q represents the ring $\mathbb{Z}_q[x]/(x^N+1)$, where $N = 256$ and $q = 3329$. Another parameter k is set to be 2, 3 or 4, which is in accordance with the three different security levels. That is, Kyber512, Kyber768, and Kyber1024, respectively. In Kyber all the secret keys and error vectors are sampled from a centered binomial distribution $\mathbf{B}_\eta$. In Kyber512 $\eta = 3$, and in Kyber768 and Kyber1024 $\eta = 2$. Here $\mathbf{B}_\eta$ is generated using $\sum_{i=1}^{\eta}(a_i - b_i)$, where a_i and b_i are independently randomly sampled from $\{0, 1\}$.

NewHope. Similarly, we present a CPA-secure version of NewHope in Fig. 3, which also includes three parts. Here $\mathcal{R}_q$ is the residue ring $\mathbb{Z}_q[x]/(x^N+1)$ with $N = 512$ in NewHope512 and 1024 in NewHope1024. The parameter q is always set as 12289.

Alice		**Bob**
1. ▷NewHope. CPAPKE. KeyGen()		
1.1 Generate matrix $\mathbf{a} \in \mathcal{R}_q$		
1.2 Sample $\mathbf{s}_A, \mathbf{e}_A \in \mathbf{B}_8$		2. $\mathbf{m} \xleftarrow{\$} \{0,1\}^{256}$
1.3 $\mathbf{P}_A \leftarrow \mathbf{a} \circ \mathbf{s}_A + \mathbf{e}_A$		3. ▷NewHope. CPAPKE. Enc($\mathbf{P}_A, \mathbf{m}$)
1.4 Output: $(\mathbf{s}_A, \mathbf{P}_A)$	$\xrightarrow{\mathbf{P}_A}$	3.1 Generate matrix $\mathbf{a} \in \mathcal{R}_q$
		3.2 Sample $\mathbf{s}_B, \mathbf{e}_B, \mathbf{e}'_B \in \mathbf{B}_8$
		3.3 $\mathbf{P}_B \leftarrow \mathbf{a} \circ \mathbf{s}_B + \mathbf{e}_B$
		3.4 $v_b \leftarrow \mathbf{H}_1(\mathbf{m})$
5. ▷NewHope. CPAPKE. Dec($\mathbf{s}_A, \mathbf{P}_B, \bar{\mathbf{c}}$)		3.5 $\mathbf{k} \leftarrow$Encode(v_b)
5.1 $\mathbf{c}' \leftarrow$ Decompress($\bar{\mathbf{c}}$)		3.6 $\mathbf{c} \leftarrow \mathbf{P}_A \circ \mathbf{s}_B + \mathbf{e}'_B + \mathbf{k}$
5.2 $\mathbf{k}' \leftarrow \mathbf{c}' - \mathbf{P}_B \circ \mathbf{s}_A$	$\xleftarrow{(\mathbf{P}_B, \bar{\mathbf{c}})}$	3.7 $\bar{\mathbf{c}} \leftarrow$ Compress($\mathbf{c}$)
5.3 $v_A \leftarrow$ Decode($\mathbf{k}'$)		3.8 Output: $(\mathbf{P}_B, \bar{\mathbf{c}})$
5.4 Output: v_A		4. $K_B \leftarrow \mathbf{H}_2(v_b \| (\mathbf{P}_B, \bar{\mathbf{c}}))$
6. $K_A \leftarrow \mathbf{H}_2(v_A \| (\mathbf{P}_B, \bar{\mathbf{c}}))$		

Fig. 3. The CPA version of NewHope

2.2 Model of Key Mismatch Attacks

In a key mismatch attack, Alice's public key P_A is reused. The adversary $\mathcal{A}$ impersonates as Bob to recover the secret key of Alice with the help of an Oracle that can decide if the two shared keys match or not.

More precisely, to show how the attack works, we build an Oracle $\mathcal{O}$ that simulates Alice's KEM.Dec part. As shown in Algorithm 2, the Oracle $\mathcal{O}$'s input P includes the parameters P_B, $\bar{c}$ chosen by the adversary and the shared key

K_B. The output of $\mathcal{O}$ is 1 or 0. To be specific, with the received P_B, $\bar{c}$, $\mathcal{O}$ calls the function Dec(P) and gets the shared key K_A as the return. If the shared keys K_A and K_B match, $\mathcal{O}$ outputs 1, otherwise the output is 0.

Algorithm 2 The Oracle and key mismatch attack

◇ **Oracle** $\mathcal{O}(P)$

Input: $P := (P_B, \bar{c}, K_B)$

Output: 0 or 1

```
1: K_A ← KEM.Dec(P_B, c̄)
2: if K_A = K_B then
3:     Return 1
4: else
5:     Return 0
6: end if
```

◇ **key mismatch attack**

Input: Alice's P_A and Oracle $\mathcal{O}$

Output: 0 or 1

```
7: s'_A ← A^O(P_A)
8: if s'_A = s_A then
9:     Return 1
10: else
11:     Return 0
12: end if
```

3 Lower Bounds for the Average Number of Queries for the Key Mismatch Attacks

For the key mismatch attacks on lattice-based KEMs, the adversary $\mathcal{A}$'s goal is to recover each coefficient of Alice's secret key $\mathbf{s}_A$ by accessing the oracle $\mathcal{O}$ multiple times.

For simplicity, we assume the adversary recovers Alice's secret key $\mathbf{s}_A$ one coefficient block by one coefficient block. A coefficient block can be either one coefficient of $\mathbf{s}_A$ or a subset of all the coefficients of $\mathbf{s}_A$. Usually, for KEMs that do not employ Encode/Decode functions, such as Kyber, a coefficient block is set to be only one coefficient. For KEMs that employ Encode/Decode functions, such as NewHope, a coefficient block contains v coefficients of $\mathbf{s}_A$ where v is defined as in Algorithm 1, since one coefficient relates to v coefficients of $\mathbf{s}_A$.

Note that the number of the queries to the oracle is obviously a key index to evaluate the efficiency of the attack. In fact, even in practice, the bottleneck of the efficiency of the attacks is also to determine if the two shared keys match or not. Therefore, it is important to indicate the optimal lower bound of the number of queries to mount a mismatch attack successfully.

3.1 Lower Bound by Optimal Binary Recovery Tree

In this subsection, we describe how to find the bounds of key mismatch attacks, which can be regarded as a problem of finding a binary tree with minimum weighted depth.

Recall that the adversary $\mathcal{A}$ recovers Alice's secret key $\mathbf{s}_A$ one coefficient block by one coefficient block, where a coefficient block can be either one coefficient of $\mathbf{s}_A$ or several coefficients of $\mathbf{s}_A$. Let $\mathbf{S} = \{\mathbf{S}_0, \mathbf{S}_1, \cdots, \mathbf{S}_{n-1}\}$ be the set of all the possible values for one coefficient block. For example, the coefficients of $\mathbf{s}_A$ in Kyber are drawn from $\{-2, -1, 0, 1, 2\}$. Since there are no Encode/Decode functions, we try to recover the coefficients of $\mathbf{s}_A$ one by one and hence $\mathbf{S} = \{-2, -1, 0, 1, 2\}$. In LAC, the coefficients of $\mathbf{s}_A$ are selected from $\{-1, 0, 1\}$. Since D-2 lattice is used to encode, we would like to recover every coefficient block which contains 2 coefficients of $\mathbf{s}_A$ due to the decryption, which yields that $\mathbf{S} = \{(0,0), (0,1), (1,0), (-1,0), (0,-1), (1,1), (-1,-1), (1,-1), (-1,1)\}$.

For any coefficient block $\mathbf{s}_A^b$ of $\mathbf{s}_A$, denote by P_i the probability that $\mathbf{s}_A^b = \mathbf{S}_i$ where $\mathbf{s}_A$ is generated from the distribution χ, that is, $P_i = \text{Prob}(\mathbf{s}_A^b = \mathbf{S}_i | \mathbf{s}_A \leftarrow \chi)$ for $i = 0, 1, \cdots, n-1$. Without loss of generality, we assume that $P_0 \geq P_1 \geq \cdots \geq P_{n-1}$. Then, it holds that $\sum_{i=0}^{n-1} P_i = 1$.

In a key mismatch attack, the adversary $\mathcal{A}$ needs to query the Oracle with properly selected parameters for several times to recover every coefficient block, which may be $\mathbf{S}_i$ with probability P_i. Denote by Q_i the number of queries $\mathcal{A}$ needs to determine the coefficient block when it is exactly $\mathbf{S}_i$. Then the average (expected) number of queries required to recover one coefficient block is obviously:

$$E_{\mathcal{A}}(\mathbf{S}) = \sum_{i=0}^{n-1} P_i Q_i.$$

Our goal is to minimize $E_{\mathcal{A}}(\mathbf{S})$ by running over the set of all possible attack strategies under our model.

Binary Recovery Tree. Our key idea to get a lower bound of minimum of $E(S)$ is to associate every attack with a binary recovery tree (BRT).

Define the BRT associated with $\mathbf{S} = \{\mathbf{S}_0, \mathbf{S}_1, \cdots, \mathbf{S}_{n-1}\}$ as below: it is a rooted binary tree with a root node and n leaf nodes, where every $\mathbf{S}_i$ occupies a leaf node. For every node that has child nodes, denote by 1 its left child node and by 0 its right child node.

Note that to recover any coefficient block for any attack, the adversary $\mathcal{A}$ can get a binary sequence of returned values from the Oracle. Denote by $\bar{s}_i$ the corresponding returned binary sequence when the coefficient block is exactly $\mathbf{S}_i$. It is obvious that each coefficient block $\mathbf{S}_i$ can be recovered by a unique binary sequence $\bar{s}_i$ and for any $i \neq j$, $\bar{s}_i$ must not be the prefix of $\bar{s}_j$. Otherwise, it would not suffice to identify $\mathbf{S}_i$ uniquely. This means that we can construct a BRT $T_{\mathcal{A}}$ associated with $\mathbf{S} = \{\mathbf{S}_0, \mathbf{S}_1, \cdots, \mathbf{S}_{n-1}\}$, where for every i, the binary string consisting of the nodes on the path from the root node to the leaf node $\mathbf{S}_i$ is exactly the binary sequence $\bar{s}_i$. The length of $\bar{s}_i$ is of course Q_i as defined above, also known as the depth $\text{depth}_{T_{\mathcal{A}}}(\mathbf{S}_i)$ of leaf node $\mathbf{S}_i$. Then

$$E_{\mathcal{A}}(\mathbf{S}) = \sum_{i=0}^{n-1} P_i Q_i = \sum_{i=0}^{n-1} P_i \cdot \text{depth}_{T_{\mathcal{A}}}(\mathbf{S}_i).$$

It seems still hard to find the minimum of $E_{\mathcal{A}}(\mathbf{S})$ since we should consider all the binary recovery trees corresponding to the possible attacks under our model.

However, it presents an obvious way to compute a lower bound of the minimum, just by enlarging the set of BRTs corresponding to the attacks to the set of all the possible BRTs.

Then, we can transform the problem of finding the lower bound of the optimal value of $E_{\mathcal{A}}(\mathbf{S})$ to the problem of finding a binary recovery tree to minimize

$$E(\mathbf{S}) = \sum_{i=0}^{n-1} P_i \cdot \text{depth}_T(\mathbf{S}_i).$$

We call the tree with the minimum weighted depth, i.e. $\min E(\mathbf{S})$, the optimal BRT. Therefore, it is enough to construct an optimal BRT to find the lower bound for recovering the secret key with fewest number of queries.

A well known method to find the optimal binary recovery tree is the Huffman coding [36,38]. The basic idea of Huffman coding is to combine two symbols with the lowest probabilities in each step. Specifically, we first find the two $\mathbf{S}_i$'s with the lowest probabilities, for example, P_{n-1} and P_{n-2}. Then the problem has transformed into solving the problem with $n-1$ weights $\{P_0, P_1, \ldots, P_{n-3}, P_{n-2} + P_{n-1}\}$. By repeating this process, we can finally solve the problem and find the optimal BRT to get $\min E(\mathbf{S})$ in time $O(n \log n)$, as well as the E(#Queries).

Algorithm 3 Huffman codes

◇ Building a Huffman Tree

```
Input: P_0, ..., P_{n-1}
Output: HuffTree T
for i = 0 → n − 1 do
    Insert leafnode T[i]
    T[i].weight = P[i]
end for
for i = 0 → n − 1 do
    for j = 0 → n + i − 1 do
        Find two nodes x_1 and x_2 with the smallest weight and no parent
    end for
    Combine x_1 and x_2, and insert the new node into T[n + i]
end for
```

◇ Huffman Coding

```
Input: HuffTree T
Output: Huffman code C
E(S) = 0
for i = 0 → n − 1 do
    C[i].length = 0
    j = i
    while T[j].parent exist do
        if T[j].lchild = j then
            C[i].code[C[i].length] = 0
        else
            C[i].code[C[i].length] = 1
        end if
        C[i].length + +
        j = T[j].parent
    end while
    E(S)+ = C[i].length * T[i].weight
end for
```

Therefore, our proposed method for calculating the bound can be summarized as follows: First, list $\mathbf{S}_0, \mathbf{S}_1, \ldots, \mathbf{S}_{n-1}$ and their corresponding probabilities $\{P_0, P_1, \ldots, P_{n-1}\}$ in the descending order. Then, construct the optimal BRT using Huffman coding. The constructed optimal BRT leads us to the $\min E(\mathbf{S})$ and the E(#Queries). The process of building the Huffman code to obtain the corresponding $\min E(\mathbf{S})$ is shown in Algorithm 3.

To prove our main theorem, we first present the following lemma, which is a special case of the famous Kraft inequality (See Theorem 5.2.2, [20]).

Lemma 1. *(Kraft equality) For any* $n \geq 1$, $(\text{depth}_T(\boldsymbol{S}_0), \cdots, \text{depth}_T(\boldsymbol{S}_{n-1}))$ *is the sequence of depths in a rooted binary tree if and only if*

$$\sum_{i=0}^{n-1} 2^{-\text{depth}_T(\boldsymbol{S}_i)} = 1. \tag{1}$$

Further, we obtain the following result.

Theorem 1. *In our key mismatch attack model, the proposed method finds bounds for minimum average number of queries in launching the key mismatch attacks. To be precise, given* $\boldsymbol{S} = \{\boldsymbol{S}_0, \boldsymbol{S}_1, \cdots, \boldsymbol{S}_{n-1}\}$ *and its corresponding probabilities* $\{P_0, P_1, \cdots, P_{n-1}\}$ *in each lattice-based KEM,* $\min E(\boldsymbol{S})$ *calculated by the optimal BRT is a lower bound for the minimum average number of queries. Moreover, set* $H(\boldsymbol{S})$ *the Shannon entropy for* $\boldsymbol{S}$*, then we have*

$$H(\boldsymbol{S}) \leq \min\ \text{E}(\mathbf{S}) < H(\boldsymbol{S}) + 1.$$

Proof. Our first result comes from the facts in Section 5.8 of [20]. That is, it is impossible to find any other code with a lower expected length than the code constructed by Huffman coding. To obtain the $\min\ \text{E}(\mathbf{S})$, we use the Lagrange multipliers. From Lemma 1, we let

$$L = \sum_{i=0}^{n-1} P_i \cdot \text{depth}_T(\mathbf{S}_i) + \lambda(\sum_{i=0}^{n-1} 2^{-\text{depth}_T(\mathbf{S}_i)} - 1).$$

By differentiating with respect to $\text{depth}_T(\mathbf{S}_i)$ and letting the derivative be 0, we have

$$\frac{\partial L}{\partial \text{depth}_T(\mathbf{S}_i)} = P_i - \lambda \cdot 2^{-\text{depth}_T(\mathbf{S}_i)} \log_e 2 = 0.$$

That is $2^{-\text{depth}_T(\mathbf{S}_i)} = \frac{P_i}{\lambda \log_e 2}$. Substituting this into Eq. (1), we obtain $\sum_{i=0}^{n-1} \frac{P_i}{\lambda \log_e 2} = 1$. Thus we have $\lambda \log_e 2 = 1$, which leads to $P_i = 2^{-\text{depth}_T(\mathbf{S}_i)}$. Therefore, the optimum solution occurs when $\text{depth}_T(\mathbf{S}_i) = \lceil -\log_2 P_i \rceil$. Here $\lceil x \rceil$ means the smallest integer greater than or equal to x, due to the fact that $\text{depth}_T(\mathbf{S}_i)$ should be integers. Since $x \leq \lceil x \rceil < x + 1$, we then conclude that $H(\mathbf{S}) \leq \min\ \text{E}(\mathbf{S}) < H(\mathbf{S}) + 1$.

In [9], it has been proved that $H(\mathbf{S}) \leq \min\ \text{E}(\mathbf{S})$. From our perspective, this can be easily obtained from the optimality of Huffman codes.

Remark 1. One may have the idea that it is safe to implement the CPA-secure version and reuse the keys fewer times than the proposed bound. In fact it is still dangerous to do so, even reusing the key far below the bound. First of all, our bound is on the average number of needed queries, which means that there may exist attacks with fewer number of queries for certain keys. Secondly, what we talk about is recovering the full key, but obviously the recovery of the partial key also leaks information about the key, significantly decreasing the bit-security. Therefore, it is still not safe to reuse the keys in a CPA-secure KEM.

3.2 Lower Bounds for Key Mismatch Attacks on NIST Candidates

Lower Bounds for Kyber. In this subsection, we take Kyber1024 as an example to show how to find the optimal BRT to get the bound. Kyber1024 uses centered binomial distribution $\mathcal{B}_\eta$ with $\eta = 2$ and has no Encode/Decode functions, which means $S = \{-2, -1, 0, 1, 2\}$. We set $\mathbf{S}_0 = 0$, $\mathbf{S}_1 = 1$, $\mathbf{S}_2 = -1$, $\mathbf{S}_3 = 2$ and $\mathbf{S}_4 = -2$.

l_{rs}	rs	$\mathbf{S}_i$	Probability				
2	11	0	0.375	0.375	0.375	0.625	1
2	10	1	0.25	0.25	0.375	0.375	
2	01	-1	0.25	0.25	0.25		
3	001	2	0.0625	0.125			
3	000	-2	0.0625				

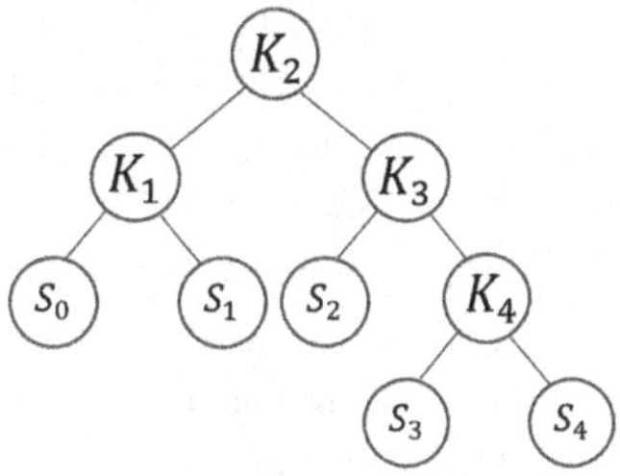

Fig. 4. Finding the optimal BRT for Kyber1024 by using Huffman coding

As shown in Fig. 4, we first list the occurrence probabilities of $\mathbf{S}_i$ in the descending order. Since $\mathbf{S}_3$ and $\mathbf{S}_4$ occur with the smallest probabilities, we create a subtree that contains them as leaf nodes. By repeatedly doing so, finally we can get an optimal BRT as also shown in Fig. 4. The corresponding $\bar{s}$ represents how to encode each $\mathbf{S}_i$, while $l_{\bar{s}}$ is the code length.

The resulting $\min E(\mathbf{S}) = 2.125$, which is the minimum number of queries needed for recovering each coefficient. Note that the Shannon entropy $H(\mathbf{S})$ is

$$H(\mathbf{S}) = \sum_{i=0}^{4} P_i \log \frac{1}{P_i} = 2.03,$$

which is in accordance with our Theorem 1. Hence, the bounds for recovering the full private key of Kyber768 and Kyber1024 with $\eta = 2$ are 1632 and 2176, respectively. Similarly, it can be concluded that the bound is 1216 for Kyber512 with $\eta = 3$.

Lower Bounds for NewHope. One of the main differences between Kyber and NewHope is that Kyber does not use Encode/Decode functions, while NewHope uses both Encode/Decode and Compress/Decompress functions. In NewHope, the secret key is sampled from centered binomial distribution $\mathbf{B}_\eta$ with parameter $\eta = 8$, so the coefficients of the secret key are integers in $[-8, 8]$.

Table 1. Lower bounds for key mismatch attacks on lattice-based NIST KEMs.

Schemes	$\mathbf{s}_A$ & $\mathbf{e}$ Ranges	Encode Decode	Comp Decomp	Unknowns	E(#Queries) Bounds
NewHope512	[−8, 8]	✓	✓	512	1568
NewHope1024				1024	3127
Kyber512	[−3, 3]	/	✓	512	1216
Kyber768	[−2, 2]			768	1632
Kyber1024				1024	2176
LightSaber	[−5, 5]	/	✓	512	1412
Saber	[−4, 4]			768	1986
FireSaber	[−3, 3]			1024	2432
Frodo640	[−12, 12]	/	✓	5120	18,227
Frodo976	[−10, 10]			7808	25,796
Frodo1344	[−6, 6]			10,752	27,973
NTRU hps4096821	[−1, 1]	/	/	821	1369
NTRU hrss701				701	1183
NTRU Prime sntrup857				857	1574
NTRU Prime ntrulpr857				857	1553

Recall that NewHope512 uses D-2 Encode/Decode functions, while in NewHope-1024 D-4 Encode/Decode functions are used. Therefore, in NewHope512, $\mathbf{S}_i = (s_{i,1}, s_{i,2})$ where $s_{i,1},\ s_{i,2} \in [-8, 8]$. In total there are 289 possibilities about each $\mathbf{S}_i$. So here we let $n = 289$. Then, we can also build the optimal BRT for NewHope512 using Huffman coding, and the min $E(\mathbf{S}) = 6.124$. Since we can recover two coefficients in $\mathbf{s}_A$ at one time, the resulted E(#Queries)=1568. For NewHope1024, there are a total of $83,521$ possible $\mathbf{S}_i$, that is, $n = 83,521$. Similarly, we have E(#Queries)= 3127 for NewHope1024.

Lower bounds for other NIST Candidates. Similarly, we can obtain bounds for other LWE-based KEMs as well as NTRU and NTRU Prime in the second category. In Table 1, we present the lower bounds for key mismatch attacks against the following second or third round NIST candidates: NewHope, Kyber, FrodoKEM, Saber, NTRU and NTRU Prime. For every candidate, we report the ranges of $\mathbf{s}_A$ & $\mathbf{e}$ and the number of unknowns, and whether the Encode/Decode and Compress/Decompress functions are employed (✓) or not (/). We also report the minimum average number of queries in our proposed bounds. For other NIST candidate KEMs, we report their results in Table 7 in Appendix A.

4 Improved Key Mismatch Attacks on NIST Candidates

We would like to point out that for some KEMs, there is still a huge gap in terms of number of queries between our theoretical bound and practical attacks, such as Frodo640. Since we have built an optimal BRT for each KEM, in the following we show how the optimal BRT helps us improve the practical attacks.

4.1 Improved Practical Attacks on Kyber

We take Kyber1024 as an example to show how to launch the practical key mismatch attack. First, we build an Oracle that simulates Alice's Kyber.KEM.Dec(), the same as that in Algorithm 2. The inputs of the oracle $\mathcal{O}$ are $\mathbf{P}_B$, $(\mathbf{c}_1, \mathbf{c}_2)$ and K_B.

In a key mismatch attack, Alice's public key $\mathbf{P}_A$ is reused, and the goal of the adversary $\mathcal{A}$ is to recover Alice's secret key $\mathbf{s}_A$. Therefore, $\mathcal{A}$ needs to choose the appropriate parameters $\mathbf{P}_B$ and $(\mathbf{c}_1, \mathbf{c}_2)$ to access $\mathcal{O}$, so that he can determine $\mathbf{s}_A$ based on $\mathcal{O}$'s return. Without loss of generality, assume that $\mathcal{A}$ wants to recover $\mathbf{s}_A[0]$. We next show the basic idea of our attack.

First of all, $\mathcal{A}$ selects a 256-bit $\mathbf{m}$ as $(1,0, \cdots, 0)$. Then he sets $\mathbf{P}_B = \mathbf{0}$, except $\mathbf{P}_B[0] = \lceil \frac{q}{32} \rfloor$. After calculating $\mathbf{c}_1 = \mathbf{Compress}_q(\mathbf{P}_B, 2^{d_{\mathbf{P}_B}})$, $\mathcal{A}$ sets $\mathbf{c}_2 = \mathbf{0}$, except that $\mathbf{c}_2[0] = h$, where h will be determined later.

With $(\mathbf{c}_1, \mathbf{c}_2)$, the Oracle calculates $\mathbf{u}_A = \mathbf{Decompress}_q(\mathbf{c}_1, 2^{d_{\mathbf{P}_B}})$, $\mathbf{v}_A = \mathbf{Decompress}_q(\mathbf{c}_2, 2^{d_{\mathbf{v}_B}})$ and

$$\mathbf{m}'[0] = \mathbf{Compress}_q((\mathbf{v}_A - \mathbf{s}_A^T\mathbf{u}_A)[0], 1) = \left\lceil \frac{2}{q}\left(\mathbf{v}_A[0] - (\mathbf{s}_A^T\mathbf{u}_A)[0]\right) \right\rfloor \bmod 2.$$

Since $\mathbf{v}_A[0] = \lceil \frac{q}{32} h \rfloor$ and $(\mathbf{s}_A^T\mathbf{u}_A)[0] = \mathbf{s}_A^T[0]\mathbf{u}_A[0] = \mathbf{s}_A^T[0] \lceil \frac{q}{32} \rfloor$, it holds that $\mathbf{m}'[0] = \left\lceil \frac{2}{q}\left(\lceil \frac{q}{32} h \rfloor - \mathbf{s}_A^T[0] \lceil \frac{q}{32} \rfloor\right) \right\rfloor \bmod 2$.

Therefore, it allows us to determine $\mathbf{s}_A^T[0]$ by choosing proper value for h. For example, by letting $h = 8$, we have the following result: If $\mathbf{s}_A^T[0] \in [-2, -1]$, $\mathbf{m}'[0] = 1$, then the oracle will output 1. Otherwise, if $\mathbf{s}_A^T[0] \in [0, 2]$, $\mathbf{m}'[0] = 0$, then the oracle outputs 0. In this way, we can distinguish which subinterval (or subset) $\mathbf{s}_A^T[0]$ belongs to by only one query. Similarly, by choosing a different value for h, we may determine another subinterval that $\mathbf{s}_A^T[0]$ belongs to. Once the intersection of the determined subintervals has only one element, we can determine the value of $\mathbf{s}_A^T[0]$ exactly. However, our goal is to query the Oracle as few as possible, which asks us to choose h more carefully.

From the optimal BRT in Sect. 3.2, to approach the bound we need to determine $\mathbf{S}_i$ with high occurrence probability with as few numbers of queries as possible. In fact, this also suggests us the ideal way to choose h, that is, choosing h such that the oracle outputs different values when $\mathbf{s}_A^T[0]$ belongs to different sets of descendants, left or right, for every node in the optimal BRT. Of course, such h may not exist. However, the optimal BRT does reveal some clues.

Following the optimal BRT, we show how to choose h for every State in our improved attack and how the States change according to the output of the

Oracle in Kyber512, Kyber768 and Kyber1024, respectively in Table 2. Our key mismatch attack always starts from State 1, and then the choice of h in the next State depends on the current Oracle's output. In each State, when the adversary gets a returned value from the Oracle, he can narrow the range of $\mathbf{s}_A[0]$ until the exact value of $\mathbf{s}_A[0]$ is determined.

Table 2. The choice of h and the States

		State 1	State 2	State 3	State 4
Kyber512	h	2	3	4	1
	$\mathcal{O} \to 0$	State 2	State 3	$\mathbf{s}_A[0] = 2$	$\mathbf{s}_A[0] = -1$
	$\mathcal{O} \to 1$	State 4	$\mathbf{s}_A[0] = 0$	$\mathbf{s}_A[0] = 1$	$\mathbf{s}_A[0] = -2$
Kyber768	h	4	5	6	3
	$\mathcal{O} \to 0$	State 2	State 3	$\mathbf{s}_A[0] = 2$	$\mathbf{s}_A[0] = -1$
	$\mathcal{O} \to 1$	State 4	$\mathbf{s}_A[0] = 0$	$\mathbf{s}_A[0] = 1$	$\mathbf{s}_A[0] = -2$
Kyber1024	h	8	9	10	7
	$\mathcal{O} \to 0$	State 2	State 3	$\mathbf{s}_A[0] = 2$	$\mathbf{s}_A[0] = -1$
	$\mathcal{O} \to 1$	State 4	$\mathbf{s}_A[0] = 0$	$\mathbf{s}_A[0] = 1$	$\mathbf{s}_A[0] = -2$

Table 3. $\mathbf{S}_i$ and its corresponding $\bar{s}$, $l_{\bar{s}}$

i	0	1	2	3	4
$\mathbf{S}_i$	0	1	−1	2	−2
$\bar{s}$	01	001	10	000	11
$l_{\bar{s}}$	2	3	2	3	2

As an example, we show how the adversary $\mathcal{A}$ determines $\mathbf{s}_A[0]$ for Kyber1024 in details.

1. The key mismatch attack starts from State 1, and $\mathcal{A}$ sets $h = 8$ first. Then $\{\mathbf{S}_0, \mathbf{S}_1, \mathbf{S}_2, \mathbf{S}_3, \mathbf{S}_4\}$ can be divided into two parts based on the returned value of the first oracle:
   - If $\mathcal{O} \to 0$: $\mathbf{s}_A[0]$ belongs to $\{\mathbf{S}_0, \mathbf{S}_1, \mathbf{S}_3\}$, and goes to State 2.
   - If $\mathcal{O} \to 1$: $\mathbf{s}_A[0]$ belongs to $\{\mathbf{S}_2, \mathbf{S}_4\}$, and State 4 will be executed.
2. If $\mathcal{A}$ comes to State 2, he goes on setting $h = 9$:
   - If $\mathcal{O} \to 0$: $\mathbf{s}_A[0]$ belongs to $\{\mathbf{S}_1, \mathbf{S}_3\}$, then goes to State 3.
   - If $\mathcal{O} \to 1$: $\mathcal{A}$ can determine $\mathbf{s}_A[0] = \mathbf{S}_0 = 0$.
3. In State 3, $\mathcal{A}$ sets $h = 10$:
   - If $\mathcal{O} \to 0$: $\mathcal{A}$ determines $\mathbf{s}_A[0] = \mathbf{S}_3 = 2$.
   - If $\mathcal{O} \to 1$: $\mathcal{A}$ determines $\mathbf{s}_A[0] = \mathbf{S}_1 = 1$.
4. When $\mathcal{A}$ is in State 4, he sets $h = 7$:
   - If $\mathcal{O} \to 0$: $\mathcal{A}$ finds that $\mathbf{s}_A[0] = \mathbf{S}_2 = -1$.
   - If $\mathcal{O} \to 1$: $\mathcal{A}$ finds that $\mathbf{s}_A[0] = \mathbf{S}_4 = -2$.

Based on the above process, we can construct $\bar{s}$, $l_{\bar{s}}$ for $\{\mathbf{S}_0, \mathbf{S}_1, \mathbf{S}_2, \mathbf{S}_3, \mathbf{S}_4\}$, as shown in Table 3. For example, if $\mathbf{s}_A[0] = \mathbf{S}_1 = 1$, we come to State 1 first, and the oracle outputs 0. Then we go to State 2 and the oracle outputs 0. Now we are in State 3 and the output is 1. Therefore we can get $\bar{s} = 001$. We can see that in this way we decide $\mathbf{S}_i$ with larger occurrence probability by as fewer queries as possible. We can also observe that the way we find $\bar{s}$ is similar to our optimal BRT.

Similarly, to recover $\mathbf{s}_A[i]$ when $i \neq 0$, $\mathcal{A}$ only needs to set $\mathbf{P}_B = 0$ except $\mathbf{P}_B[n-i] = -\lceil \frac{q}{32} \rfloor$ at first.

Now we can calculate the average number of queries needed to recover each coefficient in $\mathbf{s}_A$ as $\frac{3}{8} \times 2 + \frac{1}{4} \times (2+3) + \frac{1}{16} \times (2+3) = 2.31$. Therefore, the corresponding numbers of average queries needed in Kyber1024 and Kyber768 are 2365.44, 1774.08 respectively. Similarly, we can get the average number of queries on Kyber512, which is 1312.06. Compared with the bound in Table 1, there is only a gap less than 9%.

In [49], the authors proposed three different methods to perform key mismatch attacks on Kyber. For their best method, the queries are 2475, 1855 and 1401. Therefore, our improved practical key mismatch attack on Kyber is better than that in [49].

4.2 Improved Key Mismatch Attacks on Saber

There are three versions of Saber, the LightSaber, Saber, and FireSaber. Here we take the attack on FireSaber as an example. The attacks on LightSaber and Saber are similar. The adversary chooses $P_B = h$ and $c_m = k$, and the selection of each h_i/k_i ($i = 1, \ldots, 10$ in LightSaber; $i = 1, \ldots, 8$ in Saber; $i = 1, \ldots, 6$ in FireSaber) is shown in Table 4.

Table 4. Selection of h_i/k_i in the practical key mismatch attacks on Saber

i	1	2	3	4	5	6	7	8	9	10
LightSaber	2/60	1/69	1/35	1/23	0/50	0/40	2/30	2/20	2/15	2/12
Saber	4/28	3/37	3/36	3/18	3/12	4/27	4/13	4/9		
FireSaber	17/7	16/2	16/4	8/125	4/95	2/76				

The following procedure shows how to use h_i/k_i in Table 4 to recover $\mathbf{s}_A[0]$.

1. We set $h = h_1$ and $k = k_1$ first, then $\mathbf{S}_i$ ($i = 0, \ldots, 6$) can be divided into two parts based on the returned value of the first Oracle:
   - If $\mathcal{O} \rightarrow 0$: $\mathbf{s}_A[0]$ belongs to $\{\mathbf{S}_1, \mathbf{S}_3, \mathbf{S}_5\}$, and turn to step 4.
   - If $\mathcal{O} \rightarrow 1$: $\mathbf{s}_A[0]$ belongs to $\{\mathbf{S}_0, \mathbf{S}_2, \mathbf{S}_4, \mathbf{S}_6\}$, then step 2 and step 3 will be executed.
2. If the oracle returns 1 when we set $h = h_1$ and $k = k_1$, then we set $h = h_2$ and $k = k_2$:
   - If $\mathcal{O} \rightarrow 0$: We can determine $\mathbf{s}_A[0] = \mathbf{S}_0$.
   - If $\mathcal{O} \rightarrow 1$: $\mathbf{s}_A[0]$ belongs to $\{\mathbf{S}_2, \mathbf{S}_4, \mathbf{S}_6\}$, and go to step 3.
3. Next, we select different parameters $h = h_3$, $k = k_3$ and $h = h_4$, $k = k_4$ (the specific values of h_i/k_i are shown in Table 4) and repeat operations in step 2 until we can know which of $\{\mathbf{S}_2, \mathbf{S}_4, \mathbf{S}_6\}$ is equal to $\mathbf{s}_A[0]$.
4. Similarly, we select different parameters $h = h_5$, $k = k_5$ and $h = h_6$, $k = k_6$ in Table 4 and repeat operations in steps 2 and 3 until we can know which of $\{\mathbf{S}_1, \mathbf{S}_3, \mathbf{S}_5\}$ is $\mathbf{s}_A[0]$.

4.3 Improved Key Mismatch Attacks on FrodoKEM

There are three versions of FrodoKEM, the Frodo640, Frodo976, and Frodo1344. Here we take the attack on Frodo1344 as an example. The attacks on Frodo640 and Frodo976 are similar. In Frodo1344, $\mathbf{S}_i \in [-6, 6]$, the selection of h_i ($i \in [0, 12]$) is shown in Table 5.

Table 5. Selection of h_i in practical key mismatch attacks on FrodoKEM

i	1	2	3	4	5	6
h_i	2^{12}	$2^{12}-2$	$2^{12}-1$	$2^{12}-3$	$2^{12}-4$	$2^{12}-5$
i	7	8	9	10	11	12
h_i	$2^{12}-6$	$2^{12}-7$	$2^{12}-8$	$2^{12}-9$	$2^{12}-10$	$2^{12}-11$

Next, we introduce how to use h_i in Table 5 to recover $\mathbf{s}_A[0]$.

1. We set $h = h_1$ first, then $\mathbf{S}_i (i \in [0, 12])$ can be divided into two parts based on the returns value of the first Oracle:
   - If $\mathcal{O} \to 0$: $\mathbf{s}_A[0]$ belongs to $\{\mathbf{S}_0, \mathbf{S}_2, \mathbf{S}_4, \mathbf{S}_6, \mathbf{S}_8, \mathbf{S}_{10}, \mathbf{S}_{12}\}$, and then step 2 and step 3 will be executed.
   - If $\mathcal{O} \to 1$: $\{\mathbf{S}_1, \mathbf{S}_3, \mathbf{S}_5, \mathbf{S}_7, \mathbf{S}_9, \mathbf{S}_{11}\}$
2. If the oracle returns 0 when we set $h = h_1$, then we set $h = h_2$:
   - If $\mathcal{O} \to 0$: We can determine $\mathbf{s}_A[0] = \mathbf{S}_0$.
   - If $\mathcal{O} \to 1$: $\mathbf{s}_A[0]$ belongs to $\{\mathbf{S}_2, \mathbf{S}_4, \mathbf{S}_6, \mathbf{S}_8, \mathbf{S}_{10}, \mathbf{S}_{12}\}$, then we will proceed step 3.
3. Next, we select different parameter $h = h_2, \cdots, h_7$ (the specific values of h_i are shown in Table 5. Repeat operations in step 2 until we can know which of $\{\mathbf{S}_2, \mathbf{S}_4, \mathbf{S}_6, \mathbf{S}_8, \mathbf{S}_{10}, \mathbf{S}_{12}\}$ is $\mathbf{s}_A[0]$.
4. Similarly, we select different parameter $h = h_8, \cdots, h_{12}$ in Table 5 and repeat operations in steps 2 and 3 until we can know which of $\{\mathbf{S}_1, \mathbf{S}_3, \mathbf{S}_5, \mathbf{S}_7, \mathbf{S}_9, \mathbf{S}_{11}\}$ is $\mathbf{s}_A[0]$.

4.4 Improved Practical Attacks on Other NIST Candidates

Similarly, we can also improve the key mismatch attacks on NewHope, LAC, and Round5. The details are given in Appendix B, where we show how the adversary chooses the parameters in each scheme, and how to determine $\mathbf{s}_A$ according to the returns of the oracle.

An interesting question is, can we construct an attack to force the Oracle to output the string that is exactly the same as suggested by the optimal BRT? In this way, certainly we can find an optimal practical attack that reaches the theoretical lower bound. Unfortunately, due to the restriction of concrete schemes, we may not find such parameters to launch the attack since they may not exist at all. For example, if we want to achieve the lower bounds against Kyber1024 using Huffman coding, we need to select the parameter $\mathbf{K}_2$ according to Fig. 4, in this way the range of the secret key is divided into two sub-intervals: $\{0, 1\}$ and $\{-1, 2, -2\}$. However, in our improved practical attacks, the parameter $\mathbf{K}_2$ we choose can only divide the range of the secret key into two adjacent sub-intervals, namely $\{-2, -1\}$ and $\{0, 1, 2\}$, or $\{-2, -1, 0\}$ and $\{1, 2\}$. This is the reason why the number of queries needed in our improved practical attacks is close to the bound, but not exactly the same.

5 Improved Side-Channel Assisted Chosen Ciphertexts Attacks on CCA-Secure NIST KEM Candidates

As described above, the CPA-secure KEM candidates are vulnerable to key reuse attacks. However, it is well known that the NIST candidates are CCA-secure by applying some well-known transformation such as FO transformation [29]. To be specific, FO transform mainly consists of two parts. First, Alice decrypts Bob's ciphertext $\bar{c}$ to obtain m' and a seed by calling KEM.CPA.Dec. Then she re-encrypts m' and the seed to get c'. If $\bar{c} = c'$, she continues to calculate the shared key, otherwise she rejects the ciphertext $\bar{c}$. This mechanism of decrypting and then re-encrypting in the CCA-secure KEM protects the validity of the ciphertext, returning failure when an invalid ciphertext is detected. Thus Alice always rejects these malicious chosen ciphertexts and the adversary cannot gain any meaningful information, which also means that our attacks above will not work when these cryptosystems are correctly deployed. However, at CHES 2020, Ravi et al. [50] showed that chosen ciphertexts attacks on CCA-secure NIST candidate KEMs can also be launched with the help of side channel information. Therefore, our proposed method can be directly used to further improve the efficiency of these attacks.

Ravi et al.'s key observation is that, we can use the side channel information to bypass the restrictions of FO transform to obtain useful match or mismatch information about decryption outputs of chosen ciphertexts, making it possible to successfully attack CCA-secure cryptosystems. In other words, Ravi et al.'s chosen ciphertext attack is almost the same as the key mismatch attack, except that the adversary can actively know whether the shared message matches or not by physically accessing to devices performing decapsulation.

Algorithm 4 The Oracle and SCA-assisted chosen ciphertext attack

$\diamond$ **Oracle** $\mathcal{O}_s(P, m_0, m_1)$
Input: $P := (\mathbf{c}_1, \mathbf{c}_2)$, m_0, m_1
Output: 0 or 1
1: $\mathcal{W} \leftarrow$ SCA(KEM.CCA.Dec(P))
2: **if** $\Gamma_0 \geq \Gamma_1$ **then Return** 1
3: **else Return** 0
4: **end if**

$\diamond$ **Chosen ciphertext attack**
Input: Alice's P_A and Oracle $\mathcal{O}_s$
Output: 0 or 1
5: $\mathbf{s}'_A \leftarrow \mathcal{A}^{\mathcal{O}_s}(P_A)$
6: **if** $\mathbf{s}'_A = \mathbf{s}_A$ **then Return** 1
7: **else Return** 0
8: **end if**

In Ravi et al.'s side-channel attack (SCA), they mainly utilize Welch's t-test based template approach [30], which consists of two stages. The first is the pre-processing stage including how to generate a template for each class, while the second stage involves the template matching operation. In the first stage, we need to collect 50 measurements of $\mathcal{T} = \mathcal{T}_0 \cup \mathcal{T}_1$. Here, $\mathcal{T}_0$ and $\mathcal{T}_1$ correspond to the failure and success of KEM.CCA.Dec(), respectively. To get $\mathcal{T}_0$, we directly set $\mathbf{m}' = \mathbf{0}$ instead of calling the decryption part KEM.CPA.Dec() in KEM.CCA.Dec(), and then collect the corresponding 50 measurements. Similarly, we can get $\mathcal{T}_1$ by setting $\mathbf{m}' = \{1, 0, \ldots, 0\}$. Then we calculate their respective means denoted as $m_0 = (\sum_{i=1}^{50} \mathcal{T}_0[i])/50$ and $m_1 = (\sum_{i=1}^{50} \mathcal{T}_1[i])/50$. In the second stage, according to the results of m_0 and m_1, when we collect a wave $\mathcal{W}$ from KEM.CCA.Dec(), we can distinguish which class the wave $\mathcal{W}$ belongs to. Specifically, we need to compute the sum-of-squared difference Γ_* of the wave $\mathcal{W}$ with m_* as follows:

$$\Gamma_0 = (\mathcal{W} - m_0)^T \cdot (\mathcal{W} - m_0), \Gamma_1 = (\mathcal{W} - m_1)^T \cdot (\mathcal{W} - m_1).$$

If $\Gamma_0 \geq \Gamma_1$, $\mathcal{W}$ belongs to Γ_1, otherwise it belongs to Γ_0. When $\mathcal{W}$ belongs to Γ_0, we know that $\mathbf{m}' = \mathbf{0}$, which is the same as the principle of the mismatch situation in the key mismatch attack aforementioned. Similarly, if $\mathcal{W}$ belongs to Γ_1, it is consistent with the match situation in key mismatch attack.

Based on the above analysis, we can build an Oracle $\mathcal{O}_s$ that simulates Alice's KEM.CCA.Dec part, which is depicted in Algorithm 4. In the following we take Kyber1024 as an example to show our detailed attacks. But we need to emphasize that our method is applicable to other CCA-secure NIST candidates. For Kyber1024 we choose the parameters ($\mathbf{c}_1$, $\mathbf{c}_2$) exactly the same as listed in Table 2, to launch our chosen ciphertext attack. Here we show how the adversary $\mathcal{A}$ determines $\mathbf{s}_A[0] = 0$ with only 2 queries, and the rest are similar.

In the pre-processing stage, $\mathcal{A}$ collects two sets of 50 measurements in advance and computes their respective means. Then $\mathcal{A}$ gets two means m_0 and m_1. For the chosen ciphertext attack stage, starting from State 1 in Table 2, $\mathcal{A}$ sets $\mathbf{P}_B = 0$ except $\mathbf{P}_B[0] = \lceil \frac{q}{32} \rfloor$. After computing $\mathbf{c}_1 = \mathbf{Compress}_q(\mathbf{P}_B, 2^{d_{\mathbf{P}_B}})$, $\mathcal{A}$ sets $\mathbf{c}_2 = \mathbf{0}$, except that $\mathbf{c}_2[0] = 2$ at the first time. If the first output of $\mathcal{O}_s$ is 0, then State 1 switches to State 2. Next, $\mathcal{A}$ sets $\mathbf{c}_2[0] = 3$, if the second output of $\mathcal{O}_s$ is 1 and $\mathcal{A}$ can determine $\mathbf{s}_A[0] = 0$.

In summary, our improved attack can be applied to attack CCA-secure NIST KEM candidates just as Ravi et al.'s chosen ciphertexts attack.

However, Ravi et al. had to brute-forcedly select the parameters, which is not efficient for secret key with larger coefficients. Therefore, our proposed optimal BRT approach can be directly used to select better parameters and significantly reduce the needed number of queries with high efficiency. Specifically, Ravi et al. only gave the detailed description of attacks against Kyber512 in the second round, where the secret key $\mathbf{s}_A$ is sampled from centered binomial distribution $\mathbf{B}_\eta$ with $\eta = 2$. Thus, in their attack the needed queries for each coefficient is 5. Since $n = 256$, $k = 2$, the total number of queries for Kyber512 is 2560. In order to make a fair comparison with their results, we also apply our improved attack to the second round of Kyber. By adopting our proposed optimal BRT approach, we only need 1182.72 queries on average, reducing the number of queries by 53.79% correspondingly. Secondly, in Ravi et al.'s attack, to retrieve coefficient -2 the selected parameters $(\mathbf{c}_1, \mathbf{c}_2) = (415, 3)$. Through our analysis 415 is too large, which is the reason why their attack cannot succeed with a 100% probability.

In our paper we consider Kyber in the third round, where the private key of Kyber512 ranges from -3 to 3. All the results can be found at Table 6.

Similarly, we can also improve Ravi et al.'s method with our improved key mismatch attacks on other NIST candidates. In [50], for NewHope512, and NewHope1024, the total number of queries is 6945 and 26624, respectively. According to our results in Table 6, we reduce the number of queries for NewHope512 and NewHope1024 by 76.1% and 88.06%, respectively.

In [54], there is another interesting side-channel attack, namely the fault-injection attack, against the NIST KEMs. We find that their main idea is to construct a plaintext-checking oracle by injecting a fault first and then recover the private key by employing the key mismatch attack directly. Hence, we believe our results can also be applied to improve their attacks.

6 Experiments

In this section, we conduct experiments on the above improved attacks to confirm their correctness and efficiency. All our improved key mismatch attacks are implemented on a desktop equipped with two 3 GHz Intel Xeon E5-2620 CPUs and a 64 GB RAM. Our code is based on the C reference implementations of the NIST candidates, and we have made it public[1]. Note that first our attack is against the CPA-secure KEMs for Kyber, we directly call the Kyber.CPAPKE.KeyGen() to launch the attack. For schemes like Saber and FrodoKEM, we remove the FO transform in their CCA version. Since the improved key mismatch attacks and the SCA-assisted selection ciphertext attack share similar processes on the NIST candidate KEMs, as shown in Algorithm 5, we use Kyber1024 as an example to illustrate the details of these attacks.

In the experiment we generate 1000 different secret keys $\mathbf{s}_A$ and recover them separately. We use *queries* to represent the number of times the adversary needs to access the oracle to recover a complete $\mathbf{s}_A$. The experimental results given in Table 6 are the average number of times the adversary needs to access the oracle to recover these 1000 different $\mathbf{s}_A$.

In Table 6, we present our experimental results. For each scheme, we list the lower bound of the minimum average number of queries by our BRT method, the expected number of queries for our improved attacks (Bold), the average number of queries for our improved attacks in our experiments, as well as the number of queries of other existing results (Italic). We use "–" to mean that no result is given.

[1] https://github.com/AHaQY/Key-Mismatch-Attack-on-NIST-KEMs.

Algorithm 5 Pseudocode of improved key mismatch attack on Kyber1024

```
◇ Generate reused key pair
(s_A, P_A) ← Kyber.CPA.Gen()
◇ Recover s_A
Set m = 0, except m[0] = 1
Set queries = 0
for i = 0 → 3 do
    for j = 0 → 255 do
        Set P_B = 0
        if j = 0 then
            P_B[0] = ⌈q/32⌋
        else
            P_B[256 − j] = −⌈q/32⌋
        end if
        c_1 = Compress_q(P_B, d_{P_B})
        Set round = 0
        while round < 4 do
            round ++
            Set c_2 = 0, except c_2[0] = h
            t = O(c_1, c_2)
            queries ++
            if A recovers s_A[i][j] then
                Break
            else Continue
            end if
        end while
        if round == 4 then
            Cannot recover s_A[i][j]
        end if
    end for
end for
```

Table 6. Key mismatch attacks against lattice-based NIST KEMs.

Schemes	E(#Queries)			
	Lower Bounds	**Our improved attacks**		*Existing*
		Theory	Experiments	
Kyber512	1216	**1312**	1311	*1401* (Round 2) [49]
Kyber768	1632	**1774**	1777	*1855* [49]
Kyber1024	2176	**2365**	2368	*2475* [49]
LightSaber	1412	**1460**	1476	*2048* [37]
Saber	1986	**2091**	2095	–
FireSaber	2432	**2642**	2622	–
Frodo640	18,227	**18,329**	18,360	*65,536* [37]
Frodo976	25,796	**26,000**	26,078	–
Frodo1344	27,973	**29,353**	29,378	–
NewHope512	1568	**1660**	1660	–
NewHope1024	3127	**3180**	3180	*3197* [52]

It can be seen that our improved attacks approach the lower bound in most cases and our experiments almost perfectly match the theoretical results in our improved attack. That is, the difference between the improved attack and our experiments is less than 1.2%. As we can see in Table 6, the experimental results of our improved approach are very close to the theoretical bounds. In general, there is less than 8.2% gap between our experiments and the theoretical bounds.

Compared with other existing attack, we can see that our improved attack on Kyber is slightly better than that in [49], since for Kyber the gap between the lower bounds and practice is small. For Frodo640 and LightSaber, we have reduced the number of queries by 71.99 % and 27.93%, respectively, compared to the results in [37]. Our result on NewHope1024 is slightly better than that of [52]. For LAC256, we greatly decrease the number of queries in comparison with the work of Wang et al. [53]. Using our improved method, the results of LAC128 and LAC192 are also better than the current results [31,53]. The details are shown in Appendix B.

7 Conclusion and Discussions

In this paper, we have developed a unified method to calculate the minimum number of required queries in launching key mismatch attacks against lattice-based NIST candidate KEMs. The bound is calculated through constructing an optimal BRT, which is further used to guide us in improving the practical attacks. By using BRT method, our improved attack can significantly reduce the needed number of queries. An interesting problem is whether our proposed method applies to the similar attacks against other post-quantum cryptosystems such as HQC, which also advance to the third round of NIST's PQC standardization progress.

From the analysis of our proposed attacks, we find that the ranges of the coefficients in the secret key and their corresponding probabilities, as well as the employment of Encode/Decode functions are the most important factors in evaluating their key mismatch resilience. More specifically, the larger the range of the coefficients, the more queries are needed. For example, neither Kyber nor Saber use the Encode/Decode functions, and their number of unknowns are the same, the only difference is the range of their coefficients in secret keys. The range of coefficients in Saber is larger than that of Kyber, which leads to more queries in recovering Saber's secret key.

The occurrence probabilities corresponding to the coefficients are another factor. For example, for LAC192 and LAC256, the only difference between them is the occurrence probabilities corresponding to the coefficients. More specifically, in LAC192 the occurrence probability of 0 is greater than that of 0 in LAC256, and the probability of other coefficients is less than that in LAC256. This results in larger number of queries needed to recover the secret keys of LAC256 than that in LAC192. Whether or not the Encode/Decode functions are used also affects the number of queries needed. NewHope512 and NewHope1024 use D-2 and D-4 functions, respectively, which allows them to recover two and four coefficients at the same time. This also greatly reduces the number of queries needed to recover the coefficients. However, we need to emphasize that these factors only increase complexities of launching the key mismatch attack, but cannot stop the attack.

Acknowledgment. Chi Cheng is the corresponding author. The authors would like to thank Michael Naehrig, Muyan Shen, and the anonymous reviewers for their kind help. The research in this paper was partially supported by the National Natural Science Foundation of China (NSFC) under Grant no. s 62172374, 61672029, and 61732021, and Guangxi Key Laboratory of Trusted Software (no. KX202038). Y. Pan was supported by National Key Research and Development Program of China (No. 2018YFA0704705) and NSFC (No. 62032009). J. D. would like to thank CCB Fintech Co. Ltd for partially sponsoring the work with grant No. KT2000040.

A Bounds for other candidates

We list our lower bounds for key mismatch attacks against LAC, Round5 and Three Bears in Table 7. For each scheme, we give the ranges of coefficients, number of unknowns, and whether the Encode/Decode and Compress/Decompress are employed or not. We also report the average number of queries in our proposed bounds.

Table 7. Key mismatch attacks against LAC, Round5 and Three Bears

Schemes	$\mathbf{s}_A$ & $\mathbf{e}$ Ranges	Encode Decode	Comp Decomp	Unknowns	E(#Queries) Bounds
LAC128	[−1, 1]	✓	/	512	553
LAC192				1024	1106
LAC256				1024	1398
Round5 R5ND_1	[−1, 1]	/	✓	618	722
Round5 R5ND_3				786	1170
Round5 R5ND_5				1018	1446
BabyBear	[−1, 1]	/	✓	320	520
MamaBear	[−2, 2]			320	680
PapaBear	[−3, 3]			320	738

B Improved practical key mismatch attacks

In this section, according to the proposed bounds, we discuss how to launch the practical key mismatch attacks on NewHope, LAC and Round5.

B.1 Improved key mismatch attacks on NewHope

In a key mismatch attack on NewHope, we build an Oracle $\mathcal{O}$ to simulate the process of NewHope.KEM.Dec(). The inputs of $\mathcal{O}$ are $(\mathbf{P}_B, \overline{\mathbf{c}})$ and K_B. The

Oracle honestly executes the decryption to get K_A. Then it, compares K_A and K_B, if they are equal, it returns 1, otherwise it returns 0.

As far as we know, the best practical key mismatch attack on NewHope1024 given in [52] needs 3197 queries, which is still higher than our theoretical bound 3127. Based on it, we propose a method that can further decrease the number of queries to 3180. Here we take NewHope1024 as an example to show how to launch the attack.

Main idea. Our improved attack method is on the basis of Mehlhorn's Rule II in Nearly Optimal Binary Search Tree [42], i.e., for every given probability range, we always select the root in a way that the differences between sums of weights of its left subtree and right subtree are as small as possible.

In a key mismatch attack, we assume that Alice's public key $\mathbf{P}_A$ is always reused, and the adversary $\mathcal{A}$'s target is to get the secret key $\mathbf{s}_A$ of Alice. In order to achieve the target, $\mathcal{A}$ needs to set proper parameters.

Recall that NewHope1024 uses D-4 encoding, which means 4 coefficients $\mathbf{s}_A[i]$, $\mathbf{s}_A[i+256]$, $\mathbf{s}_A[i+512]$, $\mathbf{s}_A[i+768]$ are operated at a time. We assume that the adversary $\mathcal{A}$ wants to recover the *i-th* quadruplet, then he needs to properly select v_b, and parameters $(\mathbf{P}_B, \overline{\mathbf{c}})$.

In our improved attack, in Step 1 by precomputing the probabilities of all the quadruplets, along with the outputs of Oracle corresponding to selected parameters $(\mathbf{P}_B, \bar{\mathbf{c}})$ and all the quadruplets, $\mathcal{A}$ can choose the proper parameters which relate each quadruplet to a leaf node in a binary tree. Finally, in Step 2 by repeatedly querying the Oracle and getting the corresponding sequence of returned values, $\mathcal{A}$ can decide the quadruplets.

Step1: The pre-computation phase. In this step, the adversary $\mathcal{A}$ needs to compute the probabilities of all the quadruplets, along with the outputs of Oracle corresponding to selected parameters $(\mathbf{P}_B, \overline{\mathbf{c}})$ and all the quadruplets which is denoted as O_A, and constructs a corresponding binary recovery tree.

In the following, we construct the corresponding nearly optimal binary recovery tree T. Here, a nearly optimal binary tree means a binary tree in which the sum of the probabilities of quadruplets of the left subtree and the right subtree should be as equal as possible. We require T to be nearly optimal since in this way we can recursively divide all the possible quadruplets into almost equal two parts with lower time complexity.

We set the sum of the probabilities of quadruplets of a non-leaf node's left subtree and the right subtree as p_0 and p_1, respectively. The nearly optimal binary recovery tree T should satisfy the following properties.

1. For each non-leaf node, its corresponding p_0 and p_1 should be as equal as possible.
2. For each non-leaf node, if the Oracle returns 0, it corresponds to the left subtree of the current node, otherwise it corresponds to its right subtree.

First, we traverse the precomputing O_A to find one appropriate parameter $P = (\mathbf{P}_B, \overline{\mathbf{c}})$ which satisfies the above two properties. The construction of tree T starts from the root node with index $i = 0$. After obtaining the appropriate parameter P, we insert the root node and P into the 0-*th* position in T. Then we recursively build the left subtree and the right subtree for the root node, respectively. Finally, all the possible quadruplets are stored in the leaf nodes, and parameters $\mathbf{P}_B$ and $\overline{\mathbf{c}}$ are stored in the non-leaf nodes.

Step2: The recovery phase. In this step, the adversary $\mathcal{A}$ tries to decide the quadruplet according to the precomputed binary tree T.

Algorithm 6 Determining each quadruplet

```
Input: T
Output: the quadruplet
Set node = T.root
while node is not a leaf node do
    Set P the parameter stored in the node
    v = Oracle(P)
    if v = 0 then
        node = node.leftnode
    else
        node = node.rightnode
    end if
end while
Return the quadruplet stored in the node
```

We show how the adversary $\mathcal{A}$ decides the *i-th* quadruplet in Algorithm 6. Specifically, $\mathcal{A}$ first starts from the root node of the precomputed binary tree T, and sets P as the parameters stored in the root node. Then, he accesses the Oracle, if it returns 0, $\mathcal{A}$ accessed the left subtree of the root node, otherwise $\mathcal{A}$ accessed the right subtree of the root node. Next, $\mathcal{A}$ repeats the following two steps until the current node he accesses is a leaf node.

1. $\mathcal{A}$ judges whether the current node is a leaf node, and if it is, he directly returns the value of the quadruplet stored in the node. Otherwise, he sets P as the parameters stored in the current node, and accesses the Oracle again.
2. If the Oracle returns 0, he sets $node = node.leftnode$, otherwise $node = node.rightnode$.

Parameter Choices: The total number of queries depend on the precomputed binary tree T. Recall that in Step1, when we construct the binary tree T, we need to compute the probabilities of all the quadruplets and O_A, the latter is associated with selected parameters $(\mathbf{P}_B, \overline{\mathbf{c}})$, thus the selected parameters determines the number of queries.

Hypothesis 1. *The adversary $\mathcal{A}$ sets $v_b = \{1, 0, 0, \dots, 0\}$, $\mathbf{P}_B = gx^{-i}$, $\overline{\mathbf{c}} = \sum_{j=0}^{3} ((l_j + 4) \bmod 8) x^{256j}$. Then the goal of $\mathcal{A}$ is to choose $(\mathbf{P}_B, \overline{\mathbf{c}})$ such that $v_a = Decode(Decompress(\overline{\mathbf{c}} - \mathbf{P}_B \circ \mathbf{s}_A)) = \{b, 0, 0, \dots, 0\}$, where $b \in \{0, 1\}$.*

Table 8. The relationship between g, success probability of Hypothesis 1, and average number of queries on NewHope1024

g	[0, 383]	[384, 512]	[384, 534]	[384, 768]	[384, 819]
Success probability (%)	100	99.999	99.999	94.577	85.811
E(#Queries)	3574.953	3179.215	3206.605	3174.853	3174.085

Moreover, while selecting parameters $(\mathbf{P}_B, \overline{\mathbf{c}})$, $\mathcal{A}$ needs to guarantee that Hypothesis 1 holds with nearly 100% probability. Otherwise when the output of Oracle is 0, $\mathcal{A}$ does not know whether the mismatch is due to the 0-*th* position or other positions.

In order to get the best parameter, we traverse and compute the success rate of Hypothesis 1 through the whole value interval of g, and show the relationship among $g \in [0, 819]$, the success probability of Hypothesis 1 and the average number of queries in Table 8 above. Considering the success probability and the number of queries, we finally decide the optimal interval of parameter g, i.e. $[384, 512]$. In Step2, while selecting parameter $g \in [384, 512]$, the average number of queries needed by the adversary to get each quadruplet is 12.41881, and there are 256 unknown quadruplets in a secret key $\mathbf{s}_A$. Therefore, in total we need 3179.21536 queries to completely recover $\mathbf{s}_A$.

B.2 Improved key mismatch attacks on LAC

Although there are three versions of LAC with different security levels, the parameters in the proposed key mismatch attacks are the same. In the attack, the adversary needs to modify three parameters: $\mathbf{e}_B[0]$, $\mathbf{e}'_B[vb-1]$ and $\mathbf{e}'_B[2vb-1]$. Here, $vb = l_v = 400$, and l_v is a parameter set in LAC. And next we will show how to recover $\mathbf{s}_A[0]$.

1. We set $\mathbf{e}_B[0] = 124$, $\mathbf{e}'_B[vb-1] = 1$ and $\mathbf{e}'_B[2vb-1] = 1$ first, then $\{\mathbf{S}_0, \mathbf{S}_1, \mathbf{S}_2, \mathbf{S}_3, \mathbf{S}_4, \mathbf{S}_5, \mathbf{S}_6, \mathbf{S}_7, \mathbf{S}_8\}$ can be divided into two parts based on the returned value of the first Oracle:
   - If $\mathcal{O} \to 0$: $\mathbf{s}_A[0]$ belongs to $\{\mathbf{S}_3, \mathbf{S}_4, \mathbf{S}_5, \mathbf{S}_6, \mathbf{S}_7, \mathbf{S}_8\}$, next step 2, step 3 and step 5 will be executed.
   - If $\mathcal{O} \to 1$: $\mathbf{s}_A[0]$ belongs to $\{\mathbf{S}_0, \mathbf{S}_1, \mathbf{S}_2\}$, then go to step 4 and step 5.
2. If the oracle returns 0 in step 1, then we set $\mathbf{e}_B[0] = 124$, $\mathbf{e}'_B[vb-1] = 0$ and $\mathbf{e}'_B[2vb-1] = 0$:
   - If $\mathcal{O} \to 0$: $\mathbf{s}_A[0]$ belongs to $\{\mathbf{S}_5, \mathbf{S}_6, \mathbf{S}_7, \mathbf{S}_8\}$, next step 3 will be proceeded.
   - If $\mathcal{O} \to 1$: $\mathbf{s}_A[0]$ belongs to $\{\mathbf{S}_3, \mathbf{S}_4\}$, and next turn to step 5.
3. If the oracle returns 0 in step 2, then we set $\mathbf{e}_B[0] = 63$, $\mathbf{e}'_B[vb-1] = 63$ and $\mathbf{e}'_B[2vb-1] = 63$:
   - If $\mathcal{O} \to 0$: $\mathbf{s}_A[0]$ belongs to $\{\mathbf{S}_7, \mathbf{S}_8\}$, next go to step 5.
   - If $\mathcal{O} \to 1$: $\mathbf{s}_A[0]$ belongs to $\{\mathbf{S}_5, \mathbf{S}_6\}$, next go to step 5.
4. If the oracle returns 1 in step 1, then we set $\mathbf{e}_B[0] = 125$, $\mathbf{e}'_B[vb-1] = 0$ and $\mathbf{e}'_B[2vb-1] = 0$:

- If $\mathcal{O} \rightarrow 0$: $\mathbf{s}_A[0]$ belongs to $\{\mathbf{S}_1, \mathbf{S}_2\}$, then turn to step 5.
- If $\mathcal{O} \rightarrow 1$: We can determine $\mathbf{s}_A[0] = \mathbf{S}_0$.

5. Similarly we only need to distinguish the two coefficients in $\{\mathbf{S}_7, \mathbf{S}_8\}$, $\{\mathbf{S}_5, \mathbf{S}_6\}$, $\{\mathbf{S}_3, \mathbf{S}_4\}$, and $\{\mathbf{S}_1, \mathbf{S}_2\}$. As long as the appropriate parameters are selected, only one query is needed.

B.3 Improved key mismatch attacks on Round5

Round5 does not use D-2 Encode/Decode functions. Although there are three different versions of Round5 R5ND with different security levels, their attack process is the same, except that the parameters $P_B = h$ ($h = h_1$ or h_2) chosen by the adversary are different. Specifically, the adversary selects h_1/h_2 as $44/-44$, $120/-120$ and $144/113$, and the process of recovering $\mathbf{s}_A[0]$ is shown as follows.

1. We set $h = h_1$ first, then $\{\mathbf{S}_0, \mathbf{S}_1, \mathbf{S}_2\}$ can be divided into two parts based on the returned value of the first Oracle:
   - If $\mathcal{O} \rightarrow 0$: We can determine $\mathbf{s}_A[0] = \mathbf{S}_2$.
   - If $\mathcal{O} \rightarrow 1$: $\mathbf{s}_A[0]$ belongs to $\{\mathbf{S}_0, \mathbf{S}_1\}$.
2. When $h = h_1$, if the oracle returns 0 then we go on setting $h = h_2$:
   - If $\mathcal{O} \rightarrow 0$: $\mathbf{s}_A[0] = \mathbf{S}_0$.
   - If $\mathcal{O} \rightarrow 1$: $\mathbf{s}_A[0] = \mathbf{S}_1$.

References

1. Ajtai, M.: Generating hard instances of lattice problems. In: Proceedings of the Twenty-Eighth Annual ACM Symposium on Theory of Computing, pp. 99–108. ACM (1996)
2. Alagic, G., et al.: Status Report on the First Round of the NIST Post-Quantum Cryptography Standardization Process. US Department of Commerce, National Institute of Standards and Technology (2019). https://nvlpubs.nist.gov/nistpubs/ir/2019/NIST.IR.8240.pdf
3. Alkim, E., et al.: NewHope: algorithm specification and supporting documentation - version 1.03 (2019). https://newhopecrypto.org/data/NewHope_2019_07_10.pdf
4. Alkim, E., et al.: Frodokem learning with errors key encapsulation: algorithm specification and supporting documentation. Submission to the NIST post-quantum project (2019). https://frodokem.org/files/FrodoKEM-specification-20190702.pdf
5. Alkim, E., Ducas, L., Pöppelmann, T., Schwabe, P.: NewHope without reconciliation. IACR Cryptology ePrint Archive (2016). https://www.cryptojedi.org/papers/newhopesimple-20161217.pdf
6. Alkim, E., Ducas, L., Pöppelmann, T., Schwabe, P.: Post-quantum key exchange-a new hope. In: 25th USENIX Security Symposium (USENIX Security 16), pp. 327–343 (2016)
7. Avanzi, R., et al.: CRYSTALS-Kyber: algorithm specification and supporting documentation (version 2.0). Submission to the NIST post-quantum project (2019). https://pq-crystals.org/kyber
8. Baan, H., et al.: Round5: merge of round2 and HILA5 algorithm specification and supporting documentation. Submission to the NIST post-quantum project (2019). https://round5.org/Supporting_Documentation/Round5_Submission.pdf

9. Băetu, C., Durak, F.B., Huguenin-Dumittan, L., Talayhan, A., Vaudenay, S.: Misuse attacks on post-quantum cryptosystems. In: Ishai, Y., Rijmen, V. (eds.) EUROCRYPT 2019. LNCS, vol. 11477, pp. 747–776. Springer, Cham (2019). https://doi.org/10.1007/978-3-030-17656-3_26
10. Bauer, A., Gilbert, H., Renault, G., Rossi, M.: Assessment of the key-reuse resilience of NewHope. In: Matsui, M. (ed.) CT-RSA 2019. LNCS, vol. 11405, pp. 272–292. Springer, Cham (2019). https://doi.org/10.1007/978-3-030-12612-4_14
11. Bernstein, D.J., Groot Bruinderink, L., Lange, T., Panny, L.: HILA5 pindakaas: on the CCA security of lattice-based encryption with error correction. In: Joux, A., Nitaj, A., Rachidi, T. (eds.) AFRICACRYPT 2018. LNCS, vol. 10831, pp. 203–216. Springer, Cham (2018). https://doi.org/10.1007/978-3-319-89339-6_12
12. Bernstein, D.J., Chuengsatiansup, C., Lange, T., van Vredendaal, C.: NTRU prime: reducing attack surface at low cost. In: Adams, C., Camenisch, J. (eds.) SAC 2017. LNCS, vol. 10719, pp. 235–260. Springer, Cham (2018). https://doi.org/10.1007/978-3-319-72565-9_12
13. Bernstein, D.J., Chuengsatiansup, C., Lange, T., van Vredendaal, C.: NTRU prime: round 2. Submission to the NIST post-quantum project (2019). https://ntruprime.cr.yp.to/nist/ntruprime-20190330.pdf
14. Bindel, N., Stebila, D., Veitch, S.: Improved attacks against key reuse in learning with errors key exchange. IACR Cryptology EPrint Archive (2020). https://eprint.iacr.org/2020/1288.pdf
15. Bleichenbacher, D.: Chosen ciphertext attacks against protocols based on the RSA encryption standard PKCS #1. In: Krawczyk, H. (ed.) CRYPTO 1998. LNCS, vol. 1462, pp. 1–12. Springer, Heidelberg (1998). https://doi.org/10.1007/BFb0055716
16. Bos, J., et al.: CRYSTALS-Kyber: a CCA-secure module-lattice-based KEM. In: 2018 IEEE European Symposium on Security and Privacy (EuroS&P), pp. 353–367. IEEE (2018). https://eprint.iacr.org/2017/634
17. Bos, J.W., Costello, C., Naehrig, M., Stebila, D.: Post-quantum key exchange for the TLS protocol from the ring learning with errors problem. In: 2015 IEEE Symposium on Security and Privacy, pp. 553–570. IEEE (2015)
18. Chen, C., et al.: NTRU algorithm specifications and supporting documentation. Submission to the NIST post-quantum project (2019)
19. Chen, L., et al.: Report on post-quantum cryptography. US Department of Commerce, National Institute of Standards and Technology (2016)
20. Cover, T.M.: Elements of Information Theory. Wiley, Hoboken (1999)
21. Cramer, R., Shoup, V.: Design and analysis of practical public-key encryption schemes secure against adaptive chosen ciphertext attack. SIAM J. Comput. **33**(1), 167–226 (2003)
22. D'Anvers, J.P., Karmakar, A., Roy, S.S., Vercauteren, F.: SABER: Mod-LWR based KEM algorithm specification and supporting documentation. Submission to the NIST post-quantum project (2019). https://www.esat.kuleuven.be/cosic/publications/article-3055.pdf
23. D'Anvers, J.P., Tiepelt, M., Vercauteren, F., Verbauwhede, I.: Timing attacks on error correcting codes in post-quantum schemes. In: Proceedings of ACM Workshop on Theory of Implementation Security Workshop, pp. 2–9 (2019)
24. Diffie, W., Hellman, M.: New directions in cryptography. IEEE Trans. Inf. Theory **22**(6), 644–654 (1976)
25. Ding, J., Alsayigh, S., Saraswathy, R., Fluhrer, S., Lin, X.: Leakage of signal function with reused keys in RLWE key exchange. In: 2017 IEEE International Conference on Communications (ICC), pp. 1–6. IEEE (2017)

26. Ding, J., Branco, P., Schmitt, K.: Key exchange and authenticated key exchange with reusable keys based on RLWE assumption. IACR Cryptology EPrint Archive (2020). https://eprint.iacr.org/2019/665.pdf
27. Ding, J., Fluhrer, S., Rv, S.: Complete attack on RLWE key exchange with reused keys, without signal leakage. In: Susilo, W., Yang, G. (eds.) ACISP 2018. LNCS, vol. 10946, pp. 467–486. Springer, Cham (2018). https://doi.org/10.1007/978-3-319-93638-3_27
28. Ding, J., Xie, X., Lin, X.: A simple provably secure key exchange scheme based on the learning with errors problem. IACR Cryptology EPrint Archive (2012). https://eprint.iacr.org/2012/688.pdf
29. Fujisaki, E., Okamoto, T.: Secure integration of asymmetric and symmetric encryption schemes. In: Wiener, M. (ed.) CRYPTO 1999. LNCS, vol. 1666, pp. 537–554. Springer, Heidelberg (1999). https://doi.org/10.1007/3-540-48405-1_34
30. Gilbert Goodwill, B.J., Jaffe, J., Rohatgi, P., et al.: A testing methodology for side-channel resistance validation. In: NIST Non-Invasive Attack Testing Workshop, vol. 7, pp. 115–136 (2011)
31. Greuet, A., Montoya, S., Renault, G.: Attack on lac key exchange in misuse situation. IACR Cryptology EPrint Archive (2020). https://eprint.iacr.org/2020/063
32. Gyongyosi, L., Imre, S.: A survey on quantum computing technology. Comput. Sci. Rev. **31**, 51–71 (2019)
33. Hall, C., Goldberg, I., Schneier, B.: Reaction attacks against several public-key cryptosystem. In: Varadharajan, V., Mu, Y. (eds.) ICICS 1999. LNCS, vol. 1726, pp. 2–12. Springer, Heidelberg (1999). https://doi.org/10.1007/978-3-540-47942-0_2
34. Hamburg, M.: Post-quantum cryptography proposal: threebears. Submission to the NIST post-quantum project (2019). https://www.shiftleft.org/papers/threebears/threebears-spec.pdf
35. Hoffstein, J., Pipher, J., Silverman, J.H.: NTRU: a ring-based public key cryptosystem. In: Buhler, J.P. (ed.) ANTS 1998. LNCS, vol. 1423, pp. 267–288. Springer, Heidelberg (1998). https://doi.org/10.1007/BFb0054868
36. Huffman, D.A.: A method for the construction of minimum-redundancy codes. Proc. IRE **40**(9), 1098–1101 (1952)
37. Huguenin-Dumittan, L., Vaudenay, S.: Classical misuse attacks on NIST round 2 PQC. In: Conti, M., Zhou, J., Casalicchio, E., Spognardi, A. (eds.) ACNS 2020. LNCS, vol. 12146, pp. 208–227. Springer, Cham (2020). https://doi.org/10.1007/978-3-030-57808-4_11
38. Knuth, D.E.: The Art of Computer Programming, vol. 3. Pearson Education, London (1997)
39. Liu, C., Zheng, Z., Zou, G.: Key reuse attack on NewHope key exchange protocol. In: Lee, K. (ed.) ICISC 2018. LNCS, vol. 11396, pp. 163–176. Springer, Cham (2019). https://doi.org/10.1007/978-3-030-12146-4_11
40. Lu, X., et al.: LAC: lattice-based cryptosystems algorithm specification and supporting documentation. Submission to the NIST post-quantum project (2019). https://eprint.iacr.org/2018/1009.pdf
41. Lyubashevsky, V., Peikert, C., Regev, O.: On ideal lattices and learning with errors over rings. In: Gilbert, H. (ed.) EUROCRYPT 2010. LNCS, vol. 6110, pp. 1–23. Springer, Heidelberg (2010). https://doi.org/10.1007/978-3-642-13190-5_1
42. Mehlhorn, K.: Nearly optimal binary search trees. Acta Informatica **5**(4), 287–295 (1975)
43. Menezes, A., Ustaoglu, B.: On reusing ephemeral keys in Diffie-Hellman key agreement protocols. Int. J. Appl. Cryptogr. **2**(2), 154–158 (2010)

44. Moody, D.: Post quantum cryptography standardization: announcement and outline of NIST's call for submissions. In: PQCrypto 2016, Fukuoka, Japan (2016). https://csrc.nist.gov/Presentations/2016/Announcement-and-outline-of-NIST-s-Call-for-Submis
45. Moody, D., et al.: Status Report on the Second Round of the NIST Post-Quantum Cryptography Standardization Process. US Department of Commerce, National Institute of Standards and Technology (2020). https://nvlpubs.nist.gov/nistpubs/ir/2020/NIST.IR.8309.pdf
46. Okada, S., Wang, Y., Takagi, T.: Improving key mismatch attack on NewHope with fewer queries. IACR Cryptol. ePrint Arch. **2020**, 585 (2020)
47. Peikert, C.: Lattice cryptography for the internet. In: International Workshop on Post-Quantum Cryptography, pp. 197–219 (2014)
48. Qin, Y., Cheng, C., Ding, J.: A complete and optimized key mismatch attack on NIST candidate newhope. In: Sako, K., Schneider, S., Ryan, P.Y.A. (eds.) ESORICS 2019. LNCS, vol. 11736, pp. 504–520. Springer, Cham (2019). https://doi.org/10.1007/978-3-030-29962-0_24
49. Qin, Y., Cheng, C., Ding, J.: An efficient key mismatch attack on the NIST second round candidate kyber. IACR Cryptology EPrint Archive (2019). https://eprint.iacr.org/2019/1343
50. Ravi, P., Roy, S.S., Chattopadhyay, A., Bhasin, S.: Generic side-channel attacks on CCA-secure lattice-based PKE and KEMs. IACR Trans. Cryptogr. Hardw. Embedd. Syst., 307–335 (2020)
51. Regev, O.: On lattices, learning with errors, random linear codes, and cryptography. J. ACM **56**(6), 1–40 (2009)
52. Vacek, J., Václavek, J.: Key mismatch attack on newhope revisited. Technical report, Cryptology ePrint Archive, Report 2020/1389 (2020)
53. Wang, K., Zhang, Z., Jiang, H.: Key recovery under plaintext checking attack on LAC. In: Nguyen, K., Wu, W., Lam, K.Y., Wang, H. (eds.) ProvSec 2020. LNCS, vol. 12505, pp. 381–401. Springer, Cham (2020). https://doi.org/10.1007/978-3-030-62576-4_19
54. Xagawa, K., Ito, A., Ueno, R., Takahashi, J., Homma, N.: Fault-injection attacks against NIST's post-quantum cryptography round 3 KEM candidates. IACR Cryptology EPrint Archive (2021). https://ia.cr/2021/840
55. Zhang, X., Cheng, C., Ding, R.: Small leaks sink a great ship: an evaluation of key reuse resilience of PQC third round finalist NTRU-HRSS. ICICS2021 (2021, accepted). https://ia.cr/2021/168

Post-Quantum Cryptography

Gladius: LWR Based Efficient Hybrid Public Key Encryption with Distributed Decryption

Kelong Cong[1(✉)], Daniele Cozzo[1(✉)], Varun Maram[2(✉)], and Nigel P. Smart[1,3(✉)]

[1] imec-COSIC, KU Leuven, Leuven, Belgium
kelong.cong@esat.kuleuven.be, {daniele.cozzo,nigel.smart}@kuleuven.be
[2] ETH Zurich, Zurich, Switzerland
vmaram@inf.ethz.ch
[3] University of Bristol, Bristol, UK

Abstract. Standard hybrid encryption schemes based on the KEM-DEM framework are hard to implement efficiently in a distributed manner whilst maintaining the CCA security property of the scheme. This is because the DEM needs to be decrypted under the key encapsulated by the KEM, before the whole ciphertext is declared valid. In this paper we present a new variant of the KEM-DEM framework, closely related to Tag-KEMs, which sidesteps this issue. We then present a post-quantum KEM for this framework based on Learning-with-Rounding, which is designed specifically to have fast distributed decryption. Our combined construction of a hybrid encryption scheme with Learning-with-Rounding based KEM, called Gladius, is closely related to the NIST Round 3 candidate called Saber. Finally, we give a prototype distributed implementation that achieves a decapsulation time of 4.99 s for three parties.

1 Introduction

The potential development of quantum computers means that we need to rethink which algorithms are going to be used for public key encryption and signatures; resulting in the subarea called post-quantum cryptography. The early days of post-quantum cryptography looked at how to build basic primitives such as simple public key encryption or signatures. However, now we realise that our existing (pre-quantum) public key algorithms often offer more than what is offered by basic public key primitives. For example one may have group signatures, identity-based encryption, or proofs-of-knowledge of the secret key, etc. In this work, we look at distributed decryption for IND-CCA *hybrid* public key encryption.

Even in the context of pre-quantum cryptography, distributed decryption for hybrid systems is problematic for many schemes, as to maintain security one would need to apply a distributed decryption procedure to the symmetric component, which is rather expensive. This problem, of the difficulty of constructing threshold IND-CCA encryption/encapsulation schemes Π_p, was first pointed out

M. Tibouchi and H. Wang (Eds.): ASIACRYPT 2021, LNCS 13093, pp. 125–155, 2021.
https://doi.org/10.1007/978-3-030-92068-5_5

in [37] and then elaborated upon in [48,49]. The problem being that Π_p would seem to require a publicly checkable CCA test. For historical (i.e. impractical) CCA secure public key encryption schemes such as Naor-Yung [41] and Dolev-Dwork-Naor [25] the check is simply the verification of a zero-knowledge proof, and is thus publicly verifiable.

However, for almost all practical encryption schemes the check is non-public and thus requires often expensive machinery to deploy in a threshold manner. In [48,49] Shoup and Gennaro present two schemes (called TDH1 and TDH2) which are IND-CCA and are based on the discrete logarithm problem, for which an efficient threshold decryption algorithm is possible. Both schemes bear a strong resemblance to Cramer-Shoup encryption [17]. These two constructions are however non-hybrid encryption mechanisms, but can be turned into hybrid threshold schemes using the Tag-KEM framework [1].

Our first contribution is to provide two transforms (one secure in the ROM and one secure in the QROM) which supports distributed decryption for hybrid encryption schemes. Our transform is closely related to the previous REACT [43] transform, the Tag-KEM framework [1], or the second hybrid-variant of the Fujisaki-Okamoto transform [27]. The key take away from our (general) hybrid construction is that the DEM component can be a generic one-time IND-CPA encryption scheme, and the KEM component can be either a *rigid*[1] deterministic OW-CPA secure public key encryption scheme or (with a minor modification) a *rigid* OW-PCA-secure[2] probabilistic scheme. In the case of public-key encryption schemes which are not perfectly correct, i.e. they exhibit decryption errors, we require an additional hardness assumption.

As our second contribution, to utilize our hybrid construction in the post-quantum setting we build a *rigid* deterministic encryption scheme which has a relatively efficient distributed decryption procedure based on the standard (or module) Learning-with-Rounding (LWR) problem. Our scheme is competitive (in terms of execution time and parameters) with Saber, the Learning-with-Rounding based submission in the third round of the NIST competition. Indeed the module-LWR version of our scheme has almost exactly the same parameters as Saber[3], meaning that any run-times for Saber in hybrid encryption mode will be similar to the run-times for our scheme.

Due to the similarity with Saber we name our constructions of a hybrid encryption scheme, which has an efficient distributed decryption operation, based on Learning-with-Rounding, after the Roman sword Gladius; which came in four basic forms: A large one called Gladius–Hispaniensis, a smaller 'standard' one called Gladius–Pompeii, and two related ones called Gladius–Mainz and

[1] A scheme is defined to be rigid if decryption of a 'ciphertext', which is not the output of an encryption operation, always returns $\perp$.

[2] A scheme is said to be PCA (plain-check attack) secure if it is secure in the presence of an oracle which allows the adversary to check whether a given ciphertext encrypts a given plaintext.

[3] Although there is an issue of having comparable security for these parameters, due to our reliance on LWE in the key generation phase, see Table 1 for more details.

Gladius–Fulham. In addition, we give in the full version a pre-quantum hybrid scheme based on ElGamal encryption and the gap-Diffie–Hellman assumption, along with a methodology to perform a distributed hybrid decryption.

Of the three lattice based finalists in Round 3 of the NIST competition two of them, Crystals-Kyber [47], and Saber [22], all construct a hybrid encryption scheme by first building an IND-CPA encryption scheme, and then creating an IND-CCA hybrid scheme using the Fujisaki-Okamoto transform [26]. The problem with the Fujisaki-Okamoto design pattern is that the decryption procedure needs to perform a hash to obtain the random coins used for encryption. In the threshold setting this is a problem as one needs to hash both the DEM key k and the DEM value itself (or the message) in the Fujisaki-Okamoto transform to perform the re-encryption; and this must be done *before* one reveals k and m to the decrypting parties. The hash function used for re-encryption also needs to produce the random values used in encryption, which can be a complicated process to perform in a threshold manner for the lattice based schemes; especially if this involves sampling discrete Gaussians or other distributions which are not 'native' to whichever underlying methodology one is using to perform the threshold decryption.

The other remaining lattice based finalist in Round 3, NTRU [54], also builds a traditional KEM, with the difference that the KEM does not require re-encryption. However, NTRU builds a traditional KEM, which requires the DEM to be implemented in a threshold manner so as to maintain the CCA security. Thus threshold variants of all the remaining Round 3 lattice based schemes will be problematic if one wishes to maintain CCA security of the threshold variant.

Of the Round-2 lattice-based systems which did not progress to be finalists in Round-3, FrodoKEM [40], Round 5 [28], LAC [38], NewHope [45], and ThreeBears [30], also follow the Fujisaki-Okamoto pattern, bar NTRUprime [10]. NTRUprime differs from the previous ones in that it is based on a *rigid* deterministic base encryption scheme which is then turned into a KEM using [24, Section 6]. However, the underlying rigid deterministic encryption scheme still requires re-encryption to be secure, and as we remarked above this causes problems for thresholdizing the scheme.

1.1 Prior Work and Our Contribution

Threshold Decryption: As stated at the beginning our main goal is to provide an efficient threshold decryption procedure for a post-quantum *hybrid* encryption algorithm. We do this by providing an algorithm which is efficient, within a generic MPC framework, to perform distributed decryption. Thus, on the assumption the algorithm we implement is correct, the security of said algorithm follows from the security of the base MPC framework.

In [8] a *non-hybrid* lattice based encryption scheme is given. But the security of the underlying encryption scheme is only IND-CPA (although an actively secure distributed decryption protocol for the IND-CPA scheme is given). In [13] a generic procedure for obtaining an abitrary threshold variant of any functionality, however the construction makes use of Fully Homomorphic Encryption and is not practical.

In an earlier work [35] on distributing the decryption for a Round-1 NIST candidate which was based on Ring-LWE, namely LIMA, a distributed decryption operation was given for a basic (non-hybrid) encryption scheme. An outline for the hybrid scheme was given, but the instantiation would not preserve the CCA security guarantees of the hybrid construction, i.e. the method presented was *not* secure.

From a performance perspective the problem with the distributed decryption of LIMA was that it is a scheme based on the Fujisaki-Okamoto transform. As mentioned above the secure evaluation of the hash function and re-encryption operation is costly in the distributed setting. But this is not the only problem with [35], the decryption procedure itself is rather complicated in that it requires rounding of integers, for example. In [35] these two technical complexities meant the protocol (to be fast) was only a 3-party protocol with one dishonest party. The distributed decryption of a single non-hybrid LIMA encryption would take 4.2 s, with a similar time for the *insecure* hybrid KEM distributed decapsulation.

Traditionally, in the non-hybrid encryption setting, threshold decryption is preferred using the least amount of interaction, for example see [36,48,49]. Our threshold decryption procedure for our post-quantum hybrid scheme utilizes explicitly generic MPC techniques; thus it definitely does not minimize the level of interaction between the parties needed. An open problem would be to develop a methodology, or scheme, which can utilize the minimal amount of communication possible.

We note that there has been some work on threshold post-quantum signature schemes, e.g. [15,16,23], but the techniques and issues are rather different from those employed and discussed here.

Hybrid Encryption: Hybrid encryption is the standard method to encrypt large message via a public key scheme. The actual message is encrypted via a standard block cipher in a secure AEAD mode, such as AES-GCM. Then the one-time symmetric key for this symmetric encryption scheme is transferred to the recipient using a public key methodology. The traditional method of combining the public key encryption scheme $\Pi_p = (\mathcal{K}_p, \mathcal{E}_p, \mathcal{D}_p)$, with message space $\mathcal{M}_p$, and symmetric key encryption scheme $\Pi_s = (\mathcal{K}_s, \mathcal{E}_s, \mathcal{D}_s)$ into a hybrid scheme $\Pi_h = (\mathcal{K}_h, \mathcal{E}_h, \mathcal{D}_h)$ is called KEM-DEM [18]. Where $\mathcal{K}_\star, \mathcal{E}_\star$ and $\mathcal{D}_\star$ are the various schemes key-generation, encryption and decryption algorithms respectively.

The KEM-DEM method of [18] requires Π_s to be a (one-time) IND-CCA symmetric cipher[4] and an IND-CCA KEM scheme Π_p (a KEM is a public key scheme designed to encrypt only symmetric keys). The scheme Π_p encrypts the key k for Π_s, and then Π_s is used to encrypt the message using the key k. In particular the encryption algorithm, outputting (c_1, c_2) for $\mathcal{E}_h$ is along the lines of

$$k \leftarrow \mathcal{M}_p, \quad \mathsf{k} \leftarrow H(k), \quad c_1 \leftarrow \mathcal{E}_p(\mathsf{pk}, k), \quad c_2 \leftarrow \mathcal{E}_s(\mathsf{k}, m).$$

[4] One time meaning that the attacker does not get access to an encryption oracle.

However, there is a problem with this construction when one looks for a distributed variant of the decryption algorithm. Even if the decryption algorithm of the KEM Π_p has an efficient distributed decryption operation one cannot derive an efficient distributed hybrid cipher as the decryption of the scheme Π_s needs to be executed also in a distributed manner. Executing Π_s in a distributed manner for standard symmetric encryption scheme is possible, but very inefficient for long messages.

One obvious way to get around this problem is for the distributed decryption operation for the hybrid cipher Π_h to output k in the clear after the Π_p part has been executed, enabling the decryption using Π_s to be done in the clear. We call such a hybrid scheme 'leaky', as the decryption algorithm leaks the underlying symmetric key even if the symmetric component does not decrypt correctly. This intuitively seems attractive, however it breaks the IND-CCA security of the hybrid scheme Π_h via a trivial attack.

The most popular generic transform to turn a public key encryption scheme into a hybrid scheme in the KEM-DEM paradigm is the Fujisaki-Okamoto transform [26,27]. This comes in two forms, either (from [26])

$$k \leftarrow \mathcal{M}_p, \quad \mathsf{k} \leftarrow H(k), \quad c_1 \leftarrow \mathcal{E}_p(\mathsf{pk}, k; G(k, m)), \quad c_2 \leftarrow \mathcal{E}_s(\mathsf{k}, m),$$

or (from [27])

$$k \leftarrow \mathcal{M}_p, \quad \mathsf{k} \leftarrow H(k), \quad c_2 \leftarrow \mathcal{E}_s(\mathsf{k}, m), \quad c_1 \leftarrow \mathcal{E}_p(\mathsf{pk}, k; G(k, c_2)),$$

where G is a hash function which produces the random coins needed by the encryption algorithm $\mathcal{E}_p$. The authors of [26,27] show that this hybrid scheme, assuming some (mild) technical conditions on the encryption algorithm, is IND-CCA if Π_p is OW-CPA and Π_s is IND-CPA. Note, for the first variant one needs to decyrpt c_2 before one can verify the c_1 component, as the decryption operation $\mathcal{D}_p$ requires re-encryption to perform the necessary CCA checks. Because of this, the first Fujisaki-Okamoto hybrid construction can never be securely "leaky".

The second Fujisaki-Okamoto variant has been proved secure in the quantum random-oracle model in [53], where the scheme Π_p is assumed to be 'well-spread', perfectly correct and OW-CPA secure. This second Fujisaki-Okamoto variant can be considered as a variant of the Tag-KEM framework of [1]. The Tag-KEM framework gives another hybrid construction, which works (roughly speaking in the simplest instance) in the following manner

$$\mathsf{k} \leftarrow \mathcal{K}_s, \quad c_2 \leftarrow \mathcal{E}_s(\mathsf{k}, m), \quad c_1 \leftarrow \mathcal{E}_p(\mathsf{pk}, \mathsf{k} \| G(c_2))$$

where G is a hash function. This hybrid construction is secure if Π_p is IND-CCA secure and Π_s is one-time IND-CPA secure.

Note in [31] a QROM proof of the non-hybrid encryption version of the Fujisaki-Okamoto transform is given, that this is for the public key scheme given by $c \leftarrow \mathcal{E}_p(\mathsf{pk}, m; G(m))$. However, unlike in [53], the encryption scheme is not assumed to be perfectly correct.

One of the applications of the Tag-KEM framework mentioned in [1] is that of threshold hybrid public key encryption. Their argument is as follows. Since the one-time-pad is one-time IND-CPA secure, outputting m already leaks k. Thus revealing the value k before applying the decryption of c_2 cannot break security, as that would contradict their main theorem. Thus one can apply threshold decryption to obtain the decryption of c_1, leak the key k and then decrypt c_2 in the clear as long as Π_s is the one-time-pad encryption scheme. Unfortunately, the authors of [1] require an IND-CCA secure Π_p.

The authors of [1] provide other constructions requiring weaker properties of Π_p, but each one adds its own complications. Indeed if one thinks of the hash function G, in our construction below, applied to c_1, c_2 and k as a MAC function applied to c_1 and c_2 with key k, then their 'weak KEM+MAC' construction is identical to ours.

In [7] a construction of CCA secure Tag-based encryption which has threshold decryption is discussed. Their generic methodology uses one-time signatures and a concrete instantiation is given based on the decisional bilinear Diffie–Hellman assumption in pairing groups. Another construction of a threshold tag-KEM in the Random Oracle model based on the RSA problem is given in [32].

The solution we propose is to utilize the following modification to the Cramer-Shoup basic construction. Our main construction, which we call Hybrid_1, outputs a ciphertext of the form (c_1, c_2, c_3) where, for a hash function G modelled as a random oracle,

$$k \leftarrow \mathcal{M}_p, \quad \mathsf{k} \leftarrow H(k), \quad c_1 \leftarrow \mathcal{E}_p(\mathsf{pk}, k), \quad c_2 \leftarrow \mathcal{E}_s(\mathsf{k}, m), \quad c_3 \leftarrow G(c_1, c_2, k).$$

The distributed decryption algorithm checks the c_3 component and then 'leaks' the key k in the clear, enabling k to be produced and hence m decrypted from the c_2 component. We show that this scheme is IND-CCA secure, even with this form of leaky decryption, if the scheme Π_p is *rigid*, *deterministic* and OW-CPA, or rigid, randomized and OW-PCA secure, and the scheme Π_s is one-time IND-CPA secure. If the scheme Π_p is not perfectly correct then we require the additional hardness assumption that it is hard for the adversary to construct a message/ciphertext pair (m, c) such that $c = \mathcal{E}_p(\mathsf{pk}, m)$, but $\mathcal{D}_p(\mathsf{sk}, c) = \perp$. We also require in this case that the probability of the encryption scheme having collisions, i.e. two messages which encrypt to the same ciphertext, is negligible when this probability is computed over the space of all possible public/private key pairs.

When Π_p is randomized and OW-PCA, one needs to include c_1 into the hash function G so as to avoid attacks related to re-randomization of the output of $\mathcal{E}_p$. In this latter case, of randomized OW-PCA encryption scheme Π_p, our construction looks most closely related to the REACT transform, from [43], which encrypts via

$$k \leftarrow \mathcal{M}_p, \quad \mathsf{k} \leftarrow H(k), \quad c_1 \leftarrow \mathcal{E}_p(\mathsf{pk}, k), \quad c_2 \leftarrow \mathcal{E}_s(\mathsf{k}, m), \quad c_3 \leftarrow G(k, m, c_1, c_2).$$

The authors of [43] show that REACT is secure assuming Π_p OW-PCA secure and the scheme Π_s is IND-CPA secure. The REACT transform has a similar problem with the standard KEM-DEM construction above in that it requires c_2 to be decrypted before the check is applied, i.e. m is needed as an input to G.

In the case when Π_p is rigid and deterministic one can drop the component c_1 from the input to G. So our hybrid construction simplifies to

$$k \leftarrow \mathcal{M}_p, \quad \mathsf{k} \leftarrow H(k), \quad c_1 \leftarrow \mathcal{E}_p(\mathsf{pk}, k), \quad c_2 \leftarrow \mathcal{E}_s(\mathsf{k}, m), \quad c_3 \leftarrow G(c_2, k).$$

In this case one can think of our construction as precisely the second Fujisaki-Okamoto construction utilizing the OW-CPA, 'well-spread' public key encryption scheme with encryption algorithm given by

$$\mathcal{E}'_p(\mathsf{pk}, k; r) = (\mathcal{E}_p(\mathsf{pk}, k), r).$$

Thus our construction in this case would be automatically secure in the QROM if one considers only normal decryption oracle queries (i.e. ones which do not leak the key k); assuming that the techniques used in [31] for dealing with non-perfectly correct schemes could be extended to the proof in [53].

However, this hybrid construction seems hard to prove QROM secure when one requires threshold decryption, unless one picks the DEM operation to be a one-time pad encryption scheme. To obtain a full QROM secure efficient hybrid construction with distributed decryption we present a second hybrid construction which adds a ciphertext component, by hashing k with a second hash function H' which has domain and codomain equal to $\mathcal{M}_p$, as well as hashing k via another hash function H'', before passing the result into G; namely we compute

$$\begin{gathered} k \leftarrow \mathcal{M}_p, \ \mathsf{k} \leftarrow H(k), \ \mu \leftarrow H'(k), \\ c_1 \leftarrow \mathcal{E}_p(\mathsf{pk}, k), \ c_2 \leftarrow \mathcal{E}_s(\mathsf{k}, m), \ c_3 \leftarrow G(c_2, \mu), \ c_4 \leftarrow H''(k). \end{gathered}$$

This construction, which we call Hybrid_2, is proved secure, in the QROM, using the techniques of [51].

Most of our technical difficulties arise from the fact we want both efficient distributed decryption and an efficient DEM operation. If we take an AES-based DEM then the output of the hash function H will be a bit vector in $\{0,1\}^{|\mathsf{k}|}$. But the input k will be 'native' to the underlying public key scheme, and thus in general an element of a set such as $\mathbb{F}_p^n$, for some modulus p. This means H needs to map from one arithmetic domain to another. It is to avoid needing to do this in a secure way during distributed decryption that we 'leak' the key k and not the key k. This problem does not occur with the hash function G as we are free to select the hash function so that it can be evaluated securely. In our QROM construction using the c_4 component we need to evaluate H' and H'' securely before releasing k, but this can be done as efficiently as evaluating G, by selecting the hash functions H' and H'' in an appropriate way.

Learning-with-Rounding: After detailing our main hybrid constructions we go on to discuss how one can instantiate a suitable KEM in the post-quantum setting. For this we utilize the Learning-With-Rounding (LWR) based deterministic encryption algorithm first presented in [52], and then refined in [4]. This is itself inspired by the trapdoor LWE key generation procedure introduced by Micciancio and Peikert [39]. We present an explicit construction, including suggested parameters sizes, and compare the resulting scheme with current NIST PQ-candidates such as Saber [22]. Our basic construction utilizes the fact that LWR encryption is deterministic in nature.

To prove our main hybrid constructions secure we need to assume, for our most efficient construction, a new hard problem, which we dub the Large-Vector-Problem (LVP) problem. Informally, this problem says that for a given LWE key $(A, A \cdot R_1 + R_2)$ with $A \in \mathbb{Z}_q^{n \times n}$ uniformly randomly chosen and $R_1, R_2 \in \mathbb{Z}_q^{n \times n}$ but with 'small' entries, it is hard to find a small vector $\mathbf{m}$ such that $R_1 \cdot \mathbf{m}$ is 'relatively big'. This is needed to establish our scheme satisfies a property that we call $\perp$-Aware. The $\perp$-Aware property captures the difficulty of an adversary $\mathcal{A}$, given the public key pk, to come up with a plaintext/ciphertext pair (m, c) such that $c = \mathcal{E}(\mathsf{pk}, m)$ but $\mathcal{D}(\mathsf{sk}, c) = \perp$; i.e. a ciphertext which is a valid encryption, but which does not decrypt correctly.

The Gladius Family of Hybrid Ciphers: Combining our LWR-based rigid deterministic OW-PCA encryption scheme with our hybrid constructions we obtain a post-quantum secure hybrid cipher, which supports efficient distributed decryption. We can actually derive many variants depending on the choice of Hybrid_1 or Hybrid_2, the choice of the DEM, and the choice of using plain LWR or Module-LWR. We focus on four specific variants of this construction; Gladius–Hispaniensis (based on Hybrid_1 and plain LWR), Gladius–Pompeii and Gladius–Mainz (based on Hybrid_1 and Module-LWR), and Gladius–Fulham (based on Hybrid_2 and Module-LWR).

Gladius–Hispaniensis, Gladius–Pompeii and Gladius–Fulham all assume *any* one-time IND-CPA secure DEM. For Gladius–Hispaniensis and Gladius–Pompeii we obtain (expected) security in the QROM when the scheme is considered as a standard hybrid encryption scheme, and security in the ROM when we consider the scheme in the threshold setting (due to the additional leakage required). The expected QROM security, which we denote by QROM*, comes from the fact that Zhandry's proof [53], for the second Fujisaki–Okamoto transform, only applies to perfectly correct schemes. We also present a third variant Gladius–Mainz (see the full version) which provides QROM* security in the threshold setting, but this requires the DEM to be a one-time-pad (OTP), and requires a more expensive distributed decryption algorithm. Our fourth variant, Gladius–Fulham, utilizes the second hybrid transform mentioned above, but can achieve full QROM security (including for non-perfectly correct schemes Π_p) even when one allows the leakage from the decryption oracle required in a distributed decryption operation.

In summary the properties of our four schemes are given by the following table, where ✓* in the QROM column refers to the above QROM* caveat. We also note in the table how many secure hash function operations need to be executed by the distributed decryption algorithm.

	Hard Problem	Hybrid	DEM	Standard QROM Secure	Threshold QROM Secure	Threshold ROM Secure	No. Secure Hashes
Gladius–Hispaniensis	LWR	1	Generic	✓*	✗	✓	1
Gladius–Pompeii	Module-LWR	1	Generic	✓*	✗	✓	1
Gladius–Mainz	Module-LWR	1	OTP	✓*	✓*	✓	1
Gladius–Fulham	Module-LWR	2	Generic	✓	✓	✓	3

Open Questions: Our work leads to a number of new interesting areas of research. On a theoretical level we leave open the problem of establishing $\perp$ $-\mathsf{Aware}$ security for our Gladius construction when q is a power of two (since we focus on q prime for threshold reasons) and also on a theoretical level to prove our conjecture related to the hardness of the LVP problem. On a practical level one could examine other ways of using our Hybrid construction to build efficient threshold post-quantum encryption schemes, or remove the need to use generic MPC; which comes about mainly due to the need to execute a hash function for key derivation and to perform the necessary rounding operations.

2 Preliminaries

Learning-with-Errors and Learning-with-Rounding: We let σ denote a standard deviation, and we let $\mathcal{D}_\sigma$ denote a distribution which 'looks like' a discrete Gaussian distribution with standard deviation σ. In practice this can be generated by the NewHope methodology [3], namely if we have $\sigma = \sqrt{(B+1)/2}$ then we sample from $\mathcal{D}_\sigma$ by generating $2 \cdot B + 2$ random bits (b_i, b'_i) for $i = 0, \ldots, B$, and then generating a sample by computing $\sum_{i=0}^{B}(b_i - b'_i)$.

Given a secret vector $\mathbf{s} \in \mathbb{Z}_q^d$ (for some integer q), then a Learning-with-Errors (LWE) sample is a pair $(A, A \cdot \mathbf{s} + \mathbf{e})$ where $A \in \mathbb{Z}_q^{m \times d}$ is chosen uniformly at random and $\mathbf{e} \leftarrow \mathcal{D}_\sigma$. The decision LWE problem is to distinguish LWE samples from uniformly random samples $(A, \mathbf{u})$, for $\mathbf{u} \leftarrow \mathbb{Z}_q^m$, we denote this problem by $\mathsf{LWE}_{q,(m,d),\sigma}$. The search LWE problem is to recover the secret vector $\mathbf{s}$ from a set of LWE samples. For suitable choices of the parameters both these problems are known to be equivalent and assumed to be hard. Suitable parameters to ensure hardness given known attack algorithms can be found using Albrecht's *LWE-estimator* tool[5].

For integers p and q we define the following map

$$\lfloor x \rceil_p : \begin{cases} \mathbb{Q} \longrightarrow & \mathbb{Z}_p \\ x \longmapsto & \lceil x \cdot p/q \rfloor \pmod p \end{cases}$$

where $\lfloor \cdot \rceil$ is the round to nearest integer function, with rounding towards zero in the case of values of the form $i/2$ for i an odd integer. If the input value $x \in (-q/2, \ldots, q/2] \subset \mathbb{Z}$ then the final reduction modulo p is only required

[5] https://bitbucket.org/malb/lwe-estimator/src/master/.

(if p does not divide q) when the rounding ends up being outside the interval $(-p/2, \ldots, p/2]$, which happens with probability about $1/p$, resulting in needing a single addition of p to accomplish the reduction modulo p.

Given a secret vector $\mathbf{s} \in \mathbb{Z}_q^d$, then a Learning-with-Rounding (LWR) sample is a pair $(A, \lfloor A \cdot \mathbf{s} \rceil_p)$ where $A \in \mathbb{Z}_q^{m \times d}$ is chosen uniformly at random. The decision LWR problem is to distinguish LWR samples from uniformly random samples $(A, \lfloor \mathbf{u} \rceil_p)$, for $\mathbf{u} \leftarrow \mathbb{Z}_q^d$, we denote this problem by $\mathsf{LWR}_{q,p,(m,d)}$. The search problem is similarly defined as the problem of recovering $\mathbf{s}$ from a number of LWR samples.

Relation Between (Module-) LWE and (Module-) LWR: In the full version we extend these notions to the case of Learning-with-Rounding over modules.

The search (Module-) LWE and (Module-) LWR problems are linked theoretically by the following theorem [12, Theorem 1 and 2][6].

Theorem 2.1. *Let p, q, n, d, m and B be integers such that $q > 2 \cdot p \cdot B$. For every algorithm* Learn *there is an algorithm* Learn' *such that*

$$\Pr_{A,\mathbf{s},\mathbf{e}}[\mathsf{Learn}'(A, A \cdot \mathbf{s} + \mathbf{e}) = \mathbf{s}] \geq \Pr_{A,\mathbf{s},\mathbf{e}}[\mathsf{Learn}(A, \lfloor A \cdot \mathbf{s} + \mathbf{e} \rceil_p) = \mathbf{s}]$$
$$\geq \frac{\Pr_{A,\mathbf{s}}[\mathsf{Learn}(A, \lfloor A \cdot \mathbf{s} \rceil_p) = \mathbf{s}]^2}{(1 + 2 \cdot p \cdot B/q)^{n \cdot m \cdot d}}$$

where $A \leftarrow \mathcal{R}_q^{m \times d}$, the noise $\mathbf{e}$ is independent over all m coordinates, B-bounded and balanced in each coordinate, and $\mathbf{s} = (s_i) \in \mathcal{R}_q^d$ is chosen from any distribution such that $s_i \in \mathcal{R}_q^*$ for some i.

Note, the first inequality is not from [12] but it is immediate. To apply this result, we would take $B = \mathfrak{c} \cdot \sigma$, for some suitable constant $\mathfrak{c}$.

The fact that the square of the LWR advantage is bounded by the LWE advantage implies that one will need larger parameters to bound the LWR advantage by a given value, than to bound the LWE advantage by the same value. Thus using this theoretical reduction will result in very large parameters indeed. To avoid the problem with the above reduction submissions to the NIST Post-Quantum cryptography competition based on LWR, such as Saber [21,22], estimate their parameters by using the best attack scenario. In other words the security is estimated using Albrecht's LWE-estimator directly, or by assuming the above theorem is an exact inequality between the various one-way advantages.

This approach is examined in detail in [2], where to utilize Albrecht's tool the authors need to translate the LWR parameters into LWE parameters. In [2] this is done by setting the LWE standard deviation to be

$$\sigma = \sqrt{\frac{(q/p)^2 - 1}{12}}.$$

[6] The result in [12] is only given for normal and Ring LWE/LWR, but extending the result to the module variants is immediate.

Asymmetric and Symmetric Encryption: An asymmetric encryption scheme is a triple of algorithms $\Pi = (\mathcal{K}, \mathcal{E}, \mathcal{D})$, all of which are probabilistic polynomial time (PPT) algorithms. We let $\mathcal{M}$ denote the plaintext space of Π, $\mathcal{C}$ the ciphertext space and $\mathcal{R}$ the space of random coins of Π. The key generation algorithm $\mathcal{K}$ takes as input 1^t, where t is a security parameter and outputs a public/private key pair $(\mathsf{pk}, \mathsf{sk})$. A symmetric encryption scheme is one in which $\mathsf{pk} = \mathsf{sk}$. The standard security definitions are given in the full version.

The algorithm $\mathcal{E}(\mathsf{pk}, m; r)$ takes a message $m \leftarrow \mathcal{M}$, a public key pk and random coins $r \leftarrow \mathcal{R}$ and returns a ciphertext c. The decryption algorithm $\mathcal{D}(\mathsf{sk}, c)$ recovers the message m or returns the special symbol $\perp$. For correctness we require

$$\Pr\Big[\ \mathcal{D}(\mathsf{sk}, c) = m \ :\ (\mathsf{pk}, \mathsf{sk}) \leftarrow \mathcal{K}(1^t),\ m \leftarrow \mathcal{M},\ r \leftarrow \mathcal{R},\ c \leftarrow \mathcal{E}(\mathsf{pk}, m; r)\ \Big] \\ = 1 - \delta,$$

where δ is an exponentially small probability of decryption failure. If $\delta = 0$ we say the scheme is perfectly correct. A public key scheme will be called *deterministic* if $\mathcal{R}$ contains only the empty string (or equivalently one element), otherwise it will be called *randomized.*

A scheme which is not perfectly correct can exhibit two forms of decryption failures; either two messages could map under encryption to the same ciphertext or a valid ciphertext could decrypt to $\perp$. For the first case we say an encryption scheme is δ_c-Collision Free if

$$\Pr_{(\mathsf{sk},\mathsf{pk}) \leftarrow \mathcal{K}(1^t)}\Big[\ \exists\ m_1, m_2 \in \mathcal{M},\ \ \exists\ r_1, r_2 \in \mathcal{R}\ \ : \\ m_1 \neq m_2,\ \ \mathcal{E}(\mathsf{pk}, m_1; r_1) = \mathcal{E}(\mathsf{pk}, m_2; r_2)\ \Big] = \delta_c.$$

A perfectly correct encryption scheme is 0-Collision Free.

For the second case of decryption failure we consider the following game, which we call $\perp$-Aware. The adversary $\mathcal{A}$ is given the public key pk and is required to come up with a plaintext/ciphertext pair (m, c) such that $c = \mathcal{E}(\mathsf{pk}, m)$ but $\mathcal{D}(\mathsf{sk}, c) = \perp$. We define

$$\mathsf{Adv}_{\Pi,\mathcal{A}}^{\perp-\mathsf{Aware}}(t) = \Pr\Big[\ \ (\mathsf{pk}, \mathsf{sk}) \leftarrow \mathcal{K}(1^t),\ (m, c) \leftarrow \mathcal{A}(\mathsf{pk})\ \ : \\ c = \mathcal{E}(\mathsf{pk}, m),\ \ \mathcal{D}(\mathsf{sk}, c) = \perp\ \ \Big]$$

and say that Π is $\perp$-Aware if $\mathsf{Adv}_{\Pi,\mathcal{A}}^{\perp-\mathsf{Aware}}(t)$ is a negligible function of t for all PPT $\mathcal{A}$. Note, if Π is perfectly correct then $\mathsf{Adv}_{\Pi,\mathcal{A}}^{\perp-\mathsf{Aware}}(t) = 0$.

An asymmetric encryption scheme is said to be *rigid*, see [11] (where the definition is given just for deterministic schemes, but the generalization to probabilistic schemes is immediate) if

$$\Pr\Big[\ (\mathsf{pk}, \mathsf{sk}) \leftarrow \mathcal{K}(1^t),\ c \leftarrow \mathcal{C} \setminus \mathcal{C}^{\perp},\ \exists r \in \mathcal{R},\ \ :\ \mathcal{E}(\mathsf{pk}, \mathcal{D}(\mathsf{sk}, c); r) = c\ \Big] = 1,$$

where $\mathcal{C}^{\perp} \subset \mathcal{C}$ is the set of all ciphertexts $c \in C$ for which $\mathcal{D}(\mathsf{sk}, c) = \perp$. The effect of rigidity is that unless c is the output of $\mathcal{E}(\mathsf{pk}, m; r)$ for some m and r, then decryption will always return $\perp$. ElGamal is an example of a perfectly correct, rigid probabilistic scheme as every ciphertext pair $(c_1 = g^r, c_2 = m \cdot h^r)$ corresponds to the encryption of some message.

If we let $\|X\|$ be the infinity norm on the probability space X of a finite set S, then the min-entropy of X is $-\log \|X\|$. A randomized asymmetric encryption scheme is said to be γ-spread if

$$-\log \max_{y \in \{0,1\}^*} \Pr\left[r \leftarrow \mathcal{R} : y = \mathcal{E}(\mathsf{pk}, m; r)\right] \geq \gamma$$

for all $(\mathsf{pk}, \mathsf{sk})$ output by $\mathcal{K}$ and all $m \in \mathcal{M}$. A scheme is said to be *well-spread* if $\gamma = \omega(\log t)$. This basically means that the probability of a specific ciphertext occurring is negligibly small.

Note, if the set $\mathcal{R}$ is suitably large then we can turn a deterministic scheme Π_p into a randomized well-spread scheme Π_p' by setting $\mathcal{E}_p'(\mathsf{pk}, k; r) = (\mathcal{E}_p(\mathsf{pk}, k), r)$. It is from this observation, the QROM* security in the standard hybrid (non-leaky) encryption model for our construction based on deterministic public key encryption, mentioned in the introduction, follows.

Encryption With Distributed Decryption: Given a set $\mathcal{P} = \{\mathcal{P}_1, \ldots, \mathcal{P}_n\}$ of parties, we consider access structures A consisting of a monotonically increasing set of subsets of $2^{\mathcal{P}}$. A set S is said to be qualified if $S \in A$, and unqualified otherwise. Given an encryption scheme $\Pi = (\mathcal{K}, \mathcal{E}, \mathcal{D})$ we say that the scheme admits a distributed decryption functionality for an access structure A, if there are two n-party protocols $\Pi_{\mathcal{K}}$ and $\Pi_{\mathcal{D}}$. The protocol $\Pi_{\mathcal{K}}$ produces some data sk_i for each party, called the secret key shares. The protocol $\Pi_{\mathcal{D}}$ on input of an agreed ciphertext c from all parties in $S \in A$, and the value sk_i from all parties in S, will output the value $m = \mathcal{D}(\mathsf{sk}, c)$.

The distributed decryption protocols are said to be secure (in the IND-ATK sense) if an unqualified set of adversarial parties cannot, while interacting with a qualified set of parties, break the IND-ATK security of the underlying encryption scheme. This security definition can be made more formal by saying that the distributed decryption protocol should act like an ideal decryption functionality. See [48,49] for a specific instantiation.

We shall assume an actively secure MPC protocol for the access structure A, and will then construct an algorithm which implements the algorithm $\mathcal{D}$ within the MPC protocol. Thus it automatically becomes a distributed protocol $\Pi_{\mathcal{D}}$ for the decryption functionality, and its security is inherited from the underlying MPC protocol. The challenging part is to develop the encryption scheme and the specific instantiation of $\mathcal{D}$ to enable the underlying MPC system to provide an efficient distributed implementation.

By using a generic MPC functionality, as opposed to a specific protocol, we restrict ourselves to the threshold case where *all* parties have to be involved in the computation; but where security is maintained against an adversary controlling a given threshold. This is in contrast to the models proposed in [48,49] which allow for a subset of the key-share holding parties to participate.

KEM-DEM Philosophy: A central tenet when using public key encryption in practice, is that one never encrypts a large message with a public key algorithm. Instead one encrypts the actual message with a fast symmetric key algorithm, such as AES-GCM, and then the symmetric key is transferred to the recipient using a public key scheme. Thus producing a *hybrid* encryption scheme. In this way the symmetric key is only used once in the symmetric cipher, and thus we do not need a fully secure AEAD scheme but the weaker notion of a DEM, and the public key scheme is only needed to transport a single random key (and not a message) leading to the simpler public key construction of a KEM. See [18] for an extensive discussion, with the standard definitions and proofs.

$\mathcal{K}_h(1^t)$:	$\mathcal{E}_h(\mathsf{pk}, m)$:	$\mathcal{D}_h(\mathsf{sk}, (c_1, c_2))$:
$(\mathsf{pk}, \mathsf{sk}) \leftarrow \mathcal{K}_p(1^t)$	$k \leftarrow \mathcal{M}_p$	$k \leftarrow \mathcal{D}_p(\mathsf{sk}, c_1)$
Return $(\mathsf{pk}, \mathsf{sk})$	$r \leftarrow \mathcal{R}_p, r' \leftarrow \mathcal{R}_s$	If $k = \perp$ then return $\perp$
	$\mathsf{k} \leftarrow H(k)$.	$\mathsf{k} \leftarrow H(k)$.
	$c_1 \leftarrow \mathcal{E}_p(\mathsf{pk}, k; r)$	$m \leftarrow \mathcal{D}_s(\mathsf{k}, c_2)$
	$c_2 \leftarrow \mathcal{E}_s(\mathsf{k}, m; r')$	Return m
	Return (c_1, c_2)	

Fig. 1. The standard KEM-DEM construction

We let $\Pi_p = (\mathcal{K}_p, \mathcal{E}_p, \mathcal{D}_p)$ denote an IND-CCA public key encryption scheme with message space $\mathcal{M}_p$, ciphertext space $\mathcal{C}_p$, and space of random coins $\mathcal{R}_p$, and let $\Pi_s = (\mathcal{K}_s, \mathcal{E}_s, \mathcal{D}_s)$ denote an IND-CCA symmetric key encryption scheme (which recall for us is always one-time and hence a DEM) with message space $\mathcal{M}_s = \{0,1\}^*$. From these two components one can construct a KEM-DEM encryption scheme for arbitrary long messages as follows: We first define a hash function $H : \mathcal{M}_p \longrightarrow \mathcal{K}_s$ where by abuse of notation by $\mathcal{K}_s$ we mean the key space of Π_s. We can then define a hybrid encryption scheme $\Pi_h = (\mathcal{K}_h, \mathcal{E}_h, \mathcal{D}_h)$ in Fig. 1.

Naive Threshold KEM-DEM: The goal of our work is to produce threshold public key encryption for long messages; namely we would want to share the decryption key amongst a set of entities so that a given subset needs to come together to decrypt. Clearly we would not want the extra expense of the threshold decryption to impact when encrypting very large messages. Thus we would want to use something akin to the KEM-DEM philosophy, with the main message being encrypted and decrypted via a fast cipher such as AES-GCM.

Finding KEM-like constructions which admit distributed decryption protocols is relatively easy. However, whilst it is possible to execute AES in a threshold manner, see e.g. [33,44], the performance for long messages is prohibitive. Thus distributed DEMs are much harder to obtain. For this reason we would like to apply the decryption of the large message 'in the clear', but this implies that the decryption algorithm will need to 'leak' the decryption key k of the DEM component. In particular this key will leak irrespective of whether the DEM decrypts correctly or not; since the decrypting parties need to obtain the DEM key before it is known whether the key is valid for the DEM.

$\mathcal{D}_h(\mathsf{sk}, (c_1, c_2))$:
  $k \leftarrow \mathcal{D}_p(\mathsf{sk}, c_1)$
  If $k = \perp$ then return $(\perp, \perp)$
  $\mathsf{k} \leftarrow H(k)$.
  $m \leftarrow \mathcal{D}_s(\mathsf{k}, c_2)$
  Return (k, m)

Fig. 2. Decryption functionality for standard distributed KEM-DEM

Our decryption algorithm functionality, and thus the functionality of any decryption oracle given to an adversary, would therefore be of the form in Fig. 2. This provides an immediate attack in the standard IND-CCA model on the hybrid construction. An adversary takes the target ciphertext (c_1^*, c_2^*), submits (c_1^*, c_2) to the decryption oracle for a random value c_2. With high probability, they will receive $(k, \perp)$. Then, they can use k to obtain k and thus decrypt c_2^*, and so win the security game. It is to avoid this attack that we modify the KEM-DEM framework in the next section.

Generic Multi-Party Computation: Our methodology uses a *generic* actively-secure-with-abort MPC functionality defined via Linear Secret Sharing (LSS) over a finite field $\mathbb{F}_q$. Note, we could utilize in the case when q is not a prime in our main Gladius construction a ring $\mathbb{Z}_q$, but for the purposes of this paper we restrict to q being a prime in our used MPC methodology; see the full version. for a discussion of the issues when q is a power of two. This means that inputs of the parties remain private throughout the execution of the protocol, and when a set of adversaries deviate from the protocol, honest parties will catch this with overwhelming probability and then abort the protocol. This should be compared to passively secure protocols which offer a much weaker guarantee that security is only preserved if all parties follow the precise protocol steps correctly. We present in Fig. 3 the base MPC functionality. Despite using a generic underlying protocol, our protocol ends up being surprisingly efficient. This is because we carefully designed Gladius to be both efficient in a distributed and a non-distributed manner.

To ease notation we denote a variable $x \in \mathbb{F}_q$ stored within the MPC functionality via $\langle x \rangle$, and write addition and multiplication of shares as $\langle x \rangle + \langle y \rangle$ and $\langle x \rangle \cdot \langle y \rangle$. We extend the notation to vectors and matrices in the obvious way via $\langle \mathbf{x} \rangle$ and $\langle A \rangle$. If $\langle \mathbf{x} \rangle$ is a shared vector we let $\langle x_i \rangle$ denote the shared entries, and if $\langle A \rangle$ is a shared matrix we let $\langle A^{(i,j)} \rangle$ denote the shared entries; with a similar notation for vectors and matrices of non-shared values.

Operations for Secure Computation, $\mathcal{F}_{\mathsf{MPC}}$.

The functionality runs with $\mathcal{P} = \{\mathsf{P}^1, \ldots, \mathsf{P}^n\}$ and an ideal adversary $\mathcal{A}$, that statically corrupts a set A of parties. Given a set I of valid identifiers, all values are stored in the form $(varid, x)$, where $varid \in I$.

Initialize: On input $(init, p)$ from all parties, the functionality stores $(domain, p)$,

Input: On input $(input, \mathsf{P}^i, varid, x)$ from P^i and $(input, \mathsf{P}^i, varid, ?)$ from all other parties, with $varid$ a fresh identifier, the functionality stores $(varid, x)$.

Add: On command $(add, varid_1, varid_2, varid_3)$ from all parties (if $varid_1, varid_2$ are present in memory and $varid_3$ is not), the functionality retrieves $(varid_1, x)$, $(varid_2, y)$ and stores $(varid_3, x + y)$.

Multiply: On input $(multiply, varid_1, varid_2, varid_3)$ from all parties (if $varid_1, varid_2$ are present in memory and $varid_3$ is not), the functionality retrieves $(varid_1, x)$, $(varid_2, y)$ and stores $(varid_3, x \cdot y)$.

Output: On input $(output, varid, i)$ from all honest parties (if $varid$ is present in memory), the functionality retrieves $(varid, y)$ and outputs it to the environment. The functionality waits for an input from the environment. If this input is Deliver then y is output to all players if $i = 0$, or y is output to player i if $i \neq 0$. If the adversarial input is not equal to Deliver then all players abort.

Fig. 3. Operations for secure computation, $\mathcal{F}_{\mathsf{MPC}}$.

The cost model for LSS-based MPC protocols is such that addition of such shared entities is 'for free', whereas multiplication consumes resources (typically communication). Many MPC protocols in this setting, such as [9,20,34,50], work in an offline/online manner. In this setting the multiplication not only consumes communication resources in the online phase, but also consumes some correlated randomness (so-called Beaver triples) from the offline phase. However, an advantage of these offline/online models is that one can prepare other forms of correlated randomness in the offline phase; such as shares of random bits $\langle b \rangle$ with an unknown $b \in \{0, 1\}$. In our algorithms below we will write this as $\langle b \rangle \leftarrow \mathsf{Bits}()$. If we sample a shared random element in $\mathbb{F}_q$, we will denote this by $\langle x \rangle \leftarrow \mathbb{F}_q$. To open an element we will write $x \leftarrow \mathbf{Output}(\langle x \rangle)$ when it is output to all players.

MPC Friendly Hash Functions. Rescue: Our LWR-based construction of a hybrid cipher with efficient distributed decryption will make use of an MPC-friendly hash function, such as those in [5,29]. These hash function constructions are sponge-based, and there are two types; those suitable for MPC over characteristic two fields (StarkAD and Vision) and those suitable for MPC over large prime fields (Poseidon and Rescue). In this paper, we concentrate on the Rescue design from [5], which seems more suited to our application.

Rescue has a state of $t = r + c$ finite field elements in $\mathbb{F}_q$, for a prime q. The initial state of the sponge is defined to be the vector of t zero elements. A message is first mapped into $n = d \cdot r$ elements in $\mathbb{F}_q$, $m_0, m_1, \ldots, m_{n-1}$. The elements are absorbed into the sponge in d absorption phases, where r elements are absorbed in each phase. At each phase a permutation $f : \mathbb{F}_q^t \longrightarrow \mathbb{F}_q^t$ is applied resulting in a state $s_0, \ldots, s_{t-1}$. At the end the absorption the r values $s_c, \ldots, s_{t-1}$ are output from the state. This process can then be repeated, with more data absorbed and then squeezed out. Thus we are defining a map $H : \mathbb{F}_q^n \longrightarrow \mathbb{F}_q^r$.

Each primitive call f in the Rescue sponge is performed by executing a round function rnds times. The round function is parametrized by a (small prime) value α, an MDS matrix $M \in \mathbb{F}_q^{t \times t}$ and two step constants $\mathbf{k}_i, \mathbf{k}'_i \in \mathbb{F}_q^t$. The value α is chosen to be the smallest prime such that $\gcd(q-1, \alpha) = 1$. The round function applies exponentiation by $1/\alpha$, followed by application of the MDS matrix, followed by addition of the round constant $\mathbf{k}_i$, followed by exponentiation by α, followed by a further application of the MDS matrix, followed by addition of the round constant $\mathbf{k}'_i$. See [14] for a discussion of implementing Rescue in an MPC system, albeit for a large prime characteristic q of more than 256-bits. In our application q will be in the region of 21-bits.

3 Generic Hybrid Constructions

We let $\Pi_p = (\mathcal{K}_p, \mathcal{E}_p, \mathcal{D}_p)$ denote a OW-CPA secure, rigid, deterministic (resp. a OW-PCA secure, rigid and randomized) public key encryption scheme with message space $\mathcal{M}_p$ and ciphertext space $\mathcal{C}_p$ which is OW-CPA secure. We let $\Pi_s = (\mathcal{K}_s, \mathcal{E}_s, \mathcal{D}_s)$ denote a (one-time) IND-CPA symmetric key encryption scheme with message space $\mathcal{M}_s = \{0,1\}^*$ and ciphertext space $\mathcal{C}_s \subset \{0,1\}^*$. Again by abuse of notation we let $\mathcal{K}_s$ also denote the key space of Π_s.

3.1 Hybrid$_1$ Construction

For this construction we define two hash functions

$$H : \mathcal{M}_p \longrightarrow \mathcal{K}_s,$$

$$G : \begin{cases} \{0,1\}^* \times \mathcal{M}_p \longrightarrow \{0,1\}^{|G|} & \text{If } \Pi_p \text{ is deterministic} \\ \mathcal{C}_p \times \{0,1\}^* \times \mathcal{M}_p \longrightarrow \{0,1\}^{|G|} & \text{If } \Pi_p \text{ is randomized} \end{cases}$$

Note, G is defined to take elements in $\mathcal{M}_p$ as the last entry for efficiency reasons (see below). We can then define our first hybrid encryption scheme $\Pi_h = (\mathcal{K}_h, \mathcal{E}_h, \mathcal{D}_h)$ in Fig. 4. Notice how the decryption function 'leaks' the key k which is encrypted by the deterministic function even when the decryption function $\mathcal{D}_s$ fails. This will allow us, in our threshold decryption operation, to also leak this key before the algorithm $\mathcal{D}_s$ is called, enabling $\mathcal{D}_s$ to be applied in the clear. The only question though is whether leaking this key is secure. The attack described from the last section does not apply, as the invalid ciphertext is already rejected by the testing for the correct value of G, which does not leak k if the test fails. In what follows we call this check the G-check.

$\mathcal{K}_h(1^t)$:
  $(\mathsf{pk}, \mathsf{sk}) \leftarrow \mathcal{K}_p(1^t)$
  Return $(\mathsf{pk}, \mathsf{sk})$

$\mathcal{E}_h(\mathsf{pk}, m)$:
  $k \leftarrow \mathcal{M}_p$
  $\mathsf{k} \leftarrow H(k)$
  $r \leftarrow \mathcal{R}_s$
  $c_1 \leftarrow \mathcal{E}_p(\mathsf{pk}, k)$
  $c_2 \leftarrow \mathcal{E}_s(\mathsf{k}, m; r)$
  $c_3 \leftarrow G(c_2, k)$
    (resp. $c_3 \leftarrow G(c_1, c_2, k)$)
  Return (c_1, c_2, c_3)

$\mathcal{D}_h(\mathsf{sk}, (c_1, c_2, c_3))$:
  $k \leftarrow \mathcal{D}_p(\mathsf{sk}, c_1)$
  If $k = \perp$ then return $(\perp, \perp)$.
  $t \leftarrow G(c_2, k)$
    (resp. $t \leftarrow G(c_1, c_2, k)$)
  If $t \neq c_3$ then return $(\perp, \perp)$.
  $\mathsf{k} \leftarrow H(k)$.
  $m \leftarrow \mathcal{D}_s(\mathsf{k}, c_2)$
  Return (k, m).

Fig. 4. Hybrid_1 construction

As remarked in the introduction the variant of the hybrid construction which utilizes a deterministic Π_p can be seen as a special form of the second Fujisaki-Okamoto hybrid construction; assuming the space $\mathcal{M}_p$ is exponentially large to ensure the resulting 'randomized' public key scheme is well-spread. Thus, the above hybrid construction is secure not only in the ROM, but also in the QROM, when we do not leak the secret key k during the decryption process and when Π_p is perfectly correct.

In the standard random oracle model, the following theorem (proved in the full version) shows that first hybrid construction is secure in a model in which the key k does leak during decryption as above, and where we combine it with a generic one-time IND-CPA DEM.

Theorem 3.1. *If H and G are modelled as random oracles then if $\mathcal{A}$ is an IND-CCA adversary against Π_h then there is an OW-CPA adversary (resp. OW-PCA) adversary $\mathcal{B}$ against the deterministic (resp. randomized) rigid public key scheme Π_p, which is δ_c-Collision Free, a (one-time) IND-CPA adversary $\mathcal{C}$ against Π_s, and a $\perp$-*Aware *adversary $\mathcal{D}$ against Π_p such that*

$$\mathsf{Adv}_{\Pi_h,\mathcal{A}}^{\mathsf{ind-cca}}(t) \leq \mathsf{Adv}_{\Pi_p,\mathcal{B}}^{\mathsf{ow-cpa}}(t) + \mathsf{Adv}_{\Pi_s,\mathcal{C}}^{\mathsf{ind-cpa}}(t) + q_d \cdot \mathsf{Adv}_{\Pi_p,\mathcal{D}}^{\perp-\mathsf{Aware}}(t) + \frac{1}{|\mathcal{M}_p|} + \frac{2 \cdot q_d + q_G^2}{2^{|G|}} + \delta_c$$

where q_d (resp. q_G) is an upper bound on the number of decryption oracle (resp. G-oracle) queries and the decryption oracle queries made to the hybrid scheme leak the key k as above.

3.2 Hybrid_2 Construction

Our second hybrid construction focuses solely on the case of Π_p being a rigid deterministic OW-CPA public key encryption scheme, we show that the generic hybrid transform, given in Fig. 5, which uses the four hash functions,

$$H : \mathcal{M}_p \longrightarrow \mathcal{K}_s,$$

$$H', H'' : \mathcal{M}_p \longrightarrow \mathcal{M}_p$$
$$G : \{0,1\}^* \times \mathcal{M}_p \longrightarrow \{0,1\}^{|G|}$$

is secure in the QROM. Namely we have the following theorem (proved in the full version)

Theorem 3.2. *If G, H, H' and H'' are modelled as quantum random oracles then if $\mathcal{A}$ is an IND-CCA adversary against Π_h then there is a (one-time) IND-CPA adversary $\mathcal{B}$ against Π_s, a $\perp$-Aware adversary $\mathcal{C}$ against the deterministic rigid public key scheme Π_p – which is δ_c-Collision Free and δ being the probability of its decryption failure for a uniformly random message – and OW-CPA adversaries $\mathcal{D}$ and $\mathcal{E}$ against Π_p such that*

$$\mathsf{Adv}^{\mathsf{ind-cca}}_{\Pi_h,\mathcal{A}}(t) \leq \mathsf{Adv}^{\mathsf{ind-cpa}}_{\Pi_s,\mathcal{B}}(t) + \delta$$
$$+ 4q_1\sqrt{\frac{q_3}{\sqrt{|\mathcal{M}_p|}} + \frac{q_d}{2^{|G|}} + \delta' + \mathsf{Adv}^{\mathsf{ow-cpa}}_{\Pi_p,\mathcal{D}}(t) + 2q_2\sqrt{\delta' + \mathsf{Adv}^{\mathsf{ow-cpa}}_{\Pi_p,\mathcal{E}}(t)}}$$

for $q_1 = q_H + q_{H'} + 2q_d$, $q_2 = q_{H''} + q_d$, $q_3 = 2(q_G + q_d + 1)$ and

$$\delta' = \delta_c + q_d \cdot \mathsf{Adv}^{\perp-\mathsf{Aware}}_{\Pi_p,\mathcal{C}}(t) + \frac{1}{|\mathcal{M}_p|},$$

where q_d, q_G, q_H, $q_{H'}$ and $q_{H''}$ are respective upper bounds on the number of decryption oracle, G-oracle, H-oracle, H'-oracle and H''-oracle queries and the decryption oracle queries made to the hybrid scheme leak the key k as above.

$\mathcal{K}_h(1^t)$:	$\mathcal{E}_h(\mathsf{pk}, m)$:	$\mathcal{D}_h(\mathsf{sk}, (c_1, c_2, c_3, c_4))$:
$(\mathsf{pk}, \mathsf{sk}) \leftarrow \mathcal{K}_p(1^t)$ Return $(\mathsf{pk}, \mathsf{sk})$	$k \leftarrow \mathcal{M}_p$ $\mathsf{k} \leftarrow H(k)$ $\mu \leftarrow H'(k)$ $r \leftarrow \mathcal{R}_s$ $c_1 \leftarrow \mathcal{E}_p(\mathsf{pk}, k)$ $c_2 \leftarrow \mathcal{E}_s(\mathsf{k}, m; r)$ $c_3 \leftarrow G(c_2, \mu)$ $c_4 \leftarrow H''(k)$ Return (c_1, c_2, c_3, c_4)	$k \leftarrow \mathcal{D}_p(\mathsf{sk}, c_1)$ If $k = \perp$ then return $(\perp, \perp)$. $t \leftarrow H''(k)$ If $t \neq c_4$ then return $(\perp, \perp)$. $\mu \leftarrow H'(k)$ $t' \leftarrow G(c_2, \mu)$ If $t' \neq c_3$ then return $(\perp, \perp)$. $\mathsf{k} \leftarrow H(k)$. $m \leftarrow \mathcal{D}_s(\mathsf{k}, c_2)$ Return (k, m).

Fig. 5. Hybrid_2 construction

3.3 Threshold Variant

Assuming there are protocols $\Pi_{\mathcal{K}_p}$ and $\Pi_{\mathcal{D}_p}$ which implement the base public key encryption scheme in a threshold manner a threshold variant of our above constructions are therefore immediate. We simply apply the threshold decryption operation to c_1^*, keeping the result in a shared form. The parties then securely evaluate G (or G, H' and H'' in our second hybrid construction). Our distributed decryption operation for our Hybrid_1 construction Π_h would then consist of the following steps, with a similar methodology for Hybrid_2 (which would also require a secure evaluation of H' and H'')

1. Absorb c_2 (resp. c_1 and c_2) into G in the clear.
2. Apply $\Pi_{\mathcal{D}_p}$ to obtain a distributed decryption operation, keeping the result k in shared form.
3. Securely absorb these shares of k into the sponge G.
4. Securely evaluate the squeezing of G to obtain t in the clear.
5. Reject the ciphertext if $c_3 \neq t$.
6. Open k to all players.
7. Compute $\mathsf{k} = H(k)$ in the clear
8. Compute $m = \mathcal{D}_s(\mathsf{k}, c_2)$ in the clear and output it.

We notice that if we use a sponge-like function for G, such as Rescue [5] (see the full version) or SHA-3, then in the clear we can insert the first arguments for G (c_1 and c_2) during a distributed decryption, as they are public. Thus we only need to execute a secure distributed version of G for the final absorption of k, and then the squeezing phase to obtain c_3.

4 The Large Vector Problem (LVP)

We also need to give a new hardness assumption, which we call LVP. This is needed in order to establish the $\perp$-Aware property of our encryption scheme; namely that it is hard for an adversary $\mathcal{A}$, given the public key pk, to come up with a plaintext/ciphertext pair (m, c) such that $c = \mathcal{E}(\mathsf{pk}, m)$ but $\mathcal{D}(\mathsf{sk}, c) = \perp$; i.e. a ciphertext which is a valid encryption, but which does not decrypt correctly.

Consider the following experiment. The challenger constructs a matrix $A_1 \in \mathbb{Z}_q^{n \times n}$ uniformly at random, and then selects $R_1, R_2 \in \mathbb{Z}_q^{n \times n}$ with entries selected from the distribution $\mathcal{D}_\sigma$. The challenger constructs $A_2 = A_1 \cdot R_1 + R_2$ and gives the pair (A_1, A_2) to the adversary $\mathcal{A}$. The adversary's goal is to come up with a vector $\mathbf{m} \in [-1/2, \ldots, 1/2]^n$ such that

$$\|R_1 \cdot \mathbf{m}\|_\infty \geq \mathfrak{c} \cdot \sigma \cdot \sqrt{n}/2$$

for some constant $\mathfrak{c}$. We define the advantage of an adversary $\mathcal{A}$ against this hard problem as

$$\begin{aligned}\mathsf{Adv}_{\mathcal{A}}^{\mathsf{LVP}}(n, \mathfrak{c}, \sigma) = \Pr\Big[&A_1 \leftarrow \mathbb{Z}_q^{n \times n},\ R_1, R_2 \leftarrow \mathcal{D}_\sigma^{n \times n},\ A_2 = A_1 \cdot R_1 + R_2, \\ &\mathbf{m} \leftarrow \mathcal{A}(A_1, A_2)\ :\ \|R_1 \cdot \mathbf{m}\|_\infty \geq \mathfrak{c} \cdot \sigma \cdot \sqrt{n}/2\Big].\end{aligned}$$

We note that (see the full version for details) the probability that there are *no solutions at all* to the above problem (when we sample over all secret keys R_1 and R_2) is $1 - n \cdot \mathsf{erfc}(\mathfrak{c})$. Thus the probability that there are **ANY** solutions to this problem is already very small if $\mathfrak{c}$ is large enough. Thus for randomly chosen R_1 and $\mathfrak{c}$ large enough, the adversary already has an impossible task (i.e. information theoretically impossible) in solving LVP. If we set $\mathfrak{c} = 9.3$ (resp. 13.2) this would give us a bound on the advantage of (approximately) 2^{-128} (resp. 2^{-256}).

We note that if one can solve the search-LWE problem for the pair (A_1, A_2) then finding such a $\mathbf{m}$ is potentially trivial (if such a $\mathbf{m}$ exists). In the 'unlucky' event that there is a solution, since R_1 is hidden (due to search-LWE being hard), the adversary is left with outputting a small vector and 'hoping' it works.

We would like to use a smaller constant than $\mathfrak{c} = 9.3$ (resp. 13.2). Assuming a solution exists and sampling over all keys, the only plausible attack (due to R_1 being hidden by LWE) is for the adversary to select a message at random and hope it solves the problem. Suppose the adversary selects a message with entries in the range $[-v/2+u, \ldots, u+v/2]$ for $u \in [0, 1/2)$ and $v < 1-2 \cdot u$. The n random variables given by the entries of $R_1 \cdot \mathbf{m}$ will still have mean zero (as the entries of R_1 are pulled from a symmetric distribution of mean zero), but they will have variance given by $V = n \cdot \sigma^2 \cdot \left(u^2 + v^2/12\right)$. Thus with probability $\mathsf{erfc}(\mathfrak{c}')$ the adversary will obtain a value of size greater than $\mathfrak{c}'\sqrt{V}$. To win the game (assuming a solution exists) thus requires

$$\mathfrak{c}' \geq \frac{\mathfrak{c}}{2 \cdot \sqrt{u^2 + v^2/12}}.$$

The right hand side of this last equation is minimized when $u = 1/2, v = 0$ and thus we have $\mathfrak{c}' > \mathfrak{c}$. But this assumes a solution exists, thus our final probability for the attack to work is given by $n \cdot \mathsf{erfc}(\mathfrak{c})^2$. If this was the best possible attack then this would mean we would have $\mathsf{Adv}_{\mathcal{A}}^{\mathsf{LVP}}(n, \mathfrak{c}, \sigma) \leq n \cdot \mathsf{erfc}(\mathfrak{c})^2$. Indeed, we conjecture that the hardness of this problem is indeed given by $\mathsf{Adv}_{\mathcal{A}}^{\mathsf{LVP}}(n, \mathfrak{c}, \sigma) \leq n \cdot \mathsf{erfc}(\mathfrak{c})^2$, and assuming this allows us to obtain smaller parameters for our Gladius scheme.

Conjecture 4.1 (LVP Hardness Conjecture). We have $\mathsf{Adv}_{\mathcal{A}}^{\mathsf{LVP}}(n, \mathfrak{c}, \sigma) \leq n \cdot \mathsf{erfc}(\mathfrak{c})^2$.

5 Gladius–Hispaniensis: Plain LWR Based Encryption

According to Wikipedia the *Gladius–Hispaniensis* was the earliest and heaviest of the different types of Gladii that we know about; it is thus fitting we reserve this name for our encryption scheme based on standard LWR. The scheme is defined in Fig. 6 and is parametrized by values $t, p, q, n, \ell, \sigma, \epsilon$. We define the message space $\mathcal{M}$ to be the set $\mathbb{Z}_t^n$. From these parameters we define $\mu \in \mathbb{Z}$ and $\psi \in (-1/2, 1/2]$ via

$$\frac{p \cdot \ell}{q} = \left\lfloor \frac{p \cdot \ell}{q} \right\rceil + \psi = \mu + \psi. \tag{1}$$

The Gladius–Hispaniensis Deterministic Encryption Scheme Π_p.

Key Generation: $\mathcal{K}_p$.
1. $R_1, R_2 \leftarrow \mathcal{D}_\sigma^{n\times n}$, i.e. two $n \times n$ matrices with coefficients sampled from $\mathcal{D}_\sigma$.
2. $A_1 \leftarrow \mathbb{Z}_q^{n\times n}$
3. $A_2 \leftarrow A_1 \cdot R_1 + R_2 + G$, where G is the gadget matrix $\ell \cdot I_n$.
4. $\mathsf{pk} \leftarrow (A_1, A_2)$.
5. $\mathsf{sk} \leftarrow (\mathsf{pk}, R_1)$.
6. Return $(\mathsf{pk}, \mathsf{sk})$).

Encryption: $\mathcal{E}_p(\mathsf{pk}, \mathbf{m})$.
1. $\mathbf{c}_1 \leftarrow \lfloor \mathbf{m}^\mathsf{T} \cdot A_1 \rceil_p$.
2. $\mathbf{c}_2 \leftarrow \lfloor \mathbf{m}^\mathsf{T} \cdot A_2 \rceil_p$.
3. Return $(\mathbf{c}_1, \mathbf{c}_2)$.

Decryption: $\mathcal{D}_p(\mathsf{sk}, (\mathbf{c}_1, \mathbf{c}_2))$.
1. $\mathbf{w}^\mathsf{T} \leftarrow \mathbf{c}_2 - \mathbf{c}_1 \cdot R_1 \pmod q$
2. $\mathbf{e}^\mathsf{T} \leftarrow \mathbf{w}^\mathsf{T} \pmod p$.
3. $\mathbf{v}^\mathsf{T} \leftarrow \mathbf{e}^\mathsf{T} \pmod \mu$.
4. $\mathbf{m}^\mathsf{T} \leftarrow (\mathbf{e}^\mathsf{T} - \mathbf{v}^\mathsf{T})/\mu$.
5. $(\mathbf{c}'_1, \mathbf{c}'_2) \leftarrow \mathcal{E}_p(\mathsf{pk}, \mathbf{m})$.
6. If $\mathbf{c}_1 \neq \mathbf{c}'_1$ or $\mathbf{c}_2 \neq \mathbf{c}'_2$ return $\perp$.
7. Return $\mathbf{m}^\mathsf{T}$.

Fig. 6. The Gladius–Hispaniensis deterministic encryption scheme Π_p.

Note when μ and p are powers of two, say $\mu = 2^\nu$ and $p = 2^\pi$, and $t = 2$ then lines 3 and 4 of the decryption procedure in Fig. 6 becomes $m_i \leftarrow w_i^{(\nu)} \oplus w_i^{(\nu+1)}$, where $\mathbf{m} = (m_i)$ and $\mathbf{w} = (w_i)$ and $w_i^{(j)}$ is the j-th bit of w_i. This is again a useful simplification in our distributed decryption procedure, thus we will assume that μ and p are powers of two.

See the full version, where we discuss the criteria which need to be satisfied to ensure correctness of decryption, and security of this construction. We found the parameters in Table 1 using this analysis. Note we are only able to establish our $\perp$-Aware property (assuming the LVP-problem is hard) when q is a prime, an interesting open question would be to establish this for the parameter sets where q is a power-of-two.

The above describes solely the KEM-like component Π_p of our hybrid construction from Sect. 3. The DEM-like component Π_s can be any (one-time) IND-CPA cipher; for example a one-time pad or AES in CTR-mode. The remaining item to define is the associated hash function G (and in the case of using Hybrid_2 the hash functions H' and H''). Recall G takes the ciphertext c_2 output from the DEM, and the key k which the KEM encapsulates, and produces the hash result $G(c_2, k)$. Here we focus solely on the case of prime q variants of Gladius.

In our construction, to aid distributed decryption, we construct G as in Fig. 7, assuming we take the message modulus $t = 2$ in our above construction. Minor tweaks are needed in the case when $t \neq 2$. The construction makes use of Rescue with rate r satisfying $r \geq 2 \cdot \kappa / \lfloor \log_2 q \rfloor$, as well as SHA-3. The combined hash function can clearly be treated as a random oracle if one assumes SHA-3 and

Table 1. Gladius–Hispaniensis parameters (based on plain LWR), and the associated LWE, LWR and $\perp$ −Aware security. For the first five parameter sets with q prime we establish $\perp$ −Aware assuming Conjecture 4.1, for the second two $\perp$ −Aware security is established unconditionally since B_V is always less than $\mu/2$. For the $q = 2^k$ parameters we cannot establish $\perp$ −Aware security

	n	t	q	p	ℓ	σ	μ	LWE	LWR security		$\perp$ −Aware security	
								Security	Theoretical	Best-attack	$\mathfrak{c}'$	Adv^{-1}
prime q	971	2	$2^{21}-9$	2^9	2^{19}	$\sqrt{1/2}$	128	$2^{128.3}$	$2^{61.25}$	$2^{465.7}$	5.673	2^{89}
	1024	2	$2^{21}-9$	2^9	2^{19}	$\sqrt{1/2}$	128	$2^{135.7}$	$2^{64.78}$	$2^{492.7}$	5.523	2^{84}
	1982	2	$2^{23}-15$	2^{10}	2^{21}	$\sqrt{1/2}$	256	$2^{256.6}$	$2^{125.3}$	$2^{465.7}$	8.036	2^{183}
	2048	2	$2^{23}-15$	2^{10}	2^{21}	$\sqrt{1/2}$	256	$2^{266.0}$	$2^{129.9}$	$2^{975.5}$	7.906	2^{176}
	4096	2	$2^{26}-5$	2^{11}	2^{21}	$\sqrt{1/2}$	512	$2^{519.0}$	$2^{256.2}$	2^{2034}	11.247	2^{361}
prime q	4096	2	$2^{25}-39$	2^{11}	2^{23}	$\sqrt{1/2}$	512	$2^{537.0}$	$2^{263.8}$	2^{1951}	N/A	2^{∞}
	8192	2	$2^{27}-39$	2^{12}	2^{25}	$\sqrt{1/2}$	1024	$2^{1098.0}$	$2^{542.4}$	2^{3918}	N/A	2^{∞}
$q=2^k$	710	2	2^{14}	2^{10}	2^{11}	$\sqrt{1/2}$	128	$2^{128.9}$	$2^{550.1}$	$2^{187.6}$	–	–
	1024	2	2^{14}	2^{10}	2^{12}	$\sqrt{1/2}$	256	$2^{188.4}$	$2^{792.1}$	$2^{274.8}$	–	–
	1437	2	2^{15}	2^{11}	2^{12}	$\sqrt{1/2}$	256	$2^{256.6}$	$2^{1115.}$	$2^{366.1}$	–	–
	2048	2	2^{15}	2^{11}	2^{12}	$\sqrt{1/2}$	256	$2^{376.6}$	$2^{1584.}$	$2^{535.3}$	–	–

Rescue are themselves random oracles. In the final distributed decryption variant only lines 5 and 6 need to be performed in a secure manner (which are based on Rescue, which is an MPC-friendly hash function). Thus irrespective of how long the initial message is which is being encrypted, the number of applications of Rescue which need to be performed securely is given by $\lceil w/r \rceil + 1$. If we take parameters $\kappa = 128$, $n = 1024$ and $q = 2^{21} - 9$ then we have $r = 13$, $w = 52$ and the number of secure rounds of Rescue is five in order to absorb the key k and produce the output $G(c_2, k)$. For the case of Hybrid_2 we select H' and H'' based on Rescue as well.

For q a power-of-two a different methodology will be required. We know of no MPC-friendly hash function defined over rings of the form $\mathbb{Z}_{2^k}$. Thus for the case of power-of-two values of q it would seem one would need to use a standard sponge-based hash function (such as SHA-3), which would not be as amenable to threshold implementation via a generic MPC methodology.

6 Distributed Decryption of Gladius

In this section we present how to perform distributed decryption of the hybrid cipher obtained from our generic construction composed with Gladius. For ease of implementation we select parameters for which q is prime, $p = 2^{\pi}$ and $\mu = 2^{\nu}$ are powers of two, and the message space modulus is $t = 2$. Although this section focuses on the simpler standard LWR variant (Gladius–Hispaniensis) and not on the Ring-LWR variants (Gladius–Pompeii, Gladius–Mainz and Gladius–Fulham, see the full version), the procedure is virtually identical in all cases.

We use an MPC system defined for the q prime case for our experiments, as this is the only case for which we have both a full proof of security and a suitable MPC-friendly hash function (Rescue). Selecting q prime also means we

The Hash Function $G(c_2, k)$.

On input of c_1, c_2 and $k \in \{0,1\}^n$.

1. Apply the SHA-3 hash function to c_2 to obtain a $2 \cdot \kappa$-bit string $\mathbf{s}$.
2. Parse $\mathbf{s}$ into r bit-strings $(s_1, \ldots, s_r)$ each of length $\lfloor \log_2 q \rfloor$. This is possible due to the choice of r.
3. Treat each s_i as an element of $\mathbb{F}_q$ and absorb the set $(s_1, \ldots, s_r)$ into a fresh Rescue state. This requires one application of the Rescue absorption phase. Note, this is done in the clear during threshold decryption as c_1 and c_2 are public.
4. Take the bit string $k \in \{0,1\}^n$ and parse again into bit-strings of length $\lfloor \log_2 q \rfloor$. This will produce $w = \lceil n / \lfloor \log_2 q \rfloor \rceil$ bit-strings $k_1, \ldots, k_w$, each of which we think of as elements in $\mathbb{F}_q$.
5. The w finite field elements $k_1, \ldots, k_w$ are absorbed into the Rescue state, this will require $\lceil w/r \rceil$ executions of the Rescue function. Since during distributed decryption k is not known at this stage, this needs to be carried out securely.
6. Finally the output is obtained by squeezing out r output field elements from Rescue using a single application of the Rescue function.

Fig. 7. The hash function $G(c_2, k)$.

can utilize an existing library such as SCALE-MAMBA [6], for not only the underlying MPC system, but also many of the necessary sub-routines which our distributed decryption method requires. In the full version we discuss changes to the algorithms which would be needed if future work could establish a secure variant in the case when q is a power of two (including a suitable MPC-friendly hash function for this case).

We first present our distributed Key Generation protocol Π_{KeyGen}. Since the key generation method is based on Learning-with-Errors, with the error distribution coming from the NewHope distribution with $\sigma = 1/\sqrt{2}$, we can utilize the simple method described in [35,46]. This is described in Fig. 8.

Protocol for Distributed Key Generation Π_{KeyGen}.

1. For $i, j \in [1, \ldots, n]$
   - $\langle b \rangle, \langle b' \rangle, \langle c \rangle, \langle c' \rangle \leftarrow \mathsf{Bits}()$.
   - $\langle R_1^{(i,j)} \rangle \leftarrow \langle b \rangle - \langle b' \rangle$.
   - $\langle R_2^{(i,j)} \rangle \leftarrow \langle c \rangle - \langle c' \rangle$.
   - $A_1^{(i,j)} \leftarrow \mathbb{F}_q$.
2. $\langle A_2 \rangle \leftarrow A_1 \cdot \langle R_1 \rangle + \langle R_2 \rangle + G$.
3. $A_2 \leftarrow \mathbf{Output}(\langle A_2 \rangle)$.
4. $\mathsf{pk} \leftarrow (A_1, A_2)$.
5. $\mathsf{sk} \leftarrow (A_1, A_2, \langle R_1 \rangle)$.

Fig. 8. Protocol for distributed key generation Π_{KeyGen}.

The distributed decryption procedure itself is more complex. It makes use of the following protocols from other works, e.g. [19,42]. In each of these protocols we *can* run the protocol with clear entries. For example $\mathsf{BitDecomp}(a)$ will form the bit decomposition of an integer a, but here we also need to specify how many bits we require. Since a may not necessarily be reduced in the range $(-q/2, \ldots, q/2)$. Thus we would write $\mathsf{BitDecomp}(a, t)$ to obtain t bits.

- $\langle \mathbf{a} \rangle \leftarrow \mathsf{BitDecomp}(\langle a \rangle)$: Given a secret shared value $\langle a \rangle$ with $a \in \mathbb{F}_q$ this procedure produces a vector of shared bits $\langle \mathbf{a} \rangle = (\langle a_0 \rangle, \ldots, \langle a_{\lfloor \log_2 q \rfloor} \rangle)$ such that $a = \sum_i a_i \cdot 2^i$. Note this means a is in the non-centred interval $[0, \ldots, q)$. The method we use is from [42], which is itself built upon the work in [19].
- $\langle \mathbf{c} \rangle \leftarrow \mathsf{BitAdd}(\langle \mathbf{a} \rangle, \langle \mathbf{b} \rangle)$: Given shared bits $\langle \mathbf{a} \rangle$ and $\langle \mathbf{b} \rangle$ this executes a binary adder to produce the vector of shared bits $\langle \mathbf{c} \rangle$ such that $\sum_i c_i \cdot 2^i = \sum_i (a_i + b_i) \cdot 2^i$. This algorithm is also presented in [19]. Note this returns one bit more than the maximum of the lengths of $\langle \mathbf{a} \rangle$ and $\langle \mathbf{b} \rangle$.
- $\langle \mathbf{c} \rangle \leftarrow \mathsf{BitNeg}(\langle \mathbf{a} \rangle)$: This performs the two-complement negative of the bit vector $\langle \mathbf{a} \rangle$. It flips the bits of $\langle \mathbf{a} \rangle$ to produce $\langle \bar{\mathbf{a}} \rangle$, and then executes the function $\mathsf{BitAdd}(\langle \bar{\mathbf{a}} \rangle, \mathbf{1})$, where $\mathbf{1} = \mathsf{BitDecomp}(1, |\bar{\mathbf{a}}|)$ is the bit-vector of the correct length representing the integer one.
- $\langle c \rangle \leftarrow \mathsf{BitLT}(\langle \mathbf{a} \rangle, \langle \mathbf{b} \rangle)$: This computes the single bit output $\langle c \rangle$ of the comparison $\sum_i a_i \cdot 2^i < \sum_i b_i \cdot 2^i$. Again we use the method from [19].

When running $\mathsf{BitDecomp}(\langle a \rangle)$ on a secret shared value the run time is not deterministic, it needs to loop to produce a shared value which is uniformly distributed modulo q. It does this by rejection sampling; where the probability of rejecting a sample is given by

$$\frac{2^{\lceil \log_2 q \rceil} - q}{2^{\lceil \log_2 q \rceil}}.$$

This is another reason to select q to be close to a power-of-two, as well as to ensure μ is a power of two.

In Fig. 10 we divide our distributed decryption procedure into four phases: KEM Decapsulate, KEM Validity Check, the Hash-Check (for the checking of the DEM component) and finally the Message Extraction. As we select μ and p to be powers of two the first stage is relatively straightforward given we can implement $\mathsf{BitDecomp}(\langle a \rangle)$. There is a minor complication due to the need to map the bit-decomposition into the centred interval but this is easily dealt with using the sub-routine in Fig. 9. The third stage complexity depends on the choice of the underlying hash function G; our choice of G from Sect. 5 using SHA-3 and Rescue combined was to ensure this step is as efficient as possible. Due to our hybrid design the final step can be performed in the clear; which is not possible for other hybrid schemes.

Thus, the main complexity of the decryption procedure is the second stage, namely the KEM Validity Check, as for this we need to re-encrypt the message

Subroutine $\mathsf{Centre}(\langle x \rangle)$

1. $\langle \mathbf{b} \rangle \leftarrow \mathsf{BitDecomp}(\langle x \rangle)$; recall the bit-decomposition produces a value in the non-centred interval.
2. $\langle \mathbf{b}' \rangle \leftarrow \mathsf{BitAdd}(\langle \overline{\mathbf{b}} \rangle, q+1)$; i.e. $b' = q - u_i$ over the integers.
3. $\langle \mathbf{b}'' \rangle \leftarrow \mathsf{BitNeg}(\langle \mathbf{b}' \rangle)$; i.e. $b'' = -b' \pmod{2^{\lceil \log_2 q \rceil} - \pi}$ if we compute to $\lceil \log_2 q \rceil - \pi$ bits.
4. $\langle f \rangle \leftarrow \mathsf{BitLT}(\langle \mathbf{b} \rangle, q/2)$; i.e. is $b < q/2$?
5. $\langle \mathbf{a} \rangle \leftarrow \langle f \rangle \cdot \langle \mathbf{b} \rangle + (1 - \langle f \rangle) \cdot \langle \mathbf{b}'' \rangle$. This is again done bitwise. This results in $\mathbf{a}$ being the bit representation of the centred value of u_i modulo q represented in $\lceil \log_2 q \rceil$ bits.
6. Return $\langle \mathbf{a} \rangle$.

Fig. 9. Subroutine $\mathsf{Centre}(\langle x \rangle)$

and check the result is equal to the KEM ciphertext component. We need to verify equations of the following form

$$c = \lfloor \langle x \rangle \rceil_p = \left\lfloor \frac{p}{q} \cdot \langle x \rangle \right\rceil \pmod p$$

where c is publicly given, but the value $\langle x \rangle$ cannot be opened to the parties. We write the equation, over the integers, as $c = \frac{p}{q} \cdot \langle x \rangle + \epsilon + p \cdot v$, where $\epsilon \in (-1/2, 1/2]$, $v \in \{0, 1\}$ and we think of the shared value $\langle x \rangle$ being in the centred representation modulo q. The value v is equal to one only if the reduction modulo p in the LWR equation needs to move the rounded value $-p/2$ to $p/2$. This happens when

$$x \leq \frac{q}{p}\left(\frac{1}{2} - \frac{p}{2}\right) = \frac{q \cdot (1-p)}{2 \cdot p}.$$

This means we simply need to compute the bit representation $\langle \mathbf{s} \rangle$ of the value $|q \cdot c - p \cdot \langle x \rangle - p \cdot q \cdot \langle v \rangle|$ over the integers and then check the result is less than $q/2$. The last check can be performed using the $\mathsf{BitLT}(\langle \mathbf{s} \rangle, q/2)$ algorithm mentioned above.

But to compute the bit representation of $\langle \mathbf{s} \rangle$ we need the bit representation of the modulo q centred value $\langle x \rangle$. However, the $\mathsf{BitDecomp}$ routine only produces the bit-decomposition in the non-centred interval of a value modulo q. We could use the method from the first stage and apply the Centre sub-routine. However, this is inefficient as on its own it requires two calls to BitAdd (one explicitly to BitAdd and one implicitly in the call to BitNeg). The procedure BitAdd is our most expensive subroutine so we want to minimize the number of calls to this.

Thus instead we proceed as follows: If we think of the value $\langle x \rangle$ as the reduction in the centred interval, and $\langle u \rangle$ as the value in the non-centred interval then we have $x = u - b \cdot q$, where b is the bit given by $b = 1 - (u \leq q/2)$. We write $\langle \mathbf{u} \rangle$ for the corresponding shared bit decomposition of u. We can then re-write the equation for determining v above in terms of u, as opposed to x, as $v = b \cdot \left(u \leq \frac{q \cdot (p+1)}{(2 \cdot p)}\right)$. We note that $v = 0$ when $b = 0$, which is important in what follows.

Protocol for Distributed Decryption Π_{Dec}.

Input: A ciphertext $c_1 = (\mathbf{c}_1, \mathbf{c}_2), c_2, c_3$, the public key (A_1, A_2) and the secret key in shared form $\langle R_1 \rangle$.

KEM Decapsulation:
1. $\langle \mathbf{x} \rangle \leftarrow \mathbf{c}_2 - \mathbf{c}_1 \cdot \langle R_1 \rangle$.
2. For $i \in [1, \ldots, n]$
   - $\langle \mathbf{w} \rangle \leftarrow \mathsf{Centre}(\langle x_i \rangle)$.
   - $\langle k_i \rangle \leftarrow \langle w_i^{(\nu)} \rangle \oplus \langle w_i^{(\nu+1)} \rangle = \langle w_i^{(\nu)} \rangle + \langle w_i^{(\nu+1)} \rangle - 2 \cdot \langle w_i^{(\nu)} \rangle \cdot \langle w_i^{(\nu+1)} \rangle$.

KEM Validity Check:
1. $\langle \mathbf{y} \rangle \leftarrow \langle \mathbf{k} \rangle \cdot (A_1 \| A_2)$.
2. $\langle z \rangle \leftarrow 1$.
3. For $i \in [1, \ldots, 2 \cdot n]$
   - $\langle \mathbf{u} \rangle \leftarrow \mathsf{BitDecomp}(\langle y_i \rangle)$.
   - $\langle b \rangle \leftarrow 1 - \mathsf{BitLT}(\mathbf{u}, q/2)$.
   - $\langle v \rangle \leftarrow \langle b \rangle \cdot \mathsf{BitLT}(\langle \mathbf{u} \rangle, q \cdot (p+1)/(2 \cdot p))$. This computes the adjustment bit for dealing with the wrap around modulo p. Note, this can only apply when $a < 0$.
   - $\langle \mathbf{u}' \rangle \leftarrow \langle \mathbf{u} \rangle \ll \pi$; i.e. shift left by π bits, where $p = 2^{\pi}$. Hence $u' = p \cdot u$ over the integers, represented in $\lceil \log_2 q \rceil + \pi$ bits.
   - $\langle \mathbf{w} \rangle \leftarrow \mathsf{BitAdd}(\langle \mathbf{u}' \rangle, 2^{\lceil \log_2 q \rceil + \pi} - c_i \cdot q)$. Here $c_i = \mathbf{c}_1^{(i)}$ if $i \leq n$ and $\mathbf{c}_2^{(i-n)}$ otherwise. This produces $w = p \cdot u - c_i \cdot q$ over the integers with $\lceil \log_2 q \rceil + \pi$ bits.
   - $\langle \mathbf{f} \rangle \leftarrow \mathsf{BitAdd}(\langle \mathbf{w} \rangle, (\langle b \rangle - \langle v \rangle) \cdot (-p \cdot q))$. This applies the adjustment when $b = 1$ and $v = 0$. We now have $f = p \cdot u_i - (b - v) \cdot p \cdot q - c_i \cdot q$ over the integers with $\lceil \log_2 q \rceil + \pi$ bits.
   - $\langle \mathbf{f}' \rangle \leftarrow \mathsf{BitNeg}(\langle \mathbf{f} \rangle)$, hence $f' = -f$ over the integers.
   - $\langle g \rangle \leftarrow \langle f_{\pi + \lceil \log_2 q \rceil - 1} \rangle$; i.e. the sign bit of f.
   - $\langle \mathbf{s} \rangle \leftarrow \langle g \rangle \cdot \langle \mathbf{f}' \rangle + (1 - \langle g \rangle) \cdot \langle \mathbf{f} \rangle$. Again a bitwise operation computing $s = |f|$ as an integer.
   - $\langle j \rangle \leftarrow \mathsf{BitLT}(\langle \mathbf{s} \rangle, q/2)$; is one if this coefficient is OK.
   - $\langle z \rangle \leftarrow \langle z \rangle \cdot \langle j \rangle$; is one if the ciphertext is OK up to this point.
4. $z \leftarrow \textbf{Output}(\langle z \rangle)$
5. If $z \neq 1$ then return $\perp$.

Hash Check:
1. $\langle t \rangle \leftarrow G(c_2, \langle \mathbf{k} \rangle)$.
2. $t \leftarrow \textbf{Output}(\langle t \rangle)$.
3. If $t \neq c_3$ then return $\perp$.

Message Extaction:
1. $k \leftarrow \textbf{Output}(\langle \mathbf{k} \rangle)$.
2. $\mathsf{k} \leftarrow H(k)$.
3. $m \leftarrow \mathcal{D}_s(\mathsf{k}, c_2)$
4. If $m = \perp$ then return $\perp$.
5. Return m.

Fig. 10. Protocol for distributed decryption Π_{Dec}.

We then rewrite the equation for $\langle \mathbf{s} \rangle$ as

$$\left| p \cdot \langle \mathbf{u} \rangle - p \cdot q \cdot (\langle b \rangle - \langle v \rangle) - c_i \cdot q \right|$$

The bit representation of $p \cdot \langle \mathbf{u} \rangle$ can be determined by simply shifting bits, as p is a power-of-two. The bit representation of $-p \cdot q \cdot (\langle b \rangle - \langle v \rangle)$ can be determined by bit-wise multiplications as $b - v \in \{0, 1\}$ by construction. From these observations we can produce a method for Stage 2 which requires three calls to BitAdd, as opposed to the naive method which would go through Centre which would require four calls to BitAdd.

Security Discussion and Implementation: As remarked previously the security of our implementation follows from the security of the underlying MPC protocol. By using SCALE-MAMBA [6] we can obtain active security, and the above sub-procedures are all provided as built in functions. In addition, the large local only operations in KEM Decapsulation (line 1) and KEM Validity Check (line 1) can be carried out efficiently in C++ using the SCALE `LOCAL_FUNCTION` operation. This enables one to perform complex local only operations, i.e. complex linear functions, natively in C++ as opposed to needing them to be implemented with the MPC system (which adds a lot of overhead).

We implemented our distributed decryption procedure in the case of Shamir sharing within SCALE-MAMBA. This is because the Shamir implementation module allows the MPC sub-system to be instantiated over any finite field $\mathbb{F}_q$. In using a full threshold access structure one would need (with SCALE-MAMBA as currently implemented) to select a prime q which is FHE friendly; so as to enable the SHE scheme at the basis of SPDZ [20] to be instantiated. None of the q values in the various parameter sets for Gladius are FHE friendly; not even the Gladius-Pompeii variants which have $q - 1$ divisible by a large power of two. In our experiments, each party ran on a machine with a Intel(R) Core(TM) i9-9900 CPU at 3.10 GHz and 128 GB of memory. The machines were connected in a local network using a 10 GB switch.

For three parties, tolerating a threshold of one dishonest party, we obtained a run time for the first three phases of 1.19, 3.62, and 0.18 s respectively; for our parameter set of $q = 2^{21} - 9$ and $n = 1024$ in the plain LWR setting. Making a total decapsulation time of 4.99 s in 136491 rounds of communication. Whilst this might at first sight seem slower than the 4.20 s reported for LIMA in [35] the results are incomparable. Recall, the method in [35] to perform distributed decapsulation is insecure, as indeed would be any distributed decapsulation of any algorithm making use of the traditional KEM-DEM construction.

In our second experiment, we used the parameter set of $q = 2^{23} - 15$ and $n = 2048$, which has a better $\perp$ $-$Aware security of 2^{176}. We obtained a run time for three phases of 7.16, 19.1 and 0.99 s, respectively; which amounts to a total of 27.3 s and 274157 rounds of communication.

Acknowledgment. We would like to thank Alexandra Boldyreva for clarifying some issues with the PRIV definition of security for deterministic encryption, Frederik Vercauteren for clarifying some issues in relation to Learning-with-Rounding, Andrej Bogdanov for clarifying issues related to the theoretical reductions between LWE and LWR, and Ward Beullens on comments on an earlier draft. This work was supported in part by CyberSecurity Research Flanders with reference number VR20192203, by ERC Advanced Grant ERC-2015-AdG-IMPaCT, by the Defense Advanced Research Projects Agency (DARPA) and Space and Naval Warfare Systems Center, Pacific (SSC Pacific) under contract No. FA8750-19-C-0502, and by the FWO under an Odysseus project GOH9718N. Any opinions, findings and conclusions or recommendations expressed in this material are those of the author(s) and do not necessarily reflect the views of the ERC, DARPA, the US Government or the FWO. The U.S. Government is authorized to reproduce and distribute reprints for governmental purposes notwithstanding any copyright annotation therein.

References

1. Abe, M., Gennaro, R., Kurosawa, K.: Tag-KEM/DEM: a new framework for hybrid encryption. J. Cryptol. **21**(1), 97–130 (2008)
2. Albrecht, M.R., et al.: Estimate all the LWE, NTRU schemes! In: Catalano, D., De Prisco, R. (eds.) SCN 2018. LNCS, vol. 11035, pp. 351–367. Springer, Cham (2018). https://doi.org/10.1007/978-3-319-98113-0_19
3. Alkim, E., Ducas, L., Pöppelmann, T., Schwabe, P.: Post-quantum key exchange - a new hope. In: Holz, T., Savage, S. (eds.) USENIX Security 2016, pp. 327–343. USENIX Association (2016)
4. Alwen, J., Krenn, S., Pietrzak, K., Wichs, D.: Learning with rounding, revisited - new reduction, properties and applications. In: Canetti, R., Garay, J.A. (eds.) CRYPTO 2013. LNCS, vol. 8042, pp. 57–74. Springer, Heidelberg (2013). https://doi.org/10.1007/978-3-642-40041-4_4
5. Aly, A., Ashur, T., Ben-Sasson, E., Dhooghe, S., Szepieniec, A.: Design of symmetric-key primitives for advanced cryptographic protocols. Cryptology ePrint Archive, Report 2019/426 (2019). https://eprint.iacr.org/2019/426
6. Aly, A., et al.: SCALE and MAMBA v1.9: documentation (2020). https://homes.esat.kuleuven.be/~nsmart/SCALE/Documentation.pdf
7. Arita, S., Tsurudome, K.: Construction of threshold public-key encryptions through tag-based encryptions. In: Abdalla, M., Pointcheval, D., Fouque, P.-A., Vergnaud, D. (eds.) ACNS 2009. LNCS, vol. 5536, pp. 186–200. Springer, Heidelberg (2009). https://doi.org/10.1007/978-3-642-01957-9_12
8. Bendlin, R., Damgård, I.: Threshold decryption and zero-knowledge proofs for lattice-based cryptosystems. In: Micciancio, D. (ed.) TCC 2010. LNCS, vol. 5978, pp. 201–218. Springer, Heidelberg (2010). https://doi.org/10.1007/978-3-642-11799-2_13
9. Bendlin, R., Damgård, I., Orlandi, C., Zakarias, S.: Semi-homomorphic encryption and multiparty computation. In: Paterson, K.G. (ed.) EUROCRYPT 2011. LNCS, vol. 6632, pp. 169–188. Springer, Heidelberg (2011). https://doi.org/10.1007/978-3-642-20465-4_11
10. Bernstein, D.J., Chuengsatiansup, C., Lange, T., van Vredendaal, C.: NTRU Prime. Technical report, National Institute of Standards and Technology (2019). https://csrc.nist.gov/projects/post-quantum-cryptography/round-2-submissions

11. Bernstein, D.J., Persichetti, E.: Towards KEM unification. Cryptology ePrint Archive, Report 2018/526 (2018). https://eprint.iacr.org/2018/526
12. Bogdanov, A., Guo, S., Masny, D., Richelson, S., Rosen, A.: On the hardness of learning with rounding over small modulus. In: Kushilevitz, E., Malkin, T. (eds.) TCC 2016, Part I. LNCS, vol. 9562, pp. 209–224. Springer, Heidelberg (2016). https://doi.org/10.1007/978-3-662-49096-9_9
13. Boneh, D., Gennaro, R., Goldfeder, S., Jain, A., Kim, S., Rasmussen, P.M.R., Sahai, A.: Threshold cryptosystems from threshold fully homomorphic encryption. In: Shacham, H., Boldyreva, A. (eds.) CRYPTO 2018, Part I. LNCS, vol. 10991, pp. 565–596. Springer, Cham (2018). https://doi.org/10.1007/978-3-319-96884-1_19
14. Bonte, C., Smart, N.P., Tanguy, T.: Thresholdizing HashEdDSA: MPC to the Rescue. Cryptology ePrint Archive, Report 2020/214 (2019). https://eprint.iacr.org/2020/214
15. Cozzo, D., Smart, N.P.: Sharing the LUOV: threshold post-quantum signatures. In: Albrecht, M. (ed.) IMACC 2019. LNCS, vol. 11929, pp. 128–153. Springer, Cham (2019). https://doi.org/10.1007/978-3-030-35199-1_7
16. Cozzo, D., Smart, N.P.: Sashimi: cutting up CSI-fish secret keys to produce an actively secure distributed signing protocol. In: Ding, J., Tillich, J.-P. (eds.) PQCrypto 2020. LNCS, vol. 12100, pp. 169–186. Springer, Cham (2020). https://doi.org/10.1007/978-3-030-44223-1_10
17. Cramer, R., Shoup, V.: A practical public key cryptosystem provably secure against adaptive chosen ciphertext attack. In: Krawczyk, H. (ed.) CRYPTO 1998. LNCS, vol. 1462, pp. 13–25. Springer, Heidelberg (1998). https://doi.org/10.1007/BFb0055717
18. Cramer, R., Shoup, V.: Design and analysis of practical public-key encryption schemes secure against adaptive chosen ciphertext attack. SIAM J. Comput. **33**(1), 167–226 (2003)
19. Damgård, I., Fitzi, M., Kiltz, E., Nielsen, J.B., Toft, T.: Unconditionally secure constant-rounds multi-party computation for equality, comparison, bits and exponentiation. In: Halevi, S., Rabin, T. (eds.) TCC 2006. LNCS, vol. 3876, pp. 285–304. Springer, Heidelberg (2006). https://doi.org/10.1007/11681878_15
20. Damgård, I., Pastro, V., Smart, N., Zakarias, S.: Multiparty computation from somewhat homomorphic encryption. In: Safavi-Naini, R., Canetti, R. (eds.) CRYPTO 2012. LNCS, vol. 7417, pp. 643–662. Springer, Heidelberg (2012). https://doi.org/10.1007/978-3-642-32009-5_38
21. D'Anvers, J.-P., Karmakar, A., Sinha Roy, S., Vercauteren, F.: Saber: module-LWR based key exchange, CPA-secure encryption and CCA-secure KEM. In: Joux, A., Nitaj, A., Rachidi, T. (eds.) AFRICACRYPT 2018. LNCS, vol. 10831, pp. 282–305. Springer, Cham (2018). https://doi.org/10.1007/978-3-319-89339-6_16
22. D'Anvers, J.P., Karmakar, A., Roy, S.S., Vercauteren, F.: SABER. Technical report, National Institute of Standards and Technology (2019). https://csrc.nist.gov/projects/post-quantum-cryptography/round-2-submissions
23. De Feo, L., Meyer, M.: Threshold schemes from isogeny assumptions. In: Kiayias, A., Kohlweiss, M., Wallden, P., Zikas, V. (eds.) PKC 2020, Part II. LNCS, vol. 12111, pp. 187–212. Springer, Cham (2020). https://doi.org/10.1007/978-3-030-45388-6_7
24. Dent, A.W.: A designer's guide to KEMs. In: Paterson, K.G. (ed.) Cryptography and Coding 2003. LNCS, vol. 2898, pp. 133–151. Springer, Heidelberg (2003). https://doi.org/10.1007/978-3-540-40974-8_12
25. Dolev, D., Dwork, C., Naor, M.: Non-malleable cryptography (extended abstract). In: 23rd ACM STOC, pp. 542–552. ACM Press, May 1991

26. Fujisaki, E., Okamoto, T.: Secure integration of asymmetric and symmetric encryption schemes. In: Wiener, M. (ed.) CRYPTO 1999. LNCS, vol. 1666, pp. 537–554. Springer, Heidelberg (1999). https://doi.org/10.1007/3-540-48405-1_34
27. Fujisaki, E., Okamoto, T.: Secure integration of asymmetric and symmetric encryption schemes. J. Cryptol. **26**(1), 80–101 (2013)
28. Garcia-Morchon, O., et al.: Round5. Technical report, National Institute of Standards and Technology (2019). https://csrc.nist.gov/projects/post-quantum-cryptography/round-2-submissions
29. Grassi, L., Kales, D., Khovratovich, D., Roy, A., Rechberger, C., Schofnegger, M.: Starkad and Poseidon: New hash functions for zero knowledge proof systems. Cryptology ePrint Archive, Report 2019/458 (2019). https://eprint.iacr.org/2019/458
30. Hamburg, M.: Three Bears. Technical report, National Institute of Standards and Technology (2019). https://csrc.nist.gov/projects/post-quantum-cryptography/round-2-submissions
31. Hofheinz, D., Hövelmanns, K., Kiltz, E.: A modular analysis of the Fujisaki-Okamoto transformation. In: Kalai, Y., Reyzin, L. (eds.) TCC 2017, Part I. LNCS, vol. 10677, pp. 341–371. Springer, Cham (2017). https://doi.org/10.1007/978-3-319-70500-2_12
32. Ishihara, T., Aono, H., Hongo, S., Shikata, J.: Construction of threshold (hybrid) encryption in the random oracle model: how to construct secure threshold tag-KEM from weakly secure threshold KEM. In: Pieprzyk, J., Ghodosi, H., Dawson, E. (eds.) ACISP 2007. LNCS, vol. 4586, pp. 259–273. Springer, Heidelberg (2007). https://doi.org/10.1007/978-3-540-73458-1_20
33. Keller, M., Orsini, E., Rotaru, D., Scholl, P., Soria-Vazquez, E., Vivek, S.: Faster secure multi-party computation of AES and DES using lookup tables. In: Gollmann, D., Miyaji, A., Kikuchi, H. (eds.) ACNS 2017. LNCS, vol. 10355, pp. 229–249. Springer, Cham (2017). https://doi.org/10.1007/978-3-319-61204-1_12
34. Keller, M., Orsini, E., Scholl, P.: MASCOT: faster malicious arithmetic secure computation with oblivious transfer. In: Weippl, E.R., Katzenbeisser, S., Kruegel, C., Myers, A.C., Halevi, S. (eds.) ACM CCS 2016, pp. 830–842. ACM Press, October 2016
35. Kraitsberg, M., Lindell, Y., Osheter, V., Smart, N.P., Talibi Alaoui, Y.: Adding distributed decryption and key generation to a ring-LWE based CCA encryption scheme. In: Jang-Jaccard, J., Guo, F. (eds.) ACISP 2019. LNCS, vol. 11547, pp. 192–210. Springer, Cham (2019). https://doi.org/10.1007/978-3-030-21548-4_11
36. Libert, B., Yung, M.: Non-interactive CCA-secure threshold cryptosystems with adaptive security: new framework and constructions. In: Cramer, R. (ed.) TCC 2012. LNCS, vol. 7194, pp. 75–93. Springer, Heidelberg (2012). https://doi.org/10.1007/978-3-642-28914-9_5
37. Lim, C.H., Lee, P.J.: Another method for attaining security against adaptively chosen ciphertext attacks. In: Stinson, D.R. (ed.) CRYPTO 1993. LNCS, vol. 773, pp. 420–434. Springer, Heidelberg (1994). https://doi.org/10.1007/3-540-48329-2_36
38. Lu, X., et al.: LAC. Technical report, National Institute of Standards and Technology (2019). https://csrc.nist.gov/projects/post-quantum-cryptography/round-2-submissions
39. Micciancio, D., Peikert, C.: Trapdoors for lattices: simpler, tighter, faster, smaller. In: Pointcheval, D., Johansson, T. (eds.) EUROCRYPT 2012. LNCS, vol. 7237, pp. 700–718. Springer, Heidelberg (2012). https://doi.org/10.1007/978-3-642-29011-4_41

40. Naehrig, M., et al.: FrodoKEM. Technical report National Institute of Standards and Technology (2019). https://csrc.nist.gov/projects/post-quantum-cryptography/round-2-submissions
41. Naor, M., Yung, M.: Public-key cryptosystems provably secure against chosen ciphertext attacks. In: 22nd ACM STOC, pp. 427–437. ACM Press, May 1990
42. Nishide, T., Ohta, K.: Multiparty computation for interval, equality, and comparison without bit-decomposition protocol. In: Okamoto, T., Wang, X. (eds.) PKC 2007. LNCS, vol. 4450, pp. 343–360. Springer, Heidelberg (2007). https://doi.org/10.1007/978-3-540-71677-8_23
43. Okamoto, T., Pointcheval, D.: REACT: rapid enhanced-security asymmetric cryptosystem transform. In: Naccache, D. (ed.) CT-RSA 2001. LNCS, vol. 2020, pp. 159–174. Springer, Heidelberg (2000). https://doi.org/10.1007/3-540-45353-9_13
44. Pinkas, B., Schneider, T., Smart, N.P., Williams, S.C.: Secure two-party computation is practical. In: Matsui, M. (ed.) ASIACRYPT 2009. LNCS, vol. 5912, pp. 250–267. Springer, Heidelberg (2009). https://doi.org/10.1007/978-3-642-10366-7_15
45. Poppelmann, T., et al.: NewHope. Technical report, National Institute of Standards and Technology (2019). https://csrc.nist.gov/projects/post-quantum-cryptography/round-2-submissions
46. Rotaru, D., Smart, N.P., Tanguy, T., Vercauteren, F., Wood, T.: Actively secure setup for SPDZ. Cryptology ePrint Archive, Report 2019/1300 (2019). https://eprint.iacr.org/2019/1300
47. Schwabe, P., et al.: CRYSTALS-KYBER. Technical report, National Institute of Standards and Technology (2019). https://csrc.nist.gov/projects/post-quantum-cryptography/round-2-submissions
48. Shoup, V., Gennaro, R.: Securing threshold cryptosystems against chosen ciphertext attack. In: Nyberg, K. (ed.) EUROCRYPT 1998. LNCS, vol. 1403, pp. 1–16. Springer, Heidelberg (1998). https://doi.org/10.1007/BFb0054113
49. Shoup, V., Gennaro, R.: Securing threshold cryptosystems against chosen ciphertext attack. J. Cryptol. **15**(2), 75–96 (2002)
50. Smart, N.P., Wood, T.: Error detection in monotone span programs with application to communication-efficient multi-party computation. In: Matsui, M. (ed.) CT-RSA 2019. LNCS, vol. 11405, pp. 210–229. Springer, Cham (2019). https://doi.org/10.1007/978-3-030-12612-4_11
51. Targhi, E.E., Unruh, D.: Post-quantum security of the Fujisaki-Okamoto and OAEP transforms. In: Hirt, M., Smith, A. (eds.) TCC 2016, Part II. LNCS, vol. 9986, pp. 192–216. Springer, Heidelberg (2016). https://doi.org/10.1007/978-3-662-53644-5_8
52. Xie, X., Xue, R., Zhang, R.: Deterministic public key encryption and identity-based encryption from lattices in the auxiliary-input setting. In: Visconti, I., De Prisco, R. (eds.) SCN 2012. LNCS, vol. 7485, pp. 1–18. Springer, Heidelberg (2012). https://doi.org/10.1007/978-3-642-32928-9_1
53. Zhandry, M.: How to record quantum queries, and applications to quantum indifferentiability. In: Boldyreva, A., Micciancio, D. (eds.) CRYPTO 2019, Part II. LNCS, vol. 11693, pp. 239–268. Springer, Cham (2019). https://doi.org/10.1007/978-3-030-26951-7_9
54. Zhang, Z., et al.: NTRUEncrypt. Technical report, National Institute of Standards and Technology (2019). https://csrc.nist.gov/projects/post-quantum-cryptography/round-2-submissions

Lattice-Based Group Encryption with Full Dynamicity and Message Filtering Policy

Jing Pan[1,2], Xiaofeng Chen[1,2(✉)], Fangguo Zhang[3,4], and Willy Susilo[5]

[1] State Key Laboratory of Integrated Service Networks (ISN), Xidian University, Xi'an 710071, China
jinglap@aliyun.com, xfchen@xidian.edu.cn
[2] State Key Laboratory of Cryptology, P.O. Box 5159, Beijing 100878, China
[3] School of Computer Science and Engineering, Sun Yat-sen University, Guangzhou 510006, China
isszhfg@mail.sysu.edu.cn
[4] Guangdong Province Key Laboratory of Information Security Technology, Guangzhou 510006, China
[5] Institute of Cybersecurity and Cryptology, School of Computing and Information Technology, University of Wollongong, Wollongong, NSW 2522, Australia
wsusilo@uow.edu.au

Abstract. Group encryption (GE) is a fundamental privacy-preserving primitive analog of group signatures, which allows users to decrypt specific ciphertexts while hiding themselves within a crowd. Since its first birth, numerous constructions have been proposed, among which the schemes separately constructed by Libert et al. (Asiacrypt 2016) over lattices and by Nguyen et al. (PKC 2021) over coding theory are post-quantum secure. Though the last scheme, at the first time, achieved the full dynamicity (allowing group users to join or leave the group in their ease) and message filtering policy, which greatly improved the state-of-affairs of GE systems, its practical applications are still limited due to the rather complicated design, inefficiency and the weaker security (secure in the random oracle model). In return, the Libert et al.'s scheme possesses a solid security (secure in the standard model), but it lacks the previous functions and still suffers from inefficiency because of extremely using lattice trapdoors. In this work, we re-formalize the model and security definitions of fully dynamic group encryption (FDGE) that are essentially equivalent to but more succinct than Nguyen et al.'s; Then, we provide a generic and efficient zero-knowledge proof method for proving that a binary vector is *non-zero* over lattices, on which a proof for the Prohibitive message filtering policy in the lattice setting is first achieved (yet in a simple manner); Finally, by combining appropriate cryptographic materials and our presented zero-knowledge proofs, we achieve the first lattice-based FDGE scheme in a simpler manner, which needs no any lattice trapdoor and is proved secure in the standard model (assuming interaction during the proof phase), outweighing the existing post-quantum secure GE systems in terms of functions, efficiency and security.

Keywords: Lattice cryptography · Group encryption · Full dynamicity · Message filtering · Zero-knowledge

M. Tibouchi and H. Wang (Eds.): ASIACRYPT 2021, LNCS 13093, pp. 156–186, 2021.
https://doi.org/10.1007/978-3-030-92068-5_6

1 Introduction

Group encryption (GE), introduced by Kiayias, Tsiounis and Yung (KTY) [21] as the natural encryption analog of group signature (GS) that was first conceptualized by Chaum and van Heyst [16], is a fundamental anonymity primitive that allows anonymizing valid decryptors within a population of certified users. Since the pioneering work [21], GE has found a wide range of applications (see, e.g., [21,25,35]) in filtering malformed encrypted emails, building oblivious retriever storage systems, trusted third parties as well as hierarchical group signatures [42]. Because of the duality, these two primitives share some common design ideas in offering user memberships and generating anonymous signatures/ciphertexts.

In the design of these two anonymity primitives, to build a group of certified users is a key component. In general, there are three types of groups optional for GS: The simplest choice is the static group [6], in which the group population is fixed at the setup phase and the public/private key pairs of group members are assigned by the group manager (GM) as memberships; The partially dynamic group [7,22,40] is then introduced to support dynamic and concurrent user enrollments but deny membership revocation. In such a group, a prospective user generates a key pair on his own, and then becomes a valid group member only when his application for joining the group is accepted by the GM, who computes a signature on user's public key and returns it back as the membership. Despite an essential functionality, support for membership revocation is quite challenging to realize in an efficient manner, since it requires that the signing algorithm is disabled for revoked users and no significant increase for workloads of other parties (i.e., managers, non-revoked users and verifiers) is seen. To address this problem, several approaches [8,11,12,36] have been suggested, resulting into the fully dynamic groups [9], where membership revocation is additionally allowed.

Unlike the context of group signature, the GE always uses the partially dynamic group in its design since its first formalization [21] for security reasons. This type of group allows prospective users dynamically and concurrently to join the group, but any valid application for revoking membership is rejected, which is quite unsatisfactory in the realistic world. In fact, group signatures with full dynamicity have attracted much attention and have been constructed both on pairing assumptions [28,33] and lattice assumptions [31]. To change this situation, in PKC 2021, Nguyen et al. [35] first considered the full dynamicity in the context of group encryption and proposed a code-based instantiation secure in the random oracle model. In their design, they also first considered the message filtering policies which are quite useful for practical applications of GE systems. However, their formalization of FDGE is adapted directly from that of fully dynamic group signature [9] and hard to understand. Moreover, the construction is rather complicated and inefficient even in the random oracle model. Therefore, it is encouraging to design a group encryption that captures the full dynamicity, message filtering policy and a solid security in a relatively simple manner.

Our Contributions. Motivated by the above discussion, we reconsider the full dynamicity in the context of group encryption, and propose a lattice-based instantiation in a simpler manner that shares the same functions as the existing FDGE scheme [35] and meanwhile outweighs all available post-quantum secure schemes [25,35] in terms of functions, efficiency and security. Our contributions are summarized as follows:

- By introducing appropriate ingredients into the KTY model that supports dynamic user enrollments but denies membership revocations, we re-formalize the model and security requirements of FDGE that are essentially equal to but more succinct and understandable than the currently existing model.
- We provide a generic and efficient zero-knowledge proof method for demonstrating that some binary vector is *non-zero* over lattices, on which we first achieve a lattice-based proof (also generic and efficient) for Prohibitive message filtering policy. Both proofs will serve for our subsequent construction.
- By making use of appropriate cryptographic materials and the presented zero-knowledge proofs, we achieve the first lattice-based group encryption secure in the standard model and with full dynamicity in a free-of-trapdoor manner, which meets our formalized model and outweighs all existing post-quantum secure GE schemes in terms of functions and efficiency.

Related Work. The privacy-preserving cryptography has been an extremely active research area in the last decades. As one of the fundamental anonymity primitives, group encryption thus has attracted noticeable attention in recent years. The relevant concepts and definitions were first introduced by Kiayias, Tsiounis and Yung [21], who also then put forth a modular design consisting of zero-knowledge proofs, digital signatures (e.g., [13]) and anonymous CCA2-secure public-key encryptions (e.g., [37]). Later, Cathalo et al. [15] designed a non-interactive scheme in the standard model for the goal of optimizing the number of rounds. Similarly, over weaker assumptions, Aimani et al. [1] proposed more practical schemes by utilizing succinct approaches to protect the identity of group members. For sake of balancing better privacy vs. safety, Libert et al. [29] supposed a variant with public traceability to specific ciphertexts, which was inspired from traceable signatures [20]. Further, to strengthen secrecy, Izabachène et al. [19] constructed traceable variants that are free of subliminal channels, stressing confidentiality, anonymity and traceability. However, all these instantiations are proposed over number-theoretic assumptions and are vulnerable under quantum attacks. This situation has been unchanged until Libert et al. [25] proposed the currently only existing lattice-based scheme recently.

What should be noted out is that, all the group encryptions discussed above only offer partial dynamicity that allows concurrent user enrollments but denies membership revocations, which is quite unsatisfactory in the most realistic applications. To end this situation, more currently, Nguyen et al. [35] proposed a fully dynamic group encryption scheme secure in the random oracle from coding theory, where they also achieved the message filtering policies. However, their model is directly adapted from that of fully dynamic group signature [9] and is tedious. Moreover, the proposed scheme is rather complicated and inefficient together with provable security in the random oracle model. This motivates us to construct a fully dynamic group encryption, in a simple manner, that share practical functions similar to the scheme [35] while obtaining high efficiency and solid security (against quantum attacks).

Organization. In the forthcoming sections, we briefly recall the needed lattice techniques and cryptographic blocks in Sect. 2. The formalized model of FDGE is given in Sect. 3. Section 4 describes our new techniques used for demonstrating inequalities of binary vectors and the underlying zero-knowledge argument system. In Sect. 5, we describe our scheme that captures all desired properties, of which analysis is given. Finally, Sect. 6 concludes our work.

2 Preliminaries

Notations. For any positive integers $n \geq k$, we denote the set $\{1, ..., n\}$ by $[n]$, the set $\{k, ..., n\}$ by $[k, n]$. All vectors are written as bold lower-case letters in the column form, and matrices as bold upper-case letters. For $\mathbf{b} \in \mathbb{R}^n$ and $\mathbf{B} \in \mathbb{R}^{n \times m}$ with columns $(\mathbf{b}_i)_i$, their Euclidean l_2 norms are respectively written as $\|\mathbf{b}\|$ and $\|\mathbf{B}\| = \max_{i \leq m} \|\mathbf{b}_i\|$. If a given set S is finite, we let $U(S)$ to denote the uniform distribution over it and use $x \hookleftarrow D$ to represent the sampling action according to the distribution D. For two same-size binary vectors $\mathbf{x}$ and $\mathbf{y}$, we use $d_H(\mathbf{x}, \mathbf{y})$ to denote their Hamming distance, which is equal to l_1 norm $\|\mathbf{x} \oplus \mathbf{y}\|_1$.

2.1 Lattices and Computational Problems

As in [14,18], we use the notations L to denote lattices defined by $\Lambda_q^{\perp}(\mathbf{A}) := \{\mathbf{e} \in \mathbb{Z}^m | \ \mathbf{A} \cdot \mathbf{e} = \mathbf{0}^n \bmod q\}$ or $\Lambda_q^{\mathbf{u}}(\mathbf{A}) := \{\mathbf{e} \in \mathbb{Z}^m | \ \mathbf{A} \cdot \mathbf{e} = \mathbf{u} \bmod q\}$ w.l.o.g., where $\mathbf{A} \in \mathbb{Z}_q^{n \times m}$. Accordingly, use the notation $\mathcal{D}_{L,\sigma,\mathbf{c}}$ to denote the discrete Gaussian distributions of the support L, center $\mathbf{c} \in \mathbb{R}^m$ and parameter $\sigma > 0$, which is defined by $\mathcal{D}_{L,\sigma,\mathbf{c}}(\mathbf{x}) = \frac{\rho_{\sigma,\mathbf{c}}(\mathbf{x})}{\rho_{\sigma,\mathbf{c}}(L)}$ for each $\mathbf{x} \in L$ where $\rho_{\sigma,\mathbf{c}}(\mathbf{x}) = \exp(-\pi\|\mathbf{x} - \mathbf{c}\|^2/\sigma^2)$ is the Gaussian function over $\mathbb{R}^m$. When $\mathbf{c} = \mathbf{0}$, we also write the Gaussian distributions as $\mathcal{D}_{L,\sigma}$ for short. The following fact ensures that the outputs of the discrete Gaussian distribution are always short.

Lemma 1. ([3]) *Given any $L \subseteq \mathbb{R}^n$ and $\sigma > 0$, $\Pr_{\mathbf{b} \hookleftarrow D_{L,\sigma}}[\|\mathbf{b}\| \leq \sqrt{n}\sigma] \geq 1 - 2^{-\Omega(n)}$.*

For appropriate parameters, the syndrome $\mathbf{u} = \mathbf{A} \cdot \mathbf{e}$ with $\mathbf{A} \in \mathbb{Z}_q^{n \times m}$ and $\mathbf{e} \in \mathbb{Z}_q^m$ is nearly uniform over $\mathbb{Z}_q^n$.

Lemma 2. ([18]) *Given positive integers n, q with q prime, let $m \geq 2n \log q$ and $s \geq \omega(\sqrt{\log m})$. Then for any $\mathbf{A} \hookleftarrow U(\mathbb{Z}_q^{n \times m})$, the distribution of the syndrome $\mathbf{u} = \mathbf{A} \cdot \mathbf{e} \bmod q$ is within negligible distance to the uniform distribution over $\mathbb{Z}_q^n$, where $\mathbf{e} \hookleftarrow D_{\mathbb{Z}^m,s}$.*

The computational lattice problems and associated hardness claims used in this work are stated as follows.

Definition 1 (SIS). *Given appropriate positive integers* n, m, q, β, *the* $\mathsf{SIS}_{n,m,q,\beta}$ *problem is defined as: for any* $\mathbf{A} \hookleftarrow U(\mathbb{Z}_q^{n\times m})$, *search a non-zero vector* $\mathbf{x} \in \mathbb{Z}^m$ *such that* $\mathbf{A}\cdot\mathbf{x} = \mathbf{0}$ *and* $\|\boldsymbol{x}\| \le \beta$.

By choosing appropriate parameters, the standard worst-case lattice problem SIVP_γ can be reduced to the average-case $\mathsf{SIS}_{n,m,q,\beta}$ problem. Such an example is followed by setting $m, \beta = \mathsf{poly}(n)$; $q \ge \sqrt{n}\beta$ and $\gamma = \widetilde{\mathcal{O}}(\sqrt{n}\beta)$ (e.g., [2,18,32]).

Definition 2 (LWE). *Given appropriate positive integers* n, m, q, *and a probability distribution on* $\mathbb{Z}$ *denoted as* χ. *For secret* $\mathbf{s} \in \mathbb{Z}_q^n$, *define* $\mathbf{A}_{\mathbf{s},\chi}$ *as the distribution generated by sampling* $\mathbf{a} \hookleftarrow U(\mathbb{Z}_q^n)$ *and* $e \hookleftarrow \chi$, *and returning* $(\mathbf{a}, \mathbf{a}^{\mathrm{T}}\cdot \mathbf{s}{+}e) \in \mathbb{Z}_q^n \times \mathbb{Z}_q$. *The goal of* $\mathsf{LWE}_{n,q,\chi}$ *is to distinguish* m *samples from* $\mathbf{A}_{\mathbf{s},\chi}$ *and* m *samples from* $U(\mathbb{Z}_q^n \times \mathbb{Z}_q)$, *respectively.*

For prime power q, one can build a discrete integer distribution χ bounded by $B \ge \sqrt{n}\omega(\log n)$, for which there exists an efficient reduction from the $\mathsf{SIVP}_{\widetilde{\mathcal{O}}(nq/B)}$ problem to the $\mathsf{LWE}_{n,q,\chi}$ problem (e.g., [10,38,39]).

2.2 LNWX Lattice-Based Accumulators

The LNWX accumulator [31] is an updatable variant opposed to the static counterpart [26], and we will use it in our construction to achieve dynamic group users enrollments and membership revocations. The accumulator is built on a family of hash functions $\mathcal{H} = \{h_{\mathbf{A}} | \mathbf{A} \in \mathbb{Z}_q^{n\times m}\}$ with $\mathbf{A} = [\mathbf{A}_0|\mathbf{A}_1] \in \mathbb{Z}_q^{n\times m}$ which hash $(\mathbf{u}_0, \mathbf{u}_1) \in (\{0,1\}^{nk})^2$ into $h_{\mathbf{A}}(\mathbf{u}_0, \mathbf{u}_1) = \mathsf{bin}(\mathbf{A}_0\cdot\mathbf{u}_0 + \mathbf{A}_1\cdot\mathbf{u}_1 \bmod q) \in \{0,1\}^{nk}$. Its security is ensured by the hardness of the SIS problem.

Informally, as in [4,12,36], the accumulator is defined by the algorithms $(\mathsf{TSetup}, \mathsf{TAcc}, \mathsf{TWitness}, \mathsf{TVerify}, \mathsf{TUpdate})$. Namely, for a Merkle-tree with $N = 2^\ell$ leaves, algorithm TSetup takes a random $\mathbf{A} \in \mathbb{Z}_q^{n\times m}$ to form a hash function $h_{\mathbf{A}}$; Algorithm TAcc accumulates all values $R = \{\mathbf{d}_0, ..., \mathbf{d}_{N-1}\}$ of each length nk on leaves into the root $\mathbf{u}$ via the recursive computations shown as $\mathbf{u}_{b_1,...,b_i} = h_{\mathbf{A}}(\mathbf{u}_{b_1,...,b_i,0}, \mathbf{u}_{b_1,...,b_i,1})$ for any node at depth $i \in [\ell]$ and $\mathbf{u} = h_{\mathbf{A}}(\mathbf{u}_0, \mathbf{u}_1)$, where $(b_1, ..., b_i) \in \{0,1\}^i$; Algorithm $\mathsf{TWitness}$ returns $\perp$ if $\mathbf{d} \notin R$, otherwise computes the witness $w = \big((j_1, ..., j_\ell), (\mathbf{u}_{j_1,...,j_{\ell-1},\bar{j}_\ell}, ..., \mathbf{u}_{j_1,\bar{j}_2}, \mathbf{u}_{\bar{j}_1})\big) \in \{0,1\}^\ell \times \big(\{0,1\}^{nk}\big)^\ell$ demonstrating that $\mathbf{d} = \mathbf{d}_j \in R$ for some $j \in [0, N-1]$ with $\mathsf{bin}(j) = (j_1, ..., j_\ell)$, where $\bar{b}$ denotes the bit $1 - b$ for a chosen bit b; Then, given a witness $w = \big((j_1, ..., j_\ell), (\mathbf{w}_\ell, ..., \mathbf{w}_1)\big) \in \{0,1\}^\ell \times \big(\{0,1\}^{nk}\big)^\ell$, and set $\mathbf{v}_\ell = \mathbf{d}$, algorithm $\mathsf{TVerify}$ computes the path $\mathbf{v}_{\ell-1}, ..., \mathbf{v}_0 \in \{0,1\}^{nk}$ via the recursive formula $\mathbf{v}_i = \bar{j}_{i+1}\cdot h_{\mathbf{A}}(\mathbf{v}_{i+1}, \mathbf{w}_{i+1}) + j_{i+1}\cdot h_{\mathbf{A}}(\mathbf{w}_{i+1}, \mathbf{v}_{i+1})$ for any $j \in [0, N-1]$ and $i \in [\ell - 1]$ with initial setting $\mathbf{u} = \mathbf{v}_0$; Finally, when a value at position j is replaced by $\mathbf{p}$, algorithm $\mathsf{TUpdate}(\mathsf{bin}(j), \mathbf{p})$ efficiently updates the accumulator by simply updating the hash values of nodes on path from the specific leaf to the root, then the algorithm $\mathsf{TWitness}$ outputs the updated paths and maintains other values unchanged.

2.3 GPV Dual Encryption

The GPV encryption presented in [18] features the public-key anonymity and is efficient because of being free of lattice trapdoors. We now recall a variant that would be used in our construction. Choose positive integers n and $q \geq 2$ and set $k = \lfloor \log q \rfloor$ and $m = 2nk$. Select a random public matrix $\mathbf{A} \in \mathbb{Z}_q^{n \times m}$. Given a Gaussian parameter σ, a Gaussian distribution $D_{\mathbb{Z}^m,\sigma}$ and an error distribution χ^m, one samples a short matrix $\mathbf{E}$ from $D_{\mathbb{Z}^m,\sigma}^m$ as the secret key sk, and computes a corresponding public matrix $\mathbf{U} = \mathbf{A} \cdot \mathbf{E} \in \mathbb{Z}_q^{n \times m}$ as the public key pk. To encrypt a message $\mathbf{m} \in \{0,1\}^m$, one samples a random vector $\mathbf{s} \hookleftarrow U(\{0,1\}^n)$ and two random vectors $\mathbf{x}, \mathbf{y} \hookleftarrow \chi^m$ to compute the ciphertext $\mathbf{c} = (\mathbf{c}_1, \mathbf{c}_2)$ as: $\mathbf{c}_1 = \mathbf{A}^\top \cdot \mathbf{s} + \mathbf{x}, \mathbf{c}_2 = \mathbf{U}^\top \cdot \mathbf{s} + \mathbf{y} + \mathbf{m} \cdot \lfloor \frac{q}{2} \rceil$. When the decryptor wants to recover the message $\mathbf{m}$, he uses the preserved key $\mathsf{sk} = \mathbf{E}$ to compute $\lfloor (\mathbf{c}_2 - \mathbf{E}^\top \cdot \mathbf{c}_1)/\frac{q}{2} \rceil$.

2.4 Zero-Knowledge Argument of Knowledge

A zero-knowledge argument system of knowledge (ZKAoK) is a two-party interactive protocol, where a prover $\mathcal{P}$ triggers a proof to convince the verifier $\mathcal{V}$ that he knows a witness of the specific statement while not revealing any additional information. More formally, given an NP relation defined by a set of statements-witnesses $R = \{(y, w)\} \in \{0,1\}^* \times \{0,1\}^*$, the associated ZKAoK is defined via an interactive game $\langle \mathcal{P}, \mathcal{V} \rangle$ with completeness δ_c and soundness error δ_s as:

- Completeness. For any given $(y, w) \in R$, $\Pr[\langle \mathcal{P}(y, w), \mathcal{V}(y) \rangle \neq 1] \leq \delta_c$.
- Soundness. Given any $(y, w) \notin R, \forall$ PPT $\widehat{\mathcal{P}}$: $\Pr[\langle \widehat{\mathcal{P}}(y, w), \mathcal{V}(y) \rangle = 1] \leq \delta_s$.

In the lattice setting, the Stern-like argument system [41] is a generic framework with statistical ZK property and soundness 2/3, and has been widely applied in the constructions of advanced cryptographic schemes [23,25,26,30]. Its key idea is to use "decomposition-extension-permutation" techniques to transform the targeted NP relations into those suitable for the framework, which in general increases double to four times communication cost and makes the system quite inefficient in practice together with soundness 2/3. In this work, we use a currently presented framework referred as Yang et al.'s argument system [43] which uses novel techniques to capture the computational ZK property and an inverse polynomial soundness. Let us recall it below.

The Abstraction of the Argument System. The desired ZKAoK system provided in Sect. 4 is covered within the following abstraction:

$$R = \{(\mathbf{M}, \mathbf{y}), (\mathbf{x}) : \mathbf{M} \cdot \mathbf{x} = \mathbf{y} \wedge \mathbf{x} \in \mathsf{cond}\}, \tag{1}$$

where $\mathbf{M}, \mathbf{y}$ are the public matrix and vector, respectively, and the vector $\mathbf{x}$ is the secret witness, additionally cond represents the set of conditions that $\mathbf{x}$ should satisfy, which covers all possible constraints such as short vectors, quadratic relations. Actually, the set cond is always equally represented by a set $\mathcal{M} = \{(h, i, j)\}$ consisting of index tuples of $\mathbf{x}$ that satisfy the relation $\mathbf{x}[h] = \mathbf{x}[i] \cdot \mathbf{x}[j]$.

3 Model and Security Requirements of Fully Dynamic Group Encryption

In this section, by introducing a time factor and a group updating algorithm into the KTY model [21], also taking less oracles than that of [35], we provide the formalized model and security definitions of the fully dynamic group encryption (FDGE) primitive, which are appropriately upgraded and modified from the KTY model [21] that is only suitable for partially dynamic groups.

Like the KTY model [21], the FDGE also involves several parties: a group manager (GM) that managers a group of users, an opening authority (OA) that is empowered to revoke the anonymity of recipients should the misbehavior arise, and a set of prospective users as well as a sender producing well-formed ciphertexts for certified group members. In the forthcoming model, users join/leave the group under the permission of GM who can regularly edit and publish authentic group information info_τ at growing epoch τ, thereby anyone can learn the knowledge about changes of the group including, current/excluded group members. Additionally, by comparing two group information info_{τ_1} and info_{τ_2} under the convention that $\tau_1 < \tau_2$ if info_{τ_1} is published before info_{τ_2}, one can even identify revoked users at the recent epoch. The formalized fully dynamic group encryption is defined via the following tuple of algorithms:

- $\mathsf{SETUP}(\lambda)$: This algorithm consists of three procedures and generates group public key $\mathsf{gpk} = (\mathsf{pp}, \mathsf{pk}_{\mathsf{GM}}, \mathsf{pk}_{\mathsf{OA}})$ as follows:
  - $\mathsf{SETUP}_{\mathsf{init}}(1^\lambda)$: On input the security parameter λ, output public parameters pp.
  - $\mathsf{SETUP}_{\mathsf{GM}}(\mathsf{pp})$: Given pp, output the GM's key pair $(\mathsf{pk}_{\mathsf{GM}}, \mathsf{sk}_{\mathsf{GM}})$.
  - $\mathsf{SETUP}_{\mathsf{OA}}(\mathsf{pp})$: Given pp, output a key pair $(\mathsf{pk}_{\mathsf{OA}}, \mathsf{sk}_{\mathsf{OA}})$ for the OA.

  An interaction occurs between the GM and the OA, successfully creating group public key gpk at its end, while the GM initializes the group information info and the registration table **reg**.
- $\mathsf{UKGEN}(\mathsf{pp})$: On input pp, this algorithm produces a user key pair $(\mathsf{pk}_{\mathsf{U}}, \mathsf{sk}_{\mathsf{U}})$.
- $\langle \mathsf{JOIN}(\mathsf{sk}_{\mathsf{U}}), \mathsf{ISSUE}(\mathsf{sk}_{\mathsf{GM}})\rangle(\mathsf{info}_\tau, \mathsf{gpk}, \mathsf{pk}_{\mathsf{U}})$: This is an interaction run by the GM and a prospective user at epoch τ, whose successful completion enrolls a new group member with an identifier uid and makes the algorithm JOIN and algorithm ISSUE store group member secret key $\mathsf{sk}[\mathsf{uid}]$ and public key certificate $\mathsf{cert}_{\mathsf{pk}_{\mathsf{U}}}$ in the table **reg** with same index, respectively.
- $\mathsf{GUPDATE}(\mathsf{gpk}, \mathsf{sk}_{\mathsf{GM}}, \mathsf{info}_{\tau_{\mathrm{current}}}, \mathcal{S}, \mathbf{reg})$: Given $\mathsf{gpk}, \mathsf{sk}_{\mathsf{GM}}, \mathsf{info}_{\tau_{\mathrm{current}}}$, table **reg**, a set $\mathcal{S}$ of active users to be removed, GM runs this algorithm to generate new group information $\mathsf{info}_{\tau_{\mathrm{current}}+1}$ and update the table **reg**, while advancing the epoch and outputting $\perp$ if there is no change to the group.
- $\langle \mathcal{G}_r, \mathcal{R}, \mathsf{sample}_{\mathcal{R}}\rangle(\mathsf{pp})$: Given pp, procedure $\mathsf{sample}_{\mathcal{R}}$ samples a statement-witness pair $(x, w) \in \mathcal{R}$ by using the key pair $(\mathsf{pk}_{\mathcal{R}}, \mathsf{sk}_{\mathcal{R}})$ itself produced by procedure $\mathcal{G}_r$, where $\mathsf{sk}_{\mathcal{R}}$ may be empty in the most of real realizations.

- $\mathsf{ENC}(\mathsf{gpk}, \mathsf{pk_U}, \mathsf{cert_U}, \mathsf{info}_\tau, x, w, L)$: This algorithm is executed by sender to compute a group encryption Ψ on witness w with a label L under some public key $\mathsf{pk_U}$. It returns $\perp$ if the target group user is inactive at epoch τ.
- $\mathsf{DEC}(\mathsf{sk_U}, \Psi, L)$: The target receiver decrypts the ciphertext Ψ via this algorithm.
- $\mathsf{OPEN}(\mathsf{sk_{OA}}, \mathsf{info}_\tau, \mathbf{reg}, \Psi, L)$: This algorithm is run by OA to return an identity uid of a group member who has secret information to decrypt the ciphertext together with a proof π attributing Ψ to user uid or to return $(\perp, \pi)$ if it fails to trace the receiver.
- $\langle \mathcal{P}(\mathsf{pk_U}, \mathsf{cert_U}, w, coins_\Psi), \mathcal{V}(\pi_\Psi)\rangle(\mathsf{gpk}, \mathsf{info}_\tau, x, \Psi, L)$: This is an interactive procedure run between sender and verifier which, given inputs, convinces verifier that the ciphertext Ψ is well-formed and is actually generated for one of active group members at epoch τ.

  For security requirements, as in [21], the FDGE scheme considers *correctness*, *message secrecy*, *anonymity* and *soundness*, whose definitions are given via corresponding experiments below, respectively.

Correctness asks that a ciphertext generated by a genuine sender is always decrypted successfully by algorithm DEC, and that procedure OPEN can always identify the receiver, as well as produces a proof that can be accepted by verifier.

Definition 3. *The correctness is satisfied if the following experiment returns* 1 *with negligible probability.*

<u>Experiment $\mathbf{Exp}^{\mathsf{corr}}(\lambda)$</u>

$\mathsf{pp} \leftarrow \mathsf{SETUP_{init}}(1^\lambda)$; $(\mathsf{pk}_\mathcal{R}, \mathsf{sk}_\mathcal{R}) \leftarrow \mathcal{G}_\mathcal{R}(1^\lambda)$; $(x, w) \leftarrow \mathsf{sample}_\mathcal{R}(\mathsf{pk}_\mathcal{R}, \mathsf{sk}_\mathcal{R})$;
$(\mathsf{pk_{GM}}, \mathsf{sk_{GM}}) \leftarrow \mathsf{SETUP_{GM}}(\mathsf{pp})$; $(\mathsf{pk_{OA}}, \mathsf{sk_{OA}}) \leftarrow \mathsf{SETUP_{OA}}(\mathsf{pp})$;
$\langle \mathsf{pk}, \mathsf{sk}, \mathsf{cert_{pk}} | \mathsf{uid}, \mathsf{pk}, \mathsf{cert_{pk}}, \mathsf{info}_\tau\rangle \leftarrow \langle \mathsf{J_{user}}, \mathsf{J_{GM}}(\mathsf{sk_{GM}})\rangle(\mathsf{pk_{GM}}, \mathsf{info}_\tau)$;
if $\mathsf{IsActive}(\mathsf{info}_\tau, \mathbf{reg}, \mathsf{uid}) = 0$, return 0.
$\Psi \leftarrow \mathsf{ENC}(\mathsf{pk_{GM}}, \mathsf{pk_{OA}}, \mathsf{pk}, \mathsf{cert_{pk}}, \mathsf{info}_\tau, w, L)$;
$\pi_\Psi \leftarrow \mathcal{P}(\mathsf{pk_{GM}}, \mathsf{pk_{OA}}, \mathsf{pk}, \mathsf{cert_{pk}}, \mathsf{info}_\tau, x, w, \Psi, L, coins_\Psi)$.
if $\big((w \neq \mathsf{DEC}(\mathsf{sk}, \Psi, L)) \vee (\mathsf{pk} \neq \mathsf{OPEN}(\mathsf{sk_{OA}}, \mathsf{info}_\tau, \mathbf{reg}, \Psi, L))$
$\quad \vee (\mathcal{V}(\mathsf{pk_{GM}}, \mathsf{pk_{OA}}, \mathsf{info}_\tau, x, \Psi, L, \pi_\Psi) = 0)\big)$ then return 0 else return 1.

Message Secrecy demands that it is difficult for any PPT adversary to distinguish a ciphertext generated by a random plaintext from a one done by a specific relation pair, even if the adversary can corrupt all parties except the honest receiver via accessing to the following stateful and stateless oracles:

- $\mathsf{DEC}(\mathsf{sk}, \cdot)$: is a stateless decryption oracle with a restriction not to decrypt a ciphertext-label pair (Ψ, L) termed as $\mathsf{DEC}^{\neg\langle\Psi, L\rangle}$.
- $\mathsf{CH}^b_{\mathsf{ror}}(\lambda, \mathsf{pk}, \tau, w, L)$: is a one-time oracle used for generating real-or-random challenge ciphertexts according to the choice of coin b at epoch τ. It returns $(\Psi, coins_\Psi)$ with $\Psi \leftarrow \mathsf{ENC}(\mathsf{pk_{GM}}, \mathsf{pk_{OA}}, \mathsf{pk}, \mathsf{cert_{pk}}, \mathsf{info}_\tau, w, L)$ if $b = 1$. Otherwise, return $(\Psi, coins_\Psi)$ with $\Psi \leftarrow \mathsf{ENC}(\mathsf{pk_{GM}}, \mathsf{pk_{OA}}, \mathsf{pk}, \mathsf{cert_{pk}}, \mathsf{info}_\tau, w', L)$ where w' is a uniformly random plaintext of length $\mathcal{O}(\lambda)$ sampled in the plaintext space, and $coins_\Psi$ represents the random coins used to compute Ψ.

- $\mathsf{PROVE}^b_{\mathcal{P},\mathcal{P}'}(\mathsf{pk_{GM}},\mathsf{pk_{OA}},\mathsf{pk},\mathsf{cert_{pk}},\mathsf{info}_\tau,x,w,\Psi,L,coins_\Psi)$: is a stateful oracle that generates an actual proof π_Ψ or a simulated proof π'_Ψ for epoch τ by running the real prover $\mathcal{P}$ when $b=1$ and running the simulator $\mathcal{P}'$ else wise. It can be invoked a polynomial number times.

The usage of these oracles describes a experiment where the whole system is under the control of adversary except the member chosen as recipient. It shows the advantage of the adversary in mounting the attack against message secrecy.

Definition 4. *The message secrecy is achieved if, for any* PPT *adversary, the absolute difference of probability of outputting* 1 *between the following experiments* $\mathbf{Exp}^{\mathsf{sec}-1}_{\mathcal{A}}(\lambda)$ *and* $\mathbf{Exp}^{\mathsf{sec}-0}_{\mathcal{A}}(\lambda)$ *is negligible.*

Experiment $\mathbf{Exp}^{\mathsf{sec}-b}_{\mathcal{A}}(\lambda)$

$\mathsf{pp} \leftarrow \mathsf{SETUP_{init}}(1^\lambda)$; $(\mathsf{aux},\mathsf{pk_{GM}},\mathsf{pk_{OA}}) \leftarrow \mathcal{A}(\mathsf{pp})$;
$\langle \mathsf{pk},\mathsf{sk},\mathsf{cert_{pk}}|\mathsf{info}_\tau,\mathsf{aux}\rangle \leftarrow \langle \mathsf{J_{user}},\mathcal{A}(\mathsf{aux})\rangle(\mathsf{pk_{GM}},\mathsf{info}_\tau)$;
$(\mathsf{aux},x,w,L,\mathsf{pk}_\mathcal{R}) \leftarrow \mathcal{A}^{\mathsf{DEC}(\mathsf{sk},\cdot)}(\mathsf{aux})$; if $(x,w)\notin\mathcal{R}$ then return 0;
$b \hookleftarrow \{0,1\}$; $(\Psi,coins_\Psi) \leftarrow \mathsf{CH}^b_{\mathsf{ror}}(\lambda,\mathsf{pk},\tau,w,L)$;
$b' \leftarrow \mathcal{A}^{\mathsf{PROVE}^b_{\mathcal{P},\mathcal{P}'}(\mathsf{pk_{GM}},\mathsf{pk_{OA}},\mathsf{pk},\mathsf{cert_{pk}},\mathsf{info}_\tau,x,w,\Psi,L,coins_\Psi),\mathsf{DEC}^{\neg\langle\Psi,L\rangle}(\mathsf{sk},\cdot)}(\mathsf{aux},\Psi)$;
Return b'.

Anonymity requires that it is infeasible for any PPT adversary to distinguish ciphertexts computed under two valid public keys of its choice, even if it controls the entire system except the OA and two well-behaved users via accessing the following oracles:

- $\mathsf{CH}^b_{\mathsf{anon}}(\mathsf{pk_{GM}},\mathsf{pk_{OA}},\mathsf{pk}_0,\mathsf{pk}_1,\mathsf{info}_\tau,w,L)$: is a challenge oracle that returns a pair $(\Psi,coins_\Psi)$ consisting of a ciphertext $\Psi \leftarrow \mathsf{ENC}(\mathsf{pk_{GM}},\mathsf{pk_{OA}},\mathsf{pk}_b,\mathsf{cert}_{\mathsf{pk}_b},\mathsf{info}_\tau,w,L)$ and the coin tosses $coins_\Psi$ used for generating Ψ when a plaintext w and two possible public keys $\mathsf{pk}_0,\mathsf{pk}_1$ are given.
- $\mathsf{USER}(\mathsf{pk_{GM}},\tau)$: is a stateful oracle that simulates two instantiations of $\mathsf{J_{user}}$ via valid certificates $\{\mathsf{cert}_{\mathsf{pk}_b}\}^1_{b=0}$ supplied by adversarial GM in string keys at epoch τ, where honest outputs termed as $\{(\mathsf{pk}_b,\mathsf{sk}_b,\mathsf{cert}_{\mathsf{pk}_b})\}^1_{b=0}$ are stored.
- $\mathsf{OPEN}(\mathsf{sk_{OA}},\mathsf{info}_\tau,\mathbf{reg},\cdot)$: is a stateless oracle that executes opening operation on behalf of OA for the received ciphertext and reveals the identity of the receiver.

These above oracles can be used in a experiment that models the anonymity property, which reveals the advantage of adversary in this attack game.

Definition 5. *The* FDGE *scheme satisfies anonymity if, for any* PPT *adversary, the absolute difference of probability of outputting* 1 *between the following experiments* $\mathbf{Exp}^{\mathsf{anon}-1}_{\mathcal{A}}(\lambda)$ *and* $\mathbf{Exp}^{\mathsf{anon}-0}_{\mathcal{A}}(\lambda)$ *is negligible.*

Experiment $\mathbf{Exp}^{\mathsf{anon}-b}_{\mathcal{A}}(\lambda)$

$\mathsf{pp} \leftarrow \mathsf{SETUP_{init}}(1^\lambda)$; $(\mathsf{pk_{OA}},\mathsf{sk_{OA}}) \leftarrow \mathsf{SETUP_{OA}}(\mathsf{pp})$;
$(\mathsf{aux},\mathsf{pk_{GM}}) \leftarrow \mathcal{A}(\mathsf{pp},\mathsf{pk_{OA}})$; $\mathsf{aux} \leftarrow \mathcal{A}^{\mathsf{USER}(\mathsf{pk_{GM}},\tau),\mathsf{OPEN}(\mathsf{sk_{OA}},\mathsf{info}_\tau,\mathbf{reg},\cdot)}(\mathsf{aux})$;

if keys $\neq (\mathsf{pk}_0, \mathsf{sk}_0, \mathsf{cert}_{\mathsf{pk}_0}, \mathsf{pk}_1, \mathsf{sk}_1, \mathsf{cert}_{\mathsf{pk}_1}, \mathsf{info}_{\mathcal{T}})$ (aux) then return 0;
$(\mathsf{aux}, x, w, L, \mathsf{pk}_{\mathcal{R}}) \leftarrow \mathcal{A}^{\mathsf{OPEN}(\mathsf{sk}_{\mathsf{OA}}, \mathsf{info}_{\mathcal{T}}, \tau, \cdot), \mathsf{DEC}(\mathsf{sk}_0, \cdot), \mathsf{DEC}(\mathsf{sk}_1, \cdot)}(\mathsf{aux})$;
if $(x, w) \notin \mathcal{R}$ return 0; $b \hookleftarrow \{0,1\}$; $(\Psi, coins_\Psi) \leftarrow \mathsf{CH}^b_{\mathsf{anon}}(\mathsf{pk}_{\mathsf{GM}}, \mathsf{pk}_{\mathsf{OA}}, \mathsf{pk}_0, \mathsf{pk}_1, \mathsf{info}_{\mathcal{T}}, w, L)$;
$b' \leftarrow \mathcal{A}^{\mathcal{P}(\mathsf{pk}_{\mathsf{GM}}, \mathsf{pk}_{\mathsf{OA}}, \mathsf{pk}_b, \mathsf{cert}_{\mathsf{pk}_b}, \mathsf{info}_{\mathcal{T}}, x, w, \Psi, L, coins_\Psi), \mathsf{OPEN}^{\neg\langle\Psi,L\rangle}(\mathsf{sk}_{\mathsf{OA}}, \mathsf{info}_{\mathcal{T}}, \mathbf{reg}, \cdot), \mathsf{DEC}^{\neg\langle\Psi,L\rangle}(\mathsf{sk}_0, \cdot), \mathsf{DEC}^{\neg\langle\Psi,L\rangle}(\mathsf{sk}_1, \cdot)}(\mathsf{aux}, \Psi)$. Return b'.

Soundness requires that it is infeasible for any PPT adversary to produce a convincing valid ciphertext that opens to unregistered group member or invalid public key, even if it can choose OA's key, and is given access to the REG oracle. In the following, database, $\mathcal{PK}$ and $\mathcal{C}$ are respectively used to represent the sets of registered public keys, valid keys and valid ciphertexts.

Definition 6. *An* FDGE *scheme is sound if, for any* PPT *adversary, the experiment below returns* 1 *with negligible probability.* Experiment $\mathbf{Exp}^{\mathsf{sound}}_{\mathcal{A}}(\lambda)$

$\mathsf{pp} \leftarrow \mathsf{SETUP}_{\mathsf{init}}(1^\lambda)$; $(\mathsf{pk}_{\mathsf{OA}}, \mathsf{sk}_{\mathsf{OA}}) \leftarrow \mathsf{SETUP}_{\mathsf{OA}}(\mathsf{pp})$;
$(\mathsf{pk}_{\mathsf{GM}}, \mathsf{sk}_{\mathsf{GM}}) \leftarrow \mathsf{SETUP}_{\mathsf{GM}}(\mathsf{pp})$;
$(\mathsf{pk}_{\mathcal{R}}, x, \Psi, \pi_\Psi, \mathsf{pk}_{\mathsf{GM}}, \mathsf{aux}, \mathsf{info}_{\mathcal{T}}) \leftarrow \mathcal{A}^{\mathsf{REG}(\mathsf{sk}_{\mathsf{GM}}, \cdot)}(\mathsf{pp}, \mathsf{pk}_{\mathsf{GM}}, \mathsf{pk}_{\mathsf{OA}}, \mathsf{sk}_{\mathsf{OA}}, \mathsf{info}_{\mathcal{T}})$;
if $\mathcal{V}(\Psi, L, \pi_\Psi, \mathsf{pk}_{\mathsf{GM}}, \mathsf{pk}_{\mathsf{OA}}, \mathsf{info}_{\mathcal{T}}) = 0$ return 0;
$\mathsf{pk} \leftarrow \mathsf{OPEN}(\mathsf{sk}_{\mathsf{OA}}, \mathsf{info}_{\mathcal{T}}, \mathbf{reg}, \Psi, L)$; if($(\mathsf{pk} \notin \mathsf{database}) \vee (\mathsf{pk} \notin \mathcal{PK}) \vee (\Psi \notin \mathcal{C}^{x, L, \mathsf{pk}_{\mathcal{R}}, \mathsf{pk}_{\mathsf{GM}}, \mathsf{pk}_{\mathsf{OA}}, \mathsf{pk}})$) then return 1 else return 0.

To meet the above security requirement that pk must belong to the language of valid public keys, we use the Gaussian short vectors as shown in Sect. 5.1 to generate dense space for public keys, which simplifies our definitions.

4 The Underlying Zero-Knowledge Layer

In this section, we first introduce the needed decomposition techniques in Sect. 4.1. Then, we provide two generic and efficient zero-knowledge proofs for inequality relations of binary vectors (one is for *non-zero* binary vectors, and the other is for Hamming distance) that can work well in any lattice-based ZK framework and serve for our argument system. Finally, based on the techniques prepared in previous sections, we establish the argument system in Sect. 4.3 in the Yang et al.'s framework [43] recalled in Sect. 2.4. The argument system obtains great efficiency gains compared to that run in the Stern-type framework [41] since our system avoids using the "decomposition-extension-permutation" techniques (which at least increases the witness size double to four times) and also avoids repeating the protocol hundreds times (which incurs a drastic increase in communication cost) towards a negligible soundness as in [41].

4.1 Warm-Up: Decompositions

We briefly recall several decomposition techniques from [24,30] that would be used in constructing our argument system. We start with the integer decomposition function, i.e., for any non-negative integer i, let $\delta_i = \lceil \log(i+1) \rceil$, define

$\mathsf{bin}(i) = (i^{(1)}, ..., i^{(\delta_i)})^\top \in \{0,1\}^{\delta_i}$ and $\mathbf{g}_{\delta_i} = (1, 2, ..., 2^{\delta_i - 1})$, then it follows that $i = \sum_{j=1}^{\delta_i} 2^{j-1} \cdot i^{(j)} = \mathbf{g}_{\delta_i} \cdot \mathsf{bin}(i)$.

To decompose any integer $i \in [0, \beta]$ for a positive integer β, set $\delta_\beta := \lceil \log_2(\beta+1) \rceil$ and compute an integer sequence $\{\beta_1, ..., \beta_{\delta_\beta}\}$ via $\beta_j = \lfloor \frac{\beta + 2^{j-1}}{2^j} \rfloor, \forall j \in [1, \delta_\beta]$. Then, we have $i = \sum_{j=1}^{\delta_\beta} \beta_j \cdot i^{(j)} = \mathbf{g}'_{\delta_\beta} \cdot \mathsf{bin}'(\beta)$, where $\mathbf{g}'_{\delta_\beta} = (\beta_1, ..., \beta_{\delta_\beta})$ and $\mathsf{bin}'_\beta(i) = (i^{(1)}, ..., i^{(\delta_\beta)}) \in \{0,1\}^{\delta_\beta}$ which is a binary tuple computed in an interactive manner. This defines an integer decomposition function as $\mathsf{idec}_\beta(i) = (i^{(1)}, ..., i^{(\delta_\beta)})^\top \in \{0,1\}^{\delta_\beta}$ for any integer $i \in [0, \beta]$. Combining with $\mathbf{H}_{\mathsf{m},\beta} = \mathbf{I}_\mathsf{m} \otimes \mathbf{g}'_{\delta_\beta}$, we can similarly define decomposition functions for vectors and matrices (see, [25,26]):

- $\mathsf{vdec}_{\mathsf{m},\beta} : [0,\beta]^\mathsf{m} \to \{0,1\}^{\mathsf{m}\delta_\beta}$ maps any β-bounded non-negative vector $\mathbf{v} = (v_1, ..., v_\mathsf{m})^\top$ to $(\mathsf{idec}_\beta(v_1)^\top \| \ ... \ \| \mathsf{idec}_\beta(v_\mathsf{m})^\top)^\top$ by applying $\mathsf{idec}_\beta(\cdot)$ to each entry of $\mathbf{v}$, which holds that $\mathbf{H}_{\mathsf{m},\beta} \cdot \mathsf{vdec}_{\mathsf{m},\beta}(\mathbf{v}) = \mathbf{v}$.
- $\mathsf{mdec}_{n,m,q} : \mathbb{Z}_q^{m \times n} \to \{0,1\}^{nm\delta_{q-1}}$ maps a matrix $\mathbf{X} = [\mathbf{x}_1 | \ ... \ | \mathbf{x}_n] \in \mathbb{Z}_q^{m \times n}$ to the size-$nm\delta_{q-1}$ binary vector $(\mathsf{vedc}_{m,q-1}(\mathbf{x}_1)^\top \| \ ... \ \| \mathsf{vedc}_{m,q-1}(\mathbf{x}_n)^\top)^\top$ by imposing $\mathsf{vdec}_{m,q-1}(\cdot)$ on the each column of $\mathbf{X}$ and concatenating the obtained binary vectors in the increasing order of the indexes of columns.

We note that, hereunder this section, when needing to decompose a bounded-β vector $\mathbf{v} \in [-\beta, \beta]^\mathsf{m}$, we will first lift it to $\mathbf{v} + \boldsymbol{\beta} \in [0, 2\beta]^\mathsf{m}$, then perform $\mathsf{vdec}_{\mathsf{m},2\beta}(\cdot)$ on the transformed vector where $\boldsymbol{\beta} = (\beta, ..., \beta)$ consists of m's β, with taking appropriate modifications for the involved matrices and vectors. This transformation-and-decomposition strategy will be quite useful for the construction of our ZK argument system.

4.2 Proving Inequality Relations for Binary Vectors

In this section, we first provide a ZK proof for demonstrating a binary vector $\mathbf{p}$ is *non-zero* (used to demonstrate a group user is activated) that can efficiently work well in any lattice-based ZK framework, on which we construct a ZK proof for the Prohibitive message filtering policy (used to demonstrate the validity of the encrypted witness) which is achieved over lattices at the first time and is generic and efficient. Startlingly, our proof methods can be extended to prove inequalities of general vectors, thus it is independent of interest.

Proving Binary Vectors $\mathbf{p} \neq \mathbf{0}$. Let n, q be positive integers with $n < q$ and $\mathbf{p} \in \{0,1\}^n$, our aim is to prove the secret $\mathbf{p} \neq \mathbf{0}$ in the Yang et al.'s framework [43]. Actually, this problem has been solved in the Stern-like framework [31] in spite of inefficiency and worse usability (i.e., it can not work in the Yang et al.'s framework [43]), where the system was established by appending $n-1$ "dummy" entries to extend the targeted vector $\mathbf{p} \in \{0,1\}^n$ to $\mathbf{p}' \in \{0,1\}^{2n-1}$ of Hamming weight n exactly and running the Stern-like protocol. To handle the task in the Yang et al.'s framework [43], one may find a possible solution in [27] where numerous lattice-based range arguments were developed to prove private integer relations such as $X \in [\alpha, \beta]$ for public integers $\alpha, \beta \geq 0$. But the techniques used there are invalid in proving that one knows at least a private X_j among a given set $\{X_1, ..., X_n\}$ each of which is bounded by $[\alpha_i, \beta_i]$ with $i \in [n]$ satisfies that $\alpha_j < X_j \leq \beta_j$, which essentially generalizes our problem when setting $\mathbf{p} = (X_1, ..., X_n)^\top$ and $\alpha_i = 0$ and $\beta_i = 1$ for all $i \in [n]$. We now develop new techniques to address this problem.

An important observation is that, the task to prove $\mathbf{p} \neq \mathbf{0}$ is equivalent to that proving that there is at least an entry of $\mathbf{p}$ is > 0. To end this, intuitively, it suffices to prove the $\mathbf{p}$'s Hamming weight is ≥ 1. In the following, we provide two efficient solutions, where the first is somewhat tedious, and then second is succinct and will be applied in the construction of our argument system.

Let $\mathbf{J}_n = (1, ..., 1)^\top \in \mathbb{Z}_q^n$ of which all entries are 1's. Suppose that the Hamming weight of binary vector $\mathbf{p}$ is ≥ 1, then we can establish our argument system by proving that one knows a complementary binary vector $\mathbf{q} \in \{0,1\}^n$ with Hamming weight $\leq n-1$ such that $\mathbf{p} + \mathbf{q} = \mathbf{J}_n \bmod q$. The inequality can be solved by decomposing $\mathbf{J}_n^\top \cdot \mathbf{q}$ via the vector $\mathbf{g}'_{\delta_\beta}$ with setting $\beta = n-1$ as in Sect. 4.1. Then, it suffices for a prover to prove that he knows private vectors $\mathbf{p}, \mathbf{q} \in \{0,1\}^n$ and $\mathbf{q}' \in \{0,1\}^{\delta_{n-1}}$ such that the following conditions hold:

$$\begin{cases} \mathbf{p} + \mathbf{q} = \mathbf{J}_n \bmod q, \\ \mathbf{J}_n^\top \cdot \mathbf{q} = \mathbf{g}'_{\delta_{n-1}} \cdot \mathbf{q}' \bmod q. \end{cases} \tag{2}$$

Note that the above solution not only works well in the Yang et al.'s framework [43] but does well in the Stern-like framework [31], and is more efficient when used in the previous framework. In fact, to further achieve efficiency gains, we can directly go to prove the Hamming weight of $\mathbf{p}$ is ≥ 1, i.e., go to prove $\mathbf{J}_n^\top \cdot \mathbf{p} \geq 1$. Interestingly, we observe that the proof for this relation can be reduced to that one knows a secret non-negative integer $b \leq n-1$ such that $\mathbf{J}_n^\top \cdot \mathbf{p} = 1 + b$. Combining with the decomposition techniques defined in Sect. 4.1, we equally write the relation as (assuming a private vector $\mathbf{q} \in \{0,1\}^{\delta_{n-1}}$)

$$\mathbf{J}_n^\top \cdot \mathbf{p} - \mathbf{g}'_{\delta_{n-1}} \cdot \mathbf{q} = 1 \bmod q. \tag{3}$$

The last above solution is more efficient since it saves 50% size compared to the previous one, and both present solutions are generic and more efficient when working in [43] than that of [31]. Besides, our solutions can be readily extended to prove that one knows a private $\mathbf{x}$ having l_∞ or l_2 norm bounded by $[\alpha, \beta]$ with integers $\alpha, \beta \geq 0$.

Proving Bounded Hamming Distance. In general, there two commonly used message filtering policies termed as "Permisive" and "Prohibitive". Our task is to establish the argument system for the latter, and that for previous is trivial and is omitted in this work. Given positive integers $m \geq t \geq d$, and binary vectors $\mathbf{m} \in \{0,1\}^m$ and $\mathbf{y}_i \in \{0,1\}^t$ with $i \in [m-t+1]$, we use $\mathbf{y}_i \sqsubset \mathbf{m}$ to mean that $\mathbf{y}_i$ is a substring of $\mathbf{m}$, i.e., there exist strings $\mathbf{x}_i, \mathbf{z}_i \in \{0,1\}^{\leq m-t}$

such that $[\mathbf{x}_i^\top|\mathbf{y}_i^\top|\mathbf{z}_i^\top]^\top = \mathbf{m}$. Actually, the relation $\mathbf{y}_i \sqsubset \mathbf{m}$ is equivalent to the equality $\mathbf{B}_i \cdot \mathbf{m} = \mathbf{y}_i$ where $\mathbf{B}_i \in \mathbb{Z}_q^{t\times m}$ is a public matrix of the form $[\mathbf{0}|\mathbf{I}_t|\mathbf{0}]$. Now we define the message filtering policy "Prohibitive" used in this work:

$$R_{\mathsf{prohi}} = \{((\mathbf{s}_i)_{i=1}^{\mathrm{e}}, \mathbf{m}) \in (\{0,1\}^t)^e \times \{0,1\}^m : d_H(\mathbf{s}_i, \mathbf{y}) \geq d, \forall i \in [e], \forall \mathbf{y} \sqsubset \mathbf{m})\}.$$

To build an argument system for the relation R_{prohi}, we begin with building a system for the simple relation $d_H(\mathbf{x}, \mathbf{y}) \geq d$ with $\mathbf{x}, \mathbf{y} \in \{0,1\}^n$ being public and secret. In the context of lattices, the proof is needed to be proceeded in mod q (involved with the dimension n for security, e.g., $q \geq \sqrt{n}$) instead of mod 2, which is always an open problem. Now we use a novel idea to address it. For any $x, y \in \{0,1\}$, we observe that $x \oplus y = x + y - 2x \cdot y$, which follows that $\mathbf{x} \oplus \mathbf{y} = \mathbf{x} + \mathbf{y} - 2(x_1 \cdot y_1, ..., x_n \cdot y_n)\top$ for binary vectors $\mathbf{x} = (x_1, ..., x_n)^\top$ and $\mathbf{y} = (y_1, ..., y_n)^\top$. Then, the task to prove $d_H(\mathbf{x}, \mathbf{y}) \geq d$ can be reduced to proving $\|\mathbf{x}+\mathbf{y}-2(x_1 \cdot y_1, ..., x_n \cdot y_n)^\top\|_1 \geq d$. By extending the proof method just developed above, in the setting of mod q, our task is reduced to proving that we hold a secret vector $\mathbf{z} \in \{0,1\}^{\delta_{n-d}}$ such that the following equation holds:

$$\mathbf{J}_n^\top \cdot (\mathbf{x} + \mathbf{y} - 2(x_1 \cdot y_1, ..., x_n \cdot y_n)^\top) - \mathbf{g}'_{\delta_{n-d}} \cdot \mathbf{z} = d \bmod q.$$

Based on the above result, for each $i \in [e], j \in [m - t + 1]$, let $\mathbf{s}_i = (s_{i,1}, ..., s_{i,t})^\top$, $\mathbf{y}_j = \mathbf{B}_j \cdot \mathbf{m}$ with $\mathbf{y}_j = (y_{j,1}, ..., y_{j,t})$ and $\mathbf{B}_{j,1}^\top, ..., \mathbf{B}_{j,t}^\top$ be the row vectors of $\mathbf{B}_j$ (which essentially ensures that $y_{j,k} = \mathbf{B}_{j,k}^\top \cdot \mathbf{m}$). Then, the task to prove the relation R_{prohi} is equal to proving that one knows secret vectors $\mathbf{z}_{i,j} \in \{0,1\}^{\delta_{m-d}}$ such that $(\forall i \in [e], j \in [m - t + 1])$:

$$\mathbf{J}_n^\top \cdot (\mathbf{s}_i + \mathbf{B}_j \cdot \mathbf{m} - 2(s_{i,1} \cdot \mathbf{B}_{j,1}^\top, ..., s_{i,t} \cdot \mathbf{B}_{j,t}^\top)^\top \cdot \mathbf{m}) - \mathbf{g}'_{\delta_{m-d}} \cdot \mathbf{z}_{i,j} = d \bmod q. \quad (4)$$

Then, let $\mathbf{B}_{i,j} = \mathbf{J}_n^\top \cdot (\mathbf{B}_j - 2(s_{i,1} \cdot \mathbf{B}_{j,1}^\top, ..., s_{i,t} \cdot \mathbf{B}_{j,t}^\top)^\top) \in \mathbb{Z}_q^{1\times m}$ and $d_{i,j} = d + \mathbf{J}_n^\top \cdot \mathbf{s}_i \in \mathbb{Z}_q$, which is followed by $\mathbf{B}_{[i]} = [\mathbf{B}_{i,1}^\top, ..., \mathbf{B}_{i,m-t+1}^\top]^\top \in \mathbb{Z}_q^{(m-t+1)\times m}$ and $\mathbf{B} = [\mathbf{B}_{[1]}^\top, ..., \mathbf{B}_{[e]}^\top]^\top \in \mathbb{Z}_q^{(m-t+1)e\times m}$. Accordingly, build $\mathbf{z}_{[i]} = [\mathbf{z}_{i,1}^\top, ..., \mathbf{z}_{i,m-t+1}^\top]^\top \in \mathbb{Z}_q^{(m-t+1)\delta_{m-d}}$, $\mathbf{z} = [\mathbf{z}_{[1]}^\top, ..., \mathbf{z}_{[e]}^\top]^\top \in \mathbb{Z}_q^{(m-t+1)e\delta_{m-d}}$, and $\mathbf{d}_{[i]} = [d_{i,1}, ..., d_{i,m-t+1}]^\top \in \mathbb{Z}_q^{m-t+1}$ and $\mathbf{d} = [\mathbf{d}_{[1]}^\top, ..., \mathbf{d}_{[e]}^\top]^\top \in \mathbb{Z}_q^{(m-t+1)e}$. Combining with the definition $\mathbf{I}_{\mathbf{g}'} = \mathbf{I}_{(m-t+1)e} \otimes \mathbf{g}'_{\delta_{m-d}}$, the relation R_{prohi} is equally written as:

$$[\mathbf{B}, \mathbf{I}_{\mathbf{g}'}] \cdot \begin{pmatrix} \mathbf{m} \\ \mathbf{z} \end{pmatrix} = \mathbf{d} \bmod q. \quad (5)$$

Run the above result in the Yang et al.'s framework [43], then the argument for bounded Hamming distance is established. It is seen that the above proof method is also generic and efficient.

4.3 The Underlying ZKAoK

We now state our argument system under the abstract framework provided in [43] as recalled in Sect. 2.4 for a wide of lattice relations to fulfill our intricate task.

Given the same settings of parameters as in Sect. 5.1, let $\mathsf{bin}(j) = (j_1, ..., j_\ell) \in \{0,1\}^\ell$, $\mathbf{j} = \mathsf{bin}(j)^\top$, $\mathbf{A} = [\mathbf{A}_1|\mathbf{A}_2]$ and $\mathbf{a}_{j,i} = \mathsf{mdec}_{n,m,q}(\mathbf{U}_{j,i}^\top)$ for each $i \in \{1,2\}$. As in [26,31], take the operator $\mathsf{ext}(\cdot,\cdot)$ to express $\mathsf{ext}(b, \mathbf{v}) = \begin{pmatrix} \bar{b} \cdot \mathbf{v} \\ b \cdot \mathbf{v} \end{pmatrix}$. Our protocol can be summarized as follows:

Public Input: Matrices $\mathbf{A}$, $\mathbf{G}$, $\mathbf{F}$, $\mathbf{B}$, $\mathbf{A}_{\mathsf{rec}}$, $\mathbf{A}_{\mathsf{oa}}$, $\mathbf{U}_{\mathsf{oa},1}$, $\mathbf{U}_{\mathsf{oa},2}$, $\mathbf{I}'_{\mathbf{g}}$, and vectors $\mathbf{u}_\tau$, $\mathbf{J}_{nk}$, $\mathbf{g}'_{\delta_{nk-1}}$, $\{\mathbf{c}^{(1)}_{\mathsf{rec},i}, \mathbf{c}^{(2)}_{\mathsf{rec},i}, \mathbf{c}^{(1)}_{\mathsf{oa},i}, \mathbf{c}^{(2)}_{\mathsf{oa},i}\}_{i\in\{1,2\}}$, $\mathbf{d}$.

Prover's Goal: Prove possession of the secret inputs in the following system

$$\begin{cases} \mathbf{j} = (j_1, ..., j_\ell)^\top, (\mathbf{p}_j, (\mathbf{w}_\ell^{(j)}, ..., \mathbf{w}_1^{(j)})) \in (\{0,1\}^{nk})^{\ell+1} \text{ with } \mathbf{p}_j \neq \mathbf{0}, \\ \mathbf{q}_j \in \{0,1\}^{\delta_{nk-1}}, \mathbf{a}_{j,1}, \mathbf{a}_{j,2} \in \{0,1\}^{nmk}, \\ \mathbf{m} \in \{0,1\}^m, \mathbf{z} \in \{0,1\}^{(m-t+1)e\delta_{m-d}}, \\ i = 1,2 : \mathbf{s}_{\mathsf{rec},i}, \mathbf{s}_{\mathsf{oa},i} \in \{0,1\}^n, \\ \mathbf{x}_{\mathsf{rec},i}, \mathbf{y}_{\mathsf{rec},i}, \mathbf{x}_{\mathsf{oa},i} \in [-B,B]^m, \mathbf{y}_{\mathsf{oa},i} \in [-B,B]^\ell \end{cases} \tag{6}$$

such that the following system of modular linear equations holds:

$$\begin{cases} \mathbf{G} \cdot \mathbf{u}_\tau = \mathbf{A} \cdot \mathsf{ext}(j_1, \mathbf{v}_1^{(j)}) + \mathbf{A} \cdot \mathsf{ext}(\bar{j}_1, \mathbf{w}_1^{(j)}) \bmod q, \mathbf{v}_\ell^{(j)} = \mathbf{p}_j, \\ i \in [1, \ell-1] : \\ \mathbf{0} = \mathbf{A} \cdot \mathsf{ext}(j_{i+1}, \mathbf{v}_{i+1}^{(j)}) + \mathbf{A} \cdot \mathsf{ext}(\bar{j}_{i+1}, \mathbf{w}_{i+1}^{(j)}) + (-\mathbf{G}) \cdot \mathbf{v}_i^{(j)} \bmod q, \\ 1 = \mathbf{J}_{nk}^\top \cdot \mathbf{p}_j + (-\mathbf{g}'_{\delta_{nk-1}}) \cdot \mathbf{q}_j \bmod q, \\ \mathbf{0} = \mathbf{G} \cdot \mathbf{p}_j + (-\mathbf{F}) \cdot (\mathbf{a}_{j,1}^\top \| \mathbf{a}_{j,2}^\top)^\top \bmod q, \\ r = \{1,2\} : \mathbf{c}^{(1)}_{\mathsf{rec},r} = \mathbf{A}_{\mathsf{rec}}^\top \cdot \mathbf{s}_{\mathsf{rec},r} + \mathbf{x}_{\mathsf{rec},r} \bmod q, \\ \mathbf{c}^{(2)}_{\mathsf{rec},r} = \mathbf{U}_{j,r}^\top \cdot \mathbf{s}_{\mathsf{rec},r} + \mathbf{y}_{\mathsf{rec},r} + \mathbf{m} \cdot \lfloor \frac{q}{2} \rceil \bmod q, \\ \mathbf{d} = [\mathbf{B}, \mathbf{I}'_{\mathbf{g}}] \cdot [\mathbf{m}^\top, \mathbf{z}^\top]^\top \bmod q, \\ \mathbf{c}^{(1)}_{\mathsf{oa},r} = \mathbf{A}_{\mathsf{oa}}^\top \cdot \mathbf{s}_{\mathsf{oa},r} + \mathbf{x}_{\mathsf{oa},r} \bmod q, \\ \mathbf{c}^{(2)}_{\mathsf{oa},r} = \mathbf{U}_{\mathsf{oa},r}^\top \cdot \mathbf{s}_{\mathsf{oa},r} + \mathbf{y}_{\mathsf{oa},r} + \mathbf{j} \cdot \lfloor \frac{q}{2} \rceil \bmod q, \end{cases} \tag{7}$$

To proceed the proof, we first build two argument systems Π_1 suitable for accumulator values problem and plain encryption, and Π_2 suitable for encryption with hidden matrices, respectively, then establish the final system Π_{GE} which covers all the above involved relations. The concrete steps are made as follows:

Build System Π_1. This system covers $(\ell + 6)$ equations consisting of the first $(\ell + 2)$ and the last four ones from the above equation system (7). Our task is to construct a ZKAoK system for the following relation:

$$R_1 = \{(\mathbf{M}_1, \mathbf{y}_1), (\mathbf{x}_1) : \mathbf{M}_1 \cdot \mathbf{x}_1 = \mathbf{y}_1 \wedge \mathbf{x}_1 \in \mathsf{cond}_1\}. \tag{8}$$

In the above, the matrix $\mathbf{M}_1$ consists of the involved public matrices and vectors $\{\mathbf{A}, \mathbf{G}, \mathbf{J}_{nk}, \mathbf{g}'_{\delta_{nk-1}}, \mathbf{F}, \mathbf{A}_{\mathsf{oa}}, \mathbf{U}_{\mathsf{oa},1}, \mathbf{U}_{\mathsf{oa},2}\}$ by an appropriate arrangement, and vectors $\mathbf{x}_1$ and $\mathbf{y}_1$ are similarly made by private inputs $\{\mathbf{j}, \{\mathbf{v}_i\}_i, \{\mathbf{w}_i\}_i, \mathbf{p}_j, \mathbf{q}_j, \mathbf{q}'_j, \{\mathbf{s}_{\mathsf{oa},i}\}_i, \{\mathbf{x}_{\mathsf{oa},i}\}_i, \{\mathbf{y}_{\mathsf{oa},i}\}_i\}$ and public vectors $\{\mathbf{G} \cdot \mathbf{u}_\tau, \mathbf{J}_{nk}, \{\mathbf{c}^{(1)}_{\mathsf{oa},i},$

$\mathbf{c}^{(2)}_{\mathsf{oa},i}\}_i\}$, and the cond_1 is the set of conditions that the private inputs should meet given in system (6). We now describe the constructions of desired variables.

We achieve our goal by a sequence of steps. Let $\mathbf{b}_1, \mathbf{b}_2$ be constant vectors, respectively, of the form $\mathbf{b}_1 = (B, ..., B)^\top \in \mathbb{Z}_q^m$ and $\mathbf{b}_2 = (B, ..., B)^\top \in \mathbb{Z}_q^\ell$. Then, conduct the following.

1. Transform the inputs bounded by some positive integer to ones with non-negative entries. Concretely, for each $i \in \{1, 2\}$, set $\mathbf{x}'_{\mathsf{oa},i} = \mathbf{x}_{\mathsf{oa},i} + \mathbf{b}_1 \in [0, 2B]^m$, and $\mathbf{y}'_{\mathsf{oa},i} = \mathbf{y}_{\mathsf{oa},i} + \mathbf{b}_2 \in [0, 2B]^\ell$.
2. Decompose the above newly transformed vectors $\mathbf{x}'_{\mathsf{oa},i}, \mathbf{y}'_{\mathsf{oa},i}$. For each $i \in \{1, 2\}$, apply the operator $\mathsf{vdec}(\cdot)$ defined in Sect. 4.1 to the above targeted vectors to produce binary vectors $\mathbf{x}''_{\mathsf{oa},i}, \mathbf{y}''_{\mathsf{oa},i}$ of size $m\delta_{2B}$ and $\ell\delta_{2B}$, respectively, such that $\mathbf{x}'_{\mathsf{oa},i} = \mathbf{H}_{m,2B} \cdot \mathbf{x}''_{\mathsf{oa},i}$ and $\mathbf{y}'_{\mathsf{oa},i} = \mathbf{H}_{\ell,2B} \cdot \mathbf{y}''_{\mathsf{oa},i}$.
3. Modify the involved public vectors accordingly. For each $i \in \{1, 2\}$, set $\mathbf{c}^{(1)'}_{\mathsf{oa},i} = \mathbf{c}^{(1)}_{\mathsf{oa},i} + \mathbf{b}_1$ and $\mathbf{c}^{(2)'}_{\mathsf{oa},i} = \mathbf{c}^{(2)}_{\mathsf{oa},i} + \mathbf{b}_2$.
4. Rewrite the first ℓ equations. For each $i \in [1, \ell]$, by $\mathbf{A} = [\mathbf{A}_1|\mathbf{A}_2]$ and the operator $\mathsf{ext}(\cdot, \cdot)$, we have $\mathbf{A} \cdot \mathsf{ext}(j_i, \mathbf{v}_i^{(j)}) + \mathbf{A} \cdot \mathsf{ext}(\bar{j}_i, \mathbf{w}_i^{(j)}) = \mathbf{A}_1 \cdot \mathbf{v}_i + (\mathbf{A}_2 - \mathbf{A}_1) \cdot j_i \mathbf{v}_i + \mathbf{A}_2 \cdot \mathbf{w}_i + (\mathbf{A}_1 - \mathbf{A}_2) \cdot j_i \mathbf{w}_i$. Let $\mathbf{A}_{(1,2)} = [\mathbf{A}_1|\mathbf{A}_2 - \mathbf{A}_1|\mathbf{A}_2|\mathbf{A}_1 - \mathbf{A}_2]$, $\mathbf{A}_{[1,2]} = [-\mathbf{G}|\mathbf{0}_3|\mathbf{A}_1|\mathbf{A}_2 - \mathbf{A}_1|\mathbf{A}_2|\mathbf{A}_1 - \mathbf{A}_2]$ (where $\mathbf{0}_3$ means a block of form $[\mathbf{0}|\mathbf{0}|\mathbf{0}] \in (\mathbb{Z}_q^{n\times m})^3$) and $\mathbf{u}' = [(\mathbf{G}\cdot\mathbf{u}_\tau)^\top|\mathbf{0}^\top]^\top$, set a matrix $\mathbf{A}_{[1,\ell]} = \begin{pmatrix} \mathbf{A}_{(1,2)} \\ \mathbf{A}_{[1,2]} \\ \ddots \end{pmatrix}$ consisting of a $\mathbf{A}_{(1,2)}$ and $(\ell - 1)$'s $\mathbf{A}_{[1,2]}$ such that, for each $i \in [2, \ell - 1]$, the component $-\mathbf{G}$ from the i-th block $\mathbf{A}_{[1,2]}$ and the component $\mathbf{A}_1$ from the last block $\mathbf{A}_{(1,2)}$ or from the last $\mathbf{A}_{[1,2]}$ are in the same column. Accordingly, for each $i \in [1, \ell]$, we set $\mathbf{x}_{i,\mathbf{v}_i,\mathbf{w}_i} = [\mathbf{v}_i^\top|(j_i\mathbf{v}_i)^\top|\mathbf{w}_i^\top|(j_i\mathbf{w}_i)^\top]^\top$, and further set $\mathbf{x}_{\ell,\mathbf{v},\mathbf{w}} = [\mathbf{x}^\top_{1,\mathbf{v}_1,\mathbf{w}_1}|\cdots|\mathbf{x}^\top_{\ell,\mathbf{v}_\ell,\mathbf{w}_\ell}]^\top$, which gives that $\mathbf{u}' = \mathbf{A}_{[1,\ell]} \cdot \mathbf{x}_{\ell,\mathbf{v},\mathbf{w}}$.

After the above treatments, the targeted system is equally changed as:

$$\begin{cases} \mathbf{u}' = \mathbf{A}_{[1,\ell]} \cdot \mathbf{x}_{\ell,\mathbf{v},\mathbf{w}}, \\ 1 = \mathbf{J}_{nk}^\top \cdot \mathbf{p}_j + (-\mathbf{g}'_{\delta_{nk-1}}) \cdot \mathbf{q}_j, \\ \mathbf{0} = \mathbf{G} \cdot \mathbf{p}_j + (-\mathbf{F}) \cdot [\mathbf{a}_{j,1}^\top|\mathbf{a}_{j,2}^\top]^\top \bmod q, \\ i \in \{1,2\} : \mathbf{c}^{(1)'}_{\mathsf{oa},i} = \mathbf{A}_{\mathsf{oa}} \cdot \mathbf{s}_{\mathsf{oa},i} + \mathbf{H}_{m,2B} \cdot \mathbf{x}''_{\mathsf{oa},i} \bmod q, \\ \mathbf{c}^{(2)'}_{\mathsf{oa},i} = \mathbf{U}_{\mathsf{oa},i}^\top \cdot \mathbf{s}_{\mathsf{oa},i} + \mathbf{H}_{\ell,2B} \cdot \mathbf{y}''_{\mathsf{oa},i} + \mathbf{j} \cdot \lfloor \frac{q}{2} \rfloor \bmod q. \end{cases} \tag{9}$$

Basing on the above preparations, we obtain the desired variables as follows:

1. Build the public matrix $\mathbf{M}_1$ and the public vector $\mathbf{y}_1$. Set $\mathbf{A}' := \mathbf{A}_{[1,\ell-1]}, \mathbf{A}'_1 := \mathbf{A}_2 - \mathbf{A}_1, \mathbf{A}'_2 := \mathbf{A}_1 - \mathbf{A}_2, \mathbf{I}'_\ell := \lfloor \frac{q}{2} \rfloor \cdot \mathbf{I}_\ell$, $\mathbf{g}' := -\mathbf{g}'_{\delta_{nk-1}}$, $\mathbf{F}' := -\mathbf{F}$, $\mathbf{G}' := -\mathbf{G}$ and $\mathbf{H}'_k := \mathbf{H}_{k,2B}$ with $k \in \{\ell, m\}$. Use the matrices in (9) to construct the desired matrix $\mathbf{M}_1$ and vector $\mathbf{y}_1$ as (here we abuse notation and use $[\mathbf{A}'^\top|\mathbf{G}'^\top]^\top$ to represent that the matrix $\mathbf{G}'$ and the component $\mathbf{A}_1$ from the last row of $\mathbf{A}'$ are in the same column)

$$\begin{pmatrix} \mathbf{0} & \mathbf{A}' & 0_3 & \mathbf{0} & \mathbf{0} & \mathbf{0} & \mathbf{0} & \mathbf{0} & \mathbf{0} & \mathbf{0} & \mathbf{0} & \mathbf{0} & \mathbf{0} & \mathbf{0} & \mathbf{0} & \mathbf{0} \\ \mathbf{0} & \mathbf{G}' & 0_3 & \mathbf{A}_1 & \mathbf{A}_1' & \mathbf{A}_2 & \mathbf{A}_2' & \mathbf{0} & \mathbf{0} & \mathbf{0} & \mathbf{0} & \mathbf{0} & \mathbf{0} & \mathbf{0} & \mathbf{0} & \mathbf{0} \\ \mathbf{0} & \mathbf{0} & 0_3 & \mathbf{0} & \mathbf{0} & \mathbf{0} & \mathbf{0} & \mathbf{J}_{nk}^\top & \mathbf{g}' & \mathbf{0} & \mathbf{0} & \mathbf{0} & \mathbf{0} & \mathbf{0} & \mathbf{0} & \mathbf{0} \\ \mathbf{0} & \mathbf{0} & 0_3 & \mathbf{0} & \mathbf{0} & \mathbf{0} & \mathbf{0} & \mathbf{0} & \mathbf{0} & \mathbf{A}_{\mathsf{oa}} & \mathbf{H}_m' & \mathbf{0} & \mathbf{0} & \mathbf{0} & \mathbf{0} & \mathbf{0} \\ \mathbf{I}_\ell' & \mathbf{0} & 0_3 & \mathbf{0} & \mathbf{0} & \mathbf{0} & \mathbf{0} & \mathbf{0} & \mathbf{0} & \mathbf{U}_{\mathsf{oa},1}^\top & \mathbf{0} & \mathbf{H}_\ell' & \mathbf{0} & \mathbf{0} & \mathbf{0} & \mathbf{0} \\ \mathbf{0} & \mathbf{0} & 0_3 & \mathbf{0} & \mathbf{0} & \mathbf{0} & \mathbf{0} & \mathbf{0} & \mathbf{0} & \mathbf{0} & \mathbf{0} & \mathbf{0} & \mathbf{A}_{\mathsf{oa}} & \mathbf{H}_m' & \mathbf{0} & \mathbf{0} \\ \mathbf{I}_\ell' & \mathbf{0} & 0_3 & \mathbf{0} & \mathbf{0} & \mathbf{0} & \mathbf{0} & \mathbf{0} & \mathbf{0} & \mathbf{0} & \mathbf{0} & \mathbf{0} & \mathbf{U}_{\mathsf{oa},2}^\top & \mathbf{0} & \mathbf{H}_\ell' & \mathbf{0} \\ \mathbf{0} & \mathbf{0} & 0_3 & \mathbf{G} & \mathbf{0} & \mathbf{0} & \mathbf{0} & \mathbf{0} & \mathbf{0} & \mathbf{0} & \mathbf{0} & \mathbf{0} & \mathbf{0} & \mathbf{0} & \mathbf{0} & \mathbf{F}' \end{pmatrix}, \begin{pmatrix} \mathbf{u}' \\ 1 \\ \mathbf{c}_{\mathsf{oa},1}^{(1)'} \\ \mathbf{c}_{\mathsf{oa},1}^{(2)'} \\ \mathbf{c}_{\mathsf{oa},2}^{(1)'} \\ \mathbf{c}_{\mathsf{oa},2}^{(2)'} \\ \mathbf{0} \end{pmatrix}.$$

2. Build the private input $\mathbf{x}_1$. Arrange the modified private inputs shown in the system (9), establish the desired private vector $\mathbf{x}_1 = (\mathbf{j}^\top, \mathbf{x}_{\ell,\mathbf{v},\mathbf{w}}^\top, \mathbf{q}_j^\top, \mathbf{s}_{\mathsf{oa},1}^\top, \mathbf{x}_{\mathsf{oa},1}''^\top, \mathbf{y}_{\mathsf{oa},1}''^\top, \mathbf{s}_{\mathsf{oa},2}^\top, \mathbf{x}_{\mathsf{oa},2}''^\top, \mathbf{y}_{\mathsf{oa},2}''^\top, \mathbf{a}_{j,1}^\top, \mathbf{a}_{j,2}^\top)^\top$ with size n_1, where $n_1 = \ell + 2n + \delta_{nk-1} + 2(m+\ell)\delta_{2B} + 4\ell nk + 2nmk$.
3. Build the set of conditions cond_1. Let $\mathcal{M}_1$ be the set of triple indexes (h, i, l) of $\mathbf{x}_1$ with $h, i, l \in [n_1]$ such that $\mathbf{x}_1[h] = \mathbf{x}_1[i] \cdot \mathbf{x}_1[l]$. The set $\mathcal{M}_1$ is equivalent to the set cond_1. We now state the structure of $\mathcal{M}_1$:
   a. Observe that all entries of $\mathbf{x}_1$ are binary, we note that the choices $(h, i, l) = (i, i, i)_{i \in [n_1]}$ are in the set $\mathcal{M}_1$.
   b. Now consider the corresponding choices of $\mathcal{M}_1$ for $j_i \mathbf{v}_i, j_i \mathbf{w}_i$ for all $i \in [\ell]$: for $j_i \mathbf{v}_i$, the choices consist of $(h, i, l) = (\ell + (4i' - 3)nk + l', i', \ell + (4i' - 4)nk + l')_{i' \in [\ell], l' \in [nk]}$. Whereas, for $j_i \mathbf{w}_i$, the desired indexes are given by $(h, i, l) = (\ell + (4i' - 1)nk + l', i', \ell + (4i' - 2)nk + l')_{i' \in [\ell], l' \in [nk]}$.

This constructs the argument system Π_1 for the relation R_1, and by running the protocol in Sect. 4.3, the desired argument system is obtained.

Build System Π_2. This system covers the remaining five equations from the system (7). Our task is to construct a similar ZKAoK system for the following relation:

$$R_2 = \{(\mathbf{M}_2, \mathbf{y}_2), (\mathbf{x}_2) : \mathbf{M}_2 \cdot \mathbf{x}_2 = \mathbf{y}_2 \wedge \mathbf{x}_2 \in \mathsf{cond}_2\}. \tag{10}$$

As in the above system Π_1, the involved variables are respectively defined. We take similar strategies to proceed the present task.

1. For each $i \in \{1, 2\}$, transform the private inputs $\mathbf{x}_{\mathsf{rec},i}, \mathbf{y}_{\mathsf{rec},i}$ to ones that only have non-negative entries. Concretely, set $\mathbf{x}_{\mathsf{rec},i}' = \mathbf{x}_{\mathsf{rec},i} + \mathbf{b}_1, \mathbf{y}_{\mathsf{rec},i}' = \mathbf{y}_{\mathsf{rec},i} + \mathbf{b}_1, \in [0, 2B]^m$.
2. Decompose the above newly generated vectors. For each $i \in \{1, 2\}$, impose the function $\mathsf{vdec}(\cdot)$ on these vectors, respectively, to yield size-$m\delta_{2B}$ binary vectors $\mathbf{x}_{\mathsf{rec},i}''$ and $\mathbf{y}_{\mathsf{rec},i}''$ such that $\mathbf{x}_{\mathsf{rec},i}' = \mathbf{H}_{m,2B} \cdot \mathbf{x}_{\mathsf{rec},i}'', \mathbf{y}_{\mathsf{rec},i}' = \mathbf{H}_{m,2B} \cdot \mathbf{y}_{\mathsf{rec},i}''$.

3. Change the corresponding public matrices and vectors. Consider the decomposition of $\mathbf{U}_{j,i}^{\top} \cdot \mathbf{s}_{\mathsf{rec},i}$ with $i = 1, 2$. Let $\mathbf{U}_{j,i}^{\top} = [\mathbf{u}_{j,i}^{(1)\top}|...|\mathbf{u}_{j,i}^{(n)\top}] \in \mathbb{Z}_q^{m\times n}$ and $\mathbf{s}_{\mathsf{rec},i} = (s_{\mathsf{rec},i}^{(1)}, ..., s_{\mathsf{rec},i}^{(n)})^{\top} \in \{0,1\}^n$. In light of operators $\mathsf{vdec}(\cdot)$ and $\mathsf{mdec}(\cdot)$, we have $\mathbf{U}_{j,i}^{\top} \cdot \mathbf{s}_{\mathsf{rec},i} = \Sigma_{t=1}^{n} \mathbf{u}_{j,i}^{(t)\top} \cdot s_{\mathsf{rec},i}^{(t)} = \Sigma_{t=1}^{n} \mathbf{H}_{m,q-1} \cdot \mathbf{a}_{j,i}^{(t)} \cdot s_{\mathsf{rec},i}^{(t)} = \mathbf{H}_{m,q-1} \cdot \mathbf{s}_{\mathsf{rec},i,mk}^{\top} \cdot \mathbf{a}_{j,i}$, where $\mathbf{a}_{j,i}^{(t)} \in \{0,1\}^{mk}$ is the binary decomposition of the vector $\mathbf{u}_{j,i}^{(t)\top}$ and $\mathbf{s}_{\mathsf{rec},i,mk} = (\overbrace{s_{\mathsf{rec},i}^{(1)}, ..., s_{\mathsf{rec},i}^{(1)}}^{mk's\ \text{times}}, ..., \overbrace{s_{\mathsf{rec},i}^{(n)}, ..., s_{\mathsf{rec},i}^{(n)}}^{mk's\ \text{times}})^{\top}$. Additionally, for all $i = 1, 2$, set vectors as: $\mathbf{c}_{\mathsf{rec},i}^{(1)'} = \mathbf{c}_{\mathsf{rec},i}^{(1)} + \mathbf{b}_1$ and $\mathbf{c}_{\mathsf{rec},i}^{(2)'} = \mathbf{c}_{\mathsf{rec},i}^{(2)} + \mathbf{b}_1$.

After making the above treatments, the targeted system is equally changed as:

$$\begin{cases} i \in \{1,2\} : \mathbf{c}_{\mathsf{rec},i}^{(1)'} = \mathbf{A}_{\mathsf{rec}}^{\top} \cdot \mathbf{s}_{\mathsf{rec},i} + \mathbf{H}_{m,2B} \cdot \mathbf{x}_{\mathsf{rec},i}'' \bmod q, \\ \mathbf{c}_{\mathsf{rec},i}^{(2)'} = \mathbf{H}_{m,q-1} \cdot \mathbf{s}_{\mathsf{rec},i,mk}^{\top} \cdot \mathbf{a}_{j,i} + \mathbf{H}_{m,2B} \cdot \mathbf{y}_{\mathsf{rec},i}'' + \mathbf{m} \cdot \lfloor \frac{q}{2} \rceil \bmod q, \\ \mathbf{d} = [\mathbf{B}, \mathbf{I}_{\mathbf{g}}'] \cdot [\mathbf{m}^{\top}, \mathbf{z}^{\top}]^{\top} \bmod q, \end{cases} \tag{11}$$

This proceeds the following constructions of variables.

1. For simplicity, let $\mathbf{H}_m'' = \mathbf{H}_{m,q-1}$ and $\mathbf{I}_m' = \lfloor \frac{q}{2} \rfloor \mathbf{I}_m$. Similar to what in system Π_1, build the public matrix $\mathbf{M}_2$ and the public vector $\mathbf{y}_2$ as

$$\begin{pmatrix} \mathbf{0} & \mathbf{A}_{\mathsf{rec}}^{\top} & \mathbf{0} & \mathbf{H}_m' & \mathbf{0} & \mathbf{0} & \mathbf{0} & \mathbf{0} & \mathbf{0} & \mathbf{0} & \mathbf{0} \\ \mathbf{0} & \mathbf{0} & \mathbf{H}_m'' & \mathbf{0} & \mathbf{H}_m' & \mathbf{0} & \mathbf{0} & \mathbf{0} & \mathbf{0} & \mathbf{I}_m' & \mathbf{0} \\ \mathbf{0} & \mathbf{0} & \mathbf{0} & \mathbf{0} & \mathbf{0} & \mathbf{A}_{\mathsf{rec}}^{\top} & \mathbf{0} & \mathbf{H}_m' & \mathbf{0} & \mathbf{0} & \mathbf{0} \\ \mathbf{0} & \mathbf{0} & \mathbf{0} & \mathbf{0} & \mathbf{0} & \mathbf{0} & \mathbf{H}_m'' & \mathbf{0} & \mathbf{H}_m' & \mathbf{I}_m' & \mathbf{0} \\ \mathbf{0} & \mathbf{0} & \mathbf{0} & \mathbf{0} & \mathbf{0} & \mathbf{0} & \mathbf{0} & \mathbf{0} & \mathbf{0} & \mathbf{B} & \mathbf{I}_{\mathbf{g}}' \end{pmatrix} \text{ and } \begin{pmatrix} \mathbf{c}_{\mathsf{rec},1}^{(1)'} \\ \mathbf{c}_{\mathsf{rec},1}^{(2)'} \\ \mathbf{c}_{\mathsf{rec},2}^{(1)'} \\ \mathbf{c}_{\mathsf{rec},2}^{(2)'} \\ \mathbf{d} \end{pmatrix}.$$

2. Build the private input $\mathbf{x}_2$. According to the public variables $\mathbf{M}_2$ and $\mathbf{y}_2$ above, we build the private vector $\mathbf{x}_2 = (\mathbf{a}_{j,1}^{\top}, \mathbf{a}_{j,2}^{\top}, \mathbf{s}_{\mathsf{rec},1}^{\top}, (\mathbf{s}_{\mathsf{rec},1,mk}^{\top} \cdot \mathbf{a}_{j,1})^{\top}, \mathbf{x}_{\mathsf{rec},1}''^{\top}, \mathbf{y}_{\mathsf{rec},1}''^{\top}, \mathbf{s}_{\mathsf{rec},2}^{\top}, (\mathbf{s}_{\mathsf{rec},2,mk}^{\top} \cdot \mathbf{a}_{j,2})^{\top}, \mathbf{x}_{\mathsf{rec},2}''^{\top}, \mathbf{y}_{\mathsf{rec},2}''^{\top}, \mathbf{m}^{\top}, \mathbf{z}^{\top})^{\top}$ which has size $n_2 = m + 2n + 2m(k + nk + 2\delta_{2B}) + (m - t + 1)e\delta_{m-d}$.
3. Consider the set of conditions cond_2. Similarly, let $\mathcal{M}_2$ be the set of triple indexes (h, i, l) of $\mathbf{x}_2$ with $h, i, l \in [n_2]$ such that $\mathbf{x}_2[h] = \mathbf{x}_2[i] \cdot \mathbf{x}_2[l]$. It can be seen that the defined set of indexes is equal to the original set cond_2. Now we present the structure of set $\mathcal{M}_2$:
   a. Observe that all components of $\mathbf{x}_2$ are binary vectors, which gives that such indexes $(h, i, l) = (i, i, i)$ with $i \in [n_2]$ are in cond_2.
   b. In addition, the hidden matrix constraint in the original system is equally to the conditions $\mathbf{s}_{\mathsf{rec},i,mk}^{\top} \mathbf{a}_{j,i} = s_{\mathsf{rec},i,mk}^{\top} \cdot \mathbf{a}_{j,i}$ for each $i \in \{1,2\}$ as in system (11). This allows us to compute another choice of indexes $(h, i, l) = (2nmk + n + (i' - 1)mk + l', 2nmk + i', l')_{i' \in [n], l' \in [mk]} \cup (3nmk + 2n + 2m\delta_{2B} + (i' - 1)mk + l', 3nmk + n + 2m\delta_{2B} + i', nmk + l')_{i' \in [n], l' \in [mk]}$.

This completes the task of constructing argument system Π_2 by running the protocol given in Sect. 4.3.

Build System Π_{GE}. The final system is the desired one which covers the system Π_1 and the system Π_2 simultaneously, whose definition is shown as follows:

$$R_{\mathsf{GE}} = \{(\mathbf{M}, \mathbf{y}), (\mathbf{x}) : \mathbf{M} \cdot \mathbf{x} = \mathbf{y} \wedge \mathbf{x} \in \mathsf{cond}\}. \tag{12}$$

To build the system, we write $\mathbf{M}_1 = [\mathbf{M}_{1,1}|\mathbf{M}_{1,2}]$ and $\mathbf{M}_2 = [\mathbf{M}_{2,1}|\mathbf{M}_{2,2}]$, then build $\mathbf{M} = \begin{pmatrix} \mathbf{M}_{1,1} & \mathbf{M}_{1,2} & \mathbf{0} \\ \mathbf{0} & \mathbf{M}_{2,1} & \mathbf{M}_{2,2} \end{pmatrix}$, where the blocks $\mathbf{M}_{1,2}$ and $\mathbf{M}_{2,1}$ respectively represent the last column and the first column of $\mathbf{M}_1$ and $\mathbf{M}_2$. Accordingly, we build $\mathbf{x} = \begin{pmatrix} \mathbf{x}_1 \\ \mathbf{x}_2/\{[\mathbf{a}_{j,1}^\top|\mathbf{a}_{j,2}^\top]^\top\} \end{pmatrix}$, $\mathbf{y} = \begin{pmatrix} \mathbf{y}_1 \\ \mathbf{y}_2 \end{pmatrix}$ and $\mathsf{cond} = \mathsf{cond}_1 \cap \mathsf{cond}_2$, then a system that is suitable for the framework established in [43] is obtained. Now the family $\mathcal{M}$ of triples corresponding to the set cond is somewhat modified, i.e., $\mathcal{M} = \mathcal{M}_1 \cup \mathcal{M}_2'$, where $\mathcal{M}_2' = \{(h, i, l)\} = \{(i, i, i)\}_{i \in [n_1+1, n_1+n_2-2nmk]} \cup (n_1 + n + (i'-1)mk + l', n_1 + i', n_1 - 2nmk + l')_{i' \in [n], l' \in [mk]} \cup (n_1 + nmk + 2n + 2m\delta_{2B} + (i'-1)mk + l', n_1 + nmk + n + 2m\delta_{2B} + i', n_1 - nmk + l')_{i' \in [n], l' \in [mk]}$. Then, the prover runs an interactive protocol with the verifier as shown in [43], and the desired ZKAoK system is established.

5 Our Fully Dynamic Lattice-Based Group Encryption

This section describes how to make use of the LNWX accumulator [31], GPV dual encryption [18] and the ZKAoK system built in Sect. 4 to construct our fully dynamic lattice-based group encryption in a relatively simple manner. In our design, this scheme first achieves the "Prohibitive" message filtering policy in the lattice setting and is free of lattice trapdoors throughout the design, resulting into great efficiency gains. All of these efforts yield a much more practical group encryption, also secure against the potential quantum attacks. We now briefly interpret the overview of our techniques.

Our inspiration begins with a main observation that, by using an updatable accumulator [31], one can directly upgrade the static group signature scheme [26] to one offering full dynamicity [31] at a reasonable cost, where the GM creates and revokes group membership via altering the hash value $\mathbf{p}$ of user's public key (*non-zero* for activated users and $\mathbf{0}$ otherwise). Following the idea, combining with the GPV dual encryption [18], we consider: For a group of $N = 2^\ell$ members, given $\mathbf{A}_{\mathsf{rec}} \in \mathbb{Z}_q^{n \times m}$, users sample two random short matrices $\mathbf{E}_{j,1}, \mathbf{E}_{j,2} \in \mathbb{Z}_q^{m \times m}$ from a given Gaussian distribution to generate nearly uniform $\mathbf{U}_{j,i} = \mathbf{A} \cdot \mathbf{E}_{j,i} \in \mathbb{Z}_q^{n \times m}$ with $i \in \{1, 2\}$, resulting secret/public key pairs $(\mathsf{sk}_j, \mathsf{pk}_j) = (\mathbf{E}_{j,1}, (\mathbf{U}_{j,1}, \mathbf{U}_{j,2}))$ with hash values $\mathbf{p}_j = \mathsf{bin}(\mathbf{F} \cdot [\mathbf{a}_{j,1}^\top|\mathbf{a}_{j,2}^\top]^\top) \in \{0,1\}^{nk}$ where $\mathbf{a}_{j,i} = \mathsf{mdec}_{n,m,k}(\mathbf{U}_{j,i}^\top) \in \{0,1\}^{nmk}$. Then, the manager builds an efficiently updatable tree on top of values $\mathbf{p}_0, \cdots, \mathbf{p}_{N-1}$ and publishes the tree root $\mathbf{u}$ as well as the witness for the fact $\mathbf{p}_j$ was accumulated in $\mathbf{u}$. Particularly, the GM conducts: (i)-For an invalid user who has not joined the group or has been excluded from the group, set the j-th leaf value $\mathbf{p}_j$ as $\mathbf{0}$; (ii)-For a valid user who joins the group and has not left the group, set the corresponding value as $\mathbf{p}_j$, the hash value of the public key pk_j; (iii)-With these rules, the GM can build an efficiently updatable tree with comparative complexity $\mathcal{O}(\log N)$, for which he only needs to alter the values at specific leaves and along their paths to the root rather than to reconstruct the whole tree when group information changes. These executions guarantee that all active users (with $\mathbf{p} \neq \mathbf{0}$) in the given epoch can be accumulated into the dynamic root while no any inactive user cannot, which effectively separates active users who can receive the valid ciphertexts from those who cannot in any growing epoch.

When moving to the stage of generating a group encryption, the sender fetches the public key $(\mathbf{U}_{j,1}, \mathbf{U}_{j,2})$ and the associated membership witness $w^{(j)}$ of the target group member from group information, then samples a witness in light of the given Prohibitive message filtering policy and computes the ciphertext (we apply the Naor-Yung transformation technique [34] for CCA-2 security) and an associated proof which shows that the ciphertext is well-formed and $\mathbf{p}_j \neq \mathbf{0}$. In order for the proof to work in the Yang et al.'s ZK framework [43], we use the proof techniques we just provided in Sect. 4.2 and then resort to the argument system built in Sect. 4.3.

We also note that the dynamicity described in [31] is de facto limited to once enrollment and once revocation. To realize stronger dynamicity that users are allowed to join or leave the group at will, some modifications on procedures $\langle \mathsf{JOIN}, \mathsf{ISSUE} \rangle$ and GUPDATE are needed. Concretely, we take some significant modifications for the procedures of user registering and user leaving, such that group users indeed obtain the expected dynamicity as long as their reasonable applications are accepted by the GM.

5.1 Description of the Scheme

As in [35], we assume that our scheme allows encrypting witness $\mathbf{m} \in \{0,1\}^m$ that meets both message filtering policies termed as Permissive[1] and Prohibitive (shown in Sect. 4.2), which use constraints stronger than those used in [21,25]. For simplicity, we only take the latter policy in our scheme. Procedures of constructing the FDGE scheme are shown as follows.

- $\mathsf{SETUP}_{\mathsf{init}}$ (1^λ): This algorithm conducts the following:
  - Set the possibly maximum number of group users as $N = 2^\ell = \mathsf{poly}(\lambda)$.
  - Select integer $n = \mathcal{O}(\lambda)$ and prime $q = \widetilde{\mathcal{O}}(n^2)$. Let $k = \lceil \log q \rceil$, $m = 2nk$.
  - Pick a discrete distribution χ over $\mathbb{Z}$ of the bound $B = \sqrt{n}\omega(\log n)$.
  - Select a Gaussian parameter $\sigma = \Omega(\sqrt{n \log q} \log n)$, and build a discrete Gaussian distribution $D_{\mathbb{Z},\sigma}$ with upper bound $\beta = \sigma \cdot \omega(\log n)$.
  - Take public parameters $\mathsf{pp}_{\mathsf{COM}}$ for the homomorphic commitment scheme like [5] which serves as a key building block in the construction of the interactive game $\langle \mathcal{P}, \mathcal{V} \rangle$.
  - Pick a random matrix $\mathbf{F} \hookleftarrow \mathbb{Z}_q^{n \times 2nmk}$ which hashes users' public keys from $\mathbb{Z}_q^{n \times 2m}$ to $\mathbb{Z}_q^n$.

[1] It is defined as $R_{\mathsf{permi}} = \{((\mathbf{s}_i)_{i=1}^e, \mathbf{m}) \in (\{0,1\}^t)^e \times \{0,1\}^m : \exists i \in [e] \text{s.t.} \mathbf{s}_i \sqsubset \mathbf{m}\}$.

- Set a gadget matrix $\mathbf{G} = \mathbf{I}_n \otimes \mathbf{g}_k$ with the definition given in Sect. 4.1. Pick matrices $\mathbf{A}_{\mathsf{rec}}, \mathbf{A}_{\mathsf{oa}} \hookleftarrow U(\mathbb{Z}_q^{n\times m})$ that will be used to generate public keys for group users and the opening authority, respectively.

Output

$$\mathsf{pp} = \{N, \ell, \lambda, n, q, k, m, B, \chi, \sigma, \beta, \mathsf{pp}_{\mathsf{COM}}, \mathbf{F}, \mathbf{G}, \mathbf{A}_{\mathsf{rec}}, \mathbf{A}_{\mathsf{oa}}\}.$$

- $\mathsf{SETUP}_{\mathsf{GM}}$ (pp): This algorithm picks a random matrix $\mathbf{A} = [\mathbf{A}_1|\mathbf{A}_2] \hookleftarrow \mathbb{Z}_q^{n\times m}$ consisting of two same-size matrices, and samples $\mathsf{sk}_{\mathsf{GM}} \hookleftarrow \{0,1\}^m$ and computes $\mathsf{pk}_{\mathsf{GM}} = \mathbf{A} \cdot \mathsf{sk}_{\mathsf{GM}}$, resulting a key pair $(\mathsf{pk}_{\mathsf{GM}}, \mathsf{sk}_{\mathsf{GM}})$ for the GM. Here, we take $\mathsf{pk}_{\mathsf{GM}}$ as an identifier of the group and assume that only the GM (i.e., the party holding $\mathsf{sk}_{\mathsf{GM}}$) can edit and publish the group information.
- $\mathsf{SETUP}_{\mathsf{OA}}$ (pp): This procedure samples two short secret matrices $\mathbf{E}_{\mathsf{oa},i}$ with $i \in \{1,2\}$ from the distribution $D^{\ell}_{\mathbb{Z}^m,\sigma}$ to generate two corresponding matrices $\mathbf{U}_{\mathsf{oa},i} = \mathbf{A}_{\mathsf{oa}} \cdot \mathbf{E}_{\mathsf{oa},i} \in \mathbb{Z}_q^{n\times \ell}$, which forms the secret key $\mathsf{sk}_{\mathsf{OA}} = \mathbf{E}_{\mathsf{oa},1} \in \mathbb{Z}_q^{m\times \ell}$ and the public key $\mathsf{pk}_{\mathsf{OA}} = (\mathbf{U}_{\mathsf{oa},1}, \mathbf{U}_{\mathsf{oa},2}) \in (\mathbb{Z}_q^{n\times \ell})^2$ for the OA.
When GM receives $\mathsf{pk}_{\mathsf{OA}}$ sent from the OA, it executes the following:
    1. Build table **reg**: $=(\{\mathbf{reg}[j][i]\}_{j\in[0,N-1], i\in\{1,2\}})$ initialized as $\mathbf{reg}[j][1] = \mathbf{0}^{nk}$ and $\mathbf{reg}[j][2] = 0$. Note that the former records the user's registered public key, while the latter stores the epoch at which an execution of joining protocol is performed.
    2. Build a Merkle tree $\mathcal{T}$ on top of $\{\mathbf{reg}[j][1]\}_{j\in[0,N-1]}$ whose initial values are zero and then changed with users' public keys by the GM when one successfully joins the group or the group executes an updating operation.
    3. Set the counter of users $c := 0$.

    Then, GM outputs $\mathsf{gpk} = (\mathsf{pp}, \mathsf{pk}_{\mathsf{GM}}, \mathsf{pk}_{\mathsf{OA}})$ and publicizes the initial group information $\mathsf{info} = \emptyset$, while $\mathcal{T}$ as well as c is kept by him self.
- $\mathsf{UKGEN}(\mathsf{pp})$: For each $j \in [0, N-1]$ and each $i \in \{1,2\}$, user U_j samples two secret matrices $\mathbf{E}_{j,i}$ from the Gaussian distribution $D^m_{\mathbb{Z}^m,\sigma}$ to generate two corresponding public matrices $\mathbf{U}_{j,i} = \mathbf{A}_{\mathsf{rec}} \cdot \mathbf{E}_{j,i} \in \mathbb{Z}_q^{n\times m}$, which forms the secret key $\mathsf{sk}_j = \mathbf{E}_{j,1} \in \mathbb{Z}_q^{m\times m}$ and the public key $\mathsf{pk}_j = (\mathbf{U}_{j,1}, \mathbf{U}_{j,2}) \in (\mathbb{Z}_q^{n\times m})^2$. Then, the user computes a hash value $\mathbf{p}_j = \mathsf{bin}(\mathbf{F} \cdot (\mathbf{a}_{j,1}^\top || \mathbf{a}_{j,2}^\top)^\top) \in \{0,1\}^{nk}$ with $\mathbf{a}_{j,i} = \mathsf{mdec}_{n,m,q}(\mathbf{U}_{j,i}^\top) \in \{0,1\}^{nmk}$ for each $i \in \{1,2\}$. We note that all honestly generated pk_j's are non-zero and pairwise distinct, since the probability that users take zero-matrix $\mathbf{U}_{j,i}$ or same matrix (i.e., $\mathbf{U}_{j,i} = \mathbf{U}_{j',i'}$ for some $j \neq j'$ or $i \neq i'$), or finds a collision for hash function $\mathbf{F}$ is negligible (due to the assumed hardness of the SIS problem).
- $\langle\mathsf{JOIN}(\mathsf{sk}); \mathsf{ISSUE}(\mathsf{sk}_{\mathsf{GM}})\rangle(\mathsf{gpk}, \mathsf{pk}, \mathsf{info}_\tau)$: Let $\mathcal{S}_0$ be a set of indexes i of which associated public keys of group users are zero, with the initialization $\{\mathbf{reg}[j][1]\}$. When a user holding key pair $(\mathsf{pk}, \mathsf{sk})$ with binary hash $\mathbf{p}$ wants to join the group at the epoch τ, he sends $\mathbf{p}$ to the GM who proceeds the following procedures with him after the request is accepted:
    1. GM picks a random $j \in \mathcal{S}_0$ and sets a member identifier $\mathsf{bin}(j) \in \{0,1\}^{\ell}$ for the user, and executes the following:
        - Update $\mathcal{T}$ by running procedure $\mathsf{TUpdate}_{\mathbf{A}}(\mathsf{bin}(j), \mathbf{p}_j)$.

  - Register the user to table **reg** as $\mathbf{reg}[j][1] := \mathbf{p}_j$.
  - Update the set $\mathcal{S}_0 := \mathcal{S}_0 - \{j\}$, increase the counter $c := c + 1$.
2. When specific enrollment requests at a same epoch are ending, basing on the above updated results (note that the update process is essentially like that of running algorithm $\mathsf{TAcc}_{\mathbf{A}}(\cdot)$ on $\mathbf{reg}[\cdot][1] = \{\mathbf{reg}[j][1]\}_j$ for the generation of root value $\mathbf{u}$, thus same results are led), the GM runs algorithm $\mathsf{TWitness}_{\mathbf{A}}(\mathbf{reg}[\cdot][1], \mathbf{p}_j)$ to output a witness

$$w^{(j)} = ((j_1, ..., j_\ell) \in \{0,1\}^\ell, (\mathbf{w}_\ell^{(j)}, ..., \mathbf{w}_1^{(1)}) \in (\{0,1\})^\ell)$$

to the fact that $\mathbf{p}_j$ is accumulated in $\mathbf{u}$.
3. User checks the validity of $w^{(j)}$ by algorithm $\mathsf{TVerify}_{\mathbf{A}}(\mathbf{u}, \mathbf{p}_j, w^{(j)})$ and outputs $\perp$ if it is unaccepted. Otherwise, set $\mathsf{wit}_j = (\mathbf{u}, w^{(j)})$ as the witness of pk_j being accumulated into the root $\mathbf{u}$, which plays the similar role to a certificate of public key issued by the GM.

- $\mathsf{GUPDATE}(\mathsf{gpk}, \mathsf{sk}_{\mathsf{GM}}, \mathsf{info}_{\tau_{\mathrm{current}}}, \mathcal{S}, \mathbf{reg})$: GM updates the group information while advancing the epoch by running this algorithm as follows.
  1. Let $\mathcal{S}$ be a set of verified public keys of group users to be removed. If $\mathcal{S} = \emptyset$, go to Step 2. Otherwise, let $\mathcal{S} = \{\mathbf{reg}[j_i][1]\}_{i=1}^r$ for some $r \in [1, N]$ and $j_i \in [0, N-1]$ for all $i \in [r]$, then GM runs $\mathsf{TUpdate}_{\mathbf{A}}(\mathsf{bin}(j_i), \mathbf{0}^{nk})$ to update the tree $\mathcal{T}$, followed by $\mathcal{S}_0 := \mathcal{S}_0 \bigcup \mathcal{S}$.
  2. By construction, each zero-value leaf in $\mathcal{T}$ corresponds to an inactive user, i.e., one that is revoked or has not yet got membership. This means that only active users capable of decrypting well-formed ciphertexts generated in the new epoch τ_{new} will have *non-zero* hash values of public keys $\{\mathbf{p}_j\}_j$, that are accumulated in the root $\mathbf{u}_{\tau_{\mathrm{new}}}$ of the updated tree.
  For each j, let $w^{(j)} \in \{0,1\}^\ell \times (\{0,1\}^{nk})^\ell$ be the witness showing that $\mathbf{p}_j$ is accumulated in $\mathbf{u}_{\tau_{\mathrm{new}}}$. GM publishes the updated group information:

$$\mathsf{info}_{\tau_{\mathrm{new}}} = \left(\mathbf{u}_{\tau_{\mathrm{new}}}, \{w^{(j)}\}_j\right).$$

  As described below, in order to verify ciphertexts bound to epoch τ, the verifier only needs to download the first component $\mathbf{u}_\tau$ of size $\widetilde{\mathcal{O}}(\lambda)$ bits. Meanwhile, to compute a well-formed ciphertext, it is sufficient for sender to download the witness of size $\widetilde{\mathcal{O}}(\ell\lambda)$ of some active user.
- $\langle \mathcal{G}_r, \mathsf{sample}_{\mathcal{R}} \rangle$: Algorithm $\mathcal{G}_r$ outputs parameters (t, e) for the $\mathsf{Prohibitive}$ policy to form $(\mathsf{pk}_{\mathcal{R}}, \mathsf{sk}_{\mathcal{R}}) = ((t, e), \varepsilon)$. Then algorithm $\mathsf{sample}_{\mathcal{R}}$ takes $\mathsf{pk}_{\mathcal{R}}$ as input, and returns a set $\{\mathbf{s}_1, ..., \mathbf{s}_e\} \in (\{0,1\}^t)^e$ and a witness $\mathbf{m} \in \{0,1\}^m$ such that they hold for the relation R_{prohi} (i.e., meet the Eq. (5)).
- $\mathsf{ENC}(\mathsf{pk}_{\mathsf{GM}}, \mathsf{pk}_{\mathsf{OA}}, \mathsf{pk}_j, \mathsf{wit}_j, \mathsf{info}_\tau, \{\mathbf{s}_i\}_{i=1}^e, \mathbf{m}, L)$: To encrypt the sampled witness $\mathbf{m}$ with the group information info_τ at epoch τ, sender first checks whether a witness associated with $\mathsf{bin}(j)$ is contained in info_τ. If it is not this case, return $\perp$. Otherwise, the sender downloads $\mathbf{u}_\tau$ and some witness $(\mathsf{bin}(j), (\mathbf{w}_\ell, ..., \mathbf{w}_1))$ from info_τ, then parses $\mathsf{pk}_{\mathsf{OA}}$ as $(\mathbf{U}_{\mathsf{oa},1}, \mathbf{U}_{\mathsf{oa},2})$ and wit_j as $(\mathbf{u}_\tau, w^{(j)})$ for some $j \in [0, N-1]$, and proceeds as follows.

1. Encrypt the witness $\mathbf{m} \in \{0,1\}^m$ under U_j's public key $\mathsf{pk}_j \in (\mathbb{Z}_q^{n\times m})^2$. For each $i \in \{1,2\}$, randomly take a tuple $(\mathbf{s}_{\mathsf{rec},i}, \mathbf{x}_{\mathsf{rec},i}, \mathbf{y}_{\mathsf{rec},i}) \in U(\{0,1\}^n) \times (\chi^m)^2$ to form the private parameter set $\mathsf{rand}_{\mathsf{rec}} = (\mathbf{s}_{\mathsf{rec},i}, \mathbf{x}_{\mathsf{rec},i}, \mathbf{y}_{\mathsf{rec},i})_{i\in\{1,2\}}$. Compute the corresponding ciphertext $\mathbf{c}_{\mathsf{rec},i} = (\mathbf{c}^{(1)}_{\mathsf{rec},i}, \mathbf{c}^{(2)}_{\mathsf{rec},i}) \in (\mathbb{Z}_q^m)^2$ as
$$\mathbf{c}^{(1)}_{\mathsf{rec},i} = \mathbf{A}^\top_{\mathsf{rec}} \cdot \mathbf{s}_{\mathsf{rec},i} + \mathbf{x}_{\mathsf{rec},i} \bmod q, \mathbf{c}^{(2)}_{\mathsf{rec},i} = \mathbf{U}^\top_{j,i} \cdot \mathbf{s}_{\mathsf{rec},i} + \mathbf{y}_{\mathsf{rec},i} + \mathbf{m} \cdot \lfloor \frac{q}{2} \rceil, \quad (13)$$
which follows the ciphertext $\mathbf{c}_{\mathsf{rec}} = (\mathbf{c}_{\mathsf{rec},1}, \mathbf{c}_{\mathsf{rec},2}) \in (\mathbb{Z}_q^m \times \mathbb{Z}_q^m)^2$.
2. Encrypt the user identifier $\mathbf{j} \in \{0,1\}^\ell$ of user U_j by taking similar operations as above. First take a random tuple $(\mathbf{s}_{\mathsf{oa},i}, \mathbf{x}_{\mathsf{oa},i}, \mathbf{y}_{\mathsf{oa},i}) \in U(\{0,1\}^n) \times \chi^m \times \chi^\ell$ for each $i \in \{1,2\}$, which forms the private randomness set $\mathsf{rand}_{\mathsf{oa}} = (\mathbf{s}_{\mathsf{oa},i}, \mathbf{x}_{\mathsf{oa},i}, \mathbf{y}_{\mathsf{oa},i})_i$. Compute the corresponding ciphertext $\mathbf{c}_{\mathsf{oa},i} = (\mathbf{c}^{(1)}_{\mathsf{oa},i}, \mathbf{c}^{(2)}_{\mathsf{oa},i}) \in (\mathbb{Z}_q^m \times \mathbb{Z}_q^\ell)$ as
$$\mathbf{c}^{(1)}_{\mathsf{oa},i} = \mathbf{A}^\top_{\mathsf{oa}} \cdot \mathbf{s}_{\mathsf{oa},i} + \mathbf{x}_{\mathsf{oa},i} \bmod q, \mathbf{c}^{(2)}_{\mathsf{oa},i} = \mathbf{U}^\top_{\mathsf{oa},i} \cdot \mathbf{s}_{\mathsf{oa},i} + \mathbf{y}_{\mathsf{oa},i} + \mathbf{j} \cdot \lfloor \frac{q}{2} \rceil, \quad (14)$$
which follows the identity ciphertext $\mathbf{c}_{\mathsf{oa}} = (\mathbf{c}_{\mathsf{oa},1}, \mathbf{c}_{\mathsf{oa},2}) \in (\mathbb{Z}_q^m \times \mathbb{Z}_q^\ell)^2$.

Finally, put the above ciphertexts together, we obtain the ciphertext $\Psi = (\mathbf{c}_{\mathsf{rec}}, \mathbf{c}_{\mathsf{oa}})$ and the state information $coins_\Psi = (\mathsf{rand}_{\mathsf{rec}}, \mathsf{rand}_{\mathsf{oa}})$.

- $\mathsf{DEC}(\mathsf{sk}_j, \Psi, L)$: This algorithm takes the following steps to decrypt Ψ:
  1. Parse the secret key sk_j as $\mathbf{E}_{j,1}$ and the ciphertext Ψ as $(\mathbf{c}_{\mathsf{rec}}, \mathbf{c}_{\mathsf{oa}})$.
  2. Use the secret key $\mathbf{E}_{j,1}$ to proceed the decryption of $\mathbf{c}_{\mathsf{rec}}$ as
  $$\mathbf{m} = \left\lfloor \left(\mathbf{c}^{(2)}_{\mathsf{rec},1} - \mathbf{E}^\top_{j,1} \cdot \mathbf{c}^{(1)}_{\mathsf{rec},1}\right) / \left\lfloor \frac{q}{2} \right\rceil \right\rceil. \quad (15)$$
  Then, output $\mathbf{m}$ if it satisfies the relation R_{prohi}. Otherwise, return $\perp$.
- $\mathsf{OPEN}(\mathsf{sk}_{\mathsf{OA}}, \mathsf{info}_\tau, \mathbf{reg}, \Psi, L)$: This algorithm decrypts the ciphertext $\mathbf{c}_{\mathsf{oa}} = (\mathbf{c}_{\mathsf{oa},1}, \mathbf{c}_{\mathsf{oa},2})$ by proceeding the following steps:
  1. Parse the secret key $\mathsf{sk}_{\mathsf{oa}}$ as $\mathbf{E}_{\mathsf{oa},1}$ and the ciphertext Ψ as $(\mathbf{c}_{\mathsf{rec}}, \mathbf{c}_{\mathsf{oa}})$.
  2. To reveal the targeted recipient, use $\mathbf{E}_{\mathsf{oa},1}$ to decrypt the $\mathbf{c}_{\mathsf{oa},1}$ as
  $$\mathbf{j}' = \left\lfloor \left(\mathbf{c}^{(2)}_{\mathsf{oa},1} - \mathbf{E}^\top_{\mathsf{oa},1} \cdot \mathbf{c}^{(1)}_{\mathsf{oa},1}\right) / \left\lfloor \frac{q}{2} \right\rceil \right\rceil. \quad (16)$$
  3. Check that whether the group information info_τ includes a witness containing $\mathbf{j}'$ or not, and return $\perp$ if it is not this case.
  4. Let $j' \in [0, N-1]$ be the integer whose binary decomposition is $\mathbf{j}'$, if $\mathbf{reg}[j'][1] = \mathbf{0}^{nk}$ in table $\mathbf{reg}$, then return $\perp$.
- $\langle \mathcal{P}(\mathsf{pk}_j, \mathsf{wit}_j, \mathbf{m}, coins_\Psi), \mathcal{V}(\pi_\Psi)\rangle(\mathsf{gpk}, \mathsf{info}_\tau, \{\mathbf{s}_i\}_{i=1}^e, \Psi, L)$: Given the common inputs $\mathsf{gpk}, \mathsf{info}_\tau, \{\mathbf{s}_i\}_{i=1}^e, \Psi$ and L. The prover's secret inputs consist of a witness $\mathbf{m} \in \{0,1\}^m$, $\mathsf{pk}_j = (\mathbf{U}_{j,1}, \mathbf{U}_{j,2}) \in (\mathbb{Z}_q^{n\times m})^2$, certificate $\mathsf{wit}_j = (\mathbf{u}_\tau, w^{(j)})$ and random coins $coins_\Psi = (\mathbf{s}_{\mathsf{rec},i}, \mathbf{x}_{\mathsf{rec},i}, \mathbf{y}_{\mathsf{rec},i}; \mathbf{s}_{\mathsf{oa},i}, \mathbf{x}_{\mathsf{oa},i}, \mathbf{y}_{\mathsf{oa},i})_{i\in\{1,2\}}$, while the verifier takes π_Ψ as its private input.
  The prover constructs a zero-knowledge argument system π_Ψ to convince the verifier that the secret inputs he makes satisfy the following conditions (details of which are shown in Sect. 4):

- $\mathbf{G}\cdot\mathbf{p}_j = \mathbf{F}\cdot(\mathbf{a}_{j,1}^\top||\mathbf{a}_{j,2}^\top)^\top \bmod q$.
- $\mathsf{TVerify}_{\mathbf{A}}(\mathbf{u},\mathbf{p}_j,w^{(j)}) = 1$ and $\mathbf{p}_j \neq \mathbf{0}$.
- Witness $\mathbf{m}$ satisfies the relation R_{prohi} defined in Sect. 4.2.
- For each $i\in\{0,1\}$, vectors $\mathbf{s}_{\mathsf{rec},i},\mathbf{s}_{\mathsf{oa},i}$ are of the form $\{0,1\}$, and vectors $\mathbf{x}_{\mathsf{rec},i},\mathbf{y}_{\mathsf{rec},i},\mathbf{x}_{\mathsf{oa},i},\mathbf{y}_{\mathsf{oa},i}$ have infinity B-bounded norm.
- Equations of (13) and (14) hold.

Correctness. The correctness of the proposed group encryption follows from correctly decrypting the GPV dual ciphertexts, which may cause some decryption errors. Indeed, during the decryption procedure of $\mathsf{DEC}(\mathsf{sk}_j,\Psi,L)$, we have:

$$\mathbf{c}_{\mathsf{rec},1}^{(2)} - \mathbf{E}_{j,1}^\top\cdot\mathbf{c}_{\mathsf{rec},1}^{(1)} = \mathbf{y}_{\mathsf{rec},1} - \mathbf{E}_{j,1}^\top\cdot\mathbf{x}_{\mathsf{rec},1} + \mathbf{m}\cdot\left\lfloor\frac{q}{2}\right\rfloor. \tag{17}$$

Note that $\|\mathbf{x}_{\mathsf{rec},1}\|_\infty$ and $\|\mathbf{y}_{\mathsf{rec},1}\|_\infty$ both have upper bound B, and $\|\mathbf{E}_{j,1}\|_\infty$ is bounded by β. Then $\|\mathbf{y}_{\mathsf{rec},1} - \mathbf{E}_{j,1}^\top\cdot\mathbf{x}_{\mathsf{rec},1}\|_\infty \leq B + m\beta B$ and is further bounded by $\widetilde{\mathcal{O}}(n^{1.5})$ which is smaller than $q/5 = \widetilde{\mathcal{O}}(n^2)$. As a result, the decryption algorithm returns $\mathbf{m}$ with overwhelming probability. This gives the correctness of $\mathsf{DEC}(\mathsf{sk}_j\ ,\Psi,L)$. For $\mathsf{OPEN}(\mathsf{sk}_{\mathsf{OA}},\Psi,L)$, a similar analysis is proceeded and $\|\mathbf{y}_{\mathsf{oa},1} - \mathbf{E}_{\mathsf{oa},1}^\top\cdot\mathbf{x}_{\mathsf{oa},1}\|_\infty$ is also bounded by $\widetilde{\mathcal{O}}(n^{1.5})$.

Finally, we argue that if a sender honestly follows all the prescribed algorithms for the specific certified group user, valid witness-vectors to be used in the protocol $\langle\mathcal{P},\mathcal{V}\rangle$ are able to be computed and the present proof is accepted by the verifier, thanks to the completeness of the argument system in Sect. 4.3.

5.2 Analysis of the Scheme

Security Analysis. We provide provable security analysis for our scheme under the SIS and LWE hardness assumptions via the classical reduction methods. These security results and associated proofs are shown in the following.

Theorem 1. *The anonymity is satisfied if the $\mathsf{LWE}_{n,q,\chi}$ assumption holds.*

Proof. We prove the anonymity using a sequence of indistinguishable games, where we begin with running the experiment $\mathbf{Exp}_{\mathcal{A}}^{\mathsf{anon}-0}$ and end with the experiment $\mathbf{Exp}_{\mathcal{A}}^{\mathsf{anon}-1}$ from Definition 5 to show that the advantage for the adversary succeeding in the last game is negligible. For simplicity, hereunder we take PPT algorithms $\mathcal{A}$ and $\mathcal{B}$ as the adversary and challenger, respectively, and denote by W_i the event that the adversary $\mathcal{A}$ returns $b'=1$ in game i.

Game 1: This is the real experiment $\mathbf{Exp}_{\mathcal{A}}^{\mathsf{anon}-0}$ except that $\mathcal{B}$ retains $\mathbf{E}_{\mathsf{oa},2}$, which makes no any difference in the adversary's view since $\mathbf{E}_{\mathsf{oa},2}$ is not used in the following real experiment. Concretely, the challenger $\mathcal{B}$ publicizes the parameters pp containing $\mathbf{A}_{\mathsf{rec}},\mathbf{A}_{\mathsf{oa}}\in\mathbb{Z}^{n\times m},\mathbf{F}\in\mathbb{Z}_q^{n\times 2nmk}$ as a part, and sends the opening public key $\mathsf{pk}_{\mathsf{OA}} = (\mathbf{U}_{\mathsf{oa},1},\mathbf{U}_{\mathsf{oa},2})\in(\mathbb{Z}_q^{n\times m})^2$ to $\mathcal{A}$ who certifies the honest group members on behalf of GM by invoking the USER oracle. Specially, after receiving two users' public keys $\mathsf{pk}_0 = (\mathbf{U}_{0,1},\mathbf{U}_{0,2})\in(\mathbb{Z}_q^{n\times m})^2$ and $\mathsf{pk}_1 =$

$(\mathbf{U}_{1,1}, \mathbf{U}_{1,2}) \in (\mathbb{Z}_q^{n\times m})^2$ of challenger's choice, $\mathcal{A}$ registers the keys in the table **reg** and conducts a number of queries w.r.t. opening and decryption algorithms, whose response is handled by $\mathcal{B}$ by using $\mathsf{sk}_{\mathsf{OA}} = \mathbf{E}_{\mathsf{oa},1}$ and $\mathsf{sk}_0 = \mathbf{E}_{0,1}, \mathsf{sk}_1 = \mathbf{E}_{1,1}$. Then, the adversary moves to the challenge phase to provide a valid witness $\mathbf{m} \in \{0,1\}^m$ satisfying the Prohibitive for challenge. In return, the challenger takes the bit $b = 0$ and computes a group encryption $\Psi^* = (\mathbf{c}^*_{\mathsf{rec}}, \mathbf{c}^*_{\mathsf{oa}})$ of the witness $\mathbf{m}$ under $\mathsf{pk}_b = (\mathbf{U}_{b,1}, \mathbf{U}_{b,2})$, and the user identity $\mathbf{j}_b = \mathbf{j}_0$ under $\mathsf{pk}_{\mathsf{oa}} = (\mathbf{U}_{\mathsf{oa},1}, \mathbf{U}_{\mathsf{oa},2})$ with $\mathbf{c}_{\mathsf{oa}} = (\mathbf{c}_{\mathsf{oa},1}, \mathbf{c}_{\mathsf{oa},2})$, which follows real proofs $\pi^*_{\Psi^*}$ of Ψ^* and queries of opening and decryption under the natural restrictions of the security definition. When $\mathcal{A}$ halts, it returns a bit $b' \in \{0,1\}$ and the challenger $\mathcal{B}$ returns 1 iff $b' = b$. Otherwise, $\mathcal{B}$ outputs 0 indicating that the adversary fails in this game, which gives the success probability $\Pr[W_1 = 1]$.

Game 2: This game is like Game 1 except one change in executing the ciphertext opening oracle $\mathsf{OPEN}(\mathsf{sk}_{\mathsf{oa}}, .)$. Concretely, $\mathcal{B}$ uses $\mathbf{E}_{\mathsf{oa},2} \in \mathbb{Z}_q^{m\times \ell}$ instead of $\mathsf{sk}_{\mathsf{oa}} = \mathbf{E}_{\mathsf{oa},1} \in \mathbb{Z}_q^{m\times \ell}$ to decrypt $\mathbf{c}_{\mathsf{oa}}$ among the ciphertext $\Psi = (\mathbf{c}_{\mathsf{rec}}, \mathbf{c}_{\mathsf{oa}})$. It can be seen that, in the $\mathcal{A}$'s view, this game is the same as Game 1 until the event F_1 that $\mathcal{A}$ queries the opening oracle $\mathsf{OPEN}(\mathsf{sk}_{\mathsf{oa}}, .)$ for a ciphertext $\Psi = (\mathbf{c}_{\mathsf{rec}}, \mathbf{c}_{\mathsf{oa},1}, \mathbf{c}_{\mathsf{oa},2})$ where $\mathbf{c}_{\mathsf{oa},1}, \mathbf{c}_{\mathsf{oa},2}$ encrypt two distinct ℓ-size identities. By the soundness of our argument presented in Sect. 4.3, $\Pr[W_2] - \Pr[W_1]$ is bounded by $\Pr[F_1]$ which itself is bounded by $\mathbf{Adv}^{\mathsf{sound}}_{\mathcal{B}}(\lambda)$.

Game 3: This game is identical to Game 2 except a modification in the generation of proofs $\pi^*_{\Psi^*}$. Instead of employing the real random coins $coins^*_{\Psi} = (\{\mathbf{s}^*_{\mathsf{rec},i}\}_i, \{\mathbf{x}^*_{\mathsf{rec},i}\}_i, \{\mathbf{y}^*_{\mathsf{rec},i}\}_i, \{\mathbf{s}^*_{\mathsf{oa},i}\}_i, \{\mathbf{x}^*_{\mathsf{oa},i}\}_i, \{\mathbf{y}^*_{\mathsf{oa},i}\}_i)$ used for Ψ^* to generate proofs, we employ the zero-knowledge simulator of argument system described in Sect. 4.3 once invoking $\mathsf{PROVE}^b_{\mathcal{P},\mathcal{P}'}$ after the challenge phase (note that, given trusted public parameters, the computationally indistinguishable simulation is achieved via the techniques [17] without increasing the number of rounds). Here the computational ZK property ensures that, for any PPT adversary, the change is unnoticed: $|\Pr[W_3] - \Pr[W_2]| \in \mathsf{negl}(\lambda)$.

Game 4: This game is same as Game 3 except that we modify the generation of $\Psi^* = (\mathbf{c}^*_{\mathsf{rec}}, \mathbf{c}^*_{\mathsf{oa}})$ with $\mathbf{c}^*_{\mathsf{oa}} = (\mathbf{c}^*_{\mathsf{oa},1}, \mathbf{c}^*_{\mathsf{oa},2})$ by encrypting a random size-ℓ identity $\mathbf{j}_1$ as $\mathbf{c}^*_{\mathsf{oa},1}$, while still retaining $\mathbf{c}^*_{\mathsf{oa},2}$ for the encryption of the index $\mathbf{j}_0$ corresponding to user U_0. By the semantic security of GPV dual encryption [18] (assuming the hardness of LWE problem) for public key $\mathsf{pk}_{\mathsf{oa}} = (\mathbf{U}_{\mathsf{oa},1}, \mathbf{U}_{\mathsf{oa},2})$, this game is identical to Game 3, i.e., $|\Pr[W_4] - \Pr[W_3]| \leq \mathbf{Adv}^{\mathsf{LWE}}(\lambda)$.

Game 5: This game makes one change by switching back to the application of $\mathbf{E}_{\mathsf{oa},1} \in \mathbb{Z}_q^{m\times \ell}$ for the $\mathsf{OPEN}(\mathsf{sk}_{\mathsf{oa}}, \cdot)$ queries with discarding $\mathbf{E}_{\mathsf{oa},2}$, and the modification is invariant to the adversary except the event F_2, where the queries to the DEC for a valid ciphertext Ψ containing $\mathbf{c}^*_{\mathsf{oa},1}, \mathbf{c}^*_{\mathsf{oa},2}$ encrypting distinct ℓ-size identities $\mathbf{j}_0$ and $\mathbf{j}_1$, happens. But, the occurrence of F_2 implies that the simulation soundness of the underlying ZKAoK system used to generate Π_{GE} is broken. This results into $|\Pr[W_5 = 1] - \Pr[W_4 = 1]| \leq \mathbf{Adv}^{\mathsf{sound}}_{\Pi_{\mathsf{GE}}}(\lambda) = \mathsf{negl}(\lambda)$.

Game 6: Here, this experiment performs a modification to the Game 5 only by taking $\mathbf{c}_{\mathsf{oa},2}$ as the encryption of $\mathbf{j}_1$ for the challenge ciphertext $\Psi^* = (\mathbf{c}^*_{\mathsf{rec}}, \mathbf{c}^*_{\mathsf{oa}})$

with $\mathbf{c}^*_{\mathsf{oa}} = (\mathbf{c}^*_{\mathsf{oa},1}, \mathbf{c}^*_{\mathsf{oa},2})$. Note that this change is unnoticed to $\mathcal{A}$ due to the semantic security the encryption shares for public key $\mathbf{U}_{\mathsf{oa},2}$, and also for the application of $\mathbf{E}_{\mathsf{oa},1}$ to the OPEN, we have $|\Pr[W_6 = 1] - \Pr[W_5 = 1]| = \mathsf{negl}(\lambda)$.

Game 7: This experiment generates a real proof for ciphertext $\Psi^* = (\mathbf{c}^*_{\mathsf{rec}}, \mathbf{c}^*_{\mathsf{oa}})$ instead of using simulated proof, which is the only modification different from Game 6. The computational zero-knowledgeness of the underlying ZKAoK system makes the difference between Game 6 and Game 7 negligible, i.e., $\Pr[W_6 = 1] \approx \Pr[W_7 = 1]$. This is actually the experiment $\mathbf{Exp}^{\mathsf{anon}-1}_{\mathcal{A}}(\lambda)$, which directly leads that $\Pr[W_7 = 1] = \mathbf{Exp}^{\mathsf{anon}-1}_{\mathcal{A}}(\lambda)$. By these above games, we have $|\mathbf{Exp}^{\mathsf{anon}-1}_{\mathcal{A}}(\lambda) - \mathbf{Exp}^{\mathsf{anon}-0}_{\mathcal{A}}(\lambda)| = \mathsf{negl}(\lambda)$. This proves the anonymity. □

Theorem 2. *The message secrecy is satisfied if the* $\mathsf{LWE}_{n,q,\chi}$ *assumption holds.*

Proof. In a similar manner to that used in proving Theorem 1, we complete the proof via a sequence of indistinguishable games in which the first one is exactly the experiment $\mathbf{Exp}^{\mathsf{sec}-1}_{\mathcal{A}}$ which generates a real ciphertext and an associated real proof while the last one is the experiment $\mathbf{Exp}^{\mathsf{sec}-0}_{\mathcal{A}}$ that outputs a random ciphertext and an associated simulated proof. For simplicity, we use $\mathcal{A}, \mathcal{B}$ to represent the adversary and challenger, respectively. In addition, we also denote by W_i the event that the adversary $\mathcal{A}$ returns $b' = 1$ in game i.

Game 1: This is the real experiment $\mathbf{Exp}^{\mathsf{sec}-1}_{\mathcal{A}}$ except that $\mathcal{B}$ retains $\mathbf{E}_{j,2}$, which makes no any difference in the adversary's view since $\mathbf{E}_{j,2}$ is not used in the following real experiment. Concretely, $\mathcal{A}$ is first fed with public parameters pp including $\mathbf{A}_{\mathsf{rec}} \in \mathbb{Z}_q^{n\times m}$ by challenger. Then, under its whole control, the adversary generates public keys $\mathsf{pk}_{\mathsf{OA}} = (\mathbf{U}_{\mathsf{oa},1}, \mathbf{U}_{\mathsf{oa},2}) \in (\mathbb{Z}_q^{n\times m})^2$ and $\mathsf{pk}_{\mathsf{GM}}$, and triggers the JOIN protocol with the challenger to register and certify the public key $\mathsf{pk}_j = (\mathbf{U}_{j,1}, \mathbf{U}_{j,2}) \in (\mathbb{Z}_q^{n\times m})^2$ for some honest receiver of the challenger's choice. After that, the adversary $\mathcal{A}$ makes a polynomial number of queries to DEC oracle which is faithfully handled by the challenger using $\mathbf{E}_{j,1}$. Then, $\mathcal{A}$ provides a valid witness $\mathbf{m} \in \{0,1\}^m$ satisfying the Prohibitive for challenge. Subsequently, the challenger take $b = 1$ and computes a ciphertext $\Psi^* = (\mathbf{c}^*_{\mathsf{rec}}, \mathbf{c}^*_{\mathsf{oa}})$ which contains a group encryption of the real plaintext $\mathbf{m}$ under pk_j and returns it back as a challenger ciphertext. Then, a polynomial number of real proofs $\pi^*_{\Psi^*}$ which are associated with the challenge ciphertext Ψ^* are followed, and the decryption oracle with obvious restrictions is further granted. After doing this, $\mathcal{A}$ halts this game and outputs its guess bit $b' \in \{0,1\}$.

Game 2: This game is identical to Game 1 except one change in handling the ciphertext decryption oracle $\mathsf{DEC}(\mathsf{sk}_j, .)$. Concretely, $\mathcal{B}$ uses $\mathbf{E}_{j,2} \in \mathbb{Z}_q^{m\times m}$ instead of $\mathsf{sk}_j = \mathbf{E}_{j,1} \in \mathbb{Z}_q^{m\times m}$ to decrypt $\mathbf{c}_{\mathsf{rec}}$ among the ciphertext $\Psi = (\mathbf{c}_{\mathsf{rec}}, \mathbf{c}_{\mathsf{oa}})$. In the $\mathcal{A}$'s view, this game is the same as Game 1 until the event F_3 that $\mathcal{A}$ queries a ciphertext $\Psi = (\mathbf{c}_{\mathsf{rec},1}, \mathbf{c}_{\mathsf{rec},2}, \mathbf{c}_{\mathsf{oa}})$ where $\mathbf{c}_{\mathsf{rec},1}, \mathbf{c}_{\mathsf{rec},2}$ encrypts two distinct m-size messages. By the soundness of our argument presented in Sect. 4.3, $\Pr[W_2] - \Pr[W_1]$ is bounded by $\Pr[F_3] \leq \mathbf{Adv}^{\mathsf{sound}}_{\mathcal{B}}(\lambda)$.

Game 3: This game is like Game 2 except a modification in generating proofs $\pi^*_{\Psi^*}$. Instead of employing the real random coins $coins^*_{\Psi} = (\{\mathbf{s}^*_{\mathsf{rec},i}\}_i, \{\mathbf{x}^*_{\mathsf{rec},i}\}_i, \{\mathbf{y}^*_{\mathsf{rec},i}\}_i, \{\mathbf{s}^*_{\mathsf{oa},i}\}_i, \{\mathbf{x}^*_{\mathsf{oa},i}\}_i, \{\mathbf{y}^*_{\mathsf{oa},i}\}_i)$ used for Ψ^* to generate proofs, we rather to apply the zero-knowledge simulator presented in Sect. 4.3 once invoking $\mathsf{PROVE}^{b}_{\mathcal{P},\mathcal{P}'}$ after the challenge phase (i.e., given trusted public parameters, the computationally indistinguishable simulation is achieved with the techniques [17]). Here the computational ZK property ensures that, for any PPT adversary, the change is unnoticed: $|\Pr[W_3] - \Pr[W_2]| \in \mathsf{negl}(\lambda)$.

Game 4: In this game, we modify the generation of $\Psi^* = (\mathbf{c}^*_{\mathsf{rec}}, \mathbf{c}^*_{\mathsf{oa}})$ with $\mathbf{c}^*_{\mathsf{rec}} = (\mathbf{c}^*_{\mathsf{rec},1}, \mathbf{c}^*_{\mathsf{rec},2})$ by encrypting a random size-m message $\mathbf{m}' \in R_{\mathsf{pro}}$ as $\mathbf{c}^*_{\mathsf{rec},1}$, while still retaining $\mathbf{c}^*_{\mathsf{rec},2}$ for the encryption of $\mathbf{m} \in R_{\mathsf{pro}}$. By the semantic security of GPV dual encryption [18] (under the hardness assumption of the LWE problem) for public key $\mathsf{pk}_j = (\mathbf{U}_{j,1}, \mathbf{U}_{j,2})$, this game is identical to Game 3, i.e., $|\Pr[W_4] - \Pr[W_3]| \leq \mathbf{Adv}^{\mathsf{LWE}}(\lambda)$.

Game 5: This game makes one change by switching back to the application of $\mathbf{E}_{j,1} \in \mathbb{Z}_q^{m\times m}$ for the $\mathsf{DEC}(\mathsf{sk}_j, \cdot)$ queries with discarding $\mathbf{E}_{j,2}$, and the modification is invariant to the adversary except the event F_4, where the queries to the DEC for a valid ciphertext Ψ containing $\mathbf{c}^*_{\mathsf{rec},1}, \mathbf{c}^*_{\mathsf{rec},2}$ encrypting distinct messages satisfied the R_{Pro} relation, happens. But, the occurrence of F_4 implies that the simulation soundness of the underlying ZKAoK system used to generate Π_{GE} is broken. This results into $|\Pr[W_5 = 1] - \Pr[W_4 = 1]| \leq \mathbf{Adv}^{\mathsf{sound}}_{\Pi_{\mathsf{GE}}}(\lambda) = \mathsf{negl}(\lambda)$.

Game 6: Here, this experiment performs a modification to the Game 5 only by taking $\mathbf{c}_{\mathsf{rec},2}$ as the encryption of $\mathbf{m}' \in R_{\mathsf{Pro}}$ for the challenge ciphertext $\Psi^* = (\mathbf{c}^*_{\mathsf{rec}}, \mathbf{c}^*_{\mathsf{oa}})$ with $\mathbf{c}^*_{\mathsf{rec}} = (\mathbf{c}^*_{\mathsf{rec},1}, \mathbf{c}^*_{\mathsf{rec},2})$. Note that this change is unnoticed to $\mathcal{A}$ due to the semantic security the encryption shares for public key $\mathbf{U}_{j,2}$, and also for the application of $\mathbf{E}_{j,1}$ to the DEC, we have $|\Pr[W_6 = 1] - \Pr[W_5 = 1]| = \mathsf{negl}(\lambda)$.

Game 7: Here, this experiment generates a real proof for ciphertext $\Psi^* = (\mathbf{c}^*_{\mathsf{rec}}, \mathbf{c}^*_{\mathsf{oa}})$ instead of using simulated proof, which is the only modification different to Game 6. The computational zero-knowledgeness of the underlying ZKAoK system makes the difference between Game 6 and Game 7 negligible, i.e., $\Pr[W_6 = 1] \approx \Pr[W_7 = 1]$. This is actually the experiment $\mathbf{Exp}^{\mathsf{sec}-0}_{\mathcal{A}}(\lambda)$, which directly leads that $\Pr[W_7 = 1] = \mathbf{Exp}^{\mathsf{sec}-0}_{\mathcal{A}}(\lambda)$. Thus, we have $|\mathbf{Exp}^{\mathsf{sec}-1}_{\mathcal{A}}(\lambda) - \mathbf{Exp}^{\mathsf{sec}-0}_{\mathcal{A}}(\lambda)| = \mathsf{negl}(\lambda)$, which proves the message security. □

Theorem 3. *The scheme is sound assuming that the SIS assumption holds.*

Proof. It suffices for us to prove these facts: for a given message filtering policy Prohibitive, a ciphertext $\Psi^* = (\mathbf{c}_{\mathsf{rec}^*}, \mathbf{c}_{\mathsf{oa}^*})$, a Label L and an associated with proof Ψ^*, the public key associated with the identity revealed by the adversary is valid, certified, unique and the provided ciphertext Ψ^* is encrypted under this key. By the Lemma 2, the distribution of public keys is uniform, which ensures the public key is dense. In other words, the public is valid. In addition, the public key is unique since an occurring collision breaks the injective property of the mapping $\mathbf{F} \cdot [\mathbf{a}_1^\top | \mathbf{a}_2^\top]$. Thus, we only need to prove the other two cases.

a. The public key is certified (activated). If not, for some $j \in [0, N-1]$, there is an associated binary vector $\mathbf{p}_j \neq \mathbf{0}$ being accumulated into the published root value $\mathbf{u}$, but it is not equal to any value $\mathsf{bin}(\mathbf{F} \cdot [\mathbf{a}_1^\top | \mathbf{a}_2^\top])$, which contradicts the security of the accumulator.

b. The ciphertext is actually an encryption of witness $\mathbf{m}$ under this public key. If not, this event implies a breach in the computational soundness of our argument system and the binding property of the commitment scheme, which breaks the assumed hardness of the SIS problem. □

Efficiency Analysis. It can be seen that all algorithms used for the construction of the present group encryption are polynomially effective. The efficiency evaluation of the scheme is shown as follows.

- The public key of GM is a vector with bit-size $\widetilde{\mathcal{O}}(\lambda)$, and that of OA and users are respectively a matrix of bit-size $\widetilde{\mathcal{O}}(\lambda^2)$.
- The GM's secret key is given by a bit string of size $\widetilde{\mathcal{O}}(\lambda)$, and the secret keys of OA and users are respectively a small-norm matrix of bit size $\widetilde{\mathcal{O}}(\lambda^2)$.
- The ciphertext Ψ consists of $\mathbf{c}_{\mathsf{rec}} = (\mathbf{c}_{\mathsf{rec},1}, \mathbf{c}_{\mathsf{rec},2}) \in (\mathbb{Z}_q^m \times \mathbb{Z}_q^m)^2$ and $\mathbf{c}_{\mathsf{oa}} = (\mathbf{c}_{\mathsf{oa},1}, \mathbf{c}_{\mathsf{oa},2}) \in (\mathbb{Z}_q^m \times \mathbb{Z}_q^\ell)^2$, which leads the total bit size $\widetilde{\mathcal{O}}(\lambda + \ell)$.
- The communication cost of the protocol $\langle \mathcal{P}, \mathcal{V} \rangle$ largely relies on the bit-size of witness $\mathbf{x}$ with size $n_2 = m + 2n + 2m(k + nk + 2\delta_{2B}) + (m - t + 1)e\delta_{m-d}$ shown in Sect. 4.3, which leads $\widetilde{\mathcal{O}}(\lambda^2)$ bit-size.

In Table 1, given a security parameter λ, let $N = 2^\ell$, κ and Σ be the group size, the number of protocol repetitions and a one-time signature, respectively, we give a somewhat rough comparison between our scheme and the currently existing post-quantum secure group encryption schemes [25] (lattice-based variant) and [35] (code-based variant) in terms of functionality, efficiency and security. In the solid security, the full dynamicity is achieved with a highly reasonable cost: the GM only needs to update values of size $\widetilde{\mathcal{O}}(\ell\lambda)$ when group information changes.

Table 1. Comparison between schemes [25,35] and ours

Scheme	GM		OA		U		Ciph.	Commu.	Dynam.	Model
	pk	sk	pk	sk	pk	sk				
[25]	$\widetilde{\mathcal{O}}(\ell\lambda^2)$	$\widetilde{\mathcal{O}}(\lambda^2)$	$\widetilde{\mathcal{O}}(\lambda^2)$	$\widetilde{\mathcal{O}}(\lambda^2)$	$\widetilde{\mathcal{O}}(\lambda^2)$	$\widetilde{\mathcal{O}}(\lambda^2)$	$\widetilde{\mathcal{O}}(\lambda) + \lvert\Sigma\rvert$	$\kappa\widetilde{\mathcal{O}}(\lambda^2)$	partial	Std.
[35]	$\widetilde{\mathcal{O}}(\lambda)$	$\widetilde{\mathcal{O}}(\lambda)$	$\widetilde{\mathcal{O}}(\lambda^2)$	$\widetilde{\mathcal{O}}(\lambda^2)$	$\widetilde{\mathcal{O}}(\lambda^2)$	$\widetilde{\mathcal{O}}(\lambda^2)$	$\widetilde{\mathcal{O}}(\lambda^2)$	$\kappa\widetilde{\mathcal{O}}(\lambda^2)$	full	RO.
Ours	$\widetilde{\mathcal{O}}(\lambda)$	$\widetilde{\mathcal{O}}(\lambda)$	$\widetilde{\mathcal{O}}(\lambda^2)$	$\widetilde{\mathcal{O}}(\lambda^2)$	$\widetilde{\mathcal{O}}(\lambda^2)$	$\widetilde{\mathcal{O}}(\lambda^2)$	$\widetilde{\mathcal{O}}(\lambda)$	$\widetilde{\mathcal{O}}(\lambda^2)$	full	Std.

To better understand the advantage of our design, we also give a slightly concrete efficiency comparison between our scheme and the post-quantum safe schemes [25] and [35] for a same group size $N = 2^{10}$ toward the 80-bit security. By using the security analysis techniques shown in [35, 43, and references therein], we choose the trade-off parameters as $(n, q) = (2795, 1125899906842679 \approx 2^{50})$, $(n, k_1, t_1, k_2, t_2, m, t_m, p, t, k) = (8192, 7997, 7, 7711, 18, 2^{38}, 279, 1024, 64, 10)$ and $(n, q, t, e, d) = (222, 524309 \approx 2^{19}, 64, 10, 10)$ for these schemes and ours, respectively. The results are shown in Table 2 where all the sizes of keys, ciphertexts and communication cost are almost highly superior than those of previous schemes. Particularly, our scheme obtains the drastic efficiency gains compared to [25] due to the free-of-trapdoor design. Besides, the group update cost of [35] and ours is 10.00 KB and 5.15 KB, respectively.

Table 2. Efficiency comparison between schemes [25,35] and ours

	GM		OA		U		Ciph.	Commu.
	pk	sk	pk	sk	pk	sk		
[25]	68.60 GB	482.55 GB	2.37 GB	38.86 GB	2.37 GB	38.86 GB	2.36 TB	3728 TB
[35]	1.00 KB	32.00 GB	15.62 MB	46.86 MB	15.06 MB	45.24 MB	4.00 KB	66107 TB
Ours	0.54 KB	1.08 KB	10.85 KB	129.50 KB	9.40 MB	112.30 MB	0.13 MB	10.32 GB

6 Conclusion

In this paper, we provide a re-formalized definition and security model of FDGE that is essentially equal to but more succinct than that of [35]. Then, we provide two generic and efficient zero-knowledge proof methods for demonstrating the inequalities of binary vectors, which can be readily extended to the case of general vectors. Finally, combining the appropriate cryptographic materials and the proof techniques just presented, we achieve the first lattice-based group encryption system which meanwhile offers the full dynamicity and the message filtering policy. Our scheme is constructed in a simpler manner and nearly outweighs the post-quantum secure ones [25,35] in terms of functions, efficiency and security.

Acknowledgement. This work has been supported by National Cryptography Development Fund (No. MMJJ20180110), National Natural Science Foundation of China (No. 61960206014), (No. 62121001) and (No. 61972429), and Guangdong Major Project of Basic and Applied Basic Research (No. 2019B030302008).

References

1. El Aimani, L., Joye, M.: Toward practical group encryption. In: Jacobson, M., Locasto, M., Mohassel, P., Safavi-Naini, R. (eds.) ACNS 2013. LNCS, vol. 7954, pp. 237–252. Springer, Heidelberg (2013). https://doi.org/10.1007/978-3-642-38980-1_15
2. Ajtai, M.: Generating hard instances of the short basis problem. In: Wiedermann, J., van Emde Boas, P., Nielsen, M. (eds.) ICALP 1999. LNCS, vol. 1644, pp. 1–9. Springer, Heidelberg (1999). https://doi.org/10.1007/3-540-48523-6_1
3. Banaszczyk, W.: New bounds in some transference theorems in the geometry of numbers. Mathematische Annalen **296**(1), 625–635 (1993)
4. Barić, N., Pfitzmann, B.: Collision-free accumulators and fail-stop signature schemes without trees. In: Fumy, W. (ed.) EUROCRYPT 1997. LNCS, vol. 1233, pp. 480–494. Springer, Heidelberg (1997). https://doi.org/10.1007/3-540-69053-0_33
5. Baum, C., Damgård, I., Lyubashevsky, V., Oechsner, S., Peikert, C.: More efficient commitments from structured lattice assumptions. In: Catalano, D., De Prisco, R. (eds.) SCN 2018. LNCS, vol. 11035, pp. 368–385. Springer, Cham (2018). https://doi.org/10.1007/978-3-319-98113-0_20
6. Bellare, M., Micciancio, D., Warinschi, B.: Foundations of group signatures: formal definitions, simplified requirements, and a construction based on general assumptions. In: Biham, E. (ed.) EUROCRYPT 2003. LNCS, vol. 2656, pp. 614–629. Springer, Heidelberg (2003). https://doi.org/10.1007/3-540-39200-9_38

7. Bellare, M., Shi, H., Zhang, C.: Foundations of group signatures: the case of dynamic groups. In: Menezes, A. (ed.) CT-RSA 2005. LNCS, vol. 3376, pp. 136–153. Springer, Heidelberg (2005). https://doi.org/10.1007/978-3-540-30574-3_11
8. Boneh, D., Shacham, H.: Group signatures with verifier-local revocation. In: CCS, pp. 168–177. ACM (2004)
9. Bootle, J., Cerulli, A., Chaidos, P., Ghadafi, E., Groth, J.: Foundations of fully dynamic group signatures. In: Manulis, M., Sadeghi, A.-R., Schneider, S. (eds.) ACNS 2016. LNCS, vol. 9696, pp. 117–136. Springer, Cham (2016). https://doi.org/10.1007/978-3-319-39555-5_7
10. Brakerski, Z., Langlois, A., Peikert, C., Regev, O., Stehlé, D.: Classical hardness of learning with errors. In: STOC, pp. 575–584. ACM (2013)
11. Bresson, E., Stern, J.: Efficient revocation in group signatures. In: Kim, K. (ed.) PKC 2001. LNCS, vol. 1992, pp. 190–206. Springer, Heidelberg (2001). https://doi.org/10.1007/3-540-44586-2_15
12. Camenisch, J., Lysyanskaya, A.: Dynamic accumulators and application to efficient revocation of anonymous credentials. In: Yung, M. (ed.) CRYPTO 2002. LNCS, vol. 2442, pp. 61–76. Springer, Heidelberg (2002). https://doi.org/10.1007/3-540-45708-9_5
13. Camenisch, J., Lysyanskaya, A.: A signature scheme with efficient protocols. In: Cimato, S., Persiano, G., Galdi, C. (eds.) SCN 2002. LNCS, vol. 2576, pp. 268–289. Springer, Heidelberg (2003). https://doi.org/10.1007/3-540-36413-7_20
14. Cash, D., Hofheinz, D., Kiltz, E., Peikert, C.: Bonsai trees, or how to delegate a lattice basis. In: Gilbert, H. (ed.) EUROCRYPT 2010. LNCS, vol. 6110, pp. 523–552. Springer, Heidelberg (2010). https://doi.org/10.1007/978-3-642-13190-5_27
15. Cathalo, J., Libert, B., Yung, M.: Group encryption: non-interactive realization in the standard model. In: Matsui, M. (ed.) ASIACRYPT 2009. LNCS, vol. 5912, pp. 179–196. Springer, Heidelberg (2009). https://doi.org/10.1007/978-3-642-10366-7_11
16. Chaum, D., van Heyst, E.: Group signatures. In: Davies, D.W. (ed.) EUROCRYPT 1991. LNCS, vol. 547, pp. 257–265. Springer, Heidelberg (1991). https://doi.org/10.1007/3-540-46416-6_22
17. Damgård, I.: Efficient concurrent zero-knowledge in the auxiliary string model. In: Preneel, B. (ed.) EUROCRYPT 2000. LNCS, vol. 1807, pp. 418–430. Springer, Heidelberg (2000). https://doi.org/10.1007/3-540-45539-6_30
18. Gentry, C., Peikert, C., Vaikuntanathan, V.: Trapdoors for hard lattices and new cryptographic constructions. In: STOC, pp. 197–206. ACM (2008)
19. Izabachène, M., Pointcheval, D., Vergnaud, D.: Mediated traceable anonymous encryption. In: Abdalla, M., Barreto, P.S.L.M. (eds.) LATINCRYPT 2010. LNCS, vol. 6212, pp. 40–60. Springer, Heidelberg (2010). https://doi.org/10.1007/978-3-642-14712-8_3
20. Kiayias, A., Tsiounis, Y., Yung, M.: Traceable signatures. In: Cachin, C., Camenisch, J.L. (eds.) EUROCRYPT 2004. LNCS, vol. 3027, pp. 571–589. Springer, Heidelberg (2004). https://doi.org/10.1007/978-3-540-24676-3_34
21. Kiayias, A., Tsiounis, Y., Yung, M.: Group encryption. In: Kurosawa, K. (ed.) ASIACRYPT 2007. LNCS, vol. 4833, pp. 181–199. Springer, Heidelberg (2007). https://doi.org/10.1007/978-3-540-76900-2_11
22. Kiayias, A., Yung, M.: Secure scalable group signature with dynamic joins and separable authorities. Int. J. Secur. Netw. **1**(1/2), 24–45 (2006)
23. Langlois, A., Ling, S., Nguyen, K., Wang, H.: Lattice-based group signature scheme with verifier-local revocation. In: Krawczyk, H. (ed.) PKC 2014. LNCS,

vol. 8383, pp. 345–361. Springer, Heidelberg (2014). https://doi.org/10.1007/978-3-642-54631-0_20
24. Libert, B., Ling, S., Mouhartem, F., Nguyen, K., Wang, H.: Signature schemes with efficient protocols and dynamic group signatures from lattice assumptions. In: Cheon, J.H., Takagi, T. (eds.) ASIACRYPT 2016. LNCS, vol. 10032, pp. 373–403. Springer, Heidelberg (2016). https://doi.org/10.1007/978-3-662-53890-6_13
25. Libert, B., Ling, S., Mouhartem, F., Nguyen, K., Wang, H.: Zero-knowledge arguments for matrix-vector relations and lattice-based group encryption. In: Cheon, J.H., Takagi, T. (eds.) ASIACRYPT 2016. LNCS, vol. 10032, pp. 101–131. Springer, Heidelberg (2016). https://doi.org/10.1007/978-3-662-53890-6_4
26. Libert, B., Ling, S., Nguyen, K., Wang, H.: Zero-knowledge arguments for lattice-based accumulators: logarithmic-size ring signatures and group signatures without trapdoors. In: Fischlin, M., Coron, J.-S. (eds.) EUROCRYPT 2016. LNCS, vol. 9666, pp. 1–31. Springer, Heidelberg (2016). https://doi.org/10.1007/978-3-662-49896-5_1
27. Libert, B., Ling, S., Nguyen, K., Wang, H.: Lattice-based zero-knowledge arguments for integer relations. In: Shacham, H., Boldyreva, A. (eds.) CRYPTO 2018. LNCS, vol. 10992, pp. 700–732. Springer, Cham (2018). https://doi.org/10.1007/978-3-319-96881-0_24
28. Libert, B., Peters, T., Yung, M.: Scalable group signatures with revocation. In: Pointcheval, D., Johansson, T. (eds.) EUROCRYPT 2012. LNCS, vol. 7237, pp. 609–627. Springer, Heidelberg (2012). https://doi.org/10.1007/978-3-642-29011-4_36
29. Libert, B., Yung, M., Joye, M., Peters, T.: Traceable group encryption. In: Krawczyk, H. (ed.) PKC 2014. LNCS, vol. 8383, pp. 592–610. Springer, Heidelberg (2014). https://doi.org/10.1007/978-3-642-54631-0_34
30. Ling, S., Nguyen, K., Stehlé, D., Wang, H.: Improved zero-knowledge proofs of knowledge for the ISIS problem, and applications. In: Kurosawa, K., Hanaoka, G. (eds.) PKC 2013. LNCS, vol. 7778, pp. 107–124. Springer, Heidelberg (2013). https://doi.org/10.1007/978-3-642-36362-7_8
31. Ling, S., Nguyen, K., Wang, H., Xu, Y.: Lattice-based group signatures: achieving full dynamicity with ease. In: Gollmann, D., Miyaji, A., Kikuchi, H. (eds.) ACNS 2017. LNCS, vol. 10355, pp. 293–312. Springer, Cham (2017). https://doi.org/10.1007/978-3-319-61204-1_15
32. Micciancio, D., Peikert, C.: Hardness of SIS and LWE with small parameters. In: Canetti, R., Garay, J.A. (eds.) CRYPTO 2013. LNCS, vol. 8042, pp. 21–39. Springer, Heidelberg (2013). https://doi.org/10.1007/978-3-642-40041-4_2
33. Nakanishi, T., Fujii, H., Hira, Y., Funabiki, N.: Revocable group signature schemes with constant costs for signing and verifying. In: Jarecki, S., Tsudik, G. (eds.) PKC 2009. LNCS, vol. 5443, pp. 463–480. Springer, Heidelberg (2009). https://doi.org/10.1007/978-3-642-00468-1_26
34. Naor, M., Yung, M.: Public-key cryptosystems provably secure against chosen ciphertext attacks. In: ACM, pp. 427–437. ACM (1990)
35. Nguyen, K., Safavi-Naini, R., Susilo, W., Wang, H., Xu, Y., Zeng, N.: Group encryption: full dynamicity, message filtering and code-based instantiation. In: Garay, J.A. (ed.) PKC 2021. LNCS, vol. 12711, pp. 678–708. Springer, Cham (2021). https://doi.org/10.1007/978-3-030-75248-4_24
36. Nguyen, L.: Accumulators from bilinear pairings and applications. In: Menezes, A. (ed.) CT-RSA 2005. LNCS, vol. 3376, pp. 275–292. Springer, Heidelberg (2005). https://doi.org/10.1007/978-3-540-30574-3_19

37. Paillier, P.: Public-key cryptosystems based on composite degree residuosity classes. In: Stern, J. (ed.) EUROCRYPT 1999. LNCS, vol. 1592, pp. 223–238. Springer, Heidelberg (1999). https://doi.org/10.1007/3-540-48910-X_16
38. Peikert, C.: Public-key cryptosystems from the worst-case shortest vector problem: extended abstract. In: STOC, pp. 333–342. ACM (2009)
39. Regev, O.: On lattices, learning with errors, random linear codes, and cryptography. In: STOC, pp. 84–93. ACM (2005)
40. Sakai, Y., Schuldt, J.C.N., Emura, K., Hanaoka, G., Ohta, K.: On the security of dynamic group signatures: preventing signature hijacking. In: Fischlin, M., Buchmann, J., Manulis, M. (eds.) PKC 2012. LNCS, vol. 7293, pp. 715–732. Springer, Heidelberg (2012). https://doi.org/10.1007/978-3-642-30057-8_42
41. Stern, J.: A new paradigm for public key identification. IEEE Trans. Inf. Theory **42**(6), 1757–1768 (1996)
42. Trolin, M., Wikström, D.: Hierarchical group signatures. In: Caires, L., Italiano, G.F., Monteiro, L., Palamidessi, C., Yung, M. (eds.) ICALP 2005. LNCS, vol. 3580, pp. 446–458. Springer, Heidelberg (2005). https://doi.org/10.1007/11523468_37
43. Yang, R., Au, M.H., Zhang, Z., Xu, Q., Yu, Z., Whyte, W.: Efficient lattice-based zero-knowledge arguments with standard soundness: construction and applications. In: Boldyreva, A., Micciancio, D. (eds.) CRYPTO 2019. LNCS, vol. 11692, pp. 147–175. Springer, Cham (2019). https://doi.org/10.1007/978-3-030-26948-7_6

A New Variant of Unbalanced Oil and Vinegar Using Quotient Ring: QR-UOV

Hiroki Furue[1(✉)], Yasuhiko Ikematsu[2(✉)], Yutaro Kiyomura[3(✉)], and Tsuyoshi Takagi[1(✉)]

[1] The University of Tokyo, Tokyo, Japan
{furue-hiroki261,takagi}@g.ecc.u-tokyo.ac.jp
[2] Kyushu University, Fukuoka, Japan
ikematsu@imi.kyushu-u.ac.jp
[3] NTT Social Informatics Laboratories, Tokyo, Japan
yutaro.kiyomura.vs@hco.ntt.co.jp

Abstract. The unbalanced oil and vinegar signature scheme (UOV) is a multivariate signature scheme that has essentially not been broken for over 20 years. However, it requires the use of a large public key; thus, various methods have been proposed to reduce its size. In this paper, we propose a new variant of UOV with a public key represented by block matrices whose components correspond to an element of a quotient ring. We discuss how it affects the security of our proposed scheme whether or not the quotient ring is a field. Furthermore, we discuss their security against currently known and newly possible attacks and propose parameters for our scheme. We demonstrate that our proposed scheme can achieve a small public key size without significantly increasing the signature size compared with other UOV variants. For example, the public key size of our proposed scheme is 85.8 KB for NIST's Post-Quantum Cryptography Project (security level 3), whereas that of compressed Rainbow is 252.3 KB, where Rainbow is a variant of UOV and is one of the third-round finalists of the NIST PQC project.

Keywords: Post-quantum cryptography · Multivariate public key cryptography · Unbalanced oil and vinegar · Quotient ring

1 Introduction

Currently used public key cryptosystems such as RSA and ECC can be broken in polynomial time using a quantum computer executing Shor's algorithm [34]. Thus, there has been growing interest in post-quantum cryptography (PQC), which is secure against quantum computing attacks. Research on PQC has thus been accelerating, and the U.S. National Institute for Standards and Technology (NIST) has initiated a PQC standardization project [26].

Multivariate public key cryptography (MPKC), based on the difficulty of solving a system of multivariate quadratic polynomial equations over a finite field (the multivariate quadratic ($\mathcal{MQ}$) problem), is regarded as a strong candidate

M. Tibouchi and H. Wang (Eds.): ASIACRYPT 2021, LNCS 13093, pp. 187–217, 2021.
https://doi.org/10.1007/978-3-030-92068-5_7

for PQC. The $\mathcal{MQ}$ problem is NP-complete [20] and is thus likely to be secure in the post-quantum era.

The unbalanced oil and vinegar signature scheme (UOV) [23], a multivariate signature scheme proposed by Kipnis et al. at EUROCRYPT 1999, has withstood various types of attacks for approximately 20 years. UOV is a well-established signature scheme owing to its short signature and short execution time. Rainbow [13], a multilayer UOV variant, was selected as a third-round finalist in the NIST PQC project [29]. However, both UOV and Rainbow have public keys much larger than those of other PQC candidates, for example, lattice-based signature schemes. Indeed, Rainbow has the largest public key among the third-round-finalist signature schemes, and NIST's report [29] states that Rainbow is unsuitable as a general-purpose signature scheme owing to this problem.

The CRYSTALS-DILITHIUM [25] lattice-based signature scheme is also a third-round finalist in the NIST PQC project. It is based on the hardness of the module learning with errors (MLWE) problem [8]. As is well known, LWE [32] is a confidential hard problem in cryptography, and the MLWE problem is a generalization of it using a module comprising vectors over a ring. This illustrates that a natural way to develop an efficient multivariate scheme with a small public key is to improve confidential schemes such as UOV and Rainbow in MPKC by investigating further algebraic theory.

There are three main research approaches to developing a UOV variant with a small public key. One is to use the compression technique developed by Petzoldt et al. [30]. This technique can be applied to various UOV variants and is based on the fact that a part of a public key can be arbitrarily chosen before determining the secret key. This indicates that a part of a public key can be generated using a seed of a pseudo-random number generator. The version of Rainbow using this technique and a secret key compression technique is called "compressed Rainbow" in the third-round finalist NIST PQC project [12]. The second approach is to use the lifted unbalanced oil and vinegar (LUOV) [6] that uses polynomials over a small field as a public key, whereas the signature and message spaces are defined over an extension field. This results in a small public key. LUOV was thus selected as a candidate in the second round of the NIST PQC project [28]. However, several of its parameters were broken using the new attack proposed by Ding et al. [15]. The third approach is to use the block-anti-circulant UOV (BAC-UOV) developed by Szepieniec et al. and presented at SAC 2019 [35]. Its public key is represented by block-anti-circulant matrices, where every block is an anti-circulant matrix. As such a matrix can be constructed by its first-row vector, BAC-UOV has a smaller public key. However, the public key has a special structure; that is, block-anti-circulant-matrices can be transformed into the diagonal concatenation of two smaller matrices. This enabled Furue et al. [18] to devise a structural attack on BAC-UOV, that has less complexity than the asserted one. The attack is based on the fact that the anti-circulant matrices of size ℓ used in BAC-UOV can be represented using an element of the quotient ring $\mathbb{F}_q[x]/(x^\ell - 1)$, where $\mathbb{F}_q$ is a finite field, and $x^\ell - 1$ is reducible.

Our Contribution. In this paper, we present a new UOV variant using an arbitrary quotient ring called QR-UOV. In QR-UOV, a public key is represented by block matrices in which every component corresponds to an element of a quotient ring $\mathbb{F}_q[x]/(f)$. More precisely, we use an injective ring homomorphism from the quotient ring $\mathbb{F}_q[x]/(f)$ to the matrix ring $\mathbb{F}_q^{\ell \times \ell}$, where $f \in \mathbb{F}_q[x]$ is a polynomial with $\deg f = \ell$. In this study, image Φ_g^f of the homomorphism for $g \in \mathbb{F}_q[x]/(f)$ is called the *polynomial matrix* of g. From this homomorphism, we can compress the ℓ^2 components in Φ_g^f to ℓ elements of $\mathbb{F}_q$ because the polynomial matrix Φ_g^f is determined by the ℓ coefficients of g. This can be considered as a generalization of BAC-UOV [35], which is the case for $f = x^\ell - 1$. Utilizing the elements of a quotient ring in block matrices is similar to the MLWE problem [8] because the MLWE problem uses elements of a ring in vectors. Namely, we can consider that the research undertaken to obtain from UOV to QR-UOV (including BAC-UOV) corresponds to that obtained from LWE to MLWE. Therefore, as with the MLWE problem, this type of research deserves more attention than passing notice.

To construct the QR-UOV, we must consider the symmetry of the polynomial matrices Φ_g^f. In UOV, the public key $\mathcal{P} = (p_1, \ldots, p_m)$, which comprises quadratic polynomials p_i, is obtained by composing a central map $\mathcal{F} = (f_1, \ldots, f_m)$ and a linear map $\mathcal{S}$, that is, $\mathcal{P} = \mathcal{F} \circ \mathcal{S}$. Then, the corresponding matrices $P_1, \ldots, P_m$ of the public key $\mathcal{P}$ are given by $P_i = S^\top F_i S$, where $F_1, \ldots, F_m$, and S are matrices corresponding to $\mathcal{F}$ and $\mathcal{S}$, respectively. If we choose $F_1, \ldots, F_m$, and S as block matrices, where the components are polynomial matrices Φ_g^f, the polynomial matrices must be stable under the transpose operation, namely, $(\Phi_g^f)^\top = \Phi_{g'}^f$ for some g'. Otherwise, $P_1, \ldots, P_m$ are not block matrices of Φ_g^f, and we cannot reduce the public key size using them. Polynomial matrices Φ_g^f are generally unstable under the transpose operation; therefore, we cannot directly use polynomial matrices Φ_g^f to construct an efficient UOV variant. To solve this problem, we introduce the concept of an $\ell \times \ell$ invertible matrix W such that $W\Phi_g^f$ is symmetric for any $g \in \mathbb{F}_q[x]/(f)$; that is, $W\Phi_g^f$ is stable under the transpose operation. In Theorem 1, we prove that there exists such symmetric W for any quotient ring $\mathbb{F}_q[x]/(f)$. Therefore, from equations

$$(\Phi_{g_1}^f)^\top (W\Phi_{g_2}^f)\Phi_{g_1}^f = (W\Phi_{g_1}^f)^\top \Phi_{g_2}^f \Phi_{g_1}^f = W\Phi_{g_1 g_2 g_1}^f,$$

we can construct a UOV variant using the quotient ring $\mathbb{F}_q[x]/(f)$ by choosing $F_1, \ldots, F_m$ as block matrices using $W\Phi_g^f$ and S as a block matrix with Φ_g^f.

Moreover, we should consider how the choice of f affects the security of the QR-UOV. Furue et al. [18] broke BAC-UOV by transforming its anti-circulant matrices into diagonal concatenations of two smaller matrices. This transformation is obtained from the decomposition $x^\ell - 1 = (x - 1)(x^{\ell-1} + \cdots + 1)$. Therefore, we investigate the relationship between the irreducibility of the polynomial f used to generate the quotient ring $\mathbb{F}_q[x]/(f)$ and the existence of such a transformation for symmetric matrices $W\Phi_g^f$. In Theorem 2 herein, we show that if f is irreducible (*i.e.*, $\mathbb{F}_q[x]/(f)$ is a field), then there is no such transformation for matrices $W\Phi_g^f$, indicating that such an f is resistant to Furue et al.'s structural attack [18].

Based on these considerations regarding the symmetry of $W\Phi_g^f$ and the choice of f, we derive the quotient-ring UOV (QR-UOV). It uses $\mathbb{F}_q[x]/(f)$ generated by an irreducible polynomial f, which is resistant to Furue et al.'s structural attack [18]. We investigated its performance against both currently known and possible attacks. The currently known attacks include the direct attack, UOV attack [24], reconciliation attack [14], and intersection attack [5]. Possible attacks are derived from (1) pull-back techniques and (2) lifting techniques. In (1), the UOV, reconciliation, and intersection attacks are executed over the quotient ring $\mathbb{F}_q[x]/(f)$ by pulling $W\Phi_g^f$ back to g. In (2), we prove that by lifting the base field $\mathbb{F}_q$ to the extension field $\mathbb{F}_{q^\ell}$, the QR-UOV public key can be transformed into the diagonal concatenation of some smaller matrices: as is done in the structural attack on BAC-UOV. After applying such a transformation over $\mathbb{F}_{q^\ell}$, we execute the four currently known attacks.

Finally, by considering these currently known and possible attacks, we can select the appropriate parameters for the QR-UOV. We stress that the security of major MPKCs such as UOV and Rainbow has no computational reduction to the underlying MQ problem, and their security is usually evaluated by all known attacks. We follow this research direction in our security analysis of the proposed scheme, and we present the following secure parameters in accordance with the I, III, and V security levels of the NIST PQC project [27]. These parameters achieve a small public key, and the sizes of the public keys are approximately 30%–50% of those of compressed Rainbow [12]. For example, the public key size is 85.8 KB for security level III, whereas that of compressed Rainbow is 252.3 KB. The signature sizes with the proposed parameters are almost the same as those of Rainbow, except for security level I.

Organization. The remainder of this paper is organized as follows. In Sect. 2, we explain the construction of multivariate signature schemes, plain UOV, BAC-UOV, and an attack on BAC-UOV. In Sect. 3, we introduce the polynomial matrices of a quotient ring as a generalization of the circulant matrices. In Sect. 4, we describe the proposed signature scheme QR-UOV. In Sect. 5, we analyze the security of the proposed scheme. We present our proposed parameters and compare the performance of our scheme with that of Rainbow in Sect. 6. We conclude the paper in Sect. 7 by summarizing the key points and suggesting possible future work.

2 Preliminaries

In this section, we first explain the $\mathcal{MQ}$ problem and general signature schemes based on this problem. Subsequently, we review the construction of UOV [23]. We then describe the construction of BAC-UOV [35] and finally explain Furue et al.'s structural attack [18] on BAC-UOV.

2.1 Multivariate Signature Schemes

Let $\mathbb{F}_q$ be a finite field with q elements, and let n and m be two positive integers. For a system of quadratic polynomials $\mathcal{P} = (p_1(x_1, \dots, x_n), \dots, p_m(x_1, \dots, x_n))$ in n variables over $\mathbb{F}_q$ and $\mathbf{y} \in \mathbb{F}_q^m$, the problem of obtaining a solution $\mathbf{x} \in \mathbb{F}_q^n$ to $\mathcal{P}(\mathbf{x}) = \mathbf{y}$ is called the $\mathcal{M}Q$ problem. Garey and Johnson [20] proved that this problem is NP-complete if $n \approx m$, and thus, it is considered to have the potential to resist quantum computer attacks.

Next, we briefly explain the construction of the general multivariate signature schemes. First, an easily invertible quadratic map $\mathcal{F} = (f_1, \dots, f_m) : \mathbb{F}_q^n \to \mathbb{F}_q^m$, called a *central map*, is generated. Next, two invertible linear maps $\mathcal{S} : \mathbb{F}_q^n \to \mathbb{F}_q^n$ and $\mathcal{T} : \mathbb{F}_q^m \to \mathbb{F}_q^m$ are randomly chosen to hide the structure of $\mathcal{F}$. The public key $\mathcal{P}$ is then provided as a polynomial map:

$$\mathcal{P} = \mathcal{T} \circ \mathcal{F} \circ \mathcal{S} : \mathbb{F}_q^n \to \mathbb{F}_q^m. \tag{1}$$

The secret key comprises $\mathcal{T}$, $\mathcal{F}$, and $\mathcal{S}$. The signature is generated as follows: Given a message $\mathbf{m} \in \mathbb{F}_q^m$ to be signed, compute $\mathbf{m}_1 = \mathcal{T}^{-1}(\mathbf{m})$, and obtain a solution $\mathbf{m}_2$ to the equation $\mathcal{F}(\mathbf{x}) = \mathbf{m}_1$. This gives the signature $\mathbf{s} = \mathcal{S}^{-1}(\mathbf{m}_2) \in \mathbb{F}_q^n$ for the message. Verification is performed by confirming whether $\mathcal{P}(\mathbf{s}) = \mathbf{m}$.

2.2 Unbalanced Oil and Vinegar Signature Scheme

Let v be a positive integer and $n = v + m$. For variables $\mathbf{x} = (x_1, \dots, x_n)$ over $\mathbb{F}_q$, we call $x_1, \dots, x_v$ *vinegar variables* and $x_{v+1}, \dots, x_n$ *oil variables*. In the UOV scheme, a central map $\mathcal{F} = (f_1, \dots, f_m) : \mathbb{F}_q^n \to \mathbb{F}_q^m$ is designed such that each f_k $(k = 1, \dots, m)$ is a quadratic polynomial of the form

$$f_k(x_1, \dots, x_n) = \sum_{i=1}^{n} \sum_{j=1}^{v} \alpha_{i,j}^{(k)} x_i x_j, \tag{2}$$

where $\alpha_{i,j}^{(k)} \in \mathbb{F}_q$. A linear map $\mathcal{S} : \mathbb{F}_q^n \to \mathbb{F}_q^n$ is then randomly chosen. Next, the public key map $\mathcal{P} : \mathbb{F}_q^n \to \mathbb{F}_q^m$ is computed using $\mathcal{P} = \mathcal{F} \circ \mathcal{S}$. The linear map $\mathcal{T}$ in Eq. (1) is not required because it does not help hide the structure of $\mathcal{F}$. Thus, the secret key comprises $\mathcal{F}$ and $\mathcal{S}$.

Next, we explain the inversion of the central map $\mathcal{F}$. Given $\mathbf{y} \in \mathbb{F}_q^m$, we first choose random values $a_1, \dots, a_v$ in $\mathbb{F}_q$ as the vinegar variables. Then, we can efficiently obtain a solution $(a_{v+1}, \dots, a_n)$ for the equation $\mathcal{F}(a_1, \dots, a_v, x_{v+1}, \dots, x_n) = \mathbf{y}$ because this is a linear system of m equations in m oil variables. If there is no solution to this equation, we choose new random values $a'_1, \dots, a'_v$, and repeat the procedure. Eventually, we obtain the solution $\mathbf{x} = (a_1, \dots, a_v, a_{v+1}, \dots, a_n)$ to $\mathcal{F}(\mathbf{x}) = \mathbf{y}$. In this manner, we execute the signing process explained in Subsect. 2.1.

We assume that the characteristic of $\mathbb{F}_q$ is odd in the following. For each $1 \le i \le m$, there exists an $n \times n$ symmetric matrix F_i such that $f_i(\mathbf{x}) = \mathbf{x} \cdot F_i \cdot \mathbf{x}^\top$.

From Eq. (2), F_i has the form

$$\begin{pmatrix} *_{v\times v} & *_{v\times m} \\ *_{m\times v} & 0_{m\times m} \end{pmatrix}. \tag{3}$$

Let P_i $(i = 1, \ldots, m)$ be an $n\times n$ symmetric matrix P_i such that $p_i(\mathbf{x}) = \mathbf{x}\cdot P_i \cdot \mathbf{x}^\top$. Then, taking the $n \times n$ matrix S such that $\mathcal{S}(\mathbf{x}) = S \cdot \mathbf{x}^\top$, we have

$$P_i = S^\top F_i S, \quad (i = 1, \ldots, m) \tag{4}$$

from $\mathcal{P} = \mathcal{F} \circ \mathcal{S}$. We call F_i and P_i the representation matrices of f_i and p_i, respectively.

2.3 Block-Anti-circulant UOV

As mentioned above, the block-anti-circulant (BAC) UOV [35] is a variant of UOV. The public key is shortened by representing it using block-anti-circulant matrices. In this subsection, we describe the construction of BAC-UOV.

In a circulant matrix, each row vector is rotated by one element to the right relative to the preceding row vector. In an anti-circulant matrix, each row vector is rotated by one element to the left relative to the preceding row vector. A circulant matrix X and an anti-circulant matrix Y with size ℓ take the following forms:

$$X = \begin{pmatrix} a_0 & a_1 & \ldots & a_{\ell-2} & a_{\ell-1} \\ a_{\ell-1} & a_0 & \ldots & a_{\ell-3} & a_{\ell-2} \\ \vdots & \vdots & \ddots & \vdots & \vdots \\ a_2 & a_3 & \ldots & a_0 & a_1 \\ a_1 & a_2 & \ldots & a_{\ell-1} & a_0 \end{pmatrix}, Y = \begin{pmatrix} a_0 & a_1 & \ldots & a_{\ell-2} & a_{\ell-1} \\ a_1 & a_2 & \ldots & a_{\ell-1} & a_0 \\ \vdots & \vdots & \ddots & \vdots & \vdots \\ a_{\ell-2} & a_{\ell-1} & \ldots & a_{\ell-4} & a_{\ell-3} \\ a_{\ell-1} & a_0 & \ldots & a_{\ell-3} & a_{\ell-2} \end{pmatrix}.$$

In addition, a matrix is called a block-circulant matrix A or a block-anti-circulant matrix B with block size ℓ if every $\ell \times \ell$ block in A or B is a circulant matrix or an anti-circulant matrix, as follows ($N \in \mathbb{N}$):

$$A = \begin{pmatrix} X_{11} & \ldots & X_{1N} \\ \vdots & \ddots & \vdots \\ X_{N1} & \ldots & X_{NN} \end{pmatrix}, B = \begin{pmatrix} Y_{11} & \ldots & Y_{1N} \\ \vdots & \ddots & \vdots \\ Y_{N1} & \ldots & Y_{NN} \end{pmatrix},$$

where X_{ij} is an $\ell\times\ell$ circulant matrix, and Y_{ij} is an $\ell\times\ell$ anti-circulant matrix. For these block matrices, it holds that products AB and BA are block-anti-circulant matrices.

In BAC-UOV, the number of vinegar variables v and the number of equations m are set to be divisible by block size ℓ. The representation matrices $F_1, \ldots, F_m$ for the central map $\mathcal{F}$ are chosen as block-anti-circulant matrices with a block size ℓ, and the matrix S for the linear map $\mathcal{S}$ is chosen as a block-circulant matrix with block size ℓ. The representation matrices $P_1, \ldots, P_m$ for the public key $\mathcal{P} = \mathcal{F} \circ \mathcal{S}$ are computed using $P_i = S^\top F_i S$ $(i = 1, \ldots, m)$ and are block-anti-circulant matrices.

Owing to the structure of block-anti-circulant matrices, the $n \times n$ matrices $P_1, \ldots, P_m$ can be represented using only the first row of each block. Therefore, they can be represented by using only mn^2/ℓ elements in the finite field $\mathbb{F}_q$, which is one ℓ-th the size of the public key of the plain UOV. That is, the public key was smaller than that of the plain UOV.

2.4 Structural Attack on BAC-UOV

In 2020, Furue et al. proposed an attack on BAC-UOV that breaks the security of the proposed parameter sets [18]. The attack utilizes the property of the anti-circulant matrix, wherein the sum of the elements of one row (column) is the same as those of the other rows (columns).

We define an $\ell \times \ell$ matrix L_ℓ such that $(L_\ell)_{1i} = (L_\ell)_{i1} = 1\,(1 \le i \le \ell)$, $(L_\ell)_{ii} = -1\,(2 \le i \le \ell)$, and the other elements are equal to 0, where for a matrix A, $(A)_{ij}$ denotes the ij-component of A, namely

$$L_\ell := \ell\left\{\overbrace{\begin{pmatrix} 1 & 1 & \ldots & 1 \\ 1 & -1 & & \\ \vdots & & \ddots & \\ 1 & & & -1 \end{pmatrix}}^{\ell}\right. .$$

Subsequently, for an $\ell \times \ell$ anti-circulant matrix Y, we have

$$L_\ell^\top Y L_\ell = \begin{pmatrix} *_{1\times 1} & 0_{1\times(\ell-1)} \\ 0_{(\ell-1)\times 1} & *_{(\ell-1)\times(\ell-1)} \end{pmatrix}. \tag{5}$$

Let $L_\ell^{(N)}$ be an $n \times n$ block diagonal matrix constructed by concatenating L_ℓ diagonally N times:

$$L_\ell^{(N)} := N\left\{\overbrace{\begin{pmatrix} L_\ell & & \\ & \ddots & \\ & & L_\ell \end{pmatrix}}^{N}\right. ,$$

where $N := n/\ell$. Then, for an $n \times n$ block-anti-circulant matrix B with block size ℓ, the matrix $(L_\ell^{(N)})^\top B L_\ell^{(N)}$ is a block matrix in which each block is in the form of Eq. (5). Furthermore, a permutation matrix L' exists such that:

$$(L_\ell^{(N)} L')^\top B (L_\ell^{(N)} L') = \left(\begin{array}{c|c} *_{N\times N} & 0_{N\times(\ell-1)N} \\ \hline 0_{(\ell-1)N\times N} & *_{(\ell-1)N\times(\ell-1)N} \end{array}\right). \tag{6}$$

Therefore, the representation matrices $P_1, \ldots, P_m$ for the public key $\mathcal{P}$ of BAC-UOV can all be transformed into the form of (6) by using $L_\ell^{(N)} L'$. The UOV attack [24] can then be executed on only the upper-left $N \times N$ submatrices of the obtained matrices with little complexity. By using the transformed public key, we can reduce the number of variables appearing in the public equations $\mathcal{P}(\mathbf{x}) = \mathbf{m}$ for a message $\mathbf{m}$. This reduces the complexity of the attack by approximately 20% compared with the best existing attack on UOV. This attack can be executed only if there exists a transformation on the public key, as given by Eq. (6).

3 Polynomial Matrices of Quotient Ring

In this section, we introduce polynomial matrices as a generalization of the circulant and anti-circulant matrices used in BAC-UOV [35] and describe a method for converting polynomial matrices into symmetric matrices that can be applied to the UOV scheme. Furthermore, we discuss whether such generalized matrices can be transformed, as shown in Eq. (5).

3.1 Polynomial Matrices and Their Symmetrization

Let ℓ be a positive integer and $f \in \mathbb{F}_q[x]$ with $\deg f = \ell$. For any element g of the quotient ring $\mathbb{F}_q[x]/(f)$, we can uniquely define an $\ell \times \ell$ matrix Φ_g^f over $\mathbb{F}_q$ such that

$$\left(1\ x \cdots x^{\ell-1}\right) \Phi_g^f = \left(g\ xg \cdots x^{\ell-1}g\right). \tag{7}$$

From this equation, we have

$$x^{j-1}g = \sum_{i=1}^{\ell} \left(\Phi_g^f\right)_{ij} \cdot x^{i-1} \quad (1 \leq j \leq \ell),$$

and $\left(\Phi_g^f\right)_{ij}$ is the coefficient of x^{i-1} in $x^{j-1}g$. We call such a matrix Φ_g^f the *polynomial matrix* of g. The following lemma can be easily derived from this definition:

Lemma 1. *For any $g_1, g_2 \in \mathbb{F}_q[x]/(f)$, we have*

$$\Phi_{g_1}^f + \Phi_{g_2}^f = \Phi_{g_1+g_2}^f, \quad \Phi_{g_1}^f \Phi_{g_2}^f = \Phi_{g_1 g_2}^f.$$

That is, the map $g \mapsto \Phi_g^f$ is an injective ring homomorphism from $\mathbb{F}_q[x]/(f)$ to the matrix ring $\mathbb{F}_q^{\ell \times \ell}$.

An $\ell \times \ell$ polynomial matrix Φ_g^f can be represented by only ℓ elements in $\mathbb{F}_q$, because Φ_g^f is determined by the ℓ coefficients of $g \in \mathbb{F}_q[x]/(f)$. We let the algebra of the matrices $A_f := \left\{\Phi_g^f \in \mathbb{F}_q^{\ell \times \ell} \mid g \in \mathbb{F}_q[x]/(f)\right\}$. This is a subalgebra in the matrix algebra $\mathbb{F}_q^{\ell \times \ell}$ from Lemma 1. Similarly, for a matrix $W \in \mathbb{F}_q^{\ell \times \ell}$, any matrix in $WA_f := \{W\Phi_g^f \in \mathbb{F}_q^{\ell \times \ell} \mid g \in \mathbb{F}_q[x]/(f)\}$ can also be represented by only ℓ elements in $\mathbb{F}_q$.

As shown in Eq. (4) in Subsect. 2.2, the transpose appears in the computation of the representation matrices P_i for the public key. Thus, to use polynomial matrices Φ_g^f in the UOV scheme, we need WA_f to be stable under the transpose operation for some W. Thus, to construct our proposed scheme, we need an explicit family of f and W such that WA_f is stable under the transpose operation. In the following theorem, we prove that there exists an invertible matrix W for any f.

Theorem 1. *Let $f \in \mathbb{F}_q[x]$ with $\deg f = \ell$. Then, there exists an invertible matrix $W \in \mathbb{F}_q^{\ell\times\ell}$ such that WX is a symmetric matrix for any $X \in A_f$.*

Proof. Let $\phi : \mathbb{F}_q[x]/(f) \to \mathbb{F}_q$ be a nonzero linear map. We define W such that the ij-component of W is equal to $\phi(x^{i+j-2})$. Then, for any $g \in \mathbb{F}_q[x]/(f)$, we have the following:

$$\begin{aligned}
(W\Phi_g^f)_{ij} &= \sum_{k=1}^{\ell} \phi(x^{i+k-2})(\Phi_g^f)_{kj} \\
&= \phi\left(\sum_{k=1}^{\ell} x^{i+k-2}(\Phi_g^f)_{kj}\right) \\
&= \phi\left(x^{i-1}\left(\sum_{k=1}^{\ell} x^{k-1}(\Phi_g^f)_{kj}\right)\right) \\
&= \phi(x^{i-1}x^{j-1}g) \qquad (\because (7)) \\
&= \phi(x^{i+j-2}g) \\
&= (W\Phi_g^f)_{ji}.
\end{aligned}$$

This equation shows that $W\Phi_g^f$ is symmetric.

If we define ϕ such that $\phi(a_0 + a_1x + \cdots + a_{\ell-1}x^{\ell-1}) = a_{\ell-1}$, then W is of the following form:

$$\begin{pmatrix} 0 & & 1 \\ & \iddots & \\ 1 & & * \end{pmatrix},$$

and hence W is invertible. This indicates that there exists one invertible matrix W constructed using the above method. □

As stated in Subsect. 3.2 below, from a security perspective, f must be irreducible in our scheme. Furthermore, from the perspective of simplicity, f should have only a few nonzero terms. As there are no irreducible binomials f with $\deg f = \ell$ for many ℓ, trinomials f are considered suitable for our scheme. The following example shows that there are some trinomials f and suitable W for symmetrization purposes.

Table 1. Degree ℓ such that there exist no irreducible trinomials of the form $x^\ell - ax^i - 1$ among $2 \le \ell \le 30$ for $\mathbb{F}_q = \mathbb{F}_7$.

$\mathbb{F}_q$	$\mathbb{F}_7$
ℓ	$6, 15, 30$

Example 1. We assume that $f = x^\ell - ax^i - 1$ $(a \in \mathbb{F}_q, 1 \le i \le \ell - 1)$. If $W \in \mathbb{F}_q^{\ell \times \ell}$ is constructed using a linear map $\phi : \mathbb{F}_q[x]/(f) \to \mathbb{F}_q$ such that $\phi(a_0 + a_1 x + \cdots + a_{\ell-1}x^{\ell-1}) = a_{i-1}$, then we can represent the matrix W as

$$W = \begin{pmatrix} J_i & \\ & J_{\ell-i} \end{pmatrix},$$

where $J_i := \begin{pmatrix} & & 1 \\ & \cdot^{\cdot^{\cdot}} & \\ 1 & & \end{pmatrix}$ denotes the anti-identity matrix of size i. From Theorem 1, WX becomes a symmetric matrix for any $X \in A_f$.

The polynomial f must be irreducible in our scheme; thus, we conducted several experiments to confirm the irreducibility of $x^\ell - ax^i - 1$. We treated the finite field $\mathbb{F}_q = \mathbb{F}_7$, which is used for our proposed scheme as described below, and checked whether there exists an irreducible polynomial $f \in \mathbb{F}_q[x]$ in the form $x^\ell - ax^i - 1$ for $2 \le \ell \le 30$. We found an irreducible polynomial $x^\ell - ax^i - 1$ for sufficiently many $2 \le \ell \le 30$. Table 1 shows the degree ℓ such that there exists *no* irreducible polynomials of the above form.

Finally, if we choose $f = x^\ell - 1$ and a linear map $\phi : \mathbb{F}_q[x]/(f) \to \mathbb{F}_q$ such that $\phi(a_0 + a_1 x + \cdots + a_{\ell-1}x^{\ell-1}) = a_{\ell-1}$, then $W = J_\ell$ and $W\Phi_g^f$ is an anti-circulant matrix. Thus, this choice corresponds exactly to BAC-UOV [35], and Theorem 1 can be regarded as describing the generalization of anti-circulant matrices.

3.2 Effect of Irreducibility of f

In this subsection, we discuss the relation between the irreducibility of polynomial f used to generate the quotient ring $\mathbb{F}_q[x]/(f)$ and the existence of transformation on symmetric matrices $W\Phi_g^f$ into the diagonal concatenation of smaller matrices. This is because, as stated in Subsect. 2.4, the proposed parameters of BAC-UOV were broken by using the transformation of Eq. (5) on anti-circulant matrices obtained from the decomposition $x^\ell - 1 = (x - 1)(x^{\ell-1} + \cdots + 1)$.

In the following theorem, we show that if f is irreducible, there does not exist a transformation such as Eq. (5) on symmetric matrices $W\Phi_g^f$.

Theorem 2. *Let $f \in \mathbb{F}_q[x]$ be an irreducible polynomial with* $\deg f = \ell$ *and W be an invertible matrix such that every element of WA_f is a symmetric matrix. Subsequently, there is no invertible matrix $L \in \mathbb{F}_q^{\ell \times \ell}$ and $i, j \in \{1, \ldots, \ell\}$ such that for any $X \in WA_f$,*

$$(L^\top X L)_{ij} = 0.$$

Proof. We assume that there exists a matrix $L \in \mathbb{F}_q^{\ell\times\ell}$ and $i, j \in \{1, \dots, \ell\}$ satisfying the above condition. Let ℓ_i be the i-th column vector of $W^\top L$, and ℓ_j be the j-th column vector of L. Then, we have $\ell_i^\top \Phi_h^f \ell_j = 0$ for any $h \in \mathbb{F}_q[x]/(f)$.

Now, we define a linear isomorphism $V_1 : \mathbb{F}_q[x]/(f) \to \mathbb{F}_q^\ell$ such that

$$V_1(a_0 + a_1x + \cdots + a_{\ell-1}x^{\ell-1}) = (a_0, a_1, \dots, a_{\ell-1})^\top,$$

and $V_1(g)$ is equal to the first column vector of Φ_g^f. Furthermore, we define a linear map $V_2 : \mathbb{F}_q[x]/(f) \to \mathbb{F}_q^\ell$ such that $V_2(g)$ is equal to the first column vector of $(\Phi_g^f)^\top$. If $V_2(g) = \mathbf{0}$, then Φ_g^f is not invertible by the definition of V_2. Because A_f is a field, Φ_g^f is the zero matrix, namely, $g = 0$. As a result, V_2 is an isomorphism.

Let $g_i := V_2^{-1}(\ell_i)$ and $g_j := V_1^{-1}(\ell_j)$. Clearly, $(\Phi_{g_i}^f \Phi_h^f \Phi_{g_j}^f)_{11} = \ell_i^\top \Phi_h^f \ell_j = 0$ for any $h \in \mathbb{F}_q[x]/(f)$. If we take $h = (g_i g_j)^{-1}$, then

$$0 = (\Phi_{g_i}^f \Phi_{(g_i g_j)^{-1}}^f \Phi_{g_j}^f)_{11} = I_{11} = 1.$$

This is a contradiction. Therefore, Theorem 2 holds. □

From this theorem, we choose an irreducible polynomial as the f of A_f used in our proposed variant, which is described in Sect. 4.

Remark 1. In this remark, we discuss the transformation of elements of WA_f with reducible f by using Theorems 4 and 5 in Appendix A. Theorem 4 shows that if f is decomposed into distinct irreducible polynomials, WA_f are transformed into a concatenation of two smaller submatrices. In fact, the transformation, as in Eq. (5) in the structural attack on BAC-UOV, corresponds to the transformation described in Theorem 4. If f is divisible by a squared polynomial, Theorem 5 shows that the representation matrices can be transformed by executing a change of variables into a special form wherein the lower-right $(n/\ell) \times (n/\ell)$ block is a zero block, similar to the representation matrices of the central map (Eq. (3)).

4 Our Proposal: Quotient-Ring UOV (QR-UOV)

In this section, we present our proposed UOV variant, QR-UOV, which is constructed by applying the polynomial matrices described in Subsect. 3.1.

4.1 Description

Let ℓ be a positive integer and v, m be multiples of ℓ such that $v > m$. Set $n := v + m$ and $N := n/\ell$.

Let $f \in \mathbb{F}_q[x]$ be an irreducible polynomial with $\deg f = \ell$ and W be an invertible matrix such that every element of WA_f is symmetric. There exist f and W satisfying the above condition for many ℓ, as shown by Theorem 1 and the discussion in Subsect. 3. We define subspace $A_f^{(N)}$ in $\mathbb{F}_q^{n\times n}$ containing $n \times n$ matrices as

$$\begin{pmatrix} X_{11} & \dots & X_{1N} \\ \vdots & \ddots & \vdots \\ X_{N1} & \dots & X_{NN} \end{pmatrix},$$

where every $X_{ij} \in \mathbb{F}_q^{\ell\times\ell}$ $(i, j \in \{1, \dots, N\})$ is an element of A_f. Furthermore, we define an $n \times n$ block diagonal matrix $W^{(N)}$ constructed by concatenating W diagonally N times:

$$W^{(N)} := \begin{pmatrix} W & & \\ & \ddots & \\ & & W \end{pmatrix}.$$

For these matrices, we obtain the following proposition:

Proposition 1. *For $X \in A_f^{(N)}$ and $Y \in W^{(N)} A_f^{(N)}$, we have*

$$X^\top Y X \in W^{(N)} A_f^{(N)}.$$

Proof. We prove this proposition for $N = 1$. Let $X := \Phi_{g_1}^f$ and $Y := W\Phi_{g_2}^f$. Owing to the symmetry of WA_f and W (because Φ_1^f is the identity matrix),

$$\begin{aligned} X^\top Y X &= (\Phi_{g_1}^f)^\top (W\Phi_{g_2}^f)(\Phi_{g_1}^f) \\ &= (\Phi_{g_1}^f)^\top W^\top \Phi_{g_2}^f \Phi_{g_1}^f \\ &= W\Phi_{g_1}^f \Phi_{g_2}^f \Phi_{g_1}^f \\ &= W\Phi_{g_1 \cdot g_2 \cdot g_1}^f. \end{aligned}$$

For $N \geq 2$, the statement is proven similarly. □

Using this proposition, we can construct a quotient-ring UOV (QR-UOV), which is a variant of UOV using polynomial matrices.

Key Generation

- Choose an irreducible polynomial $f \in \mathbb{F}_q[x]$ with $\deg f = \ell$ and $W \in \mathbb{F}_q^{\ell\times\ell}$ such that every element in WA_f is symmetric.
- Choose F_i $(i = 1, \dots, m)$ from $W^{(N)} A_f^{(N)}$ such that the lower-right $m \times m$ submatrices are zero matrices.
- Choose an invertible matrix S from $A_f^{(N)}$ randomly.
- Compute $P_i = S^\top F_i S$ $(i = 1, \dots, m)$.

Then, we obtain that P_i $(i = 1, \dots, m)$ are elements of $W^{(N)} A_f^{(N)}$ from Proposition 1. The signing and verification processes were the same as those for the plain UOV. In QR-UOV, the cardinality of the finite field q is set to be odd because if q is even, then the coefficients corresponding to the non-diagonal components of every diagonal block are zero owing to the symmetry of every block $W\Phi_g^f$.

Remark 2. We can apply the polynomial matrices of a quotient ring to both UOV and Rainbow.

4.2 Improved QR-UOV

In this subsection, we explain two improved methods used in the NIST third-round proposal of Rainbow [12]. First, the secret key $\mathcal{S}$ is limited to a specific compact form, which was first proposed by Czypek et al. [11]. The second replaces a large part of the public key with a small seed for pseudo-random number generation (PRNG).

In the plain UOV, the matrix S of the secret linear map $\mathcal{S}$ can be restricted to a special form:

$$S = \begin{pmatrix} I_{v\times v} & S' \\ 0_{m\times v} & I_{m\times m} \end{pmatrix}, \tag{8}$$

where S' is a $v \times m$ matrix because it does not affect the security. In QR-UOV, S is chosen in $A_f^{(N)}$, and the identity and zero matrices are elements of A_f. Therefore, S is written as in Eq. (8), where S' is a block matrix in which every component is an element of A_f. This limits the secret key to a specific compact form.

The second method is based on Petzoldt et al.'s compression technique [30]. The version of Rainbow using this technique and a secret key compression technique is called "compressed Rainbow" in the third-round finalist NIST PQC project [12]. The representation matrices P_i $(i = 1, \ldots, m)$ of the public key map are written in the form

$$P_i = \begin{pmatrix} P_{i,1} & P_{i,2} \\ P_{i,2}^\top & P_{i,3} \end{pmatrix},$$

where $P_{i,1}$, $P_{i,2}$, and $P_{i,3}$ are $v \times v$, $v \times m$, and $m \times m$ matrices, respectively, and $P_{i,1}$ and $P_{i,3}$ are symmetric matrices. Similarly, the representation matrices F_i $(i = 1, \ldots, m)$ of the central map in Eq. (3) are written in the form

$$F_i = \begin{pmatrix} F_{i,1} & F_{i,2} \\ F_{i,2}^\top & 0_{m\times m} \end{pmatrix},$$

where $F_{i,1}$ and $F_{i,2}$ are $v \times v$ and $v \times m$ matrices, respectively, and $F_{i,1}$ is a symmetric matrix. Then, as we have

$$S^{-1} = \begin{pmatrix} I_{v\times v} & -S' \\ 0_{m\times v} & I_{o\times o} \end{pmatrix},$$

the representation matrices F_i, P_i $(i = 1, \ldots, m)$, and S hold the following equation:

$$\begin{pmatrix} F_{i,1} & F_{i,2} \\ F_{i,2}^\top & 0_{m\times m} \end{pmatrix} = \begin{pmatrix} I_{v\times v} & 0_{v\times m} \\ -S'^\top & I_{o\times o} \end{pmatrix} \begin{pmatrix} P_{i,1} & P_{i,2} \\ P_{i,2}^\top & P_{i,3} \end{pmatrix} \begin{pmatrix} I_{v\times v} & -S' \\ 0_{m\times v} & I_{o\times o} \end{pmatrix}.$$

By computing the right-hand side, we obtain

$$\begin{aligned} F_{i,1} &= P_{i,1}, \\ F_{i,2} &= -P_{i,1}S' + P_{i,2}, \\ 0_{m\times m} &= S'^{\top} P_{i,1} S' - P_{i,2}^{\top} S' - S'^{\top} P_{i,2} + P_{i,3}. \end{aligned} \tag{9}$$

In the improved key generation step, $P_{i,1}$, $P_{i,2}$ $(i = 1, \ldots, m)$, and S' are first generated from seeds $\mathbf{s}_{pk}$ and $\mathbf{s}_{sk}$, respectively, using PRNG. Next, $P_{i,3}$ $(i = 1, \ldots, m)$ is computed using

$$P_{i,3} = -S'^{\top} P_{i,1} S' + P_{i,2}^{\top} S' + S'^{\top} P_{i,2},$$

from Eq. (9): As a result, the public key is composed of $m \times m$ matrices $P_{i,3}$ $(i = 1, \ldots, m)$ and the seed $\mathbf{s}_{pk}$ for $P_{i,1}$, $P_{i,2}$ $(i = 1, \ldots, m)$. This compression technique significantly reduces the public key size of QR-UOV.

Finally, we compare the public key size of plain QR-UOV with that of the improved QR-UOV. The public key of plain QR-UOV is represented by $P_{i,1}$, $P_{i,2}$, and $P_{i,3}$ $(i = 1, \ldots, m)$, and that of the improved QR-UOV uses a seed $\mathbf{s}_{pk}$ and $P_{i,3}$ $(i = 1, \ldots, m)$. Thus, the number of elements in $\mathbb{F}_q$ needed to represent the public key of the plain QR-UOV is

$$mn(n + \ell)/2\ell,$$

whereas that of the improved QR-UOV is

$$m^2(m + \ell)/2\ell.$$

5 Security Analysis

In this section, we first analyze the security of QR-UOV against four currently known attacks on plain UOV. We then discuss possible attacks on the quotient ring obtained by pulling submatrices $W\Phi_g^f$ back to g in the quotient ring. Finally, we consider the execution of possible attacks obtained by lifting the base field $\mathbb{F}_q$ to an extension field $\mathbb{F}_{q^\ell}$ and transforming the public key system over the extension field.

5.1 Currently Known Attacks on Plain UOV

In this subsection, we consider QR-UOV as the plain UOV described in Subsect. 2.2 and describe the execution of four currently known attacks on UOV: the direct attack, UOV attack [24], reconciliation attack [14], and intersection attack [5].

Direct Attack. Given a quadratic polynomial system $\mathcal{P} = (p_1, \ldots, p_m)$ in n variables over $\mathbb{F}_q$ and $\mathbf{m} \in \mathbb{F}_q^m$, the direct attack algebraically solves the system $\mathcal{P}(\mathbf{x}) = \mathbf{m}$. For UOV, the number of variables n is larger than the number of equations m; therefore, $n - m$ variables can be specified with random values without disturbing the existence of a solution with high probability.

One of the best-known approaches for algebraically solving the quadratic system is the hybrid approach [4], which randomly guesses k ($k = 0, \ldots, n$) variables before computing a Gröbner basis [9]. The guessing process is repeated until a solution is obtained. Well-known algorithms for computing Gröbner bases include F4 [16], F5 [17], and XL [10]. The complexity of this approach for a classical adversary is estimated as follows:

$$\min_k \left(O\left(q^k \cdot 3 \cdot \binom{m-k}{2} \cdot \binom{d_{reg}+m-k}{d_{reg}}^2 \right) \right), \tag{10}$$

where d_{reg} is the so-called degree of regularity of the system. The degree of regularity d_{reg} for a certain class of polynomial systems called *semi-regular systems* [1–3] is known to be the degree of the first non-positive term in the following series [3]:

$$\frac{\left(1-z^2\right)^m}{(1-z)^{m-k}}. \tag{11}$$

Empirically, the public key system of UOV is considered to be a semi-regular system. Therefore, this series (11) can be used to estimate the degree of regularity.

On the other hand, the complexity of a quantum direct attack is estimated to be

$$\min_k \left(O\left(q^{k/2} \cdot 3 \cdot \binom{m-k}{2} \cdot \binom{d_{reg}+m-k}{d_{reg}}^2 \right) \right), \tag{12}$$

by using Grover's algorithm [21].

Thomae and Wolf [36] proposed a technique for reducing the number of variables and equations when $n > m$. For the $n \times n$ representation matrices P_i of the public key, the technique chooses a new matrix S' such that every upper-left $m \times m$ submatrix of ${S'}^\top P_i S'$ ($i = 1, \ldots, \alpha$) is diagonal, where $\alpha = \lfloor \frac{n}{m} \rfloor - 1$. We can then reduce the $(n - m + \alpha)$ variables and α equations and thereby obtain a quadratic system with $m - \alpha$ variables and equations. This technique can be fully applied only to quadratic systems that are over finite fields of even characteristics. Furthermore, Thomae and Wolf show that the technique can be applied to odd characteristic cases with sufficiently small α, whereas the technique empirically makes the direct attack faster on the resulting systems in odd characteristics cases with large α. Therefore, from a security perspective, it is not extreme that we consider this technique to be applicable to odd characteristic cases.

In Table 2, for a QR-UOV public key system, we compare the theoretical d_{reg} and experimental d_{reg}. The theoretical d_{reg} is the degree of regularity obtained

Table 2. Theoretical and experimental degree of regularity of public key system of QR-UOV obtained using the Magma algebra system [7].

(q, v, m, ℓ, k)	Theoretical d_{reg}	Experimental d_{reg}
$(7, 24, 12, 3, 0)$	13	13
$(7, 24, 12, 3, 1)$	7	7
$(7, 24, 12, 3, 2)$	6	6
$(7, 30, 15, 3, 0)$	16	16
$(7, 30, 15, 3, 1)$	8	9
$(7, 30, 15, 3, 2)$	7	7

by Eq. (11), assuming that the system is semi-regular. The experimental d_{reg} is the highest degree among the step degrees, where nonzero polynomials are generated in experiments of the direct attack using the Magma algebra system [7]. In our experiment, m was set to sufficiently large values so that our computation for one parameter was performed within one day, and v is set equal to $2m$, while q and ℓ are set to the values given in Subsect. 6.1. For the public key of the QR-UOV with $(v + m)$ variables and m equations, we fix the last v variables and execute the hybrid approach by fixing k variables additionally. That is, the direct attack is executed on the system of m equations in $m - k$ variables. These results demonstrate that the degrees of regularity obtained experimentally were the same as those obtained theoretically.

Remark 3. In the case of $(q, v, m, \ell, k) = (7, 30, 15, 3, 1)$ in Table 2, the experimental d_{reg} is larger than the theoretical d_{reg}. However, our experiment shows that the experimental d_{reg} of the same size randomized quadratic system of m equations in $(m - k)$ variables over $\mathbb{F}_7$ is not different from our experimental d_{reg} of $(q, v, m, \ell, k) = (7, 30, 15, 3, 1)$.

UOV Attack. The UOV attack [24] obtains a linear map $\mathcal{S}' : \mathbb{F}_q^n \to \mathbb{F}_q^n$ such that every component of $\mathcal{F}' := \mathcal{P} \circ \mathcal{S}'$ has the form of Eq. (2). This $\mathcal{S}'$ is called the *equivalent key*. The UOV attack obtains the subspace $\mathcal{S}^{-1}(\mathcal{O})$ of $\mathbb{F}_q^n$, where $\mathcal{O}$ is the oil subspace defined as

$$\mathcal{O} := \left\{(0, \ldots, 0, \alpha_1, \ldots, \alpha_m)^\top \mid \alpha_i \in \mathbb{F}_q\right\}.$$

This subspace $\mathcal{S}^{-1}(\mathcal{O})$ can induce an equivalent key. To obtain $\mathcal{S}^{-1}(\mathcal{O})$, the UOV attack chooses two invertible matrices W_i, W_j from the set of linear combinations of $P_1, \ldots, P_m$. Then, it probabilistically recovers a part of the subspace $\mathcal{S}^{-1}(\mathcal{O})$ by computing the invariant subspace of $W_i^{-1}W_j$. The complexity of the UOV attack is estimated to be

$$O\left(q^{v-m-1} \cdot m^4\right).$$

Grover's algorithm can be used to reduce the complexity for a quantum adversary to

$$O\left(q^{\frac{v-m-1}{2}} \cdot m^4\right).$$

Reconciliation Attack. The reconciliation attack [14] also obtains, similar to the UOV attack, an equivalent key $\mathcal{S}'$. The reconciliation attack treats every component of the matrix S' as a variable and solves the quadratic system of equations obtained using $({S'}^\top P_i S')[v+1:n,\, v+1:n] = 0_{m\times m}$ $(i=1,\dots,m)$, where $X[a:b,\, c:d]$ denotes a $(b-a+1)\times(d-c+1)$ submatrix of X, where the upper-left component has index (a,b). This attack can be decomposed into a series of steps; in the first step, a system of m quadratic equations in v variables is solved. In the case of the plain UOV, where $v > m$, the complexity is greater than that of solving a quadratic system of v equations in v variables. Therefore, we estimate the complexity of the reconciliation attack as that of the direct attack on a quadratic system with v variables and v equations, which is obtained by Eqs. (10) and (12) as $m = v$. If $v \le m$, then the complexity of the reconciliation attack is the same as that of solving a quadratic system of m equations in v variables. As a result, we estimate the complexity of the reconciliation attack as the direct attack on the quadratic system with v variables and $\max\{m, v\}$ equations.

Intersection Attack. In [5], Beullens proposed a new attack against UOV, called the intersection attack.

The intersection attack attempts to obtain an equivalent key by recovering the subspace $\mathcal{S}^{-1}(\mathcal{O})$ of $\mathbb{F}_q^n$. The intersection attack solves the following equations for $\mathbf{y} \in \mathbb{F}_q^n$:

$$\begin{cases} (W_i\mathbf{y})^\top P_k (W_i\mathbf{y}) = 0 \\ (W_j\mathbf{y})^\top P_k (W_j\mathbf{y}) = 0 \\ (W_i\mathbf{y})^\top P_k (W_j\mathbf{y}) = 0 \end{cases} \tag{13}$$

where W_i, W_j are two invertible matrices chosen from a set of linear combinations of the public key $P_1, \dots, P_m$. In the case where $n < 3m$, the solution space obtained from Eq. (13) is of the $(3m-n)$ dimensions. Thus, its complexity is equivalent to that of solving the quadratic system with $n-(3m-n) = 2n-3m$ variables and $(3m-2)$ equations. In contrast, in the case where $n \ge 3m$, the intersection attack becomes a probabilistic algorithm for solving the system (13) with n variables and $(3m-2)$ equations with a probability of approximately $q^{-n+3m-1}$. Therefore, its complexity is estimated by q^{n-3m+1} times the complexity of solving the quadratic system with n variables and $(3m-2)$ equations.

Remark 4. In [5], Beullens proposed a new attack against Rainbow, called a rectangular MinRank attack. This attack uses non-full-rank property of Rainbow and thus does not affect the security of our proposed scheme.

5.2 Pull-Back Attacks over Quotient Ring

In this subsection, we explain a technique for executing four currently known attacks on QR-UOV by utilizing the block structure derived from the quotient ring. For every block submatrix $W\Phi_g^f$ of the representation matrices of the public key, we can execute the UOV attack [24], reconciliation attack [14], and intersection attack [5] in the quotient ring $\mathbb{F}_q[x]/(f)$ by replacing $W\Phi_g^f$ with g.

We define a map $G_1 : W^{(N)}A_f^{(N)} \to (\mathbb{F}_q[x]/(f))^{N\times N}$ such that given $X \in W^{(N)}A_f^{(N)}$, $(G_1(X))_{ij}$ is equal to $g \in \mathbb{F}_q[x]/(f)$ if the ij-block of X is $W\Phi_g^f$. Furthermore, we define $G_2 : A_f^{(N)} \to (\mathbb{F}_q[x]/(f))^{N\times N}$ such that $G_2(X) = G_1(W^{(N)} \cdot X)$ for $X \in A_f^{(N)}$. In the following, we consider the execution of the four currently known attacks described in Subsect. 5.1 on $G_1(P_1), \dots, G_1(P_m)$, which is called the pull-back technique.

First, we consider the complexity of the pull-back UOV attack, which is the UOV attack on the transformed representation matrices $G_1(P_1), \dots, G_1(P_m)$. If we obtain an equivalent key S' for the transformed matrices by executing the UOV attack over $\mathbb{F}_q[x]/(f)$, then $G_2^{-1}(S') \in \mathbb{F}_q^{n\times n}$ is an equivalent key over $\mathbb{F}_q$. The complexities of the pull-back UOV attack for a classical and quantum attacker are

$$O\left(q^{v-m-\ell} \cdot (m/\ell)^4\right), \quad O\left(q^{\frac{v-m-\ell}{2}} \cdot (m/\ell)^4\right),$$

which are approximately the same values as for the plain UOV attack.

Second, the pull-back reconciliation attack is the reconciliation attack on UOV with v/ℓ vinegar variables and m equations. As we stated in Subsect. 5.1, the complexity is estimated to be that of the direct attack on a quadratic system with v/ℓ variables and $\max\{m, v/\ell\}$ equations over $\mathbb{F}_q[x]/(f)$.

Third, we discuss applying the pull-back technique to the intersection attack. The pull-back intersection attack can also be seen as the intersection attack on UOV with v/ℓ vinegar variables and m equations in $\mathbb{F}_q[x]/(f)$. From the discussion in Subsect. 5.1, when $n < 3m$, the complexity of the pull-back intersection attack is equivalent to that of solving the quadratic system with $(2n - 3m)/\ell$ variables and $(3m - 2)$ equations in $\mathbb{F}_q[x]/(f)$. In contrast, in the case where $n \geq 3m$, the complexity of the pull-back intersection attack is estimated by $q^{n-3m+\ell}$ times the complexity of solving the quadratic system with n/ℓ variables and $(3m - 2)$ equations.

Finally, for the direct attack, as vectors $\mathbf{x}$ and $\mathbf{m}$ of $\mathcal{P}(\mathbf{x}) = \mathbf{m}$ cannot be represented over the quotient ring $\mathbb{F}_q[x]/(f)$, the direct attack cannot be executed on $G_1(P_1), \dots, G_1(P_m)$.

5.3 Lifting Attacks over Extension Field

As stated in Theorem 2, there does not exist a transformation on the representation matrices $P_1, \dots, P_m$ of QR-UOV into the diagonal concatenation of smaller matrices, such as the form of Eq. (6) used in the structural attack on BAC-UOV by executing a change of variables over $\mathbb{F}_q$. However, as we prove below, such a transformation exists in the public key of QR-UOV over the extension field $\mathbb{F}_{q^\ell}$. In this subsection, we explain a technique for transforming the public key over $\mathbb{F}_{q^\ell}$ and how this affects the four currently known attacks on UOV.

Theorem 3. *With the same notation as in Theorem 2,*

(i) There exists an invertible matrix $L \in \mathbb{F}_{q^\ell}^{\ell\times\ell}$ *such that* $L^{-1}\Phi_g^f L$ *is diagonal for any* $g \in \mathbb{F}_q[x]/(f)$.
(ii) The matrix L *described in (i) satisfies the condition that* $L^\top X L$ *is diagonal for any* $X \in WA_f$.
(iii) If there exists $\mathbf{y} \in \mathbb{F}_{q^\ell}^\ell$ *such that* $\mathbf{y}^\top X\mathbf{y} = 0$ *for any* $X \in WA_f$*, then* $\mathbf{y} = \mathbf{0}$.

(The proof is provided in the appendix.)

First, Theorem 3 shows that the polynomial matrix can be diagonalized over $\mathbb{F}_{q^\ell}$. Subsequently, it indicates that $P_1, \dots, P_m$ of QR-UOV can be transformed into block diagonal matrices for which the block size is $N \times N$ by executing a change of variables over $\mathbb{F}_{q^\ell}$. Let $L^{(N)}$ be an $n \times n$ block diagonal matrix with block size ℓ ($n = \ell \cdot N$), for which the N diagonal blocks are L. Then, $(L^{(N)})^\top P_i L^{(N)}$ ($i = 1, \dots, m$) become block matrices wherein every component is in a diagonal form. Furthermore, there exists a permutation matrix L' such that $(L^{(N)}L')^\top P_i(L^{(N)}L')$ is a block diagonal matrix with block size N, and let $\bar{L} := L^{(N)}L'$. Finally, this theorem states that there does not exist a change in variables over $\mathbb{F}_{q^\ell}$ such that it directly recovers the structure of the central map of UOV.

Next, we consider the complexities of the lifting UOV, reconciliation, and intersection attacks which are the UOV attack [24], reconciliation attack [14], and intersection attack [5] on $\bar{L}^\top P_i\bar{L}$ ($i = 1, \dots, m$). The transformed matrices $\bar{L}^\top P_i\bar{L}$ can be represented by $(\bar{L}^{-1}S\bar{L})^\top(\bar{L}^\top F_i\bar{L})\,(\bar{L}^{-1}S\bar{L})$. Then, $\bar{L}^\top F_i\bar{L}$ is the diagonal concatenation of ℓ smaller matrices, similar to $\bar{L}^\top P_i\bar{L}$. Furthermore, $\bar{L}^{-1}S\bar{L}$ is also the diagonal concatenation of ℓ smaller matrices from (i) in Theorem 3. Then, owing to the structure of F_i, every diagonal block of $\bar{L}^\top F_i\bar{L}$ has an $m/\ell \times m/\ell$ zero block, similar to F_i. Therefore, each diagonal block of $\bar{L}^\top P_i\bar{L}$ has the same form as the matrix representing the public key of UOV with v/ℓ vinegar variables and m/ℓ oil variables over $\mathbb{F}_{q^\ell}$. The lifting technique executes currently known attacks on one of such diagonal blocks. Consequently, the complexity of the lifting UOV attack on each block over $\mathbb{F}_{q^\ell}$ is $O(q^{v-m-\ell} \cdot (m/\ell)^4)$, and the complexity of the lifting reconciliation attack on each block is estimated to be that of the direct attack on a quadratic system with v/ℓ variables and $\max\{m, v/\ell\}$ equations over $\mathbb{F}_{q^\ell}$. Furthermore, we can apply the lifting technique to the intersection attack. In the case where $n < 3m$, the complexity of the lifting intersection attack on each block over $\mathbb{F}_{q^\ell}$ is estimated to be the complexity of solving the quadratic system with $(2n-3m)/\ell$ variables and $(3m-2)$ equations over $\mathbb{F}_{q^\ell}$. In contrast, in the case where $n \geq 3m$, the complexity is estimated by $q^{n-3m+\ell}$ times the complexity of solving the quadratic system with n/ℓ variables and $(3m-2)$ equations over $\mathbb{F}_{q^\ell}$.

Note that the complexities of the lifting UOV, reconciliation, and intersection attacks in this subsection are the same as those of the pull-back UOV, reconciliation, and intersection attacks in Subsect. 5.2, respectively.

Next, we consider the direct attack on $\bar{L}^\top P_i\bar{L}$ ($i = 1, \dots, m$). Although in Subsect. 5.1, we use the technique proposed by Thomae and Wolf [36] in the

Table 3. Theoretical and experimental degree of regularity obtained by executing the lifting direct attack using the Magma algebra system [7].

(q, v, m, ℓ, k)	Theoretical d_{reg}	Experimental d_{reg}
$(7, 24, 12, 3, 0)$	13	13
$(7, 24, 12, 3, 1)$	7	7
$(7, 24, 12, 3, 2)$	6	5
$(7, 30, 15, 3, 0)$	16	15
$(7, 30, 15, 3, 1)$	8	8
$(7, 30, 15, 3, 2)$	7	7

plain direct attack, we cannot use this technique in the lifting direct attack. If we use this technique before the linear transformation using $\bar{L}$ over $\mathbb{F}_{q^\ell}$, the representation matrices cannot be diagonalized because the linear transformation executed in this technique breaks the block structure of QR-UOV. We thus use the technique after block-diagonalizing over $\mathbb{F}_{q^\ell}$. If $n > m$, the cardinality of the solution is generally $\mathbb{F}_q^v$. However, because the system is solved over $\mathbb{F}_{q^\ell}$, the cardinality of the obtained solution changes to $\mathbb{F}_{q^\ell}^v$. Therefore, the probability that the obtained solution is in $\mathbb{F}_q^n$ is very low; therefore, this technique is inefficient. In conclusion, there is no effective way to execute the direct attack on $\bar{L}^\top P_i \bar{L}$ using Thomae and Wolf's technique.

Therefore, we consider the lifting direct attack without using Thomae and Wolf's technique, in which we fix the v values before block-diagonalizing over $\mathbb{F}_{q^\ell}$. We then obtain a solution in $\mathbb{F}_q^n$ because the solution is uniquely determined with high probability. This means that we can execute the direct attack on a block-diagonalized system without reducing the probability of obtaining a solution in $\mathbb{F}_q^n$. Table 3 summarizes the results of experiments investigating the degree of regularity of the block-diagonalized public key system of QR-UOV using the Magma algebra system [7]. In our experiment, v is set to be equal to $2m$. For the representation matrices $P_1, \ldots, P_m$ of the public key of the QR-UOV with $(v+m)$ variables and m equations, after transforming the system like $\bar{L}^\top P_i \bar{L}$, we fix the last v variables and execute the hybrid approach by fixing k variables additionally. That is, the direct attack is executed on the system of m equations in $m - k$ variables. In Table 3, the theoretical d_{reg} is the degree of regularity obtained by Eq. (11), assuming that the system is semi-regular, and the experimental d_{reg} is the highest degree among the step degrees, where non-zero polynomials are generated in experiments of the direct attack using the Magma algebra system [7]. The results show that the experimental d_{reg} was smaller than the theoretical d_{reg} by at most one. Therefore, we estimate the complexity of the lifting direct attack by replacing q and d_{reg} in Eqs. (10) and (12) with q^ℓ and $d_{reg} - 1$, respectively. In this estimation, the degree of regularity becomes one degree smaller, but the base field $\mathbb{F}_q$ is lifted to the extension field $\mathbb{F}_{q^\ell}$.

6 Proposed Parameters and Comparison

In this section, we propose specific parameters for three security levels of the NIST PQC project [27] and compare the performance of the improved QR-UOV with that of compressed Rainbow [12].

6.1 Proposed Parameters

In this subsection, we describe the parameters selected for the improved QR-UOV described in Subsect. 4.2. Our proposed parameters are set to satisfy the security levels I, III, and V of the NIST PQC project [27] to enable comparison with the performance of compressed Rainbow [12]. The parameters for the improved QR-UOV are the order of finite fields q, number of vinegar variables v, number of oil variables (equations) m, block size of the representation matrices ℓ, and polynomial used to generate the quotient ring f. We set q as odd from a security perspective. The integer v is mainly determined by the complexity of the pull-back and lifting reconciliation attacks described in Subsects. 5.2 and 5.3, and m is determined by that of the plain direct attack. We use $\ell = 3$ because a large ℓ increases the signature and execution time. From Theorem 2, we choose irreducible polynomials f in the form of $x^\ell - ax^i - 1$ described in Example 1. In summary, we propose the following parameters for improved QR-UOV:

$$\begin{aligned}
\text{QR-UOV I}: &\quad (q, v, m, \ell, f) = (7, 189, 72, 3, x^3 - 3x - 1),\\
\text{QR-UOV III}: &\quad (q, v, m, \ell, f) = (7, 291, 111, 3, x^3 - 3x - 1),\\
\text{QR-UOV V}: &\quad (q, v, m, \ell, f) = (7, 411, 162, 3, x^3 - 3x - 1).
\end{aligned}$$

Next, we show that these parameters of QR-UOV I, III, and V satisfy the security levels I, III, and V of the NIST PQC project, respectively. Here, security levels I, III, and V indicate that a classical attacker needs more than 2^{143}, 2^{207}, and 2^{272} classical gates to break the parameters, whereas a quantum attacker needs more than 2^{74}, 2^{137}, and 2^{202} quantum gates, respectively [27]. The number of gates required for an attack against the NIST third-round proposal version of Rainbow [12] can be computed using

$$\#\text{gates} = \#\text{field multiplication} \cdot (2 \cdot (\log_2 q)^2 + \log_2 q).$$

Next, we consider the complexity of each attack described in Sect. 5 on the proposed parameters. Table 4 shows the complexity of the plain direct, UOV, reconciliation, and intersection attacks described in Subsect. 5.1, the pull-back UOV, reconciliation, and intersection attacks described in Subsect. 5.2, and the lifting direct, UOV, reconciliation, and intersection attacks described in Subsect. 5.3. (See each subsection for a concrete method of estimating the complexity of each attack). This table does not include the complexity of "the pull-back direct attack" because we cannot execute the direct attack on the pulled back public key system, as stated in Subsect. 5.2. For each parameter set, the upper entry shows the number of classical gates, whereas the lower entry shows the number of quantum gates.

Table 4. The complexity of the plain attacks in Subsect. 5.1, the pull-back attacks in Subsect. 5.2, and lifting attacks in Subsect. 5.3 on the proposed parameters of QR-UOV in Subsect. 6.1. Here, "dir", "UOV", "rec", and "int" denote the direct attack, UOV attack, reconciliation attack, and intersection attack, respectively. The bold font indicates the lowest complexity among all attacks at the same security level.

Parameter (q, v, m, ℓ)	Attack model	$\log_2(\#\text{gates})$										
		Plain				Pull-back			Lifting			
		dir	UOV	rec	int	UOV	rec	int	dir	UOV	rec	int
QR-UOV I (7,189,72,3)	Classical	152	355	373	679	346	**149**	242	210	346	**149**	242
	Quantum	**91**	192	252	411	186	148	175	182	186	148	175
QR-UOV III (7,291,111,3)	Classical	224	534	555	1022	525	**214**	351	311	525	**214**	351
	Quantum	**140**	283	371	616	277	213	250	267	277	213	250
QR-UOV V (7,411,162,3)	Classical	317	730	768	1394	721	**279**	446	440	721	**279**	446
	Quantum	**205**	382	511	844	376	275	316	376	376	275	316

For example, the complexity of the direct attack for level I is 155 classical gates and 106 quantum gates. Furthermore, the values in bold indicate the complexity of the best attack against each parameter set. The lowest complexity among all attacks is the pull-back and lifting reconciliation attacks in the classical case, whereas that is the direct attack in the quantum case. As a result, this table shows that the proposed parameters satisfy the requirements for each security level.

Remark 5. Similar to the proposed parameters for Rainbow [12], our proposed parameters for security levels I, III, and V also satisfy security levels II, IV, and VI of the NIST PQC project [27].

Remark 6. In [19], Furue et al. improved Thomae and Wolf's technique for solving the $\mathcal{MQ}$ problem in the case where $n > m$. Furthermore, Hashimoto made the method more efficient in [22]. By using these results, the complexities of the plain direct attack on QR-UOV I, III, and V are reduced from 2^{155}, 2^{227}, and 2^{320} to 2^{152}, 2^{224}, and 2^{317} in the classical case and from 2^{106}, 2^{155}, and 2^{216} to 2^{91}, 2^{140}, and 2^{205} in the quantum case, respectively. In Table 4, we take the above reduced values.

6.2 Comparison with Rainbow

In Table 5, we compare the public key and signature size for our proposed improved QR-UOV parameters with those for compressed Rainbow [12] for security levels I, III, and V. As for compressed Rainbow in the third-round proposal [12], the public key includes a 256-bit seed $\mathbf{s}_{pk}$, and the signature includes a 128 bit *salt*, which is a random binary vector for EUF-CMA security [33]. The secret key can be generated from two 256-bit seeds, $\mathbf{s}_{sk}$ and $\mathbf{s}_{pk}$. For example, the public key size of the improved QR-UOV for level I is 23.8 KB, which is approximately half that of compressed Rainbow. As a result, the public key size of the

Table 5. Comparison of public key and signature size of compressed Rainbow with those of QR-UOV. We use parameters for compressed Rainbow in [12], and parameters for the improved QR-UOV in Subsect. 4.2. The unit of the public key size is kilobyte (KB) but that of the signature size is byte (B).

Security level	Scheme	Parameters	Public key size (KB)	Signature size (B)
I	Compressed Rainbow I	$(q, v_1, o_1, o_2) = (16, 36, 32, 32)$	57.4	66.0
	QR-UOV I	$(q, v, m, \ell) = (7, 189, 72, 3)$	**23.8**	**113.9**
III	Compressed Rainbow III	$(q, v_1, o_1, o_2) = (256, 68, 32, 48)$	252.3	164.0
	QR-UOV III	$(q, v, m, \ell) = (7, 291, 111, 3)$	**85.8**	**166.8**
V	Compressed Rainbow V	$(q, v_1, o_1, o_2) = (256, 96, 36, 64)$	511.2	212.0
	QR-UOV V	$(q, v, m, \ell) = (7, 411, 162, 3)$	**264.3**	**230.9**

improved QR-UOV can be reduced by approximately 50%–70% compared with that of compressed Rainbow at the cost of a small increase in signature size. We stress that the Rainbow team [31] did not update the parameters of the compressed Rainbow by considering the intersection attack and the rectangular MinRank attack proposed by Beullens [5].

Although the public key size could be further reduced by setting the block size ℓ larger, enlarging the block size would likely increase the signature size and increase the execution time.

7 Conclusion

We proposed a new variant of UOV, which is a well-established multivariate signature scheme that has not been broken for over 20 years. Our proposed QR-UOV scheme uses a quotient ring $(\mathbb{F}_q[x]/(f))$ to reduce the public key size. Although multivariate signature schemes are promising candidates for post-quantum cryptography, and a UOV variant called Rainbow was selected as a third-round finalist in the NIST post-quantum cryptography (PQC) project, a disadvantage of UOV variants, including Rainbow, is that they have a large public key. Research on reducing the size of the UOV public key is important for post-quantum cryptography. In this paper, we present a new approach for achieving such a reduction.

Our proposed QR-UOV scheme features a small public key and a reasonable signature size. In particular, using the proposed parameters, the public key size of the improved QR-UOV can be reduced approximately 50%–70% compared with that of compressed Rainbow, a third-round finalist in the NIST PQC project, without significantly increasing the signature size. To construct QR-UOV, we defined polynomial matrices Φ_g^f ($g \in \mathbb{F}_q[x]/(f)$) and introduced the concept of a matrix W such that $W\Phi_g^f$ is symmetric. QR-UOV utilizes polynomial matrices Φ_g^f in block matrices. Moreover, we proved that if the polynomial f used to generate the quotient ring is irreducible, then QR-UOV is resistant to attacks that can break the block-anti-circulant UOV. We also analyzed the security of QR-UOV against four currently known attacks on plain UOV and possible attacks on the quotient ring. We stress that utilizing the elements of a quotient ring in block matrices is similar to the MLWE problem: a generalization of the LWE using a module comprising vectors over a ring.

Improving the efficiency of QR-UOV is an important problem. The Rainbow UOV variant has a multilayer structure and is efficient and secure. Extending QR-UOV to a comparable, efficient, and secure multilayer version of the QR-Rainbow will be a challenging task. We need to carefully analyze the security of the QR-Rainbow against various attacks by considering its multilayer structure. Another possible way to improve the efficiency is to exploit a better choice of the polynomial f. In this study, we simply used a simple trinomial for the first construction of QR-UOV; we expect to obtain another family of polynomials that can produce more efficient operations.

Acknowledgments. This work was supported by JST CREST Grant Number JPMJCR14D6 and JPMJCR2113, Japan, and JSPS KAKENHI Grant Number JP21J20391 and JP19K20266, Japan.

Appendix A: Transformation on Polynomial Matrix from a Reducible Polynomial

First, we discuss the case in which f is reducible and decomposed into distinct irreducible polynomials.

Theorem 4. *Let $f \in \mathbb{F}_q[x]$ be a reducible polynomial with $\deg f = \ell$ and W be an invertible matrix such that every element of WA_f is a symmetric matrix. If $f = f_1 \cdots f_k$ ($k \in \mathbb{N}$), where $f_1, \ldots, f_k$ are distinct and irreducible, and $\deg f_1 \leq \cdots \leq \deg f_k$, then there exists an invertible matrix $L \in \mathbb{F}_q^{\ell\times\ell}$ and $i \in \{1, \ldots, \ell-1\}$ such that for any $X \in WA_f$,*

$$L^\top XL = \begin{pmatrix} *_{i\times i} & 0_{i\times(\ell-i)} \\ 0_{(\ell-i)\times i} & *_{(\ell-i)\times(\ell-i)} \end{pmatrix}. \tag{14}$$

Proof. We first prove that every element of $A_f W^{-1}$ is symmetric. For any $g \in \mathbb{F}_q[x]/(f)$,

$$\begin{aligned}(\Phi_g^f W^{-1})^\top &= W^{-\top}(\Phi_g^f)^\top \\ &= W^{-\top}(\Phi_g^f)^\top W W^{-1} \\ &= W^{-\top}(W\Phi_g^f)^\top W^{-1} \quad (\because W \text{ is symmetric.}) \\ &= W^{-\top} W \Phi_g^f W^{-1} \\ &= \Phi_g^f W^{-1}.\end{aligned}$$

Therefore, every element of $A_f W^{-1}$ is symmetric.

As f is reducible, there exists $a, b \in \mathbb{F}_q[x]/(f)$ such that $a \cdot b = 0$. Then, for any $g \in \mathbb{F}_q[x]/(f)$,

$$\begin{aligned}(\Phi_a^f W^{-1})^\top (W\Phi_g^f)(\Phi_b^f W^{-1}) &= \Phi_{a\cdot g\cdot b}^f W^{-1} \\ &= \Phi_0^f W^{-1} = 0_{\ell\times\ell}.\end{aligned}$$

We assume that $L \in \mathbb{F}_q^{\ell\times\ell}$ is designed such that the first i column vectors of L are chosen from the column vector space of $\Phi_a^f W^{-1}$, and the other $(\ell - i)$ column vectors of L are chosen from the column vector space of $\Phi_b^f W^{-1}$. Then, Eq. (14) explicitly holds from the above equation.

We next show that there exists an invertible such an invertible matrix L. We take $a = f_1$ and $b = f_2 \cdots f_k$ (here, $f_1, \ldots, f_k$ are seen as elements of $\mathbb{F}_q[x]/(f)$.) and prove that $\operatorname{rank} \Phi_a^f = \deg b$ ($\operatorname{rank} \Phi_b^f = \deg a$). We use the bijective map V_1 used in the proof of Theorem 2. From Eq. (7), for any $c \in \mathbb{F}_q[x]/(f)$,

$$a \cdot c = 0 \Leftrightarrow \Phi_a^f \cdot V_1(c) = \mathbf{0}.$$

As there is no $c \in \mathbb{F}_q[x]/(f)$ such that $a \cdot c = 0$ and $\deg c < \deg b$, the first $\deg b$ column vectors are linearly independent. Furthermore, as $\Phi_a^f \cdot V_1(b) = \mathbf{0}$, $\Phi_a^f \cdot V_1(xb) = \mathbf{0}, \ldots, \Phi_a^f \cdot V_1(x^{\deg a - 1} b) = \mathbf{0}$, we have $\operatorname{rank} \Phi_a^f = \deg b$. Similarly, it is proved that $\operatorname{rank} \Phi_b^f = \deg a$.

Next, we design $L \in \mathbb{F}_q^{\ell\times\ell}$ such that the first $\deg b$ column vectors of L are bases of the column vector space of $\Phi_a^f W^{-1}$ and the other $(\ell - \deg b)$ $(= \deg a)$ column vectors of L are bases of the column vector space of $\Phi_b^f W^{-1}$.

Finally, we prove that the column vector spaces of $\Phi_a^f W^{-1}$ and $\Phi_b^f W^{-1}$ have no intersection, that is, the column vector spaces of Φ_a^f and Φ_b^f have no intersection. If this statement holds, then L constructed using this approach is invertible. We assume that the column vector spaces of Φ_a^f and Φ_b^f have an intersection. Then, there exist two vectors $\mathbf{x}, \mathbf{y} \in \mathbb{F}_q^\ell$ such that the last $(\ell - \deg b)$ elements of $\mathbf{x}$ and the last $(\ell - \deg a)$ elements of $\mathbf{y}$ are zero, and $\Phi_a^f \mathbf{x} = \Phi_b^f \mathbf{y}$ because the first $\deg b$ ($\deg a$) vectors of Φ_a^f (Φ_b^f) are linearly independent. From the definition of Φ_g^f, $aV_1^{-1}(\mathbf{x}) = bV_1^{-1}(\mathbf{y})$, $\deg(V_1^{-1}(\mathbf{x})) < \deg b$, and $\deg(V_1^{-1}(\mathbf{y})) < \deg a$. However, this contradicts that $f_1, \ldots, f_k$ are distinct and irreducible. Therefore, the column vector spaces of Φ_a^f and Φ_b^f have no intersections. □

Next, we discuss another case where f is reducible.

Theorem 5. *With the same notation as in Theorem 4, if there exists $f' \in \mathbb{F}_q[x]$ such that $f'^2 \mid f$, there exists an invertible matrix $L \in \mathbb{F}_q^{\ell \times \ell}$ such that, for any $X \in WA_f$,*

$$(L^\top XL)_{\ell\ell} = 0.$$

Proof. From this assumption, there exists $a \in \mathbb{F}_q[x]/(f)$ such that $a^2 = 0$. Therefore, for any $g \in \mathbb{F}_q[x]/(f)$,

$$\begin{aligned}(\Phi_a^f W^{-1})^\top (W\Phi_g^f)(\Phi_a^f W^{-1}) &= \Phi_{a \cdot g \cdot a}^f W^{-1} \\ &= 0_{\ell \times \ell},\end{aligned}$$

and $\Phi_a^f W^{-1}$ is symmetric. We suppose that $L \in \mathbb{F}_q^{\ell \times \ell}$ is an invertible matrix, wherein the ℓ-th column vector is chosen from the column vectors of $\Phi_a^f W^{-1}$. From the above equation, the (ℓ, ℓ) component of $L^\top (W\Phi_g^f)L$ is zero for any $g \in \mathbb{F}_q[x]/(f)$. □

Appendix B: Proof of Theorem 3 in Subsect. 5.3

Theorem 3. *With the same notation as in Theorem 2,*

(i) There exists an invertible matrix $L \in \mathbb{F}_{q^\ell}^{\ell \times \ell}$ such that $L^{-1}\Phi_g^f L$ is diagonal for any $g \in \mathbb{F}_q[x]/(f)$.
(ii) The matrix L described in (i) satisfies the condition that $L^\top XL$ is diagonal for any $X \in WA_f$.
(iii) If there exists $\mathbf{y} \in \mathbb{F}_{q^\ell}^\ell$ such that $\mathbf{y}^\top X\mathbf{y} = 0$ for any $X \in WA_f$, then $\mathbf{y} = \mathbf{0}$.

Proof. First, we prove statement 1. The characteristic polynomial of Φ_x^f is equal to f for $x \in \mathbb{F}_q[x]/(f)$. As f is irreducible over $\mathbb{F}_q[x]$, f is separable, and its roots are distinct in $\mathbb{F}_{q^\ell}[x]$. Therefore, the eigenvalues of Φ_x^f are distinct in $\mathbb{F}_{q^\ell}$, and there exists $L \in \mathbb{F}_{q^\ell}^{\ell \times \ell}$ such that $L^{-1}\Phi_x^f L$ is diagonal. Furthermore, Φ_1^f is the identity matrix, and $\Phi_{x^i}^f$ $(i = 2, \ldots, \ell - 1)$ can be diagonalized using L:

$$\begin{aligned}L^{-1}\Phi_{x^i}^f L &= L^{-1}(\Phi_x^f \cdots \Phi_x^f)L \\ &= (L^{-1}\Phi_x^f L) \cdots (L^{-1}\Phi_x^f L).\end{aligned}$$

Then, for any $g \in \mathbb{F}_q[x]/(f)$, $L^{-1}\Phi_g^f L$ becomes diagonal because A_f is spanned by $\{\Phi_1^f, \Phi_x^f, \ldots, \Phi_{x^{\ell-1}}^f\}$ over $\mathbb{F}_q$.

Next, we prove statement 2 by using the following lemma.

Lemma 2. *With the same notation as in Theorem 2, for $L \in \mathbb{F}_{q^\ell}^{\ell \times \ell}$ described in Theorem 3, $L^\top WL$ is diagonal.*

Proof. Since $W\Phi_g^f$ is symmetric,

$$W\Phi_g^f = (W\Phi_g^f)^\top = (\Phi_g^f)^\top W^\top.$$

Furthermore, because W is symmetric, we have

$$(\Phi_g^f)^\top = W\Phi_g^f W^{-1}. \tag{15}$$

As $L^{-1}\Phi_g^f L$ is symmetric,

$$\begin{aligned} L^{-1}\Phi_g^f L &= L^\top(\Phi_g^f)^\top L^{-\top} \\ &= L^\top W\Phi_g^f W^{-1}L^{-\top} \quad (\because (15)) \\ &= (L^\top WL)(L^{-1}\Phi_g^f L)(L^\top WL)^{-1}. \end{aligned}$$

Then, $L^\top WL$ and $L^{-1}\Phi_g^f L$ are commutative. As $L^{-1}\Phi_g^f L$ is diagonal, and the diagonal components are distinct, $L^\top WL$ is diagonal. □

For any $g \in \mathbb{F}_q[x]/(f)$, we can transform $L^\top W\Phi_g^f L$:

$$L^\top W\Phi_g^f L = (L^\top WL)(L^{-1}\Phi_g^f L).$$

From statement 1 and Lemma 2, $L^\top W\Phi_g^f L$ are diagonal.

Finally, we prove statement 3. Let $\mathbf{y} := L^{-1}\mathbf{x}$; then,

$$\begin{aligned} \mathbf{x}^\top W\Phi_g^f\mathbf{x} &= (L\mathbf{y})^\top W\Phi_g^f(L\mathbf{y}) \\ &= \mathbf{y}^\top(L^\top WL)(L^{-1}\Phi_g^f L)\mathbf{y}. \end{aligned}$$

If we define the diagonal components of $L^{-1}\Phi_x^f L$ as $\theta_1, \dots, \theta_\ell$ (the roots of f in $\mathbb{F}_{q^\ell}$), the diagonal components of $L^{-1}\Phi_g^f L$ are equal to $g(\theta_1), \dots, g(\theta_\ell)$. If $\mathbf{y}' := \left(y_1^2 \dots y_\ell^2\right)^\top$,

$$\begin{aligned} &\mathbf{y}^\top(L^\top WL)(L^{-1}\Phi_g^f L)\mathbf{y} = 0 \\ \Leftrightarrow &\left(g(\theta_1) \cdots g(\theta_\ell)\right)(L^\top WL)\mathbf{y}' = 0 \end{aligned} \tag{16}$$

since $L^\top WL$ is diagonal.

Let $g_1, \dots, g_\ell$ be the basis of $\mathbb{F}_q[x]/(f)$ over $\mathbb{F}_q$, then, satisfying Eq. (16) for any $g \in \mathbb{F}_q[x]/(f)$ is equivalent to

$$\begin{pmatrix} g_1(\theta_1) & \dots & g_1(\theta_\ell), \\ \vdots & \ddots & \vdots \\ g_\ell(\theta_1) & \dots & g_\ell(\theta_\ell) \end{pmatrix}(L^\top WL)\mathbf{y}' = \mathbf{0}. \tag{17}$$

In addition, $g_1, \dots, g_\ell$ form the basis of $\mathbb{F}_{q^\ell}[x]/(f)$ over $\mathbb{F}_{q^\ell}$, and

$$\begin{aligned} \mathbb{F}_{q^\ell}[x]/(f) &\cong \mathbb{F}_{q^\ell}[x]/(x-\theta_1) \oplus \mathbb{F}_{q^\ell}[x]/(x-\theta_2) \oplus \dots \oplus \mathbb{F}_{q^\ell}[x]/(x-\theta_\ell), \\ &\cong \mathbb{F}_{q^\ell}^\ell. \end{aligned}$$

Table 6. Performance of the improved QR-UOV in Subsect. 4.2 in Magma algebra system [7].

Parameter	(q, v, m, ℓ)	Key generation	Signature generation	Verification
QR-UOV I	$(7, 189, 72, 3)$	0.06 s	0.04 s	0.01 s
QR-UOV III	$(7, 291, 111, 3)$	0.17 s	0.13 s	0.05 s
QR-UOV V	$(7, 411, 162, 3)$	0.45 s	0.33 s	0.11 s

Therefore, $(g_i(\theta_1) \cdots g_i(\theta_\ell))$ $(i = 1, \dots, \ell)$ are linearly independent, and

$$\begin{aligned}(17) &\Leftrightarrow \mathbf{y}' = \mathbf{0} \\ &\Leftrightarrow \mathbf{y} = \mathbf{0} \\ &\Leftrightarrow \mathbf{x} = \mathbf{0}.\end{aligned}$$

□

Appendix C: Performance in Magma

Here, we present the execution times for key generation, signature generation, and verification of the improved QR-UOV in Subsect. 4.2. All experiments were performed on a MacBook Pro with a 2.4-GHz quad-core, Intel Core i5 CPU, and the Magma algebra system (V2.24-82) [7]. Table 6 shows the average times for 100 runs using the improved QR-UOV scheme described in Subsect. 4.2 and our proposed parameters for levels I, III, and V of the NIST PQC project. All timings are in second. These are not optimized implementations.

In the key generation step, we first generate two 32-bit seeds ($\mathbf{s}_{sk}$ and $\mathbf{s}_{pk}$) by using the Magma `Random` command. We then use the Magma `SetSeed` command as a pseudo-random number generator to generate part of the public and secret keys. (In Subsect. 6.2, we stated that the size of the two seeds is 256 bits; however, we use two 32-bit seeds because the size of the input for `SetSeed` is at most 32 bits.) Next, we generate a secret key using the method described in Subsect. 4.2. In the signature generation step, we recover the public and secret keys from the two seeds and perform the procedure explained in Subsect. 2.2. The signature is generated in the same manner as a signature is generated in the compressed Rainbow [12]. In the verification step, we generate the public key from the $\mathbf{s}_{pk}$ seed and follow the procedure explained in Subsect. 2.1. In the signature generation and verification steps, we need to compute the product of a vector and matrices $W\Phi_g^f$ or Φ_g^f, which is made more efficient using the structure of the polynomial matrix.

For example, in Table 6, the execution times of the key generation, signature generation, and verification steps of QR-UOV for level I are 0.06 s, 0.04 s, and 0.01 s, respectively. In most cases, our performance is approximately one order of magnitude slower than that of compressed Rainbow [12]. It should be noted that their implementation is in C, and ours is in Magma, and the signing and verification times of compressed Rainbow are dominated by the use of a cryptographic hash function which is not used in the implementation of QR-UOV.

References

1. Bardet, M.: Étude des systèms algébriques surdéterminés. Applications aux codes correcteurs et à la cryptographie. Ph.D. thesis, Université Pierre et Marie Curie-Paris VI (2004)
2. Bardet, M., Faugère, J.-C., Salvy, B.: Complexity of Gröbner basis computation for semi-regular overdetermined sequences over $\mathbb{F}_2$ with solutions in $\mathbb{F}_2$. Research Report, INRIA (2003)
3. Bardet, M., Faugère, J.-C., Salvy, B., Yang, B.-Y.: Asymptotic behavior of the index of regularity of quadratic semi-regular polynomial systems. In: 8th International Symposium on Effective Methods in Algebraic Geometry (2005)
4. Bettale, L., Faugère, J.-C., Perret, L.: Hybrid approach for solving multivariate systems over finite fields. J. Math. Cryptol. **3**, 177–197 (2009)
5. Beullens, W.: Improved cryptanalysis of UOV and rainbow. In: Canteaut, A., Standaert, F.-X. (eds.) EUROCRYPT 2021. LNCS, vol. 12696, pp. 348–373. Springer, Cham (2021). https://doi.org/10.1007/978-3-030-77870-5_13
6. Beullens, W., Preneel, B.: Field lifting for smaller UOV public keys. In: Patra, A., Smart, N.P. (eds.) INDOCRYPT 2017. LNCS, vol. 10698, pp. 227–246. Springer, Cham (2017). https://doi.org/10.1007/978-3-319-71667-1_12
7. Bosma, W., Cannon, J., Playoust, C.: The Magma algebra system. I. The user language. J. Symbol. Comput. **24**(3–4), 235–265 (1997)
8. Brakerski, Z., Gentry, C., Vaikuntanathan, V.: (Leveled) fully homomorphic encryption without bootstrapping. In: ITCS 2012, pp. 309–325. ACM (2012)
9. Buchberger, B.: Ein algorithmus zum auffinden der basiselemente des restklassenringes nach einem nulldimensionalen polynomideal. Ph.D. thesis, Universität Innsbruck (1965)
10. Courtois, N., Klimov, A., Patarin, J., Shamir, A.: Efficient algorithms for solving overdefined systems of multivariate polynomial equations. In: Preneel, B. (ed.) EUROCRYPT 2000. LNCS, vol. 1807, pp. 392–407. Springer, Heidelberg (2000). https://doi.org/10.1007/3-540-45539-6_27
11. Czypek, P., Heyse, S., Thomae, E.: Efficient implementations of MQPKS on constrained devices. In: Prouff, E., Schaumont, P. (eds.) CHES 2012. LNCS, vol. 7428, pp. 374–389. Springer, Heidelberg (2012). https://doi.org/10.1007/978-3-642-33027-8_22
12. Ding, J., et al.: Rainbow signature schemes proposal for NIST PQC project (round 3 version)
13. Ding, J., Schmidt, D.: Rainbow, a new multivariable polynomial signature scheme. In: Ioannidis, J., Keromytis, A., Yung, M. (eds.) ACNS 2005. LNCS, vol. 3531, pp. 164–175. Springer, Heidelberg (2005). https://doi.org/10.1007/11496137_12
14. Ding, J., Yang, B.-Y., Chen, C.-H.O., Chen, M.-S., Cheng, C.-M.: New differential-algebraic attacks and reparametrization of rainbow. In: Bellovin, S.M., Gennaro, R., Keromytis, A., Yung, M. (eds.) ACNS 2008. LNCS, vol. 5037, pp. 242–257. Springer, Heidelberg (2008). https://doi.org/10.1007/978-3-540-68914-0_15
15. Ding, J., Zhang, Z., Deaton, J., Schmidt, K., Vishakha, FNU.: New attacks on lifted unbalanced oil vinegar. In: Second PQC Standardization Conference 2019, NIST (2019)

16. Faugère, J.-C.: A new efficient algorithm for computing Gröbner bases (F4). J. Pure Appl. Algebra **139**(1–3), 61–88 (1999)
17. Faugère, J.-C.: A new efficient algorithm for computing Gröbner bases without reduction to zero (F5). In: ISSAC 2002, pp. 75–83. ACM (2002)
18. Furue, H., Kinjo, K., Ikematsu, Y., Wang, Y., Takagi, T.: A structural attack on block-anti-circulant UOV at SAC 2019. In: Ding, J., Tillich, J.-P. (eds.) PQCrypto 2020. LNCS, vol. 12100, pp. 323–339. Springer, Cham (2020). https://doi.org/10.1007/978-3-030-44223-1_18
19. Furue, H., Nakamura, S., Takagi, T.: Improving Thomae-Wolf algorithm for solving underdetermined multivariate quadratic polynomial problem. In: Cheon, J.H., Tillich, J.-P. (eds.) PQCrypto 2021 2021. LNCS, vol. 12841, pp. 65–78. Springer, Cham (2021). https://doi.org/10.1007/978-3-030-81293-5_4
20. Garey, M.-R., Johnson, D.-S.: Computers and Intractability: A Guide to the Theory of NP-completeness. Freeman, W.H, San Francisco (1979)
21. Grover, L.-K.: A fast quantum mechanical algorithm for database search. In: STOC 1996, pp. 212–219. ACM (1996)
22. Hashimoto, Y.: Minor improvements of algorithm to solve under-defined systems of multivariate quadratic equations. IACR Cryptology ePrint Archive: Report 2021/1045 (2021)
23. Kipnis, A., Patarin, J., Goubin, L.: Unbalanced oil and vinegar signature schemes. In: Stern, J. (ed.) EUROCRYPT 1999. LNCS, vol. 1592, pp. 206–222. Springer, Heidelberg (1999). https://doi.org/10.1007/3-540-48910-X_15
24. Kipnis, A., Shamir, A.: Cryptanalysis of the oil and vinegar signature scheme. In: Krawczyk, H. (ed.) CRYPTO 1998. LNCS, vol. 1462, pp. 257–266. Springer, Heidelberg (1998). https://doi.org/10.1007/BFb0055733
25. Lyubashevsky, V., et al.: CRYSTALS-DILITHIUM signature schemes proposal for NIST PQC project (round 2 version)
26. NIST: post-quantum cryptography CSRC. https://csrc.nist.gov/Projects/post-quantum-cryptography/post-quantum-cryptography-standardization
27. NIST: submission requirements and evaluation criteria for the post-quantum cryptography standardization process (2016). https://csrc.nist.gov/CSRC/media/Projects/Post-Quantum-Cryptography/documents/call-for-proposals-final-dec-2016.pdf
28. NIST: Status report on the first round of the NIST post-quantum cryptography standardization process. NIST Internal Report 8240, NIST (2019)
29. NIST: Status report on the second round of the NIST post-quantum cryptography standardization process. NIST Internal Report 8309, NIST (2020)
30. Petzoldt, A., Bulygin, S., Buchmann, J.: CyclicRainbow – a multivariate signature scheme with a partially cyclic public key. In: Gong, G., Gupta, K.C. (eds.) INDOCRYPT 2010. LNCS, vol. 6498, pp. 33–48. Springer, Heidelberg (2010). https://doi.org/10.1007/978-3-642-17401-8_4
31. The Rainbow Team: Response to recent paper by Ward Beullens (2020). https://troll.iis.sinica.edu.tw/by-publ/recent/response-ward.pdf
32. Regev, O.: On lattices, learning with errors, random linear codes, and cryptography. In: STOC 2005, pp. 84–93. ACM (2005)
33. Sakumoto, K., Shirai, T., Hiwatari, H.: On provable security of UOV and HFE signature schemes against chosen-message attack. In: Yang, B.-Y. (ed.) PQCrypto 2011. LNCS, vol. 7071, pp. 68–82. Springer, Heidelberg (2011). https://doi.org/10.1007/978-3-642-25405-5_5
34. Shor, P.W.: Polynomial-time algorithms for prime factorization and discrete logarithms on a quantum computer. SIAM J. Comput. **26**(5), 1484–1509 (1997)

35. Szepieniec, A., Preneel, B.: Block-anti-circulant unbalanced oil and vinegar. In: Paterson, K.G., Stebila, D. (eds.) SAC 2019. LNCS, vol. 11959, pp. 574–588. Springer, Cham (2020). https://doi.org/10.1007/978-3-030-38471-5_23
36. Thomae, E., Wolf, C.: Solving underdetermined systems of multivariate quadratic equations revisited. In: Fischlin, M., Buchmann, J., Manulis, M. (eds.) PKC 2012. LNCS, vol. 7293, pp. 156–171. Springer, Heidelberg (2012). https://doi.org/10.1007/978-3-642-30057-8_10

Shorter Lattice-Based Group Signatures via "Almost Free" Encryption and Other Optimizations

Vadim Lyubashevsky[1(✉)], Ngoc Khanh Nguyen[1,2(✉)], Maxime Plancon[1,2(✉)], and Gregor Seiler[1,2(✉)]

[1] IBM Research Europe, Zurich, Switzerland
{nkn,mpl,grs}@zurich.ibm.com
[2] ETH Zurich, Zurich, Switzerland

Abstract. We present an improved lattice-based group signature scheme whose parameter sizes and running times are independent of the group size. The signature length in our scheme is around 200KB, which is approximately a 3X reduction over the previously most compact such scheme, based on any quantum-safe assumption, of del Pino et al. (CCS 2018). The improvement comes via several optimizations of some basic cryptographic components that make up group signature schemes, and we think that they will find other applications in privacy-based lattice cryptography.

Keywords: Lattice cryptography · Group signatures · Zero-knowledge

1 Introduction

The eventual coming of quantum computers, combined with the ongoing shift to decentralization, makes designing efficient quantum-safe privacy-based primitives a highly pertinent problem. One of the more elementary privacy-preserving primitives is a group signature, and constructing such schemes has often been seen as an important stepping stone towards constructing more expressive primitives.

In a group signature scheme, the setup authority gives out individual signing keys s_i to users with identities m_i. User m_i can then utilize s_i to create a signature σ on a message μ of his choosing. There is also an entity called the Opener (or Group Manager) who is able to derive the identity m_i of the user who created σ. A basic group signature scheme has the following security properties:

1. Anonymity. The adversary who knows all the signing keys s_i cannot distinguish between signatures produced by user m_i or $m_{i'}$, for i, i' of the adversary's choosing.
2. Traceability. The adversary who possesses signing keys to all users in some set S, and the Opener's secret key, cannot create a valid signature that the Opener will decrypt to some identity $m_i \notin S$ or to $\perp$ (i.e. decryption will fail).

Supported by the SNSF ERC Transfer Grant CRETP2-166734 FELICITY and the EU H2020 ERC Project 101002845 PLAZA.

M. Tibouchi and H. Wang (Eds.): ASIACRYPT 2021, LNCS 13093, pp. 218–248, 2021.
https://doi.org/10.1007/978-3-030-92068-5_8

While there exist fairly efficient group signatures based on standard assumptions (e.g. [CS97]), most of the early work in trying to construct lattice-based group signatures were efficient only in an asymptotic sense with concrete signature sizes being around 50 MB (e.g. [GKV10, LLNW16]). More recently, some concretely efficient schemes appeared that lowered the signature sizes to a little over 1 MB (c.f. [BCN18]), and the scheme with the smallest signature size, in which the parameters and computational complexity of signing and verifying do not depend on the group size, was proposed by del Pino et al. [dPLS18] in 2018, where signature sizes are approximately 580 KB.

Starting in 2019, the efficiency of lattice-based zero-knowledge proofs, which are important components of group signatures, has improved by several orders of magnitude (c.f. [YAZ+19, BLS19, ESLL19, ESS+19, ALS20, ENS20, LNS20]). The improvements have been dramatic-enough that one can now create sophisticated systems like lattice-based confidential transactions (i.e. a Monero-like payment system based on the hardness of lattice problems) where the communication complexity of a transaction is under 30 KB [EZS+19, LNS21b].

Using these same techniques, [EZS+19] improved on the efficiency of group signatures for the special case where the group size is not too large. While the signature size is smaller, the signing, verification, and opening times are linear in the number of group members. When the group size is $\approx 2^{10}$, the signature size is around 60KB and the scheme is reasonably efficient. The computational complexity of the scheme becomes prohibitive, however, as the group size approaches 2^{20} members.

It is interesting that despite the recent progress in zero-knowledge proofs, there haven't been any improvements in general group signature constructions whose complexities are independent of the group size. One reason for this lack of progress might be that the techniques used in [dPLS18] are quite different than what has been improved upon. For example, a key component in that scheme an ABB-like [ABB10] selectively-secure signature scheme that uses the Micciancio-Peikert trapdoor generation procedure [MP12], which has not been improved upon since it was first introduced. Furthermore, the utilized zero-knowledge proof in [dPLS18] requires proving equations of the form $\boldsymbol{A}\boldsymbol{s} = \boldsymbol{t} \pmod q$, where $\boldsymbol{s}$ has very large coefficients, on the order of $\sqrt{q}$. Most of the improvements in ZK proof constructions, on the other hand, only improved upon proofs of the above equation when $\boldsymbol{s}$ has small (e.g. $-1/0/1$) coefficients. And of course the state of the art of lattice-based encryption also hasn't changed since 2018.

In this work, we improve the group signature scheme in [dPLS18] by approximately a 3X factor in the signature size. Our construction follows the framework from [dPLS18] and the signature size improvement comes from moderate improvements to many parts of that protocol. Since some of those parts are quite generic, we believe that our improvements could also find applications in other privacy-based protocols, including group signatures that satisfy stronger security notions (e.g. dynamic, corrupt setup authority, etc.). We will now give a high level overview of our signing algorithm and relate it to what was the state of the art in [dPLS18].

1. The prover $\mathcal{P}$ chooses a masking parameter $\boldsymbol{y}$ (from some specified distribution), creates $\boldsymbol{w} = \boldsymbol{A}'\boldsymbol{y}$ and sends $\boldsymbol{w}$ to the verifier
2. The verifier chooses a random challenge c
3. The prover computes $\boldsymbol{z} = c\boldsymbol{s} + \boldsymbol{y}$, performs rejection sampling to make sure $\boldsymbol{z}$ does not leak information about $\boldsymbol{s}$, and sends $\boldsymbol{z}$ to the verifier (or restarts).
4. The verifier accepts if $\|\boldsymbol{z}\|$ is small and $\boldsymbol{A}'\boldsymbol{z} = \boldsymbol{w} + c\boldsymbol{u}$.

Fig. 1. Zero Knowledge Proof of Knowledge of low-norm $\bar{s}, \bar{c}$ that satisfy $\boldsymbol{A}'\bar{\boldsymbol{s}} = \bar{c}\boldsymbol{u}$, when the prover has knowledge of $\boldsymbol{s}$ satisfying $\boldsymbol{A}'\boldsymbol{s} = \boldsymbol{u}$.

1.1 The Scheme of [dPLS18] and Our Improvements

The master public key of the setup authority consists of a random matrix $\boldsymbol{A} \in \mathcal{R}_q^{\alpha \times 2\alpha}$ and $\boldsymbol{B} = \boldsymbol{A}\boldsymbol{R} \in \mathcal{R}_q^{\alpha \times 3\alpha}$, where $\boldsymbol{R}$ is the master secret key and consists of polynomials in $\mathcal{R}_q$ with small coefficients, and a random polynomial vector $\boldsymbol{u} \in \mathcal{R}_q^{2\alpha}$. In our scheme, the ring $\mathcal{R}_q$ is fixed to be $\mathbb{Z}_q[X]/(X^{128}+1)$, for $q \approx 2^{64}$, and the security of the scheme is based on the Module-SIS/Module-LWE problems and varies with α. This is similar to the setup in [dPLS18], except there the security was based on Ring-LWE.

The secret key of a user with identity $m \in \mathcal{R}_q$ is a low-norm vector $\boldsymbol{s}$ satisfying

$$\left[\boldsymbol{A} \middle| \, \boldsymbol{B} + m\boldsymbol{G}\right] \boldsymbol{s} = \boldsymbol{u}, \tag{1}$$

where $\boldsymbol{G}$ is a "gadget matrix" which, together with the trapdoor matrix $\boldsymbol{R}$, is used to create such an $\boldsymbol{s}$ using the sampling algorithm of [MP12].

When creating a signature on a message μ, the signer needs to prove knowledge of $\boldsymbol{s}$ and m that satisfy this equation and to also to create an encryption to this same m under the public key of the opening authority.[1] As is often the case in lattice cryptography, it is more efficient to give a relaxed proof of (1) showing knowledge of an $\bar{\boldsymbol{s}}$ with a slightly larger norm, and a small $\bar{c}$ satisfying

$$\left[\boldsymbol{A} \middle| \, \boldsymbol{B} + m\boldsymbol{G}\right] \bar{\boldsymbol{s}} = \bar{c}\boldsymbol{u}. \tag{2}$$

The above is very similar in form to the basic lattice-based ZK relaxed proof that one uses to construct Schnorr-like signature schemes (c.f. [Lyu09, Lyu12, DKL+18]). The idea in those schemes is that a signer with a secret key $\boldsymbol{s}$ satisfying $\boldsymbol{A}'\boldsymbol{s} = \boldsymbol{u}$, where $\boldsymbol{A}'$ and $\boldsymbol{u}$ are public, can prove knowledge of $\bar{\boldsymbol{s}}$ and $\bar{c}$ satisfying $\boldsymbol{A}'\bar{\boldsymbol{s}} = \bar{c}\boldsymbol{u}$ as described in Fig. 1. It's a proof of knowledge because by rewinding the prover at step (2), the verifier can create a second equality $\boldsymbol{A}'\boldsymbol{z}' = \boldsymbol{w} + c'\boldsymbol{u}$, and subtract to obtain $\boldsymbol{A}'\bar{\boldsymbol{z}} = \bar{c}\boldsymbol{u}$, where $\bar{\boldsymbol{z}} = \boldsymbol{z} - \boldsymbol{z}'$ and $\bar{c} = c - c'$.

One could hope to use the same approach for creating a proof for (2), but there is an important difference that doesn't allow a direct application of the

[1] The message μ enters the signature as an input to a hash function that is used to convert the interactive proof into a non-interactive one via the Fiat-Shamir transform.

same proof technique. In (2), the matrix on the left side is not public, as it contains the secret identity m. The verifier would therefore have no way to perform the verification in step (4) of the above procedure. The solution in [dPLS18] was to commit to the vectors $m\boldsymbol{G}$ using a BDLOP commitment [BDL+18] and then replace the value $m\boldsymbol{G}$ with the commitment. Via some homomorphic properties of this commitment scheme, one can combine a zero-knowledge proof of the commitment with the zero-knowledge proof of (2) (with the modified left side) to conclude something similar to (2). The main downside of that approach is that the proof of knowledge for the commitment and (2) are both "relaxed", and therefore there is an additional $\bar{c}$ term that ends up multiplying into an extracted value and increasing the size of the extracted solution.

An improved proof of (2)**.** As part of our improved protocol, we propose a simpler and more efficient technique for proving (2). The verification in step (4) of Fig. 1 requires all the involved elements to be known to the verifier. If they are not known (as $\boldsymbol{A}' := [\boldsymbol{A}|\ \boldsymbol{B} + m\boldsymbol{G}]$ will not be), then what we can instead do is to create a commitment to the part of $\boldsymbol{A}'$ that is unknown, and also a commitment to $\boldsymbol{w}$ (this is necessary to keep the unknown part of $\boldsymbol{A}'$ hidden, and so in the first step, the prover sends the commitment to $\boldsymbol{w}$ instead of $\boldsymbol{w}$ itself), and then instead of the verifier doing the verification check himself, the prover sends him a zero-knowledge proof that $\boldsymbol{A}'\boldsymbol{z} = \boldsymbol{w} + c\boldsymbol{u}$. If we use the BDLOP commitment scheme and the above equation is linear over the ring $\mathcal{R}_q$, then proving this relation does not add anything extra over just proving knowledge of the committed values.

To go back to our example, if we create a BDLOP commitment of m and $\boldsymbol{w}$, then the equation $[\boldsymbol{A}|\ \boldsymbol{B} + m\boldsymbol{G}]\ \boldsymbol{z} = \boldsymbol{w} + c\boldsymbol{u}$ is indeed linear over $\mathcal{R}_q$ in the committed values m and $\boldsymbol{w}$. Thus sending this proof proves knowledge of $\bar{\boldsymbol{s}}$ and $\bar{c}$ satisfying (2) because one can do the extraction exactly in the same manner as for the protocol in Fig. 1.

Proving Knowledge that the identity m is in a "Special" Set. It is important for the security of our scheme, which will eventually be shown to be as hard to break as forging the ABB signature scheme, that the identity m comes from a set $S \subset \mathcal{R}_q$ which satisfies that for $m \neq m' \in S$, $m - m'$ is invertible in $\mathcal{R}_q$, and that $|S|$ is small. The security reduction of the ABB signature scheme loses a factor $|S|$, one should ideally not have S be too large.[2] A good compromise is therefore having $|S| = q \approx 2^{64}$ and one can define it to be all polynomials in $\mathcal{R}_q$ of degree 0 (i.e. the integers modulo q). Now one needs to prove that m is indeed of this form. This is somewhat surprisingly a non-trivial problem, and in [dPLS18], this proof was performed by showing that m is fixed under two specific automorphisms, and therefore must be an integer. But these "automorphism stability" proofs increased the size of the BDLOP opening proofs (unlike the linear relation proofs).

[2] While it's insecure for $S = \mathcal{R}_q$, it's unclear whether the size of S actually affects the real security of the scheme or it's just an artefact of the proof.

In our current construction, we instead use the recent advances in ZK proofs for proving multiplicative relations over $\mathcal{R}_q$ [ALS20], as well as linear relations over the NTT coefficients [ENS20], of polynomials committed using BDLOP commitments. The tools from [ALS20, ENS20] are quite powerful and the proof that a committed value is an integer follows quite easily (there may even be multiple equally good ways of doing it), but we give a sketch of one such approach anyway. If $m \in \mathcal{R}_q$ is an integer, then $\mathsf{NTT}(m)$ contains m in all the slots. In other words,

$$\mathsf{NTT}(m) = \begin{bmatrix} 1 & 2 & 4 & 8 & \dots \\ 1 & 2 & 4 & 8 & \dots \\ \dots & \dots & \dots & \dots & \dots \\ 1 & 2 & 4 & 8 & \dots \end{bmatrix} \cdot \mathsf{NTT}(m_{bin}),$$

where $m_{bin} \in \mathcal{R}_q$ is a polynomial all of whose NTT coefficients are 0/1. The idea is then to include a commitment to the polynomial m_{bin} into the BDLOP commitment that we already use for proving (2), and then the above relation can pe proved using the techniques from [ENS20]. To prove that m_{bin} has 0/1 NTT coefficients, we give a proof that $(m_{bin}) \cdot (1 - m_{bin}) = 0$ by using the multiplicative proof from [ALS20].[3]

Because we were already using a BDLOP commitment, committing to an extra $\mathcal{R}_q$ polynomial and doing the above two proofs only adds a few extra kilobytes to the entire proof system.

Encryption (and Proof) of m almost for free. Our final improvement relates to the encryption procedure. A group signature scheme requires the signer to encrypt his identity m under the opener's public key and give a zero-knowledge proof that the encryption is the same m that was used in the proof of (2). A significant saving in the size of our signature, as compared to [dPLS18], is that we show how the encryption and the proof of knowledge that the encryption is valid can already be mostly included in the commitment of m that we created when proving (2).

The BDLOP commitment to a message $m \in \mathcal{R}_q$, and other things that need to be included (e.g. the m_{bin} described in the previous section, the $\boldsymbol{w}$ needed for the proof of (2), some "garbage terms" that need to be committed to as part of the proofs, etc.) is of the form

$$\begin{bmatrix} \boldsymbol{A}_0 \\ \boldsymbol{b}_1^T \\ \vdots \end{bmatrix} \cdot \boldsymbol{r} + \begin{bmatrix} \boldsymbol{0} \\ m \\ \vdots \end{bmatrix} = \begin{bmatrix} \boldsymbol{t}_0 \\ t_1 \\ \vdots \end{bmatrix}, \tag{3}$$

[3] Observe that we cannot use m_{bin} as our identity because the set of polynomials with 0/1 NTT coefficients is not closed under subtraction – hence this conversion is necessary.

where $\boldsymbol{A}_0$ and $\boldsymbol{b}_1$ are random.[4] The important thing to note in the commitment scheme is that if we want to commit to an element in $\mathcal{R}_q$, then t_1 is just an element of the ring. On the other hand, the length of the vector $\boldsymbol{t}_0$ needs to be large for the security (binding property) of the commitment scheme. So if $\mathcal{R}_q$ is a 128-dimensional ring, the size of $\boldsymbol{t}_0$ could be 20 - 30 X larger than t_1.

Another thing to notice is that (3) looks very similar to a Regev-type encryption scheme [Reg09]. In particular, if $\boldsymbol{b}_1^T = \boldsymbol{s}_1^T \boldsymbol{A}_0 + \boldsymbol{e}_1^T$ (where $\boldsymbol{e}_1^T$ has small coefficients) then one could "decrypt" by computing $t_1 - \boldsymbol{s}_1^T \boldsymbol{t}_0 = \boldsymbol{e}_1^T \boldsymbol{r} + m$. So if $\boldsymbol{b}_1^T$ is part of the opener's public key, one can use the BDLOP commitment both for committing to m for the proof of (2) and for encrypting m! The main savings comes from the fact that we do not need to send two polynomial vectors of the form $\boldsymbol{t}_0$, one for the encryption and one for the commitment. If the opener uses $\boldsymbol{A}_0$ as part of his (Module)-LWE public key, then the same $\boldsymbol{t}_0$ can be used for both, which results in a substantial saving. Since the binding property of the commitment scheme only depends on $\boldsymbol{A}_0$, a malicious opener cannot do anything except possibly construct $\boldsymbol{b}_1$ such that it does not hide m – but a malicious opener can anyway always construct a malformed public key that does the same thing. So there is no disadvantage to combining the commitment and the encryption scheme into one.

We are, however, not quite yet done. One issue that needs to be taken care of is that from (3), the opener can recover $t_1 - \boldsymbol{s}_1^T \boldsymbol{t}_0 = \boldsymbol{e}_1^T \boldsymbol{r} + m$, where $\boldsymbol{e}_1^T \boldsymbol{r}$ has small coefficients; but this does not allow him to recover m because m is an arbitrary integer in $\mathbb{Z}_q$. In order for the opener to be able to recover m, we need to employ an encryption scheme implicit in Gentry et al. [GSW13] which allows for encryptions of arbitrary-size messages. In particular, in addition to encrypting m, the prover will also have to encrypt $\sqrt{q}m$ (it's really $\lfloor \sqrt{q} \rceil$, but we will omit the $\lfloor \cdot \rceil$ for the sake of readability) as $\boldsymbol{b}_2^T \boldsymbol{r} + \sqrt{q}m = t_2$, where $\boldsymbol{b}_2^T = \boldsymbol{s}_2^T \boldsymbol{A}_0 + \boldsymbol{e}_2^T$. Then to decrypt, the decryptor uses his secret keys $\boldsymbol{s}_1^T, \boldsymbol{s}_2^T$ as before, to obtain

$$u_1 = \boldsymbol{e}_1^T \boldsymbol{r} + m = \epsilon_1 + m \pmod q$$
$$u_2 = \boldsymbol{e}_2^T \boldsymbol{r} + \sqrt{q}m = \epsilon_2 + \sqrt{q}m \pmod q,$$

and then compute $u_2 - \sqrt{q}u_1 = \epsilon_2 - \sqrt{q}\epsilon_1 \pmod q$. If the size of $\epsilon_1, \epsilon_2 < \sqrt{q}/4$, then no reduction modulo q takes place in the preceding equation. And furthermore, ϵ_1 and ϵ_2 can be easily recovered by computing the previous equation modulo $\sqrt{q}$. And then one can recover m. So in order to have the commitment scheme which commits to arbitrary-sized ring elements also be an encryption scheme, the prover just needs to create an additional commitment to $\sqrt{q}m$ (which is very cheap because it's just one ring element), and do a BDLOP linear proof over $\mathcal{R}_q$ that the commitments to m and $\sqrt{q}m$ are related by a factor of $\sqrt{q}$ (which does not add anything to the proof size).

[4] Sometimes to save on computation time, the vector $\boldsymbol{A}_0$ and $\boldsymbol{b}_1$ can contain some polynomials that are just 0 or 1 (see [BDL+18]), but in our case we will need them to be uniformly random.

1. The prover generates masking vector $\boldsymbol{y}$ and computes $\boldsymbol{w} = \left[\boldsymbol{A} \middle| \ \boldsymbol{B} + m\boldsymbol{G}\right] \boldsymbol{y}$
2. The prover creates a BDLOP commitment f to $(m, m\sqrt{q}, m_{bin}, \boldsymbol{w})$, and sends f to the verifier.
3. The verifier picks a random challenge c and sends it to the prover.
4. The prover computes $\boldsymbol{z} = c\boldsymbol{s} + \boldsymbol{y}$ and performs rejection sampling to make sure that the distribution of $\boldsymbol{z}$ is independent of $\boldsymbol{s}$.
5. The prover creates the following ZK proofs on the values committed in f:
   - BDLOP proof of knowledge of the committed values
   - BDLOP linear proof that $\left[\boldsymbol{A} \middle| \ \boldsymbol{B} + m\boldsymbol{G}\right] \boldsymbol{z} = \boldsymbol{w} + c\boldsymbol{u}$.
   - BDLOP proof that $\sqrt{q}$ times the first committed value equals the second
   - Multiplicative proof that $m_{bin} \cdot (m_{bin} - 1) = 0$
   - Linear proof that $\begin{bmatrix} 1 & 2 & 4 & 8 & \dots \\ 1 & 2 & 4 & 8 & \dots \\ \dots & \dots & \dots & \dots & \dots \\ 1 & 2 & 4 & 8 & \dots \end{bmatrix} \cdot \mathsf{NTT}(m_{bin}) = \mathsf{NTT}(m)$.
6. The prover sends $\boldsymbol{z}$ and all the proofs to the verifier.
7. The verifier checks that $\|\boldsymbol{z}\|$ is small and that all the proofs are valid.

Fig. 2. The interactive protocol allowing a prover with identity m and low-norm polynomial vector $\boldsymbol{s}$ satisfying (1) to prove knowledge of low-norm $\bar{\boldsymbol{s}}$ and $\bar{c}$ satisfying (2). Additionally, the BLDOP proof of knowledge of the committed values implies a proof of knowledge of $\bar{\boldsymbol{r}}$, $\bar{c}$ satisfying (4), which can be used by the opener to recover m. The commitments to some "garbage terms" and other extraneous terms that are required for the scheme to work are omitted from this high level description. To convert this interactive protocol to a signing algorithm for the group signature, one applies the Fiat-Shamir transform and puts the message μ to be signed as an input to the hash function.

There is still a second issue. When doing a proof of knowledge for the BDLOP commitment as in (3) (with the additional $\boldsymbol{b}_2^T$ line), the prover does not actually prove this equation. Instead, he gives a "relaxed" proof (analogously to (2)) showing the existence of a low-norm vector $\bar{\boldsymbol{r}}$ and polynomial $\bar{c}$ satisfying

$$\begin{bmatrix} \boldsymbol{A}_0 \\ \boldsymbol{b}_1^T \\ \boldsymbol{b}_2^T \\ \vdots \end{bmatrix} \cdot \bar{\boldsymbol{r}} + \bar{c} \begin{bmatrix} \boldsymbol{0} \\ m \\ \sqrt{q}m \\ \vdots \end{bmatrix} = \bar{c} \begin{bmatrix} \boldsymbol{t}_0 \\ t_1 \\ t_2 \\ \vdots \end{bmatrix}. \tag{4}$$

Because the opener does not know $\bar{c}$, he cannot perform decryption as above. He can, however, perform a decryption of the type described in [LN17] where decryption involves guessing an element c' from the challenge space and then trying to decrypt using it and the proof produced by the prover by constructing a $\bar{c} = c - c'$ and essentially testing whether (4) is satisfied. This is also the decryption algorithm that was used in the group signatures of [dPLS18] and [EZS+19]. The encryption scheme used in [LN17] was the Regev scheme where the messages were small, but we prove that the same technique is also applicable in our case where the message is arbitrary in $\mathcal{R}_q$.

We summarize the high-level signing algorithm in Fig. 2. The real algorithm described in Fig. 5 includes the concrete "garbage terms" that one needs to include as part of the proof of all the parts we described, and also a modification to the public key that is necessary for the security proof to go through. Specifically, instead of the public key being $[\boldsymbol{A}|\ \boldsymbol{B} = \boldsymbol{AR}\,]$, it is of the form $[\boldsymbol{A}|\ \boldsymbol{AR} \mid \boldsymbol{B}']$ where $\boldsymbol{B}'$ is a random matrix and serves no real purpose in the signing procedure. The reason for its inclusion is that proving security of the scheme requires doing game hops between the public key being $[\boldsymbol{A}|\ \boldsymbol{AR}]$ and $[\boldsymbol{A}|\ \boldsymbol{AR} + m^*\boldsymbol{G}]$ for an arbitrary message m. While these two public keys are indistinguishable based on the Module-LWE assumption, the game hops also require the extractor to be able to produce valid signatures – and so some trapdoor needs to always be present. The only way that we know how to do such game hops is to embed a second trapdoor into $\boldsymbol{B}'$ so that the extractor can always sign even when he loses access to the trapdoor $\boldsymbol{AR}$. It's interesting to note that if the parameters were set such that $\boldsymbol{AR}$ were statistically-close to uniform, then we would not need to use a computational assumption and could simply replace $\boldsymbol{AR}$ with $\boldsymbol{AR}+m^*\boldsymbol{G}$. But imposing that $\boldsymbol{AR}$ is statistically-close to uniform would make the overall parameters significantly worse than just adding the useless $\boldsymbol{B}'$ to the public key (and thus also increasing the dimension of the vector $\boldsymbol{s}$ in (1)). If one chooses to remove this matrix $\boldsymbol{B}'$ from the public key, one could save approximately 15% in the size of the signature from the parameter computation in Sect. 4.2. Removing the need for such a $\boldsymbol{B}'$ in the security proof (without affecting parameters) is a very good open problem.

1.2 Reducing the Public Key Size by Using Multiple Rings

For optimal efficiency of the protocol in Fig. 2, we would like to create commitments of elements in a small ring, as certain parts of the proof are linear in the ring size. Working over small rings, however, has a negative effect on the public key size of the group signature scheme. The matrix $\boldsymbol{B}$ comprising the public key contains a trapdoor, and therefore, unlike the $\boldsymbol{A}$ and the $\boldsymbol{A}_0$ in (4), it cannot be generated from a small seed. One therefore needs to store the entire matrix $\boldsymbol{B}$ as part of the public key. In our sample instantiation (Table 1), the matrix $\boldsymbol{B}$ consists of $\alpha \times 3\alpha$ d-dimensional polynomials. Since the modulus we're working with is $\approx 2^{64}$, $\alpha = 24$, and $d = 128$, storing this matrix requires $128 \cdot 3\alpha^2 \cdot 64$ bits, which is more than 1.7 MB.

Since the security of the scheme is determined by the total dimension over $\mathbb{Z}$ of the matrix $\boldsymbol{B}$, which is αd, it would be more advantageous to work over a larger ring, while having a smaller α. For example, if we instead set $d = 1024$, and $\alpha = 3$, the total dimension over $\mathbb{Z}$ of the matrix remains the same, yet the cost of storing it goes down to 216 KB. And if we wanted to increase security to have $\alpha d = 4096$, we could set $\alpha = 1$ and $d = 4096$, and end up needing under 100 KB to represent $\boldsymbol{B}$. Having a larger αd, though, would increase the signature size.[5] In short, we want d to be small in order for the proofs to be more compact, but we want d to be large in order to have a small public key.

It turns out that we can have the best of both worlds. That is, we can still use small (e.g. 128-degree) rings for the commitment scheme in (3), while using larger rings in equations that use the non-compressible public key (1). The interaction between the committed elements in (3) and the equation in (1) is through the BDLOP proof of $[\boldsymbol{A}|\ \boldsymbol{B}+m\boldsymbol{G}]\ \boldsymbol{z} = \boldsymbol{w} + c\boldsymbol{u}$, where m and $\boldsymbol{w}$ are in committed form and all the other variables are public. If the smaller ring S is a sub-ring of the larger one R (e.g. $S = \mathbb{Z}[X]/(X^d+1)$ and $R = \mathbb{Z}[X]/(X^{dk}+1)$), then one can show that there is a ring homomorphism between R and S^k, for an appropriately-defined multiplication over S^k. In other words, whatever relation that we need to prove over R can be proved by showing that some corresponding relations over S hold true. Therefore we can use BDLOP commitments over S to prove relations over R at no extra cost. For simplicity, we describe our protocols in this paper entirely over the small ring S, and give details about how one can express relations over R in S in the full version of the paper.

2 Preliminaries

2.1 Notation

Let q be an odd prime. We write $x \leftarrow S$ when $x \in S$ is sampled uniformly at random from the finite set S and similarly $x \leftarrow D$ when x is sampled according to the distribution D. For $a < b$ and $n \in \mathbb{N}$, we define $[a,b] := \{a, a+1\ldots, b\}$ and $[n] := [1,n]$. Given two functions $f, g : \mathbb{N} \to [0,1]$, we write $f(\mu) \approx g(\mu)$ if $|f(\mu) - g(\mu)| < \mu^{-\omega(1)}$. A function f is negligible if $f \approx 0$. We write $\mathsf{negl}(n)$ to denote an unspecified negligible function in n.

For a power of two d, denote $\mathcal{R}$ and $\mathcal{R}_q$ respectively to be the rings $\mathbb{Z}[X]/(X^d+1)$ and $\mathbb{Z}_q[X]/(X^d+1)$. Unless stated otherwise, lower-case letters denote elements in $\mathcal{R}$ or $\mathcal{R}_q$ and bold lower-case letters represent column vectors with coefficients in $\mathcal{R}$ or $\mathcal{R}_q$. We also write bold upper-case letters for matrices in $\mathcal{R}$ or $\mathcal{R}_q$.

For an element $w \in \mathbb{Z}_q$, we write $\|w\|_\infty$ to mean $|w \bmod^{\pm} q|$. Define the ℓ_∞ and ℓ_p norms for $w = w_0 + w_1 X + \ldots + w_{d-1}X^{d-1} \in \mathcal{R}$ as follows:

$$\|w\|_\infty = \max_j \|w_j\|_\infty, \quad \|w\|_p = \sqrt[p]{\|w_0\|_\infty^p + \ldots + \|w_{d-1}\|_\infty^p}.$$

If $w = (w_1, \ldots, w_m) \in \mathcal{R}^k$, then

$$\|\boldsymbol{w}\|_\infty = \max_j \|w_j\|_\infty, \quad \|\boldsymbol{w}\|_p = \sqrt[p]{\|w_1\|^p + \ldots + \|w_k\|^p}.$$

By default, we denote $\|\boldsymbol{w}\| := \|\boldsymbol{w}\|_2$.

[5] In principle, d does not need to be a power-of-2, but then we could not work with the very convenient polynomial rings $\mathbb{Z}[X]/(X^d+1)$. We think that the slight saving in the public key size is not worth the extra hassle of working aver different rings, and so we only consider power-of-2 d.

2.2 Cyclotomic Rings

Suppose q splits into l prime ideals of degree d/l in $\mathcal{R}$. This means $X^d + 1 \equiv \varphi_1 \dots \varphi_l \pmod{q}$ with irreducible polynomials φ_j of degree d/l modulo q. We assume that $\mathbb{Z}_q$ contains a primitive $2l$-th root of unity $\zeta \in \mathbb{Z}_q$ but no elements whose order is a higher power of two, i.e. $q - 1 \equiv 2l \pmod{4l}$. Therefore, we have

$$X^d + 1 \equiv \prod_{j \in \mathbb{Z}_l} \left(X^{\frac{d}{l}} - \zeta^{2j+1} \right) \pmod{q}. \tag{5}$$

Let $\mathcal{M}_q := \{p \in \mathbb{Z}_q[X] : \deg(p) < d/l\}$ be the $\mathbb{Z}_q$-module of polynomials of degree less than d/l. We define the Number Theoretic Transform (NTT) of a polynomial $p \in \mathcal{R}_q$ as follows:

$$\mathsf{NTT}(p) := \begin{bmatrix} \hat{p}_0 \\ \vdots \\ \hat{p}_{l-1} \end{bmatrix} \in \mathcal{M}_q^l \text{ where } \mathsf{NTT}(p)_j = \hat{p}_j = p \bmod (X^{\frac{d}{l}} - \zeta^{2j+1}).$$

Furthermore, we expand the definition of NTT to vectors of polynomials $\boldsymbol{p} \in \mathcal{R}_q^k$, where the NTT operation is applied to each coefficient of $\boldsymbol{p}$, resulting in a vector in $\mathcal{M}_q^{kl}$.

We also define the inverse NTT operation. Namely, for a vector $\vec{v} \in \mathcal{M}_q^l$, $\mathsf{NTT}^{-1}(\vec{v})$ is the polynomial $p \in \mathcal{R}_q$ such that $\mathsf{NTT}(p) = \vec{v}$.

Let $\vec{v} = (v_0, \dots, v_{l-1}), \vec{w} = (w_0, \dots, w_{l-1}) \in \mathcal{M}_q^l$. Then, we define the component-wise product $\vec{v} \circ \vec{w}$ to be the vector $\vec{u} = (u_0, \dots, u_{l-1}) \in \mathcal{M}_q^l$ such that

$$u_j = v_j w_j \bmod (X^{\frac{d}{l}} - \zeta^{2j+1})$$

for $j \in \mathbb{Z}_l$. By definition, we have the following property of the inverse NTT operation:

$$\mathsf{NTT}^{-1}(\vec{v}) \cdot \mathsf{NTT}^{-1}(\vec{w}) = \mathsf{NTT}^{-1}(\vec{v} \circ \vec{w}).$$

Similarly, we define the *inner product* as in [LNS21b]:

$$\langle \vec{v}, \vec{w} \rangle = \sum_{j=0}^{l-1} \left(v_j w_j \bmod (X^{\frac{d}{l}} - \zeta^{2j+1}) \right).$$

We point out that this operation is not an inner product in the strictly mathematical sense (e.g. it is not linear). Nevertheless, it has a few properties which are characteristic for an inner product. For instance, given arbitrary vectors $\vec{x}, \vec{y}, \vec{z} \in \mathcal{M}_q^l$ and scalar $c \in \mathbb{Z}_q$ we have: $\langle \vec{x}, \vec{y} \rangle = \langle \vec{y}, \vec{x} \rangle$ (symmetry), $\langle \vec{x} + \vec{y}, \vec{z} \rangle = \langle \vec{x}, \vec{z} \rangle + \langle \vec{y}, \vec{z} \rangle$ (distributive law) and $\langle c\vec{x}, \vec{y} \rangle = c\langle \vec{x}, \vec{z} \rangle$. We also remark that the definition of $\langle \cdot, \cdot \rangle$ depends on the factors of $X^d + 1$ modulo q.

We generalise the newly introduced operations to work for vectors $\vec{v} = (\vec{v}_1, \dots, \vec{v}_k)$ and $\vec{w} = (\vec{w}_1, \dots, \vec{w}_k) \in \mathcal{M}_q^{kl}$ of length being a multiple of l in the usual way. In particular $\langle \vec{v}, \vec{w} \rangle = \sum_{i=1}^{k} \langle \vec{v}_i, \vec{w}_i \rangle$.

Eventually, for a matrix $A \in \mathcal{M}_q^{n \times kl}$ with rows $\vec{a}_1, \ldots, \vec{a}_n \in \mathcal{M}_q^{kl}$ and a vector $\vec{v} \in \mathcal{M}_q^{kl}$, we define the matrix-vector operation:

$$A\vec{v} = \begin{pmatrix} \langle \vec{a}_1, \vec{v} \rangle \\ \vdots \\ \langle \vec{a}_n, \vec{v} \rangle \end{pmatrix} \in \mathcal{M}_q^n.$$

In proving linear relations, we will need the following two lemmas.

Lemma 2.1. *([LNS21b]). Let $n, k \in \mathbb{N}$. Then, for any $A \in \mathcal{M}_q^{nl \times kl}, \vec{v} \in \mathcal{M}_q^{nl}$ and $\vec{s} \in \mathbb{Z}_q^{kl}$ we have*

$$\langle A\vec{s}, \vec{v} \rangle = \langle \vec{s}, A^T \vec{v} \rangle.$$

Lemma 2.2. *([ENS20]). Let $p = p_0 + p_1 X + \ldots + p_{d-1} X^{d-1} \in \mathcal{R}_q$. Then,*

$$\frac{1}{l} \sum_{i=0}^{l} \mathsf{NTT}(p)_i = \sum_{i=0}^{d/l-1} p_i X^i.$$

2.3 Challenge Space

Let $\mathcal{C} := \{-1, 0, 1\}^d \subset \mathcal{R}_q$ be the challenge set of ternary polynomials with coefficients $-1, 0, 1$. We define the following probability distribution $C : \mathcal{C} \to [0, 1]$. The coefficients of a challenge $c \leftarrow C$ are independently identically distributed with $\Pr(0) = 1/2$ and $\Pr(1) = \Pr(-1) = 1/4$. We write ω such that $\Pr_{c \leftarrow C}(\|c\|_1 \leq \omega) \leq 2^{-\lambda}$.

Consider the coefficients of the polynomial $c \bmod (X^{d/l} - \zeta^{2j+1})$ for $c \leftarrow C$. Then, all coefficients follow the same distribution over $\mathbb{Z}_q$. Let us write Y for the random variable over $\mathbb{Z}_q$ that follows this distribution. Attema et al. [ALS20] give an upper bound on the maximum probability of Y.

Lemma 2.3. *Let the random variable Y over $\mathbb{Z}_q$ be defined as above. Then for all $x \in \mathbb{Z}_q$,*

$$\Pr(Y = x) \leq \frac{1}{q} + \frac{2l}{q} \sum_{j=0}^{l-1} \prod_{i=0}^{l-1} \left| \frac{1}{2} + \frac{1}{2} \cos\left(2\pi(2j+1)y\zeta^i/q\right) \right|. \tag{6}$$

In particular, [ALS20,ENS20] computed that for $q \approx 2^{32}$, the maximum probability for each coefficient of $c \bmod X^{d/l} - \zeta^{2j+1}$ is around $2^{-31.4}$. In general, we will call this probability p.

An immediate consequence of Lemma 2.3 is that polynomial $c \leftarrow C$ is invertible in $\mathcal{R}_q$ with overwhelming probability as long as parameters q, d, l are selected so that $q^{-d/l}$ is negligible.

2.4 Module-SIS and Module-LWE Problems

Security of the [BDL+18] commitment scheme used in our protocols relies on the well-known computational lattice problems, namely Module-LWE (MLWE) and Module-SIS (MSIS) [LS15]. Both problems are defined over $\mathcal{R}_q$.

Definition 2.4. ($\mathsf{MSIS}_{\kappa,m,B}$). *Given* $\boldsymbol{A} \leftarrow \mathcal{R}_q^{\kappa\times m}$, *the* Module-SIS *problem with parameters* $\kappa, m > 0$ *and* $0 < B < q$ *asks to find* $\boldsymbol{z} \in \mathcal{R}_q^m$ *such that* $\boldsymbol{Az} = \boldsymbol{0}$ *over* $\mathcal{R}_q$ *and* $0 < \|\boldsymbol{z}\| \leqslant B$. *An algorithm* Adv *is said to have advantage* ϵ *in solving* $\mathsf{MSIS}\kappa, m, B$ *if*

$$\Pr\left[0 < \|\boldsymbol{z}\| \leqslant B \wedge \boldsymbol{Az} = \boldsymbol{0} \,\middle|\, \boldsymbol{A} \leftarrow \mathcal{R}_q^{\kappa\times m};\ \boldsymbol{z} \leftarrow \mathsf{Adv}(\boldsymbol{A})\right] \geqslant \epsilon.$$

Definition 2.5. ($\mathsf{MLWE}_{m,\lambda,\chi}$). *The* Module-LWE *problem with parameters* $m, \lambda > 0$ *and an error distribution* χ *over* $\mathcal{R}$ *asks the adversary* Adv *to distinguish between the following two cases: 1)* $(\boldsymbol{A}, \boldsymbol{As} + \boldsymbol{e})$ *for* $\boldsymbol{A} \leftarrow \mathcal{R}_q^{m\times\lambda}$, *a secret vector* $\boldsymbol{s} \leftarrow \chi^\lambda$ *and error vector* $\boldsymbol{e} \leftarrow \chi^m$, *and 2)* $(\boldsymbol{A}, \boldsymbol{b}) \leftarrow \mathcal{R}_q^{m\times\lambda} \times \mathcal{R}_q^m$. *Then,* Adv *is said to have advantage* ϵ *in solving* $\mathsf{MLWE}_{m,\lambda,\chi}$ *if*

$$\begin{aligned}\Big|\Pr\left[b = 1 \,\middle|\, \boldsymbol{A} \leftarrow \mathcal{R}_q^{m\times\lambda};\ \boldsymbol{s} \leftarrow \chi^\lambda;\ \boldsymbol{e} \leftarrow \chi^m;\ b \leftarrow \mathsf{Adv}(\boldsymbol{A}, \boldsymbol{As} + \boldsymbol{e})\right]& \\ - \Pr\left[b = 1 \,\middle|\, \boldsymbol{A} \leftarrow \mathcal{R}_q^{m\times\lambda};\ \boldsymbol{b} \leftarrow \mathcal{R}_q^m;\ b \leftarrow \mathsf{Adv}(\boldsymbol{A}, \boldsymbol{b})\right]\Big| &\geqslant \epsilon. \end{aligned} \tag{7}$$

2.5 Probability Distributions

In this paper we sample the coefficients of the random polynomials in the commitment scheme using the distribution χ on $\{-1, 0, 1\}$ where ± 1 both have probability $5/16$ and 0 has probability $6/16$ identically as in e.g. [BLS19, ALS20, ENS20]. We also write S_μ the uniform distribution over the set $\{x \in \mathcal{R}_q \mid \|x\|_\infty \leq \mu\}$.

Discrete Gaussian distribution. We now define the discrete Gaussian distribution used for the rejection sampling.

Definition 2.6. *The* discrete Gaussian distribution *on* $\mathbb{Z}^\ell$ *centered around* $\vec{v} \in \mathbb{Z}^\ell$ *with standard deviation* $\mathfrak{s} > 0$ *is given by*

$$D^\ell_{\vec{v},\mathfrak{s}}(\vec{z}) = \frac{e^{-\|\vec{z}-\vec{v}\|^2/2\mathfrak{s}^2}}{\sum_{\vec{z}'\in\mathbb{Z}^\ell} e^{-\|\vec{z}'\|^2/2\mathfrak{s}^2}}.$$

When it is centered around $\boldsymbol{0} \in \mathbb{Z}^\ell$ *we write* $D^\ell_{\mathfrak{s}} = D^\ell_{\vec{0},\mathfrak{s}}$

We will use the following tail bound, which follows from [Ban93, Lemma 1.5 (i)].

Lemma 2.7. *Let* $\boldsymbol{z} \leftarrow D^{\ell d}_{\mathfrak{s}}$. *Then*

$$\Pr\left[\|\boldsymbol{z}\|_2 \leq \mathfrak{s}\sqrt{2\ell d}\right] \geq 1 - 2^{-\log(e/2)\ell d/4}.$$

2.6 Rejection Sampling

In lattice-based zero-knowledge proofs, the prover will want to output a vector $\boldsymbol{z}$ whose distribution should be independent of a secret randomness vector $\boldsymbol{r}$, so that $\boldsymbol{z}$ cannot be used to gain any information on the prover's secret. During the protocol, the prover computes $\boldsymbol{z} = \boldsymbol{y} + c\boldsymbol{r}$ where $\boldsymbol{r}$ is the randomness used to commit to the prover's secret, $c \leftarrow C$ is a challenge polynomial, and $\boldsymbol{y}$ is a "masking" vector. In order to remove the dependency of $\boldsymbol{z}$ on $\boldsymbol{r}$, one applies *rejection sampling* [Lyu12].

Lemma 2.8. (Rejection Sampling). *Let $V \subseteq \mathcal{R}^\ell$ be a set of polynomials with norm at most T and $\rho\colon V \to [0,1]$ be a probability distribution. Now, sample $\boldsymbol{v} \leftarrow \rho$ and $\boldsymbol{y} \leftarrow D_{\mathfrak{s}}^{\ell d}$, set $\boldsymbol{z} = \boldsymbol{y}+\boldsymbol{v}$, and run $b \leftarrow \mathsf{Rej}_0(\boldsymbol{z}, \boldsymbol{v}, \mathfrak{s})$ as defined in Fig. 3. Then, the probability that $b = 0$ is at least $(1 - 2^{-100})/M$ and the distribution of $(\boldsymbol{v}, \boldsymbol{z})$, conditioned on $b = 0$, is within statistical distance of $2^{-100}/M$ of the product distribution $\rho \times D_{\mathfrak{s}}^{\ell d}$.*

$\mathsf{Rej}_0(\vec{z}, \vec{v}, \mathfrak{s})$

$u \leftarrow [0,1)$
If $u > \frac{1}{M} \cdot \exp\left(\frac{-2\langle \vec{z}, \vec{v}\rangle + \|\vec{v}\|^2}{2\mathfrak{s}^2}\right)$
  return 1
Else
  return 0

$\mathsf{Rej}_1(\vec{z}, \vec{v}, \mathfrak{s})$

If $\langle \vec{z}, \vec{v}\rangle < 0$
  return 1
$u \leftarrow [0,1)$
If $u > \frac{1}{M} \cdot \exp\left(\frac{-2\langle \vec{z}, \vec{v}\rangle + \|\vec{v}\|^2}{2\mathfrak{s}^2}\right)$
  return 1
Else
  return 0

Fig. 3. Two rejection sampling algorithms: the one used generally in previous works [Lyu12] (left) and the one proposed recently in [LNS21a] (right).

We recall how parameters $\mathfrak{s}$ and M in Lemma 2.8 are selected. Concretely, the repetition rate M is chosen to be an upper-bound on[6]:

$$\frac{D_{\mathfrak{s}}^{\ell d}(\boldsymbol{z})}{D_{\boldsymbol{v},\mathfrak{s}}^{\ell d}(\boldsymbol{z})} = \exp\left(\frac{-2\langle \boldsymbol{z}, \boldsymbol{v}\rangle + \|\boldsymbol{v}\|^2}{2\mathfrak{s}^2}\right) \leq \exp\left(\frac{24\mathfrak{s}\|\boldsymbol{v}\| + \|\boldsymbol{v}\|^2}{2\mathfrak{s}^2}\right) = M. \quad (8)$$

For the inequality we used the tail bound which says that with probability at least $1 - 2^{100}$ we have $|\langle \boldsymbol{z}, \boldsymbol{v}\rangle| < 12\mathfrak{s}\|\boldsymbol{v}\|$ for $\boldsymbol{z} \leftarrow D_{\mathfrak{s}}^{\ell d}$ [Ban93, Lyu12]. Hence, by setting $\mathfrak{s} = 11\|\boldsymbol{v}\|$ we obtain $M \approx 3$.

2.7 BDLOP Commitment Scheme

We recall the BDLOP commitment scheme from [BDL+18]. Suppose that we want to commit to a message vector $\boldsymbol{m} = (m_1, \ldots, m_n) \in \mathcal{R}_q^n$ for $n \geqslant 1$ and that module ranks of κ and λ are required for MSIS and MLWE security, respectively. Then, in the key generation, a matrix $\boldsymbol{A}_0 \leftarrow \mathcal{R}_q^{\kappa \times (\kappa+\lambda+n)}$ and vectors

[6] Here, the inner product is over $\mathbb{Z}$, i.e. $\langle \boldsymbol{z}, \boldsymbol{v}\rangle = \langle \vec{z}, \vec{v}\rangle$ where vectors $\vec{z}, \vec{v}$ are polynomial coefficients of $\boldsymbol{z}$ and $\boldsymbol{v}$ respectively.

$\boldsymbol{b}_1, \ldots, \boldsymbol{b}_n \leftarrow \mathcal{R}_q^{\kappa+\lambda+n}$ are generated and output as public parameters. Note that one could choose to generate $\boldsymbol{A}_0, \boldsymbol{a}_1, \ldots, \boldsymbol{a}_n$ in a more structured way as in [BDL+18] since it saves some computation. However, for readability, we write the commitment matrices in the "Knapsack" form as above. In our case, the hiding property of the commitment scheme is established via the duality between the Knapsack and MLWE problems. We refer to [EZS+19, Appendix C] for a more detailed discussion.

To commit to the message $\boldsymbol{m}$, we first sample $\boldsymbol{r} \leftarrow \chi^{d\cdot(\kappa+\lambda+n)}$. Now, there are two parts of the commitment scheme: the binding part and the message encoding part. In particular, we compute

$$\boldsymbol{t}_0 = \boldsymbol{A}_0\boldsymbol{r} \bmod q,$$
$$t_i = \boldsymbol{a}_i^T\boldsymbol{r} + m_i \bmod q,$$

for $i \in [n]$, where $\boldsymbol{t}_0$ forms the binding part and each t_i encodes a message polynomial m_i. In this paper, when we write that we compute a BDLOP commitment to a vector $\vec{m} = (\vec{m}_1, \ldots, \vec{m}_n) \in \mathcal{M}_q^{nl}$, we mean that we commit to the vector of polynomials $\boldsymbol{m} = (\mathsf{NTT}^{-1}(\vec{m}_1), \ldots, \mathsf{NTT}^{-1}(\vec{m}_n)) \in \mathcal{R}_q^n$ as above.

Next, we define the notion of a weak opening of the commitment [ALS20].

Definition 2.9. *A* weak opening *for the commitment $\boldsymbol{t} = \boldsymbol{t}_0 \parallel t_1 \parallel \cdots \parallel t_n$ consists of a polynomial $\bar{c} \in \mathcal{R}_q$, a randomness vector $\boldsymbol{r}^*$ over $\mathcal{R}_q$ and messages $m_1^*, \ldots, m_n^* \in \mathcal{R}_q$ such that*

$$\|\bar{c}\|_1 \leq 2d \text{ and } \bar{c} \text{ is invertible over } \mathcal{R}_q$$
$$\|\bar{c}\boldsymbol{r}^*\|_2 \leq 2\beta,$$
$$\boldsymbol{A}_0\boldsymbol{r}^* = \boldsymbol{t}_0,$$
$$\boldsymbol{a}_i^T\boldsymbol{r}^* + m_i^* = t_i \text{ for } i \in [n].$$

Attema et al. [ALS20] show that the commitment scheme is still binding with respect to weak openings if $\mathsf{MSIS}_{\kappa, 8d\beta}$ is hard.

3 The Group Signature

A group signature is composed of four algorithms. The first one, which we write KeyGen is run by the group manager and is described in Fig. 4. In the end of this algorithm, the group manager generated a group public key, his own group manager secret and secret keys for all group members. The second one is the signature. The group member of identity m was given his secret key, which he will prove knowledge of (among other statements) in the signature. The signature is a non-interactive version of the zero-knowledge proof π described on Fig. 5. Third, the verification is simply the verification of π. Finally, the last algorithm GSdec described in Algorithm 1 allows the group manager to reveal the identity at the origin of a signature. We will write $\sqrt{q}$ (respectively $\sqrt[3]{q}$) the integer $\lfloor\sqrt{q}\rceil$ (respectively $\lfloor\sqrt[3]{q}\rceil$) for the sake of readability.

3.1 All-in-One Interactive Zero-Knowledge Proof

In this subsection, we introduce a single zero-knowledge proof that encompasses all the proofs needed for our group signature scheme. From a high level, π proves the following statements

1. Knowledge of an identity m
2. Knowledge of the secret key of m
3. The decryption of the identity of the prover is m.

Intuitively, these three statements are required to capture the security notions of a group signature.

Each of these statements is proven by gathering more elementary zero-knowledge proofs from [LNS20, ALS20, BDL+18]. More specifically, we take $\mathcal{I}$ the set of identities to be $\{0, 1, \ldots, 2^d - 1\} \subset \mathcal{R}_q$ the set of degree zero polynomials of $\mathcal{R}_q$ i.e. $\mathbb{Z}_q$; such that the binary representation of m also fits in length as an element of $\mathcal{R}_q$. The prover will commit to m, but also to $m_{\text{bin}} = \mathsf{NTT}^{-1}(\mathsf{binary}(m))$ the inverse NTT of the binary representation of m. This way, we need to prove two things : 1) m_{bin}'s NTT is binary 2) we have the linear relation

$$\mathbf{Q}\,\mathsf{NTT}(m_{\text{bin}}) = \mathsf{NTT}(m), \text{ where } \mathbf{Q} = \begin{bmatrix} 1\;2\;4 \ldots 2^{d-1} \\ 1\;2\;4 \ldots 2^{d-1} \\ \vdots\;\vdots\;\vdots \qquad \vdots \\ 1\;2\;4 \ldots 2^{d-1} \end{bmatrix}.$$

For 1), this proof is done using the product proof from [ALS20]. For 2), we use the so called unstructured linear proof from [LNS20]. Notice that since all the NTT coefficients of m are proven to be equal, m has to be an integer. On top of that, since its binary representation has length d, we indeed prove that $m \in \mathcal{I}$.

Proving knowledge of the short $\mathbf{s}_1^m, \mathbf{s}_2^m, \mathbf{s}_3^m$ is done in two steps. The relation that these secret vectors verify is $\mathbf{A}\mathbf{s}_1^m + (\mathbf{B} + m\mathbf{G})\mathbf{s}_2^m + \mathbf{B}'\mathbf{s}_3^m$, where the identity m is multiplied with the so called *gadget matrix* :

$$\mathbf{G} = \mathbf{I}_\alpha \otimes [1\;\sqrt[3]{q}\;\sqrt[3]{q}^2] = \begin{bmatrix} 1\;\sqrt[3]{q}\;\sqrt[3]{q}^2 & & \\ & 1\;\sqrt[3]{q}\;\sqrt[3]{q}^2 & \\ & & \ddots \end{bmatrix}$$

The matrix $[\mathbf{A}|\mathbf{B} + m\mathbf{G}|\mathbf{B}']$ depends on the committed identity m and we can therefore not directly use the linear proof from [BDL+18]. To circumvent this problem, instead of sending some $\mathbf{w} = \mathbf{A}\mathbf{y}_1 + (\mathbf{B} + m\mathbf{G})\mathbf{y}_2 + \mathbf{B}'\mathbf{y}_3$ as in the BDLOP linear proof, we commit to this $\mathbf{w}$ and give a BDLOP linear proof that $\mathbf{A}\mathbf{z}_1 + (\mathbf{B} + m\mathbf{G})\mathbf{z}_2 + \mathbf{B}'\mathbf{z}_3 = \mathbf{w} + c\mathbf{u}$. This statement is indeed linear in the two committed values m and $\mathbf{w}$.

The encryption of the identity m is part of the commitments. In a nutshell, the group manager plants his decryption key in the public commitment matrix

Decryption secret keys

$\mathbf{h}_1, \mathbf{h}_2 \leftarrow S_\mu^\kappa,\ \mathbf{e}_1, \mathbf{e}_2 \leftarrow S_\mu^{\kappa+\lambda+\alpha+5}$

Commitment public parameters

$(\mathbf{A}_0, \mathbf{A}_1, \mathbf{a}_2, \mathbf{a}_3, \mathbf{a}_4) \leftarrow \mathcal{R}_q^{\kappa\times(\kappa+\lambda+\alpha+5)} \times \mathcal{R}_q^{\alpha\times(\kappa+\lambda+\alpha+5)} \times (\mathcal{R}_q^{\kappa+\lambda+\alpha+5})^3$

$\mathbf{t}_1 = \mathbf{A}_0^T\mathbf{h}_1 + \mathbf{e}_1,\ \mathbf{t}_2 = \mathbf{A}_0^T\mathbf{h}_2 + \mathbf{e}_2$

Group signature group manager key and public parameters

$\mathbf{R} \leftarrow \{x \in \mathcal{R}_q^{\alpha\times\alpha} \mid \|x\|_\infty \leqslant 1\}^{2\times 3}$

$\mathbf{A} \leftarrow \mathcal{R}_q^{\alpha\times 2\alpha}, \mathbf{B} = \mathbf{AR}, \mathbf{B}' \leftarrow \mathcal{R}_q^{\alpha\times 3\alpha}$

$(\mathbf{s}_1^{\mathsf{gm}}, \mathbf{s}_2^{\mathsf{gm}}, \mathbf{s}_3^{\mathsf{gm}}) \leftarrow D_\sigma^{2d\alpha} \times D_\sigma^{3d\alpha} \times D_\sigma^{3d\alpha}$

$$\mathbf{u} = \begin{bmatrix}\mathbf{A} | \mathbf{B} | \mathbf{B}'\end{bmatrix}\begin{bmatrix}\mathbf{s}_1^{\mathsf{gm}} \\ \mathbf{s}_2^{\mathsf{gm}} \\ \mathbf{s}_3^{\mathsf{gm}}\end{bmatrix}$$

Group members secret keys

$\forall m \in \mathcal{I}$, use GPV trapdoor to sample $(\mathbf{s}_1^m, \mathbf{s}_2^m, \mathbf{s}_3^m)$ such that

$$\begin{bmatrix}\mathbf{A} | \mathbf{B} + m\mathbf{G} | \mathbf{B}'\end{bmatrix}\begin{bmatrix}\mathbf{s}_1^m \\ \mathbf{s}_2^m \\ \mathbf{s}_3^m\end{bmatrix} = \mathbf{u}$$

Fig. 4. KeyGen() :

during the key generation. This way, it allows the commitment to m by the prover to also be (part of) a ciphertext for the group manager to decrypt. The encryption involves two *commitments*, one to m and one to $\sqrt{q}m$. To prove that the ciphertext is valid[7] reduces to proving the knowledge of the short randomness $\mathbf{r}$ in the commitment scheme and the linear relation between the committed m and $\sqrt{q}m$. The latter proofs almost come for free : the opening proof is anyway necessary for the other proofs, and the linear proof is very cheap since these committed values are polynomials from $\mathcal{R}_q$.

Theorem 3.1. *The interactive proof π from Fig. 5 is complete, sound and zero-knowledge.*

More precisely, if the prover follows Fig. 5 and does not abort, an honest verifier will output 1 *with overwhelming probability.*

There exists a simulator $\mathcal{S}$ that without access to secret information outputs a distribution that is, under the MLWE *assumption for parameters $(\kappa, \kappa+\lambda+\alpha+5, S_\mu)$ and $(\kappa+\alpha+5, \lambda, \chi)$, indistinguishable from the actual interaction.*

Let $B_2 \geq 8\omega^2\sigma'\sqrt{2(\kappa+\lambda+\alpha+5)d}$. If ϵ is the success probability of the prover and T its runtime, then there exists an extractor $\mathcal{E}$ that with rewindable blackbox access to this prover finds with probability $\geq 1/8$, in time $O(T/\epsilon)$,

[7] I.e that the group manager can decrypt it and recover the identity m.

Prover | Verifier

Identity $m, \mathsf{sk} = (\mathbf{s}_1, \mathbf{s}_2, \mathbf{s}_3)$

$(\mathbf{y}_1, \mathbf{y}_2, \mathbf{y}_3, \mathbf{y}_4) \leftarrow D_\sigma^{2d\alpha} \times D_\sigma^{3d\alpha} \times D_\sigma^{3d\alpha} \times D_{\sigma'}^{(\kappa+\lambda+\alpha+5)d}$

$$\mathbf{w} = \left[\mathbf{A} | \ \mathbf{B} + m\mathbf{G} | \ \mathbf{B}'\right] \begin{bmatrix} \mathbf{y}_1 \\ \mathbf{y}_2 \\ \mathbf{y}_3 \end{bmatrix}$$

$g \leftarrow (\mathbf{0}_{d/l} | \mathbb{Z}_q^{d/l \times (l-1)})$

$$\mathbf{f} = \begin{bmatrix} \mathbf{A}_0 \\ \mathbf{A}_1 \\ \mathbf{a}_2 \\ \mathbf{a}_3 \\ \mathbf{a}_4 \\ \mathbf{t}_1 \\ \mathbf{t}_2 \end{bmatrix} \mathbf{r} + \begin{bmatrix} 0 \\ \mathbf{w} \\ \mathbf{a}_3^T \mathbf{y}_4 (2m_{\text{bin}} - 1) \\ m_{\text{bin}} \\ g \\ m \\ \sqrt{q} m \end{bmatrix}$$

$\mathbf{t} = \mathbf{A}_0 \mathbf{y}_4$

$v_2 = \sqrt{q} \mathbf{t}_1^T \mathbf{y}_4 - \mathbf{t}_2^T \mathbf{y}_4$

$v_3 = (\mathbf{a}_3^T \mathbf{y}_4)^2 + \mathbf{a}_2^T \mathbf{y}_4$

$\xrightarrow{\mathbf{f},\ \mathbf{t},\ v_2,\ v_3}$ $c \leftarrow C, \ \phi \leftarrow \mathcal{M}_q^l$

$\xleftarrow{c, \phi}$

$\mathbf{z}_1 = \mathbf{y}_1 + c\mathbf{s}_1$

$\mathbf{z}_2 = \mathbf{y}_2 + c\mathbf{s}_2$

$\mathbf{z}_3 = \mathbf{y}_3 + c\mathbf{s}_3$

$\mathsf{Rej}_0(\mathbf{z}_1, c\mathbf{s}_1, \sigma), \mathsf{Rej}_0(\mathbf{z}_2, c\mathbf{s}_2, \sigma), \mathsf{Rej}_0(\mathbf{z}_3, c\mathbf{s}_3, \sigma)$

$\mathbf{v}_1 = \mathbf{A}_1^T \mathbf{y}_4 - \mathbf{G}\mathbf{z}_2 \mathbf{t}_1^T \mathbf{y}_4$

$v_4 = \left(\mathbf{a}_4^T + \mathbf{a}_3^T \mathsf{NTT}^{-1}\left(\mathbf{Q}^T \phi\right) + \mathbf{t}_1^T \mathsf{NTT}^{-1}(\phi)\right) \mathbf{y}_4$

$j = g + m_{\text{bin}} \mathsf{NTT}^{-1}\left(\mathbf{Q}^T \phi\right) - m\mathsf{NTT}^{-1}(\phi)$

$\xrightarrow{\mathbf{z}_1, \mathbf{z}_2, \mathbf{z}_3, v_1, j, v_4}$ $e \leftarrow C$

$\xleftarrow{e}$

$\mathbf{z}_4 = \mathbf{y}_4 + e\mathbf{r}$

$\mathsf{Rej}_0(\mathbf{z}_4, e\mathbf{r}, \sigma')$ $\xrightarrow{\mathbf{z}_4}$

return $\mathsf{verify}()$

Fig. 5. Interactive proof π

Accept if :

$$\|\mathbf{z}_1\|_2 \overset{?}{\leqslant} \sigma\sqrt{4\alpha d},\ \|\mathbf{z}_2\|_2 \overset{?}{\leqslant} \sigma\sqrt{6\alpha d},\ \|\mathbf{z}_3\|_2 \overset{?}{\leqslant} \sigma\sqrt{6\alpha d} \tag{9}$$

$$\text{and } \|\mathbf{z}_4\|_2 \overset{?}{\leqslant} \sigma'\sqrt{2(\kappa+\lambda+\alpha+5)d} \tag{10}$$

$$\text{and } \mathbf{A}_0\mathbf{z}_4 \overset{?}{=} \mathbf{t} + e\mathbf{f}_0 \tag{11}$$

$$\text{and } \sqrt{q}\mathbf{t}_1^T\mathbf{z}_4 - \mathbf{t}_2^T\mathbf{z}_4 \overset{?}{=} v_2 + e(\sqrt{q}f_5 - f_6) \tag{12}$$

$$\text{and } \left[e\mathbf{A} |\ e\mathbf{B} - \mathbf{t}_1^T\mathbf{z}_4\mathbf{G} |\ e\mathbf{B}'\right]\begin{bmatrix}\mathbf{z}_1\\ \mathbf{z}_2\\ \mathbf{z}_3\end{bmatrix} + \mathbf{A}_1^T\mathbf{z}_4 \overset{?}{=} \mathbf{v}_1 + ce\mathbf{u} + e(\mathbf{f}_1 - \mathbf{G}\mathbf{z}_2 f_5) \tag{13}$$

$$\text{and } (\mathbf{a}_3^T\mathbf{z}_4 - ef_3)(\mathbf{a}_3^T\mathbf{z}_4 - ef_3 - e) + \mathbf{a}_2^T\mathbf{z}_4 - ef_2 \overset{?}{=} v_3 \tag{14}$$

$$\text{and } e(j - f_4 + \mathsf{NTT}^{-1}\left(\mathbf{Q}^T\phi\right) f_3 - \mathsf{NTT}^{-1}(\phi) f_5)$$
$$\overset{?}{=} \mathbf{a}_4^T\mathbf{z}_4\mathbf{a}_3^T\mathbf{z}_4\mathsf{NTT}^{-1}\left(\mathbf{Q}^T\phi\right) - \mathbf{t}_1^T\mathbf{z}_4\mathsf{NTT}^{-1}(\phi) - v_4 \tag{15}$$

$$\text{and } j_0, \ldots, j_{d/l-1} \overset{?}{=} 0 \tag{16}$$

Fig. 6. verify(π) where π is the proof on Fig. 5

either a solution to $\mathsf{MSIS}_{\kappa,\kappa+\lambda+\alpha+5,B_2}$ *or* $\bar{m} \in \mathcal{I}$, $\bar{\mathbf{s}}_1, \bar{\mathbf{s}}_2, \bar{\mathbf{s}}_3$ *of norms lower than respectively* $4\sigma\sqrt{\alpha d}$, $2\sigma\sqrt{6\alpha d}$, $2\sigma\sqrt{6\alpha d}$ *and* $\bar{c} \in \bar{\mathcal{C}}$ *such that*

$$[\mathbf{A} |\ \mathbf{B} + \bar{m}\mathbf{G} |\ \mathbf{B}'] \begin{bmatrix}\bar{\mathbf{s}}_1\\ \bar{\mathbf{s}}_2\\ \bar{\mathbf{s}}_3\end{bmatrix} = \bar{c}\mathbf{u}.$$

Proof. Completeness. Completeness follows from equations in the soundness proof. More precisely, if the prover follows honestly his part in the protocol Fig. 5, then it follows from Eqs. (24) to (27), (30) and (31)[8] that the verifier shall always accept all conditions on Eqs. (11)–(14). Moreover, from Lemma 3.2 of [BLS19], the verifier will accept the conditions on Eqs. (9) and (10) with overwhelming probability.

Soundness. We construct an extractor $\mathcal{E}$ that with rewindable blackbox access to the prover recovers short vectors $\bar{\mathbf{s}}_1, \bar{\mathbf{s}}_2, \bar{\mathbf{s}}_3, \bar{\mathbf{z}}_4$ and polynomials $\bar{m}, \bar{c}, \bar{e}$ such that:

[8] Equation (31) holds because g's first d/l coefficients are set to be 0.

$$\begin{bmatrix}\mathbf{A} | \ \mathbf{B} + \bar{m}\mathbf{G} | \ \mathbf{B}'\end{bmatrix} \begin{bmatrix}\bar{\mathbf{s}}_1 \\ \bar{\mathbf{s}}_2 \\ \bar{\mathbf{s}}_3\end{bmatrix} = \bar{c}\mathbf{u} \tag{17}$$

$$\bar{m} \in \mathcal{I} \tag{18}$$

$$\bar{e}\mathbf{f}_0 = \mathbf{A}_0\bar{\mathbf{z}}_4 \tag{19}$$

$$\bar{e}f_5 = \mathbf{t}_1^T\bar{\mathbf{z}}_4 + \bar{e}\bar{m} \tag{20}$$

$$\bar{e}f_6 = \mathbf{t}_2^T\bar{\mathbf{z}}_4 + \bar{e}\sqrt{q}\bar{m} \tag{21}$$

First, we prove that from two transcripts $(\mathbf{f}, j, g, \mathbf{t}, \mathbf{v}, c, \phi, \mathbf{z}_1, \mathbf{z}_2, \mathbf{z}_3, e, \mathbf{z}_4)$ and $(\mathbf{f}, j, g, \mathbf{t}, \mathbf{v}, c, \phi, \mathbf{z}_1, \mathbf{z}_2, , \mathbf{z}_3, e', \mathbf{z}_4')$, the extractor can recover vectors $\bar{\mathbf{r}}, \bar{\mathbf{w}}$ and a polynomial $\bar{m}$ such that in addition to Eqs. (20) and (21), we have:

$$\begin{bmatrix}\mathbf{A} | \ \mathbf{B} + \bar{m}\mathbf{G} | \ \mathbf{B}'\end{bmatrix} \begin{bmatrix}\mathbf{z}_1 \\ \mathbf{z}_2 \\ \mathbf{z}_3\end{bmatrix} = \bar{\mathbf{w}} + c\mathbf{u}. \tag{22}$$

Let $\bar{\mathbf{z}}_4 = \mathbf{z}_4 - \mathbf{z}_4'$, $\bar{e} = e - e'$ and $\bar{r} = \bar{e}^{-1}\bar{\mathbf{z}}_4$. The extractor defines the messages in the commitment as follows:

$$\begin{bmatrix}\bar{\mathbf{w}} \\ \overline{\mathsf{garb}} \\ \bar{m} \\ \bar{m}' \\ \overline{m_{\text{bin}}} \\ \bar{g}\end{bmatrix} = \begin{bmatrix}\mathbf{f}_1 \\ f_2 \\ f_3 \\ f_4 \\ f_5 \\ f_6\end{bmatrix} - \begin{bmatrix}\mathbf{A}_1^T \\ \mathbf{a}_2^T \\ \mathbf{a}_3^T \\ \mathbf{a}_4^T \\ \mathbf{t}_1^T \\ \mathbf{t}_2^T\end{bmatrix} \bar{\mathbf{r}}. \tag{23}$$

The extractor further defines $\bar{\mathbf{y}}_4 = \mathbf{z}_4 - e\bar{\mathbf{r}}$ and $\bar{\mathbf{y}}_4' = \mathbf{z}_4 - e'\bar{\mathbf{r}}$. Equation (19) follows from taking the difference of Eq. (11) for both transcripts and Equation (20) follows from the definition of $\bar{m}$ in Eq. (23). We substitute $f_5, f_6, \mathbf{z}_4$ in Equation (12) for both transcripts and we obtain :

$$v_2 - (\sqrt{q}\mathbf{t}_1^T\bar{\mathbf{y}}_4 - \mathbf{t}_2^T\bar{\mathbf{y}}_4) + e(\sqrt{q}\bar{m} - \bar{m}') = 0 \tag{24}$$

$$v_2 - (\sqrt{q}\mathbf{t}_1^T\bar{\mathbf{y}}_4 - \mathbf{t}_2^T\bar{\mathbf{y}}_4) + e'(\sqrt{q}\bar{m} - \bar{m}') = 0. \tag{25}$$

We take the difference of both equations and we have $\bar{m}' = \sqrt{q}\bar{m}$, and hence Eq. (21). Now, we plug in the expressions of $\mathbf{f}_1, f_5, \mathbf{z}_4$ in Eq. (13) for both transcripts, and we obtain :

$$e\begin{bmatrix}\mathbf{A} | \mathbf{B} + \bar{m}\mathbf{G} | \ \mathbf{B}'\end{bmatrix} \begin{bmatrix}\mathbf{z}_1 \\ \mathbf{z}_2 \\ \mathbf{z}_3\end{bmatrix} = e(\bar{\mathbf{w}} + c\mathbf{u}) + \mathbf{v}_1 - \mathbf{A}_1^T\bar{\mathbf{y}}_4 - \mathbf{t}_1^T\bar{\mathbf{y}}_4\mathbf{G}\mathbf{z}_2 \tag{26}$$

$$e'\begin{bmatrix}\mathbf{A} | \mathbf{B} + \bar{m}\mathbf{G} | \ \mathbf{B}'\end{bmatrix} \begin{bmatrix}\mathbf{z}_1 \\ \mathbf{z}_2 \\ \mathbf{z}_3\end{bmatrix} = e'(\bar{\mathbf{w}} + c\mathbf{u}) + \mathbf{v}_1 - \mathbf{A}_1^T\bar{\mathbf{y}}_4 - \mathbf{t}_1^T\bar{\mathbf{y}}_4\mathbf{G}\mathbf{z}_2. \tag{27}$$

Again, we take the difference and we conclude Eq. (22).

We will now prove that with overwhelming probability, $\overline{m_{\text{bin}}}, \bar{m}$ are such that

$$\mathbf{Q}\,\mathsf{NTT}\left(\overline{m_{\text{bin}}}\right) = \mathsf{NTT}\left(\bar{m}\right) \tag{28}$$

$$\overline{m_{\text{bin}}}(\overline{m_{\text{bin}}} - 1) = 0. \tag{29}$$

First, we claim that the prover is committed to unique $\bar{\mathbf{y}}_4$ and $\bar{\mathbf{r}}$, that are therefore independent of the challenge. From Lemma 4.1 of [ALS20], if the prover breaks this commitment[9], then $\mathcal{B}$ finds an $\mathsf{MSIS}_{\kappa,\kappa+\alpha+\lambda+5,B_2}$ solution for $\mathbf{A}_1$. Otherwise, we have that

$$\mathbf{z}_4 = \bar{\mathbf{y}}_4 + e\bar{\mathbf{r}} \text{ and } \mathbf{z}_4' = \bar{\mathbf{y}}_4 + e'\bar{\mathbf{r}},$$

and $\bar{\mathbf{y}}_4, \bar{m_{\text{bin}}}, \bar{\mathsf{garb}}$ are independent of the challenge.

Next, we show that $\overline{m_{\text{bin}}}$ verifies Eq. (29). We substitute f_2, f_3 and $\mathbf{z}_4$ with respectively $\mathbf{a}_3^T\bar{\mathbf{r}} + \overline{m_{\text{bin}}}$, $\mathbf{a}_2^T\bar{\mathbf{r}} + \bar{\mathsf{garb}}$ and $\bar{\mathbf{y}}_4 + e\bar{\mathbf{r}}$ in Eq. (14), and we obtain :

$$\mathbf{a}_2^T\bar{\mathbf{y}}_4 - v_3 + (\mathbf{a}_3^T\bar{\mathbf{y}}_4)^2 + e(\mathbf{a}_3^T\bar{\mathbf{y}}_4(2\overline{m_{\text{bin}}} - 1) - \overline{\mathsf{garb}}) + e^2\overline{m_{\text{bin}}}(\overline{m_{\text{bin}}} - 1) = 0. \tag{30}$$

Since we claimed that (unless the extractor finds an MSIS solution for $\mathbf{A}_1$) $\bar{m_{\text{bin}}}, \bar{\mathsf{garb}}$ and $\bar{\mathbf{y}}_4$ do not depend on e, we can claim that the expression on the left of Eq. (30) is a degree 2 polynomial in e. If Eq. (29) does not hold, then there exists a prime ideal $(X^{d/l} + \zeta)$ such that Eq. (30) mod $(X^{d/l} + \zeta)$ is a degree 2 polynomial in e over the field $\mathcal{R}_q/(X^{d/l} + \zeta)$. This polynomial has at most two roots in this field, say x_1, x_2. Assuming independence, it follows from Lemma 2.3 that the probability that $e \mod (X^{d/l} + \zeta)$ is either of these roots is at most $\frac{2}{q^{d/l}} + O(\epsilon)$, where ϵ is the error term from Lemma 2.3. This probability is negligible, hence we conclude Eq. (29).

We finally prove that $\mathsf{NTT}\left(\overline{m_{\text{bin}}}\right)$ is binary. We just shown that the extracted $\overline{m_{\text{bin}}}$ is such that $\overline{m_{\text{bin}}}(\overline{m_{\text{bin}}} - 1) = 0$. Let $X^{d/l} - \zeta$ be any of the irreducible factors of $X^d + 1 \mod q$. We have the following:

$$\begin{aligned} \overline{m_{\text{bin}}}(\overline{m_{\text{bin}}} - 1) &= 0 \\ \mathsf{NTT}\left(\overline{m_{\text{bin}}}(\overline{m_{\text{bin}}} - 1)\right) &= 0 \\ \mathsf{NTT}\left(\overline{m_{\text{bin}}}\right) \circ \left(\mathsf{NTT}\left(\overline{m_{\text{bin}}}\right) - 1\right) &= 0. \end{aligned}$$

Since $\mathbb{Z}_q[X]/(X^{d/l} - \zeta)$ is a field, we either have $\overline{m_{\text{bin}}} \mod (X^{d/l} - \zeta) = 0$ or $\overline{m_{\text{bin}}} \mod (X^{d/l} - \zeta) = 1$. This holds for all the NTT coefficients, from which we conclude Eq. (18).

---

[9] That is to say $\bar{\mathbf{y}}_4 \neq \bar{\mathbf{y}}_4'$.

We just proved that $\overline{m_{\text{bin}}}$ is the inverse NTT vector of a binary element of $\mathcal{R}_q$. We then prove that this element is the binary representation of $\bar{m}$ via Eq. (28). To do so, we notice that by taking the difference of Eq. (15) for both transcripts and plugging the expressions of $\overline{m_{\text{bin}}}, \bar{m}, \bar{g}$, the extractor finds that the latter variables are such that

$$\jmath = \bar{g} + \overline{m_{\text{bin}}} \mathsf{NTT}^{-1}\left(\mathbf{Q}^T \phi\right) - \bar{m} \mathsf{NTT}^{-1}(\phi). \tag{31}$$

Equation (16) says that the first d/l coefficients of $\jmath$ are 0. On the other hand, using Lemmas 2.1 and 2.2, we have

$$l \sum_{i=0}^{d/l-1} \jmath_i = \sum_{i=0}^{d/l-1} g_i + \langle \mathbf{Q}\, \mathsf{NTT}\left(\overline{m_{\text{bin}}}\right) - \mathsf{NTT}\left(\bar{m}\right), \phi \rangle,$$

where the latter equality is over $\mathbb{Z}_q^l$. If $\mathbf{Q}\, \mathsf{NTT}\left(\overline{m_{\text{bin}}}\right) - \mathsf{NTT}\left(\bar{m}\right) \neq 0$, then since the challenge ϕ is uniformly random, so is $\langle \mathbf{Q}\, \mathsf{NTT}\left(\overline{m_{\text{bin}}}\right) - \mathsf{NTT}\left(\bar{m}\right), \phi \rangle$. Notice that g was committed to by the prover prior to its knowledge of ϕ, and therefore, the probability that Eq. (31) holds without Eq. (28) being true is $\frac{1}{q^{d/l}}$. Since this probability is negligible, we conclude Eq. (28).

Finally, to prove that $\bar{m}$ is a valid identity, we notice that Eq. (28) yields that all NTT coefficients of $\bar{m}$ are equal. Together with the fact that $\overline{m_{\text{bin}}}$ is binary, this yields that $\mathsf{NTT}(\bar{m}) = (\bar{m}, \ldots, \bar{m})$, and it follows that $\bar{m} \in \mathcal{I}$.

We now prove that $\mathcal{E}$ can extract $\bar{\mathbf{s}}_1, \bar{\mathbf{s}}_2, \bar{\mathbf{s}}_3$ that together with the previously extracted $\bar{m}$ (that, we showed, verifies Eq. (18) and (20)) verifying Eq. (17). The extractor acquires 4 transcripts

$$\begin{aligned}
&(\mathbf{f}, \mathbf{t}, \mathbf{v}, c, \phi, \jmath, \mathbf{z}_1, \mathbf{z}_2, \mathbf{z}_3, e, \mathbf{z}_4) \\
&(\mathbf{f}, \mathbf{t}, \mathbf{v}, c, \phi, \jmath, \mathbf{z}_1, \mathbf{z}_2, \mathbf{z}_3, e', \mathbf{z}_4') \\
&(\mathbf{f}, \mathbf{t}, \mathbf{v}_1', v_2, v_3, v_4', c', \phi, \jmath, \mathbf{z}_1', \mathbf{z}_2', \mathbf{z}_3', e'', \mathbf{z}_4'') \\
&(\mathbf{f}, \mathbf{t}, \mathbf{v}_1', v_2, v_3, v_4', c', \phi, \jmath, \mathbf{z}_1', \mathbf{z}_2', \mathbf{z}_3', e^{(3)}, \mathbf{z}_4^{(3)}).
\end{aligned}$$

We proceed to describe how the extractor gets those transcripts and what his success probability is. Let ϵ be the probability of a deterministic prover to produce a proof that passes verification. The extractor first runs $\frac{\log 10}{\epsilon}$ times the prover, or until the prover returns a valid transcript $(\mathbf{f}, \mathbf{t}, \mathbf{v}, c, \phi, \jmath, \mathbf{z}_1, \mathbf{z}_2, \mathbf{z}_3, e, \mathbf{z}_4)$. If the prover fails to do so, $\mathcal{E}$ aborts. Next, $\mathcal{E}$ runs the prover $\frac{\log 10}{\epsilon/2 - C(c)}$ times, answering the same challenge c (and ϕ) in the first verifier interaction, and challenges $e' \leftarrow C$ in the second verifier interaction. Again, if the prover fails to produce a valid transcript, $\mathcal{E}$ aborts. Otherwise, $\mathcal{E}$ then receives a second transcript $(\mathbf{f}, \mathbf{t}, \mathbf{v}, c, \phi, \jmath, \mathbf{z}_1, \mathbf{z}_2, \mathbf{z}_3, e', \mathbf{z}_4')$. Thirdly, $\mathcal{E}$ runs the prover on fresh challenges (c', ϕ', e'') with the only condition that $c' \neq c$ for a total of $\frac{\log 10}{\epsilon - C(c)}$ times. Unless the prover provided a valid transcript $(\mathbf{f}, \mathbf{t}, \mathbf{v}_1', v_2, v_3, v_4', c', \phi', \jmath, \mathbf{z}_1', \mathbf{z}_2', \mathbf{z}_3', e'', \mathbf{z}_4'')$, $\mathcal{E}$ aborts. Finally, $\mathcal{E}$ repeats the second step: $\mathcal{E}$ runs the prover on c', ϕ' with fresh $e^{(3)} \leftarrow C \backslash \{e''\}$ for a total of $\frac{\log 10}{\epsilon/2 - C(e'')}$ times.

We now calculate the probability that $\mathcal{E}$ never aborts and indeed acquires the 4 transcripts. The extractor has 4 opportunities to abort and thus not receive 4 transcripts from the prover. We write $\mathbf{abort}_i$ the event where $\mathcal{E}$ acquires the first $i-1$ transcripts but aborts when done trying to get the i-th. Since the failure probability of the prover for one iteration is $1-\epsilon$, $\Pr(\mathbf{abort}_1) = (1-\epsilon)^{\log 10/\epsilon} \leq \exp(-\epsilon)^{\log 10/\epsilon}$, and finally $\Pr(\mathbf{abort}_1) \leq 1/10$. For $\mathcal{E}$ to abort in step 2, $\mathcal{E}$ must have received a first transcript for challenges c, ϕ, e. From the heavy-rows lemma [OO98], the probability that the (c, ϕ) row is heavy[10] is at least 1/2. Moreover, from the definition of a heavy row, the success probability of the prover when (c, ϕ) yields a heavy row is at least $\epsilon' = \epsilon/2 - \Pr_{c' \leftarrow C}(c' = c)$. Therefore, we have $\Pr(\mathbf{abort}_2) \leq (1-\epsilon')^{\log 10/\epsilon'} + 1/2 \leq 3/5$. Similarly, we have $\Pr(\mathbf{abort}_3) \leq 1/10$, and $\Pr(\mathbf{abort}_4) \leq 3/5$. The probability that $\mathcal{E}$ never aborts is the product of $1 - \Pr(\mathbf{abort}_i)$ for $i = 1, 2, 3, 4$, which is given by $81/625 \geq 1/8$.

Using the previous result on both the first pair and the second pair of transcripts, the extractor finds $\bar{\mathbf{r}}, \bar{m}, \bar{\mathbf{w}}$ and $\bar{\mathbf{r}}', \bar{m}', \bar{\mathbf{w}}'$ that verify Eqs. (18)–(21). Since $\bar{\mathbf{r}}\bar{e}' - \bar{\mathbf{r}}'\bar{e}$ is small[11], then $(\bar{\mathbf{r}}, \bar{m}, \bar{\mathbf{w}}) = (\bar{\mathbf{r}}', \bar{m}', \bar{\mathbf{w}}')$. The extractor defines $\bar{\mathbf{s}}_1 = \mathbf{z}_1 - \mathbf{z}_1', \bar{\mathbf{s}}_2 = \mathbf{z}_2 - \mathbf{z}_2', \bar{\mathbf{s}}_3 = \mathbf{z}_3 - \mathbf{z}_3', \bar{c} = c - c'$. Then, using Eq. (21), $\bar{\mathbf{s}}_1, \bar{\mathbf{s}}_2, \bar{\mathbf{s}}_3, \bar{c}$ verify Eq. (17), and therefore the protocol is sound.

Zero-knowledge. We define the simulator $\mathcal{S}$ as follows:

1. Generate $c \leftarrow C, \phi \leftarrow \mathcal{M}_q^l, e \leftarrow C$
2. Generate $(\mathbf{z}_1, \mathbf{z}_2, \mathbf{z}_3, \mathbf{z}_4) \leftarrow D_\sigma^{2d\alpha} \times D_\sigma^{3d\alpha} \times D_\sigma^{3d\alpha} \times D_{\sigma'}^{(\kappa+\lambda+\alpha+5)d}$
3. Generate $\mathbf{f} \leftarrow \mathcal{R}_q^{\kappa+\alpha+5}, \mathbf{r} \leftarrow \chi^{\kappa+\lambda+\alpha+5}$
4. Generate $j \leftarrow (\mathbf{0}_{d/l} | \mathbb{Z}_q^{d/l \times (l-1)})$
5. Set $\mathbf{v}, \mathbf{t}$ so Eqs. (11)–(14) hold
6. Output $(\mathbf{f}, \mathbf{t}, j, \mathbf{v}, \mathbf{z}_1, \mathbf{z}_2, \mathbf{z}_3, \mathbf{z}_4, c, \phi, e)$

To conclude zero-knowledge for π, we show that the distribution output by $\mathcal{S}$ is indistinguishable from the distribution of a non-aborting accepting transcript from Fig. 5. The variables c, ϕ, e are distributed exactly as in the procedure. The vectors $(\mathbf{z}_1, \mathbf{z}_2, \mathbf{z}_3, \mathbf{z}_4)$ in non-aborting proofs follow a distribution independent to c, ϕ, e that is indistinguishable ([BLS19], Lemma 3.2) of $D_\sigma^{2d\alpha} \times D_\sigma^{3d\alpha} \times D_\sigma^{3d\alpha} \times D_{\sigma'}^{(\kappa+\lambda+\alpha+5)d}$, which is their distribution in the output of $\mathcal{S}$.

Under the hardness of $\mathsf{MLWE}_{\kappa+\lambda+\alpha+5,\kappa,S_\mu}$, $\mathbf{t}_1, \mathbf{t}_2$ are indistinguishable from uniform. Under the hiding property of the commitment scheme, which in turn relies

[10] Challenges (c, ϕ) are in a *heavy row* when the success probability of the prover conditionned on the first challenges to be these c, ϕ is at least $\epsilon/2$. We refer to [OO98] for further detail.

[11] Otherwise, $\bar{\mathbf{r}}\bar{e}' - \bar{\mathbf{r}}'\bar{e}$ is a solution for MSIS for $\mathbf{A}_0$ of norm at most $8\omega^2\sigma'\sqrt{2(\kappa+\lambda+\alpha+5)d}$.

on the hardness of $\mathsf{MLWE}_{\kappa+\alpha+5,\lambda,\chi}$, the distribution of $\mathbf{f}$ in honestly generated transcripts is indistinguishable from uniform, which is its distribution in the output of the simulator $\mathcal{S}$.

Equation (11) uniquely determines $\mathbf{t} = \mathbf{A}_0\mathbf{z}_4 - e\mathbf{f}_0$ from $\mathbf{z}_4, e, \mathbf{f}_0$. Similarly, all the coordinates of $\mathbf{v}$ are uniquely determined by the sampled variables of $\mathcal{S}$ from Eqs. (12) to (15). To summarize, the variables that $\mathcal{S}$ samples follow a distribution indistinguishable from the one from the actual interaction and the other variables are binded by the verification equations in the accepting transcripts, from which we conclude zero-knowledge.

3.2 Decryption

The verifiable encryption scheme of our group signature scheme is hidden in the commitment scheme. The group manager sets the commitment public vectors for m and $\sqrt{q}m$ to be $\mathbf{t}_1 = \mathbf{A}_0^T\mathbf{h}_1 + \mathbf{e}_1, \mathbf{t}_2 = \mathbf{A}_0^T\mathbf{h}_2 + \mathbf{e}_2$, where $\mathbf{h}_1, \mathbf{h}_2, \mathbf{e}_1, \mathbf{e}_2$ are the group manager decryption secret key. The idea of the encryption is the following: the ciphertext is of the form

$$\mathbf{A}_0\mathbf{r} = \mathbf{u}_0 \tag{32}$$

$$\mathbf{t}_1^T\mathbf{r} + m = u_1 \tag{33}$$

$$\mathbf{t}_1^T\mathbf{r} + \sqrt{q}m = u_2. \tag{34}$$

The steps to decrypt using the secrets $\mathbf{h}_1, \mathbf{h}_2, \mathbf{e}_1, \mathbf{e}_2$ are as follows. Compute $x_1 = u_1 - \mathbf{h}_1^T\mathbf{u}_0 = \mathbf{h}_1^T\mathbf{r} + m, x_2 = u_2 - \mathbf{h}_2^T\mathbf{u}_0 = \mathbf{h}_2^T\mathbf{r} + \sqrt{q}m$. Then, compute $\sqrt{q}x_1 - x_2 = (\sqrt{q}\mathbf{h}_1^T - \mathbf{h}_2^T)\mathbf{r}$. If this latter polynomial has all its coefficients less than $q/2$, then this equality holds over the integers. Moreover, if we take the parameters such that $\mathbf{h}_1^T\mathbf{r} \leq \sqrt{q}$, then we have $k = \sqrt{q}x_1 - x_2 \mod \sqrt{q} = -\mathbf{h}_1^T\mathbf{r}$. To finish, we have $m = (x_2 + k)/\sqrt{q}$, provided that $(\sqrt{q}\mathbf{h}_1^T - \mathbf{h}_2^T)\mathbf{r} \leq q/2$ and $\mathbf{h}_1^T\mathbf{r} \leq \sqrt{q}$.

The problem is that the proof that the ciphertext is valid given through π does not ensure Eqs. (32)–(34) but rather a relaxed proof that there exists a $\bar{e} \in \bar{\mathcal{C}}$ and $\bar{r}$ such that

$$\mathbf{A}_0\bar{\mathbf{r}} = \bar{e}\mathbf{u}_0$$

$$\mathbf{t}_1^T\bar{\mathbf{r}} + \bar{e}m = \bar{e}u_1$$

$$\mathbf{t}_1^T\bar{\mathbf{r}} + \bar{e}\sqrt{q}m = \bar{e}u_2.$$

We use a similar technique as [LN17,dPLS18]. The idea is that the group manager is given a proof π for a challenge e. The soundness of the proof ensures that there exists another challenge e' such that with $\bar{e} = e - e'$ (and notations from π) : $(\bar{e}\mathbf{f}_0, \bar{e}f_5, \bar{e}f_6)$ is a valid ciphertext. The known technique that we use to tackle this is to try and decrypt $(\bar{e}\mathbf{f}_0, \bar{e}f_5, \bar{e}f_6)$ for a random second challenge $e' \leftarrow C$. Possibly not any challenge e' yields a decryption to the right message m. What [LN17] shown for their verifiable encryption scheme is that a simple test condition can 1) reject the challenges e' that do not yield a decryption to

m 2) Not reject too many challenges so the decryption runtime is reasonable. We have a similar result for our decryption, where the condition on Line 6 plays this role, where both correctness of the decryption and 'reasonable' runtime are stated in Lemma 3.2.

Algorithm 1 Decryption algorithm $\mathsf{GSdec}(\pi, \mathbf{h}_1, \mathbf{h}_2, \mathbf{e}_1, \mathbf{e}_2)$:

1: $e' \leftarrow C$
2: $\bar{e} = e - e'$
3: $x_1 = f_5 - \mathbf{h}_1^T \mathbf{f}_0$
4: $x_2 = f_6 - \mathbf{h}_2^T \mathbf{f}_0$
5: $k = \bar{e}(\sqrt{q}x_1 - x_2) \mod \sqrt{q}$
6: **if** $\|\bar{e}(\sqrt{q}x_1 - x_2)\|_\infty \leq \frac{q}{4\omega}$ **then**
7:     **return** $(\bar{e}x_2 + k)/(\sqrt{q}\bar{e})$
8: **else** go to Line 1
9: **end if**

Lemma 3.2. *If the verification of a proof π from Fig. 5 passes, then Algorithm 1 on input π and the group manager secret key returns a unique decryption in expected running-time at most $O(h_2)$, where h_2 is the number of queries to the second random oracle made by the prover to generate a signature. For an honest prover, the expected number of iterations is $\sqrt{3}$.*

Proof. The proof is deferred to the full version of the paper.

4 Security and Parameters

In this section, prove the two security notions required for a group signature, that is, anonymity and traceability. Afterwards, we propose a set of parameters for the group signature that achieve a signature size of rougly 203 KB.

4.1 Security

Throughout this subsection, we will write $\epsilon_{\mathcal{A}}^{G}$ the success probability of an adversary $\mathcal{A}$ against a game G. The proof for traceability is done in two steps: we reduce the traceability of our scheme to a hybrid trace^* game, and then reduce the latter to lattice problems. The trace^* game (more formally defined in the full version of the paper) is informally defined as follows. The challenger $\mathcal{B}$ runs KeyGen honestly, except for the following steps:

1. The public matrix $[\mathbf{A}|\mathbf{B}|\mathbf{B}']$ is crafted such that $\mathbf{A}$ is uniformly random, $\mathbf{B} = \mathbf{AR} - m^*\mathbf{G}$ where $\mathbf{R}$ is generated as in KeyGen and $m^* \leftarrow \mathcal{I}$ is a uniformly random identity, and $\mathbf{B}' = \mathbf{AR}'$ where $\mathbf{R}'$ is distributed as $\mathbf{R}$.
2. The vector $\mathbf{u}$ is defined as $\mathbf{u} = \mathbf{As}_1 + \mathbf{ARs}_2 + \mathbf{AR}'\mathbf{s}_3$, and thus corresponds to the identity m^*.

Similarly as in the traceability game for our scheme, the adversary can query secret keys, signatures and the random oracles.

Lemma 4.1. *Let $\mathcal{A}$ be an adversary to the traceability game for our scheme. Let* ZK *be the zero-knowledge game for* π*. We have*

$$\epsilon_{\mathcal{A}}^{\mathsf{traceability}} \leq 5\epsilon_{\mathcal{A}}^{\mathsf{MLWE}_{\alpha,\alpha,S_1}} + \epsilon_{\mathcal{A}}^{\mathsf{ZK}} + \epsilon_{\mathcal{A}}^{\mathsf{trace*}}.$$

The proof is deferred to the full version of the paper.

Lemma 4.2. *let $\mathcal{A}$ be an adversary that runs in time T and has success probability ϵ against the* $\mathsf{trace*}$ *game. Let h_1 (respectively h_2) be the number of queries that $\mathcal{A}$ can make to the first random oracle (respectively to the second random oracle), $B \geq 4\sigma\sqrt{d\alpha}(1+2\omega)(3d\alpha+1)$ and $B_2 \geq 8\omega^2\sigma'\sqrt{2d(\kappa+\lambda+\alpha+5)}$. Then, there exists an adversary $\mathcal{B}$ that runs in time $O(T/\epsilon)$ and that has probability at least $1/(8|\mathcal{I}|)$ to find either a solution to $\mathsf{MSIS}_{\alpha,2\alpha,B}$ or to $\mathsf{MSIS}_{\kappa,\kappa+\lambda+\alpha+5,B_2}$.*

Proof. Let $\mathcal{A}$ be an adversary. We assume that with at most h_1 queries to the first random oracle, h_2 queries to the second random oracle and Q queries to the signing algorithm, $\mathcal{A}$ has a probability ϵ of successfully outputing a forgery. Let $\mathcal{B}$ be an algorithm that can query $\mathcal{A}$. The goal of $\mathcal{B}$ is to either solve $\mathsf{MSIS}_{\alpha,2\alpha,B}$ for some matrix $\mathbf{X} \in \mathcal{R}_q^{\alpha\times 2\alpha}$, or solve $\mathsf{MSIS}_{\kappa,\kappa+\lambda+\alpha+5,B_2}$ for some matrix $\mathbf{Y}$.

Description of $\mathcal{B}$:

Given the instances of MSIS, $\mathcal{B}$ sets the public parameters of the scheme honestly, except for the following steps. The public matrix $\mathbf{A}$ is set as $\mathbf{A} = \mathbf{X}$, and $\mathbf{B} = \mathbf{XR} - m\mathbf{G}^T$ for some uniformly random guess m of the identity that the adversary is going to impersonate. The public commitment matrix $\mathbf{A}_0$ is set as $\mathbf{Y}$. The parameters of this game are identical to the $\mathsf{trace*}$ game, therefore provided that $\mathcal{B}$ can answer secret key signature queries, $\mathcal{A}$ shall have a probability ϵ to output a forgery. Note that on top of his knowledge of the trapdoors $\mathbf{R}, \mathbf{R}'$, $\mathcal{B}$ knows the honestly generated secret vector $\mathbf{s}_1^{\mathsf{gm}}, \mathbf{s}_2^{\mathsf{gm}}, \mathbf{s}_3^{\mathsf{gm}}$ and defines u as

$$u = \begin{bmatrix}\mathbf{X} | \; \mathbf{XR} | \; \mathbf{AR}'\end{bmatrix} \begin{bmatrix}\mathbf{s}_1^{\mathsf{gm}} \\ \mathbf{s}_2^{\mathsf{gm}} \\ \mathbf{s}_3^{\mathsf{gm}}\end{bmatrix}.$$

To answer a secret key query for an identity $m' \neq m^*$ from $\mathcal{A}$, $\mathcal{B}$ uses his knowledge of the trapdoor $\mathbf{R}$ to sample a valid secret key $(\mathbf{s}_1^{m'}, \mathbf{s}_2^{m'}, \mathbf{s}_3^{m'})$ such that

$$\begin{bmatrix}\mathbf{X} | \; \mathbf{XR} + (m' - m^*)\mathbf{G} | \; \mathbf{AR}'\end{bmatrix} \begin{bmatrix}\mathbf{s}_1^{m'} \\ \mathbf{s}_2^{m'} \\ \mathbf{s}_3^{m'}\end{bmatrix} = u.$$

If $\mathcal{A}$ queries the secret key for m^*, $\mathcal{B}$ is unable to use its trapdoor $\mathbf{R}$ so he returns $(\mathbf{s}_1^{\mathsf{gm}}, \mathbf{s}_2^{\mathsf{gm}}, \mathbf{s}_3^{\mathsf{gm}})$.

To answer $\mathcal{A}$'s signing queries, $\mathcal{B}$ will run the simulator $\mathcal{S}$ from the zero-knowledge property of π. From Theorem 3.1, the distribution of the transcripts that $\mathcal{B}$ sends to $\mathcal{A}$ is computationally indistinguishable from the actual distribution of the transcripts from the signature, and therefore $\mathcal{A}$ can indeed be provided with as many as Q signing queries.

When $\mathcal{A}$ is ready to produce forgeries, $\mathcal{B}$ will follow the transcript-acquisition from the extractor $\mathcal{E}$ of the soundness of π. More precisely, $\mathcal{B}$ has a probability at least $1/8$ to get 4 forged signatures from $\mathcal{A}$ in time $O(T/\epsilon)$: 2 different second challenges e per first different challenges c, ϕ. We reuse the notations from the extraction.

Next, $\mathcal{B}$ will proceed as $\mathcal{E}$ and recover either a solution to $\mathsf{MSIS}_{\kappa,\kappa+\lambda+\alpha+5,B_2}$ - or recover vectors $\bar{\mathbf{s}}_1, \bar{\mathbf{s}}_2, \bar{\mathbf{s}}_3, \bar{\mathbf{r}}$ and polynomials $m, \bar{c}$ such that $m \in \mathcal{I}$ and $\mathbf{X}\bar{\mathbf{s}}_1 + (\mathbf{XR} + (m - m^*)\mathbf{G})\bar{\mathbf{s}}_2 + \mathbf{XR}'\bar{\mathbf{s}}_3 = \mathbf{u}$, which completes the proof either way.

From Lemma 3.2, the decryption of all of $\mathcal{A}$'s forgeries are the same $m \in \mathcal{I}$. Since $\mathcal{A}$ is playing the trace^* game, we assume that he never queried nor received the secret key for identity m. With probability $|\mathcal{I}|^{-1}$, $\mathcal{B}$'s uniformly random guess m^* is indeed the identity that $\mathcal{A}$ impersonates. If this did not happen, then $\mathcal{B}$ fails and aborts. From now on, we assume that $m = m^*$. On one hand, $\mathcal{B}$ received from $\mathcal{A}$ short vectors that satisfy $\mathbf{X}(\bar{\mathbf{s}}_1 + \mathbf{R}\bar{\mathbf{s}}_2 + \mathbf{R}'\bar{\mathbf{s}}_3) = \bar{c}u$. On the other hand, $\mathcal{B}$ knows $(\mathbf{s}_1^{\mathsf{gm}}, \mathbf{s}_2^{\mathsf{gm}}, \mathbf{s}_3^{\mathsf{gm}})$ verifying $\mathbf{X}(\mathbf{s}_1^{\mathsf{gm}} + \mathbf{R}\mathbf{s}_2^{\mathsf{gm}} + \mathbf{R}\mathbf{s}_3^{\mathsf{gm}}) = u$. In other words, $\bar{\mathbf{s}}_1 - \bar{c}\mathbf{s}_1^{\mathsf{gm}} + \mathbf{R}(\bar{\mathbf{s}}_2 - \bar{c}\mathbf{s}_2^{\mathsf{gm}}) + \mathbf{R}'(\bar{\mathbf{s}}_3 - \bar{c}\mathbf{s}_3^{\mathsf{gm}})$ is a solution to MSIS for the given random matrix $\mathbf{X}$ of size with overwhelming probability at most $4\sigma\sqrt{d\alpha}(1 + 2\omega)(3d\alpha + 1)$.

Theorem 4.3. *The group signature scheme, where the signature is the Fiat-Shamir transform of π defined in Fig. 5 is untraceable and anonymous.*

More precisely for anonymity, the advantage of an adversary $\mathcal{A}$ against the anonymity game is upper bounded by $2^{99}/M + 2\epsilon_{\mathcal{A}}^{\mathsf{MLWE}}$.

For traceability, with $B \geq 4\sigma\sqrt{d\alpha}(1 + 2\omega)(3d\alpha + 1)$ and

$$B_2 \geq 8\omega^2\sigma'\sqrt{2d(\kappa + \lambda + \alpha + 5)},$$

the success probability $\epsilon_{\mathcal{A}}^{\mathsf{traceability}}$ of an adversary $\mathcal{A}$ against the traceability game is upper bounded by

$$3\epsilon_{\mathcal{A}}^{\mathsf{MLWE}_{\alpha,\alpha,S_1}} + 8|\mathcal{I}| \max(\epsilon_{\mathcal{A}}^{\mathsf{MSIS}_{\alpha,2\alpha,B}}, \epsilon_{\mathcal{A}}^{\mathsf{MSIS}_{\kappa,\kappa+\lambda+\alpha+5,B_2}}).$$

The proof is deferred to the full version of the paper.

4.2 Parameters

Similarly as in [dPLS18], we apply the Fiat-Shamir transformation [FS86] on the interactive protocol in Fig. 5 to obtain a group signature. We first compute sizes for our signature and then propose several common optimisations.

To begin with, we set $(q, d, l) = (\approx 2^{64}, 128, 64)$ so that $q^{-d/l} \approx \mathsf{p}^{d/l} \approx 2^{-128}$. Next, we aim for the repetition rate of our protocol to be 27 as in [dPLS18].

Hence, we set M such that $M^2 = 27^{12}$, i.e. $M = 3^{3/2}$. We compute an upper-bound T_s on $\|c(\boldsymbol{s}_1\|\boldsymbol{s}_2\|\boldsymbol{s}_3)\|$, where $c \leftarrow C$, as follows. Recall that using a trapdoor sampling similar to [dPLS18], coefficients of vectors $\boldsymbol{s}_i$ follow a discrete Gaussian distribution with standard deviation $\mathfrak{s}_{tr} \leq 2(3\sqrt{\alpha d}+1)\sqrt{\lceil q^{1/3}\rceil^2+1}$ (see [dPLS18, Sect. 2.6] for more details). Hence, by Lemma 2.7 with an overwhelming probability we have

$$\|c(\boldsymbol{s}_1\|\boldsymbol{s}_2\|\boldsymbol{s}_3)\|^2 = \sum_{i=1}^{3} \|c\boldsymbol{s}_i\|^2 \leq \sum_{i=1}^{3} (d\|\boldsymbol{s}_i\|)^2 \leq 16 d^2 \mathfrak{s}_{tr}^2 \alpha d.$$

Thus, we set $T_s = 8(3\sqrt{\alpha d}+1)d\sqrt{\lceil q^{1/3}\rceil^2+1}\sqrt{\alpha d}$ and $\sigma = 8T_s$ in order to have $M = 3^{3/2}$ (as in Eq. 8).

Let T_r be an upper-bound on $\|e\boldsymbol{r}\|$ where e is the challenge in Fig. 5. We apply the exact method as in [LNS21a, Appendix C]. Namely, we use the observation that

$$\|e\boldsymbol{r}\|^2 \leq d \left\| \sum_{i=1}^{\ell} \sigma_{-1}(r_i) r_i \right\|_1$$

where $\boldsymbol{r} = (r_1, \ldots, r_{\kappa+\lambda+\alpha+5})$ and σ_{-1} is the Galois automorphism $\sigma_{-1} : X \longmapsto X^{-1}$. Then, we heuristically choose T_r so that the expression on the right-hand side is less than T_r^2 with probability at least 99%. Similarly as before, we set $\mathfrak{s}' = 8T_r$.

In Fig. 1 we choose parameters $\kappa, \lambda, \alpha, \mu$ so that the MSIS and MLWE problems described in the previous subsections are hard. For a fair comparison with [dPLS18], we measure the hardness with the root Hermite factor δ and aim for $\delta \approx 1.0036$.

We now turn to computing the signature size. As "full-sized" elements of $\mathcal{R}_q$ we have $\boldsymbol{f}$ and j (it is missing d/l coefficients but this has negligible impact on the sizes). Therefore, we have in total $\kappa + \alpha + 5 + 1$ full elements of $\mathcal{R}_q$ which give us

$$(\kappa + \alpha + 6) d \log q \text{ bits.}$$

What we have left are vectors of short polynomials $\boldsymbol{z}_1, \boldsymbol{z}_2, \boldsymbol{z}_3$ and $\boldsymbol{z}_4$. Since they come from a discrete Gaussian distribution with standard deviation $\mathfrak{s}$ and $\mathfrak{s}'$ respectively, with high probability we can upper-bound their coefficients by $6\mathfrak{s}$ and $6\mathfrak{s}'$ [Lyu12]. Thus, they require at most:

$$8\alpha d \log(12\mathfrak{s}) + (\kappa + \lambda + \alpha + 5) d \log(12\mathfrak{s}') \text{ bits.}$$

Finally, the challenges c, e cost at most $4 \cdot d = 512$ bits.

Various Optimisations. First, we apply the rejection strategy introduced [LNS21a] for $\boldsymbol{z}_4$. Namely, we use the algorithm Rej_1 defined in Fig. 3 instead of Rej_0. Consequently, we manage to significantly reduce the standard deviation

[12] Recall that in Fig. 5 we run four rejection algorithms. However, for efficiency purposes we can merge the ones for $\boldsymbol{z}_1, \boldsymbol{z}_2, \boldsymbol{z}_3$ since they follow the same standard deviation σ.

$\mathfrak{s}'$ at a cost of leaking one bit of the randomness $\boldsymbol{r}$. This is fine in our case since each new signature requires a fresh randomness vector.

We cannot use the rejection approach from [LNS21a] for $\boldsymbol{z}_1, \boldsymbol{z}_2, \boldsymbol{z}_3$ since each signature would reveal some more information about secret vectors $\boldsymbol{s}_i$. In order to reduce the standard deviation σ, we will use Bimodal Gaussians [DDLL13] instead. We remark that this technique is not new and it was recently used in e.g. [LNS21b, Sect. 1.5] and [LNS21a, Appendix B].

Concretely, we additionally commit to a randomly chosen sign $b \in \{-1, 1\}$:

$$f_8 = \boldsymbol{a}_5^T \boldsymbol{r} + b.$$

Then, we send $\boldsymbol{z}_i = \boldsymbol{y} + bc\boldsymbol{s}_i$ for $i = 1, 2, 3$ and later prove that

$$\begin{bmatrix} \boldsymbol{A} | \ \boldsymbol{B} + m\boldsymbol{G} | \ \boldsymbol{B}' \end{bmatrix} \begin{bmatrix} \mathbf{z}_1 \\ \mathbf{z}_2 \\ \mathbf{z}_3 \end{bmatrix} = \boldsymbol{w} + bc\boldsymbol{u}$$

where BDLOP commitments to m, b and $\boldsymbol{w}$ are given. Furthermore, we need to prove that f_8 is a commitment to -1 or 1. First, we prove that $(b+1)(b-1) = 0$ over $\mathcal{R}_q$. This implies that the NTT coefficients of b are either -1 or 1. Next, we show that all coefficients of b are the same, i.e. the NTT vector $\vec{b} = \mathsf{NTT}(b)$ of b satisfies $V\vec{b} = \vec{0}$ where

$$V = \begin{pmatrix} 1 & -1 & 0 & \dots & 0 \\ 0 & 1 & -1 & \dots & 0 \\ \vdots & \vdots & \vdots & \ddots & \vdots \\ -1 & 0 & 0 & \dots & 1 \end{pmatrix} \in \mathbb{Z}_q^{l \times l}.$$

Since we already prove linear and multiplicative relations in Fig. 5, the additional proofs for b do not affect the total signature size. Hence, we manage to decrease the standard deviation σ at a cost of committing to one more polynomial b. Eventually, with the aforementioned optimisations, we manage to decrease the standard deviations to $\sigma = 0.7T_s$ and $\sigma' = 0.7T_r$. Thanks to these modifications, the extracted MSIS solution from the traceability game has Euclidean norm at most 2^{61} which is less than q.

With the given parameters, we obtain a group signature of size around 203 KB which is around a factor of three improvement over [dPLS18].

Table 1. Group signature parameters.

q	d	l	κ	λ	α	μ
$\approx 2^{64}$	128	64	20	24	24	127

References

[ABB10] Agrawal, S., Boneh, D., Boyen, X.: Efficient lattice (H)IBE in the standard model. In: Gilbert, H. (ed.) EUROCRYPT 2010. LNCS, vol. 6110, pp. 553–572. Springer, Heidelberg (2010). https://doi.org/10.1007/978-3-642-13190-5_28

[ALS20] Attema, T., Lyubashevsky, V., Seiler, G.: Practical product proofs for lattice commitments. In: Micciancio, D., Ristenpart, T. (eds.) CRYPTO 2020. LNCS, vol. 12171, pp. 470–499. Springer, Cham (2020). https://doi.org/10.1007/978-3-030-56880-1_17

[Ban93] Banaszczyk, W.: New bounds in some transference theorems in the geometry of numbers. Math. Ann. **296**(1), 625–635 (1993)

[BCN18] Boschini, C., Camenisch, J., Neven, G.: Floppy-sized group signatures from lattices. In: Preneel, B., Vercauteren, F. (eds.) ACNS 2018. LNCS, vol. 10892, pp. 163–182. Springer, Cham (2018). https://doi.org/10.1007/978-3-319-93387-0_9

[BDL+18] Baum, C., Damgård, I., Lyubashevsky, V., Oechsner, S., Peikert, C.: More efficient commitments from structured lattice assumptions. In: Catalano, D., De Prisco, R. (eds.) SCN 2018. LNCS, vol. 11035, pp. 368–385. Springer, Cham (2018). https://doi.org/10.1007/978-3-319-98113-0_20

[BLS19] Bootle, J., Lyubashevsky, V., Seiler, G.: Algebraic techniques for short(er) exact lattice-based zero-knowledge proofs. In: Boldyreva, A., Micciancio, D. (eds.) CRYPTO 2019. LNCS, vol. 11692, pp. 176–202. Springer, Cham (2019). https://doi.org/10.1007/978-3-030-26948-7_7

[CS97] Camenisch, J., Stadler, M.: Efficient group signature schemes for large groups. In: Kaliski, B.S. (ed.) CRYPTO 1997. LNCS, vol. 1294, pp. 410–424. Springer, Heidelberg (1997). https://doi.org/10.1007/BFb0052252

[DDLL13] Ducas, L., Durmus, A., Lepoint, T., Lyubashevsky, V.: Lattice signatures and bimodal gaussians. In CRYPTO **1**, 40–56 (2013)

[DKL+18] Ducas, L., Kiltz, E., Lepoint, T., Lyubashevsky, V., Schwabe, P., Seiler, G., Stehlé, D.: Crystals-dilithium: a lattice-based digital signature scheme. IACR Trans. Cryptogr. Hardw. Embed. Syst. **2018**(1), 238–268 (2018)

[dPLS18] del Pino, R., Lyubashevsky, V., Seiler, G.: Lattice-based group signatures and zero-knowledge proofs of automorphism stability. In: ACM Conference on Computer and Communications Security, pp. 574–591. ACM (2018)

[ENS20] Esgin, M.F., Nguyen, N.K., Seiler, G.: Practical exact proofs from lattices: new techniques to exploit fully-splitting rings. In: Moriai, S., Wang, H. (eds.) ASIACRYPT 2020. LNCS, vol. 12492, pp. 259–288. Springer, Cham (2020). https://doi.org/10.1007/978-3-030-64834-3_9

[ESLL19] Esgin, M.F., Steinfeld, R., Liu, J.K., Liu, D.: Lattice-based zero-knowledge proofs: new techniques for shorter and faster constructions and applications. In: Boldyreva, A., Micciancio, D. (eds.) CRYPTO 2019. LNCS, vol. 11692, pp. 115–146. Springer, Cham (2019). https://doi.org/10.1007/978-3-030-26948-7_5

[ESS+19] Esgin, M.F., Steinfeld, R., Sakzad, A., Liu, J.K., Liu, D.: Short lattice-based one-out-of-many proofs and applications to ring signatures. In: Deng, R.H., Gauthier-Umaña, V., Ochoa, M., Yung, M. (eds.) ACNS 2019. LNCS, vol. 11464, pp. 67–88. Springer, Cham (2019). https://doi.org/10.1007/978-3-030-21568-2_4

[EZS+19] Esgin, M.F., Zhao, R.K., Steinfeld, R., Liu, J.K., Liu, D.: MatRiCT: efficient, scalable and post-quantum blockchain confidential transactions protocol. In: CCS, pp. 567–584. ACM (2019)

[FS86] Fiat, A., Shamir, A.: How To prove yourself: practical solutions to identification and signature problems. In: Odlyzko, A.M. (ed.) CRYPTO 1986. LNCS, vol. 263, pp. 186–194. Springer, Heidelberg (1987). https://doi.org/10.1007/3-540-47721-7_12

[GKV10] Gordon, S.D., Katz, J., Vaikuntanathan, V.: A group signature scheme from lattice assumptions. In: Abe, M. (ed.) ASIACRYPT 2010. LNCS, vol. 6477, pp. 395–412. Springer, Heidelberg (2010). https://doi.org/10.1007/978-3-642-17373-8_23

[GSW13] Gentry, C., Sahai, A., Waters, B.: Homomorphic encryption from learning with errors: conceptually-simpler, asymptotically-faster, attribute-based. In: Canetti, R., Garay, J.A. (eds.) CRYPTO 2013. LNCS, vol. 8042, pp. 75–92. Springer, Heidelberg (2013). https://doi.org/10.1007/978-3-642-40041-4_5

[LLNW16] Libert, B., Ling, S., Nguyen, K., Wang, H.: Zero-knowledge arguments for lattice-based accumulators: logarithmic-size ring signatures and group signatures without trapdoors. In: Fischlin, M., Coron, J.-S. (eds.) EUROCRYPT 2016. LNCS, vol. 9666, pp. 1–31. Springer, Heidelberg (2016). https://doi.org/10.1007/978-3-662-49896-5_1

[LN17] Lyubashevsky, V., Neven, G.: One-shot verifiable encryption from lattices. In: Coron, J.-S., Nielsen, J.B. (eds.) EUROCRYPT 2017. LNCS, vol. 10210, pp. 293–323. Springer, Cham (2017). https://doi.org/10.1007/978-3-319-56620-7_11

[LNS20] Lyubashevsky, V., Nguyen, N.K., Seiler, G.: Practical lattice-based zero-knowledge proofs for integer relations. In: CCS, pp. 1051–1070. ACM (2020)

[LNS21a] Lyubashevsky, V., Nguyen, N.K., Seiler, G.: Shorter lattice-based zero-knowledge proofs via one-time commitments. In: Garay, J.A. (ed.) PKC 2021. LNCS, vol. 12710, pp. 215–241. Springer, Cham (2021). https://doi.org/10.1007/978-3-030-75245-3_9

[LNS21b] Lyubashevsky, V., Nguyen, N.K., Seiler, G.: SMILE: set membership from ideal lattices with applications to ring signatures and confidential transactions. In: Malkin, T., Peikert, C. (eds.) CRYPTO 2021. LNCS, vol. 12826, pp. 611–640. Springer, Cham (2021). https://doi.org/10.1007/978-3-030-84245-1_21

[LS15] Langlois, A., Stehlé, D.: Worst-case to average-case reductions for module lattices. Des. Codes Crypt. **75**(3), 565–599 (2014). https://doi.org/10.1007/s10623-014-9938-4

[Lyu09] Lyubashevsky, V.: Fiat-Shamir with aborts: applications to lattice and factoring-based signatures. In: Matsui, M. (ed.) ASIACRYPT 2009. LNCS, vol. 5912, pp. 598–616. Springer, Heidelberg (2009). https://doi.org/10.1007/978-3-642-10366-7_35

[Lyu12] Lyubashevsky, V.: Lattice signatures without trapdoors. In: Pointcheval, D., Johansson, T. (eds.) EUROCRYPT 2012. LNCS, vol. 7237, pp. 738–755. Springer, Heidelberg (2012). https://doi.org/10.1007/978-3-642-29011-4_43

[MP12] Micciancio, D., Peikert, C.: Trapdoors for lattices: simpler, tighter, faster, smaller. In: Pointcheval, D., Johansson, T. (eds.) EUROCRYPT 2012. LNCS, vol. 7237, pp. 700–718. Springer, Heidelberg (2012). https://doi.org/10.1007/978-3-642-29011-4_41

[OO98] Ohta, K., Okamoto, T.: On concrete security treatment of signatures derived from identification. In: Krawczyk, H. (ed.) CRYPTO 1998. LNCS, vol. 1462, pp. 354–369. Springer, Heidelberg (1998). https://doi.org/10.1007/BFb0055741

[Reg09] Regev, O.: On lattices, learning with errors, random linear codes, and cryptography. J. ACM **56**(6), 1–40 (2009)

[YAZ+19] Yang, R., Au, M.H., Zhang, Z., Xu, Q., Yu, Z., Whyte, W.: Efficient lattice-based zero-knowledge arguments with standard soundness: construction and applications. In: Boldyreva, A., Micciancio, D. (eds.) CRYPTO 2019. LNCS, vol. 11692, pp. 147–175. Springer, Cham (2019). https://doi.org/10.1007/978-3-030-26948-7_6

Séta: Supersingular Encryption from Torsion Attacks

Luca De Feo[1,11](✉), Cyprien Delpech de Saint Guilhem[2](✉), Tako Boris Fouotsa[3](✉), Péter Kutas[4,5](✉), Antonin Leroux[6,7,11](✉), Christophe Petit[5,8](✉), Javier Silva[9](✉), and Benjamin Wesolowski[10,12](✉)

[1] IBM Research Europe, Zürich, Switzerland
asiacrypt21@defeo.lu
[2] imec-COSIC, KU Leuven, Leuven, Belgium
cyprien.delpechdesaintguilhem@kuleuven.be
[3] Università Degli Studi Roma Tre, Rome, Italy
takoboris.fouotsa@uniroma3.it
[4] Eötvös Loránd University, Budapest, Hungary
[5] University of Birmingham, Birmingham, UK
p.kutas@bham.ac.uk
[6] DGA, Paris, France
[7] LIX, CNRS, Ecole Polytechnique, Institut Polytechnique de Paris, Palaiseau, France
antonin.leroux@polytechnique.org
[8] Université Libre de Bruxelles, Brussels, Belgium
christophe.petit@ulb.be
[9] Universitat Pompeu Fabra, Barcelona, Spain
[10] Univ. Bordeaux, CNRS, Bordeaux INP, IMB, Talence, France
benjamin.wesolowski@math.u-bordeaux.fr
[11] INRIA, Rocquencourt, France
[12] INRIA, IMB, Talence, France

Abstract. We present *Séta* (To be pronounced [ʃeːtɒ] meaning "walk" in Hungarian.), a new family of public-key encryption schemes with post-quantum security based on isogenies of supersingular elliptic curves. It is constructed from a new family of trapdoor one-way functions, where the inversion algorithm uses Petit's so called *torsion attacks* on SIDH to compute an isogeny between supersingular elliptic curves given an endomorphism of the starting curve and images of torsion points. We prove the OW-CPA security of Séta and present an IND-CCA variant using the post-quantum OAEP transformation. Several variants for key generation are explored together with their impact on the selection of parameters, such as the base prime of the scheme. We furthermore formalise an "uber" isogeny assumption framework which aims to generalize computational isogeny problems encountered in schemes including SIDH, CSDIH, OSIDH and ours. Finally, we carefully select parameters to achieve a balance between security and run-times and present experimental results from our implementation.

M. Tibouchi and H. Wang (Eds.): ASIACRYPT 2021, LNCS 13093, pp. 249–278, 2021.
https://doi.org/10.1007/978-3-030-92068-5_9

1 Introduction

Isogeny-based cryptography. Recent years have seen an increasing interest in cryptosystems based on supersingular isogeny problems as appropriate candidates for post-quantum cryptography. The latter has received greater focus due to the recent standardization process initiated by NIST.[1]

More precisely, the central problem of isogeny-based cryptography is, given two elliptic curves, to compute an isogeny between them. For the right choice of parameters, the best quantum algorithms for solving this problem still run in exponential time [5]. Variants of this problem have been used to build primitives such as hash functions [10], encryption schemes [2,23], key encapsulation mechanism (KEM)s [2] and signatures [16,21].

Encryption schemes. The first key agreement and public-key encryption (PKE) scheme based on isogenies of ordinary elliptic curves was independently discovered by Couveignes [15] and Rostovtsev and Stolbunov [34,37]. It follows a "Diffie–Hellman-like" structure: Alice and Bob start from a public curve E_0 and choose random secret isogenies φ_A, φ_B to reach curves E_A, E_B. They then send the curves to each other and finally use their respective secrets to arrive at a common curve E_{AB}. It is then immediate to transform the key agreement into a CPA-secure PKE by following El Gamal's blueprint.

In 2011, Jao and De Feo [23] introduced SIDH, a key agreement protocol based on isogenies of supersingular curves, inspired both by the Couveignes–Rostovtsev–Stolbunov scheme and by the hash function of Charles, Goren and Lauter [10]. In the supersingular case, however, isogenies do not have a natural commutative property, meaning that, for example, the result of applying Bob's isogeny φ_B to Alice's curve E_A cannot be meaningfully defined without some extra constraints. To solve this, Jao and De Feo proposed sending additional information in the protocol in the form of images of torsion points under the secret isogenies. With the help of these points, they ensured that each party could evaluate their secret isogeny on the other's curve.

However, the isogeny problem upon which the security of the scheme is based now differs from the original problem in certain ways. Most importantly, the adversary has access to the image of certain torsion points under a secret isogeny. Galbraith, Petit, Shani and Ti [20] were the first to exploit this extra information in an active attack showing that one cannot use static keys in SIDH. Then, two further works studied the generic problem of finding isogenies if the action of the isogeny on some torsion is known [17,33]. These look at two different scenarios:

1. The starting curve is $E_0 : y^2 = x^3 + x$;
2. The starting curve is chosen by the adversary;

Let p be a prime number; for simplicity we restrict to supersingular elliptic curves defined over $\mathbb{F}_{p^2}$. Let A be the degree of some secret isogeny φ and

[1] U.S. Department of Commerce, National Institute of Standards and Technology, Post-Quantum Cryptography project, 2016. Available at https://csrc.nist.gov/projects/post-quantum-cryptography, last retrieved September 13th, 2019.

let B be the order of a torsion group on which the action of φ is known. In the first case [17] gives a polynomial-time algorithm to compute φ whenever $B > \sqrt{p}A^2$. In the second case it shows how to construct special starting curves (called *backdoor curves*) for which backdoor information is known, in the form of an endomorphism of the curve, which enables a polynomial-time algorithm to compute φ whenever $B > A^2$.

In SIDH one has $A \approx B \approx \sqrt{p}$ so these algorithms do not lead to an attack. However [17] also shows that, if an adversary is allowed to choose the starting curve, then even in the SIDH setting it is possible to mount key-recovery attacks which take exponential time, yet are faster than known algorithms [17, Corollary 32]. In anticipation of potential further cryptanalysis progress, it is desirable to design alternative cryptographic protocols that rely on different isogeny problems. An example of this is the CSIDH scheme [9] (and its variants [19,31]), a key agreement protocol that relies on the original isogeny problem, but is restricted to supersingular elliptic curves over $\mathbb{F}_p$, and can be solved in quantum subexponential time.

These results show that any relaxation of the assumptions used in building isogeny-based PKE schemes and KEMs is of interest from a theoretical point of view, and could become crucial if further cryptanalysis progress occurs.

Our contributions. Our main contribution is to turn the attack described in [17] into a PKE by using the special starting curves mentioned above as public keys. The associated secret key can be derived from an endomorphism of the curve with a specific minimal polynomial. More precisely, one can use any special curve whose endomorphism ring has a particular quadratic order embedded into it. Using such a starting curve, one can design a PKE where a message corresponds to an isogeny and a ciphertext contains the codomain of the isogeny together with images of the torsion points under the isogeny. Decryption is then performed using the algorithm which recovers the secret isogeny using the techniques developed in [33] and [17].

Choosing parameters for our scheme is not obvious due to the following reason. Even though trapdoor curves can be constructed in polynomial time, in practice this can be very costly. This is acceptable for a backdoor, but not for a PKE for which key generation should be routine computation. The expensive step is to generate a supsersingular elliptic curve with a prescribed endomorphism ring. We utilize techniques from SQISign [16] where one uses special primes to substantially speed up the procedure of generating starting curves. Furthermore, the worst-case complexity of torsion-point attacks is dependent on the number of prime factors of the isogeny degree. We therefore impose extra conditions on the quadratic order to avoid timing attacks that this could imply.

We also present variants for constructing backdoor curves which allow for slightly different decryption mechanisms. Namely one can either construct the starting curve directly and then compute a backdoor, or instead choose a secret backdoor curve first and then apply a secret walk to it. We discuss trade-offs between security, key size and speed in this context.

We emphasize that just knowing the equation of the starting curve and a description of the quadratic order embedded in it does not seem to be helpful without the concrete knowledge of an endomorphims realizing this embedding. We formalize this idea in what we call the *uber isogeny problem* or $\mathfrak{O}$-UIP (Problem 5.1): suppose that one knows that a certain quadratic order $\mathfrak{O}$ is embedded in the endomorphism ring of two curves E_0, E_s, and that and that a concrete embedding of E_0 is also given in input, the problem is to find an isogeny between E_0 and E_S corresponding to a $\mathfrak{O}$-ideal. The formulation of this $\mathfrak{O}$-UIP is inspired from the key recovery problem in CSIDH [9, Problem 10]. We show that SIDH, OSIDH [12] and our PKE scheme also rely implicitly on various instances of this assumption. We also provide an analysis on the difficulty of this problem.

Finally, we present an implementation of our scheme which includes searching for an appropriate base prime and measuring key generation and encryption/decryption speeds. Written in C, our implementation reuses some of the codebase of SQISign and improves the efficiency of several steps crucial for Séta computations.

In Sect. 2 we recall basic properties of supersingular elliptic curves and the SIDH protocol. Furthermore, we discuss backdoor curves (which in this context we rename as trapdoor curves) in more detail. In Sect. 3 we introduce our one-way function and PKE Séta. In Sect. 4 we show how one can generate keys efficiently for Séta. In Sect. 5 we introduce the uber isogeny assumption, discuss its relation to other studied isogeny problems and provide some analysis of its hardness. In Sect. 6 we provide details of our implementation.

2 Preliminaries

We denote the computational security parameter by λ. We write PPT for probabilistic polynomial time. The notation $y \leftarrow \mathcal{A}(x; r)$ means that the algorithm $\mathcal{A}$, with input x and randomness r, outputs y. The notation Pr[sampling : event] means the probability of the event on the right happening after sampling elements as specified on the left. Given a set $\mathcal{S}$, we denote sampling a uniformly random element x of $\mathcal{S}$ by $x \xleftarrow{\$} \mathcal{S}$. A probability distribution X has min-entropy $H_\infty(X) = b$ if any event occurs with probability at most 2^{-b}. Given an integer $n = \prod_i \ell_i^{e_i}$, where the ℓ_i are its prime factors, we say that n is *B-powersmooth* if $\ell_i^{e_i} < B$ for all i. We denote by $\mathbb{Z}_n$ the set of residue classes modulo n.

2.1 Quaternion Algebras and Endomorphism Rings of Supersingular Elliptic Curves

A quaternion algebra is a four-dimensional central simple algebra over a field K. When the characteristic of K is not 2, then A admits a basis $1, i, j, ij$ such that $i^2 = a,\ j^2 = b, ij = -ji$ where $a, b \in K\backslash\{0\}$. The numbers a, b characterise the quaternion algebra up to isomorphism, thus we denote the aforementioned algebra by the pair (a, b). A quaternion algebra is either a division ring or it is isomorphic to $M_2(K)$, the algebra of 2×2 matrices over K.

Let A be a quaternion algebra over $\mathbb{Q}$. Then $A \otimes \mathbb{Q}_p$ is a quaternion algebra over $\mathbb{Q}_p$ (the field of p-adic numbers) and $A \otimes \mathbb{R}$ is a quaternion algebra over the real numbers. A is said to split at p (resp. at ∞) if $A \otimes \mathbb{Q}_p$ (resp. $A \otimes \mathbb{R}$)

is a full matrix algebra. Otherwise it is said to ramify at p (resp. at ∞). A quaternion algebra over $\mathbb{Q}$ is split at every but finitely many places, and the list of these places defines the quaternion algebra up to isomorphism. An order in a quaternion algebra over $\mathbb{Q}$ is a four-dimensional $\mathbb{Z}$-lattice which is also a subring containing the identity (it is the non-commutative generalization of the ring of integers in number fields). A maximal order is an order that is maximal with respect to inclusion.

The endomorphism ring of a supersingular elliptic curve over $\mathbb{F}_{p^2}$ is a maximal order in the quaternion algebra $B_{p,\infty}$, which ramifies at p and at ∞. Moreover, for every maximal order in $B_{p,\infty}$ there exists a supersingular elliptic curve whose endomorphism ring is isomorphic to it.

It is easy to see that, when $p \equiv 3 \pmod 4$, this quaternion algebra is isomorphic to the quaternion algebra $(-p, -1)$. In that case, the integral linear combinations of $1, i, \frac{ij+j}{2}, \frac{1+i}{2}$ form a maximal order $\mathcal{O}_0$ which corresponds to an isomorphism class of supersingular curves, namely the class of curves with j-invariant 1728 (e.g. the curve $E : y^2 = x^3 + x$). It is easy to see that all elements $ai + bj + cij + d$ with $a, b, c, d \in \mathbb{Z}$ are contained in $\mathcal{O}_0$.

2.2 Class Group Action on the Set of Supersingular Curves

We briefly recall the main definitions and properties related to the class group of quadratic imaginary orders and their link with supersingular elliptic curves. We say that a curve E admits an embedding of a quadratic imaginary order $\mathfrak{O}$, if there exists a subring of $\mathrm{End}(E)$ that is isomorphic to $\mathfrak{O}$. We say this embedding is *primitive* or *optimal* if this isomorphism cannot be extended to a super-order of $\mathfrak{O}$. We write $\mathcal{E}_{\mathfrak{O}}$ for the set of supersingular elliptic curves admitting a primitive embedding of $\mathfrak{O}$ (up to isomorphisms). Following [12], we also call a primitive embedding of $\mathfrak{O}$ in $\mathrm{End}(E)$ an $\mathfrak{O}$*-orientation* on E. Through the usual Deuring correspondence, $\mathfrak{O}$-ideals can be identified with isogenies. For any such ideal $\mathfrak{a}$, we write $\varphi_{\mathfrak{a}} : E \to \mathfrak{a} \star E$ for the corresponding isogeny. The property that $\mathfrak{a} \star E \cong \mathfrak{b} \star E$ when $\mathfrak{a}$ and $\mathfrak{b}$ are in the same ideal class proves that $\star$ defines a group action of the class group $\mathrm{Cl}(\mathfrak{O})$ on $\mathcal{E}_{\mathfrak{O}}$. The class number $h(\mathfrak{O})$ is the cardinality of $\mathrm{Cl}(\mathfrak{O})$. In full generality, we cannot say much more on $\#\mathcal{E}_{\mathfrak{O}}$ than the classical Proposition 2.1.

Proposition 2.1. *Let K be a quadratic imaginary field and let $\mathfrak{O}$ be a quadratic order inside K. When p does not split in K, the number of distinct embeddings of $\mathfrak{O}$ inside maximal orders of the quaternion algebra $\mathcal{B}_{p,\infty}$ is exactly* $\mathrm{Cl}(\mathfrak{O})$. *In particular, $\#\mathcal{E}_{\mathfrak{O}} \leq h(\mathfrak{O})$.*

In general, Proposition 2.1 does not help in estimating $\#\mathcal{E}_{\mathfrak{O}}$ precisely because we do not know how to estimate the number of different embeddings of $\mathfrak{O}$ into the same maximal order in $\mathcal{B}_{p,\infty}$. We provide examples of cases where more precise properties can be stated in Sects. 5.2 and 5.3.

When p splits in the field K, then $\mathcal{E}_{\mathfrak{O}}$ is empty (the curves admitting an $\mathfrak{O}$-orientation are ordinary). In the remaining of this article, we consider that we are never in this case to simplify the notations and statements.

Any quadratic order $\mathfrak{O}$ can be written as $\mathfrak{O} = \mathbb{Z} + f\mathfrak{O}_0$ where $\mathfrak{O}_0$ is another quadratic order (not necessarily distinct from $\mathfrak{O}$) and f is often called the conductor of $\mathfrak{O}$. When the conductor is one, we say that the quadratic order is *maximal*. In [29], it was shown that these conductors can be tied to isogenies.

Proposition 2.2. *Let $\mathfrak{O} = \mathbb{Z} + f\mathfrak{O}_0$ be a quadratic order and let E be a supersingular curve defined over $\mathbb{F}_{p^2}$. If E is in $\mathcal{E}_{\mathfrak{O}}$, then there exists an isogeny of degree f between E and a supersingular curve $E_0 \in \mathcal{E}_{\mathfrak{O}_0}$. Conversely, when there exists an isogeny of degree f between E and a supersingular curve $E_0 \in \mathcal{E}_{\mathfrak{O}_0}$, then E is in $\mathcal{E}_{\mathbb{Z}+f'\mathfrak{O}_0}$ for some f' dividing f.*

In Proposition 2.2, we say that the isogeny $\varphi : E_0 \to E$ of degree f is *descending* when $f' = f$. Let $\varphi : E_0 \to E$ be a descending isogeny of degree f, the embedding of $\mathfrak{O}$ in $\mathrm{End}(E)$ in Proposition 2.2 is obtained with endomorphisms of the form $[d] + \varphi \circ \alpha_0 \circ \hat{\varphi}$ with $d \in \mathbb{Z}$ and α_0 in the embedding of $\mathfrak{O}_0$ inside $\mathrm{End}(E_0)$. Similar endomorphisms are constructed in torsion point attacks against SIDH variants [27,33], and they underlie the decryption mechanism of the Séta encryption scheme.

2.3 SIDH and SIKE

Here we give a high level description of SIDH and SIKE. We start with the original SIDH protocol of Jao and De Feo [23]. In the setup one chooses two small primes ℓ_A, ℓ_B and a prime p of the form $p = \ell_A^{e_A}\ell_B^{e_B}f - 1$, where f is a small cofactor and e_A and e_B are large (in SIKE [2] they use $\ell_A^{e_A} = 2^{216}$, $\ell_B^{e_B} = 3^{137}$ and $f = 1$). Let E be a fixed supersingular curve, for example, assuming $p = 3 \bmod 4$, the elliptic curve with j-invariant 1728.[2] Let P_A, Q_A be a basis of $E[\ell_A^{e_A}]$ and let P_B, Q_B be a basis of $E[\ell_B^{e_B}]$. The protocol is as follows:

1. Alice chooses a random cyclic subgroup of $E[\ell_A^{e_A}]$ generated by $A = [x_A]P_A + [y_A]Q_A$ and Bob chooses a random cyclic subgroup of $E[\ell_B^{e_B}]$ generated by $B = [x_B]P_B + [y_B]Q_B$.
2. Alice computes the isogeny $\varphi_A : E \to E/\langle A\rangle$ and Bob computes the isogeny $\varphi_B : E \to E/\langle B\rangle$.
3. Alice sends the curve $E/\langle A\rangle$ and the points $\varphi_A(P_B)$ and $\varphi_A(Q_B)$ to Bob, and Bob similarly sends $(E/\langle B\rangle, \varphi_B(P_A), \varphi_B(Q_A))$ to Alice.
4. Alice and Bob both use the images of the torsion points to compute the shared secret which is the curve $E/\langle A, B\rangle$ (e.g. Alice can compute $\varphi_B(A) = [x_A]\varphi_B(P_A) + [y_A]\varphi_B(Q_A)$ and $E/\langle A, B\rangle = E_B/\langle\varphi_B(A)\rangle$).

This key exchange protocol also leads to a PKE scheme in the same way as the Diffie–Hellman key exchange leads to ElGamal encryption. Let Alice's private key be the isogeny $\varphi_A : E \to E/\langle A\rangle$ and her public key be the curve $E/\langle A\rangle$ together with the images of the torsion points $\varphi_A(P_B)$ and $\varphi_A(Q_B)$. Encryption and decryption work as follows:

---

[2] Jao and De Feo do not specify a particular curve, and recommend to pick one using Bröker's algorithm [8], however there appears to be no advantage in doing so, and thus SIKE opts for $j = 1728$ for simplicity.

1. To encrypt a bitstring m, Bob chooses a random subgroup generated by $B = [x_B]P_B + [y_B]Q_B$ and computes the corresponding isogeny $\varphi_B : E \to E/\langle B \rangle$. He computes the shared secret $E \to E/\langle A, B \rangle$ and hashes the j-invariant of $E/\langle A, B \rangle$ to a binary string s. The ciphertext corresponding to m is the tuple $(E/\langle B \rangle, \varphi_B(P_A), \varphi_B(Q_A), c := m \oplus s)$
2. In order to decrypt Bob's message, Alice computes $E/\langle A, B \rangle$ and from this information computes s. Then she retrieves the message by computing $c \oplus s$.

This PKE scheme is IND-CPA secure [2,23]. In the SIKE submission [2], it is transformed using the constructions in [22, Section 3] to produce an IND-CCA secure KEM in the random oracle model (ROM).

2.4 Trapdoor Curves

Let E_1, E_2 be supersingular elliptic curves over $\mathbb{F}_{p^2}$ and let $\phi : E_1 \to E_2$ be an isogeny of degree D. First we recall the following algorithmic problem:

Problem 2.3 (SSI-T). Let D and N be smooth coprime integers. Let $\phi : E_1 \to E_2$ be a secret isogeny of degree D. Assume that we know the action of ϕ on $E_1[N]$. Compute ϕ.

Remark 2.4. The SSI-T problem is a generalization of the CSSI introduced in [23] (Problem 5.6) where D and N are prime powers of the same size.

The SSI-T problem makes sense for any D, N which are coprime and sufficiently smooth. However, in many cases the size of the input is superlinear in p thus has no practical relevance. Thus from now on we restrict to instances where the D and N-torsion are efficiently representable:

Definition 2.5. *Let N be an integer and let p be a prime number. Let E be a supersingular elliptic curve defined over $\mathbb{F}_{p^2}$. We call $E[N]$ efficiently representable if representing points in $E[N]$ requires polynomial space in $\log p = O(\lambda)$.*

Remark 2.6. In particular $E[N]$ is efficiently representable whenever N is powersmooth or N divides $p^c - 1$ for some small c. In this paper we will mainly consider instances where N is smooth and divides $p^2 - 1$.

We recall (slightly modified version of) [17, Theorem 3] how finding a certain endomorphism of E_2 relates to finding the secret isogeny ϕ:

Theorem 2.7. *Let $\phi : E_1 \to E_2$ be a secret isogeny of degree D. Assume that $E[N]$ and $E[D]$ are efficiently representable for any supersingular curve E and that the action of ϕ on $E_1[N]$ is given. Suppose furthermore, that we know $\theta \in \mathrm{End}(E_1)$ and $d, e \in \mathbb{Z}$ such that the trace of θ is 0 and $\deg(\phi \circ \theta \circ \hat{\phi} + [d]) = N^2 e$. Let M be the largest divisor of D such that $E_2[M] \subset \ker(\phi \circ \theta \circ \hat{\phi}) \cap E_2[D]$. Let k be the number of distinct prime divisors of M. Then we can compute ϕ in time $O^*(2^k \sqrt{e})$.*

Proof. We sketch the proof of the theorem. Let $\tau = \phi \circ \theta \circ \hat{\phi} + [d]$. Then if $\ker(\tau)$ is cyclic, then $\tau = \psi' \circ \eta \circ \psi$ where $\deg(\psi) = \deg(\psi') = N$ and $\deg(\eta) = e$ and the kernels of ψ and ψ' are cyclic. In [17, Theorem 3] it is shown that $\ker(\tau)$ is always cyclic if N is odd and if N is even then $\tau = \psi' \circ \eta \circ \psi \circ [K]$ where $\deg(\psi) = \deg(\psi') = N/K$, $\deg(\eta) = e$ and $K = 1$ or $K = 2$.

Then one can compute ψ and K using the torsion point information and ψ' using the observation that $\ker(\hat{\psi}') = \tau(E_2[B])$. The isogeny η can be computed by a meet-in-the-middle algorithm. Once τ is computed, one can compute ϕ by looking at $G = \ker(\phi \circ \theta \circ \hat{\phi}) \cap E_2[D]$. If $M = 1$ then G is cyclic and can be recomputed easily. If not, then one can use [Sect. 4.3][33] to recover τ. The cost of this step is $O^*(2^k)$ where k is the number of prime factors of M.

Remark 2.8. Theorem 2.7 in particular implies that one can recover ϕ in $O^*(\sqrt{e})$ whenever the number of distinct prime divisors of D (and hence M) is smaller than $\log\log p$. In Sect. 3.3, we introduce a condition on the quadratic order $\mathbb{Z}[\theta]$ to ensure that M is always equal to 1.

The key ingredient to Theorem 2.7 is the knowledge of θ. When $M = 1$ (which will be the case for the concrete inversion procedure in Algorithm 1), all we really need is the action of θ on $E_1[N]$. Indeed, from the sketch of proof of Theorem 2.7, we see that in that case θ is only used to compute the kernel of the two isogenies ψ and ψ' of degree N. These kernels are computed by evaluating the N-torsion $\tau = \phi \circ \theta \circ \hat{\phi} + [d]$ which can be done with the action of θ and ϕ on $E_1[N]$.

Note the action of θ on $E_1[N]$ is hard to recover from E_1 only. This motivates a notion of (D, N)-trapdoor T to encompass any kind of information that enables the computation described in the proof of Theorem 2.7.

Definition 2.9. *Let p be a prime number and let D and N be coprime smooth integers. Then a tuple (E, T) is called a (D, N)-trapdoor curve if one can use T to solve any instance of the SSI-T problem (with parameters D, N, p) with starting curve E in polynomial time. We sometimes call T the trapdoor.*

In [17] the authors introduces a polynomial-time algorithm for constructing (D, N)-trapdoor curves whenever $N > D^2$ and the number of prime divisors of $D < \log\log p$. The main idea is to reproduce the set-up of Theorem 2.7. Thus, if one can construct a supersingular elliptic curve E together with an endomorphism $\theta \in \mathrm{End}(E)$ verifying the requirements of Theorem 2.7, and compute the action of this endomorphism θ on $E[N]$, then one can solve SSI-T in polynomial time (by finding an e which is sufficiently small).

The conditions put on θ in Theorem 2.7 are essentially conditions on the minimal polynomial of θ, meaning that every trace zero element in the quaternion algebra whose norm is $\frac{B^2 e - d^2}{A^2}$ can be used as a suitable θ. This implies that potential (D, N)-trapdoor curves are obtained from curves in $\mathcal{E}_{\mathfrak{O}}$ for quadratic order $\mathfrak{O}$ of the form $\mathbb{Z}\left(\sqrt{\frac{N^2 e - d^2}{D^2}}\right)$.

We briefly sketch how θ can be generated. Since $\mathrm{Tr}(\theta) = 0$, it can be written as $ci + bj + aij$ over $\mathcal{B}_{p,\infty}$. Then the degree of τ is $D^2(p^2a + p^2b + c^2) + d^2$. Observe that a, b, c can be rational numbers but since θ is an integral element its norm $p^2a^2 + p^2b^2 + c^2$ must be an integer. So one has to find d, e such that $N^2e - d^2$ is divisible by D^2 and is positive.

This can be achieved when $N > D^2$. Let $\Delta = N^2e - d^2$. Then one has to find a rational solution to the equation $p^2a^2 + p^2b^2 + c^2 = \Delta$, which exists whenever Δ is a quadratic residue modulo p (if that is not the case one chooses a different d and e). A solution can be found using Denis Simon's algorithm [36]. From there, we can find a maximal order $\mathcal{O}$ containing θ and then compute a supersingular elliptic curve whose endomorphism ring is isomorphic to $\mathcal{O}$ (see Algorithm 3 in Sect. 4.2). After that, the action of θ on the N-torsion can be found using an explicit representation of $\mathcal{O}$. All these operations can be done in polynomial time (see Algorithms 2 and 3 for more details), leading to the following theorem:

Theorem 2.10. *Let p be a prime number and let D and N be smooth coprime integers such that $N > D^2$ and the number of distinct prime divisors of D is smaller than $\log\log p$. Then there exists a polynomial-time algorithm which outputs a (D, N)-trapdoor curve E with the following information:*

- *The j-invariant of E.*
- *Integers d, e with $e = O(\log(p))$.*
- *A basis P, Q of $E[N]$ and the points $\theta(P), \theta(Q)$ for a trace 0 endomorphism θ such that $\deg([D]\theta + [d]) = N^2e$.*

3 Séta Trapdoor One Way Function and Public Key Encryption Scheme

In this section we describe a general trapdoor one-way function where the main idea is to turn the attacks from [17] into a trapdoor mechanism.

We first generalise the CGL hash function and we describe a trapdoor subfamily of this generalization. We then provide more details on key generation, evaluation and inversion. We finally describe the Séta public key encryption scheme and its CCA version.

3.1 Generalised Charles-Goren-Lauter Hash Function

We generalise the CGL hash function family introduced in [10]. To select a hash function from this family, one selects a j-invariant $j \in \mathcal{J}_p$ which canonically fixes a curve $E/\mathbb{F}_{p^2}$ with $j(E) = j$. There are $\ell + 1$ isogenies of degree ℓ connecting E to other vertices. These $\ell + 1$ vertices can be ordered in a canonical way and a canonical one of them can be ignored. Then, given a message $m = b_1 b_2 \ldots b_n$, with $b_i \in [\ell]$, hashing starts by choosing a degree-ℓ isogeny from E according to symbol b_1 to arrive at a first curve E_1. Not allowing backtracking, there are then only ℓ isogenies out of E_1 and one is chosen according to b_2 to arrive at a second curve E_2. Continuing in the same way, m determines a unique walk of length n. The output of the CGL hash function h_j is then the j-invariant of the final curve in the path, i.e. $h_j(m) := j(E_n)$, where the walk starts at vertex j and is defined as above. We see that starting at a different vertex j' results in a different hash function $h_{j'}$.

We modify this hash function family in three ways. First, we consider a generalisation where we do not ignore one of the $\ell+1$ isogenies from the starting curve E. That is, we take inputs $m = b_1 b_2 \dots b_n$ where $b_1 \in [\ell+1]$ and $b_i \in [\ell]$ for $2 \leq i \leq n$; this introduces a one-to-one correspondence between inputs and cyclic isogenies of degree ℓ^n originating from E.

Secondly, we consider a generalisation where the walk takes place over multiple graphs G_{ℓ_i}. Given an integer $D = \prod_{i=1}^n \ell_i^{e_i}$ where the ℓ_i are prime factors, we introduce the notation $\mu(D) := \prod_{i=1}^n (\ell_i + 1) \cdot \ell_i^{e_i - 1}$. We then take the message m to be an element of

$$[\mu(D)] = \left\{ (m_1, \dots, m_n) \,\middle|\, \begin{array}{l} m_i = b_{i1} b_{i2} \dots b_{ie_i}, b_{i1} \in [\ell_i + 1], b_{ij} \in [\ell_i] \\ \text{for } 2 \leq j \leq e_i, \text{ for } 1 \leq i \leq n \end{array} \right\}$$

where each m_i is hashed along the graph G_{ℓ_i}. To ensure continuity, the j-invariants are chained along the hash functions, that is, we write $j_i = h_{j_{i-1}}(m_i)$, where j_{i-1} is the hash of m_{i-1}. Thus, only $j = j_0$ parameterizes the overall hash function. As before, this generalization returns the final j-invariant $j_n = h_{j_{n-1}}(m_n)$ as the hash of m.

Thirdly, we also modify the CGL hash function to return the images of two canonically defined torsion points P_j and Q_j of order N under the D-isogeny $\varphi_m : E_j \to E_{j_n}$.

We call the resulting hash function family *generalized CGL* or G-CGL, and we denote it by $\mathcal{H}^{p,D,N}$, namely

$$\mathcal{H}^{p,D,N} = \left\{ h_j^{D,N} : m \mapsto (j(E_n), \varphi_m(P_j), \varphi_m(Q_j)) \mid j \in \mathcal{J}_p \right\}.$$

3.2 A Trapdoor Function Family from the G-CGL Family

Given p, D and N, let $\mathcal{J}_{T,p} \subset \mathcal{J}_p$ be the set of j-invariants of (D, N)-trapdoor curves defined over $\mathbb{F}_{p^2}$ (see Definition 2.9). By definition of a trapdoor curve, for any $j_T \in \mathcal{J}_{T,p}$, the hash function $h_{j_T}^{D,N}$ can be inverted using the trapdoor information. We hence obtain the following family of trapdoor functions:

$$\mathcal{F}_T^{p,D,N} = \left\{ f_{j_T}^{D,N} : m \mapsto (j(E_n), \varphi_m(P_{j_T}), \varphi_m(Q_{j_T})) \mid j_T \in \mathcal{J}_{T,p} \right\},$$

where $f_{j_T}^{D,N} := h_{j_T}^{D,N}$.

Injectivity. We observe that, for a proper choice of parameters, the functions are injective.

Lemma 3.1. *Let $N^2 > 4D$. Then for any $j_T \in \mathcal{J}_{T,p}$, $f_{j_T}^{D,N}$ is injective.*

Proof. Let $N^2 > 4D$ and $j_T \in \mathcal{J}_{T,p}$, suppose that a function $f_{j_T}^D$ is not injective, i.e. that there are two distinct isogenies φ and φ' of degree D from E_{j_T} to E_c, corresponding to two distinct messages, with the same action on $E_{j_T}[N]$, implied by the colliding images of P_{j_T} and Q_{j_T}. Then, following [30, Section 4], their difference is also an isogeny between the same curves whose kernel contains the entire N-torsion. This, together with [35, Lemma V.1.2], implies that $4D \geq \deg(\varphi - \varphi') \geq N^2$. Taking $N^2 > 4D$ ensures that in fact $\varphi = \varphi'$ and therefore that $f_{j_T}^{D,N}$ is injective. □

One-wayness. One-wayness of our function family relies on Problem 3.2 below. This problem is a variant of the CSSI problem introduced in [23], with the difference that the starting j-invariant is chosen at random from $\mathcal{J}_{T,p}$ (instead of being fixed) and only the min-entropy of the distribution is specified.

Problem 3.2 (Trapdoor computational supersingular isogeny (TCSSI) problem). Given p and integers D and N, let j_T be a uniformly random element of $\mathcal{J}_{T,p}$ and $\varphi_m : E_{j_T} \to E_m$ be a random isogeny of degree D sampled from a distribution X with min-entropy $H_\infty(X) = O(\lambda)$. Let $\{P_{j_T}, Q_{j_T}\}$ be a basis of the torsion group $E_{j_T}[N]$. Given $E_{j_T}, P_{j_T}, Q_{j_T}, E_m, \varphi_m(P_{j_T})$ and $\varphi_m(Q_{j_T})$, compute φ_m.

Lemma 3.3. *Let j_T be a uniformly random element of $\mathcal{J}_{T,p}$. Then the function $f_{j_T}^{D,N} \in \mathcal{F}_T^{p,D,N}$ is (quantum) one-way under the (quantum) hardness of Problem 3.2.*

Proof. It is easy to check that the distribution of isogenies resulting from hashing a uniform $m^* \xleftarrow{\$} [\mu(D)]$ has the required entropy; hence the reduction is immediate. □

3.3 Inversion

In this section, we concretely show how to use methods from [17] to invert a given function $f_{j_T}^{D,N} \in \mathcal{F}_T^{p,D,N}$ with trapdoor information T. We assume that D is odd and that $\gcd(D, N) = 1$. We take E_{j_T} a supersingular curve inside $\mathcal{E}_{\mathfrak{O}}$ where $\mathfrak{O}$ is the quadratic order $\mathbb{Z}[\sqrt{(N^2e - d^2)/D^2}]$ for some integers d, e. We write θ for the endomorphism of $\mathrm{End}(E_{j_T})$ such that $\mathbb{Z}[\theta] \cong \mathfrak{O}$. Let us also take a basis P_{j_T}, Q_{j_T} of $E_{j_T}[N]$. If we define T as $e, d, P_{J_T}, Q_{j_T}, \theta(P_{j_T}), \theta(Q_{j_T})$, then E_{j_T}, T is a (D, N)-trapdoor curve as produced in Theorem 2.10.

To make the inversion mechanism efficient on all inputs, we require the additional condition that the discriminant Δ of $\mathfrak{O}$ is a quadratic nonresidue modulo every prime divisor of D. The concrete statement can be found in Lemma 3.4. We explain how to generate $E_{j,T}$, $\mathfrak{O}$ and T in Sects. 4.1 and 4.2. We are given (j_m, P_m, Q_m) as the output of $f_{j_T}^{D,N}$ for some input m, which we want to recover. Let the isogeny corresponding to m be denoted by ϕ_m. We assume that $P_m = \phi_m(P_{j_T})$ and $Q_m = \phi_m(Q_{j_T})$. Let $\tau := \phi_m \circ \theta \circ \hat{\phi}_m + [d]$ and let $G := \ker(\tau - [d]) \cap E_m[D]$.

Algorithm 1 Computing inverses

Require: $j_T \in \mathcal{J}_{T,p}$, a trapdoor T and c.

Ensure: $m \in [\mu(D)]$ such that $f_{j_T}^{D,N}(m) = \mathsf{c}$.

1: Parse c as $(j_m, P_m, Q_m) \in \mathbb{F}_{p^2} \times (\overline{\mathbb{F}_{p^2}})^2 \times (\overline{\mathbb{F}_{p^2}})^2$.
2: Parse T as $e, d, P_{J_T}, Q_{j_T}, \theta(P_{j_T}), \theta(Q_{j_T})$.
3: Compute the canonical curve E_m having j-invariant j_m.
4: Let $\tau = \phi_m \circ \theta \circ \hat{\phi}_m + [d] \in \mathrm{End}(E_m)$. ▷ Choices of θ and d ensure $\deg \tau = N^2 e$.
5: Compute τ as described in the proof of Theorem 2.7.
6: Compute $\ker(\phi_m \circ \theta \circ \hat{\phi}_m) \cap E_m[D] = \ker(\tau - [d]) \cap E_m[D] = \ker(\hat{\phi}_m)$.
7: Compute $\ker(\phi_m)$ using $\ker(\hat{\phi}_m)$.
8: **return** $m \in [\mu(D)]$ that corresponds to $\ker(\phi_m)$.

Lemma 3.4. *If* $\Delta = \mathrm{Disc}\,\mathfrak{O}$ *is a non-quadratic residue, the group* G *is cyclic and equal to* $\ker(\hat{\phi})$.

Proof. It is clear that $\ker(\hat{\phi}_m) \subset G$ since it is contained in $\ker(\phi_m \circ \theta \circ \hat{\phi}_m)$ and in $E_m[D]$ as well. We now show that G is cyclic. Let M be the largest divisor of D such that $E_m[M] \subset G$. Then ϕ_m can be decomposed as $\phi_{D/M} \circ \phi_M$. Then by [33, Lemma 5] the kernel of ϕ_M is fixed by θ. In the proof of [33, Lemma 6] it is shown that a subgroup of $E_{j_T}[M]$ can only be fixed by an endomorphism θ if $\mathrm{Tr}(\theta)^2 - 4\deg(\theta) = \mathrm{Disc}\,\mathbb{Z}[\theta] = \Delta$ is a square modulo M. Thus, the quadratic residuosity condition on Δ ensures that $M = 1$ which implies that G is cyclic. The order of G is a divisor of D since G is cyclic and every element of G has order dividing D. However, G contains $\ker(\hat{\phi}_m)$ which is a group of order D. This implies that $G = \ker(\hat{\phi}_m)$. □

The group $G = \ker(\hat{\phi})$ can be computed by solving a double discrete logarithm problem, which is efficient as D is smooth. We summarize the steps needed for inverting the one-way function in Algorithm 1.

In [17] it is shown that Algorithm 1 runs in polynomial time whenever $E_m[D]$ is efficiently representable and $\Delta = \mathrm{Disc}\,\mathbb{Z}[\theta]$ is as in Lemma 3.4.

3.4 Séta Public Key Encryption

We now build Séta, a Public Key Encryption scheme using the trapdoor one-way function family of Sect. 3.2, and we show that it is OW-CPA secure. Concretely, we define the Séta PKE scheme as the tuple $(\mathsf{KGen}, \mathsf{Enc}, \mathsf{Dec})$ of PPT algorithms described below.

Parameters. Let λ denote the security parameter. Let p be a prime such that $p^2 - 1 = DNf$ where D, N are smooth integers and f is a small co-factor such that $2^{2\lambda} < D$, $D^2 < N$. We let $\mathsf{params} = (\lambda, p, D, N)$.

Key generation. The $\mathsf{KGen}(\mathsf{params})$ algorithm proceeds as follows:

1. Compute a uniformly random (D, N)-trapdoor supersingular elliptic curve (E_{j_T}, T) defined over $\mathbb{F}_{p^2}$ using Algorithms 2 and 3 (see Sect. 4).
2. Set $\mathsf{pk} := (j_T)$ and $\mathsf{sk} := T$.
3. Return $(\mathsf{pk}, \mathsf{sk})$.

Encryption. The $\mathsf{Enc}(\mathsf{params}, \mathsf{pk}, m)$ algorithm proceeds as follows. For a given $m \in \{0,1\}^{n_m}$, where $n_m = \lfloor \log_2 \mu(D) \rfloor$, first cast m as an integer in the set $[\mu(D)]$ and then:

1. Parse $\mathsf{pk} = j_T \in \mathcal{J}_{T,p}$.
2. Compute $(j_m, P_m, Q_m) \leftarrow f_{j_T}^{D,N}(m)$.
3. Return $\mathsf{c} = (j_m, P_m, Q_m)$.

Decryption. The $\mathsf{Dec}(\mathsf{params}, \mathsf{pk}, \mathsf{sk}, \mathsf{c})$ algorithm proceeds as follows:

1. Given $\mathsf{params}, \mathsf{sk}$ and c, parse c as $(j_c, P_c, Q_c) \in \mathbb{F}_{p^2} \times (\overline{\mathbb{F}_{p^2}})^2 \times (\overline{\mathbb{F}_{p^2}})^2$; if that fails, return $\perp$.
2. Follow Algorithm 1 to recover $\tilde{m} \in [\mu(D)]$; if this fails, set $\tilde{m} = \perp$.
3. If $\perp$ was recovered, return $\perp$.
4. Otherwise, from $\tilde{m} \in [\mu(D)]$, recover $m \in \{0,1\}^{n_m}$ and return it.

Theorem 3.5. *Let p be a prime, let D and N be integers such that $D^2 < N$. Suppose that the output distribution of Algorithm 3 is statistically close to uniform. Let E_{j_T} be an output of Algorithm 3. If Problem 3.2 with p, D, N, E_{j_T} and X such that $H_\infty(X) = \lambda$ is hard for quantum PPT adversaries, then the PKE scheme above is quantum one-way chosen-plaintext attack (OW-CPA) secure.*

Proof. Let $\mathcal{M} = \{0,1\}^{n_m}$ denote the message space of the encryption scheme, with $n_m = O(\lambda)$. We see that a randomly sampled $m \xleftarrow{\$} \mathcal{M}$ directly embedded as an integer $m \in [\mu(D)]$ yields a distribution Y with min-entropy $H_\infty(Y) \geq \lambda$ on isogenies of degree D starting from E_{j_T}. The challenge of opening a given ciphertext c then reduces to recovering the secret isogeny of Problem 3.2 with $X = Y$. □

3.5 IND-CCA Encryption Scheme

We obtain an IND-CCA secure PKE scheme by applying the generic post-quantum OAEP transformation [38, Section 5] (see Appendix A) to Séta, for which we prove that our function $f_{j_T}^{D,N}$ is quantum partial-domain one-way.

Definition 3.6. *Let k_1, k_0 and n_c be integers. A family $\mathcal{F}$ of functions $f : \{0,1\}^{\lambda+k_1} \times \{0,1\}^{k_2} \to \{0,1\}^{n_c}$ is* partial domain one-way *if for any polynomial time adversary $\mathcal{A}$, the following advantage is negligible in λ:*

$$\mathrm{Adv}_\lambda(\mathcal{A}) = \Pr\left[s' = s; s' \leftarrow \mathcal{A}(1^\lambda, y), y \leftarrow f(s,t), (s,t) \xleftarrow{\$} A \times B, f \leftarrow \mathcal{F}\right]$$

Lemma 3.7. *Let j_T be a uniformly random element of $\mathcal{J}_{T,p}$. The function $f_{j_T}^{D,N}$ defined in Sect. 3.2 is a quantum partial-domain one-way function, under the hardness of Problem 3.2.*

Proof. We note that in our case, partial domain inversion is the same as domain inversion where only the first part of the path is required. More precisely, factor D as $D_1 \cdot D_2$ such that $\gcd(D_1, D_2) = 1$, $2^{\lambda+k_1} \leq \mu(D_1)$ and $2^{k_0} \leq \mu(D_2)$ (where $\lambda + k_0 + k_1$ is the bit-length of input strings) and then embed each of s and t into $\mu(D_1)$ and $\mu(D_2)$ respectively. Then we can set $f_{j_T}^{D,N}(s,t) := f_{j_1}^{D_2,N}(t)$ where $(j_1, P_1, Q_1) = f_{j_T}^{D_1,N}(s)$ and $f_{j_1}^{D_2,N}$ uses $\{P_1, Q_1\}$ as basis of $E_{j_1}[N]$. Since $2^{\lambda+k_1} \leq \mu(D_1)$, then recovering s from $y = f_{j_T}^{D,N}(s,t)$ is hard under the same assumption as Theorem 3.5 with D replaced by D_1. □

Theorem 3.8 (**[38], Theorem 2**)**.** *If $f_{j_T}^{D,N}$ is a quantum partial-domain one-way function, then the OAEP-transformed scheme is IND-CCA secure in the quantum random oracle model (QROM).*

4 Key Generation Variants

In this section we describe various methods for generating keys for Séta. We first describe Algorithm 2, which can generate integers d, e so that $\Delta = \operatorname{Disc} \mathfrak{O}$, where $\mathfrak{O} = \mathbb{Z}[\sqrt{(N^2e - d^2)/D^2}]$, satisfies the quadratic residuosity conditions imposed Sect. 3.3. Then, we present two options for generating a uniformly random supersingular elliptic curve inside $\mathcal{E}_{\mathfrak{O}}$ together with the remaining part of the trapdoor information T. Algorithm 3 treats the generic case, and Algorithm 4 focuses on computing a (DD_s, N)-trapdoor curve from a (D, N)-trapdoor curve and a random walk of degree D_s.

4.1 Computing the Trapdoor Information

We recall that the required condition is that $\Delta = \operatorname{Disc} \mathfrak{O} = -4\frac{N^2e-d^2}{D^2}$ must be negative and a quadratic non-residue modulo every prime dividing D and also modulo p. For simplicity, we fix $e = 1$ and look for d of a special form. This is described in Algorithm 2.

Lemma 4.1. *If d, e is the output of Algorithm 2, then $\frac{N^2e-d^2}{D^2}$ is a quadratic non-residue modulo all ℓ_i.*

Proof. Let r_i, s_{ℓ_i}, T and u be as in Algorithm 2. Let r be an integer such that $r \equiv r_i \pmod{\ell_i}$. Then we show that for every i, the integer $\frac{-N^2e+(D^2r+u)^2}{D^2}$ is not a quadratic residue modulo ℓ_i which implies that $-\frac{N^2e-d^2}{D^2}$ is not a quadratic residue modulo every ℓ_i since $T\ell + r \equiv r_i \pmod{\ell_i}$ for every integer ℓ. We have that

$$\frac{-N^2e + (D^2r + u)^2}{D^2} = \frac{-N^2e + u^2}{D^2} + D^2r^2 + 2ur.$$

Algorithm 2 Computing the integers d, e

Require: D, N, p as above. Let S be the product of primes dividing D.
Ensure: (d, e) such that $-\frac{N^2e-d^2}{D^2} < 0$ is a quadratic non-residue modulo every prime dividing D and is a quadratic non-residue modulo p.

```
1: Set e = 1.
2: Find u such that u^2 ≡ N^2 e (mod D^2).
3: for every prime ℓ_i dividing D do
4:     Let s_{ℓ_i} be a quadratic non-residue modulo ℓ_i.
5:     r_i ← (s_{ℓ_i} − (−N^2 e + u^2)/D^2)(2u)^{−1} (mod ℓ_i).
6: Compute a residue r modulo S with the property that r ≡ r_i (mod ℓ_i).
7: ℓ ← 0.
8: d ← D^2(Sℓ + r) + u.
9: A ← (N^2 e − d^2)/D^2.
10: if A < 0 then
11:     return ⊥
12: if A is not a square modulo p then
13:     ℓ ← ℓ + 1.
14:     go to Step 8.
15: return (d, e)
```

By our choice of r we have that

$$\frac{-N^2e+u^2}{D^2} + D^2r^2 + 2ur \equiv \frac{-N^2e+u^2}{D^2} + 2ur_i \equiv s_{\ell_i} \pmod{\ell_i},$$

which is a quadratic nonresidue by the choice of s_{ℓ_i}. □

Lemma 4.2. *Let S be the product of all primes dividing D. If $N > D^2S$, then Algorithm 2 returns a correct pair (d, e) with probability higher than $1-2^{-\frac{N}{SD^2}+1}$ under plausible heuristic assumption.*

Proof. Since u is found by solving an equation modulo D^2, we obtain $u < D^2$. Similarly we have $r < S$. Under plausible heuristic assumptions, we can estimate to $1/2$ the probability that the quadratic reduosity condition on A is satisfied. Thus, we obtain a bound on the failure probability by counting how many values ℓ can be tried before A becomes negative. With the conservative bound that $D^2r + u \approx D^2S$, we obtain that we can try $\frac{N-D^2S}{DS^2}$ different values for small d, which gives the result.

Correctness of the result follows from Lemma 4.1.

4.2 Trapdoor Curve Generation

Now we focus on generating a random supersingular elliptic curve whose endomorphism ring contains an embedding of $\mathfrak{O} = \mathbb{Z}[\sqrt{(N^2e - d^2)/D^2}$ for d, e outputs of Algorithm 2. In [17, Section 5.1] it is discussed how one can generate a specific curve inside $\mathcal{E}_{\mathfrak{O}}$. Essentially, this is achieved by computing a maximal order $\mathcal{O}$ containing the suborder $\mathfrak{O}$ (with [40, Algorithm 7.9]) and then computing a supersingular elliptic curve whose endomorphism ring is isomorphic to $\mathfrak{O}$ (with [18, Algorithm 12]). This procedure can be made concretely efficient with the algorithms from [16] under some conditions on the prime p that partly underlie the choice of prime described in Sect. 6.2. However, this procedure is essentially deterministic, so an adversary knowing the quadratic order $\mathfrak{O}$ can just recompute the same trapdoor curve. The point of this subsection is to show how to randomize the procedure.

We obtain randomization by first generating a curve with the deterministic procedure and then applying the action of a random class group element to derive another random curve with the same embedding. This operation would be costly if it required to compute a lot of isogenies. However, we can do it over the quaternions at a negligible cost before applying the translation algorithm from maximal orders to elliptic curves.

For concrete randomization, we use the fact (see [24]) that there exists a bound B (polynomial in p) for which the graph whose vertices are curves in $\mathcal{E}_{\mathfrak{O}}$ and edges are isogenies of prime degree smaller than B is an expander graph. The fast mixing property of expander graphs implies that the distribution of curves obtained after a random walk of fixed length quickly converges to the uniform distribution as the length of the walk grows. More precisely, for any δ we can find a length ε (logarithmic in the size of the graph and δ) for which the statistical distance between the random walk distribution and the uniform distribution is less than δ. So once the length ε (corresponding to a sufficiently small δ) has been set, for any starting curve E_0 in $\mathcal{E}_{\mathfrak{O}}$ the curve $\prod_{i=1}^{n} \mathfrak{l}_i^{\varepsilon_i} \star E_0$ where $\mathfrak{l}_1, \ldots, \mathfrak{l}_n$ are prime ideals above the n prime $\ell_1, \ldots, \ell_n$ smaller than B that are split in $\mathfrak{O}$ and $(\varepsilon_1, \ldots, \varepsilon_n)$ is uniformly random among the vectors in $\mathbb{Z}^n$ such that $\sum_{i=1}^{n} |\varepsilon_i| = \varepsilon$, is statistically close to a uniformly random element in $\mathcal{E}_{\mathfrak{O}}$. This result underlies Algorithm 3.

Proposition 4.3. *Algorithm 3 is correct and terminates in polynomial time.*

Proof. All the sub-algorithms run in polynomial-time and by choice of B and ε, the number of iterations in the loop is also polynomial.

It is easy to verify that the ideal I corresponds through the Deuring correspondence to the isogeny $\varphi_{\mathfrak{l}_i}$. Thus, our method simulates a random walk over the graph that we described at the beginning of this section. For the reasons explained there, the curve E_{j_T} obtained in the end is statistically close to a random element in $\mathcal{E}_{\mathfrak{O}}$. □

Algorithm 3 Generating the trapdoor curve from a quadratic order $\mathfrak{O}$

Require: A prime p, an integer N, a quadratic order $\mathfrak{O}$, a bound B, a length ε.

Ensure: A uniformly random curve $E_{j_T} \in \mathcal{E}_{\mathfrak{O}}$, a basis P_{j_T}, Q_{j_T} of $E_{j_T}[N]$, and $\theta(P_{j_T}), \theta(Q_{j_T})$ with $\theta \in \mathrm{End}(E_{j_T})$ such that $\mathbb{Z}[\theta] \cong \mathfrak{O}$.

1: Find a max. order $\mathcal{O} \subset \mathcal{B}_{p,\infty}$ with $\mathfrak{O}$ embedded in $\mathcal{O}$ with the alg. from [17].
2: Compute $\ell_1, \ldots, \ell_n$ the n primes split in $\mathfrak{O}$ smaller than B.
3: Select a random vector $(\varepsilon_1, \ldots, \varepsilon_n)$ in $\mathbb{Z}^n$ with L_1 norm equal to ε.
4: Set $\mathcal{O}_{j_T} = \mathcal{O}$.
5: **for** $1 \le i \le n$ **do**
6:     Compute $\alpha_i \in \mathfrak{O}$ such that $\mathfrak{l}_i = \mathfrak{O}\langle \alpha_i, \ell_i \rangle$ is a prime ideal above ℓ_i.
7:     **for** $1 \le j \le |\varepsilon_i|$ **do**
8:         Compute the ideal $I = \mathcal{O}_{j_T}\langle \alpha_i, \ell_i \rangle$.
9:         Set $\mathcal{O}_{j_T}$ as the right order of I.
10: Compute the curve E_{j_T} from $\mathfrak{O}_{j_T}$ with [18, Algorithm 12].
11: Compute a canonical basis P_{j_T}, Q_{j_T} of $E_{j_T}[N]$.
12: Select the correct element $\theta \in \mathcal{O}_{j_T}$ such that $\mathfrak{O} \cong \mathbb{Z}[\theta]$.
13: Use the representation of $\mathcal{O}_{j_T}$ obtained from the execution of [18, Algorithm 12] to compute $\theta(P_{j_T}), \theta(Q_{j_T})$.
14: **return** $E_{j_T}, P_{j_T}, Q_{j_T}$ of $E_{j_T}[N], \theta(P_{j_T}), \theta(Q_{j_T})$.

4.3 Constraints on the Prime

In Séta, we compute and evaluate isogenies of degree D and N. Hence we always require that D and N are smooth and that the DN-torsion groups are efficiently representable, i.e., that they are defined on extensions of $\mathbb{F}_{p^2}$ of small degree. For example, if we require that $E[DN] \subset E(\mathbb{F}_{p^4})$, then DN must divide $p^2 - 1$. The smoothness bound B_1 of D impacts the efficiency of encryption and the smoothness bound B_2 of N impacts the efficiency of decryption. For a given security level λ, we require $2^{2\lambda} < D$ in order to protect the scheme against the meet-in-middle attack.

Since we have the range $D^2 < D^2 S < D^3$ depending on the value of S (product of primes dividing D), and that Lemma 4.2 implies that $N > D^2 S$ then we can estimate that the value DN will be between $2^{6\lambda}$ and $2^{8\lambda}$. If we want DN dividing $p^2 - 1$, we can estimate that the minimum size for the prime p will be between 3λ and 4λ bits. The actual size will depend on the size of $(p^2 - 1)/DN$.

Besides encryption and decryption, key generation also restricts the types of primes to be used in Séta. Indeed, Step 10 and Step 13 of Algorithm 3 use [18, Algorithm 12], which in turn uses the KLTP Algorithm [26]. Although this algorithm runs in polynomial time, it is not practical in general; the variant introduced in [16] achieves much greater efficiency, provided that $p^2 - 1$ is of the form $p^2 - 1 = l^f N_2 f_2$, where ℓ is a small prime, $N_2 > p^{3/2}$ is a smooth integer co-prime to ℓ and f_2 is a cofactor. We refer to [16, §8] for more details; a concrete method to select Séta-friendly primes is described in Sect. 6.2.

Algorithm 4 Computing a (D, N)-trapdoor curve from a (D_sD, N)-trapdoor curve where $D_s \approx 2^{2\lambda}$ is a smooth integer

Require: a (D_sD, N)-trapdoor curve (E_{j_T}, T) where $T = (\theta(P_{j_T}), \theta(Q_{j_T}), d, e)$.
Ensure: a (D, N)-trapdoor curve (E_s, T').
1: Sample a uniformly random isogeny $\phi_s : E_{\theta,j} \to E_s$ of degree D_s .
2: Compute $T' = (\theta'(P_s), \theta'(Q_s), d, e)$ where $\theta' = \phi_s \circ \theta \circ \widehat{\phi_s}$ and $\{P_s, Q_s\}$ is a canonical basis of $E_s[N]$..
3: **return** (E_s, T')

4.4 Alternative Key Generation

We describe an alternative method for computing trapdoor curves and suggest a variant of the key generation algorithm for Séta. The main idea is to perform a random secret walk from a publicly available trapdoor curve. The method relies on the following proposition.

Proposition 4.4. *Let p be a prime, let D_s, D and N be three smooth integers. Let (E_{j_T}, T) where $T = (\theta(P_{j_T}), \theta(Q_{j_T}), d, e)$ be a (D_sD, N)-trapdoor curve. Let $\phi_s : E_{j_T} \to E_s$ be an isogeny of degree D_s. Set $T' = (\theta'(P_s), \theta'(Q_s), d, e)$ where $\theta' = \phi_s \circ \theta \circ \widehat{\phi_s}$ and $\{P_s, Q_s\}$ is a canonical basis of $E_s[N]$. Then (E_s, T') is a (D, N)-trapdoor curve.*

Proof. Since we know the action of θ on the torsion group $E_{j_T}[N]$ and ϕ_s, then we can efficiently evaluate $\theta' = \phi_s \circ \theta \circ \widehat{\phi_s}$ on $E_s[N]$. Since (E_{j_T}, T) is a (D_sD, N)-trapdoor curve, then $\mathrm{Tr}(\theta) = 0$ and $\widehat{\theta} = -\theta$. Hence

$$\mathrm{Tr}(\theta') = \phi_s \circ \theta \circ \widehat{\phi_s} + \widehat{\phi_s \circ \theta \circ \widehat{\phi_s}} = \phi_s \circ \theta \circ \widehat{\phi_s} - \phi_s \circ \theta \circ \widehat{\phi_s} = 0.$$

It follows that

$$\deg([D]\theta' + [d]) = D^2 \deg(\theta') + d^2 = D^2 D_s^2 \deg(\theta) + d^2 = N^2 e.$$

By Theorem 2.10, (E_s, T') is a (D, N)-trapdoor curve. □

Relying on Proposition 4.4, Algorithm 4 computes (D, N)-trapdoor curves when given a (D_sD, N)-trapdoor curve.

Lemma 4.5. *Algorithm 4 is correct and runs in polynomial time.*

Proof. The correctness of Algorithm 4 follows from Proposition 4.4. Step 1 of Algorithm 4 consists of a degree D_s isogeny computation. Since D_s is smooth, then Step 1 runs in polynomial time. Step 2 consists of an evaluation of $\phi_s \circ \theta \circ \widehat{\phi_s}$ on P_s and Q_s. One evaluate $\widehat{\phi_s}(P_s)$ and express it as a linear combination of P_{j_T} and Q_j to recover $\theta\left(\widehat{\phi_s}(P_s)\right)$, then on evaluates $\phi_s\left(\theta\left(\widehat{\phi_s}(P_s)\right)\right)$. Similarly, one evaluates $\phi_s\left(\theta\left(\widehat{\phi_s}(Q_s)\right)\right)$. All these steps run in polynomial time since D_s and N are smooth integers.

A variant of the Séta setup and key generation is described as follows.

Parameters. Let λ denote the security parameter. Let p be a prime such that $p^2 - 1 = D_s D N f$ where D_s, D, N are smooth integers and f is a small co-factor such that $2^{2\lambda} < D \approx D_s$, $D_s^2 D^2 < N$. Compute a $(D_s D, N)$-trapdoor curve (E_{j_T}, T) using Algorithm 3. We let $\mathsf{params} = (\lambda, p, D_s, D, N, E_{j_T}, T)$.

Key generation. The $\mathsf{KGen}(\mathsf{params})$ algorithm proceeds as follows:

1. Compute a random (D, N)-trapdoor curve (E_s, T') using Algorithm 4 with (E_{j_T}, T) as input.
2. Set $\mathsf{pk} := (j_s)$ and $\mathsf{sk} := T'$.
3. Return $(\mathsf{pk}, \mathsf{sk})$.

The advantage of this variant is the fact the key generation algorithm does not use Algorithm 3, hence most of the requirements on p enumerated in Sect. 4.3 can be relaxed. This implies having more freedom in the choice of D and N, for which we could opt for powers of very small primes. Mostly, less good SQISign primes would be admissible for this variant, which is not the case in the original Séta described in Sect. 3.4, since its key generation uses Algorithm 3 which requires good Séta primes in order to be practically efficient. This variant is hence a good alternative to the Séta key generation, given the fruitless search of good cryptographic size SQI-Sign primes.

On the other hand, using less good SQISign primes implies that generating the $(D_s D, N)$-trapdoor curve (E_{j_T}, T) in the parameters generation is less efficient. But since this parameter generation is run once and for all, then this does not constitute a considerable drawback.

The main drawback of this key generation method is the considerably large size of the base prime p. In fact, p needs to satisfy $p^2 - 1 = D_s D N f$ where f is a small co-factor, and $D_s \approx D \approx 2^{2\lambda}$ such that attacking the isogeny $\phi_s : E_{j_T} \to E_s$ or $\phi_m : E_s \to E_m$ are equivalent with respect to the meet in the middle attack. Considering the fact that $N > (D_s D)^2$, then $N > 2^{8\lambda}$ and $2^{12\lambda} < D_s D N \leq p^2 - 1$, as opposed to $2^{6\lambda} < ND < p^2 - 1$ in Séta (see Sect. 4.3). It follows that the bit size of $p^2 - 1$ practically doubles when we use Algorithm 4 for key generation.

5 "Uber" Isogeny Assumption

In this section, we introduce a generic framework, which we label *Uber Isogeny assumption* in analogy to [7], aiming at generalizing isogeny computation problems encountered in the main families of isogeny-based schemes such as SIDH [23], CSIDH [9], OSIDH [12] and Séta (presented in this work).

The uber isogeny problem does not directly underlie the security of these various schemes (in the sense that no formal reduction is yet known). However, for each of these protocols there exists a set of parameters for which if one can solve the uber isogeny problem, then one can break the scheme. At a higher-level, our new problem can be seen as a generic key recovery problem.

By introducing this new assumption our goal is twofold. First, we highlight the proximity between the various isogeny schemes and we provide a common target for cryptanalysis. Second, the generic attack that we describe in Sect. 5.3 gives a lower-bound on the security of any future scheme whose security may be related to our uber assumption in a similar manner as SIDH, CSIDH, OSIDH and Séta.

5.1 The New Generic Problem

The principal mathematical structure behind the uber isogeny problem is the group action at the heart of the CSIDH protocol and all the following works. In the isogeny setting, these group actions emerge through class groups of quadratic orders. The main definitions and properties were introduced in Sect. 2.2.

Problem 5.1 ($\mathfrak{O}$-Uber Isogeny Problem ($\mathfrak{O} - UIP$)). Let $p > 3$ be a prime and let $\mathfrak{O}$ be a quadratic order of discriminant Δ. Given $E_0, E_s \in \mathcal{E}_{\mathfrak{O}}$ and an explicit embedding of $\mathfrak{O}$ into $\mathrm{End}(E_0)$ (i.e. the knowledge of $\alpha_0 \in \mathrm{End}(E_0)$ such that $\mathbb{Z}[\alpha_0] \cong \mathfrak{O}$), find a powersmooth ideal $\mathfrak{a}$ of norm coprime with Δ such that $[\mathfrak{a}] \in \mathrm{Cl}(\mathfrak{O})$ is such that $E_s \cong \mathfrak{a} * E_0$.

Remark 5.2. In Problem 5.1, the powersmoothness condition on the norm is to ensure that the resulting isogeny can always be computed in polynomial time. In some special cases where the form of the prime p enables to compute some smooth isogenies in polynomial time, this condition might be relaxed a little bit.

5.2 Relation with Various Isogeny-Based Constructions

We start with the link with CSIDH [9] which is quite obvious. We state the CSIDH key recovery problem below [9, Problem 10].

Problem 5.3. Given two supersingular elliptic curves E, E_0 defined over F_p with the same F_p-rational endomorphism ring $\mathfrak{O}$, find an ideal $\mathfrak{a}$ of $\mathfrak{O}$ such that $[\mathfrak{a}] \star E = E_0$. This ideal must be represented in such a way that the action of $\mathfrak{a}$ on any curve can be evaluated efficiently, for instance a could be given as a product of ideals of small norm.

Proposition 5.4. *When $p = 3 \bmod 4$ and $\Delta = -4p$, Problem 5.1 is equivalent to the CSIDH key recovery Problem 5.3.*

Proof. In the case of CSIDH, the curves admitting an embedding of $\mathbb{Z}[\sqrt{-p}] \cong \mathbb{Z}[\pi]$ in their endomorphism rings are the curves defined over $\mathbb{F}_p$ (i.e. left stable by π the Frobenius morphism). Then, it is quite clear that Problem 5.1 is equivalent to Problem 5.3.

The OSIDH protocol [12] is a generalization of CSIDH where $\mathbb{Z}[\pi]$ is replaced by a larger class of quadratic orders. The link between OSIDH and Problem 5.1 is also straightforward. Let us fix some notations[3] for this protocol and briefly

[3] These notations do not exactly agree with the ones introduced in [12] because we want to hightlight the link with our $\mathfrak{O}$-IOP.

recall the principle. The OSIDH key exchange protocol starts from a descending chain of ℓ-isogenies of size n that we write $\varphi_0 : F_0 \to E_0$ where F_0 admits a $\mathfrak{O}_0$-orientation (i.e. an embedding of $\mathfrak{O}_0$ inside $\text{End}(E_0)$. From there, φ_0 induces an $\mathfrak{O}$-orientation on E_0. The secret keys of Alice and Bob are $\mathfrak{O}$-ideals $\mathfrak{a}, \mathfrak{b}$ whose action on E_0 will lead to curves $E_A = \mathfrak{a} * E_0$ and $E_B = \mathfrak{b} * E_0$. These curves have also a $\mathfrak{O}$-orientation which implies the existence of ℓ^n-isogenies $\varphi_A : F_0 \to E_A$ and $\varphi_B : F_0 \to E_B$ as in Proposition 2.2. Alice public key will be E_A together with some torsion points (which will allow Bob to compute $\mathfrak{b} \star E_A$).

Proposition 5.5. *When $\mathfrak{O}_0$ is a quadratic order of class number* 1 *and $\mathfrak{O} = \mathbb{Z} + \ell^n \mathfrak{O}_0$, then if there exists a PPT algorithm that can break Problem 5.1, there is a PPT algorithm that can recover the keys of the OSIDH protocol presented in [12].*

Proof. From the definition of the group action of $\text{Cl}(\mathfrak{O})$ on the curves having an $\mathfrak{O}$-orientation (see [12]), finding a smooth ideal $\mathfrak{c}$ such that $E_A = \mathfrak{c} * E_0$ is enough to recover the secret key.

Note that we do not have equivalence in Proposition 5.5 because the OSIDH public keys include more information than just curves. This will be the same for SIDH and Proposition 5.7.

For SIDH, we write[4] F_0 for the common starting curve. In SIDH, recovering the secret key from the public key is equivalent to the computational supersingular isogeny problem (CSSI), see [23] that we state in Problem 5.6.

Problem 5.6. Let ℓ_A be a small prime number and $A = \ell_A^{e_A}$ for some exponent e_A. Let $\varphi_A : F_0 \to E_A$ be an isogeny whose kernel is $\langle [m_A]P_A + [n_A]Q_A \rangle$, where m_A and n_A are chosen at random from $\mathbb{Z}/A\mathbb{Z}$ (where at least one is in $\mathbb{Z}/A\mathbb{Z}^\times$. Given E_A and the values $\varphi_A(P_B), \varphi_A(Q_B)$ for P, B, Q_B a basis of $F_0[B]$ find a generator R_A of $\ker \varphi_A$.

The proposition below requires a bit more work as the link between SIDH and group actions is less obvious.

Proposition 5.7. *Assume that F_0 admits an $\mathfrak{O}_0$-orientation with $\mathfrak{O}_0$ a maximal quadratic order of class number* 1. *If there exists a PPT algorithm solving Problem 5.1 for $\mathfrak{O} = \mathbb{Z} + A'\mathfrak{O}_0$ where A' divides A, then there exists a PPT algorithm that breaks the CSSI problem with overwhelming probability.*

Proof. First, note that A is chosen so that the kernel points of A-isogenies have a polynomial-size representation. Then, since A is also smooth, the discrete logarithms can be solved in polynomial time in the A-torsion and isogenies of degree A can be computed in polynomial time.

For the rest of this proof, let us write α the endomorphism of F_0 such that $\mathbb{Z}[\alpha]$ realizes the embedding of $\mathfrak{O}_0$ inside $\text{End}(F_0)$.

[4] Once again, we highlight that these notations are unusual and were chosen to emphasize the link with Problem 5.1.

If the curve E_A is A-isogenous to F_0, then E_A admits an embedding of $\mathbb{Z} + A\mathfrak{O}_0$. This embedding is not necessarily primitive but we know there exists A' dividing A such that $\mathfrak{O} = \mathbb{Z}+A'\mathfrak{O}_0$ admits a primitive embedding in $\mathrm{End}(E_A)$ (see Proposition 2.2). Conversely, since the class number of $\mathfrak{O}_0$ is 1, then any $\mathbb{Z} + A'\mathfrak{O}_0$-orientation on E_A implies the existence of an A'-isogeny between E_A and F_0. Let us write $\varphi_{A'} : F_0 \to E_A$ this isogeny of degree A'. Then φ_A, the secret isogeny in Problem 5.6 is the composition of φ_A with an endomorphism θ_A of $\mathfrak{O}_0$ of degree A/A'. Since A/A' is a power of ℓ_A, there are two possibilities for θ_A. Thus, the difficulty lies in recovering $\varphi_{A'}$.

We can generate a curve E_0 in $\mathcal{E}_{\mathbb{Z}+A'\mathfrak{O}_0}$ by generating $\varphi_0 : F_0 \to E_0$ a descending isogeny of degree A'. Any ideal $\mathfrak{a}$ such that $E_A = \mathfrak{a} * E_0$ can be interpreted as an isogeny $\varphi_\mathfrak{a} : E_0 \to E_A$ of degree $n(\mathfrak{a})$. The proof is concluded by the fact that $\ker \hat{\varphi}_{A'} = \varphi_\mathfrak{a}(\ker \hat{\varphi}_0)$, which we prove below. Once $\ker \hat{\varphi}_{A'}$ has been computed, is easy to recover $\ker \varphi_{A'} = \hat{\varphi}_{A'}(E_A[A'])$ and find a solution to the CSSI as we explained above.

To prove $\ker \hat{\varphi}_{A'} = \varphi_\mathfrak{a}(\ker \hat{\varphi}_0)$, we need to understand how the fact that $\mathfrak{a}$ is an $\mathfrak{O}$-ideal translates on the action of $\varphi_\mathfrak{a}$ on $\hat{\varphi}_0$. As explained in Proposition 2.2 and the following paragraph, the embedding of $\mathfrak{O}$ in E_0 (resp. E_A) is obtained as $\mathbb{Z}[\varphi_0 \circ \alpha \circ \hat{\varphi}_0] = \mathbb{Z}[\theta_0]$ (resp. $\mathbb{Z}[\varphi_{A'} \circ \alpha \circ \hat{\varphi}_{A'}] = \mathbb{Z}[\theta_{A'}]$). By definition of $\mathfrak{a}$ being an $\mathfrak{O}$-ideal, we have that $\varphi_\mathfrak{a}(\ker \theta_0) = \ker \theta_A$. Thus, we need to prove that $\ker \theta_0 \cap E_0[A'] = \ker \hat{\varphi}_0$ and $\ker \theta_{A'} \cap E_A[A'] = \ker \hat{\varphi}_A$ (note that this property is exactly what underlies the inversion mechanism in Sect. 3.3). We will do it for θ_0, the property for $\theta_{A'}$ holds for the exact same reasons. It is clear from the definition of $\theta_0 = \varphi_0 \circ \alpha \circ \hat{\varphi}_0$ that we have $\ker \hat{\varphi}_0 \subset \ker \theta_0$. Let us take $P \in E_A[A'] \setminus \ker \hat{\varphi}_0$, then $Q = \hat{\varphi}_0(P) \in \ker \varphi_0 \setminus \langle 0 \rangle$. If we assume that $P \in \ker \theta_0$, it implies that $\alpha(Q) \in \ker \varphi_0$. Since $\ker \varphi_0$ is cyclic, we have that $\alpha(Q) = \lambda Q$ for some $\lambda \in \mathbb{Z}$. This contradicts the fact that φ_0 is descending. Indeed, if we write φ_Q, the isogeny of kernel generated by Q, we have $\varphi_0 = \psi_0 \circ \varphi_Q$ for some isogeny φ_Q and the condition $\alpha(Q) = \lambda Q$ implies that φ_Q is not descending and so φ_0 would not be descending, which is a contradiction. Thus, we have proven that $\ker \theta_0 \cap E_0[A'] = \ker \hat{\varphi}_0$ and this concludes the proof asexplained above.

We refer to Sect. 3 for the full details and notations about Séta. We write $\mathfrak{O} \cong \mathbb{Z}[\sqrt{(N^2e - d^2)/D^2}] \cong \mathbb{Z}[\theta]$ and assume that $e, d, \mathfrak{O}$ are public. This assumption is plausible as the procedure described in Algorithm 2 is essentially deterministic.

Proposition 5.8. *If there exists a PPT algorithm solving Problem 5.1 for $\mathfrak{O}$, then there exists a PPT algorithm that takes a Séta public key E_s and recovers a trapdoor T such that E_{j_T}, T is a (D, N)-trapdoor curve.*

Proof. Let E_{j_T} be a Séta public key. By applying Algorithm 3 in $\mathfrak{O}$ and adding the integers e, d a (D, N)-trapdoor curve E_0, T_0 can be found in polynomial time with $E_0 \in \mathcal{E}_\mathfrak{O}$. Thus, we can apply the PPT solver for Problem 5.1 on E_0 and E_{j_T} to compute an isogeny $\varphi_\mathfrak{a} : E_0 \to E_{j_T}$ corresponding to a $\mathfrak{O}$ ideal $\mathfrak{a}$. If we write $\theta_0 \in \mathrm{End}(E_0)$ and $\theta \in \mathrm{End}(E_{j_T})$ the endomorphisms such that $\mathfrak{O} \cong \mathbb{Z}[\theta_0] \cong \mathbb{Z}[\theta]$. Then, by definition of $\mathfrak{O}$-ideals, we have that $\theta \circ \varphi_\mathfrak{a} = \varphi_\mathfrak{a} \circ$. So if $T_0 =$

$e, d, P_0, Q_0, \theta_0(P_0), \theta_0(Q_0)$, then $T = e, d\varphi_{\mathfrak{a}}(P_0), \varphi_{\mathfrak{a}}(Q_0), \varphi_{\mathfrak{a}}(\theta_0(P_0)), \varphi_{\mathfrak{a}}(\theta_0(Q_0))$ is such that E_{j_T}, T is a (D, N)-trapdoor curve.

We finish this section by proving that some instances of Problem 5.1 are related to the more generic isogeny problem of finding a smooth isogeny between any two supersingular curves (Problem 5.9 below). For that it suffices to show that there exists some quadratic order that is embedded inside the endomorphism ring of any supersingular curve.

Problem 5.9. Let $p > 3$, be a prime number. Given E_1,E_2 two distinct supersingular curves over $\mathbb{F}_{p^2}$. Find $\varphi : E_1 \to E_2$, an isogeny of powersmooth degree.

Proposition 5.10. *There is an absolute constant $c > 0$ such that the following holds. Let $\mathfrak{O}$ be a quadratic order of conductor ℓ^e inside $\mathfrak{O}_0$ a maximal quadratic order, such that ℓ is inert in $\mathfrak{O}_0$, and $e \geq c \log_\ell(p)$. If there exists a PPT algorithm that can break Problem 5.1, then there is a PPT algorithm that breaks Problem 5.9.*

Proof. From the fact that the ℓ-isogeny graph is Ramanujan, and the rapid mixing of non-backtracking random walks in expander graphs [1], we deduce that for $e = \Omega(\log_\ell(p))$, there exists a non-backtracking path of degree ℓ^e between any two supersingular curves in the graph.

In particular, if E_0 is any $\mathfrak{O}_0$-orientable curve, there exists a cyclic isogeny of degree ℓ^e from E_0 to any other E, and since ℓ is inert in $\mathfrak{O}_0$, this isogeny must be a sequence of descending isogenies. This implies that any E is $\mathfrak{O}$-orientable. Thus, if we write E_1 and E_2, the two curves in the generic isogeny problem, then we can construct a middle curve E_0 with an explicit embedding of $\mathfrak{O}$, then use the PPT algorithm to find paths between E_0, E_1 and E_0, E_2, and finally concatenate the two paths to obtain a path between E_1 and E_2 of powersmooth degree.

5.3 Analysis of the Uber Isogeny Assumption

In this section we investigate the complexity of solving Problem 5.1. We are going to see that there are various special cases leading to various complexities.

We start by giving a generic estimate which can be seen as the worst case complexity.

A first upper bound: exhaustive search. The simplest method to solve Problem 5.1 is to apply an exhaustive search, for instance by selecting a set of small primes ℓ_i all split in $\mathfrak{O}$ and trying all combinations of $\prod \mathfrak{l}_i^{e_i} \star E_0$ until one is isomorphic to E_s, where each $\mathfrak{l}_i$ is a prime ideal above ℓ_i. The expected running time of this algorithm is in $O(\#\mathcal{E}_{\mathfrak{O}})$. The best generic bound on the size of this set is given in Proposition 2.1.

The classical estimate $h(\mathfrak{O}) = \Theta(\sqrt{\Delta})$ gives a first upper-bound on the complexity to solve Problem 5.1. In particular, it shows that solving Problem 5.1 is easy when the discriminant Δ is small. However, when Δ grows, it is harder to estimate how this bound reflects on the actual complexity of the problem.

There are some special cases for which we can be a bit more precise than Proposition 2.1. For instance, when the discriminant are short, the following Theorem from Kaneko [25] can be applied to derive a precise statement.

Theorem 5.11. *Take two distinct quadratic orders $\mathfrak{O}_1, \mathfrak{O}_2$ of discriminants Δ_1, Δ_2 embedded optimally in the same maximal order inside the quaternion algebra ramified exactly at p and ∞. If we have $\mathbb{Q}(\sqrt{\Delta_1}) \cong \mathbb{Q}(\sqrt{\Delta_2})$, then $\Delta_1\Delta_2 \geq p^2$.*

Applying Theorem 5.11 to the discriminants $\Delta \leq p$, we see that there cannot be two distinct embeddings of $\mathfrak{O}$ inside the same maximal order, thus proving that $\#\mathcal{E}_{\mathfrak{O}} = h(\mathfrak{O})$. Thus, in that case, we know that the exhaustive search method described above has asymptotic complexity $\Theta(\sqrt{\Delta})$.

Another example is given in the proof of Proposition 5.10, where we saw that there are some values of Δ for which we know that $\mathcal{E}_{\mathfrak{O}}$ is exactly the set of supersingular curves. More generally, the link between the conductor of $\mathfrak{O}$ and isogenies (Proposition 2.2) allows us to obtain some better estimates on the size of $\mathcal{E}_{\mathfrak{O}}$ by using the expander properties of isogeny graphs.

The case of CSIDH. (Proposition 5.4) has received a lot of attention from the community ([6,9,11,32] since it was the first scheme that naturally fits into this framework. In fact, there are improvements over the exhaustive search strategy in both the classical and quantum settings. The main ingredient behind these speed-ups is the ability for anyone to obtain a concrete embedding (through the Frobenius morphism) of $\mathfrak{O} = \mathbb{Z}[\sqrt{-p}]$ inside $\mathrm{End}(E)$ for any $E \in \mathcal{E}_{\mathfrak{O}}$. In particular, computing $\mathfrak{a} \star E$ becomes easy for any $E \in \mathcal{E}_{\mathfrak{O}}$ when $\mathfrak{a}$ has smooth norm. In the classical setting, this implies a quadratic speed-up over the generic exhaustive search by using a meet-in-the-middle technique (see [9]). In the quantum setting, the speed-up is even more radical, as it creates a malleability oracle (see [28]) that reduces CSIDH's security to an instance of the hidden shift problem which can be solved in quantum sub-exponential time as described in [6,32] for instance.

Note that neither of these attacks can be used in the generic case as it seems hard to obtain this malleability oracle for other group actions. For instance, in OSIDH [12] the public keys are made of a curve E and some torsion points to make possible the computation of $\mathfrak{a} \star E$ for some secret ideal $\mathfrak{a}$. These additional torsion points are not needed in CSIDH because they can be easily computed.

Smooth conductor inside a maximal quadratic order. A better algorithm also exists when the conductor f of $\mathfrak{O}$ is smooth. By Proposition 2.2, there exists an isogeny of degree f between any curve $E \in \mathcal{E}_{\mathfrak{O}}$ and any curve in $\mathcal{E}_{\mathfrak{O}_0}$, where $\mathfrak{O}_0$ is the quadratic maximal order containing $\mathfrak{O}$. Let E_0, E_s given by in an instance of Problem 5.1, and let us write $\varphi_0 : F_0 \to E_0$ and $\varphi_s : F_s \to E_s$ the two isogenies of degree f.

The alternative resolution method enumerates through all possible $F_s = \mathfrak{a}_0 \star F_0$ in $\mathcal{E}_{\mathfrak{O}_0}$ then tries to find φ_s of degree f. Since f is smooth, we can apply a meet-in-the-middle technique to reduce this part to $O(\sqrt{f})$. Once $\varphi_s : F_s \to E_s$ and a $\mathfrak{O}_0$-ideal $\mathfrak{a}_0$ such that $F_s = \mathfrak{a}_0 \star F_0$ has been found, we can compute a $\mathfrak{O}$-ideal such that $E_s = \mathfrak{a} \star E_0$ as described in [12, Section 5.1].

If we write $\Delta = f^2 \Delta_0$ where Δ_0 is the fundamental discriminant of $\mathfrak{O}_0$. The complexity of this algorithm is $\Theta(\sqrt{f}\sqrt{\Delta_0})$ which is better than $\Theta(\sqrt{\Delta}) = \Theta(f\sqrt{\Delta_0})$.

Other cases. When we are not in one of the above cases, there is no known improvement over the exhaustive search (classically or quantumly). Thus, the presumed security entirely relies on the size of $\mathcal{E}_{\mathfrak{O}}$. In that regard, the cases where the conductor of $\mathfrak{O}$ is big might give more confidence in the difficulty of Problem 5.1 as the size of $\mathcal{E}_{\mathfrak{O}}$ is tied to the number of isogenies of a given degree between distinct pair of curves. In comparison, the distribution of embeddings of a maximal quadratic order of big discriminant (i.e. above the bound in Theorem 5.11) have been less studied. As of yet, there are no reason to believe that there exists such quadratic orders that would be embedded in only a small portion of all the supersingular curves but not enough work has been done on the question to reach a definitive conclusion.

6 Implementation

We implemented the version of Séta where the starting curve (E_{j_T}, T) is a (D, N)-trapdoor curve, i.e., the secret key does not contain a random walk, as described in Sect. 4.2. Our implementation is written in pure C, reusing large parts of the codebase of SQISign[5]; in particular we depend on GMP 6.2.1 for integer arithmetic, Pari 2.13 for quaternion arithmetic [39], and we adapt the so called `velusqrt` code for isogeny evaluation [4][6]. Our code is avaible at https://github.com/seta-isogeny-encryption/seta.

6.1 Main Building Blocks

Key generation consists of two parts. Finding a suitable θ in its quaternion form and then finding a supersingular elliptic curve whose endomorphism ring contains θ. The difficult part of this procedure in practice is a subroutine for finding a supersingular elliptic curve whose endomorphism ring is isomorphic to a particular maximal order $\mathcal{O}$. For this step we reused a substantial amount of the code used for SQISign [16].

Encryption consists in the evaluation of an isogeny of degree D at points of order N. In order to make this efficient we choose parameters where D has small prime factors and both D and N divide $p^2 - 1$ to avoid using extension fields.

[5] https://github.com/SQISign/sqisign.

[6] https://velusqrt.isogeny.org/software.html.

Decryption also uses evaluations of isogenies, but here isogenies of degree N are evaluated. Furthermore, decryption requires some linear algebra modulo D (when computing the intersection $\ker(\tau - [d]) \cap E_m[D]$) and modulo N (when computing the isogenies ψ and ψ'). In these steps one uses subroutines for solving discrete logarithms but due to N and D being smooth, this step is negligible compared to other computations.

6.2 Prime Search

To efficiently implement Séta, it is necessary to select a prime satisfying the many constraints mentioned in Sect. 4.3. To maximise efficiency of encryption and decryption, while maintaining reasonably efficient key generation, we opted to search for a prime satisfying the following constraints: (1) $p^2 - 1 = DN$, with both D and N smooth; (2) $D \approx 2^{2\lambda}$ and $N \approx 2^{4\lambda}$; and (3) D has as few prime factors as possible.

There are currently three known techniques to search for primes such that $p^2 - 1$ is smooth, all discussed in [14]. Of these, the most apt to satisfy the constraint that D has few prime factors was introduced by Costello in [13]: fix an exponent $n > 1$, and sieve the space of integers $p = 2x^n - 1$ until one is found such that both $p + 1 = 2x^n$ and $p - 1 = 2(x^n - 1)$ are smooth.

Thanks to this technique, D can be taken as a factor of $p + 1$, and has thus much fewer prime factors than a generic smooth prime of the same size. The drawback of the technique is that, as n increases, the search space decreases, to the point where no smooth integers may be found.

Concretely, for $\lambda = 128$, we fixed $n = 12$ and we sieved within the space $2^{32} < x < 2^{33}$, i.e., $2^{385} < p < 2^{397}$. This yielded four primes with largest factor bounded by 2^{25}, and three with bound 2^{26}, corresponding to $x = 4679747572, 4845958752, 4966654633, 5114946480, 6334792777, 8176556533, 8426067021$. Unfortunately, the search space was fully explored, meaning that no better primes exist for $n = 12$.

The relatively large smoothness bounds negatively affect performance of all algorithms in Séta. Unfortunately, it appears to be difficult to find better primes given current knowledge. Even dropping the constraint on the number of prime factors of D, the best algorithms known today can hardly beat a 2^{20} smoothness bound for a prime of 384 bits [14, Table 3].

6.3 Experimental Results

We ran experiments on a 4.00 GHz Quad-Core Intel Core i7, using a single core. We used the prime $p = 2 \cdot 8426067021^{12} - 1$, and the smooth factors

$$\begin{aligned}
D =& 43^{12} \cdot 84719^{11}, \\
N =& 3^{21} \cdot 5 \cdot 7 \cdot 13 \cdot 17 \cdot 19 \cdot 23 \cdot 73 \cdot 257^{12} \cdot 313 \cdot 1009 \cdot 2857 \cdot 3733 \cdot 5519 \cdot 6961 \\
& \cdot 53113 \cdot 499957 \cdot 763369 \cdot 2101657 \cdot 2616791 \cdot 7045009 \cdot 11959093 \\
& \cdot 17499277 \cdot 20157451 \cdot 33475999 \cdot 39617833 \cdot 45932333.
\end{aligned}$$

The key generation was ran only once, and took 10.43 h. The encryption procedure took 4.63 s, and the decryption took 10.66 min, averaged over six runs. The decryption time is almost entirely devoted to the evaluation of isogenies of degrees the largest factors of N.

7 Further Work and Conclusion

The efficiency of the scheme essentially depends on the prime factorization of D. We have managed to keep all computations within $\mathbb{F}_{p^2}$ but D still has large prime factors. In principle, one can construct trapdoor curves whenever $N > D^2$ so in particular when ND divides $p-1$ and $N = 2^k, D = 3^l$. The bottleneck here is the generation of the trapdoor curve which is rather inefficient, despite its polynomial complexity. Note that generating the curve does not affect the speed of encryption and decryption, it only affects the speed of key generation. Thus if one devised a more efficient version of the KLPT algorithm which speeds up the maximal order to elliptic curve mapping algorithm, then one could derive a much more efficient scheme. We estimate that in the best case, one could get a scheme which is only 5 times slower than SIDH. Another interesting research direction is whether one could build upon our Séta scheme and derive more advanced primitives. The framework of Séta has certain advantages in this context when compared to SIDH. First, Séta is based on a trapdoor one-way function which could be useful in building signature schemes. Second, SIDH-based constructions are more likely to need a trusted setup to avoid backdoor curve attacks such as the one described in [3, Section 6]. Finally, public key validation is easy in the context of Séta which could be used to build non-interactive key exchange or counteract fault attacks.

This work presents the OW-CPA PKE scheme Séta, built upon a generalized version of the isogeny-based CGL hash function family. To do so, we made use of a "torsion-point attack" against SIDH-like schemes [33] and transformed this into a decryption mechanism which recovers a message encrypted as a secret isogeny between a trapdoor starting curve and a final ciphertext curve. An IND-CCA variant is constructed using the post-quantum OAEP transform and both security properties are proven to reduce to the TCSSI problem, derived from the CSSI problem introduced in [23]. We then discussed the key generation in terms of computing trapdoor information, the corresponding curve generation, and of the constraints that this does or does not place on the base prime of the scheme; we also proposed an alternative method for these computations. Of independent interest, we formalized the "uber isogeny asumption" and discussed its relation with existing isogeny-based schemes, such as CSIDH, OSDIH and SIDH, before analyzing its complexity. Finally, we presented implementation results for both the search of a well-suited base prime and for key-generation, encryption and decryption experiments.

Acknowledgments. We would like to thank the anonymous reviewers for their remarks and suggestions. Péter Kutas and Christophe Petit's work was supported by EPSRC grant EP/S01361X/1. Péter Kutas was also supported by the Ministry of Innovation and Technology and the National Research, Development and Innovation Office within the Quantum Information National Laboratory of Hungary. Cyprien Delpech de Saint Guilhem's work was supported by ERC Advanced Grant ERC-2015-AdG-IMPaCT, by DARPA under contract No. HR001120C0085, and by CyberSecurity Research Flanders with reference number VR20192203.

A Post-quantum OAEP transformation

We present here the post-quantum OAEP generic transformation we used in Sect. 3.5.

Let

$$f : \{0,1\}^{\lambda+k_1} \times \{0,1\}^{k_0} \to \{0,1\}^{n_c}$$

be an invertible injective function. The function f is the public key of the scheme, its inverse f^{-1} is the secret key. The scheme makes use of three hash functions

$$G : \{0,1\}^{k_0} \to \{0,1\}^{k-k_0},$$
$$H : \{0,1\}^{k-k_0} \to \{0,1\}^{k_0},$$
$$H' : \{0,1\}^{k} \to \{0,1\}^{k},$$

modelled as random oracles, where $k = \lambda + k_0 + k_1$. Given those, the encryption scheme is defined as follows:

- Enc: given a message $m \in \{0,1\}^\lambda$, choose $r \xleftarrow{\$} \{0,1\}^{k_0}$ and set

  $$s = m||0^{k_1} \oplus G(r), \qquad t = r \oplus H(s),$$
  $$c = f(s,t), \qquad d = H'(s||t),$$

  and output the ciphertext (c, d).
- Dec: given a ciphertext (c, d), use the secret key to compute $(s,t) = f^{-1}(c)$. If $d \neq H'(s||t)$ output $\perp$. Otherwise, compute $r = t \oplus H(s)$ and $\overline{m} = s \oplus G(r)$. If the last k_1 bits of $\overline{m}$ are 0, output the first n bits of $\overline{m}$, otherwise output $\perp$.

References

1. Alon, N., Benjamini, I., Lubetzky, E., Sodin, S.: Non-backtracking random walks mix faster. Commun. Contemporary Math. **9**(04), 585–603 (2007)
2. Azarderakhsh, R., et al.: Supersingular isogeny key encapsulation, Joost Renes (2020)
3. Basso, A., Kutas, P., Merz, S.P., Petit, C., Sanso, A.: Cryptanalysis of an oblivious PRF from supersingular isogenies. Cryptology ePrint Archive, Report 2021/706 (2021)
4. Bernstein, D.J., de Feo, L., Leroux, A., Smith, B.: Faster computation of isogenies of large prime degree. Open Book Ser. **4**(1), 39–55 (2020)

5. Biasse, J.-F., Jao, D., Sankar, A.: A quantum algorithm for computing isogenies between supersingular elliptic curves. In: Meier, W., Mukhopadhyay, D. (eds.) INDOCRYPT 2014. LNCS, vol. 8885, pp. 428–442. Springer, Cham (2014). https://doi.org/10.1007/978-3-319-13039-2_25
6. Bonnetain, X., Schrottenloher, A.: Quantum security analysis of CSIDH. In: Canteaut, A., Ishai, Y. (eds.) EUROCRYPT 2020. LNCS, vol. 12106, pp. 493–522. Springer, Cham (2020). https://doi.org/10.1007/978-3-030-45724-2_17
7. Boyen, X.: The uber-assumption family. In: Galbraith, S.D., Paterson, K.G. (eds.) Pairing 2008. LNCS, vol. 5209, pp. 39–56. Springer, Heidelberg (2008). https://doi.org/10.1007/978-3-540-85538-5_3
8. Bröker, R.: Constructing supersingular elliptic curves. J. Comb. Number Theor. **1**(3), 269–273 (2009)
9. Castryck, W., Lange, T., Martindale, C., Panny, L., Renes, J.: CSIDH: an efficient post-quantum commutative group action. In: Peyrin, T., Galbraith, S. (eds.) ASIACRYPT 2018. LNCS, vol. 11274, pp. 395–427. Springer, Cham (2018). https://doi.org/10.1007/978-3-030-03332-3_15
10. Charles, D.X., Lauter, K.E., Goren, E.Z.: Cryptographic hash functions from expander graphs. J. Cryptol. **22**(1), 93–113 (2009)
11. Chávez-Saab, J., Chi-Domınguez, J.J., Jaques, S., Rodrıguez-Henrıquez, F.: The SQALE of CSIDH: square-root vélu quantum-resistant isogeny action with low exponents. Technical report, Cryptology ePrint Archive, Report 2020/1520 2020. https://eprint.iacr.org (2020)
12. Colò, L., Kohel, D.: Orienting supersingular isogeny graphs. J. Math. Cryptol. **14**(1), 414–437 (2020)
13. Costello, C.: B-SIDH: supersingular isogeny Diffie-Hellman using twisted torsion. Technical report, Cryptology ePrint Archive, Report 2019/1145, 2019. https://eprint.iacr.org/2019/1145 (2019)
14. Costello, C., Meyer, M., Naehrig, M.: Sieving for twin smooth integers with solutions to the Prouhet-Tarry-Escott problem. Cryptology ePrint Archive, Report 2020/1283 (2020)
15. Couveignes, J.-M.: Hard homogeneous spaces. IACR Cryptology ePrint Archive 2006, vol. 291 (1999)
16. De Feo, L., Kohel, D., Leroux, A., Petit, C., Wesolowski, B.: SQISign: compact post-quantum signatures from quaternions and isogenies. In: Moriai, S., Wang, H. (eds.) ASIACRYPT 2020. LNCS, vol. 12491, pp. 64–93. Springer, Cham (2020). https://doi.org/10.1007/978-3-030-64837-4_3
17. de Quehen, V., et al.: Improved torsion point attacks on SIDH variants. arXiv e-prints, page arXiv:2005.14681, May 2020
18. Eisenträger, K., Hallgren, S., Lauter, K., Morrison, T., Petit, C.: Supersingular isogeny graphs and endomorphism rings: reductions and solutions. In: Nielsen, J.B., Rijmen, V. (eds.) EUROCRYPT 2018. LNCS, vol. 10822, pp. 329–368. Springer, Cham (2018). https://doi.org/10.1007/978-3-319-78372-7_11
19. Fouotsa, I.B., Petit, C.: InSIDH: a Simplification of SiGamal. Cryptology ePrint Archive, Report 2021/218 (2021). https://eprint.iacr.org/2021/218
20. Galbraith, S.D., Petit, C., Shani, B., Ti, Y.B.: On the security of supersingular isogeny cryptosystems. In: Cheon, J.H., Takagi, T. (eds.) ASIACRYPT 2016. LNCS, vol. 10031, pp. 63–91. Springer, Heidelberg (2016). https://doi.org/10.1007/978-3-662-53887-6_3
21. Galbraith, S.D., Petit, C., Silva, J.: Identification protocols and signature schemes based on supersingular isogeny problems. J. Cryptol. **33**(1), 130–175 (2020)

22. Hofheinz, D., Hövelmanns, K., Kiltz, E.: A modular analysis of the Fujisaki-Okamoto transformation. IACR Cryptology ePrint Archive 2017, vol. 604 (2017)
23. Jao, D., De Feo, L.: Towards quantum-resistant cryptosystems from supersingular elliptic curve isogenies. In: Yang, B.-Y. (ed.) PQCrypto 2011. LNCS, vol. 7071, pp. 19–34. Springer, Heidelberg (2011). https://doi.org/10.1007/978-3-642-25405-5_2
24. Jao, D., Miller, S.D., Venkatesan, R.: Expander graphs based on grh with an application to elliptic curve cryptography. J. Number Theor. **129**(6), 1491–1504 (2009)
25. Kaneko, M.: Supersingular j-invariants as singular moduli mod p. Osaka J. Math. **26**(4), 849–855 (1989)
26. Kohel, D., Lauter, K., Petit, C., Tignol, J.P.: On the quaternion ℓ-isogeny path problem. LMS J. Comput. Math. **17**(A), 418–432 (2014)
27. Kutas, P., Martindale, C., Panny, L., Petit, C., Stange, K.E.: Weak instances of SIDH variants under improved torsion-point attacks. IACR Cryptology ePrint Archive 2020, vol. 633 (2020)
28. Kutas, P., Merz, S.-P., Petit, C., Weitkämper, C.: One-way functions and malleability oracles: Hidden shift attacks on isogeny-based protocols. IACR Cryptology ePrint Archive 2021, vol. 282 (2021)
29. Love, J., Boneh, D.: Supersingular curves with small noninteger endomorphisms. Open Book Ser. **4**(1), 7–22 (2020)
30. Martindale, C., Panny, L.: How to not break SIDH. Cryptology ePrint Archive, Report 2019/558 (2019). https://eprint.iacr.org/2019/558
31. Moriya, T., Onuki, H., Takagi, T.: SiGamal: a supersingular isogeny-based PKE and its application to a PRF. In: Moriai, S., Wang, H. (eds.) ASIACRYPT 2020. LNCS, vol. 12492, pp. 551–580. Springer, Cham (2020). https://doi.org/10.1007/978-3-030-64834-3_19
32. Peikert, C.: He gives C-Sieves on the CSIDH. In: Canteaut, A., Ishai, Y. (eds.) EUROCRYPT 2020. LNCS, vol. 12106, pp. 463–492. Springer, Cham (2020). https://doi.org/10.1007/978-3-030-45724-2_16
33. Petit, C.: Faster algorithms for isogeny problems using torsion point images. In: Takagi, T., Peyrin, T. (eds.) ASIACRYPT 2017. LNCS, vol. 10625, pp. 330–353. Springer, Cham (2017). https://doi.org/10.1007/978-3-319-70697-9_12
34. Rostovtsev, A., Stolbunov, A.: Public-key cryptosystem based on isogenies. IACR Cryptology ePrint Archive 2006, vol. 145 (2006)
35. Silverman, J.H.: The arithmetic of elliptic curves, vol. 106. Springer Science & Business Media (2009)
36. Simon, D.: Quadratic equations in dimensions 4, 5 and more. Preprint (2005)
37. Stolbunov, A.: Constructing public-key cryptographic schemes based on class group action on a set of isogenous elliptic curves. Adv. Math. Comm. **4**(2), 215–235 (2010)
38. Targhi, E.E., Unruh, D.: Post-quantum security of the fujisaki-okamoto and OAEP transforms. In: Hirt, M., Smith, A. (eds.) TCC 2016. LNCS, vol. 9986, pp. 192–216. Springer, Heidelberg (2016). https://doi.org/10.1007/978-3-662-53644-5_8
39. The PARI Group, Université de Bordeaux. PARI/GP version `2.12.0` (2021). http://pari.math.u-bordeaux.fr/
40. Voight, J.: Identifying the matrix ring: algorithms for quaternion algebras and quadratic forms. In: Quadratic and Higher Degree Forms, pp. 255–298. Springer, New York (2013). https://doi.org/10.1007/978-1-4614-7488-3_10

SHealS and HealS: Isogeny-Based PKEs from a Key Validation Method for SIDH

Tako Boris Fouotsa[1](✉) and Christophe Petit[2,3](✉)

[1] Università Degli Studi Roma Tre, Rome, Italy
takoboris.fouotsa@uniroma3.it
[2] Université Libre de Bruxelles, Brussels, Belgium
[3] University of Birmingham's School of Computer Science, Birmingham, UK

Abstract. In 2016, Galbraith et al. presented an adaptive attack on the SIDH key exchange protocol. In SIKE, one applies a variant of the Fujisaki-Okamoto transform to force Bob to reveal his encryption key to Alice, which Alice then uses to re-encrypt Bob's ciphertext and verify its validity. Therefore, Bob can not reuse his encryption keys. There have been two other proposed countermeasures enabling static-static private keys: k-SIDH and its variant by Jao and Urbanik. These countermeasures are relatively expensive since they consist in running multiple parallel instances of SIDH.

In this paper, firstly, we propose a new countermeasure to the GPST adaptive attack on SIDH. Our countermeasure does not require key disclosure as in SIKE, nor multiple parallel instances as in k-SIDH. We translate our countermeasure into a key validation method for SIDH-type schmes. Secondly, we use our key validation to design HealSIDH, an efficient SIDH-type static-static key interactive exchange protocol. Thirdly, we derive a PKE scheme SHealS using HealSIDH. SHealS uses larger primes compared to SIKE, has larger keys and ciphertexts, but only 4 isogenies are computed in a full execution of the scheme, as opposed to 5 isogenies in SIKE. We prove that SHealS is IND-CPA secure relying on a new assumption we introduce and we conjecture its IND-CCA security. We suggest HealS, a variant of SHealS using a smaller prime, providing smaller keys and ciphertexts.

As a result, HealSIDH is a practically efficient SIDH based (interactive) key exchange incorporating a "direct" countermeasure to the GPST adaptive attack.

Keywords: Post-quantum cryptography · SIDH · SIKE · Adaptive attacks · HealSIDH · SHealS · HealS

1 Introduction

The general isogeny computational problem is the following: given two isogenous elliptic curves E and E', compute an isogeny from E to E'. This hard problem was used by J. M. Couveignes [8], Rostovtsev and Stolbunov [27] to

M. Tibouchi and H. Wang (Eds.): ASIACRYPT 2021, LNCS 13093, pp. 279–307, 2021.
https://doi.org/10.1007/978-3-030-92068-5_10

design a key exchange protocol using ordinary isogenies, and by Charles, Goren and Lauter [5] to design a cryptographic hash function using supersingular isogenies. The CRS (Couveignes-Rostovtsev-Stolbunov) key exchange scheme is less practical in general and is vulnerable to a sub-exponential quantum attack [6].

In 2011, Jao and De Feo proposed SIDH [20] that uses isogenies of supersingular elliptic curves. SIDH is efficient and it is not vulnerable to the sub-exponential quantum attack presented in [6]. Nevertheless, a recent paper by Kutas et al. [21] proves that hidden-shift like attacks apply to variants of SIDH with considerably overstretched parameters. The isogeny computational problem underlying the security of SIDH is believed to be hard to break, even when using a quantum computer. SIKE [19] (which is the state of art implementation of SIDH [13,20]) is the only isogeny-based Key Encapsulation Mechanism (KEM) submitted to the NIST post-quantum standardization process. Even though SIKE is not the most efficient candidate among KEMs in this competition, SIKE provides the most compact keys and ciphertexts. This has certainly contributed to its selection for the third round of the competition as an alternate candidate [24].

Contrarily to the ordinary case where isogenies commute, supersingular isogenies do not commute in general. In order to solve this issue in SIDH, the images of some well-chosen torsion points through the secret isogeny are computed and included in the public keys.

In 2016, Galbraith et al. [17] exploited this information to develop adaptive attacks on SIDH when one party has a static secret key. The main idea of the attack is that Bob replaces the images of the torsion points in his public key by malicious ones and obtains some information on Alice's static secret when looking at the obtained shared secret. Repeating this process a polynomial number of times, Bob totally recovers Alice's private key.

In SIKE, the attack is avoided by applying a variant [18] of the Fujisaki-Okamoto transform [15]. This transform forces Bob to reveal his encryption key to Alice. Two countermeasures enabling static-static key exchange have been proposed: k-SIDH [1] and a variant by Jao and Urbanik [30]. These schemes essentially consist in running k^2 parallel instances of SIDH with each party having k SIDH private keys, hence each party computes about k^2 isogenies. In [11] and in [2], it is shown that variants of the adaptive attacks still apply to these schemes, and that the attacks are exponential in k in general. Hence one needs a relatively large k, say $k = 46$ as suggested by [11], for these schemes to be secure. For $k = 46$, about $46^2 = 2116$ isogenies are computed in k-SIDH, hence the scheme is arguably not practical. To the best of our knowledge, there exists no practically efficient method to counter the adaptive attack on SIDH without revealing the encryption key and using re-encryption to verify the validity of the ciphertext.

CSIDH [4] is the perfect post-quantum alternative to the classical Diffie-Hellman key exchange due to its analogy to the later primitive. Meanwhile, its quantum security has been considerably degraded recently [3,7,25] and remains to be precisely estimated. CSIDH was originally instantiated with a 512 bit prime, but due to analysis of its actual quantum security, in [7] it is suggested to use primes of up to 4000 bits to achieve the NIST level 1 security. The increase of the prime size impacts the efficiency of the scheme.

Contributions. The contributions of this paper are fourfold.

Firstly, we propose a new countermeasure to the GPST adaptive attack on SIDH. The main idea is that Bob enable Alice to verify that his torsion points were honestly generated. Consider an SIDH setting, let $\phi_A : E_0 \to E_A$ and $\phi'_A : E_B \to E_{BA}$ be Alice's secret isogenies, $\phi_B : E_0 \to E_B$ and $\phi'_B : E_A \to E_{AB}$ be Bob's secret isogenies in an SIDH instance. In Sect. 3, we prove that if Bob publishes the action of ϕ_B on $E_0[\ell_A^{2e_A}]$ and that of ϕ'_B on $E_A[\ell_A^{2e_A}]$, then Alice can exploit this information to verify Bob's public key validity. Working with SIDH parameters where $p = \ell_A^{e_A}\ell_B^{e_B}f$, the torsion points of order $\ell_A^{2e_A}$ and $\ell_B^{2e_B}$ would be defined over extensions of $\mathbb{F}_{p^2}$ of degree roughly $\ell_A^{e_A}$ and $\ell_B^{e_B}$ respectively. We hence increase the field characteristic to $p = \ell_A^{2e_A}\ell_B^{2e_B}f - 1$ (where f is a small co-factor) such that the later torsion groups are defined over $\mathbb{F}_{p^2}$. Also, we set the starting curve E_0 to be a random supersingular curve with unknown endomorphism ring to avoid improved torsion points attacks. We hence obtain an efficient key validation method which does not require key disclosure and re-encryption, as it is the case in SIKE.

Secondly, we incorporate this key validation method into a key exchange scheme: HealSIDH (**Healed SIDH**). Let $p = \ell_A^{2e_A}\ell_B^{2e_B}f - 1$ as required by the countermeasure, let $\phi_A : E_0 \to E_A$, $\phi'_A : E_B \to E_{BA}$, and $\phi_B : E_0 \to E_B$, $\phi'_B : E_A \to E_{AB}$ be Alice's and Bob' secret isogenies respectively. Alice reveals the action of ϕ_A on $E_0[\ell_B^{2e_B}]$ and that of ϕ'_A on $E_B[\ell_B^{2e_B}]$. Analogously, Bob reveals the action of ϕ_B on $E_0[\ell_A^{2e_A}]$ and that of ϕ'_B on $E_A[\ell_A^{2e_A}]$. Revealing the action of ϕ'_A and ϕ'_B on torsion points implies revealing points on the shared curve $E_{AB} = E_{BA}$. To avoid this, each party canonically generates a basis of the corresponding subgroup and reveals the coordinates of the points in this canonical basis. HealSIDH is an order of magnitude more efficient compared to k-SIDH (the existing countermeasure to the adaptive attack on SIDH) since only four isogenies are computed in HealSIDH while more than k^2 (with $46 \leq k$) of them are computed in k-SIDH. The security of HealSIDH against key recovery relies on Problem 4 which is a variant of the Supersingular Isogeny Computational Diffie-Hellman Problem (SSICDHP), Problem 1.

Thirdly, we design a PKE scheme using HealSIDH. Our PKE scheme is named SHealS: **S**tatic-static key **Heal**ed **S**IKE. The idea in SHealS is to use the points to encrypt the plaintext, in such a way that the receiver solves a discrete logarithm problem in a group of smooth order to recover the plaintext. A similar idea is used in SiGamal [23] and SimS [14], but our design is different. SHealS uses primes two times larger (in terms of bit size) compared to SIKE primes, has larger keys and ciphertexts, but only 4 isogenies are computed and evaluated on torsion points in a full execution (KeyGeneration + Encryption + Decryption) of the scheme, as opposed to 5 isogenies in SIKE, among which 3 isogenies are evaluated on torsion points while the remaining two are not. For this reason, we believe SHealS efficiency is comparable to that of SIKE, but only an optimised implementation of SHealS would help evaluate the exact timings and do a more precise efficiency comparison. The main advantage of SHealS over SIKE is the reuse of encryption keys. In fact, since there is no key disclosure, the encryption key can remain static for a given user. Moreover, this user can use this same key as a private key in the SHealS PKE setting. We prove that SHealS is IND-CPA secure relying on one new assumption we introduce. Despite not being able to come up with a succinct proof of IND-CCA security, we conjecture that SHealS is IND-CCA secure and provide arguments to support our conjecture.

Lastly, we suggest HealS, a variant of SHealS using a smaller prime, providing the same security level, smaller keys and ciphertexts. The size of the prime used in HealS is only 1.5 times that of the prime used in SIKE. This yields a speed-up over SHealS, smaller keys and ciphertexts; hence reducing the efficiency and key sizes gap between SHealS and SIKE. The drawback of HealS compared to SHealS is that private keys can not be used as encryption keys.

As a result, beside CSIDH whose quantum security remains to be precisely estimated, HealSIDH is a new efficient interactive post-quantum key exchange scheme enabling static-static key setting. Moreover, we believe the fact that there is no key disclosure in SHealS and HealS makes of them promising PKE schemes.

Related work. While this work was under submission, an SIDH Proof of Knowledge mechanism [12] was published online by De Feo et al. This mechanism enable any party in an SIDH instance to prove that his public key was honestly generated. The proof attached to the public key is obtained by performing an SIDH-type signature on the public key to proof the knowledge of the secret isogeny and the correctness of the torsion points. For this reason, the proof is relatively large ($O(\lambda^2)$), computing and verifying the proof are relatively time consuming compared to our schemes. Nevertheless, their proof enables the design of an SIDH based NIKE while our key exchange HealSIDH is interactive.

Outline. The remaining of this paper is organized as follows: in Sect. 2, we recall some generalities about PKE schemes, elliptic curves and isogenies. We briefly present SIDH, the improved torsion points attacks and the GPST adaptive attack. We end Sect. 2 by describing existing countermeasures to the GPST adaptive attacks. Section 3 is devoted to our countermeasure. In Sect. 4 we present HealSIDH key exchange and in Sect. 5 we construct the SHealS PKE scheme. In Sect. 6, we provide a concrete instantiation of HealSIDH and SHealS, and provide a high level comparison to k-SIDH and SIKE respectively. In Sect. 7, we present HealS and in Sect. 8 we conclude the paper.

2 Preliminaries

2.1 Public Key Encryption

We recall standard security definitions related to public key encryption.

Definition 1 (PKE). *A Public Key Encryption scheme $\mathcal{P}_\lambda$ is a triple of PPT algorithms (*$\mathsf{KeyGeneration}$, $\mathsf{Encryption}$, $\mathsf{Decryption}$*) that satisfy the following.*

1. *Given a security parameter λ as input, the key generation algorithm* KeyGeneration *outputs a public key pk, a private key sk and a plaintext space $\mathcal{M}$.*
2. *Given a plaintext $\mu \in \mathcal{M}$ and a public key pk as inputs, the encryption algorithm* Encryption *outputs a ciphertext* $\mathsf{c} = \mathsf{Encryption}_{pk}(\mu)$.
3. *Given a ciphertext* c *and sk as inputs, the decryption algorithm* Decryption *outputs a plain text* $= \mathsf{Decryption}_{sk}(\mathsf{c})$.

Definition 2 (Correctness). *A PKE scheme $\mathcal{P}_\lambda$ is correct if for any pair of keys (pk, sk) and for every plaintext $\mu \in \mathcal{M}$,*

$$\mathsf{Decryption}_{sk}\left(\mathsf{Encryption}_{pk}(\mu)\right) = \mu.$$

Definition 3 (IND-CPA Secure). *A PKE scheme $\mathcal{P}_\lambda$ is IND-CPA secure if for every PPT adversary $\mathcal{A}$,*

$$Pr\left[b = b^* \,\middle|\, \begin{array}{l}(pk, sk) \leftarrow \mathsf{KeyGeneration}(\lambda), \mu_0, \mu_1 \leftarrow \mathcal{M}, \\ b \xleftarrow{\$} \{0,1\}, \mathsf{c} \leftarrow \mathsf{Encryption}_{pk}(\mu_b), b^* \leftarrow \mathcal{A}(pk, \mathsf{c})\end{array}\right] = \frac{1}{2} + \mathsf{negl}(\lambda).$$

Definition 4 (IND-CCA secure). *A PKE scheme $\mathcal{P}_\lambda$ is IND-CCA secure if for every PPT adversary $\mathcal{A}$,*

$$Pr\left[b = b^* \,\middle|\, \begin{array}{l}(pk, sk) \leftarrow \mathsf{KeyGeneration}(\lambda), \mu_0, \mu_1 \leftarrow \mathcal{A}^{O(\cdot)}(pk, \mathcal{M}), \\ b \xleftarrow{\$} \{0,1\}, \mathsf{c} \leftarrow \mathsf{Encryption}_{pk}(\mu_b), b^* \leftarrow \mathcal{A}^{O(\cdot)}(pk, \mathsf{c})\end{array}\right] = \frac{1}{2} + \mathsf{negl}(\lambda),$$

where $O(\cdot)$ is a decryption oracle that when given a ciphertext $\mathsf{c}' \neq \mathsf{c}$, *outputs* $\mathsf{Decryption}_{sk}(\mathsf{c}')$ *or $\perp$ if the ciphertext* c' *is invalid.*

2.2 Elliptic Curves and Isogenies

An elliptic curve is a rational smooth curve of genus one with a distinguished point at infinity. Elliptic curves can be seen as commutative groups with respect to a group addition having the point at infinity as neutral element. When an elliptic curve E is defined over a finite field $\mathbb{F}_q$, the set of $\mathbb{F}_q$-rational points $E(\mathbb{F}_q)$ of E is a subgroup of E. For every integer N coprime with q, the N-torsion subgroup $E[N]$ of E is isomorphic to $\mathbb{Z}_N \oplus \mathbb{Z}_N$.

An isogeny from E to E' is a rational map from E to E' which is also a group morphism. The kernel of an isogeny is always finite and entirely defines the isogeny up to powers of the Frobenius. Given a finite subgroup G of E, there exists a Frobenius free isogeny of domain E having kernel G, called a separable isogeny. Its degree is equal to the size of its kernel. The co-domain of this isogeny is denoted by E/G. The isogeny and the co-domain E/G can be computed from the knowledge of the kernel using Vélu's formulas [28] whose efficiency depends on the smoothness of the isogeny degree.

An endomorphism of an elliptic curve E is an isogeny from E to E. The group structure of E is closely related to that of its endomorphism ring. When E is defined over a finite field, the endomorphism ring of E is either an order in a quadratic field, in which case we say E is ordinary, or a maximal order in a quaternion algebra in which case we say E is supersingular. The generic isogeny problem is harder to solve for supersingular curves (for which the best attacks are exponential) than ordinary curves (for which there exists a sub-exponential attack [6]). SIDH is based on supersingular isogenies.

2.3 SIDH

The SIDH scheme is defined as follows.

Setup. Let $p = \ell_A^{e_A}\ell_B^{e_B} - 1$ be a prime such that $\ell_A^{e_A} \approx \ell_B^{e_B} \approx \sqrt{p}$. Let E_0 be a supersingular curve defined over $\mathbb{F}_{p^2}$. Set $E_0[\ell_A^{e_A}] = \langle P_A, Q_A\rangle$ and $E_0[\ell_B^{e_B}] = \langle P_B, Q_B\rangle$. The public parameters are E_0, p, ℓ_A, ℓ_B, e_A, e_B, P_A, Q_A, P_B, Q_B.

KeyGeneration. The secret key sk_A of Alice is a uniformly random integer α sampled from $\mathbb{Z}_{\ell_A^{e_A}}$. Compute the cyclic isogeny $\phi_A : E_0 \to E_A = E_0/\langle P_A + [\alpha]Q_A\rangle$. The public key of Alice is the tuple $\mathsf{pk}_A = (E_A, \phi_A(P_B), \phi_A(Q_B))$. Analogously, Bob's secret key sk_B is a uniformly random integer β sampled from $\mathbb{Z}_{\ell_B^{e_B}}$ and his public key is $\mathsf{pk}_B = (E_B, \phi_B(P_A), \phi_B(Q_A))$ where $\phi_B : E_0 \to E_B = E_0/\langle P_B + [\beta]Q_B\rangle$.

KeyExchange. Upon receiving (E_B, R_a, S_a), Alice checks that $e(R_a, S_a) = e(P_A, Q_A)^{\ell_B^{e_B}}$, if not she aborts. She computes the isogeny $\phi'_A : E_B \to E_{BA} = E_B/\langle R_a + [\alpha]S_a\rangle$. Her shared key is $j(E_{BA})$. Similarly, upon receiving (E_A, R_b, S_b), Bob checks that $e(R_b, S_b) = e(P_B, Q_B)^{\ell_A^{e_A}}$, if not he aborts. He computes the isogeny $\phi'_B : E_A \to E_{AB} = E_A/\langle R_b + [\beta]S_b\rangle$. His shared key is $j(E_{AB})$.

The correctness of the key exchange follows from the fact that

$$E_A/\langle \phi_A(P_B) + [\beta]\phi_A(Q_B)\rangle \simeq E_0/\langle P_A + [\alpha]Q_A, P_B + [\beta]Q_B\rangle \simeq E_B/\langle \phi_B(P_A) + [\alpha]\phi_B(Q_A)\rangle.$$

The security of the SIDH key exchange protocol against shared key recovery relies on Problem 1. Furthermore, Problem 2 states that it is difficult to distinguish the shared secret from a random supersingular elliptic curve.

Problem 1 (Supersingular Isogeny Computational Diffie-Hellman). Given E_0, P_A, Q_A, P_B, Q_B, E_A, $\phi_A(P_B)$, $\phi_A(Q_B)$, E_B, $\phi_B(P_A)$, $\phi_B(Q_A)$ (defined as in SIDH), compute E_{AB}.

Problem 2 (Supersingular Isogeny Decisional Diffie-Hellman). Given E_0, P_A, Q_A, P_B, Q_B, E_A, $\phi_A(P_B)$, $\phi_A(Q_B)$, E_B, $\phi_B(P_A)$, $\phi_B(Q_A)$ (defined as in SIDH) and a random supersingular curve E, distinguish between $E = E_{AB}$ and $E \neq E_{AB}$.

An IND-CPA secure PKE from SIDH. One canonically derives a PKE schemes from SIDH as follows. Let $H : \mathbb{F}_{p^2} \rightarrow \{0,1\}^n$ be a cryptographic hash function.

$\mathsf{KeyGeneration}$. Alice generates her key pair exactly as in SIDH.
$\mathsf{Encryption}$. Let m be a plaintext. Bob generates a random integer $\beta \in \mathbb{Z}_{\ell_B^{e_B}}$ and executes the SIDH key exchange using Alice's public key to obtain $\mathsf{c}_0 = (E_B, \phi_B(P_A), \phi_B(Q_A))$ and $j_{AB} = j(E_{AB})$. The returned ciphertext is $(\mathsf{c}_0, \mathsf{c}_1 = H(j_{AB}) \oplus \mathsf{m})$.
$\mathsf{Decryption}$. Given a ciphertext $(\mathsf{c}_0, \mathsf{c}_1)$, Alice completes the underlying SIDH key exchange to obtain $j_{BA} = j(E_{BA})$ and recovers the plaintext $\mathsf{m} = \mathsf{c}_1 \oplus H(j_{BA})$.

The above scheme is IND-CPA secure assuming Problem 2 is hard [13], but it is not IND-CCA since it is vulnerable to the GPST adaptive attack [17] that we present later in Sect. 2.5.

2.4 Passive Torsion Point Attacks on SIDH

The direct key recovery attack (attacking one party's secret key) in SIDH translates into solving the following *Supersingular Isogeny Problem.*

Problem 3. Let A and B be two integers such that $\gcd(A, B) = 1$. Let E_0 be a supersingular elliptic curve defined over $\mathbb{F}_{p^2}$. Set $E_0[B] = \{P, Q\}$ and let $\phi : E_0 \rightarrow E_A$ be a random isogeny of degree A. Given E_0, E_A, P, Q, $\phi(P)$ and $\phi(Q)$, compute ϕ.

The difference between Problem 3 and the general isogeny problem is the fact that the action of ϕ on the group $E_0[B]$ is revealed. In 2017, Petit [26] exploited these torsion point images to design an algorithm that solves Problem 3 for a certain choice of unbalanced ($A \ll B$) parameters when the endomorphism ring of the starting curve E_0 is public. Petit's attack has recently been considerably improved by de Quehen et al. [10]. We refer to [10] for more details.

To counter the attack in unbalanced SIDH instances, one sets the starting curve E_0 to be a random supersingular curve with unknown endomorphism ring. We don't know how to generate random supersingular elliptic curves for which the endomorphism ring is unknown (also to the party generating the curve). This is considered as an open problem [9]. Hence one generally relies on a trusted party to generate a random curve which is then used as a public parameter of the scheme. This will be the case for the schemes presented in this paper.

2.5 GPST Adaptive Attack

In SIDH [13] one does a pairing-based check on the torsion points $\phi_B(P_A)$ and $\phi_B(Q_A)$ returned by a potentially malicious Bob. Let E be a supersingular elliptic curve, let N be an integer and let μ_N be the group of N-roots of unity. Let $e_N : E[N] \times E[N] \rightarrow \mu_N$ be the Weil pairing [16]. Let $\phi : E \rightarrow E'$ be an isogeny of degree M, then for $P, Q \in E[N]$,

$$e_N(\phi(P), \phi(Q)) = e_N(P, Q)^M$$

where the first pairing is computed on E' and the second one on E.
In SIDH, given (E_B, R, S) returned by Bob as public key, Alice checks if

$$e_{\ell_A^{e_A}}(R, S) = e_{\ell_A^{e_A}}(P_A, Q_A)^{\ell_B^{e_B}}.$$

As we will see below, this verification does not assure that the points R, S were honestly generated. More precisely, the pairing verification does not capture the GPST adaptive attack.

The GPST Adaptive Attack. The main idea of the Galbraith et al. adaptive attack [17] is that if Bob manipulates the torsion points $\phi_B(P_A)$ and $\phi_B(Q_A)$ conveniently, then he can get some information about Alice's private key α given that he knows if the secret curve computed by Alice is equal to E_{AB} or not. Hence in the attack scenario, Bob needs to have access to the later information. This access is provided to Bob through a key exchange oracle:

$$O(E, R, S, E') \text{ which returns 1 if } j(E') = j(E/\langle R + [\alpha]S\rangle) \text{ and 0 otherwise}$$

If one supposes that $\ell_A = 2$ and $e_A = n$, then after each query, Bob recovers one bit of

$$\alpha = \alpha_0 + 2^1\alpha_1 + 2^2\alpha_2 + \cdots + 2^{n-1}\alpha_{n-1}.$$

The attack recovers the first $n-2$ bits of α using $n-2$ oracle queries, and it recovers the two remaining bits by brute force. We refer to [17] for more details.

2.6 Existing Countermeasures to the GPST Adaptive Attacks

The previous section has highlighted the need for a "better" key validation method for SIDH-type schemes. We now present SIKE and k-SIDH, that are currently the two main countermeasures to the GPST attack on SIDH.

SIKE (Supersingular Isogeny Key Encapsulation). Our description is more general compared to that submitted to the third round of the NIST competition [19], and it does not include key compression features. In the following scheme, G, H and F are hash functions and n is an integer, we refer to [19] for more details.

Setup. As in SIDH.

KeyGeneration. Generate a secret key $\mathsf{sk} = \alpha \in \mathbb{Z}_{\ell_A^{e_A}}$ and a public key $\mathsf{pk} = (E_A, \phi_A(P_B), \phi_A(Q_B))$ as in SIDH. Sample a uniformly random integer $s \in \{0,1\}^n$ and return $(s, \mathsf{sk}, \mathsf{pk})$.

Encapsulation. Sample a uniformly random integer m from $\{0,1\}^n$. Compute $\beta = G(m||\mathsf{pk}) \in \mathbb{Z}_{\ell_B^{e_B}}$ and compute $\mathsf{c}_0 = (E_B, \phi_B(P_A), \phi_B(Q_A))$ and E_{AB} as in the SIDH, together with $\mathsf{c}_1 = F(j(E_{AB})) \oplus m$ and $K = H(m||(\mathsf{c}_0, \mathsf{c}_1))$ and return $((\mathsf{c}_0, \mathsf{c}_1), K)$.

Decapsulation. From $(\mathsf{c}_0, \mathsf{c}_1)$, compute E_{BA} as in SIDH and $m' = \mathsf{c}_1 \oplus F(j(E_{BA}))$.

Re-encrypt m' to obtain $\mathsf{c}_0' = (E_B', \psi_B(P_A), \psi_B(Q_A))$. If $\mathsf{c}_0 = \mathsf{c}_0'$, return $K = H(m'||(\mathsf{c}_0, \mathsf{c}_1))$, else return $K = H(s||(\mathsf{c}_0, \mathsf{c}_1))$.

In SIKE, the adaptive attacks are not applicable since during the decapsulation, Alice recomputes Bob's encryption key $\beta' = G(m'||\mathsf{pk}) \in \mathbb{Z}_{\ell_B^{e_B}}$ and checks if the obtained key leads to the curve and torsion points sent by Bob, this enables her to detect maliciously generated public keys. Therefore, the scheme requires key disclosure to the recipient. This is a common drawback to all post-quantum PKEs engaged in the NIST standardization process. In fact, as noticed in [1, §1], these schemes use ephemeral keys or indirect validation techniques that would expose one's key in the static-static setting.

Other countermeasures to the GPST attack. As a countermeasure to the GPST attack, Azarderakhsh et al. introduced k-SIDH [1]. In k-SIDH, Alice's private key is a tuple $\alpha = (\alpha_1, \cdots, \alpha_k) \in (\mathbb{Z}_{\ell_A}^{e_A})^k$ and Bob's private key is a tuple $\beta = (\beta_1, \cdots, \beta_k) \in (\mathbb{Z}_{\ell_B}^{e_B})^k$. Alice and Bob simultaneously run k^2 SIDH key exchange instances corresponding to the k^2 couples of Alice and Bob's SIDH private keys (α_i, β_j), $1 \le i, j \le k$. The shared secret is then obtained by applying a key derivation function to the corresponding k^2 SIDH shared secrets. The scheme quickly becomes impractical as k grows.

In [30], Jao and Urbanik propose a variant of k-SIDH that they expected to be more efficient. Their variant exploits non trivial automorphisms of the starting curve E_0 when this supersingular curve has j-invariant 0 or 1728 to reduce the number k of SIDH instances in k-SIDH. For example, in the case where the starting supersingular curve E_0 has j-invariant 0, there exists a non trivial automorphism η_6 of E_0 of order 6. Given a finite subgroup $G \subset E_0$, the curves E_0/G, $E_0/\eta_6(G)$ and $E_0/\eta_6^2(G)$, are isomorphic but it is not the case for the isogenies $E_0 \to E_0/G$, $E_0 \to E_0/\eta_6(G)$ and $E_0 \to E_0/\eta_6^2(G)$. Hence when performing a key exchange, these three isogenies will lead to three distinct SIDH shared keys. Hence with $\alpha' = (\alpha_1, \cdots, \alpha_{k'}) \in (\mathbb{Z}_{\ell_A}^{e_A})^{k'}$ and $\beta' = (\beta_1, \cdots, \beta_{k'}) \in (\mathbb{Z}_{\ell_B}^{e_B})^{k'}$, Alice and Bob can derive $3k'^2$ SIDH shared secrets contrarily to k'^2 for k-SIDH.

In [11], Dobson et al. show that the GPST attack can be adapted to k-SIDH. Nevertheless, the cost of the attack (number of queries to the key exchange oracle) grows exponentially with k. Dobson et al.'s attack does not directly apply to the Jao-Urbanik variant of k-SIDH. In [2], Basso et al. present an adaptation of this attack to the Jao-Urbanik variant. Moreover, they prove that considering their attack, for the same security level, k-SIDH is more efficient compared to the Jao-Urbanik variant. From these two attacks, one concludes that for k-SIDH and the Jao-Urbanik variant to be secure against adaptive attacks, one needs k to be relatively large ([11] suggests $k = 46$ for about 128 bits of security), consequently the schemes become less practical.

To sum up, as countermeasures to the GPST adaptive attack, SIKE imposes key disclosure while k-SIDH comes with a considerable efficiency drawback. We address this in the next section by providing a new countermeasure which is more efficient compared to k-SIDH and without key disclosure.

3 A New Countermeasure to the GPST Adaptive Attack

In this section, we describe a mechanism which enables Alice, when using a static key, to decide on the correctness of the torsion points returned by BoB. We translate this point correctness mechanism into a new key validation method.

3.1 Overview

In our scenario, like in SIKE, we suppose that the initiator of the communication (Bob) has to prove the validity of his torsion points to the other party (Alice). Let E_0, P_A, Q_A, P_B, Q_B, E_A, $\phi_A(P_B)$, $\phi_A(P_B)$ be the public parameters and Alice's public key in an SIDH instance. For simplicity, we suppose that the degree of Alice's isogeny is 2^a and that the degree of Bob's isogeny is 3^b for some integers a and b. In SIDH, Bob computes a cyclic isogeny $\phi_B : E_0 \to E_B$ of degree 3^b together with the images $\phi_B(P_A)$ and $\phi_B(Q_A)$ of P_A and Q_A. We say that the torsion points $R, S \in E_B[2^a]$ returned by Bob are *correct* if $R = [\lambda]\phi_B(P_A)$ and $S = [\lambda]\phi_B(Q_A)$ for some $\lambda \in \mathbb{Z}/2^a\mathbb{Z}^\times$. We establish a Points Correctness Verification (PCV) mechanism for Alice to determine if the torsion points computed by Bob are correct.

We start with an observation of Leonardi [22]: *"in an honest SIDH, $\phi_{A'} \circ \phi_B = \phi_{B'} \circ \phi_A$"*. Composing by $\widehat{\phi_{A'}}$ on the left, we get

$$[2^a] \circ \phi_B = \widehat{\phi_{A'}} \circ \phi_{B'} \circ \phi_A. \tag{1}$$

Let $P_2, Q_2 \in E_0[2^{2a}]$ be points such that $[2^a]P_2 = P_A$ and $[2^a]Q_2 = Q_A$. Then

$$\begin{cases} \phi_{A'} \circ \phi_B(P_2) = \phi_{B'} \circ \phi_A(P_2) \\ \phi_{A'} \circ \phi_B(Q_2) = \phi_{B'} \circ \phi_A(Q_2), \end{cases} \tag{2}$$

hence

$$\begin{cases} \phi_B(P_A) = \phi_B([2^2]P_2) = \widehat{\phi_{A'}} \circ \phi_{B'} \circ \phi_A(P_2) \\ \phi_B(Q_A) = \phi_B([2^a]Q_2) = \widehat{\phi_{A'}} \circ \phi_{B'} \circ \phi_A(Q_2) \end{cases} \tag{3}$$

Equation 3 suggests that if Alice can successfully check the equalities in Eq. 2, then she can verify if Bob's torsion points are correct.

The idea of the PCV mechanism is that instead of revealing the action of $\phi_B : E_0 \to E_B$ on the 2^a-torsion sub-group of E_0, Bob reveals the action of ϕ_B on the 2^{2a}-torsion sub-group of E_0 and the action of $\phi'_B : E_A \to E_{AB}$ on the 2^{2a}-torsion sub-group of E_A. In our PCV mechanism, Bob's public key (when honestly computed) is $(E_B, \phi_B(P_2), \phi_B(Q_2))$. The action of $\phi'_B : E_A \to E_{AB}$ on the 2^{2a}-torsion sub-group of E_A is provided by canonically generating a new 2^{2a}-torsion basis $\{R_A, S_A\}$ of E_A and revealing $R_{ab} = \phi'_B(R_A)$ and $S_{ab} = \phi'_B(S_A)$.

At this point, Bob can be malicious in the following three ways:

1. honestly compute $R_a = \phi_B(P_2)$ and $S_a = \phi_B(Q_2)$, and maliciously compute $R_{ab} = \phi'_B(R_A)$ and $S_{ab} = \phi'_B(S_A)$;
2. maliciously compute $R_a = \phi_B(P_2)$ and $S_a = \phi_B(Q_2)$, and honestly compute $R_{ab} = \phi'_B(R_A)$ and $S_{ab} = \phi'_B(S_A)$;
3. maliciously compute $R_a = \phi_B(P_2)$ and $S_a = \phi_B(Q_2)$, and maliciously compute $R_{ab} = \phi'_B(R_A)$ and $S_{ab} = \phi'_B(S_A)$.

In the first two cases, we say that Bob is *partially point-malicious* and in the third case we say that Bob is *doubly point-malicious.*

Remark 1. We use the term *point-malicious* to highlight the fact that we focus only on the correctness of the torsion points outputted by BoB, not on the validity of the Bob's entire public key. Hence we are supposing that ϕ_B and ϕ'_B are cyclic isogenies of degree 3^b and only the torsion point were maliciously evaluated.

When Bob is partially point-malicious, then either the right hand term or the left hand term in Eq. 2 is correctly computed by Alice. Hence the partial point-maliciousness of Bob would be detected since the other term of the equation would be different. Concretely, we have the following theorem.

Theorem 1. *Let E_0, P_A, Q_A, P_B, Q_B, E_A, $\phi_A(P_B)$, $\phi_A(P_B)$ be the public parameters and Alice's public key in an SIDH instance. Let $P_2, Q_2 \in E_0[2^{2a}]$ such that $[2^a]P_2 = P_A$ and $[2^a]Q_2 = Q_A$. Let (E_B, R_a, S_a) be Bob's public key. Moreover, let $\{R_A, S_A\}$ be a canonical basis of $E_A[2^{2a}]$ and let $\{R_{ab}, S_{ab}\}$ be its image through $\phi'_B : E_A \to E_{AB}$ outputted by Bob. Write $\phi_A(P_2) = [e_1]R_A + [f_1]S_A$ and $\phi_A(Q_2) = [e_2]R_A + [f_2]S_A$. Let us suppose that Bob is eventually partially point-malicious and let $\psi'_A : E_B \to E_B/\langle [2^a]R_a + [\alpha][2^a]S_a \rangle$ be the isogeny computed by Alice.*
If $e_{2^{2a}}(R_a, S_a) = e_{2^{2a}}(P_2, Q_2)^{3^b}$, $[e_1]R_{ab} + [f_1]S_{ab} = \psi'_A(R_a)$ and $[e_2]R_{ab} + [f_2]S_{ab} = \psi'_A(S_a)$, then Bob's torsion points are correct.

Proof. Noticing that $[e_1]R_{ab} + [f_1]S_{ab}$ stands for $\phi'_B \circ \phi_A(P_2)$ and $\psi'_A(R_a)$ for $\phi'_A \circ \phi_B(P_2)$, while $[e_2]R_{ab} + [f_2]S_{ab}$ stands for $\phi'_B \circ \phi_A(Q_2)$ and $\psi'_A(S_a)$ for $\phi'_A \circ \phi_B(Q_2)$, the theorem follows from the previous discussion. □

Remark 2. The points $\phi_A(P_2), \phi_A(Q_2) \in E_A[2^{2a}]$ are secret (known only by Alice). In fact their knowledge is equivalent to the knowledge of Alice's secret since $[2^a]P_2 = P_A$ and $[2^a]Q_2 = Q_A$.

For the third case where Bob is *doubly point-malicious*, we provide a more involved mathematical proof in the next paragraph.

3.2 The Main Theorem

In the previous section, we make use of points of order 2^{2a} or 3^{2b}. In SIDH parameters where $p = 2^a 3^b f - 1$, these points are defined over a large extension field of degree roughly $2^a \approx 3^b$. To make our key validation efficient, we use primes of the form $p = 2^{2a}3^{2b}f - 1$. Moreover, we evaluate isogenies of degree 2^a on points of order $3^{2b} \approx 2^{2a}$. To avoid improved torsion points attacks or any variant of it, we set the starting curve E_0 to be a random supersingular curve with unknown endomorphism ring. Figure 1 summarizes the key validation mechanism hence obtained.

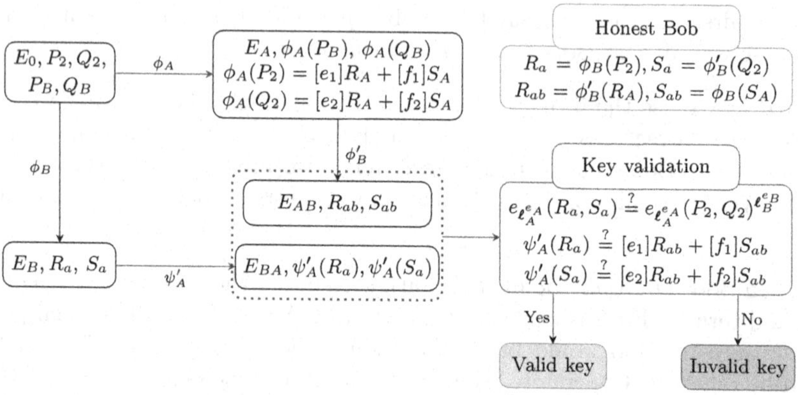

Fig. 1. Key validation mechanism for SIDH-type schemes. The curve E_0 is a random supersingular elliptic curve with unknown endomorphism ring defined over $\mathbb{F}_{p^2}$ where $p = 2^{2a}3^{2b}f - 1$.

We prove the following Theorem.

Theorem 2. *Let $p = 2^{2a}3^{2b}f - 1$ and let E_0 be a random supersingular elliptic curve with unknown endomorphism ring defined over $\mathbb{F}_{p^2}$. Let E_0, P_A, Q_A, P_B, Q_B, E_A, $\phi_A(P_B)$, $\phi_A(P_B)$ be the public parameters and Alice's public key in an SIDH instance. Let P_2, $Q_2 \in E_0[2^{2a}]$ such that $[2^a]P_2 = P_A$ and $[2^a]Q_2 = Q_A$. Let (E_B, R_a, S_a) be Bob's public key. Moreover, let $\{R_A, S_A\}$ be a canonical basis of $E_A[2^{2a}]$ and let $\{R_{ab}, S_{ab}\}$ be its image through $\phi'_B : E_A \to E_{AB}$ outputted by Bob. Write $\phi_A(P_2) = [e_1]R_A + [f_1]S_A$ and $\phi_A(Q_2) = [e_2]R_A + [f_2]S_A$. Let $\psi'_A : E_B \to E_B/\langle [2^a]R_a + [\alpha][2^a]S_a\rangle$ be the second isogeny computed by Alice during the key exchange.*

If $e_{2^{2a}}(R_a, S_a) = e_{2^{2a}}(P_2, Q_2)^{3^b}$, $[e_1]R_{ab} + [f_1]S_{ab} = \psi'_A(R_a)$ and $[e_2]R_{ab} + [f_2]S_{ab} = \psi'_A(S_a)$, then Bob's torsion points are correct.

Proof. Let us suppose that Bob is possibly doubly point-malicious, say

$$\left|\begin{array}{l} R_a = [x]\phi_B(P_2) + [y]\phi_B(Q_2) \\ S_a = [z]\phi_B(P_2) + [t]\phi_B(Q_2) \\ R_{ab} = [x']\phi'_B(R_A) + [y']\phi'_B(S_A) \\ S_{ab} = [z']\phi'_B(R_A) + [t']\phi'_B(S_A) \end{array}\right.$$

for some integers x, y, z, t, x', y', z' and t' modulo 2^{2a}.

Let us suppose that $e_{2^{2a}}(R_a, S_a) = e_{2^{2a}}(P_2, Q_2)^{3^b}$, $[e_1]R_{ab}+[f_1]S_{ab} = \phi'_A(R_a)$ and $[e_2]R_{ab} + [f_2]S_{ab} = \phi'_A(S_a)$. We prove that $x = t = x' = t' = \pm 1$ and $y = z = y' = z' = 0$, which implies that Bob's torsion points are correct. Let

$$\phi'_A : E_B \to E_{BA} = E_B/\langle \phi_B(P_A) + [\alpha]\phi_B(Q_A)\rangle = E_B/\langle [2^a]\phi_B(P_2) + [\alpha][2^a]\phi_B(Q_2)\rangle$$

be the isogeny that ought to be computed by Alice if Bob's torsion points were correct and let

$$\psi'_A : E_B \to E_B/\langle [2^a]R_a + [\alpha][2^a]S_a\rangle$$

be the isogeny effectively computed by Alice. We distinguish two cases.

Case 1: $\phi'_A \neq \psi_A$. Then $E_{AB} \neq E_B/\langle [2^a]R_a + [\alpha][2^a]S_a\rangle$ with overwhelming probability. In fact, if $E_{AB} = E_B/\langle [2^a]R_a + [\alpha][2^a]S_a\rangle$ with $\phi'_A \neq \psi_A$, then $\phi'_A \circ \widehat{\psi_A}$ is an endomorphism of E_{AB} of degree $2^{2a} \approx \sqrt{p}$. Since E_0 is a random supersingular curve, then the curve E_{AB} which is $2^a 2^b$ isogenous to E_0 can be assimilated to a random supersingular curve. Hence the probability that E_{AB} admits an endomorphism of degree $2^{2a} \approx \sqrt{p}$ is negligible.

Hence $R_{ab}, S_{ab} \notin E_B/\langle [2^a]R_a + [\alpha][2^a]S_a\rangle$. Therefore $[e_1]R_{ab} + [f_1]S_{ab} \neq \psi_A(R_a)$ and $[e_2]R_{ab}+[f_2]S_{ab} \neq \psi_A(S_a)$ since they are points on different curves.

Case 2: $\phi'_A = \psi_A$. Then Alice computes

$$\begin{aligned}
\psi_A(R_a) = \phi'_A(R_a) &= \phi'_A([x]\phi_B(P_2) + [y]\phi_B(Q_2)) \\
&= \phi'_B \circ \phi_A([x]P_2 + [y]Q_2) \\
&= \phi'_B([x]\phi_A(P_2) + [y]\phi_A(Q_2)) \\
&= \phi'_B\left([x]([e_1]R_A + [f_1]S_A) + [y]([e_2]R_A + [f_2]S_A)\right) \\
&= \phi'_B\left([xe_1 + ye_2]R_A + [xf_1 + yf_2]S_A\right) \\
&= [xe_1 + ye_2]\phi'_B(R_A) + [xf_1 + yf_2]\phi'_B(S_A)
\end{aligned}$$

and

$$\begin{aligned}
\psi_A(S_a) = \phi'_A(S_a) &= \phi'_A([z]\phi_B(P_2) + [t]\phi_B(Q_2)) \\
&= \phi'_A \circ \phi_B([z]P_2 + [t]Q_2) \\
&= \phi'_B([z]\phi_A(P_2) + [t]\phi_A(Q_2)) \\
&= \phi'_B\left([z]([e_1]R_A + [f_1]S_A) + [t]([e_2]R_A + [f_2]S_A)\right) \\
&= \phi'_B\left([ze_1 + te_2]R_A + [zf_1 + tf_2]S_A\right) \\
&= [ze_1 + te_2]\phi'_B(R_A) + [zf_1 + tf_2]\phi'_B(S_A)
\end{aligned}$$

On the other hand, Alice computes

$$[e_1]R_{ab} + [f_1]S_{ab} = [x'e_1 + z'f_1]\phi'_B(R_A) + [y'e_1 + t'f_1]\phi'_B(S_A)$$

and

$$[e_2]R_{ab} + [f_2]S_{ab} = [x'e_2 + z'f_2]\phi'_B(R_A) + [y'e_2 + t'f_2]\phi'_B(S_A)$$

The integers x, y, z, t, x', y', z' and t' need to satisfy

$$\begin{cases} \psi_A(R_a) = [e_1]R_{ab} + [f_1]S_{ab} \\ \psi_A(S_a) = [e_2]R_{ab} + [f_2]S_{ab} \end{cases}$$

i.e.

$$\begin{cases} [xe_1 + ye_2]\phi'_B(R_A) + [xf_1 + yf_2]\phi'_B(S_A) = [x'e_1 + z'f_1]\phi'_B(R_A) + [y'e_1 + t'f_1]\phi'_B(S_A) \\ [ze_1 + te_2]\phi'_B(R_A) + [zf_1 + tf_2]\phi'_B(S_A) = [x'e_2 + z'f_2]\phi'_B(R_A) + [y'e_2 + t'f_2]\phi'_B(S_A) \end{cases}$$

i.e.

$$\begin{cases} xe_1 + ye_2 = x'e_1 + z'f_1 \\ xf_1 + yf_2 = y'e_1 + t'f_1 \\ ze_1 + te_2 = x'e_2 + z'f_2 \\ zf_1 + tf_2 = y'e_2 + t'f_2 \end{cases} \mod 2^{2a}$$

i.e.

$$\begin{bmatrix} e_1 & e_2 & 0 & 0 \\ f_1 & f_2 & 0 & 0 \\ 0 & 0 & e_1 & e_2 \\ 0 & 0 & f_1 & f_2 \end{bmatrix} \begin{bmatrix} x \\ y \\ z \\ t \end{bmatrix} = \begin{bmatrix} e_1 & 0 & f_1 & 0 \\ 0 & e_1 & 0 & f_1 \\ e_2 & 0 & f_2 & 0 \\ 0 & e_2 & 0 & f_2 \end{bmatrix} \begin{bmatrix} x' \\ y' \\ z' \\ t' \end{bmatrix} \mod 2^{2a} \tag{4}$$

From Remark 2, the knowledge of e_1, e_2, f_1 and f_2 is equivalent to the knowledge of Alice's private isogeny ϕ_A. Hence Bob does not have access neither to the matrix

$$M_1 = \begin{bmatrix} e_1 & e_2 & 0 & 0 \\ f_1 & f_2 & 0 & 0 \\ 0 & 0 & e_1 & e_2 \\ 0 & 0 & f_1 & f_2 \end{bmatrix} \in \mathcal{M}_2(\mathbb{Z}/2^{2a}\mathbb{Z}) \quad \text{nor} \quad M_2 = \begin{bmatrix} e_1 & 0 & f_1 & 0 \\ 0 & e_1 & 0 & f_1 \\ e_2 & 0 & f_2 & 0 \\ 0 & e_2 & 0 & f_2 \end{bmatrix} \in \mathcal{M}_2(\mathbb{Z}/2^{2a}\mathbb{Z}).$$

The solutions of Eq. 4 that are independent of M_1 and M_2 satisfy

$$y = z = y' = z' = 0, \quad x = t = x' = t'.$$

Since $e_{2^{2a}}(R_a, S_a) = e_{2^{2a}}([a]\phi_B(P_2), [a]\phi_B(Q_2)) = e_{2^{2a}}(\phi_B(P_2), \phi_B(Q_2))^{a^2}$, then from the pairing equation $e_{2^{2a}}(R_a, S_a) = e_{2^{2a}}(P_2, Q_2)^{3^b}$, a needs to satisfy $a^2 = 1$, hence $a = \pm 1$.
We finally get $a = d = a' = d' = \pm 1$ and $b = c = b' = c' = 0$.

□

Remark 3. A formal proof of Theorem 1 can be obtained from that of Theorem 2 by setting $x = 1 = t$, $y = 0 = z$ or $x' = 1 = t'$, $y' = 0 = z'$ at the beginning of the proof depending on the points on which Bob decides to be partially point-malicious.

Remark 4. Bob can use the same key validation method to detect a malicious Alice. We set the isogeny degrees to powers of 2 and 3 just for simplicity. The key validation method generalises to any SIDH-like setup.

4 The HealSIDH (Healed SIDH) Key Exchange Protocol

We now propose a variant of SIDH key exchange protocol which makes use of the GPST adaptive attack countermeasure we have just described. We first give the general idea behind the construction, then we concretely describe the key exchange and we finally discuss the underlying Diffie-Hellman-type hard problems.

4.1 An Overview of HealSIDH

The idea behind HealSIDH is to incorporate the key validation mechanism described in Sect. 3 in the SIDH key exchange.

Set $p = 2^{2a}3^{2b}f - 1$ such that $2^a \approx 3^b$, $E_0[2^{2a}] = \langle P_2, Q_2 \rangle$, $E_0[3^{2b}] = \langle P_3, Q_3 \rangle$, $P_A = [2^a]P_2$, $Q_A = [2^a]Q_2$, $P_B = [3^b]P_3$ and $Q_B = [3^b]Q_3$. Alice's secret is an integer α sampled uniformly from $\mathbb{Z}/2^a\mathbb{Z}$ while Bob's secret is an integer β sampled uniformly from $\mathbb{Z}/3^b\mathbb{Z}$. Alice computes $\phi_A : E_0 \to E_A = E_0/\langle P_A + [\alpha]Q_A \rangle$ together with $\phi_A(P_2)$, $\phi_A(Q_2)$, $\phi_A(P_B)$ and $\phi_A(Q_B)$. She canonically generates the basis $\{R_A, S_A\}$ of $E_A[2^{2a}]$ and solves for e_1, f_1, e_2 f_2 such that $\phi_A(P_2) = [e_1]R_A + [f_1]S_A$ and $\phi_A(Q_2) = [e_2]R_A + [f_2]S_A$. Her public key is $(E_A, \phi_A(P_B), \phi_A(Q_B))$ and her secret key is $(\alpha, e_1, f_1, e_2, f_2)$. Bob does the same to obtain a public key $(E_B, \phi_B(P_A), \phi_B(Q_A))$ and a secret key $(\beta, g_1, h_1, g_2, h_2)$.

If Bob wishes to establish a shared secret with Alice, he retrieves Alice's public key (E_A, R_b, S_b), computes $\phi'_B : E_A \to E_{AB} = E_A/\langle [3^b]R_b + [\beta][3^b]S_b \rangle$ together with $\phi'_B(R_A)$, $\phi'_B(S_A)$, $\phi'_B(R_b)$ and $\phi'_B(S_b)$. The yet to be confirmed shared secret is the j-invariant j_{AB} of E_{AB}. He sends $(\phi'_B(R_A), \phi'_B(S_A))$ to Alice.

Upon receiving $(\phi'_B(R_A), \phi'_B(S_A))$, Alice retrieves Bob's public key tuple (E_B, R_a, S_a). She computes $\phi'_A : E_B \to E_{BA} = E_B/\langle [2^a]R_a + [\alpha][2^a]S_a \rangle$ together with $\phi'_A(R_B)$, $\phi'_A(S_B)$, $\phi'_A(R_a)$ and $\phi'_A(S_a)$. She then computes R_{ba} and $\widehat{\phi'_A}(\phi'_B(S_A))$.
If $e_{2^{2a}}(R_a, S_a) \neq e_{2^{2a}}(P_2, Q_2)^{3^b}$ or $[e_1]\phi'_B(R_A) + [f_1]\phi'_B(S_A) \neq \phi'_A(R_a)$ or $[e_2]\phi'_B(R_A) + [f_2]\phi'_B(S_A) \neq \phi'_A(S_a)$, Alice aborts. Otherwise, she sends $\phi'_A(R_B)$ and $\phi'_A(S_B)$ to Bob and keeps the j-invariant j_{BA} of E_{BA} as the shared secret.

Upon receiving $\phi'_A(R_B)$ and $\phi'_A(S_B)$, Bob does the key validation check. If $e_{3^{2b}}(R_b, S_b) \neq e_{3^{2b}}(P_3, Q_3)^{2^a}$ or $[g_1]\phi'_A(R_B) + [h_1]\phi'_A(S_B) \neq \phi'_B(R_b)$ or $[g_2]\phi'_A(R_B) + [h_2]\phi'_A(S_B) \neq \phi'_B(S_b)$, Bob aborts . If not he successfully takes j_{AB} as the shared secret.

Practically, if Bob reveals the points $\phi'_B(R_A)$ and $\phi'_B(S_A)$, or Alice reveals $\phi'_A(R_B)$ and $\phi'_A(S_B)$, then an adversary can recover the curve E_{AB} since for $P \in E_{AB}$, the Montgomery coefficient $A_{E_{AB}}$ of E_{AB} satisfies

$$A_{E_{AB}} = \frac{y(P)^2 - x(P)^3 - x(P)}{x(P)^2}.$$

We avoid this by exploiting the ideas used in SIKE [19] for key compression: represent a point $P \in E[N]$ by its coordinates in a basis of $E[N]$ which can be canonically computed.

4.2 HealSIDH Key Exchange

Instead of revealing the points $\phi'_B(R_A)$ and $\phi'_B(S_A)$, Bob canonically generates a basis $\{R_{AB}, S_{AB}\}$ of $E_{AB}[2^{2a}]$ and computes $e_3, f_3, e_4, f_4 \in \mathbb{Z}_{2^{2a}}$ such that

$$\phi'_B(R_A) = [e_3]R_{AB} + [f_3]S_{AB} \text{ and } \phi'_B(S_A) = [e_4]R_{AB} + [f_4]S_{AB}.$$

Similarly, Alice canonically generates a basis $\{R_{BA}, S_{BA}\}$ of $E_{BA}[3^{2b}]$ and computes $g_3, h_3, g_4, h_4 \in \mathbb{Z}_{3^{2b}}$ such that

$$\phi'_A(R_B) = [g_3]R_{BA} + [h_3]S_{BA} \text{ and } \phi'_A(S_B) = [g_4]R_{BA} + [h_4]S_{BA}.$$

Concretely, the HealSIDH Key Exchange is entirely described in Fig. 2.

Lemma 1. *HealSIDH is correct.*

Proof. Follows from the correctness of SIDH and Theorem 2. □

Remark 5. Two parties Alice and Bob need to run the key validation only once, during their first communication. In the subsequent communications between the two parties there is no need to revalidate the keys.

4.3 Security of HealSIDH

We present the Computational Diffie-Hellman-type problem underlying the security of HealSIDH. We argue that the Decisional variant of this problem is not hard.

Problem 4 (HealSIDH-CDHP). Let $p = 2^{2a}2^{2b}f - 1$ and E_0 a supersingular curve defined over $\mathbb{F}_{p^2}$ with unknown endomorphism ring. Let $E_0[2^{2a}] = \langle P_2, Q_2\rangle$, $E_0[3^{2b}] = \langle P_3, Q_3\rangle$, $P_A = [2^a]P_2$, $Q_A = [2^a]Q_2$, $P_B = [3^b]P_3$, $Q_B = [3^b]Q_3$. Let $\phi_A : E_0 \to E_A$, $\phi_B : E_0 \to E_B$, $\phi'_A : E_B \to E_{BA}$ and $\phi'_B : E_A \to E_{AB}$ be secret isogenies as described in SIDH-type schemes. Let $E_A[2^{2a}] = \langle R_A, S_A\rangle$, $E_B[3^{2b}] = \langle R_B, S_B\rangle$, $E_{AB}[2^{2a}] = \langle R_{AB}, S_{AB}\rangle$, $E_{AB}[3^{2b}] = \langle R_{BA}, S_{BA}\rangle$. Let $e_3, f_3, e_4, f_4 \in \mathbb{Z}_{2^{2a}}$ and $g_3, h_3, g_4, h_4 \in \mathbb{Z}_{3^{2b}}$ such that $\phi'_A(R_B) = [g_3]R_{BA} + [h_3]S_{BA}$, $\phi'_A(S_B) = [g_4]R_{BA} + [h_4]S_{BA}$, $\phi'_B(R_A) = [e_3]R_{AB} + [f_3]S_{AB}$ and $\phi'_B(S_A) = [e_4]R_{AB} + [f_4]S_{AB}$.

Given E_0, P_2, Q_2, P_3, Q_3, E_A, $\phi_A(P_2)$, $\phi_A(Q_3)$, R_A, S_A, E_B, $\phi_B(P_2)$, $\phi_B(Q_2)$, R_B, S_B, e_3, f_3, e_4, f_4, g_3, h_3, g_4, h_4, compute E_{AB}.

The main differences between Problem 4 and Problem 1 are as follows:

- the action of the secret isogeny ϕ_A (resp. ϕ_B) of degree 2^a (resp. 3^b) on $E_0[3^{2b}]$ (resp. $E_0[2^{2a}]$) is revealed;
- in addition to image points through ϕ_A as in SIDH, the coordinates of some image points through ϕ'_A (resp. ϕ'_B) in a canonical basis are revealed.

With respect to the first point, we reveal the action of isogenies of degree $A \approx p^{1/4}$ on a B-torsion subgroup where $B \approx p^{1/2}$. Since the endomorphism ring of the curve E_0 is unknown, then HealSIDH is protected against improved torsion attacks [10].

With respect to the second point, the coordinates g_3, h_3, g_4, h_4 of $\phi'_A(R_B)$ and $\phi'_A(S_B)$ in a canonical basis of $E_{BA}[3^{2b}]$, and the coordinates e_3, f_3, e_4, f_4 of $\phi'_B(R_A)$ and $\phi'_B(S_A)$ in a canonical basis of $E_{BA}[2^{2a}]$ are revealed. We don't see how this could affect the hardness of Problem 4.

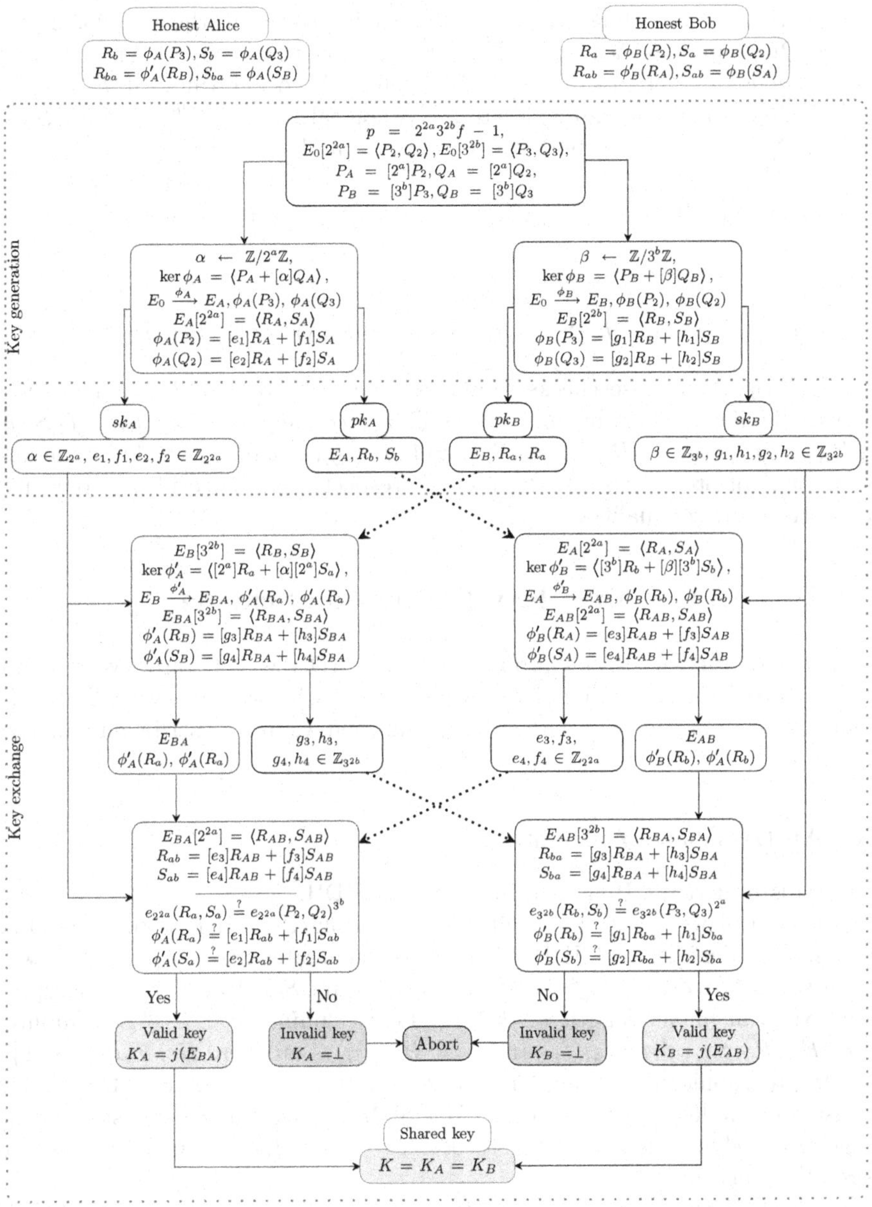

Note: the basis $\{R_A, S_A\}$, $\{R_B, S_B\}$, $\{R_{AB}, S_{AB}\}$ and $\{R_{BA}, S_{BA}\}$ are canonically generated.

Fig. 2. HealSIDH interactive key exchange. E_0 is a random supersingular curve.

Nevertheless, revealing these coordinates implies that the decisional version of Problem 4 is not hard. In fact, suppose that you are given a random supersingular elliptic curve E and you wish to determine if $E = E_{BA}$ or $E \neq E_{BA}$. Then you can generate the canonical bases $E[3^{2b}] = \langle R_{BA}, S_{BA} \rangle$ and $E[2^{2a}] = \langle R_{AB}, S_{AB} \rangle$, perform the pairing checks

$$e_{2^{2a}}\left([e_3]R_{AB} + [f_3]S_{AB}, [e_4]R_{AB} + [f_4]S_{AB}\right) \stackrel{?}{=} e_{2^{2a}}(R_A, S_A)^{3^b}$$

and

$$e_{3^{2b}}\left([g_3]R_{BA} + [h_3]S_{BA}, [g_4]R_{BA} + [h_4]S_{BA}\right) \stackrel{?}{=} e_{3^{2b}}(R_B, S_B)^{2^a}.$$

If $E = E_{AB}$, then these checks would be successful. If $E \neq E_{AB}$, then these checks will fail with overwhelming probability since the points $[e_3]R_{AB}+[f_3]S_{AB}$, $[e_4]R_{AB}+[f_4]S_{AB}$, $[g_3]R_{BA}+[h_3]S_{BA}$ and $[g_4]R_{BA}+[h_4]S_{BA}$ would be random points of E of order 2^{2a}, 2^{2a}, 3^{2b} and 3^{2b} respectively; hence likely would not satisfy the pairing equalities.

5 SHealS: A Public Key Encryption Scheme

Even though the DDH-type problem for HealSIDH is not hard, we still use HealSIDH to design a secure public key encryption scheme, which we call SHealS. We first give an overview of our construction, then we fully describe and analyze it.

5.1 An Overview of SHealS

Our aim is to derive a PKE scheme from HealSIDH.

A canonical way to design a PKE scheme from HealSIDH is to proceed as follows. Consider the HealSIDH setting. Alice generates her key pair $(\mathsf{sk}_A, \mathsf{pk}_A)$ where $\mathsf{sk}_A = (\alpha, e_1, f_1, e_2, f_2)$ and $\mathsf{pk}_A = (E_A, R_b, S_b)$. In order to encrypt a plaintext m of binary length n, Bob randomly samples $\beta \in \mathbb{Z}/3^b\mathbb{Z}$, computes $\mathsf{c}_0 = (E_B, R_a, S_a, e_3||f_3||e_4||f_4)$ and $\mathsf{c}_1 = H(j_{AB}) \oplus \mathsf{m}$ where $H : \mathbb{F}_{p^2} \to \{0,1\}^n$ is a cryptographic hash function. The ciphertext is $\mathsf{c} = (\mathsf{c}_0, \mathsf{c}_1)$. Decryption consists in completing the underlying HealSIDH key exchange using sk_A and c_0. If the key exchange is successful, recover $\mathsf{m} = \mathsf{c}_1 \oplus H(j_{BA})$ using the shared secret E_{BA}, else $\mathsf{m} = \perp$.

As shown in the following lemma, the resulting PKE scheme is not IND-CCA secure.

Lemma 2. *Let* $\mathsf{m} \in \{0,1\}^n$ *be a plaintext and let* $k \geq 1$ *be an integer such that the* k^{th} *bit of* m *(the coefficient of* 2^{k-1} *in the 2-adic expansion of* m*) is* 0. *If* $\mathsf{c} = (\mathsf{c}_0, \mathsf{c}_1)$ *is a ciphertext for* m*, then* $\mathsf{c}' = (\mathsf{c}_0, \mathsf{c}_1 \oplus 2^{k-1})$ *is a ciphertext for* $\mathsf{m} + 2^{k-1}$.

Proof. Since the kth bit of m is 0, then $\mathsf{m} + 2^{k-1} = \mathsf{m} \oplus 2^{k-1}$. Hence

$$\mathsf{c}_1 \oplus 2^{k-1} = \mathsf{m} \oplus H(j_{AB}) \oplus 2^{k-1} = (\mathsf{m} \oplus 2^{k-1}) \oplus H(j_{AB}) = (\mathsf{m} + 2^{k-1}) \oplus H(j_{AB}).$$

Therefore $\mathsf{c}' = (\mathsf{c}_0, \mathsf{c}_1 \oplus 2^{k-1})$ is a ciphertext for $\mathsf{m} + 2^{k-1}$. □

This IND-CCA attack applies to all PKE schemes in which the ciphertext is of the form $(\mathsf{c}_0, H(s) \oplus \mathsf{m})$ where s and c_0 are independent of m. We choose to use points to encrypt the plaintext, as in SiGamal [23] and SimS [14].

5.2 SHealS Public Key Encryption Scheme

The plaintext space is changed to $\mathcal{M} = \mathbb{Z}_{2^{2a}}^{\times}$, the set invertible elements in the ring of integers modulo 2^{2a}. The ciphertext of a given plaintext $\mathsf{m} \in \mathcal{M}$ is $\mathsf{c} = (\mathsf{c}_0, \mathsf{c}_1)$ where $\mathsf{c}_0 = (E_B, R_a, S_a)$, $\mathsf{c}_1 = H(j_{AB}) \oplus (\mathsf{m}e_3 || \mathsf{m}f_3 || \mathsf{m}e_4 || \mathsf{m}f_4)$ and $H : \mathbb{F}_{p^2} \rightarrow \{0,1\}^{8a}$ is a cryptographic hash function.

Note that scaling e_3, f_3, e_4 and f_4 by m is equivalent to scaling the points $[e_3]R_{AB} + [f_3]S_{AB}$ and $[e_4]R_{AB} + [f_4]S_{AB}$ by $[\mathsf{m}]$. This enables Alice to recover m by solving a discrete logarithm instance in a group of order 2^{2a}.

Concretely, Fig. 3 entirely describes SHealS PKE.

Lemma 3. *SHealS PKE is correct.*

Proof. Follows from the correctness of HealSIDH.

Remark 6. In SHealS, since there is no key disclosure, Bob can reuse his encryption key β to encrypt other plaintexts. Moreover, since the 3^{2b} torsion points are readily available, he can use the same β as a static private key.

5.3 Security Analysis

We prove that SHealS is IND-CPA secure relying on Assumption 1. Next we discuss the IND-CCA security of SHealS. We conjecture that SHealS is IND-CCA secure and provide arguments to support our conjecture.

Assumption 1 *Let* E_0, P_2, Q_2, P_A, Q_A, P_3, Q_3, P_B, Q_B, E_A, R_A, S_A, $\phi_A(P_3)$, $\phi_A(Q_3)$, E_B, $\phi_B(P_2)$, $\phi_B(Q_2)$ *the public parameters and keys of an HealSIDH instance. Set* $E_{AB}[2^{2a}] = \langle R_{AB}, S_{AB} \rangle$ *where the basis* $\{R_{AB}, S_{AB}\}$ *is canonically generated, let* $\mathcal{B}_0 = \{\phi'_B(R_A), \phi'_B(S_A)\}$ *and let* $\mathcal{B}_1 = \{R, S\}$ *be a uniformly random basis of* $E_{AB}[2^{2a}]$ *such that* $e_{2^{2a}}(R, S) = e_{2^{2a}}(R_A, S_A)^{3^b}$. *Set* $\phi'_B(R_A) = [e_{03}]R_{AB} + [f_{03}]S_{AB}$, $\phi'_B(S_A) = [e_{04}]R_{AB} + [f_{04}]S_{AB}$, $R = [e_{13}]R_{AB} + [f_{13}]S_{AB}$ *and* $S = [e_{14}]R_{AB} + [f_{14}]S_{AB}$. *For any PPT algorithm* $\mathcal{A}$,

$$Pr\left[b = b^* \left| \begin{array}{l} b \xleftarrow{\$} \{0,1\}, \\ b^* \leftarrow \mathcal{A}\begin{pmatrix} E_A, \phi_A(P_3), \phi_A(Q_3), E_B, \phi_B(P_2), \\ \phi_B(Q_2), E_{AB}, e_{b3}||f_{b3}||e_{b4}||f_{b4} \end{pmatrix} \end{array} \right. \right] = \frac{1}{2} + \mathsf{negl}(\lambda).$$

Theorem 3. *If Assumption 1 holds, then SHealS is IND-CPA secure.*

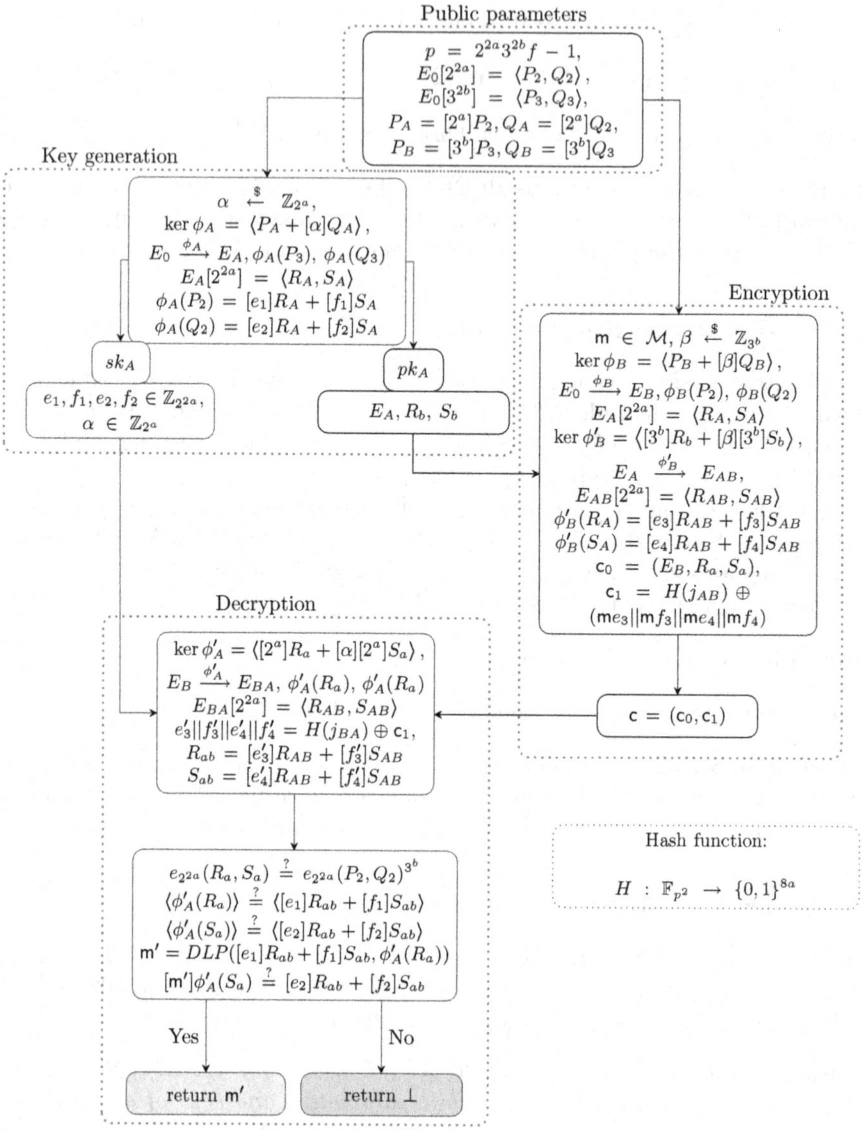

Fig. 3. SHealS PKE. E_0 is a supersingular curve with unknown endomorphism ring.

Proof. Analogous to the proof of [14, Theorem 3]. □

Concretely, Assumption 1 states that given E_A, $\phi_A(P_3)$, $\phi_A(Q_3)$, E_B, $\phi_B(P_2)$, $\phi_B(Q_2)$, E_{AB}, it is difficult to distinguish the images points $\phi'_B(R_A), \phi'_B(S_A)$ of a basis $\{R_A, S_A\}$ of $E_A[2^{2a}]$ through ϕ'_B and a uniformly random basis $\{R, S\}$ of $E_{AB}[2^{2a}]$ such that $e_{2^{2a}}(R, S) = e_{2^{2a}}(R_A, S_A)^{3^b}$.

Concerning the IND-CCA security of SHealS, one may be tempted to use a knowledge of exponnent type as Fouotsa and Petit did to prove the IND-CCA security of SimS [14]. But this type of assumption does not hold for SIDH type schemes. In fact, one can not see SIDH as an analog to the classic Diffie-Hellman as it is the case in CSIDH. In CSIDH, the secret isogeny can have any degree in a well chosen key space. But in SIDH, the degree of the secret isogeny is fixed. This eliminates the idea of assimilating the secret isogenies in SIDH to "exponents".

We have not been able to come up with a succinct proof of IND-CCA security for SHealS, but we argue that SHealS is not vulnerable to any known attack on SIDH type schemes since we have countered the GPST adaptive attack [17] and possible variants of it, and the improved torsion points attacks [10,26]. Note that we do not take side channel attacks into consideration in this analysis. We hence state the following conjecture and leave it's proof or its invalidation for future work.

Conjecture 4 *SHealS is IND-CCA secure.*

6 Concrete Instantiations and Comparisons: HealSIDH Vs K-SIDH; SHealS Vs SIKE

6.1 Concrete Instantiation

We performed a basic Sagemath [29] proof-of-concept implementation of our key validation method, HealSIDH and SHealS. We use the prime $p_{870} = 2^{432}3^{274}10 - 1$ where $a = 216$ and $b = 137$ as in SIKEp434 [19, §1.6]. Hence we expect SHealSp870 and SIKEp434 on one hand, HealSIDHp870 and k-SIDHp434 on the other hand, to provide the same security level.

The proof-of-concept implementation of SHealS is very basic and unoptimized, hence it cannot serve as a reference when comparing SHealS and SIKE in terms of efficiency. In the following paragraph, we do a high level comparison between SHealS and SIKE. We argue that the efficiency of an optimized implementation of SHealS is comparable to that of SIKE (considering instances providing the same security level).

6.2 SHealS vs SIKE

We provide a high level comparison between SHealS and SIKE and argue that SHealS's efficiency is close to that of SIKE. In what follows, we suppose that in both SIKE and SHealS, an SIDH-type public key (E, P, Q) is represented by (x_P, x_Q, x_{P-Q}) as specified in [19]. Let λ be a security parameter, and let p_h and p_s respectively be the HealSIDH (or SHealS) prime and the SIKE prime providing λ bits of security. It follows that $\lceil \log p_s \rceil \approx 4\lambda$ and $\lceil \log p_h \rceil \approx 8\lambda$.
Design. At the design level, in SHealS, the encryption public key is validated through a "direct" key validation mechanism while in SIKE, the validation is done through re-encryption. For this reason, the number of isogenies computed in

SIKE (KeyGeneration + Encapsulation + Decapsulation) is 5 while only 4 isogenies are computed in SHealS (KeyGeneration + Encryption + Decryption). Nevertheless, all the 4 isogenies in SHealS are evaluated on torsion points as well, while only 3 of the 5 isogenies in SIKE are evaluated on torsion points. In SHealS, a trusted party is needed for the generating the starting curve E_0.
Security. SHealS's IND-CCA security is conjectured while that of SIKE is inheritated from a variant Fujisaki-Okamoto transform [18].
Keys Sizes. In SIKE and SHealS, the secret key is α and $(\alpha, e_1, f_1, e_2, f_2)$ respectively. Since e_1, f_1, e_2, f_2 lie in $\mathbb{Z}/2^{2a}\mathbb{Z}$, then their bitsize is twice that of $\alpha \in \mathbb{Z}_{2^a}$. Hence the secret key of HealSIDH is 9 times larger compared to that of SIKE. The public key in SIKE and SHealS are both of the form (x_P, x_Q, x_{P-Q}). Hence in SIKE the public key has roughly $3(2\lceil\log p_s\rceil) = 6\lceil\log p_s\rceil \approx 24\lambda$ bits while in SHealS it has roughly $3(2\lceil\log p_h\rceil) = 6\lceil\log p_h\rceil \approx 48\lambda$ bits. Therefore, the size of the public key in SHealS is roughly twice that of the public key in SIKE.
For the ciphertext, the bitsize of c_0 in SHealS is twice that of c_0 in SIKE, while the bit size of c_1 in ShealS is $8a = 16\lambda$, opposed to $n \in \{128, 192, 256\}$ in SIKE. It follows that the size of SHealS ciphertexts is about 2.45 times that of SIKE ciphertexts.
Efficiency. As mentioned before, only 4 isogenies are computed in SHealS while 5 isogenies are computed in SIKE. Meanwhile, the prime used in SHealS is twice as large as SIKE prime. And, in SHealS, the isogenies $\phi'_A : E_B \to E_{BA}$ and $\phi'_B : E_A \to E_{AB}$ are evaluated on two torsion points each, which is not the case in SIKE. Without an advanced implementation of SHealS, it is difficult to provide a precise efficiency comparison between both schemes.

We summarize the comparison in Table 1. Let λ be a desired security level.

Table 1. High level comparison between SHealSIDH and SIKE.

	SIKE	SHealS
Field characteristic size	$\approx 4\lambda$	$\approx 8\lambda$
Private key size	$\approx 2\lambda$	$\approx 18\lambda$
Public key size	$\approx 24\lambda$	$\approx 48\lambda$
Ciphertext size	$\approx 26\lambda$	$\approx 64\lambda$
KeyGen (isog. comp.)	1	1
Encaps/Encrypt (isog. comp.)	2	2
Decaps/Decrypt (isog. comp.)	2	1
Adaptive attacks	No	No (conjecture)
Key disclosure	Yes	No
Encryption key reuse	No	Yes
Key validation method used	Re-encryption	Key val. method in § 3

6.3 HealSIDH vs K-SIDH

To the best of our knowledge, the only existing post-quantum key exchange schemes enabling static-static key setting prior to this work[1] were CSIDH [4], k-SIDH [1] and its variant by Jao and Urbanik [30]. As highlighted in Sect. 2.6, Basso et al. [2] showed that k-SIDH is preferable to the later variant from an efficiency vs security point of view. We provide a high level comparison between HealSIDH and k-SIDH since both are countermeasures to the GPST adaptive attacks.

Design. At the design level, HealSIDH comes with an incorporated key validation method, while k-SIDH mitigates the GPST adaptive attacks by running many parallel SIDH intances. This implies that more than k^2 isogenies are computed in k-SIDH (full execution of the key exchange) while only 4 isogenies are computed in HealSIDH. Nevertheless, There are two rounds in HealSIDH, as opposed to one round in k-SIDH. Note that the starting curve in HealSIDH is generated by a trusted party, which is not the case in k-SIDH.

Security. Security wise, HealSIDH is not vulnerable to the GPST adaptive attacks since it incorporates a countermeasure. In k-SIDH, one does not eliminate the attack completely, but one increases its cost in such a way that it becomes exponential in k.

Keys sizes. From the comparison made in Sect. 6.2, the secret key in HealSIDH has roughly 18λ bits. In k-SIDH, the size of the secret key is k times that of a SIKE secret key, hence $2k\lambda$. The public keys in HealSIDH have roughly 48λ bits while in k-SIDH they have about $24k\lambda$ bits.

Efficiency. As mentioned before, only 4 isogenies are computed in HealSIDH. In k-SIDH, roughly $2k^2 + 2k$ isogenies are computed. Even though the HealSIDH prime size is twice that of the k-SIDH prime, k-SIDH is still an order of magnitude less efficient compared to HealSIDH because of the relatively large number of isogenies computed.

Table 2 provides a high level comparison between HealSIDH and k-SIDH. We refer to [1] for more details on k-SIDH.

7 HealS (Healed SIKE): Improving the Efficiency of SHealS

From the comparison in Sect. 6.2, one concludes that the prime size, the key and ciphertext sizes in SHealS are at least twice that in SIKE. In this section, our aim is to improve on this prime, key and ciphertext sizes.

---

[1] While this work was under submission, a proof of isogeny knowledge [12] was published online. We will provide a concrete comparison with this construction in later versions of this paper that we will make available on the IACR eprint database.

Table 2. High level comparison between HealSIDH and k-SIDH ($46 \leq k$).

	HealSIDH	k-SIDH
Field characteristic size	$\approx 8\lambda$	$\approx 4\lambda$
Private key size	$\approx 18\lambda$	$\approx 2k\lambda$
Public key size	$\approx 48\lambda$	$\approx 24k\lambda$
KeyGen	1	k
Key exchange	2	$2k^2$
Adaptive attacks	No	Exp. in k
Static-static key	Yes	Yes
NIKE	No	Yes

7.1 HealS Public Key Encryption

Having a closer look at ShealS, one notices that since Bob does not run a key validation on Alice's public key in the PKE encryption scheme, then it is not a requisite to have the 3^{2b}-torsion points defined over $\mathbb{F}_{p^2}$. Hence when the parameters are chosen for a PKE scheme purpose only, the prime p can be relaxed to $p = 2^{2a}3^b f - 1$ where $2^a \approx 3^b$ and f is a small cofactor. Most of the scheme remains unchanged. Concretely, HealS is SHealS with a prime of the form $p = 2^{2a}3^b f - 1$.

While the base prime change when going from SHealS to HealS comes with considerable speed-up and considerable improvement on key and ciphertext sizes (see Sect. 7.2), one should notice that Bob can no more use his encryption key as secret key when receiving encrypted messages. In fact, in order to encrypt a plaintext for Bob, one needs to compute the images of torsion points of order 3^{2b}. For HealS primes, these torsion points are defined over large extensions since $p = 2^{2a}3^b f - 1$. Nevertheless, Bob can reuse the same encryption key β to encrypt other messages to other parties or the same party, only he can not use it as decryption key. This technical difference motivated us to rename the instance HealS instead of keeping the name SHealS. Appendix A provides more details about the KeyGeneration, Encryption and Decryption algorithms in HealS.

7.2 Concrete Instantiation and Comparison with SIKE

We instantiate HealS with the prime $p_{650} = 2^{432}3^{137} - 1$ where $a = 216$ and $b = 137$ as in SIKEp434 [19, §1.6]. Hence HealSp650 and SIKEp434 are expected to provide the same security level.

We summarise a high level comparison between HealS and SIKE in Table 3. We also include SHealS in this table to highlight the advantages of HealS when compared to SHealS.

Table 4 compares the key and ciphertext sizes of our PKE with some NIST finalists KEMs. We notice that the key sizes in HealS are more compact compared

Table 3. High level comparison between HealS, SHealS and SIKE.

	SIKE	SHealS	HealS
Field characteristic size	$\approx 4\lambda$	$\approx 8\lambda$	$\approx 6\lambda$
Private key size	$\approx 2\lambda$	$\approx 18\lambda$	$\approx 18\lambda$
Public key size	$\approx 24\lambda$	$\approx 48\lambda$	$\approx 36\lambda$
Ciphertext size	$\approx 26\lambda$	$\approx 64\lambda$	$\approx 48\lambda$
KeyGen (isog. comp.)	1	1	1
Encaps/Encrypt (isog. comp.)	2	2	2
Decaps/Decrypt (isog. comp.)	2	1	1
Adaptive attacks	No	No (conj.)	No (conj.)
Key disclosure	Yes	No	No
Encryption key reuse	No	Yes	Yes
Key validation method used	Re-encryption	Key val. method in Sect. 3	

to these finalists. The ciphertext size in HealS is close to that of Kyber, NTRU and Saber, while being considerably larger compared to that of Classic McEliece.

Table 4. Key and ciphertext sizes comparison between HealS and the four NIST finalists KEMs Kyber, NTRU, Classic McEliece and Saber, for 128 bits of security (NIST level 1).

	HealS	Kyber	NTRU	Classic McEliece	Saber
sk	288	1632	935	6492	1568
pk	576	800	699	261120	672
c	768	768	699	128	736

8 Conclusion

In this paper, we introduced an efficient countermeasure to the GPST adaptive attack which does not require key disclosure nor re-encryption. Next, we used this countermeasure to design an efficient static-static key interactive exchange scheme: HealSIDH. HealSIDH is not vulnerable to the GPST adaptive attacks. We derive an IND-CPA secure PKE scheme with conjectured IND-CCA security SHealS from HealSIDH. The full execution of SHealS contains only 4 isogeny computations while that of SIKE contains 5 isogeny computations. For this reason, even though SHealS uses larger parameters and has larger keys, we expect its efficiency to be comparable to that of SIKE. In order to optimize the efficiency, keys and ciphertexts sizes, we suggest HealS, a variant of SHealS using a smaller prime. The main difference between SHealS and HealS is that in SHealS, a party can use his private key as encryption key when encrypting ciphertexts for other parties.

Moreover, we provided a high level comparison between HealSIDH and k-SIDH on one hand, and between SHealS, HealS and SIKE on the other hand. HealSIDH is an order of magnitude more efficient compared to k-SIDH and the keys in k-SIDH are about k times bigger compared to those of HealSIDH. The advantages of SHealS and HealS over SIKE are

- no encryption key disclosure to the recipient during encryption;
- incorporated key validation method (no re-encryption during decryption);
- encryption key reuse.

In order to evaluate the concrete efficiency of the schemes constructed in this paper, an advanced implementation of SHealS and HealS is needed. We leave this task to follow-up work. We believe the design of SHealS leaves room for considerable optimisations. These may come from the implementation, from variants of the key validation method or from redesigning the schemes.

Furthermore, there are possibly existing isogeny-based schemes that would benefit from our key validation method. Also the key validation may enables the design of new isogeny-based primitives. We also leave such an investigation for future work.

Acknowledgements. We would like to express our sincere gratitude to the anonymous reviewers for their helpful comments and suggestions. Christophe Petit was supported by EPSRC grant EP/S01361X/1.

A HealS PKE

The HealS Public Key Encryption scheme is detailed in Fig. 4.

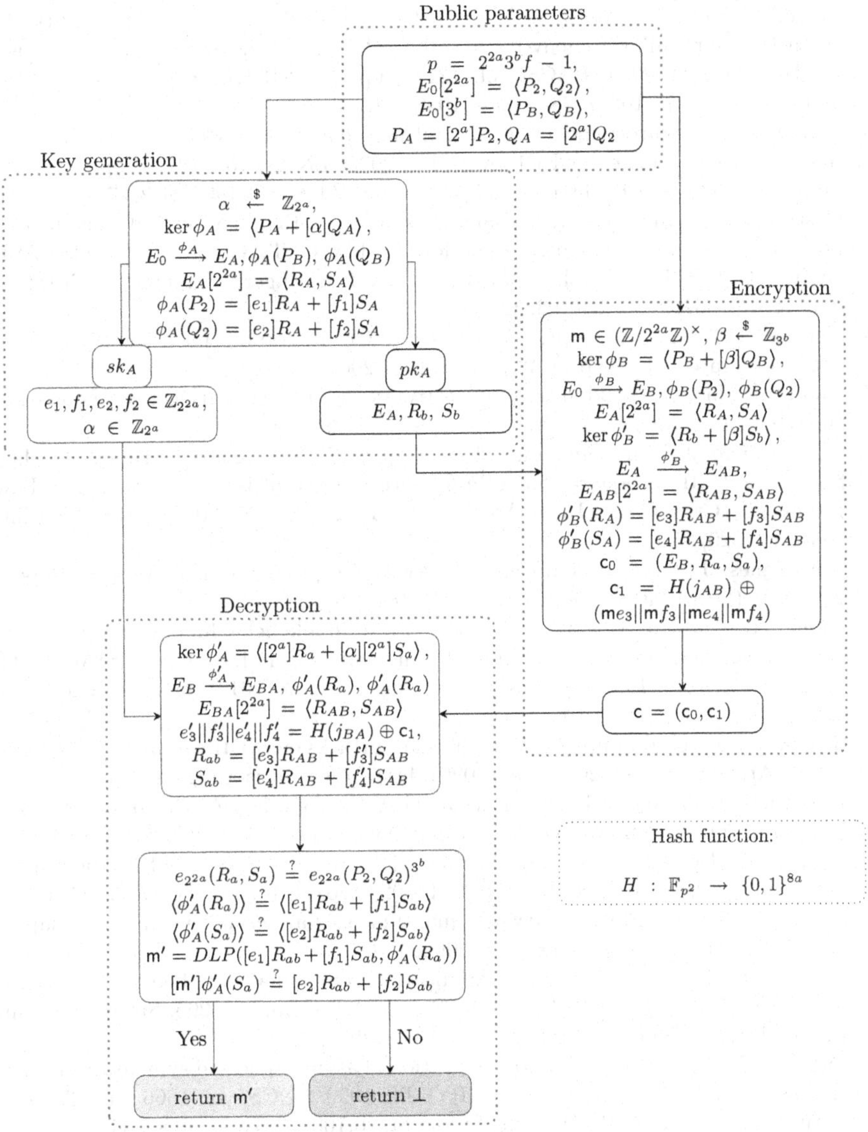

Fig. 4. HealS PKE.

References

1. Azarderakhsh, R., Jao, D., Leonardi, C.: Post-quantum static-static key agreement using multiple protocol instances. In: Adams, C., Camenisch, J. (eds.) SAC 2017. LNCS, vol. 10719, pp. 45–63. Springer, Cham (2018). https://doi.org/10.1007/978-3-319-72565-9_3

2. Basso, A., Kutas, P., Merz, S.-P., Petit, C., Weitkämper, C.: On adaptive attacks against jao-urbanik's isogeny-based protocol. In: Nitaj, A., Youssef, A. (eds.) AFRICACRYPT 2020. LNCS, vol. 12174, pp. 195–213. Springer, Cham (2020). https://doi.org/10.1007/978-3-030-51938-4_10
3. Bonnetain, X., Schrottenloher, A.: Quantum security analysis of CSIDH. In: Canteaut, A., Ishai, Y. (eds.) EUROCRYPT 2020. LNCS, vol. 12106, pp. 493–522. Springer, Cham (2020). https://doi.org/10.1007/978-3-030-45724-2_17
4. Castryck, W., Lange, T., Martindale, C., Panny, L., Renes, J.: CSIDH: an efficient post-quantum commutative group action. In: Peyrin, T., Galbraith, S. (eds.) ASIACRYPT 2018. LNCS, vol. 11274, pp. 395–427. Springer, Cham (2018). https://doi.org/10.1007/978-3-030-03332-3_15
5. Charles, D.X., Lauter, K.E., Goren, E.Z.: Cryptographic hash functions from expander graphs. J. Cryptol. **22**(1), 93–113 (2009)
6. Childs, A., Jao, D., Soukharev, V.: Constructing elliptic curve isogenies in quantum subexponential time. J. Math. Cryptol. **8**(1), 1–29 (2014)
7. Chávez-Saab, J., Chi-Domínguez, J.-J., Jaques, S., Rodríguez-Henríquez, F.: The SQALE of CSIDH: Square-root vélu Quantum-resistant isogeny Action with Low Exponents. Cryptology ePrint Archive, Report 2020/1520 (2020). https://eprint.iacr.org/2020/1520
8. Couveignes, J.M.: Hard homogeneous spaces. Cryptology ePrint Archive, Report 2006/291 (2006). https://eprint.iacr.org/2006/291
9. De Feo, L., Masson, S., Petit, C., Sanso, A.: Verifiable delay functions from supersingular isogenies and pairings. In: Galbraith, S.D., Moriai, S. (eds.) ASIACRYPT 2019. LNCS, vol. 11921, pp. 248–277. Springer, Cham (2019). https://doi.org/10.1007/978-3-030-34578-5_10
10. de Quehen, V., et al.: Improved torsion point attacks on SIDH variants. Cryptology ePrint Archive, Report 2020/633 (2020). https://eprint.iacr.org/2020/633
11. Dobson, S., Galbraith, S.D., LeGrow, J., Ti, Y.B., Zobernig, Z.: An adaptive attack on 2-sidh. Int. J. Comput. Math. Comput. Syst. Theor. **5**(4), 282–299 (2020)
12. De Feo, L., Dobson, S., Galbraith, S.D., Zobernig, L.: Sidh proof of knowledge. Cryptology ePrint Archive, Report 2021/1023 (2021). https://ia.cr/2021/1023
13. De Feo, L., Jao, D., Plût, J.: Towards quantum-resistant cryptosystems from supersingular elliptic curve isogenies, pp. 209–247 (2014)
14. Fouotsa, T.B., Petit, C.: SimS: a simplification of SiGamal. In: Cheon, J.H., Tillich, J.-P. (eds.) PQCrypto 2021 2021. LNCS, vol. 12841, pp. 277–295. Springer, Cham (2021). https://doi.org/10.1007/978-3-030-81293-5_15
15. Fujisaki, E., Okamoto, T.: Secure integration of asymmetric and symmetric encryption schemes. In: Wiener, M. (ed.) CRYPTO 1999. LNCS, vol. 1666, pp. 537–554. Springer, Heidelberg (1999). https://doi.org/10.1007/3-540-48405-1_34
16. Steven, D.: Galbraith. Mathematics of Public Key Cryptography, Cambridge University Press (2012)
17. Galbraith, S.D., Petit, C., Shani, B., Ti, Y.B.: On the security of supersingular isogeny cryptosystems. In: Cheon, J.H., Takagi, T. (eds.) ASIACRYPT 2016. LNCS, vol. 10031, pp. 63–91. Springer, Heidelberg (2016). https://doi.org/10.1007/978-3-662-53887-6_3
18. Hofheinz, D., Hövelmanns, K., Kiltz, E.: A modular analysis of the fujisaki-okamoto transformation. In: Kalai, Y., Reyzin, L. (eds.) TCC 2017. LNCS, vol. 10677, pp. 341–371. Springer, Cham (2017). https://doi.org/10.1007/978-3-319-70500-2_12
19. Jao, D., et al.: Supersingular Isogeny Key Encapsulation, 1 October 2020. https://sike.org/files/SIDH-spec.pdf

20. Jao, D., De Feo, L.: Towards quantum-resistant cryptosystems from supersingular elliptic curve isogenies. In: Yang, B.-Y. (ed.) PQCrypto 2011. LNCS, vol. 7071, pp. 19–34. Springer, Heidelberg (2011). https://doi.org/10.1007/978-3-642-25405-5_2
21. Kutas, P., Merz, S.P., Petit, C., Weitkämper, C.: One-way functions and malleability oracles: Hidden shift attacks on isogeny-based protocols. IACR Cryptol. ePrint Arch., 2021:282 (2021)
22. Leonardi, C.: A note on the ending elliptic curve in sidh. Cryptology ePrint Archive, Report 2020/262 (2020). https://eprint.iacr.org/2020/262
23. Moriya, T., Onuki, H., Takagi, T.: SiGamal: a supersingular isogeny-based PKE and its application to a PRF. In: Moriai, S., Wang, H. (eds.) ASIACRYPT 2020. LNCS, vol. 12492, pp. 551–580. Springer, Cham (2020). https://doi.org/10.1007/978-3-030-64834-3_19
24. National Institute of Standards and Technology: Post quantum Cryptography Standardization, December 2016. https://csrc.nist.gov/Projects/Post-Quantum-Cryptography/Post-Quantum-Cryptography-Standardization
25. Peikert, C.: He gives c-sieves on the CSIDH. In: Canteaut, A., Ishai, Y. (eds.) EUROCRYPT 2020. LNCS, vol. 12106, pp. 463–492. Springer, Cham (2020). https://doi.org/10.1007/978-3-030-45724-2_16
26. Petit, C.: Faster algorithms for isogeny problems using torsion point images. In: Takagi, T., Peyrin, T. (eds.) ASIACRYPT 2017. LNCS, vol. 10625, pp. 330–353. Springer, Cham (2017). https://doi.org/10.1007/978-3-319-70697-9_12
27. Rostovtsev, A., Stolbunov, A.: Public-key cryptosystem based on isogenies. IACR Cryptol. ePrint Arch. 2006, vol. 145 (2006)
28. Silverman, J.H.: The arithmetic of elliptic curves, vol. 106. Springer Science & Business Media (2009)
29. The Sage Developers. SageMath, the Sage Mathematics Software System (Version 9.0) (2020). https://www.sagemath.org
30. Urbanik, D., Jao, D.: New techniques for SIDH-based NIKE. J. Math. Cryptol. **14**(1), 120–128 (2020)

Advanced Encryption and Signatures

Adaptive Security via Deletion in Attribute-Based Encryption: Solutions from Search Assumptions in Bilinear Groups

Rishab Goyal[1(✉)], Jiahui Liu[2(✉)], and Brent Waters[2,3(✉)]

[1] MIT, Cambridge, MA, USA
goyal@utexas.edu
[2] University of Texas at Austin, Austin, TX, USA
{jiahui,bwaters}@cs.utexas.edu
[3] NTT Research, Sunnyvale, CA, USA

Abstract. One of the primary research challenges in Attribute-Based Encryption (ABE) is constructing and proving cryptosystems that are adaptively secure. To date the main paradigm for achieving adaptive security in ABE is dual system encryption. However, almost all such solutions in bilinear groups rely on (variants of) either the subgroup decision problem over composite order groups or the decision linear assumption. Both of these assumptions are decisional rather than search assumptions and the target of the assumption is a source or bilinear group element. This is in contrast to earlier selectively secure ABE systems which can be proven secure from either the decisional or search Bilinear Diffie-Hellman assumption. In this work we make progress on closing this gap by giving a new ABE construction for the subset functionality and prove security under the Search Bilinear Diffie-Hellman assumption.

We first provide a framework for proving adaptive security in Attribute-Based Encryption systems. We introduce a concept of ABE with deletable attributes where any party can take a ciphertext encrypted under the attribute string $x \in \{0,1\}^n$ and modify it into a ciphertext encrypted under any string $x' \in \{0,1,\perp\}^n$ where x' is derived by replacing any bits of x with $\perp$ symbols (i.e. "deleting" attributes of x). The semantics of the system are that any private key for a circuit C can be used to decrypt a ciphertext associated with x' if none of the input bits read by circuit C are $\perp$ symbols and $C(x') = 1$.

R. Goyal—Work done in part while at UT Austin supported by IBM PhD Fellowship, and at the Simons Institute for the Theory of Computing supported by Simons-Berkeley research fellowship. Research supported in part by NSF CNS Award #1718161, an IBM-MIT grant, and by the Defense Advanced Research Projects Agency (DARPA) under Contract No. HR00112020023. Any opinions, findings and conclusions or recommendations expressed in this material are those of the author(s) and do not necessarily reflect the views of the United States Government or DARPA.

B. Waters—Supported by NSF CNS-1908611, CNS-1414082, DARPA SafeWare, Packard Foundation Fellowship, and Simons Investigator Award.

M. Tibouchi and H. Wang (Eds.): ASIACRYPT 2021, LNCS 13093, pp. 311–341, 2021.
https://doi.org/10.1007/978-3-030-92068-5_11

We show a pathway for combining ABE with deletable attributes with constrained pseudorandom functions to obtain adaptively secure ABE building upon the recent work of Tsabary [30]. Our new ABE system will be adaptively secure and be a ciphertext-policy ABE that supports the same functionality as the underlying constrained PRF as long as the PRF is "deletion conforming". Here we also provide a simple constrained PRF construction that gives subset functionality.

Our approach enables us to access a broader array of Attribute-Based Encryption schemes support deletion of attributes. For example, we show that both the Goyal et al. (GPSW) [19] and Boyen [6] ABE schemes can trivially handle a deletion operation. And, by using a hardcore bit variant of GPSW scheme we obtain an adaptively secure ABE scheme under the *Search* Bilinear Diffie-Hellman assumption in addition to pseudo random functions in NC1. This gives the first adaptively secure ABE from a *search* assumption as all prior work relied on decision assumptions over source group elements.

1 Introduction

Attribute-Based Encryption (ABE), since its introduction by Sahai and Waters [29], has significantly propelled the concept of secure communication. The traditional notion of Public Key Encryption (PKE) [11,14,28] was meant to enable a one-to-one private communication channel with a specific targeted user over an insecure network. ABE, on the other hand, provides a more fine-grained access control over plaintext delivery where it allows the encryptor to specify a policy f which is attached to the ciphertext. In such systems, each user decryption key is associated with an attribute string x such that it can recover the encrypted message only when $f(x) = 1$, that is when the policy f accepts the attribute x.[1]

Since its inception in 2005, the notion of Attribute-Based Encryption has received tremendous amount of attention. Initial developments in the context of provably secure ABE constructions as well as new proof techniques were driven by bilinear map-based realizations. The earliest such constructions (e.g. [19,29]) were proven secure under only a relaxed notion of security called *selective* security where an attacker is required to declare the descriptor f^* that will be associated with the challenge ciphertext at the beginning of the game, i.e. even *before* seeing the public parameters. This relaxation enabled the use of a so-called "partitioning" strategy for proving security. Intuitively, availability of the challenge descriptor f^* to the reduction algorithm, before it needs to sample the system public-secret parameters, enables the reduction algorithm to shape its view of the system parameters into a *partition.* Such a partitioned view of the parameters allows the reduction algorithm to generate a secret key sk_x for every attribute x as long as $f^*(x) = 0$ (that is, whenever f^* rejects the attribute x), while simultaneously being able to translate a distinguishing attack on a challenge ciphertext

[1] For readers familiar with the notions of "ciphertext-policy" ABE and "key-policy" ABE, we will be using the ciphertext-policy vernacular in the sequel.

associated with f^* into breaking a number theoretic assumption. Unfortunately, such a partitioning strategy does not naturally translate [25] to the case of full or adaptive security where an attacker gets to choose the challenge function f^* after it sees the public parameters as well as makes a polynomial number of secret key queries. In this scenario the best known partitioning-style reductions will simply have to guess the function f^* to be chosen by the attacker and abort the reduction if the guess does not align with the actual choice of the attacker. This guessing approach incurs a security loss in the reduction proportional to the number of functions to choose from, and thus necessitates the use of a subexponentially secure variant of the underlying number theoretic assumption.

The shortcomings of the partitioning paradigm suggested the need for a new set of proof techniques for attaining adaptive security. The most well-known proof technique in that direction is Waters' dual system methodology [31] which led to the first adaptively secure ABE scheme whose security was proven under a static assumption by Lewko et al. [22]. Their approach allowed for adaptive security by moving beyond partitioning proofs.[2] Subsequently, several other works achieved adaptive security in ABE systems with various desiderata [2,23,24,26,32]. One prominent trait of all these dual system solutions is that they almost exclusively rely on (variants of) the decision subgroup decision assumption or the decision linear assumption. Briefly, the decision linear assumption over a prime order bilinear group $\mathbb{G}$ states that given $g, v, w, v^a, w^b \in \mathbb{G}$ it is hard to distinguish between g^{a+b} and a random group element in $\mathbb{G}$. This is a potentially stronger assumption due to the facts that (1) it is decisional and (2) the target of the assumption g^{a+b} is in the bilinear group.[3] In contrast earlier selectively secure schemes (such as [19,29]) can be proven secure under the Search Bilinear Diffie-Hellman assumption which states that given g, g^a, g^b, g^c it is difficult to compute $e(g,g)^{abc}$. In our work we work toward closing this gap by constructing new ABE systems provably secure from search assumptions.

We start by building upon a recent breakthrough due to Tsabary [30] for proving adaptively secure ABE systems from the Learning with Errors (LWE) assumption [27]. Until this work all prior ABE systems (that go beyond Identity-Based Encryption) from the LWE assumption (e.g. [4,6,15,16]) relied on a partitioning argument and were thus selectively secure. Tsabary's ABE construction is for the family of subset predicates where both private keys and ciphertexts are associated with subsets over $[N]$ and a secret key for subset S can decrypt a ciphertext for subset T iff $S \subseteq T$.[4] While the subset predicate class is rather limited in comparison to the functionalities mentioned earlier, the work is remarkable given the lack of progress towards realizing adaptive security from LWE for

[2] Notably, earlier works of Gentry [12] and Gentry-Halevi [13] moved beyond partitioning for IBE and Hierarchical IBE.

[3] If $e : \mathbb{G} \times \mathbb{G} \to \mathbb{G}_T$ is a bilinear map, then we refer to elements in $\mathbb{G}$ as being in the source group or bilinear group.

[4] Tsabary actually presents their construction as realizing t-CNF for any constant t. However, this can be viewed as a special application of ABE for subsets. For this reason we will interpret their construction in terms of subset semantics for the purposes of this introduction.

so many years. (It was known [8,17] how to prove security in a slightly weaker model where the attacker sees the public parameters, but is not allowed any private key queries before committing to f^*; however, these works do not appear to give any further insight into achieving full/adaptive security.)

Tsabary's idea is to start with a *selectively* secure Attribute-Based Encryption scheme with certain special partial evaluation properties, and combine it with an *adaptively* secure Constrained Pseudorandom Function (CPRF) [5,7,21] that satisfies complementary "conforming" properties. Intuitively, the central idea in the work can be interpreted as a mechanism to leverage adaptive security of the CPRF for proving adaptive security of the resulting ABE system, while relying on the underlying selectively secure ABE scheme mostly for the encryption-decryption capability. Tsabary cleverly executed the above idea, and showed that combining these primitives in the right manner the resulting ABE system is adaptively secure, and the policy class it supports matches the constraint class of the underlying CPRF. For instantiating the entire framework, Tsabary derived a simple construction for constrained PRFs for subset constraints with requisite conforming properties from CPRF construction by [9], thereby giving an adaptively secure ABE scheme for subset predicates.

The framework requires the starting selectively secure ABE system to support partial ciphertext evaluation. Such a partial computation feature is not supported in many existing ABE systems, with the Boneh et al. [4] construction being the only known construction providing requisite capability. In particular, none of the bilinear map schemes such as [19], or the simpler (albeit less powerful) LWE-based ABE scheme of Boyen [6] support partial evaluation.

This Work. In this work, we provide a framework to both broaden and simplify the adaptively secure ABE transformation. At the core of our work is the observation that while [30] relies on the partial ciphertext evaluation framework of Boneh et al. [4], there is hardly any computation performed on the ciphertext. Concretely, the transformation the partial evaluation performed on the ciphertext exactly corresponds to the CPRF constrain operation. Now in a CPRF scheme for subset constraints over a universe of elements $[N]$, the CPRF master key msk consists of $N+1$ regular PRF keys $k_0, k_1, \ldots, k_N$. And, to evaluate the CPRF on a set $S \subseteq [N]$, the evaluator computes the following:

$$\mathsf{CPRF}(\mathsf{msk}, S) = F(k_0, S) \bigoplus_{i \in S} F(k_i, S).$$

For constraining the master key to a constraint set $T \subseteq [N]$ such that evaluation works on all input sets $S \subseteq T$, all we need to do is "delete" all the regular PRF keys k_j for which $j \notin T$—thus no elaborate computation is required in constraining the key.

Our work builds around this key insight wherein we introduce the complementary notions of ABE with *deletable attributes* and *deletion conforming* CPRFs. At a high level, a *key-policy* ABE with deletable attributes allows encryption to a non-binary attribute string $x \in \{0, 1, \perp\}^n$, where $\perp$ represents a "deleted" attribute. The semantics of such an ABE scheme are that a user decryption key for a policy circuit C can decrypt the ciphertext associated with attribute x as long as the circuit C does not *touch* any of the deleted input wires and $C(x) = 1$.[5] Moreover, any user given just the public parameters can take a ciphertext ct for attribute string x and produce another ciphertext ct' encrypting the same message but for an attribute string x', where x' is the same as x except it can have some further attribute bits deleted (i.e., changed to $\perp$s). Armed with these abstractions we are able to compile these into an adaptively secure ciphertext-policy ABE scheme using a transformation that follows [30] in spirit.

The potential benefits of our approach are twofold. First, we show that the framework of ABE with deletable attributes encompasses a much broader range of ABE systems. Notably, this includes the early bilinear map based GPSW construction [19] as well as the LWE-based scheme of Boyen [6].[6] As it turns out, showing that these schemes support attribute deletion is extremely simple—e.g., in GPSW one just has to literally "delete" ciphertext components associated with the corresponding attributes. Furthermore, following this paradigm leads to the first fully secure ABE scheme from a search problem in bilinear map setting. This is done by applying a very minor tweak to original GPSW which is to hide the message under a hardcore bit. With this tweak, we can show that the resulting scheme is adaptively secure under the *Search* Bilinear Diffie-Hellman (BDH) assumption [3] in addition to assuming pseudorandom functions in NC1 which is a minicrypt assumption. We also note that pseudorandom functions in NC1 are implied by the Bilinear decisional Diffie-Hellman assumption; thus we can alternatively base our security entirely on that assumption. We emphasize that all prior work on adaptively secure ABE from bilinear maps relied on *decision* assumptions over the source group.

A second (and perhaps more nuanced) benefit of trading off partial evaluation for deletion is in simplicity. Given that deletion is a more restricted operation arguing security is inherently simpler when we only perform deletion on input wires, compared to arbitrary partial circuit evaluation. We remark that there can be a tradeoff in the direction of functionality. While our construction using deletion matches the subset functionality given in [30], it is entirely possible that in the future we may find a larger class of functionalities that are supported by

[5] Here by not touching an input wire, we mean that the circuit must not read/depend upon that particular input wire.

[6] We recently learned of the existence of an attack [1] on Boyen's ABE scheme. We still include the proof that it is deletable to demonstrate wider applicability of our framework, but do not claim extension of Boyen's scheme as an instantiation from LWE. To instantiate our framework under LWE, we believe that one could show the [4] scheme to be deletable.

a partial computation framework and not by deletion. Doing so is an intriguing open question.

1.1 Technical Overview

Following the framework developed in [30], our work provides a mechanism to leverage adaptive security of a constrained PRF for upgrading the security of an ABE system from selective to adaptive. Concretely, we show that starting with a selectively secure *key-policy* ABE (KP-ABE) system that permits attribute deletion, we could pair it with an adaptively secure CPRF scheme to build an adaptively secure *ciphertext-policy* ABE (CP-ABE) system. Such a pairing mandates the CPRF scheme to satisfy certain special properties that we refer to as deletion conforming. The transformation flips the semantics of the underlying ABE system from key-policy to ciphertext-policy, and the constraint class associated with the CPRF maps directly to the predicate class for the resulting ciphertext-policy ABE system.

We now provide an overview of our framework and techniques. The overview is broken into four parts—first, we introduce the concept of attribute deletion for key-policy ABE systems; second, we define the complementary notion of deletion conforming CPRFs, and describe a simple construction for the family of subset constraints; third, we show how these aformentioned KP-ABE and CPRFs systems (for the right functionalities) be combined to construct an adaptively secure CP-ABE scheme; and lastly, we provide two concrete instantiations for KP-ABE with deletable attributes from standard assumptions.

A Key-Policy ABE with Deletable Attributes. We begin by informally introducing the concept of attribute deletion with formal definitions provided in Sect. 3. Recall that in the key-policy setting, the semantics of an ABE scheme are that every ciphertext ct_x is associated with an attribute string $x \in \{0,1\}^n$, while every secret decryption key sk_C is associated with a policy circuit $C : \{0,1\}^n \to \{0,1\}$. Here the functionality provided by the scheme is that decryption recovers the encrypted messages whenever the policy circuit accepts the attribute (i.e., $C(x) = 1$). An ABE system with deletable attributes provides two additional capabilities—(1) the encryption algorithm can now compute ciphertexts for non-binary attribute strings $x \in \{0,1,\perp\}^n$ as well, where the '$\perp$' symbol is interpreted as an '*unset*' attribute bit, (2) given any ciphertext ct_x, one can publicly reduce it to another ciphertext $\mathsf{ct}_{x'}$ encrypting the same message with the associated attribute string x' so long as x' can be obtained by having some attribute bits of x deleted (i.e., changed from *set* to *unset*).

Formally, such schemes have a special Delete algorithm that take as input the public parameters pp, a ciphertext ct_x, and an index set $\mathcal{I} \subseteq [n]$ and it outputs a modified ciphertext ct'. Here the set $\mathcal{I}$ denotes the indices of attribute bits that the user wants to delete, and let $\mathsf{Restrict}(x, \mathcal{I})$ denote the string x' that is obtained by deleting attribute bits of x that lie in set $\mathcal{I}$. The correctness requirement in presence of attribute deletion is expanded as follows: a secret key sk_C can decrypt a ciphertext ct_x if the circuit C does not *read* any of the *unset* input wires in attribute x, and evaluating C on x outputs 1. (For example, consider the following circuit: $C(x) = x_2 \oplus x_3$, where x_i denotes the i-th bit of x. For such a circuit C, we have that a corresponding secret key sk_C can not be used to decrypt a ciphertext ct_x whenever either $x_2/x_3 = \perp$, or $x_2 \oplus x_3 \neq 1$. That is, if $x_2 = x_3 \neq \perp$, then decryption succeeds irrespective of how other attribute bits are set.)

For security, such schemes must satisfy a special deletion indistinguishability property (in addition to the regular IND-CPA security). Briefly, deletion indistinguishability states that the distributions of ciphertexts generated by either running the encryption algorithm directly, or the encryption algorithm followed by the deletion algorithm should be computationally indistinguishable as long as they encrypt the same message and w.r.t. the same attribute string. That is, we have the following:

$$\{\mathsf{Delete}(\mathsf{pp}, \mathsf{Enc}(\mathsf{pp}, m, x), \mathcal{I})\} \approx_c \{\mathsf{Enc}(\mathsf{pp}, m, x')\}, \qquad \text{where } x' = \mathsf{Restrict}(x, \mathcal{I}).$$

Here the distributions must remain indistinguishable even if the distinguisher gets the ABE master key.

Intuitively, the goal of such a deletable key-policy ABE system is to enable arbitrary attribute deletion on ciphertexts while extending the usual policy circuit evaluation functionality over to partial/incomplete input strings. Typically, evaluating circuits on incomplete inputs is regarded as an invalid operation, but here our abstraction relies on the fact that as long as all the input wires actually used by the circuit are set (i.e., are 0/1), then we could still legally evaluate the circuit and define its output for partial inputs. As we describe later on, such a attribute deletion framework is already powerful enough for realizing adaptive security in ABE systems for subset predicates.

Deletion Conforming CPRFs. A regular constrained PRF (CPRF) [5,7,21] consists of a pseudorandom function (PRF) $\mathsf{CPRF}(\cdot, \cdot)$ with a key msk. The constrained property states that given master key msk, there is a way to generate a constrained key ck_f for any constraint function f such that $\mathsf{CPRF}(\mathsf{msk}, x) = \mathsf{CPRF}(\mathsf{ck}_f, x)$ whenever $f(x) = 1$. Also, the standard constrained pseudorandomness property states that an attacker cannot distinguish PRF evaluations $\mathsf{CPRF}(\mathsf{msk}, x_i)$ from uniformly random values on all inputs x_i for which $f(x_i) = 0$, even after it gets to see the constrained key ck_f. The CPRF scheme is said to be adaptively secure if the adversary can choose the challenge constraint function f after making polynomially many PRF evaluation queries. In this work, similar to [30], we instead require the CPRF to achieve adaptive key simulation security. Key simulation property states that there exists an efficient key simulation algorithm KeySim such that an attacker cannot distinguish a simulated key $\widetilde{\mathsf{ck}}_f \leftarrow \mathsf{KeySim}(f)$ from a honestly constrained key ck_f for any adaptively chosen challenge constraint f as long as all its PRF evaluation queries x_i are not satisfied by the constraint f, i.e. $f(x_i)$ for all evaluation queries x_i. Tsabary provided a CPRF construction for subset constraints which satisfies both adaptive pseudorandomness and key simulation security properties.[7] As a side contribution, in the main body we show that the standard constrained pseudorandomness already implies key simulation security.

Inspired by our deletable attribute framework for ABE systems, we define the notion of deletion conforming CPRFs, or DCCPRF in short. Intuitively, it states a CPRF system is deletion conforming if any constrained key ck_f in such a scheme can be *deterministically* computed by simply "deleting" specific bits of the master key msk (i.e., replacing some bits of the master key with the special $\perp$ symbol). Additionally, it must be the case that the PRF evaluation algorithm for any given input x be simplified into a circuit C_x such that evaluating C_x on a master key msk and a constrained key ck_f matches on all valid inputs (i.e., all x such that $f(x) = 1$). Here evaluating the circuit on a constrained key is defined similar to that for partial inputs as in the deletable KP-ABE setting, since a constrained key could have partially *unset* key bits (i.e., contain $\perp$ symbols). All these notions are formally defined later in Sect. 4.

As mentioned previously, here we construct a deletion conforming CPRF for subset constraints. A subset constraint family is defined over a universe of elements $[N] := \{1, \ldots, N\}$, where input to the PRF is a set $S \subseteq [N]$ (which could be represented as an N-bit binary string), and each constraint function is associated with another set $T \subseteq [N]$ such that an input set S satisfies the constraint iff $S \subseteq T$. A CPRF scheme for such a constraint family can be built using a combinatorial strategy as introduced in [9], where the CPRF master key msk consists of $N+1$ regular PRF keys $k_0, k_1, \ldots, k_N$, and the CPRF output on a set S is computed by first selecting all PRF keys k_i such that the associated index $i \in S$, which is then followed by independent PRF evaluation under all selected keys and finally XORing all the evaluations together.[8] Concretely, the evaluator proceeds as follows:

$$\mathsf{CPRF}(\mathsf{msk}, S) = F(k_0, S) \bigoplus_{i \in S} F(k_i, S).$$

Note that a constrained key for a subset T can be simply set as the corresponding subset of underlying PRF keys, that is $\mathsf{ck}_T = \{k_0\} \cup \{k_i\}_{i \in T}$. Observe that for every input set S satisfying the constraint set T (i.e., $S \subseteq T$), the constrained key ck_T already contains the necessary PRF keys for performing the PRF evaluation, thus correctness of evaluation for constrained keys follows immediately. Next, the proof of adaptive constrained pseudorandomness security follows from a simple observation that a reduction algorithm can simply guess an index $i \in \{0, 1, \ldots, N\}$ which is meant to denote the index of the regular PRF key that is not required for answering the constrained key query, but is needed for evaluating the CPRF on the challenge input. Since N is a polynomial, thus such a reduction strategy gives a proof of adaptive security with just polynomial security loss.

---

[7] As we pointed out before, Tsabary gives a construction for t-CNF (for constant t) constraint functions, but this can be viewed as a special case of subset constraints.

[8] In the construction the master key consists of $N+1$ PRF keys instead of N keys just so that pseudorandomness holds for empty set as well.

Finally, to complete our overview of CPRFs, we just need to argue that our CPRF construction satisfies the desired deletion conforming properties. This mostly follows by inspection of our aformentioned construction thereby aligning with our goal of simplicity and precision. Concretely, note that a constrained key ck_T can simply be deterministically obtained by "deleting" all the regular PRF keys k_i for which $i \notin T$. Also, for any input set S, the corresponding CPRF evaluation circuit can be described as: first, it reads the input wires (encoding the appropriate PRF key) corresponding to set S, and then evaluates the circuit $F(\cdot, S)$ on each block of input wires, which is finally followed up by XORing them together. Observe that since this circuit does not even read/touch the input wires corresponding to PRF keys k_i for which $i \notin S$, thus evaluating the circuit on a master key msk and constrained key ck_T is well-defined and gives the same output whenever $S \subseteq T$. Thus, this completes the proof sketch for the above CPRF to be deletion conforming. More details on our construction are provided in the full version.

Building Adaptively Secure Ciphertext-Policy ABE. Moving on to our main transformation, our approach is to decouple the adaptivity and functionality (delivering the message to users) requirements of a CP-ABE scheme, and deal with them separately. Following Tsabary's paradigm, we rely on our deletion conforming CPRFs for enabling the reduction algorithm to be able to answer the adaptive key queries, while still using the selectively secure deletable KP-ABE system for guaranteeing that the message is hidden. At a very high level, the idea is to handle the adaptivity problem outside of the underlying KP-ABE system, while using its attribute deletion capabilities to compute the CP-ABE challenge ciphertext from a KP-ABE challenge ciphertext that was selectively obtained. Below we sketch our transformation.

The public parameters of the CP-ABE system contains the deletable (KP-)ABE parameters $\texttt{del.pp}$, while the master secret key consists of a DCCPRF master key $\texttt{prf.msk}$ as well as the deletable ABE master key $\texttt{del.msk}$. Recall that in a CP-ABE system, each secret key is associated with an attribute string $x \in \{0,1\}^N$. To sample a secret key for attribute x, the key generator first computes a tag value t as the CPRF evaluation with input x, i.e. $t = \mathsf{CPRF}(\texttt{prf.msk}, x)$. Let C_x denote the simplified explicit circuit that performs the CPRF evaluation on input x, i.e. $C_x(\mathsf{key}) = \mathsf{CPRF}(\mathsf{key}, x)$. The key generator then creates a policy circuit $f_{x,t}$, given the tag value t and circuit description C_x, as:

$$f_{x,t}(z) = \begin{cases} 1 & \text{if } C_x(z) \neq t, \\ 0 & \text{otherwise.} \end{cases}$$

The (CP-ABE) secret key sk_x for attribute x now corresponds to a (KP-ABE) secret key for the above policy circuit, i.e. $\mathsf{sk}_x = \texttt{del.sk}_{f_{x,t}}$. To encrypt a message m under a policy circuit g, the encryptor first samples a *simulated* constrained key $\widetilde{\texttt{prf.sk}_g}$ with g being used as the constraint function, and then it computes the ciphertext as an KP-ABE encryption of message m with attribute string set as sk_g. The resulting decryption algorithm is exactly the decryption algorithm of the underlying KP-ABE scheme.

First, note that, by the deletion conforming properties, evaluating C_x is well-defined and accurately matches the corresponding CPRF output on every accepting constrained key. Thus with this observation we get that correctness of the above construction follows from the fact that whenever $g(x) = 1$, then $f_{x,t}(\widetilde{\mathtt{prf}.\mathsf{sk}_g}) = 1$ with all but negligible probability, since $C_x(\widetilde{\mathtt{prf}.\mathsf{sk}_g}) = t = C_x(\mathtt{prf}.\mathsf{msk})$ happens only with negligible probability by pseudorandomness of the underlying CPRF.

Next we describe the intuition behind the proof of adaptive security. Note that initially the challenge ciphertext for policy g^* with message m is computed as KP-ABE encryption of message m with a simulated CPRF constrained key $\widetilde{\mathtt{prf}.\mathsf{sk}_{g^*}}$ as the attribute string. As a first step, we instead switch this to be a honestly constrained key $\mathtt{prf}.\mathsf{sk}_{g^*} = \mathsf{Constrain}(\mathtt{prf}.\mathsf{msk}, g^*)$. Since the CPRF satisfies the adaptive key simulation property, thus this change will be indistinguishable. Note that it is important that the CPRF is adaptively secure for this reduction to work since to answer the pre-challenge key queries, the reduction algorithm needs to query for the respective CPRF evaluations. Next, by the deletion conforming property of the constrained PRF scheme, we have that the constrained key $\mathtt{prf}.\mathsf{sk}_{g^*}$ can be computed by simply deleting certain specific key bits of the master key $\mathtt{prf}.\mathsf{msk}$. Let $\mathcal{I}_{g^*}$ denote such a set of indices, i.e. $\mathtt{prf}.\mathsf{sk}_{g^*} = \mathsf{Restrict}(\mathtt{prf}.\mathsf{msk}, \mathcal{I}_{g^*})$. By relying on the deletion indistinguishability property of the KP-ABE scheme, we get that the challenge ciphertext can instead be computed as first encrypting the message m under attribute string $\mathtt{prf}.\mathsf{msk}$, and then deleting the attribute bits as specified by set $\mathcal{I}_{g^*}$ by running the KP-ABE deletion algorithm. Finally, since the attribute string $\mathtt{prf}.\mathsf{msk}$ is sampled at the beginning of the security game, thus $\mathtt{prf}.\mathsf{msk}$ can be selectively specified to the KP-ABE challenger thereby allowing us to argue that the message is also hidden. Our construction and its proof is formally provided in Sect. 6.

Perfect Correctness? Although at first glance it may seem that imperfect correctness is an inherent and unavoidable feature of the above framework, we show in the full version that this is not the case where we provide an alternate construction which is perfectly correct. Very briefly, our idea is to have two deletable ABE sub-systems working in parallel, instead of just one, where both the ciphertexts and secret keys contain two copies (one under each ABE sub-system). The only difference is that while sampling a secret key under both the systems independently, the key generator uses two distinct tag values, where one of the tag values is computed as is now, whereas the other tag value will be its complement. Such a trick gets around the imperfect correctness problem since it can never happen that $C_x(\widetilde{\mathtt{prf}.\mathsf{sk}_g}) = t_0$ as well as $C_x(\widetilde{\mathtt{prf}.\mathsf{sk}_g}) = t_1$ where t_0, t_1 are the complementary tag pairs. It turns out that the proof of adaptive security now is more involved, as we need to first use the existing proof structure to erase the information about the challenge message from the first deletable ABE subciphertext, then we would have to undo correlations created between parts of the challenge ciphertext and secret keys, and finally use a similar proof structure to erase the information about the challenge message from the second deletable ABE sub-ciphertext as well.

Another Interpretation. Abstractly, the deletion paradigm described above can be interpreted as a mechanism to selectively activate the trapdoors embedded inside the secret keys such that whenever trapdoor is activated then the challenger can simulate the secret keys for all possible attributes. The property such simulated keys satisfy is that they are indistinguishable from honestly sampled secret keys as long as the challenge policy does not accept the corresponding key attribute. On a more intuitive level, one could also observe some similarities between the above framework and the Dual System methodology [31], where switching from a simulated CPRF key to an honestly constrained CPRF key could be comparable to moving from a *normal* to a *semi-functional* ciphertext, and the secret keys are already sampled in the semi-functional mode.

Deleting Attributes in [6,19]. Finally, we show that existing ABE schemes by Goyal et al. (GPSW) [19] from bilinear maps, and by Boyen [6] from LWE[9] already lie in the class of ABE schemes with deletable attributes, thereby displaying the generality of our framework. Below we give an overview of our deletion algorithms. More details are provided later in Sect. 7, where we also show that a KP-ABE scheme with deletable attributes for monotonic access structures can be generically upgraded to non-monotonic log-depth circuits (i.e., $\mathbf{NC}^1$).

Deletions in [19]. First, we look at the bilinear map based ABE construction by GPSW. They proposed a KP-ABE scheme for monotone access structures and proved its security under the Decisional Bilinear Diffie-Hellman (DBDH) assumption that can also be readily adapted to a scheme provably secure under the Search Bilinear Diffie-Hellman assumption. The public parameters in the GPSW scheme contain n group elements in the base group $\{T_i\}_{i \in [n]}$ and one group element in the target group K, where n denotes the length of the attributes. A ciphertext encrypting a message m under an attribute $x \in \{0,1\}^n$ is of the following form:

$$\mathsf{ct} = (m \cdot K^s, \{T_i^s\}_{i \in [n]: x_i = 1}),$$

where s is a random exponent. Basically the term T_i^s encodes the i-th bit of the attribute, and during decryption the algorithm pairs the ciphertext component T_i^s with a corresponding key component (iff the policy circuit reads the i-th input wire) and performs a polynomial interpolation in the exponent to reconstruct the masking term K^s.

Our observation is that to delete an attribute bit, say j, one could simply drop the term T_j^s from ciphertext (if it exists). Multiple attribute bits could be deleted analogously. As long as the policy circuit does not read the deleted

[9] We want to remind the reader the existence of an attack [1] on Boyen's ABE scheme. Deletions in Boyen's scheme are merely provided for illustrative purposes in the full version.

input wire, the correctness for deleted ciphertexts follows immediately from the correctness of GPSW scheme itself. Similarly, to encrypt a message m under a non-binary attribute string $x \in \{0, 1, \perp\}^n$, we simply treat each $\perp$ symbol as a 0 bit, and therefore do not encode it in the ciphertext. Clearly, the distributions of freshly computed ciphertexts and deleted ciphertexts (encrypting the same message m and attribute x) are identical, thus deletion indistinguishability for GPSW is merely a statistical property. Combining this with the fact that GPSW provides selective IND-CPA security, we obtain that GPSW augmented with the deletion procedure is KP-ABE scheme with deletable attributes. Later in the full version [18] we also describe a hardcore bit variant of the above scheme whose security relies on the Computational Bilinear Diffie-Hellman (CBDH) assumption.

Deletions in [6]. Next, we look at the LWE-based ABE construction by Boyen. Boyen's scheme is also for monotone access structures and its security relies on the LWE assumption. The public parameters in Boyen's scheme consist $\ell + 1$ matrices of appropriate dimensions $(\mathbf{A}_0, \{\mathbf{A}_i\}_{i \in [\ell]})$ and a vector $\mathbf{u}$, where ℓ denotes the length of the attributes. Now a ciphertext ct encrypting a message bit msg under an attribute $x \in \{0,1\}^\ell$ is of the following form $\mathsf{ct} = (c_0, \mathbf{c}_{1,0}, \mathbf{c}_{1,1}, \ldots, \mathbf{c}_{1,\ell})$, where

$$c_0 = \mathbf{s}^\top \cdot \mathbf{u} + \nu_0 + \lfloor \frac{q}{2} \rfloor \cdot \mathsf{msg},$$

$$\forall i \in [0, \ell], \quad \mathbf{c}_{1,i} = \begin{cases} \mathbf{s}^\top \cdot \mathbf{A}_i + \nu_{1,i} & \text{if } i = 0 \text{ or } x_i = 1, \\ \nu_{1,i} & \text{otherwise.} \end{cases}$$

and $\mathbf{s}$ is a random secret vector, and $\nu_0, \{\nu_{1,i}\}_{i \in [\ell]}$ are sampled i.i.d. according to the LWE noise distribution. Here the vector $\mathbf{c}_{1,i}$ encodes the i-th bit of the attribute, and during decryption the algorithm combines the ciphertext component $\mathbf{c}_{1,i}$ with a corresponding key component (iff the policy circuit reads the i-th input wire).

For deleting attributes in Boyen's scheme, instead of dropping the respective ciphertext component, we replace with freshly sampled noise. Concretely, to delete an attribute bit, say j, we replace the vector $\mathbf{c}_{1,j}$ in the ciphertext with a freshly sampled noise vector $\nu'_{1,i}$. Multiple attribute bits could be deleted analogously.[10] And as for our augmented GPSW scheme, during encryption we treat each $\perp$ symbol as a 0 bit, and the correctness and deletion indistinguishability of the resultant follows either immediately from Boyen's scheme or by inspection.

Recent Independent Work. Recently, Katsumata, Nishimaki, Yamada, and Yamakawa (KNYY) [20] gave an exciting construction showing how to expand the framework of [30] to encompass an inner product encryption and Fuzzy IBE functionality within the LWE setting. An important insight was showing that a

[10] We could also drop the deleted ciphertext components instead of replacing them with LWE noise, however for ensuring consistency with Boyen's scheme we keep it this way.

specific cryptosystem could relax the earlier conforming property to just functional equivalence and thus leverage a particular constrained PRF of [10] to achieve greater functionality.

In contrast, our work shows how to relax the conforming property to deletion so that it is realizable in a broader setting that includes bilinear maps. But we show that is still sufficient to maintain the t-CNF functionality. KNYY show that in the LWE setting one can strengthen the framework to handle a broader class of LWE specific constrained PRFs. The works were performed independently.

Comparing Techniques with [30]. We conclude by giving some further technical comparisons between our framework and the earlier work of Tsabary [30] that we build upon. Our work follows a similar pathway which is to leverage adaptive security of constrained PRFs (with special properties) inside a key-policy ABE scheme (with special properties) to achieve an adaptively secure ciphertext-policy ABE scheme, but differences lie in the flavour of these special properties required from the underlying constrained PRF and key-policy ABE systems. Tsabary started with the LWE-based ABE construction of Boneh et al. [4], and using the homomorphic properties of the underlying ABE scheme, Tsabary developed a framework for partial ciphertext evaluation and a circuit splitting/composition abstraction, wherein the ABE scheme allows a user to encrypt messages under *partially evaluated* attributes such that they are indistinguishable from *partially evaluated* ciphertexts encrypting same message under the original (unevaluated) attribute. Concretely, [30] relies on the fact that for any attribute x and circuit C, one could compute ciphertexts of the form: $\mathsf{ct}_0 = \mathsf{Enc}(\mathsf{pp}, m, x)$, $\mathsf{ct}_1 = \mathsf{Enc}(\mathsf{pp}, m, C(x))$ such that given a secret key $\mathsf{sk}_{\widetilde{C}}$ for some circuit $\widetilde{C}$ s.t. $\widetilde{C}(x) = 1$, a user can not only decrypt ciphertexts of the form ct_0, but it can also decrypt ciphertexts of the form ct_1 as long as there exists another circuit C' with the semantics that $\widetilde{C}(\cdot) = C'(C(\cdot))$ that the decryptor knows. Here the equality between the circuit $\widetilde{C}$ and the composition of C, C' mandates the resultant 'gate-by-gate' circuit descriptions must be *identical*. With such an ABE scheme with these special properties as the centerpiece, [30] built a constrained PRF that conforms with the necessary circuit splitting/composition semantics. Very briefly, [30] required that the PRF evaluation circuit with the input hardwired can be split into two sub-circuits such that one of those sub-circuits can be used during generating the CP-ABE ciphertext. Combining all these things in an extremely careful manner gives the desired result of an adaptively secure CP-ABE scheme for subset policies.

Our approach, on the other hand, is to skip the entire partial evaluation and circuit splitting/composition framework, and instead go with a simpler abstraction of input deletion while also demanding (as part of our definitional framework) an explicit descriptions for all the circuits used throughout the analysis.

2 Preliminaries

Notation. Let PPT denote probabilistic polynomial-time. We denote the set of all positive integers upto n as $[n] := \{1, \ldots, n\}$. Also, we use $[0, n]$ to denote the set of all non-negative integers upto n, i.e. $[0, n] := \{0\} \cup [n]$. Throughout this paper, unless specified, all polynomials we consider are positive polynomials. For any finite set S, $x \leftarrow S$ denotes a uniformly random element x from the set S. Similarly, for any distribution $\mathcal{D}$, $x \leftarrow \mathcal{D}$ denotes an element x drawn from distribution $\mathcal{D}$. The distribution $\mathcal{D}^n$ is used to represent a distribution over vectors of n components, where each component is drawn independently from the distribution $\mathcal{D}$.

For any $n \in \mathbb{N}$, string $x \in \{0, 1, \perp\}^n$ and index set $\mathcal{I} \subseteq [n]$, let $\mathsf{Restrict}(x, \mathcal{I})$ denote the string $\widetilde{x} \in \{0, 1, \perp\}^n$ such that

$$\forall i \in [n], \quad \widetilde{x}_i = \begin{cases} x_i & \text{if } j \notin \mathcal{I}, \\ \perp & \text{otherwise.} \end{cases}$$

where x_i and $\widetilde{x}_i$ denote the ith elements of strings x and $\widetilde{x}$, respectively. For any string $x \in \{0, 1, \perp\}^n$, let $\mathsf{BotSet}(x)$ denote the subset of indices in $[n]$ such that for every $i \in \mathsf{BotSet}(x)$, $x_i = \perp$ and for every $i \notin \mathsf{BotSet}(x)$, $x_i \in \{0, 1\}$. Formally, $\mathsf{BotSet}(x) := \{i \in [n] : x_i = \perp\}$.

Circuit Notation. Also, throughout the paper we use the circuit model of computation. Consider any circuit $C : \{0, 1\}^n \rightarrow \{0, 1\}$ that takes n-bits of input and outputs a single bit. For any circuit C, we define $\mathsf{Unsupported}(C) \subseteq [n]$ to be set of indices $i \in [n]$ such that the circuit C does not use on the ith input wire (i.e., C does not read the ith input bit).[11]

Lastly, we use CEval to denote an "expanded" notion of circuit evaluation. The algorithm CEval takes as input a circuit $C : \{0, 1\}^n \rightarrow \{0, 1\}^m$, and a string $x \in \{0, 1, \perp\}^n$, and it first checks that $\mathsf{BotSet}(x) \subseteq \mathsf{Unsupported}(C)$. If the check fails, it outputs the all-zeros string 0^m; otherwise it evaluates the circuit C on string x, and outputs the same result as the circuit which is $C(x)$. Note that evaluating the circuit C on string x (that could possibly contain non-binary input bits) is well-defined in the last step, since the evaluator CEval only runs the circuit C after its checks that $\mathsf{BotSet}(x) \subseteq \mathsf{Unsupported}(C)$, and thus we know that if the check succeeds then all the input wires/bits read by circuit C are defined and not set as $\perp$. Formally, CEval can be defined as:

$$\mathsf{CEval}(C, x) = \begin{cases} C(x) & \text{if } \mathsf{BotSet}(x) \subseteq \mathsf{Unsupported}(C), \\ 0^m & \text{otherwise.} \end{cases}$$

Due to space constraints, we move the definition of regular pseudorandom functions to the full version.

[11] Note that our definition of the *unsupported indices* for a circuit C is very restrictive. Concretely, we say that an index $i \in \mathsf{Unsupported}(C)$ *iff* as per the circuit description of C the ith input wire is unused/untouched. For instance, consider two circuits $C, \widetilde{C}$ which takes length 2-bit strings as inputs: $C(x) = (x_1 \vee \neg x_1) \wedge x_2$ and $\widetilde{C}(x) = x_2$. Here $\mathsf{Unsupported}(C) = \emptyset$ and $\mathsf{Unsupported}(\widetilde{C}) = \{1\}$, i.e. circuits $C, \widetilde{C}$ have different unsupported indices even though they are functionally identical. This is because as per the circuit description of C, it does use both input wires/bits; whereas $\widetilde{C}$ ignores the first input wire/bit.

3 Key Policy Attribute-Based Encryption with Deletable Attributes

In this section, we introduce the notion of Key Policy Attribute-Based Encryption (KP-ABE) with deletable attributes. First, we provide the syntax, and later describe our definitions for KP-ABE with deletable attributes.

Syntax. A key-policy attribute based encryption (KP-ABE) scheme with deletable attributes for a class of circuits $\mathcal{C} = \{\mathcal{C}_n\}_{n \in \mathbb{N}}$ and message space $\mathcal{M}$ consists of the following PPT algorithms:

$\mathsf{Setup}(1^\lambda, 1^n) \rightarrow (\mathsf{pp}, \mathsf{msk})$. On input the security parameter λ and attribute length n, the setup algorithm outputs a set of public parameters pp, and master secret key msk.

$\mathsf{KeyGen}(\mathsf{msk}, f) \rightarrow \mathsf{sk}_f$. On input the master secret key msk and a circuit $f \in \mathcal{C}_n$, the key generation algorithm outputs a predicate key sk_f.

$\mathsf{Enc}(\mathsf{pp}, x, m) \rightarrow \mathsf{ct}$. On input the public parameters pp, an attribute string $x \in \{0, 1, \perp\}^n$, and a message $m \in \mathcal{M}$, the encryption algorithm outputs a ciphertext ct. Note that here the attribute string x is possibly a non-binary string as it could contain $\perp$ symbols.

$\mathsf{Dec}(\mathsf{sk}_f, \mathsf{ct}) \rightarrow m/\mathtt{fail}$. On input a secret key sk_f and a ciphertext ct, the decryption algorithm either outputs a message m or a special string `fail` (to denote decryption failure).

$\mathsf{Delete}(\mathsf{pp}, \mathsf{ct}, \mathcal{I}) \rightarrow \mathsf{ct}'$. On input of the public parameters pp, a ciphertext ct and a set of indices $\mathcal{I} \subseteq [n]$, the deletion algorithm outputs a modified ciphertext ct'.

We require such an ABE scheme to satisfy the following properties.

Correctness. Intuitively, it says that the above scheme is correct if decrypting a ciphertext, which was either directly computed using the encryption algorithm or generated by the ciphertext deletion algorithm, outputs the correct message as long as the policy circuit accepts the attribute associated with the ciphertext.

Formally, an KP-ABE scheme with deletable attributes is said to be correct if for all $\lambda, n \in \mathbb{N}$, $f \in \mathcal{C}_n$, $m \in \mathcal{M}$, $x_0 \in \{0, 1, \perp\}^n$ and a sequence of indices sets $\mathcal{I}_1, \mathcal{I}_2 \cdots, \mathcal{I}_k \subseteq [n]$, for any $k \geq 0$, the following holds:

$$\mathsf{CEval}(f, x_k) = 1 \implies \Pr\left[\mathsf{Dec}(\mathsf{sk}_f, \mathsf{ct}_k) = m : \begin{array}{c} (\mathsf{pp}, \mathsf{msk}) \leftarrow \mathsf{Setup}(1^\lambda, 1^n) \\ \mathsf{sk}_f \leftarrow \mathsf{KeyGen}(\mathsf{msk}, f), \mathsf{ct}_0 \leftarrow \mathsf{Enc}(\mathsf{pp}, x_0, m) \\ (\forall i \in [k])\ \mathsf{ct}_i \leftarrow \mathsf{Delete}(\mathsf{pp}, \mathsf{ct}_{i-1}, \mathcal{I}_i) \end{array}\right] = 1,$$

where x_k is defined by the following sequence of operations: $x_i \leftarrow \mathsf{Restrict}(x_{i-1}, \mathcal{I}_i)$ for all $i \in [k]$.

Security. For security, we have two requirements. First, we require the scheme to provide standard semantic security as for standard ABE schemes. Here we consider both selective and adaptive IND-CPA security definitions. Second, we introduce a notion of indistinguishability for ciphertexts with deleted attributes, in which the adversary cannot distinguish between a ciphertext modified by the Delete algorithm and a ciphertext directly encrypted from the same message with respect to the same attribute string after deletion. Formally, they are defined as below.

Definition 3.1 (Adaptive IND-CPA Security). *A KP-ABE scheme is adaptively secure if for every stateful admissible PPT adversary $\mathcal{A}$, there exists a negligible function* $\mathsf{negl}(\cdot)$ *such that for all $\lambda, n \in \mathbb{N}$, the following holds*

$$\Pr\left[\mathcal{A}^{\mathsf{KeyGen}(\mathsf{msk},\cdot)}(\mathsf{ct}) = b : \begin{array}{c} (\mathsf{pp}, \mathsf{msk}) \leftarrow \mathsf{Setup}(1^\lambda, 1^n) \\ ((m_0, m_1), x^* \in \{0,1\}^n) \leftarrow \mathcal{A}^{\mathsf{KeyGen}(\mathsf{msk},\cdot)}(1^\lambda, 1^n, \mathsf{pp}) \\ b \leftarrow \{0,1\}; \mathsf{ct} \leftarrow \mathsf{Enc}(\mathsf{pp}, x^*, m_b) \end{array}\right] \leq \frac{1}{2} + \mathsf{negl}(\lambda),$$

where the adversary $\mathcal{A}$ is admissible as long as every secret key query f made by $\mathcal{A}$ to the oracle $\mathsf{KeyGen}(\mathsf{msk},\cdot)$ *satisfies the condition that $f(x^*) = 0$. Here x^* is the challenge attribute chosen by $\mathcal{A}$. Note that the adversary must choose x^* as a binary string, that is it must not contain any $\perp$ symbols.*[12]

Definition 3.2 (Selective IND-CPA Security). *A KP-ABE scheme is said to be* selectively *secure if in the above security game (see Definition 3.1), the adversary must instead declare the challenge attribute $x^* \in \{0,1\}^n$ at the beginning of the game, that is even before it receives the public paramters* pp *from the challenger.*

Definition 3.3 (Deletion Indistinguishability). *A KP-ABE scheme with deletable attributes satisfies deletion indistinguishability property if for every stateful PPT adversary $\mathcal{A}$, there exists a negligible function* $\mathsf{negl}(\cdot)$, *such that for all $\lambda, n \in \mathbb{N}$, the following holds*

$$\Pr\left[\mathcal{A}(\mathsf{ct}_b) = b : \begin{array}{c} (\mathsf{pp}, \mathsf{msk}) \leftarrow \mathsf{Setup}(1^\lambda, 1^n),\ b \leftarrow \{0,1\} \\ (m, x \in \{0,1,\perp\}^n, \mathcal{I} \subseteq [n]) \leftarrow \mathcal{A}(1^\lambda, 1^n, \mathsf{pp}, \mathsf{msk}) \\ \widetilde{\mathsf{ct}} \leftarrow \mathsf{Enc}(\mathsf{pp}, x, m),\ \mathsf{ct}_0 \leftarrow \mathsf{Delete}(\mathsf{pp}, \widetilde{\mathsf{ct}}, \mathcal{I}) \\ \widetilde{x} \leftarrow \mathsf{Restrict}(x, \mathcal{I}),\ \mathsf{ct}_1 \leftarrow \mathsf{Enc}(\mathsf{pp}, \widetilde{x}, m) \end{array}\right] \leq \frac{1}{2} + \mathsf{negl}(\lambda).$$

Note that the attribute vector x chosen by the adversary $\mathcal{A}$ can contain $\perp$ symbols.

4 Constrained PRFs: Defining Deletion Conformity

In this section, we first recall the notion of constrained PRFs (CPRFs) [5,7,21], and later introduce our notion of *deletion conforming* CPRFs.

Syntax. A constrained PRF (CPRF) for constraint class $\mathcal{F} = \{\mathcal{F}_N\}_{N \in \mathbb{N}}$ consists of three PPT algorithms (Setup, Constrain, Eval) with the following syntax:

---

[12] Note that since x^* does not contain $\perp$ symbols, thus $f(x^*)$ is always well-defined and we do not need define the admissibility constraint as $\mathsf{CEval}(f, x^*) = 0$ instead.

$\mathsf{Setup}(1^\lambda, 1^N) \to \mathsf{msk}$. On input the security parameter λ and input length N, the setup algorithm outputs a master secret key $\mathsf{msk} \in \{0,1\}^k$. Let $k = k(\lambda, N)$ denote the length of secret key, where $k(\cdot,\cdot)$ is an a-priori fixed polynomial.

$\mathsf{Constrain}(\mathsf{msk}, f) \to \mathsf{sk}_f$. On input a constraint function $f \in \mathcal{F}_N$ and master secret key msk, the constrain algorithm outputs a constrained key sk_f.

$\mathsf{Eval}(\mathsf{sk}, x) \to y$. The evaluation algorithm takes as input a (possibly constrained) secret key sk and a string $x \in \{0,1\}^N$, and outputs a string y. Let $m = m(\lambda, N)$ denote the length of the output string y for some polynomial $m(\cdot,\cdot)$.[13]

Correctness of CPRF Evaluation. A CPRF scheme is said to be correct if for all $\lambda, N \in \mathbb{N}$, $f \in \mathcal{F}_N$, and $x \in \{0,1\}^N$, the following holds:

$$f(x) = 1 \implies \Pr\left[\mathsf{Eval}(\mathsf{msk}, x) = \mathsf{Eval}(\mathsf{sk}_f, x) : \begin{array}{c}\mathsf{msk} \leftarrow \mathsf{Setup}(1^\lambda, 1^N)\\ \mathsf{sk}_f \leftarrow \mathsf{Constrain}(\mathsf{msk}, f)\end{array}\right] = 1$$

Security. Next, we recall the notion of single-key adaptive pseudorandomness security for constrained PRFs. Later on we also define the notion of key simulation security as defined in [30].

Definition 4.1 (Adaptive single-key constrained pseudorandomness). *We say that a* $\mathsf{CPRF} = (\mathsf{Setup}, \mathsf{Constrain}, \mathsf{Eval})$ *satisfies adaptive single-key constrained pseudorandomness security if for any stateful admissible PPT adversary* $\mathcal{A}$ *there exists a negligible function* $\mathsf{negl}(\cdot)$, *such that for all* $\lambda, N \in \mathbb{N}$, *the following holds:*

$$\Pr\left[\mathcal{A}^{\mathsf{Eval}(\mathsf{msk},\cdot),\mathsf{Constrain}(\mathsf{msk},\cdot)}(r_b) = b : \begin{array}{c}\mathsf{msk} \leftarrow \mathsf{Setup}(1^\lambda, 1^N),\ b \leftarrow \{0,1\}\\ x^* \leftarrow \mathcal{A}^{\mathsf{Eval}(\mathsf{msk},\cdot),\mathsf{Constrain}(\mathsf{msk},\cdot)}(1^\lambda, 1^N)\\ r_0 \leftarrow \{0,1\}^m,\ r_1 = \mathsf{Eval}(\mathsf{msk}, x^*)\end{array}\right] \le \frac{1}{2} + \mathsf{negl}(\lambda).$$

Here the adversary $\mathcal{A}$ *is said to be admissible as long as it satisfies the following conditions—(1) it makes at most one query to the constrain oracle* $\mathsf{Constrain}(\mathsf{msk}, \cdot)$, *and its queried function* f *must be such that* $f(x^*) = 0$, *(2) it must not send* x^* *as one of its evaluation queries to* $\mathsf{Eval}(\mathsf{msk}, \cdot)$.

The above pseudorandomness security could be extended to collusion-resistant notions where the adversary could make polynomially many constrain queries, however in this work we only require single-key security. Next, we define key simulation security for CPRFs.

Definition 4.2 (Adaptive key simulation). *We say that a* $\mathsf{CPRF} = (\mathsf{Setup}, \mathsf{Constrain}, \mathsf{Eval})$ *satisfies adaptive key simulation security if there exists a PPT algorithm* KeySim *such that for any stateful admissible PPT adversary* $\mathcal{A}$,

13 Here we consider a single PRF evaluation algorithm that could take as input a master key as well as a constrained key. Thus, both the master and constrained keys are of same length k. Note that one could instead split it into two separate evaluation algorithms, however for ease of exposition we avoid it.

there exists a negligible function $\mathsf{negl}(\cdot)$*, such that for all* $\lambda, N \in \mathbb{N}$*, the following holds:*

$$\Pr\left[\mathcal{A}^{\mathsf{Eval}(\mathsf{msk},\cdot)}(sk_b) = b : \begin{array}{c} \mathsf{msk} \leftarrow \mathsf{Setup}(1^\lambda, 1^N),\ b \leftarrow \{0,1\} \\ f^* \leftarrow \mathcal{A}^{\mathsf{Eval}(\mathsf{msk},\cdot)}(1^\lambda, 1^N) \\ \mathsf{sk}_0 \leftarrow \mathsf{KeySim}(1^\lambda, 1^N, f^*),\ \mathsf{sk}_1 \leftarrow \mathsf{Constrain}(\mathsf{msk}, f^*) \end{array}\right] \leq \frac{1}{2} + \mathsf{negl}(\lambda).$$

Here the adversary $\mathcal{A}$ *is said to be admissible if all its evaluation queries* $x \in \{0,1\}^N$ *satisfy the condition that* $f^*(x) = 0$*. That is, none of the queried inputs are satisfied by the constraint* f^**.*

Non-colliding Property. A constrained PRF CPRF that satisfies key simulation security (Definition 4.2) is said to be *non-colliding* if there exists a negligible function $\mathsf{negl}(\cdot)$ such that for all $\lambda, N \in \mathbb{N}$, every input $x \in \{0,1\}^N$, constraint function $f \in \mathcal{F}_N$, the following holds:

$$\Pr\left[\mathsf{Eval}(\mathsf{msk}, x) = \mathsf{Eval}(\mathsf{sk}'_f, x) : \begin{array}{c} \mathsf{msk} \leftarrow \mathsf{Setup}(1^\lambda, 1^N) \\ \mathsf{sk}'_f \leftarrow \mathsf{KeySim}(1^\lambda, 1^N, f) \end{array}\right] \leq \mathsf{negl}(\lambda).$$

Later on in the full version, we show that if the CPRF satisfies (0-key) pseudorandomness security, then it also satisfies the non-colliding property as long as the output length of the PRF is large enough. Additionally, we also show that the adaptive single-key constrained pseudorandomness security in fact implies adaptive key simulation security.

4.1 Deletion Conforming CPRFs

Now we define the deletion conforming property for CPRFs. Intuitively, it states that a constrained key in such a CPRF scheme must be deterministically computable by simply deleting specific bits of the master key (i.e., replacing some bits of the master key with a special $\perp$ symbol). Formally we define it below.

Definition 4.3 (Deletion Conforming CPRF). *We say that a constrained PRF scheme* CPRF = (Setup, Constrain, Eval) *for a function class* $\mathcal{F} = \{\mathcal{F}_N\}_{N\in\mathbb{N}}$ *is a* deletion conforming *CPRF if the constrain algorithm* Constrain *is deterministic, and there exists two polynomial time algorithms* (CircuitGen, DeleteFunc) *with the following syntax and properties:*

$\mathsf{CircuitGen}(1^\lambda, 1^N, x) \rightarrow C_x$. *The circuit generation algorithm is a* deterministic *algorithm that takes as input the security parameter* λ*, length parameter* N*, and input string* $x \in \{0,1\}^N$*. It outputs the description of a circuit* C_x*.*

$\mathsf{DeleteFunc}(1^\lambda, 1^N, f) \rightarrow \mathcal{I}_f$. *The key deletion algorithm is a* deterministic *algorithm that takes as input the security parameter* λ*, length parameter* N*, and a constraint function* $f \in \mathcal{F}_N$*. It outputs a set of indices* $\mathcal{I}_f \subseteq [k]$*, where* k *denotes the length of the master secret key.*

We say that DCCPRF = (Setup, Constrain, Eval, CircuitGen, DeleteFunc) *is a deletion conforming CPRF if for all* $\lambda, N \in \mathbb{N}$*, every function* $f \in \mathcal{F}_N$*, input* $x \in \{0,1\}^N$*, and master key* $\mathsf{msk} \leftarrow \mathsf{Setup}(1^\lambda, 1^N)$*, the following properties are satisfied.*

1. ***Function deletion property:*** $\mathsf{Constrain}(\mathsf{msk}, f) = \mathsf{Restrict}(\mathsf{msk}, \mathcal{I}_f)$, *where index set* $\mathcal{I}_f$ *is computed as* $\mathcal{I}_f = \mathsf{DeleteFunc}(1^\lambda, 1^N, f)$.
2. ***Circuit evaluation property:*** *Let* $C_x = \mathsf{CircuitGen}(1^\lambda, 1^N, x)$. *It states that* $\mathsf{Eval}(\mathsf{msk}, x) = C_x(\mathsf{msk})$ *irrespective of whether* $f(x) = 0/1$, *and* $\mathsf{Eval}(\mathsf{sk}_f, x) = \mathsf{CEval}(C_x, \mathsf{sk}_f)$ *whenever* $f(x) = 1$ *where* $\mathsf{sk}_f = \mathsf{Constrain}(\mathsf{msk}, f)$ *or* $\mathsf{sk}_f \leftarrow \mathsf{KeySim}(1^\lambda, 1^N, f)$.

Here recall that the Restrict *and* CEval *operations are as defined in Sect. 2—* $\mathsf{Restrict}(s, \mathcal{I})$ *denotes a string after replacing the bits in* s *with indices corresponding to indices in set* $\mathcal{I}$ *with* $\perp$*; and* $\mathsf{CEval}(C, x)$ *denotes evaluating the circuit* C *on input* x*, but setting the circuit output to be the all zeros string* 0^m *if the circuit* C *depends on the input wires whose indices have* $\perp$ *symbol in* x.

5 Ciphertext Policy Attribute-Based Encryption

In this section, we recall the notion of Ciphertext Policy Attribute-Based Encryption (CP-ABE). First, we provide the syntax and definitions, and later define the predicate class we study in this work.

Syntax. A ciphertext-policy attribute based encryption (CP-ABE) scheme for a class of predicates $\mathcal{F} = \{\mathcal{F}_N\}_{N \in \mathbb{N}}$ and message space $\mathcal{M}$ consists of the following PPT algorithms:

$\mathsf{Setup}(1^\lambda, 1^N) \rightarrow (\mathsf{pp}, \mathsf{msk})$. On input the security parameter λ and attribute length N, the setup algorithm outputs a set of public parameters pp, and master secret key msk.

$\mathsf{KeyGen}(\mathsf{msk}, x) \rightarrow \mathsf{sk}_x$. On input the master secret key msk and a key attribute $x \in \{0,1\}^N$, the key generation algorithm outputs a predicate key sk_x.

$\mathsf{Enc}(\mathsf{pp}, f, m) \rightarrow \mathsf{ct}$. On input the public parameters pp, a predicate $f \in \mathcal{F}_N$, and a message $m \in \mathcal{M}$, the encryption algorithm outputs a ciphertext ct.

$\mathsf{Dec}(\mathsf{sk}_x, \mathsf{ct}) \rightarrow m/\mathtt{fail}$. On input a secret key sk_x and a ciphertext ct, the decryption algorithm either outputs a message m or a special string `fail` (to denote decryption failure).

Correctness. A CP-ABE scheme is said to be correct if for all $\lambda, N \in \mathbb{N}$, $f \in \mathcal{F}_N$, $m \in \mathcal{M}$, $x \in \{0,1\}^N$, the following holds:

$$f(x) = 1 \Longrightarrow \Pr\left[\mathsf{Dec}(\mathsf{sk}_x, \mathsf{ct}) = m : \begin{array}{c} (\mathsf{pp}, \mathsf{msk}) \leftarrow \mathsf{Setup}(1^\lambda, 1^N) \\ \mathsf{sk}_x \leftarrow \mathsf{KeyGen}(\mathsf{msk}, x),\ \mathsf{ct} \leftarrow \mathsf{Enc}(\mathsf{pp}, x, m) \end{array}\right] = 1.$$

Security. For security, we require the scheme to achieve adaptive security (see Definition 3.1). Note that the admissibility condition for the adversary $\mathcal{A}$ in the security game is modified as follows. The adversary $\mathcal{A}$ is admissible as long as every secret key query $x \in \{0,1\}^N$ made by $\mathcal{A}$ to the oracle $\mathsf{KeyGen}(\mathsf{msk}, \cdot)$ satisfies the condition that $f^*(x) = 0$, where f^* is the challenge predicate chosen by $\mathcal{A}$.

6 Building Adaptively Secure CP-ABE

In this section, we build an adaptively secure CP-ABE scheme from a selectively secure KP-ABE scheme with deletable attributes DelABE and a single-key adaptively secure deletion conforming CPRF scheme DCCPRF.

6.1 Construction

Let $\mathsf{DelABE} = (\mathsf{DelABE.Setup}, \mathsf{DelABE.KeyGen}, \mathsf{DelABE.Enc}, \mathsf{DelABE.Dec}, \mathsf{DelABE.Delete})$ be a KP-ABE scheme with deletable attributes for predicate class $\mathcal{C} = \{\mathcal{C}_n\}_{n\in\mathbb{N}}$, and $\mathsf{DCCPRF} = (\mathsf{PRF.Setup}, \mathsf{PRF.Constrain}, \mathsf{PRF.Eval}, \mathsf{PRF.CircuitGen}, \mathsf{PRF.DeleteFunc}, \mathsf{PRF.KeySim})$ be a deletion conforming CPRF for constraint class $\mathcal{F} = \{\mathcal{F}_N\}_{N\in\mathbb{N}}$. We require the predicate class $\mathcal{C}$ to be sufficiently expressive such that it contains circuits which perform comparison on top of a circuit generated by the $\mathsf{PRF.CircuitGen}$ algorithm. The requirement will become evident after the construction.

Below we describe our CP-ABE scheme $\mathsf{ABE} = (\mathsf{Setup}, \mathsf{KeyGen}, \mathsf{Enc}, \mathsf{Dec})$ for predicate class $\mathcal{F} = \{\mathcal{F}_N\}_{N\in\mathbb{N}}$.

$\mathsf{Setup}(1^\lambda, 1^N) \to (\mathsf{pp}, \mathsf{msk})$. The setup algorithm first runs DCCPRF setup to generate the corresponding master secret key: $\mathtt{prf}.\mathsf{msk} \leftarrow \mathsf{PRF.Setup}(1^\lambda, 1^N)$. Let $k = k(\lambda, N)$ denote the length of the master secret key $\mathtt{prf}.\mathsf{msk}$. Next, it runs the deletable ABE setup algorithm $\mathsf{DelABE.Setup}$ to get deletable ABE public parameters and master secret key as: $(\mathtt{del}.\mathsf{msk}, \mathtt{del}.\mathsf{pp}) \leftarrow \mathsf{DelABE.Setup}(1^\lambda, 1^k)$.
It sets public parameters and master key as $\mathsf{pp} = \mathtt{del}.\mathsf{pp}, \mathsf{msk} = (\mathtt{prf}.\mathsf{msk}, \mathtt{del}.\mathsf{msk})$.

$\mathsf{KeyGen}(\mathsf{msk}, x) \to \mathsf{sk}$. Let $\mathsf{msk} = (\mathtt{prf}.\mathsf{msk}, \mathtt{del}.\mathsf{msk})$. The key generation algorithm first computes $t = \mathsf{PRF.Eval}(\mathtt{prf}.\mathsf{msk}, x)$ and generates a circuit $C_x : \{0,1\}^k \to \{0,1\}^m$ as $C_x = \mathsf{PRF.CircuitGen}(x)$. Next, it creates the following circuit $(f_{x,t} : \{0,1\}^k \to \{0,1\})$

$$f_{x,t}(z) = \begin{cases} 1 & \text{if } C_x(z) \neq t, \\ 0 & \text{otherwise.} \end{cases} \tag{1}$$

Finally, the algorithm runs the deletable ABE key generation to sample the secret key sk as $\mathsf{sk} \leftarrow \mathsf{DelABE.KeyGen}(\mathtt{del}.\mathsf{msk}, f_{x,t})$.

$\mathsf{Enc}(\mathsf{pp}, f, m) \to \mathsf{ct}$. The encryption algorithm runs the CPRF key simulation to generate a simulated key as $\mathsf{sk}'_f \leftarrow \mathsf{PRF.KeySim}(1^\lambda, 1^N, f)$. Next, it runs the deletable ABE encryption algorithm with attribute sk'_f as $\mathsf{ct} \leftarrow \mathsf{DelABE.Enc}(\mathsf{pp}, m, \mathsf{sk}'_f)$, and outputs ciphertext ct.

$\mathsf{Dec}(\mathsf{sk}, \mathsf{ct}) \to m/\mathtt{fail}$. The decryption algorithm runs the deletable ABE decryption as $z = \mathsf{DelABE.Dec}(\mathsf{sk}, \mathsf{ct})$, and outputs z as decryption output.

6.2 Correctness and Efficiency

We start by proving that our construction satisfies the CP-ABE correctness condition, and also discuss the efficiency of the resulting scheme. First, we prove correctness.

Lemma 6.1 (Correctness). *If the deletable KP-ABE scheme* DelABE *satisfies correctness, and the deletion conforming CPRF scheme* DCCPRF *satisfies non-colliding and circuit evaluation properties, then the CP-ABE scheme* ABE *described above is correct.*

Proof. We show that the scheme decrypts correctly with all but negligible probability. In the full version, we will discuss how to boost the imperfect correctness to perfect correctness.

Fix any security parameter λ and attribute length N. For every predicate $f \in \mathcal{F}_N$, message $m \in \mathcal{M}$, and attribute $x \in \{0,1\}^N$, we have that the decryption algorithm Dec, on inputs ciphertext ct and secret key sk, simply outputs $z = \mathsf{DelABE.Dec}(\mathsf{sk}, \mathsf{ct})$. Consider $(\mathtt{del}.\mathsf{msk}, \mathtt{del}.\mathsf{pp})$ and $\mathtt{prf}.\mathsf{msk}$ to be the deletable KP-ABE and CPRF parameters sampled during setup. Note that the ciphertext ct is computed as $\mathsf{ct} \leftarrow \mathsf{DelABE.Enc}(\mathtt{del}.\mathsf{pp}, m, \mathsf{sk}'_f)$, where $\mathsf{sk}'_f \leftarrow \mathsf{PRF.KeySim}(1^\lambda, 1^N, f)$. Also, the secret key sk is sampled as $\mathsf{sk} \leftarrow \mathsf{DelABE.KeyGen}(\mathtt{del}.\mathsf{msk}, f_{x,t})$, where $t = \mathsf{PRF.Eval}(\mathtt{prf}.\mathsf{msk}, x)$ and $f_{x,t}$ is as defined in the construction. First, observe that by correctness of the deletable KP-ABE scheme, if $\mathsf{CEval}(f_{x,t}, \mathsf{sk}'_f) = 1$, then the decryption algorithm outputs message m correctly, i.e. $z = m$. Thus, to complete the completeness argument, we just need to show that whenever $f(x) = 1$, then $\mathsf{CEval}(f_{x,t}, \mathsf{sk}'_f) = 1$ as well with all but negligible probability (over the choice of random coins used during setup and encryption).

Recall that circuit $f_{x,t}(\mathsf{sk}'_f) = 1$ if and only if $C_x(\mathsf{sk}'_f) \neq t$, where $C_x = \mathsf{PRF.CircuitGen}(x)$. Now if $f(x) = 1$, by the circuit evaluation property of deletion conforming CPRF, we get that $C_x(\mathsf{sk}'_f) = \mathsf{PRF.Eval}(\mathsf{sk}'_f, x)$. Since $t = \mathsf{PRF.Eval}(\mathtt{prf}.\mathsf{msk}, x)$, thus by the non-colliding property, we know that the event $C_x(\mathsf{sk}'_f) = t$ happens with only negligible probability. Therefore, whenever $f(x) = 1$, the decryption algorithm outputs message m with all but negligible probability. This completeness the correctness argument. □

Next, we state the depth of the circuit $f_{x,t}$ for which we run the KP-ABE key generation algorithm.

Lemma 6.2 (Circuit depth). *For every* $\lambda, N \in \mathbb{N}$, *predicate* $f \in \mathcal{F}_N$ *and attribute* $x \in \{0,1\}^N$, *we have that* $\mathsf{depth}(f_{x,t}) = \mathsf{depth}(C_x) + O(\log \lambda)$.

Proof. This follows immediately from our construction. Note that the circuit depth of $f_{x,t}$ is depth of C_x plus the depth of a circuit to check equality on two strings in $\{0,1\}^m$. Since m is a polynomial in the security parameter λ, and equality check on two strings in $\{0,1\}^m$ can be efficiently performed in depth $O(\log m) = O(\log \lambda)$ using XOR gates and OR gates, thus the lemma follows. □

6.3 Security

Next, we prove that the CP-ABE scheme constructed above is adaptively secure. Formally, we prove the following.

Theorem 6.3. *If the deletion KP-ABE scheme* DelABE *satisfies selective IND-CPA security and deletion indistinguishability (Definitions 3.2 and 3.3), and the deletion conforming CPRF scheme* DCCPRF *satisfies adaptive key simulation security, and circuit evaluation and function deletion properties (Definitions 4.2 and 4.3), then the CP-ABE scheme* ABE *satisfies adaptive IND-CPA security as per Definition 3.1.*

Proof. We prove the security via a sequence of hybrid games. We will first define the sequence of hybrid games, and then show that they are indistinguishable for any PPT adversary.

Game 0. This corresponds to the original adaptive IND-CPA security game.

- **Setup Phase.** The challenger runs $\mathtt{prf.msk} \leftarrow \mathsf{PRF.Setup}(1^\lambda, 1^N)$ and $(\mathtt{del.msk}, \mathtt{del.pp}) \leftarrow \mathsf{DelABE.Setup}(1^\lambda, 1^k)$. Next, it sets $\mathsf{pp} = \mathtt{del.pp}$ and $\mathsf{msk} = (\mathtt{prf.msk}, \mathtt{del.msk})$ and sends pp to the adversary $\mathcal{A}$.
- **Pre-Challenge Query Phase.** The adversary $\mathcal{A}$ makes polynomially many key queries on attributes it chooses. For each key query on attribute $x \in \{0,1\}^N$, the challenger proceeds as follows:
  1. It computes $t = \mathsf{PRF.Eval}(\mathtt{prf.msk}, x)$, and generates a circuit $C_x : \{0,1\}^k \to \{0,1\}^m$ as $C_x = \mathsf{PRF.CircuitGen}(1^\lambda, 1^N, x)$. Next, it creates a circuit $f_{x,t}$ as described in Eq. (1).
  2. Then it computes a secret key as $\mathsf{sk} \leftarrow \mathsf{DelABE.KeyGen}(\mathtt{del.msk}, f_{x,t})$, and sends sk to $\mathcal{A}$.
- **Challenge Phase.** $\mathcal{A}$ sends two messages (m_0, m_1) and a predicate function $f^* \in \mathcal{F}_N$ as its challenge to the challenger. The challenger responds with ciphertext ct^* to $\mathcal{A}$, where ct^* is computed as follows:
  1. The challenger generates a simulated key as $\mathsf{sk}_{f^*} \leftarrow \mathsf{PRF.KeySim}(1^\lambda, 1^N, f^*)$.
  2. Next, it chooses a random bit $b \leftarrow \{0,1\}$, and computes the challenge ciphertext as $\mathsf{ct}^* \leftarrow \mathsf{DelABE.Enc}(\mathtt{del.pp}, \mathsf{sk}'_{f^*}, m_b)$.
- **Post-Challenge Query Phase.** This is identical to the pre-challenge query phase.
- **Guess.** The adversary $\mathcal{A}$ finally sends the guess b', and wins if $b = b'$.

Game 1. This game is identical to **Game 0** except that in the **Challenge Phase** step **1**, the challenger encrypts the challenge ciphertext to a *real constrained PRF key* with respect to challenge function f^* instead of the simulated key.

- **Challenge Phase.** $\mathcal{A}$ sends two messages (m_0, m_1) and a predicate function $f^* \in \mathcal{F}_N$ as its challenge to the challenger. The challenger responds with ciphertext ct^* to $\mathcal{A}$, where ct^* is computed as follows:
  1. The challenger generates a constrained key as $\mathsf{sk}_{f^*} \leftarrow \mathsf{PRF.Constrain}(\mathtt{prf.msk}, f^*)$.

Game 2. This game is identical to **Game 1** except that in the **Challenge Phase** step **1**, the challenger generates the real constrained PRF key sk_{f^*} with respect to f^* directly using the PRF.DeleteFunc and Restrict algorithms on the PRF master secret key $\mathtt{prf}.\mathsf{msk}$.

- **Challenge Phase.** $\mathcal{A}$ sends two messages (m_0, m_1) and a predicate function $f^* \in \mathcal{F}_N$ as its challenge to the challenger. The challenger responds with ciphertext ct^* to $\mathcal{A}$, where ct^* is computed as follows:
  1. The challenger first computes a set of indices $\mathcal{I}_{f^*} := \mathsf{PRF.DeleteFunc}(1^\lambda, 1^N, f^*)$, and then it computes the constrained key as $\mathsf{sk}_{f^*} = \mathsf{Restrict}(\mathtt{prf}.\mathsf{msk}, \mathcal{I}_{f^*})$.

Game 3. This game is identical to **Game 2** except that in the **Challenge Phase** step **2**, the challenger encrypts the message to the *PRF master secret key* $\mathtt{prf}.\mathsf{msk}$ and then uses DelABE.Delete to modify the ciphertext according the indices set $\mathcal{I}_{f^*}$.

- **Challenge Phase.** $\mathcal{A}$ sends two messages (m_0, m_1) and a predicate function $f^* \in \mathcal{F}_N$ as its challenge to the challenger. The challenger responds with ciphertext ct^* to $\mathcal{A}$, where ct^* is computed as follows:
  1. The challenger first computes a set of indices $\mathcal{I}_{f^*} := \mathsf{PRF.DeleteFunc}(1^\lambda, 1^N, f^*)$.
  2. Next, it chooses a random bit $b \leftarrow \{0,1\}$, and computes a KP-ABE ciphertext as $\mathsf{ct}' \leftarrow \mathsf{DelABE.Enc}(\mathtt{del}.\mathsf{pp}, \mathtt{prf}.\mathsf{msk}, m_b)$. Then it computes challenge ciphertext as $\mathsf{ct}^* \leftarrow \mathsf{DelABE.Delete}(\mathtt{del}.\mathsf{pp}, \mathsf{ct}', \mathcal{I}_{f^*})$.

Analysis. Next, we show by a sequence of lemmas that no PPT adversary can distinguish between any two adjacent games with non-negligible advantage. In the last game, we show that the advantage of any PPT adversary is negligible. This completes the proof of adaptive security of our CP-ABE scheme ABE.

Let $\mathcal{A}$ denote the PPT attacker playing the adaptive IND-CPA security game with the ABE challenger. In the sequel, we denote the advantage of adversary $\mathcal{A}$ in **Game** i as $\mathsf{Adv}^i_{\mathcal{A}}(\lambda) = \Pr[\mathcal{A} \text{ wins in Game } i] - \frac{1}{2}$, where recall that $\mathcal{A}$ wins in **Game** i if it guesses the challenger's bit b correctly.

Lemma 6.4. *Assuming the key simulation security of the deletion conforming CPRF* DCCPRF *holds, then for any PPT adversary $\mathcal{A}$, there exists a negligible function* $\mathsf{negl}_1(\cdot)$, *such that for all* $\lambda, N \in \mathbb{N}$, *we have that* $\mathsf{Adv}^0_{\mathcal{A}}(\lambda) - \mathsf{Adv}^1_{\mathcal{A}}(\lambda) \leq \mathsf{negl}_1(\lambda)$.

Proof. Suppose there exists an adversary $\mathcal{A}$ and a non-negligible function $\epsilon(\cdot)$ such that $\mathsf{Adv}^0_{\mathcal{A}}(\lambda) - \mathsf{Adv}^1_{\mathcal{A}}(\lambda) \geq \epsilon(\lambda)$, then we construct a reduction algorithm $\mathcal{B}$ such that $\mathcal{B}$ has non-negligible advantage in the *key simulation game* of the deletion conforming CPRF. Below we describe our reduction algorithm $\mathcal{B}$.

- In the setup phase, the key simulation challenger $\mathcal{K}$ runs $\mathsf{PRF.Setup}$, and $\mathcal{B}$ runs $\mathsf{DelABE.Setup}$ to sample a key pair as $(\mathtt{del.pp}, \mathtt{del.msk}) \leftarrow \mathsf{DelABE.Setup}(1^\lambda, 1^k)$. $\mathcal{B}$ then sends $\mathtt{del.pp}$ to $\mathcal{A}$ as the public parameters.
- In the pre-challenge query phase, when $\mathcal{A}$ sends a key query on attribute x to $\mathcal{B}$, $\mathcal{B}$ sends x to the key simulation challenger $\mathcal{K}$ as its PRF evaluation query. $\mathcal{K}$ answers $\mathcal{B}$ with t, where $t = \mathsf{PRF.Eval}(\mathtt{prf.msk}, x)$. $\mathcal{B}$ uses t and x to generate circuit C_x and circuit $f_{x,t}$ as in Game 0; then it computes the secret key $\mathsf{sk} \leftarrow \mathsf{DelABE.KeyGen}(\mathtt{del.msk}, f_{x,t})$, and sends sk to $\mathcal{A}$ as the secret key for attribute x.
- In the challenge phase, $\mathcal{A}$ sends the predicate function f^* and messages m_0, m_1 to the reduction algorithm $\mathcal{B}$. $\mathcal{B}$ then forwards f^* to $\mathcal{K}$ as its challenge constraint function. Let sk_{f^*} denote $\mathcal{K}$'s response. $\mathcal{B}$ chooses as random bit $b \leftarrow \{0, 1\}$, and computes the challenge ciphertext as $\mathsf{ct}^* \leftarrow \mathsf{DelABE.Enc}(\mathtt{del.pp}, \mathsf{sk}_{f^*}, m_b)$, and sends ct^* to $\mathcal{A}$.
- The post-challenge phase is identical to the pre-challenge query phase. Finally, $\mathcal{A}$ outputs its guess b', and if $b = b'$ then $\mathcal{B}$ outputs 0 as its guess (to denote that sk_{f^*} was a simulated key). Otherwise, $\mathcal{B}$ outputs 1 as its guess.

First, note that $\mathcal{A}$ must be an admissible adversary in the CP-ABE security game, thus it must hold that $f^*(x) = 0$ for all attributes x queried by $\mathcal{A}$. Therefore, $\mathcal{B}$ is also an admissible adversary in the key simulation game since it also satisfies condition that $f^*(x) = 0$ for all inputs x queried by $\mathcal{B}$. Next, observe that if the challenger $\mathcal{K}$ samples sk_{f^*} as a simulated key, then $\mathcal{B}$ perfectly simulates Game 0 for $\mathcal{A}$, otherwise it simulates Game 1. Thus, $\mathcal{B}$'s advantage in the key simulation game is at least $\epsilon(\lambda)$, which is non-negligible and contradicts the key simulation security. □

Lemma 6.5. *Assuming the function deletion property of the deletion conforming CPRF* DCCPRF *holds, then for any adversary $\mathcal{A}$, parameters $\lambda, N \in \mathbb{N}$, we have that* $\mathsf{Adv}^1_{\mathcal{A}}(\lambda) = \mathsf{Adv}^2_{\mathcal{A}}(\lambda)$.

Proof. This follows immediately from the function deletion property. Recall that function deletion property states that for all $\lambda, N \in \mathbb{N}$, every constraint function $f^* \in \mathcal{F}_N$, and master key $\mathtt{prf.msk} \leftarrow \mathsf{PRF.Setup}(1^\lambda, 1^N)$, we have that:

$$\Pr\left[\mathsf{sk}^{(1)}_{f^*} = \mathsf{sk}^{(2)}_{f^*} : \begin{array}{r} \mathcal{I}_{f^*} = \mathsf{PRF.DeleteFunc}(1^\lambda, 1^N, f^*) \\ \mathsf{sk}^{(1)}_{f^*} = \mathsf{PRF.Constrain}(\mathtt{prf.msk}, f^*) \\ \mathsf{sk}^{(2)}_{f^*} = \mathsf{Restrict}(\mathtt{prf.msk}, \mathcal{I}_{f^*}) \end{array}\right] = 1.$$

Note that $\mathsf{sk}^{(1)}_{f^*}$ and $\mathsf{sk}^{(2)}_{f^*}$ exactly correspond to the CPRF keys as generated in **Game 1** and **Game 2**, respectively. Since they are identical, thus the adversary's advantage is also identical in these two games. □

Lemma 6.6. *Assuming the deletion indistinguishability security of the deletable KP-ABE* DelABE *holds, then for any PPT adversary $\mathcal{A}$, there exists a negligible function* $\mathsf{negl}_2(\cdot)$, *such that for all $\lambda, N \in \mathbb{N}$, we have that* $\mathsf{Adv}^2_{\mathcal{A}}(\lambda) - \mathsf{Adv}^3_{\mathcal{A}}(\lambda) \leq \mathsf{negl}_2(\lambda)$.

Proof. Suppose there exists an adversary $\mathcal{A}$ and a non-negligible function $\epsilon(\cdot)$ such that $\mathsf{Adv}^2_{\mathcal{A}}(\lambda) - \mathsf{Adv}^3_{\mathcal{A}}(\lambda) \geq \epsilon(\lambda)$, then we construct a reduction algorithm $\mathcal{B}$ such that $\mathcal{B}$ has non-negligible advantage in the *deletion indistinguishability game* of the deletable KP-ABE. Below we describe our reduction algorithm $\mathcal{B}$.

- In the setup phase, the deletion indistinguishability challenger $\mathcal{D}$ runs $\mathsf{DelABE.Setup}$ and sends the deletable ABE parameters $(\mathtt{del}.\mathsf{pp}, \mathtt{del}.\mathsf{msk})$ to $\mathcal{B}$. $\mathcal{B}$ then samples a CPRF master key as $\mathtt{prf}.\mathsf{msk} \leftarrow \mathsf{PRF.Setup}(1^\lambda, 1^N)$, and sends $\mathtt{del}.\mathsf{pp}$ to $\mathcal{A}$ as the CP-ABE public parameters.
- In the pre-challenge query phase, $\mathcal{A}$ sends a key query on attribute x to $\mathcal{B}$. $\mathcal{B}$ first evaluates the CPRF as $t = \mathsf{PRF.Eval}(\mathtt{prf}.\mathsf{msk}, x)$, and uses t and x to generate circuits C_x and $f_{x,t}$ as in Game 2. It then computes the secret key $\mathsf{sk} \leftarrow \mathsf{DelABE.KeyGen}(\mathtt{del}.\mathsf{msk}, f_{x,t})$, and sends sk to $\mathcal{A}$ as the secret key for attribute x.
- In the challenge phase, $\mathcal{A}$ sends the predicate function f^* and messages m_0, m_1 to $\mathcal{B}$. The reduction algorithm $\mathcal{B}$ samples a random bit $b \leftarrow \{0,1\}$, and computes a set of indices $\mathcal{I}_{f^*} = \mathsf{PRF.DeleteFunc}(1^\lambda, 1^N, f^*)$, and sends $(m_b, \mathtt{prf}.\mathsf{msk}, \mathcal{I}_{f^*})$ to the deletion challenger $\mathcal{D}$. Let ct^* denote the challenger's response. $\mathcal{B}$ forwards ct^* to $\mathcal{A}$ as its challenge ciphertext.
- The post-challenge phase is identical to the pre-challenge query phase. Finally, $\mathcal{A}$ outputs its guess b', and if $b = b'$ then $\mathcal{B}$ outputs 0 as its guess (to denote that ct^* was a freshly encrypted ciphertext). Otherwise, $\mathcal{B}$ outputs 1 as its guess.

Note that if the challenger $\mathcal{D}$ computes ct^* by first restricting the attribute to the constrained key and then encrypting it directly using the KP-ABE encryption algorithm, then $\mathcal{B}$ perfectly simulates Game 2 for $\mathcal{A}$, otherwise it simulates Game 3. Thus, $\mathcal{B}$'s advantage in the deletion indistinguishability game is at least $\epsilon(\lambda)$, which is non-negligible and contradicts the deletion indistinguishability security. □

Lemma 6.7. *Assuming the selective IND-CPA security of the deletable KP-ABE* DelABE *holds and the deletion conforming CPRF* DCCPRF *satisfies circuit evaluation property, then for any PPT adversary $\mathcal{A}$, there exists a negligible function* $\mathsf{negl}_3(\cdot)$*, such that for all $\lambda, N \in \mathbb{N}$, we have that* $\mathsf{Adv}^3_{\mathcal{A}}(\lambda) \leq \mathsf{negl}_3(\lambda)$.

Proof. Suppose there exists an adversary $\mathcal{A}$ and a non-negligible function $\epsilon(\cdot)$ such that $\mathsf{Adv}^3_{\mathcal{A}}(\lambda) \geq \epsilon(\lambda)$, then we construct a reduction algorithm $\mathcal{B}$ such that $\mathcal{B}$ has non-negligible advantage in the *selective IND-CPA game* of the deletable KP-ABE. Below we describe our reduction algorithm $\mathcal{B}$.

- In the setup phase, $\mathcal{B}$ first samples a CPRF master key as $\mathtt{prf}.\mathsf{msk} \leftarrow \mathsf{PRF.Setup}(1^\lambda, 1^N)$, and sends $\mathtt{prf}.\mathsf{msk}$ as its challenge attribute to the selective IND-CPA challenger $\mathcal{D}$. The challenger runs $\mathsf{DelABE.Setup}$ and sends the deletable public parameters $\mathtt{del}.\mathsf{pp}$ to $\mathcal{B}$. $\mathcal{B}$ simply forwards $\mathtt{del}.\mathsf{pp}$ to $\mathcal{A}$ as the CP-ABE public parameters.

- In the pre-challenge query phase, when $\mathcal{A}$ sends a key query on attribute x to $\mathcal{B}$, $\mathcal{B}$ computes $t_x = \mathsf{PRF.Eval}(\mathtt{prf.msk}, x)$ and generates the circuit f_{x,t_x} using x and t_x. Next, $\mathcal{B}$ sends secret key query on predicate f_{x,t_x} to the challenger $\mathcal{D}$. $\mathcal{D}$ replies $\mathcal{B}$'s query with sk and $\mathcal{B}$ forwards sk to $\mathcal{A}$ as the secret key for attribute x.
- In the challenge phase, $\mathcal{A}$ sends the predicate function f^* and messages m_0, m_1 to $\mathcal{B}$. $\mathcal{B}$ sends (m_0, m_1) to $\mathcal{D}$. Let ct' denote the KP-ABE challenge ciphertext sent by $\mathcal{D}$. $\mathcal{B}$ first computes the index set $\mathcal{I}_{f^*} = \mathsf{PRF.DeleteFunc}(1^\lambda, 1^N, f^*)$, and then computes challenge ciphertext as $\mathsf{ct}^* \leftarrow \mathsf{DelABE.Delete}(\mathtt{del.pp}, \mathsf{ct}', \mathcal{I}_{f^*})$. $\mathcal{B}$ sends ct^* to $\mathcal{A}$ as its challenge ciphertext.
- The post-challenge phase is identical to the pre-challenge query phase. Finally, $\mathcal{A}$ outputs its guess b', and $\mathcal{B}$ outputs the same bit b' as its guess.

First, note that for each key query on attribute x made by $\mathcal{A}$, we have that $C_x(\mathtt{prf.msk}) = \mathsf{PRF.Eval}(\mathtt{prf.msk}, x)$. This follows from the circuit evaluation property of the deletion conforming CPRF. Since $t_x = \mathsf{PRF.Eval}(\mathtt{prf.msk}, x)$, thus by definition of the circuit f_{x,t_x} (see Eq. (1)), we have that $f_{x,t_x}(\mathtt{prf.msk}) = 0$ for every attribute x. Thus, the reduction algorithm $\mathcal{B}$ is an admissible adversary in the selective IND-CPA game. Next, observe that $\mathcal{B}$ perfectly simulates Game 3 for $\mathcal{A}$, therefore $\mathcal{B}$'s advantage in the selective IND-CPA game is at least $\epsilon(\lambda)$, which is non-negligible and contradicts the selective IND-CPA security of the deletable KP-ABE system. □

Combining Lemmas 6.4 to 6.7, the Theorem 6.3 follows. □

7 Deletable ABE from Standard Assumptions

In this section we show that [19] is already a KP-ABE scheme with deletable attributes. First, we show that the KP-ABE schemes for monotone access structures in [19] have efficient deletion algorithms such that the resulting scheme satisfies both the semantic security as well deletion indistinguishability properties. Later on, we briefly elaborate the well-known approach for building a KP-ABE scheme for $\mathbf{NC}^1$ (i.e., log-depth circuits) from any KP-ABE scheme for monotone access structures, and describe that it preserves the deletion property of the underlying system.

7.1 Deletable ABE from Bilinear Maps Via [19]

Goyal et al. (GPSW) [19] proposed a KP-ABE scheme for monotone access structures and proved its security under the Decisional Bilinear Diffie-Hellman (DBDH) assumption [3]. Here we show that the GPSW scheme, described in [19, Section 4], is also a deletable KP-ABE scheme for the same predicate class. Let $\mathsf{GPSW} = (\mathsf{Setup}, \mathsf{KeyGen}, \mathsf{Enc}, \mathsf{Dec})$ represent the KP-ABE construction provided in [19, Section 4]. Formally, they proved the following.

Theorem 7.1 ([19, Theorem 1, Paraphrased]). *If the Decisional Bilinear Diffie-Hellman (DBDH) assumption holds, then the scheme* GPSW *is a selective IND-CPA secure scheme as per Definition 3.2.*

Now we describe a simple deletion algorithm for the GPSW scheme, and argue that the augmented GPSW scheme satisfies all the required properties described in Sect. 3. We start by briefly discussing some notational changes that we make to the GPSW syntax.

Notation. For consistency with our ABE definitions, we interpret the attribute string as a bit string $x \in \{0,1\}^n$, where as is the GPSW construction [19, Section 4] the attribute was parsed as a set of subset of the attribute universe $\mathcal{U} = \{1, 2, \ldots, n\}$. Here n denotes the length of the attributes selected during system setup. Note that this is mostly a syntactic change, and does not affect the GPSW scheme in any significant way.

Below we recall the Setup and Enc algorithms as provided in [19, Section 4], and also describe our Delete algorithm.

$\mathsf{Setup}(1^\lambda, 1^n) \to (\mathsf{pp}, \mathsf{msk})$. The setup algorithm chooses a bilinear group $\mathbb{G}_1$ of prime order p. Let g denote the generator of the group $\mathbb{G}_1$, and $e : \mathbb{G}_1 \times \mathbb{G}_1 \to \mathbb{G}_2$ be associated the bilinear map. It chooses a random key exponent $\alpha \in \mathbb{Z}_p$, and also chooses a random exponent per bit position of the attribute, that is $t_i \leftarrow \mathbb{Z}_p$ for $i \in [n]$.
It outputs the public parameters and master secret key as $\mathsf{pp} = (g, e(g,g)^\alpha, \{g^{t_i}\}_{i \in [n]})$ and $\mathsf{msk} = (\alpha, \{t_i\}_{i \in [n]})$.[14]

$\mathsf{Enc}(\mathsf{pp}, x, m) \to \mathsf{ct}$. The encryption algorithm parses the public parameters as $\mathsf{pp} = (g, K, \{T_i\}_{i \in [n]})$, and an attribute $x \in \{0,1\}^n$. It chooses a random exponent $s \in \mathbb{Z}_p$, and publishes the ciphertext as

$$\mathsf{ct} = (x, m \cdot K^s, \{T_i^s\}_{i \in [n] : x_i = 1}).$$

Encrypting to Attributes with $\perp$ Symbols. First, note that in the GPSW encryption algorithm the input attribute string x is a binary string, that is $x \in \{0,1\}^n$. However, in our deletable ABE framework, we allow the encryptor to choose attributes with $\perp$ symbols, thus the attribute string x now lies in $\{0,1,\perp\}^n$ instead of $\{0,1\}^n$. Now our augmented encryption algorithm is identical to the above encryption algorithm, that is the ciphertext is computed as

$$\mathsf{ct} = (x, m \cdot K^s, \{T_i^s\}_{i \in [n] : x_i = 1}).$$

Note that previously the algorithm does not compute T_i^s for all i wherever $x_i = 0$. Now the augmented encryption algorithm also does not compute T_i^s for all i wherever $x_i = \perp$. That is, it treats $\perp$ symbols as a 0 bit during encryption. Therefore, the deletion algorithm can simply *delete* the T_i^s terms from the ciphertext wherever $i \in \mathcal{I}$ to compute a corresponding deleted ciphertext. Formally, we describe it below.

[14] The parameters also contain the bilinear map parameters, but here we don't explicitly write it for simplicity.

$\mathsf{Delete}(\mathsf{pp}, \mathsf{ct}, \mathcal{I}) \rightarrow \mathsf{ct}'$. The algorithm parses the ciphertext as $\mathsf{ct} = (x, E', \{E_i\}_{i\in[n]:x_i=1})$. It sets the output ciphertext ct' as

$$\mathsf{ct}' = (\mathsf{Restrict}(x, \mathcal{I}), E', \{E_i\}_{i\in[n]\setminus\mathcal{I}:\ x_i=1}).$$

Deletion Indistinguishability. First, we show that the augmented GPSW scheme $\mathsf{AugGPSW} = (\mathsf{Setup}, \mathsf{KeyGen}, \mathsf{Enc}, \mathsf{Dec}, \mathsf{Delete})$ satisfies the deletion indistinguishability property. Below we prove a much stronger statement which in turn implies deletion indistinguishability. Intuitively, we argue that, for every choice of system parameters, the distribution of a freshly encrypted ciphertext and a (corresponding) deleted ciphertext are *identical.*

Lemma 7.2. *For every $\lambda, n \in \mathbb{N}$, parameters $(\mathsf{pp}, \mathsf{msk}) \leftarrow \mathsf{Setup}(1^\lambda, 1^n)$, attribute $x \in \{0,1\}^n$, message $m \in \mathcal{M}$, and index set $\mathcal{I} \in [n]$, the following two distributions are identical:*

$$\mathcal{D}_1 = \left\{\mathsf{ct} : \begin{array}{c} x' = \mathsf{Restrict}(x, \mathcal{I}) \\ \mathsf{ct} \leftarrow \mathsf{Enc}(\mathsf{pp}, x', m) \end{array}\right\}, \qquad \mathcal{D}_2 = \left\{\mathsf{ct}' : \begin{array}{c} \mathsf{ct} \leftarrow \mathsf{Enc}(\mathsf{pp}, x, m) \\ \mathsf{ct}' \leftarrow \mathsf{Delete}(\mathsf{pp}, \mathsf{ct}, \mathcal{I}) \end{array}\right\}.$$

That is, $\mathcal{D}_1 \equiv \mathcal{D}_2$.

Proof. The proof of this lemma immediately follows by inspection of the encryption and deletion algorithms described above. Consider any λ, n, key pair $(\mathsf{pp}, \mathsf{msk})$, attribute x, message m and index set $\mathcal{I}$. First, note that the distributions $\mathcal{D}_1$ and $\mathcal{D}_2$ can be expanded as follows:

$$\mathcal{D}_1 = \{(x', m \cdot K^s, \{T_i^s\}_{i\in S_1}) : x' = \mathsf{Restrict}(x, \mathcal{I}), s \leftarrow \mathbb{Z}_p, S_1 = \{i \in [n] : x'_i = 1\}\},$$
$$\mathcal{D}_2 = \{(x', m \cdot K^s, \{T_i^s\}_{i\in S_2}) : x' = \mathsf{Restrict}(x, \mathcal{I}), s \leftarrow \mathbb{Z}_p, S_2 = \{i \in [n] \setminus \mathcal{I} : x_i = 1\}\}.$$

Recall by definition of $\mathsf{Restrict}$, we have that $x'_i = 1$ if and only if $x_i = 1$ and $i \notin \mathcal{I}$. Therefore, it follows that $\mathcal{D}_1 \equiv \mathcal{D}_2$. □

Correctness. Note that since a deleted ciphertext is *identically* distributed to a freshly encrypted ciphertext, and also GPSW is a perfectly correct ABE scheme, thus correctness of our $\mathsf{AugGPSW}$ scheme follows.

Selective IND-CPA Security. Note that even though in our scheme, attribute vectors could contain $\perp$ symbols (i.e., lie in $\{0, 1, \perp\}^n$), the IND-CPA attacker is only allowed to specify a binary string as a challenge attribute (i.e., it must lie in $\{0,1\}^n$) in the selective security game (Definition 3.2). Therefore, the selective IND-CPA security proof of $\mathsf{AugGPSW}$ follows from selective IND-CPA security proof of GPSW.

Hence, combining above facts, Lemma 7.2 and Theorem 7.1, we obtain the following:

Theorem 7.3. *If the Decisional Bilinear Diffie-Hellman (DBDH) assumption holds, then the scheme* $\mathsf{AugGPSW}$ *is a KP-ABE scheme with deletable attributes that satisfies selective IND-CPA security as well as deletion indistinguishability (Definitions 3.2 and 3.3).*

Also, later on in the full version we describe how to get deletable ABE from Computational Bilinear Diffie-Hellman (CBDH) assumption. It follows from a straightforward use of hardcore predicate on top of the GPSW scheme.

7.2 Deletable ABE: Monotonic Access Structures to $\mathbf{NC}^1$

Suppose we start with a KP-ABE scheme for arbitrary polynomial-sized monotone boolean formulas, then there is a well-known folklore transformation that gives us a KP-ABE scheme for log-depth circuits ($\mathbf{NC}^1$) generically from the underlying scheme. The idea can be described as follows. First, the key generation algorithm, on input a log-depth (non-monotone) circuit C, generates a polynomial-sized (non-monotone) boolean formula f_C that evaluates the same circuit. (Note that size of the formula f_C grows exponentially with the depth of circuit C, thus the same transformation does not work for larger depth circuits.) Now the formula f_C is a possibly *non-monotone* boolean formula, thus it could apply negation ($\neg$) gates on non-atomic formulae. Next, one using De Morgan's identities can translate the non-monotone boolean formula f_C into another formula $\widetilde{f_C}$ such that in the description of formula $\widetilde{f_C}$, negation gates are only applied on input wires. In other words, formula $\widetilde{f_C}$ can alternatively be interpreted as a monotone boolean formula being applied on the literals. (Recall that a literal is an atomic formula or its negation, i.e. either an input wire or its negation). With this observation, one could use KP-ABE scheme for monotone boolean formulas to obtain a KP-ABE scheme for $\mathbf{NC}^1$.

A more concrete description of above transformation is provided later in the full version.

References

1. Agrawal, S., Biswas, R., Nishimaki, R., Xagawa, K., Xie, X., Yamada, S.: Attacks on Boyen's attribute-based encryption scheme in TCC 2013. Pers. Commun. (2020)
2. Attrapadung, N.: Dual system encryption via doubly selective security: framework, fully secure functional encryption for regular languages, and more. In: Nguyen, P.Q., Oswald, E. (eds.) EUROCRYPT 2014. LNCS, vol. 8441, pp. 557–577. Springer, Heidelberg (2014). https://doi.org/10.1007/978-3-642-55220-5_31
3. Boneh, D., Franklin, M.: Identity-based encryption from the Weil pairing. In: Kilian, J. (ed.) CRYPTO 2001. LNCS, vol. 2139, pp. 213–229. Springer, Heidelberg (2001). https://doi.org/10.1007/3-540-44647-8_13
4. Boneh, D., et al.: Fully key-homomorphic encryption, arithmetic circuit ABE and compact garbled circuits. In: Nguyen, P.Q., Oswald, E. (eds.) EUROCRYPT 2014. LNCS, vol. 8441, pp. 533–556. Springer, Heidelberg (2014). https://doi.org/10.1007/978-3-642-55220-5_30
5. Boneh, D., Waters, B.: Constrained pseudorandom functions and their applications. In: Sako, K., Sarkar, P. (eds.) ASIACRYPT 2013. LNCS, vol. 8270, pp. 280–300. Springer, Heidelberg (2013). https://doi.org/10.1007/978-3-642-42045-0_15
6. Boyen, X.: Attribute-based functional encryption on lattices. In: Sahai, A. (ed.) TCC 2013. LNCS, vol. 7785, pp. 122–142. Springer, Heidelberg (2013). https://doi.org/10.1007/978-3-642-36594-2_8

7. Boyle, E., Goldwasser, S., Ivan, I.: Functional signatures and pseudorandom functions. In: Krawczyk, H. (ed.) PKC 2014. LNCS, vol. 8383, pp. 501–519. Springer, Heidelberg (2014). https://doi.org/10.1007/978-3-642-54631-0_29
8. Brakerski, Z., Vaikuntanathan, V.: Circuit-ABE from LWE: unbounded attributes and semi-adaptive security. In: Robshaw, M., Katz, J. (eds.) CRYPTO 2016. LNCS, vol. 9816, pp. 363–384. Springer, Heidelberg (2016). https://doi.org/10.1007/978-3-662-53015-3_13
9. Davidson, A., Katsumata, S., Nishimaki, R., Yamada, S.: Constrained PRFs for bit-fixing (and more) from OWFs with adaptive security and constant collusion resistance. Cryptology ePrint Archive, Report 2018/982 (2018)
10. Davidson, A., Katsumata, S., Nishimaki, R., Yamada, S., Yamakawa, T.: Adaptively secure constrained pseudorandom functions in the standard model. In: Micciancio, D., Ristenpart, T. (eds.) CRYPTO 2020. LNCS, vol. 12170, pp. 559–589. Springer, Cham (2020). https://doi.org/10.1007/978-3-030-56784-2_19
11. Diffie, W., Hellman, M.E.: New directions in cryptography (1976)
12. Gentry, C.: Practical identity-based encryption without random oracles. In: Vaudenay, S. (ed.) EUROCRYPT 2006. LNCS, vol. 4004, pp. 445–464. Springer, Heidelberg (2006). https://doi.org/10.1007/11761679_27
13. Gentry, C., Halevi, S.: Hierarchical identity based encryption with polynomially many levels. In: TCC (2009)
14. Goldwasser, S., Micali, S.: Probabilistic encryption. J. Comput. Syst. Sci. **28**(2), 270–299 (1984)
15. Gorbunov, S., Vaikuntanathan, V., Wee, H.: Attribute-based encryption for circuits. In: STOC (2013)
16. Gorbunov, S., Vaikuntanathan, V., Wee, H.: Predicate encryption for circuits from LWE. In: Gennaro, R., Robshaw, M. (eds.) CRYPTO 2015. LNCS, vol. 9216, pp. 503–523. Springer, Heidelberg (2015). https://doi.org/10.1007/978-3-662-48000-7_25
17. Goyal, R., Koppula, V., Waters, B.: Semi-adaptive security and bundling functionalities made generic and easy. In: Hirt, M., Smith, A. (eds.) TCC 2016. LNCS, vol. 9986, pp. 361–388. Springer, Heidelberg (2016). https://doi.org/10.1007/978-3-662-53644-5_14
18. Goyal, R., Liu, J., Waters, B.: Adaptive security via deletion in attribute-based encryption: solutions from search assumptions in bilinear groups. Cryptology ePrint Archive, Report 2021/343 (2021). https://ia.cr/2021/343
19. Goyal, V., Pandey, O., Sahai, A., Waters, B.: Attribute-based encryption for fine-grained access control of encrypted data. In: CCS 2006 (2006)
20. Katsumata, S., Nishimaki, R., Yamada, S., Yamakawa, T.: Adaptively secure inner product encryption from LWE. In: Moriai, S., Wang, H. (eds.) ASIACRYPT 2020 (2020)
21. Kiayias, A., Papadopoulos, S., Triandopoulos, N., Zacharias, T.: Delegatable pseudorandom functions and applications. In: CCS (2013)
22. Lewko, A., Okamoto, T., Sahai, A., Takashima, K., Waters, B.: Fully secure functional encryption: attribute-based encryption and (hierarchical) inner product encryption. In: Gilbert, H. (ed.) EUROCRYPT 2010. LNCS, vol. 6110, pp. 62–91. Springer, Heidelberg (2010). https://doi.org/10.1007/978-3-642-13190-5_4
23. Lewko, A., Waters, B.: Decentralizing attribute-based encryption. In: Paterson, K.G. (ed.) EUROCRYPT 2011. LNCS, vol. 6632, pp. 568–588. Springer, Heidelberg (2011). https://doi.org/10.1007/978-3-642-20465-4_31

24. Lewko, A., Waters, B.: New proof methods for attribute-based encryption: achieving full security through selective techniques. In: Safavi-Naini, R., Canetti, R. (eds.) CRYPTO 2012. LNCS, vol. 7417, pp. 180–198. Springer, Heidelberg (2012). https://doi.org/10.1007/978-3-642-32009-5_12
25. Lewko, A., Waters, B.: Why proving HIBE systems secure is difficult. In: Nguyen, P.Q., Oswald, E. (eds.) EUROCRYPT 2014. LNCS, vol. 8441, pp. 58–76. Springer, Heidelberg (2014). https://doi.org/10.1007/978-3-642-55220-5_4
26. Okamoto, T., Takashima, K.: Fully secure functional encryption with general relations from the decisional linear assumption. In: Rabin, T. (ed.) CRYPTO 2010. LNCS, vol. 6223, pp. 191–208. Springer, Heidelberg (2010). https://doi.org/10.1007/978-3-642-14623-7_11
27. Regev, O.: On lattices, learning with errors, random linear codes, and cryptography. In: STOC (2005)
28. Rivest, R.L., Shamir, A., Adleman, L.M.: A method for obtaining digital signatures and public-key cryptosystems. Commun. ACM **21**(2), 120–126 (1978)
29. Sahai, A., Waters, B.: Fuzzy identity-based encryption. In: Cramer, R. (ed.) EUROCRYPT 2005. LNCS, vol. 3494, pp. 457–473. Springer, Heidelberg (2005). https://doi.org/10.1007/11426639_27
30. Tsabary, R.: Fully secure attribute-based encryption for t-CNF from LWE. In: Boldyreva, A., Micciancio, D. (eds.) CRYPTO 2019. LNCS, vol. 11692, pp. 62–85. Springer, Cham (2019). https://doi.org/10.1007/978-3-030-26948-7_3
31. Waters, B.: Dual system encryption: realizing fully secure IBE and HIBE under simple assumptions. In: Halevi, S. (ed.) CRYPTO 2009. LNCS, vol. 5677, pp. 619–636. Springer, Heidelberg (2009). https://doi.org/10.1007/978-3-642-03356-8_36
32. Wee, H.: Dual system encryption via predicate encodings. In: TCC (2014)

Public Key Encryption with Flexible Pattern Matching

Élie Bouscatié[1,2](✉), Guilhem Castagnos[2](✉), and Olivier Sanders[1](✉)

[1] Orange Labs, Applied Crypto Group, Cesson-Sévigné, France
olivier.sanders@orange.com
[2] Université de Bordeaux, INRIA, CNRS, IMB UMR 5251, 33405 Talence, France
elie.bouscatie@orange.com, guilhem.castagnos@math.u-bordeaux.fr

Abstract. Many interesting applications of pattern matching (*e.g.* deep-packet inspection or medical data analysis) target very sensitive data. In particular, spotting illegal behaviour in internet traffic conflicts with legitimate privacy requirements, which usually forces users (*e.g.* children, employees) to blindly trust an entity that fully decrypts their traffic in the name of security.

The compromise between traffic analysis and privacy can be achieved through searchable encryption. However, as the traffic data is a stream and as the patterns to search are bound to evolve over time (*e.g.* new virus signatures), these applications require a kind of searchable encryption that provides more flexibility than the classical schemes. We indeed need to be able to search for patterns of variable sizes in an arbitrary long stream that has potentially been encrypted prior to pattern identification. To stress these specificities, we call such a scheme a stream encryption supporting pattern matching.

Recent papers use bilinear groups to provide public key constructions supporting these features [3,13]. These solutions are lighter than more generic ones (*e.g.* fully homomorphic encryption) while retaining the adequate expressivity to support pattern matching without harming privacy more than needed. However, all existing solutions in this family have weaknesses with respect to efficiency and security that need to be addressed. Regarding efficiency, their public key has a size linear in the size of the alphabet, which can be quite large, in particular for applications that naturally process data as bytestrings. Regarding security, they all rely on a very strong computational assumption that is both interactive and specially tailored for this kind of scheme.

In this paper, we tackle these problems by providing two new constructions using bilinear groups to support pattern matching on encrypted streams. Our first construction shares the same strong assumption but dramatically reduces the size of the public key by removing the dependency on the size of the alphabet, while nearly halving the size of the ciphertext. On a typical application with large patterns, our public key is two order of magnitude smaller than the one of previous schemes, which demonstrates the practicality of our approach. Our second construction manages to retain most of the good features of the first one while exclusively relying on a simple (static) variant of DDH, which solves the security problem of previous works.

Keywords: Pattern matching · Searchable encryption

M. Tibouchi and H. Wang (Eds.): ASIACRYPT 2021, LNCS 13093, pp. 342–370, 2021.
https://doi.org/10.1007/978-3-030-92068-5_12

1 Introduction

The increasing outsourcing of IT services allows companies to shift the burden of managing their own infrastructure to some third parties but comes with many challenges regarding privacy. Traditional encryption is of no help here as it would prevent these third parties from providing their services. This has led cryptographers to propose countless encryption algorithms that are compatible with some sets of functions, meaning that it is possible to evaluate these functions directly on the ciphertexts, without having to decrypt the latter.

1.1 Related Works

As a rule of thumb, versatile systems supporting a large set of functions (*e.g.* [6, 15]) are the most complex ones, which has led to the design of encryption schemes supporting a very specific function. One of the most prominent examples of this approach is the one of searchable encryption (*e.g.* [1,4,12,18,22]) where some entities have the ability to decide whether a ciphertext C contains a given pattern (also called keyword) without decrypting C. Put differently, the ciphertext leaks nothing but the presence (or absence) of the pattern. The popularity of this type of encryption stems from the variety of applications that only need the ability to search a pattern (*e.g.*, DPI: deep packet inspection [13,21], external storage [8], etc.) combined with the efficiency of most cryptographic schemes supporting this feature. However, the fact that the latter are all presented as *searchable encryption* schemes does not mean that they are similar. Actually, this is quite the opposite as illustrated, for example, by the construction in [8] and the one in [13].

Here, the differences lie not only in the choice of the security model or the computational assumption underlying the construction, as it is usually the case in cryptography, but also in the ability to index data before encryption. In the case of external storage [8], it indeed seems reasonable to assume that each data of a database can be associated with a set of appropriate keywords that will be processed to ensure efficient queries on the encrypted database. Conversely, the use-case of DPI of Internet traffic [13,21] can hardly assume indexation of sent data. One should rather assume in this case that the data are encrypted on-the-fly without being able to pre-process them. Moreover, as pointed out in [13], there might be no obvious set of keywords to associate with the transmitted data. Finally, in this case, the searched pattern/keyword can be located anywhere in the encrypted stream, which precludes standard searchable encryption schemes (*e.g.* [1]): We do not want to decide if a ciphertext C encrypts a given pattern W but, instead, if C encrypts a message that contains W as a substring, which is fundamentally different.

In this regard, the case of encrypted traffic, that we study in this paper, is clearly the most complex one. To emphasize the difference with the scenarios compatible with indexation, we will talk of *Stream* Encryption supporting *Pattern Matching* (SEPM).

More specifically, we will consider a simple but versatile use-case where a *receiver* relies on a *service provider* to analyse the encrypted traffic he receives from a *sender*. We assume that this service requires to perform pattern matching on the traffic, which is actually the case for several applications (*e.g.* DPI). As the service provider is not fully trusted[1], we do not want to share the decryption key with it. Instead, the service provider will receive from the receiver specific trapdoors that allow it to detect the presence of some patterns within the encrypted streams.

To rehabilitate standard searchable encryption schemes, the first approach to solve this problem was based on tokenization (*e.g.* [10,21]), a technique that consists in splitting the stream to encrypt into overlapping substrings of some fixed length ℓ. Each substring S is then encrypted using a searchable encryption scheme whereas trapdoors are issued for patterns W of size ℓ. Thanks to the property of searchable encryption, one can indeed decide if $S = W$, which solves our problem as long as all searched patterns have the same size ℓ. Unfortunately, this approach inherently suffers from at least one of the following downsides, as explained in [13]: lack of expressivity if one considers only one possible substring length ℓ, lack of privacy if one splits the genuine patterns into several subpatterns of the same size or lack of efficiency if one repeats the process for each possible pattern length.

One could solve the expressivity issue by using instead predicate/functional encryption with some additional privacy features, such as *e.g.* anonymous predicate encryption [16] or hidden vector encryption [7]. A symmetric alternative was also recently proposed in [17]. Unfortunately, these solutions inherently require to provide a trapdoor for each possible position of a given pattern within the stream, which is a real problem in our case as the stream can be of any length. As explained in [13], one would then have to define a sufficiently large upper bound on this length and then generate a very large number of trapdoors (*e.g.* 1 billion for a 1 GB stream) for *each* pattern. In the symmetric setting, one could leverage efficient schemes (*e.g.* [17,23]) to argue that each trapdoor can be relatively small but, in this case, a new key (and hence new trapdoors) must be generated for each communication, which quickly becomes cumbersome. More generally, the public key setting seems more suitable in our case as it allows to generate universal trapdoors that can be used to analyse the traffic with any sender.

To circumvent all these problems, the authors of [13] proposed a new approach that allows to search patterns of any size with constant-size trapdoor. Intuitively, the core idea of this scheme is to encrypt the stream character by character by generating group elements whose exponent is $\alpha_b z^i$ where α_b is a secret encoding of the character b and z^i is a secret monomial encoding the position i of this character within the stream. Aggregating these elements leads to polynomials that can be identified with appropriate trapdoors. Unfortunately, these nice features come at the cost of three major weaknesses:

[1] More specifically, the service provider is trusted to provide the requested service but it should only learn the information necessary to carry out its task.

1. The security of [13] requires secrecy of all the elements α_b and z cited above. As the sender needs this information to encrypt the stream, the solution chosen by the authors is to provide the group elements $g^{\alpha_b z^i}$ in the public key for every possible position i and character b in the alphabet. The size of the public key thus significantly increases with the ones of the stream and of the alphabet, which quickly becomes cumbersome.
2. The polynomial construction of the trapdoors uses coefficients that have to be fresh, at least for different occurrences of the same character. The consequence is that the number of pairings needed for a test at some position is linear in the maximum occurrence of a same symbol in the pattern, which significantly increases the computational cost of the pattern detection procedure.
3. The security analysis of [13] was only made under a very strong, ad-hoc interactive assumption (i-GDH) that is likely to be necessary, as explained by the authors.

Very recently, [3] addresses some of the problems above by introducing a fragmentation approach that consists in splitting the stream into non-overlapping fragments $\mathcal{F}_h$ and into other non-overlapping fragments $\overline{\mathcal{F}}_h$ that straddle the former. This technique will be explained in more details in Sect. 4.1 but intuitively this is done in such a way that any searched pattern is entirely contained by a fragment $\mathcal{F}_h$ or $\overline{\mathcal{F}}_h$. The main advantage of this technique, that can actually be applied to [13] or any similar schemes, is that it reduces the problem of encrypting large strings to the one of encrypting several small fragments, which significantly reduces the size of the public key.

Based on this fragmentation approach, the authors of [3] propose a construction that allows to test the presence of one pattern at one position for a constant cost of 2 pairings. Moreover the dependency of the public key on the length of the string is replaced by a fixed upper bound on the length of the keywords to be searched, which is indeed much smaller in the context of DPI. But this construction uses twice as many ciphertext elements as in [13] and shares several features with it, including the fact that security still relies on the interactive i-GDH assumption and that the public key depends linearly on the size of the alphabet. The authors of [3] also consider the notion of pattern privacy, meaning that the trapdoors should not reveal the corresponding pattern but, as already noted in [13], it is very hard to retain this property for this kind of schemes, which leads to a security model in [3] that seems a bit contrived. Moreover, in the asymmetric setting that we consider here, this property can only be achieved for patterns originating from a high min-entropy set as in [5]. A look at some open-source list of patterns[2] shows that this assumption does not hold, at least for the DPI use-case. In this paper, we will therefore not consider this outlying property that would only make our security model more complex.

[2] *e.g.* https://github.com/coreruleset/coreruleset.

1.2 Our Contributions

If we sum up the state-of-the-art of SEPM, there are two main areas of progress: performance and security. We propose to improve both with two related constructions that solve the previous problems one after the other.

Improving Efficiency. From the efficiency standpoint, we note that [3] manages to reduce the size of the public key and the complexity of the detection procedure, compared to [13], but at the cost of ciphertexts containing twice as many elements. Moreover, if L is the size of the fragments and $\mathcal{S}$ is the plaintext alphabet (that is, we encrypt strings of characters $b \in \mathcal{S}$) the public key of [3] is essentially of size $L|\mathcal{S}|$, which remains quite important for many use-cases. For example, in the DPI context, it is natural to consider bytestrings which means that $|\mathcal{S}| = 256$. At first sight, it could be tempting to consider smaller alphabets, *e.g.*, bits instead of bytes, but this would lead to larger fragments that would result in a significant expansion of the ciphertext (eight-fold if we use bits instead of bytes) and that would reduce the gain regarding the public key.

In our first construction, we completely depart from the polynomial approach used in [3, 13] to fully leverage the fragmentation approach. More specifically, we note that the geometric basis z^i introduced in [13] and taken over by [3] is no longer required thanks to fragmentation. This allows us to design a new construction that looks more natural and that reduces the size of the ciphertext to nearly half the one in [3]. Interestingly, the resulting ciphertexts are essentially signatures on the characters to encrypt for some aggregatable signature scheme [19]. Intuitively, aggregatability of the signatures will ensure correctness of the construction as one will be able to combine different ciphertext elements to reconstruct (encrypted) patterns that can be tested with the appropriate trapdoors. At the same time, unforgeability of the signatures will ensure non-malleability of the ciphertexts and hence security of the whole construction.

Moreover, thanks to our approach, we can replace the secret character encoding α_b used in previous works by public elements of $\mathbb{Z}_p$ (that act as the signed messages for [19]), which leads to shorter public keys that no longer depend on the size of the alphabet.

Table 1 highlights the benefits of our first construction compared to the state-of-the-art. Although the gain consists in some multiplicative factors that could get lost in a $O(\cdot)$ notation, we stress that these factors have important consequences in practice. For example, if we take over the concrete parameters considered in [3], we show in Sect. 6 that we end up with a public key of 1.92 MB instead of 247 MB. For real-world applications, there is a significant difference between these two sizes as the latter would probably be impractical for many use-cases.

Improving Security. Our first construction only focuses on efficiency but does not consider the issue of previous works regarding security, namely the reliance on interactive ad-hoc assumptions. Actually, it still requires the i-GDH assumption, which is not very satisfying.

In our second construction, we tackle this problem by designing a scheme relying on a static assumption, EXDH, that is a simple variant of the DDH assumption. Actually, this assumption has already been used to construct an e-cash system in [11], which gives more confidence in the hardness of the underlying computational problem.

Here, the main difficulty is to modify our original scheme so as to rely on this static assumption while limiting the impact on the performance. This is particularly difficult because we consider a very strong security model where the adversary is able to query any trapdoor that does not allow to trivially succeed in the security experiment. In particular, we allow the adversary to query trapdoors that match the challenge streams, which makes simulation much harder, as we will explain in Sect. 4.

We nevertheless manage to deal with these various queries with a simple assumption by essentially adding two elements per character in the ciphertext. Regarding the size of the latter, this brings us back to the state-of-the-art [3] but our second construction has two main advantages. Firstly, it retains a short public key that still does not depend on the size of the alphabet. Secondly, it relies on a static assumption, which is a significant improvement over other schemes.

Summary of Contributions. Table 1 provides a comparison between our constructions and [3,13] with respect to the main metrics of such schemes. A more detailed complexity analysis can be found in Sect. 6.

This table shows that our first construction yields significantly shorter public keys while roughly halving the size of the ciphertext compared to [3]. It is done without decreasing the performance of the Test procedure (*i.e.* patterns detection). This is therefore the most suitable solution if one favours efficiency.

Our second construction reports lesser performance (but still better than the state-of-the-art for several metrics) but relies on a static computational assumption, which is noticeable compared to previous constructions. This is the current best solution if one favours security.

Table 1. Comparison with related works. The scalars $|S|$ and n denote respectively the number of elements in the plaintext alphabet and the length of the traffic to encrypt. L stands for the length of the longest pattern queried in SEST and for an upper bound on this value in the other schemes.

		Schemes			
		SEST ([13])	AS^{3}E([3])	Sect. 4.3	Sect. 4.4
Public Key	(nb. elements)	$n(\|S\|+1)$	$2L(\|S\|+1)$	$\mathbf{4L}$	$\mathbf{6L}$
Ciphertext	(nb. elements)	$2n$	$4n$	$\mathbf{2n+\frac{n}{L}}$	$4n+\frac{n}{L}$
Trapdoor	(nb. elements)	$L+2$	$2L$	$2L$	$3L$
Test	(nb. pairings)	$n(L+2)$	$2n$	$2n$	$3n$
Computational assumption		interactive	interactive	interactive	**static**

Outline. In Sect. 2 we provide the necessary background on bilinear groups along with the description of the computational assumptions used in our paper. Section 3 is dedicated to the syntax and the security model of SEPM. Our constructions are described in Sect. 4 and then proven secure in Sect. 5. Finally, we give a complexity analysis in Sect. 6.

2 Preliminaries

2.1 Bilinear Groups

Our construction requires bilinear groups whose definition is recalled below.

Definition 1. *Bilinear groups are a set of three groups $\mathbb{G}_1$, $\mathbb{G}_2$, and $\mathbb{G}_T$ of prime order p along with a map, called pairing, $e : \mathbb{G}_1 \times \mathbb{G}_2 \to \mathbb{G}_T$ that is*

1. *bilinear: for any $g \in \mathbb{G}_1, \widetilde{g} \in \mathbb{G}_2$, and $a, b \in \mathbb{Z}_p$, $e(g^a, \widetilde{g}^b) = e(g, \widetilde{g})^{ab}$;*
2. *non-degenerate: for any $(g, \widetilde{g}) \in \mathbb{G}_1 \times \mathbb{G}_2$, $(g, \widetilde{g}) \neq (1_{\mathbb{G}_1}, 1_{\mathbb{G}_2})$, $e(g, \widetilde{g}) \neq 1_{\mathbb{G}_T}$;*
3. *efficient: for any $g \in \mathbb{G}_1$ and $\widetilde{g} \in \mathbb{G}_2$, $e(g, \widetilde{g})$ can be efficiently computed.*

As most recent cryptographic papers, we only consider bilinear groups of prime order with *type 3* pairings [14], meaning that no efficiently computable homomorphism is known between $\mathbb{G}_1$ and $\mathbb{G}_2$.

2.2 Decisional Assumptions

We now introduce the decisional assumptions underlying the security of our constructions.

Definition 2 (i-GDH assumption [13]**).** *Let r, s, t, c and κ be five positive integers and $\mathtt{R} \in \mathbb{Z}_p[X_1, \ldots, X_c]^r, \mathtt{S} \in \mathbb{Z}_p[X_1, \ldots, X_c]^s$ and $\mathtt{T} \in \mathbb{Z}_p[X_1, \ldots, X_c]^t$ be three tuples of multivariate polynomials over $\mathbb{Z}_p$. For any polynomial $f \in \mathbb{Z}_p[X_1, \ldots, X_c]$, we say that f is dependent on $< \mathtt{R}, \mathtt{S}, \mathtt{T} >$ if there are $\{a_j\}_{j=1}^s \in \mathbb{Z}_p^s \setminus \{(0, \ldots, 0)\}$, $\{b_{i,j}\}_{i,j=1}^{i=r,j=s} \in \mathbb{Z}_p^{r \cdot s}$ and $\{c_k\}_{k=1}^t \in \mathbb{Z}_p^t$ such that*

$$f \sum_i a_j S^{(j)} = \sum_{i,j} b_{i,j} R^{(i)} S^{(j)} + \sum_k c_k T^{(k)}.$$

Let $\mathcal{O}^{\mathtt{R}}$ (resp. $\mathcal{O}^{\mathtt{S}}$ and $\mathcal{O}^{\mathtt{T}}$) be oracles that, on input $\{\{a_{i_1,\ldots,i_c}^{(k)}\}_{i_1,\ldots,i_c=0}^{d_k}\}_{k=1}^{\kappa}$, add the polynomials $\{\sum_{i_1,\ldots,i_c} a_{i_1,\ldots,i_c}^{(k)} \prod_j X_j^{i_j}\}_{k=1}^{\kappa}$ to $\mathtt{R}$ (resp. $\mathtt{S}$ and $\mathtt{T}$).

Let $(\chi_1, \ldots, \chi_c) \xleftarrow{\$} \mathbb{Z}_p^c$ be a secret vector and $q_{\mathtt{R}}$ (resp. $q_{\mathtt{S}}$ and $q_{\mathtt{T}}$) be the number of queries to $\mathcal{O}^{\mathtt{R}}$ (resp. $\mathcal{O}^{\mathtt{S}}$) (resp. $\mathcal{O}^{\mathtt{T}}$). The i-GDH *assumption states that, given the values $\{g^{R^{(i)}(\chi_1,\ldots,\chi_c)}\}_{i=1}^{r+\kappa q_{\mathtt{R}}}$, $\{\widetilde{g}^{S^{(i)}(\chi_1,\ldots,\chi_c)}\}_{i=1}^{s+\kappa q_{\mathtt{S}}}$ and $\{e(g, \widetilde{g})^{T^{(i)}(\chi_1,\ldots,\chi_c)}\}_{i=1}^{t+\kappa q_{\mathtt{T}}}$, it is hard to decide whether $\zeta = g^{f(\chi_1,\ldots,\chi_c)}$ or ζ uniform in $\mathbb{G}_1$ if f is independent of $< \mathtt{R}, \mathtt{S}, \mathtt{T} >$.*

This strong assumption has been introduced in [13] and used in a subsequent work [3]. We only use it in our first protocol and show how to replace it by the following static assumption in our second protocol.

Definition 3 (EXDH assumption [11]). *Given* $g, g^a, g^{ab}, g^c \in \mathbb{G}_1$ *and* $\widetilde{g}, \widetilde{g}^a, \widetilde{g}^b \in \mathbb{G}_2$, *it is hard to decide whether* $\zeta = g^{abc}$ *or* ζ *is uniform in* $\mathbb{G}_1$.

This assumption was used in [11] to construct an e-cash system. In that work, it was called the weak-EXDH assumption because the authors also consider a stronger variant of this assumption. In this paper, we simply call it the EXDH assumption as we only need this weak variant. It only holds for type 3 bilinear groups.

3 Stream Encryption Supporting Pattern Matching (SEPM)

Notation. For two integers $a < b$, we let $[\![a, b[\![= \{i \in \mathbb{N} : a \leq i < b\}$, or simply $[\![b[\![$ if $a = 0$. For a finite set S, we use the notation $x \overset{\$}{\leftarrow} S$ to say that x is chosen uniformly at random in S.

In this paper, we consider entities exchanging data that are represented as sequences of characters that we call *strings*. These characters may originate from different sets/alphabets (*e.g.* $\{0, 1\}$ for bitstrings, $\{0, 1\}^8$ for bytestrings, etc.) but for sake of simplicity we assume that each of them can be associated with a unique element of $\mathbb{Z}_p$, for some large prime p. For most cases, this mapping ϕ is straightforward, for example:

- $\{0, 1\} \overset{\phi}{\rightarrow} \mathbb{Z}_p$ with $\phi(b) = b \in \mathbb{Z}_p$
- $\{0, 1\}^8 \overset{\phi}{\rightarrow} \mathbb{Z}_p$ with $\phi(b_7, \ldots, b_0) = \sum_{i=0}^{7} b_i 2^i \in \mathbb{Z}_p$

In the worst case, it is always possible to define a correspondence table so we can consider strings of elements of $\mathbb{Z}_p$ without loss of generality. Finally, as in previous works (*e.g.* [3,13]), we will consider a wildcard character $\star$ that matches all characters. Therefore, all data considered in this paper are assumed to be strings of characters in $\mathbb{Z}_p \cup \{\star\}$. For a string $W = (w_0, \ldots, w_{\ell-1}) \in (\mathbb{Z}_p \cup \{\star\})^\ell$ of length $\ell \in \mathbb{N}$, we let $\mathsf{supp}(W) = \{j \in [\![\ell[\![: w_j \neq \star\}$.

3.1 Definition

We adapt the syntax and security of SEST [13] by setting an upper bound L on the length of the keywords for which trapdoors may be issued. Contrary to that work, our syntax does not require to define an upper bound on the length of the stream to be encrypted.

A stream encryption scheme that supports pattern matching (SEPM) is defined by 5 algorithms that we call `Setup`, `Keygen`, `Issue`, `Encrypt` and `Test`. The first three of these are run by an entity called the receiver, while `Encrypt` is run by a sender and `Test` by a gateway.

- $\texttt{Setup}(1^\lambda, L)$: This probabilistic algorithm takes as input a security parameter λ and an upper bound L on the length of the keywords for which trapdoors may be issued. It returns the public parameters *pp* that will be considered as an implicit input of all other algorithms and so will be omitted.
- $\texttt{Keygen}()$: This probabilistic algorithm run by the receiver returns a key pair $(\mathsf{sk}, \mathsf{pk})$. The former value is secret and only known to the receiver, while the latter is public.
- $\texttt{Issue}(W, \mathsf{sk})$: This probabilistic algorithm takes as input the receiver's secret key along with a string $W = (w_0, \ldots, w_{\ell-1}) \in (\mathbb{Z}_p \cup \{\star\})^\ell$ of any size $\ell \leq L$ and returns a trapdoor TD_W.
- $\texttt{Encrypt}(M, \mathsf{pk})$: This probabilistic algorithm takes as input the receiver's public key along with a string $M = (m_0, \ldots, m_{n-1}) \in \mathbb{Z}_p^n$ of any size n and returns a ciphertext C.
- $\texttt{Test}(C, W, \mathsf{TD}_W)$: This deterministic algorithm takes as input a ciphertext C encrypting a string $M = (m_0, \ldots, m_{n-1}) \in \mathbb{Z}_p^n$ of any size n along with a trapdoor TD_W for a string $W = (w_0, \ldots, w_{\ell-1}) \in (\mathbb{Z}_p \cup \{\star\})^\ell$ of any size $\ell \leq L$. It returns the set (potentially empty) $\mathsf{Match} \subset [\![n[\![$ of all indexes i s.t. for all $k \in \mathsf{supp}(W)$, $w_k = m_{i+k}$.

As in recent schemes, [3,13], and more generally in searchable encryption, [1,7], our definition of SEPM does not consider a decryption algorithm: this functionality can easily be added by also encrypting the stream under a conventional encryption scheme. However, decryption could be performed in an SEPM by issuing a trapdoor for all characters of $\mathbb{Z}_p$ and running the $\texttt{Test}$ algorithm on the ciphertext for each of them.

3.2 Security Model

Correctness. As in [1], we divide correctness into two parts. The first one stipulates that the $\texttt{Test}$ algorithm run on (C, W, TD_W) will always return i if W matches M at index i (no false negatives). More formally, this means that, for any string M of size n and any W of length $\ell \leq min(n, L)$:

$$(\forall k \in \mathsf{supp}(W), m_{i+k} = w_k) \\ \Rightarrow \Pr[i \in \texttt{Test}(\texttt{Encrypt}(M, \mathsf{pk}), W, \texttt{Issue}(W, \mathsf{sk}))] = 1,$$

where the probability is taken over the set of key-pairs $(\mathsf{sk}, \mathsf{pk})$.

The second part of the correctness property requires that false positives (*i.e.*, when the $\texttt{Test}$ algorithm returns i despite the fact that W doesn't match M at this position) only occur with negligible probability. More formally, this means that, for any string M of size n and any W of length $\ell \leq min(n, L)$:

$$(\exists k \in \mathsf{supp}(W), m_{i+k} \neq w_k) \\ \Rightarrow \Pr[i \in \texttt{Test}(\texttt{Encrypt}(M, \mathsf{pk}), W, \texttt{Issue}(W, \mathsf{sk}))] = \mu(\lambda)$$

where the probability is taken over the set of key-pairs $(\mathsf{sk}, \mathsf{pk})$ and μ is a negligible function.

Selective Indistinguishability (sIND-CPA). We use the notion of selective indistinguishability defined in [13] which is adapted to be consistent with the slight modifications we introduce in the syntax.

Informally, this notion requires that no adversary $\mathcal{A}$, having committed to $M^{(0)}$ and $M^{(1)}$ before seeing pk, can decide whether a ciphertext C encrypts $M^{(0)}$ or $M^{(1)}$, even with access to an oracle returning a trapdoor TD_W for any queried string W that does not allow to trivially distinguish these two strings. This is formally defined by the experiment $\mathtt{Exp}_{\mathcal{A}}^{sind-cpa}(1^\lambda, L)$ described in Fig. 1. Here, $\mathcal{O}\mathtt{Issue}$ returns $\mathsf{TD}_W \leftarrow \mathtt{Issue}(W, \mathsf{sk})$ when queried on $W = (w_0, \dots, w_{\ell-1})$ with $\ell \leq L$, unless there are $i \in [\![n-\ell[\![$ and $b \in \{0,1\}$ with

$$(\forall k \in \mathsf{supp}(W), m_{i+k}^{(b)} = w_k) \wedge (\exists k \in \mathsf{supp}(W), m_{i+k}^{(1-b)} \neq w_k).$$

This is a natural restriction as TD_W would allow to trivially win this experiment for such W. We nevertheless stress that $\mathcal{O}\mathtt{Issue}$ can be queried with patterns W matching *both* $M^{(0)}$ and $M^{(1)}$. Finally, we require that $M^{(0)}$ and $M^{(1)}$ be of the same size because the corresponding ciphertexts would be trivially distinguishable otherwise. This restriction could however be lifted by using some padding technique to generate constant-size ciphertexts.

$\mathtt{Exp}_{\mathcal{A}}^{sind-cpa}(1^\lambda, L)$

1. $pp \leftarrow \mathtt{Setup}(1^\lambda, L)$
2. $(M^{(0)}, M^{(1)}) \leftarrow \mathcal{A}$, with $M^{(b)} = (m_0^{(b)}, \dots, m_{n-1}^{(b)})$ for $b \in \{0,1\}$ and $n \in \mathbb{N}$
3. $\mathsf{pk} \leftarrow \mathtt{Keygen}()$
4. $\beta \xleftarrow{\$} \{0,1\}$
5. $C \leftarrow \mathtt{Encrypt}(M^{(\beta)}, \mathsf{pk})$
6. $\beta' \leftarrow \mathcal{A}^{\mathcal{O}\mathtt{Issue}}(C, \mathsf{pk})$
7. **If** $\beta = \beta'$ then **return** 1, **else return** 0.

Fig. 1. sIND-CPA Security Game

We define the advantage of an adversary $\mathcal{A}$ in $\mathtt{Exp}_{\mathcal{A}}^{sind-cpa}(1^\lambda, L)$ as

$$\mathtt{Adv}_{\mathcal{A}}^{sind-cpa}(1^\lambda, L) = \left| \Pr[\mathtt{Exp}_{\mathcal{A}}^{sind-cpa}(1^\lambda, L) = 1] - \frac{1}{2} \right|.$$

A stream encryption scheme that is searchable for pattern matching is sIND-CPA secure if this advantage is negligible for any polynomial-time adversary.

4 Our Constructions

Before explaining how our constructions work, we first recall the fragmentation technique introduced in [3] that we slightly simplify for ease of exposition.

4.1 Fragmentation

Let n be the length of the string to be encrypted and $L \geq 2$ be the upper bound on the length of the patterns to search. We set $d_{\mathcal{F}} := L - 1$ and $s_{\mathcal{F}} := 2d_{\mathcal{F}}$. We suppose for simplicity that there exists an integer $n_{\mathcal{F}}$ such that $n = (2n_{\mathcal{F}}+1)d_{\mathcal{F}}$. Note that we can always fulfil this requirement by adding dummy characters to the string to encrypt. See also the remark at the end of this subsection.

For all $h \in [\![n_{\mathcal{F}}[\![$, we call $\mathcal{F}_h = [\![s_{\mathcal{F}}h, s_{\mathcal{F}}(h+1)[\![$ a *fragment* and we call $\overline{\mathcal{F}}_h = [\![s_{\mathcal{F}}h + d_{\mathcal{F}}, s_{\mathcal{F}}(h+1) + d_{\mathcal{F}}[\![$ an *overlined fragment*. Hence, $n_{\mathcal{F}}$ is the *number* of fragments (or overlined ones), $s_{\mathcal{F}}$ is their *length* and $d_{\mathcal{F}}$ is the *offset* between fragments and overlined ones.

A remarkable property of this construction is that for any integer $\ell \leq L$ and any index $i \in [\![n - \ell[\![$, the set of ℓ consecutive integers $[\![i, i+\ell[\![$ is contained in at least an (overlined) fragment.

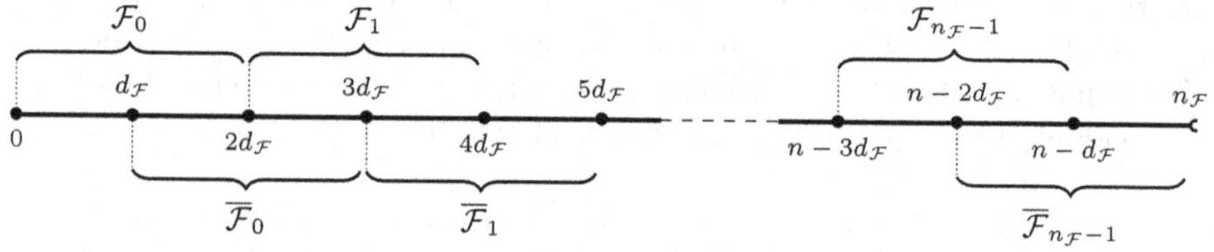

Fig. 2. Fragmentation of $[\![n[\![$ with $n = (2n_{\mathcal{F}} + 1)d_{\mathcal{F}}$

For all $i \in [\![n[\![$, we define $\mathbf{frag}(i), \mathsf{pos}(i), \overline{\mathbf{frag}}(i)$ and $\overline{\mathsf{pos}}(i)$ by

$$i = s_{\mathcal{F}}\mathbf{frag}(i) + \mathsf{pos}(i), \text{ with } 0 \leq \mathsf{pos}(i) < s_{\mathcal{F}}$$
$$i - L = s_{\mathcal{F}}\overline{\mathbf{frag}}(i) + \overline{\mathsf{pos}}(i), \text{ with } 0 \leq \overline{\mathsf{pos}}(i) < s_{\mathcal{F}}.$$

In other words, $(\mathbf{frag}(i), \mathsf{pos}(i))$ is the (quotient, remainder) pair of the euclidean division of i by $s_{\mathcal{F}}$ and so is $(\overline{\mathbf{frag}}(i), \overline{\mathsf{pos}}(i))$ for the division of $i - L$ by $s_{\mathcal{F}}$. Thus, $\mathbf{frag}(i)$ (resp. $\overline{\mathbf{frag}}(i)$) is the index of the fragment that contains i and $\mathsf{pos}(i)$ (resp. $\overline{\mathsf{pos}}(i)$) is the position of i inside $\mathcal{F}_{\mathbf{frag}(i)}$ (resp. $\overline{\mathcal{F}}_{\overline{\mathbf{frag}}(i)}$).

Remarks. A benefit of this fragmentation approach is that one does not need to define a bound on the length of the strings to encrypt. One can indeed encrypt strings of arbitrary length by processing each fragment independently. Conversely, [13] requires to define a maximal length n at the setup phase. Technically, it would be possible in [13] to split the string to encrypt into fragments of size n so as to be able to support strings of any size. Unfortunately, this would harm correctness of the resulting scheme because patterns straddling two fragments would be undetectable. In this respect, the fragmentation approach is perfectly suited to stream encryption.

Another remark is that, with this fragmentation approach, the precise knowledge of n and the number of fragment $n_{\mathcal{F}}$ is not needed in practice to encrypt the data. Theses values are indeed only necessary for formal definition of our construction so as to correctly index each fragment. As a result one can drop in practice the condition $n = (2n_{\mathcal{F}}+1)d_{\mathcal{F}}$, and process data as a stream cipher without using dummy characters: one can pause encryption in the middle of a fragment and resume it accordingly. However, for ease of exposition, we will suppose in the following that n is known at encryption time and that $n = (2n_{\mathcal{F}}+1)d_{\mathcal{F}}$.

4.2 Intuition of Our Constructions

As we explain in the introduction, the goal of our paper is twofold: we want to propose a new scheme with a better complexity than the one of [3] but also to rely on a much more reasonable computational assumption. This will be done in two steps. In the first step, we only focus on efficiency and propose a very simple construction that still requires an interactive assumption. In the second step, we show how one can tweak the previous construction to rely on a static assumption without significantly impacting performance.

First Construction. Let us first show how we can simplify the AS^{3}E protocol of Bkakria *et al.* [3] so that the size of the encryption is nearly halved, all other things being equal. In [3], each character m_i is essentially encrypted as $\{C_i, \overline{C}_i, C'_i, \overline{C}'_i\}$ with

- $C_i = (g^{z^{\mathsf{pos}(i)}})^{a_{\mathsf{frag}(i)}}$ and $C'_i = (g^{\alpha'_{m_i}(\alpha_{m_i} z)^{\mathsf{pos}(i)}})^{a_{\mathsf{frag}(i)}}$, where α'_{m_i} and α_{m_i} are secret values representing the character m_i, z is secret and $a_{\mathsf{frag}(i)}$ is a random scalar common to the whole fragment $\mathcal{F}_{\mathsf{frag}(i)}$;
- $\overline{C}_i$ and $\overline{C}'_i$ are generated similarly but for the overlined fragment $\mathcal{F}_{\mathsf{frag}(i)}$ containing i.

This construction is thus clearly reminiscent of [13] where m_i would be encrypted as $C_i = (g^{z^{\mathsf{pos}(i)}})^{a_{\mathsf{frag}(i)}}$ and $C'_i = (g^{\alpha'_{m_i}(z)^{\mathsf{pos}(i)}})^{a_{\mathsf{frag}(i)}}$ if one used fragmentation in the original scheme. However, the use of monomials ($z^{\mathsf{pos}(i)}$) whose degree depends on the position of the character within the stream was necessary in [13] to achieve a specific property, namely the ability to shift trapdoor (that is, a trapdoor can be used at *any* position). As we discuss in the introduction, the fragmentation technique makes this property less interesting. Actually the schemes proposed by Bkakria *et al.* do not achieve this property (they provide a trapdoor for each possible position of the pattern), which questions the interest of keeping the same structure as in [13].

By getting rid of this z element, it is possible to replace, for each fragment $\mathcal{F}_h$, the $s_{\mathcal{F}}$ elements C_i by a single element $C_h = g^{a_h}$ bearing the randomness a_h used for all elements C'_i with $i \in \mathcal{F}_h$ (i.e. $\mathsf{frag}(i) = h$), which roughly halves the size of the ciphertext. We can also simplify this way the elements C'_i by setting $C'_i = (g^{\alpha_{\mathsf{pos}(i),m_i}})^{a_{\mathsf{frag}(i)}}$ where $\alpha_{\mathsf{pos}(i),m_i}$ is a secret scalar encoding both the character m_i and its position $\mathsf{pos}(i)$ within the fragment.

We give the shape of such an encryption for very small fragments. When this technique is used to encrypt a message $M = (m_0, m_1, \ldots, m_{13})$ with fragments of size $s_{\mathcal{F}} = 4$, the sender chooses random elements a_0, a_1, a_2 and $\overline{a}_0, \overline{a}_1, \overline{a}_2$ to encrypt the fragments of M as follows:

$$M = (\overbrace{m_0, m_1, \rlap{$\underbrace{}_{\overline{a}_0}$}m_2, m_3}^{a_0}, \overbrace{m_4, m_5, \rlap{$\underbrace{}_{\overline{a}_1}$}m_6, m_7}^{a_1}, \overbrace{m_8, m_9, \rlap{$\underbrace{\phantom{m_{10}, m_{11}, m_{12}, m_{13}}}_{\overline{a}_2}$}m_{10}, m_{11}}^{a_2}, m_{12}, m_{13}).$$

The resulting ciphertext C is then:

C_0				C_1				C_2					
C'_0	C'_1	C'_2	C'_3	C'_4	C'_5	C'_6	C'_7	C'_8	C'_9	C'_{10}	C'_{11}	`Null`	`Null`
`Null`	`Null`	$\overline{C}'_2$	$\overline{C}'_3$	$\overline{C}'_4$	$\overline{C}'_5$	$\overline{C}'_6$	$\overline{C}'_7$	$\overline{C}'_8$	$\overline{C}'_9$	$\overline{C}'_{10}$	$\overline{C}'_{11}$	$\overline{C}'_{12}$	$\overline{C}'_{13}$
		$\overline{C}_0$				$\overline{C}_1$				$\overline{C}_2$			

Once we have reduced the size of the ciphertext, we focus on the one of the public key, which contained in [3] about $2L(|\mathcal{S}|+1)$ elements for an alphabet $\mathcal{S}$ of size $|\mathcal{S}|$. As we explain in Sect. 3, we can associate each character of the alphabet with an element of $\mathbb{Z}_p$. One could then try to set $C'_i = ((g^{\alpha_{\mathsf{pos}(i)}})^{m_i})^{a_{\mathsf{frag}(i)}}$ where $\alpha_{\mathsf{pos}(i)}$ would only encode the position $\mathsf{pos}(i)$ and where $m_i \in \mathbb{Z}_p$ is the character to encrypt, but such a scheme would suffer from malleability. Indeed, by raising C'_i to the power m_j/m_i one could transform a ciphertext encrypting m_i into a ciphertext encrypting m_j and so could use, for example, a legitimate trapdoor for m_j to detect m_i. In other words, a SEPM scheme cannot be secure if it is malleable. Our first construction solves this problem by setting $C'_i = (g^{x_{\mathsf{pos}(i)}}(g^{y_{\mathsf{pos}(i)}})^{m_i})^{a_{\mathsf{frag}(i)}}$ where $x_{\mathsf{pos}(i)}$ and $y_{\mathsf{pos}(i)}$ are secret values specific to the position $\mathsf{pos}(i)$. One can indeed note that C'_i is essentially a PS signature [19] on m_i generated with secret keys $(x_{\mathsf{pos}(i)}, y_{\mathsf{pos}(i)})$. Non-malleability of the ciphertext thus intuitively results from the unforgeability of PS signatures.

In this regard, it seems logical that the security of our first construction relies on a strong computational assumption (PS signatures were essentially proven in the generic group model). Following [3,13], we indeed prove security under the i-GDH assumption from [13], which is not really satisfactory. The goal of our second construction is to retain as much as possible the core idea (and thus the efficiency) of our new protocol while relying on a more reasonable assumption.

Second Construction. To understand why the previous construction is unlikely to rely on a static assumption, we need to briefly explain how its `Test` procedure works. As we have explained, a ciphertext element C'_i encrypting a character m_i at index i is a group element $g^{a_{\mathsf{frag}(i)}} \in \mathbb{G}_1$ raised to a power $x_{\mathsf{pos}(i)} + m_i y_{\mathsf{pos}(i)}$. By multiplying these C'_i together for $i \in \mathcal{I}$, where $\mathcal{I}$ is a subset of a fragment $\mathcal{F}_h$, we get the $C_h \in \mathbb{G}_1$ element raised to the power $\sum_{i \in \mathcal{I}}(x_{\mathsf{pos}(i)} + m_i y_{\mathsf{pos}(i)})$. By providing a mirror element in $\mathbb{G}_2$, that is, an element $\widetilde{g}^{\sum_{i \in \mathcal{I}}(x_{\mathsf{pos}(i)} + m_i y_{\mathsf{pos}(i)})}$ for some $\widetilde{g} \in \mathbb{G}_2$, we can easily check if the ciphertexts

$\{C_i'\}_{i\in\mathcal{I}}$ encrypt $\{m_i\}_{i\in\mathcal{I}}$ thanks to the bilinearity of the pairing. Of course, there are still several issues to address (we in particular need to prevent trapdoor forgeries) but the core idea remains the same.

The problem we face with such a construction is to deal with any trapdoor query in the security proof. The constraints we place on the $\mathcal{O}\mathtt{Issue}$ oracle in Sect. 3.2 are indeed very mild so we must be able to generate trapdoors for almost all possible patterns. Moreover, as our scheme has public keys, these trapdoors must be valid since the adversary could test them on patterns that it has encrypted itself. Concretely, this means that, in our proof, our simulator must be able to generate the elements $\widetilde{g}^{\sum_{i\in\mathcal{I}}(x_{\mathsf{pos}(i)}+m_i y_{\mathsf{pos}(i)})}$ for almost all possible values of m_i.

Clearly, we would like some static assumption providing each pair $\{\widetilde{g}^{x_{\mathsf{pos}(i)}}, \widetilde{g}^{y_{\mathsf{pos}(i)}}\}$ separately. Unfortunately, this cannot work in our case. Indeed, the proof uses a standard hybrid strategy where, at each step, the element $C_{i^*}' = (g^{x_{\mathsf{pos}(i^*)}}(g^{y_{\mathsf{pos}(i^*)}})^{m_i})^{a_{\mathsf{frag}(i^*)}}$ encrypting the i^*-th character is replaced by a random element. Given $\{\widetilde{g}^{x_{\mathsf{pos}(i^*)}}, \widetilde{g}^{y_{\mathsf{pos}(i^*)}}\}$, one could trivially detect this substitution because the ciphertext also contains $g^{a_{\mathsf{frag}(i^*)}}$. This is why our first construction, along with [3,13], uses the i-GDH assumption that is tailored to this kind of schemes. This interactive assumption indeed provides an oracle that can answer any trapdoor query by providing exactly the requested element $\widetilde{g}^{\sum_{i\in\mathcal{I}}(x_{\mathsf{pos}(i)}+m_i y_{\mathsf{pos}(i)})}$. This way, the simulation is perfect without having to worry about how these elements are computed concretely.

As the pair $\{\widetilde{g}^{x_{\mathsf{pos}(i^*)}}, \widetilde{g}^{y_{\mathsf{pos}(i^*)}}\}$ must remain unknown, a better strategy is to generate the pairs $\{\widetilde{g}^{x_{\mathsf{pos}(i)}}, \widetilde{g}^{y_{\mathsf{pos}(i)}}\}$, for $i \neq i^*$, in such a way that the sum $\sum_{i\in\mathcal{I}}(x_{\mathsf{pos}(i)} + m_i y_{\mathsf{pos}(i)})$ can be computed without the knowledge of $x_{\mathsf{pos}(i^*)}$ and $y_{\mathsf{pos}(i^*)}$. More concretely, this means that the pairs $(x_{\mathsf{pos}(i)}, y_{\mathsf{pos}(i)})$, for $i \neq i^*$, must be able to cancel $(x_{\mathsf{pos}(i^*)}, y_{\mathsf{pos}(i^*)})$ and so should be generated from the same secret value (let us call it A) defining an instance of the computational problem we have to solve. Unfortunately, here again, we pay the price of the strong security model we consider in Sect. 3.2.

Indeed, as we allow the adversary to query trapdoors for patterns matching the challenge ciphertext (contrarily to, *e.g.*, [20]), all the ciphertext elements, except C_{i^*}', must be well formed. This means that it should be possible to essentially compute $g^{Aa_{\mathsf{frag}(i^*)}}$ to generate C_i', for $i \neq i^*$ but, in the meantime, it should be impossible to distinguish $g^{Aa_{\mathsf{frag}(i^*)}}$ from randomness to ensure the validity of our hybrid argument in position i^*.

To address this problem, without weakening our security model, we choose to slightly modify our trapdoors by randomizing them with two different random values s_1 and s_2. Concretely, our trapdoors will be of the form

$$\widetilde{g}^{\sum_{i\in\mathcal{I}}[s_1(x_{\mathsf{pos}(i)}+m_i y_{\mathsf{pos}(i)})+s_2 z_{\mathsf{pos}(i)}]},$$

for some new scalars $z_{\mathsf{pos}(i)}$ that will be defined by our public key. The only price to pay is an increase in the size of the ciphertext that must now contain two elements per position to match these two random values.

Intuitively, these two scalars will provide enough flexibility to cancel the elements $x_{\mathsf{pos}(i^*)}$ and $y_{\mathsf{pos}(i^*)}$ without falling back on the previous problem. More specifically, they will allow us to consider a slightly more complex computational problem where $A = ab$, for some secret a and b, which allows us to construct $(x_{\mathsf{pos}(i)}, y_{\mathsf{pos}(i)})$ from a or b but not $A = ab$. This way, the challenge ciphertext can be simulated without making the underlying computational problem trivial. Moreover, the latter (called EXDH assumption, see Sect. 2) remains a simple variant of the DDH assumption, which gives more confidence in its hardness, in particular because it was already used in a previous paper [11] to design an e-cash system.

In the end, our second construction manages to be proven under a static assumption at the cost of a small increase in the ciphertext and trapdoors sizes, compared to our first contribution. We believe this is a significant improvement over the state-of-the-art [3,13] that required a tailored assumption.

4.3 Our First Protocol

- $\mathtt{Setup}(1^\lambda, L)$: Let $(\mathbb{G}_1, \mathbb{G}_2, \mathbb{G}_T, p, e)$ be the description of type 3 bilinear groups. This algorithm selects $g \in \mathbb{G}_1 \backslash \{1_{\mathbb{G}_1}\}$, $\widetilde{g} \in \mathbb{G}_2 \backslash \{1_{\mathbb{G}_2}\}$ and returns as public parameters $pp \leftarrow (\mathbb{G}_1, \mathbb{G}_2, \mathbb{G}_T, p, e, g, \widetilde{g}, d_{\mathcal{F}} := L-1, s_{\mathcal{F}} := 2d_{\mathcal{F}})$.
- $\mathtt{Keygen}()$: This algorithm chooses $x_k, y_k \xleftarrow{\$} \mathbb{Z}_p$ for all $k \in [\![s_{\mathcal{F}}[\![$ and returns $\mathsf{sk} := \{(x_k, y_k)\}_{k \in [\![s_{\mathcal{F}}[\![}$ and $\mathsf{pk} := \{(g^{x_k}, g^{y_k})\}_{k \in [\![s_{\mathcal{F}}[\![}$.
- $\mathtt{Encrypt}(M, \mathsf{pk})$: This algorithm parses M as $(m_0, \ldots, m_{n-1}) \in \mathbb{Z}_p^n$ and pk as $\{(X_k, Y_k)\}_{k \in [\![s_{\mathcal{F}}[\![}$, selects $a_h, \overline{a}_h \xleftarrow{\$} \mathbb{Z}_p$ for all $h \in [\![n_{\mathcal{F}}[\![$, where $n_{\mathcal{F}}$ is defined as in Section 4.1, *i.e.*, $n = (2n_{\mathcal{F}}+1)d_{\mathcal{F}}$, and returns the ciphertext $C := \{\{C_h, \overline{C}_h\}_{h \in [\![n_{\mathcal{F}}[\![}, \{(C'_i, \overline{C}'_i)\}_{i \in [\![n[\![}\}$ generated as follows:

$C_h := g^{a_h}$, for $h \in [\![n_{\mathcal{F}}[\![$	$\overline{C}_h := g^{\overline{a}_h}$, for $h \in [\![n_{\mathcal{F}}[\![$
For $i \in [\![n - d_{\mathcal{F}}[\![$ **:**	**For** $i \in [\![d_{\mathcal{F}}, n[\![$ **:**
$C'_i := (X_{\mathsf{pos}(i)}(Y_{\mathsf{pos}(i)})^{m_i})^{a_{\mathsf{frag}(i)}}$	$\overline{C}'_i := (X_{\overline{\mathsf{pos}}(i)}(Y_{\overline{\mathsf{pos}}(i)})^{m_i})^{\overline{a}_{\overline{\mathsf{frag}}(i)}}$
For $i \in [\![n - d_{\mathcal{F}}, n[\![$ **:**	**For** $i \in [\![d_{\mathcal{F}}[\![$ **:**
$C'_i :=$ `Null`	$\overline{C}'_i :=$ `Null`

- $\mathtt{Issue}(W, \mathsf{sk})$: On $W = (w_0, \ldots, w_{\ell-1}) \in (\mathbb{Z}_p \cup \{\star\})^\ell$, $\mathsf{sk} = \{(x_k, y_k)\}_{k \in [\![s_{\mathcal{F}}[\![}$, $\ell \leq L$, it runs:

  For $\delta \in [\![s_{\mathcal{F}} - \ell + 1[\![$:

  $$s \xleftarrow{\$} \mathbb{Z}_p,\ \widehat{W} = (\widehat{w}_0, \ldots, \widehat{w}_{s_{\mathcal{F}}-1}) := (\overbrace{\star, \ldots, \star}^{\delta}, w_0, \ldots, w_{\ell-1}, \overbrace{\star, \ldots, \star}^{s_{\mathcal{F}}-\ell-\delta})$$

  $$S := s \sum_{k \in \mathsf{supp}(\widehat{W})} (x_k + y_k \widehat{w}_k),\quad \mathsf{td}_{W,\delta} := \{\widetilde{g}^s, \widetilde{g}^S\}$$

  Return $\mathsf{TD}_W := \{\mathsf{td}_{W,\delta}\}_{\delta \in [\![s_{\mathcal{F}} - \ell + 1[\![}$
- $\mathtt{Test}(C, W, \mathsf{TD}_W)$: This algorithm uses $\mathsf{TD}_W = \{\mathsf{td}_{W,\delta}\}_{\delta \in [\![s_{\mathcal{F}} - \ell + 1[\![}$ to test whether the string $W \in (\mathbb{Z}_p \cup \{\star\})^\ell$ matches the message M encrypted by C as follows:

```
Match := ∅
For i ∈ ⟦n − ℓ⟦:
  If ⟦i, i + ℓ⟦ ⊂ F_frag(i):
    Get the trapdoor element td_{W,pos(i)} = {T1, T2} from TD_W
    If e( ∏_{k∈supp(W)} C'_{i+k} , T1 ) = e(C_frag(i), T2):
      Match := Match ∪ {i}
  Else:   #now we know that ⟦i, i + ℓ⟦ ⊂ F̄_{frag(i)‾}
    Get the trapdoor td_{W,pos(i)‾} = {T1, T2} from TD_W ;
    If e( ∏_{k∈supp(W)} C̄'_{i+k} , T1 ) = e(C̄_{frag(i)‾}, T2):
      Match := Match ∪ {i}
Return Match
```

Correctness. We first show that if M contains a pattern W at position i, then i is necessarily contained in the subset returned by Test(C, W, TD_W). Here, we assume that $i \in [\![n-\ell[\![$ is such that $[\![i, i+\ell[\![\subset \mathcal{F}_{\mathsf{frag}(i)}$. Otherwise, we would have $[\![i, i+\ell[\![\subset \overline{\mathcal{F}}_{\overline{\mathsf{frag}}(i)}$ and adapting the following argument to this case would be straightforward.
The Issue algorithm ensures that, at some point, a trapdoor element $\mathsf{td}_{W,\mathsf{pos}(i)} = \{T_1, T_2\}$ was generated for

$$\widehat{W} = (\widehat{w}_0, \ldots, \widehat{w}_{s_\mathcal{F}-1}) := (\overbrace{\star, \ldots, \star}^{\mathsf{pos}(i)}, w_0, \ldots, w_{\ell-1}, \overbrace{\star, \ldots, \star}^{s_\mathcal{F}-\ell-\mathsf{pos}(i)}).$$

To show that the index i is added by Test in Match, we must show that the pairing equation is satisfied. By non-degeneracy of the pairing, this is equivalent to showing that the following equation on the exponents of $e(g, \widetilde{g})$ holds:

$$s \sum_{k\in\mathsf{supp}(W)} a_{\mathsf{frag}(i+k)}(x_{\mathsf{pos}(i+k)} + y_{\mathsf{pos}(i+k)} m_{i+k}) = a_{\mathsf{frag}(i)} s \sum_{k\in\mathsf{supp}(\widehat{W})} x_k + y_k \widehat{w}_k$$

As $[\![i, i+\ell[\![\subset \mathcal{F}_{\mathsf{frag}(i)}$, we have for all $k \in \mathsf{supp}(W)$, $\mathsf{frag}(i+k) = \mathsf{frag}(i)$ and $\mathsf{pos}(i+k) = \mathsf{pos}(i) + k$. Thus after simplification, we have to show the equivalent equation:

$$\sum_{k\in\mathsf{supp}(W)} x_{\mathsf{pos}(i)+k} + y_{\mathsf{pos}(i)+k} m_{i+k} = \sum_{k\in\mathsf{supp}(\widehat{W})} x_k + y_k \widehat{w}_k. \qquad (1)$$

Formally, the fact that W is contained at index $i \in [\![n-\ell[\![$ in M means that $m_{i+k} = w_k$ for all $k \in \mathsf{supp}(W)$. Hence the LHS of (1) is equal to

$$\sum_{k\in\mathsf{supp}(W)} x_{\mathsf{pos}(i)+k} + y_{\mathsf{pos}(i)+k} w_k.$$

As $\widehat{w}_{\mathsf{pos}(i)+k} = w_k$ for all $k \in \mathsf{supp}(W)$, we get that this sum equals

$$\sum_{k \in \mathsf{supp}(W)} x_{\mathsf{pos}(i)+k} + y_{\mathsf{pos}(i)+k} \widehat{w}_{\mathsf{pos}(i)+k}.$$

Finally, we note that $\mathsf{supp}(\widehat{W}) = \{\mathsf{pos}(i) + k\}_{k \in \mathsf{supp}(W)}$. We can then re-index the sum above to get

$$\sum_{k \in \mathsf{supp}(\widehat{W})} x_k + y_k \widehat{w}_k,$$

which proves (1). Thus the pairing equality holds and `Test` returns a set containing i. In other words, there is no false negative in our system.

Now, let us assume that W is *not* contained in M at position i. If `Test` returns a set containing i, then the reasoning above implies that we would have:

$$\sum_{k \in \mathsf{supp}(W)} x_{\mathsf{pos}(i)+k} + y_{\mathsf{pos}(i)+k} m_{i+k} = \sum_{k \in \mathsf{supp}(W)} x_{\mathsf{pos}(i)+k} + y_{\mathsf{pos}(i)+k} w_k,$$

which means that:

$$\sum_{k \in \mathsf{supp}(W)} y_{\mathsf{pos}(i)+k}(m_{i+k} - w_k) = \sum_{\substack{k \in \mathsf{supp}(W) \\ m_{i+k} \neq w_k}} y_{\mathsf{pos}(i)+k}(m_{i+k} - w_k) = 0. \tag{2}$$

Since M does not contain W at position i, there exists at least one $k \in \mathsf{supp}(W)$ such that $w_k \neq m_{i+k}$ so the last sum above is not empty. As the $\{y_k\}_{k \in [\![s_{\mathcal{F}} [\![}$ are chosen uniformly at random independently of M and W, Eq. (2) holds with negligible probability $1/p$ (the probability that a non-zero linear form evaluates to 0). This means that we can also dismiss the occurrence of false positives.

Note that one could consider a stronger model of correctness, where an adversary intends to bypass the detection system. In this case, as the public key contains the g^{y_k}'s, the adversary gains access to some information on the y_k's which are thus not independent of M and W and the above reasoning fails. However, one could easily transform an adversary managing to find a message M and a pattern W such that Eq. (2) holds, into an algorithm that solve the discrete logarithm problem. As a result, we will have this stronger notion of correctness under the discrete logarithm assumption in $\mathbb{G}_1$.

4.4 Our Second Protocol

- `Setup`$(1^\lambda, L)$: Let $(\mathbb{G}_1, \mathbb{G}_2, \mathbb{G}_T, p, e)$ be the description of type 3 bilinear groups. This algorithm selects $g \in \mathbb{G}_1 \backslash \{1_{\mathbb{G}_1}\}$, $\widetilde{g} \in \mathbb{G}_2 \backslash \{1_{\mathbb{G}_2}\}$ and returns as public parameters $pp \leftarrow (\mathbb{G}_1, \mathbb{G}_2, \mathbb{G}_T, p, e, g, \widetilde{g}, d_{\mathcal{F}} := L - 1, s_{\mathcal{F}} := 2d_{\mathcal{F}})$.
- `Keygen`$()$: This algorithm chooses $x_k, y_k, z_k \xleftarrow{\$} \mathbb{Z}_p$ for all $k \in [\![s_{\mathcal{F}} [\![$ and returns $\mathsf{sk} = \{(x_k, y_k, z_k)\}_{k \in [\![s_{\mathcal{F}} [\![}$ and $\mathsf{pk} = \{(g^{x_k}, g^{y_k}, g^{z_k})\}_{k \in [\![s_{\mathcal{F}} [\![}$.

- $\texttt{Encrypt}(M, \mathsf{pk})$: This algorithm parses M as $(m_0, \ldots, m_{n-1}) \in \mathbb{Z}_p^n$ and pk as $\{(X_k, Y_k, Z_k)\}_{k \in [\![s_{\mathcal{F}}[\![}$, selects $a_h, \overline{a}_h \xleftarrow{\$} \mathbb{Z}_p$ for all $h \in [\![n_{\mathcal{F}}[\![$, where $n_{\mathcal{F}}$ is defined as in Section 4.1, *i.e.*, $n = (2n_{\mathcal{F}} + 1)d_{\mathcal{F}}$, and returns the ciphertext $C = \{\{C_h, \overline{C}_h\}_{h \in [\![n_{\mathcal{F}}[\![}, \{(C'_{i,1}, C'_{i,2}, \overline{C}'_{i,1}, \overline{C}'_{i,2})\}_{i \in [\![n[\![}\}$ generated as follows:

$C_h = g^{a_h}$, for $h \in [\![n_{\mathcal{F}}[\![$	$\overline{C}_h = g^{\overline{a}_h}$, for $h \in [\![n_{\mathcal{F}}[\![$
For $i \in [\![n - d_{\mathcal{F}}[\![$:	**For** $i \in [\![d_{\mathcal{F}}, n[\![$:
$C'_{i,1} = (X_{\mathsf{pos}(i)}(Y_{\mathsf{pos}(i)})^{m_i})^{a_{\mathsf{frag}(i)}}$	$\overline{C}'_{i,1} = (X_{\overline{\mathsf{pos}}(i)}(Y_{\overline{\mathsf{pos}}(i)})^{m_i})^{\overline{a}_{\overline{\mathsf{frag}}(i)}}$
$C'_{i,2} = (Z_{\mathsf{pos}(i)})^{a_{\mathsf{frag}(i)}}$	$\overline{C}'_{i,2} = (Z_{\overline{\mathsf{pos}}(i)})^{\overline{a}_{\overline{\mathsf{frag}}(i)}}$
For $i \in [\![n - d_{\mathcal{F}}, n[\![$:	**For** $i \in [\![d_{\mathcal{F}}[\![$:
$C'_{i,1} = C'_{i,2} = \texttt{Null}$	$\overline{C}'_{i,1} = \overline{C}'_{i,2} = \texttt{Null}$

- $\texttt{Issue}(W, \mathsf{sk})$: On $W = (w_0, \ldots, w_{\ell-1}) \in (\mathbb{Z}_p \cup \{\star\})^\ell$, $\mathsf{sk} = \{(x_k, y_k, z_k)\}_{k \in [\![s_{\mathcal{F}}[\![}$, $\ell \leq L$, it runs:

  For $\delta \in [\![s_{\mathcal{F}} - \ell + 1[\![$:

  $s_1, s_2 \xleftarrow{\$} \mathbb{Z}_p$, $\widehat{W} = (\widehat{w}_0, \ldots, \widehat{w}_{s_{\mathcal{F}}-1}) := (\overbrace{\star, \ldots, \star}^{\delta}, w_0, \ldots, w_{\ell-1}, \overbrace{\star, \ldots, \star}^{s_{\mathcal{F}}-\ell-\delta})$

  $S = s_1 \sum_{k \in \mathsf{supp}(\widehat{W})} [x_k + y_k \widehat{w}_k] + s_2 \sum_{k \in \mathsf{supp}(\widehat{W})} z_k$, $\mathsf{td}_{W,\delta} = \{\widetilde{g}^{s_1}, \widetilde{g}^{s_2}, \widetilde{g}^{S}\}$

  Return $\mathsf{TD}_W = \{\mathsf{td}_{W,\delta}\}_{\delta \in [\![s_{\mathcal{F}}-\ell+1[\![}$
- $\texttt{Test}(C, W, \mathsf{TD}_W)$: This algorithm uses $\mathsf{TD}_W = \{\mathsf{td}_{W,\delta}\}_{\delta \in [\![s_{\mathcal{F}}-\ell+1[\![}$ to test whether the string $W \in (\mathbb{Z}_p \cup \{\star\})^\ell$ matches the message M encrypted by C as follows:

  $\mathsf{Match} := \emptyset$

  For $i \in [\![n - \ell[\![$:

  If $[\![i, i+\ell[\![\subset \mathcal{F}_{\mathsf{frag}(i)}$:

  Get the trapdoor element $\mathsf{td}_{W,\mathsf{pos}(i)} = \{T_1, T_2, T_3\}$ from TD_W

  If $e\left(\prod_{k \in \mathsf{supp}(W)} C'_{i+k,1} \;,\; T_1\right) \cdot e\left(\prod_{k \in \mathsf{supp}(W)} C'_{i+k,2} \;,\; T_2\right) = e\big(C_{\mathsf{frag}(i)}, T_3\big)$:

  $\mathsf{Match} = \mathsf{Match} \cup \{i\}$

  Else: `#now we know that` $[\![i, i+\ell[\![\subset \overline{\mathcal{F}}_{\mathsf{frag}(i)}$

  Get the trapdoor $\mathsf{td}_{W,\overline{\mathsf{pos}}(i)} = \{T_1, T_2, T_3\}$ from TD_W ;

  If $e\left(\prod_{k \in \mathsf{supp}(W)} \overline{C}'_{i+k,1} \;,\; T_1\right) \cdot e\left(\prod_{k \in \mathsf{supp}(W)} \overline{C}'_{i+k,2} \;,\; T_2\right) = e\big(\overline{C}_{\overline{\mathsf{frag}}(i)}, T_3\big)$:

  $\mathsf{Match} = \mathsf{Match} \cup \{i\}$

  Return Match

The correctness of this protocol is similar to the one of the first protocol.

5 Security Analysis

The security of our protocols is stated by the following theorem, proved in this section.

Theorem 1.

- *The scheme described in Sect. 4.3 is* sIND-CPA *secure under the* i-GDH *assumption.*
- *The scheme described in Sect. 4.4 is* sIND-CPA *secure under the* EXDH *assumption.*

5.1 Proof Strategy

The proof of the theorem above follows the same strategy for both protocols but will rely on very different arguments according to the construction. Let $M^{(0)} = (m_0^{(0)}, \ldots, m_{n-1}^{(0)})$ and $M^{(1)} = (m_0^{(1)}, \ldots, m_{n-1}^{(1)})$ be the two strings returned by $\mathcal{A}$ at the beginning of the game. Our proof uses a sequence of games to argue that the advantage of $\mathcal{A}$ is negligible. This is a standard hybrid argument, in which at each game hop we randomize another element of the challenge ciphertext. However, due to the peculiarities of the fragmentation technique, we will have to consider the following two sets:

$$\mathcal{I}_{\neq} = \{i \in [\![n - d_{\mathcal{F}}[\![: m_i^{(0)} \neq m_i^{(1)}\} \text{ and } \overline{\mathcal{I}}_{\neq} = \{i \in [\![d_{\mathcal{F}}, n[\![: m_i^{(0)} \neq m_i^{(1)}\}.$$

In this proof we will denote the elements of $\mathcal{I}_{\neq}$ (resp. $\overline{\mathcal{I}}_{\neq}$) as $\{i_1, \ldots, i_{|\mathcal{I}_{\neq}|}\}$ (resp. $\{i'_1, \ldots, i'_{|\overline{\mathcal{I}}_{\neq}|}\}$). For $j = 1, \ldots, |\mathcal{I}_{\neq}|$, we let $\mathcal{I}_{\neq}^{(j)} = \{i_1, \ldots, i_j\}$ and $\mathcal{I}_{\neq}^{(0)} = \emptyset$. We define $\overline{\mathcal{I}}_{\neq}^{(j)}$ similarly. Finally, to harmonize the proofs of our protocols, we will introduce the notation $\mathbf{C}'_i$, for $i \in [\![n - d_{\mathcal{F}}[\![$, where:

- $\mathbf{C}'_i = [C'_i]$ in our first protocol;
- $\mathbf{C}'_i = [C'_{i,1}, C'_{i,2}]$ in our second protocol.

This way, we can refer to the first element of $\mathbf{C}'_i$ as $\mathbf{C}'_i[1]$. We define similarly $\overline{\mathbf{C}}'_i$. We can now define the following sequence of games.

- $\mathbf{game}_{0,1}$ denotes the $\mathbf{Exp}_{\mathcal{A}}^{sind-cpa}$ game, as described in algorithm 1;
- for $j = 1, \ldots, |\mathcal{I}_{\neq}|$:
  - $\mathbf{game}_{j-1,2}$, which is the same game as $\mathbf{game}_{j-1,1}$ except that, for the second protocol, $\mathbf{C}'_{i_j}[2]$ is replaced by a random element of $\mathbb{G}_1$;
  - $\mathbf{game}_{j,1}$, which is the same game as $\mathbf{game}_{j-1,1}$ except that *all elements* of $\mathbf{C}'_{i_j}$ are replaced by random elements of $\mathbb{G}_1$.
- for $j = |\mathcal{I}_{\neq}| + 1, \ldots, |\mathcal{I}_{\neq}| + |\overline{\mathcal{I}}_{\neq}|$:
  - $\mathbf{game}_{j-1,2}$, which is the same game as $\mathbf{game}_{j-1,1}$ except that $\overline{\mathbf{C}}'_{i'_{j-|\mathcal{I}_{\neq}|}}[2]$ is replaced by a random element of $\mathbb{G}_1$;

- $\mathbf{game}_{j,1}$, which is the same game as $\mathbf{game}_{j-1,1}$ except that *all elements* of $\overline{\mathbf{C}}'_{i'_{j-|\mathcal{I}_{\neq}|}}$ are replaced by random elements of $\mathbb{G}_1$.

In the case of our first protocol, one can note that $\mathbf{game}_{j,1}$ and $\mathbf{game}_{j,2}$ are the same.

Let $\mathbb{S}_j$ be the probability of success of $\mathcal{A}$ in $\mathbf{game}_{j,1}$. We can write :

$$\begin{aligned}\mathtt{Adv}_{\mathcal{A}}^{sind-cpa}(1^\lambda, n) &= \left|\Pr[\mathbf{Exp}_{\mathcal{A}}^{sind-cpa}(1^\lambda, n) = 1] - \frac{1}{2}\right| \\ &\leq \sum_{j=1}^{|\mathcal{I}_{\neq}|+|\overline{\mathcal{I}}_{\neq}|} \left|\mathbb{S}_{j,1} - \mathbb{S}_{j-1,1}\right| + \left|\mathbb{S}_{|\mathcal{I}_{\neq}|+|\overline{\mathcal{I}}_{\neq}|,1} - \frac{1}{2}\right|\end{aligned}$$

Ultimately, in the last game, the challenge ciphertext contains no information about $m_i^{(\beta)}$, for all i such that $m_i^{(0)} \neq m_i^{(1)}$. Thus, an adversary playing this game can only succeed with probability $\frac{1}{2}$ and we then have $|\mathbb{S}_{|\mathcal{I}_{\neq}|+|\overline{\mathcal{I}}_{\neq}|,1} - \frac{1}{2}| = 0$.

We conclude this proof using the following theorems.

Theorem 2. *For our first construction,* $|\mathbb{S}_{j,1} - \mathbb{S}_{j-1,1}|$ *is negligible under the* i-GDH *assumption, for all* $j \in \{1, \ldots, |\mathcal{I}_{\neq}| + |\overline{\mathcal{I}}_{\neq}|\}$.

Theorem 3. *For our second construction,* $|\mathbb{S}_{j,1} - \mathbb{S}_{j-1,1}|$ *is negligible under the* EXDH *assumption, for all* $j \in \{1, \ldots, |\mathcal{I}_{\neq}| + |\overline{\mathcal{I}}_{\neq}|\}$.

We only give proofs of these theorems for $j = 1, \ldots, |\mathcal{I}_{\neq}|$ as these proofs readily extend to the cases $j = |\mathcal{I}_{\neq}| + 1, \ldots, |\mathcal{I}_{\neq}| + |\overline{\mathcal{I}}_{\neq}|$.

In these proofs, to simplify notations, we let $i^* := i_j$ be the j-th index of $\mathcal{I}_{\neq}$, and we let $\widehat{M} = (\widehat{m}_0, \ldots, \widehat{m}_{s_{\mathcal{F}}-1})$ be the substring of $M^{(\beta)}$ corresponding to the fragment containing i^*.

5.2 Proof of Theorem 2

In our simulation, we set an upper bound q on the number of trapdoor queries that the adversary is allowed to make. The i-GDH instance from which we make our reduction has $c = 2n_{\mathcal{F}} + (q+2)s_{\mathcal{F}}$ variables called

$$\{\{a_h, \overline{a}_h\}_{h \in [\![n_{\mathcal{F}}[\![}, \{(x_k, y_k)\}_{k \in [\![s_{\mathcal{F}}[\![}, \{s_t\}_{t \in [\![qs_{\mathcal{F}}[\![}\}$$

and a secret evaluation $(\chi_1, \ldots, \chi_c) \xleftarrow{\$} \mathbb{Z}_p^c$ of these variables.

Initially, $\mathtt{R} = \{\{a_h, \overline{a}_h\}_{h \in [\![n_{\mathcal{F}}[\![}, \{(x_k, y_k)\}_{k \in [\![s_{\mathcal{F}}[\![}\}, \mathtt{S}, \mathtt{T} = \emptyset$ and

$$f = a_{\mathsf{frag}(i^*)}(x_{\mathsf{pos}(i^*)} + y_{\mathsf{pos}(i^*)}\widehat{m}_{\mathsf{pos}(i^*)}).$$

The simulator has oracle access to $\mathcal{O}^{\mathsf{R}}, \mathcal{O}^{\mathsf{S}}$ and $\mathcal{O}^{\mathsf{T}}$ to add $\kappa = 2$ polynomials at a time to these sets. At any moment, the simulator knows the elements in the current set $\{g^{R(\chi_1,\dots,\chi_c)}, \widetilde{g}^{S(\chi_1,\dots,\chi_c)}, e(g,\widetilde{g})^{T(\chi_1,\dots,\chi_c)}\}_{R\in\mathsf{R},S\in\mathsf{S},T\in\mathsf{T}}$.
For some polynomial P we say

$$\textit{the simulator uses } \mathcal{O}^{\mathsf{R}} \textit{ to get } g^{P(\chi_1,\dots,\chi_c)}$$

to say that it uses $\mathcal{O}^{\mathsf{R}}$ to add the polynomial P to R and so now it knows $g^{P(\chi_1,\dots,\chi_c)}$ (resp. $\widetilde{g}^{P(\chi_1,\dots,\chi_c)}$).
Likewise, for some polynomials P, Q we say

$$\textit{the simulator uses } \mathcal{O}^{\mathsf{S}} \textit{ to get } \widetilde{g}^{P(\chi_1,\dots,\chi_c)} \textit{ and } \widetilde{g}^{Q(\chi_1,\dots,\chi_c)}$$

to say that it uses $\mathcal{O}^{\mathsf{S}}$ to add the polynomials $\{P, Q\}$ to S so now it knows $g^{P(\chi_1,\dots,\chi_c)}$ and $\widetilde{g}^{Q(\chi_1,\dots,\chi_c)}$).
In the description of our simulator, we use the names of a variable $a_h, \overline{a}_h, x_k, y_k$ or s_t for its secret random evaluation χ_j by abuse of notation while in the proof of independency we really consider them as variables.
Finally, the simulator knows the i-GDH challenge ζ.

Key Generation. The simulator implicitly defines the secret key as $\mathsf{sk} = \{(x_k, y_k)\}_{k\in[\![s_{\mathcal{F}}[\![}$ by setting the public key to $\mathsf{pk} = \{(g^{x_k}, g^{y_k})\}_{k\in[\![s_{\mathcal{F}}[\![}$ as the polynomials x_k, y_k are initially in R.

Trapdoor Generation. The adversary can make at most q trapdoor queries to our simulator. To generate a trapdoor TD, the simulator has to generate at most $s_{\mathcal{F}}$ trapdoor elements td. Let $\widehat{W}$ be the fragment-sized pattern corresponding to the t-th trapdoor element td for some $t \leq s_{\mathcal{F}}q$. The simulator uses $\mathcal{O}^{\mathsf{S}}$ to get $\widetilde{g}^{s_t}$ and $\widetilde{g}^{S_t}$ where

$$S_t = s_t \sum_{k\in\mathsf{supp}(\widehat{W})} (x_k + y_k\widehat{w}_k)$$

and sets $\mathsf{td} = \{\widetilde{g}^{s_t}, \widetilde{g}^{S_t}\}$.

Challenge Generation. The simulator sets the challenge cyphertext as follows:

- $C_h = g^{a_h}$ and $\overline{C}_h = g^{\overline{a}_h}$ for $h \in [\![n_{\mathcal{F}}[\![$ as the polynomials $a_h, \overline{a}_h$ are initially in R.
- it uses $\mathcal{O}^{\mathsf{R}}$ to get valid $C'_i = g^{a_{\mathsf{frag}(i)}(x_{\mathsf{pos}(i)}+y_{\mathsf{pos}(i)}m_i^{(\beta)})}$ for $i \notin \mathcal{I}_{\neq}^{(j)}$
- $C'_i \xleftarrow{\$} \mathbb{G}_1$ for $i \in \mathcal{I}_{\neq}^{(j-1)}$ and $C'_{i^*} = \zeta$
- it uses $\mathcal{O}^{\mathsf{R}}$ to get valid $\overline{C}'_i = g^{\overline{a}_{\overline{\mathsf{frag}}(i)}(x_{\overline{\mathsf{pos}}(i)}+y_{\overline{\mathsf{pos}}(i)}m_i^{(\beta)})}$ for $i \in [\![d_{\mathcal{F}}, n[\![$.

If $\zeta = g^f$, then C'_{i^*} is a valid element and the simulator is playing $\mathbf{game}_{j-1,1}$. Else, C'_{i^*} is a random element from $\mathbb{G}_1$ and the simulator is playing game $\mathbf{game}_{j,1}$. An adversary able to distinguish $\mathbf{game}_{j-1,1}$ from $\mathbf{game}_{j,1}$ is thus able to break the i-GDH assumption if the polynomial $f = a_{\mathsf{frag}(i^*)}(x_{\mathsf{pos}(i^*)} + y_{\mathsf{pos}(i^*)}\widehat{m}_{\mathsf{pos}(i^*)})$ is independent from the sets R, S and T (after all the queries made by the simulator), which remains to prove.

Proof of Independence. This is done by showing that

$$a_{\mathsf{frag}(i^*)}(x_{\mathsf{pos}(i^*)} + y_{\mathsf{pos}(i^*)}\widehat{m}_{\mathsf{pos}(i^*)}) \sum_j b_j S^{(j)} = \sum_{i,j} c_{i,j} R^{(i)} S^{(j)} + \sum_k d_k T^{(k)}$$

implies $b_j = 0$ for $j = 0, \ldots, |\mathtt{S}| - 1$.

Since $\mathtt{T} = \emptyset$, we may already remove the last sum. Since the factor $a_{\mathsf{frag}(i^*)}$ only appears in the set $\mathtt{R}$ and more specifically as the $\mathbf{frag}(i^*)$-th element of the initial set $\{a_h\}_{h \in n_{\mathcal{F}}}$ and in the outputs of $\mathcal{O}^{\mathtt{R}}$, we can discard the other terms in the right hand side of the equation (and divide each member by $a_{\mathsf{frag}(i^*)}$). We reformulate the remaining coefficients as $b_{\mathsf{pos}(i^*),t}, b'_{\mathsf{pos}(i^*),t}, c_t, c'_t, b_{k,t}$ and $b'_{k,t}$ for $k \in [\![s_{\mathcal{F}} [\![\setminus \{\mathsf{pos}(i^*)\}$ and $1 \leq t \leq q_{\mathtt{S}}$ so the previous equality can be written as:

$$(x_{\mathsf{pos}(i^*)} + y_{\mathsf{pos}(i^*)}\widehat{m}_{\mathsf{pos}(i^*)}) \sum_{t=1}^{q_{\mathtt{S}}} \left[b_{\mathsf{pos}(i^*),t} s_t + b'_{\mathsf{pos}(i^*),t} S_t \right] =$$

$$= \sum_{t=1}^{q_{\mathtt{S}}} [c_t s_t + c'_t S_t] - \sum_{\substack{k=0 \\ k \neq \mathsf{pos}(i^*)}}^{s_{\mathcal{F}}-1} \left[(x_k + y_k \widehat{m}_k) \sum_{t=1}^{q_{\mathtt{S}}} \left[b_{k,t} s_t + b'_{k,t} S_t \right] \right].$$

This equation can also be written as:

$$\sum_{k=0}^{s_{\mathcal{F}}-1} \left[(x_k + y_k \widehat{m}_k) \sum_{t=1}^{q_{\mathtt{S}}} \left[b_{k,t} s_t + b'_{k,t} S_t \right] \right] = \sum_{t=1}^{q_{\mathtt{S}}} [c_t s_t + c'_t S_t]$$

and we show that if it holds, then $b_{\mathsf{pos}(i^*),t} = b'_{\mathsf{pos}(i^*),t} = 0$ for $t = 1, \ldots, q_{\mathtt{S}}$. Let's fix $1 \leq t \leq q_{\mathtt{S}}$. If we only keep the terms in s_t, we get :

$$\sum_{k=0}^{s_{\mathcal{F}}-1} \left[(x_k + y_k \widehat{m}_k)(b_{k,t} s_t + b'_{k,t} S_t) \right] = c_t s_t + c'_t S_t. \tag{3}$$

-We show that $\boxed{b'_{\mathsf{pos}(i^*),t} = 0}$: Keeping only the terms in Eq. (3) with total degree 2 in $\{x_k\}_{k \in [\![s_{\mathcal{F}} [\![}$ shows that:

$$\sum_{k=0}^{s_{\mathcal{F}}-1} x_k b'_{k,t} S_t = 0.$$

Simplifying by S_t in this equality shows that $\sum_{k=0}^{s_{\mathcal{F}}-1} x_k b'_{k,t} = 0$ and by independance of the variables $\{x_k\}_{k \in [\![s_{\mathcal{F}} [\![}$, we have $b'_{k,t} = 0$ for all $k \in [\![s_{\mathcal{F}} [\![$ and in particular, $b'_{\mathsf{pos}(i^*),t} = 0$.

-We show that $\boxed{b_{\mathsf{pos}(i^*),t} = 0}$: If we focus on the terms in Eq. (3) with total degree 1 in $\{x_k, y_k\}_{k \in [\![s_{\mathcal{F}} [\![}$, we get:

$$\sum_{k=0}^{s_{\mathcal{F}}-1} \left[(x_k + y_k \widehat{m}_k)(b_{k,t} s_t) \right] = c'_t S_t.$$

As $S_t = s_t \sum_{k\in\mathsf{supp}(\widehat{W})} (x_k + y_k\widehat{w}_k)$, where $\widehat{W} = (\widehat{w}_0, \ldots, \widehat{w}_{s_\mathcal{F}-1})$ is the t-th fragment-sized pattern processed by our simulator, this means, after simplifying by s_t:

$$\sum_{k=0}^{s_\mathcal{F}-1} [(x_k + y_k\widehat{m}_k)b_{k,t}] = c'_t \sum_{k\in\mathsf{supp}(\widehat{W})} (x_k + y_k\widehat{w}_k). \quad (4)$$

Keeping only the terms in $\{x_k\}_{k\in[\![s_\mathcal{F}[\![}$ in equation (4) shows that:

$$\sum_{k=0}^{s_\mathcal{F}-1} x_k b_{k,t} = c'_t \sum_{k\in\mathsf{supp}(\widehat{W})} x_k.$$

The independence of the variables $\{x_k\}_{k\in[\![s_\mathcal{F}[\![}$ shows that, for all $k \in [\![s_\mathcal{F}[\![$,

$$b_{k,t} = \begin{cases} c'_t & \text{if } k \in \mathsf{supp}(\widehat{W}), \\ 0 & \text{if not.} \end{cases}$$

We study the two following cases to conclude the proof:

- **if** $\boxed{c'_t = 0 \text{ or } \mathsf{pos}(i^*) \notin \mathsf{supp}(\widehat{W})}$, then we can already conclude that $b_{\mathsf{pos}(i^*),t}=0$;
- **else,** $\boxed{c'_t \neq 0 \text{ and } \mathsf{pos}(i^*) \in \mathsf{supp}(\widehat{W})}$ and we show a contradiction with the natural restriction placed on patterns in this game.

Indeed, in this last case we can Eq. (4) as:

$$c'_t \sum_{k\in\mathsf{supp}(\widehat{W})} (x_k + y_k\widehat{m}_k) = c'_t \sum_{k\in\mathsf{supp}(\widehat{W})} (x_k + y_k\widehat{w}_k).$$

We simplify by c'_t and keep the terms in $\{y_k\}_{k\in[\![s_\mathcal{F}[\![}$:

$$\sum_{k\in\mathsf{supp}(\widehat{W})} y_k\widehat{m}_k = \sum_{k\in\mathsf{supp}(\widehat{W})} y_k\widehat{w}_k.$$

The independence of the variables $\{y_k\}_{k\in[\![s_\mathcal{F}[\![}$ shows that, in this case, $\widehat{m}_k = \widehat{w}_k$ for all $k \in \mathsf{supp}(\widehat{W})$. This concretely means that $M^{(\beta)}$ contains W. However, we also have $\mathsf{pos}(i^*) \in \mathsf{supp}(\widehat{W})$. As, by definition of $i^* \in \mathcal{I}_{\neq}$, $m_{i^*}^{(\beta)} \neq m_{i^*}^{(1-\beta)}$, this means that $M^{(1-\beta)}$ does *not* contain W, which contradicts the restriction placed on patterns. This last case thus cannot occur, which concludes our proof.

5.3 Proof of Theorem 3

In the case of our second protocol, we need to proceed in two steps by using the intermediate games $\mathbf{game}_{j-1,2}$.

Lemma 1. *The difference* $|\mathbb{S}_{j-1,2} - \mathbb{S}_{j-1,1}|$ *is negligible under the* EXDH *assumption.*

Proof. Let $(g, g^a, g^{ab}, g^c, \zeta, \widetilde{g}, \widetilde{g}^a, \widetilde{g}^b) \in \mathbb{G}_1^5 \times \mathbb{G}_2^3$ be a EXDH instance.

Key Generation. The simulator generates random scalars $\{(u_k, v_k, v'_k, t_k)\}_{k\in[\![s_\mathcal{F}[\![}$ and implicitly sets the secret key $\mathsf{sk} = \{(x_k, y_k, z_k)\}_{k\in[\![s_\mathcal{F}[\![}$ with, for all $k \in [\![s_\mathcal{F}[\![$,

$$x_k = v_k + au_k\widehat{m}_k$$
$$y_k = v'_k - au_k$$
$$z_k = t_k \text{ if } k \neq \mathsf{pos}(i^*) \text{ and } z_{\mathsf{pos}(i^*)} = t_{\mathsf{pos}(i^*)} + ab.$$

Indeed, the simulator is able to compute the corresponding public key pk using g^a and g^{ab}. Note that the distribution of this public key is identical to the distribution of a regular public key.

Trapdoor Generation. To generate a trapdoor element $\mathsf{td}_{W,\delta} = \{T_1, T_2, T_3\}$ for a keyword W and an offset $\delta \in [\![s_\mathcal{F} - \ell + 1[\![$, the simulator sets

$$\widehat{W} = (\widehat{w}_0, \ldots, \widehat{w}_{s_\mathcal{F}-1}) := (\underbrace{\star, \ldots, \star}_{\delta}, w_0, \ldots, w_{\ell-1}, \underbrace{\star, \ldots, \star}_{s_\mathcal{F}-\ell-\delta})$$

and proceeds as follows:

- Case 1: $\widehat{w}_{\mathsf{pos}(i^*)} = \star$

  The simulator chooses $s_1, s_2 \xleftarrow{\$} \mathbb{Z}_p$ and returns $T_1 = \widetilde{g}^{s_1}, T_2 = \widetilde{g}^{s_2}$

  $$T_3 = \left(\prod_{k\in\mathsf{supp}(\widehat{W})} (\widetilde{g}^{x_k}(\widetilde{g}^{y_k})^{\widehat{w}_k})^{s_1}\right)\left(\prod_{k\in\mathsf{supp}(\widehat{W})} (\widetilde{g}^{z_k})^{s_2}\right).$$

  This last element T_3 can be computed from $\widetilde{g}^a$ as done for the public key. As $\mathsf{pos}(i^*)$ is not in the support of $\widehat{W}$, we do not need the element $\widetilde{g}^{ab}$ (which is not provided in the EXDH challenge).
- Case 2: $\widehat{w}_{\mathsf{pos}(i^*)} \neq \star$

  Let $J = \{k \in \mathsf{supp}(\widehat{W}) : \widehat{w}_k \neq \widehat{m}_k\}$. The condition on issued trapdoors and the definition of $i^* \in \mathcal{I}_{\neq}$ imply that this set is not empty, as seen at the end of proof of Theorem 2.

  The simulator selects $r, s_2 \xleftarrow{\$} \mathbb{Z}_p$ and implicitely sets

  $$s_1 = -bs_2\left(\sum_{k\in J} u_k(\widehat{m}_k - \widehat{w}_k)\right)^{-1} + r.$$

  For all $k \in [\![s_\mathcal{F}[\![$, u_k is uniformly distributed and the view of the adversary is independent of these variables: they only appear in x_k and y_k where they are perfectly masked by v_k and v'_k. As a result, one has $\sum_{k\in J} u_k(\widehat{m}_k - \widehat{w}_k) = 0$ with negligible probability $1/p$.
  Then, the simulator returns $T_1 = \widetilde{g}^{s_1}, T_2 = \widetilde{g}^{s_2}$ using $\widetilde{g}^b$ and

  $$T_3 = \left(\prod_{k\in\mathsf{supp}(\widehat{W})} (\widetilde{g}^{s_1})^{v_k + v'_k\widehat{w}_k}\right)\left(\prod_{k\in J} (\widetilde{g}^a)^{ru_k(\widehat{m}_k - \widehat{w}_k)}\right)\left(\prod_{k\in\mathsf{supp}(\widehat{W})} \widetilde{g}^{s_2 t_k}\right)$$

using $\widetilde{g}^a$ and $\widetilde{g}^b$.
Developing $s_1 \sum_{k\in\mathsf{supp}(\widehat{W})} x_k + y_k\widehat{w}_k + s_2 \sum_{k\in\mathsf{supp}(\widehat{W})} z_k$ shows that T_3 is correctly generated. In particular the term $\widetilde{g}^{ab}$ in $\widetilde{g}^{z_{\mathsf{pos}(i^*)}}$ cancels out thanks to the definition of x_k, y_k and s_1.
Moreover, the trapdoor element is well distributed as s_1, s_2 are well distributed.

Challenge Generation. The simulator generates the challenge ciphertext as follows:

- $C_h = \begin{cases} g^{a_h} \text{ with } a_h \xleftarrow{\$} \mathbb{Z}_p & \text{for all } h \in [\![n_{\mathcal{F}}[\![\setminus\{\mathbf{frag}(i^*)\} \\ g^c & \text{for } h = \mathbf{frag}(i^*) \end{cases}$
- $C'_{i,1} = \begin{cases} (g^{x_{\mathsf{pos}(i)}}(g^{y_{\mathsf{pos}(i)}})^{m_i^{(\beta)}})^{a_{\mathsf{frag}(i)}} & \text{for all } i \in [\![n - d_{\mathcal{F}}[\![\setminus(\mathcal{F}_{\mathbf{frag}(i^*)} \cup \mathcal{I}_{\neq}^{(j-1)}) \\ (g^c)^{v_{\mathsf{pos}(i)}+v'_{\mathsf{pos}(i)}m_i^{(\beta)}} & \text{for all } i \in \mathcal{F}_{\mathbf{frag}(i^*)} \setminus \mathcal{I}_{\neq}^{(j-1)} \\ \xleftarrow{\$} \mathbb{G}_1 & \text{for all } i \in \mathcal{I}_{\neq}^{(j-1)} \end{cases}$
- $C'_{i,2} = \begin{cases} (g^{z_{\mathsf{pos}(i)}})^{a_{\mathsf{frag}(i)}} & \text{for all } i \in [\![n - d_{\mathcal{F}}[\![\setminus(\mathcal{F}_{\mathbf{frag}(i^*)} \cup \mathcal{I}_{\neq}^{(j)}) \\ (g^c)^{t_{\mathsf{pos}(i)}} & \text{for all } i \in \mathcal{F}_{\mathbf{frag}(i^*)} \setminus \mathcal{I}_{\neq}^{(j)} \\ \xleftarrow{\$} \mathbb{G}_1 & \text{for all } i \in \mathcal{I}_{\neq}^{(j-1)} \\ (g^c)^{t_{\mathsf{pos}(i^*)}}\zeta & \text{for } i = i^* \end{cases}$
- all the overlined elements of C as in $\mathtt{Encrypt}(M^{(\beta)}, \mathsf{pk})$.

Note that either $\zeta = g^{abc}$ and the game is $\mathbf{game}_{j-1,1}$ as $C'_{i^*,2}$ is well-formed or ζ is random and the game is $\mathbf{game}_{j-1,2}$. Any adversary able to distinguish these two games can then be used against the EXDH assumption.

Lemma 2. *The difference* $|\mathbb{S}_{j,1} - \mathbb{S}_{j-1,2}|$ *is negligible under the* EXDH *assumption.*

Proof. Let $(g, g^a, g^{ab}, g^c, \zeta, \widetilde{g}, \widetilde{g}^a, \widetilde{g}^b) \in \mathbb{G}_1^5 \times \mathbb{G}_2^3$ be a EXDH instance.

Key Generation. The simulator generates random scalars $\{v_k, y_k, t_k\}_k \in [\![s_{\mathcal{F}}[\![$ and implicitly sets the secret key $\mathsf{sk} = \{(x_k, y_k, z_k)\}_{k\in[\![s_{\mathcal{F}}[\![}$ with, for all $k \in [\![s_{\mathcal{F}}[\![$,

$$x_k = v_k \text{ if } k \neq \mathsf{pos}(i^*) \text{ and } x_{\mathsf{pos}(i^*)} = v_{\mathsf{pos}(i^*)} + ab,$$
$$z_k = t_k \text{ if } k \neq \mathsf{pos}(i^*) \text{ and } z_{\mathsf{pos}(i^*)} = t_{\mathsf{pos}(i^*)} + a.$$

Indeed, the simulator is able to compute the public key pk associated with this secret key by using g^a and g^{ab}. Note that the distribution of this public key is identical to the distribution of a regular public key.

Trapdoor Generation. To issue a trapdoor element $\mathsf{td}_{W,\delta} = \{T_1, T_2, T_3\}$ for a keyword W and an offset $\delta \in [\![s_\mathcal{F} - \ell + 1[\![$, the simulator sets

$$\widehat{W} = (\widehat{w}_0, \dots, \widehat{w}_{s_\mathcal{F}-1}) := (\underbrace{\star, \dots, \star}_{\delta}, w_0, \dots, w_{\ell-1}, \underbrace{\star, \dots, \star}_{s_\mathcal{F}-\ell-\delta})$$

and proceeds as follows:

- Case 1: $\widehat{w}_{\mathsf{pos}(i^*)} = \star$
  The simulator acts exactly as in the protocol because the elements from the EXDH instance are only involved in $x_{\mathsf{pos}(i^*)}$ and $z_{\mathsf{pos}(i^*)}$.
- Case 2: $\widehat{w}_{\mathsf{pos}(i)^*} \neq \star$
  The simulator selects $r, s_1 \xleftarrow{\$} \mathbb{Z}_p$ and implicitly sets $s_2 := -bs_1 + r$. Then, it returns $T_1 = \widetilde{g}^{s_1}$, $T_2 = \widetilde{g}^{s_2}$ using $\widetilde{g}^b$ and

$$T_3 = \left(\prod_{k \in \mathsf{supp}(\widehat{W})} \widetilde{g}^{s_1(v_k + y_k \widehat{w}_k)} \right) \left(\prod_{k \in \mathsf{supp}(\widehat{W})} (\widetilde{g}^{s_2})^{t_k} \right) (\widetilde{g}^a)^r \text{ using } \widetilde{g}^a \text{ and } \widetilde{g}^b.$$

  Developping $s_1 \sum_{k \in \mathsf{supp}(\widehat{W})} [x_k + y_k \widehat{w}_k] + s_2 \sum_{k \in \mathsf{supp}(\widehat{W})} z_k$ shows that T_3 is correctly generated. Moreover, the trapdoor element is well distributed as s_1, s_2 are well distributed.

Challenge Generation. The simulator generates the challenge ciphertext as follows :

- $C_h = \begin{cases} g^{a_h} \text{ with } a_h \xleftarrow{\$} \mathbb{Z}_p & \text{for all } h \in [\![n_\mathcal{F}[\![\setminus \{\mathbf{frag}(i^*)\} \\ g^c & \text{for } h = \mathbf{frag}(i^*) \end{cases}$
- $C'_{i,1} = \begin{cases} (g^{x_{\mathsf{pos}(i)}} (g^{y_{\mathsf{pos}(i)}} m_i^{(\beta)})^{a_{\mathsf{frag}(i)}} & \text{for all } i \in [\![n - d_\mathcal{F}[\![\setminus (\mathcal{F}_{\mathsf{frag}(i^*)} \cup \mathcal{I}_{\neq}^{(j)}) \\ (g^c)^{v_{\mathsf{pos}(i)} + y_{\mathsf{pos}(i)} m_i^{(\beta)}} & \text{for all } i \in \mathcal{F}_{\mathsf{frag}(i^*)} \setminus \mathcal{I}_{\neq}^{(j)} \\ \xleftarrow{\$} \mathbb{G}_1 & \text{for all } i \in \mathcal{I}_{\neq}^{(j-1)} \\ (g^c)^{y_{\mathsf{pos}(i^*)} m_{i^*}^{(\beta)}} \zeta & \text{for } i = i^* \end{cases}$
- $C'_{i,2} = \begin{cases} (g^{z_{\mathsf{pos}(i)}})^{a_{\mathsf{frag}(i)}} & \text{for all } i \in [\![n - d_\mathcal{F}[\![\setminus (\mathcal{F}_{\mathsf{frag}(i^*)} \cup \mathcal{I}_{\neq}^{(j)}) \\ (g^c)^{t_{\mathsf{pos}(i)}} & \text{for all } i \in \mathcal{F}_{\mathsf{frag}(i^*)} \setminus \mathcal{I}_{\neq}^{(j)} \\ \xleftarrow{\$} \mathbb{G}_1 & \text{for all } i \in \mathcal{I}_{\neq}^{(j)} \end{cases}$
- all the overlined elements of C as in $\mathtt{Encrypt}(M^{(\beta)}, \mathsf{pk})$.

Note that either $\zeta = g^{abc}$ and the game is $\mathbf{game}_{j-1,2}$ as $C'_{i^*,1}$ is well-formed or ζ is random and the game is $\mathbf{game}_{j,1}$. Any adversary able to distinguish these two games can then be used against the EXDH assumption.

6 Complexity Analysis

Table 1 in Sect. 1.2 provides a comparison on some specific metrics with two relevant constructions of the state-of-the-art, namely [13] and [3]. We here provide a more comprehensive performance assessment of our constructions that we only compare to [3] as the latter outperforms [13].

6.1 Space Complexity

In this part, we focus on the size of the different elements involved in SEPM constructions. To have a common metric, we implement our bilinear groups using the BLS12-381 curve [9], yielding 48-Bytes (compressed) elements of $\mathbb{G}_1$, 96-Bytes (compressed) elements of $\mathbb{G}_2$ and 572-Bytes elements of $\mathbb{G}_T$. To provide a fair comparison, we select the same parameters as in [3] and thus consider the encryption of 1GB bytestrings where any pattern of size at most 10KB (*i.e.* $\mathrm{L} = 10000$) can be searched. The results are presented in Table 2. One can note that the results for [3] differ from those provided in the original paper. This is due in part to the use of Barreto-Naehrig curves [2] in [3] that are now deprecated. Regarding the size of the public key, the difference also stems from an error in [3] as the authors do not take into account the $|\mathcal{S}|$ factor in their computations. For bytestrings, we have $|\mathcal{S}| = 256$, which is quite significant.

Table 2 highlights the difference between our constructions and the one in [3], in particular regarding the size of the public key where ours are about 100 times smaller. Our first construction also halves the size of the ciphertext but the latter remains large. Improving this characteristic while retaining the nice features of SEPM is an open problem.

Table 2. Comparison with the state of the art

	Schemes		
	AS^{3}E ([3])	Sect. 4.3	Sect. 4.4
Public Key	247 MB	1.92 MB	2.88 MB
Ciphertext	192 GB	96 GB	192 GB
Trapdoor	1.92 MB	1.92 MB	2.88 MB

6.2 Computational Complexity

We now focus on the computational cost of the `Encrypt`, `Issue` and `Test` procedures by providing in Table 3 an estimation of the number of operations required to perform them. We set n as the length of the message to encrypt and L as the bound on the size of searchable patterns. As the treatment of wildcard and non-wildcard characters strongly differs in our `Test` procedure, we assume that the searched pattern contains c non-wildcard characters.

In our case, the encryption can be speeded up by (pre-)computing the 2^8 elements $\{(Y_k)^b\}_{k \in [\![s_{\mathcal{F}} [\![, b \in [\![2^8 [\![}$ and use the results to directly generate the ciphertext elements. Compared to the naive protocol description in Sects. 4.3 and 4.4, this saves $2n$ exponentiations.

Table 3. Comparison with the state of the art. For $i \in \{1, 2, T\}$, $\mathbf{m}_i$ (resp. $\mathbf{e}_i$) stands for one multiplication (resp. exponentiation) in $\mathbb{G}_i$ and $\mathbf{P}$ for one pairing.

	Schemes		
	AS³E ([3])	Sect. 4.3	Sect. 4.4
`Encrypt`	$4n\mathbf{e}_1$	$\left(4n + \frac{n}{L}\right)\mathbf{e}_1 + n\mathbf{m}_1$	$\left(6n + \frac{n}{L}\right)\mathbf{e}_1 + n\mathbf{m}_1$
`Issue`	$2L\mathbf{e}_2$	$2L\mathbf{e}_2$	$3L\mathbf{e}_2$
`Test`	$nc\mathbf{m}_1 + 2n\mathbf{P}$	$nc\mathbf{m}_1 + 2n\mathbf{P}$	$2nc\mathbf{m}_1 + 3n\mathbf{P} + n\mathbf{m}_T$

Our comparison shows that the performance of all these schemes is very similar and essentially requires a few exponentiations in $\mathbb{G}_1$ to encrypt one byte and 2 pairings per byte for detections. The concrete performance will obviously depend on the devices performing these computations. We nevertheless note that, for all these schemes, these computations are embarrassingly parallelizable.

Acknowledgements. The second author was supported by the French ANR ALAMBIC project ANR-16-CE39-0006. The third author is grateful for the support of the ANR through project ANR-19-CE39-0011–04 PRESTO and project ANR-18-CE-39–0019-02 MobiS5.

References

1. Abdalla, M., et al.: Searchable encryption revisited: consistency properties, relation to anonymous IBE, and extensions. J. Cryptol. **21**(3), 350–391 (2008)
2. Barreto, P.S.L.M., Naehrig, M.: Pairing-friendly elliptic curves of prime order. In: Preneel, B., Tavares, S. (eds.) SAC 2005. LNCS, vol. 3897, pp. 319–331. Springer, Heidelberg (2006). https://doi.org/10.1007/11693383_22
3. Bkakria, A., Cuppens-Boulahia, N., Cuppens, F.: Privacy-preserving pattern matching on encrypted data. In: Moriai, S., Wang, H., (eds.) *ASIACRYPT 2020, Part II*, vol. 12492 of *LNCS*, pp. 191–220. Springer, Heidelberg (2020)
4. Boneh, D., Di Crescenzo, G., Ostrovsky, R., Persiano, G.: Public key encryption with keyword search. In: Cachin, C., Camenisch, J.L. (eds.) EUROCRYPT 2004. LNCS, vol. 3027, pp. 506–522. Springer, Heidelberg (2004). https://doi.org/10.1007/978-3-540-24676-3_30
5. Boneh, D., Raghunathan, A., Segev, G.: Function-private identity-based encryption: hiding the function in functional encryption. In: Canetti, R., Garay, J.A. (eds.) CRYPTO 2013. LNCS, vol. 8043, pp. 461–478. Springer, Heidelberg (2013). https://doi.org/10.1007/978-3-642-40084-1_26

6. Boneh, D., Sahai, A., Waters, B.: Functional encryption: definitions and challenges. In: Ishai, Y. (ed.) TCC 2011. LNCS, vol. 6597, pp. 253–273. Springer, Heidelberg (2011). https://doi.org/10.1007/978-3-642-19571-6_16
7. Boneh, D., Waters, B.: Conjunctive, subset, and range queries on encrypted data. In: Vadhan, S.P. (ed.) TCC 2007. LNCS, vol. 4392, pp. 535–554. Springer, Heidelberg (2007). https://doi.org/10.1007/978-3-540-70936-7_29
8. Bossuat, A., Bost, R., Fouque, P. A., Minaud, B., Reichle, M.: Forward secure searchable encryption. In: Edgar, R., et al. (eds.) ACM CCS 2016, pp. 1143–1154. ACM Press (2016)
9. Bowe, S.: BLS12-381: new zk-SNARK elliptic curve construction (2017). electriccoin.co/blog/new-snark-curve/
10. Canard, S., Diop, A., Kheir, N., Paindavoine, M., Sabt, M.: BlindIDS: market-compliant and privacy-friendly intrusion detection system over encrypted traffic. In: Karri, R., Sinanoglu, O., Sadeghi, A., Yi, A., (eds.) ASIACCS 17, pp. 561–574. ACM Press (2017)
11. Canard, S., Pointcheval, D., Sanders, O., Traoré, J.: Divisible E-cash made practical. In: Katz, J. (ed.) PKC 2015. LNCS, vol. 9020, pp. 77–100. Springer, Heidelberg (2015). https://doi.org/10.1007/978-3-662-46447-2_4
12. Curtmola, R., Garay, J.A., Kamara, S., Ostrovsky, R.: Searchable symmetric encryption: improved definitions and efficient constructions. In: Juels, A., et al. (eds.) ACM CCS 2006, pp. 79–88. ACM Press (2006)
13. Desmoulins, N., Fouque, P., Onete, C., Sanders, O.: Pattern matching on encrypted streams. In: Peyrin, T., Galbraith, S., (eds.) *ASIACRYPT 2018, Part I*, vol. 11272 of *LNCS*, pp. 121–148. Springer, Heidelberg (2018)
14. Galbraith, S.D., Paterson, K.G., Smart, N.P.: Pairings for cryptographers. Disc. Appl. Math. **156**(16), 3113–3121 (2008)
15. Gentry, C.: Fully homomorphic encryption using ideal lattices. In: Mitzenmacher, M., (ed.) 41st ACM STOC, pp. 169–178. ACM Press (2009)
16. Katz, J., Sahai, A., Waters, B.: Predicate encryption supporting disjunctions, polynomial equations, and inner products. J. Cryptol. **26**(2), 191–224 (2013)
17. Lai, S., et al.: Practical encrypted network traffic pattern matching for secure middleboxes. IEEE Trans. Depend. Secure Comput. p. 1 (2021)
18. Leontiadis, I., Li, M.: Storage efficient substring searchable symmetric encryption. In: Proceedings of the 6th International Workshop on Security in Cloud Computing, SCC '18, pp. 3–13. Association for Computing Machinery (2018)
19. Pointcheval, D., Sanders, O.: Short randomizable signatures. In: Sako, K. (eds.) Topics in Cryptology - CT-RSA 2016. CT-RSA 2016. LNCS, vol. 9610. Springer, Cham (2016). https://doi.org/10.1007/978-3-319-29485-8_7
20. Sedghi, S., van Liesdonk, P., Nikova, S., Hartel, P., Jonker, W.: Searching keywords with wildcards on encrypted data. In: Garay, J.A., De Prisco, R. (eds.) SCN 2010. LNCS, vol. 6280, pp. 138–153. Springer, Heidelberg (2010). https://doi.org/10.1007/978-3-642-15317-4_10
21. Sherry, J., Lan, C., Popa, R. A., Ratnasamy, S.: Deep packet inspection over encrypted traffic:blindbox. In: Uhlig, S., Maennel, O., Karp, B., Padhye, J., (eds.) SIGCOMM **2015**, 213–226 (2015)
22. Song, D.X., Wagner, D., Perrig, A.: Practical techniques for searches on encrypted data. In: 2000 IEEE Symposium on Security and Privacy, pp. 44–55. IEEE Computer Society Press (2000)
23. Sun, S., et al.: Practical backward-secure searchable encryption from symmetric puncturable encryption. In: Lie, D., et al. (eds.) ACM CCS 2018, pp. 763–780. ACM Press (2018)

Bounded Collusion ABE for TMs from IBE

Rishab Goyal[1(✉)], Ridwan Syed[2(✉)], and Brent Waters[2,3(✉)]

[1] MIT, Cambridge, MA, USA
goyal@utexas.edu
[2] University of Texas at Austin, Austin, TX, USA
bwaters@cs.utexas.edu
[3] NTT Research, Sunnyvale, CA, USA

Abstract. We give an attribute-based encryption system for Turing Machines that is provably secure assuming only the existence of identity-based encryption (IBE) for large identity spaces. Currently, IBE is known to be realizable from most mainstream number theoretic assumptions that imply public key cryptography including factoring, the search Diffie-Hellman assumption, and the Learning with Errors assumption.

Our core construction provides security against an attacker that makes a single key query for a machine T *before* declaring a challenge string w^* that is associated with the challenge ciphertext. We build our construction by leveraging a Garbled RAM construction of Gentry, Halevi, Raykova and Wichs [33]; however, to prove security we need to introduce a new notion of security called iterated simulation security.

We then show how to transform our core construction into one that is secure for an a-priori bounded number $q = q(\lambda)$ of key queries that can occur either before or after the challenge ciphertext. We do this by first showing how one can use a special type of non-committing encryption to transform a system that is secure only if a single key is chosen before the challenge ciphertext is declared into one where the single key can be requested either before or after the challenge ciphertext. We give a simple construction of this non-committing encryption from public key encryption in the Random Oracle Model. Next, one can apply standard combinatorial techniques to lift from single-key adaptive security to q-key adaptive security.

1 Introduction

Attribute-based encryption (ABE) [58] provides a method for encrypting data which allows for sharing at a much finer-grained level than standard public key

R. Goyal—Work done in part while at UT Austin supported by IBM PhD Fellowship, and at the Simons Institute for the Theory of Computing supported by Simons-Berkeley research fellowship. Research supported in part by NSF CNS Award #1718161, an IBM-MIT grant, and by the Defense Advanced Research Projects Agency (DARPA) under Contract No. HR00112020023. Any opinions, findings and conclusions or recommendations expressed in this material are those of the author(s) and do not necessarily reflect the views of the United States Government or DARPA.
B. Waters—Supported by NSF CNS-1908611, CNS-1414082, DARPA SafeWare, Packard Foundation Fellowship, and Simons Investigator Award.

M. Tibouchi and H. Wang (Eds.): ASIACRYPT 2021, LNCS 13093, pp. 371–402, 2021.
https://doi.org/10.1007/978-3-030-92068-5_13

cryptography. In an ABE system one associates a ciphertext with an attribute string w when encrypting message m to form a ciphertext ct. A secret key (as issued by some authority) is associated with a predicate function f. A decryption algorithm using sk_f on the ciphertext will be able to return the message m if and only if $f(w) = 1$.

The initial and many subsequent ABE constructions (e.g. [12,43]) provided functionality for when f was a boolean formula or circuit that would operate over a fixed set of attributes. This works well for the setting when an attribute string could say represent a record that was of a fixed form, however, would not work as well in a setting where we want the attribute string structure to be less rigid and of arbitrary length. Initial progress towards resolving such issue was by Waters [60] who provided the first ABE construction for a uniform model of computation where the attribute string $w \in \{0,1\}^*$ could be an arbitrary length string and f is a Deterministic Finite Automata (DFA). A user in such a setting can decrypt a ciphertext whenever the DFA f accepts w.

Since then, ABE systems in uniform models of computation have been very well studied, with subsequent works roughly falling into the following three categories grouped by the hardness assumption.

- The ABE construction of Waters [60] for DFAs was built from bilinear maps and was collusion resistant in that it allowed for an unbounded number of private keys to be issued, but was only selectively secure in that the attacker was required to submit a challenge string w^* before seeing the public parameters of the system. Unlike constructions where the length of w is fixed by the security parameter, there is no known way of generically moving from selective to adaptive security using complexity leveraging and assuming subexponential hardness. Subsequent works [1,4,9,10,37,38] in the bilinear map setting improved upon the security arguments in this setting as well as gave "ciphertext-policy" variants of the construction.
- A second cohort of constructions [13,16,44,50] arise by constructing ABE for Turing Machines from obfuscation culminating in the work of Ananth and Sahai [8] that achieves functional encryption for Turing Machines from indistinguishability obfuscation with no a-priori bound on the input size or machine description. We refer the reader to [8] for a discussion of the tradeoffs present in prior works.
- In a third line of work, Agrawal and Singh [5] gave a construction of a single-key secure functional encryption scheme provably secure under the Learning with Errors (LWE) [56] assumption. They could prove security only when the single private key was requested before the challenge ciphertext. Additionally, in their model the encryptor had to specify the maximum time t that the Turing Machine computation is allowed to run for during decryption. The work of Gentry et al. [34] also gave a construction for single-key secure functional encryption for RAM computation from single-key secure functional encryption for circuits and garbled RAM, but the key generator not only takes the RAM program as input but the input size and run-time bound as well. Thus, the encryption algorithm could only encrypt messages of a-priori fixed length.

For unbounded collusions, Boyen and Li [15] gave constructions for DFAs from the LWE assumption and Agrawal, Maitra, and Yamada [3] did this for NFAs, but in the secret key setting. Ananth, Fan and Shi [6] give an LWE solution for unbounded collusions in the problem of constructing ABE for RAM Turing Machines. However, the maximum number of machine steps is given as a parameter to the setup algorithm and will serve as a bound for the system.

One common thread of the above works is that they all depended upon a specific number theoretic setting. Even in the case of indistinguishability obfuscation, the best known construction in the recent breakthrough work [47] relies on a careful combination of *multiple* specific algebraic assumptions.

Here we pursue a new direction of obtaining Attribute-Based Encryption for uniform computation models from general assumptions. In particular, we provide solutions that assume Identity-Based Encryption (IBE) [14,59]. We believe IBE is a good platform for this pursuit as it is known under most "mainstream" number theoretic assumptions that imply public key cryptography such as factoring, search Diffie-Hellman, and Learning with Errors [14,20,22,35].

Our Results. In this work we show how to achieve Attribute-Based Encryption for Turing Machines that is adaptively secure against any attacker that requests at most $q = q(\lambda)$ private keys where q can be any polynomial function determined at system setup. Our work is logically broken into two parts.

In the first part we develop our core construction which is an ABE system for Turing Machines secure against any poly-time attacker that requests a single key *before* declaring the attribute string w^* for a challenge ciphertext. In this system the maximum running time t of the Turing Machine is determined by the encryption algorithm as in [5].

Our approach leverages a garbled RAM construction due to Gentry, Halevi, Raykova, and Wichs (GHRW) [33] which intuitively allows a sequence of t garbled programs to run while maintaining a persistent database across invocations. We combine this with an IBE system in a spirit motivated by [22,23,27,31] which allows us to securely evaluate a Turing Machine computation that delivers the message on decryption only if the machine accepts. One challenge we encounter is that the GHRW definition of simulation security is defined as distinguishing between a real garbled RAM and a simulated one over the *whole* computation. However, this notion of simulation is not fine-grained enough for our purposes. Instead we need to introduce a notion of *iterated simulation security* where it is hard to distinguish whether the first i or $i+1$ programs were simulated, and not just indistinguishability of the entire computation. Fortunately, we were able to show that the existing GHRW construction satisfies this notion of security as well. Since the GHRW Garbled RAM itself only relies on IBE, the entire security of our construction still depends on IBE only.

The second part of our work is focused on moving from a single key system that is limited to coming before the challenge ciphertext to a q-query system that allows for key requests to come at arbitrary times. We first tackle the question of giving flexibility for when the key query is placed. To do this we use a very relaxed form of non-committing encryption [17,21,48] where the non-committing simulation property must hold when an attacker is given the secret key of a public key encryption system. (But not the randomness for encryption and key generation as in [17].) We show that this form of non-committing encryption is strong enough to transform our single key ABE system into one where the key query can come before or after the challenge ciphertext. We follow this transformation with another one to allow for q queries by applying standard combinatorial techniques. To complete the transformation we provide a simple construction for such a non-committing encryption scheme from public key encryption in the case of bounded length messages, while for unbounded messages we additionally rely on hash function modeled as a Random Oracle [11]. The non-committing encryption we consider in this work is very similar to that of receiver non-committing encryption [18].

We want to emphasize that prior to our work, all other ABE systems in uniform computation models either relied on specific algebraic assumptions, or powerful notions such as succinct function encryption and program obfuscation. That is, unlike for non-uniform models where we have numerous generic constructions (e.g., [7,39,57]) from general assumptions such as public-key encryption, it was believed that relying on algebraic manipulation or powerful encryption/obfuscation primitives might be necessary for handling uniform models where the attribute space is not statically fixed. Ours is the first work that dispels this belief. Thus, we want to highlight that one of our main take-away messages is that the central source of hardness is only full collusion resistance, and not the underlying model of computation in functional encryption.

Organization. We begin by providing a technical overview of our approach in the next section. Since our bounded collusion secure ABE system for TM predicates relies extensively on garbled RAM, thus we start by describing our notations and other standard cryptographic primitives in Sect. 2, and recalling the definition of garbled RAM along with the our proposed iterated simulation security definition in Sect. 3. In Sect. 4, we describe our main construction for ABE for TMs via the usage of IBE and garbled RAM. In the full version [42], we describe how to lift our core construction to general q-query adaptively secure scheme.

1.1 Technical Overview

The overview is split into two parts where we first describe our core construction from garbled RAM and identity-based encryption. This construction gives us 1-query secure ABE scheme for TMs where the secret key query must be made before obtaining the challenge ciphertext. In the second part, we describe how to lift the security of any ABE scheme for TMs, which guarantees security in this restricted 1-query key-selective setting, to provide general bounded collusion security via a sequence of generic black-box transformations. We conclude with some interesting open directions for further investigation.

Core construction: 1-query key-selective ABE for TMs.
As highlighted in the previous section, the aspect of ABE systems in a uniform model of computation (such as Turing Machines in our case) that makes it quite appealing is that it allows an encryptor to specify an a-priori *unbounded* length attribute during encryption while still enabling a fixed decryption key to work on all such varying length ciphertexts. From a mechnical perspective, this suggests that ciphertexts for such computation models should possess a self-reducibility feature. By this we mean that in a structural sense the ciphertext could be broadly divided into two components—one being reusable, while other being execution time-step dependent. Here we expect the reusable component to store the current state of computation during decryption, and the time-step dependent component to self-reduce, i.e. to be used piece-by-piece (with each piece annotated with an execution time-step) for updating the reusable component thereby guiding the decryption process to either the plaintext or failure depending on the predicate.

Comparing this mechnical view with that for ABE systems in a non-uniform model of computation, the stark difference comes up in the implementation of the reusable component which for non-uniform models could mostly be relegated to the predicate key instead, since each key already fixes an upper bound on the number of such re-use operations/computation steps. This restriction is very consequential both for the construction as well as proof purposes. Circumventing such unbounded reusability problems under standard cryptographic assumptions has been a difficult task so far.

Our approach is to start with the simplest goal which is of security in presence of a single key corruption where the challenge attribute as well as the TM key queried must be selectively chosen by the attacker.[1] Now we already know that the concept of garbled circuits [62] have been tremendously useful in building bounded collusion secure ABE systems in a non-uniform circuit model (and bounded collusion secure functional encryption more generally) [39,57]. A natural question is whether the same could be stated if we switch to a uniform computation model such as TMs since, despite the strengthening of the computation model, the targetted encryption primitive still provides only an all-or-nothing style guarantee.

A building block construction. First, note that plugging in TMs as the model of computation in the mechnical picture described above, we get the reusable ciphertext component to correspond to the tape of the TM being operated on, while the time-step dependent component is being used to emulate a step-by-step execution of the TM itself. Next, consider a highly simplified TM model where the number of states as well as the size of the TM tape are a-priori fixed polynomials, say N and L respectively. (Although this simplified model no longer resembles our targetted TM model of computation, this will serve as

[1] As we later show, such a core encryption scheme with such simple and weak security guarantees could be generically amplified to better and more general bounded collusion security guarantees.

a good starting point to convey the main idea which we afterwards extend to capture the more general model.) It turns out that for such a model there is a natural candidate ABE system from just plain public-key encryption and garbled circuits.

Let us start by sharing our methodology for encrypting a message m under attribute string w with time bound t.[2] At a high level, the idea is to let encryptor create a sequence of t step circuits, where each step circuit takes as input the entire state of TM (which contains the current state, location of the tape header, and the entire tape of the TM) and it performs one execution step (that is, applies one transition) and its output is the entire TM state after this execution step (that is, output state, tape header and full tape contents). Here the last step circuit simply outputs the encrypted message m if the execution lands in accepting state. An encryptor then garbles each such step circuit starting from the last one (that is, t-th step circuit first), and encodes the wire labels for the i-th garbled step circuit in the $(i-1)$-th step circuit. Now each garbled circuit must not output the wire labels in the clear, thus it instead encrypts the labels corresponding to the TM state for next step circuit under a group of carefully selected PKE public keys. The idea here is that during setup we sample a pair of PKE public-secret keys for each state transition[3], and a secret key for any TM in this system consists of a sequence of PKE secret keys corresponding to all the state transition supported by the corresponding TM.

Intuitively, a ciphertext consists of a sequence of t garbled circuits, and a secret key consists of a polynomial-sized set of PKE secret keys such that to decrypt a ciphertext, one evaluates each garbled circuit in a sequential order thereby revealing the state of the TM computation after each execution step encrypted under appropriate PKE public keys. An honest decryptor can always recover the relevant garbled circuit wires along its path of computation, and finally recovers the message if the machine accepts within the ciphertext specified time bound t. One could also provide security of this construction by a straightforward sequence of hybrids where the simulator would, instead of computing the garbled circuits honestly, replace each garbled circuit with a simulated garbled circuit one by one. And, since our assumption was the tape size and number of states to be polynomially bounded, thus this scheme is efficient (i.e., runs in polynomial time) as well.

Looking ahead, the above approach serves as a good warm-up construction for our core construction which does not suffer from the above limitations. Very briefly, we make the following observations. First, note that the above construction does not exploit the fact that a given step circuit does not need to look at the entire TM tape, but instead it needs to make changes right next to the location of tape header. Thus, instead of passing around the entire TM tape to each step circuit, we can maintain a persistent storage that contains the full TM tape while each step circuit only affects a few particular locations in the storage.

---

[2] Recall that in this work we require the encryptor to provide an upper bound on the running time of the TM.

[3] Since the number of states is polynomially bounded, thus this is efficient.

To this end, we replace our usage of garbled circuits with garbled RAMs [53] thereby bypassing the above problem. Second, we assumed that the number of states are a-priori polynomially bounded. This was mainly needed so to avoid the exponential blow-up due to the exponential state space which we could not hope to generically encode using only public-key encryption. To solve this issue, we use an identity-based encryption scheme to provide a succinct mechanism to encode the state transitions without this exponential blow-up. Similar ideas of encoding exponential size strings succinctly have been used in numerous other contexts [2,22,26,27,40].

Main construction. Before moving to a more technical description of our scheme, we fix our notation and interpretation of a TM. This will help in understanding our main construction more clearly. We consider a TM to be represented by a large set T of state transitions $\{(q^{\mathsf{in}}, b^{\mathsf{in}}, q^{\mathsf{out}}, b^{\mathsf{out}}, \mathsf{dir})\}$, where each transition is associated with an input state q^{in}, the input bit read b^{in}, the output state q^{out}, the bit to written b^{out}, and the direction dir in which the tape head moves. Also, let each state q be represented as an n-bit string.

As hinted previously, a central component of our construction is the notion of garbled RAMs. Recall that a RAM program P gets random access to a *large* memory D (upon which it can perform arbitrary reads and writes) along with a short input x, and at the end of its computation it produces an output y. Here we will be interested in multi-program versions of RAM programs where given a sequence of RAM programs $P_1, \ldots, P_\ell$ and corresponding short inputs $x_1, \ldots, x_\ell$, and an initial memory D, the programs are run in succession on their respective inputs wherein say program P_i outputs some result y_i and updates the database D which is then used by the next program P_{i+1}.

Garbled RAMs. The notion of garbled RAMs is a generalization of circuit garbling to RAM programs, where the memory owner first garbles the memory D generating a pair of garbled database $\widetilde{D}$ along with a garbling key k_D. The garbling key k_D can then be used to garble any RAM program P with respect to program index j to produce a garbled program $\widetilde{P}$ along with input labels $\{\mathsf{lab}_{i,b}\}_{i,b}$. Here the program index j is meant to capture the number of programs that have been run (including P).[4] For example, to garble the previously defined sequence of ℓ RAM programs, when the garbling party runs the program garbling procedure for program P_j it specifies index j as the program index since it wants P_j to be the j-th RAM program being evaluated in the sequence. Also, as in the case of circuit garbling, to evaluate a garbled program $\widetilde{P}$ with labels $\{\mathsf{lab}_{i,b}\}_{i,b}$ on an input x, the evaluator selects the labels corresponding to bits of x, i.e. $y = \mathsf{Eval}^{\widetilde{D}}(\widetilde{P}, \{\mathsf{lab}_{i,x_i}\}_i)$ where y is the output of running P on x with memory D. The standard security property considered in most prior works [28,29,32,33,53,54] is of static (full) simulation security wherein an adversary must not be able to

[4] For the purposes of a technical overview, we significantly simplify and relax the notation. Here we consider each program to be of fixed length, and not take time range among other things as additional inputs. Later in the main body, we define it in full generality.

distinguish a sequence of honestly garbled RAM programs and database from a simulated sequence of programs and database, where the simulator only knows the corresponding outputs $\{y_i\}_i$ of each RAM program (but not the database D, or any of the individual programs P_i, or their corresponding inputs x_i).

Core construction: *switching from garbled circuits to garbled RAMs.* With all the notation set, our main construction is very simple to follow. The setup of our system simply corresponds to sampling a IBE master public-secret key pair. (Recall that previously in our simplified building block construction, the setup was sampling a large number of PKE public-secret key pairs. As we noted then, here we use IBE instead of do the same more efficiently.) Next, to generate a secret key for a TM represented by a set T of transitions, the key generator encodes each transition $(q^{\mathsf{in}}, b^{\mathsf{in}}, q^{\mathsf{out}}, b^{\mathsf{out}}, \mathsf{dir}) \in T$ into $(n+2)$ distinct identities. (The identity-encodings we employ are the well known bit-decomposition style encodings where one encodes the output state q^{out} bit-by-bit into n strings of the form $(i, q^{\mathsf{out}}[i]) \in [n] \times \{0, 1\}$.) Here n of these IDs jointly encode the output state q^{out}, while the other two encode the output bit to written b^{out}, and the direction dir separately.

The encryption algorithm in our core construction follows a similar paradigm to that described in our building block construction with the only major change being we move to using garbled RAMs instead. Concretely, to encrypt a message m under an unbounded length attribute string $w \in \{0, 1\}^*$ with time bound t, the encryptor first creates an empty memory D of size $t + 1$.[5] It then writes the attribute w on the RAM memory D, and garbles it to get the corresponding garbled database $\widetilde{D}$. (Basically this memory is used as the tape of the TM embedded in the predicate keys during decryption.) Next, the encryptor creates a sequence of t RAM programs where the i-th program takes as input the TM state q^{in}, bit to be written b^{out}, and the direction dir that was output by the previous (i.e., $(i-1)$-th) program/TM transition. Given these inputs, the RAM program writes the bit b^{out} at the current tape header, updates the tape header location depending on dir, and encrypts the garbled labels for the next (i.e., $(i+1)$-th) RAM program under appropriate identities. (Note that here we crucially rely on our bit-decomposition style identity-encodings of the output state while encrypting the next program labels.) Thus, a ciphertext contains t such garbled RAM programs in which the programs are garbled one-by-one from the last to first since each program contains labels for the next successive garbled program. Connecting this to original mechnical viewpoint, the garbled database should be thought of as the reusable ciphertext component while the garbled programs as the time-step dependent components. During decryption, an evaluator simply decrypts the wire labels depending on the current state of its TM execution and evaluates the garbled programs to recover encryptions of the wire labels for the

[5] Since the ciphertexts need only be decryptable by keys whose corresponding TMs accept the word within time t, thus the encryptor only needs to instantiate the database with t bits of memory. To be fully accurate, we actually a little more memory for storing the TM state which we discuss later in the main body.

next program. Doing this successively, an evaluator recovers the message if its TM accepts the attribute word within the ciphertext specified time bound.

Security: *how to prove it?* Although the above simple scheme seems to be secure when an adversary makes only a single key query and that too before receiving the challenge ciphertext, proving the same seems a bit challenging. This stems from the fact that a natural proof strategy seems to be incompatible with the full simulation security guaranteed by the underlying garbled RAM scheme. To better understand this, first recall that the garbled RAM security property for multi-program version states that no adversary can distinguish between a sequence of honestly garbled RAM programs (along with half of the honestly computed corresponding garbled labels) from a sequence of simulated garbled RAM programs (again along with half of the simulated garbled labels), where the garbled labels provided depend on the input to be fed to each RAM program. Next, observe that in our construction, the RAM programs which we garble are not independent programs but instead each RAM program in our construction directly depends on the garbling of the next RAM program in the sequence (since the i-th RAM program contains labels for the $(i+1)$-th RAM program). Juxtaposing these two facts, we get that no reduction algorithm in the proof could even statically define the sequence of RAM programs it wants garbled without interacting with the garbled RAM challenger.

Thus, this circularity/interdependence prevents a natural proof strategy from working. But it turns out that the problem is a bit deeper than what one can perceive at this point. That is, suppose we could somehow make the RAM programs (that we want to garble) fully independent, the problem is that the underlying sequence of RAM programs that we want to simulate will still be executing the TM step-by-step where each program reveals the labels for the next garbled program, thus a reduction algorithm can only simulate the garbled programs one at a time, and not all at once. Let us clarify this second issue further by first suggesting a modification to our current construction to solve the first interdependence problem.

The modification to our construction for solving this interdependence problem is to sample a fresh PRF keys for each label of the garbled RAM program at the beginning, and instead of letting a RAM program output encryptions of the labels for the next program, we make each program output encryptions of the corresponding PRF keys. Once we set the underlying RAM programs this way, we garble them and to tie them together we encrypt the labels for the $(i+1)$-th RAM program under PRF keys hardwired in the i-th RAM program. Intuitively, this means evaluating the garbled RAM programs an evaluator learns encryptions of some of the PRF keys which are then used to recover the garbled labels outside of this garbled RAM structure.

Getting back to proving security, the problem we still encounter is that as a reduction algorithm it is unclear on how to simulate all the garbled RAM programs at once, since for simulation the reduction needs to able to generate the ciphertext given only half of the wire labels, but those wire labels are encrypted under PRF keys which are hardwired inside each RAM program. Therefore, for a proof to go through a reduction algorithm needs to first remove information about half of garbled labels from the ciphertexts for which it needs to remove the information about half of the corresponding PRF keys which means the reduction must be able to simulate the garbled programs instead which is what we were trying to do in the first place. This circularity stems from the fact that the garbled RAM full simulation security only guarantees security when all the garbled programs are being simulated at the same time, instead of being partially/sequentially simulated.

Strengthening garbled RAM security. To fix the above problem we introduce a stronger security notion for garbled RAMs which we call *iterated simulation security.*[6] To us, it seems a more natural notion of security for multi-program garbled RAM versions, and also captures the kind of garbled RAM security we need for our proof to go through. We describe it in detail later in Sect. 3, but very briefly it states that there exists an efficient simulator such that for any sequence of ℓ programs and inputs, it is hard to distinguish between simulations of the first i programs and inputs along with honest garblings of the remaining $\ell - i$ programs from simulations of the first $i + 1$ programs and inputs along with honest garblings of the remaining $\ell - i - 1$ programs. That is, partial executions of the multi-program garbled RAMs are also simulatable.

Plugging in the strengthened garbled RAM security property, we are able to prove security of our ABE scheme by organizing an iterated hardwiring-style proof strategy where we start by simulating the first garbled program, then remove the information about labels for the next program by relying on PRF security (and the fact that only half of the PRF keys are needed to simulate the first garbled program), and keep on interleaving garbled RAM security with PRF security to eventually remove the plaintext information whenever the underlying TM does not accept the attribute word.

In order to complete the proof, we need to construct such a garbled RAM scheme that achieves our notion of iterated simulation security. Fortunately, we were able to show that most existing garbled RAM schemes already are secure under this partial simulation framework. In the full version, we show that the IBE-based garbled RAM construction in [33] is an iterated simulation secure garbled RAM scheme.

Lifting the core construction to q-query adaptive security

After a closer look at the proof overview provided for our core construction, the reason behind our construction only enabling a proof in key-selective model (that is, where the key query must be made before receiving the challenge ciphertext) becomes apparent. Very briefly, the bottleneck is that the reduction algorithm needs to know the current state of partial TM execution while embedding the challenge ciphertext with partially simulated components. Thus, the reduction must know the TM of the key query before creating the challenge ciphertext.

[6] Although prior works [13,28,29,32–34,50,53,54] have studied other adaptive and reusable variants of garbled RAM security notions, our notion of iterated simulation security has not yet been explicitly studied previously to the best of our knowledge.

Now instead of modifying our core construction to resolve this bottleneck, we instead observe that if the adversary gets to corrupt at most one key, then we could generically amplify key-selective security in a black-box manner to adaptive security. The only tool needed for such an amplification is a relaxed notion of non-committing encryption (NCE) [17,21,48] which we call *weak* non-committing encryption (wNCE). In a wNCE system, there is an efficient simulator that could "open" the ciphertext to any message by providing a simulated secret key after already committing to the public key in the beginning. For security, it is only required that the distribution of simulated keys and ciphertext is computationally indistinguishable from the distribution generated by the real encryption protocol.[7]

Given such a weak NCE scheme, the idea is pretty straightforward. During setup, we would additionally sample a wNCE key pair, and encryption algorithm will be a simple double encryption where each (key-selective secure) ABE ciphertext will be encrypted under the wNCE system. Each predicate key now contains the wNCE secret key as well as the underlying ABE key, where during decryption, the decryptor first decrypts the outer wNCE ciphertext to learn the core ABE ciphertext which it then decrypts using the core ABE key. Now the adaptive security of this transformed scheme follows directly from wNCE simulation security and the key-selective ABE security. The idea there is that the challenge ciphertext will be computed as a simulated wNCE ciphertext instead, and when the adversary makes the post-challenge key query, then the reduction algorithm *opens* the wNCE ciphertext to the challenge ciphertext provided by the key-selective security ABE challenger, and answers the adversary's key query with a simulated wNCE secret key along with the core ABE key provided by the ABE challenger. Similar ideas were also used in [39] in the context of simulation secure functional encryption.

Since there is a very simple construction for a weak NCE scheme from regular public key encryption, this seems to suggest that any 1-query key-selective secure ABE scheme could be generically lifted to achieve 1-query adaptive security instead, however there is an important caveat. The caveat is that this weak NCE construction from PKE has public-secret keys whose sizes grow linearly with length of the messages. Recall that in our generical transformation we encrypt the key-selective ABE ciphertext using the wNCE scheme. If the size of key-selective ABE ciphertext is fixed at setup time, then the transformation goes through as is, but this is not true for ABE in uniform models of computation where the whole motivation is being able to encrypt messages under unrestricted length attributes, thus the ciphertext sizes are a-priori unbounded. This implies that for the above transformation to work in the case of ABE for TMs we need a succinct weak NCE, where by succinct we mean that the system supports encryption of unbounded length messages. To this end, we show

[7] In regular notions of non-committing encryption, the simulator must also be able to indistinguishably explain the ciphertexts by providing encryption randomness too. We do not require that, thus regard our notion as a weak NCE system. Our notion is similar to that of receiver non-committing encryption [18].

another generic transformation that takes any non-succinct weak NCE scheme and compiles it into a succinct NCE scheme albeit in the Random Oracel Model (ROM) [11]. Very briefly, the idea here is use the ROM as an *adaptive programmable* PRF to indistinguishably open simulated ciphertexts to arbitrary messages. During encryption, an encryptor chooses a random λ-bit string K which it encrypts under the non-succinct NCE scheme, and then encrypts the unbounded length message block-by-block using K as a secret key and ROM as a PRF. The simulatability of this scheme follows directly from the simulatability of the non-succinct scheme and programmability of the ROM. This is discussed in detail in the full version. We want to point out that building a succinct weak NCE scheme as described above is impossible in the standard model [55], thus adaptive security of our construction crucially relies on the usage of ROM.

Combining the above ideas, we obtain a 1-query adaptively secure ABE scheme for TMs. To conclude, we show that by using standard combinatorial techniques, the security could be improved to q-query adaptive security for any a-priori fixed polynomial $q(\cdot)$. Since we are dealing with just an ABE scheme, thus this transformation is much simpler than for other related transformations such as the one for functional encryption in [39]. For completeness, we provide it in the full version.

Related work, other suggested approaches, and future directions
Comparison with Agrawal-Singh [5]. Closest to us is the work of Agrawal-Singh [5] who construct a 1-query functional encryption scheme for Turing Machines where, like our ABE system, the encryption algorithm depends on the worst case running time of the TM. Ours and their construction share the same mechnical perspective of traversing through a sequence of garbled circuits for encrypting unbounded length inputs, however differ in overall execution since they rely on a succinct single-key FE scheme with the TM evaluation happening under the FE hood, whereas we work with more general primitives such as IBE and garbled RAM thereby our TM evaluation happens on encrypted pieces that come out as outputs of garbled RAM evaluations. The usage of a succinct single-key FE scheme has the benefit of the resulting encryption scheme being a FE scheme with short keys (and not just an ABE scheme like ours), but given the current state-of-the-art [36] it also means relying on the LWE assumption, while we rely on much weaker primitives thus are not tethered to the LWE assumption. Like our core key-selective secure ABE scheme, they also prove security in the weaker model where there is a single-key query which must be made before receiving the challenge ciphertext. Although they do not provide any follow-up transformations to improve security like us, we believe our non-committing encryption idea could also be used with their FE construction. However, extending to q-query bounded collusion security would be more tricky than our case, but might be possible to adapt a more elaborate transformation along the lines of [39].

ABE via laconic OT. Cho et al. [19] introduced the concept of laconic transfer for secure computation over large inputs. They described an application of laconic OT to non-interactively compute in the RAM setting. Although this application does not directly lead to ABE schemes that supports (RAM) Turing Machine computation, it might be possible to repurpose the underlying ideas to build ABE by going through laconic OT along with garbling techniques. One would need to be careful in executing this idea so that the description size of the Turing Machine does not need to be a-priori bounded at setup time, and this might require adjusting the definition of the corresponding primitives. Additionally, such an approach would need one to rely on laconic OT whereas we chose to focus on IBE since it is both supported by multiple number theoretic assumptions as well as there are multiple number theoretic IBE constructions that do not themselves invoke garbling and thus avoid a double layer of garbling in the eventual construction. There have been prior works [23,49] which observe that laconic OT could be replaced by IBE in certain applications, and it would be interesting to look at whether same could be done for this alternate approach. In our work, we provide a much direct construction directly from any regular IBE scheme.

Future directions. In this work we focus on proving standard semantic security of our ABE scheme, but we believe one could extend it to CCA security by either relying on the ROM, or on other generic transformations such as [51], and prove it to be a 1-sided predicate encryption scheme directly without relying on generic transformations [41,61]. An interesting open question is whether one could extend our current approach to either achieve succinctness similar to [5], or extend it to FE without relying on stronger assumptions. Another related question is whether we could avoid the ROM for amplifying the security of our core ABE scheme from key-selective to fully adaptive. It might be useful look at the graph pebbling techniques [24,25,45,46,52] to develop a more intricate hybrid structure for proving adaptive security directly. Another interesting thought might be to rely on adaptive security of garbled RAM schemes [30] instead, however it is unclear how to leverage having an adaptive garbled RAM in our setting. Briefly, the reason is that the extra adaptivity it provides is useful in cryptosystems where an attacker is able to see some of the garbled RAM programs and then somehow influence the inputs or programs for the rest of them; while in our case all the garbling program calls are bundled together in a single call to the encryption oracle. Lastly, another important question is whether these techniques could be used to build ABE systems for TMs where the encryption algorithm no longer depends on the worst case running of the TM.

2 Preliminaries

Due to space constraints, we describe our notation, the Turing machine and RAM program formalisms, and definitions of secret key encryption and identity-based encryption later in the full version.

2.1 Attribute-Based Encryption for Turing Machines

An Attribute-Based Encryption (ABE) scheme ABE for set of attribute space $\{0,1\}^*$, Turing Machines classes $\mathcal{T} = \{\mathcal{T}_\lambda\}_{\lambda\in\mathbb{N}}$, and message spaces $\mathcal{M} = \{\mathcal{M}_\lambda\}_{\lambda\in\mathbb{N}}$ consists of four polynomial time algorithms $(\mathsf{Setup}, \mathsf{KeyGen}, \mathsf{Enc}, \mathsf{Dec})$ with the following syntax:

$\mathsf{Setup}(1^\lambda) \to (\mathsf{pp}, \mathsf{msk})$. The setup algorithm takes as input the security parameter λ. It outputs the public parameters pp and the master secret key msk.
$\mathsf{KeyGen}(\mathsf{msk}, T) \to \mathsf{sk}_T$. The key generation algorithm takes as input the master secret key msk and a Turing Machine $T \in \mathcal{T}_\lambda$. It outputs a secret key sk_T.
$\mathsf{Enc}(\mathsf{pp}, m, (w,t)) \to \mathsf{ct}$. The encryption algorithm takes as input the public parameters pp, a message $m \in \mathcal{M}_\lambda$, and a pair (w,t) consisting of an attribute $w \in \{0,1\}^*$, and a positive integer time bound t. It outputs a ciphertext ct.
$\mathsf{Dec}(\mathsf{sk}_T, \mathsf{ct}) \to m/\bot$. The decryption algorithm takes as input a secret key sk_T and a ciphertext ct. It outputs either a message $m \in \mathcal{M}_\lambda$ or a special symbol $\bot$.

Correctness. We say an ABE scheme $\mathsf{ABE} = (\mathsf{Setup}, \mathsf{KeyGen}, \mathsf{Enc}, \mathsf{Dec})$ satisfies correctness if for all $\lambda \in \mathbb{N}$, $(\mathsf{pp}, \mathsf{msk}) \leftarrow \mathsf{Setup}(1^\lambda)$, $T \in \mathcal{T}_\lambda$, $m \in \mathcal{M}_\lambda$, $\mathsf{sk}_T \leftarrow \mathsf{KeyGen}(\mathsf{msk}, T)$, $t \in \mathbb{N}$, and $w \in \{0,1\}^*$ for which T accepts w within t steps, and $\mathsf{ct} \leftarrow \mathsf{Enc}(\mathsf{pp}, m, (w,t))$ we have that $\mathsf{Dec}(\mathsf{sk}_T, \mathsf{ct}) = m$.

Efficiency. We require that the algorithm $\mathsf{Setup}(1^\lambda)$ runs in time polynomial in the security parameter λ. We require that the algorithm $\mathsf{KeyGen}(\mathsf{msk}, T)$ runs in time polynomial in the security parameter λ and the size $|T|$ of T. We require that the algorithm $\mathsf{Enc}(\mathsf{pp}, m, (w,t))$ runs in time polynomial in the security parameter λ, the length $|m|$ of the message m, the length $|w|$ of the attribute w, and the time bound t. We require that the algorithm $\mathsf{Dec}(\mathsf{sk}_T, \mathsf{ct})$ runs in time polynomial in the security parameter λ and the size $|\mathsf{ct}|$ of the ciphertext ct.

Security. Next, we define the security notions we consider for ABE systems.

Definition 2.1 (adaptive security). We say an ABE scheme $\mathsf{ABE} = (\mathsf{Setup}, \mathsf{KeyGen}, \mathsf{Enc}, \mathsf{Dec})$ is fully secure if for any PPT adversary $\mathcal{A} = (\mathcal{A}_0, \mathcal{A}_1)$ there exists a negligible function $\mathrm{negl}(\cdot)$, such that for all $\lambda \in \mathbb{N}$ the following holds

$$\Pr\left[\mathcal{A}_1^{\mathsf{KeyGen}(\mathsf{msk},\cdot)}(\mathsf{st}, \mathsf{ct}) = \beta : \begin{array}{c}(\mathsf{pp}, \mathsf{msk}) \leftarrow \mathsf{Setup}(1^\lambda);\quad \beta \leftarrow \{0,1\}\\ (\mathsf{st}, m_0, m_1, (w, 1^t)) \leftarrow \mathcal{A}_0^{\mathsf{KeyGen}(\mathsf{msk},\cdot)}(\mathsf{pp}, 1^\lambda)\\ \mathsf{ct} \leftarrow \mathsf{Enc}(\mathsf{pp}, m_\beta, (w,t))\end{array}\right] \le \frac{1}{2} + \mathrm{negl}(\lambda),$$

where all Turing Machines T queried by $\mathcal{A}$ do not accept the word w within t steps.

In this work, we focus on bounded collusion security for ABE systems where the adversary is restricted to make an a-priori bounded number of key generation queries, say at most Q queries (for some polynomially bounded function $Q(\lambda)$). The definition is given below.

Definition 2.2 (Q-query adaptive security). An ABE scheme is said to be Q-query adaptively secure if in the above security game (see Definition 2.1), the adversary can make at most Q queries to the key generation oracle.

We also define the weaker notion which we call key-selective security, where the adversary to must make all key queries before it is given the challenge ciphertext. The definition is given below.

Definition 2.3 (Q-query key-selective security). An ABE scheme is said to be Q-query key-selective secure if in the above security game (see Defintion 2.1), the adversary can make at most Q queries to the key generation oracle, and all key queries must be made before getting the challenge ciphertext.

3 Garbled RAM with Iterated Simulation Security

In this section we define a notion of Garbled RAM security which abstracts out properties of Garbled RAM constructions in previous works which we will use in our construction of ABE. At a high level, our security notion, which we call Iterated Simulation Security requires that there exists an efficient simulator such that for any sequence of ℓ programs and inputs, it is hard to distinguish simulations of the first k programs and inputs along with honest garblings of the remaining $\ell - k$ programs from simulations of the first $k+1$ programs and inputs along with honest garblings of the remaining $\ell - k - 1$ programs. Our security definition will actually be a notion of security with Unprotected Memory Access (UMA), that is security in which the garbling may leak the contents of the garbled database D, and the memory access patterns access_j of the programs. We drop the label UMA in the subsequent to reduce clutter.

A Garbled RAM scheme GRAM consists of three polynomial time algorithms $(\mathsf{GData}, \mathsf{GProg}, \mathsf{Eval})$ with the following syntax:

$\mathsf{GData}(1^\lambda, D) \rightarrow (\widetilde{D}, \mathsf{k}_D)$. The data garbling algorithm takes as input the security parameter λ and a database $D \in \{0,1\}^m$. It outputs a garbled database $\widetilde{D}$ and program garbling key k_D.

$\mathsf{GProg}(1^\lambda, \mathsf{k}_D, m, P, 1^n, (t_{\mathsf{init}}, t_{\mathsf{fin}})) \rightarrow (\widetilde{P}, \{\mathsf{lab}^{\mathsf{in}}_{i,b}\}_{i\in[n],b\in\{0,1\}})$. The program garbling algorithm takes as input the security parameter λ, a program garbling key k_D, a database size m, a program P which operates on a database of size m and takes an input of length n, and time range given as a pair of an initial time t_{init} and final time t_{fin}. It outputs a garbled program $\widetilde{P}$ and a collection of input labels $\{\mathsf{lab}^{\mathsf{in}}_{i,b}\}_{i\in[n],b\in\{0,1\}}$.

$\mathsf{Eval}^{\widetilde{D}}(\widetilde{P}, \{\mathsf{lab}^{\mathsf{in}}_i\}_{i\in[n]}) \rightarrow \widetilde{y}$. The evaluation algorithm takes as input a garbled database $\widetilde{D}$, a garbled program $\widetilde{P}$, and a collection of n labels $\{\mathsf{lab}^{\mathsf{in}}_i\}_{i\in[n]}$. It outputs a value $\widetilde{y}$. As in [33], we will think of the evaluation algorithm as a RAM program operating on database $\widetilde{D}$ which is able to perform arbitrary reads and writes on $\widetilde{D}$. We slightly abuse notation, and will write

$$\mathsf{Eval}^{\widetilde{D}}((\widetilde{P_1}, \{\mathsf{lab}^{\mathsf{in},1}_i\}_{i\in[n_1]}), ..., (\widetilde{P_\ell}, \{\mathsf{lab}^{\mathsf{in},\ell}_i\}_{i\in[n_\ell]})) \rightarrow (\widetilde{y_1}, \dots, \widetilde{y_\ell})$$

to denote that for all $j \in \ell$, $\widetilde{y_j}$ is the result of the evaluation algorithm on garbled program $\widetilde{P_j}$ with labels $\{\mathsf{lab}_i^{\mathsf{in},j}\}_{i \in [n_j]}$ on garbled database $\widetilde{D}$ after running the evaluation algorithm on garbled programs $\widetilde{P_{j'}}$ with labels $\{\mathsf{lab}_i^{\mathsf{in},j'}\}_{i \in [n_{j'}]}$ in sequence on $\widetilde{D}$ for all $j' < j$ with changes made to $\widetilde{D}$ persisting across evaluations.

Correctness. Fix parameters $\lambda, \ell, m \in \mathbb{N}$, a database $D \in \{0,1\}^m$, and programs and inputs $\{(P_j, x_j \in \{0,1\}^{n_j}, n_j, t_{\mathsf{init},j}, t_{\mathsf{fin},j})\}_{j \in [\ell]}$. Let

$$(y_1, \ldots, y_\ell) \leftarrow (P_1(x_1), \ldots, P_\ell(x_\ell))^D$$

be the result of sequentially running the programs P_j on inputs x_j operating on persistent database D. We say a garbled RAM scheme $\mathsf{GRAM} = (\mathsf{GData}, \mathsf{GProg}, \mathsf{Eval})$ satisfies correctness, if for all $j \in [\ell]$ the following holds

$$\Pr\left[\widetilde{y}_j = y_j : \begin{array}{c} (\widetilde{D}, \mathsf{k}_D) \leftarrow \mathsf{GData}(1^\lambda, D) \\ \forall j \in [\ell],\ (\widetilde{P}_j, \{\mathsf{lab}_{i,b}^{\mathsf{in},j}\}_{i \in [n_j], b \in \{0,1\}}) \leftarrow \mathsf{GProg}(1^\lambda, \mathsf{k}_D, m, P_j, 1^{n_j}, (t_{\mathsf{init},j}, t_{\mathsf{fin},j})) \\ (\widetilde{y}_1, \ldots, \widetilde{y}_\ell) \leftarrow \mathsf{Eval}^{\widetilde{D}}((\widetilde{P}_1, \{\mathsf{lab}_{i,x_j[i]}^{\mathsf{in},j}\}_{i \in [n_j]}), \ldots, (\widetilde{P}_1, \{\mathsf{lab}_{i,x_j[i]}^{\mathsf{in},j}\}_{i \in [n_j]})) \end{array}\right] = 1.$$

Definition 3.1 (iterated simulation security). We say a garbled RAM scheme $\mathsf{GRAM} = (\mathsf{GData}, \mathsf{GProg}, \mathsf{Eval})$ satisfies iterated simulation security if there exists a polynomial time simulator Sim such that for any PPT adversary $\mathcal{A} = (\mathcal{A}_0, \mathcal{A}_1)$ there exists a negligible function $\mathrm{negl}(\cdot)$, such that for all $\lambda \in \mathbb{N}$, the following holds

$$\Pr\left[\mathcal{A}_1(\mathsf{st}, \mathsf{chal}) = \beta : \begin{array}{c} \beta \leftarrow \{0,1\} \\ (\mathsf{st}, k, D, \{(P_j, x_j, n_j, (t_{\mathsf{init},j}, t_{\mathsf{fin},j}))\}_{j \in [\ell]}) \leftarrow \mathcal{A}_0(1^\lambda) \\ \mathsf{chal} \leftarrow \mathsf{Exp}_{k-\beta}^\lambda(D, \{(P_j, x_j, n_j, (t_{\mathsf{init},j}, t_{\mathsf{fin},j}))\}_{j \in [\ell]}) \end{array}\right] \le \frac{1}{2} + \mathrm{negl}(\lambda),$$

where for $0 \le k \le \ell$, the output of $\mathsf{Exp}_k^\lambda(D, \{(P_j, x_j, n_j, (t_{\mathsf{init},j}, t_{\mathsf{fin},j}))\}_{j \in [\ell]})$ is defined

$$\left\{\left(\begin{array}{c} \widetilde{D}, \{(\widetilde{P}_j, \{\mathsf{lab}_i^{\mathsf{in},j}\}_i)\}_{j \in [k]}, \\ \{(\widetilde{P}_j, \{\mathsf{lab}_{i,b}^{\mathsf{in},j}\}_{i,b})\}_{j \in [k+1,\ell]} \end{array}\right) : \begin{array}{c} (\widetilde{D}, \mathsf{k}_D) \leftarrow \mathsf{GData}(1^\lambda, D) \\ \forall j > k,\ (\widetilde{P}_j, \{\mathsf{lab}_{i,b}^{\mathsf{in},j}\}_{i \in [n_j], b \in \{0,1\}}) \\ \leftarrow \mathsf{GProg}(1^\lambda, \mathsf{k}_D, |D|, P_j, 1^{n_j}, (t_{\mathsf{init},j}, t_{\mathsf{fin},j})) \\ \forall j \le k,\ (\widetilde{P}_j, \{\mathsf{lab}_i^{\mathsf{in},j}\}_{i \in [n_j], b \in \{0,1\}}) \\ \leftarrow \mathsf{Sim}(\mathsf{k}_D, 1^{n_j}, |P_j|, y_j, \mathsf{access}_j, (t_{\mathsf{init},j}, t_{\mathsf{fin},j})) \end{array}\right\}$$

where for all j, $|P_j|$ is the size of the program P_j, y_j is the result of running P_j with input x_j on the database D after having run the previous $j-1$ programs and inputs, and access_j is the memory access pattern of P_j. Note, that all the inputs to $\mathsf{Sim}(\cdot)$, can be computed from the inputs to Exp_k^λ.

Remark 3.2. As a point of comparison with the simulation security notions considered in prior works such as [33], we would want to highlight that in prior works the simulator always outputs a fully simulated execution of the garbled

RAM which must be indistinguishable from honestly garbled programs. We, on the other hand, consider indistinguishability in between these partial execution steps.

Efficiency. We require that the algorithm $\mathsf{GData}(1^\lambda, D)$ runs in time polynomial in the security parameter λ and the size $|D|$ of the database D. We require that the algorithms $\mathsf{GProg}(1^\lambda, \mathsf{k}_D, m, P, 1^n, (t_{\mathsf{init}}, t_{\mathsf{fin}}))$ and $\mathsf{Eval}^{\widetilde{D}}(\widetilde{P}, \{\mathsf{lab}_i^{\mathsf{in}}\}_{i\in[n]})$ both run in time polynomial in the security parameter λ, $\log(m)$ where m is the size of D, the size $|P|$ of P, the size n of the input taken by P, and the total number of steps $(t_{\mathsf{fin}} - t_{\mathsf{init}})$ taken by P.

4 ABE for Turing Machines

In this section we give our main construction of an ABE scheme for Turing Machines. The scheme will be for message spaces $\mathcal{M} = \{\{0,1\}^\lambda\}_{\lambda\in\mathbb{N}}$.

The primitives used by our construction are as follows. Let GRAM = (GData, GProg, Eval) be a garbled RAM scheme satisfying Iterated Simulation Security. In addition, let IBE be a secure IBE scheme which can encrypt messages of length λ, and assume there is some polynomial $n(\cdot)$ for which the identity space of IBE includes identities of length $n'(\lambda) := n(\lambda) + \lceil\log(n+2)\rceil + 2$. In the subsequent discussion we will simply write n as shorthand for $n(\lambda)$. Our scheme additionally uses a secret key encryption scheme $\mathsf{SKE} = (\mathsf{SKE.Setup}, \mathsf{SKE.Enc}, \mathsf{SKE.Dec})$. For simplicity of exposition, we assume (w.l.o.g.) that the IBE encryption algorithm takes as input λ-bits of randomness.

In our scheme, we will allow secret key queries for deterministic Turing Machines $T = (Q, \Sigma, q_{\mathsf{start}}, F, \delta)$ with the following restrictions. We assume:

- All machines have state space $Q \subset \{0,1\}^n$.
- The alphabet Σ is binary. That is $\Sigma = \{0,1\}$.
- The all 0 state 0^n is reserved as the unique start state q_{start} for all machines.
- The all 1 state 1^n is reserved as the unique accept state $q_{\mathsf{accept}} \in F$.
- The transition relation δ is a *partial* function. In particular, all machines are deterministic.

The above assumptions are essentially without loss of generality for deterministic Turing Machines. In particular, any deterministic Turing Machine with constant size alphabet and a polynomial number of states can be transformed in to a machine satisfying these assumptions with at most polynomial blowup. We will identify each machine T with the set of possible transitions it can make under δ:

$$T = \{(q^{\mathsf{in}}, b^{\mathsf{in}}, q^{\mathsf{out}}, b^{\mathsf{out}}, \mathsf{dir}) \ : \ \delta(q^{\mathsf{in}}, b^{\mathsf{in}}) = (q^{\mathsf{out}}, b^{\mathsf{out}}, \mathsf{dir})\}$$

Thus, the notation $|T|$, will simply be the cardinality of the right hand side of the above.

The secret keys of our scheme will be carefully chosen sets of identity secret keys from the IBE scheme IBE. In particular, each identity secret key will be for an identity $\mathsf{id} \in \{0,1\}^{n+\lceil\log(n)\rceil+2}$.

4.1 Construction

We now formally describe the construction of our ABE scheme, $\mathsf{ABE} = (\mathsf{Setup}, \mathsf{KeyGen}, \mathsf{Enc}, \mathsf{Dec})$.

$\mathsf{Setup}(1^\lambda) \to (\mathsf{pp}, \mathsf{msk})$. The setup algorithm chooses $(\mathsf{pp}, \mathsf{msk}) \leftarrow \mathsf{IBE.Setup}(1^\lambda)$, and outputs $(\mathsf{pp}, \mathsf{msk})$.

$\mathsf{KeyGen}(\mathsf{msk}, T) \to \mathsf{sk}_T$. Let the Turing machine T be given as the set of possible transitions it can make under its transition relation δ:

$$T = \{(q^{\mathsf{in}}, b^{\mathsf{in}}, q^{\mathsf{out}}, b^{\mathsf{out}}, \mathsf{dir}) \;:\; \delta(q^{\mathsf{in}}, b^{\mathsf{in}}) = (q^{\mathsf{out}}, b^{\mathsf{out}}, \mathsf{dir})\}$$

For each transition $(q^{\mathsf{in}}, b^{\mathsf{in}}, q^{\mathsf{out}}, b^{\mathsf{out}}, \mathsf{dir}) \in T$ the key generation algorithm samples $n+2$ identity secret keys. Let $\mathcal{ID}_T$ be the set of $(n+2)\cdot|T|$ identities described below:

$$\mathcal{ID}_T = \left\{ (q^{\mathsf{in}}, b^{\mathsf{in}}, i, \beta) \in \{0,1\}^{n'} \;:\; (q^{\mathsf{in}}, b^{\mathsf{in}}, q^{\mathsf{out}}, b^{\mathsf{out}}, \mathsf{dir}) \in T \wedge \begin{pmatrix} (i \in [n] \wedge \beta = q^{\mathsf{out}}[i]) \vee \\ (i = n+1 \wedge \beta = b^{\mathsf{out}}) \vee \\ (i = n+2 \wedge \beta = b^{\mathsf{dir}}) \end{pmatrix} \right\} \tag{1}$$

where in the above $b^{\mathsf{dir}} = 0$ if $\mathsf{dir} = L$ and $b^{\mathsf{dir}} = 1$ if $\mathsf{dir} = R$.
Next, the key generation algorithm samples an IBE secret key for each identity in $\mathcal{ID}_T$. Concretely, it chooses

$$\forall\, (q^{\mathsf{in}}, b^{\mathsf{in}}, i, \beta) \in \mathcal{ID}_T, \quad \mathsf{sk}_{(q^{\mathsf{in}}, b^{\mathsf{in}}, i, \beta)} \leftarrow \mathsf{IBE.KeyGen}(\mathsf{msk}, (q^{\mathsf{in}}, b^{\mathsf{in}}, i, \beta)).$$

Finally, the key generation algorithm sets the key to be the machine description T and the entire set of identity secret keys it chose:

$$\mathsf{sk}_T = \left(T, \left\{\mathsf{sk}_{(q^{\mathsf{in}}, b^{\mathsf{in}}, i, \beta)}\right\}_{(q^{\mathsf{in}}, b^{\mathsf{in}}, i, \beta) \in \mathcal{ID}_T}\right).$$

$\mathsf{Enc}(\mathsf{pp}, m, (w, t)) \to \mathsf{ct}$. The encryption algorithm garbles a database D along with several copies of a *step program* P. We formally describe the RAM program P in Fig. 1 before moving on to the encryption algorithm.
The encryption algorithm proceeds as follows.

1. The encryption algorithm sets a database $D \in \{0,1\}^{t+1+\lceil \log(t+1) \rceil}$. It sets the first $|w|$ bits of D to match w, and sets the remaining bits to 0. More formally,

$$D := w || 0^{t+1+\lceil \log(t+1) \rceil - |w|}$$

   where $||$ denotes concatenation. The algorithm next garbles the database $(\widetilde{D}, \mathsf{k}_D) \leftarrow \mathsf{GData}(1^\lambda, D)$.
2. For each $(i, b, j) \in [n+2] \times \{0,1\} \times [t+1]$, the algorithm samples randomness $r_{b,j}^{(i)}$ and SKE secret keys $\mathsf{K}_{i,b}^{(j)}$ as $r_{b,j}^{(i)} \leftarrow \{0,1\}^\lambda, \mathsf{K}_{i,b}^{(j)} \leftarrow \mathsf{SKE.Setup}(1^\lambda)$.
3. Let P be the RAM program described as described in Fig. 1. For each $j \in [t+1]$, the algorithm sets P_j as $P_j := P[\mathsf{pp}, \{\mathsf{K}_{i,b}^{(j)}\}_{i,b}, m, j; \{r_{b,j}^{(i)}\}_{i,b}]$.

4. Let ℓ be the number of steps P takes to run on a database of length $|D|$. For each $j \in [t+1]$, the algorithm garbles the program P_j, computing

$$(\widetilde{P_j}, \{\mathsf{lab}^{\mathsf{in},j}_{i,b}\}_{i,b}) \leftarrow \mathsf{GProg}(1^\lambda, \mathsf{k}_D, t+1+\lceil\log(t+1)\rceil, P_j, 1^{n+2}, (1+(j-1)\cdot\ell, j\cdot\ell)).$$

5. For each $(i, b, j) \in [n+2] \times \{0,1\} \times [t]$, the algorithm computes ciphertexts $\widetilde{\mathsf{ct}}^{(j)}_{i,b} \leftarrow \mathsf{SKE.Enc}(\mathsf{K}^{(j)}_{i,b}, \mathsf{lab}^{\mathsf{in},j+1}_{i,b})$.
6. Let $\{\mathsf{lab}^{\mathsf{in},1}_{i,b}\}_{i,b}$ be the set of input labels computed when garbling program P_1. Recall that the all zero state is the canonical start state. The algorithm outputs the ciphertext

$$\mathsf{ct} = (w, t, \widetilde{D}, \{\mathsf{lab}^{\mathsf{in},1}_{i,0}\}_{i\in[n+2]}, \{\widetilde{P}_j\}_{j\in[t+1]}, \{\widetilde{\mathsf{ct}}^{(j)}_{i,b}\}_{i\in[n+2],b\in\{0,1\},j\in[t]}).$$

The step program

$$P[\mathsf{pp}, \{\mathsf{K}_{i,b}\}_{(i,b)\in[n+2]\times\{0,1\}}, m, j; \{r_{i,b}\}_{(i,b)\in[n+2]\times\{0,1\}}](q^{\mathsf{in}}, b^{\mathsf{out}}, b^{\mathsf{dir}})$$

The program P operates on a database D of size $t+1+\lceil\log(t+1)\rceil$. For convenience, we will think of the database as a length $t+1$ array D' concatenated with an integer index $\mathsf{idx} \in [t+1]$ i.e $D := D'||\mathsf{idx}$. The program P has hard-coded the public parameters pp of an instance of IBE, a set of SKE secret keys $\{\mathsf{K}_{i,b}\}_{(i,b)\in[n+2]\times\{0,1\}}$, a message m, an integer $j \in [t+1]$, and a set of randomness strings $\{r_{i,b}\}_{(i,b)\in[n+2]\times\{0,1\}}$. It takes as input an n-bit state q, a bit b^{out}, and a bit b^{dir}.

1. If $j > 1$, the program reads the index idx, and then it overwrites the idx-th bit of D' with b^{out} i.e. it sets $D'[\mathsf{idx}] := b^{\mathsf{out}}$. Otherwise if $j = 1$, the program ignores the input b^{out}.
2. If $j > 1$, $\mathsf{idx} > 1$, and $b^{\mathsf{dir}} = 0$, the program overwrites idx with $\mathsf{idx} - 1$. Else if $j > 1$, $\mathsf{idx} = 1$, and $b^{\mathsf{dir}} = 0$, for each $i \in [n+2]$ and $b \in \{0,1\}$, the program re-sets $\mathsf{K}_{i,b} := \mathbf{0}$. (This instruction is to prevent decryption if the tape head tries to move left off of the tape.) Else, if $j > 1$ and $b^{\mathsf{dir}} = 1$, the program overwrites idx with $\mathsf{idx} + 1$. Else, if $j = 1$, the program ignores the input b^{dir}.
3. The program reads the bit $b^{\mathsf{in}} := D'[\mathsf{idx}]$ at the updated idx. For each pair $(i, b) \in [n+2] \times \{0,1\}$, the program computes

$$\mathsf{ct}_{i,b} := \mathsf{IBE.Enc}(\mathsf{pp}, \mathsf{K}_{i,b}, (q^{\mathsf{in}}, b^{\mathsf{in}}, i, b); r_{i,b}).$$

4. Finally, if $q^{\mathsf{in}} = \mathsf{accept}$, the program outputs $(\{\mathsf{ct}_{i,b}\}_{(i,b)\in[n+2]\times\{0,1\}}, m)$. Otherwise it outputs $(\{\mathsf{ct}_{i,b}\}_{(i,b)\in[n+2]\times\{0,1\}}, \perp)$.

Fig. 1. The step program P.

$\mathsf{Dec}(\mathsf{sk}_T, \mathsf{ct}) \to m/\bot$. The decryption algorithm parses the ciphertext and secret key as

$$\mathsf{ct} = (w, t, \widetilde{D}, \{\mathsf{lab}_i^{\mathsf{in}}\}_{i\in[n+2]}, \{\widetilde{P}_j\}_{j\in[t+1]}, \{\widetilde{\mathsf{ct}}_{i,b}^{(j)}\}_{i\in[n+2], b\in\{0,1\}, j\in[t]}),$$
$$\mathsf{sk}_T = \left(T, \left\{\mathsf{sk}_{(q^{\mathsf{in}}, b^{\mathsf{in}}, i, \beta)}\right\}_{(q^{\mathsf{in}}, b^{\mathsf{in}}, i, \beta)\in\mathcal{ID}_T}\right).$$

Let $t' \leq t$ be the maximum number of well defined transitions the machine T can make on input w within t time steps. Let

$$\{(q_j^{\mathsf{in}}, b_j^{\mathsf{in}}, q_j^{\mathsf{out}}, b_j^{\mathsf{out}}, \mathsf{dir}_j)\}_{j\in[t']}$$

be the t' transitions T makes on input w. The decryption algorithm sets $\mathbf{lab}_1 := \{\mathsf{lab}_i^{\mathsf{in}}\}_{i\in[n+2]}$, and then proceeds to evaluate the garbled RAM programs in ascending order for $j = 1$ to $j = t' + 1$ as follows:

1. The decryption algorithm evaluates the jth garbled RAM program $\widetilde{P}_j$ on the current value of the garbled database $\widetilde{D}$ with the input given by labels in $\mathbf{lab}_j$:
$$(\{\mathsf{ct}_{i,b}^{(j)}\}_{i,b}, \widetilde{y}_j) \leftarrow \mathsf{Eval}^{\widetilde{D}}(\widetilde{P}_j, \mathbf{lab}_j).$$
Note that the garbled database $\widetilde{D}$ has now been updated after running $\mathsf{Eval}(\cdot)$.
2. If $\widetilde{y}_j \neq \bot$, the algorithm breaks and exits the loop, sets $m := \widetilde{y}_j$, and outputs m.
3. Otherwise, if $\widetilde{y}_j = \bot$ it continues. Let $(q_j^{\mathsf{in}}, b_j^{\mathsf{in}}, q_j^{\mathsf{out}}, b_j^{\mathsf{out}}, \mathsf{dir}_j)$ be the jth transition T makes on input w. Also, for $i \in [n+2]$, let $b_{i,j}$ denote the following bit
$$b_{i,j} := \begin{cases} q_j^{\mathsf{out}}[i] & \text{if } i \in [n] \\ b_j^{\mathsf{out}} & \text{if } i = n+1 \\ b_j^{\mathsf{dir}} & \text{otherwise.} \end{cases}$$
where in the above $b_j^{\mathsf{dir}} = 0$ if $\mathsf{dir}_j = L$ and $b_j^{\mathsf{dir}} = 1$ if $\mathsf{dir}_j = R$. The algorithm computes the labels for the next program as follows. For $i \in [n+2]$, it decrypts the IBE and SKE ciphertexts as:
$$\mathsf{K}_{i,b_{i,j}}^{(j)} = \mathsf{IBE.Dec}(\mathsf{sk}_{(q^{\mathsf{in}}, b^{\mathsf{in}}, i, b_{i,j})}, \mathsf{ct}_{i,b_{i,j}}^{(j)}), \qquad \mathsf{lab}_{i,b_{i,j}}^{\mathsf{in}} \leftarrow \mathsf{SKE.Dec}(\mathsf{K}_{i,b_{i,j}}^{(j)}, \widetilde{\mathsf{ct}}_{i,b_{i,j}}^{(j)}).$$
4. If $j < t' + 1$, the algorithm sets the labels for the garbled program $\widetilde{P}_{j+1}$ as
$$\mathbf{lab}_{j+1} := \{\mathsf{lab}_{i,b_{i,j}}^{\mathsf{in}}\}_{i\in[n+2]}$$
and otherwise if $j = t' + 1$, the algorithm exits the loop and returns $\bot$.

4.2 Correctness

Due to space constraints, we describe the correctness proof later in the full version.

4.3 Efficiency

We discuss the efficiency of the algorithms of the above construction. Since $\mathsf{Setup}(\lambda)$ simply runs $\mathsf{IBE.Setup}(\lambda)$, the runtime is $\mathsf{poly}(\lambda)$ whenever the runtime of $\mathsf{IBE.Setup}(\lambda)$ is $\mathsf{poly}(\lambda)$. Next, the algorithm $\mathsf{KeyGen}(\mathsf{msk}, T)$ runs $\mathsf{IBE.KeyGen}(\mathsf{msk}, \cdot)$ a total of $n + 2$ times for each transition of T. Since n is bounded by $\mathsf{poly}(\lambda)$, we have that if the runtime of $\mathsf{IBE.KeyGen}(\mathsf{msk}, \cdot)$ is $\mathsf{poly}(\lambda)$ then $\mathsf{KeyGen}(\mathsf{msk}, T)$ has runtime $|T| \cdot \mathsf{poly}(\lambda)$. Next, the algorithm $\mathsf{Enc}(\mathsf{pp}, m, (w, t))$ runs $\mathsf{GData}(1^\lambda, D)$ on a database of size $O(t)$, and garbles $t+1$ copies of the step-program P. Assume $|w| \leq t$ and that each P has representation of size $\mathsf{poly}(\lambda) \cdot \mathsf{polylog(t)}$. If $\mathsf{IBE.Enc}(\mathsf{pp}, \cdot)$ has runtime $\mathsf{poly}(\lambda)$, $\mathsf{GData}(1^\lambda, D)$ has runtime $|D| \cdot \mathsf{polylog(|D|)} \cdot \mathsf{poly}(\lambda)$, and $\mathsf{GProg}(1^\lambda, \log(|D|), P, 1^n, (t_{\mathsf{init}}, t_{\mathsf{fin}}))$ has runtime $|P| \cdot \mathsf{polylog(|D|, |P|)} \cdot \mathsf{poly}(\lambda)$, then $\mathsf{Enc}(\mathsf{pp}, m, (w, t))$ has runtime $t \cdot \mathsf{polylog(t)} \cdot \mathsf{poly}(\lambda)$. Finally, the algorithm $\mathsf{Dec}(\mathsf{sk}_T, \mathsf{ct})$ evaluates a garbled program and decrypts a set of n ciphertexts of the IBE system $t' + 1$ many times, where t' is the time T takes to accept the underlying attribute w used to compute ct. Thus, if $\mathsf{IBE.Dec}(\mathsf{sk}_{\mathsf{id}}, \mathsf{ct})$ has runtime $\mathsf{poly}(\lambda)$ and if $\mathsf{Eval}^{\widetilde{D}}(\widetilde{P}, \mathbf{lab})$ has runtime $|P| \cdot \mathsf{polylog(|D|)} \cdot \mathsf{poly}(\lambda)$ then $\mathsf{Dec}(\mathsf{sk}_T, \mathsf{ct})$ has runtime $t' \cdot \mathsf{polylog(t)} \cdot \mathsf{poly}(\lambda)$ where t' is the time T takes to accept the attribute w used when computing ct and t is the time bound set at encryption time when computing ct.

4.4 Security

Next, we prove the following.

Theorem 4.1. *Let* IBE *be a secure IBE scheme,* SKE *be a secure symmetric key encryption scheme, and* GRAM *be a garbled RAM scheme satisfying Iterated Simulation Security as per Definition 3.1. Then* ABE *described above is an ABE scheme satisfying 1-query key-selective security as per Definition 2.3.*

We prove Theorem 4.1 via a sequence of hybrid games. First, we describe the games and later on prove that any two adjacent games are indistinguishable.

Game 0. This game corresponds to the original 1-query key-selective security game.

- **Setup Phase**: The challenger chooses $(\mathsf{pp}, \mathsf{msk}) \leftarrow \mathsf{IBE.Setup}(1^\lambda)$, and sends pp to the adversary. (Note that Setup in our scheme is precisely $\mathsf{IBE.Setup}$.)
- **Key Query Phase**: The adversary submits a single key query for machine T to the challenger. Let the Turing machine T be given as the set of possible transitions it can make under its transition relation δ:

$$T = \{(q^{\mathsf{in}}, b^{\mathsf{in}}, q^{\mathsf{out}}, b^{\mathsf{out}}, \mathsf{dir}) \ : \ \delta(q^{\mathsf{in}}, b^{\mathsf{in}}) = (q^{\mathsf{out}}, b^{\mathsf{out}}, \mathsf{dir})\}.$$

Let $\mathcal{ID}_T$ be the set of $(n+2) \cdot |T|$ identities as defined in Eq. (1). The challenger samples an IBE secret key for each identity in $\mathcal{ID}_T$. Concretely, it chooses

$$\forall\ (q^{\mathsf{in}}, b^{\mathsf{in}}, i, \beta) \in \mathcal{ID}_T, \quad \mathsf{sk}_{(q^{\mathsf{in}}, b^{\mathsf{in}}, i, \beta)} \leftarrow \mathsf{IBE.KeyGen}(\mathsf{msk}, (q^{\mathsf{in}}, b^{\mathsf{in}}, i, \beta)).$$

Finally, it sends the key $\mathsf{sk}_T = \left(T, \left\{\mathsf{sk}_{(q^{\mathsf{in}}, b^{\mathsf{in}}, i, \beta)}\right\}_{(q^{\mathsf{in}}, b^{\mathsf{in}}, i, \beta) \in \mathcal{ID}_T}\right)$ to $\mathcal{A}$.

- **Challenge Phase**: The adversary submits two challenge messages (m_0, m_1) and the challenge attribute and time bound $(w, 1^t)$ to the challenger. It must be the case that the machine T for which the adversary was given a secret key sk_T during the key query phase does not accept the word w within t steps. The challenger samples a bit $\beta \leftarrow \{0,1\}$, and computes the challenge ciphertext as follows.
  1. The challenger sets a database $D \in \{0,1\}^{t+1+\lceil \log(t+1) \rceil}$. It sets the first $|w|$ bits of D to match w, and sets the remaining $\lceil \log(t+1) \rceil$ bits to 0. More formally,
  $$D := w || 0^{t+1+\lceil \log(t+1) \rceil - |w|}$$
  where $||$ denotes concatenation. It next garbles the database $(\widetilde{D}, \mathsf{k}_D) \leftarrow \mathsf{GData}(1^\lambda, D)$.
  2. For each $(i,b,j) \in [n+2] \times \{0,1\} \times [t+1]$, the challenger samples randomness $r_{b,j}^{(i)}$ and SKE secret keys $\mathsf{K}_{i,b}^{(j)}$ as $r_{b,j}^{(i)} \leftarrow \{0,1\}^\lambda, \mathsf{K}_{i,b}^{(j)} \leftarrow \mathsf{SKE.Setup}(1^\lambda)$.
  3. Let P be the RAM program described as described in Fig. 1. For each $j \in [t+1]$, the challenger sets P_j as $P_j := P[\mathsf{pp}, \{\mathsf{K}_{i,b}^{(j)}\}_{i,b}, m_\beta, j; \{r_{b,j}^{(i)}\}_{i,b}]$.
  4. Let ℓ be the number of steps P takes to run on a database of length $|D|$. For each $j \in [t+1]$, the challenger garbles the program P_j, computing
  $$(\widetilde{P_j}, \{\mathsf{lab}_{i,b}^{\mathsf{in},j}\}_{i,b}) \leftarrow \mathsf{GProg}(1^\lambda, \mathsf{k}_D, t+1+\lceil \log(t+1) \rceil, P_j, 1^{n+2}, (1+(j-1)\cdot \ell, j \cdot \ell)).$$
  5. For each $(i,b,j) \in [n+2] \times \{0,1\} \times [t]$, the challenger computes ciphertexts $\widetilde{\mathsf{ct}}_{i,b}^{(j)} \leftarrow \mathsf{SKE.Enc}(\mathsf{K}_{i,b}^{(j)}, \mathsf{lab}_{i,b}^{\mathsf{in},j+1})$.
  6. Let $\{\mathsf{lab}_{i,b}^{\mathsf{in},1}\}_{i,b}$ be the set of input labels computed when garbling program P_1. Recall that the all zero state is the canonical start state. The challenger outputs the ciphertext
  $$\mathsf{ct}^* = (w, t, \widetilde{D}, \{\mathsf{lab}_{i,0}^{\mathsf{in},1}\}_{i \in [n+2]}, \{\widetilde{P_j}\}_{j \in [t+1]}, \{\widetilde{\mathsf{ct}}_{i,b}^{(j)}\}_{i \in [n+2], b \in \{0,1\}, j \in [t]}).$$
- **Guess Phase**: The adversary submits its guess β', and wins the game if $\beta = \beta'$.

Game k.1 $(1 \le k \le t+1)$. This game is defined similar to Game 0, except now the challenger simulates the first k (out of $t+1$) garbled RAM programs and the SKE ciphertexts encrypting the labels for first $k-1$ levels are also simulated (i.e., half of them contain the simulated wire label keys, while other half encrypt all zeros). Note that while setting up the garbled programs to be simulated, the challenger needs to sample the IBE ciphertexts appropriately where the IBE ciphertexts for the first $k-1$ simulated garbled programs encrypt only half of the corresponding SKE keys and the IBE ciphertexts for the k-th simulated program encrypts all the keys honestly. Below we describe it in detail highlighting the differences.

- **Challenge Phase**: The adversary submits two challenge messages (m_0, m_1) and the challenge attribute and time bound $(w, 1^t)$ to the challenger. It must be the case that the machine T for which the adversary was given a secret key sk_T during the key query phase does not accept the word w within t steps. Let $\{(q_j^{\mathsf{in}}, b_j^{\mathsf{in}}, q_j^{\mathsf{out}}, b_j^{\mathsf{out}}, \mathsf{dir}_j)\}_{j\in[t]}$ be the sequence of the first t transitions made by machine T on input w. Let $x_1 = 0^{n+2}$, and for all other j let x_j be the $(n+2)$-bit representation of $(q_{j-1}^{\mathsf{out}}, b_{j-1}^{\mathsf{out}}, b_{j-1}^{\mathsf{dir}})$. Let $D \in \{0,1\}^{t+1+\lceil\log(t+1)\rceil}$ match w in the first $|w|$ bits, and be 0 elsewhere. Let $\{\mathsf{access}_j\}_{j\in[t+1]}$ be the memory access patterns of the $t+1$ step programs P_j run on D in sequence with inputs x_j. Note that the hard-coded inputs do not affect the memory access pattern, so for all $j \in [t+1]$, access_j can be computed as a function of the machine T, the challenge attribute w, and the time bound t.
The challenger samples a bit $\beta \leftarrow \{0,1\}$, and computes the challenge ciphertext as follows.
  1. The challenger sets a database $D \in \{0,1\}^{t+1+\lceil\log(t+1)\rceil}$. It sets the first $|w|$ bits of D to match w, and sets the remaining $\lceil\log(t+1)\rceil$ bits to 0. More formally,
$$D := w||0^{t+1+\lceil\log(t+1)\rceil-|w|}$$
where $||$ denotes concatenation. It next garbles the database $(\widetilde{D}, \mathsf{k}_D) \leftarrow \mathsf{GData}(1^\lambda, D)$.
  2. For each $(i,b,j) \in [n+2] \times \{0,1\} \times [t+1]$, the challenger samples randomness $r_{b,j}^{(i)}$ and SKE secret keys $\mathsf{K}_{i,b}^{(j)}$ as $r_{b,j}^{(i)} \leftarrow \{0,1\}^\lambda, \mathsf{K}_{i,b}^{(j)} \leftarrow \mathsf{SKE.Setup}(1^\lambda)$.[8]
  3. Let P be the RAM program as described in Fig. 1. For each $j \in [k+1, t+1]$, the challenger sets P_j as $P_j := P[\mathsf{pp}, \{\mathsf{K}_{i,b}^{(j)}\}_{i,b}, m_\beta, j; \{r_{b,j}^{(i)}\}_{i,b}]$. It computes $2k(n+2)$ IBE ciphertexts as:
$$\begin{aligned}
(i,b) &\in [n+2] \times \{0,1\}, & \mathsf{ct}_{i,b}^{(k)} &\leftarrow \mathsf{IBE.Enc}(\mathsf{pp}, \mathsf{K}_{i,b}^{(k)}, (q_k^{\mathsf{in}}, b_k^{\mathsf{in}}, i, b)),\\
(i,j) &\in [n+2] \times [k-1], & \mathsf{ct}_{i,x_j[i]}^{(j)} &\leftarrow \mathsf{IBE.Enc}(\mathsf{pp}, \mathsf{K}_{i,x_j[i]}^{(j)}, (q_j^{\mathsf{in}}, b_j^{\mathsf{in}}, i, x_j[i])),\\
(i,j) &\in [n+2] \times [k-1], & \mathsf{ct}_{i,1-x_j[i]}^{(j)} &\leftarrow \mathsf{IBE.Enc}(\mathsf{pp}, \mathbf{0}, (q_j^{\mathsf{in}}, b_j^{\mathsf{in}}, i, 1-x_j[i]))
\end{aligned}$$
  4. Let ℓ be the number of steps P takes to run on a database of length $|D|$. For each $j \in [k+1, t+1]$, the challenger garbles the program P_j, computing
$$(\widetilde{P_j}, \{\mathsf{lab}_{i,b}^{\mathsf{in},j}\}_{i,b}) \leftarrow \mathsf{GProg}(1^\lambda, \mathsf{k}_D, t+1+\lceil\log(t+1)\rceil, P_j, 1^{n+2}, (1+(j-1)\cdot\ell, j\cdot\ell)).$$
For $j \in [k]$, the challenger computes a simulated program
$$(\widetilde{P_j}, \{\mathsf{lab}_i^{\mathsf{in},j}\}_{i\in[n+2]}) \leftarrow \mathsf{Sim}(1^\lambda, \mathsf{k}_D, |P|, (\{\mathsf{ct}_{i,b}^{(j)}\}_{(i,b)\in[n+2]\times\{0,1\}}, \bot), D, \{\mathsf{access}_{j'}'\}_{j'\in[t+1]})$$

[8] We point out that the challenger does not need use all the sampled random coins and secret keys anymore. However, for ease of exposition we still sample all of them as before.

5. Next, it computes the ciphertexts $\widetilde{\mathsf{ct}}_{i,b}^{(j)}$ as follows:

$$(i,b,j) \in [n+2] \times \{0,1\} \times [k,t], \quad \widetilde{\mathsf{ct}}_{i,b}^{(j)} \leftarrow \mathsf{SKE.Enc}(\mathsf{K}_{i,b}^{(j)}, \mathsf{lab}_{i,b}^{\mathsf{in},j+1}),$$
$$(i,j) \in [n+2] \times [k-1], \quad \widetilde{\mathsf{ct}}_{i,x_{j+1}[i]}^{(j)} \leftarrow \mathsf{SKE.Enc}(\mathsf{K}_{i,x_{j+1}[i]}^{(j)}, \mathsf{lab}_{i}^{\mathsf{in},j+1}),$$
$$(i,j) \in [n+2] \times [k-1], \quad \widetilde{\mathsf{ct}}_{i,1-x_{j+1}[i]}^{(j)} \leftarrow \mathsf{SKE.Enc}(\mathsf{K}_{i,1-x_{j+1}[i]}^{(j)}, \mathbf{0})$$

6. Let $\{\mathsf{lab}_i^{\mathsf{in},1}\}_i$ be the set of input labels computed when simulating program P_1. The challenger outputs the ciphertext

$$\mathsf{ct}^* = (w, t, \widetilde{D}, \{\mathsf{lab}_i^{\mathsf{in},1}\}_{i\in[n+2]}, \{\widetilde{P}_j\}_{j\in[t+1]}, \{\widetilde{\mathsf{ct}}_{i,b}^{(j)}\}_{i\in[n+2],b\in\{0,1\},j\in[t]}).$$

Game k.2 ($1 \leq k \leq t+1$). This game is defined identically to Game k.1, except now IBE ciphertexts hardwired in the k-th simulated garbled program also encrypt only half of the corresponding SKE keys (as for first $k-1$ simulated programs). Below we simply describe the change in game description when compared with previous game.

- **Challenge Phase**: The adversary submits two challenge messages (m_0, m_1) and the challenge attribute and time bound $(w, 1^t)$ to the challenger. It must be the case that the machine T for which the adversary was given a secret key sk_T during the key query phase does not accept the word w within t steps. The challenger samples a bit $\beta \leftarrow \{0,1\}$, and computes the challenge ciphertext as in Game k.1, except the following:
  3. Let P be the RAM program as described in Fig. 1. For each $j \in [k+1, t+1]$, the challenger sets P_j as $P_j := P[\mathsf{pp}, \{\mathsf{K}_{i,b}^{(j)}\}_{i,b}, m_\beta, j; \{r_{b,j}^{(i)}\}_{i,b}]$. It computes $2k(n+2)$ IBE ciphertexts as:

$$(i,j) \in [n+2] \times [k], \quad \mathsf{ct}_{i,x_j[i]}^{(j)} \leftarrow \mathsf{IBE.Enc}(\mathsf{pp}, \mathsf{K}_{i,x_j[i]}^{(j)}, (q_j^{\mathsf{in}}, b_j^{\mathsf{in}}, i, x_j[i])),$$
$$(i,j) \in [n+2] \times [k], \quad \mathsf{ct}_{i,1-x_j[i]}^{(j)} \leftarrow \mathsf{IBE.Enc}(\mathsf{pp}, \mathbf{0}, (q_j^{\mathsf{in}}, b_j^{\mathsf{in}}, i, 1-x_j[i]))$$

Game k.3 ($1 \leq k \leq t+1$). This game is defined identically to Game k.2, except now the SKE ciphertexts encrypting the garbled program labels for the $(k+1)$-th garbled program encrypt only half of the label keys (i.e., only the label keys corresponding to the k-th state transition). Below we simply describe the change in game description when compared with previous game.

- **Challenge Phase**: The adversary submits two challenge messages (m_0, m_1) and the challenge attribute and time bound $(w, 1^t)$ to the challenger. It must be the case that the machine T for which the adversary was given a secret key sk_T during the key query phase does not accept the word w within t steps. The challenger samples a bit $\beta \leftarrow \{0,1\}$, and computes the challenge ciphertext as in Game k.2, except the following:

5. Next, it computes the ciphertexts $\widetilde{\mathsf{ct}}_{i,b}^{(j)}$ as follows:

$$(i,b,j) \in [n+2] \times \{0,1\} \times [k+1,t], \quad \widetilde{\mathsf{ct}}_{i,b}^{(j)} \leftarrow \mathsf{SKE.Enc}(\mathsf{K}_{i,b}^{(j)}, \mathsf{lab}_{i,b}^{\mathsf{in},j+1}),$$
$$(i,j) \in [n+2] \times [k], \quad \widetilde{\mathsf{ct}}_{i,x_{j+1}[i]}^{(j)} \leftarrow \mathsf{SKE.Enc}(\mathsf{K}_{i,x_{j+1}[i]}^{(j)}, \mathsf{lab}_{i}^{\mathsf{in},j+1}),$$
$$(i,j) \in [n+2] \times [k], \quad \widetilde{\mathsf{ct}}_{i,1-x_{j+1}[i]}^{(j)} \leftarrow \mathsf{SKE.Enc}(\mathsf{K}_{i,1-x_{j+1}[i]}^{(j)}, \mathbf{0})$$

Analysis of game indistinguishability. We complete the proof by showing that adjacent hybrid games are indistinguishable. For any adversary $\mathcal{A}$ and game **Game s**, we denote by $\mathsf{Adv}_s^{\mathcal{A}}(\lambda)$, the probability that $\mathcal{A}$ wins in **Game s**. For ease of exposition, in the sequel we use **Game 0.3** to denote **Game 0**.

Lemma 4.2. *If* IBE *is a secure IBE scheme, then for any PPT adversary* $\mathcal{A}$ *and* $k \in [t+1]$*, we have that* $\mathsf{Adv}_{k.1}^{\mathcal{A}}(\lambda) - \mathsf{Adv}_{k.2}^{\mathcal{A}}(\lambda) \leq negl(\lambda)$ *for some negligible function* $negl(\cdot)$*.*

Proof. Suppose for contradiction that $\mathcal{A}$ is a PPT adversary for which $\mathsf{Adv}_{k.1}^{\mathcal{A}}(\lambda) - \mathsf{Adv}_{k.2}^{\mathcal{A}}(\lambda) = \epsilon$, where ϵ is non-negligible. We give a reduction $\mathcal{B}$ which uses $\mathcal{A}$ to break the security of IBE. In particular, our reduction $\mathcal{B}$ will break the multi-challenge security of IBE.

The reduction algorithm $\mathcal{B}$ plays a game with an IBE challenger. The reduction $\mathcal{B}$ samples a bit $\beta \leftarrow \{0,1\}$. The challenger chooses $(\mathsf{pp}, \mathsf{msk}) \leftarrow \mathsf{IBE.Setup}(1^\lambda)$ and sends pp to $\mathcal{B}$ who forwards it to $\mathcal{A}$. Next, $\mathcal{A}$ submits a key query for machine T to the reduction $\mathcal{B}$. Let $\mathcal{ID}_T$ denote the set of identities corresponding to machine T as per Eq. (1). $\mathcal{B}$ then makes a key query for every identity in $\mathcal{ID}_T$ to the challenger, and let S denote set containing all the secret keys sent by the challenger to $\mathcal{B}$. The reduction $\mathcal{B}$ then set $\mathsf{sk}_T = S$, and it sends sk_T to $\mathcal{A}$. Now, $\mathcal{A}$ submits two challenge messages (m_0, m_1) and the challenge attribute and time bound $(w, 1^t)$ to $\mathcal{B}$. The reduction $\mathcal{B}$ now computes the challenge ciphertext ct^* as in Game $k.1$, except for how it computes the IBE ciphertexts which constitute the output of the k-th simulated program in step 3 of the challenge phase.

Let x_k be the $n+2$ bit representation of $(q_{k-1}^{\mathsf{out}}, b_{k-1}^{\mathsf{out}}, b_{k-1}^{\mathsf{dir}})$, and let $\{\mathsf{K}_{i,b}^{(k)}\}_{(i,b)}$ be the set of SKE secret keys chosen in step 2. First, for each $i \in [n+2]$, $\mathcal{B}$ computes $\mathsf{ct}_{i,x_k[i]}^{(k)} \leftarrow \mathsf{IBE.Enc}(\mathsf{pp}, \mathsf{K}_{i,x_k[i]}^{(k)}, (q_k^{\mathsf{in}}, b_k^{\mathsf{in}}, i, x_k[i]))$. Next, it sends $\{(\mathsf{K}_{i,1-x_k[i]}^{(k)}, \mathbf{0}, (q_k^{\mathsf{in}}, b_k^{\mathsf{in}}, i, 1-x_k[i]))\}_{i\in[n+2]}$ as its challenge vector of message-identity tuples. (Recall that we are considering the multi-challenge version of IBE security.) Let $\{\mathsf{ct}_i^*\}_i$ denote the set of challenge ciphertexts received by $\mathcal{B}$. It then sets the ciphertexts $\mathsf{ct}_{i,1-x_k[i]}^{(k)}$ as $\mathsf{ct}_{i,1-x_k[i]}^{(k)} = \mathsf{ct}_i^*$ for $i \in [n+2]$. The remaining portion of the challenge ciphertext is computed as in Game $k.1$.

Finally, after sending the challenge ciphertext to $\mathcal{A}$, the adversary outputs a bit γ. If $\gamma = \beta$, then $\mathcal{B}$ guesses 0 to the challenger signalling that ciphertexts $\{\mathsf{ct}_i^*\}_i$ encrypt the PRF keys. Otherwise, $\mathcal{B}$ guesses 1 to the challenger signalling they encrypt all zeros. Observe that the reduction $\mathcal{B}$ perfectly simulates the view of Game $k.1$ and $k.2$ to $\mathcal{A}$, respectively, depending upon the challenger's bit. Note that $\mathcal{B}$ is an admissible adversary as per the multi-challenge IBE game, since the adversary $\mathcal{A}$ makes only a single key query for machine T such that T does not accept w after t steps, and the IBE keys queried by $\mathcal{B}$ are completely disjoint with the set of challenge identities. Thus, the lemma follows. ■

Lemma 4.3. *If* SKE *is a secure secret key encryption scheme, then for any PPT adversary $\mathcal{A}$ and $k \in [t+1]$, we have that $\mathsf{Adv}^{\mathcal{A}}_{k.2}(\lambda) - \mathsf{Adv}^{\mathcal{A}}_{k.3}(\lambda) \leq negl(\lambda)$ for some negligible function $negl(\cdot)$.*

Proof. We prove this lemma by sketching a sequence of $n+3$ intermediate hybrid games Game $k.2.h$, for each $h \in [0, \ldots, n+2]$. Game $k.2.h$ is defined similar to Game $k.2$, except for how the challenge ciphertext is computed. In particular in Game $k.2.h$, we change how the challenger proceeds in step 5 of computing the challenge ciphertext. Concretely, it computes the ciphertexts $\widetilde{\mathsf{ct}}^{(j)}_{i,b}$ as follows:

$$(i,b,j) \in \begin{matrix} [n+2] \times \{0,1\} \times [k+1,t] \\ \cup\, [h+1,n+2] \times \{0,1\} \times \{k\} \end{matrix}, \quad \widetilde{\mathsf{ct}}^{(j)}_{i,b} \leftarrow \mathsf{SKE.Enc}(\mathsf{K}^{(j)}_{i,b}, \mathsf{lab}^{\mathsf{in},j+1}_{i,b}),$$

$$(i,j) \in \begin{matrix} [n+2] \times [k-1] \\ \cup\, [h] \times \{k\} \end{matrix}, \quad \begin{matrix} \widetilde{\mathsf{ct}}^{(j)}_{i,x_{j+1}[i]} \leftarrow \mathsf{SKE.Enc}(\mathsf{K}^{(j)}_{i,x_{j+1}[i]}, \mathsf{lab}^{\mathsf{in},j+1}_{i}), \\ \widetilde{\mathsf{ct}}^{(j)}_{i,1-x_{j+1}[i]} \leftarrow \mathsf{SKE.Enc}(\mathsf{K}^{(j)}_{i,1-x_{j+1}[i]}, \mathbf{0}) \end{matrix}$$

In short, for each $i \leq h$, if $b \neq x_{k+1}[i]$, the encryption of label $\mathsf{lab}^{\mathsf{in},k+1}_{i,b}$ is replaced with an encryption of $\mathbf{0}$. All other steps are identical to Game $k.2$. It is immediate that Game $k.2.0$ is identical to Game $k.2$ and that Game $k.2.(n+2)$ is identical to Game $k.3$. We claim that if SKE is a secure secret key encryption scheme, that for any $\mathcal{A}$ and $h \in [n+2]$ that $\mathsf{Adv}^{\mathcal{A}}_{k.2.h}(\lambda) - \mathsf{Adv}^{\mathcal{A}}_{k.2.(h-1)}(\lambda) \leq \mathrm{negl}'(\lambda)$ for some negligible function $\mathrm{negl}'(\lambda)$. The lemma follows immediately from this claim.

Suppose for contradiction that $\mathcal{A}$ is a PPT adversary for which $\mathsf{Adv}^{\mathcal{A}}_{k.2.h}(\lambda) - \mathsf{Adv}^{\mathcal{A}}_{k.2.(h-1)}(\lambda) = \epsilon$, where ϵ is non-negligible. We give a reduction $\mathcal{B}$ which uses $\mathcal{A}$ to break the security of SKE. The reduction $\mathcal{B}$ samples a bit $\beta \leftarrow \{0,1\}$. It then chooses $(\mathsf{pp}, \mathsf{msk}) \leftarrow \mathsf{IBE.Setup}(1^\lambda)$, and forwards pp to the adversary $\mathcal{A}$. The challenger chooses $\mathsf{K} \leftarrow \mathsf{SKE.Setup}(1^\lambda)$. Next, $\mathcal{A}$ submits a key query for machine T to the reduction $\mathcal{B}$. The reduction $\mathcal{B}$ computes sk_T as in Game $k.2.(h-1)$ (equivalently $k.2$), and sends sk_T to $\mathcal{A}$. Now, $\mathcal{A}$ submits two challenge messages (m_0, m_1) and the challenge attribute and time bound $(w, 1^t)$ to $\mathcal{B}$. The reduction $\mathcal{B}$ now computes the challenge ciphertext ct^* as in Game $k.2.h$, except it computes the ciphertext $\widetilde{\mathsf{ct}}^{(k)}_{h,1-x_{k+1}[h]}$ by quering the SKE challenger on appropriate challenge messages.

Here x_k denotes the $n+2$ bit representation of $(q^{\mathsf{out}}_{k-1}, b^{\mathsf{out}}_{k-1}, b^{\mathsf{dir}}_{k-1})$. First, $\mathcal{B}$ sample all the SKE secret keys except the key $\mathsf{K}^{(k)}_{h,1-x_{k+1}[h]}$ which is implicitly set to the challenger's secret key. The reduction $\mathcal{B}$ sends the challenge messages $m_0 = \mathsf{lab}^{\mathsf{in},k+1}_{h,1-x_{k+1}[h]}$ and $m_1 = \mathbf{0}$, and let ct' denote the challenger's response. $\mathcal{B}$ now sets $\widetilde{\mathsf{ct}}^{(k)}_{h,1-x_{k+1}[h]} = \mathsf{ct}'$, while for all other $(j,i,b) \neq (k,h,1-x_{k+1}[h])$, it computes $\widetilde{\mathsf{ct}}^{(j)}_{i,b}$ as in Game $k.2.h$. The remaining portion of the challenge ciphertext is computed as in Game $k.2.h$.

Finally, after computing the challenge ciphertext ct^*, $\mathcal{B}$ sends it to $\mathcal{A}$. The adversary $\mathcal{A}$ now sends $\mathcal{B}$ its guess β''. If $\beta'' = \beta$, $\mathcal{B}$ guesses 0 to the challenger. Otherwise, $\mathcal{B}$ guesses 1 to the challenger. Observe that when $\beta' = 0$, the reduction $\mathcal{B}$ perfectly simulates the view of Game $k.2.(h-1)$ to $\mathcal{A}$. On the other hand, when $\beta' = 1$, the reduction $\mathcal{B}$ perfectly simulates the view of Game $k.2.h$ to $\mathcal{A}$. It immediately follows that $\mathcal{B}$ has advantage ϵ against the SKE challenger, which contradicts the security of SKE. This establishes the claim and thus the lemma.

Finally, after sending the challenge ciphertext to $\mathcal{A}$, the adversary outputs a bit γ. If $\gamma = \beta$, then $\mathcal{B}$ guesses 0 to the challenger signalling that ciphertext ct' was an encryption of the garbled label. Otherwise, $\mathcal{B}$ guesses 1 to the challenger signalling its encrypts all zeros. Observe that the reduction $\mathcal{B}$ perfectly simulates the view of Game $k.2.(h-1)$ and $k.2.h$ to $\mathcal{A}$, respectively, depending upon the challenger's bit. Note that $\mathcal{B}$ is an admissible adversary as per the SKE game, since the adversary $\mathcal{A}$ does not need the SKE secret key $\mathsf{K}^{(k)}_{h,1-x_{k+1}[h]}$ for preparing the challenge ciphertext as the garbled program which would have contained the key is already being simulated. Thus, the lemma follows. ■

Lemma 4.4. *If* GRAM *satisfies Iterated Simulation Security, then for any PPT adversary* $\mathcal{A}$ *and* $0 \le k \le t$, *we have that* $\mathsf{Adv}^{\mathcal{A}}_{k.3}(\lambda) - \mathsf{Adv}^{\mathcal{A}}_{k+1.1}(\lambda) \le negl(\lambda)$ *for some negligible function* $negl(\cdot)$.

Proof. Suppose for contradiction that $\mathcal{A}$ is a PPT adversary for which $\mathsf{Adv}^{\mathcal{A}}_{k.3}(\lambda) - \mathsf{Adv}^{\mathcal{A}}_{k+1.1}(\lambda) = \epsilon$, where ϵ is non-negligible. We give a reduction $\mathcal{B}$ which uses $\mathcal{A}$ to break the Iterated Simulation Security property of GRAM.

The reduction algorithm $\mathcal{B}$ plays a game with a GRAM challenger. The reduction $\mathcal{B}$ samples a bit $\beta \leftarrow \{0,1\}$. The reduction $\mathcal{B}$ then chooses $(\mathsf{pp}, \mathsf{msk}) \leftarrow \mathsf{IBE.Setup}(1^\lambda)$, and sends pp to $\mathcal{A}$. Next, $\mathcal{A}$ submits a key query for machine T to the reduction $\mathcal{B}$. The reduction $\mathcal{B}$ computes sk_T as it is computed in Game $k.3$. Then, $\mathcal{B}$ sends sk_T to $\mathcal{A}$. Now, $\mathcal{A}$ submits two challenge messages (m_0, m_1) and the challenge attribute and time bound $(w, 1^t)$ to $\mathcal{B}$. The reduction $\mathcal{B}$ now computes the challenge ciphertext ct^* as in Game $k.3$, except it simulates the $(k+1)$-th garbled program instead of computing honestly.

The reduction $\mathcal{B}$ sets up the database D as in Game $k.3$. Let $x_1 = 0^{n+2}$, and for all other j let x_j be the $n+2$ bit representation of $(q^{\mathsf{out}}_{j-1}, b^{\mathsf{out}}_{j-1}, b^{\mathsf{dir}}_{j-1})$. It samples the random coins $r^{(i)}_{b,j}$ and SKE secret keys $\mathsf{K}^{(j)}_{i,b}$ as in step 2. For each $j \in [t+1]$, the reduction $\mathcal{B}$ sets program P_j as

$$P_j := P[\mathsf{pp}, \{\mathsf{K}^{(j)}_{i,b}\}_{(i,b)}, m_\beta, j; \{r^{(i)}_{b,j}\}_{(i,b)}].$$

The reduction sends $(k+1, D, \{(P_j, x_j, n+2, (1+(j-1)\cdot\ell, j\cdot\ell))\}_j)$ to the challenger. The challenger, garbles the database D to compute $\widetilde{D}$, and then honestly garbles the programs P_j for $j \in [k+2, t+1]$, while P_{k+1} is either garbled honestly or simulated, and remaining programs $\widetilde{P_j}$, for $j \in [k]$, are simulated. Finally, the challenger sends $(\widetilde{D}, \{\widetilde{P_j}, \{\mathsf{lab}^{\mathsf{in},j}_i\}_i\}_{j\in[k+1]}, \{\widetilde{P_j}, \{\mathsf{lab}^{\mathsf{in},j}_{i,b}\}_{i,b}\}_{j\in[k+2,t+1]})$ to $\mathcal{B}$.

From this point, the reduction simply computes the challenge ciphertext as in Game $k.3$ but using the garbled database, programs, and input labels as provided by the challenger. Finally, after sending the challenge ciphertext to $\mathcal{A}$, the adversary outputs a bit γ. If $\gamma = \beta$, then $\mathcal{B}$ guesses 0 to the challenger signalling that $\widetilde{P_{k+1}}$ was honestly garbled. Otherwise, $\mathcal{B}$ guesses 1 to the challenger signalling it was simulated. Note that since the reduction $\mathcal{B}$ does not need the garbled labels for $(k+1)$-th garbled program while preparing the challenge ciphertext thus it can perfectly simulate the view of Game $k.3$ and $k+1.1$ to $\mathcal{A}$, respectively, depending upon the challenger's bit. Thus, the lemma follows. ∎

Lemma 4.5. *For any adversary, $\mathcal{A}$ we have that* $\mathsf{Adv}^{\mathcal{A}}_{t+1.1}(\lambda) = 0$.

Proof. This lemma is immediate, as in Game $t+1.1$, the challenge ciphertext consists only of simulated programs all of which are completely independent of the challenge message m_β. ∎

By combining the above lemmas, the theorem follows.

References

1. Agrawal, S., Chase, M.: Simplifying design and analysis of complex predicate encryption schemes. In: Coron, J.-S., Nielsen, J.B. (eds.) EUROCRYPT 2017. LNCS, vol. 10210, pp. 627–656. Springer, Cham (2017). https://doi.org/10.1007/978-3-319-56620-7_22
2. Agrawal, S., Maitra, M., Vempati, N.S., Yamada, S.: Functional encryption for turing machines with dynamic bounded collusion from LWE. In: Malkin, T., Peikert, C. (eds.) CRYPTO 2021. LNCS, vol. 12828, pp. 239–269. Springer, Cham (2021). https://doi.org/10.1007/978-3-030-84259-8_9
3. Agrawal, S., Maitra, M., Yamada, S.: Attribute based encryption (and more) for nondeterministic finite automata from LWE. In: Boldyreva, A., Micciancio, D. (eds.) CRYPTO 2019. LNCS, vol. 11693, pp. 765–797. Springer, Cham (2019). https://doi.org/10.1007/978-3-030-26951-7_26
4. Agrawal, S., Maitra, M., Yamada, S.: Attribute based encryption for deterministic finite automata from DLIN. In: Hofheinz, D., Rosen, A. (eds.) TCC 2019. LNCS, vol. 11892, pp. 91–117. Springer, Cham (2019). https://doi.org/10.1007/978-3-030-36033-7_4
5. Agrawal, S., Singh, I.P.: Reusable garbled deterministic finite automata from learning with errors. In: Chatzigiannakis, I., Indyk, P., Kuhn, F., Muscholl, A. (eds.) ICALP 2017 (2017)
6. Ananth, P., Fan, X., Shi, E.: Towards attribute-based encryption for RAMs from LWE: sub-linear decryption, and more. In: Galbraith, S.D., Moriai, S. (eds.) ASIACRYPT 2019. LNCS, vol. 11921, pp. 112–141. Springer, Cham (2019). https://doi.org/10.1007/978-3-030-34578-5_5
7. Ananth, P., Vaikuntanathan, V.: Optimal bounded-collusion secure functional encryption. In: Hofheinz, D., Rosen, A. (eds.) TCC 2019. LNCS, vol. 11891, pp. 174–198. Springer, Cham (2019). https://doi.org/10.1007/978-3-030-36030-6_8
8. Ananth, P., Sahai, A.: Functional encryption for Turing machines. In: Kushilevitz, E., Malkin, T. (eds.) TCC 2016. LNCS, vol. 9562, pp. 125–153. Springer, Heidelberg (2016). https://doi.org/10.1007/978-3-662-49096-9_6
9. Attrapadung, N.: Dual system encryption via doubly selective security: framework, fully secure functional encryption for regular languages, and more. In: Nguyen, P.Q., Oswald, E. (eds.) EUROCRYPT 2014. LNCS, vol. 8441, pp. 557–577. Springer, Heidelberg (2014). https://doi.org/10.1007/978-3-642-55220-5_31

10. Attrapadung, N.: Dual system encryption framework in prime-order groups via computational pair encodings. In: Cheon, J.H., Takagi, T. (eds.) ASIACRYPT 2016. LNCS, vol. 10032, pp. 591–623. Springer, Heidelberg (2016). https://doi.org/10.1007/978-3-662-53890-6_20
11. Bellare, M., Rogaway, P.: Random oracles are practical: A paradigm for designing efficient protocols. In: CCS (1993)
12. Bethencourt, J., Sahai, A., Waters, B.: Ciphertext-policy attribute-based encryption. In: IEEE Symposium on Security and Privacy, pp. 321–334 (2007)
13. Bitansky, N., et al.: Indistinguishability obfuscation for RAM programs and succinct randomized encodings. SIAM J. Comput. **47**(3), 1123–1210 (2018)
14. Boneh, D., Franklin, M.: Identity-based encryption from the Weil pairing. In: Kilian, J. (ed.) CRYPTO 2001. LNCS, vol. 2139, pp. 213–229. Springer, Heidelberg (2001). https://doi.org/10.1007/3-540-44647-8_13
15. Boyen, X., Li, Q.: Attribute-based encryption for finite automata from LWE. In: Au, M.-H., Miyaji, A. (eds.) ProvSec 2015. LNCS, vol. 9451, pp. 247–267. Springer, Cham (2015). https://doi.org/10.1007/978-3-319-26059-4_14
16. Boyle, E., Chung, K.-M., Pass, R.: On extractability obfuscation. In: Lindell, Y. (ed.) TCC 2014. LNCS, vol. 8349, pp. 52–73. Springer, Heidelberg (2014). https://doi.org/10.1007/978-3-642-54242-8_3
17. Canetti, R., Feige, U., Goldreich, O., Naor, M.: Adaptively secure multi-party computation. In: STOC 1996 (1996)
18. Canetti, R., Halevi, S., Katz, J.: Adaptively-secure, non-interactive public-key encryption. In: Kilian, J. (ed.) TCC 2005. LNCS, vol. 3378, pp. 150–168. Springer, Heidelberg (2005). https://doi.org/10.1007/978-3-540-30576-7_9
19. Cho, C., Döttling, N., Garg, S., Gupta, D., Miao, P., Polychroniadou, A.: Laconic oblivious transfer and its applications. In: Katz, J., Shacham, H. (eds.) CRYPTO 2017. LNCS, vol. 10402, pp. 33–65. Springer, Cham (2017). https://doi.org/10.1007/978-3-319-63715-0_2
20. Cocks, C.: An identity based encryption scheme based on quadratic residues. In: Honary, B. (ed.) Cryptography and Coding 2001. LNCS, vol. 2260, pp. 360–363. Springer, Heidelberg (2001). https://doi.org/10.1007/3-540-45325-3_32
21. Damgård, I., Nielsen, J.B.: Improved non-committing encryption schemes based on a general complexity assumption. In: Bellare, M. (ed.) CRYPTO 2000. LNCS, vol. 1880, pp. 432–450. Springer, Heidelberg (2000). https://doi.org/10.1007/3-540-44598-6_27
22. Döttling, N., Garg, S.: Identity-based encryption from the Diffie-Hellman assumption. In: Katz, J., Shacham, H. (eds.) CRYPTO 2017. LNCS, vol. 10401, pp. 537–569. Springer, Cham (2017). https://doi.org/10.1007/978-3-319-63688-7_18
23. Döttling, N., Garg, S.: From selective IBE to full IBE and selective HIBE. In: Kalai, Y., Reyzin, L. (eds.) TCC 2017. LNCS, vol. 10677, pp. 372–408. Springer, Cham (2017). https://doi.org/10.1007/978-3-319-70500-2_13
24. Fuchsbauer, G., Jafargholi, Z., Pietrzak, K.: A Quasipolynomial reduction for generalized selective decryption on trees. In: Gennaro, R., Robshaw, M. (eds.) CRYPTO 2015. LNCS, vol. 9215, pp. 601–620. Springer, Heidelberg (2015). https://doi.org/10.1007/978-3-662-47989-6_29
25. Fuchsbauer, G., Konstantinov, M., Pietrzak, K., Rao, V.: Adaptive security of constrained PRFs. In: Sarkar, P., Iwata, T. (eds.) ASIACRYPT 2014. LNCS, vol. 8874, pp. 82–101. Springer, Heidelberg (2014). https://doi.org/10.1007/978-3-662-45608-8_5

26. Garg, R., Goyal, R., Lu, G., Waters, B.: Dynamic collusion bounded functional encryption from identity-based encryption. Cryptology ePrint Archive, Report 2021/847 (2021). https://ia.cr/2021/847
27. Garg, S., Hajiabadi, M., Mahmoody, M., Rahimi, A.: Registration-based encryption: removing private-key generator from IBE. In: Beimel, A., Dziembowski, S. (eds.) TCC 2018. LNCS, vol. 11239, pp. 689–718. Springer, Cham (2018). https://doi.org/10.1007/978-3-030-03807-6_25
28. Garg, S., Lu, S., Ostrovsky, R.: Black-box garbled ram. In: 2015 IEEE 56th Annual Symposium on Foundations of Computer Science, pp. 210–229. IEEE (2015)
29. Garg, S., Lu, S., Ostrovsky, R., Scafuro, A.: Garbled ram from one-way functions. In: STOC (2015)
30. Garg, S., Ostrovsky, R., Srinivasan, A.: Adaptive garbled RAM from laconic oblivious transfer. In: Shacham, H., Boldyreva, A. (eds.) CRYPTO 2018. LNCS, vol. 10993, pp. 515–544. Springer, Cham (2018). https://doi.org/10.1007/978-3-319-96878-0_18
31. Garg, S., Srinivasan, A.: Garbled protocols and two-round MPC from bilinear maps. In: FOCS 2017 (2017)
32. Gentry, C., Halevi, S., Lu, S., Ostrovsky, R., Raykova, M., Wichs, D.: Garbled RAM revisited. In: Nguyen, P.Q., Oswald, E. (eds.) EUROCRYPT 2014. LNCS, vol. 8441, pp. 405–422. Springer, Heidelberg (2014). https://doi.org/10.1007/978-3-642-55220-5_23
33. Gentry, C., Halevi, S., Raykova, M., Wichs, D.: Garbled ram revisited, part i. Cryptology ePrint Archive, Report 2014/082 (2014). https://eprint.iacr.org/2014/082
34. Gentry, C., Halevi, S., Raykova, M., Wichs, D.: Outsourcing private ram computation. In: FOCS (2014)
35. Gentry, C., Peikert, C., Vaikuntanathan, V.: Trapdoors for hard lattices and new cryptographic constructions. In: STOC, pp. 197–206 (2008)
36. Goldwasser, S., Kalai, Y., Popa, R.A., Vaikuntanathan, V., Zeldovich, N.: Reusable garbled circuits and succinct functional encryption. In: STOC (2013)
37. Gong, J., Waters, B., Wee, H.: ABE for DFA from k-Lin. In: Boldyreva, A., Micciancio, D. (eds.) CRYPTO 2019. LNCS, vol. 11693, pp. 732–764. Springer, Cham (2019). https://doi.org/10.1007/978-3-030-26951-7_25
38. Gong, J., Wee, H.: Adaptively secure ABE for DFA from k-Lin and more. In: Canteaut, A., Ishai, Y. (eds.) EUROCRYPT 2020. LNCS, vol. 12107, pp. 278–308. Springer, Cham (2020). https://doi.org/10.1007/978-3-030-45727-3_10
39. Gorbunov, S., Vaikuntanathan, V., Wee, H.: Functional encryption with bounded collusions via multi-party computation. In: Safavi-Naini, R., Canetti, R. (eds.) CRYPTO 2012. LNCS, vol. 7417, pp. 162–179. Springer, Heidelberg (2012). https://doi.org/10.1007/978-3-642-32009-5_11
40. Goyal, R., Koppula, V., Waters, B.: Semi-adaptive security and bundling functionalities made generic and easy. In: Hirt, M., Smith, A. (eds.) TCC 2016. LNCS, vol. 9986, pp. 361–388. Springer, Heidelberg (2016). https://doi.org/10.1007/978-3-662-53644-5_14
41. Goyal, R., Koppula, V., Waters, B.: Lockable obfuscation. In: FOCS (2017)
42. Goyal, R., Syed, R., Waters, B.: Bounded collusion ABE for TMS from IBE. Cryptology ePrint Archive, Report 2021/709 (2021). https://ia.cr/2021/709
43. Goyal, V., Pandey, O., Sahai, A., Waters, B.: Attribute-based encryption for fine-grained access control of encrypted data. In: CCS (2006)

44. Ishai, Y., Pandey, O., Sahai, A.: Public-coin differing-inputs obfuscation and its applications. In: Dodis, Y., Nielsen, J.B. (eds.) TCC 2015. LNCS, vol. 9015, pp. 668–697. Springer, Heidelberg (2015). https://doi.org/10.1007/978-3-662-46497-7_26
45. Jafargholi, Z., Kamath, C., Klein, K., Komargodski, I., Pietrzak, K., Wichs, D.: Be adaptive, avoid overcommitting. In: Katz, J., Shacham, H. (eds.) CRYPTO 2017. LNCS, vol. 10401, pp. 133–163. Springer, Cham (2017). https://doi.org/10.1007/978-3-319-63688-7_5
46. Jafargholi, Z., Wichs, D.: Adaptive security of Yao's garbled circuits. In: Hirt, M., Smith, A. (eds.) TCC 2016. LNCS, vol. 9985, pp. 433–458. Springer, Heidelberg (2016). https://doi.org/10.1007/978-3-662-53641-4_17
47. Jain, A., Lin, H., Sahai, A.: Indistinguishability obfuscation from well-founded assumptions (2021)
48. Katz, J., Ostrovsky, R.: Round-optimal secure two-party computation. In: Franklin, M. (ed.) CRYPTO 2004. LNCS, vol. 3152, pp. 335–354. Springer, Heidelberg (2004). https://doi.org/10.1007/978-3-540-28628-8_21
49. Kitagawa, F., Nishimaki, R., Tanaka, K., Yamakawa, T.: Adaptively secure and succinct functional encryption: improving security and efficiency, simultaneously. In: Boldyreva, A., Micciancio, D. (eds.) CRYPTO 2019. LNCS, vol. 11694, pp. 521–551. Springer, Cham (2019). https://doi.org/10.1007/978-3-030-26954-8_17
50. Koppula, V., Lewko, A.B., Waters, B.: Indistinguishability obfuscation for Turing machines with unbounded memory. In: STOC (2015)
51. Koppula, V., Waters, B.: Realizing chosen ciphertext security generically in attribute-based encryption and predicate encryption. In: Boldyreva, A., Micciancio, D. (eds.) CRYPTO 2019. LNCS, vol. 11693, pp. 671–700. Springer, Cham (2019). https://doi.org/10.1007/978-3-030-26951-7_23
52. Kowalczyk, L., Wee, H.: Compact adaptively secure ABE for NC^1 from k-Lin. In: Ishai, Y., Rijmen, V. (eds.) EUROCRYPT 2019. LNCS, vol. 11476, pp. 3–33. Springer, Cham (2019). https://doi.org/10.1007/978-3-030-17653-2_1
53. Lu, S., Ostrovsky, R.: How to garble RAM programs? In: Johansson, T., Nguyen, P.Q. (eds.) EUROCRYPT 2013. LNCS, vol. 7881, pp. 719–734. Springer, Heidelberg (2013). https://doi.org/10.1007/978-3-642-38348-9_42
54. Lu, S., Ostrovsky, R.: Garbled ram revisited, part ii. Cryptology ePrint Archive, Report 2014/083 (2014). https://eprint.iacr.org/2014/083
55. Nielsen, J.B.: Separating random oracle proofs from complexity theoretic proofs: the non-committing encryption case. In: Yung, M. (ed.) CRYPTO 2002. LNCS, vol. 2442, pp. 111–126. Springer, Heidelberg (2002). https://doi.org/10.1007/3-540-45708-9_8
56. Regev, O.: On lattices, learning with errors, random linear codes, and cryptography. In: Gabow, H.N., Fagin, R. (eds.) STOC (2005)
57. Sahai, A., Seyalioglu, H.: Worry-free encryption: functional encryption with public keys. In: CCS (2010)
58. Sahai, A., Waters, B.: Fuzzy identity-based encryption. In: Cramer, R. (ed.) EUROCRYPT 2005. LNCS, vol. 3494, pp. 457–473. Springer, Heidelberg (2005). https://doi.org/10.1007/11426639_27
59. Shamir, A.: Identity-based cryptosystems and signature schemes. In: Blakley, G.R., Chaum, D. (eds.) CRYPTO 1984. LNCS, vol. 196, pp. 47–53. Springer, Heidelberg (1985). https://doi.org/10.1007/3-540-39568-7_5
60. Waters, B.: Functional encryption for regular languages. In: Safavi-Naini, R., Canetti, R. (eds.) CRYPTO 2012. LNCS, vol. 7417, pp. 218–235. Springer, Heidelberg (2012). https://doi.org/10.1007/978-3-642-32009-5_14

61. Wichs, D., Zirdelis, G.: Obfuscating compute-and-compare programs under LWE. In: FOCS (2017)
62. Yao, A.: How to generate and exchange secrets. In: FOCS, pp. 162–167 (1986)

Digital Signatures with Memory-Tight Security in the Multi-challenge Setting

Denis Diemert(✉), Kai Gellert(✉), Tibor Jager(✉), and Lin Lyu(✉)

Bergische Universität Wuppertal, Wuppertal, Germany
{denis.diemert,kai.gellert,tibor.jager,lin.lyu}@uni-wuppertal.de

Abstract. The standard security notion for digital signatures is "single-challenge" (SC) EUF-CMA security, where the adversary outputs a single message-signature pair and "wins" if it is a forgery. Auerbach *et al.* (CRYPTO 2017) introduced *memory-tightness* of reductions and argued that the right security goal in this setting is actually a stronger "multi-challenge" (MC) definition, where an adversary may output many message-signature pairs and "wins" if at least one is a forgery. Currently, no construction from simple standard assumptions is known to achieve full tightness with respect to time, success probability, and memory simultaneously. Previous works showed that memory-tight signatures cannot be achieved via certain natural classes of reductions (Auerbach *et al.*, CRYPTO 2017; Wang *et al.*, EUROCRYPT 2018). These impossibility results may give the impression that the construction of memory-tight signatures is difficult or even impossible.

We show that this impression is false, by giving the first constructions of signature schemes with full tightness in all dimensions in the MC setting. To circumvent the known impossibility results, we first introduce the notion of *canonical reductions* in the SC setting. We prove a general theorem establishing that every signature scheme with a canonical reduction is already memory-tightly secure in the MC setting, provided that it is strongly unforgeable, the adversary receives only one signature per message, and assuming the existence of a tightly-secure pseudorandom function. We then achieve memory-tight *many-signatures-per-message* security in the MC setting by a simple additional generic transformation. This yields the first memory-tightly, strongly EUF-CMA-secure signature schemes in the MC setting. Finally, we show that standard security proofs often already can be viewed as canonical reductions. Concretely, we show this for signatures from lossy identification schemes (Abdalla *et al.*, EUROCRYPT 2012), two variants of RSA Full-Domain Hash (Bellare and Rogaway, EUROCRYPT 1996), and two variants of BLS signatures (Boneh *et al.*, ASIACRYPT 2001).

1 Introduction

Work-factor-tightness. The security of many cryptosystems depends on computational hardness assumptions, where security is proven by a reduction from

Supported by the European Research Council (ERC) under the European Union's Horizon 2020 research and innovation programme, grant agreement 802823.

M. Tibouchi and H. Wang (Eds.): ASIACRYPT 2021, LNCS 13093, pp. 403–433, 2021.
https://doi.org/10.1007/978-3-030-92068-5_14

breaking the cryptosystem with respect to some security definition to breaking the hardness assumption. When such cryptosystems are concretely instantiated, cryptographic parameters such as the size of algebraic groups and moduli must be determined. If this is done in theoretically-sound way, that is, supported by the security guarantees provided by a reduction from breaking the cryptosystem to breaking the underlying assumption, then the *security loss* of the reduction has to be taken into account.

Let $\mathcal{A}$ be an adversary on a given cryptosystem with respect to a given security model, and let $\mathcal{R}$ be a reduction in a security proof that turns $\mathcal{A}$ into an algorithm solving some assumed-to-be-hard computational problem. Let $(t_{\mathcal{A}}, \epsilon_{\mathcal{A}})$ and $(t_{\mathcal{R}}, \epsilon_{\mathcal{R}})$ be the running time and advantage of $\mathcal{A}$ and $\mathcal{R}$, respectively. Then, the security loss is defined as L such that

$$L \cdot \frac{\epsilon_{\mathcal{R}}}{t_{\mathcal{R}}} = \frac{\epsilon_{\mathcal{A}}}{t_{\mathcal{A}}}$$

where $\epsilon_{\mathcal{A}}/t_{\mathcal{A}}$ and $\epsilon_{\mathcal{R}}/t_{\mathcal{R}}$ are the *work factors* of $\mathcal{A}$ and $\mathcal{R}$, respectively.[1] This is the standard approach to measure concrete security, which was established by Bellare and Ristenpart [8,9].

In the classical asymptotic setting a reduction is considered *efficient* if L is bounded by some polynomial, which may be large. However, if L is large, then a theoretically-sound concrete instantiation must compensate the security loss with larger parameters, at the cost of efficiency of the deployed cryptosystem. Often L depends on deployment parameters (such as the number of users and the number of issued signatures, for instance), which are determined by the application context. These might not be exactly known at the time of initial deployment, or they might unexpectedly encounter significant increase over time. Hence, these parameters must be chosen conservatively, based on a strict upper bounds, which may lead to overly large parameters that come with very significant performance overhead. Therefore it is desirable to have *tight* security proofs, where L is a constant, and thus independent of such deployment parameters. Such schemes can be efficiently instantiated with optimal cryptographic parameters in arbitrary application contexts, independent of the number of users, the number of issued signatures, and other application parameters. If L is a constant, then we usually call $\mathcal{R}$ a *tight* reduction. In this paper, we will refer to this notion as *work-factor-tightness*, in order to distinguish it from the notion of *memory-tightness* discussed below.

Memory-tightness. Auerbach *et al.* [4] explained that in addition to the work factor also the *memory* consumed by a reduction is relevant. This is particularly relevant when security is reduced to so-called *memory-sensitive* computational problems, where the efficiency of known algorithms depends on the amount of

[1] In the asymptotic setting, $\epsilon_{\mathcal{A}}$, $t_{\mathcal{A}}$, $\epsilon_{\mathcal{R}}$, and $t_{\mathcal{R}}$ are functions in a security parameter. In this case L is a function in the security parameter, too. In the concrete security setting the running times, success probabilities, and the security loss are real numbers.

memory that is available. This includes, for instance, known algorithms for the classical discrete logarithm problem modulo a prime number, the integer factorization problem, Learning With Errors (LWE), or Short Integer Solutions (SIS), and many more. Other problems are (currently) not considered memory-sensitive, such as the discrete logarithm problem in elliptic curve groups. However, whether a given computational problem is memory-sensitive or not may change with the discovery of new algorithms and the impact of memory on their performance. See [4] for an in-depth discussion of memory-sensitivity.

In order to address this gap, Auerbach *et al.* [4] introduced the notion of *memory-tightness*, which additionally takes the memory consumed by a reduction into account. In addition to discussing the memory-sensitivity of computational problems, they also consider the memory-tightness of finding multi-collisions for hash functions and of reductions between different security notions of digital signature schemes.

Since its introduction in 2017, the concept of memory tightness has drawn much attention and led to many follow-up works. This includes works on memory lower bounds of reductions by Wang *et al.* [51] (EUROCRYPT 2018), memory tightness of authenticated encryption by Ghoshal, Jaeger, and Tessaro [30] (CRYPTO 2020), memory tightness of hashed ElGamal by Ghoshal and Tessaro [31] (EUROCRYPT 2020), and memory tightness for key encapsulation mechanisms by Bhattacharyya [12] (PKC 2020). Hence, memory tightness is already a well-established concept in cryptography that receives broad interest.

Memory-tightly secure signatures. In the standard *existential unforgeability under chosen-message attacks* (EUF-CMA) security model, the adversary receives a public key pk and then has access to a signing oracle that, on input of any message m from the message space of the signature scheme, computes a signature $\sigma \overset{\$}{\leftarrow} \mathsf{Sign}(sk, m)$, stores m in a list $\mathcal{Q}$, and returns σ. The adversary successfully breaks the security of the signature scheme if it outputs a forgery (m^*, σ^*) such that σ^* is a valid signature for m^* with respect to pk, and $m^* \notin \mathcal{Q}$. Auerbach *et al.* call this the *single-challenge* setting, since the adversary has only one attempt to forge a signature. They also introduce a stronger *multi-challenge* security definition, where the adversary may output multiple valid message-signature pairs and it "wins" if at least one of them is a new forgery in the sense that no signature was requested for the corresponding message throughout the security experiment.

Obviously, when considering the random-access memory (RAM) model, both security notions are tightly equivalent when memory consumption is not considered. In one direction, given a multi-challenge adversary, one can simply store all message-signature pairs that the adversary has obtained from its experiment in a list. Whenever the adversary outputs a message-signature pair, it is checked whether it is contained in the list. If not, then it is a valid forgery in the single-challenge setting. The opposite direction is even more trivial. However, note that this reduction is not memory-tight, as it requires memory linear in the number of signing queries. Auerbach *et al.* even showed that it is very difficult to prove that both notions are memory-tightly equivalent, by giving an impossibility result that covers a large class of natural reductions. This result was subsequently revisited and extended by Wang *et al.* [51].

The only known construction of a signature scheme with memory-tight security proof is due to Auerbach *et al.* [4]. They show that the RSA full-domain hash signature scheme can be proven memory-tightly secure under the RSA assumption. This is already a significant result, since it introduces clever tricks to deal with a programmable random oracle in a memory-tight way. However, it is still limited, since the reduction is only memory-tight, but not work-factor-tight. This is because the tightness lower bounds from [6,19,42,43] still apply, such that a linear security loss in the number of signature queries is unavoidable.[2] Furthermore, Auerbach *et al.* only achieve memory-tightness in the weaker single-challenge setting, but not yet in the stronger multi-challenge setting. To the best of our knowledge, there exists currently no signature scheme, which has a security proof that is *fully* tight, that is, simultaneously memory-tight *and* work-factor-tight.

One main difficulty of achieving memory-tightly-secure signatures in the multi-challenge setting is to build a reduction which does not have to store the sequence of random oracle queries made by the adversary. While it seems easy to replace a random oracle with a pseudorandom function, this must be done very carefully, in particular in security proofs that "program" a random oracle, in order to achieve consistency. Here we can partially build upon techniques developed by Auerbach *et al.* [4]. Furthermore, another major difficulty in achieving security in the multi-challenge setting is to build a reduction which does not have to store the history of message-signature pairs obtained by the adversary through signing queries.

Our contributions. We summarize our contributions as follows.

- We present a sequence of transforms that give rise to the first digital signature schemes that simultaneously achieve tightness in all three dimensions: running time, success probability, and memory. The construction is efficient and yields practical signature schemes.
- On a technical level, we show how to circumvent known impossibility result by introducing the notion of "canonical reductions", which can be seen as a new "non-black-box" perspective that applies to many well-known standard reductions in security proofs for signature schemes.
- We show the applicability of this approach by considering the construction of signatures from lossy identification schemes (LID) by Abdalla *et al.* [1,2], which can be viewed as a generalization of the security proof for Katz–Wang signatures [44]. We further demonstrate the versatility of our technique by applying it to well-known signature schemes like RSA-FDH [11] (with the proof following [19] with a loss linear in the number of signing queries). Then, we additionally show that by using the technique by Katz and Wang [44] of

[2] There is also a work-factor-tight security proof for RSA full domain hash based on the Phi Hiding assumption [42,43], but this proof seems not compatible with the memory-tight implementation of the random oracle from [4].

signing the message together with an extra random bit, we can eliminate the linear security loss and achieve both memory and working factor tightness. We also show similar results for Boneh–Lynn–Shacham (BLS) signatures [14]. All of our results directly achieve *strong* unforgeability. For a comparison of our result with previous analyses of these scheme, consider Table 1.

Table 1. Comparison of our result to previous analyses of the considered schemes. All analyses are in the random oracle model. Let λ be the security parameter, let q_{H} be the number of random oracle queries, let q_{S} the number of signing queries, let e be the basis of the natural logarithm, let $|\mathbb{G}|$ be the size of the representation of a group element of a cyclic group $\mathbb{G}$ of prime order q, let $|\mathbb{Z}_N|$ denote the size of the representation of an element of $\mathbb{Z}_N$, let N be a RSA modulus, let e be a RSA public exponent, and let $|\mathbb{G}_1|$ (resp. $|\mathbb{G}_2|$) be the size of the representation of a group element of group $\mathbb{G}_1$ (resp. $\mathbb{G}_2$) of some bilinear group $(\mathbb{G}_1, \mathbb{G}_2, \mathbb{G}_T)$. Note that for comparability, we chose to instantiate the LID-based schemes with DDH. Due to collision resistance, the nonce length chosen for our transform from Sect. 4 is 2λ.

Constr.	**Proof**	**Asm.**	**Sec.**	**Sec. Loss**	**Mem. Loss**	$\|pk\|$	$\|\sigma\|$
LID-based	[1,2]	DDH	EUF-CMA	$\mathcal{O}(1)$	$\mathcal{O}(q_{\mathsf{H}} + q_{\mathsf{S}})$	$4\|\mathbb{G}\|$	$3\|\mathbb{Z}_q\|$
	Ours	DDH	msEUF-CMA	$\mathcal{O}(1)$	$\mathcal{O}(1)$	$4\|\mathbb{G}\|$	$3\|\mathbb{Z}_q\| + 2\lambda$
RSA-FDH	[18]	RSA	EUF-CMA	$\mathrm{e} \cdot q_{\mathsf{S}}$	$\mathcal{O}(q_{\mathsf{H}} + q_{\mathsf{S}})$	$\|N\| + \|e\|$	$\|\mathbb{Z}_N\|$
	[4]	RSA	EUF-CMA	$\mathrm{e} \cdot q_{\mathsf{S}}$	$\mathcal{O}(1)$	$\|N\| + \|e\|$	$\|\mathbb{Z}_N\|$
	Ours	RSA	msEUF-CMA	$\mathrm{e} \cdot q_{\mathsf{S}}$	$\mathcal{O}(1)$	$\|N\| + \|e\|$	$\|\mathbb{Z}_N\|$
RSA-FDH+	[44]	RSA	EUF-CMA	$\mathcal{O}(1)$	$\mathcal{O}(q_{\mathsf{H}} + q_{\mathsf{S}})$	$\|N\| + \|e\|$	$\|\mathbb{Z}_N\|$
	Ours	RSA	msEUF-CMA	$\mathcal{O}(1)$	$\mathcal{O}(1)$	$\|N\| + \|e\|$	$\|\mathbb{Z}_N\| + 2\lambda$
BLS	[14]	(co-)CDH	EUF-CMA	$\mathrm{e} \cdot (q_{\mathsf{S}} + 1)$	$\mathcal{O}(q_{\mathsf{H}} + q_{\mathsf{S}})$	$\|\mathbb{G}_2\|$	$\|\mathbb{G}_1\|$
	Ours	(co-)CDH	msEUF-CMA	$\mathrm{e} \cdot (q_{\mathsf{S}} + 1)$	$\mathcal{O}(1)$	$\|\mathbb{G}_2\|$	$\|\mathbb{G}_1\|$
BLS+	[44]	(co-)CDH	EUF-CMA	$\mathcal{O}(1)$	$\mathcal{O}(q_{\mathsf{H}} + q_{\mathsf{S}})$	$\|\mathbb{G}_2\|$	$\|\mathbb{G}_1\|$
	Ours	(co-)CDH	msEUF-CMA	$\mathcal{O}(1)$	$\mathcal{O}(1)$	$\|\mathbb{G}_2\|$	$\|\mathbb{G}_1\| + 2\lambda$

Our approach. Our approach can be divided into two steps.

1. At first we show how to generically transform an entire class of signature schemes from the single-challenge setting to the multi-challenge setting. During this step, it is actually useful to consider a weaker "one-signature-per-message" security notion, where an adversary may only request one (instead of many) signature per message via its signing oracle.[3]

[3] Of course, one-signature-per-message security is equivalent to standard security for signature schemes with deterministic signing algorithm, however, we are not aware of any such signature scheme which achieves tight security, not even in the classical sense that does not consider memory tightness. There are several impossibility results, showing that tightness is often difficult to achieve for such signature schemes [6,19,43].

We require that the security reduction of the underlying scheme follows a canonical pattern that is compatible with our approach to prove memory tightness. Essentially, we require that the reduction can be split into *stateless* "canonical procedures" for simulating signatures, extracting solutions from forgeries, and computing hash values (e.g., if a random oracle is needed).
The main idea is now to "de-randomize" all canonical procedures, meaning that we give all procedures access to the *same* random function but require that they otherwise behave deterministically. Note that the "one-signature-per-message" restriction helps us here, as the procedures can rely on the random function to derive randomness for one signature per message from the message by calling the random function. Giving all procedures access to the same random function, ensures consistency across procedures (e.g., a signature may need to be consistent with the simulation of a random oracle). We also show that many standard security proofs for signatures indeed can be seen as canonical reductions, so that our generic result applies.
Finally, to generically achieve memory-tightness in the multi-challenge setting, we can replace the "global random function" with a pseudorandom function. This yields a generic transform (with tightness in all dimensions) producing a signature scheme secure in the "one-signature-per-message" and multi-challenge setting.
2. In the second step we apply a simple generic transform (again, with tightness in all dimensions) that lifts any signature scheme from the "one-signature-per-message" to the standard "many-signatures-per-message" setting. To this end, any message is signed alongside a random nonce, which intuitively "expands" the set of valid signatures per message.

Applying both steps sequentially does not influence the tightness of a signature scheme in any dimension.

Related work. In the literature, "tightness" usually refers to what we call work-factor tightness in this paper. That is, running times and success probabilities are considered, but memory is not. There is a large number of research results in this area, with tightly-secure constructions of many different types of cryptosystems, including digital signatures [22,37,38,44,49], public-key encryption [7,29,37], (hierarchical) identity-based encryption [13,16], authenticated key exchange [5, 17,32,46], and symmetric encryption [34,36,41], for instance. Tight security is also increasingly considered for real-world cryptosystems, such as [20,23,34,39]. There are also various impossibility results for different types and classes of cryptosystems, such as [19,26–28,41–43,48,50], for instance.

As already mentioned, the notion of memory-tightness was only relatively recently introduced in [4]. They also introduced the single- and multi-challenge security model, and gave the first (and currently only) memory-tight security proof for a digital scheme in the weaker single-challenge setting, which however is not yet work-factor-tight. They also gave a first impossibility result, showing that a certain class of reductions cannot be used to reduce multi-challenge security to single-challenge security. Wang *et al.* [51] revisited this impossibility result and showed that multi-challenge security is impossible to achieve for a large class of reductions, unless a work-factor tightness is sacrificed. They showed a lower bound on the memory of a large class of black-box reductions from the multi-challenge unforgeability of unique signatures to any computational hardness assumption, another lower bound for restricted reductions from multi-challenge security to single-challenge security for cryptographic primitives with unique keys, and a lower bound for multi-collisions of hash functions with large domain, which extends a similar result from [4]. Bhattacharyya [12] and Ghoshal and Tessaro [31] independently considered the memory-tightness of hashed ElGamal public-key encryption. Ghoshal, Jaeger, and Tessaro [30] considered the memory-tightness of authenticated encryption.

Outline. The remainder of this paper is organized as follows. In Sect. 2, we define the computational model and the used complexity measures, alongside with standard definitions of cryptographic primitives. In Sect. 3, we present how to achieve multi-challenge security from any signature scheme secure in the single-challenge setting that follows a canonical reduction. In Sect. 4, we present our generic transform to lift any signature scheme from "one-signature-per-message" to the standard "many-signatures-per-message" setting. Finally, we show how our transforms can be applied to existing signature schemes, achieving the first fully tight signature schemes in the multi-challenge setting.

2 Preliminaries

For strings a and b, we denote the concatenation of these strings by $a \parallel b$. We denote the operation of assigning a value y to a variable x by $x := y$. If S is a finite set, we denote by $x \xleftarrow{\$} S$ the operation of sampling a value uniformly at random from set S and assigning it to variable x. For any probabilistic algorithm $\mathcal{A}$, we denote $y \leftarrow \mathcal{A}(x; r)$ the process of running $\mathcal{A}$ on input x with random coins r and assign the output to y, and we denote $y \xleftarrow{\$} \mathcal{A}(x)$ as $y \leftarrow \mathcal{A}(x; r)$ for uniformly random r.

2.1 Computational Model and Complexity Measures

In this paper, we adapt the computation model used in [4] and recall the most important aspects in this section.

Algorithms. We assume all algorithms in this paper to be random access machines (RAMs). A RAM has access to memory using words of a fixed size λ and a constant number of registers each holding a single word. If an algorithm $\mathcal{A}$ is probabilistic, then the corresponding RAM is equipped with a special instruction that fills a distinguished register with (independent) random bits. However, we do not allow the RAM to rewind random bits to access previously used random bits. That is, $\mathcal{A}$ needs to store the random bits in this case. To run algorithm $\mathcal{A}$, the RAM is executed, where the input of the algorithm is written in the RAM's memory. To denote this, we overload notation and write $x \xleftarrow{\$} \mathcal{A}(y_1, y_2, \ldots)$ to denote that random variable x takes on the value of algorithm $\mathcal{A}$ ran on inputs $y_1, y_2, \ldots$ with fresh random coins. Sometimes we also denote this random variable simply by $\mathcal{A}(y_1, y_2, \ldots)$. In case $\mathcal{A}$ is deterministic, we write $x := \mathcal{A}(y_1, y_2, \ldots)$, to denote that $\mathcal{A}$ on inputs $y_1, y_2, \ldots$ outputs x.

Oracles. In addition, algorithm $\mathcal{A}$ sometimes has access to (stateful) oracles $(\mathcal{O}_1, \mathcal{O}_2, \ldots)$. Each of these oracles also is defined by a RAM. To interact with an oracle $\mathcal{O}_i$, the RAM of algorithm $\mathcal{A}$ has three fixed regions in the memory only used for the oracle state $st_{\mathcal{O}}$, the input to the oracle and the output of the oracle. By default, these regions are empty. To query the oracle $\mathcal{O}_i$, $\mathcal{A}$ writes the query in the region of its memory reserved for the oracle input and executes a special instruction to run the RAM of $\mathcal{O}_i$ on this input together with the oracle state $st_{\mathcal{O}}$. The RAM implementing $\mathcal{O}_i$ uses its own memory and both the output and the updated oracle state $st_{\mathcal{O}}$ in the designated regions in $\mathcal{A}$'s memory. For notation, we denote that an algorithm $\mathcal{A}$ has oracle access to an algorithm *oracle* by $\mathcal{A}^{\mathcal{O}}$.

Security experiment. The security definition and proofs presented in this paper are mostly game-based. A security experiment (or game) can simply be viewed as an algorithm that runs another algorithm as subroutine, e.g., an adversary $\mathcal{A}$, and the subroutine may also be provided with a series of (stateful) oracles. As a security experiment is simply an algorithm it is also implemented by a RAM.

Complexity measures for runtime and memory consumption. We define the complexity measures for runtime and memory according to Auerbach *et al.* [4].

Runtime. Let $\mathcal{A}$ be an algorithm and Exp be a security game. We define **Time**($\mathcal{A}$) to be the runtime of $\mathcal{A}$ as the worst-case number of computation steps over all inputs of length λ and all possible random choices. In addition, we define **LocalTime**($\mathcal{A}$) to be the number of computation steps of $\mathcal{A}$ playing Exp *without* the additional steps induced by the oracle access to Exp. This quantifier allows us to precisely measure how much additional computation steps are necessary per oracle.

Memory Consumption. Let $\mathcal{A}$ be an algorithm and Exp be a security game. We define **Mem**($\mathcal{A}$) to be the memory (in λ-width words) of the code of $\mathcal{A}$ plus the worst-case number of registers used at any point during computation, over all inputs of length λ and all possible random choices. Similar to before, we define **LocalMem**($\mathcal{A}$) to be the memory required to execute Exp with algorithm $\mathcal{A}$ *without* the additional memory induced by the oracle access to Exp. This quantifier allows us to precisely measure how much additional memory is necessary per oracle.

2.2 Pseudorandom Functions

We recall the standard indistinguishability definition for pseudorandom functions. This is one of the main tools used to make reductions memory-tight.

Definition 1. *Let $\lambda \in \mathbb{N}$. Let $\mathsf{F}\colon \{0,1\}^\lambda \times \{0,1\}^* \to \mathcal{R}$ be a keyed function, where $\mathcal{R}$ is a finite set. We define the advantage of an adversary $\mathcal{A}$ in breaking the pseudorandomness of* F *as*

$$\mathsf{Adv}_{\mathsf{F}}^{\mathsf{PRF\text{-}sec}}(\mathcal{A}) := \left|\Pr\left[\mathcal{A}^{\mathsf{F}(k,\cdot)} = 1\right] - \Pr\left[\mathcal{A}^{f(\cdot)} = 1\right]\right|$$

where $k \stackrel{\$}{\leftarrow} \{0,1\}^\lambda$ and $f\colon \{0,1\}^* \to \mathcal{R}$ is a random function.

2.3 Digital Signatures

We recall the standard definition of a *digital signature scheme* by Goldwasser, Micali, and Rivest [33] and its standard security notion.

Definition 2. *A* digital signature scheme *for message space M is a triple of algorithms* $\mathsf{Sig} = (\mathsf{Gen}, \mathsf{Sign}, \mathsf{Vrfy})$ *such that*

1. Gen *is the randomized key generation algorithm generating a public (verification) key pk and a secret (signing) key sk and takes no input.*
2. $\mathsf{Sign}(sk, m)$ *is the randomized signing algorithm outputting a signature σ on input message $m \in M$ and signing key sk.*
3. $\mathsf{Vrfy}(pk, m, \sigma)$ *is the deterministic verification algorithm outputting either* 0 *or* 1.

We say that a digital signature scheme Sig *is* correct *if for any $m \in M$, and $(pk, sk) \stackrel{\$}{\leftarrow} \mathsf{Gen}$, it holds that* $\mathsf{Vrfy}(pk, m, \mathsf{Sign}(sk, m)) = 1$.

One-signature-per-message unforgeability of digital signature. We adapt the one-signature-per-message unforgeability defined by Fersch et al. [24]. First, we consider the "strong" variant of the definition given in [24], i.e., a pair (m, σ) output by the adversary is only considered a valid forgery if σ was not returned to the adversary as answer to an signing query m. In the "standard" variant, the pair is considered valid if for message m never a signature has been queried by the adversary. Second, we implement the fact that the adversary only receives one signature per message different to the original definition. Instead of aborting the whole experiment in case the adversary queries a signature for a message that it already received a signature for, we simply return the same signature to the adversary. Therefore, the adversary still gets only one signature per message, but is allowed to query a message multiple times.

We note that, for deterministic signature schemes, the one-signature-per-message security is equivalent to the many-signatures-per-message security.

Definition 3. *Let* $\mathsf{Sig} = (\mathsf{Gen}, \mathsf{Sign}, \mathsf{Vrfy})$ *be a digital signature scheme. Consider the following experiment* $\mathsf{Exp}_{\mathsf{Sig}}^{\mathsf{sEUF\text{-}CMA1}}(\mathcal{A})$ *played between a challenger and an adversary $\mathcal{A}$:*

1. *The challenger initializes the set of chosen-message queries* $\mathcal{Q} := \emptyset$*, generates a fresh key pair* $(pk, sk) \xleftarrow{\$} \mathsf{Gen}$ *and forwards* pk *to the adversary as input.*
2. *The adversary may issue queries to the following oracle adaptively:*
   - $\mathsf{Sign}(m)$*: If* $(m, \sigma) \in \mathcal{Q}$*, the challenger returns* σ*. Otherwise, it returns* $\sigma \xleftarrow{\$} \mathsf{Sign}(sk, m)$ *and adds* (m, σ) *to* $\mathcal{Q}$*.*
3. *Finally, the adversary outputs a candidate forgery* (m, σ) *and the challenger outputs* 1 *if* $\mathsf{Vrfy}(pk, m, \sigma) = 1$ *and* $(m, \sigma) \notin \mathcal{Q}$*, and 0 otherwise.*

We denote the advantage of an adversary $\mathcal{A}$ *in forging signatures for* Sig *in the* sEUF-CMA1 *security experiment by*

$$\mathsf{Adv}^{\mathsf{sEUF\text{-}CMA1}}_{\mathsf{Sig}}(\mathcal{A}) := \Pr\left[\mathsf{Exp}^{\mathsf{sEUF\text{-}CMA1}}_{\mathsf{Sig}}(\mathcal{A}) = 1\right]$$

where $\mathsf{Exp}^{\mathsf{sEUF\text{-}CMA1}}_{\mathsf{Sig}}(\mathcal{A})$ *is as defined above.*

Next, we generalize Definition 3 to the multi-challenge setting. Unforgeability in the multi-challenge setting was proposed by Auerbach et al. [4] and is a generalized version of the standard existential unforgeability against chosen-message attackers notion, in which the adversary has additional access to a "forging oracle" allowing multiple forgery attempts. The adversary wins in this setting if at least one of the forgery attempts is "valid" in the same sense as in the single challenge setting.

Definition 4. *Let* $\mathsf{Sig} = (\mathsf{Gen}, \mathsf{Sign}, \mathsf{Vrfy})$ *be a digital signature scheme. Consider the following experiment* $\mathsf{Exp}^{\mathsf{msEUF\text{-}CMA1}}_{\mathsf{Sig}}(\mathcal{A})$ *played between a challenger and an adversary* $\mathcal{A}$*:*

1. *The challenger initializes the set of chosen-message queries* $\mathcal{Q} := \emptyset$ *and the winning flag* $\mathsf{win} := 0$*. Then, it generates a fresh key pair* $(pk, sk) \xleftarrow{\$} \mathsf{Gen}$ *and forwards* pk *to the adversary as input.*
2. *The adversary may issue queries to the following oracles adaptively:*
   - $\mathsf{Sign}(m)$*: If* $(m, \sigma) \in \mathcal{Q}$ *for some* σ*, the challenger returns* σ*. Otherwise, it returns* $\sigma \xleftarrow{\$} \mathsf{Sign}(sk, m)$ *and adds* (m, σ) *to* $\mathcal{Q}$*.*
   - $\mathsf{Forge}(m, \sigma)$*: If* $\mathsf{Vrfy}(pk, m, \sigma) = 1$ *and* $(m, \sigma) \notin \mathcal{Q}$*, then set* $\mathsf{win} := 1$*.*
3. *Finally, the adversary halts and the experiment outputs* win*.*

We denote the advantage of an adversary $\mathcal{A}$ *in forging signatures for* Sig *in the* msEUF-CMA1 *security experiment by*

$$\mathsf{Adv}^{\mathsf{msEUF\text{-}CMA1}}_{\mathsf{Sig}}(\mathcal{A}) := \Pr\left[\mathsf{Exp}^{\mathsf{msEUF\text{-}CMA1}}_{\mathsf{Sig}}(\mathcal{A}) = 1\right]$$

where $\mathsf{Exp}^{\mathsf{msEUF\text{-}CMA1}}_{\mathsf{Sig}}(\mathcal{A})$ *is as defined above.*

Many-signatures-per-message unforgeability. The security notions sEUF-CMA1 and msEUF-CMA1 defined above can be generalized to the "many-signatures-per-message" setting by dropping the condition that the respective security experiments return σ if the Sign-oracle is queried with a message m such that $(m, \sigma) \in \mathcal{Q}$, i.e., a message m that was already queried before. Without this condition we obtain the standard strong existential unforgeability under chosen-message attacks (sEUF-CMA) and its multi-challenge variant (as defined in [4]) msEUF-CMA.

Adversary behavior. In this work we consider adversaries that are not necessarily well-behaved. That is, an adversary $\mathcal{A}$ may, for instance, submit a forgery (m^*, σ^*) such that σ^* was obtained by a signing query m^*. In principle, any such adversary can be converted to a well-behaved adversary by performing "sanity checks" whenever the adversary submits a forgery. This conversion, however, is not memory-tight as it leads to an increase in memory needed to store the set of chosen-message queries $\mathcal{Q}$.

Considering that there might exist adversaries that are not well-behaved but break the security of a signature scheme (e.g., by producing a forgery without knowing whether it is a fresh one), we prefer a stronger security notion and consider *any* adversary rather than restricting our proofs to a class of well-behaved adversaries. For a more detailed discussion on this topic, we refer the reader to [4, Section 2.3].

3 From the Single-Challenge Setting to the Multi-challenge Setting

In this section, we will describe a generic construction of a reduction in the multi-challenge setting, based on any "canonical" reduction in the single-challenge setting.

3.1 Non-interactive Computational Assumptions

The following definition of a non-interactive computational assumptions is based on the corresponding definition by Bader et al. [6], which is originally due to Abe et al. [3]. It captures both "search problems", such as CDH, and "decisional problems", such as DDH. We focus on *non-interactive* computational hardness assumptions, for the following reasons. First, these may be considered the most "interesting" hardness assumption when (memory) tightness is considered. Second, it makes the definitions and proofs significantly cleaner, and therefore makes it easier to understand and verify the core technical ideas and approach.

Definition 5. *A* non-interactive computational assumption *is defined as the tuple* $\Lambda = (\mathsf{InstGen}, \mathsf{V}, \mathsf{U})$*, where*

1. $(\phi, \omega) \xleftarrow{\$} \mathsf{InstGen}(1^\lambda)$*:* $\mathsf{InstGen}$ *is the probabilistic instance generation algorithm that takes as input a security parameter* 1^λ*, and outputs a problem instance* ϕ *and a witness* ω*.*
2. $0/1 := \mathsf{V}(\phi, \omega, \rho)$*:* V *is the deterministic verification algorithm that takes as input a problem instance* ϕ*, a witness* ω *and a candidate solution* ρ*, and outputs* 0 *or* 1*. We say that* ρ *is a correct solution for* ϕ *if* $\mathsf{V}(\phi, \omega, \rho) = 1$*.*
3. $\rho \xleftarrow{\$} \mathsf{U}(\phi)$*:* U *is a probabilistic algorithm that on input* ϕ *outputs a candidate solution* ρ*.*

We define the advantage of an adversary $\mathcal{R}$ *breaking* Λ *as*

$$\mathsf{Adv}_{\Lambda,\lambda}^{\mathsf{NICA}}(\mathcal{R}) := \left| \Pr\left[\mathsf{Exp}_{\Lambda,\lambda}^{\mathsf{NICA}}(\mathcal{R}) = 1\right] - \Pr\left[\mathsf{Exp}_{\Lambda,\lambda}^{\mathsf{NICA}}(\mathsf{U}) = 1\right]\right|$$

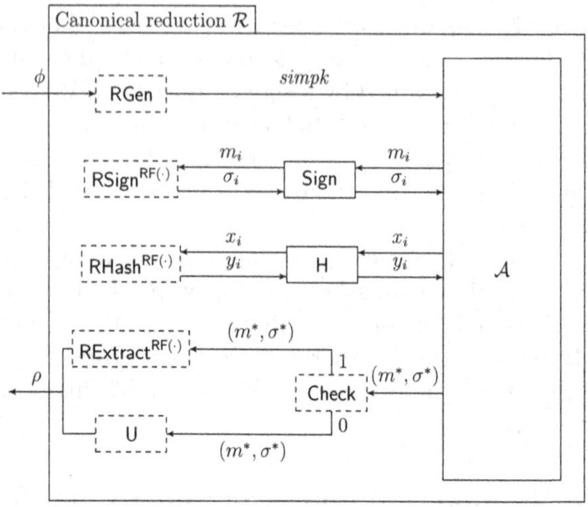

Fig. 1. Canonical reduction $\mathcal{R}$ from sEUF-CMA1-security of a signature scheme Sig to a computational assumption Λ with black-box access to an adversary $\mathcal{A}$. Check is a shorthand defined as $\mathsf{Check}(m^*, \sigma^*) = 1 \iff \mathsf{Sig.Vrfy}(simpk, m^*, \sigma^*) = 1 \wedge \sigma^* \neq \mathsf{RSign}^{\mathsf{RF}(\cdot)}(simsk, m^*)$ determining the algorithm to compute the final solution. For a complete formal definition, see Definition 6.

where the experiment $\mathsf{Exp}^{\mathsf{NICA}}_{\Lambda,\lambda}(\mathcal{A})$ *generates* $(\phi, \omega) \xleftarrow{\$} \mathsf{InstGen}(1^\lambda)$, *runs* $\rho \xleftarrow{\$} \mathcal{A}(\phi)$ *and returns* $\mathsf{V}(\phi, \omega, \rho)$.

Intuitively, U can be seen as the "trivial" solution strategy. For example, if Λ is a decisional problem, such as DDH, U usually would output a uniformly random bit such that $\Pr\left[\mathsf{Exp}^{\mathsf{NICA}}_{\Lambda,\lambda}(\mathsf{U}) = 1\right] = \frac{1}{2}$. Then, $\mathsf{Adv}^{\mathsf{NICA}}_{\Lambda,\lambda}(\mathcal{R})$ basically defines the "bit-guessing advantage" against Λ. For a search problem, such as CDH, U would output a constant symbol such that $\Pr\left[\mathsf{Exp}^{\mathsf{NICA}}_{\Lambda,\lambda}(\mathsf{U}) = 1\right] = 0$. Then, $\mathsf{Adv}^{\mathsf{NICA}}_{\Lambda,\lambda}(\mathcal{R})$ corresponds to the probability of $\mathcal{R}$ finding a solution ρ for the given problem instance ϕ.

3.2 Canonical Reductions

We introduce the notion of a *canonical reduction*, which essentially defines an abstract pattern of a reduction which is "compatible" with our approach to prove memory-tight security. Many security proofs of signature schemes can be explained as canonical reductions, we will show some concrete examples below. We focus on reductions from sEUF-CMA1-security to a non-interactive computational assumption Λ (as defined in Sect. 3.1) in both standard model and random oracle model. For an illustration of a canonical reduction, see Fig. 1.

Definition 6. *Let* Sig *be a signature scheme and let* Λ *be a non-interactive computational assumption. Let* (RGen, RF, RSign, RExtract, RHash) *be the following algorithms that are implemented by a canonical reduction:*

1. $(simpk, simsk) \xleftarrow{\$} \mathsf{RGen}(\phi)$: RGen *is the probabilistic reduction key generation algorithm that takes as input an instance* ϕ *of* Λ, *and outputs a simulated public key simpk and a simulation secret key simsk.*
2. $(r_{\mathsf{RSign}}, r_{\mathsf{RExtract}}, r_{\mathsf{RHash}}) \xleftarrow{\$} \mathsf{RF}(x)$: RF *is a stateful probabilistic algorithm simulating a truly random function with domain* $\{0,1\}^*$ *and range* $\mathsf{Coins}_{\mathsf{RSign}} \times \mathsf{Coins}_{\mathsf{RExtract}} \times \mathsf{Coins}_{\mathsf{RHash}}$ *using a lazily sampled random table, where* $\mathsf{Coins}_{\mathsf{RSign}}$, $\mathsf{Coins}_{\mathsf{RExtract}}$, *and* $\mathsf{Coins}_{\mathsf{RHash}}$ *are sets for random coins of* RSign, RExtract *and* RHash, *respectively.*[4]

Remark 7. Intuitively, RF *has the following purpose. We will below define algorithms* RSign, RExtract, *and* RHash, *which are used by the reduction to simulate signatures, extract from a forgery, and possibly to simulate a random oracle (if in the random oracle model), respectively. We require these algorithms to be* stateless *and* deterministic, *since this will be necessary for our construction of a memory-tight reduction. At the same time, we do not want the algorithms* RSign, RExtract *and,* RHash *to be completely independent of each other. For example, the simulation of a signature by* RSign *may have to be consistent with the random oracle implemented by* RHash. *We ensure this consistency by giving all oracles access to the* same *truly random function simulation algorithm* RF. *The algorithms of the canonical reduction are required to achieve consistency by only having access to* RF. *We will show below that this indeed holds for many standard security proofs for signature schemes.*

3. $\sigma := \mathsf{RSign}^{\mathsf{RF}(\cdot)}(simsk, m)$: RSign *is the deterministic signature simulation algorithm with access to the algorithm* RF *that takes as input the simulation secret key simsk and a message* m, *and outputs a simulated signature* σ.[5]
4. $\rho := \mathsf{RExtract}^{\mathsf{RF}(\cdot)}(simsk, (m^*, \sigma^*))$: RExtract *is the deterministic problem solution extraction algorithm with access to the algorithm* RF *that takes as input a forgery* (m^*, σ^*), *and outputs an extracted solution* ρ.
5. $y := \mathsf{RHash}^{\mathsf{RF}(\cdot)}(simsk, x)$: RHash *is the deterministic hash simulation algorithm with access to the algorithm* RF *that takes as input an argument* x, *and outputs a simulated hash image* y.

We call an algorithm $\mathcal{R}$ *with black-box access to any adversary* $\mathcal{A}$, *write* $\mathcal{R}^{\mathcal{A}}$, *a* (ℓ, δ)-canonical reduction *from* sEUF-CMA1 *to* Λ *if* $\mathcal{R}$ *satisfies the following properties.*

1. *The reduction* $\mathcal{R}$ *proceeds as follows:*
   (a) *When receiving a problem instance* ϕ, *the reduction* $\mathcal{R}$ *uses* $\mathsf{RGen}(\phi)$ *to simulate a public key simpk of* Sig *and generate the simulation secret key simsk, and starts* $\mathcal{A}$ *on input simpk.*

[4] We note that algorithm RF is part of the canonical reduction. Another option would be providing the canonical reduction with an external random function oracle. We choose the former characterization because it naturally includes the memory consumption of the random table when considering the overall memory consumption of the canonical reduction.

[5] Note that the output signature σ is not necessarily a valid signature of Sig with respect to *simpk*.

(b) *Whenever the adversary* $\mathcal{A}$ *issues a signing query* $\mathsf{Sign}(m)$, *the reduction simulates the signature* σ *with* $\sigma := \mathsf{RSign}^{\mathsf{RF}(\cdot)}(simsk, m)$ *and returns* σ *to* $\mathcal{A}$. *Note that* RSign *is deterministic, so even if* $\mathsf{Sign}(m)$ *is queried multiple times, the adversary always gets the same signature in return.*

(c) *In case the random oracle model (ROM) is considered, the reduction also needs to be able to simulate the random oracle. To this end, the reduction* $\mathcal{R}$ *answers a random oracle query* x *by running* $y := \mathsf{RHash}^{\mathsf{RF}(\cdot)}(simsk, x)$ *and returns* y.

(d) *When the adversary* $\mathcal{A}$ *outputs a candidate forgery* (m^*, σ^*), *the reduction* $\mathcal{R}$ *first tests whether it is a valid forgery by checking*

$$\mathsf{Sig.Vrfy}(simpk, m^*, \sigma^*) = 1 \wedge \sigma^* \neq \mathsf{RSign}^{\mathsf{RF}(\cdot)}(simsk, m^*).$$

Intuitively, the second check is the main leverage to "recognize" new signatures. If the checks pass, then we know that (m^*, σ^*) *is valid and* not *the signature that* $\mathcal{R}$ *would have simulated. Then* $\mathcal{R}$ *uses* RExtract *to extract a solution* ρ *to the underlying problem* Λ *with*

$$\rho := \mathsf{RExtract}^{\mathsf{RF}(\cdot)}(simsk, (m^*, \sigma^*)).$$

If the checks fail, $\mathcal{R}$ *runs* $\rho \xleftarrow{\$} \mathsf{U}(\phi)$. *Finally,* $\mathcal{R}$ *outputs* ρ *as the solution to the problem instance* ϕ.

2. *We require that* $\mathcal{R}$ *is a "valid" reduction from* sEUF-CMA1*-security to a non-interactive computational assumption* Λ. *That is, for any adversary* $\mathcal{A}$, *we have*

$$\mathsf{Adv}^{\mathsf{NICA}}_{\Lambda,\lambda}\left(\mathcal{R}^{\mathcal{A}}\right) \geq \frac{1}{\ell}\mathsf{Adv}^{\mathsf{sEUF\text{-}CMA1}}_{\mathsf{Sig}}(\mathcal{A}) - \delta.$$

Remark 8. If $\mathcal{R}$ is canonical, q_{S} is the upper bound of the number of Sign queries made by the adversary, q_{H} is the upper bound of the number of random oracle queries and q_{RF} is an upper bound of the number of evaluations of RF, then we obtain that

$$\begin{aligned}\mathbf{LocalTime}\left(\mathcal{R}^{\mathcal{A}}\right) \quad &\approx \mathbf{LocalTime}(\mathcal{A}) + \mathbf{Time}(\mathsf{RGen}) + q_{\mathsf{S}} \cdot \mathbf{Time}(\mathsf{RSign}) \\ &\quad + q_{\mathsf{H}} \cdot \mathbf{Time}(\mathsf{RHash}) + \mathbf{Time}(\mathsf{Sig.Vrfy}) \\ &\quad + \max\{\mathbf{Time}(\mathsf{RExtract}), \mathbf{Time}(\mathsf{U})\} + q_{\mathsf{RF}} \cdot \mathbf{Time}(\mathsf{RF}) \qquad (1)\end{aligned}$$

and that

$$\begin{aligned}\mathbf{LocalMem}\left(\mathcal{R}^{\mathcal{A}}\right) \quad &= \mathbf{LocalMem}(\mathcal{A}) + \mathbf{Mem}(\mathsf{RGen}) + \mathbf{Mem}(\mathsf{RSign}) \\ &\quad + \mathbf{Mem}(\mathsf{RHash}) + \mathbf{Mem}(\mathsf{Sig.Vrfy}) + \mathbf{Mem}(\mathsf{RExtract}) \\ &\quad + \mathbf{Mem}(\mathsf{U}) + \mathbf{Mem}(\mathsf{RF}). \qquad (2)\end{aligned}$$

Note that by design of the canonical reduction the only common state of the algorithms RGen, RSign, RHash and RExtract is the random table (whose size grows linearly with the number of different queries) in the random function simulation algorithm RF. Otherwise, these algorithms are stateless. This will be the main leverage to achieve memory-tightness, since the random function can be implemented memory-efficiently with a pseudorandom function.

3.3 Multi-challenge Security for Canonical Reductions

Next, we show how to transform any canonical reduction in the *single*-challenge setting to another reduction in the *multi*-challenge setting. Formally, consider the following theorem.

Theorem 9. *Let* Sig *be a digital signature scheme and let* Λ *be a non-interactive computational assumption. Suppose* $\mathcal{R}$ *is a* (ℓ, δ)*-canonical reduction from the* sEUF-CMA1*-security of* Sig *to* Λ *and* $\mathsf{PRF}\colon \{0,1\}^\lambda \times \{0,1\}^* \to \mathsf{Coins}_{\mathsf{RSign}} \times \mathsf{Coins}_{\mathsf{RExtract}} \times \mathsf{Coins}_{\mathsf{RHash}}$ *is a pseudorandom function. Using* $\mathcal{R}$ *and* PRF, *we can build another reduction* $\mathcal{R}'$ *from the* msEUF-CMA1*-security of* Sig *to* Λ *such that for any adversary* $\mathcal{A}'$ *attacking the* msEUF-CMA1*-security of* Sig, *there exists an adversary* $\mathcal{B}$ *so that*

$$\mathsf{Adv}^{\mathsf{NICA}}_{\Lambda,\lambda}\left(\mathcal{R}'^{\mathcal{A}'}\right) \geq \frac{1}{\ell} \cdot \mathsf{Adv}^{\mathsf{msEUF\text{-}CMA1}}_{\mathsf{Sig}}(\mathcal{A}') - \mathsf{Adv}^{\mathsf{PRF\text{-}sec}}_{\mathsf{PRF}}\left(\mathcal{B}^{\mathcal{A}'}\right) - \delta. \tag{3}$$

Furthermore,

$$\begin{aligned}\mathbf{LocalTime}(\mathcal{R}'^{\mathcal{A}'}) \approx{} & \mathbf{LocalTime}\,(\mathcal{A}') + \mathbf{Time}(\mathsf{RGen}) + (q_{\mathsf{S}} + q_{\mathsf{F}}) \cdot \mathbf{Time}(\mathsf{RSign}) \\ & + q_{\mathsf{H}} \cdot \mathbf{Time}(\mathsf{RHash}) + q_{\mathsf{F}} \cdot \mathbf{Time}(\mathsf{Sig.Vrfy}) \\ & + \max\{\mathbf{Time}(\mathsf{RExtract}), \mathbf{Time}(\mathsf{U})\} + q_{\mathsf{RF}} \cdot \mathbf{Time}(\mathsf{PRF}),\end{aligned} \tag{4}$$

$$\begin{aligned}\mathbf{LocalMem}(\mathcal{R}'^{\mathcal{A}'}) ={} & \mathbf{LocalMem}\,(\mathcal{A}') + \mathbf{Mem}(\mathsf{RGen}) + \mathbf{Mem}(\mathsf{RSign}) \\ & + \mathbf{Mem}(\mathsf{RHash}) + \mathbf{Mem}(\mathsf{Sig.Vrfy}) + \mathbf{Mem}(\mathsf{RExtract}) \\ & + \mathbf{Mem}(\mathsf{U}) + \mathbf{Mem}(\mathsf{PRF}) + 1,\end{aligned} \tag{5}$$

and

$$\begin{aligned}\mathbf{LocalTime}(\mathcal{B}^{\mathcal{A}'}) \approx{} & \mathbf{LocalTime}\,(\mathcal{A}') + \mathbf{Time}(\mathsf{RGen}) + (q_{\mathsf{S}} + q_{\mathsf{F}}) \cdot \mathbf{Time}(\mathsf{RSign}) \\ & + q_{\mathsf{H}} \cdot \mathbf{Time}(\mathsf{RHash}) + q_{\mathsf{F}} \cdot \mathbf{Time}(\mathsf{Sig.Vrfy}) \\ & + \max\{\mathbf{Time}(\mathsf{RExtract}), \mathbf{Time}(\mathsf{U})\} + \mathbf{Time}(\mathsf{InstGen}) \\ & + \mathbf{Time}(\mathsf{V}),\end{aligned}$$

$$\begin{aligned}\mathbf{LocalMem}(\mathcal{B}^{\mathcal{A}'}) ={} & \mathbf{LocalMem}\,(\mathcal{A}') + \mathbf{Mem}(\mathsf{RGen}) + \mathbf{Mem}(\mathsf{RSign}) \\ & + \mathbf{Mem}(\mathsf{RHash}) + \mathbf{Mem}(\mathsf{Sig.Vrfy}) + \mathbf{Mem}(\mathsf{RExtract}) \\ & + \mathbf{Mem}(\mathsf{U}) + \mathbf{Mem}(\mathsf{InstGen}) + \mathbf{Mem}(\mathsf{V}).\end{aligned}$$

where q_{F} *is the number of* Forge *queries made by* $\mathcal{A}'$, q_{S} *is the number of* Sign *queries made by* $\mathcal{A}'$, q_{H} *is the numbers of queries made to the random oracle*[6], *and* q_{RF} *is an upper bound of the number of evaluations of* RF.

[6] If the reduction is not in the ROM, then $q_{\mathsf{H}} = 0$ holds.

Remark 10. For any sEUF-CMA1 *adversary* $\mathcal{A}$ *and any* msEUF-CMA1 *adversary* $\mathcal{A}'$, *if we define the memory overhead of* $\mathcal{R}'$ *(*$\mathcal{R}$*) as*

$$\Delta(\mathcal{R}') := \mathbf{LocalMem}(\mathcal{R}'^{\mathcal{A}'}) - \mathbf{LocalMem}(\mathcal{A}')$$
$$\Delta(\mathcal{R}) := \mathbf{LocalMem}(\mathcal{R}^{\mathcal{A}}) - \mathbf{LocalMem}(\mathcal{A}).$$

Then, from Eq. (2) and (4), we have that,

$$\Delta(\mathcal{R}') - \Delta(\mathcal{R}) = \mathbf{Mem}(\mathsf{PRF}) + 1 - \mathbf{Mem}(\mathsf{RF}).$$

More intuitively speaking, this means that reduction $\mathcal{R}'$ *does not use memory to keep a random function* RF *whose random table grows linearly with the number of different queries, but instead it uses some small amount of memory to store a PRF key and run the PRF. Furthermore, the algorithms in* $\mathcal{R}'$ *(*RGen, RSign, RHash, RExtract, Sig.Vrfy, PRF *and* U*) are stateless and their memory usage is independent of the number of queries made by adversary. Thus, the memory overhead of* $\mathcal{R}'$, *i.e.,* $\Delta(\mathcal{R}')$ *will also be independent of the adversary, especially independent of* q_{S}.

Remark 11. Eq. (3) is equivalent to

$$\mathsf{Adv}^{\mathsf{msEUF\text{-}CMA1}}_{\mathsf{Sig}}(\mathcal{A}') \leq \ell \cdot \left(\mathsf{Adv}^{\mathsf{NICA}}_{\Lambda,\lambda}\left(\mathcal{R}'^{\mathcal{A}'}\right) + \mathsf{Adv}^{\mathsf{PRF\text{-}sec}}_{\mathsf{PRF}}\left(\mathcal{B}^{\mathcal{A}'}\right) + \delta\right).$$

It shows that the msEUF-CMA1 *security of* Sig *builds upon both the security of* NICA *and the pseudorandomness of* PRF. *If* ℓ *is a constant,* δ *is a negligible value which is independent of the number of queries made by the adversary and* PRF *is memory-tightly secure, then the* msEUF-CMA1 *security of* Sig *is tight in both working factor and memory. (See Sect. 5 for more discussions about concrete applications.)*

Proof (of Theorem 9). Since $\mathcal{R}$ is a canonical reduction, we know that there are algorithms (RGen, RSign, RExtract, RHash). Using these algorithms and a pseudorandom function, we construct another reduction $\mathcal{R}'$ which transfers any msEUF-CMA1 adversary $\mathcal{A}'$ to a hard problem solver of Λ.

Construction of $\mathcal{R}'$. The reduction $\mathcal{R}'$ receives as input an instance ϕ of Λ and simulates the experiment $\mathsf{Exp}^{\mathsf{msEUF\text{-}CMA1}}_{\mathsf{Sig}}(\mathcal{A}')$ for $\mathcal{A}'$. To this end, it first runs $(simpk, simsk) \xleftarrow{\$} \mathsf{RGen}(\phi)$ to obtain a simulated public key *simpk* for the signature scheme Sig. Note that this is exactly the same as what $\mathcal{R}$ would do.

In contrast to $\mathcal{R}$, $\mathcal{R}'$ does not simulate a random function with algorithm RF. Instead, it chooses a uniform key $k \xleftarrow{\$} \{0,1\}^{\lambda}$ for a pseudorandom function $\mathsf{PRF}\colon \{0,1\}^{\lambda} \times \{0,1\}^* \rightarrow \mathsf{Coins}_{\mathsf{RSign}} \times \mathsf{Coins}_{\mathsf{RExtract}} \times \mathsf{Coins}_{\mathsf{RHash}}$ and uses PRF as a replacement.

$\mathcal{A}'$ then receives as input the simulated public key *simpk* and gets access to the signing oracle Sign, the random oracle (if ROM is considered) and the "forgery attempt" oracle Forge. To simulate these oracles for $\mathcal{A}'$, the reduction $\mathcal{R}'$ does the following:

Sign-oracle. Upon receiving a signature query $\mathsf{Sign}(m)$ for some message $m \in M$, the reduction $\mathcal{R}'$ runs $\mathcal{R}$'s signature simulation algorithm with oracle access to PRF, i.e., $\sigma := \mathsf{RSign}^{\mathsf{PRF}(k,\cdot)}(simsk, m)$. Then it returns σ to $\mathcal{A}'$. Note that the same signature will be returned if the same message is queried multiple times since RSign is deterministic.

Random oracle. $\mathcal{R}'$ answers a random oracle query x by running RHash with oracle access to PRF, i.e., $y := \mathsf{RHash}^{\mathsf{PRF}(k,\cdot)}(simsk, x)$ and returns y.

Forge-oracle. Upon receiving a forgery attempt (m^*, σ^*), the reduction $\mathcal{R}'$ at first checks whether

$$\mathsf{Sig.Vrfy}(simpk, m^*, \sigma^*) = 1 \quad \text{and} \quad \sigma^* \neq \mathsf{RSign}^{\mathsf{PRF}(k,\cdot)}(simsk, m^*)$$

In case both checks pass, the reduction $\mathcal{R}'$ attempts to extract a solution ρ for the problem instance ϕ from the forgery at hand by running $\rho := \mathsf{RExtract}^{\mathsf{PRF}(k,\cdot)}(simsk, (m^*, \sigma^*))$. Then $\mathcal{R}'$ returns ρ and halts.
In case any of the previous two checks failed, $\mathcal{R}'$ continues to simulate $\mathcal{A}'$. If the adversary $\mathcal{A}'$ fails to output any forgery attempt (m^*, σ^*) that can pass the checks throughout the whole simulation process, $\mathcal{R}'$ runs $\rho \xleftarrow{\$} \mathsf{U}(\phi)$ and outputs ρ.

Note that $\mathcal{R}'$ proceeds exactly as $\mathcal{R}$ but it uses a pseudorandom function instead of a truly random function and it needs to handle at most q_{F} forgery attempts as opposed to just one. Therefore, the running time of $\mathcal{R}'$ is the running time of $\mathcal{R}$ as given in Remark 8, replacing $\mathbf{Time}(\mathsf{RF})$ by $\mathbf{Time}(\mathsf{PRF})$ plus the time required to simulate the additional $q_{\mathsf{F}} - 1$ Forge-queries, namely $(q_{\mathsf{F}} - 1) \cdot (\mathbf{Time}(\mathsf{Vrfy}) + \mathbf{Time}(\mathsf{RSign}))$. This yields the time given in Theorem 9.

Similarly, the memory consumption of $\mathcal{R}'$ is the memory consumed by $\mathcal{R}$ as given in Remark 8, but instead of storing the random table in RF, $\mathcal{R}'$ needs to store the function description of PRF and its corresponding key, which again yields the values given in Theorem 9. In particular, note that the memory consumed by $\mathcal{R}'^{\mathcal{A}'}$ is independent of the number of queries made by $\mathcal{A}'$, as the stateful random table is replaced with the stateless keyed PRF PRF.

We complete the proof of Theorem 9 by analyzing the advantage of $\mathcal{R}'$ as follows.

The advantage of $\mathcal{R}'^{\mathcal{A}'}$. In order to analyse the advantage of $\mathcal{R}'^{\mathcal{A}'}$, we first modify the reduction $\mathcal{R}'$ to get a new reduction $\mathcal{R}_1$. More precisely, $\mathcal{R}_1$ is exactly $\mathcal{R}'$ except that it uses a random function RF instead of a pseudorandom function PRF.

We can easily build an adversary $\mathcal{B}$ and show that

$$\mathsf{Adv}^{\mathsf{NICA}}_{\Lambda,\lambda}\left(\mathcal{R}'^{\mathcal{A}'}\right) \geq \mathsf{Adv}^{\mathsf{NICA}}_{\Lambda,\lambda}\left(\mathcal{R}_1^{\mathcal{A}'}\right) - \mathsf{Adv}^{\mathsf{PRF\text{-}sec}}_{\mathsf{PRF}}\left(\mathcal{B}^{\mathcal{A}'}\right). \tag{6}$$

The construction of $\mathcal{B}$ is straightforward. It generates the problem instance together with its witness using $(\phi, \omega) \xleftarrow{\$} \mathsf{InstGen}(1^\lambda)$. Then it simulates the above reductions and interacting with $\mathcal{A}'$ by forwarding all the input to RF/PRF to its own challenger. If the reduction outputs a solution ρ, $\mathcal{B}$ runs the algorithm V and outputs $\mathsf{V}(\phi, \omega, \rho)$. Thus, Eq. (5) holds and the running time and memory consumption of $\mathcal{B}$ follows the equations in Theorem 9.

Next we modify $\mathcal{R}_1$ again to get $\mathcal{R}_2$. $\mathcal{R}_2$ is identical to $\mathcal{R}_1$ except that it logs all the chosen message queries with their respective signatures in the set $\mathcal{Q}$ and it replaces the check in Forge-oracle from

$$\mathsf{Sig.Vrfy}(simpk, m^*, \sigma^*) = 1 \wedge \sigma^* \neq \mathsf{RSign}^{\mathsf{RF}(\cdot)}(simsk, m^*)$$

to the check

$$\mathsf{Sig.Vrfy}(simpk, m^*, \sigma^*) = 1 \wedge \sigma^* \neq \mathsf{RSign}^{\mathsf{RF}(\cdot)}(simsk, m^*) \wedge (m^*, \sigma^*) \notin \mathcal{Q}.$$

Note that the added check $(m^*, \sigma^*) \notin \mathcal{Q}$ is redundant because every (m, σ) pair in $\mathcal{Q}$ has the property that $\sigma = \mathsf{RSign}^{\mathsf{PRF}(\cdot)}(simsk, m)$. Thus, we have that

$$\mathsf{Adv}^{\mathsf{NICA}}_{\Lambda,\lambda}\left(\mathcal{R}_1^{\mathcal{A}'}\right) = \mathsf{Adv}^{\mathsf{NICA}}_{\Lambda,\lambda}\left(\mathcal{R}_2^{\mathcal{A}'}\right). \tag{7}$$

Next, we construct a single-challenge sEUF-CMA1-adversary $\widetilde{\mathcal{A}}$ that combines the multi-challenge $\mathcal{A}'$ with the check $\mathsf{Sig.Vrfy}(pk, m^*, \sigma^*) = 1 \wedge (m^*, \sigma^*) \notin \mathcal{Q}$. More precisely, after getting the public key pk, $\widetilde{\mathcal{A}}$ simulates $\mathcal{A}'$ and keep log of the set $\mathcal{Q}$ itself. Whenever $\mathcal{A}'$ submits a Forge-query, $\widetilde{\mathcal{A}}$ checks whether $\mathsf{Sig.Vrfy}(pk, m^*, \sigma^*) = 1 \wedge (m^*, \sigma^*) \notin \mathcal{Q}$. If the check does not pass, $\widetilde{\mathcal{A}}$ continues the simulation of $\mathcal{A}'$. And $\widetilde{\mathcal{A}}$ outputs the first forgery that can pass this check as its own forgery attempt. After that, $\widetilde{\mathcal{A}}$ terminates. Note that $\widetilde{\mathcal{A}}$ can perform the checks efficiently because it knows the public key pk and can log the set $\mathcal{Q}$ itself.

We can obtain an important observation on $\widetilde{\mathcal{A}}$: the game that is played between $\mathcal{R}_2$ and the multi-challenge adversary $\mathcal{A}'$ distributes identically with the game that is played between the canonical reduction $\mathcal{R}$ and the single-challenge adversary $\widetilde{\mathcal{A}}$. Thus, we have that

$$\mathsf{Adv}^{\mathsf{NICA}}_{\Lambda,\lambda}(\mathcal{R}_2^{\mathcal{A}'}) = \mathsf{Adv}^{\mathsf{NICA}}_{\Lambda,\lambda}(\mathcal{R}^{\widetilde{\mathcal{A}}}).$$

Furthermore, we know that $\widetilde{\mathcal{A}}$ wins the (single-challenge) sEUF-CMA1 game if and only if $\mathcal{A}'$ wins the (multi-challenge) msEUF-CMA1 game because of the check $\mathsf{Sig.Vrfy}(simpk, m^*, \sigma^*) = 1 \wedge (m^*, \sigma^*) \notin \mathcal{Q}$. So, we have that

$$\mathsf{Adv}^{\mathsf{sEUF\text{-}CMA1}}_{\mathsf{Sig}}(\widetilde{\mathcal{A}}) = \mathsf{Adv}^{\mathsf{msEUF\text{-}CMA1}}_{\mathsf{Sig}}(\mathcal{A}').$$

Since $\mathcal{R}$ is canonical, we have that

$$\begin{aligned}\mathsf{Adv}^{\mathsf{NICA}}_{\Lambda,\lambda}(\mathcal{R}_2^{\mathcal{A}'}) = \mathsf{Adv}^{\mathsf{NICA}}_{\Lambda,\lambda}(\mathcal{R}^{\widetilde{\mathcal{A}}}) &\geq \frac{1}{\ell}\mathsf{Adv}^{\mathsf{sEUF\text{-}CMA1}}_{\mathsf{Sig}}(\widetilde{\mathcal{A}}) - \delta \\ &= \frac{1}{\ell}\mathsf{Adv}^{\mathsf{msEUF\text{-}CMA1}}_{\mathsf{Sig}}(\mathcal{A}') - \delta.\end{aligned}$$

Combining Eq. (5) to (7), we have that

$$\mathsf{Adv}^{\mathsf{NICA}}_{\Lambda,\lambda}(\mathcal{R}'^{\mathcal{A}'}) \geq \frac{1}{\ell}\mathsf{Adv}^{\mathsf{msEUF\text{-}CMA1}}_{\mathsf{Sig}}(\mathcal{A}') - \delta - \mathsf{Adv}^{\mathsf{PRF\text{-}sec}}_{\mathsf{PRF}}(\mathcal{B}^{\mathcal{A}'}),$$

and the theorem follows. □

4 From msEUF-CMA1 Security to msEUF-CMA Security

So far we have shown how any signature scheme that can be proven sEUF-CMA1-secure (i.e., single-challenge and one-signature-per-message) via a canonical reduction to some computational problem, can be proven msEUF-CMA1-secure (i.e., *multi-challenge* and one-signature-per-message) in a memory-tight way. In this section, we extend our approach and present a generic transform, which "memory-tightly lifts" *any* signature scheme from msEUF-CMA1 security (i.e., multi-challenge and one-signature-per-message) to the desired msEUF-CMA security (i.e., multi-challenge and *many-signatures-per-message*).

Intuition. The core idea of this transform is to sign a message together with some randomly-chosen nonce n. Intuitively, this nonce "expands" the set of valid signatures for a given message. While this transform is straightforward, we see value to make it explicit.

Transform. Let $\lambda \in \mathbb{N}$ and let $\mathsf{Sig}' = (\mathsf{Gen}', \mathsf{Sign}', \mathsf{Vrfy}')$ be a signature scheme. We construct a new signature scheme $\mathsf{Sig} = (\mathsf{Gen}, \mathsf{Sign}, \mathsf{Vrfy})$ as follows:

Key Generation. Gen behaves exactly like Gen′.
Signing. Sign takes as input the secret key sk and a message m. It samples a nonce $n \xleftarrow{\$} \{0,1\}^\lambda$, computes $\sigma' \xleftarrow{\$} \mathsf{Sign}'(sk, m \,\|\, n)$, and returns $\sigma = (\sigma', n)$.
Verification. Vrfy takes as input a public key pk, a message m, and a signature $\sigma = (\sigma', n)$. It computes and returns $\mathsf{Sig}'.\mathsf{Vrfy}(pk, m \,\|\, n, \sigma')$.

Theorem 12. *From each adversary $\mathcal{A}$ breaking the* msEUF-CMA*-security of the above signature scheme* Sig *(with q_s signing queries), we can construct an adversary $\mathcal{B}$ such that* $\mathsf{Adv}^{\mathsf{msEUF\text{-}CMA}}_{\mathsf{Sig}}(\mathcal{A}) \le \mathsf{Adv}^{\mathsf{msEUF\text{-}CMA1}}_{\mathsf{Sig}'}(\mathcal{B}) + \frac{q_s^2}{2^\lambda}$ *and*

$$\mathbf{LocalTime}(\mathcal{B}) \approx \mathbf{LocalTime}(\mathcal{A}) \quad \textit{and} \quad \mathbf{LocalMem}(\mathcal{B}) = \mathbf{LocalMem}(\mathcal{A}).$$

The proof of Theorem 12 is straightforward and we provide it in the full version [21].

5 Applications

In this section, we present how the results of Sects. 3 and 4 can be used to yield memory-tight strongly unforgeable signatures in the multi-challenge and many-signatures-per-message setting. In Sect. 5.1, we present a construction based on lossy identification schemes (similar to the construction by Abdalla et al. [1]) and prove its memory-tight security using our results. Then, in Sect. 5.2, we show how existing signature schemes such as RSA-FDH [10] benefit from our result and evade the existing impossibility results of [4,51]. In the full version of this paper [21], we show similar results for the Boneh, Lynn, and Shacham signature scheme [14,15].

We note that, a pseudorandom function is required when applying our results of Sects. 3 and 4. In the standard model, we are aware of several pseudorandom functions that achieve almost tight security based on standard assumptions [40,45,47]. In the random oracle model, such a pseudorandom function exists unconditionally.

5.1 Memory-Tight Signatures from Lossy Identification Schemes

In this section, we present how to construct memory-tight strongly unforgeable signatures in the multi-challenge and many-signatures-per-message setting based on lossy identification schemes. To this end, we first present a formal definition of lossy identification schemes.

Lossy Identification Schemes. We adapt the definition of a *lossy identification scheme* [1,2].

Definition 13. *A* lossy identification scheme LID *is a tuple of algorithms*

$$\mathsf{LID} = (\mathsf{LID.Gen}, \mathsf{LID.LossyGen}, \mathsf{LID.Prove}, \mathsf{LID.Vrfy}, \mathsf{LID.Sim})$$

with the following properties.

- $(pk, sk) \xleftarrow{\$} \mathsf{LID.Gen}(1^\lambda)$ *is the normal key generation algorithm. It takes as input the security parameter and outputs a public verification key* pk *and a secret key* sk*.*
- $pk \xleftarrow{\$} \mathsf{LID.LossyGen}(1^\lambda)$ *is a lossy key generation algorithm that takes the security parameter and outputs a lossy verification key* pk*.*
- $\mathsf{LID.Prove}$ *is the prover algorithm that is split into two algorithms:*
  - $(\mathsf{cmt}, \mathsf{st}) \xleftarrow{\$} \mathsf{LID.Prove}_1(sk)$ *is a probabilistic algorithm that takes as input the secret key and returns a commitment* cmt *and a state* st.
  - $\mathsf{resp} \xleftarrow{\$} \mathsf{LID.Prove}_2(sk, \mathsf{cmt}, \mathsf{ch}, \mathsf{st})$ *is a deterministic algorithm*[7] *that takes as input the secret key, a commitment* cmt*, a challenge* ch*, a state* st*, and returns a response* resp.
- $\mathsf{LID.Vrfy}(pk, \mathsf{cmt}, \mathsf{ch}, \mathsf{resp}) \in \{0, 1\}$ *is a deterministic verification algorithm that takes a public key, and a conversation transcript (i.e., a commitment, a challenge, and a response) as input and outputs a bit, where* 1 *indicates that the proof is "accepted" and* 0 *"rejected".*

We assume that a public key pk *implicitly defines two sets, the challenge set* CSet *and the response set* RSet.

[7] As far as we know, all the instantiations of lossy identification schemes have a deterministic $\mathsf{LID.Prove}_2$ algorithm. However, if a new instantiation requires randomness, then it can be "forwarded" from $\mathsf{LID.Prove}_1$ in the state variable st. Therefore the requirement that $\mathsf{LID.Prove}_2$ is deterministic is without loss of generality, and only made to simplify our security analysis.

Definition 14. *Let* $\mathsf{LID} = (\mathsf{LID.Gen}, \mathsf{LID.LossyGen}, \mathsf{LID.Prove}, \mathsf{LID.Vrfy}, \mathsf{LID.Sim})$ *defined as above. We call* LID lossy *when the following properties hold:*

- Completeness of normal keys. *Let* $(pk, sk) \xleftarrow{\$} \mathsf{LID.Gen}(1^\lambda)$ *be a key pair and let* $(\mathsf{cmt}, \mathsf{ch}, \mathsf{resp})$ *be an honest transcript (i.e.,* $(\mathsf{cmt}, \mathsf{st}) \xleftarrow{\$} \mathsf{LID.Prove}_1(sk)$, $\mathsf{ch} \xleftarrow{\$} \mathsf{CSet}$, *and* $\mathsf{resp} \xleftarrow{\$} \mathsf{LID.Prove}_2(sk, \mathsf{cmt}, \mathsf{ch}, \mathsf{st})$*). We call* LID ρ-complete, *if*
$$\Pr[\mathsf{LID.Vrfy}(pk, \mathsf{cmt}, \mathsf{ch}, \mathsf{resp}) = 1] \geq \rho(\lambda),$$
where ρ *is a non-negligible function in* λ. *We call* LID perfectly-complete, *if it is 1-complete.*
- Simulatability of transcripts. *Let* $(pk, sk) \xleftarrow{\$} \mathsf{LID.Gen}(1^\lambda)$ *be a key pair. We call* LID ε_s-simulatable *if* LID.Sim *taking public key* pk, *a challenge* $\mathsf{ch} \in \mathsf{CSet}$ *and a response* $\mathsf{resp} \in \mathsf{RSet}$ *as input, deterministically generates a commitment* cmt *such that* $(\mathsf{cmt}, \mathsf{ch}, \mathsf{resp})$ *is a valid transcript (i.e.,* $\mathsf{LID.Vrfy}(pk, \mathsf{cmt}, \mathsf{ch}, \mathsf{resp}) = 1$*). Furthermore, if* $(\mathsf{ch}, \mathsf{resp})$ *is chosen uniformly random from* $\mathsf{CSet} \times \mathsf{RSet}$, *the distribution of the transcript* $(\mathsf{cmt}, \mathsf{ch}, \mathsf{resp})$ *is statistically indistinguishable (up to an upper bound* ε_s*) from honestly generated transcripts. If* $\varepsilon_s = 0$, *we call* LID perfectly simulatable.
- Indistinguishability of keys. *We define the advantage of an adversary* $\mathcal{A}$ *to break the key-indistinguishability of* LID *as*
$$\mathsf{Adv}_{\mathsf{LID}}^{\mathsf{IND\text{-}KEY}}(\mathcal{A}) := \left|\Pr\left[\mathcal{A}(pk) = 1\right] - \Pr\left[\mathcal{A}(pk') = 1\right]\right|,$$
where $(pk, sk) \xleftarrow{\$} \mathsf{LID.Gen}(1^\lambda)$ *and* $pk' \xleftarrow{\$} \mathsf{LID.LossyGen}(1^\lambda)$, *is negligible in* λ.
- Lossiness. *Consider the following security experiment* $\mathsf{Exp}_{\mathsf{LID}}^{\mathsf{IMPERSONATE}}(\mathcal{A})$ *described below, played between a challenger and an adversary* $\mathcal{A}$:
  1. *The challenger generates a lossy verification key* $pk \xleftarrow{\$} \mathsf{LID.LossyGen}(1^\lambda)$ *and sends it to the adversary* $\mathcal{A}$.
  2. *The adversary* $\mathcal{A}$ *may now compute a commitment* cmt *and send it to the challenger. The challenger responds with a random challenge* $\mathsf{ch} \xleftarrow{\$} \mathsf{CSet}$.
  3. *Eventually, the adversary* $\mathcal{A}$ *outputs a response* resp. *The challenger outputs* $\mathsf{LID.Vrfy}(pk, \mathsf{cmt}, \mathsf{ch}, \mathsf{resp})$.

  We call LID ε_ℓ*-lossy if no computationally unrestricted adversary* $\mathcal{A}$ *wins the above security game with probability*
$$\Pr[\mathsf{Exp}_{\mathsf{LID}}^{\mathsf{IMPERSONATE}}(\mathcal{A}) = 1] \geq \varepsilon_\ell.$$

Definition 15. *A lossy identification scheme*
$$\mathsf{LID} = (\mathsf{LID.Gen}, \mathsf{LID.LossyGen}, \mathsf{LID.Prove}, \mathsf{LID.Vrfy}, \mathsf{LID.Sim})$$
is commitment-recoverable *if* $\mathsf{LID.Vrfy}(pk, \mathsf{cmt}, \mathsf{ch}, \mathsf{resp})$ *first recomputes* $\mathsf{cmt}' = \mathsf{LID.Sim}(pk, \mathsf{ch}, \mathsf{resp})$ *and then outputs 1 if and only if* $\mathsf{cmt}' = \mathsf{cmt}$.

Remark 16. We are aware of five different lossy identification scheme instantiations and they are based on DDH [44], DSDL, Ring-LWE, Subset Sum [1, 2] and RSA [35]. As far as we know, all of them are commitment-recoverable. And the schemes based on DDH, DSDL and RSA assumption are perfectly complete and perfectly simulatable.

Memory-Tight Signatures from Lossy Identification Schemes. In the following, we present the construction of the signature scheme based on lossy identification scheme. This construction is slightly different from the construction by Abdalla et al. in [1,2] and can be seen as a variant of the Fiat-Shamir transform [25]. We show that this construction can be proven strongly unforgeable in the single challenge and one-message-per-signature setting (in the sense of sEUF-CMA1, see Definition 3) in Theorem 17. This result is not yet memory-tight, but work-factor-tight, as the reduction still needs to do book-keeping for a random function, but does not need to store the set of queried messages and there respective signatures in the set $\mathcal{Q}$ anymore. Based this result, we show how to apply Theorems 9 and 12 to yield strong unforgeability in the multi-challenge and many-signatures-per-message setting (in the sense of msEUF-CMA), which then will be fully tight, i.e., both work-factor- and memory-tight. [1,2].

Let $\mathsf{LID} = (\mathsf{LID.Gen}, \mathsf{LID.LossyGen}, \mathsf{LID.Prove}, \mathsf{LID.Vrfy})$ be a lossy identification scheme and let $\mathsf{H} : \{0,1\}^* \to \mathsf{CSet}$. Consider the following digital signature scheme $(\mathsf{Gen}, \mathsf{Sign}, \mathsf{Vrfy})$.

Key generation. Algorithm Gen samples a key pair $(pk, sk) \xleftarrow{\$} \mathsf{LID.Gen}(1^\lambda)$.

Signing. The signing algorithm Sign takes as input sk and a message $m \in \{0,1\}^*$. Then, it computes $(\mathsf{cmt}, \mathsf{st}) \xleftarrow{\$} \mathsf{LID.Prove}_1(sk)$, $\mathsf{ch} := \mathsf{H}(m, \mathsf{cmt})$ and $\mathsf{resp} := \mathsf{LID.Prove}_2(sk, \mathsf{ch}, \mathsf{cmt}, \mathsf{st})$, and outputs the signature $\sigma := (\mathsf{ch}, \mathsf{resp})$.

Verification. The verification algorithm Vrfy takes as input a public key pk, message $m \in \{0,1\}^*$, and a signature $\sigma = (\mathsf{ch}, \mathsf{resp})$. It runs the check $\mathsf{LID.Vrfy}(pk, \mathsf{cmt}, \mathsf{ch}, \mathsf{resp})$. More precisely, it first recovers

$$\mathsf{cmt} := \mathsf{LID.Sim}(pk, \mathsf{ch}, \mathsf{resp})$$

and then computes $\mathsf{ch}' := \mathsf{H}(m, \mathsf{cmt})$ Finally, the reduction outputs 1 if and only if ch equals ch'.

Compared to the signature scheme by Abdalla et al. [1,2], signature of the above scheme is a pair $(\mathsf{ch}, \mathsf{resp})$ whereas signature in [1,2] is a pair $(\mathsf{cmt}, \mathsf{resp})$ for a transcript $(\mathsf{cmt}, \mathsf{ch}, \mathsf{resp})$ of the lossy identification scheme. For a concrete instantiation based on DDH assumption, this yields a shorter signature.

Theorem 17. *Let* $\mathsf{H}\colon \{0,1\}^* \to \mathsf{CSet}$ *be modeled as a random oracle and let* LID *be a lossy identification scheme that is commitment-recoverable, perfectly complete,* ε_s*-simulatable and* ε_ℓ*-lossy.*

Then, from each adversary $\mathcal{A}$ *breaking the* sEUF-CMA1 *security of the above signature scheme, we can construct an adversary* $\mathcal{B}$ *such that*

$$\mathsf{Adv}_{\mathsf{Sig}}^{\mathsf{sEUF\text{-}CMA1}}(\mathcal{A}) \leq \mathsf{Adv}_{\mathsf{LID}}^{\mathsf{IND\text{-}KEY}}(\mathcal{B}) + \frac{1}{|\mathsf{CSet}|} + \frac{1}{|\mathsf{RSet}|} + q_{\mathsf{S}} \cdot \varepsilon_s + q_{\mathsf{H}} \cdot \varepsilon_\ell$$

and

$$\begin{aligned}\mathbf{LocalTime}(\mathcal{B}) &\leq \mathbf{LocalTime}(\mathcal{A}) + \mathbf{Time}(\mathsf{LID.LossyGen}) \\ &\quad + (q_s + q_{\mathsf{H}} + 1) \cdot \mathbf{Time}(\mathsf{RF}) + \mathbf{Time}(\mathsf{Sig.Vrfy}), \\ \mathbf{LocalMem}(\mathcal{B}) &= \mathbf{LocalMem}(\mathcal{A}) + \mathbf{Mem}(\mathsf{LID.LossyGen}) + \mathbf{Mem}(\mathsf{RF}) \\ &\quad + \mathbf{Mem}(\mathsf{Sig.Vrfy}),\end{aligned}$$

where q_{S} *is the number of* Sign*-queries issued by* $\mathcal{A}$*,* q_{F} *is the number of* Forge*-queries issued by* $\mathcal{A}$ *and* q_{H} *is the number of hash queries throughout the game.*

The proof of Theorem 17 is similar to the proof by Abdalla et al. in [1,2]. One technical difference it that, in our proof, we need to memory-tightly switch the winning condition in the sEUF-CMA1 game into the checks that a canonical reduction would do. For completeness, we provide the full proof in the full version [21].

Applying Theorem 9. Here, we show how to apply Theorem 9 to lift the security of the LID-based signature scheme to work-factor-tight *and* memory-tight security in the *multi*-challenge and one-per-message setting. To apply the theorem, we show that the adversary $\mathcal{B}$ in Theorem 17 can be "translated" into a canonical reduction $\mathcal{R}_{\mathsf{LID}}$ which satisfies Definition 6.

To this end, we define the canonical reduction $\mathcal{R}_{\mathsf{LID}}$ from sEUF-CMA1-security to the indistinguishability of keys IND-KEY to be the tuple (RGen, RF, RSign, RExtract, RHash) as follows.

RGen: On input $\phi = pk$, RGen return $(pk, \emptyset)$ where $\emptyset$ denotes the empty word in this context.

RF: On input any string $x \in \{0,1\}^*$, RF simulates a random function using a lazily sampled random table. In the following, we will omit this table and view RF as a random function. Further, for $(r_{\mathsf{RSign}}, r_{\mathsf{RHash}}) := \mathsf{RF}(x)$, we define the short-hands $r_{\mathsf{RSign}} =: \mathsf{RF}(\texttt{"sim"} \parallel x)$ and $r_{\mathsf{RHash}} =: \mathsf{RF}(\texttt{"hash"} \parallel x)$.

$\mathsf{RSign}^{\mathsf{RF}(\cdot)}$: On input *simsk* $= \emptyset$ and m, RSign outputs $\sigma = (\mathsf{ch}, \mathsf{resp})$ with $(\mathsf{ch}, \mathsf{resp}) := \mathsf{RF}(\texttt{"sim"} \parallel m)$.

$\mathsf{RExtract}^{\mathsf{RF}(\cdot)}$: On input *simsk* $= \emptyset$ and (m^*, σ^*), RExtract outputs solution $\rho = 1$. Note that by definition $\mathcal{R}_{\mathsf{LID}}$ runs RExtract only if $\mathsf{Vrfy}(pk, m^*, \sigma^*) = 1$ and $\sigma^* = (\mathsf{ch}^*, \mathsf{resp}^*) \neq \mathsf{RSign}(simsk, m^*) = \mathsf{RF}(\texttt{"sim"} \parallel m^*)$. Hence, if RExtract is run the queried forgery is valid.

$\mathsf{RHash}^{\mathsf{RF}(\cdot)}$: On input *simsk* $= \emptyset$ and x, RHash works as follows:

- If x cannot be parsed as $x = m \parallel \mathsf{cmt}$, then it returns $\mathsf{RF}(\texttt{"hash"} \parallel x)$.
- Otherwise, it parses $m \parallel \mathsf{cmt} := x$ and runs $(\mathsf{ch}, \mathsf{resp}) := \mathsf{RF}(\texttt{"sim"} \parallel m)$ and then $\mathsf{cmt}' := \mathsf{LID.Sim}(\mathsf{ch}, \mathsf{resp})$.
  - If $\mathsf{cmt} = \mathsf{cmt}'$, then it returns ch.
  - Otherwise, it returns $\mathsf{RF}(\texttt{"hash"} \parallel x)$.

According to the results of Theorem 17, we have

$$\mathsf{Adv}_{\mathsf{LID}}^{\mathsf{IND\text{-}KEY}}(\mathcal{R}_{\mathsf{LID}}^{\mathcal{A}}) \geq \mathsf{Adv}_{\mathsf{Sig}}^{\mathsf{sEUF\text{-}CMA1}}(\mathcal{A}) - \frac{1}{|\mathsf{CSet}|} - \frac{1}{|\mathsf{RSet}|} - q_{\mathsf{S}} \cdot \varepsilon_s - q_{\mathsf{H}} \cdot \varepsilon_\ell$$

where all quantities are defined as in Theorem 17 and $\mathsf{Adv}_{\mathsf{LID}}^{\mathsf{IND\text{-}KEY}}(\mathcal{R}_{\mathsf{LID}}^{\mathcal{A}}) = \mathsf{Adv}_{\mathsf{LID}}^{\mathsf{IND\text{-}KEY}}(\mathcal{B})$. Thus, $\mathcal{R}_{\mathsf{LID}}$ fulfills Definition 6, Property 2 with $\ell = 1$ and $\delta = \frac{1}{|\mathsf{CSet}|} + \frac{1}{|\mathsf{RSet}|} + q_{\mathsf{S}} \cdot \varepsilon_s + q_{\mathsf{H}} \cdot \varepsilon_\ell$.

Applying Theorem 12. It remains to lift the security of the LID-based signature scheme from the one-signature-per-message setting to the many-signatures-per-message-setting. This can easily be done, by applying the transform presented in Sect. 4. As the reduction presented in Theorem 12 preserves the memory-tightness of the one-per-message scheme Sig', we have that the transformed LID-based signature scheme is memory-tightly strongly unforgeable in the multi-challenge and many-signatures-per-message setting.

5.2 On the Memory-Tightness of RSA-FDH

Auerbach et al. [4] show that RSA-FDH can be proven memory-tightly unforgeable in the single-challenge and many-signatures-per-message setting under the RSA assumption. However, due to the existing tightness lower bounds, they did not achieve work-factor-tightness. In this subsection, we first show that RSA-FDH can be proven memory-tightly unforgeable in the *multi-challenge* setting because the reduction by Auerbach et al. satisfies our definition of a canonical reduction. Furthermore, we additionally show that with one extra random bit in the signature, we are able to achieve both memory and working factor tightness together with strong security.

We briefly recall the RSA assumption in the form of a non-interactive computational assumption.

Definition 18. *Let* GenRSA *be an algorithm that takes as input the security parameter* 1^λ *and returns* $(N = pq, e, d)$*, where* p *and* q *are distinct primes of bit length* $\lambda/2$ *and* e, d *are integers such that* $ed = 1 \bmod \phi(N)$*. The RSA assumption with respect to* GenRSA *is a non-interactive computational assumption* $\Lambda_{\mathsf{RSA}} = (\mathsf{InstGen}_{\mathsf{RSA}}, \mathsf{V}_{\mathsf{RSA}}, \mathsf{U}_{\mathsf{RSA}})$ *where*

1. $\mathsf{InstGen}_{\mathsf{RSA}}(1^\lambda)$ *runs* $(N, e, d) \stackrel{\$}{\leftarrow} \mathsf{GenRSA}(1^\lambda)$*, selects* $x \stackrel{\$}{\leftarrow} \mathbb{Z}_N$*, computes* $y = x^e \bmod N$ *and outputs a problem instance* $\phi = (N, e, y)$ *and a witness* $\omega = x$*.*
2. $\mathsf{V}_{\mathsf{RSA}}(\phi, \omega, \rho)$ *returns* 1 *if and only if* $\rho = \omega$*.*
3. $\mathsf{U}_{\mathsf{RSA}}(\phi)$ *returns a failure symbol* $\perp$*.*

Recall the RSA-FDH signature scheme [10] $\mathsf{Sig} = (\mathsf{Gen}, \mathsf{Sign}, \mathsf{Vrfy})$ as follows.

- Gen runs $(N, e, d) \stackrel{\$}{\leftarrow} \mathsf{GenRSA}(1^\lambda)$ and returns $pk = (N, e), sk = (N, d)$.

- $\mathsf{Sign}(sk, m)$ returns $\sigma = H(m)^d \bmod N$ where $H : \{0,1\}^* \rightarrow \mathbb{Z}_n$ is a hash function.
- $\mathsf{Vrfy}(pk, m, \sigma)$ returns 1 if and only if $\sigma^e = H(m) \bmod N$.

The scheme provides existential unforgeability under chosen message attacks, which can be reduced to the RSA assumption in the random oracle model as shown by [11,18]. However, these proofs are neither work-factor-tight (an inherent loss linear in the number of signature queries) nor memory-tight (implementing the random oracle). Auerbach et al. [4] were able to improve those results by proving RSA-FDH memory-tight in the single-challenge setting, based on the RSA assumption in the random oracle model. We show how to further improve this result with our techniques.

We proceed as in Sect. 5.1. That is, we first argue that RSA-FDH is strongly unforgeable under an chosen message attack in the single-challenge and one-signature-per-message setting (sEUF-CMA1-secure) under the RSA assumption in the random oracle model. From this result, we then construct the canonical reduction to show multi-challenge security. The transform presented in Sect. 4 then finally gives us many-signatures-per-message security again.

We will omit a full proof of sEUF-CMA1 security of RSA-FDH but only provide a brief sketch. The proof is very similar to the proof of EUF-CMA security presented by Auerbach et al. [4]. Note that RSA-FDH scheme is a unique signature scheme. That is, for every message m there is exactly one valid signature, namely $\sigma = \mathsf{H}(m)^d \mod N$. Thus, whenever $\mathsf{Sign}(m)$ is queried it will always return the same signature σ and the adversary will always see exactly one signature per message. Moreover, given a valid message-signature pair (m^*, σ^*), there exists no second valid signature $\sigma \neq \sigma^*$. Hence,

$$\mathsf{Adv}^{\mathsf{sEUF\text{-}CMA1}}_{\mathrm{RSA\text{-}FDH}}(\mathcal{A}) \leq \mathsf{Adv}^{\mathsf{EUF\text{-}CMA}}_{\mathrm{RSA\text{-}FDH}}(\mathcal{A}). \tag{8}$$

As we need a memory-tight reduction for RSA-FDH up to a truly random function RF, we adapt the result [4, Thm. 5] by Auerbach et al. slightly. Namely, we do not implement the random sampling with a PRF as they are doing, but by a truly random function RF that is maintained with an explicit look-up table. By standard arguments, it is easy to verify that with this adaptation it follows from [4, Thm. 5] and Eq. (8) that

$$\mathsf{Adv}^{\mathsf{sEUF\text{-}CMA1}}_{\mathrm{RSA\text{-}FDH}}(\mathcal{A}) \leq \exp(1) \cdot q_{\mathsf{S}} \cdot \mathsf{Adv}^{\mathsf{NICA}}_{\Lambda_{\mathsf{RSA}},\lambda}(\mathcal{B}) \tag{9}$$

where q_{S} denotes the number of signature queried by $\mathcal{A}$ and where $\mathcal{B}$ is identical to $\mathcal{B}_2$ in the proof of [4, Thm. 5] except that $\mathcal{B}$ uses a random function RF with a explicitly stored look-up table instead of a PRF. We have

$$\begin{aligned}\mathbf{LocalTime}(\mathcal{B}) &\approx \mathbf{LocalTime}(\mathcal{A}) + (q_{\mathsf{H}} + q_{\mathsf{S}}) \cdot \mathbf{Time}(\mathsf{RF}),\\ \mathbf{LocalMem}(\mathcal{B}) &= \mathbf{LocalMem}(\mathcal{A}) + \mathbf{Mem}(\mathsf{RF}) + 3\end{aligned}$$

where q_{H} is the number of random oracle queries and q_{S} the number of signature queries made by $\mathcal{A}$.

We define the canonical reduction $\mathcal{R}_{\mathsf{RSA}}$ from sEUF-CMA1-security to the RSA assumption as tuple (RGen, RSign, RExtract, RHash) as follows. In essence, $\mathcal{R}_{\mathsf{RSA}}$ works exactly as $\mathcal{B}$. Let $\mathsf{RF}\colon \{0,1\}^* \to \{0,1\} \times \mathbb{Z}_N$ with $\mathsf{Coins}_{\mathsf{RSign}} = \mathsf{Coins}_{\mathsf{RExtract}} = \emptyset$ and $\{0,1\} \times \mathbb{Z}_N = \mathsf{Coins}_{\mathsf{RHash}}$. Further, for $(b,r) := \mathsf{RF}(x)$, we define the short-hands $b =: \mathsf{RF}_1(x)$ and $r =: \mathsf{RF}_2(x)$. We view RF_1 as an $(1/q_{\mathsf{S}})$-biased random function similar to the biased coin used by Coron [18], i.e., $\Pr[\mathsf{RF}_1(x) = 1] = 1/q_{\mathsf{S}}$, where q_{S} is the number of signature queries issued by the adversary.

RGen: Given an RSA instance $\phi = (N,e,y)$, RGen returns $(\mathit{simpk}, \mathit{simsk}) = ((N,e),(N,e,y))$.
$\mathsf{RHash}^{\mathsf{RF}(\cdot)}$: Given $\mathit{simsk} = (N,e,y)$ and x, RHash returns $\mathsf{RF}_2(x)^e \cdot y$ if $\mathsf{RF}_1(x) = 1$. Otherwise, it returns $\mathsf{RF}_2(x)^e$.
$\mathsf{RSign}^{\mathsf{RF}(\cdot)}$: Given $\mathit{simsk} = (N,e,y)$ and m, RSign outputs a signature $\sigma = \mathsf{RF}_2(m)$ if $\mathsf{RF}_1(m) = 0$. Otherwise, the reduction aborts and terminates by outputting the failure symbol $\perp$.
$\mathsf{RExtract}^{\mathsf{RF}(\cdot)}$: Given $\mathit{simsk} = (N,e,y)$ and (m^*, σ^*), RExtract outputs a solution $\rho = \sigma^*/\mathsf{RF}_2(m)$. Note that by definition $\mathcal{R}_{\mathsf{RSA}}$ runs RExtract only if $\mathsf{Vrfy}(\mathit{simpk}, m^*, \sigma^*) = 1$ and $\sigma^* \neq \mathsf{RSign}(\mathit{simsk}, m^*)$. The validity of the signature implies that $(\sigma^*)^e = \mathsf{RHash}(\mathit{simsk}, m^*)$ and since we have $\sigma^* \neq \mathsf{RSign}(\mathit{simsk}, m^*)$, we also know that $\mathsf{RF}_1(m^*) = 1$.

Reduction $\mathcal{R}_{\mathsf{RSA}}$ works basically as $\mathcal{B}$, we have due to Eq. (9)

$$\mathsf{Adv}^{\mathsf{NICA}}_{\Lambda_{\mathsf{RSA}},\lambda}(\mathcal{R}^{\mathcal{A}}_{\mathsf{RSA}}) \geq \frac{1}{\exp(1) \cdot q_{\mathsf{S}}} \cdot \mathsf{Adv}^{\mathsf{sEUF\text{-}CMA1}}_{\mathrm{RSA\text{-}FDH}}(\mathcal{A}).$$

That is, $\mathcal{R}_{\mathsf{RSA}}$ is a $(\ell, 0)$-canonical reduction for RSA-FDH with value $\ell = 1/(\exp(1) \cdot q_{\mathsf{S}})$. The local time of $\mathcal{R}^{\mathcal{A}}_{\mathsf{RSA}}$ is $\mathbf{LocalTime}(\mathcal{R}^{\mathcal{A}}_{\mathsf{RSA}}) \approx \mathbf{LocalTime}(\mathcal{A}) + \mathbf{Time}(\mathsf{Sig.Vrfy}) + (q_{\mathsf{H}} + q_{\mathsf{S}} + 1) \cdot \mathbf{Time}(\mathsf{RF})$, and the local memory is

$$\mathbf{LocalMem}(\mathcal{R}^{\mathcal{A}}_{\mathsf{RSA}}) = \mathbf{LocalMem}(\mathcal{A}) + \mathbf{Mem}(\mathsf{RF}) + \mathbf{Mem}(\mathsf{Sig.Vrfy}) + 3.$$

Now, we can use Theorem 9 to lift the security of RSA-FDH to the multi-challenge in a memory-tight way. To this end, we can construct a reduction $\mathcal{R}'_{\mathsf{RSA}}$ from msEUF-CMA1-security of RSA-FDH to the RSA assumption as presented in the proof Theorem 9. This implies that we can construct an adversary $\mathcal{B}'$ such that

$$\mathsf{Adv}^{\mathsf{NICA}}_{\Lambda_{\mathsf{RSA}},\lambda}((\mathcal{R}'_{\mathsf{RSA}})^{\mathcal{A}'}) \geq \frac{1}{\exp(1) \cdot q_{\mathsf{S}}} \cdot \mathsf{Adv}^{\mathsf{msEUF\text{-}CMA1}}_{\mathrm{RSA\text{-}FDH}}(\mathcal{A}') - \mathsf{Adv}^{\mathsf{PRF\text{-}sec}}_{\mathsf{PRF}}(\mathcal{B}')$$

where $\mathsf{PRF}\colon \{0,1\}^\lambda \times \{0,1\}^* \to \{0,1\} \times \mathbb{Z}_N$ is a keyed function. Moreover, it holds that

$$\begin{aligned}\mathbf{LocalTime}((\mathcal{R}'_{\mathsf{RSA}})^{\mathcal{A}'}) &\approx \mathbf{LocalTime}(\mathcal{A}') + \mathbf{Time}(\mathsf{RGen}) \\ &\quad + (q_{\mathsf{S}} + q_{\mathsf{F}} + q_{\mathsf{H}}) \cdot \mathbf{Time}(\mathsf{PRF}) + q_{\mathsf{F}} \cdot \mathbf{Time}(\mathsf{Sig.Vrfy}) \\ \mathbf{LocalMem}((\mathcal{R}'_{\mathsf{RSA}})^{\mathcal{A}'}) &= \mathbf{LocalMem}(\mathcal{A}') + 4 + \mathbf{Mem}(\mathsf{Sig.Vrfy}) \\ &\quad + \mathbf{Mem}(\mathsf{PRF}).\end{aligned}$$

Thus, the reduction $\mathcal{R}'_{\mathsf{RSA}}$ is a memory-tight, but not work-factor-tight, reduction from msEUF-CMA1-security to the RSA assumption.

Note that since RSA-FDH is a unique signature scheme, the one-signature-per-message security automatically implies the many-signatures-per-message security. Thus, we do not need to apply our theorem form Sect. 4. At first glance, this result seems to contradict the memory lower bound for unique signatures established by Wang *et al.* [51, Theorem 3]. However, this is not the case as our reduction does not meet the criteria for their impossibility result to hold.[8] So we evade their lower bound and achieve memory tightness for RSA-FDH.

On the Overall Tightness of RSA-FDH. In the previous section, we have shown how RSA-FDH can be proven memory-tight in the multi-challenge and many-signatures-per-message setting. As already explained above, due to existing tightness lower bounds, plain RSA-FDH cannot be proven work-fact-tight. However, when considering a slight variant of RSA-FDH, which was proposed by Katz and Wang [44], we can apply our techniques to prove this variant fully tight. In essence, we still consider RSA-FDH, but choose a uniformly random bit b and sign $b \,\|\, m$ instead of only m. We call this scheme RSA-FDH+ and we can prove the following theorem.

Theorem 19. *For any adversary $\mathcal{A}'$, there exists a reduction $\mathcal{R}'_{\mathsf{RSA+}}$ and an adversary $\mathcal{B}'$ such that*

$$\mathsf{Adv}^{\mathsf{msEUF\text{-}CMA1}}_{\mathrm{RSA\text{-}FDH+}}(\mathcal{A}') \leq 2\mathsf{Adv}^{\mathsf{NICA}}_{\Lambda_{\mathsf{RSA}},\lambda}((\mathcal{R}'_{\mathsf{RSA+}})^{\mathcal{A}'}) + 2\mathsf{Adv}^{\mathsf{PRF\text{-}sec}}_{\mathsf{PRF}}(\mathcal{B}').$$

where $\mathsf{PRF}\colon \{0,1\}^\lambda \times \{0,1\}^* \to \{0,1\} \times \mathbb{Z}_N \times \mathbb{Z}_N$ *is a keyed PRF. Moreover, it holds that*

$$\begin{aligned}\mathbf{LocalTime}((\mathcal{R}'_{\mathsf{RSA+}})^{\mathcal{A}'}) &\approx \mathbf{LocalTime}(\mathcal{A}') + \mathbf{Time}(\mathsf{RGen}) \\ &\quad + (q_{\mathsf{S}} + q_{\mathsf{F}} + q_{\mathsf{H}}) \cdot \mathbf{Time}(\mathsf{PRF}) + q_{\mathsf{F}} \cdot \mathbf{Time}(\mathsf{Sig.Vrfy}) \\ \mathbf{LocalMem}((\mathcal{R}'_{\mathsf{RSA+}})^{\mathcal{A}'}) &= \mathbf{LocalMem}(\mathcal{A}') + \mathbf{Mem}(\mathsf{Sig.Vrfy}) + \mathbf{Mem}(\mathsf{PRF}) + 4.\end{aligned}$$

Hence, $\mathcal{R}'_{\mathsf{RSA+}}$ is a fully tight reduction (i.e., work-factor-tight and memory-tight), from msEUF-CMA1-security of RSA-FDH+ to the RSA assumption. Applying the transform of Sect. 4 and adding an additional nonce that is signed along with the message, we can further lift this result to achieve msEUF-CMA-security under the RSA assumption.

The proof of Theorem 19 follows the Katz-Wang approach. We provide the formal description of scheme RSA-FDH+ and the proof of Theorem 19 in the full version [21].

[8] More precisely, Wang *et al.* [51] define two parameters c_r and c_g, where c_r captures the work-factor loss of the reduction and c_g captures the trivial winning probability of the assumption. They require $c_g < 1/2$ and $c_r + c_g > 1/2$ for their lower bound to hold. However, we have $c_g = 0$ for the RSA assumption and $c_r = 1/(\exp(1) \cdot q_{\mathsf{S}})$ for our reduction, implying $c_r + c_g < 1/2$, which does not fall into the realm of Theorem 3 in [51].

References

1. Abdalla, M., Fouque, P.A., Lyubashevsky, V., Tibouchi, M.: Tightly-secure signatures from lossy identification schemes. In: Pointcheval, D., Johansson, T. (eds.) Advances in Cryptology 2012. EUROCRYPT 2012. LNCS, vol. 7237. Springer, Heidelberg (2012). https://doi.org/10.1007/978-3-642-29011-4_34
2. Abdalla, M., Fouque, P.A., Lyubashevsky, V., Tibouchi, M.: Tightly secure signatures from lossy identification schemes. J. Cryptol. **29**(3), 597–631 (2016)
3. Abe, M., Groth, J., Ohkubo, M.: Separating short structure-preserving signatures from non-interactive assumptions. In: Lee, D.H., Wang, X. (eds.) Advances in Cryptology 2011. LNCS, vol. 7073. Springer, Heidelberg (2011). https://doi.org/10.1007/978-3-642-25385-0_34
4. Auerbach, B., Cash, D., Fersch, M., Kiltz, E.: Memory-tight reductions. In: Katz, J., Shacham, H. (eds.) CRYPTO 2017. LNCS, vol. 10401, pp. 101–132. Springer, Cham (2017). https://doi.org/10.1007/978-3-319-63688-7_4
5. Bader, C., Hofheinz, D., Jager, T., Kiltz, E., Li, Y.: Tightly-secure authenticated key exchange. In: Dodis, Y., Nielsen, J.B. (eds.) Theory of Cryptography. TCC 2015. LNCS, vol. 9014. Springer, Heidelberg (2015). https://doi.org/10.1007/978-3-662-46494-6_26
6. Bader, C., Jager, T., Li, Y., Schage, S.: On the impossibility of tight cryptographic reductions. In: Fischlin, M., Coron, J.S. (eds.) Advances in Cryptology 2016. EUROCRYPT 2016. LNCS, vol. 9666. Springer, Heidelberg (2016). https://doi.org/10.1007/978-3-662-49896-5_10
7. Bellare, M., Boldyreva, A., Micali, S.: Public-key encryption in a multi-user setting: security proofs and improvements. In: EUROCRYPT 2000. LNCS, vol. 1807, pp. 259–274. Springer, Heidelberg (2000)
8. Bellare, M., Ristenpart, T.: Simulation without the artificial abort: simplified proof and improved concrete security for Waters' IBE scheme. In: EUROCRYPT 2009. LNCS, vol. 5479, pp. 407–424. Springer, Heidelberg (2009). https://doi.org/10.1007/978-3-642-01001-9_24
9. Bellare, M., Ristenpart, T.: Simulation without the artificial abort: simplified proof and improved concrete security for waters' IBE scheme. Cryptology ePrint Archive, Report 2009/084 (2009). eprint.iacr.org/2009/084
10. Bellare, M., Rogaway, P.: Random oracles are practical: a paradigm for designing efficient protocols. In: ACM CCS 93, pp. 62–73. ACM Press (1993)
11. Bellare, M., Rogaway, P.: The exact security of digital signatures: how to sign with RSA and Rabin. In: EUROCRYPT'96. LNCS, vol. 1070, pp. 399–416. Springer, Heidelberg (1996). https://doi.org/10.1007/3-540-68339-9_34
12. Bhattacharyya, R.: Memory-tight reductions for practical key encapsulation mechanisms. In: Kiayias, A., Kohlweiss, M., Wallden, P., Zikas, V. (eds.) PKC 2020. LNCS, vol. 12110, pp. 249–278. Springer, Cham (2020). https://doi.org/10.1007/978-3-030-45374-9_9
13. Blazy, O., Kiltz, E., Pan, J.: (Hierarchical) identity-based encryption from affine message authentication. In: CRYPTO 2014, Part I. LNCS, vol. 8616, pp. 408–425. Springer, Heidelberg (2014). https://doi.org/10.1007/978-3-662-44371-2_23
14. Boneh, D., Lynn, B., Shacham, H.: Short signatures from the Weil pairing. In: ASIACRYPT 2001. LNCS, vol. 2248, pp. 514–532. Springer, Heidelberg (2001). https://doi.org/10.1007/3-540-45682-1_30
15. Boneh, D., Lynn, B., Shacham, H.: Short signatures from the Weil pairing. J. Cryptol. **17**(4), 297–319 (2004)

16. Chen, J., Wee, H.: Fully, (almost) tightly secure IBE and dual system groups. In: CRYPTO 2013, Part II. LNCS, vol. 8043, pp. 435–460. Springer, Heidelberg (2013). https://doi.org/10.1007/978-3-642-40084-1_25
17. Cohn-Gordon, K., Cremers, C., Gjøsteen, K., Jacobsen, H., Jager, T.: Highly efficient key exchange protocols with optimal tightness. In: Boldyreva, A., Micciancio, D. (eds.) CRYPTO 2019. LNCS, vol. 11694, pp. 767–797. Springer, Cham (2019). https://doi.org/10.1007/978-3-030-26954-8_25
18. Coron, J.S.: On the exact security of full domain hash. In: CRYPTO 2000. LNCS, vol. 1880, pp. 229–235. Springer, Heidelberg (2000). https://doi.org/10.1007/3-540-44598-6_14
19. Coron, J.S.: Optimal security proofs for PSS and other signature schemes. In: EUROCRYPT 2002. LNCS, vol. 2332, pp. 272–287. Springer, Heidelberg (2002). https://doi.org/10.1007/3-540-46035-7_18
20. Davis, H., Günther, F.: Tighter proofs for the sigma and TLS 1.3 key exchange protocols. Cryptology ePrint Archive, Report 2020/1029 (2020). eprint.iacr.org/2020/1029
21. Diemert, D., Gellert, K., Jager, T., Lyu, L.: Digital signatures with memory-tight security in the multi-challenge setting. Cryptology ePrint Archive, Report 2021/1220 (2021). ia.cr/2021/1220
22. Diemert, D., Gellert, K., Jager, T., Lyu, L.: More efficient digital signatures with tight multi-user security. In: Public-Key Cryptography - PKC 2021, pp. 1–31. Springer International Publishing, Cham (2021). https://doi.org/10.1007/978-3-030-75248-4_1
23. Diemert, D., Jager, T.: On the tight security of TLS 1.3: theoretically-sound cryptographic parameters for real-world deployments. Cryptology ePrint Archive, Report 2020/726; to appear in the J. Cryptol. (2020). eprint.iacr.org/2020/726
24. Fersch, M., Kiltz, E., Poettering, B.: On the one-per-message unforgeability of (EC)DSA and its variants. In: TCC 2017, Part II. LNCS, vol. 10678, pp. 519–534. Springer, Heidelberg (2017). https://doi.org/10.1007/978-3-319-70503-3_17
25. Fiat, A., Shamir, A.: How to prove yourself: practical solutions to identification and signature problems. In: CRYPTO'86. LNCS, vol. 263, pp. 186–194. Springer, Heidelberg (1987). https://doi.org/10.1007/3-540-47721-7_12
26. Fleischhacker, N., Jager, T., Schröder, D.: On tight security proofs for Schnorr signatures. In: ASIACRYPT 2014, Part I. LNCS, vol. 8873, pp. 512–531. Springer, Heidelberg (2014). https://doi.org/10.1007/978-3-662-45611-8_27
27. Fleischhacker, N., Jager, T., Schröder, D.: On tight security proofs for Schnorr signatures. J. Cryptol. **32**(2), 566–599 (2019)
28. Garg, S., Bhaskar, R., Lokam, S.V.: Improved bounds on security reductions for discrete log based signatures. In: CRYPTO 2008. LNCS, vol. 5157, pp. 93–107. Springer, Heidelberg (2008). https://doi.org/10.1007/978-3-540-85174-5_6
29. Gay, R., Hofheinz, D., Kiltz, E., Wee, H.: Tightly CCA-secure encryption without pairings. In: EUROCRYPT 2016, Part I. LNCS, vol. 9665, pp. 1–27. Springer, Heidelberg (2016). https://doi.org/10.1007/978-3-662-49890-3_1
30. Ghoshal, A., Jaeger, J., Tessaro, S.: The memory-tightness of authenticated encryption. In: Advances in Cryptology - CRYPTO 2020–40th Annual International Cryptology Conference, CRYPTO 2020, Santa Barbara, CA, USA, August 17–21, 2020, Proceedings, Part I. LNCS, vol. 12170, pp. 127–156. Springer (2020). https://doi.org/10.1007/978-3-030-56784-2_5
31. Ghoshal, A., Tessaro, S.: On the memory-tightness of hashed ElGamal. In: EUROCRYPT 2020, Part II. LNCS, vol. 12106, pp. 33–62. Springer, Heidelberg (2020). https://doi.org/10.1007/978-3-030-45724-2_2

32. Gjøsteen, K., Jager, T.: Practical and tightly-secure digital signatures and authenticated key exchange. In: CRYPTO 2018, Part II. LNCS, vol. 10992, pp. 95–125. Springer, Heidelberg (2018). https://doi.org/10.1007/978-3-319-96881-0_4
33. Goldwasser, S., Micali, S., Rivest, R.L.: A digital signature scheme secure against adaptive chosen-message attacks. SIAM J. Comput. **17**(2), 281–308 (1988)
34. Gueron, S., Lindell, Y.: Better bounds for block cipher modes of operation via nonce-based key derivation. In: ACM CCS 2017, pp. 1019–1036. ACM Press (2017)
35. Hasegawa, S., Isobe, S.: Lossy identification schemes from decisional RSA. In: International Symposium on Information Theory and its Applications, ISITA 2014, Melbourne, Australia, pp. 143–147. IEEE (2014)
36. Hoang, V.T., Tessaro, S.: The multi-user security of double encryption. In: EUROCRYPT 2017, Part II. LNCS, vol. 10211, pp. 381–411. Springer, Heidelberg (2017). https://doi.org/10.1007/978-3-319-56614-6_13
37. Hofheinz, D., Jager, T.: Tightly secure signatures and public-key encryption. In: CRYPTO 2012. LNCS, vol. 7417, pp. 590–607. Springer, Heidelberg (2012). https://doi.org/10.1007/s10623-015-0062-x
38. Hofheinz, D., Jager, T., Knapp, E.: Waters signatures with optimal security reduction. In: PKC 2012. LNCS, vol. 7293, pp. 66–83. Springer, Heidelberg (2012). https://doi.org/10.1007/978-3-642-30057-8_5
39. Jager, T., Kakvi, S.A., May, A.: On the security of the PKCS#1 v1.5 signature scheme. In: ACM CCS 2018. pp. 1195–1208. ACM Press (2018)
40. Jager, T., Kurek, R., Pan, J.: Simple and more efficient PRFs with tight security from LWE and matrix-DDH. In: ASIACRYPT 2018, Part III. LNCS, vol. 11274, pp. 490–518. Springer, Heidelberg (2018). https://doi.org/10.1007/978-3-030-03332-3_18
41. Jager, T., Stam, M., Stanley-Oakes, R., Warinschi, B.: Multi-key authenticated encryption with corruptions: reductions are lossy. In: TCC 2017, Part I. LNCS, vol. 10677, pp. 409–441. Springer, Heidelberg (2017). https://doi.org/10.1007/978-3-319-70500-2_14
42. Kakvi, S.A., Kiltz, E.: Optimal security proofs for full domain hash, revisited. In: EUROCRYPT 2012. LNCS, vol. 7237, pp. 537–553. Springer, Heidelberg (2012). https://doi.org/10.1007/978-3-642-29011-4_32
43. Kakvi, S.A., Kiltz, E.: Optimal security proofs for full domain hash, revisited. J. Cryptol. **31**(1), 276–306 (2018)
44. Katz, J., Wang, N.: Efficiency improvements for signature schemes with tight security reductions. In: ACM CCS 2003, pp. 155–164. ACM Press (2003)
45. Lewko, A.B., Waters, B.: Efficient pseudorandom functions from the decisional linear assumption and weaker variants. In: ACM CCS 2009, pp. 112–120. ACM Press (2009)
46. Liu, X., Liu, S., Gu, D., Weng, J.: Two-pass authenticated key exchange with explicit authentication and tight security. In: ASIACRYPT 2020, Part II. LNCS, vol. 12492, pp. 785–814. Springer, Heidelberg (2020). https://doi.org/10.1007/978-3-030-64834-3_27
47. Naor, M., Reingold, O.: Number-theoretic constructions of efficient pseudo-random functions. In: 38th FOCS, pp. 458–467. IEEE Computer Society Press (1997)
48. Paillier, P., Vergnaud, D.: Discrete-log-based signatures may not be equivalent to discrete log. In: ASIACRYPT 2005. LNCS, vol. 3788, pp. 1–20. Springer, Heidelberg (2005). https://doi.org/10.1007/11593447_1
49. Schäge, S.: Tight proofs for signature schemes without random oracles. In: EUROCRYPT 2011. LNCS, vol. 6632, pp. 189–206. Springer, Heidelberg (2011). https://doi.org/10.1007/978-3-642-20465-4_12

50. Seurin, Y.: On the exact security of Schnorr-type signatures in the random oracle model. In: EUROCRYPT 2012. LNCS, vol. 7237, pp. 554–571. Springer, Heidelberg (2012). https://doi.org/10.1007/978-3-642-29011-4_33
51. Wang, Y., Matsuda, T., Hanaoka, G., Tanaka, K.: Memory lower bounds of reductions revisited. In: Nielsen, J.B., Rijmen, V. (eds.) EUROCRYPT 2018. LNCS, vol. 10820, pp. 61–90. Springer, Cham (2018). https://doi.org/10.1007/978-3-319-78381-9_3

(Compact) Adaptively Secure FE for Attribute-Weighted Sums from k-Lin

Pratish Datta[1(✉)] and Tapas Pal[1,2(✉)]

[1] NTT Research, Sunnyvale, CA 94085, USA
pratish.datta@ntt-research.com

[2] Indian Institute of Technology Kharagpur, Kharagpur 721302, West Bengal, India
tapas.pal@iitkgp.ac.in

Abstract. This paper presents the *first adaptively simulation secure* functional encryption (FE) schemes for attribute-weighted sums. In such an FE scheme, encryption takes as input N pairs of attribute $\{(x_i, z_i)\}_{i\in[N]}$ for some $N \in \mathbb{N}$ where the attributes $\{x_i\}_{i\in[N]}$ are public while the attributes $\{z_i\}_{i\in[N]}$ are private. The indices $i \in [N]$ are referred to as the slots. A secret key corresponds to some weight function f, and decryption recovers the weighted sum $\sum_{i=1}^{N} f(x_i)z_i$. This is an important functionality with a wide range of potential real life applications. In the proposed FE schemes attributes are viewed as vectors and weight functions are arithmetic branching programs (ABP). We present two schemes with varying parameters and levels of adaptive security.

(a) We first present a one-slot scheme that achieves adaptive security in the simulation-based security model against a bounded number of ciphertext queries and an arbitrary polynomial number of secret key queries both before and after the ciphertext queries. This is the best possible level of security one can achieve in the adaptive simulation-based framework. From the relations between the simulation-based and indistinguishability-based security frameworks for FE, it follows that the proposed FE scheme also achieves indistinguishability-based adaptive security against an a-priori unbounded number of ciphertext queries and an arbitrary polynomial number of secret key queries both before and after the ciphertext queries. Moreover, the scheme enjoys *compact* ciphertexts that do not grow with the number of appearances of the attributes within the weight functions.

(b) Next, bootstrapping from the one-slot scheme, we present an unbounded-slot scheme that achieves simulation-based adaptive security against a bounded number of ciphertext and pre-ciphertext secret key queries while supporting an a-priori unbounded number of post-ciphertext secret key queries. The scheme achieves public parameters and secret key sizes independent of the number of slots N and a secret key can decrypt a ciphertext for any a-priori unbounded N. Further, just like the one-slot scheme, this scheme also has the ciphertext size independent of the number of appearances of the attributes within the weight functions. However, all the parameters of the scheme, namely, the master public key, ciphertexts, and secret keys scale linearly with the bound on the number of pre-ciphertext secret key queries.

M. Tibouchi and H. Wang (Eds.): ASIACRYPT 2021, LNCS 13093, pp. 434–467, 2021.
https://doi.org/10.1007/978-3-030-92068-5_15

Our schemes are built upon asymmetric bilinear groups of prime order and the security is derived under the standard (bilateral) k-Linear (k-Lin) assumption. Our work *resolves an open problem* posed by Abdalla, Gong, and Wee in CRYPTO 2020, where they presented an unbounded-slot FE scheme for attribute-weighted sum achieving only semi-adaptive simulation security. At a technical level, our work extends the recent adaptive security framework of Lin and Luo [EUROCRYPT 2020], devised to achieve compact ciphertexts in the context of indistinguishability-based payload-hiding security, into the setting of simulation-based adaptive attribute-hiding security.

Keywords: Functional encryption · Attribute-weighted sums · Adaptive simulation security

1 Introduction

Functional Encryption: *Functional encryption* (FE), formally introduced by Boneh et al. [9] and O'Neill [26], redefines the classical encryption procedure with the motivation to overcome the limitation of the "all-or-nothing" paradigm of decryption. In a traditional encryption system, there is a single secret key such that a user given a ciphertext can either recover the whole message or learns nothing about it, depending on the availability of the secret key. FE in contrast provides fine grained access control over encrypted data by generating artistic secret keys according to the desired functions of the encrypted data to be disclosed. More specifically, in a public-key FE scheme for a function class $\mathcal{F}$, there is a setup authority which produces a master secret key and publishes a master public key. Using the master secret key, the setup authority can derive secret keys or functional decryption keys SK_f associated to functions $f \in \mathcal{F}$. Anyone can encrypt messages msg belonging to a specified message space $\mathbb{M}$ using the master public key to produce a ciphertext CT. The ciphertext CT along with a secret key SK_f recovers the function of the message $f(\mathsf{msg})$ at the time of decryption, while unable to extract any other information about msg. More specifically, the security of FE requires *collusion resistance* meaning that any polynomial number of secret keys together cannot gather more information about an encrypted message except the union of what each of the secret keys can learn individually.

FE for Attribute-Weighted Sum: Recently, Abdalla, Gong and Wee [3] proposed an FE scheme for a new class of functionalities which they termed as "attribute-weighted sums". This is a generalization of the inner product functional encryption (IPFE) [1,7]. In such a scheme, a database of N attribute-value pairs $(x_i, z_i)_{i=1,\dots,N}$ are encrypted using the master public key of the scheme, where x_i is a public attribute (e.g., demographic data) and z_i is a private attribute containing sensitive information (e.g., salary, medical condition, loans, college admission outcomes). The indices $i \in [N]$ are referred to as the *slots*. A recipient having a secret key corresponding to a weight function f can learn the attribute-weighted sum of the database, i.e., $\sum_{i=1}^{N} f(x_i)z_i$. The attribute-weighted sum functionality appears naturally in several real life applications. For instance, as discussed by Abdalla et al. [3] if we consider the weight function f as a boolean predicate, then the attribute-weighted sum functionality $\sum_{i=1}^{N} f(x_i)z_i$ would correspond to the average z_i over all users whose attribute $\boldsymbol{x}_i$ satisfies the predicate f. Important practical scenarios include average salaries of minority groups holding a particular job (z_i = salary) and approval ratings of an election candidate amongst specific demographic groups in a particular state (z_i = rating). Similarly, if z_i is boolean, then the attribute-weighted sum becomes $\sum_{i:z_i=1} f(x_i)$. This could capture for instance the number of and average age of smokers with lung cancer (z_i = lung cancer, f = numbers/age).

The work of [3] considered a more general case of the notion where the domain and range of the weight functions are vectors over some finite field $\mathbb{Z}_p$. In particular, the database consists of N pairs of public/private attribute vectors $(\boldsymbol{x}_i, \boldsymbol{z}_i)_{i=1,\ldots,N}$ which is encrypted to a ciphertext CT. A secret key SK_f generated for a weight function f allows a recipient to learn $\sum_{i=1}^{N} f(\boldsymbol{x}_i)^\top \boldsymbol{z}_i$ from CT without revealing any information about the private attribute vectors $(\boldsymbol{z}_i)_{i=1,\ldots,N}$. To handle a large database where the number of users are not a-priori bounded, Abdalla et al. further considered the notion of *unbounded-slot* FE scheme for attribute-weighted sum where the number of slots N is not fixed while generating the system parameters and any secret key SK_f can decrypt an encrypted database having an arbitrary number of slots. Another advantage of unbounded-slot FE is that the same system parameters and secret keys can be reused for different databases with variable lengths, which saves storage space and reduces communication cost significantly.

The unbounded-slot FE of [3] supports expressive function class of *arithmetic branching programs* (ABPs) which are capable of capturing boolean formulas, boolean span programs, combinatorial computations, and arithmetic span programs. The FE scheme of [3] is built in asymmetric bilinear groups of prime order and is proven secure in the simulation-based security model, which is known to be the desirable security model for FE [9,26], under the k-Linear (k-Lin)/*Matrix Diffie-Hellman* (MDDH) assumption. Moreover, their scheme enjoys ciphertext size that grows with the number of slots and the size of the private attribute vectors but is independent of the size of the public attribute vectors. Towards constructing their unbounded-slot scheme, Abdalla et al. first constructed a one-slot scheme and then bootstrap to the unbounded-slot scheme via a semi-generic transformation

However, one significant limitation of the FE scheme of [3] is that the scheme only achieves semi-adaptive security. While semi-adaptive security, where the adversary is restricted to making secret key queries only after making the ciphertext queries, may be sufficient for certain applications, it is much weaker compared to the strongest and most natural notion of adaptive security which lets the adversary request secret keys both before and after making the ciphertext queries. Thus it is desirable to have an adaptively secure scheme for this important functionality possibly supporting an unbounded number of slots.

One artifact of the standard techniques for proving adaptive security of FE schemes based on the so called dual system encryption methodology [17,18,28] is the use of a core information theoretic transition limiting the appearance of an attribute in the description of the associated functions at most once (or an a-priori bounded number of times at the expense of ciphertext and key sizes scaling with that upper bound [24,27]). Recently Kowalczyk and Wee [16] and Lin and Luo [19] presented advanced techniques to overcome the one-use restriction. However, their techniques were designed in the context of attribute-based encryption (ABE) where attributes are totally public. Currently, it is not known how to remove the one-use restriction in the context of adaptively secure FE schemes where attributes are not fully public as is the case for the attribute-weighted sum functionality. This leads us to the following open problem explicitly posed by Abdalla et al. [3]:

Open Problem. *Can we construct adaptively simulation-secure one-slot/ unbounded-slot* FE *scheme for the attribute-weighted sum functionality with the weight functions expressed as arithmetic branching programs featuring compact ciphertexts, that is, having ciphertexts that do not grow with the number of appearances of the attributes within the weight functions, from the k*-Lin *assumption?*

Our Contributions: In this work, we resolve the above open problem. More precisely, we make the following contributions.

(a) We start by presenting the *first* one-slot FE scheme for the attribute-weighted sum functionality with the weight functions represented as ABPs that achieves adaptive simulation-based security and compact ciphertexts, that is, the ciphertext size is independent of the number of appearances of the attributes within the weight functions. The scheme is secure against an adversary who is allowed to make an a-priori bounded number of ciphertext queries and an unbounded (polynomial) number of secret key queries both before and after the ciphertext queries, which is the best possible level of security one could hope to achieve in adaptive simulation-based framework [9]. Since simulation-based security also implies indistinguishability-based security and indistinguishability-based security against single and multiple ciphertexts are equivalent [9,26], the proposed FE scheme is also adaptively secure in the indistinguishability-based model against adversaries making unbounded number of ciphertext and secret key queries in any arbitrary order.

(b) We next bootstrap our one-slot scheme to an unbounded-slot scheme that also achieves simulation-based adaptive security against a bounded number of ciphertext queries and an unbounded polynomial number of secret key queries. Just like our one-slot scheme, the ciphertexts of our unbounded-slot scheme also do not depend on the number of appearances of the attributes within the weight functions. However, the caveat here is that the number of pre-ciphertext secret key queries is a priori bounded and all parameters of the scheme, namely, the master public key, ciphertexts, and secret keys scale linearly with that upper bound.

Like Abdalla et al. [3], our FE schemes are built upon asymmetric bilinear groups of prime order. We prove the security of our FE schemes based on the standard (bilateral) k-Lin/ (bilateral) MDDH assumption(s) [12]. Thus our results can be summarized as follows.

Theorem 1 (Informal). *Under the (bilateral) k*-Lin/MDDH *assumption(s), there exist adaptively simulation secure one-slot/unbounded-slot* FE *scheme* *for attribute-weighted sums against a bounded number of ciphertext and an unbounded number of secret-key queries, and having compact ciphertexts, that is, without the one-use restriction, in bilinear groups of prime order.*

The bilateral MDDH assumption is the plain MDDH assumption except that the elements are available in the exponents of both source groups of a bilinear group simultaneously. This assumption has recently been utilized in the context of achieving FE for quadratic functions in the standard model [5,30]. Unlike [3], our one-slot construction is semi-generic and is built upon two cryptographic building blocks, namely a slotted inner product functional encryption (IPFE) [19,20], which is a hybrid of a public-key IPFE and a private-key function-hiding IPFE, and an information theoretic primitive called arithmetic key garbling scheme (AKGS) [14,19]. For bootstrapping from one-slot to unbounded-slot construction we make use of the same semi-generic transformation proposed in [3], but analyze its security in the adaptive simulation-based setting as opposed to the semi-adaptive setting. Table 1 shows the current state of the art in the development of efficient attribute-hiding[1] FE schemes under standard computational assumptions.

On the technical side, our contributions lie in extending the recent framework of Lin and Luo [19]. The techniques of [19] are developed to achieve compact ciphertexts, that is, without the one-use restriction in the context of indistinguishability-based adaptively secure ABE (that is, for payload-hiding security and not attribute-hiding). In this work, we extend their techniques to overcome the one-use restriction into the context of adaptive simulation-based attribute-hiding security for the first time. The high level approach of [19] to mitigate the one-use restriction is to replace the core information theoretic step of the dual system technique with a computational step. However the application of this strategy in their framework crucially rely on the payload hiding security requirement, that is, the adversaries are not allowed to query secret keys that enable a successful decryption. In contrast, in the setting of attribute-hiding, adversaries are allowed to request secret keys enabling successful decryption and extending the technique of [19] into this context appears to be non-trivial. We resolve this by developing a three-slot variant of their framework, integrating the pre-image sampleability of the inner product functionality [10,26], and carefully exploiting the structures of the underlying building blocks, namely AKGS and slotted IPFE.

Paper Organization: We discuss detailed technical overview of our results in Sect. 2. The preliminaries, definitions and tools are provided in Sect. 3. We present our 1-key 1-ciphertext secure 1-slot FE and unbounded-key secure 1-slot FE for attribute-weighted sums in Sects. 4 and 5 respectively. The details of security reductions are given in the full version. Next, in Sect. 6, we provide an extended version of our 1-slot FE scheme, on which we apply the bootstrapping transformation from [3] leading to our unbounded-slot scheme. The formal security analysis of the scheme is deferred to the full version as well. Further, the formal definition of bilinear maps, related hardness assumptions, syntax and

[1] In this paper, by attribute-hiding, we mean the so-called "strong" attribute-hiding, as stipulated by the security definitions of FE, meaning that private attributes must remain hidden even to decryptors who are able to perform a successful decryption.

Table 1. Current State of the Art in Attribute-Hiding FE

Scheme	Functionality	Number of Slots	IND Security	SIM Security	$\lvert\mathsf{CT}\rvert$	Assumption
KSW08 [15]	$\phi_{\boldsymbol{y}\in\mathbb{Z}_p^n}:\mathbb{Z}_p^n\to\{0,1\},\phi_{\boldsymbol{y}}(\boldsymbol{z})=(\boldsymbol{z}^\top\boldsymbol{y}\stackrel{?}{=}0)$	1	$(-,\mathsf{poly},\mathsf{poly})$-AD	$\times$	$O(\lvert\boldsymbol{z}\rvert)$	2 non-standard assumptions
OT12 [22]	$\phi_{\boldsymbol{y}\in\mathbb{Z}_p^n}:\mathbb{Z}_p^n\to\{0,1\},\phi_{\boldsymbol{y}}(\boldsymbol{z})=(\boldsymbol{z}^\top\boldsymbol{y}\stackrel{?}{=}0)$	1	$(\mathsf{poly},\mathsf{poly},\mathsf{poly})$-AD	$\times$	$O(\lvert\boldsymbol{z}\rvert)$	DLIN
ABDCP15 [1]	$\phi_{\boldsymbol{y}\in\mathbb{Z}_p^n}:\mathbb{Z}_p^n\to\mathbb{Z}_p,\phi_{\boldsymbol{y}}(\boldsymbol{z})=\boldsymbol{z}^\top\boldsymbol{y}$	1	$(-,\mathsf{poly},\mathsf{poly})$-Sel	$\times$	$O(\lvert\boldsymbol{z}\rvert)$	DDH, LWE
ALS16, ALMT20 [6,7]	$\phi_{\boldsymbol{y}\in\mathbb{Z}_p^n}:\mathbb{Z}_p^n\to\mathbb{Z}_p,\phi_{\boldsymbol{y}}(\boldsymbol{z})=\boldsymbol{z}^\top\boldsymbol{y}$	1	$(\mathsf{poly},\mathsf{poly},\mathsf{poly})$-AD	$(\mathsf{poly},\mathsf{bdd},\mathsf{poly})$-Sel	$O(\lvert\boldsymbol{z}\rvert)$	DDH, DCR, LWE
Agr17 [4]	$\phi_{f\in\mathsf{GC}^{(n,n')}}:\mathbb{Z}_p^n\times\mathbb{Z}_p^{n'}\to\{0,1\},\phi_f(\boldsymbol{x},\boldsymbol{z})=(f(\boldsymbol{x})^\top\boldsymbol{z}\stackrel{?}{=}0)$	1	$(-,\mathsf{poly},\mathsf{bdd})$-S-AD	$(-,1,\mathsf{bdd})$-S-AD	$O(\lvert\boldsymbol{x}\rvert+\lvert\boldsymbol{z}\rvert)$	LWE
Wee17 [29]	$\phi_{f\in\mathcal{F}_{\mathsf{ABP}}^{(n,n')}}:\mathbb{Z}_p^n\times\mathbb{Z}_p^{n'}\to\{0,1\},\phi_f(\boldsymbol{x},\boldsymbol{z})=(f(\boldsymbol{x})^\top\boldsymbol{z}\stackrel{?}{=}0)$	1	$(-,\mathsf{poly},\mathsf{poly})$-S-AD	$(-,1,\mathsf{poly})$-S-AD	$O(\lvert\boldsymbol{x}\rvert+\lvert\boldsymbol{z}\rvert)$	k-Lin
DOT18 [10]	$\phi_{f\in\mathcal{F}_{\mathsf{ABP}}^{(n,n')}}:\mathbb{Z}_p^n\times\mathbb{Z}_p^{n'}\to\{0,1\},\phi_f(\boldsymbol{x},\boldsymbol{z})=(f(\boldsymbol{x})^\top\boldsymbol{z}\stackrel{?}{=}0)$	1	$(\mathsf{poly},\mathsf{poly},\mathsf{poly})$-AD	$(\mathsf{poly},\mathsf{bdd},\mathsf{poly})$-AD	$O(\lvert\boldsymbol{x}\rvert+\lvert\boldsymbol{z}\rvert)$	SXDLIN
ACGU20 [2]	$\phi_{(f\in(\mathsf{NC}^1)^{(n)},\boldsymbol{y}\in\mathbb{Z}_p^{n'})}:\mathbb{Z}_p^n\times\mathbb{Z}_p^{n'}\to\mathbb{Z}_p,\phi_{(f,\boldsymbol{y})}(\boldsymbol{x},\boldsymbol{z})=(f(\boldsymbol{x})\stackrel{?}{=}0)\cdot\boldsymbol{z}^\top\boldsymbol{y}$	1	$(\mathsf{poly},\mathsf{poly},\mathsf{poly})$-AD	$\times$	$O(\lvert\boldsymbol{x}\rvert+\lvert\boldsymbol{z}\rvert)$	SXDH
AGW20 [3]	$\phi_{f\in\mathcal{F}_{\mathsf{ABP}}^{(n,n')}}:\mathbb{Z}_p^n\times\mathbb{Z}_p^{n'}\to\mathbb{Z}_p,\phi_f(\boldsymbol{x},\boldsymbol{z})=f(\boldsymbol{x})^\top\boldsymbol{z}$	unbounded	$(-,\mathsf{poly},\mathsf{poly})$-AD	$(-,\mathsf{bdd},\mathsf{poly})$-S-AD	$O(\lvert\boldsymbol{z}\rvert)$	k-Lin
Wee20 [30]	$\phi_{f\in\mathcal{F}_{\mathsf{ABP}}^{(n,n_1n_2)}}:\mathbb{Z}_p^n\times(\mathbb{Z}_p^{n_1}\times\mathbb{Z}_p^{n_2})\to\mathbb{Z}_p,\phi_f(\boldsymbol{x},(\boldsymbol{z}_1,\boldsymbol{z}_2))=f(\boldsymbol{x})^\top(\boldsymbol{z}_1\otimes\boldsymbol{z}_2)$	1	$(-,\mathsf{poly},\mathsf{poly})$-S-AD	$(-,\mathsf{bdd},\mathsf{poly})$-S-AD	$O(\lvert\boldsymbol{z}_1\rvert+\lvert\boldsymbol{z}_2\rvert)$	bilateral k-Lin and k-Lin
This Work	$\phi_{f\in\mathcal{F}_{\mathsf{ABP}}^{(n,n')}}:\mathbb{Z}_p^n\times\mathbb{Z}_p^{n'}\to\mathbb{Z}_p,\phi_f(\boldsymbol{x},\boldsymbol{z})=f(\boldsymbol{x})^\top\boldsymbol{z}$	1	$(\mathsf{poly},\mathsf{poly},\mathsf{poly})$-AD	$(\mathsf{poly},\mathsf{bdd},\mathsf{poly})$-AD	$O(\lvert\boldsymbol{x}\rvert+\lvert\boldsymbol{z}\rvert)$	k-Lin
This Work	$\phi_{f\in\mathcal{F}_{\mathsf{ABP}}^{(n,n')}}:\mathbb{Z}_p^n\times\mathbb{Z}_p^{n'}\to\mathbb{Z}_p,\phi_f(\boldsymbol{x},\boldsymbol{z})=f(\boldsymbol{x})^\top\boldsymbol{z}$	unbounded	$(\mathsf{bdd},\mathsf{poly},\mathsf{poly})$-AD	$(\mathsf{bdd},\mathsf{bdd},\mathsf{poly})$-AD	$O(\lvert\boldsymbol{x}\rvert+\lvert\boldsymbol{z}\rvert+B)$	bilateral k-Lin and k-Lin

The notations used in this table have the following meanings:
- GC: General polynomial-size circuits
- ABP: Arithmetic branching programs
- IND: Indistinguishability-based security
- SIM: Simulation-based security
- AD: Adaptive security
- S-AD: Semi-adaptive security
- Sel: Selective security
- poly: Arbitrary polynomial in the security parameter
- bdd: A-priori bounded by the public parameters
- $|x|$: Size of x
- B: A bound on the number of pre-ciphertext decryption key queries

In this table, (U, V, W) signifies that the adversary is allowed to make V number of ciphertext queries in the relevant security experiment, while U and W number of decryption key queries in the pre- and post-ciphertext phases respectively.

security definition of slotted IPFE, and the details of special piecewise security of AKGS are provided in the full version. For security analysis of our 1-slot extended FE, we construct a 1-key 1-ciphertext secure 1-slot extended FE scheme which is also available in the full version. Finally, in the full version, we present our formal analysis of the bootstrapping transformation from [3].

2 Technical Overview

In this section, we present our main technical ideas. Let $\mathsf{G} = (\mathbb{G}_1, \mathbb{G}_2, \mathbb{G}_T, g_1, g_2, e)$ be a bilinear group of prime order p and $[\![a]\!]_i$ denotes g_i^a for any $a \in \mathbb{Z}_p$ and $i \in \{1, 2, T\}$, which notation can also be extended in case of vectors and matrices. At the topmost level of strategy, we follow [3] to first design an adaptively simulation-secure one-slot FE scheme and then apply a compiler to bootstrap to an unbounded-slot scheme. For the later part, we use the same compiler as the one presented in [3]. However, [3] only showed that the compiler works in the context of semi-adaptive security, that is, they show that their compiler can bootstrap a semi-adaptively secure one-slot FE scheme to a semi-adaptively secure unbounded-slot scheme. In contrast, we analyze the security of the same transformation in the context of the simulation-based adaptive security framework. We observe that in order to prove the adaptive security for the compiler, the (bilateral) k-Lin/(bilateral) MDDH assumption is needed whereas for semi-adaptive security, the plain k-Lin/MDDH was sufficient [3]. Moreover, we are only able to establish the simulation-based adaptive security for the transformation for settings where only a bounded number of secret-key queries are allowed prior to making the ciphertext queries.

The majority of our technical ideas in this paper lies in the design and analysis of our one-slot scheme which we describe first in this technical overview. Next, we would briefly explain the modifications to our one-slot scheme leading to our extended one-slot scheme, followed by explaining our analysis of the one-slot to unbounded-slot bootstrapping compiler from [3] applied on our one-slot extended FE scheme.

Recall that the adaptive simulation security of an FE scheme is proven by showing the indistinguishability between a real game with all the real algorithms and an ideal game where a simulator simulates all the ciphertexts and secret keys queried by the adversary. When an adversary makes a pre-ciphertext query for some function f, the simulator provides the secret key to the adversary. When the adversary makes a challenge ciphertext query for an attribute vector pair $(\boldsymbol{x}, \boldsymbol{z})$, the simulator receives the information of $\boldsymbol{x}$ but not $\boldsymbol{z}$. Instead it receives the functional values $f(\boldsymbol{x})^\top \boldsymbol{z}$ for all the pre-ciphertext secret keys. Based on this information, the simulator must simulate the challenge ciphertext. Finally, when an adversary makes a secret-key query for some function f after making a ciphertext query, the simulator receives f along with the functional value $f(\boldsymbol{x})^\top \boldsymbol{z}$ for that key and simulates the key based on this information.

2.1 Designing Adaptively Simulation Secure One-Slot FE Scheme

Abdalla et al. [3] built their one-slot FE scheme for attribute-weighted sums by extending the techniques devised by Wee [29] in the context of partially hiding predicate encryptions for predicates expressed as ABPs over public attributes followed by inner product evaluations over private attributes. The proof strategy of [3,29] is designed to achieve selective type security where during the security reduction, the challenge ciphertext is made completely random and then the secret keys are simulated using the functional value and the randomness used in the challenge ciphertext. In particular, its simulated secret key is divided into two parts—the first part is computed similar to the original key generation algorithm and is used for decrypting the honestly computed ciphertext whereas the second part contains the functional value and is used for decrypting the simulated ciphertext correctly. However, in the adaptive setting, we must embed the correct functional values for the functions associated with the pre-ciphertext secret keys into the challenge ciphertext and therefore the proof technique of [3,29] does not seem to extend to the adaptive setting. Datta et al. [11] designed an adaptively simulation secure predicate encryption scheme for the same class of predicates as [29], but their ciphertexts do not preserve compactness as they had to impose a read-once restriction on the attributes due to the usual information theoretic argument required in dual system encryption.

Overcoming the one-use restriction of the dual system proof techniques for adaptive security, Lin and Luo [19] developed new techniques to obtain adaptive indistinguishability secure ABE with compact ciphertexts for the class of predicates expressed as ABPs. [19] takes a semi-generic approach to design their ABE schemes. Their main idea is to replace the core information theoretic step of the dual system methodology with a computational step and thereby avoid the one-use restriction. Two main ingredients of [19] are arithmetic key garbling scheme (AKGS) which is the information theoretic component and function-hiding *slotted* inner product functional encryption (IPFE) which is the computational component. We try to adopt the techniques of [19] into our setting of simulation-based security for FE without the one-use restriction. However, a straight-forward adaptation of the [19] framework into our setting presents several challenges which we overcome with new ideas. Before describing those challenges and our ideas, we first give a high-level overview of the two primitives, namely, AKGS and function-hiding slotted IPFE.

Arithmetic Key Garbling Schemes: The notion of partial garbling scheme was proposed in [14] and recently it was further refined by [19] in the context of arithmetic computations. The refined notion is called arithmetic key garbling scheme (AKGS) which garbles a function $f : \mathbb{Z}_p^n \to \mathbb{Z}_p^{n'}$ along with two secrets $\alpha, \beta \in \mathbb{Z}_p$ so that the evaluation with an input $\boldsymbol{x} \in \mathbb{Z}_p^n$ gives the value $\alpha f(\boldsymbol{x}) + \beta$. Note that the evaluation does not reveal any information about α and β. In particular, the AKGS has the following algorithms:

- $(\boldsymbol{\ell}_1, \ldots, \boldsymbol{\ell}_{m+1}) \leftarrow \mathsf{Garble}(\alpha f(\boldsymbol{x}) + \beta; \boldsymbol{r})$: The garbling algorithm outputs $(m + 1)$ affine label functions $L_1, \ldots, L_{m+1}$, described by their coefficient vectors $\boldsymbol{\ell}_1, \ldots, \boldsymbol{\ell}_{m+1}$ over $\mathbb{Z}_p$, using the randomness $\boldsymbol{r} \in \mathbb{Z}_p^m$ where $(m + 1)$ denotes the size of the function f.

- $\gamma \leftarrow \mathsf{Eval}(f, \boldsymbol{x}, \ell_1, \ldots, \ell_{m+1})$: The linear evaluation procedure recovers $\gamma = \alpha f(\boldsymbol{x}) + \beta$ using the input $\boldsymbol{x}$ and the label function values $\ell_j = L_j(\boldsymbol{x}) = \boldsymbol{\ell}_j \cdot (1, \boldsymbol{x}) \in \mathbb{Z}_p$.

AKGS is a partial garbling process as it only hides α, β which is captured by the usual simulation security given by [14]. The simulator produces simulated labels $(\widehat{\ell}_1, \ldots, \widehat{\ell}_{m+1}) \leftarrow \mathsf{SimGarble}(f, \boldsymbol{x}, \alpha f(\boldsymbol{x}) + \beta)$ which is the same distribution as the actual label function values evaluated at input $\boldsymbol{x}$. Additionally, [19] defines *piecewise* security of AKGS that consists of two structural properties, namely *reverse sampleability* and *marginal randomness*. The partial garbling scheme for ABPs of Ishai and Wee [14] directly implies a piecewise secure AKGS for ABPs. (See Sect. 3.3 for further details.)

Function-Hiding Slotted IPFE: A private-key function-hiding inner product functional encryption (IPFE) scheme based on a bilinear group $\mathsf{G} = (\mathbb{G}_1, \mathbb{G}_2, \mathbb{G}_T, g_1, g_2, e)$ generates secret keys IPFE.SK for vectors $[\![\boldsymbol{v}]\!]_2 \in \mathbb{G}_2^n$ and produces ciphertexts IPFE.CT for vectors $[\![\boldsymbol{u}]\!]_1 \in \mathbb{G}_1^n$ using the master secret key of the system. Both the key generation and encryption algorithm perform linear operations in the exponent of the source groups $\mathbb{G}_2, \mathbb{G}_1$ respectively. The decryption recovers the inner product $[\![\boldsymbol{v} \cdot \boldsymbol{u}]\!]_T \in \mathbb{G}_T$ in the exponent of the target group. The sizes of the secret keys, IPFE.SK, and ciphertexts, IPFE.CT, in such a system grow linearly with the sizes of the vectors $\boldsymbol{v}$ and $\boldsymbol{u}$ respectively. Roughly, the function-hiding security of an IPFE ensures that no information about the vectors $\boldsymbol{v}, \boldsymbol{u}$ is revealed from IPFE.SK and IPFE.CT except the inner product value $\boldsymbol{v} \cdot \boldsymbol{u}$ which is trivially extracted using the decryption algorithm. A slotted version of IPFE introduced in [19,20] is a hybrid between a secret-key function-hiding IPFE and a public-key IPFE. The index set of the vectors $\boldsymbol{u}$ is divided into two subsets: public slots S_{pub} and private slot S_{priv} so that the vector $\boldsymbol{u}$ is written as $\boldsymbol{u} = (\boldsymbol{u}_{\mathsf{pub}} \parallel \boldsymbol{u}_{\mathsf{priv}})$. With addition to the usual (secret-key) encryption algorithm, the slotted IPFE has another encryption algorithm that uses the master public key of the system to encrypt the public slots of $\boldsymbol{u}$, i.e. vectors with $\boldsymbol{u}_{\mathsf{priv}} = \mathbf{0}$. The slotted IPFE preserves the function-hiding security with respect to the private slots only as anyone can encrypt arbitrary vectors into the public slots.

Challenges with Adapting the Framework of [19] **and Our Ideas**
We now briefly explain at a high level, the main challenges in adapting the [19] technique into our setting and our ideas to overcome those challenges.

1. To handle the pre-challenge secret-key queries, [19] formulates new properties of AKGS such as *reverse sampling* and *marginal randomness*. Using such structural properties of AKGS, their main motivation was to reversely sample the first garbling label using the challenge attribute so that it can be shifted into the ciphertext component and make the remaining labels uniformly random. This procedure works fine for arguing zero advantage for the adversary at the end of the hybrid sequence in case of ABE as functions in the queried secret keys do not vanish on the challenge attribute and hence the challenge ciphertext can never be decrypted using such secret keys available to the adversary such that the value $\alpha f(\boldsymbol{x}) + \beta$ becomes completely

random. But, FE permits the adversary to have secret keys that decrypts the challenge ciphertext, that is, we cannot afford to have $\boldsymbol{z}[t]f_t(\boldsymbol{x}) + \beta_t$ completely random. In order to handle this, we carefully integrate the techniques of *pre-image sampleability* [11,26] with the reverse sampling and marginal randomness properties of AKGS to handle the pre-challenge queries.

2. The security proof of [19] implements a version of the dual system encryption methodology [17,18,28] via the function-hiding slotted IPFE. Since the ABE is only payload hiding, the usual dual system encryption technique is sufficient for achieving adaptive security where only one hidden subspace is required. More precisely, the secret keys are made of two slots, out of which the first public slot contains the honestly computed components which may be used to decrypt any honestly computed ciphertext and the other hidden slot is used to embed its interaction with the challenge ciphertext. This dual system encryption technique has been used in several prior works [11,17–19,23–25,28]. Here, a single hidden slot is enough to handle the interaction between all ciphertext and secret-key queries since by the game restrictions, no secret key queried by the adversary can decrypt the challenge ciphertext and thus their interactions with the challenge ciphertext always result in random outputs. For our application, a portion of the attribute must be kept hidden from an adversary in the context of FE, who is allowed to have polynomially many secret keys that successfully decrypts the challenge ciphertext. The usual dual system encryption is not sufficient for our purpose. We need three hidden subspaces for our security reduction. The first hidden subspace of the challenge ciphertext is kept for handling the interactions with the post-ciphertext secret keys. The second hidden subspace is required to place the dummy vector (obtained from pre-image sampleability) which helps in simulating the interactions between the challenge ciphertext and the pre-ciphertext secret keys. The last hidden subspace is used as a temporary way station to switch each pre-ciphertext secret key from interacting with the original hidden attribute of the challenge ciphertext to interacting with the dummy attribute sampled using the pre-image sampleability. We extend the framework of [19] to implement a three-slot dual system encryption procedure for building our one-slot FE scheme.

Our One-Slot FE: We aim to design our decryption algorithm such that given a secret key for a weight function ABP $f : \mathbb{Z}_p^n \to \mathbb{Z}_p^{n'}$ with coordinate functions $f_1, \ldots, f_{n'} : \mathbb{Z}_p^n \to \mathbb{Z}_p$ and an encryption of an attribute vector pair $(\boldsymbol{x}, \boldsymbol{z}) \in \mathbb{Z}_p^n \times \mathbb{Z}_p^{n'}$, the decryption algorithm would first recover the value for each coordinate $\boldsymbol{z}[t]f_t(\boldsymbol{x})$ masked with a random scalar β_t, that is, $\boldsymbol{z}[t]f_t(\boldsymbol{x}) + \beta_t$ and then sum over all these values to obtain the desired functional value (we take the scalars $\{\beta_t\}_{t\in[n']}$ such that $\sum_{t=[n']} \beta_t = 0 \mod p$). Thus we want our key generation algorithm to use AKGS to garble the functions $\boldsymbol{z}[t]f_t(\boldsymbol{x}) + \beta_t$. Note that here, β_t is a constant but $\boldsymbol{z}[t]$ is a variable. While doing this garbling, we also want the label functions to involve either only the variables $\boldsymbol{x}$ or the variable $\boldsymbol{z}[t]$. This is because, in the construction we need to handle $\boldsymbol{x}$ and $\boldsymbol{z}[t]$ separately since $\boldsymbol{x}$ is public whereas $\boldsymbol{z}[t]$ is private. This is unlike [19] which garbles $\alpha f(\boldsymbol{x}) + \beta$ where both α, β are known constants and only $\boldsymbol{x}$ is a variable. To solve this issue, we garble an extended ABP where we extend the original ABP f_t by adding a new sink node and connecting the original sink node of f_t to this new sink node with a directed edge labeled with the variable $\boldsymbol{z}[t]$.

We also make use of a particular instantiation of AKGS given by [14] where we observe that the first m coefficient vectors $\boldsymbol{\ell}_{1,t},\ldots,\boldsymbol{\ell}_{m,t}$ are independent of $\boldsymbol{z}[t]$ and the last coefficient vector $\boldsymbol{\ell}_{m+1,t}$ involves only the variable $\boldsymbol{z}[t]$. In the setup phase, two pairs of IPFE keys (IPFE.MSK, IPFE.MPK) and ($\widehat{\mathsf{IPFE.MSK}}$, $\widehat{\mathsf{IPFE.MPK}}$) for a slotted IPFE are generated for appropriate public and private index sets. The first instance of IPFE is used to handle the public attributes $\boldsymbol{x}$, whereas the second instance for the private attributes $\boldsymbol{z}$. Let $f = (f_1,\ldots,f_{n'}) : \mathbb{Z}_p^n \to \mathbb{Z}_p^{n'}$ be a given weight function ABP such that $f_t : \mathbb{Z}_p^n \to \mathbb{Z}_p$ is the t-th coordinate ABP of f. To produce a secret-key SK_f, we proceed as follows:

- Sample vectors $\boldsymbol{\alpha},\boldsymbol{\beta}_t \leftarrow \mathbb{Z}_p^k$ such that $\sum_{t\in[n']}\boldsymbol{\beta}_t[\iota] = 0 \mod p\ \forall\iota\in[k]$
- Suppose we want to base the security of the proposed scheme under the MDDH_k assumption. Generate k instances of the garblings $(\boldsymbol{\ell}_{1,t}^{(\iota)},\ldots,\boldsymbol{\ell}_{m+1,t}^{(\iota)}) \leftarrow \mathsf{Garble}(\boldsymbol{\alpha}[\iota]\boldsymbol{z}[t]f_t(\boldsymbol{x}) + \boldsymbol{\beta}_t[\iota];\boldsymbol{r}_t^{(\iota)})$ for $\iota\in[k]$ where $\boldsymbol{r}_t^{(\iota)} \leftarrow \mathbb{Z}_p^m$. Using the instantiation of AKGS given by [14], we have that the $(m+1)$-th label functions $L_{m+1,t}^{(\iota)}$ take the form $L_{m+1,t}^{(\iota)}(\boldsymbol{z}[t]) = \boldsymbol{\alpha}[\iota]\boldsymbol{z}[t] - r_t^{(\iota)}[m]$ with $\boldsymbol{\alpha}[\iota]$ a constant.
- Compute the IPFE secret keys

$$\mathsf{IPFE.SK} = \mathsf{IPFE.KeyGen}(\mathsf{IPFE.MSK}, [\![\boldsymbol{\alpha},\mathbf{0}_{kn} \parallel 0,\mathbf{0}_n,\mathbf{0}_{n'},\mathbf{0}_{n'}]\!]_2)$$
$$\mathsf{IPFE.SK}_{j,t} = \mathsf{IPFE.KeyGen}(\mathsf{IPFE.MSK}, [\![\boldsymbol{\ell}_{j,t}^{(1)},\ldots,\boldsymbol{\ell}_{j,t}^{(k)} \parallel 0,\mathbf{0}_n,\mathbf{0}_{n'},\mathbf{0}_{n'}]\!]_2) \text{ for } j\in[m]$$
$$\widehat{\mathsf{IPFE.SK}}_{m+1,t} = \mathsf{IPFE.KeyGen}(\widehat{\mathsf{IPFE.MSK}}, [\![\boldsymbol{r}_t^{(1)}[m],\ldots,\boldsymbol{r}_t^{(k)}[m],\boldsymbol{\alpha} \parallel 0,0,0,0,0,0,0]\!]_2)$$

- Return $\mathsf{SK}_f = (\mathsf{IPFE.SK}, \{\mathsf{IPFE.SK}_{j,t}\}_{j\in[m],t\in[n']}, \{\widehat{\mathsf{IPFE.SK}}_{m+1,t}\}_{t\in[n']})$

Here, we separate public and private slots by " $\parallel$ " and $\mathbf{0}$ denotes a vector of all zero elements. Now, to produce a ciphertext CT for some attribute vectors $(\boldsymbol{x},\boldsymbol{z})$, we use the following steps:

- Sample $\boldsymbol{s} \leftarrow \mathbb{Z}_p^k$ and use the slotted encryption of IPFE to compute the ciphertexts

$$\mathsf{IPFE.CT} = \mathsf{IPFE.SlotEnc}(\mathsf{IPFE.MSK}, [\![\boldsymbol{s},\boldsymbol{s}\otimes\boldsymbol{x}]\!]_1)$$
$$\widehat{\mathsf{IPFE.CT}}_t = \mathsf{IPFE.SlotEnc}(\widehat{\mathsf{IPFE.MSK}}, [\![-\boldsymbol{s},\boldsymbol{s}\cdot\boldsymbol{z}[t]]\!]_1) \text{ for all } t\in[n']$$

where $\otimes$ denotes the tensor product.
- return $\mathsf{CT} = (\mathsf{IPFE.CT}, \{\widehat{\mathsf{IPFE.CT}}_t\}_{t\in[n']})$

Decryption first uses IPFE.Dec to compute

$$\boldsymbol{v}\cdot\boldsymbol{u} = [\![\boldsymbol{\alpha}\cdot\boldsymbol{s}]\!]_T \tag{1}$$
$$\boldsymbol{v}_{j,t}\cdot\boldsymbol{u} = [\![\sum_{\iota}\boldsymbol{s}[\iota](\boldsymbol{\ell}_{j,t}^{(\iota)}\cdot(1,\boldsymbol{x}))]\!]_T = [\![\boldsymbol{\ell}_{j,t}]\!]_T \quad \text{for } j\in[m],t\in[n'] \tag{2}$$
$$\boldsymbol{v}_{m+1,t}\cdot\boldsymbol{h}_t = [\![\sum_{\iota}\boldsymbol{s}[\iota](\boldsymbol{\alpha}[\iota]\boldsymbol{z}[t] - \boldsymbol{r}_t^{(\iota)}[m])]\!]_T = [\![\boldsymbol{\ell}_{m+1,t}]\!]_T \quad \text{for } t\in[n'] \tag{3}$$

and then apply the evaluation procedure of AKGS to get

$$\mathsf{Eval}(f_t,\boldsymbol{x},[\![\boldsymbol{\ell}_{1,t}]\!]_T,\ldots,[\![\boldsymbol{\ell}_{m+1,t}]\!]_T) = [\![(\boldsymbol{\alpha}\cdot\boldsymbol{s})\cdot\boldsymbol{z}[t]f_t(\boldsymbol{x}) + \boldsymbol{\beta}_t\cdot\boldsymbol{s}]\!]_T. \tag{4}$$

Finally, multiplying all these evaluated values and utilizing the fact $\sum_{t\in[n']} \boldsymbol{\beta}_t \cdot \boldsymbol{s} = 0$, we recover $f(\boldsymbol{x})^\top \boldsymbol{z} = \sum_{t\in[n']} \boldsymbol{z}[t] f_t(\boldsymbol{x})$.

The Simulator for Our One-Slot FE Scheme: We now describe our simulator of the adaptive game for our one-slot FE scheme. Note that the private slots on the right side of " $\|$ " will be used by the simulator and we program them during the security analysis. For the q-th secret-key query corresponding to a function $f_q = (f_{q,1}, \ldots, f_{q,n'})$, the simulator sets public slots of all the vectors $\boldsymbol{v}_q, \boldsymbol{v}_{q,j,t}$ for $j \in \{1, \ldots, m_q + 1\}$ as in the original key generation algorithm. Instead of using the linear combination of the label vectors, the simulator uses freshly sampled garblings to set the private slots. The *pre-challenge* secret key SK_{f_q} takes the form

$$\mathsf{IPFE.SK}_q = \mathsf{IPFE.KeyGen}(\mathsf{IPFE.MSK}, [\![\boldsymbol{\alpha}[\iota], \mathbf{0}_{kn} \parallel \widetilde{\alpha}_q, \mathbf{0}_n, \mathbf{0}_{n'}, \mathbf{0}_{n'}]\!]_2)$$
$$\mathsf{IPFE.SK}_{q,j,t} = \mathsf{IPFE.KeyGen}(\mathsf{IPFE.MSK}, [\![\boldsymbol{\ell}^{(1)}_{q,j,t}, \ldots, \boldsymbol{\ell}^{(k)}_{q,j,t} \parallel \widetilde{\boldsymbol{\ell}}_{q,j,t}, \mathbf{0}_{n'}, \mathbf{0}_{n'}]\!]_2) \quad \text{for } j \in [m_q]$$
$$\widehat{\mathsf{IPFE.SK}}_{q,m_q+1,t} = \mathsf{IPFE.KeyGen}(\widehat{\mathsf{IPFE.MSK}}, [\![\boldsymbol{r}^{(1)}_t[m_q], \ldots, \boldsymbol{r}^{(k)}_t[m_q], \boldsymbol{\alpha} \parallel 0, 0, \widetilde{\boldsymbol{r}}_{q,t}[m_q], \widetilde{\alpha}_q, 0, 0, 0]\!]_2)$$

where $(\widetilde{\boldsymbol{\ell}}_{q,1,t}, \ldots, \widetilde{\boldsymbol{\ell}}_{q,m_q,t}) \leftarrow \mathsf{Garble}(\widetilde{\alpha}_q \boldsymbol{z}[t] f_{q,t}(\boldsymbol{x}) + \widetilde{\beta}_{q,t}; \widetilde{\boldsymbol{r}}_{q,t}), \widetilde{\alpha}_q, \widetilde{\beta}_{q,t} \leftarrow \mathbb{Z}_p$ such that $\sum_{t\in[n']} \widetilde{\beta}_{q,t} = 0 \mod p$. We write $\mathbf{0}_\xi$ as a vector of length ξ with all zero elements. To simulate the *ciphertext* for the challenge attribute $\boldsymbol{x}^*$, the simulator uses the set of all functional values $\mathcal{V} = \{(f_q, f_q(\boldsymbol{x}^*)^\top \boldsymbol{z}^*) : q \in [Q_{\mathsf{pre}}]\}$ to compute a dummy vector $\boldsymbol{d}$ satisfying $f_q(\boldsymbol{x}^*)^\top \boldsymbol{d} = f_q(\boldsymbol{x}^*)^\top \boldsymbol{z}^*$ for all $q \in [Q_{\mathsf{pre}}]$. Since the inner product functionality is *pre-image sampleable* and both $f_q, \boldsymbol{x}^*$ are known to the simulator, a dummy vector $\boldsymbol{d}$ can be efficiently computed via a polynomial time algorithm given by O'Niell [26]. The simulated ciphertext becomes

$$\mathsf{IPFE.CT} = \mathsf{IPFE.Enc}(\mathsf{IPFE.MSK}, [\![\mathbf{0}_k, \mathbf{0}_{kn} \parallel 1, \boldsymbol{x}^*, \mathbf{0}_{n'}, \mathbf{0}_{n'}]\!]_1)$$
$$\widehat{\mathsf{IPFE.CT}}_t = \mathsf{IPFE.Enc}(\widehat{\mathsf{IPFE.MSK}}, [\![\mathbf{0}_k, \mathbf{0}_k \parallel 1, 0, -1, \boldsymbol{d}[t], 0, 0, 0]\!]_1)$$

The *post-challenge* secret-key query for the q-th function $f_q = (f_{q,1}, \ldots, f_{q,n'})$ with $q > Q_{\mathsf{pre}}$ is answered using the simulator of AKGS. In particular, we choose $\beta_{q,t} \leftarrow \mathbb{Z}_p$ satisfying $\sum_{t\in[n']} \beta_{q,t} = 0 \mod p$ and compute the simulated labels as follows:

$$(\widehat{\ell}_{q,1,1}, \ldots, \widehat{\ell}_{q,m_q+1,1}) \leftarrow \mathsf{SimGarble}(f_{q,1}, \boldsymbol{x}^*, \widetilde{\alpha}_q \cdot f_q(\boldsymbol{x}^*)^\top \boldsymbol{z}^* + \beta_{q,1}) \tag{5}$$
$$(\widehat{\ell}_{q,1,t}, \ldots, \widehat{\ell}_{q,m_q+1,t}) \leftarrow \mathsf{SimGarble}(f_{q,t}, \boldsymbol{x}^*, \beta_{q,t}) \quad \text{for } 1 < t \leq n' \tag{6}$$

Note that, for post-challenge secret keys the functional value $f_q(\boldsymbol{x}^*)^\top \boldsymbol{z}^*$ is known and hence the simulator can directly embed the value into the secret keys. The post-challenge secret key SK_{f_q} takes the form

$$\mathsf{IPFE.SK}_q = \mathsf{IPFE.KeyGen}(\mathsf{IPFE.MSK}, [\![\boldsymbol{\alpha}, \mathbf{0}_{kn} \parallel \widetilde{\alpha}_q, \mathbf{0}_n, \mathbf{0}_{n'}, \mathbf{0}_{n'}]\!]_2)$$
$$\mathsf{IPFE.SK}_{q,j,t} = \mathsf{IPFE.KeyGen}(\mathsf{IPFE.MSK}, [\![\boldsymbol{\ell}^{(1)}_{j,t}, \ldots, \boldsymbol{\ell}^{(k)}_{j,t} \parallel \ell_{q,j,t}, \mathbf{0}_n, \mathbf{0}_{n'}, \mathbf{0}_{n'}]\!]_2) \quad \text{for } j \in [m_q]$$
$$\widehat{\mathsf{IPFE.SK}}_{q,m_q+1,t} = \mathsf{IPFE.KeyGen}(\widehat{\mathsf{IPFE.MSK}}, [\![\boldsymbol{r}^{(1)}_t[m_q], \ldots, \boldsymbol{r}^{(k)}_t[m_q], \boldsymbol{\alpha} \parallel \ell_{q,m_q+1,t}, 0, 0, 0, 0, 0, 0]\!]_2)$$

Security Analysis of Our One-Slot FE Scheme: To show the adaptive simulation-based security of our FE scheme, we follow a sequence of hybrid experiments to move from the real game to the ideal game with the simulated algorithms described above. The security analysis has three steps where in the first step we apply function-hiding IPFE and MDDH assumption to use freshly sampled garblings instead of linearly combined coefficient vectors. In the second step, the dummy vector $\boldsymbol{d}$ is utilized in the challenge ciphertext to handle pre-challenge secret-key queries. Here, we need to extend the framework of [19] to implement a three slot encryption technique using function-hiding IPFE. Finally, in the third step, we use the simulator of AKGS for simulating the post-challenge secret-key queries.

Step 1

Hybrid H_0: This is the real adaptive simulation security game with all the real algorithms described above.

Hybrid H_1: Indistinguishable from H_0 by the slot-mode correctness of the IPFE where we replace the SlotEnc algorithm with the Enc algorithm of slotted IPFE.

$$\boldsymbol{u} = (\boldsymbol{s}, \boldsymbol{s} \otimes \boldsymbol{x}^* \parallel \boxed{0}, \boxed{\mathbf{0}_n}, \boxed{\mathbf{0}_{n'}}, \boxed{\mathbf{0}_{n'}}),$$

$$\boldsymbol{h}_t = (-\boldsymbol{s}, \boldsymbol{s} \cdot \boldsymbol{z}^*[t] \parallel \boxed{0}, \boxed{0}, \boxed{0}, \boxed{0}, \boxed{0}, \boxed{0}, \boxed{0}).$$

Hybrid H_2: Indistinguishable from H_1 by function-hiding IPFE

$$\begin{aligned}
\boldsymbol{v}_q &= (\ \boldsymbol{\alpha}, \quad \mathbf{0}_{kn} \parallel \boxed{\overline{\alpha}_q}, \mathbf{0}_n, \mathbf{0}_{n'}, \mathbf{0}_{n'}\ ) \\
\boldsymbol{v}_{q,j,t} &= (\ \boldsymbol{\ell}^{(1)}_{q,j,t}, \ldots, \boldsymbol{\ell}^{(k)}_{q,j,t} \parallel \boxed{\overline{\ell}_{q,j,t}}, \mathbf{0}_{n'}, \mathbf{0}_{n'}\ ) \quad \text{for } j \in [m_q] \\
\boldsymbol{u} &= (\ \boxed{\mathbf{0}_k}, \boxed{\mathbf{0}_{kn}} \parallel \boxed{1}, \boxed{\boldsymbol{x}^*}, \mathbf{0}_{n'}, \mathbf{0}_{n'}\ ) \\
\boldsymbol{v}_{q,m_q+1,t} &= (\ \boldsymbol{r}^{(1)}_t[m_q], \ldots, \boldsymbol{r}^{(k)}_t[m_q], \ \boldsymbol{\alpha} \parallel \boxed{\overline{\boldsymbol{r}}_{q,t}[m_q]}, \boxed{\overline{\alpha}_q}, 0, 0, 0, 0, 0\ ) \\
\boldsymbol{h}_t &= (\ \boxed{\mathbf{0}_k}, \boxed{\mathbf{0}_k} \parallel \boxed{-1}, \boxed{\boldsymbol{z}^*[t]}, 0, 0, 0, 0, 0\ )
\end{aligned}$$

where $\overline{\alpha}_q = \boldsymbol{\alpha}_q \cdot \boldsymbol{s}, \overline{\boldsymbol{\ell}}_{q,j,t} = \sum_\iota \boldsymbol{s}[\iota]\boldsymbol{\ell}^{(\iota)}_{q,j,t}$ and $\overline{\boldsymbol{r}}_{q,t}[m_q] = \sum_\iota \boldsymbol{s}[\iota]\boldsymbol{r}^{(\iota)}_{q,t}[m_q]$. Since the inner product values between the vectors remain the same, the indistinguishability follows from the function-hiding property of IPFE.

Hybrid H_3: Indistinguishable from H_2 by MDDH assumption

$$\begin{aligned}
\boldsymbol{v}_q &= (\ \boldsymbol{\alpha}, \quad \mathbf{0}_{kn} \parallel \boxed{\widetilde{\alpha}_q}, \mathbf{0}_n, \mathbf{0}_{n'}, \mathbf{0}_{n'}\ ) \\
\boldsymbol{v}_{q,j,t} &= (\ \boldsymbol{\ell}^{(1)}_{j,t}, \ldots, \boldsymbol{\ell}^{(k)}_{j,t} \parallel \boxed{\widetilde{\boldsymbol{\ell}}_{q,j,t}} \ \mathbf{0}_{n'}, \mathbf{0}_{n'}\ ) \quad \text{for } j \in [m_q] \\
\boldsymbol{v}_{q,m_q+1,t} &= (\boldsymbol{r}^{(1)}_t[m_q], \ldots, \boldsymbol{r}^{(k)}_t[m_q], \boldsymbol{\alpha} \parallel \boxed{\widetilde{\boldsymbol{r}}_{q,t}[m_q]}, \boxed{\widetilde{\alpha}_q}, 0, 0, 0, 0, 0)
\end{aligned}$$

where $\widetilde{\alpha}_q, \widetilde{\beta}_{q,t} \leftarrow \mathbb{Z}_p$ satisfying $\sum_{t \in [n']} \widetilde{\beta}_{q,t} = 0 \bmod p$ and $(\widetilde{\boldsymbol{\ell}}_{q,1,t}, \ldots, \widetilde{\boldsymbol{\ell}}_{q,m_q+1,t}) \leftarrow \mathsf{Garble}(\widetilde{\alpha}_q \boldsymbol{z}[t] f_{q,t}(\boldsymbol{x}) + \widetilde{\beta}_{q,t}; \widetilde{\boldsymbol{r}}_{q,t})$. The indistinguishability follows from the MDDH assumption in the source group $\mathbb{G}_2$. This completes the first step of the security analysis. In the next step, we use the dummy vector $\boldsymbol{d}$ obtained via the pre-image sampling algorithm [26] and execute our *three slot* dual system encryption variant devised by extending the framework of [19].

Step 2

Hybrid H_4: Indistinguishable from H_3 by function-hiding security of IPFE

$$\begin{aligned} \boldsymbol{v}_{q,m_q+1,t} &= (\cdots \parallel \widetilde{\boldsymbol{r}}_{q,t}[m_q],\ \widetilde{\alpha}_q,\ 0,\ 0,\ 0,\ 0,\ 0\ ) \\ \boldsymbol{h}_t &= (\cdots \parallel -1,\ \boldsymbol{z}^*[t],\ \boxed{-1},\ \boxed{\boldsymbol{d}[t]},\ \boxed{-1},\ \boxed{\boldsymbol{z}^*[t]},\ 0\ ) \end{aligned}$$

Hybrid $\mathsf{H}_{5,q}(q \in [Q_{\mathsf{pre}}])$: Indistinguishable from $\mathsf{H}_{5,(q-1)}$ via a sequence of sub-hybrids $\{\mathsf{H}_{5,q,1}, \mathsf{H}_{5,q,2}, \mathsf{H}_{5,q,3}\}$. Hybrid $\mathsf{H}_{5,0}$ coincides with H_4.

$$\begin{aligned} \boldsymbol{v}_{q',m_q+1,t} &= (\cdots \parallel 0,\ 0,\ \boxed{\widetilde{\boldsymbol{r}}_{q',t}[m_q]},\ \boxed{\widetilde{\alpha}_{q'}},\ 0,\ 0,\ 0\ ) \quad \text{for } q' \leq q \\ \boldsymbol{v}_{q',m_q+1,t} &= (\cdots \parallel \widetilde{\boldsymbol{r}}_{q',t}[m_q],\ \widetilde{\alpha}_{q'},\ 0,\ 0,\ 0,\ 0,\ 0\ ) \quad \text{for } q < q' < Q_{\mathsf{pre}} \end{aligned}$$

Hybrid $\mathsf{H}_{5,q,1}(q \in [Q_{\mathsf{pre}}])$: Indistinguishable from $\mathsf{H}_{5,(q-1)}$ by function-hiding security of IPFE.

$$\begin{aligned} \boldsymbol{v}_{q',m_q+1,t} &= (\cdots \parallel 0,\ 0,\ \widetilde{\boldsymbol{r}}_{q',t}[m_q],\ \widetilde{\alpha}_{q'},\ 0,\ 0,\ 0\ ) \quad \text{for } q' < q \\ \boldsymbol{v}_{q,m_q+1,t} &= (\cdots \parallel \boxed{0},\ \boxed{0},\ 0,\ 0,\ \boxed{\widetilde{\boldsymbol{r}}_{q,t}[m_q]},\ \boxed{\widetilde{\alpha}_q},\ 0\ ) \\ \boldsymbol{v}_{q',m_q+1,t} &= (\cdots \parallel \widetilde{\boldsymbol{r}}_{q',t}[m_q],\ \widetilde{\alpha}_{q'},\ 0,\ 0,\ 0,\ 0,\ 0\ ) \quad \text{for } q < q' < Q_{\mathsf{pre}} \end{aligned}$$

Hybrid $\mathsf{H}_{5,q,2}(q \in [Q_{\mathsf{pre}}])$: Indistinguishable from $\mathsf{H}_{5,q,1}$ by piecewise security of AKGS and function-hiding security of IPFE.

$$\boldsymbol{h}_t = (\cdots \parallel -1, \boldsymbol{z}^*[t], -1, \boldsymbol{d}[t], -1, \boxed{\boldsymbol{d}[t]}, 0)$$

In order to establish the indistinguishability between $\mathsf{H}_{5,q,1}$ and $\mathsf{H}_{5,q,2}$, we actually rely on a computational problem, namely the 1-key 1-ciphertext simulation security of a secret-key FE scheme for attribute-weighted sums where the single key query is made before making the challenge ciphertext query. This scheme is presented in Sect. 4. The security of (secret-key) one FE scheme follows from the piecewise security of AKGS and the function-hiding security of IPFE. This is the core indistinguishability step that has been information theoretic in all prior applications of the extended dual system encryption methodology for adaptive attribute-hiding security [10,22]. Built on the techniques of [19], we are able to make this core indistinguishability step computational and thus remove the one-use restriction in the context of adaptive attribute-hiding security for the first time.

Hybrid $\mathsf{H}_{5,q,3}(q \in [Q_{\mathsf{pre}}])$: Indistinguishable from $\mathsf{H}_{5,q,2}$ by function-hiding security of IPFE.

$$\begin{aligned} \boldsymbol{v}_{q',m_q+1,t} &= (\cdots \parallel 0,\ 0,\ \widetilde{\boldsymbol{r}}_{q',t}[m_q],\ \widetilde{\alpha}_{q'},\ 0,\ 0,\ 0\ ) \quad \text{for } q' < q \\ \boldsymbol{v}_{q,m_q+1,t} &= (\cdots \parallel 0,\ 0,\ \boxed{\widetilde{\boldsymbol{r}}_{q,t}[m_q]},\ \boxed{\widetilde{\alpha}_q},\ \boxed{0},\ \boxed{0},\ 0,\ ) \\ \boldsymbol{v}_{q',m_q+1,t} &= (\cdots \parallel \widetilde{\boldsymbol{r}}_{q',t}[m_q],\ \widetilde{\alpha}_{q'},\ 0,\ 0,\ 0,\ 0,\ 0,\ ) \quad \text{for } q < q' < Q_{\mathsf{pre}} \\ \boldsymbol{h}_t &= (\cdots \parallel -1,\ \boldsymbol{z}^*[t],\ -1,\ \boldsymbol{d}[t],\ -1,\ \boxed{\boldsymbol{z}^*[t]},\ 0,\ ) \end{aligned}$$

Observe that $\mathsf{H}_{5,q,3}$ coincides with $\mathsf{H}_{5,q}$.
Hybrid H_6: Indistinguishable from $\mathsf{H}_{5,Q_{\mathsf{pre}}}$ by function-hiding security of IPFE

$$\boldsymbol{h}_t = (\cdots \parallel -1, \boldsymbol{z}^*[t], -1, \boldsymbol{d}[t], \boxed{0}, \boxed{0}, 0)$$

The second step of the security analysis is now over as all the pre-challenge secret keys decrypt the challenge ciphertext using dummy vector $\boldsymbol{d}$, instead of using the private attribute $\boldsymbol{z}^*$. However, we still require $\boldsymbol{z}^*$ to be present in the vector $\boldsymbol{h}_t$ for the successful decryption of the challenge ciphertext by post-challenge secret keys since we have not yet altered the forms of the post-ciphertext secret keys. The last step of the security analysis is similar to the selective game of [3] where the simulator of AKGS is employed to remove $\boldsymbol{z}^*$ from the challenge ciphertext and functional values are directly plugged into the post-challenge secret keys.
Step 3

Hybrid H_7: Indistinguishable from H_6 by function-hiding security IPFE.

$$\boldsymbol{v}_{q,j,t} = (\cdots \parallel \boxed{\widetilde{\ell}_{q,j,t}}, \boxed{\mathbf{0}_n}, \mathbf{0}_{n'}, \mathbf{0}_{n'}) \quad \text{for } j \in [m_q], q > Q_{\mathsf{pre}}$$

$$\begin{aligned} \boldsymbol{v}_{q,m_q+1,t} &= (\cdots \parallel \boxed{\widetilde{\ell}_{q,m_q+1,t}}, \boxed{0}, 0, 0, 0, 0, 0) \quad \text{for } q > Q_{\mathsf{pre}} \\ \boldsymbol{h}_t &= (\cdots \parallel \boxed{1}, \boxed{0}, -1, \boldsymbol{d}[t], 0, 0, 0) \end{aligned}$$

Hybrid H_8: Indistinguishable from H_7 by simulation security of AKGS.

$$\boldsymbol{v}_{q,j,t} = (\cdots \parallel \boxed{\widehat{\ell}_{q,j,t}}, \mathbf{0}_n, \mathbf{0}_{n'}, \mathbf{0}_{n'}) \quad \text{for } j \in [m_q], q > Q_{\mathsf{pre}}$$

$$\boldsymbol{v}_{q,m_q+1,t} = (\cdots \parallel \boxed{\widehat{\ell}_{q,m_q+1,t}}, 0, 0, 0, 0, 0, 0) \quad \text{for } q > Q_{\mathsf{pre}}$$

In hybrid H_7, we use the honestly computed value $\widetilde{\ell}_{q,j,t} = \widetilde{L}_{q,j,t}(\boldsymbol{x}^*)$ for $j \in [m_q]$ and $\widetilde{\ell}_{q,m_q+1,t} = \widetilde{\alpha}_q \boldsymbol{z}^*[t] - \widetilde{\boldsymbol{r}}_{q,t}[m_q]$. After that, in H_8, we utilize simulator of AKGS to simulate $\widetilde{\alpha}_q \cdot \boldsymbol{z}^*[t] f_{q,t}(\boldsymbol{x}^*) + \widetilde{\beta}_{q,t}$ using $\widetilde{\ell}_{q,j,t}$.
Hybrid H_9: Statistically close to H_8

$$\boldsymbol{v}_{q,j,t} = (\cdots \parallel \boxed{\widehat{\ell}_{q,j,t}}, \mathbf{0}_n, \mathbf{0}_{n'}, \mathbf{0}_{n'}) \quad \text{for } j \in [m_q], q > Q_{\mathsf{pre}}$$

$$\boldsymbol{v}_{q,m_q+1,t} = (\cdots \parallel \boxed{\widehat{\ell}_{q,m_q+1,t}}, 0, 0, 0, 0, 0, 0) \quad \text{for } q > Q_{\mathsf{pre}}$$

Finally, we change the distribution of $\{\widetilde{\beta}_{q,t}\}$ to embed the value $\widetilde{\alpha}_q \cdot f_q(\boldsymbol{x}^*)^\top \boldsymbol{z}^* + \widetilde{\beta}_{q,1}$ into $\widehat{\ell}_{q,j,1}$ and the value $\widetilde{\beta}_{q,t}$ into $\widehat{\ell}_{q,j,1}$ for $1 < t \leq n'$, as in Eqs. 5 and 6. We observe that hybrid H_9 is exactly the same as the simulator of our FE scheme.

From One-Slot FE to One-Slot extFE: We extend our one-slot FE to an extended FE (extFE) scheme which is required for applying the compiler of [3] to bootstrap to the unbounded-slot scheme. In an extFE scheme, as opposed to just taking a weight function f as input, the key generation procedure additionally takes a vector $\boldsymbol{y}$ as input. Similarly, the encryption algorithm takes an additional vector $\boldsymbol{w}$ in addition to a usual public/private vector pair $(\boldsymbol{x}, \boldsymbol{z})$ such that

$$\mathsf{SK}_{f,\boldsymbol{y}} \leftarrow \mathsf{KeyGen}(\mathsf{MSK}, (f, \boldsymbol{y})), \quad \mathsf{CT} \leftarrow \mathsf{Enc}(\mathsf{MPK}, (\boldsymbol{x}, \boldsymbol{z} \parallel \boldsymbol{w}))$$

The decryption procedure recovers $f(\boldsymbol{x})^\top \boldsymbol{z} + \boldsymbol{y}^\top \boldsymbol{w}$ instead of $f(\boldsymbol{x})^\top \boldsymbol{z}$ like a regular one-slot scheme. The main idea is to use the linearity of the Eval algorithm of AKGS. We add an extra term $\psi_t = \nu_t \cdot (\boldsymbol{\alpha} \cdot \boldsymbol{s})\boldsymbol{y}^\top \boldsymbol{w}$ to the first garbling value $\ell_{1,t}$ so that Eq. 4 becomes

$$\begin{aligned}
&\mathsf{Eval}(f_t, \boldsymbol{x}, [\![\ell_{1,t} + \psi_t]\!]_T, \ldots, [\![\ell_{m+1,t}]\!]_T) \\
&= \mathsf{Eval}(f_t, \boldsymbol{x}, [\![\ell_{1,t}]\!]_T, \ldots, [\![\ell_{m+1,t}]\!]_T) \cdot [\![\psi_t]\!]_T \\
&= [\![(\boldsymbol{\alpha} \cdot \boldsymbol{s}) \cdot (\boldsymbol{z}[t] f_t(\boldsymbol{x}) + \nu_t \boldsymbol{y}^\top \boldsymbol{w}) + \boldsymbol{\beta}_t \cdot \boldsymbol{s}]\!]_T
\end{aligned}$$

where $\nu_t \leftarrow \mathbb{Z}_p$ for $t \in [n']$ be such that $\sum_{t \in [n']} \nu_t = 1 \bmod p$. Therefore, multiplying all the evaluated terms and using the inner product $\boldsymbol{v} \cdot \boldsymbol{u} = \boldsymbol{\alpha} \cdot \boldsymbol{s}$, as in our one-slot FE scheme, we get $[\![f(\boldsymbol{x})^\top \boldsymbol{z} + \boldsymbol{y}^\top \boldsymbol{w}]\!]_T$ using the fact that $\sum_{t \in [n']} \boldsymbol{\beta}_t \cdot \boldsymbol{s} = 0$. The security analysis is similar to our one-slot scheme.

2.2 Bootstrapping from One-Slot FE to Unbounded-Slot FE

Abdalla et al. [3] devised a compiler that upgrades the one-slot FE into an unbounded-slot FE scheme where the number of slots N can be arbitrarily chosen at the time of encryption. The transformation also preserves the compactness of ciphertexts of the underlying one-slot scheme. However, their transformation actually needs a one-slot extFE scheme as defined above.

The extFE scheme of [3] is built in a bilinear group $\mathsf{G} = (\mathbb{G}_1, \mathbb{G}_2, \mathbb{G}_T, g_1, g_2, e)$ where ciphertexts are encoded in the group $\mathbb{G}_1$ and secret keys in the group $\mathbb{G}_2$. Interestingly, the structure of the extFE scheme of [3] is such that the key generation procedure can still be run if the vector $\boldsymbol{y}$ is given in the exponent of $\mathbb{G}_2$, that is, $[\![\boldsymbol{y}]\!]_2$. The decryption, given $(\mathsf{SK}_{f,\boldsymbol{y}}, (f, [\![\boldsymbol{y}]\!]_2)), (\mathsf{CT}, \boldsymbol{x})$, recovers $[\![f(\boldsymbol{x})^\top \boldsymbol{z} + \boldsymbol{y}^\top \boldsymbol{w}]\!]_T$ without leaking any additional information about the vectors $\boldsymbol{z}, \boldsymbol{w}$. Now, the unbounded-slot FE (ubdFE) scheme follows a natural masking procedure over the original one-slot scheme. More specifically, we use N extFE encryptions to obtain ciphertexts $\{\mathsf{CT}_i\}_{i \in [N]}$ where CT_i encrypts $(\boldsymbol{x}_i, \boldsymbol{z}_i \parallel \boldsymbol{w}_i)$ with $\sum_{i \in [N]} \boldsymbol{w}_i = \boldsymbol{0} \bmod p$. The decryption procedure first computes individual sum $[\![f(\boldsymbol{x}_i)^\top \boldsymbol{z}_i + \boldsymbol{y}^\top \boldsymbol{w}_i]\!]_T$ and then multiply all the sums to learn $\sum_{i \in [N]} f(\boldsymbol{x}_i)^\top \boldsymbol{z}_i$ via solving a discrete logarithm problem (using brute force). Abdalla et al. [3] proved the semi-adaptive simulation-based security of the scheme assuming MDDH assumption in the source group $\mathbb{G}_2$. The main idea was to gradually shift the sum $\sum_{i \in [2,N]} f(\boldsymbol{x}_i)^\top \boldsymbol{z}_i$ from the last $(N-1)$ ciphertexts $\{\mathsf{CT}_i\}_{i \in [2,N]}$ to the first component of the ciphertext CT_1.

We apply the same high level strategy for proving the adaptive simulation security of the transformation. However, in order to do so, we face two main obstacles. First, the reduction must incorporate the decryption results of all the pre-ciphertext secret keys into the challenge ciphertext. Therefore, for all the pre-ciphertext secret key queries $(f, \boldsymbol{y})$, the reduction needs to know $[\![\boldsymbol{y}]\!]_1$ in order to simulate the challenge ciphertext and $[\![\boldsymbol{y}]\!]_2$ to simulate the key. The reason why $\boldsymbol{y}$ cannot be made available to the reduction in the clear at a high level, is that the shifting of the sums into the first ciphertext component CT_1 from a subsequent ciphertext component, say CT_η, once both CT_1 and CT_η are in the simulated form is to be done via a computational transition based on some MDDH-like assumption. In case of [3], there was no pre-ciphertext key queries and hence the MDDH assumption in $\mathbb{G}_2$ was sufficient. However, in our case, the MDDH assumption only in the source group $\mathbb{G}_2$ is not sufficient to shift the sum $\sum_{i\in[2,N]} f(\boldsymbol{x}_i)^\top \boldsymbol{z}_i$ to the first ciphertext component without changing the adversary's view. Thus, we consider the bilateral MDDH (bMDDH) assumption [5,12,30] which allows the vector components to be available in the exponent of both the source groups $\mathbb{G}_1, \mathbb{G}_2$.

$$\{[\![\boldsymbol{y}]\!]_1, [\![\boldsymbol{y}]\!]_2, [\![\boldsymbol{y}^\top \boldsymbol{w}_i]\!]_1, [\![\boldsymbol{y}^\top \boldsymbol{w}_i]\!]_2\} \overset{c}{\approx} \{[\![\boldsymbol{y}]\!]_1, [\![\boldsymbol{y}]\!]_2, [\![\boldsymbol{u}]\!]_1, [\![\boldsymbol{u}]\!]_2\}$$

where $\boldsymbol{u}$ is uniform.

The second and more subtle obstacle arises in handling the pre-ciphertext secret key queries in the simulated game. The simulator algorithm of [3] uses the simulator of the underlying one-slot scheme to simulate the ciphertext and secret key components for the first slot while it generates all other ciphertexts and secret key components normally. Now recall that in the simulated adaptive security game, the simulator embed the outputs of all the functions $\{f_q\}_{q\in[Q_{\mathsf{pre}}]}$, for which the pre-ciphertext secret key queries are made, on the challenge message $\{(\boldsymbol{x}_i, \boldsymbol{z}_i)\}_{i\in[N]}$, that is, the values $\{\sum_{i\in[N]} f_q(\boldsymbol{x}_i)^\top \boldsymbol{z}_i\}_{q\in[Q_{\mathsf{pre}}]}$ into the challenge ciphertext. Since the simulator is only generating the ciphertext and secret key components for the first slot in simulated format, we must embed the functional values $\{\sum_{i\in[N]} f_q(\boldsymbol{x}_i)^\top \boldsymbol{z}_i\}_{q\in[Q_{\mathsf{pre}}]}$ into the ciphertext component corresponding to the first slot. As for the one-slot scheme, we aim to make use of the pre-image sampling procedure for this embedding. However, this means we need to solve the system of equations $\{f_q(\boldsymbol{x}_1)^\top \boldsymbol{d}_1 + \boldsymbol{y}_q^\top \boldsymbol{d}_2 = \sum_{i\in[N]} f_q(\boldsymbol{x}_i)^\top \boldsymbol{z}_i\}_{q\in[Q_{\mathsf{pre}}]}$ for $(\boldsymbol{d}_1, \boldsymbol{d}_2)$. Clearly, this system of equations may not possess a solution since the right-hand side contains the sum of the functional values for all the slots while the left-hand side only involves entries corresponding to the first slot. Further, even if solution exists information theoretically, finding it out in polynomial time may not be possible given the fact that the simulator does not receive the vectors $\{\boldsymbol{y}_q\}_{q\in[Q_{\mathsf{pre}}]}$ in the clear, rather in the exponent of group elements.

In order to overcome the above problem, rather than solving the above system of equations, we instead solve the system of equations $\{f_q(\boldsymbol{x}^*)^\top \boldsymbol{d}_1 + \boldsymbol{y}_q^\top \boldsymbol{d}_2 + \boldsymbol{e}_q^\top \boldsymbol{d}_3 = \sum_{i\in[N]} f_q(\boldsymbol{x}_i)^\top \boldsymbol{z}_i\}_{q\in[Q_{\mathsf{pre}}]}$ for $(\boldsymbol{d}_1, \boldsymbol{d}_2, \boldsymbol{d}_3)$, where $\boldsymbol{e}_q$ is the q-th unit vector. Note that this system of equations can be easily solved by sampling the vectors $\boldsymbol{d}_1, \boldsymbol{d}_2$ randomly and then setting the q-th entry of the vector $\boldsymbol{d}_3$ to be $\sum_{i\in[N]} f_q(\boldsymbol{x}_i)^\top \boldsymbol{z}_i - f_q(\boldsymbol{x}^*)^\top \boldsymbol{d}_1 - \boldsymbol{y}_q^\top \boldsymbol{d}_2$ for all $q \in [Q_{\mathsf{pre}}]$. However, this strategy would necessitate the introduction of Q_{pre} many additional subspaces into the ciphertext and secret key components for the underlying one-slot extFE scheme to accommodate for $\boldsymbol{d}_3$. (Those subspaces will contain 0s in the real scheme and only become active in the security proof). This, in turn, requires setting a bound on Q_{pre}, that is, the number of pre-ciphertext secret key queries, for both the underlying extFE scheme and the resulting ubdFE scheme.

Based on the bMDDH assumption and the above pre-image sampling strategy, we are able to show that the ubdFE scheme provides adaptive simulation-based security against a bounded number of pre-ciphertext secret key queries and an arbitrary polynomial number of post-ciphertext secret key queries if the underlying extFE scheme is adaptive simulation secure against such many secret key queries. Please refer to the full version of the paper for a detailed formal exposure of the modifications and our analysis of the bootstrapping transformation.

3 Preliminaries

Notations. We denote by λ the security parameter that belongs to the set of natural number $\mathbb{N}$ and 1^λ denotes its unary representation. We use the notation $s \leftarrow S$ to indicate the fact that s is sampled uniformly at random from the finite set S. For a distribution $\mathcal{X}$, we write $x \leftarrow \mathcal{X}$ to denote that x is sampled at random according to distribution $\mathcal{X}$. A function $\mathsf{negl} : \mathbb{N} \to \mathbb{R}$ is said to be a negligible function of λ, if for every $c \in \mathbb{N}$ there exists a $\lambda_c \in \mathbb{N}$ such that for all $\lambda > \lambda_c$, $|\mathsf{negl}(\lambda)| < \lambda^{-c}$.

Let Expt be an interactive security experiment played between a challenger and an adversary, which always outputs a single bit. We assume that $\mathsf{Expt}_{\mathcal{A}}^{\mathsf{C}}$ is a function of λ and it is parametrized by an adversary $\mathcal{A}$ and a cryptographic protocol C. Let $\mathsf{Expt}_{\mathcal{A}}^{\mathsf{C},0}$ and $\mathsf{Expt}_{\mathcal{A}}^{\mathsf{C},1}$ be two such experiment. The experiments are computationally/statistically indistinguishable if for any PPT/computationally unbounded adversary $\mathcal{A}$ there exists a negligible function negl such that for all $\lambda \in \mathbb{N}$,

$$\mathsf{Adv}_{\mathcal{A}}^{\mathsf{C}}(\lambda) = |\Pr[1 \leftarrow \mathsf{Expt}_{\mathcal{A}}^{\mathsf{C},0}(1^\lambda)] - \Pr[1 \leftarrow \mathsf{Expt}_{\mathcal{A}}^{\mathsf{C},1}(1^\lambda)]| < \mathsf{negl}(\lambda)$$

We write $\mathsf{Expt}_{\mathcal{A}}^{\mathsf{C},0} \overset{c}{\approx} \mathsf{Expt}_{\mathcal{A}}^{\mathsf{C},1}$ if they are *computationally indistinguishable* (or simply *indistinguishable*). Similarly, $\mathsf{Expt}_{\mathcal{A}}^{\mathsf{C},0} \overset{s}{\approx} \mathsf{Expt}_{\mathcal{A}}^{\mathsf{C},1}$ means *statistically indistinguishable* and $\mathsf{Expt}_{\mathcal{A}}^{\mathsf{C},0} \equiv \mathsf{Expt}_{\mathcal{A}}^{\mathsf{C},1}$ means they are *identically* distributed.

For $n \in \mathbb{N}$, we denote $[n]$ the set $\{1, 2, \dots, n\}$ and for $n, m \in \mathbb{N}$ with $n < m$, we denote $[n, m]$ be the set $\{n, n+1, \dots, m\}$. We use lowercase boldface, e.g., $\boldsymbol{v}$, to denote column vectors in $\mathbb{Z}_p^n$ and uppercase boldface, e.g., $\mathbf{M}$, to denote matrices in $\mathbb{Z}_p^{n\times m}$ for $p, n, m \in \mathbb{N}$. The i-th component of a vector $\boldsymbol{v} \in \mathbb{Z}_p^n$ is written as $\boldsymbol{v}[i]$ and the (i, j)-th element of a matrix $\mathbf{M} \in \mathbb{Z}_p^{n\times m}$ is denoted by $\mathbf{M}[i, j]$. The transpose of a matrix $\mathbf{M}$ is denoted by $\mathbf{M}^\top$ such that $\mathbf{M}^\top[i, j] = \mathbf{M}[j, i]$. To write a vector of length n with all zero elements, we write $\mathbf{0}_n$ or simply $\mathbf{0}$ when the length is clear from the context. Let $\boldsymbol{u}, \boldsymbol{v} \in \mathbb{Z}_p^n$, then the inner product between the vectors is denoted as $\boldsymbol{u} \cdot \boldsymbol{v} = \boldsymbol{u}^\top \boldsymbol{v} = \sum_{i \in [n]} \boldsymbol{u}[i]\boldsymbol{v}[i] \in \mathbb{Z}_p$.

Let $f : \mathbb{Z}_p^n \to \mathbb{Z}_p$ be an affine function with coefficient vector $\mathbf{f} = (\mathbf{f}[\mathsf{const}], \mathbf{f}[\mathsf{coef}_1], \ldots, \mathbf{f}[\mathsf{coef}_n])$. Then for any $\boldsymbol{x} \in \mathbb{Z}_p^n$, we have $f(\boldsymbol{x}) = \mathbf{f}[\mathsf{const}] + \sum_{i \in [n]} \mathbf{f}[\mathsf{coef}_i]\boldsymbol{x}[i] \in \mathbb{Z}_p$.

3.1 Arithmetic Branching Program

Arithmetic Branching Program (ABP) is a computational model [21] that can be used to model boolean formula, boolean branching program or arithmetic formula through a linear time reduction with a constant blow-up in their respective sizes. In this work, we consider ABP over $\mathbb{Z}_p$.

Definition 1 (Arithmetic Branching Program). An arithmetic branching program (ABP) over $\mathbb{Z}_p^n$ is a weighted directed acyclic graph (V, E, ϕ, v_0, v_1), where V is the set of all vertices, E is the set of all edges, $\phi : E \to (\mathbb{Z}_p^n \to \mathbb{Z}_p)$ specifies an affine weight function for each edge, and $v_0, v_1 \in V$ are two distinguished vertices (called the source and the sink respectively). The in-degree of v_0 and the out-degree of v_1 are 0. It computes a function $f : \mathbb{Z}_p^n \to \mathbb{Z}_p$ given by

$$f(\boldsymbol{x}) = \sum_{P \in \mathfrak{P}} \prod_{e \in P} \phi(e)(\boldsymbol{x})$$

where $\mathfrak{P}$ is the set of all v_0-v_1 path and $e \in P$ denotes an edge in the path $P \in \mathfrak{P}$. The size of the ABP is $|V|$, the number of vertices.

We denote by $\mathcal{F}_{\mathsf{ABP}}^{(n)}$ the class of ABPs over $\mathbb{Z}_p^n$:

$$\mathcal{F}_{\mathsf{ABP}}^{(n)} = \{f | f \text{ is an ABP over } \mathbb{Z}_p^n \text{ for some prime } p \text{ and positive integer } n\}$$

The class of ABP can be extended in a coordinate-wise manner to a ABPs $f : \mathbb{Z}_p^n \to \mathbb{Z}_p^{n'}$. More precisely, an ABP $f : \mathbb{Z}_p^n \to \mathbb{Z}_p^{n'}$ has all its weight functions $\phi = (\phi_1, \ldots, \phi_{n'}) : E \to (\mathbb{Z}_p^n \to \mathbb{Z}_p^{n'})$ with each coordinate function ϕ_t for $t \in [n']$ of ϕ being an affine function in $\boldsymbol{x}$ having scalar constants and coefficients. Therefore, such a function f can be viewed as $f = (f_1, \ldots, f_{n'})$ with each coordinate function $f_t : \mathbb{Z}_p^n \to \mathbb{Z}_p$ being an ABP that has the same underlying graph structure as that of f and having $\phi_t : E \to (\mathbb{Z}_p^n \to \mathbb{Z}_p)$ as the weight functions. The class of all such functions is given by

$$\mathcal{F}_{\mathsf{ABP}}^{(n,n')} = \{f = (f_1, \ldots, f_{n'}) : \mathbb{Z}_p^n \to \mathbb{Z}_p^{(n')} | f_t \in \mathcal{F}_{\mathsf{ABP}}^{(n)} \text{ for } t \in [n']\}$$

Thus $\mathcal{F}_{\mathsf{ABP}}^{(n)}$ can alternatively be viewed as $\mathcal{F}_{\mathsf{ABP}}^{(n,1)}$.

Lemma 1 [13]. *Let* $f = (V, E, \phi, v_0, v_1) \in \mathcal{F}_{\mathsf{ABP}}^{(n,1)}$ *be an* ABP *of size* m *and* $v_0, v_2, \ldots, v_{m-1}, v_1$ *be stored topologically. Let* $\mathbf{M}$ *be a square matrix of order* $(m-1)$ *defined by*

$$\mathbf{M}[i+1, j] = \begin{cases} 0, & i > j; \\ -1, & i = j; \\ 0, & i < j, e_{i,j} = (v_i, v_j) \notin E; \\ \phi(e_{i,j}), & i < j, e_{i,j} = (v_i, v_j) \in E. \end{cases}$$

Then the entries of $\mathbf{M}$ *are affine in* $\boldsymbol{x}$ *and* $f(\boldsymbol{x}) = \det(\mathbf{M})$.

3.2 Functional Encryption for Attribute-Weighted Sum

We formally present the syntax of FE for attribute-weighted sum and define adaptive simulation security of the primitive. We consider the function class $\mathcal{F}_{\mathsf{ABP}}^{(n,n')}$ and message space $\mathcal{M} = (\mathbb{Z}_p^n \times \mathbb{Z}_p^{n'})^*$.

Definition 2 (The Attribute-Weighted Sum Functionality). For any $n, n' \in \mathbb{N}$, the class of attribute-weighted sum functionalities is defined as

$$\left\{ (\boldsymbol{x} \in \mathbb{Z}_p^n, \boldsymbol{z} \in \mathbb{Z}_p^{n'}) \mapsto \boldsymbol{f}(\boldsymbol{x})^\top \boldsymbol{z} = \sum_{t \in [n']} f_t(\boldsymbol{x}) \boldsymbol{z}[t] \mid \boldsymbol{f} = (f_1, \ldots, f_{n'}) \in \mathcal{F}_{\mathsf{ABP}}^{(n,n')} \right\}$$

Definition 3 (Functional Encryption for Attribute-Weighted Sum). An unbounded-slot FE for attribute-weighted sum associated to the function class $\mathcal{F}_{\mathsf{ABP}}^{(n,n')}$ and the message space $\mathcal{M}$ consists of four PPT algorithms defined as follows:

Setup(1^λ, 1^n, $1^{n'}$): The setup algorithm takes as input a security parameter λ along with two positive integers n, n' representing the lengths of message vectors. It outputs the master secret-key MSK and the master public-key MPK.

KeyGen(MSK, $\boldsymbol{f}$): The key generation algorithm takes as input MSK and a function $\boldsymbol{f} \in \mathcal{F}_{\mathsf{ABP}}^{(n,n')}$. It outputs a secret-key $\mathsf{SK}_{\boldsymbol{f}}$ and make $\boldsymbol{f}$ available publicly.

Enc(MPK, $(\boldsymbol{x}_i, \boldsymbol{z}_i)_{i \in [N]}$): The encryption algorithm takes as input MPK and a message $(\boldsymbol{x}_i, \boldsymbol{z}_i)_{i \in [N]} \in (\mathbb{Z}_p^n \times \mathbb{Z}_p^{n'})^*$. It outputs a ciphertext CT and make $(\boldsymbol{x}_i)_{i \in [N]}$ available publicly.

Dec(($\mathsf{SK}_{\boldsymbol{f}}$, $\boldsymbol{f}$), (CT, $(\boldsymbol{x}_i)_{i \in [N]}$)): The decryption algorithm takes as input $\mathsf{SK}_{\boldsymbol{f}}$ and CT along with $\boldsymbol{f}$ and $(\boldsymbol{x}_i)_{i \in [N]}$. It outputs a value in $\mathbb{Z}_p$.

Correctness: The unbounded-slot FE for attribute-weighted sum is said to be correct if for all $(\boldsymbol{x}_i, \boldsymbol{z}_i)_{i \in [N]} \in (\mathbb{Z}_p^n \times \mathbb{Z}_p^{n'})^*$ and $\boldsymbol{f} \in \mathcal{F}_{\mathsf{ABP}}^{(n,n')}$, we get

$$\Pr\left[\mathsf{Dec}((\mathsf{SK}_{\boldsymbol{f}}, \boldsymbol{f}), (\mathsf{CT}, (\boldsymbol{x}_i)_{i \in [N]})) = \sum_{i \in [N]} \boldsymbol{f}(\boldsymbol{x}_i)^\top \boldsymbol{z}_i : \begin{array}{l} (\mathsf{MSK}, \mathsf{MPK}) \leftarrow \mathsf{Setup}(1^\lambda, 1^n, 1^{n'}), \\ \mathsf{SK}_{\boldsymbol{f}} \leftarrow \mathsf{KeyGen}(\mathsf{MSK}, \boldsymbol{f}), \\ \mathsf{CT} \leftarrow \mathsf{Enc}(\mathsf{MPK}, (\boldsymbol{x}_i, \boldsymbol{z}_i)_{i \in [N]}) \end{array} \right] = 1$$

We consider adaptively simulation-based security of FE for attribute-weighted sum.

Definition 4. Let (Setup, KeyGen, Enc, Dec) be an unbounded-slot FE for attribute-weighted sum for function class $\mathcal{F}_{\mathsf{ABP}}^{(n,n')}$ and message space $\mathcal{M}$. The scheme is said to be adaptively simulation secure if $\mathsf{Expt}_{\mathcal{A}}^{\mathsf{Real,ubdFE}}(1^\lambda) \overset{c}{\approx} \mathsf{Expt}_{\mathcal{A}}^{\mathsf{Ideal,ubdFE}}(1^\lambda)$, where the experiments are defined as follows:

$\underline{\mathsf{Expt}_{\mathcal{A}}^{\mathsf{Real,ubdFE}}(1^\lambda)}$

1. $1^N \leftarrow \mathcal{A}(1^\lambda)$;
2. $(\mathsf{MSK}, \mathsf{MPK}) \leftarrow \mathsf{Setup}(1^\lambda, 1^n, 1^{n'})$;
3. $((\boldsymbol{x}_i^*, \boldsymbol{z}_i^*)_{i\in[N]}) \leftarrow \mathcal{A}^{\mathcal{O}_{\mathsf{KeyGen}(\mathsf{MSK},\cdot)}}(\mathsf{MPK})$;
4. $\mathsf{CT}^* \leftarrow \mathsf{Enc}(\mathsf{MPK}, (\boldsymbol{x}_i^*, \boldsymbol{z}_i^*)_{i\in[N]})$;
5. return $\mathcal{A}^{\mathcal{O}_{\mathsf{KeyGen}(\mathsf{MSK},\cdot)}}(\mathsf{MPK}, \mathsf{CT}^*)$

$\underline{\mathsf{Expt}_{\mathcal{A}}^{\mathsf{Ideal,ubdFE}}(1^\lambda)}$

1. $1^N \leftarrow \mathcal{A}(1^\lambda)$;
2. $(\mathsf{MSK}^*, \mathsf{MPK}) \leftarrow \mathsf{Setup}^*(1^\lambda, 1^n, 1^{n'}, 1^N)$;
3. $((\boldsymbol{x}_i^*, \boldsymbol{z}_i^*)_{i\in[N]}) \leftarrow \mathcal{A}^{\mathcal{O}_{\mathsf{KeyGen}_0^*(\mathsf{MSK}^*,\cdot)}}(\mathsf{MPK})$
4. $\mathsf{CT}^* \leftarrow \mathsf{Enc}^*(\mathsf{MPK}, \mathsf{MSK}^*, (\boldsymbol{x}_i^*)_{i\in[N]}, \mathcal{V})$;
5. return $\mathcal{A}^{\mathcal{O}_{\mathsf{KeyGen}_1^*(\mathsf{MSK}^*,(\boldsymbol{x}_i^*)_{i\in[N]},\cdot,\cdot)}}(\mathsf{MPK}, \mathsf{CT}^*)$

$\underline{\mathcal{O}_{\mathsf{KeyGen}(\mathsf{MSK},\cdot)}}$

1. input: f
2. output: SK_f

$\underline{\mathcal{O}_{\mathsf{KeyGen}_0^*(\mathsf{MSK}^*,\cdot)}}$

1. input: f_q for $q \in [Q_{\mathsf{pre}}]$
2. output: $\mathsf{SK}_{f_q}^*$

$\underline{\mathsf{Enc}^*(\mathsf{MPK}, \mathsf{MSK}^*, (\boldsymbol{x}_i^*)_{i\in[N]}, \cdot)}$

1. input: $\mathcal{V} = \{((f_q, \mathsf{SK}_{f_q}), \sum_{i\in[N]} f_q(\boldsymbol{x}_i^*)^\top \boldsymbol{z}_i^*) : q \in [Q_{\mathsf{pre}}]\}$
2. output: CT^*

$\underline{\mathcal{O}_{\mathsf{KeyGen}_1^*(\mathsf{MSK}^*,(\boldsymbol{x}_i^*)_{i\in[N]},\cdot,\cdot)}}$

1. input: $f_q, \sum_{i\in[N]} f_q(\boldsymbol{x}_i^*)^\top \boldsymbol{z}_i^*$ for $q > Q_{\mathsf{pre}}$
2. output: $\mathsf{SK}_{f_q}^*$

3.3 Arithmetic Key Garbling Scheme

Lin and Luo [19] introduced arithmetic key garbling scheme (AKGS). The notion of AKGS is an information theoretic primitive, inspired by randomized encodings [8] and partial garbling schemes [14]. It garbles a function $f : \mathbb{Z}_p^n \rightarrow \mathbb{Z}_p$ (possibly of size $(m+1)$) along with two secrets $z, \beta \in \mathbb{Z}_p$ and produces affine label functions $L_1, \ldots, L_{m+1} : \mathbb{Z}_p^n \rightarrow \mathbb{Z}_p$. Given f, an input $\boldsymbol{x} \in \mathbb{Z}_p^n$ and the values $L_1(\boldsymbol{x}), \ldots, L_{m+1}(\boldsymbol{x})$, there is an efficient algorithm which computes $zf(\boldsymbol{x}) + \beta$ without revealing any information about z and β.

Definition 5 (Arithmetic Key Garbling Scheme (AKGS), [14,19]). An arithmetic garbling scheme (AKGS) for a function class $\mathcal{F} = \{f\}$, where $f : \mathbb{Z}_p^n \rightarrow \mathbb{Z}_p$, consists of two efficient algorithms:

Garble($zf(\boldsymbol{x}) + \beta$): The garbling is a randomized algorithm that takes as input a description of the function $zf(\boldsymbol{x}) + \beta$ with $f \in \mathcal{F}$ and scalars $z, \beta \in \mathbb{Z}_p$ where $z, \boldsymbol{x}$ are treated as variables. It outputs $(m+1)$ affine functions $L_1, \ldots, L_{m+1} : \mathbb{Z}_p^{n+1} \rightarrow \mathbb{Z}_p$ which are called label functions that specifies how input is encoded as labels. Pragmatically, it outputs the coefficient vectors $\boldsymbol{\ell}_1, \ldots, \boldsymbol{\ell}_{m+1}$.

Eval(f, $\boldsymbol{x}$, ℓ_1, ..., ℓ_{m+1}): The evaluation is a deterministic algorithm that takes as input a function $f \in \mathcal{F}$, an input vector $\boldsymbol{x} \in \mathbb{Z}_p^n$ and integers $\ell_1, \ldots, \ell_{m+1} \in \mathbb{Z}_p$ which are supposed to be the values of the label functions at $(\boldsymbol{x}, z)$. It outputs a value in $\mathbb{Z}_p$.

Correctness: The AKGS is said to be correct if for all $f : \mathbb{Z}_p^n \to \mathbb{Z}_p \in \mathcal{F}, z, \beta \in \mathbb{Z}_p$ and $\boldsymbol{x} \in \mathbb{Z}_p^n$, we have

$$\Pr\left[\mathsf{Eval}(f, \boldsymbol{x}, \ell_1, \ldots, \ell_{m+1}) = zf(\boldsymbol{x}) + \beta : \begin{array}{l}(\boldsymbol{\ell}_1, \ldots, \boldsymbol{\ell}_{m+1}) \leftarrow \mathsf{Garble}(zf(\boldsymbol{x}) + \beta), \\ \ell_j \leftarrow L_j(\boldsymbol{x}, z) \text{ for } j \in [m+1]\end{array}\right] = 1$$

The scheme has *deterministic shape*, meaning that m is determined solely by f, independent of z, β and the randomness in Garble. The number of label functions, $(m+1)$, is called the *garbling size* of f under this scheme.

Linearity: The AKGS is said to be *linear* if the following conditions hold:

- $\mathsf{Garble}(zf(\boldsymbol{x})+\beta)$ uses a uniformly random vector $\boldsymbol{r} \leftarrow \mathbb{Z}_p^{m'}$ as its randomness, where m' is determined solely by f, independent of z, β.
- The coefficient vectors $\boldsymbol{\ell}_1, \ldots, \boldsymbol{\ell}_{m+1}$ produced by $\mathsf{Garble}(zf(\boldsymbol{x}) + \beta)$ are linear in $(z, \beta, \boldsymbol{r})$.
- $\mathsf{Eval}(f, \boldsymbol{x}, \ell_1, \ldots, \ell_{m+1})$ is linear in $\ell_1, \ldots, \ell_{m+1}$.

Simulation-Based Security: In this work, we consider linear AKGS for our application. Now, we state the usual simulation-based security of AKGS, which is similar to the security of partial garbling scheme [14].

An AKGS = (Garble, Eval) for a function class $\mathcal{F}$ is secure if there exists an efficient algorithm SimGarble such that for all $f : \mathbb{Z}_p^n \to \mathbb{Z}_p, z, \beta \in \mathbb{Z}_p$ and $\boldsymbol{x} \in \mathbb{Z}_p^n$, the following distributions are identically distributed:

$$\left\{(\boldsymbol{\ell}_1, \ldots, \boldsymbol{\ell}_{m+1}) : \begin{array}{l}(\boldsymbol{\ell}_1, \ldots, \boldsymbol{\ell}_{m+1}) \leftarrow \mathsf{Garble}(zf(\boldsymbol{x}) + \beta), \\ \ell_j \leftarrow L_j(\boldsymbol{x}, z) \text{ for } j \in [m+1]\end{array}\right\},$$

$$\left\{(\widehat{\ell}_1, \ldots, \widehat{\ell}_{m+1}) : (\widehat{\ell}_1, \ldots, \widehat{\ell}_{m+1}) \leftarrow \mathsf{SimGarble}(f, \boldsymbol{x}, zf(\boldsymbol{x}) + \beta)\right\}$$

The simulation security of AKGS is used to obtain semi-adaptive or selective security of FE for attribute-weighted sum [3], however it is not sufficient for achieving adaptive security. We consider the *piecewise* security of AKGS proposed by Lin and Luo [19] where they used it to get adaptive security for ABE.

Instantiation of AKGS [14,19]**:** We now discuss an instantiation of AKGS = (Garble, Eval) for the function class $\mathcal{F} = \mathcal{F}_{\mathsf{ABP}}^{(n,1)}$ following [14,19].

$\mathsf{Garble}(zf(\boldsymbol{x}) + \beta)$: It takes input an ABP $f : \mathbb{Z}_p^n \to \mathbb{Z}_p \in \mathcal{F}_{\mathsf{ABP}}^{(n,1)}$ of size $(m+1)$ and two secrets $z, \beta \in \mathbb{Z}_p$. The algorithm works as follows:

1. Using Lemma 1, it computes a matrix $\mathbf{M} \in \mathbb{Z}_p^{m\times m}$ such that $\det(\mathbf{M})$ is the output of the function f.
2. Next, it augments $\mathbf{M}$ into an $(m+1) \times (m+1)$ matrix $\mathbf{M}'$:

$$\mathbf{M}' = \left(\begin{array}{ccccc|c} * & * & \cdots & * & * & \beta \\ -1 & * & \cdots & * & * & 0 \\ & -1 & \cdots & * & * & 0 \\ & & \ddots & \vdots & \vdots & \vdots \\ 0 & & & -1 & * & 0 \\ \hline 0 & 0 & \cdots & 0 & -1 & z \end{array}\right) = \left(\begin{array}{c|c} \mathbf{M} & \boldsymbol{m}_1 \\ \hline \boldsymbol{m}_2^\top & z \end{array}\right)$$

3. It samples its randomness $\boldsymbol{r} \leftarrow \mathbb{Z}_p^m$ and sets $\mathbf{N} = \begin{pmatrix} \mathbf{I}_m & \boldsymbol{r} \\ \mathbf{0} & 1 \end{pmatrix}$.
4. Finally, it defines the label functions by computing

$$\widehat{\mathbf{M}} = \mathbf{M}'\mathbf{N} = \begin{pmatrix} \mathbf{M} & \mathbf{M}\boldsymbol{r} + \boldsymbol{m}_1 \\ \boldsymbol{m}_2^\top & \boldsymbol{m}_2^\top \boldsymbol{r} + z \end{pmatrix} = \left(\begin{array}{ccccc|c} & & & & & L_1(\boldsymbol{x}) \\ & & & & & L_2(\boldsymbol{x}) \\ & & \mathbf{M} & & & \vdots \\ & & & & & L_m(\boldsymbol{x}) \\ \hline 0 & 0 & \cdots & 0 & -1 & L_{m+1}(z) \end{array}\right)$$

and outputs the coefficient vectors $\boldsymbol{\ell}_1, \ldots, \boldsymbol{\ell}_{m+1}$ of $L_1, \ldots, L_{m+1}$.

Remark 1. We note down some structural properties of Garble as follows:

- The label function L_j for every $j \in [m]$ is an *affine* function of the input $\boldsymbol{x}$ and L_{m+1} is an *affine* function of z. It follows from the fact that $\mathbf{M}'$ is affine in $\boldsymbol{x}, z$ and $\mathbf{N}$ is independent of $\boldsymbol{x}, z$. Hence, the last column of the product $\mathbf{M}'\mathbf{N}$, which is the label functions $L_1, \ldots, L_{m+1}$, are affine in $\boldsymbol{x}, z$.
- The output size of Garble is determined solely by the size of f (as an ABP), hence Garble has *deterministic shape.*
- Note that Garble is *linear* in $(z, \beta, \boldsymbol{r})$, i.e., the coefficient vectors $\boldsymbol{\ell}_1, \ldots, \boldsymbol{\ell}_{m+1}$ are linear in $(z, \beta, \boldsymbol{r})$. It follows from the fact that $\mathbf{M}, \boldsymbol{m}_2$ are independent of $(z, \beta, \boldsymbol{r})$, and $\boldsymbol{r}, \boldsymbol{m}_1, z$ are linear in $(z, \beta, \boldsymbol{r})$. Hence, $\mathbf{M}\boldsymbol{r} + \boldsymbol{m}_1$, which defines the label functions $L_1, \ldots, L_m$, and $\boldsymbol{m}_2^\top \boldsymbol{r} + z$, which is the label function L_{m+1}, are linear in $(z, \beta, \boldsymbol{r})$.
- The last label function L_{m+1} is in a *special form,* meaning that it is independent of $\boldsymbol{x}, \beta$ and $\boldsymbol{r}[j < m]$. In particular, it takes the form $L_m = \boldsymbol{m}_2^\top \boldsymbol{r} + z = z - \boldsymbol{r}[m]$. Thus, the elements of the coefficient vector $\boldsymbol{\ell}_{m+1}$ are all zero except the constant term, i.e., $\boldsymbol{\ell}_m[\mathsf{const}] = z - \boldsymbol{r}[m]$ and $\boldsymbol{\ell}_m[\mathsf{coef}_i] = 0$ for all $i \in [n]$.

$\mathsf{Eval}(f, \boldsymbol{x}, \boldsymbol{\ell}_1, \ldots, \boldsymbol{\ell}_m)$: It takes input an ABP $f : \mathbb{Z}_p^n \to \mathbb{Z}_p \in \mathcal{F}_{\mathsf{ABP}}^{(n,1)}$ of size $(m+1)$, an input $\boldsymbol{x} \in \mathbb{Z}_p^n$ and $(m+1)$ labels $\ell_1, \ldots, \ell_{m+1}$. It proceeds as follows:

1. It computes the matrix $\mathbf{M}$ using Lemma 1 after substituting $\boldsymbol{x}$.
2. Next, it augments $\mathbf{M}$ to get the matrix

$$\widehat{\mathbf{M}} = \left(\begin{array}{ccccc|c} & & & & & \ell_1 \\ & & & & & \ell_2 \\ & & \mathbf{M} & & & \vdots \\ & & & & & \ell_m \\ \hline 0 & 0 & \cdots & 0 & -1 & \ell_{m+1} \end{array}\right)$$

3. It returns $\det(\widehat{\mathbf{M}})$.

For correctness of the evaluation procedure, we see that when $\ell_j = L_j(\boldsymbol{x})$ for all $j \in [m]$ and $\ell_{m+1} = L_{m+1}(z)$, Eval computes

$$\det(\widehat{\mathbf{M}}) = \det(\mathbf{M}'\mathbf{N}) = \det(\mathbf{M}')\det(\mathbf{N}) = \det(\mathbf{M}') = z\det(\mathbf{M}) + \beta = zf(\boldsymbol{x}) + \beta.$$

The determinant of $\mathbf{M}'$ is calculated via Laplace expansion in the last column.

Remark 2. Here, we observe some structural properties of Eval which we require for our application.

- If we consider the Laplace expansion of $\det(\widehat{\mathbf{M}})$ in the last column then Eval can be written as
$$\mathsf{Eval}(f, \boldsymbol{x}, \ell_1, \ldots, \ell_{m+1}) = A_1\ell_1 + A_2\ell_2 + \cdots + A_{m+1}\ell_{m+1} \tag{7}$$
where A_j is the $(j, (m+1))$-cofactor of $\widehat{\mathbf{M}}$. This shows that Eval is *linear* in $\ell_1, \ldots, \ell_{m+1}$. Due to this linearity feature, Eval can be computed in the exponent of any bilinear group. More precisely, suppose $\mathsf{G} = (\mathbb{G}_1, \mathbb{G}_2, \mathbb{G}_T, g_1, g_2, e)$ be a bilinear group then for any $i \in \{1, 2, T\}$, we have $\mathsf{Eval}(f, \boldsymbol{x}, [\![\ell_1]\!]_i, \ldots, [\![\ell_{m+1}]\!]_i) = [\![\mathsf{Eval}(f, \boldsymbol{x}, \ell_1, \ldots, \ell_{m+1})]\!]_i$.
- Now, in particular, the coefficient of ℓ_1 is $A_1 = (-1)^{2+m}(-1)^m = 1$. Therefore, for any non-zero $\delta \in \mathbb{Z}_p$, we can write
$$\delta + \mathsf{Eval}(f, \boldsymbol{x}, \ell_1, \ldots, \ell_{m+1}) = \mathsf{Eval}(f, \boldsymbol{x}, \delta, 0, \ldots, 0) + \mathsf{Eval}(f, \boldsymbol{x}, \ell_1, \ldots, \ell_{m+1}) \tag{8}$$
$$= \mathsf{Eval}(f, \boldsymbol{x}, \ell_1 + \delta, \ell_2, \ldots, \ell_{m+1}) \tag{9}$$
where Eq. 8 holds due to Eq. 7 and $A_1 = 1$; and Eq. 9 holds by the linearity of Eval. We will utilize Eq. 9 in our extended one slot FE construction.

Now, we describe the simulator of AKGS which simulates the values of label functions by using $f, \boldsymbol{x}$ and $zf(\boldsymbol{x}) + \beta$.

SimGarble(f, $\boldsymbol{x}$, $zf(\boldsymbol{x}) + \beta$): The simulator works as follows:

1. It defines a set $H = \left\{ \begin{pmatrix} \mathbf{I}_m & \boldsymbol{r} \\ \mathbf{0} & 1 \end{pmatrix} \middle| \boldsymbol{r} \in \mathbb{Z}_p^m \right\}$ which forms a matrix subgroup.
2. Following Lemma 1, it computes the matrix $\mathbf{M}$ using $f, \boldsymbol{x}$ and sets the matrix
$$\mathbf{M}'' = \left(\begin{array}{cccc|c} & & & & zf(\boldsymbol{x}) + \beta \\ & & & & 0 \\ & & \mathbf{M} & & \vdots \\ & & & & 0 \\ \hline 0 & 0 & \cdots & 0 \;\; -1 & 0 \end{array} \right)$$
which defines a left coset $\mathbf{M}''H = \{\mathbf{M}''\mathbf{N} | \mathbf{N} \in H\}$.
3. It uniformly samples a random matrix from the coset $\mathbf{M}''H$ and returns the last column of the matrix as simulated values of the label functions.

The simulation security follows from [14]. They observed that $\mathbf{M}''$ belongs to the coset $\mathbf{M}'H$ and hence by the property of cosets $\mathbf{M}''H = \mathbf{M}'H$ which proves the security. We omit the details here and state the security of AKGS in the following lemma.

Lemma 2 ([19]). *The above construction of* AKGS = (Garble, Eval) *is secure. Moreover, it is special piecewise secure.*

4 Our 1-Key 1-Ciphertext Secure 1-Slot FE

In this section, we describe our 1-slot FE scheme for the attribute-weighted sum functionality secure against a single ciphertext and secret key queries. We describe the construction for any fixed value of the security parameter λ and suppress the appearance of λ for simplicity of notations. Let (Garble, Eval) be a special piecewise secure AKGS for a function class $\mathcal{F}_{\mathsf{ABP}}^{(n,n')}$, $\mathsf{G} = (\mathbb{G}_1, \mathbb{G}_2, \mathbb{G}_T, g_1, g_2, e)$ a tuple of pairing groups of prime order p, and (SK-IPFE.Setup.SK-IPFE.KeyGen, SK-IPFE.Enc, SK-IPFE.Dec) a secret-key function-hiding SK-IPFE based on G.

Setup(1^n, $1^{n'}$): Define the index sets as follows

$$S_{\text{1-FE}} = \{\mathsf{const}, \{\mathsf{coef}_i\}_{i\in[n]}, \{\mathsf{sim}_\tau, \mathsf{sim}_\tau^*\}_{\tau\in[n']}\}, \widehat{S}_{\text{1-FE}} = \{\widehat{\mathsf{const}}, \widehat{\mathsf{coef}}, \widehat{\mathsf{sim}}^*\}$$

It generates $\mathsf{IPFE.MSK} \leftarrow \mathsf{SK\text{-}IPFE.Setup}(S_{\text{1-FE}})$ and $\widehat{\mathsf{IPFE.MSK}} \leftarrow \mathsf{SK\text{-}IPFE.Setup}(\widehat{S}_{\text{1-FE}})$. Finally, it returns $\mathsf{MSK} = (\mathsf{IPFE.MSK}, \widehat{\mathsf{IPFE.MSK}})$.

KeyGen(**MSK**, f): Let $f \in \mathcal{F}_{\mathsf{ABP}}^{(n,n')}$ be a function such that $f = (f_1, \ldots, f_{n'}) : \mathbb{Z}_p^n \times \mathbb{Z}_p^{n'} \to \mathbb{Z}_p$ where $f_1, \ldots, f_{n'} : \mathbb{Z}_p^n \to \mathbb{Z}_p$ are ABPs of size $(m+1)$. Sample $\beta_t \leftarrow \mathbb{Z}_p$ for $t \in [n']$ such that $\sum_{t\in[n']} \beta_t = 0 \mod p$. Next, sample independent random vectors $\boldsymbol{r}_t \leftarrow \mathbb{Z}_p^m$ for garbling and compute the coefficient vectors

$$(\boldsymbol{\ell}_{1,t}, \ldots, \boldsymbol{\ell}_{m,t}, \boldsymbol{\ell}_{m+1,t}) \leftarrow \mathsf{Garble}(\boldsymbol{z}[t] f_t(\boldsymbol{x}) + \beta_t; \boldsymbol{r}_t)$$

for all $t \in [n']$. Here we make use of the instantiation of the AKGS described in Sect. 3.3. From the description of that AKGS instantiation, we note that the $(m+1)$-th label function $\boldsymbol{\ell}_{m+1,t}$ would be of the form $\boldsymbol{\ell}_{m+1,t} = \boldsymbol{z}[t] - \boldsymbol{r}_t[m]$. Also all the label functions $\boldsymbol{\ell}_{1,t}, \ldots, \boldsymbol{\ell}_{m,t}$ involve only the variables $\boldsymbol{x}$ and not the variable $\boldsymbol{z}[t]$. Next, for all $j \in [m]$ and $t \in [n']$, it defines the vectors $\boldsymbol{v}_{j,t}$ corresponding to the label functions $\boldsymbol{\ell}_{j,t}$ obtained from the partial garbling:

vector	const	coef_i	sim_τ	sim_τ^*
$\boldsymbol{v}_{j,t}$	$\boldsymbol{\ell}_{j,t}[\mathsf{const}]$	$\boldsymbol{\ell}_{j,t}[\mathsf{coef}_i]$	0	0

vector	$\widehat{\mathsf{const}}$	$\widehat{\mathsf{coef}}$	$\widehat{\mathsf{sim}}^*$
$\boldsymbol{v}_{m+1,t}$	$\boldsymbol{r}_t[m]$	1	0

It generates the secret-keys as

$$\mathsf{IPFE.SK}_{j,t} \leftarrow \mathsf{SK\text{-}IPFE.KeyGen}(\mathsf{IPFE.MSK}, [\![\boldsymbol{v}_{j,t}]\!]_2) \quad \text{for } j \in [m], t \in [n']$$
$$\widehat{\mathsf{IPFE.SK}}_{m+1,t} \leftarrow \mathsf{SK\text{-}IPFE.KeyGen}(\widehat{\mathsf{IPFE.MSK}}, [\![\boldsymbol{v}_{m+1,t}]\!]_2) \quad \text{for } t \in [n']$$

It returns the secret-key as $\mathsf{SK}_f = (\{\mathsf{IPFE.SK}_{j,t}\}_{j\in[m],t\in[n']}, \{\widehat{\mathsf{IPFE.SK}}_{m+1,t}\}_{t\in[n']})$.

Enc(**MSK**, $\boldsymbol{x} \in \mathbb{Z}_p^n$, $\boldsymbol{z} \in \mathbb{Z}_p^{n'}$): It sets the vectors

vector	const	coef_i	sim_τ	sim^*_τ
$\boldsymbol{u}$	1	$\boldsymbol{x}[i]$	0	0

vector	$\widehat{\text{const}}$	$\widehat{\text{coef}}$	$\widehat{\text{sim}^*}$
$\boldsymbol{h}_t$	−1	$\boldsymbol{z}[t]$	0

for all $t \in [n']$. It encrypts the vectors as

$$\mathsf{IPFE.CT} \leftarrow \mathsf{SK\text{-}IPFE.Enc}(\mathsf{IPFE.MSK}, [\![\boldsymbol{u}]\!]_1)$$
$$\widehat{\mathsf{IPFE.CT}}_t \leftarrow \mathsf{SK\text{-}IPFE.Enc}(\widehat{\mathsf{IPFE.MSK}}, [\![\boldsymbol{h}_t]\!]_1) \quad \text{for } t \in [n']$$

and returns the ciphertext as $\mathsf{CT} = (\mathsf{IPFE.CT}, \{\widehat{\mathsf{IPFE.CT}}_t\}_{t\in[n']})$.

Dec((SK$_f$, f), (CT, $\boldsymbol{x}$)): It parses the secret-key $\mathsf{SK}_f = (\{\mathsf{IPFE.SK}_{j,t}\}_{j\in[m],t\in[n']}, \{\widehat{\mathsf{IPFE.SK}}_{m+1,t}\}_{t\in[n']})$ and the ciphertext $\mathsf{CT} = (\mathsf{IPFE.CT}, \{\widehat{\mathsf{IPFE.CT}}_t\}_{t\in[n']})$. It uses the decryption algorithm of SK-IPFE to compute

$$[\![\ell_{j,t}]\!]_T = \mathsf{SK\text{-}IPFE.Dec}(\mathsf{IPFE.SK}_{j,t}, \mathsf{IPFE.CT}) \text{ for } j \in [m], t \in [n']$$
$$[\![\ell_{m+1,t}]\!]_T = \mathsf{SK\text{-}IPFE.Dec}(\widehat{\mathsf{IPFE.SK}}_{m+1,t}, \widehat{\mathsf{IPFE.CT}}_t) \text{ for } t \in [n']$$

Next, it utilizes the evaluation procedure of AKGS and obtain a combined value

$$[\![\rho]\!]_T = \prod\nolimits_{t\in[n']} \mathsf{Eval}(f_t, \boldsymbol{x}, [\![\ell_{1,t}]\!]_T, \ldots, [\![\ell_{m+1,t}]\!]_T).$$

Finally, it returns a value ρ by solving a discrete logarithm problem. Similar to [3], we assume that the desired attribute-weighted sum lies within a specified polynomial-sized domain so that discrete logarithm can be solved via brute force.

Correctness: By the correctness of IPFE, we have $\mathsf{SK\text{-}IPFE.Dec}(\mathsf{IPFE.SK}_{j,t}, \mathsf{IPFE.CT}) = [\![\ell_{j,t}]\!]_T = [\![L_{j,t}(\boldsymbol{x})]\!]_T$ for all $j \in [m], t \in [n']$ and $\mathsf{SK\text{-}IPFE.Dec}(\widehat{\mathsf{IPFE.SK}}_{m+1,t}, \widehat{\mathsf{IPFE.CT}}_t) = [\![\ell_{m+1,t}]\!]_T = [\![\boldsymbol{z}[t] - \boldsymbol{r}_t[m]]\!]_T$ for all $t \in [n']$. Next, using the correctness of AKGS and the linearity of the Eval function, we have

$$\mathsf{Eval}(f_t, \boldsymbol{x}, [\![\ell_{1,t}]\!]_T, \ldots, [\![\ell_{m+1,t}]\!]_T) = [\![f_t(\boldsymbol{x})\boldsymbol{z}[t] + \beta_t]\!]_T$$

Therefore, we get by multiplying

$$\begin{aligned}[\![\rho]\!]_T &= \prod_{t\in[n']} \mathsf{Eval}(f_t, \boldsymbol{x}, [\![\ell_{1,t}]\!]_T, \ldots, [\![\ell_{m+1,t}]\!]_T) \\ &= [\![\sum_{t=1}^{n'} \mathsf{Eval}(f_t, \boldsymbol{x}, \ell_{1,t}, \ldots, \ell_{m+1,t})]\!]_T = [\![\sum_{t=1}^{n'} f_t(\boldsymbol{x})\boldsymbol{z}[t] + \beta_t]\!]_T = [\![f(\boldsymbol{x})^\top \boldsymbol{z}]\!]_T\end{aligned}$$

where the last equality holds since $\sum_{t\in[n']} \beta_t = 0 \mod p$.

Theorem 2. *The 1-FE scheme for attribute-weighted sum is adaptively simulation secure against a single ciphertext and secret key queries assuming the AKGS is piecewise secure and the IPFE is function hiding.*

5 Our 1-Slot FE for Attribute-Weighted Sums

In this section, we describe our 1-slot FE scheme Π_{one} for the attribute-weighted sum functionality. We describe the construction for any fixed value of the security parameter λ and suppress the appearance of λ for simplicity of notations. Let (Garble, Eval) be a special piece-wise secure AKGS for a function class $\mathcal{F}_{\mathsf{ABP}}^{(n,n')}$, $\mathsf{G} = (\mathbb{G}_1, \mathbb{G}_2, \mathbb{G}_T, g_1, g_2, e)$ a tuple of pairing groups of prime order p such that the MDDH_k assumption holds in $\mathbb{G}_2$, and (IPFE.Setup. IPFE.KeyGen, IPFE.Enc, IPFE.Dec) a slotted IPFE based on G. We construct an FE scheme for attribute-weighted sums with the message space $\mathbb{M} = \mathbb{Z}_p^n \times \mathbb{Z}_p^{n'}$.

Setup(1^n, $1^{n'}$): Define the following index sets as follows

$$S_{\mathsf{pub}} = \left\{\{\mathsf{const}^{(\iota)}\}_{\iota\in[k]}, \{\mathsf{coef}_i^{(\iota)}\}_{\iota\in[k], i\in[n]}\right\}, \widehat{S}_{\mathsf{pub}} = \left\{\widehat{\mathsf{const}}^{(\iota)}, \widehat{\mathsf{coef}}^{(\iota)}\right\}_{\iota\in[k]}$$
$$S_{\mathsf{priv}} = \left\{\mathsf{const}, \{\mathsf{coef}_i\}_{i\in[n]}, \{\mathsf{sim}_\tau, \mathsf{sim}_\tau^*\}_{\tau\in[n']}\right\},$$
$$\widehat{S}_{\mathsf{priv}} = \{\widehat{\mathsf{const}}_1, \widehat{\mathsf{coef}}_1, \widehat{\mathsf{const}}_2, \widehat{\mathsf{coef}}_2, \widehat{\mathsf{const}}, \widehat{\mathsf{coef}}, \widehat{\mathsf{sim}}^*\}.$$

It generates $(\mathsf{IPFE.MSK}, \mathsf{IPFE.MPK}) \leftarrow \mathsf{IPFE.Setup}(S_{\mathsf{pub}}, S_{\mathsf{priv}})$ and $(\widehat{\mathsf{IPFE.MSK}}, \widehat{\mathsf{IPFE.MPK}}) \leftarrow \mathsf{IPFE.Setup}(\widehat{S}_{\mathsf{pub}}, \widehat{S}_{\mathsf{priv}})$. Finally, it returns $\mathsf{MSK} = (\mathsf{IPFE.MSK}, \widehat{\mathsf{IPFE.MSK}})$ and $\mathsf{MPK} = (\mathsf{IPFE.MPK}, \widehat{\mathsf{IPFE.MPK}})$.

KeyGen(MSK, f): Let $f = (f_1, \ldots, f_{n'}) \in \mathcal{F}_{\mathsf{ABP}}^{(n,n')}$. Sample $\boldsymbol{\alpha}, \boldsymbol{\beta}_t \leftarrow \mathbb{Z}_p^k$ for $t \in [n']$ such that

$$\sum\nolimits_{t\in[n']} \boldsymbol{\beta}_t[\iota] = 0 \mod p \text{ for all } \iota \in [k]$$

Next, sample independent random vectors $\boldsymbol{r}_t^{(\iota)} \leftarrow \mathbb{Z}_p^m$ and computes

$$(\boldsymbol{\ell}_{1,t}^{(\iota)}, \ldots, \boldsymbol{\ell}_{m,t}^{(\iota)}, \boldsymbol{\ell}_{m+1,t}^{(\iota)}) \leftarrow \mathsf{Garble}(\boldsymbol{\alpha}[\iota]\boldsymbol{z}[t]f_t(\boldsymbol{x}) + \boldsymbol{\beta}_t[\iota]; \boldsymbol{r}_t^{(\iota)})$$

for all $\iota \in [k], t \in [n']$. Here we make use of the instantiation of the AKGS described in Sect. 3.3. From the description of that AKGS instantiation, we note that the $(m+1)$-th label function $\boldsymbol{\ell}_{m+1,t}^{(\iota)}$ would be of the form $\boldsymbol{\ell}_{m+1,t}^{(\iota)} = \boldsymbol{\alpha}[\iota]\boldsymbol{z}[t] - \boldsymbol{r}_t^{(\iota)}[m]$ where $\boldsymbol{\alpha}[\iota]$ is a constant. Also all the label functions $\boldsymbol{\ell}_{1,t}^{(\iota)}, \ldots, \boldsymbol{\ell}_{m,t}^{(\iota)}$ involve only the variables $\boldsymbol{x}$ and not the variable $\boldsymbol{z}[t]$. Next, for all $j \in [m]$ and $t \in [n']$, it defines the vectors $\boldsymbol{v}_{j,t}$ corresponding to the label functions $\boldsymbol{\ell}_{j,t}^{(\iota)}$ obtained from the partial garbling above as

vector	$\mathsf{const}^{(\iota)}$	$\mathsf{coef}_i^{(\iota)}$	S_{priv}
$\boldsymbol{v}$	$\boldsymbol{\alpha}[\iota]$	0	0
$\boldsymbol{v}_{j,t}$	$\boldsymbol{\ell}_{j,t}^{(\iota)}[\mathsf{const}]$	$\boldsymbol{\ell}_{j,t}^{(\iota)}[\mathsf{coef}_i]$	0

vector	$\widehat{\mathsf{const}}^{(\iota)}$	$\widehat{\mathsf{coef}}^{(\iota)}$	$\widehat{S}_{\mathsf{priv}}$
$\boldsymbol{v}_{m+1,t}$	$\boldsymbol{r}_t^{(\iota)}[m]$	$\boldsymbol{\alpha}[\iota]$	0

It generates the secret-keys as

$$\mathsf{IPFE.SK} \leftarrow \mathsf{IPFE.KeyGen}(\mathsf{IPFE.MSK}, [\![\boldsymbol{v}]\!]_2)$$
$$\mathsf{IPFE.SK}_{j,t} \leftarrow \mathsf{IPFE.KeyGen}(\mathsf{IPFE.MSK}, [\![\boldsymbol{v}_{j,t}]\!]_2) \text{ for } j \in [m], t \in [n']$$
$$\widehat{\mathsf{IPFE.SK}}_{m+1,t} \leftarrow \mathsf{IPFE.KeyGen}(\widehat{\mathsf{IPFE.MSK}}, [\![\boldsymbol{v}_{m+1,t}]\!]_2) \text{ for } t \in [n']$$

It returns $\mathsf{SK}_f = (\mathsf{IPFE.SK}, \{\mathsf{IPFE.SK}_{j,t}\}_{j\in[m],t\in[n']}, \{\widehat{\mathsf{IPFE.SK}}_{m+1,t}\}_{t\in[n']})$.

Enc(MPK, $\boldsymbol{x} \in \mathbb{Z}_p^n$, $\boldsymbol{z} \in \mathbb{Z}_p^{n'}$): It samples $\boldsymbol{s} \leftarrow \mathbb{Z}_p^k$ and set the vectors

vector	$\mathsf{const}^{(\iota)}$	$\mathsf{coef}_i^{(\iota)}$
$\boldsymbol{u}$	$\boldsymbol{s}[\iota]$	$\boldsymbol{s}[\iota]\boldsymbol{x}[i]$
vector	$\widehat{\mathsf{const}}^{(\iota)}$	$\widehat{\mathsf{coef}}^{(\iota)}$
$\boldsymbol{h}_t$	$-\boldsymbol{s}[\iota]$	$\boldsymbol{s}[\iota]\boldsymbol{z}[t]$

for all $t \in [n']$. It encrypts the vectors as

$$\mathsf{IPFE.CT} \leftarrow \mathsf{IPFE.SlotEnc}(\mathsf{IPFE.MPK}, [\![\boldsymbol{u}]\!]_1)$$
$$\widehat{\mathsf{IPFE.CT}}_t \leftarrow \mathsf{IPFE.SlotEnc}(\widehat{\mathsf{IPFE.MPK}}, [\![\boldsymbol{h}_t]\!]_1) \text{ for } t \in [n']$$

and returns the ciphertext as $\mathsf{CT} = (\mathsf{IPFE.CT}, \{\widehat{\mathsf{IPFE.CT}}_t\}_{t\in[n']})$.

Dec((SK$_f$, f), (CT, $\boldsymbol{x}$)): It parses $\mathsf{SK}_f = (\mathsf{IPFE.MSK}, \{\mathsf{IPFE.MSK}_{j,t}\}_{j\in[m],t\in[n']}, \{\widehat{\mathsf{IPFE.MSK}}_{m+1,t}\}_{t\in[n']})$ and $\mathsf{CT} = (\mathsf{IPFE.CT}, \{\widehat{\mathsf{IPFE.CT}}_t\}_{t\in[n']})$. It uses the decryption algorithm of IPFE to compute

$$[\![\mu]\!]_T = \mathsf{IPFE.Dec}(\mathsf{IPFE.SK}, \mathsf{IPFE.CT})$$
$$[\![\ell_{j,t}]\!]_T = \mathsf{IPFE.Dec}(\mathsf{IPFE.SK}_{j,t}, \mathsf{IPFE.CT}) \text{ for } j \in [m], t \in [n']$$
$$[\![\ell_{m+1,t}]\!]_T = \mathsf{IPFE.Dec}(\widehat{\mathsf{IPFE.SK}}_{m+1,t}, \widehat{\mathsf{IPFE.CT}}_t) \text{ for } t \in [n']$$

Next, it utilizes the evaluation procedure of AKGS and obtain a combined value

$$[\![\rho]\!]_T = \prod_{t\in[n']} \mathsf{Eval}(f_t, \boldsymbol{x}, [\![\ell_{1,t}]\!]_T, \ldots, [\![\ell_{m+1,t}]\!]_T).$$

Finally, it returns a value ζ from a polynomially bounded set $\mathcal{P}$ such that $[\![\rho]\!]_T = [\![\mu]\!]_T \cdot [\![\zeta]\!]_T$; otherwise $\perp$.

Correctness: By the correctness of IPFE, AKGS and the linearity of the Eval function we have

$$\begin{aligned}\mathsf{Eval}(f_t, \boldsymbol{x}, [\![\ell_{1,t}]\!]_T, \ldots, [\![\ell_{m+1,t}]\!]_T) &= [\![\sum_{\iota=1}^{k} \boldsymbol{\alpha}[\iota]\boldsymbol{s}[\iota] \cdot \boldsymbol{z}[t]f_t(\boldsymbol{x}) + \boldsymbol{\beta}_t[\iota]\boldsymbol{s}[\iota]]\!]_T \\ &= [\![\boldsymbol{\alpha} \cdot \boldsymbol{s} \cdot \boldsymbol{z}[t]f_t(\boldsymbol{x}) + \boldsymbol{\beta}_t \cdot \boldsymbol{s}]\!]_T\end{aligned}$$

Therefore, $[\![\rho]\!]_T = [\![\sum_{t=1}^{n'} \boldsymbol{\alpha} \cdot \boldsymbol{s} \cdot \boldsymbol{z}[t]f_t(\boldsymbol{x}) + \boldsymbol{\beta}_t \cdot \boldsymbol{s}]\!]_T = [\![(\boldsymbol{\alpha} \cdot \boldsymbol{s})f(\boldsymbol{x})^\top \boldsymbol{z}]\!]_T$ since $\sum_{t\in[n']} \boldsymbol{\beta}_t[\iota] = 0 \mod p$ for all $\iota \in [k]$. Also, by the correctness of IPFE we see that $[\![\mu]\!]_T = [\![\boldsymbol{\alpha} \cdot \boldsymbol{s}]\!]_T$ and hence $[\![\zeta]\!]_T = [\![f(\boldsymbol{x})^\top \boldsymbol{z}]\!]_T \in \mathcal{P}$.

Remark 3 (Multi-ciphertext Scheme). The 1-slot FE scheme Π_{one} described above is secure against adversaries that are restricted to query a single ciphertext. However, we can easily modify the FE scheme to another FE scheme that is secure for any a-priori bounded number of ciphertext queries from the adversary's end. For the extension, we introduce additional $(2n'+2)q_{\mathsf{CT}}$ private slots on each ciphertext and decryption key sides, where q_{CT} denotes the number of ciphertext queries. More specifically, we add $2n'q_{\mathsf{CT}}$ and $2q_{\mathsf{CT}}$ dimensional hidden slots to $\mathcal{S}_{\mathsf{priv}}$ and $\widehat{\mathcal{S}}_{\mathsf{priv}}$ respectively to handle the q_{CT} ciphertext queries during the security reduction. Consequently, the sizes of the master public key, secret-keys, and ciphertext would grow linearly with q_{CT}. A similar strategy can be followed to convert our extended 1-slot FE scheme (of Sect. 6) that only supports a single ciphertext query to one that is secure for any a-priori bounded number of ciphertext queries.

Theorem 3. *The 1-slot* FE *scheme* Π_{one} *for attribute-weighted sums is adaptively simulation-secure assuming the* AKGS *is piece-wise secure, the* MDDH_k *assumption holds in group* $\mathbb{G}_2$*, and the slotted* IPFE *is function hiding.*

6 Our 1-Slot Extended FE for Attribute-Weighted Sums

In this section, we describe our 1-slot extFE scheme Π_{extOne} for the attribute-weighted sum functionality. We describe the construction for any fixed value of the security parameter λ and suppress the appearance of λ for simplicity of notations. Let (Garble, Eval) be a special piecewise secure AKGS for a function class $\mathcal{F}_{\mathsf{ABP}}^{(n,n')}$, $\mathsf{G} = (\mathbb{G}_1, \mathbb{G}_2, \mathbb{G}_T, g_1, g_2, e)$ a tuple of pairing groups of prime order p such that MDDH_k assumption holds in $\mathbb{G}_2$, and (IPFE.Setup.IPFE.KeyGen, IPFE.Enc, IPFE.Dec) a slotted IPFE based on G. We construct an FE scheme for attribute-weighted sums with the message space $\mathbb{M} = \mathbb{Z}_p^n \times \mathbb{Z}_p^{n'}$.

Setup$(1^\lambda, 1^n, 1^{n'}, 1^B)$**:** Defines the following index sets as follows

$$S_{\mathsf{pub}} = \left\{\{\mathsf{const}^{(\iota)}\}_{\iota\in[k]}, \{\mathsf{coef}_i^{(\iota)}\}_{\iota\in[k],i\in[n]}, \{\mathsf{extnd}_\kappa^{(\iota)}\}_{\iota,\kappa\in[k]}\right\}, \widehat{S}_{\mathsf{pub}} = \{\widehat{\mathsf{const}}^{(\iota)}, \widehat{\mathsf{coef}}^{(\iota)}\}_{\iota\in[k]},$$
$$S_{\mathsf{priv}} = \left\{\mathsf{const}, \{\mathsf{coef}_i\}_{i\in[n]}, \{\mathsf{extnd}_{\kappa,1}, \mathsf{extnd}_{\kappa,2}, \mathsf{extnd}_\kappa\}_{\kappa\in[k]}, \{\mathsf{query}_\eta\}_{\eta\in[B]}, \{\mathsf{sim}_\tau, \mathsf{sim}_\tau^*\}_{\tau\in[n']}\right\},$$
$$\widehat{S}_{\mathsf{priv}} = \{\widehat{\mathsf{const}}_1, \widehat{\mathsf{coef}}_1, \widehat{\mathsf{const}}_2, \widehat{\mathsf{coef}}_2, \widehat{\mathsf{const}}, \widehat{\mathsf{coef}}, \widehat{\mathsf{sim}}^*\}$$

where B denotes a bound on the number of pre-ciphertext queries. It generates two pair of IPFE keys $(\mathsf{IPFE.MSK}, \mathsf{IPFE.MPK}) \leftarrow \mathsf{IPFE.Setup}(S_{\mathsf{pub}}, S_{\mathsf{priv}})$ and $(\widehat{\mathsf{IPFE.MSK}}, \widehat{\mathsf{IPFE.MPK}}) \leftarrow \mathsf{IPFE.Setup}(\widehat{S}_{\mathsf{pub}}, \widehat{S}_{\mathsf{priv}})$. Finally, it returns the master secret-key of the system as $\mathsf{MSK} = (\mathsf{IPFE.MSK}, \widehat{\mathsf{IPFE.MSK}})$ and master public-key as $\mathsf{MPK} = (\mathsf{IPFE.MPK}, \widehat{\mathsf{IPFE.MPK}})$.

KeyGen(MSK, $(\boldsymbol{f}, \boldsymbol{y})$): Let $f = (f_1, \ldots, f_{n'}) \in \mathcal{F}_{\mathsf{ABP}}^{(n,n')}$ and $\boldsymbol{y} \in \mathbb{Z}_p^k$. It samples integers $\nu_t \leftarrow \mathbb{Z}_p$ and vectors $\boldsymbol{\alpha}, \boldsymbol{\beta}_t \leftarrow \mathbb{Z}_p^k$ for $t \in [n']$ such that

$$\sum_{t\in[n']} \nu_t = 1 \text{ and } \sum_{t\in[n']} \boldsymbol{\beta}_t[\iota] = 0 \bmod p \text{ for all } \iota \in [k]$$

Next, sample independent random vectors $\boldsymbol{r}_t^{(\iota)} \leftarrow \mathbb{Z}_p^m$ and computes

$$(\boldsymbol{\ell}_{1,t}^{(\iota)}, \ldots, \boldsymbol{\ell}_{m,t}^{(\iota)}, \boldsymbol{\ell}_{m+1,t}^{(\iota)}) \leftarrow \mathsf{Garble}(\boldsymbol{\alpha}[\iota]\boldsymbol{z}[t]f_t(\boldsymbol{x}) + \boldsymbol{\beta}_t[\iota]; \boldsymbol{r}_t^{(\iota)})$$

for all $\iota \in [k], t \in [n']$. Here, we make use of the instantiation of the AKGS described in Sect. 3.3. From the description of that AKGS instantiation, we note that the $(m+1)$-th label function $\boldsymbol{\ell}_{m+1,t}^{(\iota)}$ would be of the form $\boldsymbol{\ell}_{m+1,t}^{(\iota)} = \boldsymbol{\alpha}[\iota]\boldsymbol{z}[t] - \boldsymbol{r}_t^{(\iota)}[m]$ where $\boldsymbol{\alpha}[\iota]$ is a constant. Also all the label functions $\boldsymbol{\ell}_{1,t}^{(\iota)}, \ldots, \boldsymbol{\ell}_{m,t}^{(\iota)}$ involve only the variables $\boldsymbol{x}$ and not the variable $\boldsymbol{z}[t]$. Next, for all $j \in [2, m]$ and $t \in [n']$, it defines the vectors $\boldsymbol{v}_{j,t}$ corresponding to the label functions $\boldsymbol{\ell}_{j,t}$ obtained from the partial garbling above and the vector $\boldsymbol{y}$ as

vector	$\mathsf{const}^{(\iota)}$	$\mathsf{coef}_i^{(\iota)}$	$\mathsf{extnd}_\kappa^{(\iota)}$	S_{priv}
$\boldsymbol{v}$	$\boldsymbol{\alpha}[\iota]$	0	0	0
$\boldsymbol{v}_{1,t}$	$\boldsymbol{\ell}_{1,t}^{(\iota)}[\mathsf{const}]$	$\boldsymbol{\ell}_{1,t}^{(\iota)}[\mathsf{coef}_i]$	$\boldsymbol{\alpha}[\iota]\boldsymbol{y}[\kappa]\nu_t$	0
$\boldsymbol{v}_{j,t}$	$\boldsymbol{\ell}_{j,t}^{(\iota)}[\mathsf{const}]$	$\boldsymbol{\ell}_{j,t}^{(\iota)}[\mathsf{coef}_i]$	0	0

vector	$\widehat{\mathsf{const}}^{(\iota)}$	$\widehat{\mathsf{coef}}^{(\iota)}$	$\widehat{S}_{\mathsf{priv}}$
$\boldsymbol{v}_{m+1,t}$	$\boldsymbol{r}_t^{(\iota)}[m]$	$\boldsymbol{\alpha}[\iota]$	0

It generates the secret-keys as

$$\mathsf{IPFE.SK} \leftarrow \mathsf{IPFE.KeyGen}(\mathsf{IPFE.MSK}, [\![\boldsymbol{v}]\!]_2)$$

$$\mathsf{IPFE.SK}_{j,t} \leftarrow \mathsf{IPFE.KeyGen}(\mathsf{IPFE.MSK}, [\![\boldsymbol{v}_{j,t}]\!]_2) \text{ for } j \in [m], t \in [n']$$

$$\widehat{\mathsf{IPFE.SK}}_{m+1,t} \leftarrow \mathsf{IPFE.KeyGen}(\widehat{\mathsf{IPFE.MSK}}, [\![\boldsymbol{v}_{m+1,t}]\!]_2) \text{ for } t \in [n']$$

Finally, it returns the secret-key as $\mathsf{SK}_{f,\boldsymbol{y}} = (\mathsf{IPFE.SK}, \{\mathsf{IPFE.SK}_{j,t}\}_{j\in[m],t\in[n']}, \{\widehat{\mathsf{IPFE.SK}}_{m+1,t}\}_{t\in[n']})$ and $(f, \boldsymbol{y})$.

Remark 4. We note that the vector $\boldsymbol{y}$ is only used to set $\boldsymbol{v}_{1,t}[\mathsf{extnd}_\kappa^{(\iota)}]$ and the $\mathsf{IPFE.KeyGen}$ only requires $[\![\boldsymbol{v}_{1,t}]\!]_2 \in \mathbb{G}_2^k$ to compute the secret-key $\mathsf{IPFE.SK}_{1,t}$. Therefore, the key generation process can compute the same secret-key $\mathsf{SK}_{f,\boldsymbol{y}}$ if $(f, [\![\boldsymbol{y}]\!]_2)$ is supplied as input instead of $(f, \boldsymbol{y})$ and we express this by writing $\mathsf{KeyGen}(\mathsf{MSK}, (f, [\![\boldsymbol{y}]\!]_2)) = \mathsf{KeyGen}(\mathsf{MSK}, (f, \boldsymbol{y}))$. This fact is crucially while describing our unbounded-slot FE in the full version.

Enc(MPK, $(\boldsymbol{x}, \boldsymbol{z}||\boldsymbol{w}) \in \mathbb{Z}_p^n \times \mathbb{Z}_p^{n'+k}$): It samples a random vector $\boldsymbol{s} \leftarrow \mathbb{Z}_p^k$ and sets the vectors

vector	$\mathsf{const}^{(\iota)}$	$\mathsf{coef}_i^{(\iota)}$	$\mathsf{extnd}_\kappa^{(\iota)}$
$\boldsymbol{u}$	$\boldsymbol{s}[\iota]$	$\boldsymbol{s}[\iota]\boldsymbol{x}[i]$	$\boldsymbol{s}[\iota]\boldsymbol{w}[\kappa]$

vector	$\widehat{\mathsf{const}}^{(\iota)}$	$\widehat{\mathsf{coef}}^{(\iota)}$
$\boldsymbol{h}_t$	$-\boldsymbol{s}[\iota]$	$\boldsymbol{s}[\iota]\boldsymbol{z}[t]$

for all $t \in [n']$. It encrypts the vectors as

$$\mathsf{IPFE.CT} \leftarrow \mathsf{IPFE.SlotEnc}(\mathsf{IPFE.MPK}, [\![\boldsymbol{u}]\!]_1)$$
$$\widehat{\mathsf{IPFE.CT}}_t \leftarrow \mathsf{IPFE.SlotEnc}(\widehat{\mathsf{IPFE.MPK}}, [\![\boldsymbol{h}_t]\!]_1) \text{ for } t \in [n']$$

and returns the ciphertext as $\mathsf{CT} = (\mathsf{IPFE.CT}, \{\widehat{\mathsf{IPFE.CT}}_t\}_{t\in[n']})$ and $\boldsymbol{x}$.

Dec((SK_f, $\boldsymbol{y}$, f), (CT, $\boldsymbol{x}$)): It parses the secret-key and ciphertext as $\mathsf{SK}_f = (\mathsf{IPFE.SK}, \{\mathsf{IPFE.SK}_{j,t}\}_{j\in[m],t\in[n']}, \{\widehat{\mathsf{IPFE.SK}}_{m+1,t}\}_{t\in[n']})$ and $\mathsf{CT}_{\boldsymbol{x},\boldsymbol{z}} = (\mathsf{IPFE.CT}, \{\widehat{\mathsf{IPFE.CT}}_t\}_{t\in[n']})$. It uses the decryption algorithm of IPFE to compute

$$[\![\rho]\!]_T \leftarrow \mathsf{IPFE.Dec}(\mathsf{IPFE.SK}, \mathsf{IPFE.CT})$$
$$[\![\ell_{1,t} + \psi_t]\!]_T \leftarrow \mathsf{IPFE.Dec}(\mathsf{IPFE.SK}_{1,t}, \mathsf{IPFE.CT})$$
$$[\![\ell_{j,t}]\!]_T \leftarrow \mathsf{IPFE.Dec}(\mathsf{IPFE.SK}_{j,t}, \mathsf{IPFE.CT}) \text{ for } j \in [2, m], t \in [n']$$
$$[\![\ell_{m+1,t}]\!]_T \leftarrow \mathsf{IPFE.Dec}(\widehat{\mathsf{IPFE.SK}}_{m+1,t}, \widehat{\mathsf{IPFE.CT}}_t) \text{ for } t \in [n']$$

where $\psi_t = \sum_{\iota=1}^k \boldsymbol{\alpha}[\iota]\boldsymbol{s}[\iota] \cdot \nu_t \cdot \boldsymbol{y}^\top \boldsymbol{w} = \boldsymbol{\alpha} \cdot \boldsymbol{s} \cdot \nu_t \cdot \boldsymbol{y}^\top \boldsymbol{w}$. Next, it utilizes the evaluation procedure of AKGS and obtain a combined value

$$[\![\zeta]\!]_T = \prod\nolimits_{t\in[n']} \mathsf{Eval}(f_t, \boldsymbol{x}, [\![\ell_{1,t} + \psi_t]\!]_T, \ldots, [\![\ell_{m+1,t}]\!]_T).$$

Finally, it returns a value $[\![\mu]\!]_T = [\![\zeta]\!]_T \cdot [\![\rho]\!]_T^{-1} \in \mathbb{G}_T$.

Correctness: First, the IPFE correctness implies $\mathsf{IPFE.Dec}(\mathsf{IPFE.SK}_{1,t}, \mathsf{IPFE.CT}) = [\![\ell_{1,t} + \psi_t]\!]$ where $\psi_t = \sum_{\iota=1}^k \boldsymbol{\alpha}[\iota]\boldsymbol{s}[\iota] \cdot \nu_t \cdot \boldsymbol{y}^\top \boldsymbol{w} = \boldsymbol{\alpha} \cdot \boldsymbol{s} \cdot \nu_t \cdot \boldsymbol{y}^\top \boldsymbol{w}$. Next, by the correctness of IPFE, AKGS we have

$$\begin{aligned}
&\mathsf{Eval}(f_t, \boldsymbol{x}, \ell_{1,t} + \psi_t, \ldots, \ell_{m+1,t}) \\
&= \mathsf{Eval}(f_t, \boldsymbol{x}, \ell_{1,t}, \ldots, \ell_{m+1,t}) + \mathsf{Eval}(f_t, \boldsymbol{x}, \psi_t, 0, \ldots, 0) \\
&= \mathsf{Eval}(f_t, \boldsymbol{x}, \ell_{1,t}, \ldots, \ell_{m+1,t}) + \psi_t \\
&= \sum_{\iota=1}^{k} (\boldsymbol{\alpha}[\iota]\boldsymbol{s}[\iota] \cdot \boldsymbol{z}[t] f_t(\boldsymbol{x}) + \boldsymbol{\beta}_t[\iota]\boldsymbol{s}[\iota]) + \boldsymbol{\alpha} \cdot \boldsymbol{s} \cdot \nu_t \cdot \boldsymbol{y}^\top \boldsymbol{w} \\
&= \boldsymbol{\alpha} \cdot \boldsymbol{s} \cdot (\boldsymbol{z}[t] f_t(\boldsymbol{x}) + \nu_t \cdot \boldsymbol{y}^\top \boldsymbol{w}) + \boldsymbol{\beta}_t \cdot \boldsymbol{s}
\end{aligned}$$

The first equality follows from the linearity of Eval algorithm. Therefore, multiplying all the evaluated values we have

$$\begin{aligned}
[\![\zeta]\!]_T &= \prod_{t \in [n']} \mathsf{Eval}(f_t, \boldsymbol{x}, [\![\ell_{1,t} + \psi_t]\!]_T, \ldots, [\![\ell_{m+1,t}]\!]_T) \\
&= [\![\sum_{t=1}^{n'} \boldsymbol{\alpha} \cdot \boldsymbol{s} \cdot (\boldsymbol{z}[t] f_t(\boldsymbol{x}) + \nu_t \cdot \boldsymbol{y}^\top \boldsymbol{w}) + \boldsymbol{\beta}_t \cdot \boldsymbol{s}]\!]_T = [\![\boldsymbol{\alpha} \cdot \boldsymbol{s} \cdot (f(\boldsymbol{x})^\top \boldsymbol{z} + \boldsymbol{y}^\top \boldsymbol{w})]\!]_T
\end{aligned}$$

where the last equality follows from the fact that $\sum_{t \in [n']} \nu_t = 1$ and $\sum_{t \in [n']} \boldsymbol{\beta}_t[\iota] = 0$ for all $\iota \in [k]$. Also, by the correctness of IPFE we see that $[\![\rho]\!]_T = [\![\boldsymbol{\alpha} \cdot \boldsymbol{s}]\!]_T$ and hence $[\![\mu]\!]_T = [\![f(\boldsymbol{x})^\top \boldsymbol{z} + \boldsymbol{y}^\top \boldsymbol{w}]\!]_T$.

Theorem 4. *The extended one slot* FE *scheme Π_{extOne} for attribute-weighted sum is adaptively simulation-secure against adversaries making at most B pre-ciphertext secret key queries and an arbitrary polynomial number of post-ciphertext secret key queries assuming the* AKGS *is piecewise-secure, the* MDDH_k *assumption holds in group $\mathbb{G}_2$, and the slotted* IPFE *is function hiding.*

References

1. Abdalla, M., Bourse, F., De Caro, A., Pointcheval, D.: Simple functional encryption schemes for inner products. In: Katz, J. (ed.) PKC 2015. LNCS, vol. 9020, pp. 733–751. Springer, Heidelberg (2015). https://doi.org/10.1007/978-3-662-46447-2_33
2. Abdalla, M., Catalano, D., Gay, R., Ursu, B.: Inner-product functional encryption with fine-grained access control. IACR Cryptology ePrint Archive, Report 2020/577 (2020)
3. Abdalla, M., Gong, J., Wee, H.: Functional encryption for attribute-weighted sums from k-Lin. In: Micciancio, D., Ristenpart, T. (eds.) CRYPTO 2020. LNCS, vol. 12170, pp. 685–716. Springer, Cham (2020). https://doi.org/10.1007/978-3-030-56784-2_23
4. Agrawal, S.: Stronger security for reusable garbled circuits, general definitions and attacks. In: Katz, J., Shacham, H. (eds.) CRYPTO 2017. LNCS, vol. 10401, pp. 3–35. Springer, Cham (2017). https://doi.org/10.1007/978-3-319-63688-7_1
5. Agrawal, S., Goyal, R., Tomida, J.: Multi-input quadratic functional encryption from pairings. IACR Cryptology ePrint Archive, Report 2020/1285 (2020)
6. Agrawal, S., Libert, B., Maitra, M., Titiu, R.: Adaptive simulation security for inner product functional encryption. In: Kiayias, A., Kohlweiss, M., Wallden, P., Zikas, V. (eds.) PKC 2020. LNCS, vol. 12110, pp. 34–64. Springer, Cham (2020). https://doi.org/10.1007/978-3-030-45374-9_2

7. Agrawal, S., Libert, B., Stehlé, D.: Fully secure functional encryption for inner products, from standard assumptions. In: Robshaw, M., Katz, J. (eds.) CRYPTO 2016. LNCS, vol. 9816, pp. 333–362. Springer, Heidelberg (2016). https://doi.org/10.1007/978-3-662-53015-3_12
8. Applebaum, B., Ishai, Y., Kushilevitz, E.: How to garble arithmetic circuits. In: FOCS 2011, pp. 120–129. IEEE Computer Society (2011)
9. Boneh, D., Sahai, A., Waters, B.: Functional encryption: definitions and challenges. In: Ishai, Y. (ed.) TCC 2011. LNCS, vol. 6597, pp. 253–273. Springer, Heidelberg (2011). https://doi.org/10.1007/978-3-642-19571-6_16
10. Datta, P., Okamoto, T., Takashima, K.: Adaptively simulation-secure attribute-hiding predicate encryption. In: Peyrin, T., Galbraith, S. (eds.) ASIACRYPT 2018. LNCS, vol. 11273, pp. 640–672. Springer, Cham (2018). https://doi.org/10.1007/978-3-030-03329-3_22
11. Datta, P., Okamoto, T., Takashima, K.: Adaptively simulation-secure attribute-hiding predicate encryption. IEICE Trans. Inf. Syst. **103**(7), 1556–1597 (2020)
12. Escala, A., Herold, G., Kiltz, E., Ràfols, C., Villar, J.: An algebraic framework for Diffie–Hellman assumptions. J. Cryptol. **30**(1), 242–288 (2015). https://doi.org/10.1007/s00145-015-9220-6
13. Ishai, Y., Kushilevitz, E.: Perfect constant-round secure computation via perfect randomizing polynomials. In: Widmayer, P., Eidenbenz, S., Triguero, F., Morales, R., Conejo, R., Hennessy, M. (eds.) ICALP 2002. LNCS, vol. 2380, pp. 244–256. Springer, Heidelberg (2002). https://doi.org/10.1007/3-540-45465-9_22
14. Ishai, Y., Wee, H.: Partial garbling schemes and their applications. In: Esparza, J., Fraigniaud, P., Husfeldt, T., Koutsoupias, E. (eds.) ICALP 2014. LNCS, vol. 8572, pp. 650–662. Springer, Heidelberg (2014). https://doi.org/10.1007/978-3-662-43948-7_54
15. Katz, J., Sahai, A., Waters, B.: Predicate encryption supporting disjunctions, polynomial equations, and inner products. In: Smart, N. (ed.) EUROCRYPT 2008. LNCS, vol. 4965, pp. 146–162. Springer, Heidelberg (2008). https://doi.org/10.1007/978-3-540-78967-3_9
16. Kowalczyk, L., Wee, H.: Compact adaptively secure ABE for NC^1 from k-Lin. J. Cryptol. **33**(3), 954–1002 (2019). https://doi.org/10.1007/s00145-019-09335-x
17. Lewko, A., Okamoto, T., Sahai, A., Takashima, K., Waters, B.: Fully secure functional encryption: attribute-based encryption and (hierarchical) inner product encryption. In: Gilbert, H. (ed.) EUROCRYPT 2010. LNCS, vol. 6110, pp. 62–91. Springer, Heidelberg (2010). https://doi.org/10.1007/978-3-642-13190-5_4
18. Lewko, A., Waters, B.: New techniques for dual system encryption and fully secure HIBE with short ciphertexts. In: Micciancio, D. (ed.) TCC 2010. LNCS, vol. 5978, pp. 455–479. Springer, Heidelberg (2010). https://doi.org/10.1007/978-3-642-11799-2_27
19. Lin, H., Luo, J.: Compact adaptively secure ABE from k-Lin: beyond NC^1 and towards NL. In: Canteaut, A., Ishai, Y. (eds.) EUROCRYPT 2020. LNCS, vol. 12107, pp. 247–277. Springer, Cham (2020). https://doi.org/10.1007/978-3-030-45727-3_9
20. Lin, H., Vaikuntanathan, V.: Indistinguishability obfuscation from DDH-like assumptions on constant-degree graded encodings. In: FOCS 2016, pp. 11–20. IEEE (2016)
21. Nisan, N.: Lower bounds for non-commutative computation (extended abstract). In: STOC 1991, pp. 410–418. ACM (1991)

22. Okamoto, T., Takashima, K.: Adaptively attribute-hiding (hierarchical) inner product encryption. In: Pointcheval, D., Johansson, T. (eds.) EUROCRYPT 2012. LNCS, vol. 7237, pp. 591–608. Springer, Heidelberg (2012). https://doi.org/10.1007/978-3-642-29011-4_35
23. Okamoto, T., Takashima, K.: Fully secure unbounded inner-product and attribute-based encryption. In: Wang, X., Sako, K. (eds.) ASIACRYPT 2012. LNCS, vol. 7658, pp. 349–366. Springer, Heidelberg (2012). https://doi.org/10.1007/978-3-642-34961-4_22
24. Okamoto, T., Takashima, K.: Fully secure functional encryption with general relations from the decisional linear assumption. In: Rabin, T. (ed.) CRYPTO 2010. LNCS, vol. 6223, pp. 191–208. Springer, Heidelberg (2010). https://doi.org/10.1007/978-3-642-14623-7_11
25. Okamoto, T., Takashima, K.: Efficient (hierarchical) inner-product encryption tightly reduced from the decisional linear assumption. IEICE Trans. Fundam. Electron. Commun. Comput. Sci. **96**(1), 42–52 (2013)
26. O'Neill, A.: Definitional issues in functional encryption. IACR Cryptology ePrint Archive, Report 2010/556 (2010)
27. Waters, B.: Ciphertext-policy attribute-based encryption: an expressive, efficient, and provably secure realization. In: Catalano, D., Fazio, N., Gennaro, R., Nicolosi, A. (eds.) PKC 2011. LNCS, vol. 6571, pp. 53–70. Springer, Heidelberg (2011). https://doi.org/10.1007/978-3-642-19379-8_4
28. Waters, B.: Dual system encryption: realizing fully secure IBE and HIBE under simple assumptions. In: Halevi, S. (ed.) CRYPTO 2009. LNCS, vol. 5677, pp. 619–636. Springer, Heidelberg (2009). https://doi.org/10.1007/978-3-642-03356-8_36
29. Wee, H.: Attribute-hiding predicate encryption in bilinear groups, revisited. In: Kalai, Y., Reyzin, L. (eds.) TCC 2017. LNCS, vol. 10677, pp. 206–233. Springer, Cham (2017). https://doi.org/10.1007/978-3-319-70500-2_8
30. Wee, H.: Functional encryption for quadratic functions from k-Lin, revisited. In: Pass, R., Pietrzak, K. (eds.) TCC 2020. LNCS, vol. 12550, pp. 210–228. Springer, Cham (2020). https://doi.org/10.1007/978-3-030-64375-1_8

Boosting the Security of Blind Signature Schemes

Jonathan Katz[1(✉)], Julian Loss[2], and Michael Rosenberg[1]

[1] University of Maryland, College Park, USA
micro@cs.umd.edu

[2] CISPA Helmholtz Center for Information Security, Saarbrücken, Germany

Abstract. Existing blind signature schemes that are secure for polynomially many concurrent executions of the signing protocol are either inefficient or rely on non-standard assumptions (even in the random-oracle model). We show the first efficient blind signature schemes achieving this level of security based on the RSA, factoring, or discrete logarithm assumptions (in the random-oracle model). Our core technique involves an extension and generalization of a transform due to Pointcheval (Eurocrypt'98) that allows us to convert certain blind signature schemes that are secure for (concurrently) issuing logarithmically many signatures into ones secure for (concurrently) issuing polynomially many signatures.

1 Introduction

A *blind signature scheme* [6] consists of an interactive protocol executed between a signer $\mathcal{S}$ (holding a secret key sk) and a user $\mathcal{U}$ (holding a message m and the signer's public key pk), by which $\mathcal{U}$ obtains a signature σ on m. *Blindness* ensures that $\mathcal{S}$ learns nothing about m, and in fact is even unable to link (m, σ) to the execution of the protocol in which σ was generated. *One-more unforgeability* means that if $\mathcal{U}$ executes the signing protocol ℓ times, it should be unable to generate valid signatures on more than ℓ messages. Even in the random-oracle model, known blind signature schemes that support polynomially many signatures are either inefficient [7,11,12,16,18], rely on non-standard assumptions or the algebraic group model [3,5,8,9,13,19,21], or are secure only for sequential executions of the signing protocol [2,18,19]. Known efficient schemes that rely on standard assumptions such as RSA, factoring, the hardness of computing discrete logarithms, or the hardness of SIS [1,10,15,23–25] are concurrently secure but their signature size depends linearly on the maximum amount of signatures that can be issued. Moreover, for many schemes this limitation is known to be inherent as there is an efficient attack [4,26,27] when running the scheme concurrently with shorter signatures.

J. Loss—Work done while at the University of Maryland.

M. Rosenberg—Work supported by a National Defense Science and Engineering Graduate (NDSEG) Fellowship.

M. Tibouchi and H. Wang (Eds.): ASIACRYPT 2021, LNCS 13093, pp. 468–492, 2021.
https://doi.org/10.1007/978-3-030-92068-5_16

In an effort to obtain an efficient blind signature scheme secure for issuing polynomially many signatures, Pointcheval [22] showed a transform for "boosting" the security of the Okamoto-Schnorr blind signature scheme [20,25]. Specifically, under the assumption that the Okamoto-Schnorr blind signature scheme is secure for logarithmically many sequential executions of the signing protocol (which itself can be shown to hold in the random-oracle model, based on the hardness of computing discrete logarithms), the transformed scheme is secure for polynomially many sequential executions of the signing protocol.[1] The resulting scheme, however, has a significant drawback: it requires the signer to *refuse to issue any further signatures* if a user is ever caught cheating. Thus, while the scheme could be used in a setting where the signer interacts with a *single* user repeatedly (and thus the signer would be justified in refusing to interact with that user once that user is caught cheating), the scheme is not appropriate for standard applications of blind signatures where the signer interacts with *many* users, some of whom may collude. Indeed, in the latter setting a single malicious user could easily carry out a devastating denial-of-service attack by interacting with the signer once and cheating, thus preventing the signer from issuing any further signatures. Note further that an abort by the user during an execution of the signing protocol is considered cheating, so even transient network failures during an honest execution of the protocol may lead to the same result.

1.1 Our Contributions

Inspired by Pointcheval's transform, we show a new transform for boosting the security of certain blind signature schemes. Our transform has the following advantages compared to Pointcheval's result:

1. As with Pointcheval's transform, our transform boosts security in the following sense: if the original scheme BS is secure for *logarithmically* many executions of the signing protocol, then the transformed scheme CCBS is secure for *polynomially* many executions. Importantly, however, in our case the transformed scheme CCBS does *not* require the signer to stop issuing signatures if cheating is detected.
2. Moreover, if BS is secure for (logarithmically many) *concurrent* executions of the signing protocol, then CCBS is secure for (polynomially many) concurrent executions as well. This is in contrast to Pointcheval's transform, which is not secure for concurrent executions of the signing protocol even if the original scheme is concurrently secure.

[1] We have identified a bug in Pointcheval's result, in that the transformed scheme does not satisfy blindness. This is easy to fix, though.

3. Our transform can be applied to any blind signature scheme BS constructed in a certain way from a *linear function family* [14], in contrast to Pointcheval's transform that is specific to the Okamoto-Schnorr scheme.[2] In particular, our transform can be applied to the Fiat-Shamir, Okamoto-Guillou-Quisquater, and Okamoto-Schnorr blind signature schemes, all of which can be proven secure (for logarithmically many executions) under standard assumptions in the random-oracle model. Our transform can also be applied to the Schnorr blind signature scheme, which was recently proven secure (for logarithmically many executions) in the algebraic group model [10].
4. As in Pointcheval's transform, the size of signatures in the transformed scheme CCBS is (almost) the same as in the underlying scheme BS.

Overall, then, our work gives the first efficient blind signature schemes that are secure for polynomially many concurrent executions of the signing protocol based on standard assumptions (in the random-oracle model).

1.2 Overview

In this section we give a high-level overview of our transform and its proof of security. Our treatment is deliberately informal, and we refer the reader to Sect. 3 for details of our scheme. Throughout this section we let BS be a blind signature scheme that is secure for logarithmically many executions of the signing protocol, and for which our transform applies. This in particular means that the signing protocol BS has a three-round structure in which the signer sends the first message. We denote the messages sent in each round of the protocol as R, c, and s, respectively.

Pointcheval's transform. We begin by recalling Pointcheval's transform and its proof of security. (Pointcheval's transform was only defined for the Okamoto-Schnorr scheme, but our work shows that it can be applied to a larger class of schemes.) The basic idea of Pointcheval's transform is to use 1-out-of-2 cut-and-choose to catch (in a limited sense) cheating behavior of a user $\mathcal{U}$. In more detail, the transformed scheme works roughly as follows for a user who wants to obtain a signature on a message m:

1. $\mathcal{U}$ runs two parallel executions of BS (we refer to each as a *session*) where the messages to be signed are $\mu_1 = \mathsf{H}'(m, \varphi_1)$ and $\mu_2 = \mathsf{H}'(m, \varphi_2)$, respectively. (Here, H' is a random oracle and φ_1, φ_2 are random strings.) The transformed protocol begins by having $\mathcal{U}$ send a commitment com_1 to μ_1 and its randomness for the first session, and a commitment com_2 to μ_2 and its randomness for the second session. These commitments also rely on a random oracle, which enables extraction in the proof of one-more unforgeability (see below).
2. $\mathcal{S}$ runs two executions of BS to obtain initial messages R_1, R_2, which it sends to $\mathcal{U}$.

[2] Pointcheval states that his transform can be adapted to apply to the Okamoto-Guillou-Quisquater scheme, but does not give details (or a proof).

3. $\mathcal{U}$ responds with c_1, c_2, which are the second messages of its two executions of BS.
4. $\mathcal{S}$ then chooses a uniform $I \in \{1, 2\}$ and challenges $\mathcal{U}$ to open commitment com_{3-I} and thus demonstrate that it behaved honestly in the corresponding session. If the commitment is opened correctly, then $\mathcal{S}$ sends the final message s_I for the unopened session and $\mathcal{U}$ uses BS to compute a signature on μ_I (which is defined to be a signature on m in the transformed scheme). If $\mathcal{U}$ is caught cheating, then $\mathcal{S}$ aborts and refuses to issue any more signatures (see further discussion below).

It is not difficult to show that the transformed scheme is blind if BS is blind, and so the main challenge is to prove one-more unforgeability of the transformed scheme for polynomially many executions. This is shown by reduction to the one-more unforgeability of BS for logarithmically many executions. The idea of the reduction is as follows. Each time the adversarial user $\mathcal{U}^*$ sends its commitments in the first round of the transformed protocol, the reduction uses the random-oracle queries of $\mathcal{U}^*$ to try to extract the randomness of $\mathcal{U}^*$ for both sessions. If this cannot be done for either session, then $\mathcal{U}^*$ will not succeed in the cut-and-choose (except with negligible probability) and so simulation is easy. If extraction can be done for both sessions, then the reduction will be able to simulate an execution of BS on its own, regardless of the value of I. The remaining case is when the reduction is able to extract the randomness for only one of the two sessions. (In that case, we say $\mathcal{U}^*$ *attempts to cheat.*) $\mathcal{U}^*$ can then succeed in the cut-and-choose with probability 1/2 (in which case we say $\mathcal{U}^*$ *successfully cheats*), but the reduction will be unable to simulate BS for the unopened session in that case (since it was unable to extract the randomness for that session). Instead, in this case the reduction will interact with the real signer in the underlying scheme BS, forwarding messages in the obvious way between the signer and $\mathcal{U}^*$. (One must show that a forgery by $\mathcal{U}^*$ in the transformed scheme implies that the reduction can compute a forgery in BS with high probability, but this is irrelevant for the discussion that follows.)

To complete the proof, we must argue that with overwhelming probability the reduction interacts with the signer for the underlying scheme BS only logarithmically many times. Although the formal analysis is quite involved, intuitively this holds because each time $\mathcal{U}^*$ attempts to cheat it is caught with probability 1/2. Thus, the probability that $\mathcal{U}^*$ successfully cheats t times (and thus causes the reduction to interact with the signer t times) is 2^{-t}, and hence t is super-logarithmic in the security parameter with only negligible probability. This highlights why it is essential that the signer must refuse to run any more executions of the signing protocol once it detects cheating: if it did not, then $\mathcal{U}^*$ could attempt to cheat in polynomially many executions and successfully cheat (in expectation) in half of those. Since each instance of successful cheating requires the reduction to interact with the signer in BS, this would mean that the transform would then at best be able to double the number of executions of the signing protocol that can be supported.

Our transform. We follow a template similar to Pointcheval's transform, but since we wish to support an unbounded (polynomial) number of executions of the signing protocol we need to modify things to bound the number of times an adversarial user $\mathcal{U}^*$ can successfully cheat in the cut-and-choose. Our key insight is that we can do this by using 1-out-of-N cut-and-choose, *where N increases with the number of executions.*[3] That is, we consider following Pointcheval's general approach, but in the $(N-1)$st execution of the transformed protocol we instead use *1-out-of-N cut-and-choose* on the underlying scheme BS. The probability that $\mathcal{U}^*$ can successfully cheat in the $(N-1)$st execution is now $1/N$, so even if $\mathcal{U}^*$ attempts to cheat in every one of its p executions of the transformed protocol, the expected number of times it can successfully cheat is

$$\frac{1}{2} + \frac{1}{3} + \cdots + \frac{1}{p+1} < \ln(p+1).$$

An appropriate concentration bound implies that for any polynomial p (which bounds the number of executions $\mathcal{U}^*$ runs) the probability that $\mathcal{U}^*$ successfully cheats super-logarithmically many times is negligible.

We remark that although the complexity of our signing protocol grows, the other parameters of the scheme—namely, the size of the keys, the size of the signatures, and the cost of verification—are fixed and essentially the same as in the original scheme BS. The round complexity of our signing protocol is also constant.

Comparison with generic constructions. The complexity of the signing protocol in our scheme is (roughly) N times the complexity of the signing protocol in BS, where N is linear in the number of executions. (But see footnote 3.) One might therefore wonder whether our scheme is better than a generic construction of a blind signature scheme where signing involves running a secure two-party computation (2PC) protocol for computing any (standard) signature [18]. (The details are more complex, but are unimportant for the purposes of this discussion.) This generic approach, however, has several drawbacks compared to our scheme.

1. Such a generic construction would not be concurrently secure without additional complexity and/or without assuming some form of trusted setup or non-standard hardness assumptions.
2. The efficiency of such a generic construction (even restricting attention to sequential security) is unclear, but we conservatively estimate (based on work of Jayaraman et al. [17]) that secure 2PC of an Okamoto-Schnorr signature at the 96-bit security level would have communication complexity at least $10^9\times$ that of our protocol when $N = 2$. Thus, our signing protocol would have better communication complexity for $N < 10^9$. The comparison would be even more favorable for our scheme at higher security levels.

[3] In fact, it suffices to have N depend linearly on *the number of times cheating is detected* (cf. Sect. 3.3), but we ignore this optimization in our informal overview.

3. Efficient and provably secure signature schemes rely on the random-oracle model, but secure computation of a signature would require a circuit for the hash function instantiating the random oracle. Security of the resulting protocol in this case is unclear.

Notwithstanding the above, we note that the generic approach does have two advantages compared to our scheme: First, the signer is *stateless*, whereas in our scheme the signer is required to maintain (a small amount of) state. Second, the signatures produced in the generic scheme are identical to signatures in the underlying scheme, whereas in our scheme (as in Pointcheval's) signatures include an additional random value.

Another generic construction of blind signatures is given by Fischlin [7]. Roughly, in his scheme the signer signs a commitment to m; the signature computed by the user consists of a non-interactive zero-knowledge proof of knowledge (NIZKPoK) of a signed commitment on m. Fischlin's scheme is concurrently secure. Nevertheless, the signatures produced by his scheme are much larger than standard signatures (even if SNARKs are used for the NIZKPoK); also, as with the generic construction discussed above, the concrete efficiency of this approach—especially if one wants to rely on standard assumptions—is unclear.

2 Preliminaries

We give definitions for blind signature schemes and linear function families, and recall a generic construction of blind signature schemes secure for logarithmically many signatures from the latter.

Notation. We denote the security parameter by κ. We write $a \leftarrow S$ to denote that a is drawn uniformly from set S. For a randomized algorithm $\mathcal{A}$ we write $y \leftarrow \mathcal{A}(x)$ to denote that $\mathcal{A}$ returns y when run on input x. For a positive integer N we let $[N] = \{1, \ldots, N\}$.

2.1 Blind Signatures

We define the syntax of a blind signature scheme, followed by definitions of *blindness* and *one-more unforgeability*.

Definition 1 (Blind signature scheme). *A* blind signature scheme *is a tuple of algorithms* $\mathsf{BS} = (\mathsf{Gen}, \mathcal{S}, \mathcal{U}, \mathsf{Vrfy})$ *such that:*

- *The* key-generation algorithm Gen *takes as input the security parameter* 1^κ *and outputs a public/secret key pair* $(\mathsf{pk}, \mathsf{sk})$ *as well as initial state* $\mathsf{st}_\mathcal{S}$.
- *The* signer algorithm $\mathcal{S}$ *is an interactive algorithm that takes as input a secret key* sk *and can (atomically) read/write a global variable* $\mathsf{st}_\mathcal{S}$ *during its execution. At the end of its execution, it outputs either* $\perp$ *(indicating an abort) or 1 (indicating a successful execution). When* $\mathcal{S}$ *outputs 1 at the end of an execution we call that execution* complete.

- *The* user algorithm $\mathcal{U}$ *is an interactive algorithm that takes as input a public key* pk *and a message* m. *At the end of its execution, it either outputs* $\perp$ *(indicating an abort) or a signature* σ.
- *The* verification algorithm Vrfy *takes as input a public key* pk, *a message* m, *and a signature* σ, *and outputs a bit* b *indicating "accept"* $(b = 1)$ *or "reject"* $(b = 0)$.

We require perfect correctness: for all (pk, sk) *output by* Gen *and all messages* m, *if* $\mathcal{S}(\mathsf{sk})$ *and* $\mathcal{U}(\mathsf{pk}, m)$ *execute the protocol honestly then* $\mathcal{S}$ *outputs 1 and the signature* σ *output by* $\mathcal{U}$ *satisfies* $\mathsf{Vrfy}_{\mathsf{pk}}(m, \sigma) = 1$.

The above definition allows the signer to be *stateful*, and this will be the case for our construction. For simplicity, however, we leave the state implicit in our definitions.

Definition 2 (Blindness). *For blind signature scheme* BS = (Gen, $\mathcal{S}$, $\mathcal{U}$, Vrfy) *and an adversary* $\mathcal{A}$, *consider the following experiment:*

1. $\mathcal{A}(1^\kappa)$ *outputs a public key* pk *and a pair of messages* m_0, m_1. *A uniform bit* $b \leftarrow \{0, 1\}$ *is also chosen.*
2. *Run* $\mathcal{A}^{\mathcal{U}(\mathsf{pk}, m_b), \mathcal{U}(\mathsf{pk}, m_{1-b})}(1^\kappa)$, *where* $\mathcal{A}$ *may run one execution with each of its oracles, but may arbitrarily interleave its oracle calls.*
3. *When both executions are completed, let* σ_b, σ_{1-b} *be the (local) outputs of the respective oracles. If* $\sigma_0 = \perp$ *or* $\sigma_1 = \perp$, *then* $\mathcal{A}$ *is given* $\perp$; *otherwise,* $\mathcal{A}$ *is given* σ_0, σ_1. *Finally,* $\mathcal{A}$ *outputs* b'.
4. $\mathcal{A}$ succeeds *iff* $b' = b$.

The advantage *of* $\mathcal{A}$ *is the probability that it succeeds in the above experiment minus* 1/2. *We say* BS *satisfies* blindness *if for all probabilistic polynomial-time* $\mathcal{A}$, *the advantage of* $\mathcal{A}$ *is negligible.*

The above definition allows the malicious signer to use a maliciously generated public key pk. A weaker definition that is often considered in the literature assumes pk is generated honestly using the key-generation algorithm of BS. We refer to the corresponding notion of security as *blindness for honestly generated keys*.

Definition 3 (One-more unforgeability). *Let* $\ell : \mathbb{N} \to \mathbb{N}$. *For blind signature scheme* BS = (Gen, $\mathcal{S}$, $\mathcal{U}$, Vrfy) *and adversary* $\mathcal{A}$, *consider the following experiment:*

1. *Generate keys* $(\mathsf{pk}, \mathsf{sk}) \leftarrow \mathsf{Gen}(1^\kappa)$.
2. *Run* $\mathcal{A}^{\mathcal{S}(\mathsf{sk})}(\mathsf{pk})$, *where* $\mathcal{A}$ *may initiate an arbitrary number of executions with its oracle (arbitrarily interleaving its oracle calls), so long as* $\mathcal{S}$ *completes at most* $\ell = \ell(\kappa)$ *of those executions.*
3. $\mathcal{A}$ *outputs* $\ell + 1$ *message-signature pairs* $(m_1, \sigma_1), \ldots, (m_{\ell+1}, \sigma_{\ell+1})$.
4. $\mathcal{A}$ succeeds *if all* $\{m_i\}$ *are distinct and* $\mathsf{Vrfy}_{\mathsf{pk}}(m_i, \sigma_i) = 1$ *for all* i.

BS *satisfies* ℓ-one-more unforgeability *if for all probabilistic polynomial-time* $\mathcal{A}$, *the probability that* $\mathcal{A}$ *succeeds is negligible.* BS *satisfies* one-more unforgeability *if it is* ℓ*-one-more unforgeable for all polynomial* ℓ.

The above definition allows concurrent executions of the signing protocol. A weaker definition considers only *sequential* executions. (Formally, this would mean that if $\mathcal{A}$ initiates a new session with its oracle $\mathcal{S}(\mathsf{sk})$, then the oracle terminates the currently active session.) We refer to the corresponding notion of security as *sequential (*ℓ*-)one-more unforgeability.*

2.2 Linear Function Families

A *linear function family* [14] is a tuple of probabilistic polynomial-time algorithms $\mathsf{LF} = (\mathsf{PGen}, \mathsf{F}, \Psi)$. The *parameter-generation algorithm* PGen takes as input the security parameter 1^κ and returns parameters par that, in particular, define abelian groups $\mathcal{S}$, $\mathcal{D}$, and $\mathcal{R}$ (written additively), with $|\mathcal{S}|, |\mathcal{R}| \geq 2^{2\kappa}$. (These correspond to a set of "scalars," a "domain," and a "range," respectively). We require the existence of a "scalar multiplication" map $\cdot : \mathcal{S} \times \mathcal{D} \to \mathcal{D}$ such that for all $s \in \mathcal{S}$ and $x, x' \in \mathcal{D}$ we have $s \cdot (x + x') = s \cdot x + r \cdot x'$ and $0 \cdot x = s \cdot 0 = 0$. (We stress that it is *not* necessarily the case that $(s + s') \cdot x = s \cdot x + s' \cdot x$; see further below.) We also require a map $\cdot : \mathcal{S} \times \mathcal{R} \to \mathcal{R}$ with analogous properties. Finally, it should be possible to efficiently sample uniform elements from $\mathcal{S}$ and $\mathcal{D}$.

For concreteness, the reader may want to keep in mind the linear function family where $\mathcal{S} = \mathcal{D} = \mathbb{Z}_q$ and $\mathcal{R}$ is a cyclic group $\mathbb{G}$ of prime order q (written multiplicatively). (Looking ahead to the next section, this is the linear function family that underlies the Schnorr blind signature scheme.) We have scalar multiplication maps $s \cdot x = s \cdot x \pmod{q}$ for $s, x \in \mathbb{Z}_q$ and $s \cdot g = g^s$ for $g \in \mathbb{G}$. We give other examples of linear function families in Appendix A.

The linear *evaluation function* $\mathsf{F} = \mathsf{F}_{\mathsf{par}}$ takes as input a point $x \in \mathcal{D}$ and returns an element $y \in \mathcal{R}$. We require that for all $s \in \mathcal{S}$ and $x, y \in \mathcal{D}$, it holds that $\mathsf{F}(s \cdot x + y) = s \cdot \mathsf{F}(x) + \mathsf{F}(y)$. We also assume that F has has min-entropy at least 2κ, i.e., that the min-entropy of $\mathsf{F}(x)$ is at least 2κ when x is uniform in $\mathcal{D}$. We say LF *has a pseudo torsion-free element in the kernel* if there exists $z^* \in \mathcal{D}$ such that (1) $\mathsf{F}(z^*) = 0$, and (2) for all distinct $s, s' \in \mathcal{S}$, we have $s \cdot z^* \neq s' \cdot z^*$. (Note this implies $z^* \neq 0$.)

Returning to our running example: if par includes a uniformly selected generator $g \in \mathbb{G}$ we can define $\mathsf{F}(x) = g^x$, which is clearly linear. In this example, however, the linear function family does not have a pseudo torsion-free element in the kernel.

The *distributor function* $\Psi = \Psi_{\mathsf{par}}$ takes as input an element $y \in \mathcal{R}$ and points $s, s' \in \mathcal{S}$, and outputs a point in $\mathcal{D}$. For all y in the range of F and $s, s' \in \mathcal{S}$, we require

$$(s + s') \cdot y = s \cdot y + s' \cdot y + \mathsf{F}(\Psi(y, s, s')).$$

Intuitively, the distributor function Ψ outputs a *correction term* that corrects for the fact that the group operation in $\mathcal{S}$ may not distribute over $\mathcal{R}$. (Thus, the distributor function is the zero function whenever the scalar multiplication map does distribute, as in our running example).

We define two security properties for linear function families.

Definition 4 (Preimage resistance). *For a linear function family* LF *and an adversary* $\mathcal{A}$ *consider the following experiment:*

1. *Generate parameters* $\mathsf{par} \leftarrow \mathsf{PGen}(1^\kappa)$ *and choose* $x \leftarrow \mathcal{D}$.
2. *Run* $\mathcal{A}(\mathsf{par}, \mathsf{F}(x))$ *to obtain* $x' \in \mathcal{D}$.
3. $\mathcal{A}$ succeeds *if* $\mathsf{F}(x') = \mathsf{F}(x)$.

LF *is* preimage resistant *if for all probabilistic polynomial-time* $\mathcal{A}$, *the probability that* $\mathcal{A}$ *succeeds is negligible.* LF *is* $(t, \epsilon_{\mathsf{PRE}})$-preimage resistant *if every* $\mathcal{A}$ *running in time at most t succeeds with probability at most* ϵ_{PRE} *in the above experiment.*

Definition 5 (Collision resistance). *For a linear function family* LF *and an adversary* $\mathcal{A}$ *consider the following experiment:*

1. *Generate parameters* $\mathsf{par} \leftarrow \mathsf{PGen}(1^\kappa)$.
2. *Run* $\mathcal{A}(\mathsf{par})$ *to obtain* $x_1, x_2 \in \mathcal{D}$.
3. $\mathcal{A}$ succeeds *if* $\mathsf{F}(x_1) = \mathsf{F}(x_2)$ *and* $x_1 \neq x_2$.

LF *is* collision resistant *if for all probabilistic polynomial-time* $\mathcal{A}$, *the probability that* $\mathcal{A}$ *succeeds is negligible.* LF *is* $(t, \epsilon_{\mathsf{CR}})$-collision resistant *if every* $\mathcal{A}$ *running in time at most t succeeds with probability at most* ϵ_{CR} *in the above experiment.*

The linear function family in our running example is preimage resistant if the discrete-logarithm problem is hard in $\mathbb{G}$, and trivially collision resistant (since F is a bijection).

2.3 Blind Signatures from Linear Function Families

Hauck et al. [14] showed that several blind signature schemes from the literature, including the Schnorr, Okamoto-Schnorr, Fiat-Shamir, and Okamoto-Guillou-Quisquater schemes, can be viewed as being derived from linear function families. We recall their generic construction of a blind signature scheme $\mathsf{BS}[\mathsf{LF}]$ from a linear function family LF. The secret key is a uniform element $\mathsf{sk} \leftarrow \mathcal{D}$ and the corresponding public key is $\mathsf{pk} := \mathsf{F}(\mathsf{sk})$. The signing protocol, where $\mathcal{U}$ holds a message m, proceeds as follows. (See Fig. 1.) In the first step, $\mathcal{S}$ samples $r \leftarrow \mathcal{D}$ and sends $R := \mathsf{F}(r)$ to $\mathcal{U}$. Then $\mathcal{U}$ samples blinding parameters $\alpha \leftarrow \mathcal{D}$ and $\beta \leftarrow \mathcal{S}$ that it uses to compute a "blinded commitment" $R' := R + \mathsf{F}(\alpha) + \beta \cdot \mathsf{pk}$, computes $c' := \mathsf{H}(m, R')$, and sends the blinded challenge $c := c' + \beta$ to $\mathcal{S}$. In the last round of the protocol, $\mathcal{S}$ replies with $s := r + c \cdot \mathsf{sk}$, and $\mathcal{U}$ checks that $\mathsf{F}(s) = R + c \cdot \mathsf{pk}$. (If not, $\mathcal{U}$ aborts). Finally, $\mathcal{U}$ computes $s' := s + \alpha + \Psi(\mathsf{pk}, c, -c')$ and outputs the signature $\sigma := (c', s')$. Verification is done by checking whether $c' = \mathsf{H}(m, \mathsf{F}(s') - c' \cdot \mathsf{pk})$.

If both parties follow the protocol honestly, then

$$s' = s + \alpha + \Psi(\mathsf{pk}, c, -c') = c \cdot \mathsf{sk} + r + \alpha + \Psi(\mathsf{pk}, c, -c').$$

Thus,

$$\begin{aligned}
\mathsf{F}(s') - c' \cdot \mathsf{pk} &= \mathsf{F}(c \cdot \mathsf{sk} + r + \alpha + \Psi(\mathsf{pk}, c, -c')) - c' \cdot \mathsf{pk} \\
&= c \cdot \mathsf{pk} - c' \cdot \mathsf{pk} + \mathsf{F}(\Psi(\mathsf{pk}, c, -c')) + \mathsf{F}(r) + \mathsf{F}(\alpha) \\
&= (c - c') \cdot \mathsf{pk} + \mathsf{F}(r) + \mathsf{F}(\alpha) \\
&= \beta \cdot \mathsf{pk} + R + \mathsf{F}(\alpha) \ = \ R',
\end{aligned}$$

and so verification succeeds. This demonstrates correctness of the scheme.

Hauck et al. [14] show that $\mathsf{BS}[\mathsf{LF}]$ is statistically blind for honestly generated keys. Their proof extends to full blindness (i.e., even for maliciously generated keys) when $\mathsf{BS}[\mathsf{LF}]$ corresponds to the Schnorr or Okamoto-Schnorr blind signature scheme. More interestingly, $\mathsf{BS}[\mathsf{LF}]$ is ℓ-one-more unforgeable for any $\ell = \mathcal{O}(\log \kappa)$:

Theorem 1 ([14]). *Let* $\mathsf{LF} = (\mathsf{PGen}, \mathsf{F}, \Psi)$ *be a collision-resistant linear function family with a torsion-free element in the kernel, and let* H *be modeled as a random oracle. Then* $\mathsf{BS}[\mathsf{LF}]$ *is* ℓ*-one-more unforgeable for any* $\ell = \mathcal{O}(\log \kappa)$.

Concretely, if there is an adversary against ℓ*-one-more unforgeability of* $\mathsf{BS}[\mathsf{LF}]$ *that runs in time* t*, initiates at most* $p \geq \ell$ *executions, makes at most* q_{H} *queries to* H*, and has success probability* ϵ*, then there is an adversary against collision resistance of* LF *running in time* $t' = 2t$ *and having success probability at least*

$$\epsilon' = \Omega\left(\left(\frac{\epsilon}{2} - \frac{(q_{\mathsf{H}} \cdot (p - \ell))^{\ell+1}}{|S|}\right)^3 \cdot \frac{1}{q_{\mathsf{H}}^2 \cdot \ell^3}\right).$$

Theorem 1 requires LF to have a pseudo torsion-free element in the kernel, and thus applies to the Okamoto-Schnorr, Okamoto-Guillou-Quisquater, and Fiat-Shamir blind signature schemes. (See Appendix A.) However, there are examples of other schemes matching the template of Fig. 1 that can be proven secure without relying on Theorem 1. In particular, recent work [10] has shown that the Schnorr blind signature scheme is ℓ-one-more unforgeable for any $\ell = \mathcal{O}(\log \kappa)$ in the algebraic group model under the one-more discrete logarithm assumption.

$\mathcal{S}(\mathsf{sk}, \mathsf{pk})$		$\mathcal{U}(\mathsf{pk}, m)$
$r \leftarrow \mathcal{D}$		
$R := \mathsf{F}(r)$	$\xrightarrow{R}$	$\alpha \leftarrow \mathcal{D};\ \beta \leftarrow \mathcal{S}$
		$R' := R + \mathsf{F}(\alpha) + \beta \cdot \mathsf{pk}$
		$c' := \mathsf{H}(m, R')$
	$\xleftarrow{c}$	$c := c' + \beta$
$s := r + c \cdot \mathsf{sk}$	$\xrightarrow{s}$	
		if $\mathsf{F}(s) \neq R + c \cdot \mathsf{pk}$
		abort
		$s' := s + \alpha + \Psi(\mathsf{pk}, c, -c')$
		$\sigma := (c', s')$
		output σ

Fig. 1. The signing protocol for blind signature scheme $\mathsf{BS[LF]}$, where LF is a linear function family and $\mathsf{H} : \{0,1\}^* \to \mathcal{S}$ is modeled as a random oracle.

3 Boosting Security of Blind Signatures

We now present our cut-and-choose blind signature scheme $\mathsf{CCBS[LF]}$. (We assume the reader has read the informal overview in Sect. 1.2.) As in $\mathsf{BS[LF]}$, the secret key is a uniform element $\mathsf{sk} \leftarrow \mathcal{D}$ and the corresponding public key is $\mathsf{pk} := \mathsf{F}(\mathsf{sk})$. Now, however, the signer $\mathcal{S}$ additionally maintains a counter N that is initialized to 1. The signing protocol for a message m then proceeds as follows (cf. Fig. 2):

1. $\mathcal{S}$ atomically increments its counter (see further discussion below) and sends the updated counter N to the user $\mathcal{U}$.
2. Informally, $\mathcal{U}$ runs N executions of $\mathsf{BS[LF]}$, using the "message" $\mu_i = \mathsf{H}'(m, \varphi_i)$ in the ith execution. (We refer to each execution of the underlying scheme $\mathsf{BS[LF]}$ as a *session*.) Here, $\varphi_i \in \{0,1\}^\kappa$ is a uniform string and H' is modeled as a random oracle. Thus, in the first step, for $i \in [N]$ the user chooses randomness α_i, β_i for the ith session of $\mathsf{BS[LF]}$ and sends a commitment $\mathsf{com}_i = \mathsf{H}'(\alpha_i, \beta_i, \mu_i, \gamma_i)$, where $\gamma_i \in \{0,1\}^\kappa$ is another uniform string.
3. $\mathcal{S}$ runs N sessions of $\mathsf{BS[LF]}$ to obtain initial messages $R_1, \ldots, R_N$, which it sends to $\mathcal{U}$. In response, $\mathcal{U}$ computes $c_1, \ldots, c_N$ using $\mathsf{BS[LF]}$ and the randomness it chose earlier.

4. $\mathcal{S}$ then chooses a uniform index $I \in [N]$ and sends it to $\mathcal{U}$. The user reveals $(\alpha_i, \beta_i, \mu_i, \gamma_i)$ for all $i \neq I$ (thus opening all but its Ith commitment), and $\mathcal{S}$ verifies that $\mathcal{U}$ behaved honestly in all the opened sessions. If cheating is detected, then $\mathcal{S}$ aborts the entire execution.
5. If $\mathcal{U}$ behaved honestly in the opened sessions, $\mathcal{S}$ uses $\mathsf{BS}[\mathsf{LF}]$ to compute a response $s := r_I - c_I \cdot \mathsf{sk}$ for the Ith (unopened) session.
6. $\mathcal{U}$ computes a signature (c'_I, s'_I) on μ_I using $\mathsf{BS}[\mathsf{LF}]$. It then outputs the signature (c'_I, s'_I, φ_I) on m.

A signature $\sigma = (c', s', \varphi)$ on a message m is verified by checking that (c', s') is a valid signature on $\mu = \mathsf{H}'(m, \varphi)$ in the underlying scheme $\mathsf{BS}[\mathsf{LF}]$.

The counter is used to ensure that each execution of the protocol uses a different value for the cut-and-choose parameter N. (In Sect. 3.3, we show that it is possible to do better.) In the concurrent setting, it is therefore important to ensure that the counter is incremented atomically so that this property holds across all the concurrent executions.

Theorem 2. *Let* LF *be a linear function family that is preimage resistant and let* H, H' *be modeled as random oracles. If* $\mathsf{BS}[\mathsf{LF}]$ *satisfies blindness (for honestly generated keys), then* $\mathsf{CCBS}[\mathsf{LF}]$ *satisfies blindness (for honestly generated keys). If* $\mathsf{BS}[\mathsf{LF}]$ *is (sequentially)* ℓ*-one-more unforgeable for any* $\ell \in \mathcal{O}(\log \kappa)$*, then* $\mathsf{CCBS}[\mathsf{LF}]$ *is (sequentially)* ℓ*-one-more unforgeable for any* $\ell = \mathsf{poly}(\kappa)$*.*

We separately consider blindness and one-more unforgeability in the sections that follow.

3.1 Blindness

This section is dedicated to a proof of the following:

Theorem 3. *Let* H' *be modeled as a random oracle. If* $\mathsf{BS}[\mathsf{LF}]$ *satisfies blindness (resp., blindness for honestly generated keys), then* $\mathsf{CCBS}[\mathsf{LF}]$ *satisfies blindness (resp., blindness for honestly generated keys).*

Concretely, if there is an adversary $\mathcal{A}$ *against blindness of* $\mathsf{CCBS}[\mathsf{LF}]$ *that runs in time* t*, makes at most* $q_{\mathsf{H}'}$ *queries to* H'*, uses counters* $N^{\mathsf{L}}, N^{\mathsf{R}}$ *in its executions with the user, and has advantage* ϵ*, then there is an adversary* $\mathcal{B}$ *against blindness of* $\mathsf{BS}[\mathsf{LF}]$ *that runs in time* $t' \approx t$ *and has advantage at least* $\frac{1}{N^{\mathsf{L}} \cdot N^{\mathsf{R}}} \cdot \left(\epsilon - \frac{2 \cdot (N^{\mathsf{L}} + N^{\mathsf{R}}) \cdot q_{\mathsf{H}'}}{2^{2\kappa}}\right)$.

$\mathcal{S}(\mathsf{sk}, \mathsf{pk})$; state N		$\mathcal{U}(\mathsf{pk}, m)$
atomically increment N	$\xrightarrow{N}$	for $i \in [N]$:
		$\alpha_i \leftarrow \mathcal{D}$; $\beta_i \leftarrow \mathcal{S}$
		$\varphi_i, \gamma_i \leftarrow \{0,1\}^\kappa$
		$\mu_i := \mathsf{H}'(m, \varphi_i)$
for $i \in [N]$:	$\xleftarrow{\mathsf{com}_1, \ldots, \mathsf{com}_N}$	$\mathsf{com}_i := \mathsf{H}'(\alpha_i, \beta_i, \mu_i, \gamma_i)$
$r_i \leftarrow \mathcal{D}$		
$R_i := \mathsf{F}(r_i)$	$\xrightarrow{R_1, \ldots, R_N}$	for $i \in [N]$:
		$R'_i := R_i + \mathsf{F}(\alpha_i) + \beta_i \cdot \mathsf{pk}$
		$c'_i := \mathsf{H}(\mu_i, R'_i)$
	$\xleftarrow{c_1, \ldots, c_N}$	$c_i := c'_i + \beta_i$
$I \leftarrow [N]$	$\xrightarrow{I}$	
	$\xleftarrow{\{(\alpha_i, \beta_i, \mu_i, \gamma_i)\}_{i \neq I}}$	
for $i \in [N] \setminus \{I\}$:		
$R'_i := R_i + \mathsf{F}(\alpha_i) + \beta_i \cdot \mathsf{pk}$		
if $\exists i \in [N] \setminus \{I\}$ s.t		
$\mathsf{com}_i \neq \mathsf{H}'(\alpha_i, \beta_i, \mu_i, \gamma_i)$		
or $c_i \neq \mathsf{H}(\mu_i, R'_i) + \beta_i$		
abort		
$s_I := r_I + c_I \cdot \mathsf{sk}$	$\xrightarrow{s_I}$	if $\mathsf{F}(s_I) \neq R_I + c_I \cdot \mathsf{pk}$
		abort
		$s'_I := s_I + \alpha_I + \Psi(\mathsf{pk}, c_I, -c'_I)$
		$\sigma := (c'_I, s'_I, \varphi_I)$
		output σ

Fig. 2. The signing protocol for blind signature scheme $\mathsf{CCBS}[\mathsf{LF}]$, where LF is a linear function family and $\mathsf{H} : \{0,1\}^* \to \mathcal{S}$, $\mathsf{H}' : \{0,1\}^* \to \{0,1\}^{2\kappa}$ are modeled as random oracles.

Proof. We consider the case of blindness for maliciously generated keys, but the proof holds also for honestly generated keys. Fix an adversary $\mathcal{A}$ attacking blindness of $\mathsf{CCBS}[\mathsf{LF}]$, let $\mathsf{Succ}_\mathcal{A}$ be the event that $\mathcal{A}$ succeeds, and let $\epsilon = \epsilon(\kappa)$ be the advantage of $\mathcal{A}$ so that $\Pr[\mathsf{Succ}_\mathcal{A}] = \frac{1}{2} + \epsilon$. In an execution of the experiment used to define blindness of $\mathsf{CCBS}[\mathsf{LF}]$, the adversary interacts with two instances of $\mathcal{U}$; we use superscripts L, R to denote variables used in the left and right interactions, respectively. Let $N^{\mathsf{L}}, N^{\mathsf{R}}$ be the values of the counters that $\mathcal{A}$ sends in its two interactions with $\mathcal{U}$, and let Bad be the event that $\mathcal{A}$ makes any H'-queries of the following form:

- $\mathsf{H}'(\star, \varphi_i^{\mathsf{L}})$ for $i = 1, \ldots, N^{\mathsf{L}}$ (resp., $\mathsf{H}'(\star, \varphi_i^{\mathsf{R}})$ for $i = 1, \ldots, N^{\mathsf{R}}$). (In the case of $\varphi_{I^{\mathsf{L}}}^{\mathsf{L}}, \varphi_{I^{\mathsf{R}}}^{\mathsf{R}}$, this must occur *before* those values are revealed to $\mathcal{A}$ as part of the signatures output by $\mathcal{U}$.)
- $\mathsf{H}'(\star, \star, \star, \gamma_i^{\mathsf{L}})$ for $i = 1, \ldots, N^{\mathsf{L}}$ (resp., $\mathsf{H}'(\star, \star, \star, \gamma_i^{\mathsf{R}})$ for $i = 1, \ldots, N^{\mathsf{R}}$) *before* γ_i^{L} (resp., γ_i^{R}) is sent by $\mathcal{U}$ to $\mathcal{A}$ in round 6.

In particular, since $\gamma_{I^{\mathsf{L}}}^{\mathsf{L}}$ (resp., $\gamma_{I^{\mathsf{R}}}^{\mathsf{R}}$) is not sent in round 6, event Bad occurs if $\mathcal{A}$ makes a query of the form $\mathsf{H}'(\star, \star, \star, \gamma_{I^{\mathsf{L}}}^{\mathsf{L}})$ (resp., $\mathsf{H}'(\star, \star, \star, \gamma_{I^{\mathsf{R}}}^{\mathsf{R}})$) at any point during the experiment. If $q_{\mathsf{H}'}$ denotes the number of queries $\mathcal{A}$ makes to H', it is immediate that

$$\Pr[\mathsf{Succ}_{\mathcal{A}} \wedge \overline{\mathsf{Bad}}] \geq \frac{1}{2} + \epsilon - \frac{2 \cdot (N^{\mathsf{L}} + N^{\mathsf{R}}) \cdot q_{\mathsf{H}'}}{2^{2\kappa}}.$$

We now construct an adversary $\mathcal{B}$ attacking blindness of $\mathsf{BS}[\mathsf{LF}]$. Intuitively, $\mathcal{B}$ simulates $\mathcal{A}$'s oracle calls by locally running all-but-one of the sessions of $\mathsf{BS}[\mathsf{LF}]$ honestly, and using its own oracles (which correspond to two executions of the user algorithm for $\mathsf{BS}[\mathsf{LF}]$) to simulate the remaining instance. $\mathcal{B}$ works as follows:

1. Throughout, H'-oracle calls made by $\mathcal{A}$ are handled in the natural way.[4] If event Bad occurs, $\mathcal{B}$ aborts and outputs a uniform bit.
2. $\mathcal{B}$ runs $\mathcal{A}$ to obtain pk, m_0, m_1. It then chooses uniform $\mu_0, \mu_1 \in \{0,1\}^\kappa$ and outputs $\mathsf{pk}, \mu_0, \mu_1$.
3. $\mathcal{B}$ handles the interaction of $\mathcal{A}$ with its left oracle by playing the role of $\mathcal{U}$ in an execution of $\mathsf{CCBS}[\mathsf{LF}]$, as follows:
   (a) When $\mathcal{A}$ sends N^{L}, choose uniform $i^{\mathsf{L}} \in [N^{\mathsf{L}}]$ and uniform values $\gamma_{i^{\mathsf{L}}}^{\mathsf{L}}, \varphi_{i^{\mathsf{L}}}^{\mathsf{L}}, \mathsf{com}_{i^{\mathsf{L}}}^{\mathsf{L}} \in \{0,1\}^\kappa$. For $i \in [N^{\mathsf{L}}] \setminus \{i^{\mathsf{L}}\}$, run $\mathcal{U}$ honestly to obtain $\mathsf{com}_i^{\mathsf{L}}$. Send $\mathsf{com}_1^{\mathsf{L}}, \ldots, \mathsf{com}_{N^{\mathsf{L}}}^{\mathsf{L}}$ to $\mathcal{A}$.
   (b) When $\mathcal{A}$ sends $R_1^{\mathsf{L}}, \ldots, R_{N^{\mathsf{L}}}^{\mathsf{L}}$, then $\mathcal{B}$ forwards $R_{i^{\mathsf{L}}}^{\mathsf{L}}$ to its own left oracle to receive response $c_{i^{\mathsf{L}}}^{\mathsf{L}}$. For $i \in [N^{\mathsf{L}}] \setminus \{i^{\mathsf{L}}\}$, it runs $\mathcal{U}$ honestly to obtain c_i^{L}, and then sends $c_1^{\mathsf{L}}, \ldots, c_{N^{\mathsf{L}}}^{\mathsf{L}}$ to $\mathcal{A}$.
   (c) When $\mathcal{A}$ sends I^{L}, then $\mathcal{B}$ aborts and outputs a uniform bit if $I^{\mathsf{L}} \neq i^{\mathsf{L}}$. Otherwise, it responds in the natural way.
   (d) When $\mathcal{A}$ sends the final message $s_{I^{\mathsf{L}}}^{\mathsf{L}}$, then $\mathcal{B}$ forwards this to its own left oracle.

   $\mathcal{B}$ handles the interaction of $\mathcal{A}$ with its right oracle in an exactly analogous manner.

---

[4] We do not need to model H as a random oracle; our proof holds as long as $\mathsf{BS}[\mathsf{LF}]$ is secure when using H. For this reason we do not mention how calls to H are handled.

4. When $\mathcal{B}$ is given the output of its own oracles, it does the following. If the output was $\bot$, it gives $\bot$ to $\mathcal{A}$. Otherwise, $\mathcal{B}$ is given signature (c'_0, s'_0) on μ_0 and signature (c'_1, s'_1) on μ_1; it gives $(c'_0, s'_0, \varphi^{\mathsf{L}}_{i^{\mathsf{L}}})$ and $(c'_1, s'_1, \varphi^{\mathsf{R}}_{i^{\mathsf{R}}})$ to $\mathcal{A}$ and programs $\mathsf{H}'(m_0, \varphi^{\mathsf{L}}_{i^{\mathsf{L}}}) = \mu_0$ and $\mathsf{H}'(m_1, \varphi^{\mathsf{R}}_{i^{\mathsf{R}}}) = \mu_1$. Finally, it outputs whatever bit is output by $\mathcal{A}$.

First observe that the probability of event Bad is unchanged in the above. Let Guess be the event that $I^{\mathsf{L}} = i^{\mathsf{L}}$ and $I^{\mathsf{R}} = i^{\mathsf{R}}$. If Bad does not occur by the time $\mathcal{A}$ sends the latter of I^{L} or I^{R}, then the view of $\mathcal{A}$ at that point is independent of $i^{\mathsf{L}}, i^{\mathsf{R}}$ and so $\Pr[\mathsf{Guess}] = 1/N^L N^{\mathsf{R}}$. Furthermore, if Guess occurs and Bad does not occur then the simulation provided by $\mathcal{B}$ is perfect, and $\mathcal{B}$ succeeds iff $\mathcal{A}$ succeeds. Letting $\mathsf{Succ}_{\mathcal{B}}$ be the event that $\mathcal{B}$ succeeds, we thus have

$$\begin{aligned}\Pr[\mathsf{Succ}_{\mathcal{B}}] &= \frac{1}{2} \cdot \Pr[\overline{\mathsf{Guess}} \vee \mathsf{Bad}] + \Pr[\mathsf{Succ}_{\mathcal{A}} \wedge \mathsf{Guess} \wedge \overline{\mathsf{Bad}}] \\ &\geq \frac{1}{2} + \frac{1}{N^{\mathsf{L}} \cdot N^{\mathsf{R}}} \cdot \left(\epsilon - \frac{2 \cdot (N^{\mathsf{L}} + N^{\mathsf{R}}) \cdot q_{\mathsf{H}'}}{2^{2\kappa}}\right).\end{aligned}$$

Since the advantage of $\mathcal{B}$ must be negligible (by blindness of $\mathsf{BS}[\mathsf{LF}]$), and $N^{\mathsf{L}}, N^{\mathsf{R}}, q_{\mathsf{H}'}$ are polynomial,[5] we conclude that ϵ must be negligible.

3.2 One-More Unforgeability

In this section we show:

Theorem 4. *Let* LF *be a linear function family that is preimage resistant and let* H, H' *be modeled as random oracles. If* $\mathsf{BS}[\mathsf{LF}]$ *is (sequentially)* ℓ*-one-more unforgeable for any* $\ell \in \mathcal{O}(\log \kappa)$*, then* $\mathsf{CCBS}[\mathsf{LF}]$ *is (sequentially)* ℓ*-one-more unforgeable for any* $\ell = \mathsf{poly}(\kappa)$.

Concretely, assume LF *is* $(t, \epsilon_{\mathsf{PRE}})$*-preimage resistant and there is an adversary against (sequential)* ℓ*-one-more unforgeability of* $\mathsf{CCBS}[\mathsf{LF}]$ *that runs in time* t*, initiates* p *executions, makes at most* q_{H} *queries to* H *and* $q_{\mathsf{H}'}$ *queries to* H'*, and has success probability* ϵ*. Then there is an adversary against (sequential)* λ*-one-more unforgeability of* $\mathsf{BS}[\mathsf{LF}]$*, where* $\lambda = 3\ln(p+1) + \ln(2/\epsilon)$*, that runs in time* $t' \approx t$*, initiates* p *executions, makes at most* q_{H} *queries to* H*, and has success probability at least*

$$\epsilon' = \frac{\epsilon}{2} - \frac{q_{\mathsf{H}'}^2 + p \cdot q_{\mathsf{H}'} + p^2 \cdot (p^2 + q_{\mathsf{H}})}{2^{2\kappa}} - p \cdot \epsilon_{\mathsf{PRE}}.$$

[5] Technically, we can enforce that $N^{\mathsf{L}}, N^{\mathsf{R}}$ are polynomial by requiring the counter N sent by $\mathcal{S}$ to be represented in unary (so $N^{\mathsf{L}}, N^{\mathsf{R}}$ are bounded by the running time of $\mathcal{A}$). In practice one might fix a large polynomial bound B and require $N \leq B$.

Proof. Let $\mathcal{A}$ be an adversary attacking the one-more unforgeability of $\mathsf{CCBS}[\mathsf{LF}]$ and having success probability ϵ. We let $q_{\mathsf{H}}, q_{\mathsf{H}'}$ denote the number of queries $\mathcal{A}$ makes to H, H', respectively, let ℓ denote the number of complete executions of the signing protocol run by $\mathcal{A}$, and let p denote the total number of executions of the signing protocol by $\mathcal{A}$, including ones that are aborted early by $\mathcal{S}$. (These are all polynomial in the security parameter, but we leave this dependence implicit.) For simplicity, we make some assumptions about the behavior of $\mathcal{A}$ that are without significant loss of generality; specifically, we assume that if $\mathcal{A}$ sends $\alpha_i, \beta_i, \mu_i, \gamma_i$ during an execution of the signing protocol where the corresponding message from the signer was R_i then it had previously queried $\mathsf{H}'(\alpha_i, \beta_i, \mu_i, \gamma_i)$ as well as $\mathsf{H}(\mu_i, R_i + \mathsf{F}(\alpha_i) + \beta_i \cdot \mathsf{pk})$, and that if $\mathcal{A}$ outputs a message/signature pair $(m, (c', s', \varphi))$ then it had previously queried $\mathsf{H}'(m, \varphi)$.

We prove the theorem via a sequence of hybrid experiments.

Expt G_0. This is the one-more unforgeability experiment where $\mathcal{A}$ interacts with the transformed scheme $\mathsf{CCBS}[\mathsf{LF}]$.

When $\mathcal{A}$ sends a commitment com as part of the second message of an execution of the signing protocol, we say com is *extractable* if it was previously returned as output from a query of the form $\mathsf{H}'(\alpha, \beta, \mu, \gamma)$.

Expt G_1. This experiment is identical to G_0 except that it aborts (and $\mathcal{A}$ does not succeed) if (1) at any point in the experiment, there is a collision in H' or (2) in some execution of the signing protocol, some commitment com_i sent by $\mathcal{A}$ is not extractable, but later in the same execution $I \neq i$ and the signer does not abort (so, in particular, $\mathcal{A}$ sends $\alpha_i, \beta_i, \mu_i, \gamma_i$ for which $\mathsf{H}'(\alpha_i, \beta_i, \mu_i, \gamma_i) = \mathsf{com}_i$). The probability of the first event is at most $q_{\mathsf{H}'}^2/2^{2\kappa}$. Focusing on the least $i \neq I$ in each execution of the signing protocol for which com_i is not extractable (if one exists), we see that the probability of the second event is at most $p \cdot q_{\mathsf{H}'}/2^{2\kappa}$. Hence, $\mathcal{A}$'s success probability in G_1 is at least $\epsilon - (q_{\mathsf{H}'}^2 + p \cdot q_{\mathsf{H}'})/2^{2\kappa}$.

Note that in G_1 and all subsequent experiments, as long as the experiment is not aborted, any extractable commitment com was previously returned as output from a *unique* query of the form $\mathsf{H}'(\alpha, \beta, \mu, \gamma)$. We say that α, β, μ are *associated with* com in that case.

In an execution of the signing protocol, we say $\mathcal{A}$ *successfully cheats* if the signer does not abort the execution (nor does the experiment itself abort), yet either (1) some commitment sent by $\mathcal{A}$ in that execution was not extractable or (2) for some i, the commitment com_i sent in that execution was extractable with associated values α_i, β_i, μ_i, but $c_i \neq \mathsf{H}(\mu_i, R_i + \mathsf{F}(\alpha_i) + \beta_i \cdot \mathsf{pk})$ (where R_i is the value sent by the signer in the corresponding session). In G_1, the only way $\mathcal{A}$ can successfully cheat in some execution is if $\mathcal{A}$ sends a *single* non-extractable commitment com_i and/or a single incorrect c_i in that execution, and the challenge I sent by the signer is equal to i. For an integer N, we let cheat_N be the indicator variable that is equal to 1 iff $\mathcal{A}$ successfully cheats in the (unique) execution of the signing protocol that uses cut-and-choose parameter N.

Let $\mathsf{cheat}^* = \sum_{N=2}^{p+1} \mathsf{cheat}_N$ be the number of times $\mathcal{A}$ successfully cheats in the entire experiment. By the observation made a moment ago, we have $\mathbb{E}[\mathsf{cheat}_N] \le 1/N$ for all N, and so

$$\mathbb{E}[\mathsf{cheat}^*] \le \sum_{N=2}^{p+1} \frac{1}{N} \le \ln(p+1).$$

Expt G_2. This experiment is identical to G_1 except that it aborts (and $\mathcal{A}$ does not succeed) if $\mathsf{cheat}^* > 3\ln(p+1) + \ln(2/\epsilon)$. As the cheat_N are (dominated by) independent Bernoulli variables, and cheat^* is their sum, we can apply the Chernoff bound to conclude that

$$\Pr[\mathsf{cheat}^* > 3\ln(p+1) + \ln(2/\epsilon)] \le \epsilon/2.$$

(We defer the full calculation to Appendix B). Hence, $\mathcal{A}$'s success probability in G_2 is at least $\epsilon/2 - (q_{\mathsf{H}'}^2 + p \cdot q_{\mathsf{H}'})/2^{2\kappa}$.

Expt G_3. Here, we change the way each execution of the signing protocol is run. Now, for each execution of the signing protocol—say, using cut-and-choose parameter N—first choose uniform $j \in [N]$. Then:

- For $i \in [N]$, if com_i is not extractable then compute R_i (and s_i, if needed) as before. Set $C_i := \perp$. (The purpose of C_i will be clear later.)
- For $i \in [N] \setminus \{j\}$, if com_i is extractable with associated values α_i, β_i, μ_i, then compute R_i as before and set $R_i' := R_i + \mathsf{F}(\alpha_i) + \beta_i \cdot \mathsf{pk}$. If $\mathsf{H}(\mu_i, R_i')$ is already defined (before R_i is sent to $\mathcal{A}$), the experiment aborts and $\mathcal{A}$ does not succeed. Otherwise, set $\mathsf{H}(\mu_i, R_i')$ to a uniform value and set $C_i := \mathsf{H}(\mu_i, R_i') + \beta_i$. Compute s_i (if needed) as before.
- If com_j is extractable with associated values α_j, β_j, μ_j, we refer to j as a *programmed session.* In this case, choose $r_j \leftarrow \mathcal{D}$ and $C_j \leftarrow \mathcal{S}$, compute $R_j := \mathsf{F}(r_j) + C_j \cdot (-\mathsf{pk})$ and $R_j' := R_j + \mathsf{F}(\alpha_j) + \beta_j \cdot \mathsf{pk}$, and program $\mathsf{H}(\mu_j, R_j') := C_j - \beta_j$. (This programming is done before R_j is sent to $\mathcal{A}$.) If $\mathsf{H}(\mu_j, R_j')$ is already defined, the experiment aborts (and $\mathcal{A}$ does not succeed). Later in the execution, if $I = j$ and neither the execution nor the experiment is aborted, compute and send $s_j := r_j + C_j \cdot (-\mathsf{sk}) + c_j \cdot \mathsf{sk}$, where c_j is the corresponding value sent by $\mathcal{A}$.

Ignoring for a moment the aborts introduced in this experiment, we claim that the view of the adversary in each execution of the signing protocol is identical to its view in G_2. This is immediate for all but a programmed session. But it can be verified that in a programmed session j, the joint distribution of s_j and R_j is identical to the distribution of those values in G_2. Moreover, C_j is uniform even conditioned on s_j, R_j, and so $\mathsf{H}(\mu_j, R_j')$ is programmed to be a uniform value. The latter can be seen as follows. As long as c_j has not been sent by $\mathcal{A}$, R_j is uniform, and hence so is C_j. After c_j is sent by $\mathcal{A}$, s_j and c_j together fully determine R_j as $R_j = \mathsf{F}(s_j) - c_j \cdot \mathsf{pk}$. Hence, for all values of c_j, conditioning on

s_j, R_j is the same as conditioning on only s_j. Since $s_j = r_j + C_j \cdot (-\mathsf{sk}) + c_j \cdot \mathsf{sk}$ and r_j is a uniform value, C_j is also uniform.

As for the aborts introduced in G_3, note that whenever the experiment checks whether $\mathsf{H}(\mu, R')$ is already defined it is the case that R' has min-entropy at least 2κ. (This follows because $R = \mathsf{F}(r)$ for uniform r and F has min-entropy at least 2κ.) Thus, the probability that G_3 aborts where G_2 would not is at most $p^2 \cdot (p^2 + q_{\mathsf{H}})/2^{2\kappa}$. We conclude that $\mathcal{A}$ succeeds in G_3 with probability at least $\epsilon/2 - (q_{\mathsf{H}'}^2 + p \cdot q_{\mathsf{H}'} + p^2 \cdot (p^2 + q_{\mathsf{H}}))/2^{2\kappa}$.

Expt G_4. Here, we again change each execution of the signing protocol. Consider an execution with cut-and-choose parameter N, and let $j, \{C_i\}_{i\in[N]}$ be as in the previous experiment. After $\mathcal{A}$ sends $c_1, \ldots, c_N$, if it holds that $(c_1, \ldots, c_n) = (C_1, \ldots, C_n)$ then set $I := j$; otherwise, set $I := j + 1 \pmod N$. The rest of the execution is as in G_3.

We claim that $\mathcal{A}$'s view in G_4 is identically distributed to its view in G_3, and hence its success probability is unchanged. Indeed, in any particular execution of the protocol, the value of j is independent of both the view of $\mathcal{A}$ before I is sent as well as the $\{C_i\}_{i\in[N]}$. Thus, regardless of whether $(c_1, \ldots, c_n)$ is equal to $(C_1, \ldots, C_n)$ or not, I is uniformly distributed in $[N]$ in experiment G_4 just as in experiment G_3.

In an execution of the signing protocol, we say the programmed session is *completed* if $I = j$ and the signer does not abort during the remainder of the execution of the signing protocol. Note that when the programmed session is completed, $c_j = C_j$ and hence

$$s_I = s_j = r_j + C_j \cdot (-\mathsf{sk}) + c_j \cdot \mathsf{sk} = r_j = r_I.$$

Thus, the only time sk is needed when executing the signing protocol in G_4 is when $\mathcal{A}$ successfully cheats, in which case the programmed session is not completed.

For a valid message/signature pair $(m, \sigma) = (m, (c', s', \varphi))$ output by $\mathcal{A}$, let $R' = \mathsf{F}(s') - c' \cdot \mathsf{pk}$ and $\mu = \mathsf{H}'(m, \varphi)$; we say this message/signature pair is *fake* if there is a programmed session in which H was programmed at the point (μ, R') and, if so, we associate (m, σ) with the unique such session. (There cannot be more than one programmed session where H' is programmed at the same point, or else the experiment aborts.) A fake message/signature pair can thus be associated with a particular commitment com_j having associated values $\alpha_j, \beta_j, \mu_j = \mu$ (recall that a session is only programmed if the corresponding commitment is extractable), as well as values r_j, R_j, C_j defined by the experiment. Since (c', s', φ) is a valid signature on m, we have $c' = \mathsf{H}(\mu, R')$; we also have $\mathsf{H}(\mu, R') = C_j - \beta_j$ (by definition of how programming is done) and thus $\beta_j = C_j - c'$. Therefore

$$\begin{aligned}
\mathsf{F}(s') &= R' + c' \cdot \mathsf{pk} \\
&= R_j + \mathsf{F}(\alpha_j) + \beta_j \cdot \mathsf{pk} + c' \cdot \mathsf{pk} \\
&= R_j + C_j \cdot (-\mathsf{pk}) + \mathsf{F}(\alpha_j) + (C_j - c') \cdot \mathsf{pk} + c' \cdot \mathsf{pk} \\
&= R_j + C_j \cdot (-\mathsf{pk}) + \mathsf{F}(\alpha_j) \\
&\quad + C_j \cdot \mathsf{pk} - c' \cdot \mathsf{pk} + \mathsf{F}(\Psi(\mathsf{pk}, C_j, -c')) + c' \cdot \mathsf{pk} \\
&= R_j + C_j \cdot (-\mathsf{pk}) + \mathsf{F}(\alpha_j) + C_j \cdot \mathsf{pk} + \mathsf{F}(\Psi(\mathsf{pk}, C_j, -c')) \\
&= R_j + \mathsf{F}(\alpha_j) + \mathsf{F}(\Psi(\mathsf{pk}, C_j, -c')),
\end{aligned}$$

and so

$$\mathsf{F}(s' - \alpha_j - \Psi(\mathsf{pk}, C_j, -c')) = R_j. \tag{1}$$

There is at most one fake message/signature pair associated with any programmed session (since the distinct $\{m_i\}$ in $\mathcal{A}$'s output correspond to distinct $\{\mu_i = \mathsf{H}'(m_i, \varphi_i)\}$ or else the experiment aborts), and so the number of fake pairs is at most the number of programmed sessions.

Expt G_5**.** Experiment G_5 aborts (and $\mathcal{A}$ does not succeed) if the number F of fake pairs exceeds the number of *completed*, programmed sessions. Before we bound the probability of this event, note that the number of completed, programmed sessions is at most $\ell - \mathsf{cheat}^*$; therefore, if F is at most the number of completed, programmed sessions, then if $\mathcal{A}$ succeeds the number of valid message/signature pairs that are *not* fake is

$$(\ell + 1) - F \geq (\ell + 1) - (\ell - \mathsf{cheat}^*) = \mathsf{cheat}^* + 1.$$

Claim. The probability (in G_4) that $\mathcal{A}$ succeeds and the number of fake message/signature pairs exceeds the number of completed, programmed sessions is at most $p \cdot \epsilon_{\mathsf{PRE}}$.

Proof. Let E be the event that $\mathcal{A}$ succeeds and the number of fake message/signature pairs exceeds the number of completed, programmed sessions. We construct an adversary $\mathcal{C}$ attacking preimage resistance of LF that succeeds with probability at least $\Pr[E]/p$. The claim follows.

$\mathcal{C}$ is given parameters par and a challenge $R \in \mathcal{R}$. It honestly generates $(\mathsf{pk}, \mathsf{sk})$ and runs experiment G_5 with $\mathcal{A}$ with the following exception:

- For a uniformly chosen execution of the signing protocol (say, the kth execution), $\mathcal{C}$ sets $R_j := R + C_j \cdot (-\mathsf{pk})$ in the programmed session of that execution. If in that execution, $I = j$ and s_j must be sent to the adversary (so the programmed session is to be completed), $\mathcal{C}$ aborts.

Note that when $\mathcal{C}$ does not abort, $\mathcal{C}$ never needs to use a preimage of R. At the end of the experiment, $\mathcal{C}$ aborts if E has not occurred. If E has occurred, $\mathcal{C}$ finds the first fake message/signature pair $(m, (c', s', \varphi))$ associated with a non-completed, programmed session and aborts if that pair is not associated with the programmed session in execution k. If $\mathcal{C}$ has not aborted, $\mathcal{C}$ has values

α_j, C_j, used as part of the programmed session in execution k, such that $s' - \alpha - \Psi(\mathsf{pk}, C, -c')$ is a preimage of R (using Eq. (1)). The probability that $\mathcal{C}$ does not abort is precisely $\Pr[E]/p$.

Using the above claim, we see that $\mathcal{A}$ succeeds in G_5 with probability at least $\epsilon/2 - (q_{\mathsf{H}'}^2 + p \cdot q_{\mathsf{H}'} + p^2 \cdot (p^2 + q_{\mathsf{H}}))/2^{2\kappa} - p \cdot \epsilon_{\mathsf{PRE}}$.

Bounding $\mathcal{A}$'s success probability in G_5. To conclude the proof, we show that the success probability of $\mathcal{A}$ in G_5 is negligible. We do so by defining an adversary $\mathcal{B}$ that runs $\mathcal{A}$ as a subroutine and attacks the λ-one-more unforgeability of $\mathsf{BS}[\mathsf{LF}]$, where $\lambda = 3\ln(p+1) + \ln(2/\epsilon)$. Adversary $\mathcal{B}$ works as follows:

1. $\mathcal{B}$ is given a public key pk as well as access to a signing oracle for $\mathsf{BS}[\mathsf{LF}]$ and an oracle H. It runs $\mathcal{A}$ on pk, and simulates experiment G_5 for $\mathcal{A}$ as described below. Queries that $\mathcal{A}$ makes to H' are answered by $\mathcal{B}$ with uniform values in the natural way. Queries that $\mathcal{A}$ makes to H are in general answered by simply relaying those queries to $\mathcal{B}$'s oracle H, except that in programmed sessions $\mathcal{B}$ programs H to a different value (as described in G_3).
2. $\mathcal{B}$ simulates an execution of the signing protocol for $\mathcal{A}$ using cut-and-choose parameter N as follows. $\mathcal{B}$ selects a uniform $j \leftarrow [N]$ and initiates an interaction with its signing oracle for $\mathsf{BS}[\mathsf{LF}]$. Let R^* be the value that $\mathcal{B}$ receives from its signing oracle in the first round. When $\mathcal{A}$ sends $\mathsf{com}_1, \ldots, \mathsf{com}_N$, then:
   - $\mathcal{B}$ sets $R_{j+1} := R^*$ and generates the remaining $\{R_i\}_{i \neq j+1}$ as in G_5. It then sends these values to $\mathcal{A}$.
   - $\mathcal{B}$ then continues to run the signing protocol as in G_5. If $I = j+1$ and $\mathcal{B}$ needs to send s_I (i.e., neither the current execution of the signing protocol nor the experiment itself is aborted) then $\mathcal{B}$ forwards c_I to its signing oracle for $\mathsf{BS}[\mathsf{LF}]$, and returns the response s^* to $\mathcal{A}$.
3. At the end of the experiment, if $\mathcal{A}$ outputs $\ell + 1$ valid message/signature pairs $(m, (c', s', \varphi))$ (where validity is determined relative to $\mathsf{CCBS}[\mathsf{LF}]$ and the oracles H, H' that $\mathcal{B}$ simulated for $\mathcal{A}$), then $\mathcal{B}$ aborts if the number of fake message/signature pairs exceeds the number of completed, programmed sessions. Assuming it has not aborted, $\mathcal{B}$ identifies $\mathsf{cheat}^* + 1$ valid message/signature pairs that are not fake, and for each such pair $(m, (c', s', \varphi))$ outputs $(\mathsf{H}'(m, \varphi), (c', s'))$.

The simulation provided by $\mathcal{B}$ is perfect, and thus the probability that $\mathcal{A}$ succeeds when run by $\mathcal{B}$ is exactly the probability that $\mathcal{A}$ succeeds in G_5. The number of executions of the signing protocol that $\mathcal{B}$ initiates with $\mathsf{BS}[\mathsf{LF}]$ is p, while the number that $\mathcal{B}$ completes is exactly cheat^* and so is at most $3\ln(p+1) + \ln(2/\epsilon)$. Finally, whenever $\mathcal{A}$ succeeds then for any message/signature pair $(m, (c', s', \varphi))$ output by $\mathcal{A}$ that is not fake, the message/signature pair $(\mathsf{H}'(m, \varphi), (c', s'))$ output by $\mathcal{B}$ is a valid message/signature pair relative to $\mathsf{BS}[\mathsf{LF}]$ and the oracle H provided to $\mathcal{B}$; additionally, the messages $\mathsf{H}'(m, \varphi)$ are distinct since no collisions were found in H'. We conclude that the success probability of $\mathcal{B}$ is equal to the success probability of $\mathcal{A}$ in G_5, which is negligible since $\mathsf{BS}[\mathsf{LF}]$ is secure. This completes the proof of the theorem.

3.3 Improving the Complexity of the Signing Protocol

The complexity of the signing protocol is linear in the cut-and-choose parameter N, and it is therefore important to minimize that parameter. In the scheme analyzed thus far, N is incremented each time the signing protocol is executed. Here, we argue that it suffices to increment the cut-and-choose parameter *only when cheating is detected.* Not only is this strictly better in theory (assuming at least some interactions are with honest users), but we expect that this optimization would have a significant impact on efficiency in practice where (1) the signer would likely know the identity of each user executing the protocol, and could ban any user the first time they are caught cheating, and (2) we expect that a majority of users are honest.

The discussion that follows assumes familiarity with the high-level overview from Sect. 1.2 and/or the proof of one-more unforgeability from the previous section. We focus our treatment on the sequential setting, and briefly discuss at the end how it can be extended to handle concurrent executions of the protocol.

Recall that in an execution of the signing protocol of our transformed scheme, we say the adversary *successfully cheats* if it cheats in a single session and is not caught by the signer. In a given execution using cut-and-choose parameter N, the adversary successfully cheats with probability at most $1/N$. For the proof of one-more unforgeability, it is crucial that (over the course of the entire experiment) the adversary successfully cheats at most logarithmically many times, except with negligible probability.

Let cheat_N be a random variable denoting the number of times, over the course of the entire one-more unforgeability experiment, the adversary successfully cheats when the cut-and-choose parameter is N. In the scheme analyzed thus far, each value of the cut-and-choose parameter is used only once and so $\mathbb{E}[\mathsf{cheat}_N] \leq 1/N$. Thus, assuming the attacker runs p executions of the signing protocol overall, the expected number of times the attacker successfully cheats is

$$\sum_{N=2}^{p+1} \mathbb{E}[\mathsf{cheat}_N] \leq \sum_{N=2}^{p+1} \frac{1}{N} \leq \ln(p+1).$$

Consider now what happens if we modify our scheme so that the counter is only incremented when cheating is detected. (We also assume for simplicity that the attacker cheats in exactly one session each time it runs the protocol; it is clear that this maximizes the number of times it can successfully cheat.) Then cheat_N is equal to the number of times the attacker successfully cheats (when the cut-and-choose parameter is N) before being caught. This is one less than the number of trials (when the cut-and-choose parameter is N) until the adversary is caught. (Recall that here we are assuming sequential executions of the signing protocol only.) Since the probability of being caught in each such trial is $(N-1)/N$, we now have

$$\mathbb{E}[\mathsf{cheat}_N] = \frac{N}{N-1} - 1 = \frac{1}{N-1},$$

and so if the attacker runs p executions of the signing protocol overall, the expected number of times the attacker successfully cheats is at most

$$\sum_{N=2}^{p+1} \mathbb{E}[\mathsf{cheat}_N] = \sum_{N=2}^{p+1} \frac{1}{N-1} \leq 1 + \ln p.$$

Proceeding as in[6] the proof of Theorem 4, we can show that the adversary successfully cheats at most logarithmically many times, except with negligible probability.

Handling concurrent executions. The optimization described above does not work when there may be concurrent executions of the signing protocol. (To see what goes wrong, consider the case where the adversary runs p parallel executions, all using cut-and-choose parameter $N = 2$. Then the adversary successfully cheats in roughly half those executions before the signer detects cheating and has any chance to increment the counter.) For the argument outlined above to work, the key property we need to ensure is that the adversary can successfully cheat *at most once* for each value of the cut-and-choose parameter. To enforce this, the signer just needs to make sure that any currently active executions of the signing protocol use distinct values of the cut-and-choose parameter; moreover, once cheating is detected in an execution using cut-and-choose parameter N, no subsequent executions may use cut-and-choose parameter N. So, for example, the signer can store the largest value of the cut-and-choose parameter N^* for which cheating has been detected, and then when initiating an execution of the signing protocol can use as the cut-and-choose parameter the least value $N > N^*$ that is not currently being used by any active execution.

A Additional Examples of Linear Function Families

In Sect. 2.2 we defined linear function families, and described the linear function family that underlies the Schnorr blind signature scheme. Here we recall additional examples of linear function families from the work of Hauck et al. [14].

Okamoto-Schnorr. Here, par defines a cyclic group $\mathbb{G}$ of prime order $q \geq 2^{2\kappa}$, and also includes uniformly selected generators $g_1, g_2 \in \mathbb{G}$. We let $\mathcal{S} = \mathbb{Z}_q$, $\mathcal{D} = \mathbb{Z}_q^2$, and $\mathcal{R} = \mathbb{G}$, with the scalar multiplication maps $s \cdot (x, y) = (s \cdot x, s \cdot y)$ (for $s, x, y \in \mathbb{Z}_q$) and $s \cdot g = g^s$ (for $g \in \mathbb{G}$). Defining $\mathsf{F}(x, y) := g_1^x \cdot g_2^y$, a pseudo torsion-free element in the kernel is given by $z^* = (-1, \log_{g_2} g_1)$. Since scalar multiplication between $\mathcal{S}$ and $\mathcal{R}$ is distributive, Ψ is the zero function. Finally, LF is preimage resistant and collision resistant under the discrete logarithm assumption in $\mathbb{G}$.

Okamoto-Guillou-Quisquater. Here, par contains $N = pq$ for distinct primes p, q, along with a uniform value $a \in \mathbb{Z}_N^*$ and a prime λ with

[6] As cheat_N now may take values larger than 1, we use Hoeffding's inequality instead of a Chernoff bound (which results in a slightly looser reduction).

$\gcd(\varphi(N), \lambda) = \gcd(N, \lambda) = 1$ and of size at least $2^{2\kappa}$. We define $\mathcal{S} = \mathbb{Z}_\lambda$ under addition modulo λ; define $\mathcal{R} = \mathbb{Z}_N^*$ under multiplication modulo N; and define $\mathcal{D} = \mathbb{Z}_\lambda \times \mathbb{Z}_N^*$ with group operation given by

$$(x_1, y_1) \circ (x_2, y_2) := \left(x_1 + x_2 \bmod \lambda,\ \ y_1 \cdot y_2 \cdot a^{\lfloor \frac{x_1+x_2}{\lambda} \rfloor} \bmod N\right).$$

(It can be shown [14] that this is indeed a group.) Scalar multiplication maps $s \cdot b$ for $b \in \mathcal{R}$ or $b \in \mathcal{D}$ are defined as s-fold iteration of the corresponding group operation. Moreover, define $\mathsf{F}(x, y) := a^x y^\lambda \bmod N$ and $\Psi(x, s, s') := (0, x^{\lfloor -\frac{s+s'}{\lambda} \rfloor} \bmod N)$. A pseudo torsion-free element in the kernel is given by $z^* = (\lambda - 1,\ a^{\lambda^{-1}-1} \pmod N)$, where λ^{-1} is the inverse of λ modulo $\varphi(N)$. LF is preimage resistant and collision resistant under a suitable version of the RSA assumption.

Fiat-Shamir. Here, par contains $N = pq$ for distinct primes p, q, and we define $\mathcal{S} = \mathbb{Z}_2^k$, $\mathcal{D} = \mathcal{R} = (\mathbb{Z}_N^*)^k$ for $k \geq 2^{2\kappa}$. The scalar multiplication maps are

$$(s_1, \ldots, s_k) \cdot (x_1, \ldots, x_k) = (x_1^{s_1}, \ldots, x_k^{s_k}).$$

Let $\mathsf{F}(x_1, ..., x_k) := (x_1^2 \pmod N), ..., x_k^2 \pmod N))$, and define $\Psi(\vec{x}, \vec{r}, \vec{s})$ component-wise with $\Psi(x_i, r_i, s_i) := x_i^{-(r_i > s_i + r_i \pmod 2))}$ (where $r_i > s_i + r_i \pmod 2$) denotes the predicate that returns 1 iff $r_i = s_i = 1 \pmod 2$. A pseudo torsion-free element in the kernel is $z^* = (-1, ..., -1)$. LF is preimage resistant and collision resistant under the factoring assumption.

B Deferred Calculations

Let X be a sum of independent $\{0,1\}$-random variables with $\mu = \mathbb{E}[X]$. The multiplicative Chernoff bound states that for all $\delta > 0$

$$\Pr[X \geq (1+\delta) \cdot \mu] \leq \exp\left(-\frac{\mu\delta^2}{2+\delta}\right).$$

Let $X = \mathsf{cheat}^* = \sum_{N=2}^{p+2} \mathsf{cheat}_N$. Then for any $s > \ln(p+1) \geq \mathbb{E}[\mathsf{cheat}_N]$ we have

$$\begin{aligned}\Pr[\mathsf{cheat}^* \geq s] &= \Pr\left[\mathsf{cheat}^* \geq \left(1 + \left(\frac{s}{\mu} - 1\right)\right) \cdot \mu\right] \\ &\leq \exp\left(-\frac{\mu(s/\mu - 1)^2}{2 + (s/\mu - 1)}\right).\end{aligned}$$

Using the fact that $x^2/(2+x) > x - 2$ for all $x \geq 0$, the above is at most

$$\exp\left(-\mu\left(\frac{s}{\mu} - 3\right)\right) = \exp(3\mu - s)$$

If we set $s = 3\ln(p+1) + \ln(2/\epsilon)$, the above equals $\epsilon/2$.

References

1. Abe, M., Okamoto, T.: Provably secure partially blind signatures. In: Bellare, M. (ed.) CRYPTO 2000. LNCS, vol. 1880, pp. 271–286. Springer, Heidelberg (2000). https://doi.org/10.1007/3-540-44598-6_17
2. Baldimtsi, F., Lysyanskaya, A.: Anonymous credentials light. In: Sadeghi, A.-R., Gligor, V.D., Yung, M. (eds.) ACM CCS 2013, pp. 1087–1098. ACM Press, November 2013
3. Bellare, M., Namprempre, C., Pointcheval, D., Semanko, M.: The power of RSA inversion oracles and the security of Chaum's RSA-based blind signature scheme. In: Syverson, P. (ed.) FC 2001. LNCS, vol. 2339, pp. 319–338. Springer, Heidelberg (2002). https://doi.org/10.1007/3-540-46088-8_25
4. Benhamouda, F., Lepoint, T., Loss, J., Orrù, M., Raykova, M.: On the (in)security of ROS. In: Canteaut, A., Standaert, F.-X. (eds.) EUROCRYPT 2021. LNCS, vol. 12696, pp. 33–53. Springer, Cham (2021). https://doi.org/10.1007/978-3-030-77870-5_2
5. Boldyreva, A.: Threshold signatures, multisignatures and blind signatures based on the gap-Diffie-Hellman-group signature scheme. In: Desmedt, Y.G. (ed.) PKC 2003. LNCS, vol. 2567, pp. 31–46. Springer, Heidelberg (2003). https://doi.org/10.1007/3-540-36288-6_3
6. Chaum, D.: Blind signatures for untraceable payments. In: Chaum, D., Rivest, R.L., Sherman, A.T. (eds.) Crypto'82, pp. 199–203. Plenum Press, New York (1982)
7. Fischlin, M.: Round-optimal composable blind signatures in the common reference string model. In: Dwork, C. (ed.) CRYPTO 2006. LNCS, vol. 4117, pp. 60–77. Springer, Heidelberg (2006). https://doi.org/10.1007/11818175_4
8. Fuchsbauer, G., Hanser, C., Kamath, C., Slamanig, D.: Practical round-optimal blind signatures in the standard model from weaker assumptions. In: Zikas, V., De Prisco, R. (eds.) SCN 2016. LNCS, vol. 9841, pp. 391–408. Springer, Cham (2016). https://doi.org/10.1007/978-3-319-44618-9_21
9. Fuchsbauer, G., Hanser, C., Slamanig, D.: Practical round-optimal blind signatures in the standard model. In: Gennaro, R., Robshaw, M. (eds.) CRYPTO 2015, Part II. LNCS, vol. 9216, pp. 233–253. Springer, Heidelberg (2015). https://doi.org/10.1007/978-3-662-48000-7_12
10. Fuchsbauer, G., Plouviez, A., Seurin, Y.: Blind Schnorr signatures and signed ElGamal encryption in the algebraic group model. In: Canteaut, A., Ishai, Y. (eds.) EUROCRYPT 2020, Part II. LNCS, vol. 12106, pp. 63–95. Springer, Cham (2020). https://doi.org/10.1007/978-3-030-45724-2_3
11. Garg, S., Gupta, D.: Efficient round optimal blind signatures. In: Nguyen, P.Q., Oswald, E. (eds.) EUROCRYPT 2014. LNCS, vol. 8441, pp. 477–495. Springer, Heidelberg (2014). https://doi.org/10.1007/978-3-642-55220-5_27
12. Garg, S., Rao, V., Sahai, A., Schröder, D., Unruh, D.: Round optimal blind signatures. In: Rogaway, P. (ed.) CRYPTO 2011. LNCS, vol. 6841, pp. 630–648. Springer, Heidelberg (2011). https://doi.org/10.1007/978-3-642-22792-9_36
13. Ghadafi, E.: Efficient round-optimal blind signatures in the standard model. In: Kiayias, A. (ed.) FC 2017. LNCS, vol. 10322, pp. 455–473. Springer, Cham (2017). https://doi.org/10.1007/978-3-319-70972-7_26
14. Hauck, E., Kiltz, E., Loss, J.: A modular treatment of blind signatures from identification schemes. In: Ishai, Y., Rijmen, V. (eds.) EUROCRYPT 2019, Part III. LNCS, vol. 11478, pp. 345–375. Springer, Cham (2019). https://doi.org/10.1007/978-3-030-17659-4_12

15. Hauck, E., Kiltz, E., Loss, J., Nguyen, N.K.: Lattice-based blind signatures, revisited. In: Micciancio, D., Ristenpart, T. (eds.) CRYPTO 2020, Part II. LNCS, vol. 12171, pp. 500–529. Springer, Cham (2020). https://doi.org/10.1007/978-3-030-56880-1_18
16. Hazay, C., Katz, J., Koo, C.-Y., Lindell, Y.: Concurrently-secure blind signatures without random oracles or setup assumptions. In: Vadhan, S.P. (ed.) TCC 2007. LNCS, vol. 4392, pp. 323–341. Springer, Heidelberg (2007). https://doi.org/10.1007/978-3-540-70936-7_18
17. Jayaraman, B., Li, H., Evans, D.: Decentralized certificate authorities. https://arxiv.org/abs/1706.03370
18. Juels, A., Luby, M., Ostrovsky, R.: Security of blind digital signatures. In: Kaliski, B.S. (ed.) CRYPTO 1997. LNCS, vol. 1294, pp. 150–164. Springer, Heidelberg (1997). https://doi.org/10.1007/BFb0052233
19. Kastner, J., Loss, J., Xu, J.: On pairing-free blind signature schemes in the algebraic group model (2020). https://eprint.iacr.org/2020/1071
20. Okamoto, T.: Provably secure and practical identification schemes and corresponding signature schemes. In: Brickell, E.F. (ed.) CRYPTO 1992. LNCS, vol. 740, pp. 31–53. Springer, Heidelberg (1993). https://doi.org/10.1007/3-540-48071-4_3
21. Okamoto, T.: Efficient blind and partially blind signatures without random oracles. In: Halevi, S., Rabin, T. (eds.) TCC 2006. LNCS, vol. 3876, pp. 80–99. Springer, Heidelberg (2006). https://doi.org/10.1007/11681878_5
22. Pointcheval, D.: Strengthened security for blind signatures. In: Nyberg, K. (ed.) EUROCRYPT 1998. LNCS, vol. 1403, pp. 391–405. Springer, Heidelberg (1998). https://doi.org/10.1007/BFb0054141
23. Pointcheval, D., Stern, J.: Provably secure blind signature schemes. In: Kim, K., Matsumoto, T. (eds.) ASIACRYPT 1996. LNCS, vol. 1163, pp. 252–265. Springer, Heidelberg (1996). https://doi.org/10.1007/BFb0034852
24. Pointcheval, D., Stern, J.: New blind signatures equivalent to factorization (extended abstract). In: Graveman, R., Janson, P.A., Neuman, C., Gong, L. (eds.) ACM CCS '97, pp. 92–99. ACM Press, April 1997
25. Pointcheval, D., Stern, J.: Security arguments for digital signatures and blind signatures. J. Cryptol. **13**(3), 361–396 (2000). https://doi.org/10.1007/s001450010003
26. Schnorr, C.P.: Security of blind discrete log signatures against interactive attacks. In: Qing, S., Okamoto, T., Zhou, J. (eds.) ICICS 2001. LNCS, vol. 2229, pp. 1–12. Springer, Heidelberg (2001). https://doi.org/10.1007/3-540-45600-7_1
27. Wagner, D.: A generalized birthday problem. In: Yung, M. (ed.) CRYPTO 2002. LNCS, vol. 2442, pp. 288–304. Springer, Heidelberg (2002). https://doi.org/10.1007/3-540-45708-9_19

Zero-Knowledge Proofs, Threshold and Multi-Signatures

PrORAM

Fast $O(\log n)$ Authenticated Shares ZK ORAM

David Heath(✉) and Vladimir Kolesnikov(✉)

Georgia Institute of Technology, Atlanta, GA, USA
{heath.davidanthony,kolesnikov}@gatech.edu

Abstract. We construct a concretely efficient Zero Knowledge (ZK) Oblivious RAM (ORAM) for ZK Proof (ZKP) systems based on authenticated sharings of arithmetic values. It consumes $2\log n$ oblivious transfers (OTs) of length-2σ secrets per access of an arithmetic value, for statistical security parameter σ and array size n. This is an asymptotic and concrete improvement over previous best (concretely efficient) ZK ORAM BubbleRAM of Heath and Kolesnikov ([HK20a], CCS 2020), whose access cost is $\frac{1}{2}\log^2 n$ OTs of length-2σ secrets.

ZK ORAM is essential for proving statements that are best expressed as RAM programs, rather than Boolean or arithmetic circuits.

Our construction is private-coin ZK. We integrate it with [HK20a]'s ZKP protocol and prove the resulting ZKP system secure.

We implemented PrORAM in C++. Compared to state-of-the-art BubbleRAM, PrORAM is $\approx$10$\times$ faster for arrays of size 2^{20} of 40-bit values.

Keywords: Oblivious RAM · Zero knowledge

1 Introduction

Zero Knowledge (ZK) proofs (ZKP) allow an untrusted prover $\mathcal{P}$ to convince an untrusted verifier $\mathcal{V}$ of the truth of a given statement *while revealing nothing additional.* ZKPs are foundational cryptographic objects useful in many contexts. Early ZK focused on proofs of specific statements, but more recent systems handle *arbitrary* statements, so long as the statements are encoded as circuits.

Motivation. Unfortunately, many statements are more easily and efficiently expressed as RAM machine programs rather than circuits. Indeed, most standard algorithms are formalized for RAM machines.[1] Importantly, recent work, e.g. [HK20a], shows that support for writing proof statements as arbitrary C programs is within reach. ORAM is a major cost factor in [HK20a]'s ZK virtual machine, responsible for 1/3 to 1/2 or more of the total cost, since ORAM is

[1] RAM machines reduce to circuits, but improving the reduction will allow more efficient proofs.

Supplementary Information The online version contains supplementary material available at https://doi.org/10.1007/978-3-030-92068-5_17.

M. Tibouchi and H. Wang (Eds.): ASIACRYPT 2021, LNCS 13093, pp. 495–525, 2021.
https://doi.org/10.1007/978-3-030-92068-5_17

accessed at each CPU step. An efficient ZK ORAM would greatly improve the performance of (already practical) ZK virtual machine of [HK20a].

Most ORAM research targets either (1) an untrusted server holding a client's private data or (2) the secure multiparty computation setting. ZK ORAMs have been less studied. ZK, as compared to these more explored settings, gives a crucial advantage: $\mathcal{P}$ can precompute the order in which the proof circuit will access each RAM element. Prior work [HK20a] has shown that this knowledge suffices to build a circuit-based ORAM that incurs only $\frac{1}{2}\log^2 n$ oblivious transfers (OTs) per access. While the constant factor of this approach is excellent, the $\log^2$ scaling can be costly for large RAMs.

Our work. We construct an efficient ZK ORAM that we call PrORAM. PrORAM consumes only $2\log n$ OTs per access. Note, ZK-ORAM's security has not been defined standalone; rather, its functionality and security are considered together with a complete ZKP system, e.g., in [HK20a]. We follow a similar approach: our ZK-ORAM construction is modular, but we prove security of the complete ZKP system, implementing arithmetic circuit with RAM access. Based on this, we then motivate and present a ZK ORAM definition for a specific execution environment.

Our approach. We use the [JKO13] ZK framework, which converts any sound, correct, and verifiable garbling scheme into a malicious-verifier ZKP.

1.1 High Level Intuition of Our Approach

Informally, ORAM is an object implementing a persistent memory. The RAM is initialized and accessed by a computation, such as an arithmetic circuit. ZK ORAM and the computation must together realize a secure ZKP system.

$\mathcal{P}$ and $\mathcal{V}$ evaluate the proof circuit or program by jointly processing it gate-by-gate. The validity of the proof is ensured by the fact that each circuit wire holds an *authenticated secret share* that $\mathcal{P}$ cannot forge.

Our prover $\mathcal{P}$ stores the RAM locally on her system, but the authenticated contents are masked by one-time-pad masks chosen by $\mathcal{V}$. Because $\mathcal{P}$ stores the RAM locally and because she knows the RAM access order, she can directly access each requested index. From here, the crucial problem is that each RAM slot is masked by a distinct value chosen by $\mathcal{V}$. To ensure $\mathcal{V}$, who does not know the access order, can authenticate a value read from the RAM, the value must have a mask that is *independent of the accessed index.* Thus, RAM essentially reduces to 'aligning' masks without leaking the RAM access order to $\mathcal{V}$. We arrange mask alignment by allowing $\mathcal{P}$ to authentically and obliviously permute $\mathcal{V}$'s chosen masks into a desired order.

For a RAM with n slots, a single permutation on $2n$ elements suffices to support the next n accesses. Using a permutation network, this can be achieved by $2n\log n$ OTs. Thus, each access consumes amortized $2\log n$ OTs.

1.2 Contribution

We construct a private-coin ZK ORAM, PrORAM, that uses only $2 \log n$ OTs per access, while previous ZK ORAM has cost $1/2 \log^2 n$. We instantiate our ORAM in the [JKO13] ZK framework, resulting in a ZKP protocol with 2 rounds (4 flows) of communication when using standard OT, such as [KOS15].[2]

- We present PrORAM in technical detail, and prove it correct.
- We integrate PrORAM into the arithmetic ZK protocol of [HK20a]. Thus, our construction allows proofs of arbitrary arithmetic statements encoded as circuits with access to a highly efficient RAM. Note, [HK20a]'s ZK virtual machine is a circuit; our ORAM can be directly plugged in their ZK VM.
- We formalize the resulting construction in the [JKO13] garbled-circuit based ZK proof framework and prove the system correct and secure.
- We propose a definition of ZK ORAM for a specific execution environment. Security of our ZKP system implies ZK ORAM security of PrORAM.
- We implemented our approach in `C++` and we explore its concrete performance. As compared to BubbleRAM [HK20a], a state-of-the-art ORAM for the same setting, and for size 2^{20} RAMs, PrORAM improves communication by >4× and runs >10× faster on a commodity laptop. Our more significant computation improvement follows from the fact that our algorithms are friendlier to cache than BubbleRAM's (see Sect. 9).

2 Related Work

Our contribution is an efficient ORAM for an interactive Zero Knowledge protocol. In our review of related work, we discuss both ZK protocols and ORAMs. For lack of space, we postpone the detailed discussion of related work to Supplementary Material (Sect. 10). Here we provide comparison with prior work in the setting of concretely efficient interactive ZK.

Consider the prover $\mathcal{P}$, interacting with $\mathcal{V}$, wishing to convince him, that she, $\mathcal{P}$, holds a satisfying assignment to a circuit. One line of work builds linear-sized proofs [JKO13, FNO15, HK20c, HK20a, WYKW20]. This line of work is attractive because it features costs that scale linearly in the circuit size with low constants. Thus, if $\mathcal{P}$ and $\mathcal{V}$ wish to finish a proof as fast as possible, these constructions are excellent choices.

[JKO13] was the first work to construct concretely efficient proofs of arbitrary circuits by reducing ZKPs to *garbled circuits* (GCs). Recent work [HK20a] proposed a concretely efficient (running at 2.1 KHz on a commodity laptop) ZKP system for RAM programs, and a ZK ORAM, BubbleRAM. BubbleRAM has amortized complexity $1/2 \log^2 n$ per access of an array of n elements.

[2] In our implementation, we use Ferret OT [YWL+20], which greatly improves communication. Ferret processes OTs in very large chunks, requiring additional rounds for each next chunk. This round complexity increase is small and contributes little to total runtime. E.g., in concrete terms, two added rounds give $\approx 2^{23}$ OTs.

Our ZK ORAM PrORAM is built to work with the in [HK20a]'s arithmetic protocol. PrORAM improves performance of ZK ORAM to $2 \log n$, thus asymptotically improving over BubbleRAM.

Recently, BubbleCache [HYDK21] enhanced BubbleRAM by adding multi-level ORAM caching. The idea is to "spread out" the BubbleRAM schedule and hope for the best (i.e., that the required array element won't be needed too soon, in which case a cache miss occurs, with a corresponding performance penalty). BubbleCache has worse worst-case performance than BubbleRAM, and hence PrORAM correspondingly improves over BubbleCache as well. See Sect. 9 for an expanded comparison between PrORAM and BubbleCache.

3 Notation

- $\mathcal{P}$ is the prover. We refer to $\mathcal{P}$ by she, her, hers, etc.
- $\mathcal{V}$ is the verifier. We refer to $\mathcal{V}$ by he, him, his, etc.
- σ is the statistical security parameter (e.g., 40).
- κ is the computational security parameter (e.g., 128).
- $x \in_{\$} S$ denotes that the value x is drawn uniformly from the set S.
- $\langle x, y \rangle$ denotes a pair of values where x is held by $\mathcal{V}$ and y is held by $\mathcal{P}$.
- We write $a \triangleq b$ to denote that a is *defined* to be b.
- p denotes a prime integer.
- We work with *authenticated sharings* of values held between $\mathcal{V}$ and $\mathcal{P}$. The authentic sharing of a value $x \in \mathbb{Z}_p$ is denoted by $[\![x]\!]$. We define authentic sharings and an algebra over such sharings in Sect. 4.1. A sharing consists of two *shares*, one held by $\mathcal{V}$ and one by $\mathcal{P}$.
- Authenticated sharings use uniform masks chosen by $\mathcal{V}$. It is sometimes convenient to make this mask explicit. $[\![x]\!]_M$ is an authenticated share of x that uses the mask M (see Sect. 4.3).
- We also work with standard *additive sharings*. We denote the additive sharing of a value $x \in \mathbb{Z}_p$ by $(\!|x|\!)$. Additive sharings are discussed in Sect. 4.4.
- We view RAMs as *arrays* of values, and hence work extensively with arrays:
  - In general we use capital variables to denote arrays, e.g. A.
  - When clear from context, n denotes the number of array slots. When needed for precision, we use $|A|$ to denote the number of array slots in A.
  - We consider arrays where each array *slot* may hold more than one integral value. When clear from context, s denotes the *slot size*, i.e., the number of integer values stored in each array slot.

    Flexibly sized array slots both allow arrays of complex objects and also are crucial for preventing $\mathcal{P}$ from accessing an arbitrary RAM slot rather than the program-dictated slot: we store an explicit RAM index in each slot and perform an equality check as part of the ZK proof.
  - The set $(\mathbb{Z}_p^s)^n$ denotes the prime field arrays of n slots each with size s.
  - $A[i]$ denotes the value stored in the ith slot of A. We use zero-based indexing.
  - $A[i := x]$ denotes an array update. The expression $A[i := x]$ is a new array whose contents are identical to A except that slot i is set to x.

This notation *does not* denote a program statement that mutates an array in computer memory, but rather denotes the construction of a fresh mathematical object.

- When clear from context, we extend notation over field elements to arrays. For example, if A and B are two arrays of field elements with matching length and slot size, $A + B$ denotes the array containing the pointwise addition of the contents. We similarly extend share notation to arrays, $[\![A]\!]$ denotes an array where each element is an authentic sharing. We also extend array access notation: $[\![A[i]]\!]$ is the sharing of the ith element of array A.
- If $i \leq j$, then $A[i..j]$ denotes the *subarray* of elements $A[i]..A[j-1]$. The subarray does not include the jth element. We write $A[i..]$ to denote the subarray starting from index i and containing all subsequent elements of A.
- $[\cdot]$ denotes the empty array. $[a]$ denotes an array holding only the value a.
- We sometimes *concatenate* arrays. $A \mid B$ is the composite array containing each element of A followed by each element of B.

- We work with permutations that map points in time to array locations being accessed. We represent such permutations by arrays over the natural numbers such that for a given permutation π, $\pi[t] = i$ indicates that location i is accessed at time t.
- It will be convenient to keep track of a complementary view of the access order that we refer to as a *timetable*. A timetable $\mathcal{T}$ is an array over the natural numbers such that $\mathcal{T}[i] = t$ indicates that location i was last written at time t. In general, a timetable is not a permutation.

4 Preliminaries

In this section, we present technical background to our work needed to understand our contribution. In particular, we review [HK20a]'s arithmetic ZK protocol and discuss permutation networks.

4.1 Authenticated Share Algebra

We now review authenticated secret shares and the operations they support. Our ORAM is built on this share algebra. We use [HK20a]'s efficient arithmetic protocol, where the parties operate over shares using a combination of local operations and OT. Crucially, although the parties compute using OT, each of $\mathcal{P}$'s OT inputs can be precomputed from her proof witness. Thus, all OTs can be executed in parallel, and the resulting protocol runs in constant rounds.

Authenticated Shares. In the protocol, $\mathcal{P}$ and $\mathcal{V}$ hold *authenticated sharings* of values in a field $\mathbb{Z}_p$ for a σ-bit prime p (our implementation instantiates p as $2^{40} - 87$, the largest 40 bit prime). An authenticated sharing consists of two *shares*, one held by $\mathcal{V}$ and one by $\mathcal{P}$. We denote a sharing where $\mathcal{V}$'s share is $s \in \mathbb{Z}_p$ and $\mathcal{P}$'s share is $t \in \mathbb{Z}_p$ by writing $\langle s, t\rangle$. At the start of the protocol, $\mathcal{V}$ samples a non-zero global value $\Delta \in_{\$} \mathbb{Z}_p^{\times}$. Consider a sharing $\langle X, x\Delta - X\rangle$

where $X \in \mathbb{Z}_p$ is chosen by $\mathcal{V}$. A sharing of this form is a *valid* sharing of the semantic value $x \in \mathbb{Z}_p$. We use the shorthand $[\![x]\!]$ to denote a valid sharing:

$$[\![x]\!] \triangleq \langle X, x\Delta - X \rangle$$

Sharings have two key properties:

1. $\mathcal{V}$'s share gives no information about the semantic value. This holds trivially: $\mathcal{V}$'s share is independent of x.
2. $\mathcal{P}$'s share is 'unforgeable': $\mathcal{P}$ cannot use $x\Delta - X$ to construct $y\Delta - X$ for $y \neq x$. We ensure this by hiding from $\mathcal{P}$ both the additive mask X and the authentication value Δ. This, combined with the fact that (1) the multiples of Δ are uniformly distributed over the field, and (2) the chosen prime p is large enough to achieve our desired security ensures that $\mathcal{P}$ can forge $[\![y]\!]$ only by guessing $y\Delta - X$, which only succeeds with probability $\frac{1}{p-1}$.

Opening shares. $\mathcal{P}$ must, at distinguished parts of the circuit, open her shares to $\mathcal{V}$. Let $[\![x]\!]$ be a valid authenticated sharing. When the two parties agree to open a share, we require that $\mathcal{V}$ knows the expected value x. This information is dictated by the circuit; thus $\mathcal{P}$ opening a share to $\mathcal{V}$ proves that the share represents a specific constant value. To complete the opening, $\mathcal{P}$ sends her share $x\Delta - X$ to $\mathcal{V}$, and $\mathcal{V}$ checks that the share is indeed valid (recall, $\mathcal{V}$ knows Δ and X). For complex proofs, $\mathcal{P}$ might open *many* shares to $\mathcal{V}$. Thus, [HK20a] adds a simple optimization: rather than sending each share separately, $\mathcal{P}$ instead accumulates a hash digest of all opened shares and sends this to $\mathcal{V}$. $\mathcal{V}$ can locally reconstruct the same hash and check that the two are equal. Thus, $\mathcal{P}$ sends only κ bits to open an arbitrary number of sharings.

Linear Operations. We can induce a *vector space* structure over authenticated sharings where sharings are vectors and publicly agreed constants are scalars. The vector space operations (addition, subtraction, and scaling by public constants) allow the parties to locally perform linear operations over sharings:

- To compute an authenticated sharing of a sum of shares, parties locally add their respective shares:

$$\begin{aligned}[\![x]\!] + [\![y]\!] &= \langle X, x\Delta - X \rangle + \langle Y, y\Delta - Y \rangle \\ &\triangleq \langle X + Y, (x+y)\Delta - (X+Y) \rangle = [\![x+y]\!]\end{aligned}$$

  To authentically subtract sharings, parties subtract their respective shares.
- To authentically scale a sharing by a public constant, the parties locally multiply their respective shares by the constant:

$$c[\![x]\!] = c\langle X, x\Delta - X \rangle \triangleq \langle cX, cx\Delta - cX \rangle = [\![cx]\!]$$

The parties also have access to a unit vector:

$$[\![1]\!] \triangleq \langle \Delta, 0 \rangle$$

Here, the sharing mask X is $0 - \Delta$. Note that the mask X is not known to $\mathcal{P}$ because $\mathcal{P}$ does not know Δ. With this unit vector, the parties can locally construct authenticated sharings of arbitrary publicly agreed values.

Vector-Scalar Multiplication. It is not sufficient to only consider linear operations. We also need a form of non-linear operation; we use a form of vector-scalar multiplication where the scalar is known to be in $\{0,1\}$, but is unknown to $\mathcal{V}$. (Vector-scalar multiplication where $\mathcal{P}$ chooses scalar $a \in \mathbb{Z}_p$ can be achieved by $\lceil \log p \rceil$ applications of this special form.)

Let $x \in \{0,1\}$ be held by $\mathcal{P}$ and let $y_1, ..., y_n \in \mathbb{Z}_p$ be a vector of field elements. Let the parties hold sharings $[\![y_1]\!], ..., [\![y_n]\!]$ and suppose they wish to compute $[\![xy_1]\!], ..., [\![xy_n]\!]$ (while $\mathcal{P}$'s input x is not authenticated, it could be verified later by an appropriately applied opening). First, $\mathcal{P}$ locally multiplies her shares by x. Thus the parties together hold:

$$\langle Y_1, xy_1\Delta - xY_1\rangle, ..., \langle Y_n, xy_n\Delta - xY_n\rangle$$

These intermediate sharings are invalid: the shares in the ith sharing do not sum to $y_i\Delta$. To resolve this, the parties participate in a single 1-out-of-2 OT where $\mathcal{V}$ acts as the sender. $\mathcal{V}$ uniformly draws n values $Y_i' \in_\$ \mathbb{Z}_p$ and allows $\mathcal{P}$ to choose between the following two vectors:

$$Y_1', ..., Y_n' \qquad Y_1' - Y_1, ..., Y_n' - Y_n \tag{1}$$

$\mathcal{P}$ chooses based on x and receives as output the vector $Y_1' - xY_1, ..., Y_n' - xY_n$. The parties can now compute a valid authenticated sharing for each vector index:

$$\langle Y_i', xy_i\Delta - xY_i - (Y_i' - xY_i)\rangle = \langle Y_i', xy_i\Delta - Y_i'\rangle = [\![xy_i]\!]$$

A vector-scalar multiplication of a length n vector requires a 1-out-of-2 OT of $n\lceil \log p \rceil$-bit secrets. In practice, we instantiate multiplication with the Ferret OT technique [YWL+20].

4.2 Implementing Standard Circuit Gates

Typical circuits include multiplication gates, not special vector-scalar gates where $\mathcal{P}$ chooses the scalar, as described above. There is a simple reduction from standard multiplication gates to [HK20a]'s vector-scalar multiplication gates and *opening gates* (an opening gate on input $[\![x]\!]$ simply requires $\mathcal{P}$ to open her share to $\mathcal{V}$, see Sect. 4.1): To authentically compute $[\![ab]\!]$ from inputs $[\![a]\!]$ and $[\![b]\!]$, instead compute $a'[\![1, b]\!] \mapsto [\![a', a'b]\!]$ by vector-scalar multiplication where $\mathcal{P}$ chooses a' freely, and then check that the $[\![a - a']\!] = [\![0]\!]$ using an opening gate. This check forces $\mathcal{P}$ to choose $a' = a$, and prevents her from multiplying incorrectly. We choose to keep vector-scalar gates and opening gates because these gates are highly efficient and because this reduction is simple. Each standard multiplication gate uses one vector-scalar gate and one opening gate.

Vector-scalar gates also allow $\mathcal{P}$ to provide input bits. To input $\mathcal{P}$'s private bit x, the parties compute $x[\![1]\!] = [\![x]\!]$ using a vector-scalar gate.

Other standard gates, e.g. addition and subtraction, are directly handled by the construction and do not require opening gates.

4.3 Explicit-Mask Sharings

Section 4.1 introduced an algebra over authenticated sharings. In the algebra as presented so far, we consider tuples of the form $\langle X, x\Delta - X\rangle$ where $X \in_\$ \mathbb{Z}_p$ is a uniform mask. For the purposes of our construction, it will be convenient to also consider sharings that use a *specific* mask chosen by $\mathcal{V}$. Thus, we introduce new notation for a sharing masked by a particular value:

$$[\![x]\!]_M \triangleq \langle M, x\Delta - M\rangle$$

That is, $[\![x]\!]_M$ is a sharing of x where the parties use the *specific* mask M, rather than an arbitrary mask.

We extend this notation to arrays: if A, B are equal-length arrays of $\mathbb{Z}_p$ elements, then $[\![A]\!]_B$ denotes an authentic share of A where each mask is in B:

$$[\![A[i]]\!]_B = \langle B[i], A[i]\Delta - B[i]\rangle$$

For convenience, we extend this notation so that we can mask a short array by a long array: the above array notation holds even if B is longer than A.

4.4 Standard Additive Sharings

Our construction relies on the parties' ability to manipulate secret masks chosen by $\mathcal{V}$ and unknown to $\mathcal{P}$. The algebra presented in Sect. 4.1 is not suitable, because it only supports sharings where $\mathcal{P}$ knows in cleartext each semantic value. We therefore also consider more traditional additive secret shares where neither party knows the underlying value.

Let $x \in \mathbb{Z}_p$ be an arbitrary value. In an additive share of x, $\mathcal{V}$ holds a uniform mask $M \in \mathbb{Z}_p$ and $\mathcal{P}$ holds $x - M$: together the parties hold $\langle M, x - M\rangle$. We use the shorthand $(\!|x|\!)$ to denote such a pair:

$$(\!|x|\!) \triangleq \langle X, x - X\rangle$$

The difference between authenticated sharings (Sect. 4.1) and additive sharings is that $\mathcal{P}$ does not know semantic values corresponding to additive sharings.

The parties can operate over additive sharings in the same way they can authenticated sharings: namely, we induce a vector space structure over additive sharings such that parties can add, subtract, multiply by public constants, and construct sharings of constants. Additionally, the parties can operate non-linearly by vector-scalar multiplication where $\mathcal{P}$ chooses the scalar. The needed protocol is *identical* to the vector-scalar protocol reviewed in Sect. 4.1.

Finally, $\mathcal{V}$ can construct a sharing $(\!|x|\!)$ for a value $x \in \mathbb{Z}_p$ that he chooses. To do so, $\mathcal{V}$ simply samples a uniform mask $M \in_\$ \mathbb{Z}_p$ and sends to $\mathcal{P}$ $x - M$.

4.5 Additive Sharing Permutations Programmed by $\mathcal{P}$

In our construction, $\mathcal{V}$ chooses random masks that are used to authenticate the RAM content. $\mathcal{P}$ is then given the opportunity to arrange these masks as she likes so that she can implement the RAM access order. So, we need a capability by which $\mathcal{P}$ can rearrange $\mathcal{V}$'s chosen masks. The parties thus construct additive shares of the masks which can then be manipulated by $\mathcal{P}$.

More precisely, $\mathcal{V}$ chooses an array of random masks $K \in_\$ (\mathbb{Z}_p^s)^n$, and the random masks are shared such that the parties hold $(\!|K|\!)$. Now, the parties must compute $(\!|\pi(K)|\!)$ for π chosen by $\mathcal{P}$. To apply an arbitrary permutation, we employ a particular circuit construction called a Waksman permutation network [Wak68]. This recursively constructed circuit builds a permutation of n elements from many permutations of two elements: i.e., from 'swap' gates. In our context, a swap gate allows $\mathcal{P}$ to conditionally swap two shares $(\!|a|\!)$ and $(\!|b|\!)$ based on her private bit $r \in \{0, 1\}$. Precisely, the gate is specified as follows:

$$swap(r, a, b) \triangleq \begin{cases} (a, b) & \text{if } \mathrm{r} = 0 \\ (b, a) & \text{otherwise} \end{cases}$$

To implement this gate, the parties compute a conditional difference $(\!|\delta|\!) \triangleq r(\!|a - b|\!)$ and output the pair $(\!|a - \delta, b + \delta|\!)$. A swap gate is computed by a single vector-scalar multiplication and linear operations. The gate can be computed even though $\mathcal{P}$ knows neither a nor b.

A permutation network on n elements (where n is a power of two) consumes $n \log n - n + 1$ swap gates; hence we use $n \log n - n + 1$ oblivious transfers.

5 Technical Overview

In this section, we give high level intuition sufficient to understand our approach.

ORAM is an object implementing a persistent memory array. The RAM is initialized and accessed by a computation, such as Boolean or arithmetic circuit, or a CPU built from such circuits. ZK ORAM and the computation must together realize a secure ZKP system. We formally specify the PrORAM object and its access functions, and prove correctness of its operation in Sect. 6; we prove security of our ZKP system in Sect. 7; we define (and prove) security our ZK ORAM in Sect. 7.4.

Informally, there are three attacks $\mathcal{P}$ may attempt on the RAM: 1) modify a memory value by forging an authentication code, 2) return a stale value, 3) return a valid authenticated value from a wrong location. The last attack is easily prevented by storing each array index as an authenticated value alongside the corresponding RAM element, and checking it on each access, a standard technique used, e.g., in [HK20a]. In this overview and in the formal constructions we focus on issue 1) value modification. Preventing the return of stale values is achieved by enforcing a key invariant that a valid authenticated element cannot be stored in more than one place; we point this aspect out as we discuss how to ensure value integrity.

As a thought experiment, suppose that $\mathcal{V}$ and $\mathcal{P}$ both know the array access order; we will soon remove this restriction. That is, they know *a priori* the locations of *each* array read and write. Further, suppose that each array element is stored as an authenticated secret share (Sect. 4.1) held by both parties. That is, for an array A, its value at each index i is formatted as follows:

$$[\![A[i]]\!] = \langle K[i], A[i]\Delta - K[i]\rangle,$$

where $K[i]$ is a uniform mask chosen by $\mathcal{V}$. Suppose on the jth array access, the parties wish to access array slot i. This case is easy: each player can simply read from RAM slot i in their local memory, and use the already-authenticated array element as needed in the proof.

Of course, we want to access RAM in an order unknown to $\mathcal{V}$. Here we run into a problem: on an access of position i, $\mathcal{P}$ can still read $A[i]\Delta - K[i]$ from her local array, but $\mathcal{V}$ does not have sufficient information to align the matching mask $K[i]$. Further, $\mathcal{V}$ cannot be allowed to learn the accessed position i, since this would give her information about the access order.

Instead of giving $K[i]$ to $\mathcal{V}$, we instead allow $\mathcal{V}$ to use a fresh mask $M[j]$ and convey the appropriate matching mask to $\mathcal{P}$. Specifically, we arrange that $\mathcal{P}$ will obtain $K[i] - M[j]$. Given this information, the parties compute:

$$\langle M[j], (A[i]\Delta - K[i]) + (K[i] - M[j])\rangle = \langle M[j], A[i]\Delta - M[j]\rangle = [\![A[i]]\!]$$

This authenticated secret share can be used as a wire in the ZK circuit.

The remaining task is to show *how* these mask differences are securely conveyed to $\mathcal{P}$. We present our solution in several steps. First, we present solutions that allow for RAMs with constrained access orders; these initial constructions do not allow arbitrary RAM reads/writes. Then, we use these constrained constructions as building blocks upon which we achieve general purpose RAM.

Read-once RAM. As a simplifying assumption, consider an n-element RAM that is preloaded with authenticated shares. Further, suppose the program will read each RAM slot exactly once, though the order in which these reads occur is unconstrained and is known to $\mathcal{P}$. In this case, the RAM's read order can be described by a *permutation* π on n elements that maps the time of each access to the accessed array index.

If we consider all n reads simultaneously, then our problem becomes one of delivering to $\mathcal{P}$ a sequence of n mask differences $K[i] - M[j]$, while hiding the access order from $\mathcal{V}$. To do so, $\mathcal{V}$ distributes to the two parties *additive secret shares* of the elements of the array of masks K: the parties hold $(\!|K|\!)$. Let π specify the permutation on A defining the RAM access order. The parties securely compute $(\!|\pi(K)|\!)$ using the permutation protocol described in Sect. 4.5. Informally, this permutation aligns the elements of K, which were originally in array order, with the order of accesses.

If we recall the syntax of an additive share $(\!|\pi(K)[j]|\!)$, we find that $\mathcal{P}$'s share has nearly the form that we need:

$$(\!|\pi(K)[j]|\!) = \langle Q[j], \pi(K)[j] - Q[j]\rangle = \langle Q[j], K[i] - Q[j]\rangle,$$

where $Q[j]$ is a uniform mask.

So far, the access masks M are *unconstrained.* Thus, $\mathcal{V}$ simply sets $M[j] = Q[j]$, and now each of $\mathcal{P}$'s share of the permuted array has *exactly* the form needed to align her share with that of $\mathcal{V}$. This implements read-once RAM: the parties can read an array of n elements in any order specified by $\mathcal{P}$.

swordRAM. Read-once RAM assumes that the array is preloaded with values. We also need a capability to write new RAM elements. Thus, we extend the above read-once RAM to allow for writes. However, the write capability we add is *highly constrained*: the parties must agree on and both know the order in which the array contents are written. For concreteness, we use a *sequential* write order, meaning that the jth write stores an element in the jth array slot. Array reads and writes may be arbitrarily interspersed with the restriction that each read occurs after the write to the accessed slot. As with our read-once RAM, we enforce that the program must read each array slot exactly once. We call this intermediate RAM a swordRAM (Sequential-Write, One-time ReaD RAM).

With the idea for read-once RAMs established, swordRAM is trivial. As argued in the beginning of this section, if each party knows the RAM access order, our task is easy: the parties trivially obtain matching authentication codes. Thus, swordRAM writes are simple, since both parties agree that the elements should be written sequentially, and hence the order is known to each. There is one subtlety in aligning the authentication masks used in RAM writes with the array slot masks $K[i]$, but this is easily addressed. Specifically, $\mathcal{V}$ simply sends the difference between the two masks to $\mathcal{P}$ on each RAM write.

General Purpose ZK ORAM. swordRAMs are highly restrictive. Nevertheless, there is an efficient reduction from general purpose RAM to swordRAM. We call this reduction PrORAM. A PrORAM of n elements is built on a swordRAM of $2n$ elements. There is no single one-to-one mapping from PrORAM slots to swordRAM slots. Rather, the swordRAM should be viewed as a *running log* of the PrORAM accesses; each PrORAM access corresponds to a single write and a single read in the swordRAM. At all times, we ensure that there are exactly n swordRAM slots that have been written to but not yet read, and it is exactly these n slots that hold the current PrORAM content. To track the relationship between PrORAM slots and swordRAM slots, the prover $\mathcal{P}$ maintains a cleartext data structure that we refer to as the *timetable.* A timetable $\mathcal{T}$ maps each PrORAM index i to the swordRAM slot where that element is currently stored.

The PrORAM is maintained as follows:

- To **initialize** a size-n PrORAM we perform a sequence of n writes to a fresh capacity-$2n$ swordRAM. Correspondingly, $\mathcal{P}$ initializes $\mathcal{T}$: at initialization, each PrORAM slot i is stored in swordRAM slot i.
- To **access** RAM slot i, $\mathcal{P}$ first looks up $\mathcal{T}[i]$ and reads from the corresponding swordRAM slot. Because of swordRAM's tight restrictions, this read 'exhausts' the accessed swordRAM slot, and so the parties must write back an element to the array. In the case of RAM write, the write-back element will be the written element. In the case of a RAM read, the write-back element will be the same element that was read. $\mathcal{P}$ then updates $\mathcal{T}$, indicating that PrORAM slot i is now stored in the newly written swordRAM slot.

- INPUTS: Parties agree on a swordRAM capacity n and a slot width s. $\mathcal{P}$ inputs a permutation on n elements π, denoting the order in which she wishes to read swordRAM elements.
- OUTPUTS: Let $K \in_\$ (\mathbb{Z}_p^s)^n$ be uniform masks drawn by $\mathcal{V}$. Parties output a swordRAM $([\cdot], \pi, 0, K, [\cdot], (\!|\pi(K)|\!))$.
- PROTOCOL:
  - $\mathcal{V}$ samples a length-n array of uniform values $K \in_\$ (\mathbb{Z}_p^s)^n$.
  - $\mathcal{V}$ constructs an additive sharing $(\!|K|\!)$ by sampling uniform masks $R \in_\$ (\mathbb{Z}_p^s)^n$ and sending $K - R$ to $\mathcal{P}$.
  - $\mathcal{V}$ and $\mathcal{P}$ compute $(\!|\pi(K)|\!)$ via a permutation network (see Section 4.5).
  - The swordRAM $([\cdot], \pi, 0, K, [\cdot], (\!|\pi(K)|\!))$ is now defined; the parties output their respective components.

Fig. 1. Initializing an empty capacity-n swordRAM. The parties output a swordRAM that encodes an empty array and that is ready for n writes and n reads. The n reads will happen as specified by the the access order π.

- Because the number of reads/writes to a swordRAM are bounded, we must periodically **refresh** the PrORAM. Each PrORAM access consumes one swordRAM read and one swordRAM write. After n PrORAM accesses, we exhaust all $2n$ available swordRAM writes (recall, n writes were used to initialize) and n of the available $2n$ swordRAM reads. The remaining n reads suffice for us to fetch the current PrORAM content and store it into a freshly initialized swordRAM. By doing so, we "refresh" the PrORAM and are ready for n more accesses.

The **crucial point** is that because $\mathcal{P}$ knows the entire PrORAM access order $\mathcal{O}$ in advance, she can play out the above reduction "in her head" to obtain the corresponding read order π for the underlying swordRAM. π is then used to initialize a swordRAM that will precisely service the access order $\mathcal{O}$.

Efficiency. PrORAM is efficient. Essentially the only cost is in permuting additive shares of the array K. For every n PrORAM accesses we initialize $2n$ swordRAM reads and thus consume a permutation of $2n$ masks. A permutation of $2n$ elements costs $2n \log 2n - 2n + 1$ OTs via a permutation network, and hence each PrORAM access consumes amortized $2 \log n$ OTs.

The remainder of this paper presents the above in technical detail.

6 PrORAM Formal Constructions

In this section, we present PrORAM in formal detail. Section 7 formalizes our construction's security.

- Inputs: Parties input a capacity-n swordRAM:

$$(A, \pi, r, K, [\![A]\!]_K, (\!|\pi(K)|\!))$$

Let i be the read index: $i \triangleq \pi[r]$. It is illegal to call this functionality if $i \geq w$.
- Outputs: Parties output the read value $[\![A[i]]\!]$ and the updated swordRAM:

$$(A, \pi, r+1, K, [\![A]\!]_K, (\!|\pi(K)|\!))$$

- Protocol:
  - Consider the sharing $(\!|\pi(K)[r]|\!) = (\!|K[i]|\!)$. Suppose $(\!|K[i]|\!) = \langle M, K[i] - M\rangle$. Note, $\mathcal{V}$ knows M: he simply looks up the rth element of his share of $(\!|\pi(K)|\!)$.
  - $\mathcal{P}$ fetches her share $[\![A[i]]\!]_K = A[i]\Delta - K[i]$.
  - Parties compute and output:

$$\langle M, (A[i]\Delta - K[i]) + (K[i] - M)\rangle = \langle M, A[i]\Delta - M\rangle = [\![A[i]]\!]$$

  - Parties increment r and output the updated swordRAM.

Fig. 2. Reading from a swordRAM. This procedure does not take an index as an argument. Rather, the index is defined by the permutation π chosen at initialization (cf. Fig. 1).

- Inputs: Parties input a capacity-n swordRAM:

$$(A, \pi, r, K, [\![A]\!]_{K]}, (\!|\pi(K)|\!))$$

It is illegal to call this functionality if $|A| \geq n$. The parties input a sharing of a value a with mask M: $[\![a]\!]_M$.
- Outputs: Parties output the updated swordRAM:

$$(A \mid [a], \pi, r, K, [\![A \mid [a]]\!]_K, (\!|\pi(K)|\!))$$

I.e., the parties output a swordRAM where a is appended to A.
- Protocol:
  - Let $w = |A|$. Recall, the mask for swordRAM slot w is $K[w]$ known to $\mathcal{V}$. $\mathcal{V}$ sends to $\mathcal{P}$ the mask difference $M - K[w]$.
  - $\mathcal{P}$ computes:

$$(a\Delta - M) + (M - K[w]) = a\Delta - K[w]$$

    This is $\mathcal{P}$'s share of $[\![a]\!]_{K[w]}$. $\mathcal{P}$ appends a to A and appends her share of $[\![a]\!]_{K[w]}$ to the encrypted array.
  - Both parties output the updated swordRAM.

Fig. 3. Writing to a swordRAM. Recall that writes to swordRAM are *sequential*: the shared element a is appended to the array A.

6.1 swordRAM

Recall from Sect. 5 that we decompose the problem of building a RAM into two parts: first we construct a 'sequential write, one-time read RAM' (swordRAM) that only supports one read and one write per RAM slot, and where writes must occur in sequential order. Then we build a general purpose ORAM on top of swordRAM. We therefore start by defining swordRAM. Syntactically, a capacity-n swordRAM is a six-tuple:

$$(A, \pi, r, K, [\![A]\!]_K, (\!|\pi(K)|\!))$$

Each of these elements are as follows:

- $A \in (\mathbb{Z}_p^s)^*$ denotes the cleartext array encoded by the swordRAM. As we write to the swordRAM, A will grow in length. A is known only to $\mathcal{P}$.
- π is a permutation on n elements. π denotes the *read order* of the swordRAM. π is known only to $\mathcal{P}$. Note, the read order does not fully specify the *access* order, as writes may be arbitrarily interspersed with the constraint that each element is written before it is read.
- $r \in \mathbb{N}$ denotes the number of swordRAM reads that have occurred so far. In a valid swordRAM, $r \leq |A| \leq n$. Both $\mathcal{P}$ and $\mathcal{V}$ maintain local copies of r.
- $K \in_\$ (\mathbb{Z}_p^s)^n$ is an n-element array with slots of size s, i.e. each slot K holds s values. $K[i]$ stores uniform masks used as swordRAM authenticators. $K[i]$ is drawn uniformly by $\mathcal{V}$ and is unknown to $\mathcal{P}$. We need more than one mask per swordRAM slot to support arrays of more general objects. In particular, in our RAMs we operate with value-index tuples (v, i), which allows us to perform an index check, preventing $\mathcal{P}$ from providing an invalid permutation and illegally substituting one RAM value for another.
  Although we use s masks for a single RAM slot, we are careful that any operations the parties perform are applied to the masks as a unit; hence, there is no opportunity for a cheating $\mathcal{P}$ to 'break apart' the contents within a single RAM slot.
- $[\![A]\!]_K$ is the authenticated secret sharing of A masked by K. Informally, this is the authenticated array. On a read, $\mathcal{P}$ indexes directly into this array and then aligns her share with $\mathcal{V}$'s (as described in Sect. 5).
- $(\!|\pi(K)|\!)$ is an additive secret sharing of the array K permuted according to π. These sharings are the values that $\mathcal{P}$ needs to align her shares with $\mathcal{V}$'s (as described in Sect. 5).

With syntax established, we describe operations over swordRAMs.

Initialize. Figure 1 lists the procedure for constructing a fresh swordRAM. At initialization, the encoded array A is empty (i.e., has size 0), so most of the swordRAM components are trivially initialized. The objective of initialization is to prepare for all n future reads. To do so, $\mathcal{P}$ provides as input the read order permutation π and $\mathcal{V}$ chooses a mask array K. The parties compute $(\!|\pi(K)|\!)$ via a permutation network (Sect. 4.5). This permutation provides to $\mathcal{P}$ the specific values that she needs to align her shares with $\mathcal{V}$'s on each read. We emphasize that swordRAM permutations account for almost all of our ORAM's cost.

Read. swordRAM reads (Fig. 2) are entirely local operations: indeed, initialization already properly arranged that $\mathcal{P}$ will receive the correct mask alignment values on each read. $\mathcal{P}$ directly accesses the correct index of $[\![A]\!]_K$ and then aligns her share with $\mathcal{V}$'s using $(\!|\pi(K)|\!)[r]$.

Write. swordRAM writes (Fig. 3) append values to the array A. The swordRAM authenticated array should be masked by the specific array K, but the parties write an arbitrary share $[\![a]\!]$. To properly store this value, $\mathcal{V}$ sends a difference between the mask on $[\![a]\!]$ and the target mask in K. $\mathcal{P}$ uses this value to align her share such that it can be properly appended.

As an aside, swordRAM performs no checking on the order in which $\mathcal{P}$ decides to read values: $\mathcal{P}$ freely chooses the read-order π. However, we next will perform a reduction from general purpose RAM to swordRAM. In this reduction, we explicitly include copies of each index identifier in the swordRAM. By this mechanism, the reduction fully constrains the permutation π, since the parties will check that each read yields the expected index identifier.

It will be convenient to abstract over some of the swordRAM detail. We give a shorthand for a swordRAM that encodes an array A with r remaining reads given by a read order π. Specifically we write $\rho(A, \pi, r)$:

$$\rho(A, \pi, r) \triangleq (A, \pi, r, K, [\![A]\!]_K, (\!|\pi(K)|\!))$$

where $K \in_\$ (\mathbb{Z}_p^s)^n$ is uniform and the masks on $(\!|\pi(K)|\!)$ are uniform.

6.2 swordRAM to PrORAM

Recall that we implement general purpose RAM by a reduction to swordRAM. We call this reduction PrORAM.

At a high level, a PrORAM implementing a size-n array operates in blocks of n accesses. Each block is handled by a distinct data structure, which is updated on each of the n accesses. After n accesses, we create a fresh data structure to support the next n accesses. We initialize the new structure by moving the contents of the old one, and then we retire the old data structure, and so on.

Each data structure is a capacity-$2n$ swordRAM (with accompanying metadata), which is initialized to contain the (current state of the) array A *in the canonical order* $A[0], ..., A[n-1]$. Of course, to initialize a swordRAM, we need an appropriate read order π. This permutation π must achieve two tasks: (1) it must encode the order of the next n accesses and (2) it must encode the order of the n reads needed to copy its content into the next swordRAM block *in canonical order* before being retired. That is, the first n (of the $2n$ total) reads of the capacity-$2n$ swordRAM service the n PrORAM requests for data, and the next n accesses read the array A as part of moving to the next PrORAM data structure. In total, there are $2n$ swordRAM reads, which can be encoded in a permutation π over $2n$ elements. We formally describe how to construct π based on the array's access order in Sect. 6.3.

PrORAM Syntax. We denote a PrORAM that encodes a cleartext array A with access order $\mathcal{O}$ by writing $\boxed{A, \mathcal{O}}$. A size-n PrORAM is a four-tuple:

$$\boxed{A, \mathcal{O}} \triangleq (A, \mathcal{O}, \rho(H, \pi, r), \mathcal{T})$$

These elements are as follows:

- $A \in (\mathbb{Z}_p^s)^n$ is the cleartext content of the PrORAM. A is known only to $\mathcal{P}$.
- $\mathcal{O}$ is a list of all indexes accessed by the RAM and is known as the *access order*. $\mathcal{O}$ is maintained in cleartext by $\mathcal{P}$ and is unknown to $\mathcal{V}$. $\mathcal{P}$ can precompute $\mathcal{O}$ by running the proof in cleartext and logging all RAM accesses.
  For simplicity, assume $\mathcal{O}$ initially has length that is a multiple of n. $\mathcal{P}$ can pad $\mathcal{O}$ with extra zeros to reach the next multiple of n.
  As we perform accesses, the access order shrinks: each access removes the first element of $\mathcal{O}$ to reflect that the access has already been handled.
- $\rho(H, \pi, r)$ is a capacity-$2n$ swordRAM over an array H that we refer to as the *log*. Informally, the swordRAM logs each PrORAM access. The swordRAM's remaining reads $\pi[r..]$ correspond to $\mathcal{O}$. $\rho(H, \pi, r)$ is the authenticated component of PrORAM, and PrORAM's array accesses are ultimately authenticated via the mechanisms of this swordRAM.
- $\mathcal{T}$ is the *timetable* maintained in cleartext by $\mathcal{P}$. The timetable maps each array index to the last timestep when that index was accessed. That is, for each array index i, $\mathcal{T}[i]$ is a pointer into the log denoting where $A[i]$ was last logged. The timetable is unknown to $\mathcal{V}$.

6.3 Scheduling the Underlying swordRAM

Recall, we are working with an n-element PrORAM that facilitates operations on an n-element array A. In this section, we formally describe how to derive a swordRAM read order π given a length-n PrORAM access order. Recall from Sect. 6.2 that the permutation π must account both for the block of the next n PrORAM accesses and for the reads needed to copy array contents to a fresh PrORAM such that we can support more accesses.

Figure 4 presents schedule, an algorithm that computes π, the order in which the underlying swordRAM will obliviously read the elements of the log. schedule takes as input the given access order $\mathcal{O}$. swordRAM writes are sequential, and need not be scheduled, though the read schedule does depend on writes.

As explained in Sect. 6.2, each PrORAM data structure $\boxed{A, \mathcal{O}}$ is initialized with the array A in canonical order (initialization is discussed in Sect. 6.5).

To explain schedule, we first discuss how a single PrORAM access is mapped to the swordRAM. At initialization, the underlying capacity-$2n$ swordRAM stores all n elements of A in its first n available slots; the remaining n slots are not yet written and no reads have yet been used. Suppose that $\mathcal{P}$ wishes to read PrORAM slot $A[i]$. The swordRAM's read order permutation π should reflect this access: the first entry of π should indicate that slot i is read at time 0 (i.e., $\pi[0] = i$). Recall that swordRAM slots can be read only once. Therefore,

```
schedule(O) :
  ▷ Initialize a timetable to track which element will live where.
  ▷ Initially, the swordRAM will store elements in canonical order.
  T ← [0..n]
  return schedule − suffix(O, T, n)

schedule − suffix(O, T, r) :
  π ← 0^{r+n}     ▷ Initialize an array π to hold the remaining swordRAM reads
  ▷ Schedule a swordRAM read corresponding to each tth PrORAM access.
  for t ∈ [0..r] :
    i ← O[t]     ▷ Look up the target index of the tth access.
    slot ← T[i]     ▷ Look up the swordRAM slot that holds i.
    π[t] ← slot     ▷ slot should be read on the tth swordRAM read.
    ▷ Index i will be written back into the end of the swordRAM.
    ▷ Keep track of this write in the timetable.
    T[i] ← 2n − r + t
  ▷ After all n accesses, we prepare to move elements to a fresh swordRAM.
  ▷ Thus, we schedule a read of each element in canonical order.
  for i ∈ [0..n] :
    slot ← T[i]     ▷ Look up the swordRAM slot that holds i.
    π[i + r] ← slot     ▷ slot should be read on the (i + n)th swordRAM read.
  return π
```

Fig. 4. Scheduling swordRAM accesses. schedule takes as an argument a PrORAM access order $\mathcal{O}$ and outputs a corresponding swordRAM read order permutation π. PrORAM supports schedules of arbitrary length, but schedule only sets up the next n accesses in the schedule, and hence only looks at the first n entries of $\mathcal{O}$. schedule delegates to a more general procedure schedule − suffix which generates a length $r + n$ *suffix* of a read order permutation. While this more general call is never exercised in our execution (except directly via schedule), we use it to define validity of a general PrORAM state, in which some accesses may have occurred: a valid PrORAM must have a schedule equal to one (correctly) generated by schedule − suffix.

to allow the PrORAM slot $A[i]$ to be read a second time, we must write back a value to the swordRAM. Because swordRAM writes occur sequentially, this write will place the new value into slot n. To account for this write, we should keep track of the new location of $A[i]$ which is done using a timetable $\mathcal{T}$. As a side remark, $\mathcal{T}$ is initialized to $[0, 1, ..., n-1]$, reflecting the fact that initially each element of A is stored in the swordRAM in canonical order.

Scheduling many accesses simply repeatedly applies the following basic procedure for accesses $j = 0, 1, \ldots, n-1$: Let i be the queried index on access j. We

(1) look up the location of element i in the swordRAM based on $\mathcal{T}$, (2) update π such that slot i is read at time j (i.e., $\pi[j] = i$), (3) allocate the next available swordRAM write slot as the fresh location for element i, (4) update $\mathcal{T}$ to record that element i is stored in the fresh location.

schedule (Fig. 4) implements this procedure. schedule accepts an access order $\mathcal{O}$ and outputs a permutation on $2n$ elements (encoded as an array) suitable for a swordRAM.

After allocating reads for the n accesses, schedule indicates that the last n entries in the permutation should match the current timetable. This detail is used to move the contents of an old data structure into a new one: after n accesses, we read the array contents in canonical order. The order of these last n reads is exactly what is stored in the final state of $\mathcal{T}$.

schedule highlights the key points of the reduction from RAM to swordRAM: map each array access to a swordRAM slot and continually update which array element is where. Of course, the reader must keep in mind the duality of our presentation as an iterative processing in response to queries, and the precomputed non-interactive one-shot schedule chosen before each block of n accesses.

6.4 PrORAM Validity

Before we specify PrORAM operations, we establish a validity condition that connects the PrORAM to its underlying swordRAM. This condition is the invariant that allows us to prove PrORAM is correct over many accesses.

As explained in Sect. 5, the swordRAM should be viewed as a log of the accesses to the PrORAM. PrORAM **validity** ensures that its swordRAM both (1) stores a log that properly reflects the PrORAM's current content and (2) has a read order that reflects PrORAM's future accesses.

Definition 1 (PrORAM Validity). *Let* $\boxed{A, \mathcal{O}} = (A, \mathcal{O}, \rho(H\,\pi, r), \mathcal{T})$ *be a size-n PrORAM. We say that this PrORAM is* ***valid*** *if:*

1. *For each PrORAM index i:*

$$H[\mathcal{T}[i]] = (A[i], i)$$

2. *Let* $w \triangleq |H|$ *be the number of elements written to the underlying swordRAM:*

$$\mathsf{schedule} - \mathsf{suffix}(\mathcal{O}, \mathcal{T}, n - w) = \pi[r..]$$

Less formally, these two conditions ensure the following:

1. If we look up each element's location in the timetable and then find each location in the log, then we recover the array A. This ensures that the swordRAM properly stores the array A. Note, we store each element $A[i]$ in a pair with its index i. This allows RAM accesses to check that the queried index matches the stored index, ensuring that $\mathcal{P}$ cannot substitute one RAM element for another.
2. If we construct a partial swordRAM schedule from the access order and the current timetable, then we obtain a new copy of the remaining swordRAM read order. This ensures that the remaining swordRAM reads properly reflect the array access order $\mathcal{O}$.

6.5 PrORAM Operations

Figures 5, 6 and 7 list the operations over PrORAMs:

- Figure 5 indicates how a new PrORAM is initialized. The parties select an array of n sharings $[\![A]\!]$ as the initial array state, then sequentially write these elements into a fresh swordRAM. The procedure also sets up the swordRAM schedule and $\mathcal{P}$'s timetable $\mathcal{T}$. The swordRAM schedule is set using $\mathsf{schedule}$, and at initialization each PrORAM slot lives in the corresponding swordRAM slot: $\mathcal{T}$ is initialized to $[0, 1, ..., n-1]$.
- Figure 6 indicates how the parties access a PrORAM index. To access element i, the parties first read from the underlying swordRAM and retrieve a pair $[\![A[i], i']\!]$. The parties check that $i = i'$ by opening $\mathcal{P}$'s share of $i - i'$. This check ensures that $\mathcal{P}$ cannot substitute one array value for another.
- Figure 7 is a helper procedure that allows the parties to refresh the PrORAM after every n accesses. To perform this refresh, the parties read the latest copy of every RAM slot from the swordRAM, then write these values back into a fresh swordRAM. We call the refresh procedure once every n accesses.

Crucially, each PrORAM operation preserves validity. We argue this formally in our proof of correctness.

- **Inputs:** Parties input an array of n authenticated secret shares $[\![A]\!]$ that form the initial state of the array (for example, parties might use $[\![0]\!]^n$). $\mathcal{P}$ inputs the array access order $\mathcal{O}$.
- **Outputs:** Parties output a valid initialized PrORAM:

$$(A, \mathcal{O}, \rho(H, \pi, 0), \mathcal{T})$$

where $\mathcal{T} = [0, 1, ..., n-1]$ and the log H is equal to A.
- **Protocol:**
  - $\mathcal{P}$ initializes her timetable $\mathcal{T}$ as $[0, 1, ..., n-1]$. That is, in the initial state of the PrORAM, each index i is in log slot i.
  - $\mathcal{P}$ computes $\pi \triangleq \mathsf{schedule}(\mathcal{O})$. π is the swordRAM read order.
  - Parties initialize an empty swordRAM to hold the log H; $\mathcal{P}$ uses π to perform this initialization.
  - Parties perform n writes to the swordRAM where the ith write stores the pair $[\![A[i], i]\!]$ (each i is a public constant, so the parties use the protocol's support for constants to encode these indexes). After all n writes, the swordRAM holds A in order, where each slot is explicitly marked with its index.
  - The PrORAM $(A, \mathcal{O}, \rho(A, \pi, 0), \mathcal{T})$ is now defined; the parties output their respective components.

Fig. 5. The PrORAM initialization procedure $\mathsf{initialize}$. $\mathsf{initialize}$ takes as arguments (1) an authenticated size-n array $[\![A]\!]$ and (2) an access order $\mathcal{O}$. $\mathsf{initialize}$ outputs a fresh PrORAM $\boxed{A, \mathcal{O}}$.

- INPUTS: Parties input:
  1. A size-n PrORAM $\boxed{\text{A}, \mathcal{O}}$.
  2. A shared index $[\![i]\!]$.
  3. An agreed upon function f used to update the selected element. f should be described as a circuit computable by the algebraic protocol (Section 4.1).
- OUTPUTS: Parties output:
  1. The selected value $[\![A[i]]\!]$.
  2. The updated array $\boxed{\text{A}[\text{i} := \text{f}(\text{A}[\text{i}])], \mathcal{O}[1..]}$.
- PROTOCOL:
  - Let $\boxed{\text{A}, \mathcal{O}} = (A, \mathcal{O}, \rho(H, \pi, r), \mathcal{T})$.
  - If $|H| = 2n$, parties call refresh (Figure 7) and replace the PrORAM by the output of the refresh operation.
  - Parties perform a read on $\rho(H, \pi, r)$ (Figure 2). Let $\rho(H, \pi, r+1)$ be the updated swordRAM and let $[\![x, i']\!]$ be the read value.
  - $\mathcal{P}$ opens her share of $[\![i - i']\!] = [\![0]\!]$. If $\mathcal{P}$'s share is not a share of 0, $\mathcal{V}$ aborts. This check prevents $\mathcal{P}$ from accessing an element $A[j]$ for $j \neq i$.
  - Parties jointly compute $[\![f(x)]\!]$ via the algebraic protocol.
  - Parties write $[\![(i, f(x))]\!]$ to $\rho(H, \pi, r+1)$ (Figure 3). Let $\rho(H|f(x), \pi, r+1)$ be the updated swordRAM.
  - Parties output $[\![x]\!]$.
  - Parties output $(A[i := f(A[i])], \mathcal{O}[1..], \rho(H|f(x), \pi, r+1), \mathcal{T}[i := |H|])$. That is, they output $\boxed{\text{A}[\text{i} := \text{f}(\text{A}[\text{i}])], \mathcal{O}[1..]}$, which is the PrORAM updated to include the new write.

Fig. 6. PrORAM access procedure access. access performs the following functions: (1) it looks up and outputs the queried element $[\![A[i]]\!]$, (2) it computes $[\![f(A[i]]\!]$ for arbitrary circuit-encoded function f, and (3) it writes $[\![f(A[i]]\!]$ back to the array. If $\mathcal{O}[0] \neq i$ (that is, if $\mathcal{P}$ tries to use a bad read order), then $\mathcal{V}$ will abort.

- INPUTS: Parties input a valid size-n PrORAM $(A, \mathcal{O}, \rho(H, \pi, n), \mathcal{T})$ such that $|H| = 2n$; i.e., the underlying swordRAM has no writes and n reads remaining.
- OUTPUTS: Parties output a valid, refreshed PrORAM $(A, \mathcal{O}, \rho(H', \pi', 0), \mathcal{T}')$ such that $|H'| = n$; i.e., the new underlying swordRAM has n writes and $2n$ reads remaining.
- PROTOCOL:
  - Parties perform n swordRAM reads on $\rho(H, \pi, n)$. Because of the validity condition (Definition 1) and the definition of schedule (Figure 4), these n reads fetch the array content: the parties hold $[\![A]\!]$.
  - Parties call the PrORAM initialize procedure (Figure 5) with $[\![A]\!]$ and $\mathcal{O}$ and return the resulting PrORAM.

Fig. 7. PrORAM refresh procedure. PrORAM is built on top of swordRAM which allows only a bounded number of reads/writes. To allow many PrORAM accesses, we periodically *refresh*. The refresh procedure simply reads the content of the old swordRAM into an array, then initializes a fresh PrORAM with the result.

Implementing Read and Write. access takes a general function f as an argument; accessing $A[i]$ also writes back $f(A[i])$. We quickly show that this is sufficient to implement the standard read and write array operations:

$$\mathsf{read}(\boxed{A,\ \mathcal{O}}, [\![i]\!]) \triangleq \mathsf{access}(\boxed{A,\ \mathcal{O}}, [\![i]\!], [\![x]\!] \mapsto [\![x]\!])$$
$$\mathsf{write}(\boxed{A,\ \mathcal{O}}, [\![i]\!], [\![y]\!]) \triangleq \mathsf{access}(\boxed{A,\ \mathcal{O}}, [\![i]\!], [\![x]\!] \mapsto [\![y]\!])$$

To implement read, we call access with the identity function: read simply writes back the read element. To implement write, we call access with a constant function that ignores the read element and returns the written element y.

Taking an arbitrary function is flexible. For example, we can implement an increment function that in-place updates an array slot:

$$\mathsf{increment}(\boxed{A,\ \mathcal{O}}, [\![i]\!]) \triangleq \mathsf{access}(\boxed{A,\ \mathcal{O}}, [\![i]\!], [\![x]\!] \mapsto [\![x+1]\!])$$

Thus, we can mutate an array value without using two RAM accesses.

6.6 PrORAM Formal Properties

In this section, we state PrORAM's formal properties. Due to lack of space, we defer full proofs of these properties to Supplementary Material.

initialize and access maintain validity:

Theorem 1 (Initialize Correctness). *Let $[\![A]\!]$ be an authenticated share of an array of n elements and let $\mathcal{O}$ be an arbitrary access order over n elements.*

$$\mathsf{initialize}([\![A]\!], \mathcal{O}) = \boxed{A,\ \mathcal{O}}$$

where $\boxed{A,\ \mathcal{O}}$ is a valid PrORAM.

Theorem 2 (Access Correctness). *Let $\boxed{A,\ \mathcal{O}}$ be a valid n-element PrORAM. Let $j \triangleq \mathcal{O}[0]$. Let $[\![i]\!]$ be a shared RAM index, and let f be a publicly agreed function. If $i = j$ (i.e., if the shared RAM index matches the access order), then the following holds:*

$$\mathsf{access}(\boxed{A,\ \mathcal{O}}, [\![i]\!], f) = ([\![A[i]]\!], \boxed{A[i := f(A[i])],\ \mathcal{O}[1..]}),$$

where $\boxed{A[i := f(A[i])],\ \mathcal{O}[1..]}$ is a valid PrORAM.

In short, we show that the operations update the timetable/schedule and appropriately make use of swordRAM such that validity is maintained.

PrORAM is also concretely efficient:

Theorem 3 (Access Cost). *The procedure* access *(Fig. 6) invoked on a size-n PrORAM consumes amortized $2\log n$ oblivious transfers of length 2σ secrets. Additionally, each access transmits amortized 8σ bits.*

In short, we inspect the PrORAM algorithms for communication cost, then amortize costs across each block of n accesses.

7 A Complete ZKP System and Security Proofs

Our approach to defining and proving security. PrORAM naturally integrates with ZKP systems based on authenticated shares, such as the ZKP system of [HK20a]. To *define* and prove security of a ZK ORAM construction, including our PrORAM, one needs to set up a general ZK proof environment which can generate arbitrary RAM query patterns. The ZKP system of [HK20a] provides a simple, general, and efficient environment. We embed PrORAM directly into this protocol, and state and prove the security properties of the resulting system.

We list the following benefits from taking this route:

1. We construct a *complete* PrORAM-based ZKP system.
2. [HK20a], and hence our complete system, is concretely efficient.
3. As discussed next, we can reuse the clean and powerful GC-based ZK framework of [JKO13,FNO15] to *compile a garbling scheme into a ZKP system.*
4. We obtain a simple formalism that can be easily generalized/plugged in other systems (separate proofs are required, but often may be modeled on our proof blueprint).

ZK-ORAM Definition. We stress that while we do not define ZK ORAM in *full* generality, a natural and generalizable ORAM definition emerges (see Sect. 7.4).

7.1 Casting as a Garbling Scheme

Like [HK20a], we cast our system as a Garbling Scheme (GS), and thus are able to reuse the convenient and powerful framework of [JKO13]. Their framework **plugs** a custom GS (satisfying certain requirements) into their protocol; the instantiated constant round protocol **is a malicious-verifier ZKP system**.

In the following, we derive notation from [BHR12], but include changes proposed by recent works that separate the circuit's logical description from *GC material* [HK20c,HK20b]. We explicitly include both the GC material M and the computed circuit $\mathcal{C}$ as arguments to our GS functions.

Before continuing, we discuss the correspondence of our system to a garbling scheme, as this correspondence may *a priori* be unintuitive; after all, we do not construct encryptions of logical gates which are the hallmark of garbled circuits. Nevertheless, our construction does have components that map cleanly to a GS:

Garbled input labels. In a GS, the GC evaluator receives *garbled input labels.* These labels are typically encryption keys that correspond to the logical values on the input wires. The collection of all input labels is called the *encoding* (denoted e), and in most protocols the parties run OTs to send a selection of input labels (a subset corresponding to the player's input) from the encoding to the evaluator. Our labels are more naturally understood as *authentication keys*, rather than encryption keys. We send particular authentication mask differences via OT to enable the authentic multiplication of shares (see Sect. 4.1). The collection of all OT messages used for multiplications forms our encoding e.

Garbled material. In a GS, the GC evaluator receives an extra string that does not depend on her input and is used to evaluate the GC. This string is called the *material* (denoted M), and is typically a collection of encrypted truth tables. While we do not encrypt truth tables, we do send fixed values from $\mathcal{V}$ to $\mathcal{P}$ to initialize additive shares and to execute writes to swordRAMs (see Fig. 3). The collection of these extra messages is our material M.

Garbled output label. Similar to the input encoding e, GSs also require an output decoding (denoted d). In the [JKO13] framework, d is a single, unforgeable value that indicates a proof; $\mathcal{V}$ simply checks that $\mathcal{P}$ indeed constructed d to become convinced. In our construction, the string d is the hash digest of all of $\mathcal{P}$'s opened shares (see Sect. 4.1).

Achieving verifiability. The [JKO13] framework requires a GS to be verifiable. Informally, this provides for a way to "open" the garbled function to prove that it was constructed correctly. One natural way to achieve this, which we adopt, is for all of $\mathcal{V}$'s randomness be derived from a seed S. Revealing S allows $\mathcal{P}$ to verify the garbled function. GSs and the [JKO13] framework do not provide a side channel for $\mathcal{V}$ to deliver S to $\mathcal{P}$. Therefore, we use e for this purpose: we simply XOR secret share S and append the shares to the labels of wire 1 of the circuit. This way, S remains protected until it is opened by $\mathcal{V}$.

7.2 The [JKO13] ZK Framework

To plug a construction into [JKO13]'s ZK protocol, we must prove that the construction is a **verifiable garbling scheme**. A verifiable garbling scheme is a tuple of six algorithms (see [BHR12, JKO13] for precise syntax and formalization details):

$$(\mathsf{ev}, \mathsf{Gb}, \mathsf{En}, \mathsf{Ev}, \mathsf{De}, \mathsf{Ve})$$

The first five algorithms define a garbling scheme [BHR12], while the sixth adds verifiability [JKO13].

A garbling scheme specifies the functionality computed by $\mathcal{V}$ and $\mathcal{P}$. $\mathcal{V}$ uses Gb to construct material M, input encoding e, and output decoding d. Gb is computed by walking through the agreed proof circuit $\mathcal{C}$ gate-by-gate. In our construction, we simplify Gb by ensuring that all random values are chosen according to a single pseudorandom seed. Next, $\mathcal{V}$ uses OT to encode $\mathcal{P}$'s witness according to e. En specifies what these OTs should accomplish: it maps $\mathcal{P}$'s input space to a concrete choice of encoding, specifying the particular values in e that $\mathcal{P}$ should receive for each of her inputs. Upon receiving material M and an encoded witness, $\mathcal{P}$ uses Ev to authentically compute the circuit gate-by-gate. At the end of a ZK proof, $\mathcal{P}$ constructs a particular output value which is first committed and later sent to $\mathcal{V}$. $\mathcal{V}$ then calls De, which checks that the received value is exactly equal to the output decoding d; if not, $\mathcal{V}$ aborts.

The steps described so far do not protect $\mathcal{P}$ from a cheating $\mathcal{V}$, who might maliciously construct e and M in order to leak $\mathcal{P}$'s input. Therefore, before opening her commitment, $\mathcal{P}$ rebuilds M, e, and d according to $\mathcal{V}$'s seed (which is sent after the commitment). $\mathcal{P}$ uses these reconstructed values to check that the messages received from $\mathcal{V}$ were honestly constructed. If so, she opens her commitment; if not, she aborts. Ve describes how $\mathcal{P}$ should reconstruct M, e, and d and how she should check that $\mathcal{V}$ did not cheat.

Finally, ev provides a *specification* against which the correctness of the garbling scheme can be checked: ev describes the cleartext semantics of the circuits manipulated by the GS.

A verifiable garbling scheme must be **correct**, **sound**, and **verifiable** (definitions are in Sect. 7).

7.3 Our Garbling Scheme, Its Security, and Our Main Theorem

Our garbling scheme is the arithmetic garbling scheme of [HK20a] augmented with PrORAM. The arithmetic circuit may arbitrarily issue calls to PrORAM's initialize and access functionalities (Figs. 5 and 6).

Construction 1 (Our Garbling Scheme). *Our garbling scheme is the six tuple of algorithms:*

$$(\mathsf{ev}, \mathsf{Gb}, \mathsf{En}, \mathsf{Ev}, \mathsf{De}, \mathsf{Ve})$$

described below. Circuits handled by the garbling scheme allow (1) publicly agreed constant wire values, (2) addition gates, (3) subtraction gates, (4) scalar gates (which multiply a value by a public constant), (5) vector-scalar multiplication gates (where the scalar is chosen by $\mathcal{P}$), (6) opening gates (which force $\mathcal{P}$ to prove a share represents a specific constant), (7) array initialization gates, and (8) array access gates. Circuits thus include two types of wires: (1) algebraic wires that hold values in $\mathbb{Z}_p$ and (2) array wires that hold arrays of values in $\mathbb{Z}_p$.

Our circuits do not include standard multiplication gates, but recall (from Sect. 4.2) that standard multiplication gates are easily implemented on top of vector-scalar multiplication gates and opening gates.

We describe each of our garbling scheme procedures:

ev evaluates the ZK relation in cleartext and implicitly specifies the cleartext semantics of each gate type. Our gate types have natural semantics, for example addition gates indeed add their inputs.

Gb processes the circuit gate-by-gate. As it goes, it generates random values, obtained from expansion of a pseudorandom seed S. The procedure generates the mask differences that are $\mathcal{V}$'s OT inputs (i.e. the encoding e). Additionally, Gb generates the material M: when $\mathcal{V}$ constructs additive sharings and on swordRAM writes, Gb appends the 'sent' component of the sharing to accumulated string of material. To handle opening gates, the algorithm also accumulates, as it goes, the hash of the expected opened shares (that $\mathcal{V}$ expects from $\mathcal{P}$). The final value of this hash is decoding secret d.

Gb processes arithmetic gates according to the [HK20a] protocol (see Sect. 4.1). Array access gates are processed with our ORAM construction (Figs. 5 and 6). Each of these gates is handled by running $\mathcal{V}$'s procedure.

As an additional detail, Gb includes in e two XOR secret shares of the pseudorandom seed S. We discuss this in Sect. 7.1 under **achieving verifiability**.

En describes which mask differences (for vector-scalar multiplication gates) $\mathcal{P}$ should receive according to her input. Looking at the procedure for vector-scalar multiplication (Sect. 4.1), En is the trivial mapping that indicates $\mathcal{P}$ should receive the left OT secret if her input is zero and the right OT secret otherwise (cf. Eq. 1 in Sect. 4.1).

Ev is complementary to Gb. Like Gb, it processes the circuit gate-by-gate. On vector-scalar multiplication gates, Ev consumes encoded input delivered by En. On the construction of additive sharings/swordRAM writes Ev consumes material in M. On opening gates, Ev accumulates a hash of opened shares.

Ev handles each gate by running $\mathcal{P}$'s procedures as described in Sect. 4.1 and Figs. 5 and 6.

De is a simple comparison: if the expected output d is equal to the provided hash, then the procedure accepts; otherwise it rejects (and $\mathcal{V}$ aborts).

Ve is implemented in the same manner as Gb: it uses the pseudorandom seed (included in e, see Sect. 7.1) to replay the actions of Gb. As it goes, it checks that the generated encoding e, material M, and decoding d are equal to the given values. If all values are equal, Ve accepts; otherwise it rejects (and $\mathcal{P}$ aborts).

We next formalize that Construction 1 is **correct**, **sound**, and **verifiable**. Due to lack of space, we defer full proofs of these properties to Supplementary Material. These theorems, combined with Theorem 2 from [JKO13] and theorems in Sect. 6 imply the following:

Theorem 4 (Main Theorem). *In the OT-hybrid model, assuming collision-resistant hash, and statistical security parameter σ, the framework of [JKO13] instantiated with Construction 1 is a (malicious-verifier) ZKP system with soundness $O(2^{-\sigma})$. Circuits in the resulting system may construct and access random-access arrays, and each access to an array of size n consumes amortized $2\log n$ OTs of length 2σ secrets.*

Definition 2 (Correctness). *A garbling scheme is* ***correct*** *if for all circuits $\mathcal{C}$ and all inputs i such that $\mathcal{C}(i) = 1$:*

$$(e, M, d) = \mathsf{Gb}(1^\sigma, \mathcal{C}) \implies \mathsf{Ev}(\mathcal{C}, M, \mathsf{En}(e, i), i) = d$$

Correctness enforces that GS correctly implements the specification ev.

Theorem 5. *Construction 1 is* ***correct****.*

In short, correctness follows from the correctness of [HK20a]'s arithmetic protocol and from the correctness of PrORAM (Theorems 1 and 2).

Definition 3 (Soundness). *A garbling scheme is* ***sound*** *if for all circuits $\mathcal{C}$, all inputs i such that $\mathcal{C}(i) = 0$, and all probabilistic polynomial time adversaries $\mathcal{A}$ the following probability is negligible in σ:*

$$Pr(\mathcal{A}(\mathcal{C}, M, \mathsf{En}(e, i)) = d : (e, M, d) \leftarrow \mathsf{Gb}(1^\sigma, \mathcal{C}))$$

Soundness ensures that a cheating $\mathcal{P}$ cannot forge a convincing proof.

Theorem 6 (Soundness). *Assuming the existence of collision-resistant hash functions, Construction 1 is* ***sound****.*

In short, soundness follows from the authenticity of secret shares. $\mathcal{P}$ cannot forge RAM values because each is masked by a distinct value chosen by $\mathcal{V}$.

Definition 4 (Verifiability). *A garbling scheme is* ***verifiable*** *if for all circuits $\mathcal{C}$, all inputs i such that $\mathcal{C}(i) = 1$, and all probabilistic polynomial time adversaries $\mathcal{A}$ there exists an expected polynomial time algorithm* Ext *such that the following probability is negligible in σ:*

$$Pr\left(\mathsf{Ext}(\mathcal{C}, M, e) \neq \mathsf{Ev}(\mathcal{C}, M, \mathsf{En}(e, i)) : (e, M) \leftarrow \mathcal{A}(1^\sigma, \mathcal{C}), \mathsf{Ve}(\mathcal{C}, M, e) = 1\right)$$

At a high level, in the [JKO13] protocol, $\mathcal{P}$ receives and evaluates GC and commits to her proof message. Then she is given $\mathcal{V}$'s private randomness used to construct the GC. $\mathcal{P}$ uses this randomness to check messages sent by $\mathcal{V}$. Verifiability ensures that this check is reliable in the following sense: $\mathcal{V}$ will learn nothing from the opened proof message because $\mathcal{P}$'s proof message can be reconstructed in polytime by Ext without $\mathcal{P}$'s witness. Altogether, verifiability ensures that the ZK protocol is secure against a malicious verifier.

Our construction takes a natural approach and derives all of $\mathcal{V}$'s randomness from a seed S, and then reveal S as part of the verification procedure Ve. To syntactically fit the conveyance of S into the [JKO13] framework, we include S in e. See discussion accompanying the protocol specification Construction 1. Note, opening all of $\mathcal{V}$'s private randomness is a natural protocol design decision, but is not required by the definition of verifiability (Definition 4).

Theorem 7 (Verifiability). *Construction 1 is* ***verifiable****.*

In short, verifiability follows relatively trivially from the fact that $\mathcal{V}$ chooses all randomness starting from a pseudorandom seed.

7.4 Defining ZK ORAM

As discussed before, we do not aim to define ZK ORAM in utmost generality. So far, we proved (Theorem 4) that PrORAM, integrated with the (quite general) GC-based ZKP CPU [HK20a], which can generate an arbitrary sequence of RAM accesses, results in secure and correct ZKP system. Here we explain why this is a reasonable framework to also *define* ZK ORAM with respect to specific execution environments.

Recall, MPC ORAM is often defined as a compiler that translates logical RAM/array accesses to physical memory accesses; its obliviousness property is defined by the indistinguishability of physical RAM accesses of any two programs of equal length (or, alternatively, via simulation), executed in some well-defined RAM Execution Environment (REE). The programs in a REE, e.g., can simply be defined as arbitrary sequences of logical RAM accesses. Again, MPC ORAM is said to be correct and secure, if the REE execution of the RAM program satisfies formally defined security and correctness properties.

We can follow the same definitional approach in defining ZK ORAM: We specify a REE (the GC-based ZKP CPU [HK20a]) which interfaces with the ORAM protocol using initialize and access commands and which can generate arbitrary access sequences. We then require that the REE execution of any RAM program results in a secure ZKP system.

Hence, PrORAM is proven secure with respect to the GC-based ZKP CPU of [HK20a] according to the following definition.

Definition 5 (ZK ORAM for a REE). *Let RAM Execution Environment* $\mathsf{Env}_{\mathsf{RAM}}$ *be a pair of interactive Turing machines* $\mathcal{P}$, $\mathcal{V}$, *which operate with arrays by making calls to* initialize *and* access *as described above. We say that a protocol* Z *supporting calls to* initialize *and* access *from* $\mathsf{Env}_{\mathsf{RAM}}$, *is a secure ZK ORAM, if the protocol obtained by composition of* $\mathsf{Env}_{\mathsf{RAM}}$ *and* Z *is a secure ZKP system (in particular, secure against malicious verifier* $\mathcal{V}$*).*

8 Instantiation

We implemented PrORAM in 1300 lines of C++. Our implementation uses the recent and efficient correlated Ferret OT technique [YWL+20]. Note, Ferret requires additional cryptographic assumptions: (1) learning parity with noise (LPN), (2) a tweakable correlation-robust hash function, and (3) a random oracle (RO). We use statistical security parameter $\sigma = 40$ and accordingly instantiate our prime field with modulus $p = 2^{40} - 87$, the largest 40 bit prime.

In the following section, we discuss an experimental evaluation of our implementation. All experiments were performed on a MacBook Pro laptop with an Intel Dual-Core i5 3.1 GHz processor and 8 GB of RAM. We ran our experiments on a simulated LAN network featuring 1 Gbps of bandwidth and 2 ms latency.

9 Evaluation

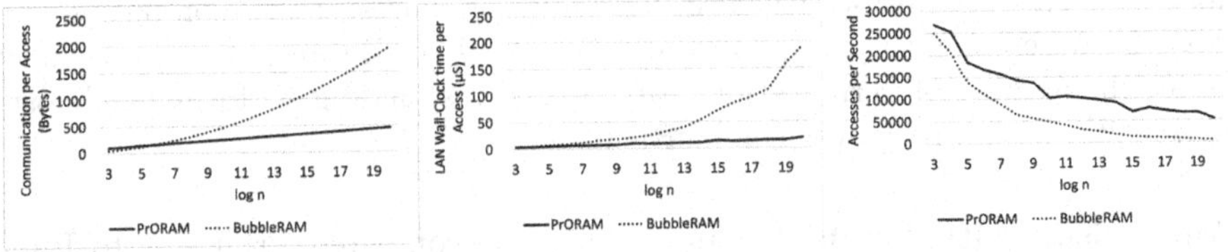

Fig. 8. Performance comparison of PrORAM against [HK20a]'s BubbleRAM. We plot performance as a function of the size of RAM n. Each experiment accessed the RAM 2^{20} times. We plot (1) the amortized communication cost of each access (left), (2) the amortized wall-clock time per access (center), and (3) the number of accesses performed per second (right). Center and right are different views of the same information.

In this section, we illustrate the performance of PrORAM by experimental evaluation. For comparison, we also ran BubbleRAM, a circuit-based ZK ORAM that was implemented as part of [HK20a]'s ZK construction. Since their construction is built on the same underlying arithmetic protocol, the comparison is direct. We emphasize that we implement both constructions in the same protocol and use the *same underlying OT protocol* (Ferret [YWL+20]); thus our experiments directly compare the ORAM techniques, not the environments they run in. Our comparison highlights the low asymptotic and concrete costs of PrORAM.

We implemented both PrORAM and BubbleRAM and used them to evaluate a circuit which accesses an array 2^{20} times on random indexes. Of course, a more realistic use case would use the RAM in the context of a more complex circuit, but our goal is only to measure performance. We varied the size of the RAM n between 2^3 slots and 2^{20} slots. Each RAM slot holds a single $\mathbb{Z}_p$ element; recall that, internally, the PrORAM also reserves an extra slot to store the index identifier. Hence, internally the PrORAM slots have width two; BubbleRAM uses the same trick and hence also has slots of width two. We measured both the total communication transmitted between $\mathcal{P}$ and $\mathcal{V}$ and the wall-clock time needed to complete the entire proof. Figure 8 plots the results of these experiments.

Communication improvement. Our communication improvement follows naturally from our improved asymptotics: BubbleRAM incurs $1/2 \log^2 n$ OTs per access while we incur only $2 \log n$. In addition to the OTs, our $\mathcal{V}$ also sends an additional eight $\mathbb{Z}_p$ elements per RAM access: four to convey shares of K to $\mathcal{P}$ before permuting and four for the two swordRAM writes.

PrORAM outperforms BubbleRAM for $n > 2^5$. At $n = 2^{20}$, communication is improved by $4.36\times$.

Wall-clock time improvement. Our wall-clock time improvement is far more dramatic than our communication improvement.

Both BubbleRAM and PrORAM primarily involve applying Waksman permutation networks to an array of shared values. However, PrORAM applies only a single permutation to prepare for n accesses. In contrast, BubbleRAM applies a permutation on *each* access (though the permutations vary in size). Waksman networks are not cache friendly. The network involves swapping (via algebra) data between disparate locations in the array of shares. Thus, computing the network causes many cache misses and is expensive. Because we significantly reduce the number of permutations, we see a corresponding performance boost. At $n = 2^{20}$, we improve over BubbleRAM by $10.6\times$.

Comparison with BubbleCache. Above, we compared PrORAM to BubbleRAM. [HYDK21] gave a practical improvement to BubbleRAM called BubbleCache. Here, we analytically compare PrORAM and BubbleCache.

BubbleCache improves BubbleRAM by exploiting data locality and by introducing the possibility of cache misses. BubbleCache incurs only $O(\log n)$ communication overhead per access, matching the asymptotic complexity of PrORAM.

Indeed, if we ignore the cost of cache misses, BubbleCache is slightly cheaper than PrORAM. E.g., for a RAM with 2^{17} words of memory, BubbleCache consumes ≈20 OTs per access while PrORAM consumes 34.

However, if there is insufficient data locality in the program execution, BubbleCache will be unable to fetch a needed data item, and the RAM will be forced to issue a cache miss. These cache misses must be handled by the surrounding ZK circuitry. PrORAM does not issue cache misses and implements a simple array interface.

This difference between the two RAMs is both quantitative and qualitative:

- Suppose we plug both RAMs into a CPU-based architecture. When using BubbleCache, we must pay overhead on the CPU cycle circuit corresponding to the cache miss rate. For example, in the [HYDK21] processor, each CPU cycle costs ≈270 OTs and reads/writes memory once. [HYDK21] found that a cache miss rate of ≈10% was relatively normal. Thus, we can allocate the extra $0.1 \times 270 = 27$ OTs to each BubbleCache read. Already, PrORAM is thus superior. Moreover, the CPU cycle circuit could be simplified since it no longer needs to account for cache misses.
- Consider implementing a proof via a specialized circuit with array accesses. I.e., suppose we do not implement a ZK CPU. Notice that it is not clear how cache misses should be handled. Indeed, a cache-missing RAM seems to force the designer to adopt a circuit structure that repeatedly performs the same computation over and over (i.e., a CPU). PrORAM, which cannot miss, can be used easily alongside simple circuits.

Acknowledgments. This work was supported in part by NSF award #1909769, by a Facebook research award, by Georgia Tech's IISP cybersecurity seed funding (CSF) award. This material is also based upon work supported in part by DARPA under Contract No. HR001120C0087. Any opinions, findings and conclusions or recommendations expressed in this material are those of the authors and do not necessarily reflect the views of DARPA.

References

[AHIV17] Ames, S., Hazay, C., Ishai, Y., Venkitasubramaniam, M.: Ligero: lightweight sublinear arguments without a trusted setup. In: Thuraisingham, B.M., Evans, D., Malkin, T., Xu, D. (eds.) ACM CCS 2017, pp. 2087–2104. ACM Press, October/November 2017

[AKL+20] Asharov, G., Komargodski, I., Lin, W.-K., Nayak, K., Peserico, E., Shi, E.: OptORAMa: optimal oblivious RAM. In: Canteaut, A., Ishai, Y. (eds.) EUROCRYPT 2020, Part II. LNCS, vol. 12106, pp. 403–432. Springer, Cham (2020). https://doi.org/10.1007/978-3-030-45724-2_14

[BBHR18] Ben-Sasson, E., Bentov, I., Horesh, Y., Riabzev, M.: Scalable, transparent, and post-quantum secure computational integrity. Cryptology ePrint Archive, Report 2018/046 (2018). https://eprint.iacr.org/2018/046

[BCG+13] Ben-Sasson, E., Chiesa, A., Genkin, D., Tromer, E., Virza, M.: SNARKs for C: verifying program executions succinctly and in zero knowledge. In: Canetti, R., Garay, J.A. (eds.) CRYPTO 2013, Part II. LNCS, vol. 8043, pp. 90–108. Springer, Heidelberg (2013). https://doi.org/10.1007/978-3-642-40084-1_6

[BCG+19] Boyle, E., Couteau, G., Gilboa, N., Ishai, Y., Kohl, L., Scholl, P.: Efficient pseudorandom correlation generators: silent OT extension and more. In: Boldyreva, A., Micciancio, D. (eds.) CRYPTO 2019, Part III. LNCS, vol. 11694, pp. 489–518. Springer, Cham (2019). https://doi.org/10.1007/978-3-030-26954-8_16

[BCGT13] Ben-Sasson, E., Chiesa, A., Genkin, D., Tromer, E.: Fast reductions from RAMs to delegatable succinct constraint satisfaction problems: extended abstract. In: Kleinberg, R.D. (ed.) ITCS 2013, pp. 401–414. ACM, January 2013

[BFH+20] Bhadauria, R., Fang, Z., Hazay, C., Venkitasubramaniam, M., Xie, R., Zhang, Y.: Ligero++: a new optimized sublinear IOP. In: Ligatti, J., Ou, X., Katz, J., Vigna, G. (ed.) ACM CCS 20, pp. 2025–2038. ACM Press, November 2020

[BHR12] Bellare, M., Hoang, V.T., Rogaway, P.: Foundations of garbled circuits. In: Yu, T., Danezis, G., Gligor, V.D. (eds.) ACM CCS 2012, pp. 784–796. ACM Press, October 2012

[CDG+17] Chase, M., et al. Post-quantum zero-knowledge and signatures from symmetric-key primitives. In: Thuraisingham, B.M., Evans, D., Malkin, T., Xu, D. (eds.) ACM CCS 2017, pp. 1825–1842. ACM Press, October/November 2017

[CFH+15] Costello, C., et al: Geppetto: versatile verifiable computation. In: 2015 IEEE Symposium on Security and Privacy, pp. 253–270. IEEE Computer Society Press, May 2015

[Ds17] Doerner, J., Shelat, A.: Scaling ORAM for secure computation. In: Thuraisingham, B.M., Evans, D., Malkin, T., Xu, D. (eds.) ACM CCS 2017, pp. 523–535. ACM Press, October/November 2017

[FNO15] Frederiksen, T.K., Nielsen, J.B., Orlandi, C.: Privacy-free garbled circuits with applications to efficient zero-knowledge. In: Oswald, E., Fischlin, M. (eds.) EUROCRYPT 2015, Part II. LNCS, vol. 9057, pp. 191–219. Springer, Heidelberg (2015). https://doi.org/10.1007/978-3-662-46803-6_7

[GMR85] Goldwasser, S., Micali, S., Rackoff, C.: The knowledge complexity of interactive proof-systems (extended abstract). In: 17th ACM STOC, pp. 291–304. ACM Press, May 1985

[GMW91] Goldreich, O., Micali, S., Wigderson, A.: Proofs that yield nothing but their validity or all languages in np have zero-knowledge proof systems. J. ACM **38**(3), 690–728 (1991)

[GO96] Goldreich, O., Ostrovsky, R.: Software protection and simulation on oblivious rams. J. ACM **43**, 01 (1996)

[HK20a] Heath, D., Kolesnikov, V.: A 2.1 KHz zero-knowledge processor with BubbleRAM. In: Ligatti, J., Ou, X., Katz, J., Vigna, G. (eds.) ACM CCS 20, pp. 2055–2074. ACM Press, November 2020

[HK20b] Heath, D., Kolesnikov, V.: Stacked garbling. In: Micciancio, D., Ristenpart, T. (eds.) CRYPTO 2020, Part II. LNCS, vol. 12171, pp. 763–792. Springer, Cham (2020). https://doi.org/10.1007/978-3-030-56880-1_27

[HK20c] Heath, D., Kolesnikov, V.: Stacked garbling for disjunctive zero-knowledge proofs. In: Canteaut, A., Ishai, Y. (eds.) EUROCRYPT 2020, Part III. LNCS, vol. 12107, pp. 569–598. Springer, Cham (2020). https://doi.org/10.1007/978-3-030-45727-3_19

[HMR15] Hu, Z., Mohassel, P., Rosulek, M.: Efficient zero-knowledge proofs of non-algebraic statements with sublinear amortized cost. In: Gennaro, R., Robshaw, M. (eds.) CRYPTO 2015, Part II. LNCS, vol. 9216, pp. 150–169. Springer, Heidelberg (2015). https://doi.org/10.1007/978-3-662-48000-7_8

[HYDK21] Heath, D., Yang, Y., Devecsery, D., Kolesnikov, V.: Zero knowledge for everything and everyone: fast ZK processor with cached ORAM for ANSI C programs. In: 2021 2021 IEEE Symposium on Security and Privacy (SP), Los Alamitos, CA, USA, pp. 1538–1556. IEEE Computer Society, May 2021

[IKOS07] Ishai, Y., Kushilevitz, E., Ostrovsky, R., Sahai, A.: Zero-knowledge from secure multiparty computation. In: Johnson, D.S., Feige, U. (eds.) 39th ACM STOC, pp. 21–30. ACM Press, June 2007

[JKO13] Jawurek, M., Kerschbaum, F., Orlandi, C.: Zero-knowledge using garbled circuits: how to prove non-algebraic statements efficiently. In: Sadeghi, A., Gligor, V.D., Yung, M. (eds.) ACM CCS 2013, pp. 955–966. ACM Press, November 2013

[KKW18] Katz, J., Kolesnikov, V., Wang, X.: Improved non-interactive zero knowledge with applications to post-quantum signatures. In: Lie, D., Mannan, M., Backes, M., Wang, X. (eds.) ACM CCS 2018, pp. 525–537. ACM Press, October 2018

[KOS15] Keller, M., Orsini, E., Scholl, P.: Actively secure OT extension with optimal overhead. In: Gennaro, R., Robshaw, M. (eds.) CRYPTO 2015, Part I. LNCS, vol. 9215, pp. 724–741. Springer, Heidelberg (2015). https://doi.org/10.1007/978-3-662-47989-6_35

[MRS17] Mohassel, P., Rosulek, M., Scafuro, A.: Sublinear zero-knowledge arguments for RAM programs. In: Coron, J.-S., Nielsen, J.B. (eds.) EUROCRYPT 2017, Part I. LNCS, vol. 10210, pp. 501–531. Springer, Cham (2017). https://doi.org/10.1007/978-3-319-56620-7_18

[RS19] Raskin, M., Simkin, M.: Perfectly secure oblivious RAM with sublinear bandwidth overhead. In: Galbraith, S.D., Moriai, S. (eds.) ASIACRYPT 2019, Part II. LNCS, vol. 11922, pp. 537–563. Springer, Cham (2019). https://doi.org/10.1007/978-3-030-34621-8_19

[SvS+13] Stefanov, E., et al.: Path ORAM: an extremely simple oblivious RAM protocol. In: Sadeghi, A., Gligor, V.D., Yung, M. (eds.) ACM CCS 2013, pp. 299–310. ACM Press, November 2013

[Wak68] Waksman, A.: A permutation network. J. ACM **15**(1), 159–163 (1968)

[WYKW20] Weng, C., Yang, K., Katz, J., Wang, X.: Wolverine: fast, scalable, and communication-efficient zero-knowledge proofs for Boolean and arithmetic circuits. Cryptology ePrint Archive, Report 2020/925 (2020). https://eprint.iacr.org/2020/925

[YWL+20] Yang, K., Weng, C., Lan, X., Zhang, J., Wang, X.: Ferret: fast extension for correlated OT with small communication. In: Ligatti, J., Ou, X., Katz, J., Vigna, G. (eds.) ACM CCS 20, pp. 1607–1626. ACM Press, November 2020

Compressed Σ-Protocols for Bilinear Group Arithmetic Circuits and Application to Logarithmic Transparent Threshold Signatures

Thomas Attema[1,2,4](✉), Ronald Cramer[1,2](✉), and Matthieu Rambaud[3](✉)

[1] CWI, Cryptology Group, Amsterdam, The Netherlands
cramer@cwi.nl, cramer@math.leidenuniv.nl
[2] Leiden University, Mathematical Institute, Leiden, The Netherlands
[3] Telecom Paris, Institut Polytechnique de Paris, Palaiseau, France
rambaud@enst.fr
[4] TNO, Cyber Security and Robustness, The Hague, The Netherlands
thomas.attema@tno.nl

Abstract. Lai et al. (CCS 2019) have shown how Bulletproof's arithmetic circuit zero-knowledge protocol (Bootle et al., EUROCRYPT 2016 and Bünz et al., S&P 2018) can be generalized to work for bilinear group arithmetic circuits directly, i.e., without requiring these circuits to be translated into arithmetic circuits.

In a nutshell, a bilinear group arithmetic circuit is a standard arithmetic circuit augmented with special gates capturing group exponentiations or pairings. Such circuits are highly relevant, e.g., in the context of zero-knowledge statements over pairing-based languages. As expressing these special gates in terms of a standard arithmetic circuit results in a significant overhead in circuit size, an approach to zero-knowledge via standard arithmetic circuits may incur substantial additional costs. The approach due to Lai et al. shows how to avoid this by integrating additional zero-knowledge techniques into the Bulletproof framework so as to handle the special gates very efficiently.

We take a different approach by generalizing *Compressed Σ-Protocol Theory* (CRYPTO 2020) from arithmetic circuit relations to bilinear group arithmetic circuit relations. Besides its conceptual simplicity, our approach has the practical advantage of reducing the communication costs of Lai et al.'s protocol by roughly a multiplicative factor 3.

Finally, we show an application of our results which may be of independent interest. We construct the first k-out-of-n threshold signature scheme (TSS) that allows for transparent setup *and* that yields threshold signatures of size logarithmic in n. The threshold signature hides the identities of the k signers and the threshold k can be dynamically chosen at aggregation time.

Keywords: Zero-knowledge · Bilinear groups · Pairings · Compressed Σ-Protocol Theory · Threshold signature schemes

M. Tibouchi and H. Wang (Eds.): ASIACRYPT 2021, LNCS 13093, pp. 526–556, 2021.
https://doi.org/10.1007/978-3-030-92068-5_18

1 Introduction

Bulletproofs [11,13] introduced an ingenious technique to compress the communication complexity of discrete logarithm (DL) based circuit zero-knowledge (ZK) protocols from linear to logarithmic. Their approach was presented as a drop-in replacement for the well-established Σ-protocol theory and it results in efficient zero-knowledge protocols for relations captured by a circuit defined over $\mathbb{Z}_q \cong \mathbb{Z}/(q\mathbb{Z})$. In [4], Bulletproofs and Σ-protocol theory were reconciled by repurposing an appropriate adaptation of Bulletproofs as a black-box compression mechanism for basic Σ-protocols. They first show how to handle linear arithmetic relations by deploying a basic Σ-protocol. Second, they show how an adaptation of Bulletproofs allows the communication complexity of the basic Σ-protocol to be compressed from linear to logarithmic. Hence, the resulting *compressed Σ-protocol* allows a prover to prove *linear* statements with a communication complexity that is *logarithmic* in the size of the witness. Finally, to handle arbitrary non-linear relations, arithmetic secret sharing based techniques [19] are deployed to *linearize* these non-linearities. Cryptographic protocol design can now follow well-established approaches from Σ-protocol theory, but with the additional black-box compression mechanism to reduce the communication complexity down to logarithmic.

These, and other, recent advances in communication-efficient circuit ZK lead to an obvious, but *indirect*, approach for efficient protocols for arbitrary relations:

1. Construct an arithmetic circuit capturing the relation;
2. Apply an efficient circuit ZK protocol to this arithmetic circuit.

However, for some relations, the associated arithmetic circuits can be large and complex. Thereby losing the conceptual simplicity and possibly even the concrete efficiency over a more *direct* approach. The work of [5], for instance, describes a number of efficiency advantages of their direct approach for proving knowledge of k discrete logarithms out of n public group elements.

Moreover, Lai et al. [35] construct a zero-knowledge proof system for directly handling relations captured by *bilinear group arithmetic circuits.* A bilinear group is a tuple $(q, \mathbb{G}_1, \mathbb{G}_2, \mathbb{G}_T, e, G, H)$, where $e : \mathbb{G}_1 \times \mathbb{G}_2 \to \mathbb{G}_T$ is a bilinear map, also called a pairing, and $\mathbb{G}_1$, $\mathbb{G}_2$ and $\mathbb{G}_T$ are groups (group operations are written additively) of prime order q generated by G, H and $e(G,H)$, respectively. A bilinear group arithmetic circuit, or a bilinear circuit, is a circuit in which each wire takes values in $W \in \{\mathbb{Z}_q, \mathbb{G}_1, \mathbb{G}_2, \mathbb{G}_T\}$ and the gates all have fan-in 2 and unbounded fan-out. Gates are either group operations, $\mathbb{Z}_q$-scalar multiplications or bilinear pairings. For more details see Sect. 6. Bilinear circuits directly capture relations encountered in, e.g., identity based encryption [41] and structure preserving signatures [2]. We note that, for a highly optimized group of order $q \approx 2^{256}$, multiplying a single group element with a $\mathbb{Z}_q$-scalar requires an arithmetic circuit with approximately 800 multiplication gates [32], instead of a single gate in the bilinear circuit model. Hence, besides conceptual simplicity there can be significant efficiency advantages of the *direct* approach over the *indirect* approach that uses generic solutions for arithmetic circuit ZK.

In this work, we focus on one application of our bilinear circuit ZK protocols: *Threshold Signature Schemes* (TSSs) [20]. A k-out-of-n TSS is a standard signature scheme, allowing each of the n players to individually sign arbitrary messages m, enriched with a public k-aggregation algorithm. The k-aggregation algorithm takes as input k signatures, issued by *any* k distinct players, on the same message m and outputs a *threshold signature* σ. A naive TSS is obtained by exhibiting the k individual signatures directly. However, this approach results in threshold signatures with size linear in the threshold k. The main goal for TSSs is to have *succinct* threshold signatures, i.e., with size sub-linear in k. The succinct TSS of [43] immediately found an application in reducing the communication complexity of consensus protocols [15]. The impact of succinctness is significant since, in consensus applications, the threshold k is of the same order of magnitude as n (typically $k = n/2$ or $k = 2n/3$). Although desirable in some applications, it is not required that a threshold signature *hides* the k-subset of signers.

1.1 Contributions

In this work, we present a novel ZK protocol for relations captured by bilinear circuits. We show that there is a generalization of the approach of [4] for arithmetic circuit relations to bilinear circuit relations. Generalizing [4], our approach is to first *compress* a basic Σ-protocol for proving linear statements about committed vectors and, second, to show how to handle arbitrary bilinear circuit relations by *linearizing* non-linearities. This leads to a conceptually simple and modular construction of ZK protocols for bilinear circuit relations.

In [5], an abstraction of the compressed Σ-protocols for proving linear relations was introduced. An appropriate instantiation of these abstract protocols immediately results in a compressed Σ-protocol for proving that a *mixed* vector $\mathbf{x} \in \mathbb{Z}_q^{n_0} \times \mathbb{G}_1^{n_1} \times \mathbb{G}_2^{n_2} \times \mathbb{G}_T^{n_T}$ satisfies a *linear* constraint defined over a bilinear circuit. The main ingredient in this instantiation is a homomorphic commitment scheme [2,35] that allows a prover to commit to such mixed vectors. However, a number of modification to this straightforward approach are warranted.

First, in contrast to the Pedersen commitment scheme for $\mathbb{Z}_q$-vectors, the commitment scheme for mixed vectors is not *compact*, i.e., the size of a commitment is not constant in the size of the committed vector. More precisely, the size of a commitment to a vector $\mathbf{x} \in \mathbb{Z}_q^{n_0} \times \mathbb{G}_1^{n_1} \times \mathbb{G}_2^{n_2} \times \mathbb{G}_T^{n_T}$ is constant in the dimensions n_0, n_1 and n_2, but it is linear in the dimension n_T. For this reason, compression should only be applied to the compact part of the commitment scheme. We handle this complication in an abstract manner by considering homomorphisms $\Psi(\mathbf{x}_1, \mathbf{x}_2)$, where the input consists of two parts and compressing is only applied to the first part $\mathbf{x}_1$.

Second, the arithmetic circuit instantiation of the abstract protocol allows for an additional reduction of the communication costs by roughly a factor 2. This technique stems from [13] and was also applied in the compressed Σ-protocols of [4]. However, it is not applicable in general, i.e., for arbitrary homomorphisms Ψ, and has therefore been omitted in the abstract framework of [5]. Here, we show how this technique can be adapted to the bilinear circuit setting. Again, and in contrast to prior works, the compact part and the non-compact part of the commitment must be treated separately.

Third, the non-compact part of the commitment scheme has an "El Gamal structure". We adapt the basic Σ-protocols, used in compressed Σ-protocol, to exploit this structure. Informally, to prove knowledge of an opening of an El Gamal commitment it is sufficient to prove knowledge of commitment randomness $\gamma \in \mathbb{Z}_q$ satisfying certain properties. Altogether, this technique reduces the constant in the linear component of the communication costs from 3 down to 1 (the other components are logarithmic).

Finally, the abstract framework of [5] only considers linear relations. To handle non-linear relations, we show how the linearization techniques from the arithmetic circuit setting of [4] can be adapted to the bilinear circuit setting.

The communication complexity of our protocols is logarithmic in n_0, n_1 and n_2, but linear in n_T. Asymptotically this is comparable to the prior work of [35]. However, we consider a strictly stronger application scenario, i.e., [35] only considers bilinear relations captured by a limited class of circuits.[1] Moreover, in comparison to [35], we improve upon the *concrete* communication costs by roughly a factor 3. More precisely, we reduce the constant in the logarithmic component of the communication costs from 16 down to 6, and the constant in the linear component from 3 down to 1. See Sect. 6.3 for a detailed comparison.

Another application of the commitment scheme of [2,35] is that it allows a prover to commit to Pedersen commitments in a pairing-based platform. This layered approach, of committing to commitments, was already suggested in [2] and it allows a prover to commit to n^2 $\mathbb{Z}_q$-coefficients using only $2n+1$ public group elements, instead of the n^2+1 public group elements required when using Pedersen commitments directly. Replacing the Pedersen commitment scheme, in circuit ZK protocols derived from Bulletproofs [11,13] or Compressed Σ-Protocol Theory [4], by this layered commitment scheme immediately gives a square root reduction in the size of the set of public parameters while leaving the logarithmic communication costs exactly the same.

An additional advantage of our approach is that we can handle linear relations directly. By contrast, Lai et al. [35] generalize the Bulletproof approach [11,13] where the pivotal protocol handles a specific non-linear inner-product relation. Applying this approach to a linear relation requires a cumbersome approach of capturing this linear relation by a set of non-linear inner-product constraints, leading to unnecessarily complicated protocols.

As an application of our compressed Σ-protocol for proving linear relations, we construct a transparent k-out-of-n threshold signature scheme (TSS) with threshold signatures that are $O(\kappa \log(n))$ bits, where κ is the security parameter. Recall that a TSS enables any set of at least k players, in a group of n, to issue a "threshold" signature on a message m, but no subset of less than k players is able to issue one. A TSS is called *transparent* if it does not require a trusted setup phase, i.e., all public parameters are random coins. Given recent advances in efficient circuit zero-knowledge, an obvious solution is to construct

[1] This is perhaps not immediate from the paper [35], but it has been confirmed by the authors. See also Sect. 6.3.

a threshold signature as a proof of knowledge attesting the knowledge of k-out-of-n signatures. With the appropriate ZK protocol this would immediately result in a transparent TSS with sublinear size threshold signatures. However, this approach requires an inefficient reduction from the corresponding threshold signature relation to a relation defined over an arithmetic circuit. More precisely, the arithmetic circuits capturing these relations are typically large.

For this reason, we follow a more *direct* approach avoiding this inefficient reduction. Namely, we append the BLS signature scheme [10] with a k-aggregation algorithm. The BLS signature scheme is defined over a bilinear group. In particular, the BLS verification algorithms naturally fit with our compressed Σ-protocols for relations defined over bilinear groups. A key feature of this signature scheme is that its signing algorithm does not contain the evaluation of a hash function. This would namely require the hash function to be expressed in terms of a (typically large) bilinear circuit. To derive the required threshold functionality, we use an appropriated adaptation of k-out-of-n proofs of partial knowledge from a recent work [5].

The compressed Σ-protocols are interactive and can be made non-interactive by the Fiat-Shamir transform [21]. In general, the Fiat-Shamir transformation of a $(2\mu+1)$-move protocol increases the knowledge error from κ to $Q^{\mu} \cdot \kappa$, where Q is the number of random oracle queries the non-interactive prover is allowed to make, i.e., the security loss is *exponential* in the number of rounds. However, for $(k_1, \ldots, k_{\mu})$-special sound protocols such as ours, it is believed that this loss is actually constant in the number of rounds. This claim was recently proven in the algebraic group model [27].

The non-interactive proofs contain precisely the messages sent from the prover to the verifier. Hence, the logarithmic proof size is inherited by the logarithmic communication complexity of the compressed Σ-protocol. More precisely, a k-out-of-n threshold signature contains $4\lceil \log_2(n) \rceil + 3$ $\mathbb{G}_T$-elements, 1 $\mathbb{G}_1$-element and 1 $\mathbb{Z}_q$-element.

The k-aggregation algorithm can be evaluated by any party with input at least k valid signatures from distinct signers. Besides the signatures, the k-aggregation algorithm only takes public input values. Moreover, the threshold k can be chosen at aggregation time independent of the set-up phase. By contrast, Shoup's construction [43] requires a different trusted setup phase for every threshold k. Since the compressed Σ-protocol is zero-knowledge, an additional property of our TSS is that a threshold signature hides the k-subset of signers $\mathcal{S}$. Our TSS does not require a trusted setup and is therefore transparent. More precisely, the players can generate their own public-private key-pairs and the Σ-protocol only requires an unstructured public random string defined by the public parameters of the commitment scheme.

1.2 Related Work

Zero-Knowledge Proof Systems. Groth and Sahai [28] were the first to consider zero-knowledge proof systems for relations defined over bilinear groups *directly*. In contrast to more standard indirect approaches, their work avoids inefficient reductions to arithmetic circuit relations. Bilinear groups have found applications in many areas of cryptography. For instance, in digital signatures, identity based encryption and efficient zero-knowledge proof systems. For this reason many relevant relations are naturally defined over bilinear groups. The goal is not only to achieve efficiency, but also modularity in the design of cryptographic protocols.

A drawback of the Groth-Sahai proof system is that its proof sizes are linear in the size of the statements. By contrast, Bulletproofs [11,13] are practically efficient DL-based proof systems for arithmetic circuit relations with logarithmic proof sizes. Their main building block is an efficient protocol for proving a specific non-linear inner-product relation. Arbitrary relations captured by an arithmetic circuit are reduced to a set of inner-product constraints. Lai et al. [35] adapted the techniques from Bulletproofs to the bilinear circuit model achieving a communication-efficient ZKP system for relations defined over bilinear circuits. More precisely, the communication complexity is logarithmic in the number of $\mathbb{Z}_q$, $\mathbb{G}_1$ and $\mathbb{G}_2$ inputs, but linear in the number of $\mathbb{G}_T$ inputs. They first reduce the bilinear circuit relation to a set of inner-products constraints, and subsequently describe protocols for proving various inner-product relations. The work of [14] improves the efficiency for a specific subset of bilinear *inner-product* relations. Hence, although these approaches avoid reductions to arithmetic circuits, they do rely on the reduction to a set of inner-product constraints.

In [4], an alternative approach for arithmetic circuit relations is described. Their pivotal protocol is a basic Σ-protocol for proving linear relations. They show how to compress the communication complexity down to logarithmic and how to handle non-linearities in arbitrary arithmetic circuit relations. This approach is compatible with standard Σ-protocol theory and avoids the need for reinventing cryptographic protocol design around non-linear inner-product relations. Here, we generalize compressed Σ-protocols to the bilinear circuit model.

Threshold Signature Schemes. Shoup's TSS [43] already achieves threshold signatures of constant size. However, his approach, and all other approaches with threshold signature sizes sub-linear in k and n are not transparent [9, 24–26,30,33,34,36]. These works require either an explicit trusted dealer, or they have implemented this trusted dealer by an MPC (or other interactive) protocol that is evaluated before messages are signed. At first glance it might seem that [24] also achieves a transparent setup. However, in their protocol the k signing players first have to run an interactive protocol before they can generate threshold signatures. This interactive protocol has to be evaluated before players can produce their inputs to the aggregation algorithm, therefore we consider this as a trusted setup.

The standard approach, introduced by Desmedt and Frankel [20], works by secret sharing the private key amongst the n players. This requires the private key to be generated by either a trusted dealer or an MPC protocol, i.e., this approach has a trusted set-up and is not transparent. Moreover, in contrast to our scheme, the threshold k should be fixed during the setup phase.

By contrast, all known *transparent* TSSs have size at least linear in the threshold k. Besides the naive implementation of simply outputting k valid signatures, there is also the following approach used by the decentralized transaction system Libra [37] and by [39]. Every player generates its own public-private key-pair. A threshold signature is computed as the sum of k individual BLS signatures, and it can be verified by running the BLS verification algorithm using the sum of the public keys of the k signers. Hence, the threshold signature should contain a list of the k signers, i.e., it is of size $O(n)$ or $O(k \log(n))$ depending on the exact encoding of this list. Moreover, these threshold signatures clearly do not hide the k-subset of signers. By contrast, Haque et al. [29] construct a transparent TSS that does hide the k-subset of signers. However, while individual signature sizes are logarithmic in n, the threshold signatures are linear in the threshold k.

Finally, a recent work [12] presents a different variant of a TSS, which they call *succinctly reconstructed distributed signatures* (SRDS). Their SRDS is most similar to the obvious approach of reducing the problem to an arithmetic circuit relation. It indeed applies a general (unspecified) SNARK in a black-box manner to achieve $O(\mathsf{polylog}(n))$-size signatures. However, their SRDS can only tolerate up to $n/3$ corruptions.

1.3 Organization of the Paper

The remainder of the paper is organized as follows. In Sect. 2, we recall basic notation and definitions regarding bilinear groups and zero-knowledge proof systems. In Sect. 3, we define a number of commitment schemes generalizing Pedersen vector commitments. In Sect. 4, we describe a compressed Σ-protocol for proving linear relations about committed vectors, with logarithmic communication complexity. In Sect. 5, as an application of our compressed Σ-protocol, we construct a novel threshold signature scheme. In Sect. 6, we describe our linearization strategy for handling non-linear relations.

2 Preliminaries

2.1 Bilinear Groups

We consider the ring $\mathbb{Z}_q \cong \mathbb{Z}/(q\mathbb{Z})$ for a prime q. Moreover, we let $\mathbb{G}_1, \mathbb{G}_2$ and $\mathbb{G}_T$ be groups of prime order q supporting discrete-log (DL) based cryptography, hence $\log(q) = O(\kappa)$ for security parameter κ. Some properties of commitment schemes used in this work rely on the stronger *Decisional Diffie-Hellman* (DDH) assumption. Therefore, we assume the DDH assumption to hold in all groups.

We write the group operations additively. Clearly, all groups $\mathbb{G}_i$ are $\mathbb{Z}_q$-modules and, for all $a \in \mathbb{Z}_q$ and $g \in \mathbb{G}_i$, the product $ag \in \mathbb{G}_i$ is well-defined. We write vectors in boldface and inner-products are defined naturally, i.e., for all $\mathbf{a} = (a_1, \dots, a_n) \in \mathbb{Z}_q^n$ and $\mathbf{g} = (g_1, \dots, g_n) \in \mathbb{G}_i^n$ we define $\langle \mathbf{a}, \mathbf{g} \rangle := \sum_{i=1}^n a_i g_i$.

Let $G \in \mathbb{G}_1$ and $H \in \mathbb{G}_2$ be generators and let $e : \mathbb{G}_1 \times \mathbb{G}_2 \to \mathbb{G}_T$ be a non-trivial bilinear mapping, i.e., e is a pairing such that $e(G, H)$ generates $\mathbb{G}_T$. Then, a tuple $(q, \mathbb{G}_1, \mathbb{G}_2, \mathbb{G}_T, e, G, H)$ defines a *bilinear group*. For vectors $\mathbf{G} \in \mathbb{G}_1^n$ and $\mathbf{H} \in \mathbb{G}_2^n$ the following inner-product is defined $e(\mathbf{G}, \mathbf{H}) := \sum_{i=1}^{n} e(G_i, H_i)$.

We say that the *Symmetrical External Diffie-Hellman* (SXDH) holds in a bilinear group $(q, \mathbb{G}_1, \mathbb{G}_2, \mathbb{G}_T, e, G, H)$, if the DDH assumption holds in both $\mathbb{G}_1$ and $\mathbb{G}_2$ [7]. By the above assumption that the DDH assumption holds in all $\mathbb{G}_i$, it follows that the SXDH assumption holds for all bilinear groups that are considered in this work. The SXDH assumption implies that there is no efficiently computable isomorphism from $\mathbb{G}_1$ to $\mathbb{G}_2$, or from $\mathbb{G}_2$ to $\mathbb{G}_1$ [3], i.e., we only consider bilinear groups of Type III [22].

2.2 Proofs of Knowledge

We recall some standard notions regarding Proofs of Knowledge (PoKs) following the notation and definitions of [4,5]. A relation R is a set of statement-witness pairs $(x; w)$. A μ-move protocol Π for relation R is an interactive protocol with μ communication rounds between a prover $\mathcal{P}$ and verifier $\mathcal{V}$. It allows $\mathcal{P}$ to convince $\mathcal{V}$ that it knows a witness w for statement x, i.e., $(x; w) \in R$. Protocol Π is also called an interactive proof for relation R. The statement x is *public input* for both $\mathcal{P}$ and $\mathcal{V}$ and the witness w is *private input* only for $\mathcal{P}$. In our protocol descriptions this is written as INPUT$(x; w)$, i.e., the public and private input are separated by a semicolon. As the output of the protocol $\mathcal{V}$ either accepts or rejects $\mathcal{P}$'s claim. The messages sent between $\mathcal{P}$ and $\mathcal{V}$ in one protocol execution are also referred to as a *conversation* or *transcript*. If $\mathcal{V}$ accepts the associated transcript, it is called accepting.

An interactive proof is said to be *public coin*, if all message from $\mathcal{V}$ are chosen uniformly at random and independent from prior messages. Interactive protocols that are public-coin can be made *non-interactive* by the Fiat-Shamir transformation [21], as proven in [8], without increasing the communication costs from $\mathcal{P}$ to $\mathcal{V}$. All interactive proofs in this work are public-coin.

Let us now describe some desirable (security) properties.

Definition 1 (Completeness). *An interactive proof Π is called perfectly* complete, *if on any input $(x; w) \in R$, the verifier $\mathcal{V}$ always accepts.*

Definition 2 (Knowledge Soundness). *An interactive proof $\Pi = (\mathcal{P}, \mathcal{V})$ is said to be knowledge sound with knowledge error $\kappa : \mathbb{N} \rightarrow [0, 1)$, if there exists a polynomial $q : \mathbb{N} \rightarrow \mathbb{N}$ and an algorithm χ (extractor) with the following properties. For each (potentially dishonest) PPT prover $\mathcal{P}^*$, for each $x \in \{0,1\}^*$, whenever $(\mathcal{P}^*, \mathcal{V})(x)$ outputs accept with probability $\epsilon(x) \geq \kappa(|x|)$, the extractor χ, given input x and rewindable oracle access to the $\mathcal{P}^*$, runs in expected polynomial time and successfully outputs a witness w for statement x with probability at least $(\epsilon(x) - \kappa(|x|))/q(|x|)$.*

Definition 3 (Proof/Argument of Knowledge). *An interactive proof that is both complete and knowledge sound is said to be a Proof or Knowledge (PoK). PoKs for which knowledge soundness only holds under computational assumptions are also referred to as Arguments of Knowledge.*

Witness extended emulation [38] gives an alternative notion for knowledge soundness, sufficient for most practical scenarios, and it is known to be implied by knowledge soundness [38]. For details we refer to [4,31,38].

We now recall a generalization of the *special-soundness* property. Special soundness is in general easier to handle than knowledge soundness. We first introduce the notion of a tree of accepting transcripts.

Definition 4 (Tree of Accepting Transcripts). *Let Π be a $(2\mu+1)$-move protocol. A $(k_1, k_2, \dots, k_\mu)$-tree of accepting transcripts for protocol Π is a set of $\prod_{i=1}^{\mu} k_i$ accepting transcripts that are arranged in the following tree structure. The nodes in this tree correspond to the prover's messages and the edges correspond to the verifier's challenges. Every node at depth i has precisely k_i children corresponding to k_i pairwise distinct challenges. Every transcript corresponds to exactly one path from the root node to a leaf node.*

Definition 5 (Special Soundness). *A $(2\mu+1)$-move protocol is said to be $(k_1, k_2, \dots, k_\mu)$-special-sound, if there exists an efficient algorithm that on input a $(k_1, k_2, \dots, k_\mu)$-tree of accepting transcripts for statement x, outputs a witness w for x. A 3-move protocol is said to be special-sound if it is 2-special-sound.*

Recently, it was shown that $(k_1, k_2, \dots, k_\mu)$-special-soundness *tightly* implies knowledge soundness [6]. Therefore, protocols that are complete and special-sound are also referred to as proofs of knowledge (PoKs).

Definition 6 (Honest Verifier Zero-Knowledge (HVZK)). *An interactive proof Π is said to be honest verifier zero-knowledge (HVZK), if there exists a PPT simulator that, on input a statement x that admits a witness w, outputs an accepting transcript, such that simulated transcripts follow exactly the same distribution as transcripts between an honest prover and an honest verifier. If the simulator proceeds by first sampling the random challenges, the protocol is said to be special honest verifier zero-knowledge (SHVZK).*

Finally, we recall that two protocols, Π_a for relation R_a and Π_b for relation R_b, are said to be *composable*, if the final message of protocol Π_a contains a witness for relation R_b [4]. In this case, the composition $\Pi_b \diamond \Pi_a$ runs Protocol Π_a but replaces the witness for relation R_b in its final message by an appropriate instantiation of Protocol Π_b. If protocol Π_a is $(k_1, \dots, k_{\mu_1})$-special-sound and protocol Π_b is $(k'_1, \dots, k'_{\mu_2})$-special-sound, then the composition $\Pi_b \diamond \Pi_a$ is easily seen to be $(k_1, \dots, k_{\mu_1}, k'_1, \dots, k'_{\mu_2})$-special-sound.

3 Commitment Schemes

Compressed Σ-protocols allow a prover to prove that a committed vector satisfies some public constraint. These protocols crucially depend on the homomorphic properties of the commitment scheme. In this section, we describe a number of homomorphic commitment schemes for committing to vector $\mathbf{x} \in \mathbb{Z}_q^{n_0} \times \mathbb{G}_1^{n_1} \times \mathbb{G}_2^{n_2} \times \mathbb{G}_T^{n_T}$ with coefficients in a bilinear group $(q, \mathbb{G}_1, \mathbb{G}_2, \mathbb{G}_T, e, G, H)$.

First, the Pedersen vector commitment scheme [40] considers the case $n_1 = n_2 = n_T = 0$, i.e., the committed vector is a $\mathbb{Z}_q$-vector. Recall that group operations are written additively.

Definition 7 (Pedersen Vector Commitment [40]**).** *Let $\mathbb{G}$ be an Abelian group of prime order q. Pedersen vector commitments to vectors $\mathbf{x} \in \mathbb{Z}_q^n$ are defined by the following setup and commitment phase:*

- *Setup:* $\mathbf{g} = (g_1, \ldots, g_n) \leftarrow_R \mathbb{G}^n$, $h \leftarrow_R \mathbb{G}$.
- *Commit:* $\text{COM} : \mathbb{Z}_q^n \times \mathbb{Z}_q \to \mathbb{G}, \quad (\mathbf{x}, \gamma) \mapsto h\gamma + \langle \mathbf{g}, \mathbf{x} \rangle$.

Abe et al. [2] constructed a similar commitment scheme that works with bilinear groups $(q, \mathbb{G}_1, \mathbb{G}_2, \mathbb{G}_T, e, G, H)$ and allows a prover to commit to vectors of group elements $\mathbf{x} \in \mathbb{G}_1^n$. A straightforward generalization shows that this approach allows a prover to commit to vectors $\mathbf{x} \in \mathbb{Z}_q^{n_0} \times \mathbb{G}_1^{n_1}$ [35]. The commitment scheme is perfectly hiding and computationally binding under the DDH assumption in $\mathbb{G}_1$. Analogously, this construction results in a commitment scheme for vectors $\mathbf{x} \in \mathbb{Z}_q^{n_0} \times \mathbb{G}_2^{n_2}$.

Definition 8 (Commitment to $(\mathbb{Z}_q, \mathbb{G}_1)$-vectors [2,35]**).** *Let $(q, \mathbb{G}_1, \mathbb{G}_2, \mathbb{G}_T, e, G, H)$ be a bilinear group and let $n_0, n_1 \geq 0$. The following setup and commitment phase define a commitment scheme for vectors in $\mathbb{Z}_q^{n_0} \times \mathbb{G}_1^{n_1}$:*

- *Setup:* $\mathbf{g} = (g_1, \ldots, g_{n_0}) \leftarrow_R \mathbb{G}_T^{n_0}$, $h \leftarrow_R \mathbb{G}_T$, $\mathbf{H} = (H_1, \ldots, H_{n_1}) \leftarrow_R \mathbb{G}_2^{n_1}$.
- *Commit:* $\text{COM} : \mathbb{Z}_q^{n_0} \times \mathbb{G}_1^{n_1} \times \mathbb{Z}_q \to \mathbb{G}_T, \ (\mathbf{x}, \mathbf{y}, \gamma) \mapsto h\gamma + \langle \mathbf{g}, \mathbf{x} \rangle + e(\mathbf{y}, \mathbf{H})$.

Remark 1. As an application of the commitment scheme of Definition 8, Abe et al. [2] mention commitments to Pedersen vector commitments. A commitment to n n-dimensional Pedersen vector commitments is namely a commitment to an n^2-dimensional $\mathbb{Z}_q$-vector. This two-tiered commitment scheme only requires $2n+1$ public group elements. By contrast, Pedersen's commitment scheme requires n^2+1 public group elements to commit to an n^2-dimensional $\mathbb{Z}_q$-vector. Replacing the Pedersen vector commitment scheme in, for example, [4,11,13] by this two-tiered commitment scheme results in arithmetic circuit ZK protocols with exactly the same communication complexity, but with a square root improvement in the size of the public parameters.

In addition, Lai et al. [35] show how this approach can be extended to construct a commitment scheme for vectors with coefficients in $\mathbb{Z}_q$, $\mathbb{G}_1$ and $\mathbb{G}_2$. In contrast to the previous commitments, a commitment to a vector $\mathbf{x} \in \mathbb{Z}_q^{n_0} \times \mathbb{G}_1^{n_1} \times \mathbb{G}_2^{n_2}$ consists of two target group elements. Informally, the reason is that, with high probability, $(S, -R) \in \mathbb{G}_1 \times \mathbb{G}_2$ is a non-trivial solution for the equation $e(x, R) + e(S, y) = 1$, where $(S, R) \in \mathbb{G}_1 \times \mathbb{G}_2$ is sampled uniformly at random. Such a solution would break the binding property of the naive generalization in which commitments consist of only one target group element. However, with high probability, there does not exist a solution $(x, y) \in \mathbb{G}_1 \times \mathbb{G}_2$ to the system of equations $e(x, R_1) + e(S_1, y) = 1$ and $e(x, R_2) + e(S_2, y) = 1$, where $(S_1, R_1), (S_2, R_2) \in \mathbb{G}_1 \times \mathbb{G}_2$ are sampled uniformly at random. For this reason, the commitments consist of two target group elements and breaking their binding property can be reduced to solving a similar system of equations. The resulting commitment scheme is described in Definition 9. It is computationally hiding under the DDH assumption in $\mathbb{G}_T$, and it is computationally binding under the SXDH assumption [35]. The scheme can be made perfectly hiding by introducing an additional randomizer $\gamma_2 \in \mathbb{Z}_q$.

Definition 9 (Commitment to $(\mathbb{Z}_q, \mathbb{G}_1, \mathbb{G}_2)$-vectors [35]). *Let $(q, \mathbb{G}_1, \mathbb{G}_2, \mathbb{G}_T, e, G, H)$ be a bilinear group and let $n_0, n_1, n_2 \geq 0$. The following setup and commitment phase define a commitment scheme for vectors in $\mathbb{Z}_q^{n_0} \times \mathbb{G}_1^{n_1} \times \mathbb{G}_2^{n_2}$:*

- *Setup:* $\mathbf{g} \leftarrow_R \mathbb{G}_T^{2\times n_0}$, $h \leftarrow_R \mathbb{G}_T^2$, $\mathbf{H} \leftarrow_R \mathbb{G}_2^{2\times n_1}$,$\mathbf{G} \leftarrow_R \mathbb{G}_1^{2\times n_2}$.
- *Commit:* $\text{COM}_1 : \mathbb{Z}_q^{n_0} \times \mathbb{G}_1^{n_1} \times \mathbb{G}_2^{n_2} \times \mathbb{Z}_q \to \mathbb{G}_T^2, \quad (\mathbf{x}, \mathbf{y}, \mathbf{z}, \gamma) \mapsto h\gamma + \langle \mathbf{g}, \mathbf{x} \rangle + e(\mathbf{y}, \mathbf{H}) + e(\mathbf{G}, \mathbf{z})$, *where*

$$h\gamma + \langle \mathbf{g}, \mathbf{x} \rangle + e(\mathbf{y}, \mathbf{H}) + e(\mathbf{G}, \mathbf{z}) := \begin{pmatrix} h_1\gamma + \langle \mathbf{g}_1, \mathbf{x} \rangle + e(\mathbf{y}, \mathbf{H}_1) + e(\mathbf{G}_1, \mathbf{z}) \\ h_2\gamma + \langle \mathbf{g}_2, \mathbf{x} \rangle + e(\mathbf{y}, \mathbf{H}_2) + e(\mathbf{G}_2, \mathbf{z}) \end{pmatrix}. \tag{1}$$

The aforementioned commitment schemes do not allow a prover to commit to elements of the target group $\mathbb{G}_T$ of the bilinear pairing $e : \mathbb{G}_1 \times \mathbb{G}_2 \to \mathbb{G}_T$. For this reason, we introduce the homomorphic commitment scheme of Definition 10. This scheme is based on the El Gamal encryption scheme [23]. The commitment scheme is unconditionally binding and hiding under the DDH assumption in $\mathbb{G}_T$.

Definition 10 (Commitment to $(\mathbb{G}_T)$-vectors [23,35]). *Let $\mathbb{G}_T$ be an Abelian group of prime order q. The following setup and commitment phase define a commitment scheme for vectors in $\mathbb{G}_T^{n_T}$:*

- *Setup:* $\mathbf{g} \leftarrow_R \mathbb{G}_T^{n_T}$, $h \leftarrow_R \mathbb{G}_T$.
- *Commit:* $\text{COM}_2 : \mathbb{G}_T^{n_T} \times \mathbb{Z}_q \to \mathbb{G}_T^{n_T+1}, \quad (\mathbf{x}, \gamma) \mapsto \begin{pmatrix} h\gamma \\ \mathbf{g}\gamma + \mathbf{x} \end{pmatrix}$.

Note that, in contrast to the schemes of Definitions 7, 8 and 9, this commitment scheme is not compact, i.e., a commitment to a vector $\mathbf{x} \in \mathbb{G}_T^{n_T}$ contains $n_T + 1$ group elements. For this reason, the compression techniques applicable to compact commitments are of no benefit for commitments to $\mathbb{G}_T$-vectors, and we will treat commitments to target group elements separately.

Altogether, for a bilinear group $(q, \mathbb{G}_1, \mathbb{G}_2, \mathbb{G}_T, e, G, H)$, we obtain the following commitment scheme:

$$\begin{aligned} \text{COM} :& \mathbb{Z}_q^{n_0} \times \mathbb{G}_1^{n_1} \times \mathbb{G}_2^{n_2} \times \mathbb{G}_T^{n_T} \times \mathbb{Z}_q^2 \to \mathbb{G}_T^{n_T+3}, \\ & (\mathbf{x}, \mathbf{y}, \gamma_1, \gamma_2) \mapsto \begin{pmatrix} \text{COM}_1(\mathbf{x}; \gamma_1) \\ \text{COM}_2(\mathbf{y}; \gamma_2) \end{pmatrix}, \end{aligned} \tag{2}$$

where $\mathbf{x} \in \mathbb{Z}_q^{n_0} \times \mathbb{G}_1^{n_1} \times \mathbb{G}_2^{n_2}$, $\mathbf{y} \in \mathbb{G}_T^{n_T}$, COM_1 is the commitment scheme from Definition 9, and COM_2 is the commitment scheme from Definition 10.

4 Compressed Σ-Protocol for Opening Homomorphisms

In this section, we describe a compressed Σ-protocol for proving that a committed vector $\mathbf{x} \in \mathbb{Z}_q^{n_0} \times \mathbb{G}_1^{n_1} \times \mathbb{G}_2^{n_2} \times \mathbb{G}_T^{n_T}$ satisfies a linear constraint $f(\mathbf{x}) = y$ captured by an arbitrary homomorphism f. We also say that this protocol allows a prover to *open* a homomorphism f.

We present our protocols in an abstract language. More precisely, let

$$\Psi \colon \mathbb{H}_1 \times \mathbb{H}_2 \to \mathbb{H}, \quad (x_1, x_2) \to \Psi(x_1, x_2),$$

be a homomorphism between $\mathbb{Z}_q$-modules. We construct a compressed Σ-protocol for proving knowledge of a pre-image $x = (x_1, x_2)$ of $y = \Psi(x)$. Instantiating this abstract protocol with $\mathbb{H}_1 = \mathbb{Z}_q^{n_0+1} \times \mathbb{G}_1^{n_1} \times \mathbb{G}_2^{n_2}$, $\mathbb{H}_2 = \mathbb{Z}_q \times \mathbb{G}_T^{n_T}$ and $\Psi = (\text{COM}_1, \text{COM}_2, f)$, where f is understood to ignore the commitment randomness in x_1 and x_2, results in exactly the desired functionality.

Prior works [5,6] have considered similar abstractions of compressed Σ-protocols. However, we adapt these approaches in order to be able to treat the compact and non-compact parts of the commitment scheme separately. More precisely, we explicitly consider homomorphism where the domain is a Cartesian product $\mathbb{H}_1 \times \mathbb{H}_2$ and apply the compression techniques only to the $\mathbb{H}_1$-part.

In Sect. 4.1, we construct a basic Σ-protocol for proving knowledge of a Ψ-pre-image. In Sect. 4.2, we describe the compression mechanism that reduces the communication complexity of a Σ-protocol. In Sect. 4.3, we introduce the compressed Σ-protocol for our abstract problem. This protocol is the recursive composition of the Σ-protocol and the compression mechanism. In Sect. 4.4 and Sect. 4.5, we describe efficiency improvements applicable to the special case where the homomorphism Ψ is defined over a bilinear group. Finally, in Sect. 4.6, we compose the different building blocks and describe our compressed Σ-protocol for opening homomorphisms on a committed vector $\mathbf{x} \in \mathbb{Z}_q^{n_0} \times \mathbb{G}_1^{n_1} \times \mathbb{G}_2^{n_2} \times \mathbb{G}_T^{n_T}$.

4.1 Basic Σ-Protocol

Protocol 0, denoted by Π_0, is a basic Σ-protocol for proving knowledge of a pre-image of a homomorphism $\Psi \colon \mathbb{H}_1 \times \mathbb{H}_2 \to \mathbb{H}$. More precisely, it is a Σ-protocol for the following relation

$$R_\Psi = \{ (y; x) : y = \Psi(x) \}. \tag{3}$$

Protocol 0 follows the generic design for q-one-way homomorphisms [17,18] and its main properties are summarized in Theorem 1. Note that this Σ-protocol does not yet rely on the special structure of the homomorphism Ψ, i.e., it does not rely on the fact that the domain of Ψ is a Cartesian product $\mathbb{H}_1 \times \mathbb{H}_2$.

Theorem 1 (Homomorphism Evaluation). *Π_0 is a Σ-protocol for relation R_Ψ. It is perfectly complete, special honest-verifier zero-knowledge and unconditionally special-sound. Moreover, the communication costs are:*

- *$\mathcal{P} \to \mathcal{V}$: 1 $\mathbb{H}$-element, 1 $\mathbb{H}_1$-element and 1 $\mathbb{H}_2$-element.*
- *$\mathcal{V} \to \mathcal{P}$: 1 $\mathbb{Z}_q$-element.*

Protocol 0. Σ-protocol Π_0 for relation R_Ψ
Σ-protocol for proving knowledge of the pre-image of a $\mathbb{Z}_q$-module homomorphism $\Psi\colon \mathbb{H}_1 \times \mathbb{H}_2 \to \mathbb{H}$.

INPUT$(y; x)$

$y = \Psi(x)$

Prover		Verifier
$r \leftarrow_R \mathbb{H}_1 \times \mathbb{H}_2$		
$t = \Psi(r)$	$\xrightarrow{t}$	
		$c \leftarrow_R \mathbb{Z}_q$
	$\xleftarrow{c}$	
$z = cx + r$		
	$\xrightarrow{z}$	$\Psi(z) \stackrel{?}{=} cy + t$

4.2 Compression Mechanism

In [4], it was observed that the final message z of Σ-protocol Π_0 is actually a witness for the statement $cy + t$ of relation R_Ψ, i.e., the final message of this Σ-protocol constitutes a *trivial proof of knowledge* for relation R_Ψ in which the witness is simply revealed. Moreover, replacing this trivial PoK by a PoK with smaller communication costs would improve the communication-efficiency of the overall protocol. Note that the alternative protocol does not have to be zero-knowledge, because the trivial PoK clearly is not.

In order to construct a more efficient PoK for relation R_Ψ, let us assume that $\mathbb{H}_1$ is the Cartesian product of a group $\mathbb{H}_0$ with itself, i.e., $\mathbb{H}_1 = \mathbb{H}_0 \times \mathbb{H}_0$. In this case, for all $x_1 \in \mathbb{H}_1$, we can write $x_1 = (x_1^L, x_1^R)$ with $x_1^L, x_1^R \in \mathbb{H}_0$.

The compression mechanism is a proof of knowledge for relation R_Ψ with communication costs smaller than the communication-costs of the trivial PoK. The main idea of this compression mechanism is that, after receiving a challenge c from the verifier, the prover *folds* the secret element $x_1 \in \mathbb{H}_1$ in half by computing the response $z = x_1^L + cx_1^R \in \mathbb{H}_0$. Note that $z \in \mathbb{H}_0$ and $x_1 \in \mathbb{H}_1 = \mathbb{H}_0 \times \mathbb{H}_0$, so this folding procedure indeed reduces the size of the witness. The cost of this reduction is that the prover has to send two "cross-terms" $a = \Psi((0, x_1^L), 0)$ and $b = \Psi_1((x_1^R, 0), 0)$ to the verifier before receiving the challenge.

This compression mechanism is an adaptation of the compression mechanisms of [4,5]. The difference with these prior works is that here the folding procedure is only applied on the first part of the secret witness, i.e., the $\mathbb{H}_1$-part. The compression mechanism, denoted by Π_1, is described in Protocol 1 and its main properties are summarized in Theorem 2.

Theorem 2 (Compression Mechanism). *Π_1 is a 3-move protocol for relation R_Ψ. It is perfectly complete and unconditionally 3-special-sound. Moreover, the communication costs are:*

- *$\mathcal{P} \to \mathcal{V}$: 2 $\mathbb{H}$-elements, 1 $\mathbb{H}_0$-element and 1 $\mathbb{H}_2$-element.*

Protocol 1. Compression Mechanism Π_1 for relation R_Ψ.

$$\text{INPUT}\,(y; x = (x_1, x_2))$$

$$y = \Psi(x)$$

Prover		Verifier
$a = \Psi((0, x_1^L), 0)$		
$b = \Psi((x_1^R, 0), 0)$	$\xrightarrow{a,b}$	
		$c \leftarrow_R \mathbb{Z}_q$
	$\xleftarrow{c}$	
$z = x_1^L + c x_1^R$		
	$\xrightarrow{z, x_2}$	$\Psi((cz, z), cx_2) \stackrel{?}{=} a + cy + c^2 b$

- $\mathcal{V} \to \mathcal{P}$: 1 $\mathbb{Z}_q$*-element.*

The proof of Theorem 2 is almost identical to the proofs of [4, Theorem 2] and [5, Theorem 2].

Proof. **Completeness** follows directly.

3-Special Soundness: Let $(a, b; c_1; z_1, x_1)$, $(a, b; c_2; z_2, x_2)$ and $(a, b; c_3; z_3, x_3)$ be three accepting transcripts for distinct challenges $c_1, c_2, c_3 \in \mathbb{Z}_q$ and with common first message (a, b). Let $\alpha_1, \alpha_2, \alpha_3 \in \mathbb{Z}_q$ be such that

$$\begin{pmatrix} 1 & 1 & 1 \\ c_1 & c_2 & c_3 \\ c_1^2 & c_2^2 & c_3^2 \end{pmatrix} \begin{pmatrix} \alpha_1 \\ \alpha_2 \\ \alpha_3 \end{pmatrix} = \begin{pmatrix} 0 \\ 1 \\ 0 \end{pmatrix}.$$

Note that, since the challenges are distinct, this Vandermonde matrix is invertible and a solution to this equation exists. Let $\bar{z} = \sum_{i=1}^{3} \alpha_i((c_i z_i, z_i), c_i x_i)$. Then, since Ψ is a homomorphism, it follows that $\Psi(\bar{z}) = y$. Hence, $\bar{z}$ is a witness for statement y of relation R_Ψ, which completes the proof. □

4.3 Abstract Compressed Σ-Protocol

The the final message (z, x_2) of Π_1 is again a witness, but now for statement $a + cy + c^2 b$ of relation $R_{\Psi'}$ where $\Psi'(z, x_2) = \Psi((cz, z), cx_2)$. Hence, if $\mathbb{H}_0$ is the Cartesian product of a group $\mathbb{H}_0'$ with itself, the compression mechanism can be applied again, i.e., instead of sending (z, x_2) the prover and verifier run an appropriately instantiated compression mechanism. In particular, if $\mathbb{H}_1 = \mathbb{H}_0^n$, the compression mechanism can be applied recursively, i.e., the first part of the witness is folded until it consists of only one $\mathbb{H}_0$ element.

The recursive composition of Σ-protocol Π_0 and compression mechanism Π_1 is a compressed Σ-protocol for relation R_Ψ. It is denoted by

$$\Pi_{\text{abs}} = \underbrace{\Pi_1 \diamond \cdots \diamond \Pi_1}_{\mu \text{ times}} \diamond \Pi_0, \tag{4}$$

where $\mu = \lceil \log_2(n) \rceil$. Note that if n is not a power of 2 it can be appended with zeros. The basic Σ-protocol requires the prover to send one $\mathbb{H}_1$-element, or equivalently n $\mathbb{H}_0$-elements. By contrast, the compressed Σ-protocol only has to send 1 $\mathbb{H}_0$-element. However, this reduction comes at the cost of sending a logarithmic number of $2\mu+3$ $\mathbb{H}$-elements. The properties of Π_{abs} are summarized in Theorem 3. Note that Π_{abs} is SHVZK because Π_0 is.

Theorem 3 (Abstract Compressed Σ-Protocol). *Let $n \in \mathbb{N}, \mu = \lceil \log_2(n) \rceil$ and $\Psi \colon \mathbb{H}_0^n \times \mathbb{H}_2 \to \mathbb{H}$ be a $\mathbb{Z}_q$-module homomorphism. Then Π_{abs} is a $2\mu + 3$-move protocol for relation R_Ψ. It is perfectly complete, special honest-verifier zero-knowledge and unconditionally 3-special-sound. Moreover, the communication costs are:*

- *$\mathcal{P} \to \mathcal{V}$: $2\mu + 1$ $\mathbb{H}$-elements, 1 $\mathbb{H}_0$-element and 1 $\mathbb{H}_2$-element.*
- *$\mathcal{V} \to \mathcal{P}$: $\mu + 1$ $\mathbb{Z}_q$-elements.*

4.4 Efficiency Improvements for Bilinear Instances

In this section, we consider the following $\mathbb{Z}_q$-module homomorphism

$$\begin{aligned} \Psi \colon \mathbb{Z}_q^{n_0+2} \times \mathbb{G}_1^{n_1} \times \mathbb{G}_2^{n_2} \times \mathbb{G}_T^{n_T} &\to \mathbb{G}_T^{n_T+3} \times \mathbb{Z}_q \times \mathbb{G}_1 \times \mathbb{G}_2 \times \mathbb{G}_T, \\ (\mathbf{x}_1, \mathbf{x}_2) &\mapsto \big(\textsc{Com}_1(\mathbf{x}_1), \textsc{Com}_2(\mathbf{x}_2), f(\mathbf{x}_1, \mathbf{x}_2)\big), \end{aligned}$$

where the vectors $\mathbf{x}_1 = (\mathbf{x}_1', \gamma_1) \in \mathbb{Z}_q^{n_0+1} \times \mathbb{G}_1^{n_1} \times \mathbb{G}_2^{n_2}$ and $\mathbf{x}_2 = (\mathbf{x}_2', \gamma_2) \in \mathbb{G}_T^{n_T} \times \mathbb{Z}_q$ both include the commitment randomness $\gamma_1, \gamma_2 \in \mathbb{Z}_q$ and the homomorphism f is understood to ignore this commitment randomness. This notation allows the commitment randomness to be treated implicitly.

Instantiating compressed Σ-protocol Π_{abs} with homomorphism Ψ allows a prover to show that a committed vector $\mathbf{x} \in \mathbb{Z}_q^{n_0} \times \mathbb{G}_1^{n_1} \times \mathbb{G}_2^{n_2} \times \mathbb{G}_T^{n_T}$ satisfies the linear constraint $f(\mathbf{x}) = \mathbf{y}$. In Sect. 4.7, it is explained why we can restrict ourselves to linear relation captured by homomorphisms with codomain $\mathbb{Z}_q \times \mathbb{G}_1 \times \mathbb{G}_2 \times \mathbb{G}_T$. This instantiation therefore immediately results in the desired *linear* functionality. However, we describe two improvements that are applicable to this specific instantiation of compressed Σ-protocol Π_{abs}.

First, we note that in this case the first message (a, b) of compression mechanism Π_1 is always of the form

$$\begin{aligned} a &= \Psi((0, x_1^L), 0) = \big(\textsc{Com}_1(0, x_1^L), \textsc{Com}_2(0), f((0, x_1^L), 0)\big), \\ b &= \Psi((x_1^R, 0), 0) = \big(\textsc{Com}_1(x_1^R, 0), \textsc{Com}_2(0), f((x_1^R, 0), 0)\big). \end{aligned}$$

Hence, the second component of both a and b equals $\textsc{Com}_2(0) = 0$ and does not have to be sent to the verifier. For this reason, we understand Π_{abs} to omit this information from the first message.

Second, we observe that in every iteration of the compression mechanism the prover has to send two evaluations of the homomorphism f to the verifier. This step can be made more efficient by a pre-processing step in which part of the evaluation of f is "incorporated into the commitment". The goal is not to hide the evaluation $y = f(\mathbf{x})$, in fact y is still public, but to reduce the overall communication complexity that is achieved after compression. Ultimately, this step will reduce a relevant constant in the communication costs of our compressed Σ-protocol by a factor 1/2. This technique was first deployed in [13] to improve the communication complexity of certain protocols [11] for inner-product relations defined over $\mathbb{Z}_q$. Here, it is generalized to our bilinear setting.

To this end, we write $f = (f_1, f_2)$ with $f_1(x) \in \mathbb{Z}_q \times \mathbb{G}_1 \times \mathbb{G}_2$ and $f_2(x) \in \mathbb{G}_T$ for all x. The reason is that the commitment scheme is not compact on the $\mathbb{G}_T$-part. Hence incorporating $f_2(x)$ into the commitment will not reduce the communication complexity of the protocol.

The pre-processing step proceeds as follows. After the verifier has sent a random challenge ρ to the prover, the problem of proving knowledge of a pre-image for Ψ is reduced to proving knowledge of a pre-image for

$$\Psi_\rho(\mathbf{x}_1, \mathbf{x}_2) = (\textsc{Com}_1(\mathbf{x}_1, \rho \cdot f_1(\mathbf{x}_1, \mathbf{x}_2)), \textsc{Com}_2(\mathbf{x}_2), f_2(\mathbf{x}_1, \mathbf{x}_2)),$$

where the domain of $\textsc{Com}_1$ has been increased from $\mathbb{Z}_q^{n_0+1} \times \mathbb{G}_1^{n_1} \times \mathbb{G}_2^{n_2}$ to $\mathbb{Z}_q^{n_0+2} \times \mathbb{G}_1^{n_1+1} \times \mathbb{G}_2^{n_2+1}$. Note that, since $\textsc{Com}_1$ is compact, the codomain of Ψ_ρ is smaller than the codomain of Ψ. Because the challenge ρ is sampled uniformly at random and the commitment scheme $\textsc{Com}_1$ is binding, the reduction is sound, i.e., a prover that knows a pre-image for Ψ_ρ must also know a pre-image for Ψ.

The reduction, denoted by Π_r, is formalized in Protocol 2 and its main properties are summarized in Lemma 1. Note that, in contrast to the previous protocols, Π_r only has *computational* soundness. Moreover, this protocol is clearly not special-honest verifier zero-knowledge; the secret witness $\mathbf{x}$ is sent to the verifier. However, since the final message of this reduction will be replaced by an appropriate compressed Σ-protocol Π_{abs}, it does not have to be SHVZK.

Protocol 2. Argument of Knowledge Π_r for R_Ψ
Reduction from relation R_Ψ to relation R_{Ψ_ρ}, where $\Psi(\mathbf{x}_1, \mathbf{x}_2) = (\textsc{Com}_1(\mathbf{x}_1), \textsc{Com}_2(\mathbf{x}_2), f(\mathbf{x}_1, \mathbf{x}_2))$.

$\textsc{Input}(z = (P_1, P_2, y_1, y_2); \mathbf{x})$

$$z = \Psi(\mathbf{x})$$
$$y_1 = f_1(\mathbf{x})$$
$$y_2 = f_2(\mathbf{x})$$

Prover		Verifier
	$\xleftarrow{\ \rho\ }$	$\rho \leftarrow_R \mathbb{Z}_q$
	$\xrightarrow{\ \mathbf{x}\ }$	
		$\Psi_\rho(\mathbf{x}) \stackrel{?}{=} z + (\textsc{Com}_1(0, \rho \cdot y_1), 0, 0)$

Lemma 1. *Π_r is a 2-move protocol for relation R_Ψ. It is perfectly complete and computationally special-sound, under the assumption that the commitment scheme* COM_1 *is binding. Moreover, the communication costs are:*

- *$\mathcal{P} \to \mathcal{V}$: 1 element of $\mathbb{Z}_q^{n_0+2} \times \mathbb{G}_1^{n_1} \times \mathbb{G}_2^{n_2} \times \mathbb{G}_T^{n_T}$.*
- *$\mathcal{V} \to \mathcal{P}$: 1 element of $\mathbb{Z}_q$.*

Proof. **Completeness** follows directly.

Special soundness: We show that there exists an efficient algorithm χ that, on input two accepting transcripts, either extracts a witness for R_ψ, or finds two different openings to the same commitment, and thereby breaks the binding property of the COM_1.

So let $(\rho, \mathbf{x})$ and $(\rho', \mathbf{x}')$ be two accepting transcripts with $\rho \neq \rho'$, then by subtracting the two verification equations and since $\text{COM}_1(\cdot)$ is a homomorphism,

$$\text{COM}_1\left(\mathbf{x} - \mathbf{x}', \rho f_1(\mathbf{x}) - \rho' f_1(\mathbf{x}')\right) = \text{COM}\left(0, (\rho - \rho')y_1, 0\right).$$

Hence, either we have extracted two different openings to the same commitment, or $\mathbf{x} = \mathbf{x}'$, $\rho f_1(\mathbf{x}) - \rho' f_1(\mathbf{x}') = (\rho - \rho')y_1$. In the latter case, it follows that $f_1(\mathbf{x}) = f_1(\mathbf{x}') = y_1$. Moreover, in this case it follows that

$$\text{COM}_1\left(\mathbf{x}_1, \rho f_1(\mathbf{x})\right) = P_1 + \text{COM}_1\left(0, \rho y_1\right),$$

which implies that $\text{COM}_1(\mathbf{x}_1) = P_1$. Hence, $\Psi(\mathbf{x}) = z$ and $\mathbf{x}$ is a witness for statement z of relation R_Ψ, which completes the proof. □

4.5 Reduced Communication for El Gamal Based Commitments

The basic Σ-protocol Π_0 of Sect. 4.1 follows the generic design for q-one-way group homomorphisms Ψ [17,18]. However, for some instantiations of Ψ this generic approach is sub-optimal as it leads to unnecessarily high communication costs. This is the case for our bilinear instantiation that makes use of the El Gamal based commitment scheme COM_2 of Definition 10,

$$\text{COM}_2 : \mathbb{G}_T^{n_T} \times \mathbb{Z}_q \to \mathbb{G}_T^{n_T+1}, \quad (\mathbf{x}, \gamma) \mapsto \begin{pmatrix} h\gamma \\ \mathbf{g}\gamma + \mathbf{x} \end{pmatrix}.$$

Here, we describe a more efficient approach tailored to the commitment scheme COM_2. Subsequently, we explain how this improvement translates to a reduction of the communication costs of our compressed Σ-protocol.

The main observation is that to open a COM_2-commitment $P = (P_1, P_2) \in \mathbb{G}_T \times \mathbb{G}_T^{n_T}$, a prover merely has to reveal $\gamma \in \mathbb{Z}_q$ with $h\gamma = P_1$. The committed vector $\mathbf{x} \in \mathbb{G}_T^{n_T}$ can be computed from the commitment P and the opening γ, i.e., $\mathbf{x} = P_2 - \mathbf{g}\gamma$. Hence, proving knowledge of a commitment opening is equivalent to proving knowledge of a discrete logarithm (in base h). The latter problem has a natural Σ-protocol with constant communication complexity. By contrast, the natural Σ-protocol for proving knowledge of a pre-image of the homomorphism COM_2 has communication costs linear in the dimension n_T of the committed vector. A straightforward extension of this protocol allows a prover to prove that the committed vector satisfies an arbitrary *linear* relation.

The resulting protocol, denoted by Π_{EG}, is a protocol for relation

$R_{EG} = \{ (P \in \mathbb{G}_T^{n_T+1}, y \in \mathbb{H}; \mathbf{x} \in \mathbb{G}_T^{n_T}, \gamma \in \mathbb{Z}_q) : P = \text{Com}_2(\mathbf{x}, \gamma), f(\mathbf{x}) = y\}$.

Its properties are summarized in Theorem 4. A detailed protocol description and the proof of Theorem 4 are given in the full version of this paper [1].

Theorem 4 (Σ-Protocol for El Gamal Based Commitments). *Π_{EG} is a Σ-protocol for relation R_{EG}. It is perfectly complete, special honest-verifier zero-knowledge and unconditionally special-sound. Moreover, the communication cost, from prover to verifier, is* 1 *element in $\mathbb{G}_T \times \mathbb{H} \times \mathbb{Z}_q$.*

4.6 Composition of the Protocols

Let Π_c be the compressed Σ-protocol obtained by instantiating Π_{abs} with homomorphism

$$\begin{aligned}\Psi \colon \mathbb{Z}_q^{n_0+2} \times \mathbb{G}_1^{n_1} \times \mathbb{G}_2^{n_2} \times \mathbb{G}_T^{n_T} &\to \mathbb{G}_T^{n_T+3} \times \mathbb{Z}_q \times \mathbb{G}_1 \times \mathbb{G}_2 \times \mathbb{G}_T, \\ (\mathbf{x}_1, \mathbf{x}_2) &\mapsto \left(\text{Com}_1(\mathbf{x}_1), \text{Com}_2(\mathbf{x}_2), f(\mathbf{x}_1, \mathbf{x}_2)\right),\end{aligned}$$

and incorporating the efficiency improvements of Sect. 4.4 and Sect. 4.5. These efficiency improvements are applicable, because we restrict ourselves to homomorphisms Ψ defined over a bilinear group. More precisely, for $\mu = \lceil \log_2 (\max(n_0 + 1, n_1, n_2)) \rceil$,

$$\Pi_c = \underbrace{\Pi_1 \diamond \cdots \diamond \Pi_1}_{\mu \text{ times}} \diamond \Pi_0 \diamond \Pi_r, \tag{5}$$

where Π_0 is understood to apply the improved Σ-protocol of Sect. 4.5 to Ψ's $\mathbb{G}_T$-part. This protocol allows a prover to prove that a committed vector $\mathbf{x} \in \mathbb{Z}_q^{n_0} \times \mathbb{G}_1^{n_1} \times \mathbb{G}_2^{n_2} \times \mathbb{G}_T^{n_T}$ satisfies a *linear* constraint $f(\mathbf{x}) = y$. The properties of Π_c are summarized in the Theorem 5. Note that, by the improvement of Sect. 4.5, the communication costs are independent of the dimension n_T of the $\mathbb{G}_T$-part of the committed vector, even though the size of the commitment is linear in n_T.

Theorem 5 (Compressed Σ-Protocol for Opening Homomorphisms). *Π_c is a $(2\mu + 4)$-move protocol for relation R_Ψ, where $\mu = \lceil \log_2 (\max(n_0 + 1, n_1, n_2)) \rceil$. It is perfectly complete, special honest-verifier zero-knowledge and computationally $(2, 2, 3, \ldots, 3)$-special-sound, under the assumption that the commitment scheme* Com$_2$ *is binding. Moreover, the communication costs are:*

- $\mathcal{P} \to \mathcal{V}$: $6\mu + 3$ *$\mathbb{G}_T$-elements,* 2 *$\mathbb{Z}_q$-elements,* 1 *$\mathbb{G}_1$-element and* 1 *$\mathbb{G}_2$-element.*
- $\mathcal{V} \to \mathcal{P}$: $\mu + 2$ *$\mathbb{Z}_q$-elements.*

Remark 2. The compressed Σ-protocols of [4], for relations defined over $\mathbb{Z}_q$, have a similar structure as Π_c. However, there a variant of the reduction Π_r is applied *after* applying the Σ-protocol. By contrast, we first apply reduction Π_r and subsequently apply the basic Σ-protocol Π_0. This adaptation yields a minor improvement as it reduces the communication costs by 3 elements.

4.7 Amortization

Standard amortization techniques apply to the basic Σ-protocol Π_0 for relation R_Ψ, and thereby also to compressed Σ-protocol Π_c. These amortization techniques allow a prover to open *many* homomorphisms on *one* commitment, or *one* homomorphism on *many* commitments, without increasing the communication costs from the prover to the verifier. For details we refer to [4, Section 5.1].

These amortization techniques allow us to restrict ourselves to homomorphisms with the codomain $\mathbb{Z}_q \times \mathbb{G}_1 \times \mathbb{G}_2 \times \mathbb{G}_T$. Namely, opening a homomorphism f with codomain $\mathbb{Z}_q^{s_0} \times \mathbb{G}_1^{s_1} \times \mathbb{G}_2^{s_2} \times \mathbb{G}_T^{s_T}$ can be casted as opening $\max(s_i)$ homomorphisms with codomain $\mathbb{Z}_q \times \mathbb{G}_1 \times \mathbb{G}_2 \times \mathbb{G}_T$.

5 Threshold Signature Schemes

In this section, we describe a threshold signature scheme (TSS), as an application of the compressed Σ-protocol Π_c for proving linear statements on committed vectors $\mathbf{x}$. Informally a k-out-of-n threshold signature can only be computed given k valid signatures issued by a k-subset of n players. We first describe the formal definition of a TSS. Subsequently, we give our construction based on the compressed Σ-protocol Π_c.

5.1 Definition and Security Model

We deviate from standard TSS definitions and aim for a strictly stronger functionality. In standard TSS definitions [9,43], a non-transparent mechanism generates a single public key and n private keys that are distributed amongst the n players. The private keys allow individual players to generate *partial* signatures on messages m. There is a public algorithm to aggregate k partial signatures into a threshold signature. The threshold signature can be verified with the public key.

By contrast, we define a TSS as an *extension* of a digital signature scheme. Our fundamental strengthening of the definitions of [9,43] and related works, is that the public and private keys are generated by the players locally. Public keys are published on a *bulletin board* and thereby publicly tied to the player's identities. This setup is thus *transparent* (called "bulletin board" in [12] and formalized as $\mathcal{F}_{CA}$ in the UC framework [16]). The players can individually sign messages by using their private keys. The aggregation algorithm now takes as input k signatures, instead of partial signatures, to generate a threshold signature.

For simplicity we assume the threshold k to be fixed. We will explain later why our construction (trivially) satisfies some stronger properties.

Let us first give a definition for the basic building block of our TSS.

Definition 11 (Digital Signature). *A digital signature scheme consists of three algorithms:*

- KEYGEN *is a randomized key generation algorithm that outputs a public-private key-pair* $(\mathsf{pk}, \mathsf{sk})$.
- SIGN *is a (possibly randomized) signing algorithm. On input a message* $m \in \{0,1\}^*$ *and a secret key* sk*, it outputs a signature* $\sigma = \text{SIGN}(\mathsf{sk}, m)$.
- VERIFY *is a deterministic verification algorithm. On input a public key* pk*, a message* m *and a signature* σ*, it outputs either* accept *or* reject.

A signature scheme is *correct* if $\text{VERIFY}(\mathsf{pk}, m, \text{SIGN}(\mathsf{sk}, m)) = \mathsf{accept}$ for all key-pairs $(\mathsf{pk}, \mathsf{sk}) \leftarrow \text{KEYGEN}$ and messages $m \in \{0,1\}^*$. If $\text{VERIFY}(\mathsf{pk}, m, \sigma) = \mathsf{accept}$ we say that σ is a *valid* signature on message m. Moreover, an adversary that does not know the secret key sk should not be able to forge a valid signature. This security property is formally captured in the widely accepted definition *Existential Unforgeability under Chosen-Message Attacks* (EUF-CMA) [9]. We assume digital signature schemes to be correct and EUF-CMA by definition.

Definition 12 (Threshold Signature). *A k-out-of-n threshold signature scheme (TSS) is a digital signature scheme* (KEYGEN, SIGN, VERIFY) *appended with two algorithms:*

- k-AGGREGATE *is a (possibly randomized) aggregation algorithm. On input* n *public keys* $(\mathsf{pk}_1, \ldots, \mathsf{pk}_n)$*,* k *signatures* $(\sigma_i)_{i\in\mathcal{S}}$ *for a k-subset* $\mathcal{S} \in \{1, \ldots, n\}$ *and a message* $m \in \{0,1\}^*$*, it outputs a threshold signature* Σ.
- k-VERIFY *is a deterministic verification algorithm. On input* n *public keys* $(\mathsf{pk}_1, \ldots, \mathsf{pk}_n)$*, a message* m *and a threshold signature* Σ*, it outputs either* accept *or* reject.

Let $\mathcal{S} \subset \{1, \ldots, n\}$ be some k-subset of indices and let $(\sigma)_{i\in\mathcal{S}}$ be signatures, such that $\text{VERIFY}(\mathsf{pk}_i, m, \sigma_i) = \mathsf{accept}$, for all $i \in \mathcal{S}$, and for some message $m \in \{0,1\}^*$. Then a TSS is *correct*, if for all $(\mathsf{pk}_1, \ldots, \mathsf{pk}_n)$, m, $\mathcal{S}$ and $(\sigma)_{i\in\mathcal{S}}$,

$$k\text{-VERIFY}\Big((\mathsf{pk}_1, \ldots, \mathsf{pk}_n), m, k\text{-AGGREGATE}\big(m, (\sigma_i)_{i\in\mathcal{S}}\big)\Big) = \mathsf{accept}.$$

If $k\text{-VERIFY}\Big((\mathsf{pk}_1, \ldots, \mathsf{pk}_n), m, \Sigma\Big) = \mathsf{accept}$ we say that Σ is a valid threshold signature. Moreover, an adversary with at most $k-1$ valid signatures on a message m should not be able to construct a valid threshold signature. This *unforgeability* property can be formalized by the following security game. Consider an adversary that is allowed to choose a subset of $k-1$ indices $\mathcal{I} \subset \{1, \ldots, n\}$ and impose the values of the keys pk_i in this subset. Assume that all remaining keys pk_i were generated honestly from KEYGEN and therefore correspond to secret keys sk_i. The adversary is allowed to query polynomially many signatures

$\sigma_i' = \text{SIGN}(sk_i, m')$ for arbitrary messages m'. The TSS is said to be *unforgeable*, if the adversary is incapable of producing a valid k-out-of-n threshold signature on some message m that has not been queried. We assume threshold signatures schemes to be correct and unforgeable by definition.

5.2 Our Threshold Signature Scheme

We follow a non-standard, but conceptually simple, approach for constructing a threshold signature scheme. The starting point of our TSS is a digital signature scheme (KEYGEN, SIGN, VERIFY) and the k-aggregation algorithm k-AGGREGATE simply produces a proof of knowledge of k valid signatures on a message m, i.e., a PoK for the following relation:

$$R_T = \{ (\mathsf{pk}_1, \dots, \mathsf{pk}_n, m; \mathcal{S}, (\sigma_i)_{i\in\mathcal{S}}) : \\ |\mathcal{S}| = k, \ \text{VERIFY}(\mathsf{pk}_i, m, \sigma_i) = \mathsf{accept}\ \forall i \in \mathcal{S}\}. \tag{6}$$

The obvious approach is to capture this relation by an arithmetic circuit, i.e., reduce it to a number of constraints defined over $\mathbb{Z}_q$, and apply a communication-efficient proof of knowledge for arithmetic circuit relations in a black-box manner. A significant drawback of this *indirect* approach is that it relies on an inefficient reduction to arithmetic circuit relations. For this reason, we follow a *direct* approach avoiding these inefficient reductions.

We instantiate our TSS with the BLS signature scheme [10] defined over a bilinear group $(q, \mathbb{G}_1, \mathbb{G}_2, \mathbb{G}_T, e, G, H)$. Let us now briefly recall the BLS signature scheme, instantiated in our n-player setting. All players i, $1 \le i \le n$, generate their own private key $u_i \in \mathbb{Z}_q$, and publish the associated public key $P_i = u_i H \in \mathbb{G}_2$. To sign a message $m \in \{0,1\}^*$, player i computes signature $\sigma_i = u_i \mathcal{H}(m) \in \mathbb{G}_1$, where $\mathcal{H}\colon \{0,1\}^* \to \mathbb{G}_1$ is some public hash function. The public verification algorithm accepts a signature σ_i if

$$e(\sigma_i, H) = e(\mathcal{H}(m), P_i). \tag{7}$$

By the bilinearity of e, all honestly generated signatures are accepted. The unforgeability follows from the co-CDH assumption [10]. Note that in [10], where $\mathbb{G}_1 = \mathbb{G}_2$, this collapses to the "gap-group" assumption.

We will be using the commitment scheme from Definition 8:

$$\text{COM} : \mathbb{Z}_q^{n_0} \times \mathbb{G}_1^{n_1} \times \mathbb{Z}_q \to \mathbb{G}_T,\ (\mathbf{x}_{\mathbb{Z}_q}, \mathbf{x}_{G_1}, \gamma) \mapsto h\gamma + \langle \mathbf{g}, \mathbf{x}_{\mathbb{Z}_q} \rangle + e(\mathbf{x}_{G_1}, \mathbf{H}).$$

This commitment scheme requires the slightly stronger DDH assumption in $\mathbb{G}_1$ to hold. Note that, in contrast to the general case considered in Sect. 4, here we do not need to be able to commit to $\mathbb{G}_2$- and $\mathbb{G}_T$-coefficients. Therefore, we can use the somewhat simpler commitment scheme of Definition 8. In particular, these commitments consist of only 1 instead of 2 $\mathbb{G}_T$-elements.

Instantiating relation R_T with the BLS signature scheme therefore results in the following relation,

$$R_{TSS} = \{(P_1, \dots, P_n, m; \mathcal{S}, (\sigma_i)_{i\in\mathcal{S}}) : |\mathcal{S}| = k,\ e(\sigma_i, H) = e(\mathcal{H}(m), P_i)\ \forall i \in \mathcal{S}\}.$$

The k-AGGREGATE algorithm simply computes a proof of knowledge for relation R_{TSS}. The main challenge is that the prover only knows k-out-of-n signatures. To handle this problem the k-out-of-n case is reduced to the n-out-of-n as follows. The k signatures are appended with $n-k$ signatures $\sigma_i = 0$ and a binary vector that allows the prover to eliminate the $n-k$ new and invalid signatures. The left hand side of the verification remains the same, while the right hand side is multiplied by corresponding coefficient of the binary vector. This approach results in a TSS with the desired properties. However, it requires the prover to prove a number of *non-linear* statements, i.e., that the committed binary vector is binary and contains at most $n-k$ zeros. Although this can be done efficiently, e.g., with the range proofs of [4], a recent result on *k-out-of-n proofs of partial knowledge* [5] gives an even more efficient solution, that completely avoids non-linearities.

The proof of partial knowledge technique allows us to reduce relation R_{TSS} to a linear relation defined over the bilinear group $(q, \mathbb{G}_1, \mathbb{G}_2, \mathbb{G}_T, e, G, H)$. Let $p(X) = 1 + \sum_{j=1}^{n-k} a_j X^j \in \mathbb{Z}_q[X]$ be the unique polynomial of degree at most $n-k$ with $p(i) = 0$ for all $i \in \{1, \dots, n\} \backslash \mathcal{S}$. Note that this polynomial defines an $(n-k, n)$ secret sharing of 1, with shares $s_i = 0$ for all $i \notin \mathcal{S}$. The k-aggregator defines $\widetilde{\sigma}_i = p(i)\sigma_i$, where $\widetilde{\sigma}_i$ is understood to be equal to 0 for $i \notin \mathcal{S}$, i.e., the secret sharing defined by $p(X)$ *eliminates* the signatures $(\sigma_i)_{i \notin \mathcal{S}}$ that the k-aggregator does not know. Subsequently, the k-aggregator commits to

$$\mathbf{x} = (a_1, \dots, a_{n-k}, \widetilde{\sigma}_1, \dots, \widetilde{\sigma}_n) \in \mathbb{Z}_q^{n-k} \times \mathbb{G}_1^n.$$

Now note that the committed vector $\mathbf{x}$ satisfies $f_i(\mathbf{x}) = f_i(a_1, \dots, a_{n-k}, \widetilde{\sigma}_1, \dots \widetilde{\sigma}_n) = e(\mathcal{H}(m), P_i)$ for all $1 \leq i \leq n$, where

$$f_i : \mathbb{Z}_q^{n-k} \times \mathbb{G}_1^n \to \mathbb{G}_T, \quad \mathbf{x} \to e(\widetilde{\sigma}_i, H) - \sum_{j=1}^{n-k} a_j i^j e(\mathcal{H}(m), P_i). \tag{8}$$

Hence, by proving that the committed vector satisfies these relations, it follows that the k-aggregator knows a non-zero polynomial $p(X)$ of degree at most $n-k$ and group elements $\widetilde{\sigma}_1, \dots \widetilde{\sigma}_n \in \mathbb{G}_1$ such that $e(\widetilde{\sigma}_i, H) = p(i) e(\mathcal{H}(m), P_i)$ for all $1 \leq i \leq n$. Therefore, the k-aggregator must know valid signatures for all indices i with $p(i) \neq 0$, and since $p(X)$ is non-zero and of degree at most $n-k$, at least k of its evaluations are non-zero. Because the mappings f_i are homomorphisms, the required proof of knowledge follows from an appropriate instantiation of compressed Σ-protocol Π_c. We apply the amortization techniques of Sect. 4.7 to prove all n relations of Eq. (8) for essentially the price of one. Moreover, we apply the Fiat-Shamir transform to make protocol Π_c non-interactive. Altogether the threshold signature contains a commitment $P \in \mathbb{G}_T$ to the vector $\mathbf{x}$ together with a non-interactive proof of knowledge π of an opening of P that satisfies the aforementioned linear constraints. The k-AGGREGATE algorithm is summarized in Algorithm 3. The associated k-verification algorithm k-VERIFY simply runs the verifier of Π_c. Correctness of the resulting threshold signature follows immediately from the completeness of Π_c, and unforgeability follows from the soundness of Π_c. The properties of the TSS are summarized in Theorem 6. Note that our TSS has some additional properties not required by the definition of Sect. 5.1. For instance, since the proof of knowledge Π_c is special honest-verifier zero-knowledge, our threshold signatures hide the k-subset $\mathcal{S}$ of signers.

Algorithm 3. k-Aggregation Algorithm k-AGGREGATE

PUBLIC INPUT : Public Keys $P_1, \ldots, P_n \in \mathbb{G}_2$
Message $m \in \{0,1\}^*$

PRIVATE INPUT : k – Subset $\mathcal{S} \subset \{1, \ldots, n\}$
Signatures $(\sigma_i)_{i \in \mathcal{S}} \in \mathbb{G}_1^k$

OUTPUT : Threshold Signature. $\Sigma = (\pi, P) \in \mathbb{Z}_q \times \mathbb{G}_1 \times \mathbb{G}_T^{4\lceil \log_2(n) \rceil + 3} \cup \{\bot\}$

1. If $\exists i \in \mathcal{S}$ such that $e(\sigma_i, H) \neq e(\mathcal{H}(m), P_i)$ output $\bot$ and abort.
2. Compute the unique polynomial $p(X) = 1 + \sum_{i=1}^{n-k} a_j X^j \in \mathbb{Z}_q[X]$ of degree at most $n-k$ such that $p(i) = 0$ for all $i \in \{1, \ldots, n\} \backslash \mathcal{S}$.
3. Compute $\widetilde{\sigma}_i := p(i)\sigma_i$ for all $i \in \mathcal{S}$ and set $\widetilde{\sigma}_i = 0$ for all $i \notin \mathcal{S}$.
4. Let $\mathbf{x} = (a_1, \ldots, a_{n-k}, \widetilde{\sigma}_1, \ldots, \widetilde{\sigma}_n) \in \mathbb{Z}_q^{n-k} \times \mathbb{G}_1^n$ and compute commitment $P = \text{COM}(\mathbf{x}, \gamma) \in \mathbb{G}_T$ for $\gamma \in \mathbb{Z}_q$ sampled uniformly at random.
5. Run the non-interactive variant of Π_c to produce a proof π attesting that the committed vector $\mathbf{x}$ satisfies $f_i(\mathbf{x}) = f_i(a_1, \ldots, a_{n-k}, \widetilde{\sigma}_1, \ldots \widetilde{\sigma}_n) = e(\mathcal{H}(m), P_i)$ for all $1 \leq i \leq n$, where f_i are homomorphisms defined in Equation 8.
6. Output commitment P and the non-interactive proof $\pi \in \mathbb{Z}_q \times \mathbb{G}_1 \times \mathbb{G}_T^{4\lceil \log_2(n) \rceil + 2}$.

Theorem 6 (Threshold Signature Scheme). *The k-out-of-n threshold signature scheme defined by the BLS signatures scheme [10] appended with the algorithms (k-AGGREGATE, k-VERIFY) is correct and unforgeable. Moreover:*

- *A threshold signature contains exactly $4\lceil \log_2(n) \rceil + 3$ $\mathbb{G}_T$-elements, 1 $\mathbb{G}_1$-element and 1 $\mathbb{Z}_q$-element.*
- *A threshold signature is zero-knowledge on the identities of the k signers.*
- *The threshold k can be chosen at aggregation time.*
- *It resists against an adaptive adversary which can replace the public keys of corrupted players.*

Proof. See the full version of this paper [1]. □

6 Generalized Circuit Zero-Knowledge Protocols

The Compressed Σ-Protocol Π_c of Sect. 4 allows a prover to prove linear statements. In this section, we show how to handle non-linear statements. Our approach is a generalization of the linearization techniques of [4], where it was shown how to linearize non-linearities in arithmetic circuit relations. More precisely, we aim to find a SHVZK PoK for proving knowledge of a witness $\mathbf{x}$ such that $C(\mathbf{x}) = 0$ for some circuit C defined over a bilinear group, i.e., a protocol for the following circuit satisfiability relation:

$$R_{cs} = \{(C; \mathbf{x}) : C(\mathbf{x}) = 0\}. \tag{9}$$

Circuits defined over a bilinear group have the following form:

$$C : \mathbb{Z}_q^{n_0} \times \mathbb{G}_1^{n_1} \times \mathbb{G}_2^{n_2} \times \mathbb{G}_T^{n_T} \rightarrow \mathbb{Z}_q^{s_0} \times \mathbb{G}_1^{s_1} \times \mathbb{G}_2^{s_2} \times \mathbb{G}_T^{s_T}.$$

These circuits are also called *bilinear group arithmetic circuits* [35] and they are composed of addition gates and the following 5 types of bilinear gates:

$$\begin{aligned}
\text{Gate}_0 &: \mathbb{Z}_q \times \mathbb{Z}_q \rightarrow \mathbb{Z}_q, & (a,b) &\rightarrow ab,\\
\text{Gate}_1 &: \mathbb{G}_1 \times \mathbb{Z}_q \rightarrow \mathbb{G}_1, & (g,a) &\rightarrow ga,\\
\text{Gate}_2 &: \mathbb{G}_2 \times \mathbb{Z}_q \rightarrow \mathbb{G}_2, & (h,a) &\rightarrow ha,\\
\text{Gate}_3 &: \mathbb{G}_T \times \mathbb{Z}_q \rightarrow \mathbb{G}_T, & (k,a) &\rightarrow ka,\\
\text{Gate}_4 &: \mathbb{G}_1 \times \mathbb{G}_2 \rightarrow \mathbb{G}_T, & (g,h) &\rightarrow e(g,h).
\end{aligned} \tag{10}$$

Each wire of C corresponds to a variable that takes values in a group $W \in \{\mathbb{Z}_q, \mathbb{G}_1, \mathbb{G}_2, \mathbb{G}_T\}$. We assume all gates to have fan-in two and unbounded fan-out. Note that these circuits are indeed generalizations of arithmetic circuits, where wires take values in $\mathbb{Z}_q$, and gates are addition or multiplication gates.

Bilinear gates taking one constant and one variable input value are linear mappings. Hence, circuits C containing no bilinear gates with two variable inputs are handled directly by the techniques from Sect. 4. In this case, $C(\mathbf{x}) = f(\mathbf{x}) + a$ for a homomorphism f and a fixed constant a. A protocol for relation R_{cs} then goes as follows:

1. The prover commits to $\mathbf{x} \in \mathbb{Z}_q^{n_0} \times \mathbb{G}_1^{n_1} \times \mathbb{G}_2^{n_2} \times \mathbb{G}_T^{n_T}$.
2. The prover and the verifier run Π_c to open the homomorphism f, i.e., the prover reveals a value y and proves that $f(\mathbf{x}) = y$.
3. The verifier checks that $y + a = 0$.

When C contains bilinear gates, we cannot express the circuit in this *linear* manner. To handle non-linearities, the prover appends the secret vector $\mathbf{x}$ with a vector aux containing auxiliary information, i.e., in the first step of the protocol the prover commits to the appended vector $(\mathbf{x}, \mathsf{aux})$. The approach is a generalization of the *secret sharing based* techniques from [4]; linearizing non-linearities.

Let $\mathbf{c}$ be the vector of wire values associated to the output wires of all the bilinear gates in $C(\mathbf{x})$. Note that $\mathbf{c}$ depends on the secret vector $\mathbf{x}$. Then, there exists a homomorphism f and a constant a, independent from $\mathbf{x}$, such that $C(\mathbf{x}) = f(\mathbf{x}, \mathbf{c}) + a$. A naive generalization of the above approach to arbitrary circuits is now obtained by taking $\mathsf{aux} = \mathbf{c}$. However, this approach does not guarantee that the committed vector $(\mathbf{x}, \mathbf{c})$ is of the appropriate form, i.e., that $\mathbf{c}$ corresponds to the outputs of bilinear gates when C is evaluated in $\mathbf{x}$.

To prove that the committed vector $(\mathbf{x}, \mathbf{c})$ is of the appropriate form the inputs and outputs of the bilinear gates are *encoded* in polynomials $f \in A[X]$ where $A \in \{\mathbb{Z}_q, \mathbb{G}_1, \mathbb{G}_2, \mathbb{G}_T\}$. We first describe some properties of these polynomials.

6.1 Polynomials over Groups of Prime Order

The $\mathbb{Z}_q$-module structure of the groups $\mathbb{G}_i$ naturally extends to their polynomial rings, i.e., $\mathbb{G}_i[X]$ is a $\mathbb{Z}_q[X]$-module for all i and the product $h(X)$ of two polynomials $f(X) \in \mathbb{Z}_q[X]$ and $g(X) \in \mathbb{G}_i[X]$ is defined naturally.

Since $\mathbb{G}_i$ is a $\mathbb{Z}_q$-module, a polynomial $f = \sum_{i=0}^n a_i X^i \in \mathbb{G}_i[X]$ defines a mapping $f : \mathbb{Z}_q \to \mathbb{G}_i$, $\rho \to f(\rho) = \sum_{i=0}^n a_i \rho^i$, called the "evaluation" mapping. Moreover, every $\rho \in \mathbb{Z}_q$ defines a mapping:

$$F_\rho : \mathbb{G}_i[X] \to \mathbb{G}_i, \quad f = \sum_{i=0}^n a_i X^i \to f(\rho) = \sum_{i=0}^n a_i \rho^i,$$

called the "evaluation at ρ" mapping, which is linear.

A bilinear gate Gate : $\mathrm{L} \times \mathrm{R} \to \mathrm{U}$ can be extended to act on polynomials:

$$\mathrm{Gate}\left(\sum_{i=0}^n a_i X^i, \sum_{j=0}^m b_j X^j\right) = \sum_{i=0}^n \sum_{j=0}^m \mathrm{Gate}(a_i, b_j) X^{i+j} \in \mathrm{U}[X]. \tag{11}$$

By the bilinearity of Gate it follows that this mapping commutes with polynomial evaluation, i.e., for all $\rho \in \mathbb{Z}_q$ it holds that $\mathrm{Gate}(f(\rho), g(\rho)) = \mathrm{Gate}(f, g)(\rho)$.

The following lemma shows that a non-zero polynomial f has at most $\deg(f)$ zeros. From this it follows that, for a fixed non-zero polynomial f and a random challenge c, the probability that $f(c) = 0$ is at most $\deg(f)/q$.

Lemma 2. *Let $f(X) \in A[X]$ be non-zero, for some $A \in \{\mathbb{Z}_q, \mathbb{G}_1, \mathbb{G}_2, \mathbb{G}_T\}$. Then $f(X)$ has at most $\deg(f)$ zeros.*

Proof. Recall that A has prime order q and let g be a generator of A. Then it is easily seen that $f(X) = f'(X)g$ for some polynomial $f'(X) \in \mathbb{Z}_q[X]$ with $\deg(f) = \deg(f')$. Moreover, since g is a generator of A, it holds that $f(a) = 0$ if and only if $f'(a) = 0$. The lemma now follows from the fact that a non-zero polynomial f' defined over the field $\mathbb{Z}_q$ has at most $\deg(f')$ zeros. □

The following lemma describes an approach for testing whether three polynomials $f(X)$, $g(X)$ and $h(X)$ satisfy a bilinear relation defined by Gate: $\mathrm{L} \times \mathrm{R} \to \mathrm{U}$. More precisely, when the bilinear relation holds in a random evaluation point $c \in \mathbb{Z}_q$ then, with high probability, it holds for the polynomials f, g and h.

Lemma 3. *Let $f(X) \in \mathrm{L}[X]$, $g(X) \in \mathrm{R}[X]$ and $h(X) \in \mathrm{U}[X]$ with $\deg(f), \deg(g) \leq n$ and $\deg(h) \leq 2n$. Then, for $d \in C \subset \mathbb{Z}_q$ sampled uniformly at random, it holds that*

$$\Pr\left(\mathrm{Gate}\left(f(d), g(d)\right) = h(d) \middle| \mathrm{Gate}\left(f(X), g(X)\right) \neq h(X)\right) \leq 2n/\left|C\right|.$$

Proof. The polynomial $h(X) - \mathrm{Gate}\left(f(X), g(X)\right) \in \mathrm{U}[X]$ has degree at most $2n$. The lemma now follows from Lemma 2. □

6.2 Linearization of Bilinear Gates

We are now ready to describe the linearization approach. To this end, for $0 \leq i \leq 4$, let m_i be the number of gates $\text{Gate}_i \colon \mathrm{L}_i \times \mathrm{R}_i \to \mathrm{U}_i$ of type i in circuit C. Then, for a circuit evaluation $C(\mathbf{x})$, we let $\mathbf{a}_i \in \mathrm{L}_i^{m_i}$ and $\mathbf{b}_i \in \mathrm{R}_i^{m_i}$ be the vectors of left and right input values of these gates. Similarly, we let $\mathbf{c}_i \in \mathrm{U}_i^{m_i}$ be the vector of output values for the gates of type i.

The protocol now goes as follows. First, for each i, the prover samples two polynomials $f_i(X) \in \mathrm{L}_i[X]_{\leq m_i}$ and $g_i(X) \in \mathrm{R}_i[X]_{\leq m_i}$ of degree at most m_i uniformly at random under the condition that $f_i(j) = a_{i,j}$ and $g_i(j) = b_{i,j}$ for all $1 \leq j \leq m_i$. Note that these polynomials define *packed Shamir secret sharings* [42] with $(m_i + 1)$-reconstruction and 1-privacy of the vectors $\mathbf{a}_i$ and $\mathbf{b}_i$, i.e., the vectors $\mathbf{a}_i$ and $\mathbf{b}_i$ can be reconstructed from any $m_i + 1$ evaluations of $f_i(X)$ and $g_i(X)$ and any single evaluation outside $\{1, \dots, m_i\}$ is independent from the vectors $\mathbf{a}_i$ and $\mathbf{b}_i$.

Second, the prover computes the polynomial $h_i(X) = \text{Gate}_i\left(f_i(X), g_i(X)\right)$. By the *strong-multiplicativity* of Shamir's secret sharing scheme, $h_i(X) \in \mathrm{U}_i[X]$ defines a packed secret sharing of the vector $\mathbf{c}_i \in \mathrm{U}_i^{m_i}$ with $2m_i + 1$ reconstruction. More precisely, $h_i(X)$ is of degree at most $2m_i$ and $h_i(j) = c_{i,j}$ for all $1 \leq j \leq m_i$. Subsequently, the prover sends a commitment to the following secret vector to the verifier:

$$\begin{aligned}\mathbf{y} = \big(&\mathbf{x}, f_0(0), g_0(0), h_0(0), \dots, h_0(2m_0), \dots,\\ &f_4(0), g_4(0), h_4(0), h_4(1), \dots, h_4(2m_4)\big).\end{aligned}$$

The vector $\mathbf{y} = (\mathbf{x}, \mathsf{aux})$ contains the vector $\mathbf{c} = (\mathbf{c}_1, \dots, \mathbf{c}_\ell)$ of the output values of all bilinear gates as a sub-vector. Hence, all wire values can be expressed as the evaluation of some public homomorphism in $\mathbf{y}$ plus a public constant value. This holds in particular for the evaluations $f_i(j)$ and $g_i(j)$ for all $1 \leq i \leq \ell$ and $1 \leq j \leq m_j$. Hence, for every i, $m_i + 1$ evaluations of f_i and g_i can be computed as affine functions evaluated in $\mathbf{y}$, i.e., $\mathbf{y}$ uniquely defines polynomials $f_i(X)$ and $g_i(X)$ of degree at most m_i. Similarly, $\mathbf{y}$ uniquely defines polynomials $h_i(X)$ of degree at most $2m_i$. By the linearity of Lagrange interpolation it follows that, in addition to the wire values, all evaluations of the polynomials $f_i(X)$, $g_i(X)$ and $h_i(X)$ can be expressed as some homomorphism evaluated in $\mathbf{y}$ plus a constant.

These properties allow the prover to convince the verifier that the vector $\mathbf{y}$ is of the appropriate form by proving that certain linear constraints hold. Namely, in the next step of the protocol, the verifier samples a random challenge $d \in \mathbb{Z}_q \backslash \{1, \dots, \max(m_i)\}$ uniformly at random and asks the prover to run protocol Π_c to open $C(\mathbf{x})$, $f_i(d)$, $g_i(d)$ and $h_i(d)$ for all $1 \leq i \leq \ell$. Note that all these values correspond to homomorphisms evaluated in the committed vector $\mathbf{y} = (\mathbf{x}, \mathsf{aux})$. To further reduce the communication costs, the amortization techniques mentioned in 4.7 are applied. Finally, the verifier verifies that $C(\mathbf{x}) = 0$ and that $\text{Gate}\left(f_i(d), g_i(d)\right) = h_i(d)$ for all $0 \leq i \leq 4$. By Lemma 3 this final verification implies that $\text{Gate}\left(f_i(X), g_i(X)\right) = h_i(X)$, and therefore that $\text{Gate}\left(a_{i,j}, b_{i,j}\right) = c_{i,j}$ for all j, with probability at least $1 - 2m_i/(q - m_i)$.

If m_i is polynomial and q is exponential in the security parameter, this probability is overwhelming. The protocol is SHVZK because the polynomials $f_i(X)$, $g_i(X)$ and $h_i(X)$ define secret sharings with 1-privacy, and because protocol Π_c is SHVZK. For a more detailed discussion we refer to [4] in which this approach is restricted to arithmetic circuits.

The resulting protocol, denoted by Π_{cs}, is described in the full version of this paper [1]. To state the properties of protocol Π_{cs} observe that

$$\mathbf{y} = (\mathbf{x}, \mathsf{aux}) \in \mathbb{Z}_q^{n_0+2m_0+6} \times \mathbb{G}_1^{n_1+2m_1+3} \times \mathbb{G}_1^{n_2+2m_2+3} \times \mathbb{G}_T^{n_T+2m_3+2m_4+3},$$

where $\mathbf{y}$ is the vector to which the prover commits in the first round of protocol Π_{cs}. For ease of notation we define the following parameters:

$$\begin{aligned} m &:= \max(m_i), \quad s := \max(s_0+6, s_1+3, s_2+3, s_T+3), \\ N &:= \max\left(n_0+2m_0+7, n_1+2m_1+3, n_2+2m_2+3\right), \\ N_T &:= n_T+2m_3+2m_4+3. \end{aligned}$$

Note that we make a distinction between the $(\mathbb{Z}_q, \mathbb{G}_1, \mathbb{G}_2)$-part, for which the commitment scheme is compact, and the $\mathbb{G}_T$-part of the vector $\mathbf{y}$. Using this notation, the properties of Π_{cs} are summarized in Theorem 7.

Theorem 7 (Circuit Zero-Knowledge Protocol for Bilinear Circuits). *Π_{cs} is a $(2\mu+7)$-move protocol for circuit relation R_{cs}, where $\mu = \lceil \log_2(N) \rceil$. It is perfectly complete, special honest-verifier zero-knowledge, under the DDH assumption in $\mathbb{G}_T$, and computationally $(2m+1, s, 2, 2, 3, \ldots, 3)$-special-sound under the SXDH assumption. Moreover, the communication costs are:*

- *$\mathcal{P} \to \mathcal{V}$: $6\mu + N_T + 9$ $\mathbb{G}_T$-elements, 4 $\mathbb{G}_1$-elements, 4 $\mathbb{G}_2$-elements and 8 $\mathbb{Z}_q$-elements.*
- *$\mathcal{V} \to \mathcal{P}$: $\mu + 4$ $\mathbb{Z}_q$-elements.*

Remark 3. Without the improvement of Sect. 4.5, for El Gamal based commitments, the prover would have to communicate $2N_T$ additional $\mathbb{G}_T$ elements in protocol Π_{cs}. Hence, this improvement causes the constant in front of the only linear term of the communication costs to be reduced from 3 down to 1.

6.3 Comparison of the Communication Costs

In this section, we compare the communication costs of our protocol Π_{cs} to the bilinear circuit ZK protocol of [35]. We note that, a rigorous comparison is difficult, for the following two reasons. First, we consider arbitrary bilinear circuits, whereas they assume certain structural properties. The communication costs stated in [35] hold only for circuits in which the gates with $\mathbb{G}_T$ outputs are output gates. Second, we consider a strictly stronger scenario in which the prover proves that the *committed* input values satisfy some bilinear relation, instead of merely proving knowledge of a satisfying input vector without being committed to this input vector, i.e., we consider a *commit-and-proof* functionality. This difference explains why their communications costs are independent of the input dimensions n_0, n_1 and n_2.

Despite these two aspects, showing that we consider a stronger application scenario, it is interesting to note that our communication costs are smaller in certain parameter regimes. From Theorem 7 it follows that our Protocol Π_{cs} requires the prover to send a total of $6\lceil\log_2(N)\rceil + N_T + 28$ elements (group and field elements) to the verifier, i.e., the communication costs associated to the $(\mathbb{Z}_q, \mathbb{G}_1, \mathbb{G}_2)$-part are logarithmic and the communications costs associated to the $\mathbb{G}_T$-part are linear. By contrast, the protocol of [35] results in a total communication cost of $16\log_2(\ell_{mix}) + 3n_T + 71$ elements, where $\ell_{mix} = 2m_0' + m_1' + m_2' + n_T m_3' + m_4'$. Here, the variable m_i' counts all gates of type i, including the ones taking a constant input value, i.e., $m_i' \geq m_i$. Hence, we have reduced the constant of the logarithmic part from 16 down to 6, and the constant of the linear part from 3 down to 1. However, when comparing the linear parts of the communication complexity, we note that there exist bilinear circuits for which $3n_T < N_T = n_T + 2m_3 + 2m_4 + 3$, e.g., circuits with $n_T = 0$ and $m_4 > 0$. Therefore, depending on the bilinear circuit our *linear* communication costs can be larger. This can partially be explained by the fact that Lai et al. [35] make structural assumptions on the bilinear circuit. For instance, they assume that only input and output wires can take values in $\mathbb{G}_T$, whereas our protocol works for arbitrary bilinear circuits.

Nevertheless, as opposed to general bilinear circuits, there are specific quadratic inner-product relations for which the approach of Lai et al. [35] can result in communication costs lower than those obtained by applying our generic approach. These relations exploit the fact that their approach reduces bilinear circuit relations to sets of inner-product constraints. These techniques are further improved in Bünz et al. [14], who focus on communication-efficient protocols for quadratic inner-product relations. By contrast, for the example of threshold signature schemes, which only rely on linear circuits, application of the latter approach would result in unnecessary overhead as compared to our compressed Σ-protocol approach.

Acknowledgments. We are grateful for the constructive and encouraging comments from Hieu Phan. We also thank Thijs Veugen for numerous helpful editorial comments. We thank Russell Lai for answering some relevant questions regarding his prior work [35] and for explaining their techniques. Thomas Attema has been supported by the Vraaggestuurd Programma Veilige Maatschappij, supervised by the Innovation Team of the Dutch Ministry of Justice and Security, and the Vraaggestuurd Programma Cyber Security, part of the Dutch Top Sector High Tech Systems and Materials programme. Ronald Cramer has been supported by ERC ADG project No 74079 (ALGSTRONGCRYPTO) and by the NWO Gravitation Programme (QSC).

References

1. Full version of this paper. IACR ePrint 2020/1147
2. Abe, M., Fuchsbauer, G., Groth, J., Haralambiev, K., Ohkubo, M.: Structure-preserving signatures and commitments to group elements. J. Cryptol. **29**(2), 363–421 (2015). https://doi.org/10.1007/s00145-014-9196-7
3. Ateniese, G., Camenisch, J., Hohenberger, S., de Medeiros, B.: Practical group signatures without random oracles. IACR ePrint 2005/385 (2005)
4. Attema, T., Cramer, R.: Compressed Σ-protocol theory and practical application to plug & play secure algorithmics. In: Micciancio, D., Ristenpart, T. (eds.) CRYPTO 2020. LNCS, vol. 12172, pp. 513–543. Springer, Cham (2020). https://doi.org/10.1007/978-3-030-56877-1_18
5. Attema, T., Cramer, R., Fehr, S.: Compressing proofs of k-out-of-n-partial knowledge. IACR ePrint 2020/753 (2020)
6. Attema, T., Cramer, R., Kohl, L.: A compressed Σ-protocol theory for lattices. In: Malkin, T., Peikert, C. (eds.) CRYPTO 2021. LNCS, vol. 12826, pp. 549–579. Springer, Cham (2021). https://doi.org/10.1007/978-3-030-84245-1_19
7. Ballard, L., Green, M., de Medeiros, B., Monrose, F.: Correlation-resistant storage via keyword-searchable encryption. IACR ePrint 2005/417 (2005)
8. Bellare, M., Rogaway, P.: Random oracles are practical: a paradigm for designing efficient protocols. In: ACM CCS 1993 (1993)
9. Boldyreva, A.: Threshold signatures, multisignatures and blind signatures based on the gap-Diffie-Hellman-group signature scheme. In: Desmedt, Y.G. (ed.) PKC 2003. LNCS, vol. 2567, pp. 31–46. Springer, Heidelberg (2003). https://doi.org/10.1007/3-540-36288-6_3
10. Boneh, D., Lynn, B., Shacham, H.: Short signatures from the Weil pairing. In: Boyd, C. (ed.) ASIACRYPT 2001. LNCS, vol. 2248, pp. 514–532. Springer, Heidelberg (2001). https://doi.org/10.1007/3-540-45682-1_30
11. Bootle, J., Cerulli, A., Chaidos, P., Groth, J., Petit, C.: Efficient zero-knowledge arguments for arithmetic circuits in the discrete log setting. In: Fischlin, M., Coron, J.-S. (eds.) EUROCRYPT 2016. LNCS, vol. 9666, pp. 327–357. Springer, Heidelberg (2016). https://doi.org/10.1007/978-3-662-49896-5_12
12. Boyle, E., Cohen, R., Goel, A.: Breaking the $O(\sqrt{n})$-bits barrier: balanced byzantine agreement with polylog bits per-party. In: To Appear in ACM PODC (2021)
13. Bünz, B., Bootle, J., Boneh, D., Poelstra, A., Wuille, P., Maxwell, G.: Bulletproofs: short proofs for confidential transactions and more. In: IEEE S&P (2018)
14. Bünz, B., Maller, M., Mishra, P., Vesely, N.: Proofs for inner pairing products and applications. IACR ePrint 2019/1177 (2019)
15. Cachin, C., Kursawe, K., Shoup, V.: Random oracles in Constantinople: practical asynchronous byzantine agreement using cryptography. J. Cryptol. **18**(3), 219–246 (2005). https://doi.org/10.1007/s00145-005-0318-0
16. Canetti, R.: Universally composable signature, certification, and authentication. In: IEEE Computer Security Foundations Workshop 2004 (2004)
17. Cramer, R.: Modular design of secure yet practical cryptographic protocols. Ph.D. thesis, CWI and University of Amsterdam (1996)
18. Cramer, R., Damgård, I.: Zero-knowledge proofs for finite field arithmetic, or: can zero-knowledge be for free? In: Krawczyk, H. (ed.) CRYPTO 1998. LNCS, vol. 1462, pp. 424–441. Springer, Heidelberg (1998). https://doi.org/10.1007/BFb0055745

19. Cramer, R., Damgård, I., Pastro, V.: On the amortized complexity of zero knowledge protocols for multiplicative relations. In: Smith, A. (ed.) ICITS 2012. LNCS, vol. 7412, pp. 62–79. Springer, Heidelberg (2012). https://doi.org/10.1007/978-3-642-32284-6_4
20. Desmedt, Y., Frankel, Y.: Threshold cryptosystems. In: Brassard, G. (ed.) CRYPTO 1989. LNCS, vol. 435, pp. 307–315. Springer, New York (1990). https://doi.org/10.1007/0-387-34805-0_28
21. Fiat, A., Shamir, A.: How to prove yourself: practical solutions to identification and signature problems. In: Odlyzko, A.M. (ed.) CRYPTO 1986. LNCS, vol. 263, pp. 186–194. Springer, Heidelberg (1987). https://doi.org/10.1007/3-540-47721-7_12
22. Galbraith, S.D., Paterson, K.G., Smart, N.P.: Pairings for cryptographers. Discret. Appl. Math **156**, 3113–3121 (2008)
23. ElGamal, T.: A public key cryptosystem and a signature scheme based on discrete logarithms. In: Blakley, G.R., Chaum, D. (eds.) CRYPTO 1984. LNCS, vol. 196, pp. 10–18. Springer, Heidelberg (1985). https://doi.org/10.1007/3-540-39568-7_2
24. Gennaro, R., Goldfeder, S.: One round threshold ECDSA with identifiable abort. IACR ePrint 2020/540 (2020)
25. Gennaro, R., Jarecki, S., Krawczyk, H., Rabin, T.: Robust threshold DSS signatures. In: Maurer, U. (ed.) EUROCRYPT 1996. LNCS, vol. 1070, pp. 354–371. Springer, Heidelberg (1996). https://doi.org/10.1007/3-540-68339-9_31
26. Gennaro, R., Jarecki, S., Krawczyk, H., Rabin, T.: Secure applications of Pedersen's distributed key generation protocol. In: Joye, M. (ed.) CT-RSA 2003. LNCS, vol. 2612, pp. 373–390. Springer, Heidelberg (2003). https://doi.org/10.1007/3-540-36563-X_26
27. Ghoshal, A., Tessaro, S.: Tight state-restoration soundness in the algebraic group model. In: Malkin, T., Peikert, C. (eds.) CRYPTO 2021. LNCS, vol. 12827, pp. 64–93. Springer, Cham (2021). https://doi.org/10.1007/978-3-030-84252-9_3
28. Groth, J., Sahai, A.: Efficient non-interactive proof systems for bilinear groups. In: Smart, N. (ed.) EUROCRYPT 2008. LNCS, vol. 4965, pp. 415–432. Springer, Heidelberg (2008). https://doi.org/10.1007/978-3-540-78967-3_24
29. Haque, A., Krenn, S., Slamanig, D., Striecks, C.: Logarithmic-size (linkable) threshold ring signatures in the plain model. IACR ePrint 2020/683 (2020)
30. Harchol, Y., Abraham, I., Pinkas, B.: Distributed SSH key management with proactive RSA threshold signatures. In: Preneel, B., Vercauteren, F. (eds.) ACNS 2018. LNCS, vol. 10892, pp. 22–43. Springer, Cham (2018). https://doi.org/10.1007/978-3-319-93387-0_2
31. Hoffmann, M., Klooß, M., Rupp, A.: Efficient zero-knowledge arguments in the discrete log setting, revisited. In: ACM CCS 2019 (2019)
32. Hopwood, D., Bowe, S., Hornby, T., Wilcox, N.: Zcash Protocol Specication - Version 2020.1.7 (2020)
33. Kokoris-Kogias, E., Spiegelman, A., Malkhi, D.: Asynchronous distributed key generation for computationally-secure randomness, consensus, and threshold signatures. In: ACM CCS 2020 (2020)
34. Komlo, C., Goldberg, I.: FROST: flexible round-optimized Schnorr threshold signatures. In: SAC 2020, pp. 34–65 (2020)
35. Lai, R.W.F., Malavolta, G., Ronge, V.: Succinct arguments for bilinear group arithmetic: practical structure-preserving cryptography. In: ACM CCS 2019, pp. 2057–2074 (2019)
36. Libert, B., Joye, M., Yung, M.: Born and raised distributively: fully distributed non-interactive adaptively-secure threshold signatures with short shares. Theor. Comput. Sci. **645**, 1–24 (2016)

37. Libra Team: State machine replication in the LibraBlockchain, version 2019–10-24 (2019)
38. Lindell, Y.: Parallel coin-tossing and constant-round secure two-party computation. J. Cryptol. **16**(3), 143–184 (2003). https://doi.org/10.1007/s00145-002-0143-7
39. Nayak, K., Ren, L., Shi, E., Vaidya, N.H., Xiang, Z.: Improved extension protocols for byzantine broadcast and agreement. In: DISC 2020, pp. 28:1–28:17 (2020)
40. Pedersen, T.P.: Non-interactive and information-theoretic secure verifiable secret sharing. In: Feigenbaum, J. (ed.) CRYPTO 1991. LNCS, vol. 576, pp. 129–140. Springer, Heidelberg (1992). https://doi.org/10.1007/3-540-46766-1_9
41. Sahai, A., Waters, B.: Fuzzy identity-based encryption. In: Cramer, R. (ed.) EUROCRYPT 2005. LNCS, vol. 3494, pp. 457–473. Springer, Heidelberg (2005). https://doi.org/10.1007/11426639_27
42. Shamir, A.: How to share a secret. Commun. ACM **22**, 612–613 (1979)
43. Shoup, V.: Practical threshold signatures. In: Preneel, B. (ed.) EUROCRYPT 2000. LNCS, vol. 1807, pp. 207–220. Springer, Heidelberg (2000). https://doi.org/10.1007/3-540-45539-6_15

Promise Σ-Protocol: How to Construct Efficient Threshold ECDSA from Encryptions Based on Class Groups

Yi Deng[1,2](✉), Shunli Ma[1,2](✉), Xinxuan Zhang[1,2](✉), Hailong Wang[1,2](✉), Xuyang Song[3](✉), and Xiang Xie[3](✉)

[1] State Key Laboratory of Information Security, Institute of Information Engineering, Chinese Academy of Sciences, Beijing, China
{deng,mashunli,zhangxinxuan,wanghailong9065}@iie.ac.cn

[2] School of Cyber Security, University of Chinese Academy of Sciences, Beijing, China

[3] Shanghai Key Laboratory of Privacy-Preserving Computation, Shanghai, China
{songxuyang,xiexiang}@matrixelements.com

Abstract. Threshold Signatures allow n parties to share the ability of issuing digital signatures so that any coalition of size at least $t+1$ can sign, whereas groups of t or fewer players cannot. The currently known class-group-based threshold ECDSA constructions are either inefficient (requiring parallel-repetition of the underlying zero knowledge proof with small challenge space) or requiring rather non-standard low order assumption. In this paper, we present efficient threshold ECDSA protocols from encryption schemes based on class groups *with neither assuming the low order assumption nor parallel repeating the underlying zero knowledge proof*, yielding a significant efficiency improvement in the key generation over previous constructions.

Along the way we introduce a new notion of *promise* Σ-protocol that satisfies only a weaker soundness called *promise extractability*. An accepting *promise* Σ-proof for statements related to class-group-based encryptions does not establish the truth of the statement but provides security guarantees (promise extractability) that are sufficient for our applications. We also show how to simulate homomorphic operations on a (possibly invalid) class-group-based encryption whose correctness has been proven via our *promise* Σ-protocol. We believe that these techniques are of independent interest and applicable to other scenarios where efficient zero knowledge proofs for statements related to class-group is required.

1 Introduction

Threshold Digital Signature Schemes [Des88] enable distributed signing amongst a group of individuals such that any subgroup which is larger than a certain predetermined size can jointly sign, whereas any group with fewer players cannot. Specifically, a t-out-of-n threshold signature scheme is a protocol that allows n parties to jointly generate a common public verification key, along with n shares

M. Tibouchi and H. Wang (Eds.): ASIACRYPT 2021, LNCS 13093, pp. 557–586, 2021.
https://doi.org/10.1007/978-3-030-92068-5_19

of the corresponding secret signing key, and allows any subgroup of at least $t+1$ parties to securely sign a given message distributedly. In addition to satisfying the standard unforgeability of signature schemes, threshold variants should provide security that no malicious party can subvert the protocol to extract another party's secret share, and no more than t cannot collude to generate a valid signature.

The Elliptic Curve Digital Signature Algorithm (ECDSA) has been widely used in various applications including TLS, DNSSec, SSH and cryptocurrencies such as Bitcoin and Ethereum. The efficiency and widespread adoptions of ECDSA make its threshold version become an active research topic recently. After the work [GJKR96] and [MR01], many improved protocols have been proposed in recent years both for the specific two-party case [Lin17, DKLs18, CCL+19] and for the more general t-out-of-n case [GGN16, BGG19, GG18, LN18, DKLs19, CCL+20]. Among these schemes, a common used primitive to study threshold ECDSA is additively homomorphic encryption such as Paillier encryption and CL encryption [CL15, CLT18]. The latter is an ElGamal-like encryption scheme based on class groups of unknown order that contain a prime-order subgroup where the discrete logarithm (DL) problem is tractable, and such a distinguished property enables the CL encryption scheme to support much larger message space than the traditional ElGamal scheme.

Protocols based on Paillier encryption. Gennaro et al. [GGN16] extended the technique of [MR01], and introduced a six-round t-out-of-n threshold signature. Boneh et al. [BGG19] optimized their extension in terms of computational efficiency, and reduced the number of rounds to four. Meanwhile Lindell [Lin17] optimized the protocol framework and proposed an efficient protocol in the two-party setting. Subsequently, Gennaro and Goldfeder[GG18, GG20], Lindell and Nof [LN18] presented efficient protocols in the multi-party case that supported efficient distributed key generation. Unfortunately, mainly due to the mismatch between the Paillier modulus and the ECDSA modulus, these schemes all require expensive zero knowledge proofs, such as costly range proofs.

Protocols based on CL encryption. Castagnos et al. [CCL+19, CCL+20] employed the CL encryption and presented bandwidth efficient protocols for the two-party case and multi-party case, respectively. The modulus, which defines the underlying message space of CL encryption, could be set as the same prime modulus as in ECDSA. Thus, these protocols are able to eliminate the expensive range proofs which are required in the Paillier-based protocols, and achieve low communication cost. However, it is challenging to design efficient zero knowledge proofs for CL ciphertexts. As discussed in Sect. 1.2, a malicious prover holding low-order elements can convince the verifier of an invalid ciphertext with high probability. In order to resist this low-order-element attack, the two-party protocol in [CCL+19] adopts a zero knowledge proof with a single bit challenge to prove the validity of a CL ciphertext, and repeats this subprotocol in parallel to achieve a negligible soundness error. To overcome the inefficiency caused by repetition, [CCL+20] proposed more efficient threshold ECDSA protocols relying on stronger and non-standard low order assumption, which essentially says that no one can find a low order element efficiently in the given class group.

On low order assumption and non-uniform security. We would like to stress that the new low order assumption on the class group of imaginary quadratic fields has been much less studied. Following the Cohen-Lenstra heuristic [Coh00], the probability that any integer d divides the order of the class group is approximately $1/d + 1/d^2$, and it seems inherent that the class group often contains low order elements. Boneh et al. [BBF18] suggested one possible approach to find low order elements in the class group. As stated in [CCL+19], computing square roots or finding elements of order 2 can be efficiently done in class groups knowing the factorization of the discriminant (which is public in the associated schemes). Recently Belabas et al. [BKSW20] show that breaking the low-order assumption is possible if the discriminant belongs to some special class of prime numbers.

We note that the low order assumption on class groups that actually contains low order elements would become false in the presence of non-uniform adversaries, which can be simply hardwired with a low order element in theory. Note that non-uniform security is implicitly required by almost all cryptographic protocols, since we often need to compose them with other protocols.

1.1 Our Contribution

In this paper, we introduce a new notion of *promise* Σ-protocol that satisfies only a weaker soundness called *promise extractability*. The *promise* Σ-protocols for statements involved in class-group-based encryptions relax the requirements of soundness but does provide security guarantees (promise extractability) that are sufficient for our applications. We also show how to simulate homomorphic operations on a (possibly invalid) class-group-based encryption whose correctness has been proven via our *promise* Σ-protocol. We believe that these techniques are of independent interests and applicable to other scenarios where efficient zero knowledge proofs for statements related to class-group is required.

Building on *promise* Σ-protocols, we present efficient two-party and multi-party threshold ECDSA from CL encryptions based on class groups with neither assuming the low order assumption nor parallel repeating the underlying zero knowledge proof. Compared to [CCL+19] (resp. [CCL+20]), in the key generation phase our two-party protocol is about 15× (resp. about 2×) faster, and about 17× (resp. 2×) less in bandwidth. Compared to [CCL+20], *without resorting to the low order assumption and strong root assumption*, our multi-party protocol removes the time-consuming interactive setup phase. It also reduces the number of expensive exponential operation in class groups of each party from $14t - 10$ in [CCL+20] to $10t - 6$ in the signing phase, where t is the threshold. Note that 40-bit soundness error is considered in the above comparison. The improvement will be much better if 128-bit soundness error is required.

1.2 Technical Overview

In this section we mainly give a high-level overview on our new techniques in the two-party ECDSA, which can be naturally extended to the multi-party case.

Before going into a technical discussion, we briefly recall the ECDSA algorithm and its threshold variant. Given a group of points of an elliptic curve $\mathbb{G}$ with a generator G of prime order p, the verification key of a ECDSA algorithm is a point $Q \in \mathbb{G}$ and the signing key is x such that $Q = x \cdot G$. To sign a message m one first hashes it using a (publicly known) hash function H, chooses a random $k \in \mathbb{Z}_p$ and computes $R = kG$, then sets $r = r_x \bmod p$ where r_x is the x-coordinate of the elliptic curve point R. The signature is $(s = (k^{-1}(\mathsf{H}(m) + rx) \bmod p, r)$.

Let us give an example of two-party ECDSA of [Lin17] to illustrate how a distributed ECDSA works. In this case, two parties $\mathcal{P}_1$ and $\mathcal{P}_2$, holding multiplicative shares x_1 and x_2 respectively, execute a coin-tossing-like protocol to generate a verification key $Q = x_1 x_2 G$, then $\mathcal{P}_1$ computes a ciphertext c_{key} of x_1 using a homomorphic encryption scheme and sends it, together with a zero knowledge proof of its correctness, to $\mathcal{P}_2$. To sign a message m, $\mathcal{P}_1$ and $\mathcal{P}_2$ choose k_1 and k_2 at random respectively, and execute another coin-tossing-like protocol to generate a point $R = k_1 k_2 G$ and set $r = r_x \bmod p$. Finally, $\mathcal{P}_2$ homomorphically computes an encryption of $s' = k_2^{-1}\mathsf{H}(m) + k_2^{-1} r x_2 x_1$ on the ciphertext c_{key} and sends the ciphertext to $\mathcal{P}_1$, who decrypts the ciphertext and obtains s', and outputs a signature $(r, s = k_1^{-1} s')$. As we mentioned before, both of the two popular Paillier and CL schemes for encrypting x_1 incur large computation/communication overheads.

Promise Σ-protocol for equality of messages. Towards achieving more efficient constructions of two-party ECDSA, our first idea is to use CL encryption scheme to encrypt x_1 and introduce a *promise* Σ-protocol for proving equality of message encoded into $Q_1 = x_1 \cdot G$ and the one encrypted in the CL ciphertext.

To better explain our new notion let us briefly describe a CL encryption scheme and see how a traditional efficient Σ-protocol fails to prove a CL ciphertext. CL encryption scheme works on a tuple of parameters of groups $(\tilde{s}, g, f, g_p, \hat{\mathcal{G}}, \mathcal{G}, \mathcal{F}, \mathcal{G}^p)$ [CL15]. The finite abelian group $\hat{\mathcal{G}}$ is of order $p\hat{s}$ where p is prime, $\hat{s}$ is unknown but with an upper bound $\tilde{s}$ and $\gcd(p, \hat{s}) = 1$. The cyclic group $\mathcal{G} := \langle g \rangle$ of order ps is a subgroup of $\hat{\mathcal{G}}$ in which the Decisional Diffie-Hellman (DDH) assumption holds and $s|\hat{s}$ is also unknown. $\mathcal{G}$ contains a unique cyclic subgroup of order p, $\mathcal{F} := \langle f \rangle$, where the DL problem is *solvable*. Group $\mathcal{G}^p := \langle g_p \rangle$ is the subgroup of p-th powers in $\mathcal{G}$ (of unknown order s). Similar to the ElGamal scheme, the public and secret keys of a CL scheme are (g_p, f, h) and d (such that $h = g_p^d$) respectively, and a ciphertext of m is of the form $(c_1, c_2) = (g_p^r, h^r f^m)$, where $r \leftarrow [0, S]$ and S chosen in practice is a rough upperbound on the unknown order s of group $\mathcal{G}^p$. Note that since the DL problem over $\mathcal{F}$ is easy, one can decrypt such a CL ciphertext even when $|m| = p$.

When applying a traditional Σ-protocol with large challenge space to prove the plaintext knowledge of a CL ciphertext, one will obtain a transcript $((a_1 =$

$g_p^{s_r}, a_2 = h^{s_r} f^{s_m}), e, (z_r = s_r + er, z_m = s_m + em \bmod p))$ where $s_r \leftarrow [0, U)$ for some sufficiently large U and $s_m \in \mathbb{Z}_p$ are randomness used to mask r and m, respectively. If this transcript is accepted, then it holds that $z_r \in [0, U+(p-1)S)$, $g_p^{z_r} = a_1 c_1^e$ and $h^{z_r} f^{z_m} = a_2 c_2^e$. However, an accepting proof does not imply the correctness of the ciphertext. That is, a traditional Σ-protocol with large challenge space does not enjoy special soundness here. For example, it is easy to see that a malicious prover P^* holding low-order elements (g', h') (g' may be equal to h') could convince the verifier of a false statement $(c_1' = g'c_1, c_2' = h'c_2)$ as long as the challenge e is divided by both the order of g' and h'. This is why the work [CCL+19] adopts a Σ-protocol with a single-bit challenge for proving knowledge of plaintext then parallelizes it to achieve a negligible soundness error.

To overcome this efficiency issue, we have $\mathcal{P}_1$ encode x_1 twice to obtain $Q_1 = x_1 \cdot G$ and a CL ciphertext c_{key} and then use a *promise* Σ-protocol (with large challenge space) to prove equality of the plaintexts. Let $c_{key} = (c_{key,1}, c_{key,2})$ be an encryption of x_1 under the public key $\mathsf{pk} = (g_p, f, h)$ of CL scheme, where $c_{key,1} = g_p^r, c_{key,2} = h^r f^{x_1}$ and r is the randomness used to encrypt x_1. Our *promise* Σ-protocol can be built from the Schnorr protocol and the above "Σ-protocol" (that does not enjoy special soundness) for CL ciphertext (see Sect. 3.1 for a detailed description).

An interesting observation on the above "Σ-protocol" for CL ciphertext is that, given two accepting transcripts (a_1, a_2, e, z_r, z_m) and $(a_1, a_2, e', z_r', z_m')$ $(e \neq e')$, one could obtain $c_{key,1}^{\tilde{e}} = g_p{}^{\tilde{z}_r}$ and $c_{key,2}^{\tilde{e}} = h^{\tilde{z}_r} f^{\tilde{z}_m}$, where $\tilde{e} = e - e' \in \mathbb{Z}_p$, $\tilde{z}_r = z_r - z_r' \in \mathbb{Z}$ and $\tilde{z}_m = z_m - z_m' \in \mathbb{Z}_p$. Since the Schnorr protocol for $Q_1 = x_1 G$ enjoys special soundness, one can extract x_1 by standard rewinding technique and deduce that, if a prover can make a verifier accept a *promise* Σ-proof for equality of plaintexts of (Q_1, c_{key}), it holds that $c_{key,2}^{\tilde{e}} = h^{\tilde{z}_r} f^{\tilde{z}_m} = h^{\tilde{z}_r} f^{\tilde{e} x_1}$. That is, we can modify $c_{key} = (c_{key,1}, c_{key,2})$ into a valid ciphertext $(c_{key,1}' = c_{key,1}^{\tilde{e}}, c_{key,2}' = c_{key,2}^{\tilde{e}})$ by picking e, e' (with $e \neq e'$) at random and setting $\tilde{e} = e - e'$. This provides us with an additional extraction strategy using the secret key sk: Given the secret key sk, one could efficiently decrypt $(c_{key,1}', c_{key,2}')$ and recover x_1 from the decrypted plaintext $\tilde{e}x_1$, and output x_1 if it satisfies $x_1 \cdot G = Q_1$.

Specifically, our *promise* Σ-protocol for equality of ciphertexts (Q_1, c_{key}) guarantees the following *promise* extractability: for any prover that makes the verifier accept with high probability,

1. With oracle access to this prover, there is an efficient extractor that extracts the message x_1 of Q_1 with probability negligibly close to 1.
2. If the public key pk are honestly generated, then there is an efficient extractor (without access to the prover) that, given the corresponding sk as input, it extracts the plaintext x_1 of Q_1 with probability negligibly close to 1.

Both properties turn out to be very useful in our constructions of two-party and multi-party ECDSA.

Simulating homomorphic operations on an invalid ciphertext. Suppose in the key generation of a two-party ECDSA $\mathcal{P}_1$ sends to $\mathcal{P}_2$ a pair (Q_1, c_{key}) which both encode x_1, along with a *promise* Σ-proof of equality of their plaintexts.

Following the framework of [Lin17,CCL+19], in the final step of a two-party signing subprotocol, $\mathcal{P}_1$ and $\mathcal{P}_2$ hold (x_1, k_1, r) and (x_2, k_2, r) respectively, and compute a signature on message m as follows. $\mathcal{P}_2$ computes $b = k_2^{-1}m'$ (where m' is the hash value of m), $a = k_2^{-1}rx_2$, and a ciphertext of $ax_1 + b$ by homomorphic operations on $(c_{key,1}, c_{key,2})$, then sends the ciphertext to $\mathcal{P}_1$, who decrypts the ciphertext and computes a signature $(r, k_1^{-1}(ax_1 + b))$.

Let us abuse notation slightly and denote by $\mathcal{P}_2(r_1)$ the last step of $\mathcal{P}_2$ in which it generates a ciphertext of $ax_1 + b$ using randomness r_1. (It is convenient to think that a and b (along with the public keys) are "hardwired" into $\mathcal{P}_2(r_1)$.) Suppose the ciphertext $(c_{key,1}, c_{key,2})$ is computed under a public key $\mathsf{pk} = (\tilde{s}, p, g_p, f, h)$ of the CL encryption scheme. As shown in [CCL+19], if the ciphertext $(c_{key,1}, c_{key,2})$ is valid, say $c_{key,1} = g_p^r$ and $c_{key,2} = h^r f^{x_1}$, then $\mathcal{P}_2(r_1)$ can compute the ciphertext $(g_p^{r_1} \cdot c_{key,1}^a, h^{r_1} f^b \cdot c_{key,2}^a)$ homomorphically. Furthermore, there is a simulator $\mathcal{S}$ that given only $s' = ax_1 + b$ (without any knowledge of a or b) simulates the honest party $\mathcal{P}_2$ by computing $(g_p^{r_2}, h^{r_2} \cdot f^{s'})$, no matter how the public key pk is generated. However, as mentioned, in order to ensure the correctness of $(c_{key,1}, c_{key,2})$, $\mathcal{P}_1$ needs to run a parallel version of the standard Σ-protocol with single bit challenge for $(c_{key,1}, c_{key,2})$ due to the low-order-element attack, which is the major efficiency bottleneck.

In our case, when using *promise* Σ-protocol for proving equality of plaintexts of (Q_1, c_{key}), as we showed, it guarantees only that the $(c_{key,1}, c_{key,2})$ satisfies $c_{key,1} = g_p^{\tilde{z}/\tilde{e}}$ and $c_{key,2} = h^{\tilde{z}/\tilde{e}} f^{x_1}$ for some $\tilde{e} \in [-p+1, p-1] \setminus \{0\}, \tilde{z} \in [-U-(p-1)S+1, U+(p-1)S-1] \setminus \{0\}$. Now if we have the same $\mathcal{P}_2$ and $\mathcal{S}$, we obtain the following two ciphertexts[1]:

$$\mathcal{P}_2(r_1): \ (g_p^{r_1} \cdot c_{key,1}^a, h^{r_1} f^b \cdot c_{key,2}^a) = (g_p^{r_1 + a\tilde{z}/\tilde{e}}, h^{r_1 + a\tilde{z}/\tilde{e}} \cdot f^{ax_1+b});$$
$$\mathcal{S}(r_2): \ (g_p^{r_2}, h^{r_2} \cdot f^{s'}).$$

We observe that it is possible for a malicious $\mathcal{P}_1^*$ to launch a low-order-element attack and tell these two ciphertexts apart. $\mathcal{P}_1^*$ chooses a $y \in \hat{\mathcal{G}}$ of low order (say, order 2) and produces an invalid ciphertext $(c_{key,1} = g_p^r, c_{key,2} = yh^r f^{x_1})$. (one can verify that there always exist $\tilde{e}$ and $\tilde{z}$ such that the above equations hold for this ciphertext.) Note also that $\mathcal{P}_1^*$ can carry out the *promise* Σ-protocol with success probability $\frac{1}{2}$. Once $\mathcal{P}_1^*$ receives the ciphertext from $\mathcal{P}_2$ as above, it can compute $y^a f^{ax_1+b}$ using his secret key and then obtain a mod 2. (Note that $a = 0$ mod 2 if and only if one can solve $y^a f^{ax_1+b}$ and obtain $ax_1 + b$ since the DL problem is tractable in group $\mathcal{F}$.) But if the ciphertext is computed by the simulator $\mathcal{S}$, then $\mathcal{P}_1^*$ always obtains $a = 0$ mod 2.

We have $\mathcal{P}_2$ randomize a in computing the ciphertext of ax_1+b to get around this issue. That is, $\mathcal{P}_2$ chooses a random t, raises $c_{key,1}$ and $c_{key,2}$ to the power $a+t$, and then computes a ciphertext $(c_{key,1}^{a+t}, f^b \cdot c_{key,2}^{a+t})$ (Note that, by introducing randomness t, we can drop $g_p^{r_1}$ and h^{r_1} here). For an honest $\mathcal{P}_1$ to decrypt and obtain $ax_1 + b$, $\mathcal{P}_2$ sends back this ciphertext along with t mod p.

[1] In our construction of the two-party protocol, $\mathcal{P}_2$ does homomorphic operations only on $(c_{key,1}, c_{key,2})$ (and not on $(C_{key,1}, C_{key,2})$) and sends back the resulting CL ciphertext.

It appears that revealing information about t would make this randomization useless. However, as we will prove in Sect. 4, as long as the random string t is sufficiently long and both $p \nmid \mathrm{ord}(g_p)$, $p \nmid \mathrm{ord}(h)$ (we denote by $\mathrm{ord}(y)$ the order of y), the above randomization actually works, i.e., the following two distributions are indistinguishable:

$$\mathcal{P}_2(t_1) : (c_{key,1}^{a+t_1}, f^b \cdot c_{key,2}^{a+t_1}, t_1 \bmod p), \text{ and } \mathcal{S}(t_2) : (c_{key,1}^{t_2}, f^{s'} \cdot c_{key,2}^{t_2}, t_2 \bmod p).$$

To make sure $p \nmid \mathrm{ord}(g_p)$ and $p \nmid \mathrm{ord}(h)$, one can have $\mathcal{P}_1$ generate a CL public key of the form $(g_0, g_p = g_0^p, h_0, h = h_0^p)$. $\mathcal{P}_2$ checks if $g_p = g_0^p$ and $h = h_0^p$ hold, and if so, it takes (g_p, h) as the public key of a standard CL encryption scheme.

Promise Σ-protocol for homomorphic operations. In the multi-party setting, in the signing phase one party needs to prove that it did the same homomorphic operations on given a linear encoding and a CL ciphertext. We also construct a *promise* Σ-protocol for proving such a statement. As before, though a *promise* Σ-proof does not guarantee the statement is true, but the *promise extractability* suffices to prove the security of our protocol.

1.3 Related Work

ECDSA based on oblivious transfer. Instead of using additively homomorphic encryption, Doerner et al. [DKLs18,DKLs19] constructed two-party and multi-party threshold ECDSA based on oblivious transfer. As a consequence, these schemes are fast in computational complexity but at the cost of increasing the bandwidth.

Concurrent work. Very recently, Yuen et al. [YCX21] optimize the underlying zero knowledge proof related to class-group encryption, and construct more efficient two-party and multi-party ECDSA protocols. However, their schemes still rely on the low order assumption and the strong root assumption and the security is proved in the generic group model.

2 Preliminaries

Notation. Let λ be the security parameter. A non-negative function $\mathsf{negl}(\lambda)$ is negligible if for every polynomial $p(\lambda)$, it holds that $\mathsf{negl}(\lambda) \leq 1/p(\lambda)$ for sufficiently large $\lambda \in \mathbb{N}$. Let $\mathsf{poly}(\lambda)$ be a polynomial of λ. PPT stands for probabilistic polynomial time. Denote $\mathrm{ord}(g)$ the order of the element g in a given group.

2.1 CL Encryption from HSM Assumption

Castagnos et al. [CCL+19] gave a specific hard subgroup membership assumption (HSM) [CLT18] which is defined in the context of a group with an easy Dlog subgroup. Their instantiation makes use of class groups of imaginary quadratic fields. We list the definitions and constructions below and refer to [CCL+19] for more details.

Definition 1 **([CCL+19]).** *Let* GenGroup *be a pair of algorithms* (Gen, Solve). *The* Gen *algorithm taking as inputs the security parameter* λ *and a prime* p *outputs a tuple* param $= (\tilde{s}, g, f, g_p, \hat{\mathcal{G}}, \mathcal{G}, \mathcal{F}, \mathcal{G}^p)$. *The set* $(\hat{\mathcal{G}}, \cdot)$ *is a finite abelian group of order* $p \cdot \hat{s}$ *where the bitsize of the unknown* $\hat{s}$ *with an upper bound* $\tilde{s}$ *is a function of* λ *and* $\gcd(p, \hat{s}) = 1$. *It is also required that one can efficiently recognise valid encodings of elements in* $\hat{\mathcal{G}}$. *The set* $(\mathcal{F}, \cdot)$ *is the unique cyclic subgroup of* $\hat{\mathcal{G}}$ *of order* p. *The set* $(\mathcal{G}, \cdot)$ *is a cyclic subgroup of* $\hat{\mathcal{G}}$ *of order* $p \cdot s$ *where* s *divides* $\hat{s}$. *By construction* $\mathcal{F} \subset \mathcal{G}$, *and, denoting* $\mathcal{G}^p := \{x^p, x \in \mathcal{G}\}$ *the subgroup of order* s *of* $\mathcal{G}$, *it holds that* $\mathcal{G} = \mathcal{G}^p \times \mathcal{F}$. *The elements* f, g_p *and* $g = f \cdot g_p$ *are respective generators of* $\mathcal{F}$, $\mathcal{G}^p$ *and* $\mathcal{G}$. *Let* $\mathcal{D}$ *(resp.* $\mathcal{D}_p$*) be a distribution over the integers such that the distribution* $\{g^x | x \leftarrow \mathcal{D}\}$ *(resp.* $\{g_p^x | x \leftarrow \mathcal{D}_p\}$*) is at distance less than* $2^{-\lambda}$ *from the uniform distribution in* $\mathcal{G}$ *(resp. in* $\mathcal{G}^p$*). The* Solve *algorithm is a deterministic polynomial time algorithm that solves the discrete logarithm problem in* F. *We suppose moreover that:*

(1) The Dlog problem is easy in $\mathcal{F}$*:*

$$\Pr\left[\begin{array}{c} \mathsf{param} \leftarrow \mathsf{Gen}(1^\lambda, p); \\ x \leftarrow \mathbb{Z}_p, y = f^x, \\ x^\star \leftarrow \mathsf{Solve}(p, \mathsf{param}, y) \end{array} : x = x^\star \right] = 1.$$

(2) The HSM problem is hard even with access to the Solve *algorithm:*

$$\Pr\left[\begin{array}{c} \mathsf{param} \leftarrow \mathsf{Gen}(1^\lambda, p); \\ x \leftarrow \mathcal{D}, x' \leftarrow \mathcal{D}_p; \\ z_0 = g^x, z_1 = g_p^{x'}; \\ b \leftarrow \{0,1\}; \\ b^\star \leftarrow \mathcal{A}(p, \mathsf{param}, z_b, \mathsf{Solve}(\cdot)) \end{array} : b = b^\star \right] \leq \frac{1}{2} + \mathsf{negl}(\lambda),$$

for arbitrary PPTadversary $\mathcal{A}$.

In practice, we will use for $\mathcal{D}_p$ the uniform distribution on $\{0, \ldots, S\}$ where $S = 2^{\lambda-2} \cdot \tilde{s}$. Following the notations of [CCL+19], we now describe a standard IND-CPA secure encryption scheme (called CL encryption) under the HSM assumption.

Definition 2. *The additively homomorphic public-key encryption scheme* CL *consists of the following algorithms.*

- $\mathsf{CL.KGen}(1^\lambda, p)$: *Let* $(\tilde{s}, g, f, g_p, \hat{\mathcal{G}}, \mathcal{G}, \mathcal{F}, \mathcal{G}^p) \leftarrow \mathsf{Gen}(1^\lambda, p)$. *Choose* $x \leftarrow \mathcal{D}_p$ *and compute* $h = g_p^x$. *Set* $\mathsf{pk} = (\tilde{s}, p, g_p, f, h)$ *and* $\mathsf{sk} = x$.
- $\mathsf{CL.Enc}_{\mathsf{pk}}(m)$: *Pick* $r \leftarrow \mathcal{D}_p$, *and output* $c = (g_p^r, h^r f^m)$.
- $\mathsf{CL.Dec}_{\mathsf{sk}}(c)$: *Parse* $c = (c_1, c_2)$, *and output* $m \leftarrow \mathsf{Solve}(c_2 / c_1^x)$.

As stated in [CCL+19], we also use the double encoding assumption to ensure the security of the presented two-party ECDSA in the case that the party $\mathcal{P}_2$ is corrupted. The intuition behinds this assumption is that given a one way function evaluated in $x \in \mathbb{Z}_p$ (in our protocol this is the elliptic curve point $Q := xG$) - no polynomial time adversary can produce two invalid CL encryptions of x.

Definition 3 (Double Encoding Assumption [CCL+19]**).** *The double encoding (DE) problem is δ_{DE}-hard for the one way function* $\mathsf{exp}_{\mathbb{G}} : x \mapsto xG$ *if for any PPT $\mathcal{A}$, it holds that:*

$$\Pr\left[\begin{array}{c} \mathsf{pp}_{\mathbb{G}} := (\mathbb{G}, G, p) \\ \mathsf{pp}_{\mathcal{G}} := (\tilde{s}, f, g_p, \mathcal{G}, \mathcal{F}, \mathcal{G}^p) \leftarrow \mathsf{Gen}(1^\lambda, p) \\ x \leftarrow \mathbb{Z}_p, Q = xG \\ (\mathit{pk}, (u_1, u_1^{\mathit{sk}} f^x), (u_2, u_2^{\mathit{sk}} f^x) \leftarrow \mathcal{A}(\mathsf{pp}_{\mathbb{G}}, \mathsf{pp}_{\mathcal{G}}, Q)) \end{array} : \begin{array}{c} u_1, u_2 \in \mathcal{G} \backslash \mathcal{G}^p \\ u_2 \cdot u_1^{-1} \in \mathcal{G} \backslash \mathcal{G}^p \\ \text{and } \mathit{pk} = g_p^{\mathit{sk}} \end{array}\right] \leq \delta_{\mathrm{DE}},$$

where $\mathbb{G}$ is a group of points of an elliptic curve with a generator G of prime order p.

The DE assumption holds if for any λ-bit prime p, δ_{DE} is negligible in λ.

2.2 Σ-Protocol

Denote $\mathcal{L}$ an NP language and $\mathcal{R}$ the associated binary relation. We say an instance x lies in $\mathcal{L}$ if and only if there exists a witness w s.t. $(x, w) \in \mathcal{R}$. Consider two-party protocols with the following pattern: The prover P taking input (x, w) computes a commitment a and hands it to V. The verifier V taking input x samples a random challenge e from a given challenge space and sends it to P. Then P responses z to V. Depending on the transcript (a, e, z), the verifier chooses to accept or reject it.

Definition 4 (Σ-protocol). *A 3-round protocol with the above form is called a Σ-protocol for an NP language $\mathcal{L}$ with an efficiently recognizable relation $\mathcal{R}$ iff. it satisfies the following properties:*

- *Completeness. If P and V behave honestly on input x and private input w to P where $(x, w) \in \mathcal{R}$, then V always accepts.*
- *Special soundness. There exists a PPT algorithm* Ext *which, given any instance $x \in L$ and two accepting transcripts (a, e, z) and (a, e', z') with $e \neq e'$, computes a witness w s.t. $(x, w) \in \mathcal{R}$.*
- *Special honest verifier zero knowledge (HVZK). There exists a PPT algorithm $\mathcal{S}$ which, taking $x \in \mathcal{L}$ and a challenge e as inputs, outputs (a, z) such that the tuple (a, e, z) is indistinguishable from an accepting transcript generated by a real protocol run between the honest $\mathsf{P}(x, w)$ and $\mathsf{V}(x)$.*

Σ-protocols can be transformed to non-interactive zero knowledge (NIZK) arguments via the Fiat-Shamir heuristic [FS87] and achieve zero knowledge in the random oracle model.

2.3 Threshold ECDSA and Its Security

Let ECDSA run on the elliptic curve group $\mathbb{G}$ of prime-order p with base point G. For a threshold t and a number of parties $n \geq t$, a (t, n)-threshold ECDSA consists of the following two interactive protocols:

IKeyGen: The interactive key generation protocol, which takes the public parameter $(\mathbb{G}, G, p)$ as input. Each party $\mathcal{P}_i$ in the end receives the public key Q and its secret key x_i. The values $x_1, \ldots, x_n$ constitute a (t, n)-threshold secret sharing of the secret signing key x.

ISign: The interactive signing protocol, which take a message m as common input as well as a private input x_i from each party. It outputs an valid signature (r, s) of m or abort the execution.

The verification algorithm Verify is the same as that of the standard ECDSA.

Simulation-Based Security and Ideal Functionalities. In this paper, we prove the security of two-party ECDSA according to the standard simulation paradigm with the ideal/real model, in the presence of static adversaries that choose which parties are corrupted before the protocol begins. The ideal/real simulation paradigm is to imagine what properties one would have in an ideal world, then a real world (constructed) protocol is said to be secure if it provides similar properties. Specifically, when proving that a constructed protocol Π achieves the simulation-based security, we always define an ideal functionality $\mathcal{F}$ executed by a trusted party to capture all the properties that need to be met. Then, we construct a simulator $\mathcal{S}$ (essentially plays the role of honest parties) that interacts with the trusted party computing $\mathcal{F}$, invokes the PPT adversary $\mathcal{A}$ internally, and simulates an execution of the real protocol. If $\mathcal{A}$ has negligible advantage to distinguish a real execution with honest parties from the simulation, then Π is considered secure.

We first describe the ECDSA ideal functionality between parties $\mathcal{P}_1, \ldots, \mathcal{P}_n$ as follows. Note that when considering two-party ECDSA, we only need to set $n = 2$.

The ECDSA Functionality $\mathcal{F}_{\text{ECDSA}}$

- Upon receiving KeyGen$(\mathbb{G}, G, p)$ from all parties $\mathcal{P}_1, \ldots, \mathcal{P}_n$, where $\mathbb{G}$ is an Elliptic-curve group of order p with generator G, then:
  1. Generate a pair of ECDSA keys (x, Q), where $x \leftarrow \mathbb{Z}_p^*$ is the secret signing key, and $Q = x \cdot G$ is the verification key.
  2. Send Q to all parties.
  3. Ignore future calls to KeyGen.
- Upon receiving Sign(sid, m) from $\mathcal{P}_1, \ldots, \mathcal{P}_n$, if KeyGen was already called and sid has not been stored, then:
  1. Compute an ECDSA signature (r, s) on m.
  2. Send (r, s) to all parties, and store (sid, m).

As in [Lin17,LN18,CCL+19], we prove the security of our protocol in a hybrid model using the ideal zero knowledge functionality $\mathcal{F}_{\text{zk}}$, and the ideal commit-and-prove functionality $\mathcal{F}_{\text{com-zk}}$.

We now describe the ideal commitment functionality $\mathcal{F}_{\text{com}}$.

The Commitment Functionality $\mathcal{F}_{\text{com}}$

- Upon receiving $(\mathsf{commit}, sid, x)$ from party $\mathcal{P}_i$ for $i \in [n]$, if sid has already been stored then ignore the message. Otherwise, store (sid, i, x) and send $(\mathsf{receipt}, sid, i)$ to all other parties $\mathcal{P}_j$ for all $j \in [n]\backslash\{i\}$.
- Upon receiving $(\mathsf{decommit}, sid, i)$ from party $\mathcal{P}_i$, if (sid, i, x) has been stored, then send $(\mathsf{decommit}, sid, i, x)$ to all other parties $\mathcal{P}_j$ for all $j \in [n]\backslash\{i\}$.

The ideal zero knowledge functionality, denoted $\mathcal{F}_{\text{zk}}$, is defined for a relation $\mathcal{R}$ by $(\emptyset, (x, \mathcal{R}(x, w))) \leftarrow \mathcal{F}_{\text{zk}}((x, w), \emptyset)$, where $\emptyset$ denotes the empty string, and $\mathcal{R}(x, w) = 1$ iff. $(x, w) \in \mathcal{R}$.
On HVZK in practice. We note that, in all previously known works in this line, the zero knowledge functionalities are realized by Σ-protocols or its NIZK version by Fiat-Shamir transformation, which achieve only honest verifier zero knowledge or zero knowledge in the random oracle model.

The Zero Knowledge Functionality $\mathcal{F}_{\text{zk}}^{\mathcal{R}}$ for Relation $\mathcal{R}$

Upon receiving $(\mathsf{prove}, sid, i, x, w)$ from party $\mathcal{P}_i$ for $i \in [n]$, if sid has already been stored then ignore the message. Otherwise, store sid and send $(\mathsf{proof}, sid, i, x, \mathcal{R}(x, w))$ to all other parties $\mathcal{P}_j$ for all $j \in [n]\backslash\{i\}$.

We also use an ideal functionality $\mathcal{F}_{\text{com-zk}}^{\mathcal{R}}$ to commit to NIZK proofs of knowledge for a relation $\mathcal{R}$. This can be achieved by having the prover commit to a NIZK proof of knowledge using the ideal commitment functionality $\mathcal{F}_{\text{com}}$.

The Committed NIZK Functionality $\mathcal{F}_{\text{com-zk}}^{\mathcal{R}}$ for Relation $\mathcal{R}$

- Upon receiving $(\mathsf{com\text{-}prove}, sid, x, w)$ from party $\mathcal{P}_i$ for $i \in [n]$, if sid has already been stored then ignore the message. Otherwise, store (sid, i, x) and send $(\mathsf{proof\text{-}receipt}, sid, i)$ to all other parties $\mathcal{P}_j$ for all $j \in [n]\backslash\{i\}$.
- Upon receiving $(\mathsf{decom\text{-}proof}, sid, i)$ from party $\mathcal{P}_i$, if (sid, i, x) has been stored, then send $(\mathsf{decom\text{-}proof}, sid, i, x, \mathcal{R}(x, w))$ to all other parties $\mathcal{P}_j$ for all $j \in [n]\backslash\{i\}$.

Game-Based Security. Following [GJKR96, CCL+20], our construction of multi-party ECDSA is secure under a game-based definition: threshold unforgeability under chosen message attacks described as follows.

Definition 5 (Threshold Signature Unforgeability [GJKR96]**).** *A* (t, n)*-threshold signature scheme* $(\mathsf{IKeyGen}, \mathsf{ISign}, \mathsf{Verify})$ *is said to be unforgeable, if* *for any PPT adversary $\mathcal{A}$ who corrupts at most t parties, given the view of the protocols* $\mathsf{IKeyGen}$ *and* ISign *on input messages $m_1, \ldots, m_k$ of its adaptive choice as well as signatures on those messages, the probability that $\mathcal{A}$ can produce a signature on any new message m ($m \notin \{m_1, \ldots, m_k\}$) is negligible.*

3 Promise Σ-Protocols

For our purpose, we *ideally* want an additively homomorphic encryption scheme over large message space and an efficient Σ-protocol to prove the validity of certain statements about ciphertexts. Unfortunately, as mentioned before, all currently known constructions are far from satisfactory: The ElGamal encryption scheme admits an efficient Σ-protocol but only supports a very small message space, while the CL encryption scheme supports large message space but does not admit an efficient Σ-protocol.

We obtain the best of both worlds using the following approach. Consider the following two *keyed* linear-homomorphic encoding schemes (we stress that these secret keys do *not necessarily* enable one to decode a codeword efficiently)[2]

- $(\mathsf{DL.Gen}, \mathsf{DL.Code})$ over elliptic curve group of prime order: $(\mathsf{pk}_0, \mathsf{sk}_0) \leftarrow \mathsf{DL.Gen}(1^\lambda)$, $cw_0 \leftarrow \mathsf{DL.Code}_{\mathsf{pk}_0}(m)$;
- $(\mathsf{CL.Gen}, \mathsf{CL.Code})$ over class group of unknown order: $(\mathsf{pk}_1, \mathsf{sk}_1) \leftarrow \mathsf{CL.Gen}(1^\lambda)$, $cw_1 \leftarrow \mathsf{CL.Code}_{\mathsf{pk}_1}(m)$.

We encode a message m twice independently, and then compose in parallel the efficient Σ-protocol for $\mathsf{DL.Code}_{\mathsf{pk}_0}$ with the efficient *insecure* Σ-protocol for $\mathsf{CL.Code}_{\mathsf{pk}_1}$ to prove that "$\mathsf{DL.Code}_{\mathsf{pk}_0}(m)$ and $\mathsf{CL.Code}_{\mathsf{pk}_1}(m)$ encode the same message m", i.e., a statement in the following language:

$$\mathcal{L} = \{(\mathsf{pk}_0, \mathsf{pk}_1, cw_0, cw_1) | \exists m \quad cw_0 = \mathsf{DL.Code}_{\mathsf{pk}_0}(m) \text{ and } cw_1 = \mathsf{CL.Code}_{\mathsf{pk}_1}(m)\}.$$

We observe that, though the composed Σ-protocol does not enjoy the special soundness, it provides some interesting security guarantees that are sufficient for our applications.

We call it *promise* Σ-protocol. Roughly, a *promise* Σ-protocol for the above statement weakens the special soundness property and promises only that one can extract the message m encoded into $\mathsf{DL.Code}_{\mathsf{pk}_0}(m)$ by rewinding a successful prover, *or*, extract certain information $\rho(m)$ (for some efficiently computable function $\rho(\cdot)$) about m using both secret keys sk_0 and sk_1 *without access to the prover.*

Definition 6 (Promise Σ-protocol). *Let λ be the security parameter and $\rho(\cdot)$ be an efficiently computable function. Let encoding schemes* $(\mathsf{DL.Gen}, \mathsf{DL.Code})$,

[2] These encoding schemes $\mathsf{DL.Code}$ and $\mathsf{CL.Code}$ may vary with applications, and may be randomized.

(CL.Gen, CL.Code) *and language* $\mathcal{L}$ *be as above. A promise* Σ*-protocol* (P, V) *for* $\mathcal{L}$ *with respect to* $\rho(\cdot)$ *is a 3-round public coin protocol (with transcript being of the form* (a, e, z)*) that satisfies the following conditions:*

- *Completeness and special honest verifier zero knowledge defined in the same way as* Σ*-protocol.*
- *Promise extractability. For any inverse polynomial* $\epsilon(\lambda)$*, any* PPT P^* *that makes the verifier accept with probability* $\epsilon(\lambda)$*, there is a* PPT *extractor* Ext *such that the following conditions hold.*
  1. *Extraction by rewinding (Special-soundness) for* $\mathsf{DL.Code}_{\mathsf{pk}_0}(m)$*. With oracle access to* P^**,* $\mathsf{Ext}^{\mathsf{P}^*}(cw_0, cw_1)$ *extracts* m *of* $\mathsf{DL.Code}_{\mathsf{pk}_0}(m)$ *with probability negligibly close to* 1*.*
  2. *Straight-line extraction for* $\mathsf{DL.Code}_{\mathsf{pk}_0}(m)$ *using secret keys. If both key pairs* $(\mathsf{pk}_0, \mathsf{sk}_0)$ *and* $(\mathsf{pk}_1, \mathsf{sk}_1)$ *are honestly generated, then given* $(\mathsf{sk}_0, \mathsf{sk}_1)$ *as input the extractor* $\mathsf{Ext}(\mathsf{sk}_0, \mathsf{sk}_1, cw_0, cw_1)$ *(without access to* P^**) extracts* $\rho(m)$ *with probability negligibly close to* 1*, where* m *is message encoded into* $\mathsf{DL.Code}_{\mathsf{pk}_0}(m)$*.*

Remark 1. Note that the promise extractability is a weaker notion than the special soundness: An accepting *promise* Σ-proof does not even guarantee the second codeword cw_1 is valid.

However, the second condition of promise extractability implies that if a prover can make the verifier accept the statement with high probability (hence there exist at least two accepting transcripts with the same first message a but different challenges $e \neq e'$), then the one who holds the honestly generated secret keys could extract $\rho(m)$.

Remark 2. As we will see, in our applications the first secret key sk_0 would not allow us to efficiently recover the message encoded into cw_0, but sk_1 would *if* cw_1 *is valid.* As explained above, since cw_1 may be invalid, our straight-line extractor will depart from the normal "decryption" procedure associated with CL.Code. Although we cannot use the first secret key sk_0 to decode cw_0, but it is useful for the straight-line extractor to check if the message extracted out is the right message (see the construction in Sect. 3.1).

Remark 3. One may use different (rewinding or straight-line) extractor in simulation strategies. Suppose that a malicious party sends out two codewords cw_0 and cw_1, along with a *promise* Σ-proof, to an honest party in a step of a protocol. In case cw_0 and cw_1 are computed under the public keys generated by the malicious party, then the *promise* Σ-proof guarantees that the malicious party "knows" the message encoded into cw_0, which can be extracted using rewinding by the simulator (playing the role of the honest party) in the security proof. Otherwise, if the corresponding public keys are generated by the honest party, then the *promise* Σ-proof promises that the codeword cw_1 is "decodable", and the simulator can use straight-line extractor (with the corresponding secret keys which are actually generated by itself in a simulation) to extract certain useful information about the message encoded into cw_0.

Theoretically, we can achieve Σ-protocol for such a statement with fully special soundness. Our *promise* Σ-protocol is motivated purely out of efficiency consideration. As we shall see, the weak notion of Σ-protocol is sufficient for our application, and it achieves much better performance than the known constructions of Σ-protocols.

Promise NIZK in the random oracle model. In practice, one can apply the Fiat-Shamir transform to our *promise* Σ-protocol to obtain a non-interactive protocol. One can verify that the resulting protocol also enjoys the *promise* extractability in the random oracle model using the forking technique from [PS96], as well as completeness and zero knowledge property.

Definition 7 (Promise NIZK). *Let λ be the security parameter and $\rho(\cdot)$ be an efficiently computable function. Let* $(\mathsf{DL.Gen}, \mathsf{DL.Code})$, $(\mathsf{CL.Gen}, \mathsf{CL.Code})$ *and language $\mathcal{L}$ be defined as above. A promise NIZK proof* (P, V) *for $\mathcal{L}$ in the random oracle model with respect to $\rho(\cdot)$ satisfies the following conditions:*

- *Completeness and zero knowledge defined in the same way as a NIZK proof.*
- *Promise extractability. For any inverse polynomial $\epsilon(\lambda)$, any PPT P^* that generates a proof with an accepted probability $\epsilon(\lambda)$, there is a PPT extractor* Ext *such that the following conditions hold.*
  1. *Extraction by rewinding for* $\mathsf{DL.Code}_{\mathsf{pk}_0}(m)$. *With oracle access to P^* and the programmability of the random oracle H,* $\mathsf{Ext}^{\mathsf{P}^*,H}(cw_0, cw_1)$ *extracts m of* $\mathsf{DL.Code}_{\mathsf{pk}_0}(m)$ *with probability negligibly close to* 1.
  2. *Straight-line extraction for* $\mathsf{DL.Code}_{\mathsf{pk}_0}(m)$ *using secret keys. If both key pairs* $(\mathsf{pk}_0, \mathsf{sk}_0)$ *and* $(\mathsf{pk}_1, \mathsf{sk}_1)$ *are honestly generated, then given* $(\mathsf{sk}_0, \mathsf{sk}_1)$ *as input the extractor* $\mathsf{Ext}(\mathsf{sk}_0, \mathsf{sk}_1, cw_0, cw_1)$ *(without access to P^*) extracts $\rho(m)$ with probability negligibly close to* 1, *where m is message encoded into* $\mathsf{DL.Code}_{\mathsf{pk}_0}(m)$.

3.1 Promise Σ-Protocol for Encryptions

In this section we first consider the following encoding schemes:

- $\mathsf{DL.Code}_G : m \to m \cdot G$, where G is a random generator of an elliptic curve group $\mathbb{G}$ of prime order p, serving the public key pk_0 (and there is no secret key).
- $\mathsf{CL.Code}_{\mathsf{pk}} : m \to \mathsf{CL.Enc}_{\mathsf{pk}}(m; r)$, i.e., $\mathsf{CL.Code}_{\mathsf{pk}}$ is the CL encryption algorithm $\mathsf{CL.Enc}$ (see Sect. 2), where pk is generated by its corresponding key generation algorithm $(\mathsf{pk}, \mathsf{sk}) \leftarrow \mathsf{CL.KGen}(1^\lambda)$.

and the following language:

$$\mathcal{L}_{\mathrm{DLCL}} = \{(G, \mathsf{pk}, Q, c) | \exists m \in \mathbb{Z}_p, r \in [0, S], s.t. \\ Q = m \cdot G \text{ and } c = \mathsf{CL.Enc}_{\mathsf{pk}}(m; r)\}.$$

We construct a *promise* Σ-protocol by composing two "Σ-protocols" for discrete logarithm and CL ciphertext in parallel. Though the latter "Σ-protocol" is insecure as mentioned before, we can still show the composed protocol is a *promise* Σ-protocol. In the following, we fix U such that $(p-1)S/U$ is negligible.

Protocol Σ^1_{prom} for proving the consistency of messages

Common input: G,$\mathsf{pk}=(\tilde{s}, p, g_p, f, h)$,$Q$, $c=(c_1, c_2)$.
P's Private input: $m \in \mathbb{Z}_p$ and $r \in [0, S]$ s.t. $Q = m \cdot G$, $c_1 = g_p^r$ and $c_2 = h^r f^m$.

1. P chooses $s_m \leftarrow \mathbb{Z}_p$ and $s_r \leftarrow [0, U)$ at random, computes $A = s_m G$, $a_1 = g_p^{s_r}$, $a_2 = h^{s_r} f^{s_m}$. P sends A, a_1, a_2 to verifier V.
2. V chooses and sends a random $e \leftarrow \mathbb{Z}_p$ to P.
3. P computes $z_m = s_m + em \bmod p$ and $z_r = s_r + er$, then sends z_m, z_r to V.
4. V outputs 1 iff. $z_r \in [0, U + (p-1)S)$, $z_m G = A + eQ$, $g_p^{z_r} = a_1 c_1^e$ and $h^{z_r} f^{z_m} = a_2 c_2^e$.

Theorem 1. *If $(p-1)S/U$ is negligible, then protocol Σ^1_{prom} is a promise Σ-protocol with respect to the identity function $\rho : m \rightarrow m$.*

The construction and security proof of protocol Σ^1_{prom} are actually subsumed by the following *promise* Σ-protocol in which the first encoding scheme is replaced with the ElGamal encryption scheme[3].

With replacement of the first encoding scheme in the above with the ElGamal key generation and encryption algorithm (EG.KGen, EG.Enc) (Note that here the secret key does not allow one to decrypt ciphertexts since the plaintext is too long), we present a *promise* Σ-protocol for the following language:

$$\mathcal{L}_{\text{EGCL}} = \{(\mathsf{pk}_0, \mathsf{pk}_1, C, c) | \exists m \in \mathbb{Z}_p, r_1 \in \mathbb{Z}_p, \text{ and } r_2 \in [0, S], s.t.\ C = \mathsf{EG.Enc}_{\mathsf{pk}_0}(m; r_1) \text{ and } c = \mathsf{CL.Enc}_{\mathsf{pk}_1}(m; r_2)\}.$$

Protocol Σ^2_{prom} for proving the equality of plaintexts

Common input: $\mathsf{pk}_0=(G, P)$,$\mathsf{pk}_1=(\tilde{s}, p, g_p, f, h)$,$C=(C_1, C_2)$, $c=(c_1, c_2)$.
P's Private input: $m \in \mathbb{Z}_p$,$r_1 \in \mathbb{Z}_p$ and $r_2 \in [0, S]$ s.t. $C_1 = r_1 G$, $C_2 = r_1 P + mG$,$c_1 = g_p^{r_2}$ and $c_2 = h^{r_2} f^m$.

1. P chooses $s_1 \leftarrow \mathbb{Z}_p$, $s_2 \leftarrow [0, U)$ and $s_m \leftarrow \mathbb{Z}_p$ at random, and computes $A_1 = s_1 G$, $A_2 = s_1 P + s_m G$, $a_1 = g_p^{s_2}$, $a_2 = h^{s_2} f^{s_m}$. P sends A_1, A_2, a_1, a_2 to verifier V.

[3] It is easy to verify that the straight-line extractor for protocol Σ^1_{prom}, similar to the one for protocol Σ^2_{prom}, does not require the knowledge of sk_0 (which does not exist in protocol Σ^1_{prom}).

2. V chooses and sends a random $e \leftarrow \mathbb{Z}_p$ to P.
3. P computes $z_1 = s_1 + er_1 \bmod p$, $z_2 = s_2 + er_2$ and $z_m = s_m + em \bmod p$, and sends z_1, z_2, z_m to V.
4. V outputs 1 if $z_2 \in [0, U + (p-1)S)$,$z_1 G = A_1 + eC_1$,$z_1 P + z_m G = A_2 + eC_2$,$g_p^{z_2} = a_1 c_1^e$ and $h^{z_2} f^{z_m} = a_2 c_2^e$.

Theorem 2. *If $(p-1)S/U$ is negligible, then protocol Σ^2_{prom} is a promise Σ-protocol with respect to the function $\rho : m \to m$.*

Proof. Completeness is obvious. Special honest verifier zero knowledge property follows from the same arguments as in [CCL+19, GPS06], which we omit here.

We now prove the *promise extractability.* Suppose there is a prover P^* that can make the honest verifier accept with probability $\epsilon(\lambda)$, we can fix a good random tape r_p^* for P^* and define $\mathcal{G'}_{r_p^*} := \{e \in \mathbb{Z}_p : \mathsf{P}^*(r_p^*) \text{ answers } e \text{ correctly}\}$, which is of size greater than $p\epsilon(\lambda)$.

By applying standard rewinding strategy to the prover $\mathsf{P}^*(r_p^*)$, we have an efficient extractor $\mathsf{Ext}^{\mathsf{P}^*(r_p^*)}$ that computes two accepting transcripts $(A_1, A_2, a_1, a_2, e, z_1, z_2, z_m)$ and $(A_1, A_2, a_1, a_2, e', z_1', z_2', z_m')$ with $e \neq e'$. From (A_1, A_2, e, z_1, z_m) and $(A_1, A_2, e', z_1', z_m')$ one can compute the plaintext $m = (z_m - z_m')/(e - e') \bmod p$ of the ElGamal ciphertext (C_1, C_2) (since the Σ-protocol for an ElGamal ciphertext satisfies special soundness).

It remains to prove the second condition of *promise extractability* holds. In this case we assume both the public keys pk_0 and pk_1 are honestly generated. Let sk_0 and sk_1 are the corresponding secret keys. From the above two accepting transcripts, we also have that $g_p^{z_2} = a_1 c_1^e, h^{z_2} f^{z_m} = a_2 c_2^e$ and $g_p^{z_2'} = a_1 c_1^{e'}, h^{z_2'} f^{z_m'} = a_2 c_2^{e'}$. Set $\tilde{z}_2 = z_2 - z_2', \tilde{z}_m = z_m - z_m', \tilde{e} = e - e'$. By $\tilde{z}_m = m\tilde{e} \bmod p$ as above, we conclude

$$g_p^{\tilde{z}_2} = c_1^{\tilde{e}}, \text{ and } h^{\tilde{z}_2} f^{m\tilde{e}} = c_2^{\tilde{e}}. \tag{1}$$

This implies that we can efficiently modify the second ciphertext (c_1, c_2) into a valid ciphertext $(c_1' = c_1^{\tilde{e}}, c_2' = c_2^{\tilde{e}})$ of the message $m\tilde{e}$. Furthermore, combining $z_m - z_m' = m\tilde{e} \bmod p$ with the first condition of *promise extractability*, we have

$$\tilde{e} \cdot (C_2 - \mathsf{sk}_0 \cdot C_1) = m\tilde{e} \cdot G \text{ and } \left(\frac{c_2}{c_1^{\mathsf{sk}_1}}\right)^{\tilde{e}} = f^{m\tilde{e}}.$$

This gives rise to the following extractor Ext that can compute the plaintext m from the two secret keys and the two ciphertexts without access to the prover P^* with probability negligibly close to 1.

Extractor $\mathsf{Ext}(\mathsf{sk}_0, \mathsf{sk}_1, (C_1, C_2), (c_1, c_2))$:

1. Run the decryption algorithm $\mathsf{CL.Dec}_{\mathsf{sk}_1}$ on input $((c_1, c_2))$, if it outputs a plaintext m such that $C_2 - \mathsf{sk}_0 \cdot C_1 = mG$, then return m (In this case (c_1, c_2) is a valid ciphertext).
2. Pick two random $e, e' \in \mathbb{Z}_p$, compute $(\frac{c_2}{c_1^{\mathsf{sk}_1}})^{e-e'}$ and run $\tilde{z}_m \leftarrow \mathsf{CL.Solve}((\frac{c_2}{c_1^{\mathsf{sk}_1}})^{e-e'})$. If $e \neq e'$ and $(e - e') \cdot (C_2 - \mathsf{sk}_0 C_1) = \tilde{z}_m G$ holds for the ElGamal ciphertext (C_1, C_2), then compute m by solving $(e - e')m = \tilde{z}_m \bmod p$ and return m; otherwise, repeat this step.

Note that if $e \neq e'$ and $(e - e') \cdot (C_2 - \mathsf{sk}_0 \cdot C_1) = \tilde{z}_m \cdot G$, then the ElGamal ciphertext is valid and we can compute the unique plaintext m from $(e - e')m = \tilde{z}_m \bmod p$. Since the size of $\mathcal{G}'_{r_p^*}$ is greater than $p\epsilon(\lambda)$, a single step 2 of Ext will output the plaintext of (C_1, C_2) with probability at least $\epsilon^2(\lambda) - \frac{1}{2^\lambda}$, and hence it will succeed in expected time at most $\mathcal{O}\left(\frac{1}{\epsilon(\lambda)^2} T\right)$, where T is the running time of a single repetition of step 2. □

3.2 Promise Σ-protocol for Homomorphic Operations

Suppose we have a tuple $(\mathsf{pk}_0, \mathsf{pk}_1, C = (C_1, C_2), c = (c_1, c_2))$ that has already been proven to be in $\mathcal{L}_{\mathrm{EGCL}}$ via the *promise* Σ-protocol Σ^2_{prom} described in the previous section. We call such a pair (C, c) *semi-equal.*

Given such a $(\mathsf{pk}_0, \mathsf{pk}_1, C = (C_1, C_2), c = (c_1, c_2))$, we consider the following encoding schemes both derived from homomorphic operations:

- $\mathsf{DL.Code}_{\mathsf{pk}'_0 = (\mathsf{pk}_0, C_1, C_2)} : (a, b) \to (aC_1 + rG, aC_2 + bG + rP)$, where $\mathsf{pk}_0 = (G, P)$ is the public key of the ElGamal encryption, r is selected randomly from $\mathbb{Z}_p$. We let the secret key corresponding to pk'_0 be the secret key of the ElGamal encryption.
- $\mathsf{CL.Code}_{\mathsf{pk}'_0 = (\mathsf{pk}_1, c_1, c_2)} : (a, b) \to (c_1^a, c_2^a f^b)$, where pk_1 is the public key of the CL encryption. We let the secret key corresponding to pk'_1 be the secret key of the CL encryption.

We now present a *promise* Σ-protocol for the following language with respect the above two schemes:

$$\mathcal{L}_{\mathsf{affine}} = \{((\mathsf{pk}_0 = (G, P), C_1, C_2), (\mathsf{pk}_1 = (\tilde{s}, p, g_p, f, h), c_1, c_2), (C'_1, C'_2), (c'_1, c'_2))| \\ \exists a \in [0, pS), b, r \in \mathbb{Z}_p, \text{s.t. } C'_1 = aC_1 + rG \wedge C'_2 = aC_2 + bG + rP \wedge c'_1 = c_1^a \wedge c'_2 = c_2^a f^b\}$$

Such a statement essentially says that the tuple $(C' = (C'_1, C'_2), c' = (c'_1, c'_2))$ is generated from $(C = (C_1, C_2), c = (c_1, c_2))$ by doing the *same* affine homomorphic operations.

The protocol proceeds as follows.

Protocol Σ^3_{prom} for correctness of homomorphic operations

Common input: $(((G,P),C_1,C_2),((\tilde{s},p,g_p,f,h),c_1,c_2),(C'_1,C'_2),(c'_1,c'_2))$.
P's Private input: $a \in [0,pS), b, r \in \mathbb{Z}_p$.

1. P randomly chooses $s_a \in [0,pU), s_b, s_r \in \mathbb{Z}_p$, and computes $A_1 = s_aC_1 + s_rG, A_2 = s_aC_2 + s_bG + s_rP, a_1 = c_1^{s_a}, a_2 = c_2^{s_a}f^{s_b}$, then sends (A_1, A_2, a_1, a_2) to V.
2. V chooses randomly $e \in \mathbb{Z}_p$ and sends it to P.
3. P computes $z_a = s_a + ea$ in $\mathbb{Z}$, $z_b = s_b + eb \bmod p$ and $z_r = s_r + er \bmod p$, then sends (z_a, z_b) to V.
4. V first checks whether $z_a \in [0, p(U + (p-1)S))$, and accepts iff. the following conditions hold: $z_aC_1 + z_rG = A_1 + eC'_1, z_aC_2 + z_bG + z_rP = A_2 + eC'_2, c_1^{z_a} = a_1{c'_1}^e, c_2^{z_a}f^{z_b} = a_2{c'_2}^e$.

Theorem 3. *If $(p-1)S/U$ is negligible, and $((C_1,C_2),(c_1,c_2))$ is a* semi-equal *pair under the encoding schemes* $\mathsf{EG.Enc}_{pk_0}$ *and* $\mathsf{CL.Enc}_{pk_1}$ *respectively, then protocol Σ^3_{prom} is a promise Σ-protocol with respect to the function $\rho_m : (a,b) \to (am + b \bmod p)$, where m is such that $(C_1,C_2) = \mathsf{EG.Enc}_{pk_0}(m)$.*

Proof. Again, here we omit the proofs of completeness and the HVZK property, and just prove the *promise extractability*.

Suppose an adversarial prover P* convinces V with a non-negligible probability, we could obtain two accepting transcripts $(A_1, A_2, a_1, a_2, e, z_a, z_b, z_r)$ and $(A_1, A_2, a_1, a_2, e', z'_a, z'_b, z'_r)$ with $e \neq e' \bmod p$ using the similar proof strategy as the previous section. Subsequently following the special soundness of the Σ-protocol for ElGamal ciphertexts, one can compute the affine factors $(a \bmod p) = (z_a - z'_a)/(e - e') \bmod p$ and $b = (z_b - z'_b)/(e - e') \bmod p$, as well as the randomness $r = (z_r - z'_r)/(e - e') \bmod p$ such that $C'_1 = aC_1 + rG$ and $C'_2 = aC_2 + bG + rP$.

We now turn to the second property of *promise extractability.* Note that from the above two accepting transcripts it yields

$$c_1^{\Delta z_a} = {c'_1}^{\Delta e}, c_2^{\Delta z_a} f^{\Delta z_b} = {c'_2}^{\Delta e}, \tag{2}$$

where $\Delta z_a = z_a - z'_a, \Delta z_b = z_b - z'_b$ and $\Delta e = e - e'$.

From the fact that $(C = (C_1,C_2), c = (c_1,c_2))$ are semi-equal, it follows from the equality (1) that $c_1^{\tilde{e}} = g_p^{\tilde{z}}, c_2^{\tilde{e}} = h^{\tilde{z}}f^{m\tilde{e}}$ for some $\tilde{e}$. Combining these two equalities with the equality (2), we have

$$g_p^{\tilde{z}\Delta z_a} = {c'_1}^{\tilde{e}\Delta e}, h^{\tilde{z}\Delta z_b} f^{(am+b)\tilde{e}\Delta e} = {c'_2}^{\tilde{e}\Delta e}. \tag{3}$$

This essentially says that one can efficiently modify the second codeword (c'_1, c'_2) into a valid codeword $(c''_1 = {c_1}^{\tilde{e}\Delta e}, c''_2 = {c'_2}^{\tilde{e}\Delta e})$ of the message $(am + b)\tilde{e}\Delta e$.

We set $\hat{e} = \tilde{e}\Delta e$ and $\hat{z} = \tilde{z}\Delta z_a$. Let $(\mathsf{sk}_0, \mathsf{sk}_1)$ be the (honest generated) secret keys of the underlying ElGamal and CL encryption scheme. Thus, combining the first condition of promise extractability and the equality (3), we have

$$(am + b)G = C_2' - \mathsf{sk}_0 \cdot C_1', {c_1'}^{\hat{e}} = g_p^{\hat{z}}, {c_2'}^{\hat{e}} = h^{\hat{z}} f^{(am+b)\hat{e}},$$

which allow us to construct a straight-line extractor $\mathsf{Ext}(\mathsf{sk}_0, \mathsf{sk}_1, \cdot)$ to extract $\rho(m) = am + b$ in the same way as in Sect. 3.1. □

We prove in the full version of this paper that the *promise* Σ-protocols described above are indeed *promise* NIZKs in the random oracle model after applying Fiat-Shamir transformation.

4 Simulating Homomorphic Operations on an Invalid Ciphertext

Recall that in the final stage of a two-party signing subprotocol of [Lin17, CCL+19], $\mathcal{P}_2$ holds (x_2, k_2, r) and computes $b = k_2^{-1}m'$ (where m' is the hash value of m), $a = k_2^{-1}rx_2$, and a ciphertext of $ax_1 + b$ by homomorphic operations on the ciphertext $(c_{key,1}, c_{key,2})$ of x_1, which it received in the key generation phase. $\mathcal{P}_2$ sends the resulting ciphertext of $ax_1 + b$ to $\mathcal{P}_1$, who decrypts the ciphertext and computes a signature $(r, k_1^{-1}(ax_1 + b))$.

In our settings, in the key generation phase $\mathcal{P}_1$ computes a pair $(Q_1, c_{key} = (c_{key,1}, c_{key,2}))$ which both encode x_1, and then runs an efficient *promise* Σ-protocol (with challenge of polynomial length) to prove the knowledge of x_1. This *promise* Σ-proof guarantees only that the $(c_{key,1}, c_{key,2})$ satisfies $c_{key,1}^{\tilde{e}} = g_p^{\tilde{z}}$ and $c_{key,2}^{\tilde{e}} = h^{\tilde{z}} f^{\tilde{e}x_1}$ for some $\tilde{e} \in [-p+1, p-1] \setminus \{0\}, \tilde{z} \in [-U-(p-1)S+1, U+(p-1)S-1] \setminus \{0\}$. As discussed in the introduction, if we have the same $\mathcal{P}_2$ as in [CCL+19], then the same simulator $\mathcal{S}$ would fail.

Instead, we have $\mathcal{P}_2$ choose a random t, raise $c_{key,1}$ and $c_{key,2}$ to the power $a+t$ (randomizing a), and then compute a ciphertext $(c_{key,1}^{a+t}, f^b \cdot c_{key,2}^{a+t})$. For an honest $\mathcal{P}_1$ to decrypt and obtain $ax_1 + b$, $\mathcal{P}_2$ sends back this ciphertext along with $t \bmod p$. Specifically, we consider the following $\mathcal{P}_2$ and $\mathcal{S}$ (think that a,b and $s' = ax_1 + b$ (along with the public keys) are "hardwired" into $\mathcal{P}_2$ and $\mathcal{S}$, respectively):

$$\mathcal{P}_2(t_1) : (c_{key,1}^{a+t_1}, f^b c_{key,2}^{a+t_1}, t_1 \bmod p), \text{ and } \mathcal{S}(t_2) : (c_{key,1}^{t_2}, f^{s'} c_{key,2}^{t_2}, t_2 \bmod p). \quad (4)$$

We now give a formal proof that, if the random string t is sufficiently long and $p \nmid \mathrm{ord}(g_p)$, $p \nmid \mathrm{ord}(h)$, then these two distributions above are statistically close. As mentioned, the last two conditions can be achieved by having $\mathcal{P}_1$ generate a public key of the CL encryption scheme of the form $(g_0, g_p = g_0^p, h_0, h = h_0^p)$. Recall the following notations and their properties:

- $\mathsf{param} := (\tilde{s}, g, f, g_p, \hat{\mathcal{G}}, \mathcal{G}, \mathcal{F}, \mathcal{G}^p)$ and S are the parameters of groups we work on, satisfying that 1) p is a prime, $|\hat{\mathcal{G}}| = p\hat{s}$ for some unknown $\hat{s} < \tilde{s}$ and $S = 2^{\lambda-2}\tilde{s}$; 2) $\gcd(p, \hat{s}) = 1$.

- $\mathsf{pk} := (\tilde{s}, p, g_p, f, h)$ is the public key such that $p \nmid \mathrm{ord}(g_p)$ and $p \nmid \mathrm{ord}(h)$. As discussed above, this property can be easily achieved even if the public key is maliciously generated.
- (x_1, a, b, s') satisfies $s' = ax_1 + b \bmod p$.
- $(c_{key,1}, c_{key,2})$ and h'. $(c_{key,1}, c_{key,2})$ is the ciphertext as above, and satisfies $c_{key,1}^{\tilde{e}} = g_p^{\tilde{z}}$ and $c_{key,2}^{\tilde{e}} = h^{\tilde{z}} f^{\tilde{e}x_1}$ for some $\tilde{e} \in [-p+1, p-1] \setminus \{0\}, \tilde{z} \in [-U-(p-1)S, U+(p-1)S] \setminus \{0\}$. h' is an arbitrary $\tilde{e}$-th root of $h^{\tilde{z}}$, which satisfies that $c_{key,2} = h' f^{x_1}$.

We define $\mathfrak{p} := (\mathsf{param}, \mathsf{pk}, x_1, a, b, s', c_{key,1}, c_{key,2}, h')$, and prove the following lemma.

Lemma 1. *Let $\mathfrak{p}$ be defined as above. Then the statistical distance between the two distributions $\{t_1 \leftarrow [0, pS) : \mathcal{P}_2(t_1)\}$ and $\{t_2 \leftarrow [0, pS) : \mathcal{S}(t_2)\}$ in (4) is exponentially small.*

Proof. From the facts that $p \nmid \mathrm{ord}(g_p)$, $p \nmid \tilde{e}$ and $c_{key,1}^{\tilde{e}} = g_p^{\tilde{z}}$, it follows $p \nmid \mathrm{ord}(g_p^{\tilde{z}})$ and $\gcd(p, \mathrm{ord}(g_p^{\tilde{z}}) = \mathrm{ord}(c_{key,1}^{\tilde{e}})) = 1$. Since

$$\mathrm{ord}(c_{key,1}^{\tilde{e}}) = \mathrm{ord}(c_{key,1}) / \gcd(\mathrm{ord}(c_{key,1}), \tilde{e}) \text{ and } p \nmid \tilde{e},$$

we have $\gcd(p, \mathrm{ord}(c_{key,1})) \le \gcd(p, \mathrm{ord}(c_{key,1}^{\tilde{e}})) \cdot \gcd(p, \gcd(\mathrm{ord}(c_{key,1}), \tilde{e})) = 1$, i.e., $p \nmid \mathrm{ord}(c_{key,1})$.

Similarly, one can deduce $p \nmid \mathrm{ord}(h')$ from the facts that $p \nmid \mathrm{ord}(h)$, $p \nmid \tilde{e}$ and $h'^{\tilde{e}} = h^{\tilde{z}}$. Observe also that $\mathrm{ord}(c_{key,1}) | p\hat{s}$ and $\mathrm{ord}(h') | p\hat{s}$, we have

$$\mathrm{ord}(c_{key,1}) | \hat{s} \text{ and } \mathrm{ord}(h') | \hat{s}. \tag{5}$$

We define the following deterministic algorithm $\mathfrak{f}$ with $\mathfrak{p}$ hardwired:

$$\mathfrak{f}_{\mathfrak{p}}(t') = (c_{key,1}^{a+t'}, h'^{a+t'} f^{ax_1 + t'x_1 + b}, t' \bmod p),$$

and observe that,

$$\begin{aligned} \mathcal{P}_2(t_1) &= (c_{key,1}^{a+t_1}, f^b \cdot c_{key,2}^{a+t_1}, t_1 \bmod p); \\ &= (c_{key,1}^{a+t_1 \bmod \hat{s}}, h'^{a+t_1 \bmod \hat{s}} \cdot f^{ax_1 + t_1 x_1 + b \bmod p}, t_1 \bmod p) = \mathfrak{f}_{\mathfrak{p}}(t_1) \end{aligned} \tag{6}$$

By defining $t_2^* := t_2 - p^{-1} pa \bmod p\hat{s}$, where p^{-1} satisfies that $p^{-1} p \equiv 1 \bmod \hat{s}$ (recall $\gcd(p, \hat{s}) = 1$), we have:

$$\begin{aligned} \mathcal{S}(t_2) &= (c_{key,1}^{t_2}, f^{s'} \cdot c_{key,2}^{t_2}, t_2 \bmod p) \\ &= (c_{key,1}^{t_2^* + p^{-1} pa \bmod \hat{s}}, h'^{t_2^* + p^{-1} pa \bmod \hat{s}} \cdot f^{ax_1 + t_2^* x_1 + b \bmod p}, t_2^* + p^{-1} pa \bmod p) \\ &= (c_{key,1}^{t_2^* + a \bmod \hat{s}}, h'^{t_2^* + a \bmod \hat{s}} \cdot f^{ax_1 + t_2^* x_1 + b \bmod p}, t_2^* \bmod p) = \mathfrak{f}_{\mathfrak{p}}(t_2^*) \end{aligned} \tag{7}$$

It is easy to verify that $\{t_1 \leftarrow [0, p\hat{s}) : \mathfrak{f}_{\mathfrak{p}}(t_1)\}$ is identical to $\{t_2 \leftarrow [0, p\hat{s}) : \mathfrak{f}_{\mathfrak{p}}(t_2^* = t_2 - p^{-1} pa \bmod p\hat{s})\}$, which implies that

$$\{t_1 \leftarrow [0, p\hat{s}) : \mathcal{P}_2(t_1)\} \equiv \{t_2 \leftarrow [0, p\hat{s}) : \mathcal{S}(t_2)\}. \tag{8}$$

Denote by D_1 the distribution $\{t_1 \leftarrow [0, pS) : t_1 \bmod p\hat{s}\}$ and by D_2 the distribution $\{t_1 \leftarrow [0, p\hat{s}) : t_1\}$. The statistical distance $\mathsf{SD}(D_1, D_2)$ between the two distributions D_1 and D_2 is

$$\mathsf{SD}(D_1, D_2) = \frac{1}{2} \sum_{t \in [0, p\hat{s})} |\Pr[t_1 \leftarrow D_1 : t_1 = t] - \Pr[t_1 \leftarrow D_2 : t_1 = t]|.$$

Suppose that $\tilde{s} = k\hat{s}$ for some $k > 1$. We have $pS = 2^{\lambda-2}p\tilde{s} = k2^{\lambda-2}p\hat{s}$, and therefore

$$\Pr_{t \in [0,p\hat{s})}[t_1 \leftarrow D_1 : t_1 = t] = \frac{\lfloor k2^{\lambda-2} \rfloor}{k2^{\lambda-2}p\hat{s}} \text{ or } \frac{\lfloor k2^{\lambda-2} \rfloor + 1}{k2^{\lambda-2}p\hat{s}} \in [\frac{1}{p\hat{s}} - \frac{1}{k2^{\lambda-2}p\hat{s}}, \frac{1}{p\hat{s}} + \frac{1}{k2^{\lambda-2}p\hat{s}}].$$

Thus, we conclude

$$\mathsf{SD}(D_1, D_2) = \frac{1}{2} \sum_{t \in [0, p\hat{s})} |\Pr[t_1 \leftarrow D_1 : t_1 = t] - \Pr[t_1 \leftarrow D_2 : t_1 = t]| < \frac{1}{k2^{\lambda-1}}.$$

Then $\mathsf{SD}(\mathfrak{f}_\mathsf{p}(D_1), \mathfrak{f}_\mathsf{p}(D_2)) \leq 1/k2^{\lambda-1}$ since the *deterministic* $\mathfrak{f}_\mathsf{p}$ doesn't amplify the statistical distance. And we have $\mathsf{SD}(\mathcal{P}_2(D_1), \mathcal{P}_2(D_2)) \leq 1/k2^{\lambda-1}$ from (6) . Similarly, the statistical distance between $\{t_2 \leftarrow [0, pS) : \mathcal{S}(t_2)\}$ and $\{t_2 \leftarrow [0, p\hat{s}) : \mathcal{S}(t_2)\}$ is also less than $1/k2^{\lambda-1}$. Combining (8), it follows

$$\mathsf{SD}(\{t_1 \leftarrow [0, pS) : \mathcal{P}_2(t_1)\}, \{t_2 \leftarrow [0, pS) : \mathcal{S}(t_2)\}) < \frac{1}{k2^{\lambda-2}}.$$

□

5 Two-Party ECDSA

We now present an efficient construction for two-party ECDSA protocol and prove its security under a simulation-based definition. We follow the framework of [Lin17, CCL+19], but apply the *promise* Σ-protocol to avoid doing parallel repetition which is the main efficiency bottleneck in [CCL+19]. Our protocol, as depicted in Fig. 1, differs from [CCL+19] as follows (labeled with colored boxes in Fig. 1):

1. $\mathcal{P}_1$ is required to generate a CL public key of the form $(g_p = \hat{g}_p^p, h = \hat{h}^p)$ to make it sure $p \nmid \mathrm{ord}(g_p)$ and $p \nmid \mathrm{ord}(h)$.
2. $\mathcal{P}_1$ proves via the *promise* Σ-protocol Σ^1_{prom} described in Sect. 3.1 that Q_1 and the CL ciphertext c_{key} encode the same message x_1, i.e., $(Q_1, c_{key}) \in \mathcal{L}_{\mathrm{DLCL}}$.
3. In the signing phase, $\mathcal{P}_2$ generates a ciphertext by homomorphic operations together with $t_p = t \bmod p$ in the same way described in Sect. 4.

We use the ideal zero knowledge functionality $\mathcal{F}_{\mathsf{zk}}$ for the following NP relation (where the parameters of the elliptic curve $(\mathbb{G}, G, p)$ are implicit public

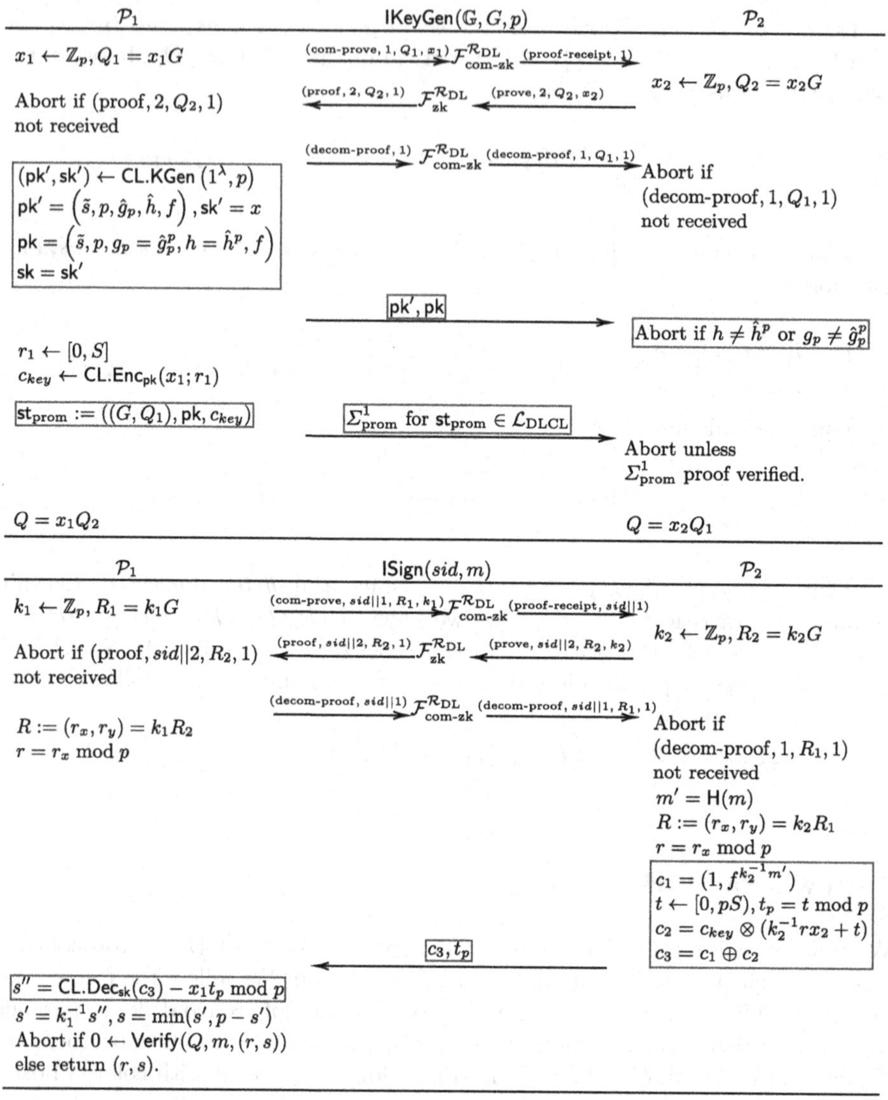

Fig. 1. Two-party ECDSA key generation and signing protocols

inputs): $\mathcal{R}_{\mathrm{DL}} = \{(Q; w) | Q = wG\}$. Functionality $\mathcal{F}_{\mathrm{zk}}$ can be efficiently instantiated by Schnorr protocol. Note that instead of using the $\mathcal{F}_{\mathrm{zk}}$-hybrid model, we use the *promise* Σ-protocol directly in our construction.

In Fig. 1 we denote by $\otimes$ and $\oplus$ the homomorphic operations, defined as $c_{key} \otimes k = (c^k_{key,1}, c^k_{key,2})$ and $c_1 \oplus c_2 = (c_{1,1} \cdot c_{2,1}, c_{1,2} \cdot c_{2,2})$, where c_{key}, c_1, c_2 are CL ciphertexts and k is an integer.

Theorem 4. *Under the DDH assumption, the HSM assumption and the Double Encoding assumption, the protocol described in Fig. 1 securely computes $\mathcal{F}_{\mathrm{ECDSA}}$ for a two-party case in the $(\mathcal{F}_{\mathrm{zk}}, \mathcal{F}_{\mathrm{com\text{-}zk}})$-hybrid model in the presence of a malicious static adversary under the simulation-based definition.*

Our construction is to some extent derived from the one in [CCL+19] except that the *promise* Σ-protocol only enjoys a *weaker* special soundness. On one hand, if the adversary $\mathcal{A}$ corrupts party $\mathcal{P}_2$ which only verifies a *promise* Σ-proof, we can simulate $\mathcal{P}_1$ in the same manner as in [CCL+19]; On the other hand, if $\mathcal{P}_1$ is corrupted by $\mathcal{A}$ who plays the role of a prover in a *promise* Σ-protocol, we could construct a simulator to generate an indistinguishable view from the adversarial perspective by leveraging the extraction by rewinding (the first property of *promise extraction*) and the technique to simulate homomorphic operations (described in Sect. 4). The detailed proof of Theorem 4 is presented in the full version of this paper.

6 Multi-party (Threshold) ECDSA

In this section, we show how to use *promise* Σ-protocols to remove the low order assumption and strong root assumption for the multi-party (threshold) ECDSA of [CCL+20]. The resulting protocol is more efficient than the one of [CCL+20] in terms of both bandwidth and computational efficiency. Our techniques also apply the multi-party protocol of [LN18] to improve bandwidth efficiency at the cost of relatively high computational complexity as in the case [CCL+20].

6.1 Improvment on [CCL+20] with *promise* Σ-protocols

In the threshold ECDSA of [CCL+20], their zero knowledge proof for proving the well-formedness of a CL ciphertext requires a random group generator g_p due to the need of strong root assumption. This leads to a costly interactive setup phase to generate such g_p. Without relying the assumption, we could remove this phase.

We modify the threshold ECDSA protocol in [CCL+20] with *promise* Σ-protocols in the following way (labeled with colored boxes in Fig. 2 and Fig. 3):

1. After generating the CL public/secret key pair $(\hat{\mathsf{pk}}_i = (\tilde{s}, p, \hat{g}_p, \hat{h}, f), \hat{\mathsf{sk}}_i)$, we have each party refresh the public key to obtain a new $\mathsf{pk}_i = (\tilde{s}, p, g_p = \hat{g}_p^p, h = \hat{h}^p, f)$ as in the two-party case, and additionally generate a public/secret key pair of $\mathsf{ElGamal}$ encryption $(\mathsf{pk}'_i, \mathsf{sk}'_i) \leftarrow \mathsf{EG.KGen}(1^\lambda)$ in the key generation and broadcast $(\mathsf{pk}'_i, \hat{\mathsf{pk}}_i, \mathsf{pk}_i)$.

2. In **Phase** 1 of the signing phase of [CCL+20], we have each party $\mathcal{P}_i$ encrypt k_i using CL encryption scheme, as well as encoding it using ElGamal encryption scheme, then use the *promise* Σ-protocol Σ^2_{prom} decsribed in Sect. 3.1 to prove the plaintexts equality.
3. In **Phase** 2 of the signing phase of [CCL+20], instead of generating a CL ciphertext $c_{k_j\gamma_i}$ of $k_j\gamma_i - \beta_{j,i} \bmod p$, $\mathcal{P}_i$, like $\mathcal{P}_2$ in its final step of the two-party signing protocol described in the previous section, homomorphically computes a CL ciphertext of $k_j\gamma_i + k_j\hat{t}_{j,i} - \beta_{j,i} \bmod p$, where $\hat{t}_{j,i}$ is selected uniformly from a sufficient large space $[0, pS)$. $\mathcal{P}_i$ generates a ciphertext $c_{k_jw_i}$ of $k_jw_i + k_jt_{j,i} - v_{j,i} \bmod p$ in the same way. And $\mathcal{P}_i$ sends $c_{k_j\gamma_i}, c_{k_jw_i}$, along with $\hat{t}_{p,ji} = \hat{t}_{j,i} \bmod p$ and $t_{p,ji} = t_{j,i} \bmod p$ (for $\mathcal{P}_j$ to derandomized the plaintexts) to $\mathcal{P}_j$.

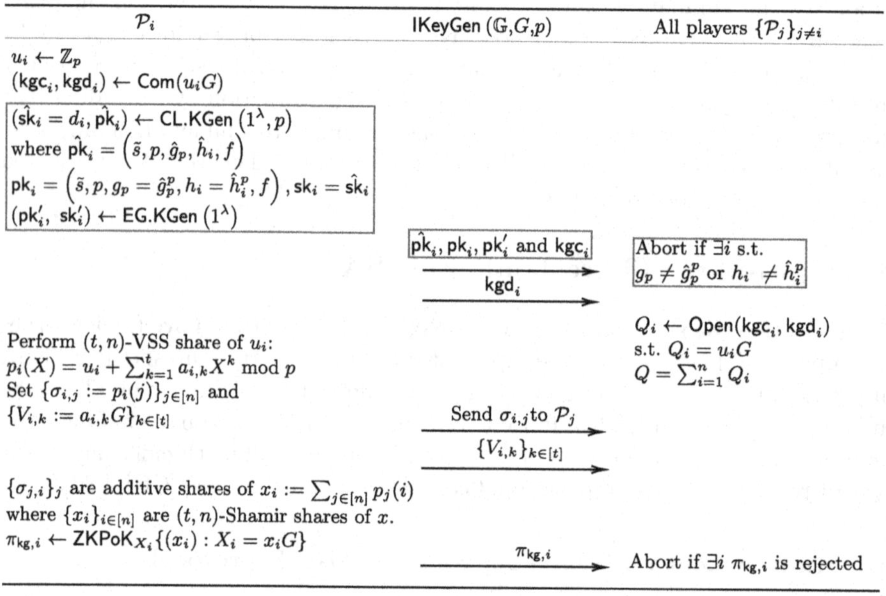

Fig. 2. Multi-party key generation protocol

Following [GG18, CCL+20], we also use cryptographic primitives such as Feldman's verifiable secret sharing (VSS) scheme and a non-malleable equivocable commitment. We refer to [GG18, CCL+20] for more details of the two schemes.

To enable a threshold signing protocol where a subset $S \subseteq [n]$ of parties collaborate to sign a message m, given the (t, n) shares $\{x_i\}_{i\in[n]}$ of x obtained in the key generation phase, each party can compute the additive shares $\{w_i\}_{i\in S}$ of x using the appropriate Lagrangian coefficients, as well as $\{W_i = w_iG\}_{i\in S}$. We also use the symbols $\otimes, \oplus$ defined in Sect. 5 to represent homomorphic operations.

$\mathcal{P}_i$	**Phase 1**	All players $\{\mathcal{P}_j\}_{j\neq i}$
$k_i, \gamma_i \leftarrow \mathbb{Z}_p, r_i \leftarrow [0,\ S]$		
$c_{k_i} \leftarrow \mathsf{CL.Enc}_{\mathsf{pk}_i}(k_i; r_i)$		
$(\mathsf{c}_i, \mathsf{d}_i) \leftarrow \mathsf{Com}(\gamma_i G)$		
$r'_i \leftarrow \mathbb{Z}_p$ $C_{k_i} \leftarrow \mathsf{EG.Enc}_{\mathsf{pk}'_i}(k_i; r'_i)$	$\mathsf{c}_i, c_{k_i}, C_{k_i}$ $\longrightarrow$	
$\mathsf{st}_i := (\mathsf{pk}_i, \mathsf{pk}'_i, C_{k_i}, c_{k_i})$	Σ^2_{prom}-proof π_i for $\mathsf{st}_i \in \mathcal{L}_{\text{EGCL}}$ $\longrightarrow$	Abort if a proof fails
	Phase 2	
$\beta_{j,i}, v_{j,i} \leftarrow \mathbb{Z}_p, B_{j,i} = v_{j,i}G$		
$t_{j,i}, \hat{t}_{j,i} \leftarrow [0, pS)$ $t_{p,ji} = t_{j,i} \bmod p, \hat{t}_{p,ji} = \hat{t}_{j,i} \bmod p$ $c_{k_j\gamma_i} \leftarrow c_{k_j} \otimes (\gamma_i + \hat{t}_{j,i}) \oplus (1, f^{-\beta_{j,i}})$ $c_{k_j w_i} \leftarrow c_{k_j} \otimes (w_i + t_{j,i}) \oplus (1, f^{-v_{j,i}})$	$c_{k_j\gamma_i}, c_{k_j w_i}, B_{j,i}, t_{p,ji}, \hat{t}_{p,ji}$ $\longrightarrow$	$\alpha_{j,i} \leftarrow \mathsf{CL.Dec}_{\mathsf{sk}_j}(c_{k_j\gamma_i}) - k_j \hat{t}_{p,ji}$ $\mu_{j,i} \leftarrow \mathsf{CL.Dec}_{\mathsf{sk}_j}(c_{k_j w_i}) - k_j t_{p,ji}$ Abort if $\mu_{j,i}G + B_{j,i} \neq k_j W_i$
$\delta_i = k_i\gamma_i + \sum_{j\neq i}(\alpha_{i,j} + \beta_{j,i})$ $\sigma_i = k_i w_i + \sum_{j\neq i}(\mu_{i,j} + v_{j,i})$		
	Phase 3	
	δ_i $\longrightarrow$	$\delta = \sum_{i\in S}\delta_i = k\gamma$
	Phase 4	
	d_i $\longrightarrow$	
$\pi_{\gamma_i} \leftarrow \mathsf{ZKPoK}_{\Gamma_i}\{(\gamma_i) : \Gamma_i = \gamma_i G\}$	π_{γ_i} $\longrightarrow$	$\Gamma_i \leftarrow \mathsf{Open}(\mathsf{c}_i, \mathsf{d}_i) = \gamma_i G$ Abort if a proof fails. $(R := (r_x, r_y)) = \delta^{-1}\left(\sum_{i\in S}\Gamma_i\right)$ and $r = r_x \bmod p$
	Phase 5	
$m' = \mathsf{H}(m), s_i = m'k_i + r\sigma_i$ $\ell_i, \rho_i \leftarrow \mathbb{Z}_p$ $V_i = s_i R + \ell_i G, A_i = \rho_i G$ $(\hat{\mathsf{c}}_i, \hat{\mathsf{d}}_i) \leftarrow \mathsf{Com}(V_i, A_i)$ $\hat{\pi}_i \leftarrow \mathsf{ZKPoK}_{(V_i,A_i)}\{(s_i, \ell_i, \rho_i) :$ $V_i = s_i R + \ell_i G \wedge A_i = \rho_i G\}$	$\hat{\mathsf{c}}_i$ $\longrightarrow$ $\hat{\mathsf{d}}_i$ $\longrightarrow$ $\hat{\pi}_i$ $\longrightarrow$	
$U_i = \rho_i V, T_i = \ell_i A$ $\left(\tilde{\mathsf{c}}_i, \tilde{\mathsf{d}}_i\right) \leftarrow \mathsf{Com}(U_i, T_i)$	$\tilde{\mathsf{c}}_i$ $\longrightarrow$ $\tilde{\mathsf{d}}_i$ $\longrightarrow$ s_i $\longrightarrow$	Abort if a proof fails $V = -m'G - rQ + \sum_{i\in S}V_i$ $A = \sum_{i\in S}A_i$ Abort if $\sum_{i\in S}T_i \neq \sum_{i\in S}U_i$ $s = \sum_{i\in S}s_i$ Abort if (r, s) is not valid, else return (r, s).

Fig. 3. Multi-party threshold signing protocol

Note that the only subprotocol of the construction of [CCL+20] that requires the low order assumption and the strong root assumption is the Σ-protocol for the correctness of CL ciphertexts. When replacing such a subprotocol with our *promise* Σ-protocol (as in the above second modification), we remove these two stronger assumptions since our *promise* Σ-protocol per se does not rely on any assumptions. Thus we have the following theorem, and leave its proof in the full version of this paper due to space constraints.

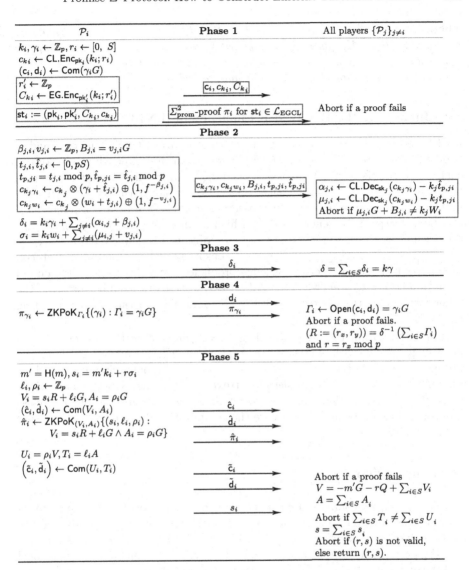

Theorem 5. *Under the assumption that the standard ECDSA is existentially unforgeable, the DDH assumption, the HSM assumption, and the assumption that* Com *is equivocable and non-malleable, then the protocol of Fig. 2 and 3 is an existentially unforgeable threshold signature scheme.*

6.2 Improving the Bandwidth Efficiency of [LN18]

Lindell and Nof [LN18] propose an efficient multi-party ECDSA but with higher bandwidth due to the usage of Paillier encryption and expensive zero knowledge range proofs in a subprotocol, called $\pi_{\mathsf{mult}}^{\mathsf{priv}}$. In the first round of the protocol each party $\mathcal{P}_i$ sends a Paillier encryption c_i of x_i (under its own public key), and receives back c_j. In the second round $\mathcal{P}_i$ selects a random $r_{i\to j}$ and homomorphically generates $c_{i\to j}$ which is an encryption of $x_j \cdot y_i + r_{i\to j}$, then sends it to $\mathcal{P}_j$. $\mathcal{P}_i$ decrypts $c_{j\to i}$ to obtain $z_{j\to i}$, and computes $z_i = \sum_{j\in[n]\setminus\{i\}} z_{j\to i} + x_i y_i - \sum_{j\in[n]\setminus\{i\}} r_{i\to j}$. To ensure the parties follow the protocol, each party provides two zero knowledge proofs for every other one at the end of each round: One zero knowledge proof for correctness of the ciphertext, and the other for proving the correctness of the homomorphic operations in generating $c_{i\to j}$.

Similarly, within the subprotocol $\pi_{\mathsf{mult}}^{\mathsf{priv}}$, we can replace the above two zero knowledge proofs with our *promise* Σ-protocol Σ_{prom}^2 and Σ_{prom}^3 described in Sect. 3 via encoding the secret message into an ElGamal ciphertext and an CL ciphertext instead of a Paillier ciphertext, which achieves better bandwidth efficiency. We stress that, due to the relatively heavy computation over class groups, this replacement will increase the computational complexity as the case in [CCL+20].

7 Comparisons

In this section, we compare implementations of our protocols with the state-of-the-art ones. For fair comparison, we implement four two-party protocols with Rust, including our protocol, the protocol in [CCL+19], its variant in [CCL+20] and the protocol in [Lin17], and two multi-party ECDSA including our protocol and the one in [CCL+20]. The elliptic curve is secp256k1 and the bit length of the discriminant of the class group is chosen as 1827, which ensures that our protocols have 128-bit security. We use Pari C library to handle arithmetic operations in class groups and Paillier encryption. The running times are measured on a single core of an Intel(R) Core(TM) i7-9700K @ 3.6GHz.

Two-Party ECDSA Protocol. In the theoretical aspect, we compare our two-party ECDSA protocol with [CCL+19] and its improved variant in [CCL+20] which reduces the repetition rounds of the zero knowledge proof to $\kappa/10$ times with soundness error $2^{-\kappa}$.

Table 1. Theoretical comparisons in computation of two-party protocols

	Keygen (#CL-Exp)	Signing (#CL-Exp)	Assumptions (related to class group)
Ours	11	3	HSM + Double Encoding
[CCL+19]	$4\kappa + 2$	5	HSM + Double Encoding
[CCL+20]	$(6\kappa)/10 + 2$	5	HSM + Double Encoding

Table 2. Theoretical comparisons in communication of two-party protocols

	Keygen (Bytes)	Signing (Bytes)
Ours	$5\lvert\mathbb{G}\rvert + 4\lvert\mathcal{G}\rvert + 8L_p + L$	$4\lvert\mathbb{G}\rvert + 2\lvert\mathcal{G}\rvert + 7L_p$
[CCL+19]	$(4+\kappa)\lvert\mathbb{G}\rvert + (2\kappa+2)\lvert\mathcal{G}\rvert + (6+\kappa)L_p + \kappa L$	$4\lvert\mathbb{G}\rvert + 2\lvert\mathcal{G}\rvert + 6L_p$
[CCL+20]	$(4+\kappa/10)\lvert\mathbb{G}\rvert + (\kappa/5+2)\lvert\mathcal{G}\rvert + (6+\kappa/10)L_p + (\kappa/10)L$	$4\lvert\mathbb{G}\rvert + 2\lvert\mathcal{G}\rvert + 6L_p$

Table 3. Concrete performance of two-party protocols

	Keygen (ms)	Signing (ms)	Keygen (Bytes)	Signing (Bytes)
Ours	967	391	1916	1046
[CCL+19] ($\kappa = 40$)	14107	442	35814	1014
[CCL+20] ($\kappa = 40$)	2275	442	4494	1014
[Lin17] ($\kappa = 40$)	6120	41	96805	1092
[CCL+19] ($\kappa = 128$)	44740	442	112374	1014
[CCL+20] ($\kappa = 128$)	6471	442	11454	1014
[Lin17] ($\kappa = 128$)	19032	41	305189	1092

The theoretical comparisions are given in Table 1 and Table 2. Since the exponential operation in class groups is much costly than in elliptic curve and dominates the computation cost, we only list the number of exponentiations in class groups, and denote it as #CL-Exp. $|\mathcal{G}|$ and $|\mathbb{G}|$ are size of group elements in $\mathcal{G}$ and $\mathbb{G}$, respectively. L, L_p are the length of the integers sampled from $\mathcal{D}_p$ and $\mathbb{Z}_p$. In our implementation, $|\mathbb{G}| = 33$ Bytes, $|\mathcal{G}| = 345$ Bytes, $L = 115$ Bytes and $L_p = 32$ Bytes.

As shown in Table 1, in the key generation phase our two-party ECDSA protocol is about 15× (resp. about 2×) faster than the protocol in [CCL+19] (resp. in [CCL+20]) when $\kappa = 40$. The improvement is about 44× (resp. about 7×) when $\kappa = 128$. Our protocol is slightly better than the ones in [CCL+19, CCL+20] in the signing phase.

Our protocol also reduces the communication cost significantly. As in Table 2, the improvement of communication is about 17× (resp. 2×) in the key generation phase compared to the protocol in [CCL+19] (resp. in [CCL+20]) when $\kappa = 40$. The improvement is about 54× (resp. about 6×) when $\kappa = 128$. The communication cost in the signing phase is almost the same.

In the concrete apsect, we compare all the four protocols. The running time and consumed bandwidth of our protocol and the protocols in [CCL+19] and [CCL+20] shown in Table 3 meet the theoretical analysis above. Further, we compare our protocol with the one in [Lin17], where Paillier modulus is chosen as 3072 to get 128-bit security. In the key generation phase, our protocol improves the computation performance by a factor about 6× (resp. 20×) when $\kappa = 40$ (resp. $\kappa = 128$). Our protocol also reduces the bandwidth by a factor about 47× (resp. 149×) when $\kappa = 40$ (resp. $\kappa = 128$).

Table 4. Theoretical comparisons in computation of multi-party protocols

	Keygen (#CL-Exp)	Signing (#CL-Exp)	Assumptions (related to class group)
Ours	$2n + 1$	$10t - 6$	HSM
[CCL+20]	$((2n - 1)\kappa)/10 + 2$	$14t - 10$	HSM + Low Order + Strong Root

Multi-Party ECDSA Protocol. The improvement of our multi-party ECDSA protocol on [CCL+20], which is essentially based on [GG18], is very obvious. Using the same notations as above, we show the theoretical comparisons in Table 4 and Table 5, and the concrete comparison in Table 6.

Table 5. Theoretical comparisons in communication of multi-party protocols

	Keygen (Bytes)	Signing (Bytes)
Ours	$((4 + t)\lvert\mathbb{G}\rvert + \lvert\mathcal{G}\rvert + 5L_p)(n - 1)$	$(17\lvert\mathbb{G}\rvert + 8\lvert\mathcal{G}\rvert + 19L_p + L)(t - 1)$
[CCL+20]	$((3 + t)\lvert\mathbb{G}\rvert + (\kappa/10 + 3)\lvert\mathcal{G}\rvert + 10L_p + (\kappa/10)L)(n - 1)$	$(9\lvert\mathbb{G}\rvert + 8\lvert\mathcal{G}\rvert + 16L_p + L)(t - 1)$

Table 6. Concrete performance of multi-party protocols

	Keygen (ms)	Signing (ms)	Keygen (Bytes)	Signing (Bytes)
Ours	$186n + 95$	$1137t - 539$	$33tn + 637n - 33t - 637$	$4044t - 4044$
[CCL+20] ($\kappa = 40$)	$739n - 163$	$1258t - 834$	$33tn + 3792n - 33t - 3792$	$3684t - 3684$
[CCL+20] ($\kappa = 128$)	$2287n - 934$	$1252t - 842$	$33tn + 7434n - 33t - 7434$	$3684t - 3684$

In terms of computational complexity, our multi-party ECDSA protocol is about 4× (resp. 12×) faster than the protocol in [CCL+20] in the key generation phase when $\kappa = 40$ (resp. $\kappa = 128$), which can be seen both in the theoretical and concrete aspects. The signing phase of our construction is slightly better than that in [CCL+20], and it is about 10% faster in the concrete aspect.

In terms of communications, since we eliminate the need of costly interactive setup phase, our protocol outperforms the one in [CCL+20] in the key generation phase for both $\kappa = 40$ and $\kappa = 128$, factors vary according to the number of parties n and the threshold t. In the signing phase the communication overhead is slightly larger while our solution remains of the same order of magnitude.

Finally, it is worth noting that all our constructions are based on HSM assumption (along with other assumptions in elliptic curve group) just as in [CCL+19], instead of using stronger and non-standard assumptions: the low order assumption and the strong root assumption as in [CCL+20].

Acknowledgments. We would like to thank the anonymous reviewers for their valuable suggestions. We are supported by the National Natural Science Foundation of China (Grant No. 61932019, No. 61772521 and No. 61772522) and the Key Research Program of Frontier Sciences, CAS (Grant No. QYZDB-SSW-SYS035).

References

[BBF18] Boneh, D., Bünz, B., Fisch, B.: A survey of two verifiable delay functions. Cryptology ePrint Archive, Report 2018/712 (2018). https://eprint.iacr.org/2018/712

[BGG19] Boneh, D., Gennaro, R., Goldfeder, S.: Using Level-1 homomorphic encryption to improve threshold DSA signatures for bitcoin wallet security. In: Lange, T., Dunkelman, O. (eds.) LATINCRYPT 2017. LNCS, vol. 11368, pp. 352–377. Springer, Cham (2019). https://doi.org/10.1007/978-3-030-25283-0_19

[BKSW20] Belabas, K., Kleinjung, T., Sanso, A., Wesolowski, B.: A note on the low order assumption in class group of an imaginary quadratic number fields. Cryptology ePrint Archive, Report 2020/1310 (2020). https://eprint.iacr.org/2020/1310

[CCL+19] Castagnos, G., Catalano, D., Laguillaumie, F., Savasta, F., Tucker, I.: Two-party ECDSA from hash proof systems and efficient instantiations. In: Boldyreva, A., Micciancio, D. (eds.) CRYPTO 2019. LNCS, vol. 11694, pp. 191–221. Springer, Cham (2019). https://doi.org/10.1007/978-3-030-26954-8_7

[CCL+20] Castagnos, G., Catalano, D., Laguillaumie, F., Savasta, F., Tucker, I.: Bandwidth-efficient threshold EC-DSA. In: Kiayias, A., Kohlweiss, M., Wallden, P., Zikas, V. (eds.) PKC 2020. LNCS, vol. 12111, pp. 266–296. Springer, Cham (2020). https://doi.org/10.1007/978-3-030-45388-6_10

[CL15] Castagnos, G., Laguillaumie, F.: Linearly homomorphic encryption from DDH. In: Nyberg, K. (ed.) CT-RSA 2015. LNCS, vol. 9048, pp. 487–505. Springer, Cham (2015). https://doi.org/10.1007/978-3-319-16715-2_26

[CLT18] Castagnos, G., Laguillaumie, F., Tucker, I.: Practical fully secure unrestricted inner product functional encryption modulo p. In: Peyrin, T., Galbraith, S. (eds.) ASIACRYPT 2018. LNCS, vol. 11273, pp. 733–764. Springer, Cham (2018). https://doi.org/10.1007/978-3-030-03329-3_25

[Coh00] Cohen, H.: A Course in Computational Algebraic Number Theory. Springer, Heidelberg (2000). https://doi.org/10.1007/978-3-662-02945-9

[Des88] Desmedt, Y.: Society and group oriented cryptography: a new concept. In: Pomerance, C. (ed.) CRYPTO 1987. LNCS, vol. 293, pp. 120–127. Springer, Heidelberg (1988). https://doi.org/10.1007/3-540-48184-2_8

[DKLs18] Doerner, J., Kondi, Y., Lee, E., Shelat, A.: Secure two-party threshold ECDSA from ECDSA assumptions. In: 2018 IEEE Symposium on Security and Privacy (SP), pp. 980–997 (2018)

[DKLs19] Doerner, J., Kondi, Y., Lee, E., Shelat, A.: Threshold ECDSA from ECDSA assumptions: the multiparty case. In: 2019 IEEE Symposium on Security and Privacy (SP), pp. 1051–1066 (2019)

[FS87] Fiat, A., Shamir, A.: How to prove yourself: practical solutions to identification and signature problems. In: Odlyzko, A.M. (ed.) CRYPTO 1986. LNCS, vol. 263, pp. 186–194. Springer, Heidelberg (1987). https://doi.org/10.1007/3-540-47721-7_12

[GG18] Gennaro, R., Goldfeder, S.: Fast multiparty threshold ECDSA with fast trustless setup. In: Proceedings of the 2018 ACM SIGSAC Conference on Computer and Communications Security, CCS 2018, pp. 1179–1194. Association for Computing Machinery, New York (2018)

[GG20] Gennaro, R., Goldfeder, S.: One round threshold ECDSA with identifiable abort. Cryptology ePrint Archive, Report 2020/540 (2020). https://eprint.iacr.org/2020/540

[GGN16] Gennaro, R., Goldfeder, S., Narayanan, A.: Threshold-optimal DSA/ECDSA signatures and an application to bitcoin wallet security. In: Manulis, M., Sadeghi, A.-R., Schneider, S. (eds.) ACNS 2016. LNCS, vol. 9696, pp. 156–174. Springer, Cham (2016). https://doi.org/10.1007/978-3-319-39555-5_9

[GJKR96] Gennaro, R., Jarecki, S., Krawczyk, H., Rabin, T.: Robust threshold DSS signatures. In: Maurer, U. (ed.) EUROCRYPT 1996. LNCS, vol. 1070, pp. 354–371. Springer, Heidelberg (1996). https://doi.org/10.1007/3-540-68339-9_31

[GPS06] Girault, M., Poupard, G., Stern, J.: On the fly authentication and signature schemes based on groups of unknown order. J. Cryptol. **19**, 463–487 (2006)

[Lin17] Lindell, Y.: Fast secure two-party ECDSA signing. In: Katz, J., Shacham, H. (eds.) CRYPTO 2017. LNCS, vol. 10402, pp. 613–644. Springer, Cham (2017). https://doi.org/10.1007/978-3-319-63715-0_21

[LN18] Lindell, Y., Nof, A.: Fast secure multiparty ECDSA with practical distributed key generation and applications to cryptocurrency custody. In: Proceedings of the 2018 ACM SIGSAC Conference on Computer and Communications Security, CCS 2018, pp. 1837–1854. Association for Computing Machinery, New York (2018)

[MR01] MacKenzie, P., Reiter, M.K.: Two-party generation of DSA signatures. In: Kilian, J. (ed.) CRYPTO 2001. LNCS, vol. 2139, pp. 137–154. Springer, Heidelberg (2001). https://doi.org/10.1007/3-540-44647-8_8

[PS96] Pointcheval, D., Stern, J.: Security proofs for signature schemes. In: Maurer, U. (ed.) EUROCRYPT 1996. LNCS, vol. 1070, pp. 387–398. Springer, Heidelberg (1996). https://doi.org/10.1007/3-540-68339-9_33

[YCX21] Yuen, T.H., Cui, H., Xie, X.: Compact zero-knowledge proofs for threshold ECDSA with trustless setup. In: Garay, J.A. (ed.) PKC 2021. LNCS, vol. 12710, pp. 481–511. Springer, Cham (2021). https://doi.org/10.1007/978-3-030-75245-3_18

The One-More Discrete Logarithm Assumption in the Generic Group Model

Balthazar Bauer[1(✉)], Georg Fuchsbauer[2(✉)], and Antoine Plouviez[3(✉)]

[1] Université de Paris, Paris, France
balthazar.bauer@ens.fr
[2] TU Wien, Vienna, Austria
georg.fuchsbauer@tuwien.ac.at
[3] Inria, ENS, CNRS, PSL, Paris, France
antoine.plouviez@ens.fr

Abstract. The one more-discrete logarithm assumption (OMDL) underlies the security analysis of identification protocols, blind signature and multi-signature schemes, such as blind Schnorr signatures and the recent MuSig2 multi-signatures. As these schemes produce standard Schnorr signatures, they are compatible with existing systems, e.g. in the context of blockchains. OMDL is moreover assumed for many results on the impossibility of certain security reductions.

Despite its wide use, surprisingly, OMDL is lacking any rigorous analysis; there is not even a proof that it holds in the generic group model (GGM). (We show that a claimed proof is flawed.) In this work we give a formal proof of OMDL in the GGM. We also prove a related assumption, the one-more computational Diffie-Hellman assumption, in the GGM. Our proofs deviate from prior GGM proofs and replace the use of the Schwartz-Zippel Lemma by a new argument.

Keywords: One-more discrete logarithm · Generic group model · Blind signatures · Multi-signatures

1 Introduction

Provable security is the prevailing paradigm in present-day cryptography. To analyze the security of a cryptographic scheme, one first formally defines what it means to break it and then gives a rigorous proof that this is infeasible assuming that certain computational problems are hard.

Classical hardness assumption like RSA and the discrete logarithm assumption in various groups have received much scrutiny over the years, but there are now myriads of less studied assumptions. This has attracted criticism [KM07,KM10], as the value of a security proof is unclear when it is by reduction from an (often newly introduced) assumption that is not well understood. A sanity check that is considered a minimum requirement for assumptions in cyclic groups is a proof in the generic group model (GGM), which guarantees that there are no efficient solvers that work for any group.

M. Tibouchi and H. Wang (Eds.): ASIACRYPT 2021, LNCS 13093, pp. 587–617, 2021.
https://doi.org/10.1007/978-3-030-92068-5_20

In this work we give the first proof that the *one-more discrete logarithm assumption*, a widely used hardness assumption, holds in the GGM. While prior proofs in the GGM have followed a common blueprint, the nature of OMDL differs from that of other assumptions and its proof requires a new approach, which we propose in this paper. We then extend our proof so that it also covers the *one-more Diffie-Hellman assumption.*

GGM. The *generic group model* [Nec94, Sho97] is an idealized model for the security analysis of hardness assumptions (as well as cryptographic schemes themselves) that are defined over cyclic groups. It models a "generic group" by not giving the adversary any group elements, but instead abstract "handles" (or *encodings*) for them. To compute the group operation, the adversary has access to an oracle which given handles for group elements X and Y returns the handle of the group element $X + Y$ (we denote groups additively).

OMDL. The one-more discrete logarithm problem, introduced by Bellare et al. [BNPS03], is an extension of the discrete logarithm (DL) problem. Instead of being given one group element X of which the adversary must compute the discrete logarithm w.r.t. some basis G, for OMDL the adversary can ask for arbitrarily many challenges X_i, all sampled independently and uniformly from the group. In addition, it has access to an oracle that returns the discrete logarithm of any group element submitted by the adversary. The adversary's goal is to compute the DL of all challenges X_i, of which there must be (at least) *one more* than the number of calls made to the DL oracle.

Applications of OMDL

BLIND SIGNATURES. Blind signature schemes [Cha82] let a user obtain a signature from a signer without the latter learning the message it signed. Their security is formalized by *one-more unforgeability*, which requires that after q signing interactions with the signer, the user should not be able to compute signatures on more than q messages.

The signatures in the *blind Schnorr signature scheme* [CP93] are standard Schnorr signatures [Sch91], which, in the form of EdDSA [BDL+12] are increasingly used in practice and considered for standardization by NIST [NIS19]. They are now used in OpenSSL, OpenSSH, GnuPG and considered to be supported by Bitcoin [WNR20], which will enable drastic scalability improvements due to signature aggregation [BDN18, MPSW19] (see below). Blind Schnorr signatures will moreover enable new privacy-preserving applications such as *blind coin swaps* and *trustless tumbler services* [Nic19].

One-more unforgeability of blind Schnorr signatures was proven by Schnorr and Jakobsson [SJ99, Sch01] directly in the GGM, also assuming the random-oracle model (ROM) and that the so-called *ROS problem* is hard. While unforgeability of blind Schnorr signatures cannot, even in the ROM, be proved from standard assumptions [FS10, Pas11, BL13], Fuchsbauer et al. [FPS20] give a proof in the *algebraic group model* (AGM) [FKL18], a model between the standard model and the GGM.

In the AGM, adversaries are assumed to be *algebraic*, meaning that for every group element Z they output, they must know a "representation" $\vec{z} = (z_1, \ldots, z_n)$ such that $Z = \sum_{i=1}^{n} z_i X_i$, where $X_1, \ldots, X_n$ are the group elements received so far. The authors prove unforgeability of blind Schnorr in the AGM+ROM assuming ROS and OMDL [FPS20].

While there has been evidence [Wag02] that the ROS problem was easier than initially assumed, Benhamouda et al. [BLL+21] recently presented a polynomial-time solver for ROS. This leads to forgeries of blind Schnorr signatures when the attacker is allowed to run *concurrent* executions of the signing protocol. To overcome these issues, Fuchsbauer et al. [FPS20] define a new signing protocol and introduce a modified ROS assumption, against which there are no known attacks. Their *Clause blind Schnorr* signature scheme is proven unforgeable in the AGM+ROM assuming hardness of their modified ROS problem and OMDL.

MULTI-SIGNATURES. *Multi-signature schemes* [IN83] allow a group of signers, each having individual verification and signing keys, to sign a message on behalf of all of them via a single signature. In recent work, Nick et al. [NRS21] present a (concurrently secure) two-round multi-signature scheme called *MuSig2* (a variant of the *MuSig* scheme [MPSW19]), which they prove secure under the OMDL assumption. The resulting signatures are ordinary Schnorr signatures (under an *aggregated* verification key, which is of the same form as a key for Schnorr); they are thus fully compatible with blockchain systems already using Schnorr. This will help ease scalability issues, as a single aggregate signature can replace a set of individual signatures to be stored on the blockchain.

Earlier, Bellare and Neven [BN06] instantiated another signature primitive called *transitive signatures* [MR02] assuming OMDL.

IDENTIFICATION SCHEMES. Bellare and Palacio [BP02] assume OMDL to prove that the Schnorr identification protocol is secure against active and concurrent attacks, and Gennaro et al. [GLSY04] use it for a batched version of the scheme. Bellare and Shoup [BS07] prove that the Schnorr identification scheme verifies *special soundness* under concurrent attack from OMDL. Bellare et al. [BNN04] assume OMDL to prove their ID-based identification protocol secure against impersonation under concurrent attacks.

NEGATIVE RESULTS. OMDL has also been assumed in numerous proofs of impossibility results. Paillier and Vergnaud [PV05] prove that unforgeability of Schnorr signatures cannot be proven under the discrete logarithm assumption. Specifically, they show that there is no *algebraic* reduction to DL in the standard model if OMDL holds. Seurin [Seu12] shows that, assuming OMDL, the security bound for Schnorr signatures by Pointcheval and Stern [PS96] using the *forking lemma* is optimal in the ROM under the DL assumption. More precisely, the paper shows that if the OMDL assumption holds, then any algebraic reduction of Schnorr signatures must lose the same factor as a proof via the forking lemma. Fischlin and Fleischhacker [FF13] generalize this impossibility result to a large class of reductions they call *single-instance reductions*, again assuming OMDL. There are further negative results on the security of Schnorr signatures that assume OMDL [GBL08,FJS14,FH17].

Finally, Drijvers et al. [DEF+19] show under the OMDL assumption that many multi-signature schemes, such as *CoSi* [STV+16], *MuSig* [MPSW19], *BCJ* [BCJ08] and *MWLD* [MWLD10], cannot be proven secure from DL or OMDL.

The Generic Security of OMDL

Despite its wide use, surprisingly, OMDL is lacking any rigorous analysis, apart from a comparison to DL in certain groups: while clearly the OMDL problem is not harder than DL, it is strictly easier in any group for which the index calculus algorithm is the best way to solve both problems [KM08,Gra10]. This does thus not apply to elliptic-curve groups, which typically underlie contemporary instantiations of schemes relying on OMDL.

The only analysis of OMDL in the GGM is a more recent proof sketch by Coretti, Dodis, and Guo [CDG18, eprint version], which we show is flawed.[1] (The authors confirmed this in personal communication.)

Their analysis follows the blueprint of earlier GGM proofs, which goes back to Shoup's [Sho97] proof of the hardness of DL in the GGM. However, as we explain below, the adversary can easily make their simulation of the GGM OMDL game fail. The particularity of OMDL compared to other assumptions, which lend themselves more easily to a GGM proof, is that via its DL oracle, the adversary can obtain information about the secret values chosen by the experiment.

Bauer et al. [BFL20] gave further evidence that the analysis of the generic security of OMDL must differ from that of other assumptions. They show that, in the algebraic group model, a large class of assumptions, captured by an extension of the *uber assumption* framework [BBG05,Boy08], is implied by the hardness of q-DLog. In this problem the adversary is given $(xG, x^2G, \ldots, x^qG)$ and must find x. While in the AGM q-DLog implies assumptions as diverse as the strong Diffie-Hellman [BB08], the gap Diffie-Hellman [OP01], and the LRSW assumption [LRSW99], this is not the case for OMDL. Using the meta-reduction technique, Bauer et al. [BFL20] show that it is impossible to prove OMDL from q-DLog, for any q, in the AGM.

This extends earlier results on q-OMDL, a parametrized variant where the adversary receives exactly q challenges. For different values of q, these assumptions are not equivalent under black-box reductions [Bro07] or algebraic reductions [BMV08] (a separation under standard white-box reductions appears to be open).

<u>PROOFS IN THE GGM.</u> To explain the challenges in proving OMDL in the GGM, we start by recalling how GGM proofs typically proceed. In the GGM the adversary does not see actual group elements of the form xG, with $x \in \mathbb{Z}_p$

[1] The authors study assumptions (including OMDL) and schemes in an extension of the GGM that models preprocessing attacks. They give a proof sketch for the security of OMDL with preprocessing. While we show that their sketch is flawed (see p. 5), their preprocessing techniques can be adapted to our proof. Their result for OMDL in the preprocessing GGM thus still holds, except for a change of the security bounds.

and G a fixed generator; instead it gets encodings $\Xi(x)$ of them, where Ξ is a random injective function. As the adversary cannot compute the encoding of $(x+y)G$ from encodings of xG and yG, it is provided with an oracle that on input $(\Xi(x), \Xi(y))$ returns $\Xi(x+y)$.

When analyzing hardness assumptions in the GGM, instead of choosing secret values in the security game, the challenger represents them by indeterminates. For concreteness, consider the GGM game for the DL assumption: the adversary is given the challenge $\Xi(x)$ and must compute the discrete logarithm $x \in \mathbb{Z}_p$. In the proof, the challenger *simulates* this game by using the variable X instead of x and encodes the *polynomial* X instead of x. That is, the challenger gives $\Xi(\mathsf{X})$ to the adversary, who is oblivious to this change. If then the adversary asks, for example, for the addition of $\Xi(1)$ and $\Xi(\mathsf{X})$, the challenger replies $\Xi(\mathsf{X}+1)$, that is, the encoding of a polynomial of degree 1.

This allows the challenger to simulate the game without actually defining a challenge. *After* the adversary output its answer, the challenger picks a value x uniformly at random, which the adversary can only guess with negligible probability. This shows generic hardness of the DL problem.

There is however a caveat: $\Xi(\mathsf{X})$ represents $\Xi(x)$, and, more generally, for any polynomial P that the adversary constructed via its queries, $\Xi(P)$ represents $\Xi(P(x))$. So the simulation would be inconsistent if for some polynomials $P \neq Q$ computed by the adversary we had $P(x) = Q(x)$. Indeed, if such a *collision* occurs, then the simulated game gives the adversary $\Xi(P) \neq \Xi(Q)$ instead of $\Xi(P(x)) = \Xi(Q(x))$.

In order to bound the probability that the simulation fails due to such collisions, the standard technique is to apply the Schwartz-Zippel Lemma, which states that for a non-zero degree-d (multivariate) polynomial $P \in \mathbb{Z}_p[\mathsf{X}_1, \ldots, \mathsf{X}_n]$ the probability that $P(x_1, \ldots, x_n) = 0$ for a uniformly chosen $\vec{x} \xleftarrow{\$} \mathbb{Z}_p^n$ is $\frac{d}{p}$.

Since x is picked uniformly *after* the adversary has defined the polynomials P and Q, the probability that $P(x) - Q(x) = 0$ is bounded by $\frac{1}{p}$. Applying this to all pairs of polynomials generated by the adversary via its group-operation oracle during the game then yields the final bound. This was precisely how Shoup [Sho97] proved the security of DL in the GGM and it was followed by many subsequent GGM proofs. The technique easily extends to games where there are several secrets $x_1, \ldots, x_n$.

<u>CHALLENGES IN THE GGM PROOF OF OMDL.</u> We follow Shoup [Sho97] in that we replace all challenges x_i in the OMDL game by corresponding polynomials $\mathsf{X}_i \in \mathbb{Z}_p[\mathsf{X}_1, \ldots, \mathsf{X}_n]$. It seems tempting to then deduce, like for DL, that the probability that $P(x_1, \ldots, x_n) = Q(x_1, \ldots, x_n)$ for any $P \neq Q$ generated during the game is at most $\frac{1}{p}$ by Schwartz-Zippel. (This is what Coretti et al. [CDG18] do in their proof sketch.) This argument however ignores the fact that, via the discrete logarithm oracle $\text{DLOG}(\cdot)$, the adversary can obtain (a lot of) information on the challenges x_i and can thereby easily cause collisions. In more detail, such a straightforward proof has the following issues:

First, in the game simulated via polynomials, the adversary's oracle DLOG($\cdot$) must be simulated carefully. For example, suppose the adversary asks for the discrete logarithm of the first challenge by querying DLOG($\Xi(\mathsf{X}_1)$). Since x_1 is not defined yet, the challenger samples it uniformly and gives it to the adversary. Now if the adversary later asks for $\Xi(\mathsf{X}_1 + 1)$ (via its group-operation oracle) and queries DLOG on it, it expects the answer $x_1 + 1$. (In [CDG18], the DLOG oracle always returns random values; the adversary can thus easily detect that it is not playing the OMDL game in the GGM.)

Second, there is a more subtle issue. Again suppose that the adversary queried DLOG($\Xi(\mathsf{X}_1)$) and was given x_1. Let $P := \mathsf{X}_1$. Using the group-operation oracle, the adversary can compute (an encoding of) the constant polynomial $Q := x_1$, that is, it can obtain $\Xi(Q)$. Since $P(x_1) = Q(x_1) = x_1$, this means that the adversary can in fact construct polynomials P and Q such that $P(x_1, \dots, x_n) = Q(x_1, \dots, x_n)$ and $P \neq Q$.

Note that this situation cannot occur in prior GGM proofs for other assumptions, because as long as there is no simulation failure, the adversary's polynomials are *independent* of $\vec{x}$, which is a prerequisite for applying Schwartz-Zippel (SZ) in the end. This standard use of SZ (followed by [CDG18]) is thus not possible for OMDL, as the adversary can, via its DLOG oracle, obtain information on the challenge $(x_1, \dots, x_n)$ even when there is no simulation failure.

All these issues persist if instead of Shoup's GGM model [Sho97], one uses Maurer's model [Mau05], which is an abstraction of the former. In his model, all (logarithms of) group elements remain in a "black box", and the adversary can ask for the creation of new entries in the box that are either the sum of existing entries or values of its choice. To capture the DLOG oracle in OMDL one would have to extend the model and allow the adversary to ask for values from the box to be revealed. Moreover, in proofs in this model [Mau05] the adversary wins as soon as it creates a collision between values in the box, which is why one can assume *non-adaptive* adversaries. However, an OMDL adversary *is* adaptive and can easily create collisions (e.g., get x_1 from the DLog oracle, then insert the constant x_1 into the black box). A new approach would thus be required.

OUR GGM PROOF OF OMDL. In our proof we simulate the OMDL game in the GGM using polynomials, but we take into account all the issues just described. That is, the challenger monitors what the adversary has learned about the challenge and defines the simulation considering this knowledge, thus preventing the adversary from trivially distinguishing the real game from the simulation.

Still, there might be simulation failures due to "bad luck", which corresponds precisely to the event whose probability previous proofs bound via Schwartz-Zippel. As OMDL requires a different approach, we propose a new lemma that bounds the probability that our simulation of the OMDL game fails. After modifying the game by aborting in case of a simulation failure, we give a formally defined sequence of game hops showing that the game is *equivalent* to a game that the adversary cannot win. Given the pitfalls in previous approaches and the intricacies outlined so far (and the importance of OMDL), we believe that such a rigorous approach is justified for OMDL.

Our first step is comparable to how Yun [Yun15] analyzed the generic security of the *multiple discrete logarithm* assumption, where the adversary must solve multiple DL challenges (but is not given a DLog oracle, which is what makes OMDL so different from other assumptions). Like Yun, we formalize the knowledge about the challenge that the adversary accumulates by affine hyperplanes in $\mathbb{Z}_p^n$.

POSSIBLE ALTERNATIVE APPROACHES. One might wonder if it was possible to nonetheless rely on the Schwartz-Zippel lemma (SZ) for proving OMDL. We have already argued that applying it once and at the end of the game, as in previous proofs, is not possible. But can SZ be used earlier in the game?

A first idea could be to apply SZ at each DLOG call. Consider a call $\mathrm{DLOG}(\Xi(\mathsf{X}_1 + \mathsf{X}_2))$, answered with a uniform $v \leftarrow \mathbb{Z}_p$. One could now formally replace the indeterminate X_1 by the expression $\mathsf{X}_2 - v$ in all polynomials P generated so far and use SZ to bound the probability that this creates a collision. A first issue is that since P is a multivariate polynomial, SZ does not directly imply a bound on $\Pr[P(\mathsf{X}_2 - v, \mathsf{X}_2, \ldots, \mathsf{X}_n) = 0]$. Indeed, $P(\mathsf{X}_2 - v, \mathsf{X}_2, \ldots, \mathsf{X}_n)$ is the evaluation of the polynomial $\hat{P}(\mathsf{X}_1) := P(\mathsf{X}_1, \mathsf{X}_2, \ldots, \mathsf{X}_n)$ for $\mathsf{X}_1 = \mathsf{X}_2 - v$, so we need to bound $\Pr[\hat{P}(\mathsf{X}_2 - v) = 0]$ for a polynomial $\hat{P}$ with coefficients in the ring $\mathbb{Z}_p[\mathsf{X}_2, \ldots, \mathsf{X}_n]$, whereas SZ is defined for polynomials over fields.

Moreover, when the query $\mathrm{DLOG}(\Xi(P(\mathsf{X}_1, \ldots, \mathsf{X}_n))$ involves a more complex polynomial than $P = \mathsf{X}_1 + X_2$ then the substitution of one variable by a linear expression of the others is even cumbersome to describe notationally. We avoid these problems in our proof by using our lemma instead of (a variant of) SZ, which also lets us keep notation simple.

Another idea would be to apply SZ each time a new encoding is computed. Indeed, assuming no collisions have occurred so far, one could use SZ to bound the probability that the new encoding introduces a collision and then proceed by induction. But the resulting proof would require one game hop for every newly computed encoding: In the j-th hybrid of this game the first j encodings are chosen all different independently of the real value of the challenge; the challenge $\vec{x}$ is picked by the game just before the $(j+1)$-th encoding, when P_{j+1} is defined. Using SZ, we can show that the probability that $P_{j+1}(\vec{x}) = P_i(\vec{x})$ for all $i \leq j$ is negligible.

However, we need to be more cautious. To prevent the attack in which the adversary queries $\mathrm{DLOG}(\Xi(\mathsf{X}_1))$, obtains x_1 and then generates the constant polynomial $P_{j+1} = x_1$, we need to adapt all polynomials defined so far to reflect the information revealed by $\mathrm{DLOG}(\cdot)$. In this example, this is easy to formalize: update every polynomial by evaluating X_1 on x_1 and replace $P_k(x_1, \mathsf{X}_2, \ldots, \mathsf{X}_n)$ by some $P'_k(\mathsf{X}_2, \ldots, \mathsf{X}_n)$; the updated challenge $\vec{x}$ would be of size $n - 1$. To generalize this, we would have to apply an affine transformation to all variables of the polynomials at each call to $\mathrm{DLOG}(\cdot)$. After as many game hops as there are queries by the adversary, we would arrive at a game in which all encodings are random and the challenge is defined after the adversary output its solution.

We believe that both approaches just sketched lead to more complicated (and error-prone) proofs than the one we propose. In our proof, in the first game hop we abort if our simulation fails and we bound this probability by our new lemma. The remaining 3 game hops are purely syntactical and do not change the adversary's winning probability.

One-More CDH

Another "one-more" assumption is the *one-more computational Diffie-Hellman* assumption [BNN04], also known as 1-*MDHP* [KM08,KM10], which is similar to the *chosen-target CDH* assumption [Bol03]. Here, the adversary receives q pairs of group elements (X, Y_i), all with the same first component $X = xG$, and its task is to compute xY_i for all i. It is given an oracle $\mathrm{CDH}_1(\cdot)$, which on input Y returns xY, and which it can query fewer than q times.

It turns out that this assumption can be proved to hold in the generic group model using standard techniques. Following the original GGM proof of DL [Sho97], we modify the simulation for the adversary from encoding logarithms to encoding polynomials in $\mathbb{Z}_p[\mathsf{X}, \mathsf{Y}_1, \ldots, \mathsf{Y}_n]$. The challenges that the adversary receives are the monomials $\mathsf{X}, \mathsf{Y}_1, \ldots, \mathsf{Y}_n$, and when the adversary queries its oracle $\mathrm{CDH}_1(\cdot)$ on an encoding of a polynomial P, it receives an encoding of $\mathsf{X}P$, i.e., its polynomial multiplied by the indeterminate X. To win this "ideal" game, the adversary must construct encodings of $(\mathsf{XY}_1, \ldots, \mathsf{XY}_n)$. Making q calls to its $\mathrm{CDH}_1(\cdot)$ oracle and using its group-operation oracle, it can only construct (encodings of) polynomials from $\mathsf{Span}(1, \mathsf{X}, \mathsf{Y}_1, \ldots, \mathsf{Y}_n, \mathsf{X}P_1, \ldots, \mathsf{X}P_q)$.

Ignoring polynomials of degree less than 2, the adversary wins the game if $\mathsf{Span}(\mathsf{XY}_1, \ldots, \mathsf{XY}_n) \subseteq \mathsf{Span}(\mathsf{X}P_1, \ldots, \mathsf{X}P_q)$. But it must also solve more challenges than it makes $\mathrm{CDH}_1(\cdot)$ oracle queries; that is $q < n$. Using a dimension argument, we deduce that the above condition cannot be satisfied, and thus the adversary cannot win this game.

This "ideal" game is indistinguishable from the real game if the adversary does not create two distinct polynomials that agree on $x, y_1, \ldots, y_n$, the secret values of the real game. Because the degree of all polynomials is upper-bounded by $q+1$, we can use the Schwartz-Zippel Lemma (as, e.g., done in [Boy08]) to upper-bound the statistical distance between the two games by $\mathcal{O}\left(\frac{(q+1)(m+q)^2}{p}\right)$, where m is the number of group operations made by the adversary. This establishes the generic security of this assumption. (An alternative is to cast the assumption as an uber-assumption in the algebraic group model and apply [BFL20, Theorem 4.1].)

The situation is quite different for a variant of the above problem, in which the first component of the challenge pairs is not fixed. That is, the adversary can request challenges, which are random pairs (X_i, Y_i) and is provided with an oracle $\mathrm{CDH}(\cdot)$, which on input any pair $(X = xG, Y)$ returns the CDH solution of X and Y, that is xY. The adversary must compute the CDH solutions of the challenge pairs while making fewer queries to $\mathrm{CDH}(\cdot)$. In this paper we will refer to this assumption as OMCDH.

For this problem the standard proof methodology in the GGM fails for the following reason. Providing the adversary with an oracle $\mathrm{CDH}_1(\cdot)$, as in the one-more Diffie-Hellman assumption with one component fixed (or a DLog oracle in OMDL) lets the adversary only construct polynomials of degree at most $q + 1$. In contrast, the CDH$(\cdot)$ oracle in OMCDH leads to a multiplication of the degrees, which enables the adversary to "explode" the degrees and makes arguments à la Schwartz-Zippel impossible, since they rely on low-degree polynomials.

To get around this problem, we prove the following, *stronger* assumption: as in OMCDH, the adversary still has to compute CDH solutions, but now it is given a discrete-logarithm oracle. This hybrid assumption implies both OMDL (for which the goal is harder) and OMCDH (in which the oracle is less powerful) and we prove it in the GGM by extending our proof of OMDL.

2 Preliminaries

GENERAL NOTATION. We denote the (closed) integer interval from a to b by $[a, b]$. A function $\mu \colon \mathbb{N} \to [0, 1]$ is *negligible* (denoted $\mu = \mathsf{negl}$) if for all $c \in \mathbb{N}$ there exists $\lambda_c \in \mathbb{N}$ such that $\mu(\lambda) \le \lambda^{-c}$ for all $\lambda \ge \lambda_c$. A function ν is *overwhelming* if $1 - \nu = \mathsf{negl}$. Given a non-empty finite set S, we let $x \xleftarrow{\$} S$ denote sampling an element x from S uniformly at random. A list $\vec{z} = (z_1, \dots, z_n)$, also denoted $(z_i)_{i \in [n]}$, is a finite sequence. The length of a list $\vec{z}$ is denoted $|\vec{z}|$. The empty list is denoted $(\,)$.

All algorithms are probabilistic unless stated otherwise. By $y \leftarrow \mathcal{A}(x_1, \dots, x_n)$ we denote running algorithm $\mathcal{A}$ on inputs $(x_1, \dots, x_n)$ and uniformly random coins and letting y denote the output. If $\mathcal{A}$ has oracle access to some algorithm ORACLE, we write $y \leftarrow \mathcal{A}^{\text{ORACLE}}(x_1, \dots, x_n)$. A *security game* $\text{GAME}_{par}(\lambda)$ indexed by a set of parameters *par* consists of a main procedure and a collection of oracle procedures. The main procedure, on input the security parameter λ, generates input on which an adversary $\mathcal{A}$ is run. The adversary interacts with the game by calling oracles provided by the game and returns some output, based on which the game computes its own output bit b, which we write $b \leftarrow \text{GAME}^{\mathcal{A}}_{par}(\lambda)$. We identify **false** with 0 and **true** with 1. As all games in this paper are computational, we define the *advantage* of $\mathcal{A}$ in $\text{GAME}_{par}(\lambda)$ as $\mathbf{Adv}^{\text{GAME}}_{par,\mathcal{A}} := \Pr[1 \leftarrow \text{GAME}^{\mathcal{A}}_{par}(\lambda)]$. We say that GAME_{par} is *hard* if $\mathbf{Adv}^{\text{GAME}}_{par,\mathcal{A}} = \mathsf{negl}$ for any probabilistic polynomial-time (p.p.t.) adversary $\mathcal{A}$.

ALGEBRAIC NOTATION. A *group description* is a tuple $\Gamma = (p, \mathbb{G}, G)$ where p is an odd prime, $\mathbb{G}$ is an abelian group of order p, and G is a generator of $\mathbb{G}$. We use additive notation for the group law and denote group elements with uppercase letters. We assume the existence of a p.p.t. algorithm GrGen which, on input the security parameter 1^λ in unary, outputs a group description $\Gamma = (p, \mathbb{G}, G)$ where p is of bit-length λ. For $X \in \mathbb{G}$, we let $\log_G(X)$ denote the discrete logarithm of X with respect to the generator G, i.e., the unique $x \in \mathbb{Z}_p$ such that $X = xG$.

For multivariate polynomials $P \in \mathbb{Z}_p[\mathsf{X}_1, \dots, \mathsf{X}_n]$ we write $\vec{\mathsf{X}} := (\mathsf{X}_1, \dots, \mathsf{X}_n)$ and $P(\vec{x}) := P(x_1, \dots, x_n)$ for $\vec{x} \in \mathbb{Z}_p^n$. We consider subspaces of $\mathbb{Z}_p[\mathsf{X}_1, \dots, \mathsf{X}_n]$:

Game $\mathrm{DL}^{\mathcal{A}}_{\mathsf{GrGen}}(\lambda)$

$(p, \mathbb{G}, G) \leftarrow \mathsf{GrGen}(1^\lambda)$
$x \xleftarrow{\$} \mathbb{Z}_p\,;\ X := xG$
$y \leftarrow \mathcal{A}(p, \mathbb{G}, G, X)$
return $(y = x)$

Game $\mathrm{OMDL}^{\mathcal{A}}_{\mathsf{GrGen}}(\lambda)$

$(p, \mathbb{G}, G) \leftarrow \mathsf{GrGen}(1^\lambda)$
$\vec{x} := ()\,;\ q := 0$
$\vec{y} \leftarrow \mathcal{A}^{\textsc{Chal},\textsc{DLog}}(p, \mathbb{G}, G)$
return $\big(\vec{y} = \vec{x}\ \wedge\ q < |\vec{x}|\big)$

Oracle $\textsc{Chal}()$

$x \xleftarrow{\$} \mathbb{Z}_p\,;\ X := xG$
$\vec{x} := \vec{x} \,\|\, (x)$
return X

Oracle $\textsc{DLog}(X)$

$q := q + 1\,;\ x := \log_G(X)$
return x

Fig. 1. The DL and the OMDL problem

Game $\mathrm{CDH}^{\mathcal{A}}_{\mathsf{GrGen}}(\lambda)$

$(p, \mathbb{G}, G) \leftarrow \mathsf{GrGen}(1^\lambda)$
$x, y \xleftarrow{\$} \mathbb{Z}_p$
$X := xG\,;\ Y := yG$
$V \leftarrow \mathcal{A}(p, \mathbb{G}, G, X, Y)$
return $(V = xyG)$

Game $\mathrm{OMCDH}^{\mathcal{A}}_{\mathsf{GrGen}}(\lambda)$

$(p, \mathbb{G}, G) \leftarrow \mathsf{GrGen}(1^\lambda)$
$\vec{Z} := ()\,;\ q := 0$
$\vec{V} \leftarrow \mathcal{A}^{\textsc{Chal},\mathrm{CDH}}(p, \mathbb{G}, G)$
return $\big(\vec{Z} = \vec{V}\ \wedge q < |\vec{Z}|\big)$

Oracle $\textsc{Chal}()$

$x, y \xleftarrow{\$} \mathbb{Z}_p$
$(X, Y) := (xG, yG)$
$\vec{Z} := \vec{Z} \,\|\, (xyG)$
return (X, Y)

Oracle $\mathrm{CDH}(X, Y)$

$q := q + 1$
$x := \log_G(X)\,;\ y := \log_G(Y)$
return xyG

Fig. 2. The CDH and the OMCDH problem

for a set $L = \{P_1, \dots, P_q\}$ of polynomials, $\mathsf{Span}(L) := \big\{\sum_{i\in[1,q]} \alpha_i P_i \mid \vec{\alpha} \in \mathbb{Z}_p^q\big\}$ is the smallest vector space containing the elements of L. If $L = \emptyset$ then $\mathsf{Span}(L) = \{0\}$. By $\mathsf{dim}(A)$ we denote the dimension of vector spaces or affine spaces.

By $\langle \vec{x}, \vec{y}\rangle = \sum_{i\in[1,n]} x_i y_i$ we denote the scalar product of vectors $\vec{x}$ and $\vec{y}$ of length n. In this work, polynomials are typically of degree 1, so we can write $P = \rho_0 + \sum_{i=1}^{n} \rho_i \mathsf{X}_i$ as a scalar product: $P(\vec{\mathsf{X}}) = \rho_0 + \langle \vec{P}, \vec{\mathsf{X}}\rangle$, where we define $\vec{P} := (\rho_i)_{i\in[1,n]}$, that is the vector of *non-constant* coefficients of P.

DISCRETE LOGARITHM AND DIFFIE-HELLMAN PROBLEMS. In Figs. 1 and 2 we recall the discrete logarithm (DL) problem and the computational Diffie-Hellman (CDH) problem and define the one-more discrete logarithm (OMDL) problem and the one-more computational Diffie-Hellman (OMCDH) problem.

3 OMDL in the GGM

3.1 A Technical Lemma

While a standard argument in GGM proofs uses the Schwartz-Zippel lemma, it does not work for OMDL, where the adversary obtains information on the challenge $\vec{x}$ *not* only when the simulation fails. So we cannot argue that $\vec{x}$ looks uniformly random to the adversary, which is a precondition for applying Schwartz-Zippel. We therefore use a different lemma, which bounds the probability that for a given polynomial P, we have $P(\vec{x}) = 0$ when $\vec{x}$ is chosen uniformly from a set $\mathcal{C}$. This set $\mathcal{C} \subseteq \mathbb{Z}_p^n$ represents the knowledge the adversary has gained on the challenge $\vec{x}$ during the OMDL game.

The Schwartz-Zippel lemma applies when $\mathcal{C} = S^n$ with S a subset of $\mathbb{Z}_p$, whereas our lemma is for the case that P has degree 1 and $\mathcal{C}$ is defined by an intersection of affine hyperplanes $\mathcal{Q}_j$ from which we remove other affine hyperplanes $\mathcal{D}_i$, that is $\mathcal{C} := \big(\bigcap_{j\in[1,q]} \mathcal{Q}_j\big)\backslash\big(\bigcup_{i\in[1,m]} \mathcal{D}_i\big)$.

We start with some notations. Consider m polynomials $D_i \in \mathbb{Z}_p[\mathsf{X}_1, \ldots, \mathsf{X}_n]$ of degree 1, and $q+1$ polynomials $Q_j \in \mathbb{Z}_p[X_1, \ldots, \mathsf{X}_n]$ also of degree 1. We can write them as

$$D_i(\vec{\mathsf{X}}) = D_{i,0} + \sum_{k=1}^{n} D_{i,k}\mathsf{X}_k = D_{i,0} + \langle \vec{D}_i, \vec{\mathsf{X}}\,\rangle \tag{1}$$

with $\vec{D}_i := (D_{i,k})_{1\le k\le n}$, and similarly for Q_j. We define the sets of roots of these polynomials, which are hyperplanes of $\mathbb{Z}_p^n$:

$$\begin{aligned} \forall i \in [1,m]: \ \mathcal{D}_i &:= \{\vec{x} \in \mathbb{Z}_p^n \mid D_i(\vec{x}) = 0\} \\ \forall j \in [1,q+1]: \ \mathcal{Q}_j &:= \{\vec{x} \in \mathbb{Z}_p^n \mid Q_j(\vec{x}) = 0\} \ . \end{aligned} \tag{2}$$

From (1), we see that the vector $\vec{D}_i$ of non-constant coefficients defines the direction of the hyperplane $\mathcal{D}_i$. It contains the coefficients of the polynomial $D_i - D_i(0) = \sum_{k=1}^{n} D_{i,k}\mathsf{X}_k$.

We define the set

$$\mathcal{C} := \Big(\bigcap_{j\in[1,q]} \mathcal{Q}_j\Big) \setminus \Big(\bigcup_{i\in[1,m]} \mathcal{D}_i\Big) , \tag{3}$$

that is, the set of points at which all Q_i's vanish but none of the D_i's do. The following lemma will be the heart of our proofs of one-more assumptions in the GGM.

Lemma 1. *Let $D_1, \ldots, D_m, Q_1, \ldots, Q_{q+1} \in \mathbb{Z}_p[\mathsf{X}_1, \ldots, \mathsf{X}_n]$ be of degree 1; let $\mathcal{C}$ be as defined in* (2) *and* (3). *Assume $\mathcal{Q}_{q+1} \cap \mathcal{C} \neq \emptyset$ and $\vec{Q}_{q+1}$ is linearly independent of $(\vec{Q}_j)_{j\in[1,q]}$. If $\vec{x}$ is picked uniformly at random from $\mathcal{C}$ then*

$$\frac{p-m}{p^2} \le \Pr\big[Q_{q+1}(\vec{x}) = 0\big] \le \frac{1}{p-m}.$$

Proof. Since $\vec{x}$ is picked uniformly in $\mathcal{C}$, we have $\Pr[\vec{x} \in \mathcal{Q}_{q+1}] = |\mathcal{Q}_{q+1} \cap \mathcal{C}|/|\mathcal{C}|$.

We first bound $|\mathcal{C}|$. We define $\mathcal{Q} := \bigcap_{j\in[1,q]} \mathcal{Q}_j$, which is thus an affine space, and let $d := \mathsf{dim}(\mathcal{Q})$ denote its dimension. Thus, $\mathcal{Q}$ contains p^d elements. We rewrite $\mathcal{C}$:

$$\mathcal{C} = \mathcal{Q} \setminus \Big(\bigcup_{i\in[1,m]} (\mathcal{D}_i \cap \mathcal{Q}) \Big) .$$

Now for a fixed $i \in [1, m]$ we bound the size of $\mathcal{D}_i \cap \mathcal{Q}$. Since the polynomial D_i has degree 1 by definition, $\mathcal{D}_i$ is a hyperplane. There are three cases: either $\mathcal{Q} \subseteq \mathcal{D}_i$, which means $\mathcal{C} = \emptyset$. This contradicts the premise of the lemma, namely $\mathcal{Q}_{q+1} \cap \mathcal{C} \neq \emptyset$. Since $\mathcal{D}_i$ is an hyperplane, the remaining cases are $\mathcal{Q} \cap \mathcal{D}_i = \emptyset$ and $\mathcal{Q} \cap \mathcal{D}_i$ has dimension $\mathsf{dim}(\mathcal{Q}) - 1 = d - 1$. In both cases $\mathcal{D}_i \cap \mathcal{Q}$ contains at most p^{d-1} elements.

When we remove the sets $(\mathcal{D}_i)_{i\in[1,m]}$ from $\mathcal{Q}$, we remove at most mp^{d-1} elements, which yields

$$p^d - mp^{d-1} \leq |\mathcal{C}| \leq p^d. \tag{4}$$

We now use the same method to bound $|\mathcal{C} \cap \mathcal{Q}_{q+1}|$. We define $\mathcal{Q}' = \mathcal{Q}_{q+1} \cap \mathcal{Q}$. Since $\vec{Q}_{q+1}$ is linearly independent of $(\vec{Q}_j)_{j\in[1,m]}$, we get $\mathsf{dim}(\mathcal{Q}') = d - 1$.

For a fixed $i \in [1, m]$, since by assumption $\mathcal{Q}_{q+1} \cap \mathcal{C} \neq \emptyset$, we can proceed as with $\mathcal{Q}$ above: either $\mathcal{Q}' \cap \mathcal{D}_i = \emptyset$ or $\mathcal{Q}' \cap \mathcal{D}_i$ has dimension $d - 2$, which yields

$$p^{d-1} - mp^{d-2} \leq |\mathcal{Q}_{q+1} \cap \mathcal{C}| \leq p^{d-1}. \tag{5}$$

Combining equations (4) and (5) we obtain the following, which concludes the proof:

$$\frac{p^{d-1} - mp^{d-2}}{p^d} \leq \frac{|\mathcal{Q}_{q+1} \cap \mathcal{C}|}{|\mathcal{C}|} \leq \frac{p^{d-1}}{p^d - mp^{d-1}}.$$

□

3.2 Proof Overview

<u>THE GENERIC GAME.</u> We prove a lower bound on the computational complexity of the OMDL game in generic groups in the sense of Shoup [Sho97]. We follow the notation developed by Boneh and Boyen [BB08] for this proof.

In the generic group model, elements of $\mathbb{G}$ are encoded as arbitrary unique strings, so that no property other than equality can be directly tested by the adversary. The adversary performs operations on group elements by interacting with an oracle called GCMP.

To represent and simulate the working of the oracles, we model the opaque encoding of the elements of $\mathbb{G}$ using an injective function $\Xi\colon \mathbb{Z}_p \to \{0,1\}^{\lceil \log_2(p) \rceil}$ where p is the group order. Internally, the simulator represents the elements of $\mathbb{G}$ by their discrete logarithms relative to a fixed generator G. This is captured by Ξ, which maps any integer a to the string $\xi := \Xi(a)$ representing $a \cdot G$. In the game we will use an encoding procedure ENC to implement Ξ.

We specify the game OMDL in the GGM in Fig. 3. In contrast to Fig. 1 there are no more group elements. The game instead maintains discrete logarithms $a \in \mathbb{Z}_p$ and gives the adversary their encodings $\Xi(a)$, which are computed by

Game $\mathrm{OMDLGGM}^{\mathcal{A}}_{\mathsf{GrGen}}(\lambda)$

$\vec{x} := ()$; $a_0 := 1$
$j := 0$; $q := 0$; $n := 0$
$\vec{y} \leftarrow \mathcal{A}^{\text{CHAL},\text{DLOG},\text{GCMP}}(\text{ENC}())$
return $(\vec{y} = \vec{x} \wedge q < n)$

Oracle CHAL()

$n := n + 1$
$x_n \xleftarrow{\$} \mathbb{Z}_p$
$j := j + 1$
$a_j := x_n$
return ENC()

Oracle DLOG(ξ)

if $\xi \notin \{\xi_i\}_{i \in [0,j]}$
  then return $\perp$
$q := q + 1$
$i := \min\{k \in [0, j] \mid \xi = \xi_k\}$
return a_i

ENC()

if $\exists i \in [0, j-1] : a_j = a_i$
  then $\xi_j := \xi_i$
else
  $\xi_j \xleftarrow{\$} \{0,1\}^{\log(p)} \setminus \{\xi_i\}_{i \in [0,j-1]}$
return ξ_j

Oracle GCMP(ξ, ξ', b)

if $\xi \notin \{\xi_i\}_{i \in [0,j]}$ **or** $\xi' \notin \{\xi_i\}_{i \in [0,j]}$
  then return $\perp$
$i := \min\{k \in [0, j] \mid \xi = \xi_k\}$
$i' := \min\{k \in [0, j] \mid \xi' = \xi_k\}$
$j := j + 1$; $a_j := a_i + (-1)^b a_{i'}$
return ENC()

Fig. 3. The OMDL game in the GGM

the procedure ENC. The challenger uses the variable j to represent the number of created group elements, which is incremented before each call to ENC. The procedure ENC then encodes the latest scalar a_j. If a_j has already been assigned a string ξ, then ENC() outputs ξ, else it outputs a random string different from all previous ones. For this, the game maintains a list $(a_i, \xi_i)_{0 \le i \le j}$ of logarithms and their corresponding encodings.

OMDLGGM initializes $j = 0$ and $a_0 = 1$, and runs the adversary on input $\xi_0 \leftarrow$ ENC() (ξ_0 is thus the encoding of the group generator). The oracle CHAL increments a counter of challenges n, samples a new value x_n and returns its encoding by calling ENC(). Since it creates a new element, it first increments j and defines the $a_j := x_n$. The oracle DLOG is called with a string ξ and returns $\perp$ if the string is not in the set of assigned strings $\{\xi_i\}_{i \in [0,j]}$. Else, it picks an index i (concretely: the smallest such index) such that $\xi_i = \xi$ and returns a_i, which is the Ξ-preimage of ξ (and thus the logarithm of the group element encoded by ξ).

The adversary also has access to the oracle GCMP for group operations, which takes as input two strings ξ and ξ' and a bit b, which indicates whether to compute the addition or the subtraction of the group elements. The oracle gets the (smallest) indexes i and i' such that $\xi = \xi_i$ and $\xi' = \xi_{i'}$, it increments j, sets $a_j := a_i + (-1)^b a_{i'}$ and returns ENC(), which computes the encoding of a_j.

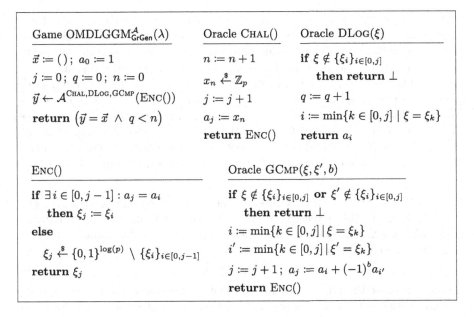

<u>PROOF OVERVIEW.</u> The goal of our proof is to simulate the game without ever computing scalars a_i by replacing them with polynomials P_i and show that with overwhelming probability this does not affect the game. Game_0 (defined by ignoring all the boxes, except the dashed ones, in Fig. 4) is the same game as OMDLGGM, except for two syntactical changes, which will be useful in the proof. The main modification is that we now make n calls to the oracle DLOG after $\mathcal{A}$ outputs its answer $\vec{y}$: for $i \in [1, n]$ we set $x_i := \text{DLOG}(\xi_{j_i})$, where indices j_i are defined in the oracle CHAL so that $a_{j_i} = x_i$; thus $\text{DLOG}(\xi_{j_i})$ always outputs $a_{j_i} = x_i$, meaning this does not affect the game. Second, as calls to DLOG increase q, we put the condition "**if** $q < n$ **then return** 0" before those calls.

<u>INTRODUCING POLYNOMIALS.</u> Game_1, defined in Fig. 4 by only ignoring the gray boxes, introduces the polynomials P_i, where $P_0 = 1$ represents $a_0 = 1$. In the n-th call to CHAL, the game defines a new polynomial $P_j = \mathsf{X}_n$, which represents the value x_n. We thus have

$$P_i(\vec{x}) = a_i \ , \tag{6}$$

and in this sense the polynomial P_i represents the scalar a_i (and thus implicitly the group element $a_i G$). The group-operation oracle maintains this invariant; when computing $a_j := a_i + (-1)^b a_{i'}$, it also sets $P_j := P_i + (-1)^b P_{i'}$.

Note that there are many ways to represent a group element aG by a polynomial. E.g., the first challenge $x_1 G$ is represented by both the polynomial X_1 and the constant polynomial x_1. Intuitively, since x_1 is a challenge, it is unknown to $\mathcal{A}$, and as long as $\mathcal{A}$ does not query $\text{DLOG}(\xi)$, with $\xi := \Xi(x_1)$, it does not know that the polynomials X_1 and x_1 represent the same group element. Game_1 introduces a list L that represents this knowledge of $\mathcal{A}$. E.g., when $\mathcal{A}$ calls $\text{DLOG}(\Xi(x_1))$, the game will append the polynomial $\mathsf{X}_1 - x_1$ to the list L. More generally, on call $\text{DLOG}(\xi_i)$ it appends $P_i - P_i(\vec{x})$ to L, which represents the fact that $\mathcal{A}$ knows that the polynomial $P_i - P_i(\vec{x})$ represents the scalar 0 and the group element $0_{\mathbb{G}}$. The list L will be used to ensure consistency when we replace scalars by polynomials in the game.

Recall that our goal is to have the challenger only deal with polynomials when simulating the game for $\mathcal{A}$. As this can be done without actually defining the challenge $\vec{x}$, the challenger could then select $\vec{x}$ *after* $\mathcal{A}$ gave its output, making it impossible for $\mathcal{A}$ to predict the right answer.

This is done in the final game Game_4, defined in Fig. 6, where the challenger is in the same position as $\mathcal{A}$: it does not know that x_1 is the answer to the challenge represented by the polynomial X_1 until $\text{DLOG}(\xi)$ is called with $\xi := \Xi(x_1)$. In fact, x_1 is not even defined before this call, and, more generally, $\vec{x}$ does not exist until the proper DLOG queries are made.

To get to Game_4, we define two intermediate games. We will modify procedure ENC so that it later deals with polynomials only (instead of their evaluations, as $\vec{x}$ will not exist). Because of this, it will be unknown whether $P_j(\vec{x}) = P_i(\vec{x})$ for some $i \in [0, j-1]$, *unless* $P_j - P_i \in \mathsf{Span}(L)$, since both the challenger and the adversary are aware that all polynomials in L evaluate to 0 at $\vec{x}$.

However, it can happen that, when $\vec{x}$ is defined later, $P_j(\vec{x}) = P_i(\vec{x})$. That is, in the original game, we would have had $a_j = a_i$, but in the final game, ENC is not aware of this. This is precisely when the simulation fails, and we abort the game. We will then bound the probability of this event, using Lemma 1.

In "typical" GGM proofs an abort happens when $P_j(\vec{x}) = P_i(\vec{x})$ and $P_j \neq P_i$. For OMDL, because the adversary might have information on the $\vec{x}$ (and the challenger is aware of this), we allow that there are $P_j \neq P_i$ for which the current knowledge on $\vec{x}$ lets us deduce $P_j(\vec{x}) = P_i(\vec{x})$. With the formalism introduced above this corresponds exactly to the situation that $P_i - P_j \in \mathsf{Span}(L)$. We introduce this abort condition in the procedure ENC in Game_1 (Fig. 4). Because in the "ideal" game Game_4 (Fig. 6), there are no more values a_i, we will express the abort condition differently (namely in oracle DLOG) and argue that the two conditions are equivalent.

<u>ELIMINATING USES OF SCALARS.</u> Using the abort condition in Game_1, we can replace some uses of the scalars a_i by their representations as polynomials P_i. This is what we do in Game_2, (Fig. 4, including all boxes *except* the dashed box), which eliminates all occurrences of a_i's. In ENC, since the game aborts when $P_j(\vec{x}) = P_i(\vec{x})$ and $P_j - P_i \notin \mathsf{Span}(L)$, and because when $P_j - P_i \in \mathsf{Span}(L)$ then $P_j(\vec{x}) = P_i(\vec{x})$, we can replace the event $P_j(\vec{x}) = P_i(\vec{x})$ by $P_j - P_i \in \mathsf{Span}(L)$. Intuitively, we can now think of ENC() as encoding the polynomial P_j instead of the scalar a_j.

We next modify the oracle DLOG. The first change is that instead of returning a_i the oracle uses $P_i(\vec{x})$, which is equivalent by (6). The second change is that on input ξ, oracle DLOG checks if $\mathcal{A}$ already knows the answer to its query, in which case it computes the answer without using $\vec{x}$. E.g., assume $\mathcal{A}$ has only made one query CHAL(), and thus $q = 0$ and $L = \emptyset$: if $\mathcal{A}$ now queries DLOG(ξ) with $\xi := \Xi(x_1)$, the oracle first checks if $P_i = \mathsf{X}_1 \in \mathsf{Span}(1, L)$, (where i is the current number of group elements seen by the adversary), which is not the case, and so it computes $v := P_i(\vec{x}) = x_1$. It then adds the polynomial $Q_1 := \mathsf{X}_1 - x_1$ to L and returns x_1. If for example $\mathcal{A}$ makes another call DLOG(ξ') with $\xi' := \Xi(2x_1+2)$, then it knows that the answer should be $2x_1 + 2$. And indeed, the oracle DLOG checks if $2\mathsf{X}_1 + 2 \in \mathsf{Span}(1, L)$, and since this is the case, it gets the decomposition

$$2\mathsf{X}_1 + 2 = (2x_1 + 2) + 2Q_1 = \alpha_0 + \alpha_1 Q_1$$

with $\alpha_0 = 2x_1 + 2$ and $\alpha_1 = 2$. The oracle uses this decomposition to compute its answer $v := \alpha_0 = 2x_1 + 2$.

More generally, on input ξ_i, the oracle DLOG checks if $P_i \in \mathsf{Span}(1, L)$. If so, it computes the answer using the decomposition of P_i in $\mathsf{Span}(1, L)$; else it uses $\vec{x}$ and outputs $a_i = P_i(\vec{x})$.

We have now arrived at a situation close to the "ideal" game, where the challenger only uses polynomials. The only uses of scalars are the abort condition in ENC (since it compares $P_j(\vec{x})$ and $P_i(\vec{x})$) and in DLOG, when computing the logarithm of an element that is not already known to $\mathcal{A}$. Towards our goal of simulating the game without defining $\vec{x}$, we modify those two parts next.

Game_0, $\boxed{\mathsf{Game}_1}$, $\boxed{\mathsf{Game}_2}$

$\vec{x} := ()$; $a_0 := 1$
$j := 0;\ q := 0;\ n := 0$
$P_0 := 1;\ L := \emptyset$
$\vec{y} \leftarrow \mathcal{A}^{\text{CHAL,DLOG,GCMP}}(\text{ENC}())$
if $q \geq n$ **then return** 0
for $i \in [1, n]$
  $x_i := \text{DLOG}(\xi_{j_i})$
return $\vec{y} = \vec{x}$

Oracle CHAL()

$n := n + 1$
$x_n \xleftarrow{\$} \mathbb{Z}_p$
$j_n := j$
$j := j + 1$
$a_j := x_n$
$P_j := \mathsf{X}_n$
return ENC()

Oracle DLOG(ξ)

if $\xi \notin \{\xi_i\}_{i \in [0,j]}$
  then return $\bot$
$i := \min\{k \in [0, j] \mid \xi = \xi_k\}$
$q := q + 1$
$v := a_i$ $\quad v := P_i(\vec{x})$
if $P_i \in \mathsf{Span}(1, L)$ **then**
  Let $(\alpha_k)_{k=0}^{q-1} \in \mathbb{Z}_p^q$ **s.t.**
    $P_i = \alpha_0 + \sum_{k=1}^{q-1} \alpha_k Q_k$
  $v := \alpha_0$
$Q_q := P_i - v$
$L = L \cup \{P_i - v\}$
return v

ENC( ) // outputs $\xi_j := \Xi(a_j)$

// Only in Game_0 and Game_1
if $\exists i \in [0, j-1] : a_j = a_i$
  then $\xi_j := \xi_i$

if $\exists i \in [0, j-1] : P_j(\vec{x}) = P_i(\vec{x})$
and $P_j - P_i \notin \mathsf{Span}(L)$
  then abort game

if $\exists i \in [0, j-1] : P_j - P_i \in \mathsf{Span}(L)$
then $\xi_j := \xi_i$

else $\xi_j \xleftarrow{\$} \{0,1\}^{\log(p)} \setminus \{\xi_i\}_{i \in [0,j-1]}$
return ξ_j

Oracle GCMP(ξ, ξ', b)

if $\xi \notin \{\xi_i\}_{i \in [0,j]}$ **or** $\xi' \notin \{\xi_i\}_{i \in [0,j]}$
  then return $\bot$
$i := \min\{k \in [0, j] \mid \xi = \xi_k\}$
$i' := \min\{k \in [0, j] \mid \xi' = \xi_k\}$
$j := j + 1$; $a_j := a_i + (-1)^b a_{i'}$
$P_j := P_i + (-1)^b P_{i'}$
return ENC()

Fig. 4. Game_0 (which only includes the dashed boxes) is the GGM version of OMDL. Game_1 (including all but the gray boxes) introduces the polynomials that represent the information that $\mathcal{A}$ obtains, and aborts when Game_0 cannot be simulated with polynomials. In Game_2 (including all but the dashed boxes) we eliminate the use of scalars (except for the abort condition) in oracles ENC and DLOG.

<u>CHANGING THE ABORT CONDITION.</u> The aim of Game_3 is precisely to modify the abort condition so that it does not use $\vec{x}$ anymore. Figure 5 recalls Game_2 and defines Game_3 by not including the dashed and the gray box. In Game_3 the challenger does not abort in the procedure ENC. This means that if $P_j - P_i \notin \mathsf{Span}(L)$ for some i, the challenger creates a string $\xi_j \neq \xi_i$ even when $P_j(\vec{x}) = P_i(\vec{x})$. This means that the simulation of the game is not correct anymore; but we will catch these inconsistencies and abort in the oracle DLOG.

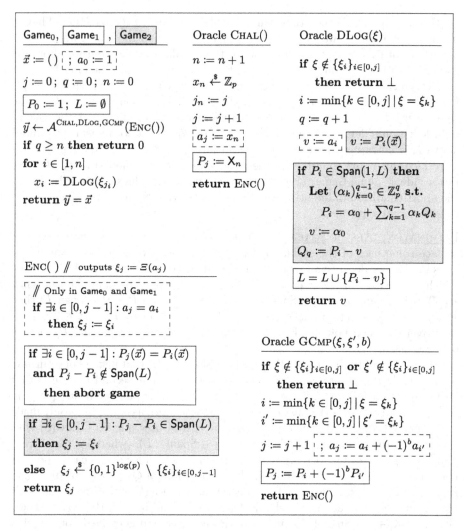

For concreteness consider the following example: let $\vec{x} = (x_1)$ and suppose $\mathcal{A}$ built the polynomials $P_{i_1} = x_1$ using the oracle GCMP and $P_{i_2} = \mathsf{X}_1$ using the oracle CHAL; suppose also that $\mathcal{A}$ has not queried DLOG yet, thus $L = \emptyset$. If $i_1 < i_2$ then Game_2 aborts on the call ENC() which encodes P_{i_2}, since $P_{i_1}(\vec{x}) = P_{i_2}(\vec{x})$ and $P_{i_2} - P_{i_1} \notin \mathsf{Span}(L)$. In contrast, in Game_3 the challenger defines $\xi_{i_1} \neq \xi_{i_2}$, which is inconsistent. But the abort will now happen during a call to DLOG.

Suppose $\mathcal{A}$ queries DLOG(ξ_{i_3}), with $\xi_{i_3} = \Xi(2\mathsf{X}_1 + 2)$. Game_3 now adds the polynomial $Q_1 = 2\mathsf{X}_1 + 2 - (2x_1 + 2) = 2(\mathsf{X}_1 - x_1)$ to L and checks for an inconsistency of this answer with all the polynomials that $\mathcal{A}$ computed. Since it finds that $P_{i_1} - P_{i_2} = x_1 - \mathsf{X}_1 \in \mathsf{Span}(L)$ but $\xi_{i_1} \neq \xi_{i_2}$, the game aborts. But Game_3 should also abort even if $\mathcal{A}$ does not query the oracle DLOG. This was precisely the reason for adding the final calls of the game to the oracle DLOG in Game_0. Since $P_{j_i} = \mathsf{X}_i$ and the challenger calls $x_i \leftarrow$ DLOG(ξ_{j_i}) for $i \in [1, n]$ at the end, the challenger makes the query DLOG(ξ_{j_1}), which adds $\mathsf{X}_1 - x_1$ to L, after which we have $P_{i_1} - P_{i_2} \in \mathsf{Span}(L)$ and therefore an abort.

More generally, in Game_3 the oracle DLOG aborts if there exists $(i_1, i_2) \in [0, j]^2$ such that $P_{i_1} - P_{i_2} \in \mathsf{Span}(L)$ and $\xi_{i_1} \neq \xi_{i_2}$. In the proof of Theorem 1 we show that this abort condition is equivalent to the abort condition in Game_2.

ELIMINATING ALL USES OF $\vec{x}$. In Game_3 the only remaining part that uses $\vec{x}$ is the operation $v := P_i(\vec{x})$ in oracle DLOG. Our final game hop will replace this by an equivalent operation. In Game_4, also presented in Fig. 5, the challenger samples v uniformly from $\mathbb{Z}_p$ instead of evaluating P_i on the challenge. In the proof of Theorem 1, we will show that since the distribution of $P_i(\vec{x})$ is uniform for a fixed P_i, this change does not affect the game.

This is the only difference between Game_4 and Game_3, but since this modification removes all uses of $\vec{x}$ for the challenger, we rewrite Game_4 explicitly in Fig. 6, where we define $\vec{x}$ only after $\mathcal{A}$ outputs $\vec{y}$. Game_4 is thus easily seen to be impossible (except with negligible probability) to win for $\mathcal{A}$. The reason is that $\mathcal{A}$ cannot make enough queries to DLOG to constrain the construction of $\vec{x}$ at the end of the game and therefore cannot predict the challenge $\vec{x}$. We now make the intuition given above formal in the following theorem.

3.3 Formal Proof

Theorem 1. *Let $\mathcal{A}$ be an adversary that solves OMDL in a generic group of prime order p, making at most m oracle queries. Then*

$$\boldsymbol{Adv}_{\mathcal{A}}^{OMDLGGM} \leq \frac{m^2}{p - m^2} + \frac{1}{p}.$$

Proof of Theorem 1. The proof will proceed as follows: we first compute the statistical distance between Game_0, which is OMDLGGM, and Game_1 (Fig. 4); we then show that Game_1, Game_2, Game_3 and Game_4 (Figs. 4 and 5) are equivalently distributed; and finally we upper-bound the probability of winning Game_4 (Fig. 6).

Game_2, $\boxed{\mathsf{Game}_3}$, $\boxed{\mathsf{Game}_4}$

$\vec{x} := ()$
$j := 0;\ q := 0;\ n := 0$
$P_0 := 1;\ L := \emptyset$
$\vec{y} \leftarrow \mathcal{A}^{\text{CHAL,DLOG,GCMP}}(\text{ENC}())$
if $q \geq n$ **then return** 0
for $i \in [1, n]$
  $x_i := \text{DLOG}(\xi_{j_i})$
return $\vec{y} = \vec{x}$

Oracle CHAL()

$j := j + 1;\ n := n + 1$
$x_n \xleftarrow{\$} \mathbb{Z}_p;\ j_n := j$
$P_j := \mathsf{X}_n$
return ENC()

ENC() // outputs ξ_j which encodes P_j

// Abort condition in Game_2 only
if $\exists i \in [0, j-1] : P_j(\vec{x}) = P_i(\vec{x})$
  and $P_j - P_i \notin \mathsf{Span}(L)$
  then abort game
if $\exists i \in [0, j-1] : P_j - P_i \in \mathsf{Span}(L)$
  then $\xi_j := \xi_i$
else
  $\xi_j \xleftarrow{\$} \{0,1\}^{\log(p)} \setminus \{\xi_i\}_{i \in [0, j-1]}$
return ξ_j

Oracle DLOG(ξ)

if $\xi \notin \{\xi_i\}_{i\in[0,j]}$ **then return** $\perp$
$i := \min\{k \in [0, j] \mid \xi = \xi_k\}$
$q := q + 1$
$v := P_i(\vec{x})$ $\boxed{;\ v \xleftarrow{\$} \mathbb{Z}_p}$
if $P_i \in \mathsf{Span}(1, L)$ **then**
  let $(\alpha_k)_{k=0}^{q-1} \in \mathbb{Z}_p^q$ **s.t.** $P_i = \alpha_0 + \sum_{k=1}^{q-1} \alpha_k Q_k$
  $v := \alpha_0$
$Q_q := P_i - v;\ L = L \cup \{P_i - v\}$

// Abort condition in Game_3 and Game_4 only
if $\exists (i_1, i_2) \in [0, j]^2 : P_{i_1} - P_{i_2} \in \mathsf{Span}(L)$
  and $\xi_{i_1} \neq \xi_{i_2}$
  then abort game
return v

Oracle GCMP(ξ, ξ', b)

if $\xi \notin \{\xi_i\}_{i\in[0,j]}$ **or** $\xi' \notin \{\xi_i\}_{i\in[0,j]}$
  then return $\perp$
$i := \min\{k \in [0, j] \mid \xi = \xi_k\}$
$i' := \min\{k \in [0, j] \mid \xi' = \xi_k\}$
$j := j + 1$
$P_j := P_i + (-1)^b P_{i'}$
return ENC()

Fig. 5. In Game_3 we move the abort condition from ENC to the oracle DLOG, so it can be checked without using scalars. The only remaining use is then "$v := P_i(\vec{x})$" in oracle DLOG. Game_4 instead pick the output x uniformly at random.

PRELIMINARY RESULTS. We start with proving three useful invariants of the polynomials P_i and the set L which are introduced in Game_1. The first one is:

$$\forall i \in [0, j] : \ P_i(\vec{x}) = a_i. \tag{7}$$

This holds in Game_1 and justifies replacing all occurrences of a_i by $P_i(\vec{x})$ in Game_2 in Fig. 5. To prove this, we show that each time the games introduce a new polynomial P_j, we have $P_j(\vec{x}) = a_j$.

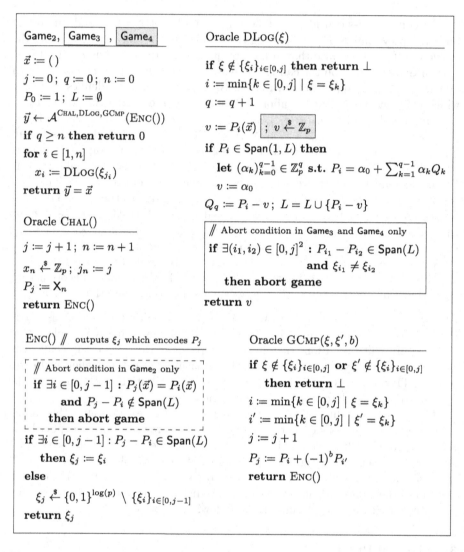

Game_4

$j := 0;\ q := 0;\ n := 0$
$P_0 := 1;\ L := \emptyset$
$\vec{y} \leftarrow \mathcal{A}^{\text{CHAL},\text{DLOG},\text{GCMP}}(\text{ENC}())$
if $q \geq n$ **then return** 0
for $i \in [1, n]$
  $x_i := \text{DLOG}(\xi_{j_i})$
return $\vec{y} = \vec{x}$

Oracle $\text{CHAL}()$

$j := j + 1;\ n := n + 1$
$P_j := \mathsf{X}_n;\ j_n := j$
return $\text{ENC}()$

Oracle $\text{DLOG}(\xi)$

if $\xi \notin \{\xi_i\}_{i \in [0,j]}$ **then return** $\bot$
$i := \min\{k \in [0, j] \mid \xi = \xi_k\}$
$q := q + 1;\ v \xleftarrow{\$} \mathbb{Z}_p$
if $P_i \in \mathsf{Span}(1, L)$ **then**
  let $(\alpha_k)_{k=0}^{q-1} \in \mathbb{Z}_p^q$ **s.t.** $P_i = \alpha_0 + \sum_{k=1}^{q-1} \alpha_k Q_k$
  $v := \alpha_0$
$Q_q := P_i - v;\ L = L \cup \{P_i - v\}$
if $\exists (i_1, i_2) \in [0, j]^2 : P_{i_1} - P_{i_2} \in \mathsf{Span}(L)$ **and** $\xi_{i_1} \neq \xi_{i_2}$
  then abort game
return v

$\text{ENC}()$ // outputs ξ_j which encodes P_j

if $\exists i \in [0, j-1] : P_j - P_i \in \mathsf{Span}(L)$
 then $\xi_j := \xi_i$
else
  $\xi_j \xleftarrow{\$} \{0,1\}^{\log(p)} \setminus \{\xi_i\}_{i \in [0, j-1]}$
return ξ_j

Oracle $\text{GCMP}(\xi, \xi', b)$

if $\xi \notin \{\xi_i\}_{i \in [0,j]}$ **or** $\xi' \notin \{\xi_i\}_{i \in [0,j]}$
  then return $\bot$
$i := \min\{k \in [0, j] \mid \xi = \xi_k\}$
$i' := \min\{k \in [0, j] \mid \xi' = \xi_k\}$
$j := j + 1$
$P_j := P_i + (-1)^b P_{i'}$
return $\text{ENC}()$

Fig. 6. Final game Game_4 does not use $\vec{x}$ in the oracles anymore. It defines the challenge $\vec{x}$ after $\mathcal{A}$ gave its output and this is what makes it simple for us to prove it is hard to win for $\mathcal{A}$.

We prove this by induction. Initially, $P_0 = 1$ and $a_0 = 1$ so the statement holds for $j = 0$. Now suppose it is true for all $i \in [0, j-1]$. We show it is true for j. Polynomial P_j can be built either by oracle CHAL or by oracle GCMP:

- In oracle CHAL, $P_j := \mathsf{X}_n$ and $a_j := x_n$ so we have $P_j(\vec{x}) = x_n = a_j$.
- In oracle GCMP, $P_j := P_i + (-1)^b P_{i'}$ and $a_j := a_i + (-1)^b a_{i'}$ so we have $P_j(\vec{x}) := P_i(\vec{x}) + (-1)^b P_{i'}(\vec{x}) = a_i + (-1)^b a_{i'} = a_j$.

This proves (7).

We next show that the following holds in Game_1, Game_2 and Game_3:

$$\forall Q \in \mathsf{Span}(L),\ Q(\vec{x}) = 0 \tag{8}$$

(in the other games either L or $\vec{x}$ are not defined). For $L = \{Q_1, \ldots, Q_q\}$ if $Q \in \mathsf{Span}(L)$ then $Q = \sum_{k=1}^{q} \alpha_k Q_k$. To show (8), it suffices to show that for all $k \in [1, q]$ we have $Q_k(\vec{x}) = 0$.

For $k \in [0, q]$, Q_k is defined during the k-th call to DLOG on some input ξ. In Game_1, the oracle finds i such that $\xi_i = \xi$ and sets $v := a_i$ and $Q_k := P_i - v$, so we get $Q_k(\vec{x}) = P_i(\vec{x}) - a_i$. Using the first result (7), we get that (8) holds. In Game_2 and Game_3 the oracle sets $v := P_i(\vec{x})$ so we directly get $Q_k(\vec{x}) = P_i(\vec{x}) - P_i(\vec{x}) = 0$

The third result we will use holds (assuming the game did not abort) in Game_1, Game_2, Game_3 and Game_4:

$$\forall j \geq 1\, \forall i \in [0, j-1] : \xi_j = \xi_i \Leftrightarrow P_j - P_i \in \mathsf{Span}(L) \; . \tag{9}$$

We first prove

$$\forall j \geq 1\, \forall i \in [0, j-1] : \;\; \xi_j = \xi_i \Rightarrow P_j - P_i \in \mathsf{Span}(L)$$

by induction. We show that this holds for $j = 1$ and all other $j > 0$ and suppose that for some $i^* \in [0, j-1]$, $\xi_j = \xi_{i^*}$. We show that $P_j - P_{i^*} \in \mathsf{Span}(L)$.

- In Game_2, Game_3 and Game_4, since ξ_j is not a new random string when it is defined, thus for some $i_1 \in [0, j-1]$ we had $P_j - P_{i_1} \in \mathsf{Span}(L)$ and so the game defined $\xi_j := \xi_{i_1}$. This implies that $\xi_{i_1} = \xi_{i^*}$, and since $i_1 < j$, using the induction hypothesis, we get that $P_{i_1} - P_{i^*} \in \mathsf{Span}(L)$ and furthermore

  $$P_j - P_{i^*} = (P_j - P_{i_1}) - (P_{i_1} - P_{i^*}) \in \mathsf{Span}(L) \; .$$

  Now the situation is simpler when $j = 1$: we must have $i_1 = i^* = 0$ so

  $$P_j - P_{i_1} = P_j - P_{i^*} = P_1 - P_0 \in \mathsf{Span}(L) \; .$$

- In Game_1 the proof is almost the same: since ξ_j is not a new random string, thus for some $i_1 \in [0, j-1]$ we had $P_j(\vec{x}) = P_{i_1}(\vec{x})$, so the game defined $\xi_j := \xi_{i_1}$. Since the game did not abort, "$P_j(\vec{x}) = P_{i_1}(\vec{x})$ **and** $P_j - P_{i_1} \notin \mathsf{Span}(L)$" does not hold, and thus $P_j - P_{i_1} \in \mathsf{Span}(L)$. From here the proof proceeds as for the other games above, and thus $P_j - P_{i^*} \in \mathsf{Span}(L)$. When $j = 1$, we have $i^* = 0$ and $P_1 - P_0 \in \mathsf{Span}(L)$, as otherwise the game aborts.

We now prove the other implication:

$$\forall j \geq 1\, \forall i \in [0, j-1] : P_j - P_i \in \mathsf{Span}(L) \Rightarrow \xi_j = \xi_i,$$

again by induction. Using the same method as before we can argue that this is true for $j = 1$. For $j > 1$, when ENC() defines ξ_j, if for some $i^* \in [0, j-1]$ we have $P_j - P_{i^*} \in \mathsf{Span}(L)$ then we show that ξ_j is assigned $\xi_j = \xi_{i^*}$.

- In Game_2, Game_3 and Game_4, since for some $i_1 \in [0, j-1] : P_j - P_{i_1} \in \mathsf{Span}(L)$, the game defines $\xi_j := \xi_{i_1}$. And since

  $$P_{i^*} - P_{i_1} = (P_{i^*} - P_j) + (P_j - P_{i_1}) \in \mathsf{Span}(L),$$

  by induction we get $\xi_{i_1} = \xi_{i^*}$ which yields $\xi_j = \xi_{i^*}$.

- In Game_1, since we know that $(P_j - P_{i^*})(\vec{x}) = 0$ from the (8), we get that for some $i_1 \in [0, j-1] : P_j(\vec{x}) = P_{i_1}(\vec{x})$. Since the game did not abort, we know that $P_j - P_{i_1} \in \mathsf{Span}(L)$, so by the same argument as before, we get $\xi_j = \xi_{i^*}$.

Game_0 TO Game_1. We now compare Game_0 to Game_1. The only difference between the two is when Game_1 aborts in the procedure ENC() on event

$$\exists i \in [0, j-1] \textbf{ such that } P_j(\vec{x}) = P_i(\vec{x}) \textbf{ and } P_j - P_i \notin \mathsf{Span}(L)\ . \qquad (10)$$

We call this event F. Since ENC is called at most m times, we get:

$$\mathbf{Adv}_{\mathcal{A}}^{\mathsf{Game}_0} \leq \mathbf{Adv}_{\mathcal{A}}^{\mathsf{Game}_1} + m \cdot \Pr[F]. \qquad (11)$$

We now upper-bound $\Pr[F]$. Before a call to ENC, the oracle defines P_j. Consider a fixed $i \in [0, j-1]$ and define $P := P_j - P_i$. We will upper-bound the probability that

$$P_j(\vec{x}) - P_i(\vec{x}) = P(\vec{x}) = 0$$

with $P := P_j - P_i \notin \mathsf{Span}(L)$.

Since $\mathcal{A}$ does not know $\vec{x}$ one might consider applying the Schwartz-Zippel lemma. But we cannot, since $\mathcal{A}$ knows information on $\vec{x}$. From $\mathcal{A}$'s point of view, $\vec{x}$ is not uniformly chosen from $\mathbb{Z}_p^n$, since it satisfies $Q(\vec{x}) = 0$ for all $Q \in L$ (using (8)). We write $L = \{Q_1, \ldots, Q_q\}$, and using the notation from Lemma 1 $Q_{q+1} := P$.

$\mathcal{A}$ also knows that if for some indexes i_1, i_2 it was given $\xi_{i_1} \neq \xi_{i_2}$ then $P_{i_1}(\vec{x}) \neq P_{i_2}(\vec{x})$. We can reformulate this by writing $D_{\vec{\imath}} = P_{i_1} - P_{i_2}$ for $\vec{\imath} \in I := \{(i_1, i_2) \in [0, j-1]^2 \mid \xi_{i_1} \neq \xi_{i_2}\}$. $\mathcal{A}$ knows that $D_{\vec{\imath}}(\vec{x}) \neq 0$. Using the notation of Lemma 1 we get that

$$\vec{x} \in \mathcal{C} := \Big(\bigcap_{j \in [1,q]} \mathcal{Q}_j \Big) \setminus \Big(\bigcup_{i \in I} \mathcal{D}_i \Big).$$

Our goal is to apply Lemma 1 to upper-bound $\Pr_{\vec{x} \leftarrow \mathcal{C}}[P(\vec{x}) = 0]$. We need to verify that the three premises of the lemma are satisfied, which are: from $\mathcal{A}$'s point of view, $\vec{x} \in \mathcal{C}$ is picked uniformly at random, $\mathcal{Q}_{q+1} \cap \mathcal{C} \neq \emptyset$ and $\vec{Q}_{q+1}$ is independent of $(\vec{Q}_i)_{i \in [1,q]}$.

$\vec{x}$ IS CHOSEN UNIFORMLY IN $\mathcal{C}$. To show this, we fix the randomness (of the challenger and the adversary) of the game (which means the order in which the ξ_i are picked is deterministic) and we consider the transcript $\pi(\vec{x})$ of what $\mathcal{A}$ sees during the game when the secret is chosen as $\vec{x}$: $\pi(\vec{x}) = (\xi_0, \ldots, \xi_{j-1}, v_1, \ldots, v_q)$ (In this transcript, the strings ξ_i are ordered and so are the v_i, but we implicitly suppose that before the query v_k there was a query v_{k-1} or ξ_{i_k} and after the query v_k there was either a query v_{k+1} or $\xi_{i'_k}$. We do not formalize this.)

The transcript π corresponds to all the output of the oracles that were given to $\mathcal{A}$: The ξ_i are the outputs of GCMP and CHAL, and the v_i are the outputs of DLOG. The transcript $\pi(\vec{x})$ only depends on the challenge $\vec{x}$. What is important to notice is that for all $\vec{y} \in \mathcal{C}$: $\pi(\vec{y}) = \pi(\vec{x})$. Indeed, if we call $\pi(\vec{y}) = (\xi'_0, \ldots, \xi'_{j-1}, v'_1, \ldots, v'_q)$ we can show by induction that $\xi'_i = \xi_i$ and $v'_k = v_k$ for all $i \in [1, j-1]$ and $k \in [1, q]$.

- Let $k \in [1, q]$; we show that $v_k = v'_k$: in both challenges $\vec{x}$ and $\vec{y}$, since the transcript $\mathcal{A}$ received is the same by the induction hypothesis, it behaves the same way and calls DLOG on input ξ. The oracle DLOG then picks $i = \min\{j \mid \xi_j = \xi\}$ which is the same in both cases by the induction hypothesis. DLOG computes $v_k = P_i(\vec{x})$ and defines $Q_i := P_i - v_k$ for the challenge $\vec{x}$ while it computes $v'_k = P_i(\vec{y})$ and $Q'_i := P_i - v'_k$ for the challenge $\vec{y}$. Now Since $\vec{y} \in \mathcal{C}$, we have in particular $\vec{y} \in \mathcal{Q}_i$, so we know that $Q_k(\vec{y}) = P_i(\vec{y}) - v_k = 0$. This gives $P_i(\vec{y}) = v'_k = v_k$ and $Q'_k = Q_k$.
- Let $k \in [1, j-1]$; we show that $\xi_k = \xi'_k$: for both challenges $\vec{x}$ and $\vec{y}$, since the transcript $\mathcal{A}$ received is the same by induction hypothesis, it behaves the same way and calls either CHAL or GCMP. In both cases the game creates a polynomial P_k and calls the procedure ENC(), for which there are two cases:
  1: $\forall i \in [0, k-1] : P_k(\vec{x}) \neq P_i(\vec{x})$. The game with challenge $\vec{x}$ outputs a new random ξ_k, which means $\xi_k \neq \xi_i$ for $i \in [1, k-1]$. Since $\vec{y} \in \mathcal{C}$, we know that for all $i \in [0, k-1]$, $\vec{y} \notin \mathcal{D}_{i,k} = \{\vec{z} \,:\, (P_i - P_k)(\vec{z}) = 0 \textbf{ and } \xi_i \neq \xi_k\}$ This means that for all $i \in [0, k-1]$, since $\xi_i \neq \xi_k$, we have $P_i(\vec{y}) \neq P_k(\vec{y})$, so the game also chooses ξ'_k as a new random string. Since we fixed the randomness of the game, we get $\xi_k = \xi'_k$.
  2: $\exists i^* \in [0, k-1] : P_k(\vec{x}) = P_{i^*}(\vec{x})$. The game defines $\xi_k := \xi_i$ for the challenge $\vec{x}$. Since the game did not abort for $k < j$, we know that $P_k - P_{i^*} \in \mathsf{Span}(L)$. Now since $L = (Q_i)_i$ and $\vec{y} \in \bigcap_{i \in [1,q]} \mathcal{Q}_i$, we also get $(P_k - P_{i^*})(\vec{y}) = 0$. So the game defines $\xi'_k := \xi'_i = \xi_i = \xi_k$, by the induction hypothesis and the preliminary result (9).

  In both cases we get that $\xi_k = \xi'_k$.

Since the transcript that $\mathcal{A}$ sees is the same for all elements in $\mathcal{C}$, $\mathcal{A}$ can only make a uniform guess on which element of $\mathcal{C}$ is the challenge. Thus from $\mathcal{A}$'s point of view, $\vec{x}$ is chosen uniformly at random in $\mathcal{C}$.

$\mathcal{Q}_{q+1} \cap \mathcal{C} \neq \emptyset$. Since $\mathcal{Q}_{q+1} = \{\vec{x} \in \mathbb{Z}_p : P(\vec{x}) = 0\}$, if we had $\mathcal{C} \cap \mathcal{Q}_{q+1} = \emptyset$, then $P(\vec{x}) \neq 0$ for all $\vec{x} \in \mathcal{C}$, and thus $\Pr_{\vec{x} \xleftarrow{\$} \mathcal{C}}[P(\vec{x}) = 0] = 0$. In this case, there is no need to upper-bound the probability, which is why we assume that $\mathcal{Q}_{q+1} \cap \mathcal{C} \neq \emptyset$.

$\vec{Q}_{q+1}$ IS INDEPENDENT OF $(\vec{Q}_i)_{i \in [1,q]}$. Recall that $\vec{P} = (p_k)_{k \in [1,n]}$ is the vector representing the polynomial $P - P(\vec{0}) = \sum_{k=1}^{n} p_k \mathsf{X}_k$. We assume that $\vec{Q}_{q+1}$ is dependent of $(\vec{Q}_i)_{i \in [1,q]}$ and then show that this contradicts the previous premise $\mathcal{Q}_{q+1} \cap \mathcal{C} \neq \emptyset$. Assume thus that for some α:

$$Q_{q+1} - Q_{q+1}(\vec{0}) = \sum_{k=1}^{q} \alpha_k \big(Q_k - Q_k(\vec{0})\big).$$

With $\alpha := Q_{q+1}(\vec{0}) + \sum_{k=1}^{q} \alpha_k Q_k(\vec{0})$ and $Q := \sum_{k=1}^{q} \alpha_k Q_k$, we can write this as $Q_{q+1} = \alpha + Q$ with $\alpha \in \mathbb{Z}_p$ and $Q \in \mathsf{Span}(L)$. Now since we are in event F, defined in (10), we have $Q_{q+1} = P \notin \mathsf{Span}(L)$, which implies $\alpha \neq 0$ (otherwise $P = Q \in \mathsf{Span}(L)$). Since $\mathcal{C} \subset \mathcal{Q}_i$ we have that for all $i \in [1, q]$ and all $\vec{x} \in \mathcal{C}$:

$Q_i(\vec{x}) = 0$, and thus $Q(\vec{x}) = 0$. From this, we have $Q_{q+1}(\vec{x}) = \alpha + Q(\vec{x}) = \alpha$. Thus, $Q_{q+1}(\vec{x}) \neq 0$ for all $\vec{x} \in \mathcal{C}$, which implies $\mathcal{C} \cap \mathcal{Q}_{q+1} = \emptyset$, which contradicts the previous assumption. We thus proved that $\vec{Q}_{q+1}$ is independent of $(\vec{Q}_i)_{i\in[1,q]}$.

APPLYING LEMMA 1. Since all its premises are satisfied, we can apply Lemma 1 and obtain:

$$\Pr_{\vec{x}\leftarrow\mathcal{C}}\left[P(\vec{x}) = 0\right] = \Pr_{\vec{x}\leftarrow\mathcal{C}}\left[Q_{q+1}(\vec{x}) = 0\right] \leq \frac{1}{p - |I|},$$

with $|I| \leq j^2 \leq m^2$. Since we need to test this with $P = P_j - P_i$ for all $i \in [0, j-1]$, we get $\Pr[F] \leq \frac{m}{p - m^2}$ and from (11):

$$\mathbf{Adv}_{\mathcal{A}}^{\mathsf{Game}_0} \leq \mathbf{Adv}_{\mathcal{A}}^{\mathsf{Game}_1} + \frac{m^2}{p - m^2}. \tag{12}$$

Game_1 TO Game_2. There are three changes in Game_2, which we show do not affect the distributions of the game. First, we replace a_i by $P_i(\vec{x})$ in oracle DLOG, which is equivalent by (7).

Second, in ENC, we replace the condition

$$\textbf{if}\ \exists i \in [0, j-1] : P_j(\vec{x}) = P_i(\vec{x})\ \textbf{then}\ \xi_j := \xi_i$$

by

$$\textbf{if}\ \exists i \in [0, j-1] : P_j - P_i \in \mathsf{Span}(L)\ \textbf{then}\ \xi_j := \xi_i.$$

We show that this new condition does not affect the output of ENC(). There are two cases for $P_j(\vec{x})$:

Case 1: $\exists i^* \in [0, j-1] : P_j(\vec{x}) = P_{i^*}(\vec{x})$. We have either
- $P_j - P_{i^*} \in \mathsf{Span}(L)$, and in this case Game_1 and Game_2 both set $\xi_j = \xi_{i^*}$ and output ξ_j using (9); or
- $P_j - P_{i^*} \notin \mathsf{Span}(L)$, meaning that both Game_1 and Game_2 abort since "$P_j - P_{i^*} \notin \mathsf{Span}(L)$ **and** $P_j(\vec{x}) = P_{i^*}(\vec{x})$" is the abort condition.

Case 2: $\forall i \in [0, j-1]\ P_j(\vec{x}) \neq P_i(\vec{x})$. Since, by 8, all polynomials in $\mathsf{Span}(L)$ vanish at $\vec{x}$, this implies $\forall i \in [0, j-1] : P_j - P_i \notin \mathsf{Span}(L)$. In this case both Game_1 and Game_2 output a random new string ξ_j.

The third change in Game_2, in the oracle DLOG, does not change the output either: in Game_1 the DLOG oracle always outputs $a_i = P_i(\vec{x})$. In Game_2, when $P_i \in \mathsf{Span}(L)$, the game uses the decomposition $P_i = \alpha_0 + \sum_{k=1}^{q-1} \alpha_k Q_k$, and since $Q_k(\vec{x}) = 0$ by (8), it outputs $P_i(\vec{x}) = \alpha_0$.

Together this yields:

$$\mathbf{Adv}_{\mathcal{A}}^{\mathsf{Game}_1} = \mathbf{Adv}_{\mathcal{A}}^{\mathsf{Game}_2}. \tag{13}$$

Game_2 TO Game_3. In this game hop we move the abort condition from the procedure ENC to the oracle DLOG. We show that the two abort conditions are equivalent, by showing the two implications of the equivalence:

IF Game_2 ABORTS THEN Game_3 ALSO ABORTS. If Game_2 aborts, it means that for a fixed index j^* the game found $i^* \in [0, j^*-1]$ such that $P_{j^*} - P_{i^*} \notin \mathsf{Span}(L)$ and $P_{j^*}(\vec{x}) = P_{i^*}(\vec{x})$. We show that Game_3 also aborts in this situation. Let $P := P_{j^*} - P_{i^*}$. At the end of Game_3 the challenger makes calls to DLOG on each challenge $P_{j_i} = \mathsf{X}_i$. This adds the corresponding polynomials $\mathsf{X}_i - x_i$ to L for all $i \in [1, n]$. With $P = P(\vec{0}) + \sum_{k=1}^{n} p_k \mathsf{X}_k$, we can write

$$P = \sum_{k=1}^{n} p_k(\mathsf{X}_k - x_k) + P(\vec{0}) + \sum_{k=1}^{n} p_k x_k.$$

Since $P(\vec{x}) = P_{j^*}(\vec{x}) - P_{i^*}(\vec{x})$, we have $P(\vec{x}) = 0$. On the other hand, by the equation above, we have $P(\vec{x}) = P(\vec{0}) + \sum_{k=1}^{n} p_k x_k$. Together, this yields $P = \sum_{k=1}^{n} p_k(\mathsf{X}_k - x_k)$, which means $P \in \mathsf{Span}(L)$ at the end of the game. At the time when Game_2 would have aborted, we had $P \notin \mathsf{Span}(L)$ and thus the game attributed two different strings $\xi_{i^*} \neq \xi_{j^*}$ to P_{i^*} and P_{j^*}, respectively. But at the end of Game_3, when L contains all $\mathsf{X}_i - x_i$ for $i \in [1, n]$, we have $P \in \mathsf{Span}(L)$. This means that one call to DLOG updated L so that $P \in \mathsf{Span}(L)$ and when this happened, since $\xi_{i^*} \neq \xi_{j^*}$, the abort condition in DLOG was satisfied and the game aborted

IF Game_3 ABORTS THEN Game_2 ALSO ABORTS. If Game_3 aborts, then on a call to DLOG we have $\exists (i_1, i_2) \in [0, j]^2$ such that $P_{i_1} - P_{i_2} \in \mathsf{Span}(L)$ and $\xi_{i_1} \neq \xi_{i_2}$. From $P_{i_1} - P_{i_2} \in \mathsf{Span}(L)$, using (8) we get $P_{i_1}(\vec{x}) = P_{i_2}(\vec{x})$. Suppose $i_1 < i_2$. The challenger in Game_2 used the procedure ENC() when the counter j was equal to i_2 to compute $\xi_{i_2} \neq \xi_{i_1}$. This means that at that moment, L contained fewer elements and we had $P_{i_2} - P_{i_1} \notin \mathsf{Span}(L)$. Since Game_2 aborts when $P_{i_1}(\vec{x}) = P_{i_2}(\vec{x})$ and $P_{i_2} - P_{i_1} \notin \mathsf{Span}(L)$, thus Game_2 aborts in this case.

Combining both implications yields

$$\mathbf{Adv}_{\mathcal{A}}^{\mathsf{Game}_2} = \mathbf{Adv}_{\mathcal{A}}^{\mathsf{Game}_3}. \tag{14}$$

Game_3 TO Game_4. The only difference between these games is in the oracle DLOG. Instead of computing $v := P_i(\vec{x})$, Game_4 picks a random $v \xleftarrow{\$} \mathbb{Z}_p$. We prove that after this modification, the distribution of the outputs of oracle DLOG remains the same. The difference between the two games occurs only when $P_i \notin \mathsf{Span}(1, L)$. Let us bound $\Pr_{\vec{x} \leftarrow \mathcal{C}}\left[P_i(\vec{x}) = v \textbf{ in } \mathsf{Game}_3\right]$, where $\vec{x} \in \mathcal{C}$ represents the information that $\mathcal{A}$ knows about $\vec{x}$, which we previously used in the first game hop.

We apply Lemma 1 again to bound this probability. Now since the game does not abort immediately when the inconsistency $P_{i_1}(\vec{x}) = P_{i_2}(\vec{x})$ and $\xi_{i_1} \neq \xi_{i_2}$ occurs, the inequalities on the strings level do not give $\mathcal{A}$ any information on what the evaluation $P_i(\vec{x})$ cannot be. This means that $\mathcal{C}$ is simpler than in the first game hop, namely

$$\mathcal{C} = \bigcap_{i \in [1,q]} \mathcal{Q}_i.$$

We define $Q_{q+1} := P_i - v$ and show that once again the three premises of Lemma 1 hold: $\vec{x} \in \mathcal{C}$ is picked uniformly at random, $\mathcal{Q}_{q+1} \cap \mathcal{C} \neq \emptyset$ and $\vec{Q}_{q+1}$ is independent of $(\vec{Q}_i)_{i\in[1,q]}$.

<u>$\vec{x}$ IS CHOSEN UNIFORMLY IN $\mathcal{C}$.</u> To show this, we again fix the randomness of the game and consider the transcript π that $\mathcal{A}$ sees during the game if a particular $\vec{x}$ is chosen: $\pi(\vec{x}) = (\xi_0, \ldots, \xi_{j-1}, v_1, \ldots, v_q)$, which contains all oracle outputs given to $\mathcal{A}$. We show that for all $\vec{y} \in \mathcal{C} : \pi(\vec{y}) = \pi(\vec{x})$. Indeed, for $\pi(\vec{y}) =: (\xi'_0, \ldots, \xi'_{j-1}, v'_1, \ldots, v'_q)$ we show by induction that $\xi'_i = \xi_i$ and $v'_k = v_k$ for all $i \in [1, j-1]$ and $k \in [1, q]$.

- Let $k \in [1, q]$; then $v_k = v'_k$ is showed exactly as in the first game hop (on page 22).
- Let $k \in [1, j-1]$; we show that $\xi_k = \xi'_k$: for both challenges $\vec{x}$ and $\vec{y}$, since the transcript $\mathcal{A}$ received is the same by induction hypothesis, $\mathcal{A}$ behaves the same way and calls either CHAL or GCMP. In both cases the game creates a polynomial P_k and calls ENC(), for which there are two cases:
  1: $\forall i \in [0, k-1] : P_k - P_i \notin \mathsf{Span}(L)$. Since this condition is independent of $\vec{x}$ and $\vec{y}$, for both the game outputs a new random string ξ_k and ξ'_k. Since we fixed the randomness of the game, we get $\xi_k = \xi'_k$.
  2: $\exists i^* \in [0, k-1] : P_k - P_{i^*} \in \mathsf{Span}(L)$. In this case the game defines $\xi_k := \xi_i$ and $\xi'_k := \xi'_i$ for both challenge $\vec{x}$ and $\vec{y}$. We get $\xi'_k := \xi'_i = \xi_i = \xi_k$ by the induction hypothesis and (9).

  In both cases we thus have $\xi_k = \xi'_k$.

As in first game hop, we conclude that $\mathcal{A}$ cannot distinguish between two different values $\vec{x} \in \mathcal{C}$ and so we can consider $\vec{x}$ to be chosen uniformly at random in $\mathcal{C}$.

<u>$\vec{Q}_{q+1}$ IS LINEARLY INDEPENDENT OF $(\vec{Q}_i)_{i\in[1,q]}$.</u> Recall that $P_i \notin \mathsf{Span}(1, L)$ and $Q_{q+1} := P_i - v$. If $\vec{Q}_{q+1}$ were linearly dependent of $(\vec{Q}_i)_{i\in[0,j]}$, then (using the same method as in the first game hop) we would have $Q_{q+1} = P_i - v = \alpha + Q$ with $\alpha \in \mathbb{Z}_p$ and $Q \in \mathsf{Span}(L)$. As this contradicts $P_i \notin \mathsf{Span}(1, L)$, we conclude that $\vec{Q}_{q+1}$ is linearly independent of $(\vec{Q}_i)_{i\in[1,q]}$.

<u>$\mathcal{Q}_{q+1} \cap \mathcal{C} \neq \emptyset$.</u> $\mathcal{C} = \bigcup_{i\in[1,q]} \mathcal{Q}_i$ is an affine space and $\vec{Q}_{q+1}$ is linearly independent of $(\vec{Q}_i)_{i\in[0,j]}$. This implies that $\mathcal{Q}_{q+1} \cap \mathcal{C}$ has dimension $\dim(\mathcal{C}) - 1$ and thus $\mathcal{Q}_{q+1} \cap \mathcal{C} \neq \emptyset$.

<u>APPLYING LEMMA 1.</u> Since its three premises are satisfied, Lemma 1 with $M := 0$ yields:

$$\Pr[\,Q_{q+1}(\vec{x}) = 0\,]_{\vec{x}\leftarrow\mathcal{C}} = \Pr_{\vec{x}\leftarrow\mathcal{C}}\left[P_i(\vec{x}) = v \textbf{ in } \mathsf{Game}_3\right] = \frac{1}{p}.$$

This means that in Game_3 the distribution of $P_i(\vec{x})$ is uniform, so the change we make does not affect the overall distribution of the game. We thus have

$$\mathbf{Adv}_{\mathcal{A}}^{\mathsf{Game}_3} = \mathbf{Adv}_{\mathcal{A}}^{\mathsf{Game}_4}. \tag{15}$$

Analysis of Game_4. We prove that $\mathcal{A}$ wins Game_4 at most with negligible probability $\frac{1}{p}$. To do this, we prove that at least one component of the vector $\vec{x}$ is picked uniformly at random *after* $\mathcal{A}$ outputs $\vec{y}$.

When $\mathcal{A}$ outputs $\vec{y}$, L contains q elements, so $\mathsf{dim}(\mathsf{Span}(L)) \leq q$. Since $q < n$, $\mathsf{Span}(1, L)$ has dimension at most $q+1$ and therefore at most n when the adversary outputs the vector $\vec{y}$. Since the dimension of $\mathsf{Span}(\mathsf{X}_1, \ldots, \mathsf{X}_n)$ is n and $1 \notin \mathsf{Span}(\mathsf{X}_1, \ldots, \mathsf{X}_n)$, we get that $\mathsf{Span}(\mathsf{X}_1, \ldots, \mathsf{X}_n)$ is not contained in $\mathsf{Span}(1, L)$. This means that there will be at least one index $i \in [1, n]$ such that $\mathsf{X}_i \notin \mathsf{Span}(1, L)$. We choose the smallest index i that verifies this. Then the oracle DLOG outputs a randomly sampled value x_i when called on ξ_{j_i}. This x_i is sampled randomly after the i-th coefficient of vector $\vec{y}$ output by $\mathcal{A}$ and we obtain: $\Pr[\vec{x} = \vec{y}] \leq \frac{1}{p}$. This yields:

$$\mathbf{Adv}_{\mathcal{A}}^{\mathsf{Game}_4} \leq \frac{1}{p}. \tag{16}$$

The theorem now follows from Eqs. (12), (13), (14), (15), and (16) □

4 OMCDH in the GGM

The OMCDH assumption (defined in Fig. 2), though similar to OMDL, is slightly more complex. In OMDL the adversary has access to a DLOG oracle and must solve DLOG challenges; in OMCDH the adversary has access to a CDH oracle and must solve CDH challenges. This CDH oracle enables the adversary to construct (encodings of) group elements corresponding to high-degree polynomials: on input $(\Xi(x), \Xi(y))$, the oracle returns $\Xi(xy)$, which in the "ideal" game is encoded as the product of the polynomials representing x and y. This makes using known proof techniques in the GGM impossible, since if their degree is not linearly bounded, $\mathcal{A}$ can build non-zero polynomials that evaluate to zero on the challenge with non-negligible probability. (E.g., $\mathsf{X}^p - \mathsf{X}$ evaluates to 0 everywhere in $\mathbb{Z}_p$.)

Given this, we can neither use the Schwartz-Zippel lemma (as it would only yield a non-negligible bound on the adversary's advantage) nor Lemma 1 (since it only applies to polynomials of degree 1). In fact, existing cryptanalysis, such as the attacks by Maurer and Wolf [MW96, Mau99]), precisely uses high-degree polynomials to break DL in groups of order p (when $p-1$ is smooth) when given a CDH oracle.

Since the GGM does not handle high-degree polynomials well, we will analyze the hardness of OMCDH by considering a *stronger* assumption instead, which we call OMCDH^{DL} and define in Fig. 7. This problem is analogous to OMCDH, except that the CDH oracle is replaced by a DLOG oracle. As the adversary has access to the same oracles as in the OMDL game, it can only build polynomials of degree at most 1, as seen in our proof of OMDL. In the full version [BFP21] we show that OMCDH^{DL} implies OMDL and that (modulo a polynomial number of group operations) OMCDH^{DL} implies OMCDH.

Game $\text{OMCDHDL}^{\mathcal{A}}_{\mathsf{GrGen}}(\lambda)$	Oracle $\textsc{Chal}()$	Oracle $\textsc{DLog}(X)$
$(p, \mathbb{G}, G) \leftarrow \mathsf{GrGen}(1^\lambda)$	$x \xleftarrow{\$} \mathbb{Z}_p\,;\ X := xG$	$q := q + 1$
$\vec{Z} := ()\,;\ q := 0$	$y \xleftarrow{\$} \mathbb{Z}_p\,;\ Y := yG$	$x := \log_G(X)$
$\vec{Z}' \leftarrow \mathcal{A}^{\textsc{Chal},\textsc{DLog}}(p, \mathbb{G}, G)$	$\vec{Z} := \vec{Z} \parallel (xyG)$	**return** x
return $\left(\vec{Z} = \vec{Z}' \ \wedge\ q < \lvert\vec{Z}\rvert\right)$	**return** (X, Y)	

Fig. 7. The OMCDH^{DL} problem

In the full version [BFP21] we formally prove the hardness of OMCDH^{DL} in the generic group model. This is done following the same strategy as for OMDL in Theorem 1 ; the games hops are the same, only the final analysis of the last game is different, since the winning condition is different, which yields a different winning probability at the end. This is summarized in Theorem 2 below.

Proposition 1 (OMCDL^{DL} implies OMCDH). *In a cyclic group of order p, let $\mathcal{A}$ be an adversary that solves OMCDH using at most m group operations and q calls to* DLOG. *Then there exists an adversary mathcalB that solves $OMCDH^{DL}$ using at most $m + 2q\lceil\log(p)\rceil$ group operations.*

The proof is straightforward; the reduction answers CDH oracle queries by making queries to its DLOG oracle.

Theorem 2. *Let $\mathcal{A}$ be an adversary that solves $OMCDH^{DL}$ in a generic group of order p, making at most m oracle queries. Then*

$$\boldsymbol{Adv}_{\mathcal{A}}^{OMCDH\text{-}GGM} \leq \frac{1}{p-1} + \frac{2m}{p} + \frac{m^2}{p - m^2}.$$

A formal proof can be found in the full version [BFP21]. Combining this with Proposition 1, we obtain the following corollary, which proves the security of OMCDH in the generic group model.

Corollary 1. *Let $\mathcal{A}$ be an adversary that solves $OMCDH^{DL}$ in a generic group of order p, making at most m oracle queries and q* CDH *oracle queries. Then*

$$\boldsymbol{Adv}_{\mathcal{A}}^{OMCDH\text{-}GGM} \leq \frac{1}{p-1} + \frac{2(m + 2q\lceil\log(p)\rceil)}{p} + \frac{(m + 2q\lceil\log(p)\rceil)^2}{p - (m + 2q\lceil\log(p)\rceil)^2}.$$

Acknowledgements. We would like to thank the reviewers for their valuable feedback. The second author is supported by the Vienna Science and Technology Fund (WWTF) through project VRG18-002. This work is funded in part by the MSR–Inria Joint Centre.

References

[BB08] Boneh, D., Boyen, X.: Short signatures without random oracles and the SDH assumption in bilinear groups. J. Cryptol. **21**(2), 149–177 (2008)

[BBG05] Boneh, D., Boyen, X., Goh, E.-J.: Hierarchical identity based encryption with constant size ciphertext. In: Cramer, R. (ed.) EUROCRYPT 2005. LNCS, vol. 3494, pp. 440–456. Springer, Heidelberg (2005). https://doi.org/10.1007/11426639_26

[BCJ08] Bagherzandi, A., Cheon, J.H., Jarecki, S.: Multisignatures secure under the discrete logarithm assumption and a generalized forking lemma. In: Ning, P., Syverson, P.F., Jha, S. (eds.) ACM CCS 2008, pp. 449–458. ACM Press (2008)

[BDL+12] Bernstein, D.J., Duif, N., Lange, T., Schwabe, P., Yang, B.-Y.: High-speed high-security signatures. J. Cryptogr. Eng. **2**(2), 77–89 (2012)

[BDN18] Boneh, D., Drijvers, M., Neven, G.: Compact multi-signatures for smaller blockchains. In: Peyrin, T., Galbraith, S. (eds.) ASIACRYPT 2018, Part II. LNCS, vol. 11273, pp. 435–464. Springer, Cham (2018). https://doi.org/10.1007/978-3-030-03329-3_15

[BFL20] Bauer, B., Fuchsbauer, G., Loss, J.: A classification of computational assumptions in the algebraic group model. In: Micciancio, D., Ristenpart, T. (eds.) CRYPTO 2020, Part II. LNCS, vol. 12171, pp. 121–151. Springer, Cham (2020). https://doi.org/10.1007/978-3-030-56880-1_5

[BFP21] Bauer, B., Fuchsbauer, G., Plouviez, A.: The one-more discrete logarithm assumption in the generic group model. Cryptology ePrint Archive, Report 2021/866 (2021). https://ia.cr/2021/866

[BL13] Baldimtsi, F., Lysyanskaya, A.: On the security of one-witness blind signature schemes. In: Sako, K., Sarkar, P. (eds.) ASIACRYPT 2013, Part II. LNCS, vol. 8270, pp. 82–99. Springer, Heidelberg (2013). https://doi.org/10.1007/978-3-642-42045-0_5

[BLL+21] Benhamouda, F., Lepoint, T., Loss, J., Orrù, M., Raykova, M.: On the (in)security of ROS. In: Canteaut, A., Standaert, F.-X. (eds.) EUROCRYPT 2021, Part I. LNCS, vol. 12696, pp. 33–53. Springer, Cham (2021). https://doi.org/10.1007/978-3-030-77870-5_2

[BMV08] Bresson, E., Monnerat, J., Vergnaud, D.: Separation results on the "one-more" computational problems. In: Malkin, T. (ed.) CT-RSA 2008. LNCS, vol. 4964, pp. 71–87. Springer, Heidelberg (2008). https://doi.org/10.1007/978-3-540-79263-5_5

[BN06] Bellare, M., Neven, G.: Multi-signatures in the plain public-key model and a general forking lemma. In: Juels, A., Wright, R.N., De Capitani di Vimercati, S. (eds.) ACM CCS 2006, pp. 390–399. ACM Press (2006)

[BNN04] Bellare, M., Namprempre, C., Neven, G.: Security proofs for identity-based identification and signature schemes. In: Cachin, C., Camenisch, J.L. (eds.) EUROCRYPT 2004. LNCS, vol. 3027, pp. 268–286. Springer, Heidelberg (2004). https://doi.org/10.1007/978-3-540-24676-3_17

[BNPS03] Bellare, M., Namprempre, C., Pointcheval, D., Semanko, M.: The one-more-RSA-inversion problems and the security of Chaum's blind signature scheme. J. Cryptol. **16**(3), 185–215 (2003)

[Bol03] Boldyreva, A.: threshold signatures, multisignatures and blind signatures based on the gap-Diffie-Hellman-group signature scheme. In: Desmedt, Y.G. (ed.) PKC 2003. LNCS, vol. 2567, pp. 31–46. Springer, Heidelberg (2003). https://doi.org/10.1007/3-540-36288-6_3

[Boy08] Boyen, X.: The uber-assumption family (invited talk). In: Galbraith, S.D., Paterson, K.G. (eds.) Pairing 2008. LNCS, vol. 5209, pp. 39–56. Springer, Heidelberg (2008). https://doi.org/10.1007/978-3-540-85538-5_3

[BP02] Bellare, M., Palacio, A.: GQ and Schnorr identification schemes: proofs of security against impersonation under active and concurrent attacks. In: Yung, M. (ed.) CRYPTO 2002. LNCS, vol. 2442, pp. 162–177. Springer, Heidelberg (2002). https://doi.org/10.1007/3-540-45708-9_11

[Bro07] Brown, D.R.L.: Irreducibility to the one-more evaluation problems: more may be less. Cryptology ePrint Archive, Report 2007/435 (2007). http://eprint.iacr.org/2007/435

[BS07] Bellare, M., Shoup, S.: Two-tier signatures, strongly unforgeable signatures, and Fiat-Shamir without random oracles. In: Okamoto, T., Wang, X. (eds.) PKC 2007. LNCS, vol. 4450, pp. 201–216. Springer, Heidelberg (2007). https://doi.org/10.1007/978-3-540-71677-8_14

[CDG18] Coretti, S., Dodis, Y., Guo, S.: Non-uniform bounds in the random-permutation, ideal-cipher, and generic-group models. In: Shacham, H., Boldyreva, A. (eds.) CRYPTO 2018, Part I. LNCS, vol. 10991, pp. 693–721. Springer, Cham (2018). https://doi.org/10.1007/978-3-319-96884-1_23

[Cha82] Chaum, D.: Blind signatures for untraceable payments. In: Chaum, D., Rivest, R.L., Sherman, A.T. (eds.) Advances in Cryptology, pp. 199–203. Springer, Boston, MA (1983). https://doi.org/10.1007/978-1-4757-0602-4_18

[CP93] Chaum, D., Pedersen, T.P.: Wallet databases with observers. In: Brickell, E.F. (ed.) CRYPTO 1992. LNCS, vol. 740, pp. 89–105. Springer, Heidelberg (1993). https://doi.org/10.1007/3-540-48071-4_7

[DEF+19] Drijvers, M., et al.: On the security of two-round multi-signatures. In: Symposium on Security and Privacy, pp. 1084–110. IEEE Computer Society Press (2019)

[FF13] Fischlin, M., Fleischhacker, N.: Limitations of the meta-reduction technique: the case of Schnorr signatures. In: Johansson, T., Nguyen, P.Q. (eds.) EUROCRYPT 2013. LNCS, vol. 7881, pp. 444–460. Springer, Heidelberg (2013). https://doi.org/10.1007/978-3-642-38348-9_27

[FH17] Fukumitsu, M., Hasegawa, S.: Impossibility of the provable security of the Schnorr signature from the one-more DL assumption in the non-programmable random oracle model. In: Okamoto, T., Yu, Y., Au, M.H., Li, Y. (eds.) ProvSec 2017. LNCS, vol. 10592, pp. 201–218. Springer, Cham (2017). https://doi.org/10.1007/978-3-319-68637-0_12

[FJS14] Fleischhacker, N., Jager, T., Schröder, D.: On tight security proofs for Schnorr signatures. In: Sarkar, P., Iwata, T. (eds.) ASIACRYPT 2014, Part I. LNCS, vol. 8873, pp. 512–531. Springer, Heidelberg (2014). https://doi.org/10.1007/978-3-662-45611-8_27

[FKL18] Fuchsbauer, G., Kiltz, E., Loss, J.: The algebraic group model and its applications. In: Shacham, H., Boldyreva, A. (eds.) CRYPTO 2018, Part II. LNCS, vol. 10992, pp. 33–62. Springer, Cham (2018). https://doi.org/10.1007/978-3-319-96881-0_2

[FPS20] Fuchsbauer, G., Plouviez, A., Seurin, Y.: Blind Schnorr signatures and signed ElGamal encryption in the algebraic group model. In: Canteaut, A., Ishai, Y. (eds.) EUROCRYPT 2020, Part II. LNCS, vol. 12106, pp. 63–95. Springer, Cham (2020). https://doi.org/10.1007/978-3-030-45724-2_3

[FS10] Fischlin, M., Schröder, D.: On the impossibility of three-move blind signature schemes. In: Gilbert, H. (ed.) EUROCRYPT 2010. LNCS, vol. 6110, pp. 197–215. Springer, Heidelberg (2010). https://doi.org/10.1007/978-3-642-13190-5_10

[GBL08] Garg, S., Bhaskar, R., Lokam, S.V.: Improved bounds on security reductions for discrete log based signatures. In: Wagner, D. (ed.) CRYPTO 2008. LNCS, vol. 5157, pp. 93–107. Springer, Heidelberg (2008). https://doi.org/10.1007/978-3-540-85174-5_6

[GLSY04] Gennaro, R., Leigh, D., Sundaram, R., Yerazunis, W.: Batching Schnorr identification scheme with applications to privacy-preserving authorization and low-bandwidth communication devices. In: Lee, P.J. (ed.) ASIACRYPT 2004. LNCS, vol. 3329, pp. 276–292. Springer, Heidelberg (2004). https://doi.org/10.1007/978-3-540-30539-2_20

[Gra10] Granger, R.: On the static Diffie-Hellman problem on elliptic curves over extension fields. In: Abe, M. (ed.) ASIACRYPT 2010. LNCS, vol. 6477, pp. 283–302. Springer, Heidelberg (2010). https://doi.org/10.1007/978-3-642-17373-8_17

[IN83] Itakura, K., Nakamura, K.: A public-key cryptosystem suitable for digital multisignatures. NEC Res. Dev. **71**, 1–8 (1983)

[KM07] Koblitz, N., Menezes, A.J.: Another look at "provable security". J. Cryptol. **20**(1), 3–37 (2007)

[KM08] Koblitz, N., Menezes, A.: Another look at non-standard discrete log and Diffie-Hellman problems. J. Math. Cryptol. **2**(4), 311–326 (2008)

[KM10] Koblitz, N., Menezes, A.: The brave new world of bodacious assumptions in cryptography. Not. Am. Math. Soc. **57**(3), 357–365 (2010)

[LRSW99] Lysyanskaya, A., Rivest, R.L., Sahai, A., Wolf, S.: Pseudonym systems. In: Heys, H., Adams, C. (eds.) SAC 1999. LNCS, vol. 1758, pp. 184–199. Springer, Heidelberg (2000). https://doi.org/10.1007/3-540-46513-8_14

[Mau99] Maurer, U.: Information-theoretic cryptography. In: Wiener, M. (ed.) CRYPTO 1999. LNCS, vol. 1666, pp. 47–65. Springer, Heidelberg (1999). https://doi.org/10.1007/3-540-48405-1_4

[Mau05] Maurer, U.: Abstract models of computation in cryptography. In: Smart, N.P. (ed.) Cryptography and Coding 2005. LNCS, vol. 3796, pp. 1–12. Springer, Heidelberg (2005). https://doi.org/10.1007/11586821_1

[MPSW19] Maxwell, G., Poelstra, A., Seurin, Y., Wuille, P.: Simple Schnorr multi-signatures with applications to Bitcoin. Des. Codes Cryptogr. **87**(9), 2139–2164 (2019). https://doi.org/10.1007/s10623-019-00608-x

[MR02] Micali, S., Rivest, R.L.: Transitive signature schemes. In: Preneel, B. (ed.) CT-RSA 2002. LNCS, vol. 2271, pp. 236–243. Springer, Heidelberg (2002). https://doi.org/10.1007/3-540-45760-7_16

[MW96] Maurer, U.M., Wolf, S.: Diffie-Hellman oracles. In: Koblitz, N. (ed.) CRYPTO 1996. LNCS, vol. 1109, pp. 268–282. Springer, Heidelberg (1996). https://doi.org/10.1007/3-540-68697-5_21

[MWLD10] Ma, C., Weng, J., Li, Y., Den, R.H.: Efficient discrete logarithm based multi-signature scheme in the plain public key mode. Des. Codes Cryptogr. **54**(2), 121–133 (2010)

[Nec94] Nechaev, V.I.: Complexity of a determinate algorithm for the discrete logarithm. Math. Notes **55**(2), 165–172 (1994)

[Nic19] Nick, J.: Blind signatures in scriptless scripts. Presentation given at Building on Bitcoin 2019 (2019). https://jonasnick.github.io/blog/2018/07/31/blind-signatures-in-scriptless-scripts/

[NIS19] NIST: Digital signature standard (DSS), FIPS PUB 186–5 (draft) (2019). https://csrc.nist.gov/publications/detail/fips/186/5/draft

[NRS21] Nick, J., Ruffing, T., Seurin, Y.: MuSig2: simple two-round Schnorr multi-signatures. In: Malkin, T., Peikert, C. (eds.) CRYPTO 2021, Part I. LNCS, vol. 12825, pp. 189–221. Springer, Cham (2021). https://doi.org/10.1007/978-3-030-84242-0_8

[OP01] Okamoto, T., Pointcheval, D.: The gap-problems: a new class of problems for the security of cryptographic schemes. In: Kim, K. (ed.) PKC 2001. LNCS, vol. 1992, pp. 104–118. Springer, Heidelberg (2001). https://doi.org/10.1007/3-540-44586-2_8

[Pas11] Pass, R.: Limits of provable security from standard assumptions. In: Fortnow, L., Vadhan, S.P. (eds.) 43rd ACM STOC, pp. 109–118. ACM Press (2011)

[PS96] Pointcheval, D., Stern, J.: Security proofs for signature schemes. In: Maurer, U. (ed.) EUROCRYPT 1996. LNCS, vol. 1070, pp. 387–398. Springer, Heidelberg (1996). https://doi.org/10.1007/3-540-68339-9_33

[PV05] Paillier, P., Vergnaud, D.: Discrete-log-based signatures may not be equivalent to discrete log. In: Roy, B. (ed.) ASIACRYPT 2005. LNCS, vol. 3788, pp. 1–20. Springer, Heidelberg (2005). https://doi.org/10.1007/11593447_1

[Sch91] Schnorr, C.P.: Efficient signature generation by smart cards. J. Cryptol. **4**(3), 161–174 (1991). https://doi.org/10.1007/BF00196725

[Sch01] Schnorr, C.P.: Security of blind discrete log signatures against interactive attacks. In: Qing, S., Okamoto, T., Zhou, J. (eds.) ICICS 2001. LNCS, vol. 2229, pp. 1–12. Springer, Heidelberg (2001). https://doi.org/10.1007/3-540-45600-7_1

[Seu12] Seurin, Y.: On the exact security of Schnorr-type signatures in the random oracle model. In: Pointcheval, D., Johansson, T. (eds.) EUROCRYPT 2012. LNCS, vol. 7237, pp. 554–571. Springer, Heidelberg (2012). https://doi.org/10.1007/978-3-642-29011-4_33

[Sho97] Shoup, V.: Lower bounds for discrete logarithms and related problems. In: Fumy, W. (ed.) EUROCRYPT 1997. LNCS, vol. 1233, pp. 256–266. Springer, Heidelberg (1997). https://doi.org/10.1007/3-540-69053-0_18

[SJ99] Schnorr, C.-P., Jakobsson, M.: Security of discrete log cryptosystems in the random oracle and the generic model (1999). https://core.ac.uk/download/pdf/14504220.pdf

[STV+16] Syta, E., et al.: Keeping authorities "honest or bust" with decentralized witness cosigning. In: Symposium on Security and Privacy, pp. 526–545. IEEE Computer Society Press (2016)

[Wag02] Wagner, D.: A generalized birthday problem. In: Yung, M. (ed.) CRYPTO 2002. LNCS, vol. 2442, pp. 288–304. Springer, Heidelberg (2002). https://doi.org/10.1007/3-540-45708-9_19

[WNR20] Wuille, P., Nick, J., Ruffing, T.: Schnorr signatures for secp256k1. Bitcoin Improvement Proposal 340 (2020). https://github.com/bitcoin/bips/blob/master/bip-0340.mediawiki

[Yun15] Yun, A.: Generic hardness of the multiple discrete logarithm problem. In: Oswald, E., Fischlin, M. (eds.) EUROCRYPT 2015, Part II. LNCS, vol. 9057, pp. 817–836. Springer, Heidelberg (2015). https://doi.org/10.1007/978-3-662-46803-6_27

Verifiably-Extractable OWFs and Their Applications to Subversion Zero-Knowledge

Prastudy Fauzi[1(✉)], Helger Lipmaa[1,2(✉)], Janno Siim[2(✉)], Michał Zając[3(✉)], and Arne Tobias Ødegaard[1(✉)]

[1] Simula UiB, Bergen, Norway
[2] University of Tartu, Tartu, Estonia
[3] Clearmatics, London, UK

Abstract. An extractable one-way function (EOWF), introduced by Canetti and Dakdouk (ICALP 2008) and generalized by Bitansky et al. (SIAM Journal on Computing vol. 45), is an OWF that allows for efficient extraction of a preimage for the function. We study (generalized) EOWFs that have a public image verification algorithm. We call such OWFs verifiably-extractable and show that several previously known constructions satisfy this notion. We study how such OWFs relate to subversion zero-knowledge (Sub-ZK) NIZKs by using them to generically construct a Sub-ZK NIZK from a NIZK satisfying certain additional properties, and conversely show how to obtain them from any Sub-ZK NIZK. Prior to our work, the Sub-ZK property of NIZKs was achieved using concrete knowledge assumptions.

1 Introduction

Extractability is a way to formalize what an algorithm *knows*. It is a notion essential to modern cryptography which dates back to the works of Goldwasser et al. [34] who proposed *proofs of knowledge*, and later formalized for interactive proofs by Bellare and Goldreich [10].[1] For non-interactive proofs, Damgård [23] proposed knowledge-of-exponent assumptions, which are non-falsifiable assumptions[2] saying that any efficient algorithm that produces group elements that satisfy a specific relation must know their discrete logarithms.

Investigating extractable primitives, Canetti and Dakdouk [19] introduced the notion of extractable one-way functions (EOWFs). These are one-way functions f such that any adversary who produces an image of f must "know" its preimage. One formalizes this by saying that for every adversary $\mathcal{A}$ that outputs a value $y \in \text{image}(f)$, there exists an extractor Ext that, given $\mathcal{A}$'s auxiliary input and randomness, can output a preimage for y under f. In the case of black-box (resp., non-black-box [7]) extractability, Ext is universal and has no access (resp., has access) to $\mathcal{A}$'s code.

---

[1] Extractability in interactive protocols is well-studied and involves a technique called *rewinding*. In this paper we focus on extractability for non-interactive protocols.

[2] Essentially, one cannot efficiently check if an adversary breaks the assumption.

M. Tibouchi and H. Wang (Eds.): ASIACRYPT 2021, LNCS 13093, pp. 618–649, 2021.
https://doi.org/10.1007/978-3-030-92068-5_21

Until the work of Bitansky *et al.* in [14], EOWFs were only known under very strong knowledge-of-exponent assumptions [13], making little attempt to justify how extraction would work. Bitansky *et al.* defined generalized extractable one-way functions (GEOWFs) and constructed a GEOWF based on sub-exponential learning with errors (or, alternatively, any delegation scheme) and non-black-box extraction, given that the auxiliary input of the adversary is bounded. They also prove that GEOWFs secure against auxiliary input of polynomially unbounded length do not exist assuming indistinguishability obfuscation (which seems an increasingly plausible assumption given recent progress [41,56]).

Extractability and SNARKs. Extractability assumptions are widely used in various flavors of non-interactive zero-knowledge (NIZK) protocols, which are useful tools in ensuring privacy and correctness of cryptographic protocols. Succinct non-interactive zero-knowledge arguments of knowledge (zk-SNARKs, [30,36,37,48]) are NIZKs that have sublinear-length proofs and are knowledge-sound (for any valid proof, the prover must "know" a witness). The knowledge-soundness property of a SNARK relies on being able to extract the witness from an adversary that outputs a valid argument. SNARKs are extremely popular due to practical applications such as verifiable computation and privacy-preserving cryptocurrencies (e.g., Zcash [11]).

An interesting question is which assumptions are necessary for SNARKs. Due to the impossibility result of Gentry and Wichs [32], any adaptively sound SNARK must rely on non-falsifiable assumptions. However, while non-falsifiable assumptions are necessary, they need not be knowledge assumptions. In fact, Bitansky et al. [13] showed that extractable collision-resistant hash functions (ECRHs) are necessary and sufficient to construct a SNARK that is adaptively sound and only privately verifiable. More precisely, they construct a designated verifier SNARK for NP from an ECRH and (an appropriate) private information retrieval, and construct a (specific variant of) ECRH from a designated verifier SNARK and a CRH. They also showed that ECRH implies EOWF.

Extractability and Subversion Zero-Knowledge. Efficient SNARKs are typically defined in the common reference string (CRS) model, where one assumes that the prover and the verifier have access to a CRS generated by a trusted third party. However, in practice, such a party usually does not exist; this is important since a malicious CRS generator may cooperate with the prover to break soundness, or with the verifier to break zero-knowledge. Thus, it is preferable to construct SNARKs, and NIZKs in general, in weaker trust models than the CRS model.

The general notion of parameter subversion has been studied in [53]. Bellare et al. [9] defined subversion zero-knowledge (Sub-ZK), where zero-knowledge holds even in the case of a dishonestly generated CRS, and constructed a Sub-ZK NIZK argument. Subsequently, [1,3,27] constructed Sub-ZK SNARKs and [2] constructed succinct Sub-ZK quasi-adaptive NIZKs [42]. As noted in [2], Sub-ZK in the CRS model is equivalent to zero-knowledge in the minimal bare public key (BPK, [20]) model where the authority is only trusted to store the public key of each party. Since auxiliary-string non-black-box NIZK is impossible in the BPK model [33], one needs to use non-auxiliary-string non-black-box techniques to achieve Sub-ZK [2]. Existing Sub-ZK NIZKs extract a CRS trapdoor from the (possibly malicious) CRS generator, and then use the CRS trapdoor to simulate the NIZK argument. Prior to our work, extraction in Sub-ZK NIZKs was done using a concrete knowledge-of-exponent assumption.

As previously mentioned, the work of Bitansky et al. [13] established that extractable collision-resistant hash functions are necessary to obtain adaptive soundness of SNARKs. A natural extension of this question is then to ask:

> Which assumptions are necessary to obtain Sub-ZK for NIZKs and SNARKs? Are those assumptions stronger than the ones required to obtain adaptive soundness of SNARKs?

1.1 Our Contributions

Inspired by (G)EOWFs, we propose a new *generic assumption*[3]: the existence of verifiably-extractable (generalized) OWFs (VE(G)OWFs). We argue that VEGOWFs are a natural extension of GEOWFs introduced by Bitansky et al. [14], and show that in fact their GEOWF construction can easily be turned into a VEGOWF. Moreover, while Bitansky et al. [14] showed that a GEOWF can be transformed into a EOWF under certain assumptions, we similarly show that any VEGOWF can be transformed into a VEOWF with no further assumptions. To circumvent the impossibility result that EOWF and similar primitives do not exist assuming indistinguishability obfuscation, our definitions include non-black-box extractability as in [14] and assume a benign distribution of auxiliary inputs as suggested in [18].

Answering the first research question, we show that VEGOWFs are vital in understanding subversion zero-knowledge. Firstly, we show that VEGOWFs allow for the transformation of any perfect NIZK with a publicly verifiable CRS into a Sub-ZK NIZK. Secondly, we show the necessity of VEGOWFs by showing that the existence of a Sub-ZK NIZK with certain properties implies that the NIZK's CRS generation algorithm must be a VEOWF. We also prove that if a NIZK has perfect zero-knowledge and well-formedness of the CRS can be efficiently verified, then we automatically obtain a statistical two-message private-coin witness-indistinguishable argument. Obtaining statistical two-message witness-indistinguishable arguments (either public or private coin) was an open question until recently [6,35,49]. Similar observations were previously made about specific Sub-ZK SNARKs in [27].

We answer the second research question by showing that the assumption corresponding to this primitive seems weaker than that of extractable collision-resistant hash functions. In particular, we show that VEGOWFs can be built either from knowledge assumption or knowledge-sound NIZKs, and we also propose candidate VEGOWFs from various signature schemes.

[3] Generic assumptions postulate the existence of a cryptographic primitive, such as OWFs and one-way permutations. Meanwhile, concrete assumptions are used for concrete constructions, such as the RSA assumption [52] for the RSA cryptosystem.

By showing connections to Sub-ZK NIZK, our work further demonstrates the importance of extractable OWFs as an independent primitive. This tool, which has not been thoroughly studied, seems to lead the way to protocols that are otherwise difficult to achieve. We encourage further study into extractable functions under weaker (or different) assumptions as there are significant differences between various non-black-box techniques.

2 Technical Overview

Extending the notions of EOWF [19] and GEOWF [14], we define *Verifiably-Extractable Generalized One-Way Functions* (VEGOWFs), show several instantiations of these and show how it is related to subversion resistant zero-knowledge. Intuitively, an EOWF f is a one-way function such that for any PPT adversary $\mathcal{A}$, there exists a PPT extractor $\mathsf{Ext}_{\mathcal{A}}$, such that if $\mathcal{A}$ outputs $y \in \text{image}(f)$, then $\mathsf{Ext}_{\mathcal{A}}$ (given access to $\mathcal{A}$'s auxiliary input) retrieves x such that $f(x) = y$. Meanwhile, a GEOWF g generalizes EOWFs by introducing a relation $\mathbf{RG}$ such that for every PPT $\mathcal{A}$, there exists an extractor $\mathsf{Ext}_{\mathcal{A}}$, such that if $\mathcal{A}$ outputs $y \in \text{image}(g)$, then $\mathsf{Ext}_{\mathcal{A}}$ (given access to $\mathcal{A}$'s auxiliary input) returns z such that $(y, z) \in \mathbf{RG}$. It is required that it is difficult for any adversary who is only given y to compute such z, i.e., $\mathbf{RG}$ is a hard relation.

2.1 Verifiably-Extractable (Generalized) OWFs

A *Verifiably-Extractable Generalized OWF* (VEGOWF) $\mathcal{G} = \{\mathsf{g_e}\}_{\mathsf{e}}$ is a GEOWF which additionally allows one to efficiently check whether extraction will succeed for a given value y. More precisely, we define a relation $\mathbf{RG}_{\mathsf{e}}$ and a set $Y_{\mathsf{Ext}} \supseteq \text{image}(\mathsf{g_e})$ such that

(i) given y one can efficiently verify whether $y \in Y_{\mathsf{Ext}}$ and
(ii) if $y \in Y_{\mathsf{Ext}}$ then there exists an extractor $\mathsf{Ext}_{\mathcal{A}}$ that given non-black-box access to $\mathcal{A}$ extracts z such that $(y, z) \in \mathbf{RG}_{\mathsf{e}}$.

Note that extraction should work even if $y \in Y_{\mathsf{Ext}} \setminus \text{image}(\mathsf{g_e})$, and in general, it might be hard to decide if $y \in \text{image}(\mathsf{g_e})$. We say that a VEGOWF is keyless if e is the security parameter λ; in this case we write $\mathbf{RG}$ instead of $\mathbf{RG}_{\mathsf{e}}$. The formal definition of VEGOWFs can be found in Sect. 4.1.

We denote both properties together as $\mathbf{RG}$-*verifiable-extractability.* The requirements for $\mathbf{RG}$-hardness remain the same as for GEOWFs. We introduce *verifiably-extractable OWFs* (VEOWF) as a special case of VEGOWFs where the corresponding relation is $\mathbf{RG}_{\mathsf{e}} = \{(\mathsf{g_e}(x), x)\}$.

Generic Transformations. We show that any VEGOWF can be transformed to a VEOWF with a simple technique that was first mentioned in [14], in a slightly different context. However, since the transformation incurs some efficiency loss, we still consider VEGOWFs to be a weaker primitive and base our subversion zero-knowledge application on VEGOWFs. We also give a construction of a VEGOWF from any GEOWF by evaluating the GEOWF on two different inputs and attaching a NIWI proof (in the plain model) that at least one of the functions was evaluated correctly. Together they give a surprising result that any GEOWF can be transformed to a VEOWF under the relatively mild assumptions (e.g., decisional linear assumption) required by the NIWI. We note that similar techniques have been previously used in specific applications. For example, [12] uses similar idea to obtain a 3-round zero-knowledge argument from any (non-verifiable) EOWF. We believe it is valuable to point out that this technique works as a general transformation. See Sect. 4.2 for more details.

Robust Combiners. We show that n VEGOWFs can be combined to a new VEGOWF, which is secure if any $t > n/2$ of the initial functions is secure. A robust combiner[26,40] for VEGOWFs is useful since many of the proposed VEGOWFs rely on strong assumptions. With combining we only need to trust that some of those strong assumptions hold without knowing which. Details are provided in Sect. 4.2.

We show several VEGOWFs and VEOWFs under various assumptions like bounded auxiliary input size, knowledge assumptions, and the random oracle.

VEGOWF from the BCPR Construction. In the first construction, we show that the keyless GEOWF $\mathcal{G}$ from [14, Fig. 4] is, in fact, a VEGOWF against any adversary with bounded auxiliary input if we assume that the used delegation scheme has efficient public CRS-verifiability. We recall that a delegation scheme DS [5] allows one to prove statements of the form "a machine $\mathcal{M}$ outputs y on input x in time t". A delegation proof π_{DS} must be faster to verify than the statement itself. The CRS-verifiability means that one can efficiently check if the DS CRS $\mathsf{crs}_{\mathsf{DS}}$ is a valid CRS.

In the BCPR construction, each function g_{e} computes a CRS $\mathsf{crs}_{\mathsf{DS}}$ for a delegation scheme DS, and then evaluates a PRG on a random value. The relation $\mathbf{RG}(y, z)$ holds for $y = (\mathsf{crs}_{\mathsf{DS}}, v)$ and $z = (\mathcal{A}, \pi_{\mathsf{DS}}, \mathsf{pad})$, if π_{DS} is a DS-proof, using $\mathsf{crs}_{\mathsf{DS}}$ as the CRS, for the statement that $\mathcal{A}$ on input 1^{λ} outputs v. (pad is a padding.) The proof of $\mathbf{RG}$-hardness is as in [14], and follows from the security of the PRG together with an argument about Kolmogorov complexity. The $\mathbf{RG}$-verifiable-extractability follows from the CRS-verifiability and completeness of the delegation scheme. See Sect. 4.3 for more details.

We note that even if the delegation scheme is not CRS-verifiable, one could still make the BCPR EOWF a VEGOWF using the generic transformation presented in Sect. 4.2.

VEGOWFs from Knowledge-of-Exponent Assumptions. Secondly, we show that many knowledge-of-exponent assumptions naturally imply VEGOWFs. For these VEGOWFs, the input key e consists of a bilinear group description and possibly some additional information.

We first construct of a VEOWF based on the Bilinear Diffie–Hellman Knowledge-of-Exponent (BDH-KE) assumption from [1] which states that if an adversary on input p (the asymmetric bilinear group description) outputs $([x]_1, [x]_2)$ for some x then he knows x.[4] Here, $\mathsf{e} = \mathsf{p}$ and $\mathsf{g}_\mathsf{p}(x) = ([x]_1, [x]_2)$.

We also construct a VEGOWF based on the Diffie–Hellman Knowledge of Exponent (DH-KE) assumption introduced in [9]. The key is a description p of a symmetric bilinear group, and $\mathsf{g}_\mathsf{p}(x, y) = [x, y, xy]_1$. The DH-KE assumption states that is possible to extract at least one of x and y. This results in a VEGOWF with respect to the relation $\mathbf{RG}_\mathsf{p}([x, y, xy]_1, z) = 1$ iff $z = x$ or $z = y$.

We discuss these and other similar VE(G)OWF constructions in Sect. 4.4.

VEGOWFs from Knowledge Sound NIZKs. Thirdly, inspired by [22,47], we build VEGOWFs using knowledge-sound NIZKs. Suppose that we have a knowledge-sound NIZK Π for a relation $\mathbf{R}$ and that $\mathbf{R}$ has an efficient sampling algorithm $\mathcal{S}$ which produces instances that are hard on average. We define $\mathsf{g}_\mathsf{e}(r_\mathcal{S}, r_\pi)$ such that it samples $(\mathsf{x}, \mathsf{w}) \leftarrow \mathcal{S}(r_\mathcal{S})$, uses r_π as random coins to generate a proof π for x, and outputs (x, π). The input e is either the CRS or a description of a hash function (in the random oracle model). We define $\mathbf{RG}_\mathsf{e}((\mathsf{x}, \pi), \mathsf{w}) = 1$ iff π satisfies NIZK verification and $(\mathsf{x}, \mathsf{w}) \in \mathbf{R}$. Since Π is knowledge-sound, we obtain $\mathbf{RG}$-verifiable-extractability by using Π's verification on (x, π). $\mathbf{RG}$-hardness is satisfied since π is simulatable and $\mathcal{S}$ produces hard instances on average.

As an interesting instantiation, if we let $\mathcal{S}$ output $([x], x)$ for a random x and use Schnorr's Σ-protocol together with the Fiat-Shamir heuristic as a NIZK, we obtain a very efficient VEOWF $\mathsf{g}_\mathsf{e}(x, r) := (\mathsf{x} = [x], a = [r], z = H([x], [r]) \cdot x + r)$ where H is a hash function and verification works by asserting that $H(\mathsf{x}, a)\mathsf{x} + a = [z]$. See Sect. 4.5 for more details.

VEGOWFs from Signature Schemes. Finally, we propose a novel heuristic for coming up with new VEGOWFs and knowledge-type assumptions in general. The intuition behind signature schemes is that only the one with (at least some) knowledge of the signing key sk can sign a message. Thus, it gives a very simple formula for looking for new VEGOWFs. Let $\Sigma = (\mathsf{KGen}, \mathsf{sign}, \mathsf{Vf})$ be a digital signature scheme. Then, $\mathsf{g}_\mathsf{p}(\mathsf{sk}) = (\mathsf{vk} = \mathsf{KGen}(\mathsf{sk}), \sigma = \mathsf{sign}(\mathsf{sk}, m = 0))$ is a candidate for a VEGOWF where p is some parameter for the signature scheme, in particular when $\mathsf{vk} \in \mathsf{KGen}$ can be efficiently tested. Of course, this is just a heuristic since at least the standard notion of existential unforgeability does not require that the signer knows the secret key.

We then proceed by going over many concrete signatures schemes and investigate the security of the corresponding VEGOWF candidate. We see that in some cases the VEGOWF is insecure (e.g., Lamport's one-time signature [46] and RSA signature), in some cases it gives a VEGOWF that we already considered before (e.g., Schnorr's signature scheme [55] and Boneh-Boyen signature [16]) and in some cases we obtain (plausibly secure) VEGOWFs that have not been considered before. In the latter set is for example the DSA signature which gives quite a unique function in a non-pairing-based group and (and a slight modification

---

[4] We use the additive notation for bilinear groups $\mathbb{G}_1, \mathbb{G}_2, \mathbb{G}_T$ where $[x]_i$ denotes xg_i using the fixed generator g_i of $\mathbb{G}_i$ described in p. A bilinear map $\bullet$ allows us to compute $[x]_1 \bullet [y]_2 = [xy]_T$.

of) the hash-and-sign lattice based signature scheme of [31], which gives the first lattice based VEGOWF candidate.

2.2 Constructing Sub-ZK NIZK from VEGOWF

We propose two generic constructions of a Sub-ZK NIZK. The first construction produces a knowledge-sound Sub-ZK NIZK from any knowledge-sound Sub-WI NIWI[5] and keyless VEGOWF. The second construction produces a sound Sub-ZK NIZK from a sound Sub-WI NIWI, a keyless extractable commitment, and a VEGOWF.

Knowledge-Sound Sub-ZK NIZK. For the first construction, we propose a knowledge-sound Sub-ZK NIZK for any NP-relation $\mathbf{R}$ using a variant of the well-known FLS disjunctive approach [25]. Namely, we use a knowledge-sound Sub-WI NIWI Π_{wi} for the composite relation $\mathbf{R}'$, where $((\mathsf{x}, \widehat{y}), (\mathsf{w}, \widehat{z})) \in \mathbf{R}'$ iff either $(\mathsf{x}, \mathsf{w}) \in \mathbf{R}$ or $(\widehat{y}, \widehat{z}) \in \mathbf{RG}$. Here $\mathcal{G} = \{\mathsf{g_e}\}$ is a keyless VEGOWF with respect to $\mathbf{RG}$ and $\widehat{y} \in Y_{\mathsf{Ext}}$ being added to Π_{wi}'s CRS. Knowledge-soundness of the new protocol will follow from the knowledge-soundness of Π_{wi} together with the $\mathbf{RG}$-hardness of $\mathcal{G}$, and subversion zero-knowledge follows from the verifiable-extractability of $\mathcal{G}$ and the Sub-WI property of Π_{wi}. This construction preserves succinctness, and thus we obtain a Sub-ZK SNARK from a keyless VEGOWF and a Sub-WI SNARK. We later note that any perfectly zero-knowledge SNARK with efficient CRS verification is automatically a Sub-WI SNARK. See Sect. 5.1 for the full details of the construction.

Sub-ZK NIZK. Secondly, we construct a Sub-ZK NIZK Π for any NP-relation $\mathbf{R}$. It similarly uses the FLS approach with a keyless VEGOWF, but additionally uses a commitment to a trapdoor. Specifically, Π implements a Sub-WI NIWI Π_{wi} for the relation $\mathbf{R}'$, where $((\mathsf{x}, c, \widehat{y}), (\mathsf{w}, \widehat{z}, \widehat{r})) \in \mathbf{R}'$ iff $(\mathsf{x}, \mathsf{w}) \in \mathbf{R}$ or $c = \mathsf{C.Com}(\widehat{z}, \widehat{r})$ such that $\mathbf{RG}(\widehat{y}, \widehat{z}) = 1$, where $\mathcal{G}$ is a keyless VEGOWF with respect to $\mathbf{RG}$ and $\mathsf{C} = (\mathsf{Com}, \mathsf{Open}, \mathsf{Vf})$ is a keyless extractable commitment scheme.

A proof in Π consists of a commitment c and a proof in Π_{wi}, so this construction is less efficient than the previous one. However, this does not rely on Π_{wi} being knowledge-sound, so the construction is still of interest. The soundness of Π follows from the soundness of Π_{wi} together with the $\mathbf{RG}$-hardness of $\mathcal{G}$ and the extractability of C. Note that Π_{wi} will already guarantee that c is a valid commitment. Therefore, we do not need the commitment itself to have an efficient image verification procedure and can obtain it from any (even non-verifiable) injective EOWF. Sub-ZK follows from the verifiable-extractability of $\mathcal{G}$, the Sub-WI property of Π_{wi} and the hiding property of C. See Sect. 5.2 for the full details of the construction.

Statistical ZAPRs with Adaptive Soundness. We observe that if a NIZK has perfect zero-knowledge and CRS-verifiability, then we immediately obtain a

[5] Although in the literature NIWI often refers to the plain model, in this context we allow for a CRS. A Sub-WI NIWI needs to remain witness indistinguishable even if the CRS is subverted. We note that any CRS-less NIWI is trivially a Sub-WI NIWI.

statistical two-message private-coin witness-indistinguishable argument. Obtaining statistical two-message witness-indistinguishable arguments that are public-coin (ZAP) or private-coin (ZAPR) was considered a significant open problem, until recent breakthroughs [6,35,49]. Note that existing Sub-ZK SNARKs [1,27] are already statistical ZAPRs with adaptive soundness. Compared to previous statistical ZAP/ZAPR constructions, the soundness of SNARKs is based on less standard assumptions, but they have much better efficiency. Similar observations about Sub-ZK SNARKs were previously made by Fuchsbauer in [27].

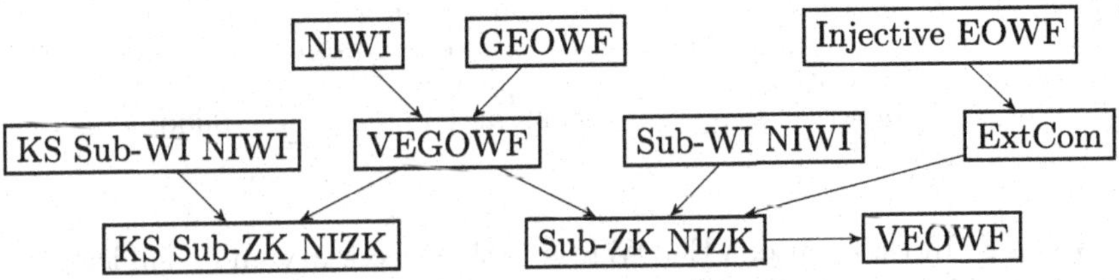

Fig. 1. Relations between argument systems and extractable functions. Multiple arrows pointing to the same node means that each source node is required to construct the destination node. KS denotes knowledge-sound.

Instantiations. The relations between our primitives are summarized in Fig. 1.

Table 1 shows a selection of instantiations for our generic constructions and compares them to previous work. We can achieve a keyless extractable commitment from any keyless injective VEOWF (or even from keyless injective EOWF if the commitment does not have to be image verifiable). In particular, this includes a VEOWF based on the symmetric discrete logarithm (SDL) assumption and the BDH-KE assumption, and a VEOWF based on the security of a non-interactive version of Schnorr's protocol.

We can construct a Sub-ZK NIZK by combining a keyless extractable commitment, a VEGOWF, and a Sub-WI NIWI. For example, we may use the Sub-WI NIWI of [39] based on DLIN or [15] based on iO and OWF. In comparison, [9] proposed a Sub-ZK NIZK which is based on the DLIN and DH-KE assumptions. We can obtain a KS Sub-ZK NIZK by combining a KS Sub-WI NIWI with a VEGOWF. In Table 1, we consider the case where we use [28] as the KS Sub-WI NIWI component, together with a VEGOWF which holds under the same assumptions. In Sect. 5.2, we also show that existing Sub-ZK SNARKs [1,27] can be slightly modified to achieve Sub-ZK from any VEGOWF rather than a specific knowledge-of-exponent assumption.

2.3 Constructing VEOWF from Sub-ZK NIZK

It turns out that not only can Sub-ZK NIZK be constructed with the help of VEGOWF, but (under certain restrictions) Sub-ZK NIZK also implies a

Table 1. Instantiations of our generic constructions in comparison to previous work. SKE denotes the Square Knowledge-of-Exponent assumption, GGM denotes the generic group model, PDH denotes the Power Diffie-Hellman assumption, PKE denotes the Power Knowledge-of-Exponent assumption, and TSDH denotes the Target Strong Diffie-Hellman assumption.

	Soundness	Knowledge Soundness	Sub-ZK
[9]	DH-KE + CDH	×	DH-KE + DLIN
Sec. 5.2	injective VEOWF	×	injective VEOWF + DLIN
Sec. 5.2	injective VEOWF	×	injective VEOWF + iO
[1]	GGM	GGM	BDH-KE
[27, Sec. 4]	q_1-PDH + q_2-PKE	q_1-PDH + q_2-PKE	SKE
[27, Sec. 5]	q_1-PDH + q_2-PKE + q_3-SDH	q_1-PDH + q_2-PKE + q_3-TSDH	SKE
[27, Sec. 6]	GGM	GGM	SKE
Sec. 5.1	DH-KE + DL	DH-KE + DL	DH-KE + DLIN

VE(G)OWF. In that sense, VEGOWF is both a necessary and a sufficient condition for achieving Sub-ZK NIZKs, similar to how ECRH (also, under certain restrictions) is a necessary and a sufficient condition for achieving a SNARK.

More technically, we consider a CRS generation function $\mathsf{KGen}_{\mathbf{R},\mathsf{p}}$ of a Sub-ZK NIZK that takes as an input a randomly sampled trapdoor td and outputs a crs. We show that this function has to be one-way if the NIZK is both computationally sound and computationally zero-knowledge. Intuitively, if one-wayness would not hold, the soundness adversary could recover td and use the simulator to construct a proof for a false statement. We additionally require that $\mathsf{KGen}_{\mathbf{R},\mathsf{p}}$ is injective to avoid the situation where one-wayness adversary computes td is which is particularly bad for simulation among all the possible preimages of crs. Verifiable-extractability property follows straightforwardly from the Sub-ZK property of the NIZK since it requires that td must be extractable. However, here we also need to make some slight restrictions. Namely, the Sub-ZK extractor should be able to extract the complete td, not only some part of it, which might still be sufficient for simulating the proof.

3 Preliminaries

Let PPT denote probabilistic polynomial-time. Let $\lambda \in \mathbb{N}$ be the security parameter. All adversaries are stateful. For an algorithm $\mathcal{A}$, let image($\mathcal{A}$) be the image of $\mathcal{A}$ (the set of valid outputs of $\mathcal{A}$), let $\mathsf{RND}_\lambda(\mathcal{A})$ denote the random tape of $\mathcal{A}$, and let $r \leftarrow_\$ \mathsf{RND}_\lambda(\mathcal{A})$ denote the random choice of values from $\mathsf{RND}_\lambda(\mathcal{A})$. We write that $y \in \mathrm{range}(\mathcal{A}(x))$ if there is non-zero probability that the algorithm $\mathcal{A}$ outputs a value y given the input x. We denote by $\mathsf{negl}(\lambda)$ an arbitrary negligible function and by $\mathsf{poly}(\lambda)$ an arbitrary polynomial function. We write $a(\lambda) \approx_\lambda b(\lambda)$ if $|a(\lambda) - b(\lambda)| = \mathsf{negl}(\lambda)$. For an NP-relation $\mathbf{R} = \{(\mathsf{x}, \mathsf{w})\}$, let $\mathcal{L}_{\mathbf{R}} := \{\mathsf{x} : \exists \mathsf{w}, (\mathsf{x}, \mathsf{w}) \in \mathbf{R}\}$ be the corresponding language.

In the pairing-based setting, we use the standard bracket notation together with additive notation, i.e., we write $[a]_\iota$ to denote ag_ι where g_ι is a fixed generator of $\mathbb{G}_\iota$ and $a \in \mathbb{Z}_p$ for some prime p. Intuitively, pairings $\bullet : \mathbb{G}_1 \times \mathbb{G}_2 \rightarrow \mathbb{G}_T$ are efficient (one-way) functions that map $([a]_1, [b]_2)$ to $[a]_1 \bullet [b]_2 = [ab]_T$.

Let $A = \{A_\lambda\}_{\lambda \in \mathbb{N}}, B = \{B_\lambda\}_{\lambda \in \mathbb{N}}$ be collections of efficiently sampleable sets, such that $|B_\lambda| > |A_\lambda|$ for each $\lambda \in \mathbb{N}$. A polynomial-time function $\mathsf{PRG}\colon A_\lambda \rightarrow B_\lambda$ is a pseudorandom generator (PRG) if its output is computationally indistinguishable from a truly random one.

3.1 (Generalized) Extractable OWF

An extractable one-way function (EOWF, [19]) g is an OWF with the property that if $\mathcal{A}$ outputs a value in the image of g, then one can extract its preimage. A generalized EOWF (GEOWF, [14]) is a function g with an associated hard relation $\mathbf{RG}$, such that given $\mathsf{g}(x)$, it is intractable to compute z such that $\mathbf{RG}(\mathsf{g}(x), z) = 1$. However, given a machine (and its auxiliary input) that computes $\mathsf{g}(x)$, it is possible to extract z such that $\mathbf{RG}(\mathsf{g}(x), z) = 1$. One obtains an EOWF when $\mathbf{RG} = \{(\mathsf{g}(x), z) : \mathsf{g}(z) = \mathsf{g}(x)\}$. Unless stated otherwise, we assume that $\mathbf{RG}$ is efficiently checkable.

Bitansky *et al.* [14] show that, assuming the existence of indistinguishability obfuscation, there do not exist EOWFs or GEOWFs with common auxiliary-input of unbounded polynomial length. However, the result does not rule out their existence when the common auxiliary input comes from some natural distribution, such as the uniform distribution. Thus, nowadays zk-SNARKs explicitly assume that the auxiliary input is benign, i.e., with overwhelming probability it does not encode a malicious obfuscation. We also make the same assumption: if no bound for the auxiliary input is given, then we assume that it is taken from a benign distribution.

We present a slight modification of the GEOWF definition of [14]. Note that hardness is required to hold even against poly-length auxiliary inputs.

Definition 1 (GEOWFs). *Let* $\mathcal{X} = \{X_\lambda\}_\lambda$, $\mathcal{Y} = \{Y_\lambda\}_\lambda$, $\mathcal{Z} = \{Z_\lambda\}_\lambda$ *and* $\mathcal{K} = \{K_\lambda\}_\lambda$ *be collections of sets indexed by* $\lambda \in \mathbb{N}$. *An efficiently computable family of functions* $\mathcal{G} = \{\mathsf{g}_\mathsf{e}\colon X_\lambda \rightarrow Y_\lambda \mid \mathsf{e} \in K_\lambda, \lambda \in \mathbb{N}\}$ *associated with an efficient (probabilistic) key sampler* $\mathsf{KeySamp}$, *is a* GEOWF *with respect to a relation* $\mathbf{RG}_\mathsf{e}(y, z)$ *on triples* $(\mathsf{e}, y, z) \in K_\lambda \times Y_\lambda \times Z_\lambda$ *if it is:*

RG-hard: *for any PPT adversary* $\mathcal{A}$ *and any* aux *sampled from a benign distribution of* $\mathsf{poly}(\lambda)$*-bit strings*

$$\Pr_{\substack{\mathsf{e} \leftarrow \mathsf{KeySamp}(1^\lambda) \\ x \leftarrow\$ X_\lambda}} [z \leftarrow \mathcal{A}(\mathsf{e}, \mathsf{g}_\mathsf{e}(x), \mathsf{aux}) : \mathbf{RG}_\mathsf{e}(\mathsf{g}_\mathsf{e}(x), z) = 1] \leq \mathsf{negl}(\lambda) \ .$$

RG-extractable: *For any PPT adversary* $\mathcal{A}$, *there exists a PPT extractor* $\mathsf{Ext}_\mathcal{A}$, *s.t. for any benign distribution* $\mathcal{D}_\lambda$ *of* $\mathsf{poly}(\lambda)$*-bit strings,*

$$\Pr_{\substack{\mathsf{e} \leftarrow \mathsf{KeySamp}(1^\lambda) \\ \mathsf{aux} \leftarrow \mathcal{D}_\lambda}} \left[\begin{matrix} y \leftarrow \mathcal{A}(\mathsf{e}; \mathsf{aux}), z \leftarrow \mathsf{Ext}_\mathcal{A}(\mathsf{e}; \mathsf{aux}) : \\ y \in \mathrm{image}(\mathsf{g}_\mathsf{e}) \wedge \mathbf{RG}_\mathsf{e}(y, z) \neq 1 \end{matrix} \right] \leq \mathsf{negl}(\lambda) \ .$$

The function is publicly verifiable *if there exists a polynomial-time tester $\mathcal{T}$ such that for any* (e, x, z), $\mathbf{RG}_{\mathsf{e}}(\mathsf{g}_{\mathsf{e}}(x), z) = \mathcal{T}(\mathsf{e}, \mathsf{g}_{\mathsf{e}}(x), z)$.

We say that a GEOWF is keyless if, for each security parameter λ, *there is only one key* $\mathsf{e} = 1^\lambda$. *For ease of notation, we simply write* g_λ *and* $\mathbf{RG}$ *in this case. A GEOWF is an EOWF if* $\mathbf{RG}_{\mathsf{e}}(\mathsf{g}_{\mathsf{e}}(x), z) = \{(\mathsf{e}, \mathsf{g}_{\mathsf{e}}(x), z) : \mathsf{g}_{\mathsf{e}}(x) = \mathsf{g}_{\mathsf{e}}(z)\}$.

Bounded Auxiliary Input. We also consider GEOWFs where the auxiliary input in $\mathbf{RG}$-extractability holds for any $\mathsf{aux} \in \{0,1\}^{\mathfrak{b}(\lambda)}$ (not just for a benign distribution) for some fixed polynomial $\mathfrak{b}$. We call these $\mathfrak{b}$-bounded GEOWFs.

3.2 BCPR GEOWF and EOWF

Bitansky *et al.* [14] show that if the common auxilliary string of the adversary and the extractor has an a priori bounded length $\mathfrak{b}(\lambda)$, then one can implement extractable one-way functions (EOWF) based on a pseudorandom generator and a universal delegation scheme [43,44]. In a universal delegation scheme, one delegates computation of some circuit M on input x to a prover, who must compute $M(x)$ and provide a proof π that he computed it correctly; any verifier that is given $(M, x, M(x), \pi)$ must be able to verify the proof in less time than computing $M(x)$ itself. One can construct universal delegation schemes under the subexponential learning with errors assumption [44] and even falsifiable assumptions [43] for languages in BPP.

BCPR GEOWF. We briefly describe the construction from [14] of a GEOWF secure against an adversary with $(\mathfrak{b}(\lambda) - \omega(1))$-bounded auxiliary input.

Fix a polynomial $\mathfrak{b}(\lambda)$. Let $\mathsf{PRG}\colon \{0,1\}^\lambda \to \{0,1\}^{\mathfrak{b}(\lambda)+\lambda}$ be a PRG. Let DS be a *universal* delegation scheme that consists of a CRS generator $\mathsf{DS.K}$, a prover $\mathsf{DS.P}$, and a verifier $\mathsf{DS.V}$. We assume that using DS, one can construct a succinct proof π_{DS} of length $\mathsf{DS.plen}(\lambda)$ that a Turing machine M on input 1^λ outputs some value v in time $T(\lambda)$, where $T(\lambda) \in (2^{\omega(\log \lambda)}, 2^{\mathsf{poly}(\lambda)})$ is some superpolynomial function. DS must satisfy that the proof verification complexity is linear in M's size and polylogarithmic in M's execution time T.

We define the function $\mathsf{g}_\lambda\colon (s, r) \mapsto (\mathsf{crs}_{\mathsf{DS}}, v)$ and the corresponding relation $\mathbf{RG}(y, z)$ as in Fig. 2, where $y = (\mathsf{crs}_{\mathsf{DS}}, v)$ and $z = (\mathsf{M}, \pi_{\mathsf{DS}}, \mathsf{pad})$ with $|z| = \mathfrak{l}(\lambda)$.

Proposition 1 ([14, Theorem 14]). *$\mathcal{G} = \{\mathsf{g}_\lambda\}_{\lambda \in \mathbb{N}}$, depicted in Fig. 2, is a GEOWF with respect to* $\mathbf{RG}$, *against* $(\mathfrak{b}(\lambda) - \omega(1))$*-bounded auxiliary input.*

This proposition relies on the security of DS and PRG. In addition, it uses a Barak-type [7] extractability paradigm (namely, the machine M is the adversary who outputs y). It is worth noting that a similar approach with a number of extra steps [14, Theorem 14] also allows one to construct a function family which is an EOWF against $(\mathfrak{b}(\lambda) - \omega(1))$-bounded auxiliary-input. We will see an adaptation of this approach in Fig. 4.2.

$\mathsf{g}_\lambda(s, r)$

$(\mathsf{crs_{DS}}, \tau) \leftarrow \mathsf{DS.K}(1^\lambda; r)$; // the generator for universal delegation
return $(\mathsf{crs_{DS}}, v \leftarrow \mathsf{PRG}(s))$;

$\mathbf{RG}(y, z)$

parse $y = (\mathsf{crs_{DS}}, v), z = (\mathsf{M}, \pi_{\mathsf{DS}}, \mathsf{pad})$;
// $|\mathsf{M}| = \mathfrak{b}(\lambda), |\pi_{\mathsf{DS}}| = \mathsf{DS.plen}(\lambda), |\mathsf{pad}| = \mathfrak{l}(\lambda) - \mathfrak{b}(\lambda) - \mathsf{DS.plen}(\lambda)$;
find the verification state τ corresponding to the reference string $\mathsf{crs_{DS}}$;
verify the statement "$\mathsf{M}(1^\lambda)$ outputs v in $T(\lambda)$ steps" by using π_{DS} (DS proof);
return 1 iff the DS verifier accepts π_{DS};

Fig. 2. BCPR GEOWF $\mathcal{G}$ (above) and the relation $\mathbf{RG}(y, z)$ (below).

3.3 NIZK and NIWI Arguments

We recall the definition of NIZK and NIWI arguments and their security properties. We assume that $\mathcal{R}$ is a relation generator that output an NP relation $\mathbf{R}$ and a parameter p (e.g., the group description). An argument system Ψ is a tuple of PPT algorithms $(\mathsf{K}, \mathsf{P}, \mathsf{V})$. The CRS generation algorithm K takes in $(\mathbf{R}, \mathsf{p})$ and outputs a crs and a trapdoor td (which may be $\perp$ if the argument does not have zero-knowledge). The prover algorithm P takes in $\mathbf{R}, \mathsf{p}, \mathsf{crs}$ and $(\mathsf{x}, \mathsf{w}) \in \mathbf{R}$ and outputs a proof π. The verifier algorithm V takes in $(\mathbf{R}, \mathsf{p}, \mathsf{crs}, \mathsf{x}, \pi)$ and outputs either 0 (rejecting the proof) or 1 (accepting the proof). A NIZK argument system will additionally have a simulator Sim that takes in $(\mathbf{R}, \mathsf{p}, \mathsf{crs}, \mathsf{td}, \mathsf{x})$ and outputs a simulated proof π for the statement x. Furthermore, a subversion resistant argument will have a CRS verification algorithm CV that take in $(\mathbf{R}, \mathsf{p}, \mathsf{crs})$ and output either 0 (by rejecting the CRS) or 1 (by accepting the CRS).

Definition 2 (Perfect Completeness [37]**).** *A non-interactive argument Ψ is* perfectly complete for $\mathcal{R}$, *if for all λ, all* $(\mathbf{R}, \mathsf{p}) \in \mathrm{range}(\mathcal{R}(1^\lambda))$, *and* $(\mathsf{x}, \mathsf{w}) \in \mathbf{R}$,

$$\Pr\left[\mathsf{crs} \leftarrow \mathsf{K}(\mathbf{R}, \mathsf{p}) : \mathsf{V}(\mathbf{R}, \mathsf{p}, \mathsf{crs}, \mathsf{x}, \mathsf{P}(\mathbf{R}, \mathsf{p}, \mathsf{crs}, \mathsf{x}, \mathsf{w})) = 1\right] = 1 \ .$$

Definition 3 (Perfect CRS Verifiability). *A non-interactive (subversion-resistant) argument Ψ is* perfectly CRS-verifiable for $\mathcal{R}$, *if for all λ and all* $(\mathbf{R}, \mathsf{p}) \in \mathrm{range}(\mathcal{R}(1^\lambda))$, $\Pr\left[(\mathsf{crs}, \mathsf{td}) \leftarrow \mathsf{K}(\mathbf{R}, \mathsf{p}) : \mathsf{CV}(\mathbf{R}, \mathsf{p}, \mathsf{crs}) = 1\right] = 1$.

Definition 4 (Computational Soundness). *Ψ is computationally (adaptively)* sound for $\mathcal{R}$, *if for every PPT $\mathcal{A}$,*

$$\Pr\left[\begin{array}{l}(\mathbf{R}, \mathsf{p}) \leftarrow \mathcal{R}(1^\lambda), (\mathsf{crs}, \mathsf{td}) \leftarrow \mathsf{K}(\mathbf{R}, \mathsf{p}), (\mathsf{x}, \pi) \leftarrow \mathcal{A}(\mathbf{R}, \mathsf{p}, \mathsf{crs}) : \\ \mathsf{x} \notin \mathcal{L}_{\mathbf{R}} \wedge \mathsf{V}(\mathbf{R}, \mathsf{p}, \mathsf{crs}, \mathsf{x}, \pi) = 1\end{array}\right] \leq \mathsf{negl}(\lambda) \ .$$

Definition 5 (Computational Knowledge Soundness). *Ψ is computationally (adaptively)* knowledge-sound for $\mathcal{R}$, *if for every PPT $\mathcal{A}$, there exists a PPT* *extractor* $\mathsf{Ext}_{\mathcal{A}}$, *such that*

$$\Pr\left[\begin{array}{l}(\mathbf{R},\mathsf{p})\leftarrow\mathcal{R}(1^\lambda),(\mathsf{crs},\mathsf{td})\leftarrow\mathsf{K}(\mathbf{R},\mathsf{p}),r\leftarrow_{\$}\mathsf{RND}_\lambda(\mathcal{A}),\\(\mathsf{x},\pi)\leftarrow\mathcal{A}(\mathbf{R},\mathsf{p},\mathsf{crs};r),\mathsf{w}\leftarrow\mathsf{Ext}_{\mathcal{A}}(\mathbf{R},\mathsf{p},\mathsf{crs};r):\\(\mathsf{x},\mathsf{w})\not\in\mathbf{R}\wedge\mathsf{V}(\mathbf{R},\mathsf{p},\mathsf{crs},\mathsf{x},\pi)=1\end{array}\right]\leq\mathsf{negl}(\lambda)\ .$$

Above we assume that the input $(\mathbf{R},\mathsf{p},\mathsf{crs};r)$ comes from a benign distribution and thus avoids the impossibility result of [14].

Definition 6 (Statistically Composable ZK). *Ψ is* statistically composable zero-knowledge for $\mathcal{R}$, *if for all* $(\mathbf{R},\mathsf{p})\in\mathrm{range}(\mathcal{R}(1^\lambda))$, *and all computationally unbounded* $\mathcal{A}$, $\varepsilon_0^{comp}\approx_\lambda\varepsilon_1^{comp}$, *where* $\varepsilon_b^{comp}=$

$$\Pr\left[\begin{array}{l}(\mathsf{crs},\mathsf{td})\leftarrow\mathsf{K}(\mathbf{R},\mathsf{p}),(\mathsf{x},\mathsf{w})\leftarrow\mathcal{A}(\mathbf{R},\mathsf{p},\mathsf{crs},\mathsf{td});\pi_0\leftarrow\mathsf{P}(\mathbf{R},\mathsf{p},\mathsf{crs},\mathsf{x},\mathsf{w});\\\pi_1\leftarrow\mathsf{Sim}(\mathbf{R},\mathsf{p},\mathsf{crs},\mathsf{td},\mathsf{x}):(\mathsf{x},\mathsf{w})\in\mathbf{R}\wedge\mathcal{A}(\pi_b)=1\end{array}\right].$$

Ψ is perfectly composable ZK for $\mathcal{R}$ *if one requires that* $\varepsilon_0^{comp}=\varepsilon_1^{comp}$. *In Theorem 8 we also consider a computational version of this definition, that is* $\mathcal{A}$ *is a PPT adversary and the input* td *is not given as input to* $\mathcal{A}$.

Definition 7 (Statistically Composable Sub-ZK [1]**).** *Ψ is* statistically composable subversion ZK (Sub-ZK) for $\mathcal{R}$, *if for any PPT subverter* $\mathcal{Z}$ *there exists a PPT* $\mathsf{Ext}_{\mathcal{Z}}$, *such that for all* $\mathbf{R}\in\mathrm{range}(\mathcal{R}(1^\lambda))$, *and all computationally unbounded* $\mathcal{A}$, $\varepsilon_0^{comp}\approx_\lambda\varepsilon_1^{comp}$, *where* $\varepsilon_b^{comp}=$

$$\Pr\left[\begin{array}{l}r\leftarrow_{\$}\mathsf{RND}_\lambda(\mathcal{Z}),(\mathsf{crs},\mathsf{aux}_{\mathcal{Z}})\leftarrow\mathcal{Z}(\mathbf{R},\mathsf{p};r),\mathsf{td}\leftarrow\mathsf{Ext}_{\mathcal{Z}}(\mathbf{R},\mathsf{p};r)\\(\mathsf{x},\mathsf{w})\leftarrow\mathcal{A}(\mathbf{R},\mathsf{p},\mathsf{crs},\mathsf{td},\mathsf{aux}_{\mathcal{Z}}),\pi_0\leftarrow\mathsf{P}(\mathbf{R},\mathsf{p},\mathsf{crs},\mathsf{x},\mathsf{w});\\\pi_1\leftarrow\mathsf{Sim}(\mathbf{R},\mathsf{p},\mathsf{crs},\mathsf{td},\mathsf{x}):(\mathsf{x},\mathsf{w})\in\mathbf{R}\wedge\mathsf{CV}(\mathbf{R},\mathsf{p},\mathsf{crs})=1\wedge\mathcal{A}(\pi_b,\mathsf{aux}_{\mathcal{Z}})=1\end{array}\right].$$

Ψ is perfectly composable Sub-ZK for $\mathcal{R}$ *if one requires that* $\varepsilon_0^{comp}=\varepsilon_1^{comp}$.

Definition 8 (Witness Indistinguishability). *Ψ is* computationally witness indistinguishable (WI) for $\mathcal{R}$, *if for any PPT* $\mathcal{A}$, $\varepsilon_0^{wi}\approx_\lambda\varepsilon_1^{wi}$, *where* $\varepsilon_b^{wi}=$

$$\Pr\left[\begin{array}{l}(\mathsf{crs},\mathsf{td})\leftarrow\mathsf{K}(\mathbf{R},\mathsf{p}),(\mathsf{x},\mathsf{w}_0,\mathsf{w}_1)\leftarrow\mathcal{A}(\mathbf{R},\mathsf{p},\mathsf{crs}),\pi_b\leftarrow\mathsf{P}(\mathbf{R},\mathsf{p},\mathsf{crs},\mathsf{x},\mathsf{w}_b):\\(\mathsf{x},\mathsf{w}_0)\in\mathbf{R}\wedge(\mathsf{x},\mathsf{w}_1)\in\mathbf{R}\wedge\mathcal{A}(\pi_b)=1\end{array}\right].$$

Ψ is perfectly WI for $\mathcal{R}$ *if one requires that* $\varepsilon_0^{wi}=\varepsilon_1^{wi}$ *for unbounded* $\mathcal{A}$. *Note that* td *above might be* $\perp$ *if* Ψ *is not zero-knowledge.*

Definition 9 (Sub-WI [9]**).** *Ψ is* computationally Sub-WI for $\mathcal{R}$, *if for any PPT subverter* $\mathcal{Z}$, $\varepsilon_0^{wi}\approx_\lambda\varepsilon_1^{wi}$, *where* $\varepsilon_b^{wi}=$

$$\Pr\left[\begin{array}{l}(\mathsf{crs},\mathsf{x},\mathsf{w}_0,\mathsf{w}_1,\mathsf{aux}_{\mathcal{Z}})\leftarrow\mathcal{Z}(\mathbf{R},\mathsf{p}),\pi_b\leftarrow\mathsf{P}(\mathbf{R},\mathsf{p},\mathsf{crs},\mathsf{x},\mathsf{w}_b):\\(\mathsf{x},\mathsf{w}_0)\in\mathbf{R}\wedge(\mathsf{x},\mathsf{w}_1)\in\mathbf{R}\wedge\mathsf{CV}(\mathbf{R},\mathsf{p},\mathsf{crs})=1\wedge\mathcal{Z}(\pi_b,\mathsf{aux}_{\mathcal{Z}})=1\end{array}\right].$$

Ψ is perfectly Sub-WI for $\mathcal{R}$ *if one requires that* $\varepsilon_0^{wi}=\varepsilon_1^{wi}$ *for an unbounded* $\mathcal{Z}$. *In case Ψ does not utilise any common string we assume* $\mathsf{CV}(\mathbf{R},\mathsf{p},\varepsilon)=1$.

4 Verifiably-Extractable Generalized OWFs

4.1 Definition

We study GEOWFs $\mathcal{G} = \{\mathsf{g_e}\}$ that come with an efficient (public) algorithm that decides whether or not extraction is going to be successful. That is, we require that there exists an extraction verification algorithm EV, such that $\mathsf{EV}(\mathsf{e}, y)$ decides whether $y \in Y_{\mathsf{Ext}} \supseteq \mathrm{image}(\mathsf{g_e})$, where extraction succeeds for any $y \in Y_{\mathsf{Ext}}$. We also require that, with overwhelming probability, extraction is successful for any adversary which outputs a value in Y_{Ext}. (Extraction *may* succeed even if $y \notin Y_{\mathsf{Ext}}$.) We call GEOWFs with such properties *Verifiably-Extractable Generalized OWFs* (VEGOWFs).

Although for some VEGOWFs it may hold that $Y_{\mathsf{Ext}} = \mathrm{image}(\mathsf{g_e})$, it is not necessarily the case. For example in the BCPR GEOWF, one is not able to decide if $y \in \mathrm{image}(\mathsf{g}_\lambda)$, because any such algorithm can be used to decide membership in image(PRG) which contradicts the security of PRG. However, as we will show, extraction is successful for any $y = (\mathsf{crs_{DS}}, v)$, where $\mathsf{crs_{DS}}$ is a valid DS CRS and v is *any* string output by an adversary with bounded auxiliary input.

Define VEGOWFs as GEOWFs where the **RG**-extractability property has been substituted with the following, stronger one. (It makes an implicit assumption that EV exists.)

RG-Verifiably-Extractable with Respect to Y_{Ext}: Let $\mathrm{image}(\mathsf{g_e}) \subseteq Y_{\mathsf{Ext}} \subseteq Y_\lambda$, and let EV be an efficient algorithm such that $\mathsf{EV}(\mathsf{e}; y) = 1$ iff $y \in Y_{\mathsf{Ext}}$. For any PPT adversary $\mathcal{A}$, there exists a PPT extractor Ext, s.t. for any benign distribution $\mathcal{D}_\lambda$ of $\mathsf{poly}(\lambda)$-bit strings,

$$\Pr_{\substack{\mathsf{e} \leftarrow \mathsf{KeySamp}(1^\lambda) \\ \mathsf{aux} \leftarrow \mathcal{D}_\lambda}} \left[\begin{array}{l} y \leftarrow \mathcal{A}(\mathsf{e}; \mathsf{aux}), z \leftarrow \mathsf{Ext}(\mathsf{e}; \mathsf{aux}) : \\ y \in Y_{\mathsf{Ext}} \wedge (y, z) \notin \mathbf{RG_e} \end{array} \right] \leq \mathsf{negl}(\lambda) \ .$$

If this definition holds for adversaries with auxiliary input length bounded by some polynomial $\mathfrak{b}(\lambda)$, we say that that the GEOWF is **RG**-*verifiably-extractable against* $\mathfrak{b}$*-bounded adversaries with respect to* Y_{Ext}.

We also require that there is a PPT algorithm t, such that for any $x \in X_\lambda$, $(\mathsf{g_e}(x), t(x)) \in \mathbf{RG_e}$, that is, given x, t computes the "witness" for $\mathsf{g_e}(x)$ in **RG**.

If there exists an algorithm ImV that decides membership in image($\mathsf{g_e}$), then the GEOWF is *image-verifiable*. Clearly, any image-verifiable GEOWF is also verifiably-extractable with respect to $Y_{\mathsf{Ext}} = \mathrm{image}(\mathsf{g_e})$. Furthermore, for an EOWF, $\mathbf{RG_e}$ only consists of pairs $(\mathsf{g_e}(x), x)$ so extraction is not possible if one is given $y \notin \mathrm{image}(\mathsf{g_e})$. Hence, for an EOWF, verifiable-extractability is the same as image-verifiability.

4.2 Generic Transformations

VEGOWF ⇒ VEOWF. Surprisingly, any VEGOWF can be transformed to a VEOWF with the transformation in Fig. 3 that adds very little overhead. The

$\mathsf{f_e}(i \in \{0,1\}^\lambda, x \in X_\lambda, y \in Y_\lambda, z \in X_\lambda)$	$\mathsf{ImV_f}(\mathsf{e}; y)$
if $i \neq 0^\lambda$ **then return** $\mathsf{g_e}(x)$; **elseif** $(y,z) \in \mathbf{RG}_\mathsf{e} \wedge \mathsf{EV_g}(\mathsf{e}; y)$ **then return** y; **else return** $\perp$;	**return** $\mathsf{EV_g}(\mathsf{e}; y) \vee y = \perp$;

Fig. 3. Transformation from a VEGOWF $\mathcal{G} = \{\mathsf{g_e}\}_\mathsf{e}$ to a VEOWF $\mathcal{F} = \{\mathsf{f_e}\}_\mathsf{e}$.

idea is to include to a VEGOWF $\mathsf{g_e}$ a branch input $i \in \{0,1\}^\lambda$. If $i \neq 0^\lambda$, which happens with an overwhelming probability, then $\mathsf{g_e}$ works as usual and outputs $\mathsf{g_e}(x)$. However, on a trapdoor branch $i = 0^\lambda$, the function uses its two extra inputs y and z. If y satisfies $\mathsf{EV_g}(\mathsf{e}; y)$ and $(y,z) \in \mathbf{RG}_\mathsf{e}$, it outputs y (or $\perp$ if the condition is not met). One-wayness follows since with overwhelming probability the function outputs $y \in \text{image}(\mathsf{g_e})$ and the preimage has to contain either x such that $\mathsf{g_e}(x) = y$ or z such that $(y,z) \in \mathbf{RG}_\mathsf{e}$. By outputting either $t(x)$ (in the first case) or z (in the other case), one breaks $\mathbf{RG}$-hardness. On the other hand, the VEOWF extractor can use the VEGOWF extractor to recover z from y when $\mathsf{EV_g}(\mathsf{e}; y) = 1$ and then return a preimage $(0^\lambda, \perp, y, z)$.

A similar transformation was introduced in [14] to obtain EOWFs from GEOWFs. However, they observed that an adversary can pick as input $(0^\lambda, \perp, y, z)$ with $(y,z) \in \mathbf{RG}_\mathsf{e}$, but $y \notin \text{image}(\mathsf{g_e})$. This makes the extraction impossible. Our construction does not run into this issue since we assume that extraction is possible when $\mathsf{EV}(\mathsf{e}; y) = 1$.

Theorem 1. *If $\mathcal{G} = \{\mathsf{g_e}\}_\mathsf{e}$ is $\mathbf{RG}$-hard and $\mathbf{RG}$-verifiably-extractable, then $\mathcal{F} = \{\mathsf{f_e}\}_\mathsf{e}$ in Fig. 3 is a VEOWF.*

GEOWFs ⇒ VEGOWF. We now consider a generic transformation from a GEOWF to a VEGOWF. One approach is to simply append a NIZK proof π which proves that the given value was computed correctly. A problem with this approach is that it would require a CRS computed by a trusted third party, which might not be desirable in a number of settings. We therefore give a modification of this approach, where we instead rely on a NIWI, which are known to exist in the plain model under various assumptions [8,15,39].

The intuition is that we create a new function $g(x,y,r) = (f(x), f(y), \pi)$ where π is a NIWI proof (created using randomness r) showing that either $f(x)$ or $f(y)$ belongs to the image of f (in which case extraction will be possible). Verifiable-extractability follows from extractability of the GEOWF as well as perfect soundness of the NIWI, and hardness will follow from the hardness of f and witness-indistinguishability of the NIWI.

Consider a GEOWF $\mathcal{F} = \{\mathsf{f_e}\}_\mathsf{e}$ with an associated relation $\mathbf{RG}$. Let $\Pi = (\mathsf{P}, \mathsf{V})$ be a perfectly sound NIWI, and let the relation $\mathbf{R}_\mathsf{e}((y_1,y_2),(x'_1,x'_2))$ hold iff $y_1 = \mathsf{f_e}(x'_1)$ or $y_2 = \mathsf{f_e}(x'_2)$. We define a VEGOWF $\mathcal{G} = \{\mathsf{g_e}\}_\mathsf{e}$ with an extraction verification algorithm EV in Fig. 4 and define the hardness relation:

$$\mathbf{RG}'_\mathsf{e}((y_1,y_2,\pi),(z_1,z_2)) := \mathbf{RG}_\mathsf{e}(y_1,z_1) \vee \mathbf{RG}_\mathsf{e}(y_2,z_2).$$

$\mathsf{g_e}(x_1, x_2, r)$	$\mathsf{EV}(\mathsf{e}; (y_1, y_2, \pi))$
$y_1 \leftarrow \mathsf{f_e}(x_1); y_2 \leftarrow \mathsf{f_e}(x_2);$ $\pi \leftarrow \mathsf{P}(\mathbf{R_e}, (\mathsf{f_e}(x_1), \mathsf{f_e}(x_2)), (x_1, x_2); r);$ **else return** $(y_1, y_2, \pi);$	**return** $\mathsf{V}(\mathbf{R_e}, (y_1, y_2), \pi);$

Fig. 4. Transformation from a GEOWF $\mathcal{F} = \{\mathsf{f_e}\}_\mathsf{e}$ to a VEGOWF $\mathcal{G} = \{\mathsf{g_e}\}_\mathsf{e}$.

Similar techniques have been used before in conjunction with EOWFs (e.g., 3-round ZK in [12]) but not, up to our knowledge, as a generic transformation. The proof of the following theorem is deferred to the full version of our paper.

Theorem 2. *If $\mathcal{F}$ is a GEOWF with respect to* $\mathbf{RG}$*, then $\mathcal{G}$ in Fig. 4 is a VEGOWF with respect to* $\mathbf{RG}'$.

A Robust Combiner. Additionally, a simple robust combiner is possible for VEGOWFs (or even for GEOWFs). Let us suppose that $\mathcal{G} = \{\mathsf{g}_{\mathsf{e}_1}\}_{\mathsf{e}_1}$, $\mathcal{F} = \{\mathsf{f}_{\mathsf{e}_2}\}_{\mathsf{e}_2}$, and $\mathcal{H} = \{\mathsf{h}_{\mathsf{e}_3}\}_{\mathsf{e}_3}$ are candidate VEGOWFs for the respective relations $\mathbf{RG}^\mathsf{g}$, $\mathbf{RG}^\mathsf{f}$, and $\mathbf{RG}^\mathsf{h}$. We do assume that the associated extraction verification algorithm always accepts when given a value in the image of each candidate, but we make no other assumption about the security of the candidates.

We define a new VEGOWF $\mathcal{T} = \{\mathsf{t_e}\}_\mathsf{e}$ by $\mathsf{t_e}(x, y, z) := (\mathsf{g}_{\mathsf{e}_1}(x), \mathsf{f}_{\mathsf{e}_2}(y), \mathsf{h}_{\mathsf{e}_3}(z))$ where $\mathsf{e} = (\mathsf{e}_1, \mathsf{e}_2, \mathsf{e}_3)$ and the relation $\mathbf{RG}_\mathsf{e}$ is

$$\left\{ \begin{array}{l} ((a, b, c), (z_1, z_2)) : ((a, z_1) \in \mathbf{RG}^\mathsf{g}_{\mathsf{e}_1} \wedge (b, z_2) \in \mathbf{RG}^\mathsf{f}_{\mathsf{e}_2}) \vee \\ ((a, z_1) \in \mathbf{RG}^\mathsf{g}_{\mathsf{e}_1} \wedge (c, z_2) \in \mathbf{RG}^\mathsf{h}_{\mathsf{e}_3}) \vee ((b, z_1) \in \mathbf{RG}^\mathsf{f}_{\mathsf{e}_2} \wedge (c, z_2) \in \mathbf{RG}^\mathsf{h}_{\mathsf{e}_3}) \end{array} \right\}.$$

We define the new extraction verification algorithm to accept when all individual extraction verification algorithms accept.

If any two of the candidates are hard for their respective relations, then $\mathcal{T}$ is $\mathbf{RG}$-hard. Similarly, if any two are extractable, then $\mathcal{T}$ is $\mathbf{RG}$-extractable. The idea can be generalized to n VEGOWFs for an arbitrary constant n, where it is sufficient that more than $n/2$ are secure. An interesting open question is to construct a robust combiner where fewer functions have to be secure.

4.3 The BCPR GEOWF is Verifiably-Extractable

We show that if a delegation scheme DS is CRS-verifiable, then the BCPR GEOWF from Fig. 2 is verifiably-extractable with respect to $Y_\mathsf{Ext} = \mathrm{image}(\mathsf{DS.K}(1^\lambda)) \times \{0,1\}^{\mathfrak{b}(\lambda)+\lambda}$. That is, z contains the code of an adversary and the DS argument, independently of whether or not $y \in \mathrm{image}(\mathsf{g}_\lambda)$.

The proof of the following theorem is very similar to the proof of Theorem 14 from [14]; we have reproduced it for the sake of completeness.

Theorem 3. *Let* DS *be a delegation scheme that has publicly verifiable proofs and CRS, and let* $\mathsf{PRG} : \{0,1\}^\lambda \to \{0,1\}^{\mathfrak{b}(\lambda)+\lambda}$ *be a PRG. Let* $\mathcal{G} = \{\mathsf{g}_\lambda\}_{\lambda \in \mathbb{N}}$ *and* $\mathbf{RG}$ *be as in Fig. 2.* $\mathcal{G}$ *is a VEGOWF for* $\mathbf{RG}$ *with respect to* $Y_\mathsf{Ext} = \mathrm{image}(\mathsf{DS.K}(1^\lambda)) \times \{0,1\}^{\mathfrak{b}(\lambda)+\lambda}$ *and* $(\mathfrak{b}(\lambda) - \omega(1))$*-bounded* aux.

Proof. **RG-hardness.** Identical to the proof of Theorem 14 in [14].

RG-verifiable-extractability. Since DS is CRS-verifiable, there exists an algorithm CV which decides if $\mathsf{crs}_{\mathsf{DS}} \in \text{image}(\mathsf{DS.K}(1^\lambda))$. On input $y = (\mathsf{crs}_{\mathsf{DS}}, v)$, the new extraction verification algorithm EV returns 1 if $\mathsf{CV}(\mathsf{crs}_{\mathsf{DS}}) = 1$ and $|v| = \mathfrak{b}(\lambda) + \lambda$.

We show that there is one universal PPT extractor Ext that can handle any PPT adversary $\mathcal{A}$ with advice of size at most $\mathfrak{b}(\lambda) - \omega(1)$. For an adversary $\mathcal{A}$ (a Turing machine) and advice $\mathsf{aux} \in \{0,1\}^{\mathfrak{b}(\lambda)-\omega(1)}$, denote by $\mathcal{A}_{\mathsf{aux}}$ the machine that, on input 1^λ, runs $\mathcal{A}(1^\lambda; \mathsf{aux})$. Assume that (i) $\mathcal{A}_{\mathsf{aux}}$ has description size at most $\mathfrak{b}(\lambda)$ and that (i) on input 1^λ, after at most $t_{\mathcal{A}} < T(\lambda)$ steps, it outputs $\mathcal{A}_{\mathsf{aux}}(1^\lambda) := y = (\mathsf{crs}_{\mathsf{DS}}, v) \in \{0,1\}^{\mathfrak{l}'(\lambda)}$. (Recall $Y_{\mathsf{Ext}} \subseteq \{0,1\}^{\mathfrak{l}'(\lambda)}$.) The extractor $\mathsf{Ext}(\mathcal{A}, \mathsf{aux}, 1^{t_{\mathcal{A}}})$ works as follows:

$\mathsf{Ext}(\mathcal{A}, \mathsf{aux}, 1^{t_{\mathcal{A}}})$

Construct $\mathcal{A}_{\mathsf{aux}}$;
$(\mathsf{crs}_{\mathsf{DS}}, v) \leftarrow \mathcal{A}_{\mathsf{aux}}(1^\lambda)$; **if** $\mathsf{EV}((\mathsf{crs}_{\mathsf{DS}}, v)) = 0$ **then return** $\perp$; **fi** ;
Compute a DS-argument π_{DS} for the fact that "$\mathcal{A}_{\mathsf{aux}}(1^\lambda) = (\mathsf{crs}_{\mathsf{DS}}, v)$";
return $z \leftarrow (\mathcal{A}_{\mathsf{aux}}, \pi_{\mathsf{DS}}, \mathsf{pad})$;

It follows directly from the perfect completeness of DS that $\mathbf{RG}(y, z) = 1$. Since this holds for any $(\mathsf{crs}_{\mathsf{DS}}, v) \in Y_{\mathsf{Ext}}$ output by an adversary with $(\mathfrak{b}(\lambda) - \omega(1))$-bounded auxiliary input, we get **RG**-verifiable-extractability. By the relative prover efficiency of the delegation scheme, the extractor's running time is polynomial in the running time $t_{\mathcal{A}}$ of the adversary. □

To instantiate the construction, we need a delegation scheme with public CRS and proof verification. Firstly, SNARKs in [1,27,51] satisfy both properties and have succinct proofs. All of them are based on non-falsifiable assumptions, however, here it is only needed that they are sound for the class P. Thus, even a tautological security assumption (the corresponding SNARK is sound for BPP) would be falsifiable. Secondly, some recent suggestions for delegation schemes [43,45] with public proof-verification are based on non-tautological falsifiable assumptions. Unfortunately, it is not immediately evident if those schemes also have CRS-verifiability. We leave the latter as an important open problem.

4.4 VEGOWFs from Knowledge-of-Exponent Assumptions

Next, we construct VEGOWFs based on knowledge-of-exponent (KE) assumptions, a logical direction partially motivated by [22, Section 3.3.1.1]. In each case, the key is a description p of an asymmetric or symmetric (in the latter case, we state it explicitly) bilinear group generated by a group generator algorithm $\mathsf{Pgen}(1^\lambda)$. Note that if the group generator Pgen is deterministic, i.e., each security parameter corresponds to a unique group, this is a keyless EOWF.

The ABLZ VEOWF from BDH-KE. The ABLZ VEOWF is based on an idea from Abdolmaleki *et al.* [1]. We define $\mathsf{g}_{\mathsf{p}}(x) := ([x]_1, [x]_2)$. The one-way property of the ABLZ EOWF is equivalent to the Symmetric Discrete Logarithm

(SDL) assumption, and extractability is equivalent to the BDH-KE assumption introduced in [1]. Finally, one can verify if $([x]_1, [y]_2) \in \text{image}(\mathsf{g_p})$ by checking that $[x]_1 \bullet [1]_1 = [1]_1 \bullet [y]_2$. We give a formal proof that this is a VEOWF in the full version of the paper. Note that this VEOWF is injective.

VEGOWF from DH-KE. Some KE assumptions from the literature lead to VEGOWFs rather than VEOWFs. The Diffie-Hellman KE (DH-KE) assumption introduced in [9] states that any adversary which produces a DDH triple $[x, y, xy]_1$ must know at least one of x and y. Given a symmetric bilinear group, this gives rise to the following VEGOWF. Define $\mathsf{g_p}(x, y) := [x, y, xy]_1$ and the relation $\mathbf{RG}_\mathsf{p}([x, y, xy]_1, z) = 1$ iff $z = x$ or $z = y$. We can verify if $[x, y, w]_1 \in \text{image}(\mathsf{g_p})$ by checking that $[x]_1 \bullet [y]_1 = [w]_1 \bullet [1]_1$. This function is **RG**-hard if the discrete logarithm problem is hard and is verifiably-extractable if the DH-KE assumption holds.

Further Examples. There are also a number of other knowledge of exponent assumptions in the literature, and these give rise to the following verifiably-extractable injective OWFs:

- $\mathsf{g}_{(\mathsf{p},[1,\alpha]_1)}(x) := [x, x\alpha]_1$ is a OWF under the discrete logarithm assumption and verifiably-extractable for symmetric pairings under the knowledge-of-exponent assumption [23].
- $\mathsf{g_p}(x) = ([1, x, \dots, x^q]_1, [1, x, \dots, x^q]_2)$ is a OWF under the q-PDL assumption [48] and verifiably-extractable under the q-PKE assumption [24].
- $\mathsf{g_p}(x) = ([x, x^2]_1, [x]_2)$ is a OWF under a well-known variant of the discrete logarithm assumption and verifiably-extractable under the square knowledge of exponent assumption [27].
- $\mathsf{g_p}(x) = ([x]_1, [1/x]_2)$ is a OWF under the inverse-exponent assumption [54] and verifiably-extractable under the tautological assumption, which we call *inverse-KE*, that it is hard to compute $[x]_1$, $[1/x]_2$ without knowing x.

4.5 VEGOWFs from Knowledge-Sound NIZK

Dakdouk [22, Section 3.3.3.2] observed that EOWFs can be constructed from the proof of knowledge (PoK) assumption of Lepinski [47] which states that a specific non-interactive Σ-protocol described in [47] is secure. We generalize this idea, and show how to use knowledge-sound NIZKs to build VEGOWFs.

Suppose that $\mathbf{R}$ is an NP relation with a sampler $\mathcal{S}_{\mathbf{R},\mathsf{p}}$ that outputs (x, w), such that (i) it is efficient to verify that (x, w) is a possible output of $\mathcal{S}_{\mathbf{R},\mathsf{p}}$, and (ii) with an overwhelming probability it is computationally hard to guess w given x. Then we say that this relation is $\mathcal{S}_{\mathbf{R},\mathsf{p}}$-hard. Such samplers (and relations) are common in cryptography, e.g., the discrete logarithm problem ($\mathsf{x} = [x]_1, \mathsf{w} = x$ for a uniformly random x) and the short integer solution problem ($\mathsf{x} = A$ is a random matrix and $\mathsf{w} = \boldsymbol{x}$ is a short integer vector such that $A\boldsymbol{x} = 0$).

Consider a knowledge-sound NIZK $\Pi = (\mathsf{KGen}, \mathsf{P}, \mathsf{V}, \mathsf{Sim})$ for a $\mathcal{S}_{\mathbf{R},\mathsf{p}}$-hard relation $\mathbf{R}$, where $\mathsf{P}, \mathsf{V}, \mathsf{Sim}$ are the prover, the verifier, and the simulator. KGen is the "key" generation algorithm, such that $\mathsf{KGen}(\mathbf{R}, \mathsf{p})$ produces an auxiliary input aux_Π, provided to P, V and Sim. If the NIZK uses a random oracle, then

aux_Π may contain the description of a hash function instantiating the random oracle. If the NIZK is CRS-based, then aux_Π contains the CRS. The following theorem shows how to construct a VEGOWF given a knowledge-sound NIZK.

Theorem 4. *Define* $\mathcal{G} := \{\mathsf{g}_{\mathbf{R},\mathsf{p},\mathsf{aux}_\Pi}\}_{\mathbf{R}\in\mathcal{R}(1^\lambda),\mathsf{p}\leftarrow\mathsf{Pgen}(1^\lambda),\mathsf{aux}_\Pi\in\mathsf{KGen}(\mathbf{R},\mathsf{p})}$*, where* $\mathsf{g}_{\mathbf{R},\mathsf{p},\mathsf{aux}_\Pi}(r_\mathcal{S}, r_\Pi)$ *sets* $(\mathsf{x},\mathsf{w}) \leftarrow \mathcal{S}_\mathbf{R}(r_\mathcal{S})$*,* π *produced by* Π*'s prover* P *for* x,w*, and then outputs* (x,π)*. Define the corresponding relation as* $\mathbf{RG}_{\mathbf{R},\mathsf{p},\mathsf{aux}_\Pi} :=$

$$\{(\widehat{y},\widehat{z}) : \widehat{y} = (\mathsf{x},\pi) \wedge \widehat{z} = \mathsf{w} \wedge \Pi.\mathsf{V} \text{ accepts } \pi \wedge (\mathsf{x},\mathsf{w}) \in \mathbf{R}\} . \tag{1}$$

If $\mathbf{R}$ *is* $\mathcal{S}_\mathbf{R}$*-hard and* Π *is zero-knowledge, then* $\mathcal{G}$ *is* $\mathbf{RG}$*-hard. If* Π *is a proof of knowledge, then* $\mathcal{G}$ *is* $\mathbf{RG}$*-verifiably-extractable.*

Proof. **RG-hardness:** Let $\mathcal{B}$ be an adversary that given $\widehat{y} = (\mathsf{x},\pi)$, where π is a proof for (x,w) returns $\widehat{z}$, such that $\mathbf{RG}_{\mathbf{R},\mathsf{p},\mathsf{aux}_\Pi}(\widehat{y},\widehat{z})$ holds with non-negligible probability. We construct an adversary $\mathcal{B}$ that breaks $\mathcal{S}_\mathbf{R}$-hardness. On input $(\mathbf{R},\mathsf{x})$, $\mathcal{B}$ sets $\mathsf{aux}_\Pi \leftarrow \mathsf{KGen}(\mathbf{R},\mathsf{p})$, runs the simulator Sim and gets a simulated proof π_Sim. Since Π is zero-knowledge, $\mathcal{B}$ outputs the same $\widehat{z} = \mathsf{w}$ (with overwhelming probability) when run on $\widehat{y} = (\mathsf{x},\pi)$ and $\widehat{y} = (\mathsf{x},\pi_\mathsf{Sim})$. Thus, $\mathcal{B}$ breaks the $\mathcal{S}_{\mathbf{R},\mathsf{p}}$-hardness of $\mathbf{R}$ with non-negligible probability.

RG-verifiable-extractability: Clearly, one can verify that $\widehat{y} \in \mathrm{image}(\mathsf{g}_{\mathbf{R},\mathsf{p},\mathsf{aux}_\Pi})$ by checking that the NIZK verifier accepts $\widehat{y} = (\mathsf{x},\pi)$, i.e., Π's verifier accepts. We use the knowledge-soundness extractor Ext from Π to build a $\mathcal{G}$ extractor $\mathsf{Ext}_\mathcal{G}$. Let $\mathcal{A}_\mathsf{ext}$ be an algorithm that on input $(\mathbf{R},\mathsf{p},\mathsf{aux}_\Pi)$ outputs $\widehat{y} \in \mathrm{image}(\mathsf{g}_{\mathbf{R},\mathsf{p},\mathsf{aux}_\Pi})$. Since $\widehat{y} \in \mathrm{image}(\mathsf{g}_{\mathbf{R},\mathsf{p},\mathsf{aux}_\Pi})$, then $\widehat{y} = (\mathsf{x},\pi)$ and Π's verifier accepts. $\mathsf{Ext}_\mathcal{G}$ runs Ext on the same input $(\mathbf{R},\mathsf{p},\mathsf{aux}_\Pi)$ given to $\mathcal{A}_\mathsf{ext}$. By knowledge-soundness, with an overwhelming probability, the Π-extractor Ext outputs w, such that $(\mathsf{x},\mathsf{w}) \in \mathbf{R}$. $\mathsf{Ext}_\mathcal{G}$ sets $\widehat{z} \leftarrow \mathsf{w}$, and succeeds with the same probability as Ext. □

For the sake of concreteness we instantiate the above result as follows. Let Σ be the non-interactive version (e.g., by using the Fiat-Shamir transform) of the well-known Schnorr's protocol for proving the knowledge of the discrete logarithm of $\mathsf{x} = [x]_1$. Let the VEGOWF key be $\mathsf{e} = (\mathbf{R},\mathsf{p},\mathsf{aux}_\Pi = H)$, where p is the system parameters (group description). Define $\mathsf{g}_\mathsf{e}(x,r) := ([x]_1, a = [r]_1, z = cx + r) = \widehat{y}$, where $c = H([x]_1,[r]_1)$. The verifier recomputes c and accepts if $[z]_1 = c\mathsf{x} + a$ and $c = H(\mathsf{x},a)$. Then $\mathbf{RG}_\mathsf{e}$-verifiable-extractability holds since Σ is knowledge-sound in the random oracle model and the algebraic group model [29]. If Σ is zero-knowledge in the random oracle model and the discrete logarithm problem is hard, g_e is also $\mathbf{RG}_\mathsf{e}$-hard. Moreover, Σ can be used to get an injective VEOWF since after the extractor extracts the witness x, it can also compute $r \leftarrow z - cx$.

4.6 VEGOWFs from Signature Schemes

We propose the following heuristic approach for finding new candidates for VEGOWFs. Suppose that $\Sigma = (\mathsf{KGen},\mathsf{sign},\mathsf{Vf})$ is a digital signature scheme. If an adversary outputs (vk,σ) such that $\mathsf{vk} \in \mathsf{KGen}$ and $\mathsf{Vf}(\mathsf{vk},\sigma,m = 0) = 1$, then there exists an extractor that can recover (some part of) sk. In other words, we follow the intuition that if someone can sign a message (say $m = 0$ for simplicity), then she must possess the secret key. Moreover, if $\mathsf{vk} \in \mathsf{KGen}$ can be efficiently verified, then we might be able obtain a VEGOWF.

Remark 1. Note that unforgeability of a signature scheme does not require that the signer *knows* the secret key. It is only important that the adversary cannot produce valid signatures for previously unsigned messages. A stronger notion of knowledge has been formalized by signatures of knowledge [21], where the signer can sign messages under any statement $\mathsf{x} \in \mathcal{L}$ if it knows the corresponding witness. In general this is a very strong notion and implies, e.g., simulation-extractable NIZKs. Therefore, we will not focus on those constructions here.

There are signature schemes which do give believable VEGOWF candidates, but there are also cases where it clearly fails. We will mention some of them here, and defer others to the full version of our paper.

Negative Example: RSA Signatures. Let H be a hash function, $\mathsf{sk} = d$ be the secret key and $\mathsf{vk} = (n, e)$ be a public key such that $de \equiv 1 \pmod{n}$. A signature of an integer m is then $\sigma = H(m)^d \mod n$, and a signature σ of a message m is valid if $\sigma^e \equiv H(m) \pmod{n}$. However, RSA signatures are also not good candidates for a VEGOWF. The adversary could easily compute $\mathsf{vk} = (n, 3)$ such that $H(0) \mod n$ is a perfect cube, then output $(\mathsf{vk}, (H(0) \mod n)^{1/3})$.

Positive Example: Boneh-Boyen Signatures. Boneh-Boyen [16] is a pairing-based signature scheme where $\mathsf{vk} = [x]_2$ and $\mathsf{sk} = x \leftarrow_\$ \mathbb{Z}_p$ and $\mathsf{sign}(\mathsf{sk}, m) = [1/(x+m)]_1$. In fact, $\mathsf{g}_\mathsf{p}(x) = (\mathsf{vk}, \mathsf{sign}(0)) = ([x]_2, [1/x]_1)$ is an asymmetric version of a VEOWF candidate mentioned in Sect. 4.4. In particular, it is verifiably-extractable under a similar tautological assumption.

Positive Example: BLS Signatures. BLS [17] is another pairing-based signature scheme where $\mathsf{vk} = [x]_2$, $\mathsf{sk} = x \leftarrow_\$ \mathbb{Z}_p$, and $\mathsf{sign}(\mathsf{sk}, m) = xH(m) = [\sigma]_1$ where H hashes into $\mathbb{G}_1$. Verification is done by checking that $[\sigma]_1[1]_2 = H(m)[x]_2$. This gives us a VEOWF candidate $\mathsf{g}_\mathsf{p}(x) = ([x]_2, xH(0))$.

Positive Example: DSA. In the DSA signature scheme,[6] we again have some discrete logarithm secure group $\mathsf{p} = (\mathbb{G}, p, g)$. The verification key is $\mathsf{vk} = g^x$ for $\mathsf{sk} = x \leftarrow_\$ \mathbb{Z}_p$, $\sigma = \mathsf{sign}(\mathsf{sk}, M \in \{0,1\}^*; r) = (u = g^r \bmod p, v = r^{-1}(H_K(m) + xu) \bmod p)$, and the verifier checks that $0 < u, v < p$ and $u = (g^{H_K(M)}\mathsf{vk}^u)^{v^{-1}} \bmod p$. DSA results in a candidate VEOWF $\mathsf{g}_{\mathsf{p},K}(x, r) = (g^x, g^r \bmod p, r^{-1}(H_K(m) + xu) \bmod p)$.

Hash-and-Sign Lattice Signatures. We recall hash-and-sign lattice-based signatures introduced by Gentry et al. [31], which relies on the hardness of the short integer solution problem. Let p be a prime, H be a hash function, and let $A \in \mathbb{Z}_p^{m \times n}$ be a randomly generated matrix. Define $L_p^\perp(A) := \{y | Ay = 0 \mod p\}$, and let T be a basis of $L_p^\perp(A)$ with short vectors. The trapdoor can be used to compute short vectors s s.t. $As = b$, for any vector b. Set $\mathsf{vk} = A$ and $\mathsf{sk} = T$.

[6] https://nvlpubs.nist.gov/nistpubs/FIPS/NIST.FIPS.186-4.pdf.

To sign a message m, one first computes $b = H(m)$, then outputs a short $s = \sigma_A(b)$ such that $As = b$. A signature σ of a message m is valid if it is short and if $A\sigma = H(m)$. However, this does not work as a VEGOWF. The adversary could easily compute s with a nice structure (e.g., a unit vector), then choose A such that $As = H(\mathbf{0})$. An easy fix is to set $b = H(A, m)$ to prevent choosing A after setting s. This results in a candidate VEOWF $\mathsf{g}_p(x) = (A, \sigma_A(H(A, \mathbf{0})))$, where x is a short basis of $L_p^{\perp}(A)$.

5 Sub-ZK NIZKs Based on VEGOWFs

We give a generic construction of a knowledge-sound Sub-ZK NIZK from any VEGOWF and any knowledge-sound Sub-WI NIWI in the CRS model. We also give a generic construction of a sound Sub-ZK NIZK from any VEGOWF, any keyless extractable commitment and any Sub-WI NIWI in the CRS model. Later, we show some interesting instantiations of these constructions.

5.1 Constructing Knowledge-Sound Sub-ZK NIZK

Let $\mathcal{G} = \{\mathsf{g}_\lambda : X_\lambda \to Y_\lambda \mid \lambda \in \mathbb{N}\}$ be a keyless VEGOWF with respect to a publicly testable relation $\mathbf{RG}$ on triples $(1^\lambda, \widehat{y}, \widehat{z})$. We construct a knowledge-sound Sub-ZK NIZK Π by using a knowledge-sound Sub-WI NIWI Π_{wi} and $\mathcal{G}$. To prove that $\mathsf{x} \in \mathcal{L}$, we use Π_{wi} to prove that $(\mathsf{x}, \widehat{y}) \in \mathcal{L}'$, where $\widehat{y} \in Y_{\mathsf{Ext}}$ is a new element in the CRS for Π, and $\mathbf{R}' := \{(\mathsf{x}_{\mathbf{R}'} = (\mathsf{x}, \widehat{y}), \mathsf{w}_{\mathbf{R}'} = (\mathsf{w}, \widehat{z})) : (\mathsf{x}, \mathsf{w}) \in \mathbf{R} \vee (\widehat{y}, \widehat{z}) \in \mathbf{RG}\}$ where $\mathcal{L} = \{\mathsf{x} \mid \exists \mathsf{w} : (\mathsf{x}, \mathsf{w}) \in \mathbf{R}\}$ and $\mathcal{L}' = \{\mathsf{x}_{\mathbf{R}'} \mid \exists \mathsf{w}_{\mathbf{R}'} : (\mathsf{x}_{\mathbf{R}'}, \mathsf{w}_{\mathbf{R}'}) \in \mathbf{R}'\}$. We assume that $\mathbf{R}$ is generated by a relation generator $\mathcal{R}(1^\lambda)$. The full construction of Π can be found in Fig. 5.

The construction yields a knowledge-sound Sub-ZK NIZK, where knowledge-soundness follows from the $\mathbf{RG}$-hardness of $\mathcal{G}$ and the knowledge-soundness of Π_{wi}, and subversion zero-knowledge is achieved by the $\mathbf{RG}$-verifiable-extractability of $\mathcal{G}$ as well as the subversion witness-indistinguishability of Π_{wi}.

Note that if $\mathbf{R}$ is implemented by a circuit of size k and $\mathbf{RG}$ is implemented by a circuit of size l, then the efficiency of Π is the same as the efficiency of Π' for the modified circuit of size $k + l$. Note also that l is independent of $\mathbf{R}$. The proof of the following theorem is deferred to the full version of our paper.

Theorem 5 (Knowledge-sound Sub-WI NIWI + VEGOWF $\Longrightarrow$ Knowledge-sound Sub-ZK NIZK). *Let Π_{wi} be a non-interactive argument for $\mathbf{R}'$ and let $\mathcal{G} = \{\mathsf{g}_\lambda\}_{\lambda \in \mathbb{N}}$ be a keyless function family with a corresponding publicly testable relation* $\mathbf{RG}$.

(1) If Π_{wi} is complete then Π is complete.
(2) If Π_{wi} is knowledge-sound for $\mathbf{R}'$ and $\mathcal{G}$ is $\mathbf{RG}$-hard then Π is knowledge-sound for $\mathbf{R}$.
(3) If Π_{wi} is Sub-WI for $\mathbf{R}'$ and $\mathcal{G}$ is $\mathbf{RG}$-verifiably-extractable, then Π is Sub-ZK for $\mathbf{R}$.

$\mathsf{K}(\mathbf{R})$

$\widehat{x} \leftarrow_{\$} X_\lambda$;
$\widehat{y} \leftarrow \mathsf{g}_\lambda(\widehat{x})$
$\mathsf{crs}' \leftarrow \mathsf{K}'(\mathbf{R})$
$\mathsf{crs} \leftarrow (\mathsf{crs}', \widehat{y})$
$\mathsf{td} \leftarrow t(\widehat{x})$
return $(\mathsf{crs}, \mathsf{td})$

$\mathsf{CV}(\mathbf{R}, \mathsf{crs})$

parse $\mathsf{crs} = (\mathsf{crs}', \widehat{y})$;
if $\mathsf{CV}(\mathbf{R}', \mathsf{crs}') = 1 \wedge \widehat{y} \in Y_{\mathsf{Ext}}$
  then return 1
  else return 0

$\mathsf{Sim}(\mathbf{R}, \mathsf{crs}, \mathsf{x}, \mathsf{td})$

parse $\mathsf{crs} = (\mathsf{crs}', \widehat{y})$;
return $\mathsf{P}'(\mathbf{R}', \mathsf{crs}', (\mathsf{x}, \widehat{y}), (\perp, \mathsf{td}))$

$\mathsf{P}(\mathbf{R}, \mathsf{crs}, \mathsf{x}, \mathsf{w})$

parse $\mathsf{crs} = (\mathsf{crs}', \widehat{y})$
return $\pi \leftarrow \mathsf{P}'(\mathbf{R}', \mathsf{crs}', (\mathsf{x}, \widehat{y}), (\mathsf{w}, \perp))$;

$\mathsf{V}(\mathbf{R}, \mathsf{crs}, \mathsf{x}, \pi)$

parse $\mathsf{crs} = (\mathsf{crs}', \widehat{y})$;
return $\mathsf{V}'(\mathbf{R}', \mathsf{crs}', (\mathsf{x}, \widehat{y}), \pi)$

Fig. 5. The Sub-ZK KS NIZK $\Pi = (\mathsf{K}, \mathsf{CV}, \mathsf{P}, \mathsf{V}, \mathsf{Sim})$, where $\Pi_{wi} = (\mathsf{K}', \mathsf{CV}', \mathsf{P}', \mathsf{V}')$ is a Sub-WI KS argument, and $\mathcal{G} = \{\mathsf{g}_\lambda\}_{\lambda \in \mathbb{N}}$ is a VEGOWF. Recall that t computes the "witness" for $\mathsf{g}_\lambda(\widehat{x})$ in **RG**.

(4) *If Π_{wi} is a Sub-WI SNARK and $\mathcal{G}$ is a VEGOWF with respect to a relation* **RG** *which takes inputs of polynomial size, then Π is a Sub-ZK SNARK.*

5.2 Constructing Sub-ZK NIZK

Next, we propose a Sub-ZK NIZK Π which only relies on Π_{wi} being sound, not knowledge-sound, but Π will also not be knowledge-sound. As part of this construction, we rely on a keyless extractable commitment scheme. We now give the definition of a keyless extractable commitment scheme, and in the full version of our paper we show how this can be constructed based on injective EOWFs.

Definition 10. *We say that $\mathsf{Com}_\lambda \colon \mathcal{M}_\lambda \times \mathcal{R}_\lambda \to \mathcal{C}_\lambda$ is a keyless extractable commitment if it satisfies the following properties.*

Computational hiding: *For any PPT adversary $\mathcal{A}$, $\varepsilon_0 \approx_\lambda \varepsilon_1$, where*

$$\varepsilon_b := \Pr\left[\begin{matrix}(m_1, m_2) \leftarrow \mathcal{A}(1^\lambda), r \leftarrow_{\$} \mathcal{R}_\lambda, c \leftarrow \mathsf{Com}_\lambda(m_b; r) : \\ m_1, m_2 \in \mathcal{M}_\lambda \wedge \mathcal{A}(c) = 1\end{matrix}\right] .$$

Perfect binding: *For any adversary $\mathcal{A}$ and $\lambda \in \mathbb{N}$,*

$$\Pr\left[\begin{matrix}(m_1, r_1, m_2, r_2) \leftarrow \mathcal{A}(1^\lambda) : \\ \mathsf{Com}_\lambda(m_1; r_1) = \mathsf{Com}_\lambda(m_2; r_2) \wedge m_1 \neq m_2\end{matrix}\right] = 0 .$$

Non-black-box extractability: *Let $\mathcal{D}$ be a family $\{D_\lambda\}_\lambda$ of efficiently sampleable distributions. We say that $\mathsf{Com}_\lambda \colon \mathcal{M}_\lambda \times \mathcal{R}_\lambda \to \mathcal{C}_\lambda$ is non-black-box extractable with respect to auxiliary distribution $\mathcal{D}$ if for any PPT adversary $\mathcal{A}$, there exists a PPT extractor $\mathsf{Ext}_\mathcal{A}$ such that,*

$$\Pr\left[\begin{matrix}\mathsf{aux} \leftarrow_{\$} D_\lambda, c \leftarrow \mathcal{A}(1^\lambda, \mathsf{aux}), m \leftarrow \mathsf{Ext}_\mathcal{A}(1^\lambda, \mathsf{aux}), \\ c \in \mathrm{image}(\mathsf{Com}_\lambda) : c = \mathsf{Com}_\lambda(m; r) \text{ for some } r \in \mathcal{R}_\lambda;\end{matrix}\right] \geq 1 - \mathsf{negl}(\lambda) .$$

$\mathsf{K}(\mathbf{R})$

$\widehat{x} \leftarrow_{\$} X_\lambda$;
$\widehat{y} \leftarrow \mathsf{g}_\lambda(\widehat{x})$;
$\mathsf{crs}' \leftarrow \mathsf{K}'(\mathbf{R}')$;
$\mathsf{crs} \leftarrow (\mathsf{crs}', \widehat{y})$;
$\mathsf{td} \leftarrow t(\widehat{x})$;
return $(\mathsf{crs}, \mathsf{td})$;

$\mathsf{CV}(\mathbf{R}, \mathsf{crs})$

parse $\mathsf{crs} = (\mathsf{crs}', \widehat{y})$;
if $\mathsf{CV}'(\mathbf{R}', \mathsf{crs}') = 1 \wedge y \in Y_{\mathsf{Ext}}$;
  then return 1
  else return 0

$\mathsf{Sim}(\mathbf{R}, \mathsf{crs}, \mathsf{td} = \widehat{z}, \mathsf{x})$

parse $\mathsf{crs} = (\mathsf{crs}', \widehat{y})$;
$r \leftarrow_{\$} \mathsf{RND}_\lambda(\mathsf{Com})$;
$c \leftarrow \mathsf{Com}(\widehat{z}; r)$;
$\pi' \leftarrow \mathsf{P}(\mathbf{R}', \mathsf{crs}', (\mathsf{x}, c, \widehat{y}), (\perp, \widehat{z}, r))$;
return $\pi \leftarrow (c, \pi')$

$\mathsf{P}(\mathbf{R}, \mathsf{crs}, \mathsf{x}, \mathsf{w})$

parse $\mathsf{crs} = (\mathsf{crs}', \widehat{y})$;
$r \leftarrow \mathsf{RND}_\lambda(\mathsf{Com})$;
$c \leftarrow \mathsf{Com}(x_\lambda; r)$ where $x_\lambda \leftarrow_{\$} X_\lambda$;
$\pi' \leftarrow \mathsf{P}'(\mathbf{R}', \mathsf{crs}', (\mathsf{x}, c, \widehat{y}), (\mathsf{w}, x_\lambda, r))$;
return $\pi \leftarrow (c, \pi')$;

$\mathsf{V}(\mathbf{R}, \mathsf{crs}, \mathsf{x}, \pi)$

parse $\pi = (c, \pi')$;
parse $\mathsf{crs} = (\mathsf{crs}', \widehat{y})$;
return $\mathsf{V}'(\mathbf{R}', \mathsf{crs}', (\mathsf{x}, c, \widehat{y}), \pi')$;

Fig. 6. The Sub-ZK NIZK $\Pi = (\mathsf{K}, \mathsf{CV}, \mathsf{P}, \mathsf{V}, \mathsf{Sim})$, where $\Pi_{wi} = (\mathsf{K}', \mathsf{CV}', \mathsf{P}', \mathsf{V}')$ is a Sub-WI NIWI, C is an extractable commitment scheme, and $\mathcal{G} = \{\mathsf{g}_\lambda\}_{\lambda \in \mathbb{N}}$ is a GEOWF.

In some cases, we may have an efficient commitment verification function ComV_λ *that outputs 1 on input* c *if and only if* $c \in \mathrm{image}(\mathsf{Com}_\lambda)$.

Let $\mathcal{G} = \{\mathsf{g}_\lambda\}_{\lambda \in \mathbb{N}}$ be a function family with associated relation $\mathbf{RG}$. Let $\mathsf{C} = (\mathsf{Com}, \mathsf{Open}, \mathsf{Vf})$ be an extractable commitment scheme. Let Π_{wi} be a NIWI argument for the relation We set $\mathsf{crs} = (\mathsf{crs}', \widehat{y})$, where crs' is the CRS of the underlying NIWI Π_{wi} for $\mathbf{R}'$ and crs is the CRS of the NIZK for $\mathbf{R}$. The argument consists of the commitment c and the Π_{wi}-argument π; see Fig. 6. The proof of the following theorem is deferred to the full version of our paper.

Theorem 6 (Sub-WI NIWI + VEGOWF + ExtCom $\Longrightarrow$ Sub-ZK NIZK). *Let* Π_{wi} *be a non-interactive argument,* C *be a commitment scheme, and* $\mathcal{G}$ *be a function family with associated publicly testable relation* $\mathbf{RG}$.

(1) If Π_{wi} *is perfectly complete then* Π *is perfectly complete.*
(2) If Π_{wi} *is sound,* C *is keyless and extractable, and* $\mathcal{G}$ *is* $\mathbf{RG}$*-hard then* Π *is sound.*
(3) If Π_{wi} *is Sub-WI,* $\mathcal{G}$ *is* $\mathbf{RG}$*-verifiably-extractable, and* C *is keyless and hiding, then* Π *is Sub-ZK.*

5.3 Instantiations and Statistical ZAPR

We show some interesting instantiations of the above construction and also make a simple, but significant, connection between Sub-ZK NIZK and ZAPs with private random coin (ZAPRs).

Firstly, we argue that there is a knowledge-sound Sub-ZK NIZK based on the DLin and DH-KE assumptions. To the best of our knowledge, the only known knowledge-sound Sub-ZK NIZKs are Sub-ZK SNARKs. Our construction therefore relies arguably on weaker assumptions.

Proposition 2. *There exists a knowledge-sound Sub-ZK NIZK based on the DLin and DH-KE assumptions with 3 group elements as the CRS and with a proof size of $\mathcal{O}(\lambda(k+l))$ where k is the circuit size and l is size of a circuit verifying the image of the DH-KE GEOWF.*

Proof. In [28] it is proven that there exists a knowledge-sound NIWI in the plain model based on the DLin and DH-KE assumptions. Since it has no CRS, it is also Sub-WI. From Sect. 4.4, there exists a VEGOWF based on the DH-KE and discrete logarithm (DL) assumptions (note that DLIN implies DL). We now apply our construction in Fig. 5 using the knowledge-sound NIWI from [28] and the VEGOWF from Fig. 4.4. It then follows from Theorem 5 that the resulting protocol is a knowledge-sound Sub-ZK NIZK. □

Let us next prove a helpful lemma that shows when NIWI is Sub-WI. The corollary follows since perfect zero knowledge implies perfect WI.

Lemma 1. *Suppose Ψ is perfectly WI for relation $\mathbf{R}$ and there exists an efficient CRS validation algorithm CV. Then Ψ is Sub-WI.*

Proof. Definition 8 for perfect WI states that for all honestly generated CRS crs (i.e., CRS in the image of $\mathsf{K}(\mathbf{R})$), instances x, and corresponding witnesses $\mathsf{w}_0, \mathsf{w}_1$, no unbounded adversary can distinguish a proof generated using either $(\mathsf{crs}, \mathsf{x}, \mathsf{w}_0)$ or $(\mathsf{crs}, \mathsf{x}, \mathsf{w}_1)$. Note that if a subverter can create a valid crs such that $\mathcal{A}$ breaks Sub-WI with probability at least $\varepsilon > 0$, the same $\mathcal{A}$ can break WI with probability at least $\varepsilon/(|\mathsf{crs}| + |\mathsf{aux}_{\mathcal{Z}}|) > 0$ by simply guessing crs and $\mathsf{aux}_{\mathcal{Z}}$. Hence assuming perfect WI, verifying that a subverter-generated CRS crs is in fact in the image of $\mathsf{K}(\mathbf{R})$ is enough to assure that perfect subversion WI holds. □

Corollary 1. *If Ψ is perfectly zero-knowledge and there exist an efficient CRS validation algorithm, then Ψ is Sub-WI.*

Therefore, the efficient SNARK constructions in [1,27], the updatable SNARKs in [38,50], and the shuffle argument in [4] are all Sub-WI. The same observation about Sub-ZK SNARKs was already made by Fuchsbauer in [27]. These arguments have a CRS validation algorithm and were already known to be Sub-ZK under a knowledge assumption. However, the above result shows that they are perfect Sub-WI *without any assumptions*. Moreover, any NIWI without a CRS is trivially Sub-WI.

Firstly, it means that [1,27] are statistical ZAPRs with adaptive soundness. The only other pairing-based ZAPR is [49] which is less efficient and uses much more advanced tools, but relies on weaker assumptions for soundness. Secondly, if we use the SNARKs of [1,27] in Fig. 5, we have Sub-ZK SNARKs from any VEGOWF rather than from a specific knowledge assumption.

Proposition 3. *Suppose there exists a perfectly zero-knowledge SNARK with an efficient CRS validation algorithm* CV *and there exists a VEGOWF. Then there exists a Sub-ZK SNARK.*

Proof. Since the given SNARK Π is perfectly ZK and has a CV algorithm, it follows from Corollary 1 that it is perfectly Sub-WI. Applying our construction in Sect. 5.1 to Π and the VEGOWF $\mathcal{G}$ to construct a new SNARK Π', it then follows from part (4) of Theorem 5 that Π' is a Sub-ZK SNARK, as desired. □

6 Characterising Sub-ZK NIZKs

We show that the CRS generation algorithm K of a NIZK is a VEOWF if and only if the NIZK is Sub-ZK. Let $\mathcal{R}$ be a relation generator, and let $\Pi = (\mathsf{K}, \mathsf{P}, \mathsf{V}, \mathsf{Sim})$ be a NIZK argument for $\mathcal{R}$. We define a family of functions $\mathcal{G}_{\mathsf{K}} = \{\mathsf{K}_{\mathbf{R},\mathsf{p}} \colon \{\mathsf{td}\} \to \{\mathsf{crs}\} \mid (\mathbf{R}, \mathsf{p}) \in \mathcal{R}(1^\lambda), \lambda \in \mathbb{N}\}$ where $\mathsf{K}_{\mathbf{R},\mathsf{p}}$ takes in a uniformly sampled trapdoor td and maps it deterministically to a crs. We assume that the distribution $(\mathsf{crs}, \mathsf{td}) \leftarrow \mathsf{KGen}(\mathbf{R}, \mathsf{p})$ is the same as $(\mathsf{crs} \leftarrow \mathsf{K}_{\mathbf{R},\mathsf{p}}(\mathsf{td}), \mathsf{td} \leftarrow_{\$} \{\mathsf{td}\})$. We use both notations interchangeably in this section.

Let us start by establishing the following straightforward connection.

Theorem 7 (VEOWF $\mathcal{G}_{\mathsf{K}} \implies$ Sub-ZK). *Suppose $\Pi = (\mathsf{K}, \mathsf{P}, \mathsf{V}, \mathsf{Sim})$ is a perfect NIZK argument. If $\mathcal{G}_{\mathsf{K}}$ is a VEOWF with image verification algorithm* ImV*, then Π is statistically composable Sub-ZK with respect to the CRS verification algorithm* $\mathsf{CV} = \mathsf{ImV}$.

Proof. Consider a subverter $\mathcal{Z}$ which outputs a CRS crs. We only need to consider the case where $\mathsf{CV}(\mathsf{crs}) = 1$ and thus $\mathsf{crs} \in \text{image}(\mathsf{K}_{\mathbf{R},\mathsf{p}})$. Since $\mathsf{K}_{\mathbf{R},\mathsf{p}}$ is a VEOWF and the subverter $\mathcal{Z}$ outputs an image of $\mathsf{K}_{\mathbf{R},\mathsf{p}}$, we know that there exists an extractor $\mathsf{Ext}_{\mathcal{Z}}$ which with overwhelming probability outputs a simulation trapdoor td. Since Π is perfect zero-knowledge, proofs $\pi_0 \leftarrow \mathsf{Sim}(\mathbf{R}, \mathsf{p}, \mathsf{td}, \mathsf{crs}, \mathsf{x})$ and $\pi_1 \leftarrow \mathsf{P}(\mathbf{R}, \mathsf{p}, \mathsf{crs}, \mathsf{x}, \mathsf{w})$ are identically distributed. □

Remark 2. The same result does not hold for statistical (or computational) NIZK since there might be a negligible number of CRSs where td does not allow simulation, which the subverter could output.

Following [37], we say that the relation generator $\mathcal{R}$ *has a $\varepsilon_{\mathcal{S}}$-hard decisional problem* if there exist two samplers $\mathcal{S}$ and $\mathcal{S}'$ such that for $(\mathbf{R}, \mathsf{p}) \leftarrow \mathcal{R}(1^\lambda)$ (1) sampler $\mathcal{S}(\mathbf{R}, \mathsf{p})$ produces $(\mathsf{x}, \mathsf{w}) \in \mathbf{R}$, and (2) $\mathcal{S}'(\mathbf{R}, \mathsf{p})$ produces $\mathsf{x} \notin \mathcal{L}_{\mathbf{R}}$. Furthermore, for some negligible $\varepsilon_{\mathcal{S}}$, it holds for all PPT adversaries $\mathcal{A}$ that $|\varepsilon_0 - \varepsilon_1| \le \varepsilon_{\mathcal{S}}$, where $\varepsilon_b = \Pr\left[(\mathbf{R}, \mathsf{p}) \leftarrow \mathcal{R}(1^\lambda), (\mathsf{x}_0, \mathsf{w}_0) \leftarrow \mathcal{S}(\mathbf{R}, \mathsf{p}), \mathsf{x}_1 \leftarrow \mathcal{S}'(\mathbf{R}, \mathsf{p}) : \mathcal{A}(\mathbf{R}, \mathsf{p}, \mathsf{x}_b) = 1\right]$.

A simple example of this is the language of Diffie-Hellman tuples where $\mathsf{p} = (\mathbb{G}, g, p) \leftarrow \mathcal{R}(1^\lambda)$ is a group description, $\mathcal{S}$ outputs $(\mathsf{x} = (g^x, g^y, g^{xy}), \mathsf{w} = (x, y))$ for random $x, y \leftarrow_{\$} \mathbb{Z}_p$, and $\mathcal{S}'$ outputs g^x, g^y, g^z for random $x, y \leftarrow_{\$} \mathbb{Z}_p$ and $z \leftarrow_{\$} \mathbb{Z}_p \setminus \{xy\}$.

Now let us establish the opposite connection between VEOWF and Sub-ZK. In general, the extractor in subversion zero-knowledge definition does not need to extract the whole preimage of the CRS function. It just needs to extract something which allows for simulation of proofs. For example, this could be only a small part of the full trapdoor. Due to this, we restrict ourselves slightly and lend the following notion from [3].

Definition 11 (Trapdoor-Extractability [3]**).** *A subversion-resistant argument* Ψ *for a relation* $\mathcal{R}$ *has trapdoor-extractability if for any PPT subverter* $\mathcal{Z}$ *there exists a PPT extractor* $\mathsf{Ext}_{\mathcal{Z}}$*, s.t. for all* λ *and* $(\mathbf{R}, \mathsf{p}) \in \mathcal{R}(1^\lambda)$*,*

$$\Pr\left[\begin{array}{l} r \leftarrow_{\$} \mathsf{RND}_\lambda(\mathcal{Z}), \mathsf{crs} \leftarrow \mathcal{Z}(\mathbf{R}, \mathsf{p}; r), \mathsf{td} \leftarrow \mathsf{Ext}_{\mathcal{Z}}(\mathbf{R}, \mathsf{p}; r) : \\ \mathsf{CV}(\mathbf{R}, \mathsf{p}, \mathsf{crs}) = 1 \wedge \mathsf{K}_{\mathbf{R},\mathsf{p}}(\mathsf{td}) \neq \mathsf{crs} \end{array}\right] \leq \mathsf{negl}(\lambda) \ .$$

Theorem 8 (Sub-ZK $\Longrightarrow$ VEOWF $\mathcal{G}_{\mathsf{K}}$). *Assume* Π *is a NIZK argument for* $\mathcal{R}$*, which has* $\varepsilon_{\mathcal{S}}$*-hard decisional problems. Let* $\mathcal{G}_{\mathsf{K}}$ *be as defined above. Assume the distribution* $\mathcal{D}_\lambda$ *is benign. Then*

1. *if (i)* $\Pi = (\mathsf{K}, \mathsf{P}, \mathsf{V}, \mathsf{Sim})$ *is perfectly complete, computationally sound, and computationally zero-knowledge, and (ii)* $\mathsf{K}_{\mathbf{R},\mathsf{p}}$ *is injective, then* $\mathcal{G}_{\mathsf{K}}$ *is a one-way function;*
2. *if* $\Pi = (\mathsf{K}, \mathsf{P}, \mathsf{V}, \mathsf{Sim}, \mathsf{CV})$ *is a statistically composable Sub-ZK argument with trapdoor extractability, then* $\mathcal{G}_{\mathsf{K}}$ *is verifiably-extractable with* $\mathcal{G}_{\mathsf{K}}.\mathsf{ImV} = \Pi.\mathsf{CV}$ *respect to auxiliary inputs* $(\mathbf{R}, \mathsf{p}, r)$ *where* $(\mathbf{R}, \mathsf{p}) \leftarrow \mathcal{R}(1^\lambda)$*,* $r \leftarrow_{\$} \{0,1\}^{\mathsf{poly}(\lambda)}$*.*

Proof. **Soundness + ZK $\Longrightarrow$ One-Wayness.** Suppose there exists a PPT adversary $\mathcal{A}$ that breaks one-wayness of $\mathcal{G}_{\mathsf{K}}$ with probability ε_{owf}. That is, for a random $(\mathbf{R}, \mathsf{p}) \leftarrow \mathsf{KeySamp}_{\mathcal{G}}(1^\lambda)$, $\mathsf{td} \leftarrow_{\$} \{\mathsf{td}\}, \mathsf{aux} \leftarrow_{\$} \mathcal{D}_\lambda$, the $\mathcal{A}(\mathbf{R}, \mathsf{p}, \mathsf{crs} = \mathsf{K}_{\mathbf{R},\mathsf{p}}(\mathsf{td}), \mathsf{aux})$ outputs td' such that $\mathsf{K}_{\mathbf{R},\mathsf{p}}(\mathsf{td}') = \mathsf{crs}$ with probability ε_{owf}.

We are going to construct a PPT adversary $\mathcal{B}$ that internally runs $\mathcal{A}$ together with an auxiliary input aux. We build the soundness adversary $\mathcal{B}$ as follows:

1. $\mathcal{B}$ gets $(\mathbf{R}, \mathsf{p}, \mathsf{crs})$ as an input;
2. $\mathcal{B}$ samples $\mathsf{aux}' \leftarrow_{\$} \mathcal{D}_\lambda$ and computes $\mathsf{td}' \leftarrow \mathcal{A}(\mathbf{R}, \mathsf{p}, \mathsf{crs}, \mathsf{aux}')$;
3. $\mathcal{B}$ outputs x such that $\mathsf{x} \leftarrow \mathcal{S}'(\mathbf{R}, \mathsf{p})$ (i.e. $\mathsf{x} \notin \mathcal{L}_{\mathbf{R}}$) along with a simulated proof $\pi \leftarrow \mathsf{Sim}(\mathbf{R}, \mathsf{p}, \mathsf{crs}, \mathsf{td}', \mathsf{x})$.

Since $\mathsf{x} \notin \mathcal{L}_{\mathbf{R}}$ by definition, it means that $\mathcal{B}$ wins the soundness game if $\mathsf{V}(\mathbf{R}, \mathsf{p}, \mathsf{crs}, \mathsf{x}, \pi) = 1$. We use games in Fig. 7 to quantify the probability that $\mathsf{V}(\mathbf{R}, \mathsf{p}, \mathsf{crs}, \mathsf{x}, \pi) = 1$ in the soundness game.

Game0: This is the original soundness game without the condition $\mathsf{x} \notin \mathcal{L}_{\mathbf{R}}$ with the adversary $\mathcal{B}$ inlined. The winning condition is just $\mathsf{V}(\mathbf{R}, \mathsf{p}, \mathsf{crs}, \mathsf{x}, \pi) = 1$.

Game1: We change Game 0 such that $\mathcal{B}$ samples a true statement-witness pair $(\mathsf{x}, \mathsf{w}) \leftarrow \mathcal{S}(\mathbf{R}, \mathsf{p})$ instead.

Game2: We modify Game 1 such that the simulator gets the real trapdoor td as an input rather than the trapdoor td' extracted by $\mathcal{A}$.

Game3: Finally, instead of simulating the proof π, we use the witness w to create an honest proof.

Let us denote the probability of Game i outputting 1 by ε_i. Firstly, it is clear that ε_0 is the probability of $\mathcal{B}$ winning (that is, outputting 1) in the soundness game since, although, we do not check the condition $\mathsf{x} \notin \mathcal{L}_{\mathbf{R}}$, it always holds for the adversary $\mathcal{B}$. We now prove that distinguishing Game 0 and Game 1 succeeds with probability at most $\varepsilon_{\mathcal{S}}$.

Game 0:	Game 1:
$(\mathbf{R}, \mathsf{p}) \leftarrow \mathcal{R}(1^\lambda)$;	$(\mathbf{R}, \mathsf{p}) \leftarrow \mathcal{R}(1^\lambda)$;
$(\mathsf{crs}, \mathsf{td}) \leftarrow \mathsf{K}(\mathbf{R}, \mathsf{p}); \mathsf{aux}' \leftarrow_{\$} \mathcal{D}_\lambda$;	$(\mathsf{crs}, \mathsf{td}) \leftarrow \mathsf{K}(\mathbf{R}, \mathsf{p}); \mathsf{aux}' \leftarrow_{\$} \mathcal{D}_\lambda$;
$\mathsf{td}' \leftarrow \mathcal{A}(\mathbf{R}, \mathsf{p}, \mathsf{crs}, \mathsf{aux}')$;	$\mathsf{td}' \leftarrow \mathcal{A}(\mathbf{R}, \mathsf{p}, \mathsf{crs}, \mathsf{aux}')$;
$\mathsf{x} \leftarrow \mathcal{S}'(\mathbf{R}, \mathsf{p})$;	$(\mathsf{x}, \mathsf{w}) \leftarrow \mathcal{S}(\mathbf{R}, \mathsf{p})$;
$\pi \leftarrow \mathsf{Sim}(\mathbf{R}, \mathsf{p}, \mathsf{crs}, \mathsf{td}', \mathsf{x})$;	$\pi \leftarrow \mathsf{Sim}(\mathbf{R}, \mathsf{p}, \mathsf{crs}, \mathsf{td}', \mathsf{x})$;
return $\mathsf{V}(\mathbf{R}, \mathsf{p}, \mathsf{crs}, \mathsf{x}, \pi)$;	**return** $\mathsf{V}(\mathbf{R}, \mathsf{p}, \mathsf{crs}, \mathsf{x}, \pi)$;

Game 2:	Game 3:
$(\mathbf{R}, \mathsf{p}) \leftarrow \mathcal{R}(1^\lambda)$;	$(\mathbf{R}, \mathsf{p}) \leftarrow \mathcal{R}(1^\lambda)$;
$(\mathsf{crs}, \mathsf{td}) \leftarrow \mathsf{K}(\mathbf{R}, \mathsf{p}); \mathsf{aux}' \leftarrow_{\$} \mathcal{D}_\lambda$;	$(\mathsf{crs}, \mathsf{td}) \leftarrow \mathsf{K}(\mathbf{R}, \mathsf{p}); \mathsf{aux}' \leftarrow_{\$} \mathcal{D}_\lambda$;
$\mathsf{td}' \leftarrow \mathcal{A}(\mathbf{R}, \mathsf{p}, \mathsf{crs}, \mathsf{aux}')$;	$\mathsf{td}' \leftarrow \mathcal{A}(\mathbf{R}, \mathsf{p}, \mathsf{crs}, \mathsf{aux}')$;
$(\mathsf{x}, \mathsf{w}) \leftarrow \mathcal{S}(\mathbf{R}, \mathsf{p})$;	$(\mathsf{x}, \mathsf{w}) \leftarrow \mathcal{S}(\mathbf{R}, \mathsf{p})$;
$\pi \leftarrow \mathsf{Sim}(\mathbf{R}, \mathsf{p}, \mathsf{crs}, \mathsf{td}, \mathsf{x})$;	$\pi \leftarrow \mathsf{P}(\mathbf{R}, \mathsf{p}, \mathsf{crs}, \mathsf{x}, \mathsf{w})$;
return $\mathsf{V}(\mathbf{R}, \mathsf{p}, \mathsf{crs}, \mathsf{x}, \pi)$;	**return** $\mathsf{V}(\mathbf{R}, \mathsf{p}, \mathsf{crs}, \mathsf{x}, \pi)$;

Fig. 7. Security games for Theorem 8.

Lemma 2. *For the probabilities* ε_0 *and* ε_1 *defined as above,* $|\varepsilon_0 - \varepsilon_1| \leq \varepsilon_{\mathcal{S}}$.

Proof. Consider the following adversary $\mathcal{C}$ against the $\varepsilon_{\mathcal{S}}$-hardness. Firstly, $\mathcal{C}$ gets as an input $(\mathbf{R}, \mathsf{p}, \mathsf{x}_b)$ where x_1 is generated by $\mathcal{S}$ and x_0 is generated by $\mathcal{S}'$. Then, $\mathcal{C}$ samples $(\mathsf{crs}, \mathsf{td}) \leftarrow \mathsf{K}(\mathbf{R}, \mathsf{p})$ and $\mathsf{aux}' \leftarrow_{\$} \mathcal{D}_\lambda$, computes $\mathsf{td}' \leftarrow \mathcal{A}(\mathbf{R}, \mathsf{p}, \mathsf{crs}, \mathsf{aux}')$, and simulates the proof $\pi \leftarrow \mathsf{Sim}(\mathbf{R}, \mathsf{p}, \mathsf{crs}, \mathsf{td}', \mathsf{x})$. It returns the answer of $\mathsf{V}(\mathbf{R}, \mathsf{p}, \mathsf{crs}, \mathsf{x}, \pi)$.

By construction, the probability that $\mathcal{C}$ outputs 1 given x_0 is ε_0 and given x_1 is ε_1. It thus follows that $|\varepsilon_0 - \varepsilon_1| \leq \varepsilon_{\mathcal{S}}$. □

Lemma 3. *Assuming that* $\mathsf{K}_{\mathbf{R},\mathsf{p}}$ *is injective,* $|\varepsilon_1 - \varepsilon_2| \leq 1 - \varepsilon_{owf}$.

Proof. The only difference between Game 1 and Game 2 is that one uses td' for simulation and the other uses td. If $\mathcal{A}$ is successful in breaking one-wayness, then $\mathsf{td} = \mathsf{td}'$ (since $\mathsf{K}_{\mathbf{R},\mathsf{p}}$ is injective) and output distributions of both games are the same. That happens with probability ε_{owf}. Outputs distributions of games can differ only when $\mathcal{A}$ fails in breaking one-wayness, which happens at most with the probability $1 - \varepsilon_{owf}$. We conclude that $|\varepsilon_1 - \varepsilon_2| \leq 1 - \varepsilon_{owf}$. □

Lemma 4. *Let* ε_{zk} *denote the maximum advantage that any PPT adversary wins in the zero-knowledge game. Then,* $|\varepsilon_2 - \varepsilon_3| \leq \varepsilon_{zk}$.

Proof. Consider the verifier V as the adversary in the zero-knowledge game. From this perspective Game 2 is the zero-knowledge game with the simulator and Game 3 is the zero-knowledge game with the honest prover given that we ignore the line $\mathsf{td}' \leftarrow \mathcal{A}(\mathbf{R}, \mathsf{p}, \mathsf{crs}, \mathsf{aux})$. It follows that $|\varepsilon_2 - \varepsilon_3| \leq \varepsilon_{zk}$. □

Using the triangle inequality, we now get that $|\varepsilon_0 - \varepsilon_3| \le \varepsilon_{\mathcal{S}} + (1 - \varepsilon_{owf}) + \varepsilon_{zk}$. Since the argument system is perfectly complete, $\varepsilon_3 = 1$ and therefore $|\varepsilon_0 - \varepsilon_3| = |\varepsilon_0 - 1| = 1 - \varepsilon_0$. Putting equations together, we get $1 - \varepsilon_0 \le \varepsilon_{\mathcal{S}} + (1 - \varepsilon_{owf}) + \varepsilon_{zk}$, which can be simplified to $\varepsilon_{owf} \le \varepsilon_0 + \varepsilon_{\mathcal{S}} + \varepsilon_{zk}$, which is negligible. □

Sub-ZK $\Longrightarrow$ Verifiable-Extractability. This part of the proof is essentially tautological. Let $\mathcal{A}$ be an adversary in the verifiable extractability game and let $\mathsf{aux} = (\mathbf{R}, \mathsf{p}, r)$ where $(\mathbf{R}, \mathsf{p}) \leftarrow \mathcal{R}(1^\lambda)$ and $r \leftarrow_{\$} \{0,1\}^{\mathsf{poly}(\lambda)}$. Suppose that $\mathcal{A}$ is Sub-ZK subverter that outputs crs such that $\mathsf{CV}(\mathbf{R}, \mathsf{p}, \mathsf{crs}) = 1$. Then according to the trapdoor extractability property, there exists a PPT extractor $\mathsf{Ext}_{\mathcal{A}}$ that on input aux, outputs with an overwhelming td such that $\mathsf{K}_{\mathbf{R},\mathsf{p}}(\mathsf{td}) = \mathsf{crs}$. Thus, verifiable extractability holds. □

Acknowledgements. Janno Siim and Helger Lipmaa were partially supported by the Estonian Research Council grant (PRG49).

References

1. Abdolmaleki, B., Baghery, K., Lipmaa, H., Zając, M.: A subversion-resistant SNARK. In: Takagi, T., Peyrin, T. (eds.) ASIACRYPT 2017, Part III. LNCS, vol. 10626, pp. 3–33. Springer, Cham (2017). https://doi.org/10.1007/978-3-319-70700-6_1
2. Abdolmaleki, B., Lipmaa, H., Siim, J., Zając, M.: On QA-NIZK in the BPK model. In: Kiayias, A., Kohlweiss, M., Wallden, P., Zikas, V. (eds.) PKC 2020, Part I. LNCS, vol. 12110, pp. 590–620. Springer, Cham (2020). https://doi.org/10.1007/978-3-030-45374-9_20
3. Abdolmaleki, B., Lipmaa, H., Siim, J., Zając, M.: On subversion-resistant SNARKs. Cryptology ePrint Archive, Report 2020/668 (2020). https://eprint.iacr.org/2020/668
4. Aggelakis, A., et al.: A non-interactive shuffle argument with low trust assumptions. In: Jarecki, S. (ed.) CT-RSA 2020. LNCS, vol. 12006, pp. 667–692. Springer, Cham (2020). https://doi.org/10.1007/978-3-030-40186-3_28
5. Aiello, W., Bhatt, S., Ostrovsky, R., Rajagopalan, S.R.: Fast verification of any remote procedure call: short witness-indistinguishable one-round proofs for NP. In: Montanari, U., Rolim, J.D.P., Welzl, E. (eds.) ICALP 2000. LNCS, vol. 1853, pp. 463–474. Springer, Heidelberg (2000). https://doi.org/10.1007/3-540-45022-X_39
6. Badrinarayanan, S., Fernando, R., Jain, A., Khurana, D., Sahai, A.: Statistical ZAP arguments. In: Canteaut, A., Ishai, Y. (eds.) EUROCRYPT 2020, Part III. LNCS, vol. 12107, pp. 642–667. Springer, Cham (2020). https://doi.org/10.1007/978-3-030-45727-3_22
7. Barak, B.: How to go beyond the black-box simulation barrier. In: 42nd FOCS, pp. 106–115. IEEE Computer Society Press (October 2001). https://doi.org/10.1109/SFCS.2001.959885
8. Barak, B., Ong, S.J., Vadhan, S.: Derandomization in cryptography. In: Boneh, D. (ed.) CRYPTO 2003. LNCS, vol. 2729, pp. 299–315. Springer, Heidelberg (2003). https://doi.org/10.1007/978-3-540-45146-4_18

9. Bellare, M., Fuchsbauer, G., Scafuro, A.: NIZKs with an untrusted CRS: security in the face of parameter subversion. In: Cheon, J.H., Takagi, T. (eds.) ASIACRYPT 2016, Part II. LNCS, vol. 10032, pp. 777–804. Springer, Heidelberg (2016). https://doi.org/10.1007/978-3-662-53890-6_26
10. Bellare, M., Goldreich, O.: On defining proofs of knowledge. In: Brickell, E.F. (ed.) CRYPTO 1992. LNCS, vol. 740, pp. 390–420. Springer, Heidelberg (1993). https://doi.org/10.1007/3-540-48071-4_28
11. Ben-Sasson, E., et al.: Zerocash: decentralized anonymous payments from bitcoin. In: 2014 IEEE Symposium on Security and Privacy, pp. 459–474. IEEE Computer Society Press (May 2014). https://doi.org/10.1109/SP.2014.36
12. Bitansky, N., et al.: The hunting of the SNARK. J. Cryptol. **30**(4), 989–1066 (2016). https://doi.org/10.1007/s00145-016-9241-9
13. Bitansky, N., Canetti, R., Chiesa, A., Tromer, E.: From extractable collision resistance to succinct non-interactive arguments of knowledge, and back again. In: Goldwasser, S. (ed.) ITCS 2012, pp. 326–349. ACM (January 2012). https://doi.org/10.1145/2090236.2090263
14. Bitansky, N., Canetti, R., Paneth, O., Rosen, A.: On the existence of extractable one-way functions. SIAM J. Comput. **45**(5), 1910–1952 (2016)
15. Bitansky, N., Paneth, O.: ZAPs and non-interactive witness indistinguishability from indistinguishability obfuscation. In: Dodis, Y., Nielsen, J.B. (eds.) TCC 2015, Part II. LNCS, vol. 9015, pp. 401–427. Springer, Heidelberg (2015). https://doi.org/10.1007/978-3-662-46497-7_16
16. Boneh, D., Boyen, X.: Short signatures without random oracles. In: Cachin, C., Camenisch, J.L. (eds.) EUROCRYPT 2004. LNCS, vol. 3027, pp. 56–73. Springer, Heidelberg (2004). https://doi.org/10.1007/978-3-540-24676-3_4
17. Boneh, D., Lynn, B., Shacham, H.: Short signatures from the Weil pairing. J. Cryptol. **17**(4), 297–319 (2004). https://doi.org/10.1007/s00145-004-0314-9
18. Boyle, E., Pass, R.: Limits of extractability assumptions with distributional auxiliary input. In: Iwata, T., Cheon, J.H. (eds.) ASIACRYPT 2015, Part II. LNCS, vol. 9453, pp. 236–261. Springer, Heidelberg (2015). https://doi.org/10.1007/978-3-662-48800-3_10
19. Canetti, R., Dakdouk, R.R.: Extractable perfectly one-way functions. In: Aceto, L., Damgård, I., Goldberg, L.A., Halldórsson, M.M., Ingólfsdóttir, A., Walukiewicz, I. (eds.) ICALP 2008, Part II. LNCS, vol. 5126, pp. 449–460. Springer, Heidelberg (2008). https://doi.org/10.1007/978-3-540-70583-3_37
20. Canetti, R., Goldreich, O., Goldwasser, S., Micali, S.: Resettable zero-knowledge (extended abstract). In: 32nd ACM STOC, pp. 235–244. ACM Press (May 2000). https://doi.org/10.1145/335305.335334
21. Chase, M., Lysyanskaya, A.: On signatures of knowledge. In: Dwork, C. (ed.) CRYPTO 2006. LNCS, vol. 4117, pp. 78–96. Springer, Heidelberg (2006). https://doi.org/10.1007/11818175_5
22. Dakdouk, R.R.: Theory and application of extractable functions. Ph.D. thesis, Yale University (2009)
23. Damgård, I.: Towards practical public key systems secure against chosen ciphertext attacks. In: Feigenbaum, J. (ed.) CRYPTO 1991. LNCS, vol. 576, pp. 445–456. Springer, Heidelberg (1992). https://doi.org/10.1007/3-540-46766-1_36
24. Danezis, G., Fournet, C., Groth, J., Kohlweiss, M.: Square span programs with applications to succinct NIZK arguments. In: Sarkar, P., Iwata, T. (eds.) ASIACRYPT 2014, Part I. LNCS, vol. 8873, pp. 532–550. Springer, Heidelberg (2014). https://doi.org/10.1007/978-3-662-45611-8_28

25. Feige, U., Lapidot, D., Shamir, A.: Multiple non-interactive zero knowledge proofs based on a single random string (extended abstract). In: 31st FOCS, pp. 308–317. IEEE Computer Society Press (October 1990). https://doi.org/10.1109/FSCS.1990.89549
26. Fischlin, M., Lehmann, A., Pietrzak, K.: Robust multi-property combiners for hash functions revisited. In: Aceto, L., Damgård, I., Goldberg, L.A., Halldórsson, M.M., Ingólfsdóttir, A., Walukiewicz, I. (eds.) ICALP 2008, Part II. LNCS, vol. 5126, pp. 655–666. Springer, Heidelberg (2008). https://doi.org/10.1007/978-3-540-70583-3_53
27. Fuchsbauer, G.: Subversion-zero-knowledge SNARKs. In: Abdalla, M., Dahab, R. (eds.) PKC 2018, Part I. LNCS, vol. 10769, pp. 315–347. Springer, Cham (2018). https://doi.org/10.1007/978-3-319-76578-5_11
28. Fuchsbauer, G., Orrù, M.: Non-interactive zaps of knowledge. In: Preneel, B., Vercauteren, F. (eds.) ACNS 2018. LNCS, vol. 10892, pp. 44–62. Springer, Cham (2018). https://doi.org/10.1007/978-3-319-93387-0_3
29. Fuchsbauer, G., Plouviez, A., Seurin, Y.: Blind Schnorr signatures and signed ElGamal encryption in the algebraic group model. In: Canteaut, A., Ishai, Y. (eds.) EUROCRYPT 2020, Part II. LNCS, vol. 12106, pp. 63–95. Springer, Cham (2020). https://doi.org/10.1007/978-3-030-45724-2_3
30. Gennaro, R., Gentry, C., Parno, B., Raykova, M.: Quadratic span programs and succinct NIZKs without PCPs. In: Johansson, T., Nguyen, P.Q. (eds.) EUROCRYPT 2013. LNCS, vol. 7881, pp. 626–645. Springer, Heidelberg (2013). https://doi.org/10.1007/978-3-642-38348-9_37
31. Gentry, C., Peikert, C., Vaikuntanathan, V.: Trapdoors for hard lattices and new cryptographic constructions. In: Ladner, R.E., Dwork, C. (eds.) 40th ACM STOC, pp. 197–206. ACM Press (May 2008). https://doi.org/10.1145/1374376.1374407
32. Gentry, C., Wichs, D.: Separating succinct non-interactive arguments from all falsifiable assumptions. In: Fortnow, L., Vadhan, S.P. (eds.) 43rd ACM STOC, pp. 99–108. ACM Press (June 2011). https://doi.org/10.1145/1993636.1993651
33. Goldreich, O., Oren, Y.: Definitions and properties of zero-knowledge proof systems. J. Cryptol. **7**(1), 1–32 (1994). https://doi.org/10.1007/BF00195207
34. Goldwasser, S., Micali, S., Rackoff, C.: The knowledge complexity of interactive proof-systems (extended abstract). In: 17th ACM STOC, pp. 291–304. ACM Press (May 1985). https://doi.org/10.1145/22145.22178
35. Goyal, V., Jain, A., Jin, Z., Malavolta, G.: Statistical zaps and new oblivious transfer protocols. In: Canteaut, A., Ishai, Y. (eds.) EUROCRYPT 2020, Part III. LNCS, vol. 12107, pp. 668–699. Springer, Cham (2020). https://doi.org/10.1007/978-3-030-45727-3_23
36. Groth, J.: Short pairing-based non-interactive zero-knowledge arguments. In: Abe, M. (ed.) ASIACRYPT 2010. LNCS, vol. 6477, pp. 321–340. Springer, Heidelberg (2010). https://doi.org/10.1007/978-3-642-17373-8_19
37. Groth, J.: On the size of pairing-based non-interactive arguments. In: Fischlin, M., Coron, J.-S. (eds.) EUROCRYPT 2016, Part II. LNCS, vol. 9666, pp. 305–326. Springer, Heidelberg (2016). https://doi.org/10.1007/978-3-662-49896-5_11
38. Groth, J., Kohlweiss, M., Maller, M., Meiklejohn, S., Miers, I.: Updatable and universal common reference strings with applications to zk-SNARKs. In: Shacham, H., Boldyreva, A. (eds.) CRYPTO 2018, Part III. LNCS, vol. 10993, pp. 698–728. Springer, Cham (2018). https://doi.org/10.1007/978-3-319-96878-0_24
39. Groth, J., Ostrovsky, R., Sahai, A.: Non-interactive zaps and new techniques for NIZK. In: Dwork, C. (ed.) CRYPTO 2006. LNCS, vol. 4117, pp. 97–111. Springer, Heidelberg (2006). https://doi.org/10.1007/11818175_6

40. Harnik, D., Kilian, J., Naor, M., Reingold, O., Rosen, A.: On robust combiners for oblivious transfer and other primitives. In: Cramer, R. (ed.) EUROCRYPT 2005. LNCS, vol. 3494, pp. 96–113. Springer, Heidelberg (2005). https://doi.org/10.1007/11426639_6
41. Jain, A., Lin, H., Sahai, A.: Indistinguishability obfuscation from well-founded assumptions. Cryptology ePrint Archive, Report 2020/1003 (2020). https://eprint.iacr.org/2020/1003
42. Jutla, C.S., Roy, A.: Shorter quasi-adaptive NIZK proofs for linear subspaces. In: Sako, K., Sarkar, P. (eds.) ASIACRYPT 2013, Part I. LNCS, vol. 8269, pp. 1–20. Springer, Heidelberg (2013). https://doi.org/10.1007/978-3-642-42033-7_1
43. Kalai, Y.T., Paneth, O., Yang, L.: How to delegate computations publicly. In: Charikar, M., Cohen, E. (eds.) 51st ACM STOC, pp. 1115–1124. ACM Press (June 2019). https://doi.org/10.1145/3313276.3316411
44. Kalai, Y.T., Raz, R., Rothblum, R.D.: How to delegate computations: the power of no-signaling proofs. In: Shmoys, D.B. (ed.) 46th ACM STOC, pp. 485–494. ACM Press (May/Jun 2014). https://doi.org/10.1145/2591796.2591809
45. Katsumata, S., Nishimaki, R., Yamada, S., Yamakawa, T.: Exploring constructions of compact NIZKs from various assumptions. In: Boldyreva, A., Micciancio, D. (eds.) CRYPTO 2019, Part III. LNCS, vol. 11694, pp. 639–669. Springer, Cham (2019). https://doi.org/10.1007/978-3-030-26954-8_21
46. Lamport, L.: Constructing digital signatures from a one-way function. Technical report SRI-CSL-98, SRI International Computer Science Laboratory (October 1979)
47. Lepinski, M.: On the existence of 3-round zero-knowledge proofs. Master's thesis, MIT, USA (2002)
48. Lipmaa, H.: Progression-free sets and sublinear pairing-based non-interactive zero-knowledge arguments. In: Cramer, R. (ed.) TCC 2012. LNCS, vol. 7194, pp. 169–189. Springer, Heidelberg (2012). https://doi.org/10.1007/978-3-642-28914-9_10
49. Lombardi, A., Vaikuntanathan, V., Wichs, D.: Statistical ZAPR arguments from bilinear maps. In: Canteaut, A., Ishai, Y. (eds.) EUROCRYPT 2020, Part III. LNCS, vol. 12107, pp. 620–641. Springer, Cham (2020). https://doi.org/10.1007/978-3-030-45727-3_21
50. Maller, M., Bowe, S., Kohlweiss, M., Meiklejohn, S.: Sonic: Zero-knowledge SNARKs from linear-size universal and updatable structured reference strings. In: Cavallaro, L., Kinder, J., Wang, X., Katz, J. (eds.) ACM CCS 2019, pp. 2111–2128. ACM Press (November 2019). https://doi.org/10.1145/3319535.3339817
51. Micali, S.: Computationally sound proofs. SIAM J. Comput. **30**(4), 1253–1298 (2000)
52. Rivest, R.L., Shamir, A., Adleman, L.M.: A method for obtaining digital signatures and public-key cryptosystems. Commun. Assoc. Comput. Mach. **21**(2), 120–126 (1978)
53. Russell, A., Tang, Q., Yung, M., Zhou, H.-S.: Cliptography: clipping the power of kleptographic attacks. In: Cheon, J.H., Takagi, T. (eds.) ASIACRYPT 2016, Part II. LNCS, vol. 10032, pp. 34–64. Springer, Heidelberg (2016). https://doi.org/10.1007/978-3-662-53890-6_2
54. Sadeghi, A.-R., Steiner, M.: Assumptions related to discrete logarithms: why subtleties make a real difference. In: Pfitzmann, B. (ed.) EUROCRYPT 2001. LNCS, vol. 2045, pp. 244–261. Springer, Heidelberg (2001). https://doi.org/10.1007/3-540-44987-6_16

55. Schnorr, C.P.: Efficient identification and signatures for smart cards. In: Brassard, G. (ed.) CRYPTO 1989. LNCS, vol. 435, pp. 239–252. Springer, New York (1990). https://doi.org/10.1007/0-387-34805-0_22
56. Wee, H., Wichs, D.: Candidate obfuscation via oblivious LWE sampling. Cryptology ePrint Archive, Report 2020/1042 (2020). https://eprint.iacr.org/2020/1042

Chain Reductions for Multi-signatures and the HBMS Scheme

Mihir Bellare(✉) and Wei Dai(✉)

Department of Computer Science and Engineering,
University of California, San Diego, USA
{mihir,wdai}@eng.ucsd.edu

Abstract. Existing proofs for existing Discrete Log (DL) based multi-signature schemes give only weak guarantees if the schemes are implemented, as they are in practice, in 256-bit groups. This is because the underlying reductions, which are mostly in the standard model and from DL, are loose. We show that relaxing either the model or the assumption suffices to obtain tight reductions. Namely we give (1) tight proofs from DL in the Algebraic Group Model, and (2) tight, standard-model proofs from well-founded assumptions other than DL. We first do this for the classical 3-round schemes, namely BN and MuSig. Then we give a new 2-round multi-signature scheme, HBMS, as efficient as prior ones, for which we do the same. These multiple paths to security for a single scheme are made possible by a framework of chain reductions, in which a reduction is broken into a chain of sub-reductions involving intermediate problems. Overall our results improve the security guarantees for DL-based multi-signature schemes in the groups in which they are implemented in practice.

1 Introduction

Usage in cryptocurrencies has lead to interest in practical, Discrete-Log-based multi-signature schemes. Proposals exist, are efficient, and are supported by proofs, BUT, the bound on adversary advantage in the proofs is so loose that the proofs fail to support use of the schemes in the 256-bit groups in which they are implemented in practice. This leaves the security of in-practice schemes unclear.

We ask, is it possible to bridge this gap to give some valuable support, in the form of tight reductions, for in-practice schemes? As long as we stay in the current paradigm, namely standard-model proofs from DL, the answer is likely NO. To make progress, we need to be willing to change either the model or the assumption. We show that in fact changing either suffices. Our approach is to give, for any scheme, many different paths to security. In particular we give (1) tight reductions from DL in the Algebraic Group Model (AGM) [17], and (2) tight, standard-model reductions from well-founded assumptions other than DL. We obtain these results via a framework in which a reduction is "factored" into a chain of sub-reductions involving intermediate problems.

M. Tibouchi and H. Wang (Eds.): ASIACRYPT 2021, LNCS 13093, pp. 650–678, 2021.
https://doi.org/10.1007/978-3-030-92068-5_22

We implement this approach first with classical 3-round schemes, giving chain reductions yielding (1) and (2) above for the BN [7] and MuSig [25] schemes. Then, in the space of 2-round schemes, we give a new, efficient scheme, called HBMS, for which we do the same. We now look at all this in more detail.

Background. A multi-signature σ on a message m can be thought of as affirming that "We, the members of this group, all, jointly, endorse m." The group is indicated by the vector $\mathbf{vk} = (\mathbf{vk}[1], \ldots, \mathbf{vk}[n])$ of individual public verification keys of its members, and can be dynamic, changing from one signature to another. Signing is done via an interactive protocol between group members; each member i begins with its own public verification key $\mathbf{vk}[i]$, its matching private signing key $\boldsymbol{sk}[i]$, and the message m, and, at the end of the interaction, they output the multi-signature σ. The latter should be compact (of size independent of the size of the group), precluding the trivial solution in which σ is a list of the individual signatures of the group members on m.

Following its suggestion in the 1980s [20], the primitive has seen much evolution [7,19,22,26,29]. Early schemes assumed all signers in the signing protocol picked their verification keys honestly. "Rogue-key attacks," in which a malicious signer picked its verification key as function of that of an honest signer, lead to an upgraded target, schemes that retain security even in the presence of adversarially-chosen verification keys. Towards this challenging end we first saw schemes either using interactive key-generation [26] or making the "knowledge of secret key" assumption [10,23]. Finally, BN [7] gave an efficient, Schnorr-based scheme in the "plain public-key" model, where security was provided even in the face of maliciously-chosen verification keys, yet no more was assumed about these keys than their having certificates as per a standard PKI.

The BN model and definition have become the preferred target; it is the one used in the schemes we discuss next, and in our scheme as well. We denote the security goal as MS-UF. In Sect. 4 we define it via a game, and define the ms-uf advantage of an adversary as its probability of winning this game.

A new wave. Applications in blockchains and cryptocurrencies —see [11] for details— have fueled a resurgence of interest in multi-signatures. The desire here is MS-UF-secure, DL-based schemes that work over standard elliptic curves such as Secp256k1 or Curve25519. (Pairing-based schemes [11] are thus precluded.) The natural candidate is BN. But the new application arena has lead to a desire for the following further features, not possessed by BN: (1) Key aggregation. There should be a way to aggregate a set of verification keys into a single, short aggregate key, relative to which signatures are verified. (2) Two rounds. A signing protocol using only 2 rounds of interaction, as opposed to the 3 used by BN.

MuSig [11,25] broke ground by adapting BN to add key aggregation. Now the effort moved to reducing the number of rounds. This proved challenging. Early proposals of two-round schemes —[2,24,35] as well as an early, two-round version of MuSig [25]— were broken by DEFKLNS [15]. To fill the gap, DEFKLNS gave a new two-round scheme, mBCJ. Other proposals followed: MuSig2 [27], MuSig-DN [28] and DWMS [1]. All these support key aggregation.

	Previous		Ours	
Scheme MS	$\mathbf{UB}^{\text{ms-uf}}_{\mathsf{MS}}(t, q, q_s, p)$	$p \approx 2^{256}$	$\mathbf{UB}^{\text{ms-uf}}_{\mathsf{MS}}(t, q, q_s, p)$	$p \approx 2^{256}$
BN [7]	$\sqrt{(q \cdot t^2)/p}$	2^{-8}	t^2/p	2^{-96}
MuSig [11, 25]	$\sqrt[4]{(q^3 \cdot t^2)/p}$	1	t^2/p	2^{-96}

Fig. 1. Bounds on ms-uf advantage for the 3-round schemes BN and MuSig. First we show prior bounds, then ours. In each case we first show the upper bound $\mathbf{UB}^{\text{ms-uf}}_{\mathsf{MS}}(t, q, q_s, p)$ as a formula, where t, q, q_s are, respectively the adversary running time, the number of its RO queries and the number of executions of the signing protocol, while prime p is the size of the underlying group $\mathbb{G}$. We then show the evaluation with $t = q = 2^{80}$, $q_s = 2^{30}$ and $p \approx 2^{256}$, to capture security over 256-bit curves Secp256k1 or Curve25519.

All the schemes discussed here come with proofs of MS-UF security based on the hardness of the DL (Discrete Log) problem in the underlying group $\mathbb{G}$, up to variations in the model (standard or AGM [17]) or the type of DL problem (plain or OMDL [6]).

<u>CURRENT BOUNDS.</u> On being informed that a scheme has a proof of security based on the hardness of the DL problem in an underlying elliptic-curve group $\mathbb{G}$, the expectation of a practitioner is that the probability that a time t attacker can violate MS-UF security is no more than the probability of successfully computing a discrete logarithm in $\mathbb{G}$, which, as per [34], is t^2/p, where p, a prime, is the size of $\mathbb{G}$. Concretely, with the 256-bit curves Secp256k1 or Curve25519 —$p \approx 2^{256}$— they would expect that a time $t \approx 2^{80}$ attacker has ms-uf advantage at most $2^{160-256} = 2^{-96}$.

But this expectation is only correct if the reduction in the proof is tight. Current proofs for DL-based multi-signature schemes are loose. With the 256-bit curves Secp256k1 or Curve25519, and for a 2^{80}-time attacker, the proof of [7] for BN can preclude only a 2^{-8} ms-uf advantage, while the proof of [11,25] for MuSig cannot even preclude a ms-uf advantage of 1, meaning there may be, per the proof, no security at all (cf. Fig. 1). For 2-round schemes, the advantage precluded by current proofs is 2^{-16} in one case, and again just 1 for the others (cf. Fig. 2). Overall, the proofs fail, by big margins, to support the parameter choices and expectations of practice.

Before continuing, let us expand on the above estimates. A proof of MS-UF security for a multi-signature scheme MS gives a formula $\mathbf{UB}^{\text{ms-uf}}_{\mathsf{MS}}(t, q, q_s, p)$ that upper bounds the ms-uf advantage of an adversary as a function of its running time t, the number q of its queries to the random oracle, and the number q_s of executions of the signing protocol in the chosen-message attack in the ms-uf game. They are shown in Figs. 1 and 2. We assume that $t \geq q \geq q_s$. To get these formulas, we first assume that the best attack against the DL problem is generic, so that a time t attacker has success probability at most t^2/p [34]. Next, we use the concrete-security results, in theorems in the papers, that give reductions from the DL problem to the MS-UF security of their scheme. The square-roots in the

Scheme	Security		Efficiency	
	$\mathbf{UB}^{\text{ms-uf}}_{\mathsf{MS}}(t,q,q_s,p)$	$p \approx 2^{256}$	Sign	Vf
mBCJ [15]	$(q_s^3 \cdot q^2 \cdot t^2)/p$	1	$T_2^{\text{me}} + T_3^{\text{me}}$	$3T_2^{\text{me}}$
MuSig-DN [28]	$\sqrt[4]{(q^3 \cdot t^2)/p}$	1	NIZK	T_2^{me}
MuSig2, $\nu \geq 4$ [27]	$\sqrt[4]{(q^3 \cdot t^2)/p}$	1	T_ν^{me}	T_2^{me}
MuSig2, $\nu = 2$ [27]	$(t^2 + q^3)/p$	2^{-16}	T_2^{me}	T_2^{me}
DWMS [1]	$t^2/p + q/\sqrt{p}$	2^{-48}	$T_2^{\text{me}} + T_{2N}^{\text{me}}$	T_2^{me}
HBMS	t^2/p	2^{-96}	T_2^{me}	T_3^{me}

Fig. 2. Bounds on ms-uf advantage for 2-round schemes. First we show bounds for prior schemes, then the bounds for our new scheme HBMS. As before, we first show the upper bound formula $\mathbf{UB}^{\text{ms-uf}}_{\mathsf{MS}}(t,q,q_s,p)$, where t, q, q_s are, respectively the adversary running time, the number of its RO queries and the number of executions of the signing protocol, while prime p is the size of the underlying group $\mathbb{G}$. We then show the evaluation with $t = q = 2^{80}$, $q_s = 2^{30}$ and $p \approx 2^{256}$, to capture security over 256-bit curves Secp256k1 or Curve25519. For MuSig2, results differ depending on a parameter ν of the scheme. We also show estimates of signing time (per signer) and verification time. Here T_n^{me} is the time to compute one n-multi-exponentiation in $\mathbb{G}$. The "NIZK" for MuSig-DN indicates that signing requires computation and verification of a NIZKs, which is (much) more expensive then other operations shown.

formulas arise from uses of forking lemmas [2,7,31]; the fourth-roots from nested use. The bounds in our Figures are approximate, dropping negligible additive terms. The proofs on which the bounds of Figs. 1 and 2 are based, are, for BN [7], MuSig [11,25], mBCJ [15], MuSig-DN [28] and MuSig2 ($\nu \geq 4$) [27], in the standard model; and for MuSig2 ($\nu = 2$) [27], DWMS [1] and HBMS, in the AGM. See [4] for details.

<u>Towards better bounds.</u> Our thesis is that proofs should provide, not merely a qualitative guarantee, but one whose bounds quantitatively support parameter choices made in practice and the indications of cryptanalysis. Accordingly we want multi-signature schemes for which we can prove tight bounds on ms-uf advantage. How are we to reach this end? Impossibility results for Schnorr signatures [21,30], on which the multi-signature schemes under consideration are based, indicate that a search for tight reductions that are both (1) in the standard model, and (2) from DL, is unlikely to succeed. We need to be flexible, and relax either (1) or (2). In fact we show that relaxing either suffices: We give (1) tight reductions from DL in the Algebraic Group Model (AGM) [17], and (2) tight, standard-model reductions from assumptions other than DL. Together, these provide valuable theoretical support for the use of practical multi-signature schemes in 256-bit groups.

AGM. The AGM considers a limited, but still large class of adversaries, called algebraic. When such an adversary queries a group element to an oracle, it provides also its representation in terms of prior group elements that the adversary has seen. Intuitively, the assumption is that the adversary "knows" how group elements it creates are represented. For elliptic curve groups, this appears to be a realistic assumption, and here the AGM captures natural and currently-known attack strategies.

When considering the merits of the AGM, an important one to keep in mind is that a proof in the AGM immediately implies a proof in the well-accepted Generic Group Model (GGM) of [34]. (So the AGM is only "better" than the GGM.) In more detail, a tight AGM reduction from DL to some problem X immediately yields a GGM bound on adversary advantage, for X, that matches the GGM bound for DL [17]. Thus, overall, tight AGM reductions provide a valuable guarantee. This is recognized by Fuchsbauer, Plouviez and Seurin [18] who use the AGM to give a tight reduction from DL to the UF security of the Schnorr signature scheme. Their result gives hope, realized here, that such reductions are possible for multi-signatures as well.

CHAIN REDUCTIONS. We achieve the above ends, and more, as follows. For each multi-signature scheme MS we consider, we give a chain of reductions, starting from DL, that we depict as

$$\mathrm{DL} = \mathrm{P}_0 \rightarrow \mathrm{P}_1 \rightarrow \cdots \rightarrow \mathrm{P}_{m-1} \rightarrow \mathrm{P}_m = \mathsf{MS} ,$$

where $\mathrm{P}_1, \ldots, \mathrm{P}_{m-1}$ are intermediate computational problems. We refer to $m \geq 1$ as the length of the chain. For each step $\mathrm{P}_{i-1} \rightarrow \mathrm{P}_i$ we provide one of the following.

1. A tight, standard-model reduction. This is the ideal and done for as many steps as possible.
2. When **1.** is not possible, we give BOTH of the following:
  2.1 A tight AGM reduction, AND ALSO
  2.2 A non-tight standard-model reduction.

Since a tight standard-model reduction implies a tight AGM one, this yields a tight AGM reduction from DL to MS, the first of our goals stated above. (A bit better, since some sub-reductions are standard-model.) For i such that the chain $\mathrm{P}_i \rightarrow \cdots \rightarrow \mathsf{MS}$ consists only of tight standard-model reductions, we have a tight, standard model proof of MS from assumption P_i, realizing our second goal, stated above, of tight standard-model reductions from assumptions other than DL. (Of course how interesting or valuable this is depends on the choice of P_i, but as discussed below, we are able to make well-founded choices.)

Finally, something not yet mentioned, that follows from **1** and **2.2** of the chain reductions, is that we always have a standard model (even if non-tight) reduction DL $\rightarrow$ MS. This means that, while adding tight AGM reductions that are valuable in practice, we are not lowering the theoretical or qualitative guarantees, these remaining as one would expect or desire.

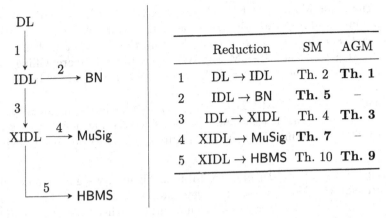

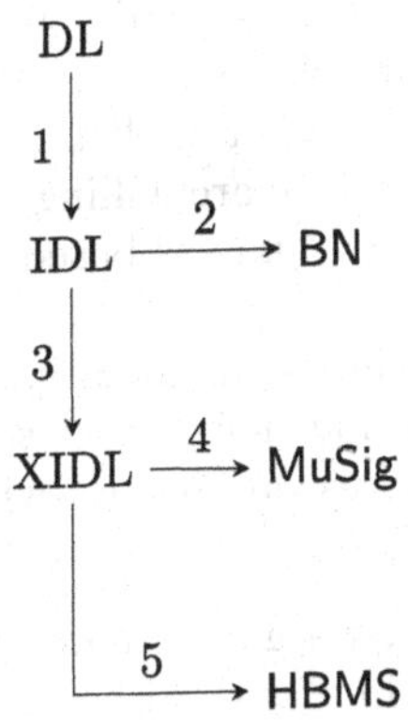

	Reduction	SM	AGM
1	DL → IDL	Th. 2	**Th. 1**
2	IDL → BN	**Th. 5**	–
3	IDL → XIDL	Th. 4	**Th. 3**
4	XIDL → MuSig	**Th. 7**	–
5	XIDL → HBMS	Th. 10	**Th. 9**

Fig. 3. Chain reductions for multi-signatures. SM stands for "Standard Model" and AGM for "Algebraic Group Model." An arrow P → Q means a reduction from P to Q; i.e. a proof that P implies Q. A boldface **Theorem Number** indicates the reduction is **tight**. A blank appears in the AGM column when a (tight) SM reduction to its left makes the AGM reduction unnecessary. Writing a MS scheme like BN, MuSig, HBMS as a point in a chain refers to MS-UF security of the scheme in question.

Chain reductions can be seen as a way to implement a modular proof framework in the style of [21], in which steps are reused across proofs for different schemes.

<u>New bounds for classical schemes.</u> We start by revisiting the classical 3-round schemes, namely BN and MuSig. Figure 3 illustrates our chains, that we now discuss.

IDL, formulated in [21] —they call it IDLOG, which we have abbreviated— is a purely group-based problem that is equivalent to the security against parallel impersonation under key-only attack (PIMP-KOA) of the Schnorr ID scheme. A tight GGM bound for IDL was shown by [21], but an AGM reduction DL → IDL does not seem to be in the literature; we fill this gap by providing it in Theorem 1. A (non-tight) standard model DL → IDL reduction is in [21], but we slightly improve it in Theorem 2.

Now our chain for BN is DL → IDL → BN. This chain has length 2. Our main result for BN is Theorem 5, which shows IDL → BN with a *tight, standard model* reduction. Putting this together with our above-mentioned tight DL → IDL AGM-reduction of Theorem 1, we get a tight DL → BN AGM-reduction. Also our tight, standard-model IDL → BN reduction says that BN is as secure as the Schnorr identification scheme, which is valuable in its own right since the latter has withstood cryptanalysis for many years.

We introduce an intermediate, purely group-based problem we call XIDL. We show IDL → XIDL with a tight AGM reduction (Theorem 3) and a (non-tight) standard-model reduction (Theorem 4).

Our chain for MuSig is DL $\rightarrow$ IDL $\rightarrow$ XIDL $\rightarrow$ MuSig. This chain has length 3. Our main result for MuSig is Theorem 7, which shows XIDL $\rightarrow$ MuSig with a *tight, standard model* reduction. Putting this together with the rest of the chain, we get a tight DL $\rightarrow$ MuSig AGM-reduction. If we are willing to view XIDL as an assumption extending IDL, we can also view MuSig as based tightly on that.

This means we show that $\mathbf{UB}^{\text{ms-uf}}_{\mathsf{MS}}(t, q, q_s, p) \leq t^2/p$ for both schemes, matching the DL bound. This is tight and optimal, since the multi-signature schemes can be broken by taking discrete-logs. Figure 1 compares our results with the prior ones.

<u>New 2-round scheme.</u> Turning to 2-round schemes, we give a new scheme, called HBMS. HBMS supports key aggregation, in line with other 2-round schemes. Our chain for our new 2-round HBMS scheme is DL $\rightarrow$ IDL $\rightarrow$ XIDL $\rightarrow$ HBMS. This chain has length 3. We show XIDL $\rightarrow$ HBMS with a tight AGM reduction (Theorem 9) and a (non-tight) standard-model reduction (Theorem 10). Putting this together with the rest of the chain, we get a tight DL $\rightarrow$ HBMS AGM-reduction, in particular showing $\mathbf{UB}^{\text{ms-uf}}_{\mathsf{MS}}(t, q, q_s, p) \leq t^2/p$, matching the DL bound. We also get a (non-tight) DL $\rightarrow$ HBMS standard-model-reduction.

Figure 2 compares HBMS with prior 2-round schemes. It shows that our improvement in security is not at the cost of efficiency. (Signing in HBMS is as efficient, or more so, than in prior schemes. For verification, MuSig-DN [28] is slightly faster, but signing in the latter is prohibitive due to the use of NIZKs.)

As the above shows, we reuse steps across different chains. Thus XIDL is an intermediate point for both MuSig and HBMS, and IDL for both BN and XIDL. This simplifies proofs and reduces effort. It also shows common elements and relations across schemes.

<u>Equivalences.</u> As discussed above, Theorem 5 shows IDL $\rightarrow$ BN with a tight, standard model reduction. We also give, in Theorem 6, a converse, namely a tight, standard-model reduction showing BN $\rightarrow$ IDL. This shows that IDL and BN are, security-wise, equivalent. Similarly, as discussed above, Theorem 7 shows MuSig $\rightarrow$ XIDL with a tight, standard model reduction, and we also give, in Theorem 8, a converse, namely a tight, standard-model reduction showing XIDL $\rightarrow$ MuSig. This shows that XIDL and MuSig are equivalent. Overall, this shows that IDL and XIDL are not arbitrary choices, but characterizations of the schemes whose consideration is necessary.

<u>Definitional contributions.</u> DEFKLNS [15] found subtle gaps in some prior proofs of security for some two-round multi-signature schemes [2,24,35]. This indicates a need for greater care in the domain of multi-signatures. We suggest that this needs to begin with *definitions*. The ones in prior work, stemming mostly from [7], suffer from some lack of detail and precision. In particular, the very *syntax* of a multi-signature scheme is not specified in detail. This results in scheme descriptions that lack in precision, and proofs that stay at a high level in part due to lack of technical language in which to give details. This in turn can lead to bugs.

To address these issues, we revisit the definitions. We start by giving a detailed syntax that formalizes the signing protocol as a stateful algorithm, run separately by each player. Details addressed include that a player knows its position in the signer list, that player identities are separate from public keys, and integration of the ROM through a parameter describing the type of ideal hash functions needed. Then we give a security definition written via a code-based game. See Sect. 4.

RELATED WORK. The interest for blockchains and cryptocurrencies, and thus our focus, is DL-based schemes over elliptic curves. There are many other multi-signature schemes, based on other hard problems. Aggregate signatures [5,12] yield multi-signatures, but these use pairings (bilinear maps). A pairing-based multi-signature scheme is also given in [11]. Lattice-based multi-signature schemes include [14,16].

As noted above, IDL [21] captures the security against parallel impersonation under key-only attack (PIMP-KOA) of the Schnorr ID scheme and thus, given the ZK property of the scheme, also its security against parallel impersonation under passive attack (PIMP-PA). "Parallel" means multiple impersonation attempts are allowed. IMP-PA, traditional security against impersonation under passive attack, is the case where just one impersonation attempt is allowed. The Reset Lemma [8] gives a standard model DL $\rightarrow$ IMP-PA reduction. This uses rewinding and is non-tight, with a square-root loss. BD [3] introduce the Multi-Base Discrete Logarithm (MBDL) problem, give a tight standard-model MBDL $\rightarrow$ IMP-PA reduction, and show that, in the GGM, the security of MBDL is the same as that of DL. An interesting open question is whether MBDL can be used as a starting point for tight reductions for multi-signature schemes. Rotem and Segev [32] give a standard model DL $\rightarrow$ IMP-PA reduction that improves the square-root-loss reduction but is still not tight.

2 Preliminaries

NOTATION. If n is a positive integer, then $\mathbb{Z}_n$ denotes the set $\{0, \ldots, n-1\}$ and $[n]$ or $[1..n]$ denote the set $\{1, \ldots, n\}$. If $\boldsymbol{x}$ is a vector then $|\boldsymbol{x}|$ is its length (the number of its coordinates), $\boldsymbol{x}[i]$ is its i-th coordinate and $[\boldsymbol{x}] = \{\, \boldsymbol{x}[i] \,:\, 1 \leq i \leq |\boldsymbol{x}| \,\}$ is the set of all its coordinates. A string is identified with a vector over $\{0, 1\}$, so that if x is a string then $x[i]$ is its i-th bit and $|x|$ is its length. By ε we denote the empty vector or string. The size of a set S is denoted $|S|$.

Let S be a finite set. We let $x \leftarrow\!\!\$\; S$ denote sampling an element uniformly at random from S and assigning it to x. We let $y \leftarrow A^{\mathrm{O}_1,\ldots}(x_1, \ldots; \rho)$ denote executing algorithm A on inputs $x_1, \ldots$ and coins ρ with access to oracles $\mathrm{O}_1, \ldots$, and letting y be the result. We let $\rho \leftarrow\!\!\$\; \mathrm{rand}(A)$ denote sampling random coins for algorithm A and assigning it to variable ρ. We let $y \leftarrow\!\!\$\; A^{\mathrm{O}_1,\ldots}(x_1, \ldots)$ be the result of $\rho \leftarrow\!\!\$\; \mathrm{rand}(A)$ followed by $y \leftarrow A^{\mathrm{O}_1,\ldots}(x_1, \ldots; \rho)$. We let $[A^{\mathrm{O}_1,\ldots}(x_1, \ldots)]$ denote the set of all possible outputs of A when invoked with inputs $x_1, \ldots$ and oracles $\mathrm{O}_1, \ldots$. Algorithms are randomized unless otherwise indicated. Running time is worst case.

GAMES. We use the code-based game playing framework of [9]. (See Fig. 4 for an example.) Games have procedures, also called oracles. Amongst these are INIT and a FIN. In executing an adversary $\mathcal{A}$ with a game Gm, procedure INIT is executed first, and what it returns is the input to $\mathcal{A}$. The latter may now call all game procedures except INIT, FIN. When the adversary terminates, its output is viewed as the input to FIN, and what the latter returns is the game output. By $\mathrm{Gm}(\mathcal{A}) \Rightarrow y$ we denote the event that the execution of game Gm with adversary $\mathcal{A}$ results in output y. We write $\Pr[\mathrm{Gm}(\mathcal{A})]$ as shorthand for $\Pr[\mathrm{Gm}(\mathcal{A}) \Rightarrow \mathsf{true}]$, the probability that the game returns true. In writing game or adversary pseudocode, it is assumed that boolean variables are initialized to false, integer variables are initialized to 0 and set-valued variables are initialized to the empty set $\emptyset$.

A procedure (oracle) with a certain name O may appear in several games. (For example, CH appears in two games in Fig. 4.) To disambiguate, we may write Gm.O for the one in game Gm.

When adversary $\mathcal{A}$ is executed with game Gm, we consider the running time of $\mathcal{A}$ as the running time of the execution of $\mathrm{Gm}(\mathcal{A})$, which includes the time taken by game procedures. By $\mathrm{Q}^{\mathrm{O}}_{\mathcal{A}}$ we denote the number of queries made by $\mathcal{A}$ to oracle O in the execution. These counts are both worst case.

GROUPS. Throughout, $\mathbb{G}$ is a group whose order, assumed prime, we denote by p. We will use multiplicative notation for the group operation, and we let $1_{\mathbb{G}}$ denote the identity element of $\mathbb{G}$. We let $\mathbb{G}^* = \mathbb{G} \setminus \{1_{\mathbb{G}}\}$ denote the set of non-identity elements, which is the set of generators of $\mathbb{G}$ since the latter has prime order. If $g \in \mathbb{G}^*$ is a generator and $X \in \mathbb{G}$, then $\mathsf{DL}_{\mathbb{G},g}(X) \in \mathbb{Z}_p$ denotes the discrete logarithm of X in base g.

ALGEBRAIC ALGORITHMS. We recall the definition of algebraic algorithms [17]. As above, fix a group $\mathbb{G}$ of prime order p, and let g be a generator. In all of our security games involving $\mathbb{G}$ and g, we assume that any inputs and outputs of game oracles that are group elements (meaning, in $\mathbb{G}$) are distinguished. In particular, it will be clear from the game pseudocode definition which components of inputs and outputs are such group elements. We say that an adversary, against game Gm, is algebraic, if, whenever it submits a group element $Y \in \mathbb{G}$ as an oracle query, it also provides, alongside, a representation of Y in terms of group elements previously returned by the game oracles (the latter including INIT). Specifically, suppose during an execution of adversary $\mathcal{A}$ with game Gm, the adversary submits a group element $Y \in G$ to game oracle O. Then, alongside, it must provide a vector $(v_0, v_1, \ldots, v_m) \in \mathbb{Z}_p^m$, called a representation of Y, such that $Y = g^{v_0} \cdot h_1^{v_1} \cdots h_m^{v_m}$, where $h_1, \ldots, h_m$ are the group elements that have been returned to the adversary by game oracles of Gm, so far. When considering an execution of game Gm with an adversary $\mathcal{A}$ that is not algebraic, we omit the writing of representations in the oracle calls.

HEDGING. Not all attacks are algebraic. The thesis of [17] is that natural ones are, and thus proving security relative to algebraic adversaries gives meaningful guarantees in practice. We adopt this here but add hedging. Recall this means that, for the same scheme, we seek both (1) A tight AGM reduction from DL, and (2) a standard-model (even if non-tight) reduction from DL. The former is used to guide and support parameter choices. The latter is viewed as at least qualitatively ruling out non-algebraic attacks.

REDUCTIONS. All our standard-model reductions are black-box and preserve algebraicness of adversaries, meaning, if the starting adversary is algebraic, so is the constructed one. This means that we can chain standard-model reductions with AGM-reductions to get overall AGM reductions.

3 Hardness of Problems in Groups

Our chain reductions exploit three computational problems related to groups: standard discrete log (DL); IDL [21]; and a new problem XIDL that we introduce. Here we give the definitions. We then show the length-2 chain DL $\rightarrow$ IDL $\rightarrow$ XIDL. We give reductions that are tight in the AGM and also give (non-tight) standard-model reductions, a total of four results. Referring to Fig. 3, we are establishing the four theorems, shown in the table, that correspond to arrows 1 and 3. For the rest of the section, we fix a group $\mathbb{G}$ of prime order p, and a generator $g \in \mathbb{G}$.

DL. We recall the standard discrete logarithm (DL) problem via game $\mathrm{Gm}^{\mathrm{dl}}_{\mathbb{G},g}$ in Fig. 4. INIT provides the adversary, as input, a random challenge group element X, and to win it must output $x' = \mathsf{DL}_{\mathbb{G},g}(X)$ to FIN. We let $\mathbf{Adv}^{\mathrm{dl}}_{\mathbb{G},g}(\mathcal{A}) = \Pr[\mathrm{Gm}^{\mathrm{dl}}_{\mathbb{G},g}(\mathcal{A})]$ be the discrete-log advantage of adversary $\mathcal{A}$.

IDL. The identification discrete logarithm (IDL) problem, introduced by KMP [21], characterizes the hardness of parallel impersonation under key-only attack (PIMP-KOA) security [21] of the Schnorr identification scheme [33]. Formally, consider the game $\mathrm{Gm}^{\mathrm{idl}}_{\mathbb{G},g,q}$ given in Fig. 4, where parameter q is a positive integer. The IDL-adversary receives a random target point X from INIT. It is additionally given access to a challenge oracle CH that can be called at most q times. The oracle takes as query a group element R (representing the commitment sent by the prover in Schnorr identification), stores it as R_i, and responds with a random challenge $c_i \leftarrow\!\!\$\ \mathbb{Z}_p$ (representing the one sent by the verifier). The adversary wins if it can produce the discrete log z (representing the final prover response) of the group element $R_i \cdot X^{c_i}$, for a choice of i, denoted I, made by the adversary. We define the IDL-advantage of $\mathcal{A}$ to be $\mathbf{Adv}^{\mathrm{idl}}_{\mathbb{G},g,q}(\mathcal{A}) = \Pr[\mathrm{Gm}^{\mathrm{idl}}_{\mathbb{G},g,q}(\mathcal{A})]$.

KMP [21] study IDL in the Generic Group Model (GGM) [34] and prove a bound matching that for DL. Here, we strengthen this to give a tight AGM reduction DL $\rightarrow$ IDL. This could be seen as implicit in part of the AGM proof of security for the Schnorr signature scheme given in [18], although they make no connection to IDL.

Theorem 1. [DL $\rightarrow$ IDL, AGM] *Let $\mathbb{G}$ be a group of prime order p with generator g. Let q be a positive integer. Let $\mathcal{A}^{\mathrm{alg}}_{\mathrm{idl}}$ be an algebraic adversary against $\mathrm{Gm}^{\mathrm{idl}}_{\mathbb{G},g,q}$. Then, adversary $\mathcal{A}_{\mathrm{dl}}$ can be constructed so that*

$$\mathbf{Adv}^{\mathrm{idl}}_{\mathbb{G},g,q}(\mathcal{A}^{\mathrm{alg}}_{\mathrm{idl}}) \leq \mathbf{Adv}^{\mathrm{dl}}_{\mathbb{G},g}(\mathcal{A}_{\mathrm{dl}}) + \frac{q}{p} .$$

Game $\mathrm{Gm}^{\mathrm{dl}}_{\mathbb{G},g}$

INIT:

$x \leftarrow\!\!\$\ Z_{|\mathbb{G}|}$; $X \leftarrow g^x$; Return X

FIN(x'):

Return $(x = x')$

Game $\mathrm{Gm}^{\mathrm{idl}}_{\mathbb{G},g,q}$

INIT:

$x \leftarrow \mathbb{Z}_{|\mathbb{G}|}$; $X \leftarrow g^x$

Return X

CH(R): // At most q queries.

$i \leftarrow i+1$; $R_i \leftarrow R$

$c_i \leftarrow\!\!\$\ \mathbb{Z}_{|\mathbb{G}|}$; Return c_i

FIN(I, z):

Return $(g^z = R_I \cdot X^{c_I})$

Game $\mathrm{Gm}^{\mathrm{xidl}}_{\mathbb{G},g,q_1,q_2}$

INIT:

$x \leftarrow \mathbb{Z}_{|\mathbb{G}|}$; $X \leftarrow g^x$

Return X

NWTAR(S): // At most q_1 queries.

$j \leftarrow j+1$; $S_j \leftarrow S$

$e_j \leftarrow\!\!\$\ \mathbb{Z}_{|\mathbb{G}|}$; $T_j \leftarrow S_j \cdot X^{e_j}$

Return e_j

CH(j_{sel}, R): // At most q_2 queries.

$i \leftarrow i+1$; $R_i \leftarrow R$; $Y_i \leftarrow T_{j_{\mathrm{sel}}}$

$c_i \leftarrow\!\!\$\ \mathbb{Z}_{|\mathbb{G}|}$; Return c_i

FIN(I, z):

Return $(g^z = R_I \cdot {Y_I}^{c_I})$

Fig. 4. Let $\mathbb{G}$ be a group of prime order $p = |\mathbb{G}|$, and let $g \in \mathbb{G}^*$ be a generator of $\mathbb{G}$. Let q, q_1, q_2 be positive integers. Top: Game defining discrete logarithm (DL) problem. Bottom left: Game defining identification logarithm (IDL) problem. Bottom right: Game defining random-target identification logarithm (XIDL) problem.

Furthermore, the running time of $\mathcal{A}_{\mathrm{dl}}$ *is about that of* $\mathcal{A}^{\mathrm{alg}}_{\mathrm{idl}}$.

The full proof is given in [4]. The idea of the proof is as follows. Since $\mathcal{A}^{\mathrm{alg}}_{\mathrm{idl}}$ is algebraic, its query R to CH is accompanied by (r_1, r_2) such that $R = g^{r_1} X^{r_2}$. Our adversary $\mathcal{A}_{\mathrm{dl}}$, who is running $\mathcal{A}^{\mathrm{alg}}_{\mathrm{idl}}$, records these as $R_i, r_{i,1}, r_{i,2}$, and responds with a random c_i. Eventually, $\mathcal{A}^{\mathrm{alg}}_{\mathrm{idl}}$ outputs I, z. Assuming it succeeds, we have $g^z = R_I \cdot X^{c_I} = g^{r_{I,1}} X^{r_{I,2}} X^{c_I}$, or $g^{z - r_{I,1}} = X^w$ where $w = (r_{I,2} + c_I) \bmod p$. Now $\mathsf{DL}_{\mathbb{G},g}(X)$ can be obtained as long as w has an inverse modulo p, meaning is non-zero. But c_I was chosen at random *after the adversary supplied* $r_{I,2}$, so the probability that w is 0 is at most $1/p$. The factor of q accounts for the adversary's having a choice of I made after receiving challenges.

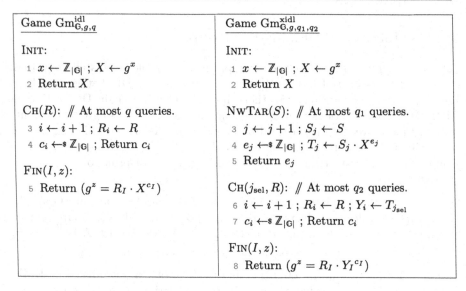

By q-IDL, we refer to IDL with parameter q. 1-IDL corresponds to IMP-KOA security of the Schnorr identification scheme, and a reduction DL $\rightarrow$ 1-IDL is obtained via the Reset Lemma of [8]. KMP show that 1-IDL $\rightarrow$ q-IDL. Overall this gives a standard model (very non-tight) DL $\rightarrow$ q-IDL reduction. However, a somewhat tighter (but still non-tight) result can be obtained when the forking lemma of [7] (which we recall as in [4].) is applied directly instead. Concretely, we give the following theorem, improving the prior reduction by a $\sqrt{q}$ factor. The proof is in [4].

Theorem 2. [DL → IDL, Standard Model] *Let $\mathbb{G}$ be a group of prime order $p = |\mathbb{G}|$, and let $g \in \mathbb{G}^*$ be a generator of $\mathbb{G}$. Let q be a positive integer. Let $\mathcal{A}_{\mathrm{idl}}$ be an adversary against the game $\mathrm{Gm}^{\mathrm{idl}}_{\mathbb{G},g,q}$. The proof constructs an adversary $\mathcal{A}_{\mathrm{dl}}$ such that*

$$\mathbf{Adv}^{\mathrm{idl}}_{\mathbb{G},g,q}(\mathcal{A}_{\mathrm{idl}}) \leq \sqrt{q \cdot \mathbf{Adv}^{\mathrm{dl}}_{\mathbb{G},g}(\mathcal{A}_{\mathrm{idl}})} + \frac{q}{p} \,. \quad (1)$$

Additionally, the running time of $\mathcal{A}_{\mathrm{dl}}$ is approximately $\mathrm{T}_{\mathcal{A}_{\mathrm{dl}}} \approx 2 \cdot \mathrm{T}_{\mathcal{A}_{\mathrm{idl}}}$.

Theorem 2 appears to yield a 1-IDL → q-IDL reduction with a bound that contradicts the lower bound claimed in [21, Corollary 4.4]. Our best guess as to an explanation is that our reduction does not meet the key and randomness preserving restrictions of [21, Corollary 4.4] or that their lower bound does not cover rewinding strategies.

XIDL. We define a new problem, random target identification discrete logarithm, abbreviated XIDL. It abstracts out the algebraic core of MuSig, and we will show that its security is equivalent to the MS-UF security of MuSig. It will also be an intermediate point in our reduction chain reaching our new HBMS scheme, thereby serving multiple purposes.

With $\mathbb{G}, p, g$ fixed as usual, XIDL is parameterized by positive integers q_1, q_2. Formally, consider the game $\mathrm{Gm}^{\mathrm{xidl}}_{\mathbb{G},g,q_1,q_2}$ given in Fig. 4. The adversary receives a randomly chosen group element X from INIT. The game maintains a list $T_1, \ldots, T_{q_1}$ of "targets." The adversary can create a target by querying the New Target oracle NWTAR with a group element S of its choosing, whence $T_j = S \cdot X^{e_j}$ is added to the list of targets, for e_j chosen randomly from $\mathbb{Z}_p$ by the game and returned to the adversary. The adversary can query the challenge oracle CH(j_{sel}, R) by supplying an index j_{sel} and a group element R. The oracle records $T_{j_{\mathrm{sel}}}$ as Y_i, and R as R_i, based on the counter i it maintains. Intuitively, CH is similar to the challenge oracle CH in IDL game, besides that our adversary here needs to specify the target $T_{j_{\mathrm{sel}}}$ it is trying to impersonate against. The adversary wins the game if it can produce the discrete log z of $R_I \cdot Y_I^{c_I}$, for an index I of its choice. The oracles NWTAR and CH are allowed to be called at most q_1 and q_2 times, respectively. We define the XIDL advantage of $\mathcal{A}$ as $\mathbf{Adv}^{\mathrm{xidl}}_{\mathbb{G},g,q_1,q_2}(\mathcal{A}) = \Pr[\mathrm{Gm}^{\mathrm{xidl}}_{\mathbb{G},g,q_1,q_2}(\mathcal{A})]$.

We show hardness of XIDL in both the AGM and the standard model, starting with the former. The theorem actually establishes the stronger DL → XIDL, tightly in the AGM.

Theorem 3. [DL → XIDL, AGM] *Let $\mathbb{G}$ be a group of order p with generator g. Let q_1, q_2 be positive integers. Let $\mathcal{A}^{\mathrm{alg}}_{\mathrm{xidl}}$ be an algebraic adversary against $\mathrm{Gm}^{\mathrm{xidl}}_{\mathbb{G},g,q_1,q_2}$. Then, adversary $\mathcal{A}_{\mathrm{dl}}$ can be constructed so that*

$$\mathbf{Adv}^{\mathrm{xidl}}_{\mathbb{G},g,q_1,q_2}(\mathcal{A}^{\mathrm{alg}}_{\mathrm{xidl}}) \leq \mathbf{Adv}^{\mathrm{dl}}_{\mathbb{G},g}(\mathcal{A}_{\mathrm{dl}}) + \frac{q_1 + q_2}{p} \,.$$

Furthermore, the running time of $\mathcal{A}_{\mathsf{dl}}$ *is about that of* $\mathcal{A}^{\mathrm{alg}}_{\mathrm{xidl}}$.

The full proof is given in [4]. Here we sketch the intuition. Since $\mathcal{A}^{\mathrm{alg}}_{\mathrm{xidl}}$ is algebraic, the j-th query to NwTar is of the form $S_j, s_{j,1}, s_{j,2}$ such that $S_j = g^{s_{j,1}}X^{s_{j,2}}$, and the i-th query to Ch is of the form $j_{\mathrm{sel}}, R_i, r_{i,1}, r_{i,2}$ such that $R_i = g^{r_{i,1}}X^{r_{i,2}}$. Let e_j, c_i denote, respectively, the responses to the j-th query to NwTar and the i-th query to Ch. Eventually, $\mathcal{A}_{\mathrm{xidl}}$ outputs I, z. Assuming it succeeds, the equation $g^z = R_I \cdot T_J^{c_I} = R_I \cdot (S_J \cdot X^{e_J})^{c_I}$ must hold, where J was the selected index j_{sel} in the I-th query to Ch. This means that $g^z = g^{r_{I,1}}X^{r_{I,2}}(g^{s_{J,1}}X^{s_{J,2}}X^{e_J})^{c_I}$, whence $g^{z-r_{I,1}-s_{J,1}\cdot c_I} = X^w$, where $w = r_{I,2} + (s_{J,2} + e_J)c_I$. As long as w is non-zero modulo p, one can solve for the value of $\mathsf{DL}_{\mathbb{G},g}(X)$. But e_J and c_I were independently chosen after the adversary supplied $s_{J,2}$ and $r_{I,2}$, respectively. The probability that there exists j such that $(s_{j,2} + e_j) = 0 \mod p$ is at most q_1/p over q_1 queries to NwTar. Assuming there is no such j, the probability that $w = 0$ is at most q_2/p, due to the q_2 queries to Ch that $\mathcal{A}^{\mathrm{alg}}_{\mathrm{xidl}}$ can make.

In the standard model, techniques in the security proof of MuSig [11,25] could be used to show DL $\rightarrow$ XIDL, which involves two applications of the Forking Lemma, leading to a fourth-root in the bound. We now show IDL $\rightarrow$ XIDL, using a single application of the forking lemma and thus with only a square-root in the bound. Combining this with Theorem 2 recovers the DL $\rightarrow$ XIDL reduction with its fourth-root.

Theorem 4. [IDL $\rightarrow$ XIDL, Standard Model] *Let* $\mathbb{G}$ *be a group of prime order* p *with generator* g. *Let* q_1, q_2 *be positive integers. Let* $\mathcal{A}_{\mathrm{xidl}}$ *be an adversary against* $\mathrm{Gm}^{\mathrm{xidl}}_{\mathbb{G},g,q_1,q_2}$. *Then, an adversary* $\mathcal{A}_{\mathrm{idl}}$ *can be constructed so that*

$$\mathbf{Adv}^{\mathrm{xidl}}_{\mathbb{G},g,q_1,q_2}(\mathcal{A}_{\mathrm{xidl}}) \leq \sqrt{q_2 \cdot \mathbf{Adv}^{\mathrm{idl}}_{\mathbb{G},g,q_1}(\mathcal{A}_{\mathrm{idl}})} + \frac{q_2}{p} .$$

Furthermore, the running time of $\mathcal{A}_{\mathrm{idl}}$ *is about twice of that of* $\mathcal{A}_{\mathrm{xidl}}$.

The full proof is given in [4]. We now sketch the intuition. Adversary $\mathcal{A}_{\mathrm{idl}}$ receives X from game $\mathrm{Gm}^{\mathrm{idl}}_{\mathbb{G},g,q_1}$ and runs adversary $\mathcal{A}_{\mathrm{xidl}}$, forwarding it X as the target point. It answers queries to $\mathcal{A}_{\mathrm{xidl}}$'s NwTar oracle using its own $\mathrm{Gm}^{\mathrm{idl}}_{\mathbb{G},g,q_1}$.Ch oracle. Specifically, the j-th query S to NwTar is responded to with $e_j \leftarrow\!\!\$\; \mathrm{Gm}^{\mathrm{idl}}_{\mathbb{G},g,q_1}.\mathrm{Ch}(S)$, and $\mathcal{A}_{\mathrm{idl}}$ additionally records the group element $T_j \leftarrow S \cdot X^{e_j}$. It simulates adversary $\mathcal{A}_{\mathrm{xidl}}$'s Ch oracle locally, meaning the i-th query $\mathrm{Ch}(j_{\mathrm{sel}}, R)$ is responded to with a fresh challenge $c_i \leftarrow\!\!\$\; \mathbb{Z}_p$. Eventually, adversary $\mathcal{A}_{\mathrm{xidl}}$ gives a response I, z. Our $\mathcal{A}_{\mathrm{idl}}$ adversary wins game $\mathrm{Gm}^{\mathrm{idl}}_{\mathbb{G},g,q_1}$ if it can produce the discrete log of T_j for any j of its choice. To do so, $\mathcal{A}_{\mathrm{idl}}$ uses rewinding, the analysis of which uses the Forking Lemma [7] that we recall in [4]. Rewinding is used to produce another response, (I', z'), from a forked execution of $\mathcal{A}_{\mathrm{xidl}}$. The Forking Lemma applies to an execution of an algorithm making queries to one oracle, but adversary $\mathcal{A}_{\mathrm{xidl}}$ has two oracles NwTar and Ch. We only "fork" $\mathcal{A}_{\mathrm{xidl}}$ on its queries to Ch. Specifically, we program oracle NwTar to behave identically compared to the first run (meaning we use previously recorded values of $e_1, \ldots$ as long as they are defined). In the second run, oracle CH is replied with $c_1, \ldots, c_{I-1}, c'_I, \ldots$, where $c'_I, \ldots$ are randomly chosen from $\mathbb{Z}_p$. Let us assume that $\mathcal{A}_{\text{idl}}$ has derived two valid responses from $\mathcal{A}_{\text{xidl}}$ using the Forking Lemma. Then it is guaranteed that $I = I'$ and $c_I \neq c'_I$. Moreover, we know the two executions of $\mathcal{A}_{\text{xidl}}$ only differ *after* the response of the I-th query to CH, so the I-th query to CH in both runs is some J, R_I. This allows our adversary to solve the equations $g^z = R_I \cdot T_J^{c_I}$ and $g^{z'} = R_I \cdot T_J^{c'_I}$ (which are guaranteed to be true if both runs succeed) to compute $\mathsf{DL}_{\mathbb{G},g}(T_J)$ and thus win the IDL game.

4 Definitions for Multi-signatures

As discussed in Sect. 1, current definitions for multi-signatures, stemming mostly from [7], suffer from some lack of detail and precision, including lack of a precise syntax. This results in scheme descriptions that also lack somewhat in precision, and to proofs that stay at a high level in part due to lack of technical language in which to give details. This could be one of the contributors to bugs in these proofs [15].

To address this, we revisit the definitions. We give a detailed syntax that formalizes the signing protocol as a stateful algorithm, run separately by each player. (The state will be maintained by the overlying game.) Details addressed include that a player knows its position in the signer list, that player identities are separate from public keys, and integration of the ROM through a parameter describing the type of ideal hash functions needed. Then we give a security definition written via a code-based game.

<u>Syntax.</u> A multi-signature scheme MS specifies algorithms MS.Kg, MS.Vf, MS.Sign, as well as a set MS.HF of functions, and an integer MS.nr, whose intent and operation is as follows:

- *Key generation.* Via $(pk, sk) \leftarrow\$ \mathsf{MS.Kg}$, the key generation algorithm generates public signature-verification key pk and secret signing key sk for a user. (Each user is expected to run this independently to get its keys.)
- *Hash functions.* MS.HF is a set of functions, from which, via $\mathsf{h} \leftarrow\$ \mathsf{MS.HF}$, one is drawn and provided to scheme algorithms (except key generation) and the adversary as the random oracle. Specifying this as part of the scheme allows the domain and range of the random oracle to be scheme-dependent.
- *Verification.* Via $d \leftarrow \mathsf{MS.Vf}^{\mathrm{H}}(\boldsymbol{pk}, m, \sigma)$, the verification algorithm deterministically outputs a decision $d \in \{\mathsf{true}, \mathsf{false}\}$ indicating whether or not σ is a valid signature on message m under a vector $\boldsymbol{pk}$ of verification keys.
- *Signing.* The signing protocol is specified by signing algorithm MS.Sign. In each round, each party, applies this algorithm to its current state st and the vector **in** of received messages from the other parties, to compute an outgoing message σ (viewed as broadcast to the other parties) and an updated state st′, written $(\sigma, \mathsf{st}') \leftarrow \mathsf{MS.Sign}^{\mathrm{H}}(\mathbf{in}, \mathsf{st})$. In the last round, σ is the signature that this party outputs. (See Fig. 5.)

– *Rounds.* The interaction consists of a fixed number $\mathsf{MS.nr}$ of rounds. (We number the rounds $0, \ldots, \mathsf{MS.nr}$. The final broadcast of the signature is not counted as in practice it is a local output.)

We say that a multi-signature scheme MS supports key aggregation if MS has two additional algorithms, $\mathsf{MS.Ag}$ and $\mathsf{MS.VfAg}$, such that the following hold: (1) Via $apk \leftarrow\$ \mathsf{MS.Ag}^{\mathrm{H}}(pk_1, \ldots, pk_n)$, the key aggregation algorithm $\mathsf{MS.Ag}$ generates an aggregate public key, (2) Via $d \leftarrow \mathsf{MS.VfAg}^{\mathrm{H}}(apk, m, \sigma)$, the aggregate verification algorithm deterministically outputs a decision $d \in \{\mathsf{true}, \mathsf{false}\}$, and (3) the verification algorithm $\mathsf{MS.Vf}$ is defined exactly as $\mathsf{MS.Vf}^{\mathrm{H}}(\boldsymbol{pk}, m, \sigma) = \mathsf{MS.VfAg}^{\mathrm{H}}(\mathsf{MS.Ag}^{\mathrm{H}}(\boldsymbol{pk}), m, \sigma)$.

Some conventions will aid further definitions and scheme descriptions. A party's state st has several parts: $\mathsf{st.n}$ is the number of parties in the current execution of the protocol; $\mathsf{st.me} \in [1..\mathsf{st.n}]$ is the party's own identity; $\mathsf{st.rnd} \in [0..\mathsf{MS.nr}]$ is the current round number; $\mathsf{st.sk}$ is the party's own signing key; $\mathsf{st.pk}$ is the $\mathsf{st.n}$-vector of all verification keys; $\mathsf{st.msg}$ is the message being signed; $\mathsf{st.rej} \in \{\mathsf{true}, \mathsf{false}\}$ is the decision to reject (not produce a signature) or accept. It is assumed and required that each invocation of $\mathsf{MS.Sign}$ leaves all of these unchanged except for $\mathsf{st.rnd}$, which it increments by 1, and $\mathsf{st.rej}$, which is assumed initialized to false and may at some point be set to true. The state can, beyond these, have other components that vary from protocol to protocol. (For example, Fig. 6 describing the BN scheme has $\mathsf{st}.\boldsymbol{R}[j], \mathsf{st}.\boldsymbol{t}[j], \mathsf{st}.\boldsymbol{z}[j], \mathsf{st}.R, \ldots$.) We write $\mathsf{st} \leftarrow \mathsf{StInit}(j, sk, \boldsymbol{pk}, m)$ to initialize st by setting $\mathsf{st.n} \leftarrow |\boldsymbol{pk}|$; $\mathsf{st.me} \leftarrow j$; $\mathsf{st.rnd} \leftarrow 0$; $\mathsf{st.sk} \leftarrow sk$; $\mathsf{st.pk} \leftarrow \boldsymbol{pk}$; $\mathsf{st.msg} \leftarrow m$; $\mathsf{st.rej} \leftarrow \mathsf{false}$. If an execution $(\sigma, \mathsf{st}') \leftarrow \mathsf{MS.Sign}^{\mathrm{H}}(\mathbf{in}, \mathsf{st})$ returns $\sigma = \bot$ then it is assumed and required that further executions starting from st' all return $\bot$ as the output message.

<u>CORRECTNESS.</u> Algorithm $\mathsf{Exec}_{\mathsf{MS}}$, shown in the left column of Fig. 5, executes the signing protocol of MS on input a vector $\boldsymbol{sk}$ of signing keys, a vector $\boldsymbol{pk}$ of matching verification keys with $|\boldsymbol{sk}| = |\boldsymbol{pk}|$, and a message m to be signed, and with access to random oracle $\mathsf{h} \in \mathsf{MS.HF}$. The number of parties n at line 1 is the number of coordinates (length) of $\boldsymbol{pk}$. The state st_j of party j at line 3 is initialized using the function StInit defined above. The loop at line 5 executes $\mathsf{MS.nr}$ rounds. Here $\boldsymbol{b}$ denotes the n-vector of currently-broadcast messages, meaning $\boldsymbol{b}[i]$ was broadcast by party i in the prior round, and the entire vector is the input to party j for the current round. At line 8, $\boldsymbol{b}$ now holds the next round of broadcasts.

The correctness game $\mathbf{G}^{\text{ms-cor}}_{\mathsf{MS},n}$ shown in the right column of Fig. 5 has only one procedure, namely FIN. We say that MS satisfies (perfect) correctness if for all positive integers n we have $\Pr[\mathbf{G}^{\text{ms-cor}}_{\mathsf{MS},n}] = 1$.

<u>UNFORGEABILITY.</u> Game $\mathbf{G}^{\text{ms-uf}}_{\mathsf{MS}}$ in Fig. 5 captures a notion of unforgeability for multi-signatures that slightly extends [7]. There is one honest player whose keys are picked at line 1, the adversary controlling all the other players. A new instance of the signing protocol is initialized by calling NS with an index k and a vector $\boldsymbol{pk}$ of verification keys that the adversary can choose, possibly dishonestly, subject only to $\boldsymbol{pk}[k]$ being the verification key pk of the honest player, as enforced by line 2. The first message of the honest player is sent out, and at

Algorithm $\mathsf{Exec}^{\mathsf{h}}_{\mathsf{MS}}(\boldsymbol{sk}, \boldsymbol{pk}, m)$:

$n \leftarrow |\boldsymbol{pk}|$
For $j = 1, \ldots, n$ do
  $\mathsf{st}_j \leftarrow \mathsf{StInit}(j, \boldsymbol{sk}[j], \boldsymbol{pk}, m)$
$\boldsymbol{b} \leftarrow (\varepsilon, \ldots, \varepsilon)$ // n-vector
For $i = 1, \ldots, \mathsf{MS.nr}$ do
  For $j = 1, \ldots, n$ do
    $(\sigma_j, \mathsf{st}_j) \leftarrow\!\!\$\ \mathsf{MS.Sign}^{\mathsf{h}}(\boldsymbol{b}, \mathsf{st}_j)$
  $\boldsymbol{b} \leftarrow (\sigma_1, \ldots, \sigma_n)$
Return σ_1

Game $\mathbf{G}^{\text{ms-cor}}_{\mathsf{MS},n}$

FIN:
$\mathsf{h} \leftarrow\!\!\$\ \mathsf{MS.HF}$
For $i = 1, \ldots, n$ do
  $(\boldsymbol{pk}[i], \boldsymbol{sk}[i]) \leftarrow\!\!\$\ \mathsf{MS.Kg}$
$\sigma \leftarrow\!\!\$\ \mathsf{Exec}^{\mathsf{h}}_{\mathsf{MS}}(\boldsymbol{sk}, \boldsymbol{pk}, m)$
$d \leftarrow \mathsf{MS.Vf}^{\mathsf{h}}(\boldsymbol{pk}, m, \sigma)$
Return d

Game $\mathbf{G}^{\text{ms-uf}}_{\mathsf{MS}}$

INIT:
$\mathsf{h} \leftarrow\!\!\$\ \mathsf{MS.HF}$; $(pk, sk) \leftarrow\!\!\$\ \mathsf{MS.Kg}$; Return pk

NS$(k, \boldsymbol{pk}, m)$:
$\boldsymbol{pk}[k] \leftarrow pk$; $u \leftarrow u + 1$; $\boldsymbol{pk}_u \leftarrow \boldsymbol{pk}$; $m_u \leftarrow m$; $\mathsf{st}_u \leftarrow \mathsf{StInit}(k, sk, \boldsymbol{pk}, m)$
$\boldsymbol{b} \leftarrow (\varepsilon, \ldots, \varepsilon)$; $(\sigma, \mathsf{st}_u) \leftarrow\!\!\$\ \mathsf{MS.Sign}^{\mathrm{H}}(\boldsymbol{b}, \mathsf{st}_u)$; Return σ

SIGN$_j(s, \boldsymbol{b})$: // $1 \le j \le \mathsf{MS.nr}$
$(\sigma, \mathsf{st}_s) \leftarrow\!\!\$\ \mathsf{MS.Sign}^{\mathrm{H}}(\boldsymbol{b}, \mathsf{st}_s)$; Return σ

H(x):
Return $\mathsf{h}(x)$

FIN$(k, \boldsymbol{pk}, m, \sigma)$:
If $(\boldsymbol{pk}[k] \ne pk)$ then Return false
If $(\boldsymbol{pk}, m) \in \{(\boldsymbol{pk}_i, m_i) : 1 \le i \le u\}$ then Return false
Return $\mathsf{MS.Vf}^{\mathrm{H}}(\boldsymbol{pk}, m, \sigma)$

Fig. 5. Top left: Procedure specifying an honest execution of the signing protocol associated with multi-signature scheme MS. **Top right:** Correctness game. **Bottom:** Unforgeability game.

this point $\mathsf{st}_u.\mathsf{rnd} = 1$. Now the adversary can run multiple concurrent instances of the signing protocol with the honest signer. Oracle H is the random oracle, simply calling h. Eventually the adversary calls FIN with a forgery index k, a vector of verification keys (subjected to $\boldsymbol{pk}[k]$ being the public key of the honest signer), a message and a claimed signature. It wins if verification succeeds and the forgery was non-trivial. The ms-uf-advantage of adversary $\mathcal{A}$ is $\mathbf{Adv}^{\text{ms-uf}}_{\mathsf{MS}}(\mathcal{A}) = \Pr[\mathbf{G}^{\text{ms-uf}}_{\mathsf{MS}}(\mathcal{A})]$.

It is convenient for (later) proofs to have a separate signing oracle SIGN$_j$ for each round $j \in [1..\mathsf{MS.nr}]$. It is required that any SIGN$_j(s, \cdot)$ satisfy $s \in [1..u]$, and that the prior round queries $\text{SIGN}_k(s, \cdot)$ for $k < j$ have already been made. It is required that for each j, s, at most one $\text{SIGN}_j(s, \cdot)$ query is ever made.

REMARKS. Our syntax and security notions for multi-signatures view a group of signers as captured by the vector (rather than the set) of their public keys. So for example, a forgery $((pk_1, pk_2), m, \sigma)$ is considered to be non-trivial even if there was a previous signing session under public keys (pk_2, pk_1) and message m. This differs from previous formalizations that work instead with sets of public keys. However, previous definition can be recovered if a canonical encoding of sets of public keys into vectors of public keys is fixed in the usage of a scheme.

5 Analysis of the BN Scheme

BN SCHEME. Let $\mathbb{G}$ be a group of prime order p. Let g be a generator of $\mathbb{G}$ and let $\ell \geq 1$ be an integer. The associated BN [7] multi-signature scheme $\mathsf{MS} = \mathsf{BN}[\mathbb{G}, g, \ell]$ is shown in detail, in our syntax, in Fig. 6. The set $\mathsf{MS.HF}$ consists of all functions h such that $\mathsf{h}(0, \cdot) : \{0,1\}^* \to \{0,1\}^\ell$ and $\mathsf{h}(1, \cdot) : \{0,1\}^* \to \mathbb{Z}_p$. For $b \in \{0,1\}$ we write $\mathrm{H}_b(\cdot)$ for $\mathrm{H}(b, \cdot)$, so that scheme algorithms, and an ms-uf adversary, will have access to oracles $\mathrm{H}_0, \mathrm{H}_1$ rather than just H.

The signing protocol has 3 rounds. In round 0, player j picks $r \leftarrow\!\!\$\ \mathbb{Z}_p$, stores g^r in its state as $\mathsf{st}.\boldsymbol{R}[j]$, computes, and stores in its state, a value $\mathsf{st}.\boldsymbol{t}[j] \leftarrow \mathrm{H}_0((j, \mathsf{st}.\boldsymbol{R}[j]))$ that we call the BN-commitment, and broadcasts the BN-commitment. (Per our syntax, what is returned is the message to be broadcast and the updated state to be retained.) Since each player does this, in round 1, player j receives the BN-commitments of the other players, storing them in vector $\mathsf{st}.\boldsymbol{t}$, and now broadcasting $\mathsf{st}.\boldsymbol{R}[j]$. In round 2, these broadcasts are received, so player j can form the vector $\mathsf{st}.\boldsymbol{R}$. At line 20, it returns $\perp$ if one of the received values fails to match its commitment. As per our conventions, when this happens, this player will always broadcast $\perp$ in the future, so for round 3 we assume lines 21 and 22 are executed. These lines create the second component $\mathsf{st}.\boldsymbol{z}[j]$ of a Schnorr signature relative to the Schnorr-commitment $\mathsf{st}.\boldsymbol{R}[j]$ defined at line 13, and the player's own secret key, the computations being modulo p. This $\mathsf{st}.\boldsymbol{z}[j]$ is broadcast, so that, in round 3, our player receives the corresponding values from the other players. At line 27 it forms their modulo-p sum z and then forms the final signature $(\mathsf{st}.R, z)$.

Our description of the signing protocol differs, from that in [7], in some details that are brought out by our syntax, for example in using explicit party identities rather than seeing these as implicit in public keys.

PRIOR BOUNDS. We recall the prior result of [7]. Let $\mathsf{MS} = \mathsf{BN}[\mathbb{G}, g, \ell]$ and let $\mathcal{A}_{\mathrm{ms}}$ be an adversary for game $\mathbf{G}^{\text{ms-uf}}_{\mathsf{MS}}$. Assume the execution of game $\mathbf{G}^{\text{ms-uf}}_{\mathsf{MS}}$ with $\mathcal{A}_{\mathrm{ms}}$ has at most q distinct queries across $\mathrm{H}_0, \mathrm{H}_1$ and at most q_{s} queries to NS. Suppose the number of parties (length of verification-key vector) in queries to NS and FIN is at most n. Let $a = 8q_{\mathrm{s}} + 1$ and $b = 2q + 16n^2 q_{\mathrm{s}}$. Let $p = |\mathbb{G}|$. Then BN [7] give a DL-adversary $\mathcal{A}_{\mathrm{dl}}$ such that

$$\mathbf{Adv}^{\text{ms-uf}}_{\mathsf{MS}}(\mathcal{A}_{\mathrm{ms}}) \leq \sqrt{(q + q_{\mathrm{s}}) \cdot \left(\mathbf{Adv}^{\mathrm{dl}}_{\mathbb{G},g}(\mathcal{A}_{\mathrm{dl}}) + \frac{a}{p} + \frac{b}{2^\ell}\right)}\,. \tag{2}$$

Kg:	$\mathsf{Vf}^{\mathrm{H}}(\boldsymbol{pk}, m, \sigma)$:

$sk \leftarrow_{\$} \mathbb{Z}_p$; $pk \leftarrow g^{sk}$
 Return (pk, sk)
	$(R, z) \leftarrow \sigma$; $(pk_1, \ldots, pk_n) \leftarrow \boldsymbol{pk}$
	 $\underline{\mathsf{BN}:}$
	   For $i = 1, \ldots, n$ do $c_i \leftarrow \mathrm{H}_1((i, R, \boldsymbol{pk}, m))$
	   Return ($g^z = R \cdot \prod_{i=1}^{n} pk_i^{c_i}$)
	 $\underline{\mathsf{MuSig}:}$
	   $apk \leftarrow \prod_i^n pk_i^{\mathrm{H}_2((i,\boldsymbol{pk}))}$
	   $c \leftarrow \mathrm{H}_1((R, apk, m))$
	   Return ($g^z = R \cdot apk^c$)

$\mathsf{Sign}^{\mathrm{H}}(\boldsymbol{b}, \mathsf{st})$:

$j \leftarrow \mathsf{st.me}$; $n \leftarrow \mathsf{st.n}$; $m \leftarrow \mathsf{st.msg}$; $sk \leftarrow \mathsf{st.sk}$; $\boldsymbol{pk} \leftarrow \mathsf{st.pk}$
If ($\mathsf{st.rnd} = 0$) then
  $\mathsf{st}.r \leftarrow_{\$} \mathbb{Z}_p$; $\mathsf{st}.\boldsymbol{R}[j] \leftarrow g^r$; $\mathsf{st}.\boldsymbol{t}[j] \leftarrow \mathrm{H}_0((j, \mathsf{st}.\boldsymbol{R}[j]))$; $\mathsf{st.rnd} \leftarrow \mathsf{st.rnd} + 1$
  Return $(\mathsf{st}.\boldsymbol{t}[j], \mathsf{st})$
If ($\mathsf{st.rnd} = 1$) then
  For all $i \neq j$ do $\mathsf{st}.\boldsymbol{t}[i] \leftarrow \boldsymbol{b}[i]$
  $\mathsf{st.rnd} \leftarrow \mathsf{st.rnd} + 1$; Return $(\mathsf{st}.\boldsymbol{R}[j], \mathsf{st})$
If ($\mathsf{st.rnd} = 2$) then
  For all $i \neq j$ do $\mathsf{st}.\boldsymbol{R}[i] \leftarrow \boldsymbol{b}[i]$
  If ($\exists i : \mathrm{H}_0((i, \mathsf{st}.R[i])) \neq \mathsf{st}.\boldsymbol{t}[i]$) then Return $(\bot, \mathsf{st})$
  $\mathsf{st}.R \leftarrow \prod_{i=1}^{n} \mathsf{st}.R[i]$
  $\underline{\mathsf{BN}:}$ $c_j \leftarrow \mathrm{H}_1((j, R, \boldsymbol{pk}, m))$; $\mathsf{st}.\boldsymbol{z}[j] \leftarrow sk \cdot c_j + \mathsf{st}.r$
  $\underline{\mathsf{MuSig}:}$
    $apk \leftarrow \prod_{i=1}^{n} \boldsymbol{pk}[i]^{\mathrm{H}_2((i,\boldsymbol{pk}))}$; $c \leftarrow \mathrm{H}_1((R, apk, m))$
    $\mathsf{st}.\boldsymbol{z}[j] \leftarrow sk \cdot \mathrm{H}_2((\mathsf{st.me}, \boldsymbol{pk})) \cdot c + \mathsf{st}.r$
  $\mathsf{st.rnd} \leftarrow \mathsf{st.rnd} + 1$; Return $(\mathsf{st}.\boldsymbol{z}[j], \mathsf{st})$
If ($\mathsf{st.rnd} = 3$) then
  For all $i \neq j$ do $\mathsf{st}.\boldsymbol{z}[i] \leftarrow \boldsymbol{b}[i]$
  $z \leftarrow \sum_{i=1}^{n} \mathsf{st}.\boldsymbol{z}[i]$; Return $((\mathsf{st}.R, z), \mathsf{st})$

Fig. 6. Algorithms of the multi-signature scheme $\mathsf{BN}[\mathbb{G}, g, \ell]$ and $\mathsf{MuSig}[\mathbb{G}, g, \ell]$, where $\mathbb{G}$ is a group of prime order p with generator g. Code that differs between the two schemes is marked explicitly. Oracle $\mathrm{H}_i(\cdot)$ is defined to be $\mathrm{H}(i, \cdot)$ for $i = 0, 1$ (BN) and $i = 0, 1, 2$ (MuSig).

The running time of $\mathcal{A}_{\mathrm{dl}}$ is twice that of the execution of game $\mathbf{G}_{\mathsf{MS}}^{\text{ms-uf}}$ with $\mathcal{A}_{\mathrm{ms}}$. BN obtain this result via their general forking lemma, which uses rewinding and accounts for the square-root in the bound.

SECURITY OF BN FROM IDL. We give a IDL $\rightarrow$ BN reduction that is *tight* and in the *standard model*. Combining this with our tight AGM reduction DL $\rightarrow$ IDL of Theorem 1 we conclude a tight AGM reduction DL $\rightarrow$ BN. However, the standard model tight IDL $\rightarrow$ BN reduction is also interesting in its own right. It says that BN is just as secure as the Schnorr identification scheme. Since the latter has been around and resisted cryptanalysis for quite some time, this is good support for the security of BN.

Theorem 5. [IDL $\rightarrow$ BN, Standard Model] *Let $\mathbb{G}$ be a group of prime order p. Let g be a generator of $\mathbb{G}$ and let $\ell \geq 1$ be an integer. Let $\mathsf{MS} = \mathsf{BN}[\mathbb{G}, g, \ell]$ be the associated BN multi-signature scheme. Let $\mathcal{A}_{\mathrm{ms}}$ be an adversary for game $\mathbf{G}^{\text{ms-uf}}_{\mathsf{MS}}$ of Fig. 5. Assume the execution of game $\mathbf{G}^{\text{ms-uf}}_{\mathsf{MS}}$ with $\mathcal{A}_{\mathrm{ms}}$ has at most q_0, q_1, q_{s} distinct queries to* $\mathrm{H}_0, \mathrm{H}_1, \mathrm{NS}$*, respectively, and the number of parties (length of verification-key vector) in queries to* NS *and* FIN *is at most n. Let $\alpha = q_{\mathrm{s}}(4q_0 + 2q_1 + q_{\mathrm{s}})$ and $\beta = q_0(q_0 + n)$. Then we construct an adversary $\mathcal{A}_{\mathrm{id}}$ for game $\mathrm{Gm}^{\mathrm{idl}}_{\mathbb{G},g,q_1}$ such that*

$$\mathbf{Adv}^{\text{ms-uf}}_{\mathsf{MS}}(\mathcal{A}_{\mathrm{ms}}) \leq \mathbf{Adv}^{\mathrm{idl}}_{\mathbb{G},g,q_1}(\mathcal{A}_{\mathrm{idl}}) + \frac{\alpha}{2p} + \frac{\beta}{2^{\ell}} \,. \tag{3}$$

The running time of $\mathcal{A}_{\mathrm{idl}}$ is about that of the execution of game $\mathbf{G}^{\text{ms-uf}}_{\mathsf{MS}}$ with $\mathcal{A}_{\mathrm{ms}}$. Furthermore, adversary $\mathcal{A}_{\mathrm{idl}}$ is algebraic if adversary $\mathcal{A}_{\mathrm{ms}}$ is.

Above, q_0 is the number of distinct queries to H_0 made, not directly by the adversary, but across the execution of the adversary in game $\mathbf{G}^{\text{ms-uf}}_{\mathsf{MS}}$, and similarly for q_1. A lower bound on q_1 is the length of $\boldsymbol{pk}$ in $\mathcal{A}_{\mathrm{ms}}$'s FIN query, so we can assume it is positive. With the above theorem, we can now derive an upperbound $\mathbf{UB}^{\text{ms-uf}}_{\mathsf{MS}}(t, q, q_{\mathrm{s}}, p)$ of the advantage of any MS adversary with running time t, making q queries to H, and q_{s} signing interactions. We take $\ell \approx \log_2(p)$ and assume that $q_{\mathrm{s}} \leq q \leq t \leq p$. Additionally, we assume that the advantage of any IDL adversary with running time t is at most t^2/p (as justified by Theorem 2). We obtain $\mathbf{UB}^{\text{ms-uf}}_{\mathsf{MS}}(t, q, q_s, p) \leq t^2/p$ as shown in Fig. 1.

The full proof of Theorem 5 is given in [4]. Here we give a sketch. The reduction adversary $\mathcal{A}_{\mathrm{idl}}$ receives a group element X from $\mathrm{Gm}^{\mathrm{idl}}_{\mathbb{G},g,q_1}$ and forwards it to adversary $\mathcal{A}_{\mathrm{ms}}$ as the target public key. In order to run adversary $\mathcal{A}_{\mathrm{ms}}$, our adversary needs to be able to simulate the signing oracles $\mathrm{NS}, \mathrm{SIGN}_1, \mathrm{SIGN}_2$ as well as random oracles H_0 and H_1 without knowing $\mathsf{DL}_{\mathbb{G},g}(X)$. We first describe how the reduction proceeds if $\mathcal{A}_{\mathrm{ms}}$ makes no queries to $\mathrm{NS}, \mathrm{SIGN}_1$ or SIGN_2, as this steps constitutes the main difference between our proof and the original proof of security for BN [7]. Adversary $\mathcal{A}_{\mathrm{idl}}$ uses the challenge oracle $\mathrm{Gm}^{\mathrm{idl}}_{\mathbb{G},g,q_1}.\mathrm{CH}$ to program the random oracle H_1 (hence CH needs to be able to be queried upto the number of times H_1 is evaluated). In particular, for each query $\mathrm{H}_1((k, R, \boldsymbol{pk}, m))$ where $\boldsymbol{pk}[k] = X$, our adversary first computes $T \leftarrow R \cdot \prod_{j \neq k} \boldsymbol{pk}[j]^{\mathrm{H}_1((j,R,\boldsymbol{pk},m))}$, then obtains $c \leftarrow\$\ \mathrm{CH}(T)$ before returning c as the return value for the query $\mathrm{H}_1((k, R, \boldsymbol{pk}, m))$. By construction, a valid forgery for $\boldsymbol{pk}, m$ is some signature $\sigma = (R, z)$ such that

$$g^z = R \cdot \prod_{i=1}^{n} \boldsymbol{pk}[i]^{\mathrm{H}_1((i,R,\boldsymbol{pk},m))} = T \cdot X^c ,$$

where the first equality is by the verification equation of BN and the second equality is by the way H_1 is programmed. This means that adversary $\mathcal{A}_{\mathsf{idl}}$ can simply forward the value of z from a valid forgery, along with the index of the CH query corresponding to the H_1 query of the forgery, to break game $\mathrm{Gm}^{\mathrm{idl}}_{\mathbb{G},g,q_1}$. Moreover, adversary $\mathcal{A}_{\mathsf{idl}}$ succeeds as long as the forgery given by $\mathcal{A}_{\mathsf{ms}}$ is valid.

It remains to show that oracles NS, SIGN_1, SIGN_2 can be simulated without knowledge of the secret key, $\mathsf{DL}_{\mathbb{G},g}(X)$. Roughly, this is done using the zero-knowledge property of the underlying Schnorr identification scheme as well as by programming the random oracles H_0 and H_1. The original proof by [7] constructs an adversary and argues that it simulates these oracles faithfully if certain bad events do not happen. We take a more careful approach and do this formally via a sequence of seven games and use the code-base game playing framework of [9]. This game sequence incurs the additive loss as indicated in (3).

CONVERSE. IDL is not merely some group problem that can be used to justify security of BN tightly; the hardness of IDL is, in fact, tightly equivalent to the MS-UF security of BN. Formally, we give below a reduction turning any adversary against IDL into a forger $\mathcal{A}_{\mathsf{ms}}$ against BN. This means that any security justification for BN must also justify the hardness of IDL.

Theorem 6. [BN $\rightarrow$ IDL, Standard Model] *Let $\mathbb{G}$ be a group of prime order p. Let g be a generator of $\mathbb{G}$ and let $\ell \geq 1$ be an integer. Let $\mathsf{MS} = \mathsf{BN}[\mathbb{G}, g, \ell]$ be the associated BN multi-signature scheme. Let q be a positive integer and $\mathcal{A}_{\mathsf{idl}}$ be an adversary against $\mathrm{Gm}^{\mathrm{idl}}_{\mathbb{G},g,q}$. Then, we can construct an adversary $\mathcal{A}_{\mathsf{ms}}$ for game $\mathbf{G}^{\mathrm{ms\text{-}uf}}_{\mathsf{MS}}$, making no queries to NS, and at most $2q$ queries to H_1, such that*

$$\mathbf{Adv}^{\mathrm{ms\text{-}uf}}_{\mathsf{MS}}(\mathcal{A}_{\mathsf{ms}}) \geq \mathbf{Adv}^{\mathrm{idl}}_{\mathbb{G},g,q}(\mathcal{A}_{\mathsf{idl}}) . \tag{4}$$

The running time of $\mathcal{A}_{\mathsf{ms}}$ is about that of $\mathcal{A}_{\mathsf{idl}}$.

Proof (Theorem 6). Consider the adversary given in Fig. 7. The adversary receives the target public key pk from the MS-UF game and samples a key pair $(pk', sk') \leftarrow_{\$} \mathsf{MS.Kg}$. The adversary will attempt to forge a signature against the vector of public keys (pk, pk'). Adversary $\mathcal{A}_{\mathsf{ms}}$ forwards $X = pk$ as the target point and runs IDL adversary $\mathcal{A}_{\mathsf{idl}}$. For each query $\mathrm{CH}(R)$ of $\mathcal{A}_{\mathsf{idl}}$, adversary $\mathcal{A}_{\mathsf{ms}}$ simulates the response as per line 4 to 6. If $\mathcal{A}_{\mathsf{idl}}$ succeeds, it must be that

$$g^z = R_I \cdot pk^{c_{I,1}} .$$

The value of z can be used to construct a forgery signature (line 3). □

6 Analysis of the MuSig Scheme

The current three-round version of MuSig has been proposed and analyzed by both [11,25]. Roughly, it is the BN scheme with added key aggregation.

$\mathcal{A}_{\rm ms}^{\rm H_1}(pk)$:

$X \leftarrow pk$; $(pk', sk') \leftarrow\!\!\$\ \mathsf{MS.Kg}()$

$(I, z) \leftarrow \mathcal{A}_{\rm xidl}^{\rm CH}(pk)$ // $g^z = R_I \cdot pk^{c_{I,1}}$

$\sigma \leftarrow (R_I, z + sk' \cdot c_{I,2} \mod p)$; Return $((pk, pk'), m_I, \sigma)$

$\textsc{Ch}(R)$:

$i \leftarrow i + 1$; $R_i \leftarrow R$; $m_i \leftarrow \langle i \rangle$

$c_{i,1} \leftarrow\!\!\$\ \mathrm{H}_1((1, R_i, (pk, pk'), m_i))$; $c_{i,2} \leftarrow\!\!\$\ \mathrm{H}_1((2, R_i, (pk, pk'), m_i))$

Return $c_{i,1}$

Fig. 7. Adversary $\mathcal{A}_{\rm ms}$ for Theorem 7. For an integer i, $\langle i \rangle$ denote the binary representation of i.

Let $\mathbb{G}$ be a group of prime order p. And let g be a generator of g and $\ell \geq 1$ be an integer. The formal specification of $\mathsf{MS} = \mathsf{MuSig}[\mathbb{G}, g, \ell]$ in our syntax is shown in Fig. 6. There are minimal differences between MuSig and BN and we only highlight the differences. The set $\mathsf{MS.HF}$ consists of all functions h such that $h(0, \cdot) : \{0,1\}^* \rightarrow \{0,1\}^\ell$ and $h(i, \cdot) : \{0,1\}^* \rightarrow \mathbb{Z}_p$ for $i = 1, 2$. Verification is done as follows. First, an aggregate key apk for the list of keys $\boldsymbol{pk} = (pk_1, \ldots, pk_n)$ is computed as $apk \leftarrow pk_1^{\mathrm{H}_2((1,\boldsymbol{pk}))} \cdots pk_n^{\mathrm{H}_2((n,\boldsymbol{pk}))}$ (line 8). Next, a single challenge is derived from the commitment R and aggregate key apk (line 9). The signature (R, z) is valid if $g^z = R \cdot apk^c$. The second round of signing also changes accordingly to generate a valid signature (line 24 and 25).

The following gives a tight, standard-model reduction XIDL $\rightarrow$ MuSig. Combining this with our tight AGM chain DL $\rightarrow$ IDL $\rightarrow$ XIDL from Theorems 1 and 3, we get a tight AGM reduction DL $\rightarrow$ MuSig.

Theorem 7. [XIDL $\rightarrow$ MuSig, Standard Model] *Let $\mathbb{G}$ be a group of prime order p. Let g be a generator of $\mathbb{G}$ and $\ell \geq 1$ be an integer. Let $\mathsf{MS} = \mathsf{MuSig}[\mathbb{G}, g, \ell]$ be the associated MuSig multi-signature scheme. Let $\mathcal{A}_{\rm ms}$ be an adversary for game $\mathbf{G}_{\mathsf{MS}}^{\text{ms-uf}}$ of Fig. 5. Assume the execution of game $\mathbf{G}_{\mathsf{MS}}^{\text{ms-uf}}$ with $\mathcal{A}_{\rm ms}$ has at most $q_0, q_1, q_2, q_{\rm s}$ distinct queries to $\mathrm{H}_0, \mathrm{H}_1, \mathrm{H}_2, \mathrm{NS}$, respectively, and the number of parties (length of verification-key vector) in queries to* NS *and* Fin *is at most n. Let $\alpha = q_{\rm s}(4q_0 + 2q_1 + q_{\rm s}) + 2q_1q_2$ and $\beta = q_0(q_0 + n)$. Then we can construct an adversary $\mathcal{A}_{\rm xidl}$ for game $\mathrm{Gm}_{\mathbb{G},g,q_2,q_1}^{\rm xidl}$ such that*

$$\mathbf{Adv}_{\mathsf{MS}}^{\text{ms-uf}}(\mathcal{A}_{\rm ms}) \leq \mathbf{Adv}_{\mathbb{G},g,q_2,q_1}^{\rm xidl}(\mathcal{A}_{\rm xidl}) + \frac{\alpha}{2p} + \frac{\beta}{2^\ell} \,. \tag{5}$$

The running time of $\mathcal{A}_{\rm xidl}$ is about that of the execution of game $\mathbf{G}_{\mathsf{MS}}^{\text{ms-uf}}$ with $\mathcal{A}_{\rm ms}$. Furthermore, adversary $\mathcal{A}_{\rm xidl}$ is algebraic if adversary $\mathcal{A}_{\rm ms}$ is.

We remark that the values of q_1 and q_2 above arise from the number of queries to H_1 and H_2 made in the execution of $\mathbf{G}_{\mathsf{MS}}^{\text{ms-uf}}(\mathcal{A}_{\rm ms})$. As a result, the appearance of q_1 and q_2 has their orders "switched" compared to in Sect. 3. With the above theorem, we can now derive an upperbound $\mathbf{UB}_{\mathsf{MS}}^{\text{ms-uf}}(t, q, q_{\rm s}, p)$ of the advantage of any MS adversary with running time t, making q queries to H, and q_s signing interactions. We take $\ell \approx \log_2(p)$ and assume that $q_s \leq q \leq t \leq p$. Additionally, we assume that the advantage of any XIDL adversary with running time t is at most t^2/p (as justified by Theorem 4). We obtain $\mathbf{UB}_{\mathsf{MS}}^{\text{ms-uf}}(t, q, q_s, p) \leq t^2/p$ as shown in Fig. 1.

We again describe the reduction at a high level and defer the full proof to [4]. First, the reduction adversary $\mathcal{A}_{\text{xidl}}$ receives group element X from game $\mathrm{Gm}^{\text{xidl}}_{\mathbb{G}g,q_2,q_1}$ and runs $\mathcal{A}_{\text{ms}}$ with the target public key set to X. Similar to the proof of Theorem 5, our adversary needs to simulate the signing oracles NS, $\mathsf{Sign}_1, \mathsf{Sign}_2$ as well as $\mathrm{H}_0, \mathrm{H}_1, \mathrm{H}_2$ without knowing $\mathsf{DL}_{\mathbb{G},g}(X)$ in order to run $\mathcal{A}_{\text{ms}}$. This again relies on the zero-knowledge property of the underlying Schnorr identification scheme and the programming of $\mathrm{H}_0, \mathrm{H}_1, \mathrm{H}_2$. This step is done formally in a game sequence in the full proof and incurs the additive loss in (5). To turn a forgery into a break against XIDL, our adversary programs H_1 and H_2 as follows. For the j-th query of $\mathrm{H}_2((k, \boldsymbol{pk}))$ where $\boldsymbol{pk}[k] = X$, the adversary first computes $S \leftarrow \prod_{i \neq k} \boldsymbol{pk}[i]^{\mathrm{H}_2((i,\boldsymbol{pk}))}$, then obtains $e_j \leftarrow\!\!\$\ \textsc{NwTar}(S)$ before returning e_j as the response for the query. We remark that this particular query of H_2 have created an aggregate public key $apk = \prod_{i=1}^{|\boldsymbol{pk}|} \boldsymbol{pk}[i]^{\mathrm{H}_2((i,\boldsymbol{pk}))} = S \cdot X^{e_j}$, which is also the value of T_j that is recorded in the game $\mathrm{Gm}^{\text{xidl}}_{\mathbb{G},g,q_2,q_1}$. For each i-th query of $\mathrm{H}_1((R, apk, m))$, the adversary first finds the index j_{sel} of the H_2-query that corresponds to the input apk, then obtains $c_i \leftarrow\!\!\$\ \textsc{Ch}(j_{\text{sel}}, R)$ before returning c_i as the response for the query. If the eventual forgery is given for these two particular queries to H_1 and H_2, meaning forgery is $\boldsymbol{pk}, m, (R, z)$ for some z, then the verification equation of the signature scheme says that $g^z = R \cdot apk^{\mathrm{H}_1((R,apk,m))}$. But this matches exactly the winning condition of $\mathrm{Gm}^{\text{xidl}}_{\mathbb{G},g,q_2,q_1}$, since $apk = T_{j_{\text{sel}}}$ and $c_i = \mathrm{H}_1((R, apk, m))$. Hence, our adversary $\mathcal{A}_{\text{xidl}}$ can simply return (i, z) to break XIDL, as long as the forgery provided by $\mathcal{A}_{\text{ms}}$ is valid.

Similar to the relation between IDL and BN, XIDL is also tightly equivalent to the MS-UF security of MuSig. In particular, we turn any adversary breaking XIDL into a forger against MuSig. This means that any security justification for MuSig must also justify the hardness of XIDL.

Theorem 8. [MuSig $\rightarrow$ XIDL, Standard Model] *Let $\mathbb{G}$ be a group of prime order p. Let g be a generator of $\mathbb{G}$ and let $\ell \geq 1$ be an integer. Let $\mathsf{MS} = \mathsf{MuSig}[\mathbb{G}, g, \ell]$ be the associated MuSig multi-signature scheme. Let q_1, q_2 be a positive integers and $\mathcal{A}_{\text{xidl}}$ be an adversary against $\mathrm{Gm}^{\text{xidl}}_{\mathbb{G},g,q_2,q_1}$. Then, we can construct an adversary $\mathcal{A}_{\text{ms}}$ for game $\mathbf{G}_{\mathsf{MS}}^{\text{ms-uf}}$, making no queries to NS, and at most $2q_1$ and $2q_2$ queries to H_1 and H_2 respectively, such that*

$$\mathbf{Adv}_{\mathsf{MS}}^{\text{ms-uf}}(\mathcal{A}_{\text{ms}}) \geq \mathbf{Adv}^{\text{xidl}}_{\mathbb{G},g,q_2,q_1}(\mathcal{A}_{\text{xidl}}) \ . \tag{6}$$

The running time of $\mathcal{A}_{\text{ms}}$ is about that of $\mathcal{A}_{\text{idl}}$.

Proof (Theorem 8). Consider the adversary given in Fig. 8. The adversary receives the target publick key pk from the MS-UF game. Adversary $\mathcal{A}_{\text{ms}}$ forwards $X = pk$ as the target point and runs XIDL adversary $\mathcal{A}_{\text{idl}}$. For each

$\mathcal{A}_{\mathrm{ms}}^{\mathrm{H}_1,\mathrm{H}_2}(pk)$:

1 $X \leftarrow pk$; $(I, z) \leftarrow \mathcal{A}_{\mathrm{xidl}}^{\mathrm{NwTar},\mathrm{Ch}}(pk)$; $J \leftarrow \mathrm{TI}[I]$

2 $\sigma \leftarrow (R_I, z)$; Return $((pk, S_J), m_I, \sigma)$

NwTar(S):

3 $j \leftarrow j + 1$; $S_j \leftarrow S$

4 $e_{j,1} \leftarrow\!\!\$\ \mathrm{H}_2((1, (pk, S)))$; $e_{j,2} \leftarrow\!\!\$\ \mathrm{H}_2((2, (pk, S)))$; $e_j \leftarrow e_{j,2}/e_{j,1} \mod p$

5 $apk_j \leftarrow pk^{e_{j,1}} S^{e_{j,2}}$; $T_j \leftarrow pk \cdot S^{e_j}$; Return e_j

Ch(j_{sel}, R):

6 $i \leftarrow i + 1$; $R_i \leftarrow R$; $m_i \leftarrow \langle i \rangle$; $\mathrm{TI}[i] \leftarrow j_{\mathrm{sel}}$

7 $c_i \leftarrow \mathrm{H}_1((apk_{j_{\mathrm{sel}}}, R, m_i)) \cdot e_{j_{\mathrm{sel}},1}$; Return c_i

Fig. 8. Adversary $\mathcal{A}_{\mathrm{ms}}$ for Theorem 7. For an integer i, $\langle i \rangle$ denote the binary representation of i.

query NwTar(S) of $\mathcal{A}_{\mathrm{xidl}}$, adversary $\mathcal{A}_{\mathrm{ms}}$ uses S as a public key to generate the aggregate key apk for the list (pk, S). By construction, the j-th target T_j for the XIDL game is related to apk_j by $apk_j = T_j^{e_{j,1}}$. For each Ch(j_{sel}, R) query of $\mathcal{A}_{\mathrm{xidl}}$, adversary $\mathcal{A}_{\mathrm{ms}}$ programs in the H_1 outputs corresponding to a forgery agaisnt the aggregate key $apk_{j_{\mathrm{sel}}}$ (line 6 and 7). By construction, if $\mathcal{A}_{\mathrm{xidl}}$ succeeds, it must be that

$$g^z = R_I \cdot T_J^{c_I} = R_I \cdot T_J^{\mathrm{H}_1((apk_J, R, m_i)) \cdot e_{J,1}} = R_I \cdot apk_J^{\mathrm{H}_1((apk_J, R, m_i))} .$$

Hence, adversary $\mathcal{A}_{\mathrm{ms}}$ produces a valid forgery at line 2. □

7 HBMS: Our New Two-Round Multi-signature Scheme

Recall that BN and MuSig are three-round schemes, and two-round schemes are desired due to blockchain applications. In this section, we introduce our new, efficient two-round multi-signature scheme supporting key-aggregation, HBMS. We first demonstrate its tight security against algebraic adversaries (Theorem 9), before justifying its security in the standard model (Theorem 10). Referring to Fig. 3, these results establish arrow 5. We refer to Fig. 2 for comparisons of HBMS against other two-round schemes.

Two-round MS scheme HBMS. The formal definition of our scheme is given in Fig. 9. HBMS has the same key generation algorithm Kg and key aggregation Ag algorithm as MuSig. We describe informally the process involved to sign a message m under a vector of public keys $\boldsymbol{pk}$. In the first round, each signer i samples s_i and r_i uniformly from $\mathbb{Z}_p$ and computes a commitment

$$T_i \leftarrow \mathrm{H}_0((\boldsymbol{pk}, m))^{s_i} \cdot g^{r_i} ,$$

MS.Kg:	$\mathsf{MS.Vf}^{\mathrm{H}_0,\mathrm{H}_1,\mathrm{H}_2}(\boldsymbol{pk}, m, \sigma)$:
$sk \leftarrow_{\$} \mathbb{Z}_p$; $pk \leftarrow g^{sk}$	$(pk_1, \ldots, pk_n) \leftarrow \boldsymbol{pk}$; $apk \leftarrow \prod_i^n pk_i^{\mathrm{H}_2((i,\boldsymbol{pk}))}$
Return (pk, sk)	$(T, s, z) \leftarrow \sigma$; $c \leftarrow \mathrm{H}_1((T, apk, m))$
	$h \leftarrow \mathrm{H}_0((\boldsymbol{pk}, m))$; Return $(g^z h^s = T \cdot apk^c)$

$\mathsf{MS.Sign}^{\mathrm{H}_0,\mathrm{H}_1,\mathrm{H}_2}(\boldsymbol{b}, \mathsf{st})$:

$j \leftarrow \mathsf{st.me}$; $n \leftarrow \mathsf{st.n}$; $m \leftarrow \mathsf{st.msg}$; $sk \leftarrow \mathsf{st.sk}$; $\boldsymbol{pk} \leftarrow \mathsf{st.pk}$
$(pk_1, \ldots, pk_n) \leftarrow \boldsymbol{pk}$; $apk \leftarrow \prod_i^n pk_i^{\mathrm{H}_2((i,\boldsymbol{pk}))}$
If $(\mathsf{st.rnd} = 0)$ then
  $\mathsf{st}.r[j] \leftarrow_{\$} \mathbb{Z}_p$; $\mathsf{st}.s[j] \leftarrow_{\$} \mathbb{Z}_p$
  $h \leftarrow \mathrm{H}_0((\boldsymbol{pk}, m))$; $\mathsf{st}.\boldsymbol{R}[j] \leftarrow g^{\mathsf{st}.r[j]}$; $\mathsf{st}.\boldsymbol{T}[j] \leftarrow \mathsf{st}.\boldsymbol{R}[j] \cdot h^{\mathsf{st}.s[j]}$
  $\mathsf{st.rnd} \leftarrow \mathsf{st.rnd} + 1$; Return $(\mathsf{st}.\boldsymbol{T}[j], \mathsf{st})$
If $(\mathsf{st.rnd} = 1)$ then
  For all $i \neq j$ do $\mathsf{st}.\boldsymbol{T}[i] \leftarrow \boldsymbol{b}[i]$
  $\mathsf{st}.T \leftarrow \prod_{i=1}^n \mathsf{st}.\boldsymbol{T}[i]$; $\mathsf{st}.c \leftarrow \mathrm{H}_1((\mathsf{st}.T, apk, m))$; $e_j \leftarrow \mathrm{H}_2((j, \boldsymbol{pk}))$
  $\mathsf{st}.z[j] \leftarrow sk \cdot c \cdot e_j + \mathsf{st}.r[j]$; $\mathsf{st}.\boldsymbol{t}[j] \leftarrow (\mathsf{st}.s[j], \mathsf{st}.z[j])$
  $\mathsf{st.rnd} \leftarrow \mathsf{st.rnd} + 1$; Return $(\mathsf{st}.\boldsymbol{t}[j], \mathsf{st})$
If $(\mathsf{st.rnd} = 2)$ then
  For all $i \neq j$ do $\mathsf{st}.\boldsymbol{t}[i] \leftarrow \boldsymbol{b}[i]$
  $(s, z) \leftarrow \sum_i^n \boldsymbol{t}[i]$; Return $((\mathsf{st}.T, s, z), \mathsf{st})$

Fig. 9. Two-round multi-signature scheme $\mathsf{MS} = \mathsf{HBMS}[\mathbb{G}, g]$ parameterized by a group $\mathbb{G}$ of prime order p with generator g.

which is sent to every other signer. In the second round, each signer receives the list of commitments $T_1, \ldots, T_n$ from each signer, and computes the aggregate value $T \leftarrow \prod_i T_i$. Each signer then computes the challenge value as $c \leftarrow \mathrm{H}_1((T, apk, m))$. To compute the reply, each signer i computes $z_i \leftarrow r_i + sk \cdot c \cdot \mathrm{H}_2((i, \boldsymbol{pk}))$ and sends (s_i, z_i) to every other signer. Finally, any signer can now compute the final signature as (T, s, z) where $s = \sum_i s_i$ and $z = \sum_i z_i$. To verify a signature (T, s, z) on $(\boldsymbol{pk}, m)$, the equation

$$g^z \cdot \mathrm{H}_0((\boldsymbol{pk}, m))^s = T \cdot apk^{\mathrm{H}_1((T, apk, m))} ,$$

must hold, where $apk = \prod_{i=1}^{|\boldsymbol{pk}|} \boldsymbol{pk}[i]^{\mathrm{H}_2((i,\boldsymbol{pk}))}$. Compared to MuSig, the verification equation of HBMS involves an additional power of $\mathrm{H}((\boldsymbol{pk}, m))$ (hence the name HBMS, or "Hash-Base Multi-Signature").

TIGHT SECURITY AGAINST ALGEBRAIC ADVERSARIES. We first show that HBMS is tightly MS-UF-secure against algebraic adversaries.

Theorem 9. [DL $\rightarrow$ HBMS, AGM] *Let $\mathbb{G}$ be a group of prime order p with generator g. Let* MS *be the* $\mathsf{HBMS}[\mathbb{G}, g]$ *scheme. Let $\mathcal{A}_{\mathrm{ms}}^{\mathrm{alg}}$ be an algebraic adversary for game $\mathbf{G}_{\mathsf{MS}}^{\text{ms-uf}}$ of Fig. 5. Assume the execution of game $\mathbf{G}_{\mathsf{MS}}^{\text{ms-uf}}$ with $\mathcal{A}_{\mathrm{ms}}$ has at most q_1, q_2 distinct queries to $\mathrm{H}_1, \mathrm{H}_2$, respectively. Then we can construct an* *adversary* $\mathcal{A}_{\rm dl}$ *for game* $\mathsf{DL}_{\mathbb{G},g}$ *such that*

$$\mathbf{Adv}^{\text{ms-uf}}_{\mathsf{MS}}(\mathcal{A}^{\rm alg}_{\rm ms}) \le \mathbf{Adv}^{\rm dl}_{\mathbb{G},g}(\mathcal{A}_{\rm dl}) + \frac{(q_1+1)q_2}{p} . \tag{7}$$

The running time of $\mathcal{A}_{\rm dl}$ *is about that of the execution of game* $\mathbf{G}^{\text{ms-uf}}_{\mathsf{MS}}$ *with* $\mathcal{A}^{\rm alg}_{\rm ms}$.

Above, a reduction is given directly from DL, and there is no multiplicative loss. As before, assuming $q_s \le q \le t \le p$ and the generic hardness of DL (advantage of t-time adversary to be at most t^2/p), we derive that $\mathbf{UB}^{\text{ms-uf}}_{\mathsf{MS}}(t, q, q_s, p) \le t^2/p$, as shown in Fig. 2.

We give the highlevel proof sketch here and defer the full proof to [4]. Let $\mathcal{A}_{\rm ms}$ be the algebraic adversary against HBMS. Our reduction adversary $\mathcal{A}_{\rm dl}$ sets its own target point X (which it needs to obtain the discrete log of) as the target public key for $\mathcal{A}_{\rm ms}$. In order to run $\mathcal{A}_{\rm ms}$, our adversary $\mathcal{A}_{\rm dl}$ needs to be able to simulate oracles NS, SIGN_1, SIGN_2 (oracles representing the honest signer) as well as random oracles $\text{H}_0, \text{H}_1, \text{H}_2$. We first tackle the problem of simulating the honest signer without knowledge of the corresponding secret key. This is done by programming of random oracle H_0. Suppose for $\boldsymbol{pk}, m$, we set $\text{H}_0((\boldsymbol{pk}, m))$ to be $h = g^{\alpha} pk^{\beta}$ for some $\alpha, \beta \ne 0 \in \mathbb{Z}_p$ (whose exact distribution will be specified later). When the adversary interacts with the honest signer, the honest signer must first provide some commitment $T \in G$ (in the output of NS), then later produce $z, s \in \mathbb{Z}_p$ (in the output of SIGN_1) such that

$$g^z h^s = T \cdot pk^c , \tag{8}$$

where $c \in \mathbb{Z}_p$ is some challenge value (that is derived using the random oracle and the responses of the adversary). To do this, our adversary set commitment $T = g^a h^b$ for $a, b \leftarrow\!\!\$\ \mathbb{Z}_p$. It shall be convenient to express pk in terms of g and h as well. Note that as long as $\beta \ne 0$, $pk = h^{(\beta^{-1})} g^{-\alpha(\beta^{-1})}$. Since both T and pk are known to be of the form $g^{\star} h^{\star}$ (where $\star$ denotes some element of $\mathbb{Z}_p$), so is the group element $T \cdot pk^c$ (for any known value of c). Hence, the right-hand side of (8) is of the form $g^z h^s$ for some values z and s that our adversary can compute, and our adversary can return them as response in the second round. Above, we noted that this works as long as $\beta \ne 0$. To guarantee this, we sample $\alpha \leftarrow\!\!\$\ \mathbb{Z}_p$ and $\beta \leftarrow\!\!\$\ \mathbb{Z}_p^*$ in H_0. It remains to check that such way of simulating the honest signer is indistinguishable from the behavior of an honest signer holding the secrete key and executing the protocol. Roughly, this is because in both cases, the triple (T, z, s) is uniformly distributed over $\mathbb{G} \times \mathbb{Z}_p^2$, subjected to the condition that Eq. (8) holds.

Now, our adversary $\mathcal{A}_{\rm dl}$ can move onto turning a forgery from $\mathcal{A}_{\rm ms}$ into a discrete logarithm for target point X. Suppose adversary $\mathcal{A}_{\rm ms}$ returns forgery $(\boldsymbol{pk}, m, (T, s, z))$. Then,

$$g^z h^s = T \cdot apk^c , \tag{9}$$

where $apk = \prod_{i=1}^{|\boldsymbol{pk}|} \boldsymbol{pk}[i]^{\text{H}_2((i, \boldsymbol{pk}))}$ and $c = \text{H}_1((T, apk, m))$. Since $\mathcal{A}_{\rm ms}$ is algebraic, our adversary $\mathcal{A}_{\rm dl}$ can rewrite Eq. (9) to the form $g^{\alpha_g} = X^{\alpha_X}$, which allows us to compute the discrete log of X as $\alpha_g \alpha_x^{-1} \mod p$, as long as α_X is not zero. The full proof upperbounds the probability that $\alpha_X = 0$ to be at most $q_1 q_2/p$. Outside of this bad event, our adversary $\mathcal{A}_{\mathrm{dl}}$ will successfully compute the value of $\mathsf{DL}_{\mathbb{G},g}(X)$ from a valid forgery.

STANDARD MODEL SECURITY OF HBMS. We reduce the security of HBMS to the hardness of XIDL, with factor q_s loss. For applications, the number of signing queries q_s is much less than adversarial hash function evaluations. As a result, even though our reduction here is non-tight, the reduction loss is smaller compared to previous results for BN, MuSig or other two round schemes (cf. Fig. 1 and 2), at the expense of assuming the hardness of XIDL. Interestingly, due to Theorem 8, our results also state that HBMS is secure as long as MuSig is (via the reduction chain MuSig $\rightarrow$ XIDL $\rightarrow$ HBMS), and this reduction again only losses a factor of q_s in the advantage.

Theorem 10. [XIDL $\rightarrow$ HBMS, Standard Model] *Let $\mathbb{G}$ be a group of prime order p with generator g. Let* MS *be the* HBMS$[\mathbb{G}, g]$ *scheme given in Fig. 9. Let $\mathcal{A}_{\mathrm{ms}}$ be an adversary for game $\mathbf{G}_{\mathsf{MS}}^{\mathrm{ms\text{-}uf}}$ of Fig. 5. Assume the execution of game $\mathbf{G}_{\mathsf{MS}}^{\mathrm{ms\text{-}uf}}$ with $\mathcal{A}_{\mathrm{ms}}$ has at most q_0, q_1, q_2, q_s distinct queries to* $\mathrm{H}_0, \mathrm{H}_1, \mathrm{H}_2, \mathrm{NS}$, *respectively. Then we can construct an adversary $\mathcal{A}_{\mathrm{xidl}}$ for game $\mathrm{Gm}_{\mathbb{G},g,q_2,q_1}^{\mathrm{xidl}}$ such that*

$$\mathbf{Adv}_{\mathsf{MS}}^{\mathrm{ms\text{-}uf}}(\mathcal{A}_{\mathrm{ms}}) \leq e(q_s+1) \cdot \mathbf{Adv}_{\mathbb{G},g,q_2,q_1}^{\mathrm{xidl}}(\mathcal{A}_{\mathrm{xidl}}) + \frac{q_1 q_2}{p}, \tag{10}$$

where e is the base of the natural logarithm. Adversary $\mathcal{A}_{\mathrm{xidl}}$ makes q_2 queries to NWTAR *and q_1 queries to* CH. *The running time of $\mathcal{A}_{\mathrm{xidl}}$ is about that of the execution of game $\mathbf{G}_{\mathsf{MS}}^{\mathrm{ms\text{-}uf}}$ with $\mathcal{A}_{\mathrm{ms}}$.*

Concretely, if we assume that XIDL is quantitatively as hard as DL, then against *any* adversary with running time t, making q evaluations of the random oracle and making at most q_s signing queries, HBMS has security $(q_s t^2 + q^2)/p \approx q_s t^2/p$.

We sketch the highlevel proof here and give the full proof in [4]. Our adversary receives the target point X from the XIDL game and sets it as the target public key for adversary $\mathcal{A}_{\mathrm{ms}}$. As before, in order to run $\mathcal{A}_{\mathrm{ms}}$, we need to simulate oracles NWTAR, SIGN$_1$, SIGN$_2$ as well as $\mathrm{H}_0, \mathrm{H}_1, \mathrm{H}_2$. Recall that in the AGM proof, we can simulate the honest signer for $\boldsymbol{pk}, m$ if we set $\mathrm{H}_0((\boldsymbol{pk}, m)) = g^\alpha h^\beta$. However, this way of programming H_0 does not facilitate in turning a forgery into a break for XIDL. Instead, we would like to program $\mathrm{H}_0((\boldsymbol{pk}, m)) = g^\alpha$ for the forgery $\boldsymbol{pk}, m$. To do this, we use a technique of Coron [13], which programs $\mathrm{H}_0((\boldsymbol{pk}, m))$ randomly in one of these two ways depending on a biased coin flip (with probability ρ of giving 1). The reduction only succeeds if correct "guesses" are made. Specifically, we need that for every $\boldsymbol{pk}, m$ that is queried to the honest signer (in NS) then $\mathrm{H}_0((\boldsymbol{pk}, m))$ must have been programmed to be $g^\alpha pk^\beta$ (for some α and β), and for the forgery $\boldsymbol{pk}, m$, it must be that $\mathrm{H}_0((\boldsymbol{pk}, m)) = g^\alpha$ (for some α). We can then optimize for the value of ρ, resulting in a multiplicative loss of $e(1 + q_s)$.

Suppose adversary $\mathcal{A}_{\mathrm{ms}}$ returns a forgery $(\boldsymbol{pk}, m, (T, s, z))$ where we have previously programmed $\mathrm{H}_0((\boldsymbol{pk}, m)) = g^{\alpha}$. The verification equation say that $g^z h^s = T \cdot apk^c$. Since h is just a power of g, the left-hand side of the verification equation is also a known power of g (specifically $g^{z+\alpha\cdot s}$). This means that our adversary $\mathcal{A}_{\mathrm{xidl}}$ can proceed exactly as the reduction for MuSig. In particular, for the j-th query of $\mathrm{H}_2((k, \boldsymbol{pk}))$ where $\boldsymbol{pk}[k] = X$, the adversary first computes $S \leftarrow \prod_{i \neq k} \boldsymbol{pk}[i]^{\mathrm{H}_2((i,\boldsymbol{pk}))}$, then obtains $e_j \leftarrow\!\!\$\ \mathrm{NwTar}(S)$ before returning e_j as the response for the query. We remark that this particular query of H_2 have created an aggregate public key $apk = \prod_{i=1}^{|\boldsymbol{pk}|} \boldsymbol{pk}[i]^{\mathrm{H}_2((i,\boldsymbol{pk}))} = S \cdot X^{e_j}$, which is also the value of T_j that is recorded in the game $\mathrm{Gm}^{\mathrm{xidl}}_{\mathbb{G},g,q_2,q_1}$. For each i-th query of $\mathrm{H}_1((T, apk, m))$, the adversary first finds the index j_{sel} of the H_2-query that corresponds to the input apk, then obtains $c_i \leftarrow\!\!\$\ \mathrm{Ch}(j_{\mathrm{sel}}, T)$ before returning c_i as the response for the query. If the eventual forgery is given for these two particular queries to H_1 and H_2, meaning forgery is $\boldsymbol{pk}, m, (T, s, z)$, then the verification equation of the signature scheme says that $g^{z+\alpha\cdot s} = T \cdot apk^{\mathrm{H}_1((T,apk,m))}$ (if we programmed $\mathrm{H}_0((\boldsymbol{pk}, m))$ to be g^{α}). Hence, our adversary $\mathcal{A}_{\mathrm{xidl}}$ can simply return $(i, z+\alpha\cdot s)$ to break XIDL, as long as the forgery provided by $\mathcal{A}_{\mathrm{ms}}$ is valid and we have made the right guesses in programming H_0.

Acknowledgments. We thank the ASIACRYPT 2021 reviewers for their careful reading and valuable comments.

Bellare was supported in part by NSF grant CNS-1717640 and a gift from Microsoft. Dai was supported in part by a Powell Fellowship and grants of the first author.

References

1. Kılınç Alper, H., Burdges, J.: Two-round trip Schnorr multi-signatures via Delinearized witnesses. In: Malkin, T., Peikert, C. (eds.) CRYPTO 2021. LNCS, vol. 12825, pp. 157–188. Springer, Cham (2021). https://doi.org/10.1007/978-3-030-84242-0_7
2. Bagherzandi, A., Cheon, J.H., Jarecki, S.: Multisignatures secure under the discrete logarithm assumption and a generalized forking lemma. In: Ning, P., Syverson, P.F., Jha, S. (eds.) ACM CCS 2008, pp. 449–458. ACM Press, Oct. (2008)
3. Bellare, M., Dai, W.: The multi-base discrete logarithm problem: tight reductions and non-rewinding proofs for Schnorr identification and signatures. In: Bhargavan, K., Oswald, E., Prabhakaran, M. (eds.) INDOCRYPT 2020. LNCS, vol. 12578, pp. 529–552. Springer, Cham (2020). https://doi.org/10.1007/978-3-030-65277-7_24
4. Bellare, M., Dai, W.: Chain reductions for multi-signatures and the HBMS scheme. Cryptology ePrint Archive, Report 2021/404 (2021)
5. Bellare, M., Namprempre, C., Neven, G.: Unrestricted aggregate signatures. In: Arge, L., Cachin, C., Jurdziński, T., Tarlecki, A. (eds.) ICALP 2007. LNCS, vol. 4596, pp. 411–422. Springer, Heidelberg (2007). https://doi.org/10.1007/978-3-540-73420-8_37
6. Bellare, M., Namprempre, C., Pointcheval, D., Semanko, M.: The one-more-RSA-inversion problems and the security of Chaum's blind signature scheme. J. Cryptol. **16**(3), 185–215 (2003)
7. Bellare, M., Neven, G.: Multi-signatures in the plain public-key model and a general forking lemma. In: Juels, A., Wright, R.N., De Capitani, S., di Vimercati (eds.) ACM CCS 2006, pp. 390–399. ACM Press, October 2006

8. Bellare, M., Palacio, A.: GQ and Schnorr identification schemes: proofs of security against impersonation under active and concurrent attacks. In: Yung, M. (ed.) CRYPTO 2002. LNCS, vol. 2442, pp. 162–177. Springer, Heidelberg (2002). https://doi.org/10.1007/3-540-45708-9_11
9. Bellare, M., Rogaway, P.: The security of triple encryption and a framework for code-based game-playing proofs. In: Vaudenay, S. (ed.) EUROCRYPT 2006. LNCS, vol. 4004, pp. 409–426. Springer, Heidelberg (2006). https://doi.org/10.1007/11761679_25
10. Boldyreva, A.: Threshold signatures, multisignatures and blind signatures based on the Gap-Diffie-Hellman-Group signature scheme. In: Desmedt, Y.G. (ed.) PKC 2003. LNCS, vol. 2567, pp. 31–46. Springer, Heidelberg (2003). https://doi.org/10.1007/3-540-36288-6_3
11. Boneh, D., Drijvers, M., Neven, G.: Compact multi-signatures for smaller blockchains. In: Peyrin, T., Galbraith, S. (eds.) ASIACRYPT 2018. LNCS, vol. 11273, pp. 435–464. Springer, Cham (2018). https://doi.org/10.1007/978-3-030-03329-3_15
12. Boneh, D., Gentry, C., Lynn, B., Shacham, H.: Aggregate and verifiably encrypted signatures from bilinear maps. In: Biham, E. (ed.) EUROCRYPT 2003. LNCS, vol. 2656, pp. 416–432. Springer, Heidelberg (2003). https://doi.org/10.1007/3-540-39200-9_26
13. Coron, J.-S.: On the exact security of full domain hash. In: Bellare, M. (ed.) CRYPTO 2000. LNCS, vol. 1880, pp. 229–235. Springer, Heidelberg (2000). https://doi.org/10.1007/3-540-44598-6_14
14. Damgård, I., Orlandi, C., Takahashi, A., Tibouchi, M.: Two-round n-out-of-n and multi-signatures and trapdoor commitment from lattices. Cryptology ePrint Archive, Report 2020/1110 (2020). https://eprint.iacr.org/2020/1110
15. Drijvers, M., et al.: On the security of two-round multi-signatures. In: 2019 IEEE Symposium on Security and Privacy, pp. 1084–1101. IEEE Computer Society Press, May 2019
16. El Bansarkhani, R., Sturm, J.: An efficient lattice-based multisignature scheme with applications to bitcoins. In: Foresti, S., Persiano, G. (eds.) CANS 2016. LNCS, vol. 10052, pp. 140–155. Springer, Cham (2016). https://doi.org/10.1007/978-3-319-48965-0_9
17. Fuchsbauer, G., Kiltz, E., Loss, J.: The algebraic group model and its applications. In: Shacham, H., Boldyreva, A. (eds.) CRYPTO 2018. LNCS, vol. 10992, pp. 33–62. Springer, Cham (2018). https://doi.org/10.1007/978-3-319-96881-0_2
18. Fuchsbauer, G., Plouviez, A., Seurin, Y.: Blind Schnorr signatures and signed ElGamal encryption in the algebraic group model. In: Canteaut, A., Ishai, Y. (eds.) EUROCRYPT 2020. LNCS, vol. 12106, pp. 63–95. Springer, Cham (2020). https://doi.org/10.1007/978-3-030-45724-2_3
19. Harn, L.: Group-oriented (t, n) threshold digital signature scheme and digital multisignature. In: IEE Proceedings-Computers and Digital Techniques, vol. 141, no. 5, pp. 307–313 (1994)
20. Itakura, K., Nakamura, K.: A public-key cryptosystem suitable for digital multisignatures. NEC Res. Dev. **71**, 1–8 (1983)
21. Kiltz, E., Masny, D., Pan, J.: Optimal security proofs for signatures from identification schemes. In: Robshaw, M., Katz, J. (eds.) CRYPTO 2016. LNCS, vol. 9815, pp. 33–61. Springer, Heidelberg (2016). https://doi.org/10.1007/978-3-662-53008-5_2

22. Li, C.-M., Hwang, T., Lee, N.-Y.: Threshold-multisignature schemes where suspected forgery implies traceability of adversarial shareholders. In: De Santis, A. (ed.) EUROCRYPT 1994. LNCS, vol. 950, pp. 194–204. Springer, Heidelberg (1995). https://doi.org/10.1007/BFb0053435
23. Lu, S., Ostrovsky, R., Sahai, A., Shacham, H., Waters, B.: Sequential aggregate signatures and multisignatures without random oracles. In: Vaudenay, S. (ed.) EUROCRYPT 2006. LNCS, vol. 4004, pp. 465–485. Springer, Heidelberg (2006). https://doi.org/10.1007/11761679_28
24. Ma, C., Weng, J., Li, Y., Deng, R.: Efficient discrete logarithm based multi-signature scheme in the plain public key model. Des. Codes Crypt. **54**(2), 121–133 (2010)
25. Maxwell, G., Poelstra, A., Seurin, Y., Wuille, P.: Simple Schnorr multi-signatures with applications to bitcoin. Des. Codes Crypt. **87**(9), 2139–2164 (2019)
26. Micali, S., Ohta, K., Reyzin, L.: Accountable-subgroup multisignatures: extended abstract. In: Reiter, M.K., Samarati, P. (eds.) ACM CCS 2001, pp. 245–254. ACM Press, November 2001
27. Nick, J., Ruffing, T., Seurin, Y.: MuSig2: simple two-round Schnorr multi-signatures. In: Malkin, T., Peikert, C. (eds.) CRYPTO 2021. LNCS, vol. 12825, pp. 189–221. Springer, Cham (2021). https://doi.org/10.1007/978-3-030-84242-0_8
28. Nick, J., Ruffing, T., Seurin, Y., Wuille, P.: MuSig-DN: Schnorr multi-signatures with verifiably deterministic nonces. In: Ligatti, J., Ou, X., Katz, J., Vigna, G. (eds.) ACM CCS 2020, pp. 1717–1731. ACM Press, November 2020
29. Ohta, K., Okamoto, T.: A digital multisignature scheme based on the Fiat-Shamir scheme. In: Imai, H., Rivest, R.L., Matsumoto, T. (eds.) ASIACRYPT 1991. LNCS, vol. 739, pp. 139–148. Springer, Heidelberg (1993). https://doi.org/10.1007/3-540-57332-1_11
30. Paillier, P., Vergnaud, D.: Discrete-log-based signatures may not be equivalent to discrete log. In: Roy, B. (ed.) ASIACRYPT 2005. LNCS, vol. 3788, pp. 1–20. Springer, Heidelberg (2005). https://doi.org/10.1007/11593447_1
31. Pointcheval, D., Stern, J.: Security arguments for digital signatures and blind signatures. J. Cryptol. **13**(3), 361–396 (2000)
32. Rotem, L., Segev, G.: Tighter security for Schnorr identification and signatures: a high-moment forking lemma for Σ-protocols. In: Malkin, T., Peikert, C. (eds.) CRYPTO 2021. LNCS, vol. 12825, pp. 222–250. Springer, Cham (2021). https://doi.org/10.1007/978-3-030-84242-0_9
33. Schnorr, C.P.: Efficient signature generation by smart cards. J. Cryptol. **4**(3), 161–174 (1991). https://doi.org/10.1007/BF00196725
34. Shoup, V.: Lower bounds for discrete logarithms and related problems. In: Fumy, W. (ed.) EUROCRYPT 1997. LNCS, vol. 1233, pp. 256–266. Springer, Heidelberg (1997). https://doi.org/10.1007/3-540-69053-0_18
35. Syta, E., et al.: Keeping authorities “honest or bust” with decentralized witness cosigning. In: 2016 IEEE Symposium on Security and Privacy, pp. 526–545. IEEE Computer Society Press, May 2016

Authenticated Key Exchange

Symmetric Key Exchange with Full Forward Security and Robust Synchronization

Colin Boyd[1(✉)], Gareth T. Davies[2(✉)], Bor de Kock[1(✉)], Kai Gellert[2(✉)], Tibor Jager[2(✉)], and Lise Millerjord[1(✉)]

[1] NTNU – Norwegian University of Science and Technology, Trondheim, Norway
{colin.boyd,bor.dekock,lise.millerjord}@ntnu.no

[2] Bergische Universität Wuppertal, Wuppertal, Germany
{davies,kai.gellert,tibor.jager}@uni-wuppertal.de

Abstract. We construct lightweight authenticated key exchange protocols based on pre-shared keys, which achieve *full* forward security and rely only on simple and efficient symmetric-key primitives. All of our protocols have rigorous security proofs in a strong security model, all have low communication complexity, and are particularly suitable for resource-constrained devices.

We describe three protocols that apply *linear* key evolution to provide different performance and security properties. *Correctness* in parallel and concurrent protocol sessions is difficult to achieve for linearly key-evolving protocols, emphasizing the need for assurance of availability alongside the usual confidentiality and authentication security goals. We introduce *synchronization robustness* as a new formal security goal, which essentially guarantees that parties can re-synchronize efficiently. All of our new protocols achieve this property.

Since protocols based on linear key evolution cannot guarantee that all concurrently initiated sessions successfully derive a key, we also propose two constructions with *non-linear* key evolution based on puncturable PRFs. These are instantiable from standard hash functions and require $O(C \cdot \log(|\mathsf{CTR}|))$ memory, where C is the number of concurrent sessions and $|\mathsf{CTR}|$ is an upper bound on the total number of sessions per party. These are the first protocols to simultaneously achieve full forward security, synchronization robustness, and concurrent correctness.

1 Introduction

Authenticated key exchange protocols based on pre-shared long-term symmetric keys (PSK-AKE) enable two parties to use a previously established symmetric

This work was supported by Deutscher Akademischer Austauschdienst (DAAD) and Norges forskningsråd (NFR) under the PPP-Norwegen programme. Colin Boyd and Lise Millerjord have been supported by NFR project number 288545. Tibor Jager and Gareth T. Davies have been supported by the European Research Council (ERC) under the European Union's Horizon 2020 research and innovation programme, grant agreement 802823.

M. Tibouchi and H. Wang (Eds.): ASIACRYPT 2021, LNCS 13093, pp. 681–710, 2021.
https://doi.org/10.1007/978-3-030-92068-5_23

key, agreed upon via out-of-band communication, to (mutually) authenticate and derive a shared session key. Prominent examples of such protocols are the PSK modes of TLS 1.3 and prior TLS versions, but these examples still make use of public-key techniques for key derivation, even if authentication uses symmetric keys. PSK-AKE protocols can be significantly more efficient than classical public-key AKE protocols, particularly when they can be constructed exclusively based on symmetric key primitives ("symmetric AKE") for both authentication and key derivation. Therefore such protocols are especially desirable for performance-constrained devices, such as battery-powered wireless IoT devices, where every computation and every transmitted bit has a negative impact on battery life. More generally, such protocols may be preferable in "closed-world" applications, such as industrial settings, where pre-sharing keys may be easier and more practical than deploying a public-key infrastructure. Furthermore, protocols based purely on symmetric-key techniques, such as hash functions and symmetric encryption, also achieve security against quantum attacks by adjusting security parameters appropriately.

Forward Security in Symmetric AKE Protocols. *Forward security* is today a standard security goal of key exchange protocols. It requires that past session keys remain secure, even if the secret long-term key material is compromised. Note that this is only achievable if past session keys are *not* efficiently computable from a current long-term key. Forward security is comparatively easily achievable if *public key* cryptography is used. For instance, a classical approach is to use *ephemeral* keys for key establishment, such as the Diffie-Hellman protocol or, more generally, a key encapsulation mechanism (KEM). *Independent* long-term keys can then be used for authentication via digital signatures or another KEM.

The only currently known way to avoid public key techniques and use only symmetric key primitives is based on the *"derive-then-evolve"* approach, where first a session key is derived from a long-term key, and then the long-term key is evolved. This key evolution prevents efficient re-computation of prior session keys which yields forward security. Both steps can be implemented with simple key derivation functions. There are two common ways to use this approach:

1. *Synchronized key evolution.* In this case, both parties evolve their long-term keys in "epochs", e.g., once per day. Note that this approach cannot achieve *"full"* forward security, but only a weaker *"delayed"* form. This is because all session keys of the current epoch can be computed from the current long-term secret, so forward security only holds for session keys of past epochs. Moreover, this approach requires synchronized clocks between parties, even to achieve correctness. For many applications this seems impractical, in particular for cheap low-performance devices, for which symmetric AKE protocols are particularly relevant.
2. *Triggered key evolution.* In this case the protocol ensures that both parties advance their key material during protocol execution. This approach directly achieves "full" forward security for every session, and therefore seems preferable. However, this apparently simple approach turns out to be much less

trivial to realize than might be expected, because both parties must remain "in sync", such that correctness is guaranteed even in presence of *concurrent* sessions or message loss due to network failures or *active attacks*. This approach has similarities with *ratcheting* [1], but there are significant differences in our setting as discussed under *Related Work* below.

Concurrency and Key-Evolving Protocols. The possibility of running concurrent protocol sessions in parallel is a standard correctness requirement for protocols, and reflected in all common AKE security models, such as the BR and CK models [8,15] and their countless variants and refinements. The main technical challenge of key evolution is to achieve full forward security while maintaining *correctness* in the presence of parallel and concurrent protocol sessions.

Even if we assume that all parties are *honest* and that all messages are transmitted *reliably* (i.e., without being dropped because of an unreliable network or influence from an adversary) this is already highly non-trivial and we do not know of any currently existing forward-secure symmetric AKE protocol which achieves *correctness* and full forward security in such a setting. The difficulty is essentially that one session might advance a key "too early" for another concurrent session to be completed, which breaks correctness. No such difficulty appears in classical forward-secure public key protocols, since long-term keys are usually *static* and different sessions use independent randomness. So it turns out that, somewhat surprisingly, forward security and correctness is more difficult to achieve for symmetric AKE.

To complicate matters even further, note that the assumption of honest parties and reliable message transmission is very strong and may not be realistic for many applications. Therefore we actually want to achieve forward security and "synchronization robustness" in the presence of an adversary which intentionally aims to *break* synchronization, e.g., by adaptively dropping or re-ordering messages. Such an adversary is attacking *availability* properties of the AKE protocol, an important aspect of security usually omitted from key exchange security models. The development of techniques to ensure availability for stateful key exchange is an unsolved foundational problem.

Our Contributions. In this work we develop several new lightweight forward-secure symmetric AKE protocols with different efficiency and correctness properties. Table 1 summarizes the main security and efficiency properties of our new protocols. This includes the first protocols that provably achieve synchronization robustness, a formal availability security notion we introduce, and correctness in the presence of concurrent sessions. More concretely we achieve the following.

Security model. We describe a security model suited to forward-secure symmetric AKE capturing entity authentication (one-sided and mutual), indistinguishability of established keys, and forward security. Our model follows a standard approach for AKE protocols based on the Bellare-Rogaway model [8], adapted to the requirements of symmetric AKE with evolving keys.

Table 1. Overview of our protocols and comparison to SAKE [4]. The number in the protocol name indicates the total number of messages per protocol run, "R only" means that only the responder authenticates its communication partner. The third column considers the communication complexity, where **C** is the number of counter values that are sent, **M** the number of MACs, and **N** the number of nonces. **Sync. Rob.** indicates the achieved level of synchronization robustness, **Bd. Gap** whether the gap between two parties is bounded (for non-concurrent executions), **CC** whether concurrent correctness is achieved, and **FS** whether full forward security is achieved.

Protocol	Auth.	(C, M, N)	Sync. Rob.	Bd. Gap	CC	FS
SAKE (5) [4]	mutual	(0, 4, 2) + ID	✗	✓	✗	✓
SAKE-AM (4) [4]	mutual	(0, 4, 2) + ID	✗	✓	✗	✓
LP3	mutual	(3, 3, 2)	weak	✓	✗	✓
LP2	mutual	(2, 2, 0)	weak	✗	✗	✓
LP1	R only	(1, 1, 0)	weak	✗	✗	✓
PP2	mutual	(1, 2, 0)	full	✓	✓	✓
PP1	R only	(1, 1, 0)	full	✓	✓	✓

Synchronization robustness. We formalize a new property called *synchronization robustness* (SR), which is trivially achieved for traditional AKE protocols with fixed long-term keys, but turns out to be a crucial feature for key-evolving protocols such as forward-secure symmetric AKE. Essentially, SR captures whether parties in a protocol can efficiently re-synchronize their states in order to complete a successful protocol run. This should even hold if an adversary controls the network and/or some of the parties.

We define two flavours. Both consider an active adversary that may execute arbitrary protocol sessions to manipulate the state of parties, and whose goal is to manipulate the state such that a subsequent protocol execution fails. In *weak* SR the 'target' protocol session must then be executed without adversarial interaction (similar to the corresponding requirement in Krawczyk's weak forward security [26]). "Full" SR allows the adversary arbitrary queries between messages of the 'target' session, even to parties of the oracles involved in the 'target' session.

Linear key evolving protocols. We define the notion of *linear key evolution*, which makes the classical "derive-then-evolve" approach concrete. We argue that protocols based on linear key evolution can only achieve weak SR and cannot achieve concurrent correctness.

We construct three different protocols (LP1, LP2, LP3, cf. Table 1), all of which achieve weak SR. Most interestingly, LP3 even achieves a "bounded gap" property, which means that no active adversary in control of the network is able to force the state of two parties to differ by more than one key evolving step, so that a party is always able to catch up quickly, if necessary. For all three protocols we show that in a setting where concurrent runs between two parties are allowed, this number of steps required to catch up is bounded in the number of concurrent runs. To this end, we apply a new approach to precisely analyze the state machine of a protocol. Furthermore, we also show two extremely lightweight protocols LP1 and LP2, which provide one-sided and mutual authentication, respectively, and where the communication complexity is only one (resp. two) MAC and one (resp. two) counter value.

Full SR and concurrent correctness. This leads to the question of whether and how full synchronization robustness and concurrent correctness (CC) can be achieved. We propose the use of puncturable pseudorandom functions (PPRFs) to apply a "non-linear" key evolving strategy, and we construct two protocols PP1 and PP2, which both achieve full SR and CC.
Since PPRFs can be efficiently instantiated from cryptographic hash functions, both protocols are extremely lightweight. PP1 achieves one-sided authentication with a single counter value and a single MAC, PP2 mutual authentication with one counter and two MACs. Furthermore, while repeated puncturing PPRFs may lead to large secret keys [3], we take advantage of the stateful nature of symmetric AKE protocols to instantiate the PPRF such that secret key size is at most *logarithmic* in the number of sessions.

Hence, we offer a versatile catalogue of lightweight and forward-secure symmetric AKE protocols with significantly stronger correctness and security properties. This includes the first protocols to achieve concurrent correctness and full synchronization robustness, or weak SR with bounded gap. Which of these protocols is best for a particular application depends on the nature of the security and functionality requirements. Further, in LP3 the parties exchange nonces: we recognize that in some applications sufficient randomness will not be available and so we prove the protocol secure for any nonce generation procedure, which could be random selection or (stateful) use of a counter.

Related Work. Bellare and Yee [9] analyzed forward security for symmetric-key primitives, specifically pseudo-random generation, message authentication codes and symmetric encryption. They provide constructions using key evolution which are similar to the linear key evolution that we employ, and their protocols use some techniques from key-evolving schemes such as prior work on forward-secure signatures [6]. Their work does not deal with key exchange.

Brier and Peyrin [14] gave a tree-based protocol for key establishment, with the stated aim of improving the DUKPT scheme defined in ANSI X9.24 [2]. The idea in DUKPT is that the client device (payment terminal) is highly constrained in terms of memory, yet needs to derive a unique key per transaction from an original pre-shared key, by applying a PRF (based on Triple-DES) to a counter and the base derivation key. Their work involves formalizing the specific problem faced in the payment terminal setting, and their scheme assumes an incorruptible server: a far weaker security model than the one that we consider. A similar security assumption was used by Le et al. [27], who presented a protocol for use in the context of Radio Frequency Identification (RFID), where the server keeps two values of the key derivation key to deal with potential synchronization loss.

Li et al. [28] analyzed the pre-shared key ciphersuites of TLS 1.2, using an adaption of the ACCE model of Jager et al. [23]. In this setting, Li et al. presented a formalization of the prior AKE-style models, but where parties could share PSK material with other parties in addition to their long-term key pairs.

Dousti and Jalili [18] presented a key exchange protocol called FORSAKES, which is based on synchronized time-based key evolution. Their protocol requires 3 messages and assumes perfect synchronicity of parties to achieve correctness, and as we have already mentioned their approach can only obtain *delayed forward security*. A discussion of delayed forward security and more generally the various challenges involved in defining forward security was given Boyd and Gellert [12].

The concept of evolving symmetric keys is reminiscent of Signal's double ratchet [1], a well-known example of a symmetric protocol with evolving keys. Signal employs a Diffie-Hellman-ratchet, which adds new key material at every step through multiple Diffie-Hellman exchanges along the way. At every step of this main ratchet a separate linear key evolving ratchet is 'branched off', which is similar to how linear evolution works in our protocols—however, a critical difference is that in our scenario we evolve the key shared across different sessions as opposed to evolving a key within one session as happens in the Signal protocol. It is this difference which leads to the complexity of managing synchronization between sessions which run concurrently. In addition to this difference, which anyway makes Signal unusable for our setting, use of Diffie-Hellman in the Signal ratchet means that there is a vector for quantum attacks, while our protocol is purely based on symmetric primitives.

Another primitive conceptually similar to PPRFs is *puncturable encryption*, which was introduced by Green and Miers in 2015 [20], and has since led to several follow-up constructions of puncturable encryption [16,17,21,30]. However, all those constructions rely on expensive public-key techniques (such as bilinear pairings) and are thus impractical in the context of this work.

Comparison with Avoine et al. [4]. In Table 1 above we have mentioned two protocols named SAKE and SAKE-AM that were presented by Avoine et al. [4] (henceforth ACF20). Their paper was the first to provide key exchange protocols that attain forward security via linear evolution. Their system assumptions are largely the same as ours, with the crucial difference that our models are equipped to capture parallel executions. The security model of ACF20 explicitly disallows concurrent sessions, which not only yields a weak security notion, but also sidesteps the major difficulty of achieving even correctness in the presence of concurrent sessions in key-evolving symmetric-key protocols. Indeed, the protocols from ACF20 completely break down when executed concurrently, allowing an adversary to prevent the parties from computing any session keys in future sessions. We consider this an unrealistic and impractical restriction for many applications. Therefore we introduce the new notion of synchronization robustness, which formally defines the ability of key-evolving protocols to deal with concurrent executions, including in adversarial environments.

We embrace the use of (explicit) counters to acquire linear key evolving protocols that are conceptually simpler and require fewer messages than those provided by ACF20, in a way that additionally provides (weak) synchronization robustness. In any protocol that uses PSK evolution to achieve forward security a party must update the key state after a successful protocol run, and in embedded devices this requires writing to persistent storage. Our protocols require the updating (writing) of one key and one counter per session, while SAKE and SAKE-AM require updating two keys. Since a sequentially evolving key can also be seen as an implicit counter, conceptually the distinction between counters and evolving keys seems to be minor. The storage overhead of our protocols compared to ACF20's protocols is the (usually 8-byte) counter, while the linear key evolving protocols in our paper and ACF20 require storage of two keys (usually 16 or 32 bytes).

We note that ACF20 remarked that the parties could use separate PSKs for concurrent executions, however this solution requires an a priori bound on the number of possible concurrent sessions that could occur and a corresponding multiplication in key storage: none of our protocols require this. Further, implementing their approach would require a modification of their protocols, since parties need to know which PSK to use, and the security of these modified protocols is not proven.

Preliminaries. We denote the security parameter as λ. For any $n \in \mathbb{N}$ let 1^n be the unary representation of n and let $[n] = \{1, \ldots, n\}$ be the set of numbers between 1 and n. We write $x \xleftarrow{\$} \mathcal{S}$ to indicate that we choose element x uniformly at random from set $\mathcal{S}$. For a probabilistic polynomial-time algorithm $\mathcal{A}$ we define $y \xleftarrow{\$} \mathcal{A}(a_1, \ldots, a_n)$ as the execution of $\mathcal{A}$ (with fresh random coins) on input $a_1, \ldots, a_n$ and assigning the output to y. The function $\texttt{NextOdd}(x)$ takes as input an integer and outputs the next odd integer greater than x, i.e. whichever element of $\{x+1, x+2\}$ is odd. Our protocols require the use of counters, and integer $|\mathsf{CTR}|$ is the largest possible counter value. Furthermore, we write $[n] \times [n] \setminus (i^*, j^*)$ as a shorthand for $\{(i,j) \in [n]^2\} \setminus \{(i^*, j^*) \text{ with } i < j\}$.

1.1 Message Authentication Codes

Throughout this paper we assume that all MACs are deterministic. This is to reduce complexity in our proofs, however most MACs used in practice are deterministic [22,25].

Definition 1 (Message Authentication Codes). *A* message authentication code *consists of three probabilistic polynomial-time algorithms* $\mathsf{MAC} = (\mathsf{KGen}, \mathsf{Mac}, \mathsf{Vrfy})$ *with key space* $\mathcal{K}_{\mathsf{MAC}}$ *and the following properties:*

- $\mathsf{KGen}(1^\lambda)$ *takes as input a security parameter* λ *and outputs a symmetric key* $\mathsf{K}^{\mathsf{MAC}} \in \mathcal{K}_{\mathsf{MAC}}$*;*

$\mathsf{G}_{\mathsf{MAC}}^{\mathsf{SEUF\text{-}CMA\text{-}}Q}(\mathcal{A})$	$\mathcal{O}_{\mathsf{Mac}}(m)$	$\mathcal{O}_{\mathsf{Vrfy}}(m,\sigma)$
$\mathsf{K}^{\mathsf{MAC}} \xleftarrow{\$} \mathsf{KGen}(1^\lambda)$	$\sigma \leftarrow \mathsf{Mac}(\mathsf{K}^{\mathsf{MAC}}, m)$	$b \leftarrow \mathsf{Vrfy}(m,\sigma)$
$\mathcal{Q}, \mathcal{V} \leftarrow \emptyset$	$\mathcal{Q} := \mathcal{Q} \cup \{(m,\sigma)\}$	**if** $b = 1$
$\mathcal{A}^{\mathcal{O}_{\mathsf{Mac}}(\cdot),\mathcal{O}_{\mathsf{Vrfy}}(\cdot,\cdot)}(1^\lambda)$	**return** σ	$\quad \mathcal{V} := \mathcal{V} \cup \{(m,\sigma)\}$
if $\exists (m,\sigma) \in \mathcal{V} \setminus \mathcal{Q}$		**return** b
$\quad$ **return** 1		
return 0		

Fig. 1. The SEUF-CMA-Q security experiment for message authentication code MAC. $\mathcal{A}$ can make Q queries to $\mathcal{O}_{\mathsf{Vrfy}}$.

- $\mathsf{Mac}(\mathsf{K}^{\mathsf{MAC}}, m)$ *takes as input a key* $\mathsf{K}^{\mathsf{MAC}} \in \mathcal{K}_{\mathsf{MAC}}$ *and a message* m. *Output is a tag* σ;
- $\mathsf{Vrfy}(\mathsf{K}^{\mathsf{MAC}}, m, \sigma)$ *takes as input a key* $\mathsf{K}^{\mathsf{MAC}} \in \mathcal{K}_{\mathsf{MAC}}$, *a message* m, *and a tag* σ. *Output is a bit* $b \in \{0,1\}$.

We call a message authentication code correct *if for all* m, *we have*

$$\Pr_{\mathsf{K}^{\mathsf{MAC}} \xleftarrow{\$} \mathsf{KGen}(1^\lambda)} \left[\mathsf{Vrfy}(\mathsf{K}^{\mathsf{MAC}}, m, \mathsf{Mac}(\mathsf{K}^{\mathsf{MAC}}, m)) = 1\right] = 1.$$

We define MAC security as strong existential unforgeability under chosen message attack, where the adversary has access to a verification oracle. In the more common version of this game, which we denote SEUF-CMA-1, the adversary must stop running after it submits its first verification query: this is a subcase of our more general definition. Bellare et al. [5] showed that in the strong unforgeability case these definitions are equivalent up to a loss factor Q.

Definition 2 (MAC Security). *The advantage of an adversary* $\mathcal{A}$ *in the* SEUF-CMA-Q *security experiment defined in Fig. 1 for message authentication code* MAC *is*

$$\mathsf{Adv}_{\mathsf{MAC}}^{\mathsf{SEUF\text{-}CMA\text{-}}Q}(\mathcal{A}) := \Pr\left[\mathsf{G}_{\mathsf{MAC}}^{\mathsf{SEUF\text{-}CMA\text{-}}Q}(\mathcal{A}) = 1\right].$$

1.2 Pseudorandom Functions

Definition 3 (Pseudorandom Functions). *A* pseudrandom function *is a deterministic function* $y = \mathsf{PRF}(k, x)$ *that takes as input some key* $k \in \mathcal{K}_{\mathsf{PRF}}$ *and some element of a domain* $\mathcal{D}_{\mathsf{PRF}}$, *and returns an element* $y \in \mathcal{R}_{\mathsf{PRF}}$.

Definition 4 (PRF Security). *The advantage of an adversary* $\mathcal{A}$ *in the* PRF-sec *security experiment defined in Fig. 2 for pseudorandom function* PRF *is*

$$\mathsf{Adv}_{\mathsf{PRF}}^{\mathsf{PRF\text{-}sec}}(\mathcal{A}) := \left|\Pr\left[\mathsf{G}_{\mathsf{PRF}}^{\mathsf{PRF\text{-}sec}}(\mathcal{A}) = 1\right] - \frac{1}{2}\right|.$$

$\mathsf{G}_{\mathsf{PRF}}^{\mathsf{PRF\text{-}sec}}(\mathcal{A})$	$\mathcal{O}_f(x)$
$b \xleftarrow{\$} \{0,1\}$	**if** $b = 1$
$k_{\mathsf{PRF}} \xleftarrow{\$} \mathcal{K}_{\mathsf{PRF}}$	$\quad y \leftarrow f(k_{\mathsf{PRF}}, x)$
$g \xleftarrow{\$} \{\mathcal{F} : \mathcal{D}_{\mathsf{PRF}} \to \mathcal{R}_{\mathsf{PRF}}\}$	**else**
$b^* \xleftarrow{\$} \mathcal{A}^{\mathcal{O}_f(\cdot)}(1^\lambda)$	$\quad y \leftarrow g(x)$
if $b^* = b$	**return** y
$\quad$ **return** 1	
return 0	

Fig. 2. The PRF-sec security experiment for pseudorandom function PRF. $\{\mathcal{F} : \mathcal{D}_{\mathsf{PRF}} \to \mathcal{R}_{\mathsf{PRF}}\}$ is the set of all functions from $\mathcal{D}_{\mathsf{PRF}}$ to $\mathcal{R}_{\mathsf{PRF}}$.

2 Authenticated Key Exchange in the Symmetric Setting

In this section we describe our model for authenticated key exchange with forward security in the symmetric setting. Our model follows the standard approach of AKE protocols based on the Bellare-Rogaway model [8], adapted to the requirements of symmetric AKE with evolving keys. This includes definitions for entity authentication (one-sided or mutual), key indistinguishability, and forward security. Furthermore, we define the property of synchronization robustness, which is a crucial feature for forward-secure symmetric key exchange protocols. Parts of our formalization take inspiration from the models of Jager et al. [23].

Differences to public-key AKE models. The most notable difference in the symmetric key setting is that each pair of parties is initialized with shared key material, which is specified before the actual protocol is run. This key material typically includes MAC keys or key derivation keys that have been established in an out-of-band communication (e.g., chosen during the manufacturing process of devices). In order to achieve forward-security via "key evolving techniques" in the symmetric key setting, we additionally have to provide (sessions of) parties with the ability to modify the party's key material. As a consequence, the shared key material of two parties will not always be equal: While one party might evolve their key before preparing the first protocol message, the responder can (at the earliest) evolve after it has received that message.

2.1 Execution Environment

We consider a set of n parties $\{P_1, \ldots, P_n\}$, where each party is a potential protocol participant. We refer to parties by P_i or by their label i if context is clear. Initially, each pair of parties (P_i, P_j) with $i \neq j$ share a common secret $\mathsf{PSK}_{i,j}$, which is the initial key material generated during protocol initialization (e.g., MAC keys or key derivation keys). Note that this key material may evolve over time and that $\mathsf{PSK}_{i,j}$ and $\mathsf{PSK}_{j,i}$ may not necessarily be equal at all times.

We model parallel executions of a protocol by equipping each party i with $q \in \mathbb{N}$ session oracles $\pi_i^1, \ldots, \pi_i^q$. Each session oracle represents a process that executes one single instance of the protocol. All oracles have access to the "global key material" PSK (including the ability to modify the key material PSK). Moreover, each oracle maintains an internal state consisting of the following variables:

Variable	Description
α	Execution state $\in \{\texttt{uninitialized}, \texttt{negotiating}, \texttt{accept}, \texttt{reject}\}$
pid	Identity of the intended partner $\in \{P_1, \ldots, P_n\}$
ρ	role $\in \{\mathsf{Initiator}, \mathsf{Responder}\}$
sk	Session key $\in \mathcal{K}_\mathsf{s} \cup \perp$ for some session key space $\mathcal{K}_\mathsf{s}$
κ	Freshness of session key $\in \{\mathsf{exposed}, \mathsf{fresh}\}$
sid	Session identifier
b	Security bit $\in \{0, 1\}$

Additionally, we assume that each oracle has an additional temporary state variable, used to store ephemeral values or the transcript of messages. As initial state of the oracle, we have $\alpha = \texttt{uninitialized}$ and $\kappa = \mathsf{fresh}$ and $b \xleftarrow{\$} \{0, 1\}$. Note that pid and ρ are set when the adversary interacts with the respective oracles and that sid and sk are defined as the protocol/adversary progresses.

As usual, if an oracle derives a session key then it will enter the execution state $\texttt{accept}$. If an oracle reaches the execution state $\texttt{reject}$, then it will no longer accept any messages. Later on when we describe protocols, the event $\texttt{Abort}$ will identify points at which this action would be triggered.

To begin any of the experiments in this section, the challenger initializes n parties $\{P_1, \ldots, P_n\}$, with each pair of parties sharing symmetric key material PSK as specified by the protocol.

An adversary interacts with session oracles π_i^s by issuing the following queries. Several of these queries add output to an oracle transcript (defined below) which is available to the adversary.

- $\mathsf{NewSessionI}(\pi_i^s, \mathsf{pid})$ initializes a new initiator session for party P_i with intended partner pid. Specifically, this query assigns pid, $\rho = \mathsf{Initiator}$ and $\alpha = \texttt{negotiating}$ to π_i^s, creates the first protocol message and adds this to transcript of π_i^s.
- $\mathsf{NewSessionR}(\pi_i^s, \mathsf{pid}, m)$ initializes a new responder session for party P_i with $\rho = \mathsf{Responder}$ and intended partner pid, and delivers a protocol message to this oracle. Specifically, it assigns pid and $\rho = \mathsf{Responder}$ to π_i^s and processes message m. The message m and consequent protocol messages (if any) are added to its transcript, and the execution state is set to $\texttt{negotiating}$.
- $\mathsf{Send}(\pi_i^s, m)$ delivers message m to oracle π_i^s. This input message, and consequent protocol messages (if any), are added to this oracle's transcript.
- $\mathsf{RevealKey}(\pi_i^s)$ reveals session key sk_i^s and sets $\pi_i^s.\kappa$ to $\mathsf{exposed}$.
- $\mathsf{Corrupt}(P_i, P_j)$ (issued to some oracle of P_i or P_j) returns $\mathsf{PSK}_{i,j}$. If the query $\mathsf{Corrupt}(P_i, P_j)$ is the τ-th query issued by $\mathcal{A}$, we say that all oracles π_i with

pid $= j$ are τ-corrupted. (i.e., party P_i becomes τ-corrupted with respect to the other party P_j). An uncorrupted oracle is considered as $+\infty$-corrupted.
- Test (π_i^s) chooses $sk_0 \xleftarrow{\$} \mathcal{K}_s$, sets $sk_1 = \pi_i^s.sk$ and returns sk_b. This oracle can only be queried once, and the query making this action is labelled τ_0.

The adversary must call NewSessionI or NewSessionR in order to specify a role and intended partner identifier for each oracle it wishes to use. Afterwards, the adversary can use the Send query to convey messages to these oracles.

2.2 AKE Security

To define entity authentication we use *matching conversations* [8] for oracle partnering, which requires a definition of an oracle's *transcript*: T_i^s is the sequence of all messages sent and received by π_i^s in chronological order. The standard definition of matching conversations, reflects that the party that sends the last message cannot be sure that the responder received that protocol message. We use this definition for entity authentication.

Note that an oracle π_i^s only has a transcript, T_i^s, if $\pi_i^s.\alpha \neq$ `uninitialized`. Transcript T_j^t is a *prefix* of T_i^s if T_j^t contains at least one message and messages in T_j^t are identical to and in the same order as the first $|\mathsf{T}_j^t|$ messages of T_i^s.

Definition 5 (Partial-transcript Matching conversations [23, Def. 3]**).** *π_i^s has a partial-transcript matching conversation to π_j^t if*

- *T_j^t is a prefix of T_i^s and π_i^s has sent the last message(s), or*
- *$\mathsf{T}_i^s = \mathsf{T}_j^t$ and π_j^t has sent the last message(s).*

However, standard matching conversations are not strong enough to define key indistinguishability in a symmetric setting and leave room for a trivial attack (intuitively, this is due to the "asynchronous evolution" of the global key material PSK). Consider an adversary that uses the above execution environment to execute some protocol between two (sessions of two) parties. The adversary forwards all messages but the last one between both parties. At this point the party that sent the last message must have reached the accept state and applied some one-way procedure to its key material PSK in order to achieve forward security. However, the other party still needs to receive the final message in order to derive the session key and update its version of the key material. If the adversary were now to use Test on the accepting party while using Corrupt on the other party, this leads to a trivial distinguishing attack in standard key indistinguishability games (e.g., in [23]). Hence, we need to introduce a slightly stronger notion of matching conversations to precisely capture when Corrupt queries are allowed: the conversation is only deemed to be matching if all messages were delivered.

Definition 6 (Guaranteed Delivery Matching conversations). *π_i^s has a guaranteed delivery matching conversation to π_j^t if $\mathsf{T}_i^s = \mathsf{T}_j^t$.*

As usual, we say that the adversary breaks entity authentication if it forces a fresh oracle to accept maliciously, and breaks key indistinguishability if it can distinguish from random an established key that it cannot trivially access.

Definition 7 (Entity Authentication). *Let Π be a protocol. Let $\mathsf{G}_{\Pi}^{\mathsf{Ent\text{-}Auth}}(\mathcal{A})$ be the following game:*

- *The challenger initializes n parties and their keys;*
- *$\mathcal{A}$ may issue queries to oracles* NewSessionI, NewSessionR, Send, RevealKey, Corrupt *and* Test *as defined above;*
- *Once $\mathcal{A}$ has concluded, the experiment outputs 1 if and only if there exists an accepting oracle π_i^s such that the following conditions hold:*
  1. *both P_i (w.r.t. P_j) and intended partner P_j (w.r.t. P_i) were not corrupted before query τ_0;*
  2. *there is no unique π_j^t, with $\rho_i^s \neq \rho_j^t$, such that π_i^s has a partial-transcript matching conversation to π_j^t.*

Define the advantage of an adversary $\mathcal{A}$ in the Ent-Auth *security experiment $\mathsf{G}_{\Pi}^{\mathsf{Ent\text{-}Auth}}(\mathcal{A})$ as*

$$\mathsf{Adv}_{\Pi}^{\mathsf{Ent\text{-}Auth}}(\mathcal{A}) := \Pr\left[\mathsf{G}_{\Pi}^{\mathsf{Ent\text{-}Auth}}(\mathcal{A}) = 1\right].$$

An oracle π_i^s accepting in the above sense 'accepts maliciously'.

Later on we separate the analysis of an initiator oracle accepting maliciously from a responder oracle accepting maliciously. Further, we will present protocols that only provide one-sided authentication: this requires separation of the AKE definition. To this end, we use the following notation:

$$\mathsf{Adv}_{\Pi}^{\mathsf{Ent\text{-}Auth}}(\mathcal{A}) = \mathsf{Adv}_{\Pi}^{\mathsf{Ent\text{-}Auth\text{-}I}}(\mathcal{A}) + \mathsf{Adv}_{\Pi}^{\mathsf{Ent\text{-}Auth\text{-}R}}(\mathcal{A}).$$

Definition 8 (Key Indistinguishability). *Let Π be a protocol. Let $\mathsf{G}_{\Pi}^{\mathsf{Key\text{-}Ind}}(\mathcal{A})$ be the following game:*

- *The challenger initializes n parties and their keys;*
- *$\mathcal{A}$ may issue queries to oracles* NewSessionI, NewSessionR, Send, RevealKey, Corrupt *and* Test *as defined above;*
- *Once $\mathcal{A}$ has output (i, s, b') to indicate its conclusion, the experiment outputs 1 if and only if there exists an oracle π_i^s such that the following holds:*
  1. *π_i^s accepts, with a unique oracle π_j^t, such that π_i^s has a partial-transcript matching conversation to π_j^t, when $\mathcal{A}$ issues its τ_0-th query;*
  2. *$\mathcal{A}$ did not issue* RevealKey *to π_i^s nor π_j^t (so $\kappa_i^s = \mathsf{fresh}$) and $\rho_i^s \neq \rho_j^t$;*
  3. *P_i (w.r.t. P_j) is τ_i-corrupted and P_j (w.r.t. P_i) is τ_j-corrupted, with $\tau_i, \tau_j > \tau_0$;*
  4. *at the point of query τ_j, oracle π_j^t had a guaranteed delivery matching conversation to π_i^s, and*
  5. *$b' = \pi_i^s.b$.*

Define the advantage of an adversary $\mathcal{A}$ in the Key-Ind *security experiment $\mathsf{G}_{\Pi}^{\mathsf{Key\text{-}Ind}}(\mathcal{A})$ as*

$$\mathsf{Adv}_{\Pi}^{\mathsf{Key\text{-}Ind}}(\mathcal{A}) := \left|\Pr\left[\mathsf{G}_{\Pi}^{\mathsf{Key\text{-}Ind}}(\mathcal{A}) = 1\right] - \frac{1}{2}\right|.$$

We assume that all adversaries in the Key-Ind game are valid, meaning that they terminate and provide an output in the correct format (i.e. $(i, s, b') \in [n] \times [q] \times \{0,1\}$). Later on in our proofs we will follow the game-hopping strategy, and in doing so we will often simplify exposition by additionally assuming adversaries that do not trigger a trivial win (in the Key-Ind game or any subsequent modifications of this game).

We define AKE security in three flavors, distinguished by the level of entity authentication that is achieved by the protocol. An adversary breaks the AKE security of a protocol if it wins either the entity authentication game, or the key indistinguishability game.

Definition 9 (Authenticated Key Exchange). *Let Π be a protocol. The advantage of an adversary $\mathcal{A}$ in terms of* AKE-M *(mutual entity authentication), resp.* AKE-I *(initiator authenticates the responder), resp.* AKE-R *(responder authenticates the initiator) is defined as follows:*

$$\mathsf{Adv}_{\Pi}^{\mathsf{AKE\text{-}M}}(\mathcal{A}) := \mathsf{Adv}_{\Pi}^{\mathsf{Key\text{-}Ind}}(\mathcal{A}) + \mathsf{Adv}_{\Pi}^{\mathsf{Ent\text{-}Auth\text{-}I}}(\mathcal{A}) + \mathsf{Adv}_{\Pi}^{\mathsf{Ent\text{-}Auth\text{-}R}}(\mathcal{A}).$$

$$\mathsf{Adv}_{\Pi}^{\mathsf{AKE\text{-}I}}(\mathcal{A}) := \mathsf{Adv}_{\Pi}^{\mathsf{Key\text{-}Ind}}(\mathcal{A}) + \mathsf{Adv}_{\Pi}^{\mathsf{Ent\text{-}Auth\text{-}I}}(\mathcal{A}).$$

$$\mathsf{Adv}_{\Pi}^{\mathsf{AKE\text{-}R}}(\mathcal{A}) := \mathsf{Adv}_{\Pi}^{\mathsf{Key\text{-}Ind}}(\mathcal{A}) + \mathsf{Adv}_{\Pi}^{\mathsf{Ent\text{-}Auth\text{-}R}}(\mathcal{A}).$$

We do not specify any protocols that provide AKE-I alone in this paper, however it is defined here for completeness.

2.3 Concurrent Execution Synchronization Robustness

We now describe a novel property for key exchange protocols. The goal is to capture, in a formal manner, how *robust* a protocol is in the event of adversarial control of the network and/or some of the parties. We seek a definition that asks: after an adversary has had control of the communication network (by executing arbitrary Send and NewSessionI/NewSessionR queries), can an honest protocol run be executed successfully? Specifically, if it is possible for the parties to lose synchronization (due to dropped messages or adversarial control) such that the parties cannot, in one protocol run, regain synchronization and compute the same key, then the protocol does not meet this property.

Our formalization follows the execution environment of the Ent-Auth and Key-Ind games described above, and allows an adversary to specify the protocol run (that it is attempting to 'interrupt') at the end of its execution by specifying two oracles. The challenger awards success if the two parties (specifically those two oracles) did not accept with the same session key. We define two flavours: a weaker version wSR in which the 'target' protocol run must be executed without any other messages interleaved, and a stronger version SR which allows arbitrary queries in between messages of the 'target' run, even to parties of the oracles involved in the 'target' run (though of course not to the two oracles).

We define an *honest protocol run* (via adversarial queries) between two oracles (with initial state `uninitialized`) as follows: a NewSessionI query was made that produced a protocol message m_1, a NewSessionR query was made to the other oracle with input message m_1, and if this query produced a protocol message m_2 then this value was given as a Send query to the other oracle, and so on, until all protocol messages have been created and delivered, if possible. In the event that any of these queries fails (returns $\bot$) the honest protocol run aborts. This honest protocol run can be thought of as a genuine attempt to execute a protocol execution.

Definition 10 ((weak) Synchronization Robustness). *Let Π be a protocol. Let $\mathsf{G}_{\Pi}^{\mathsf{wSR}}(\mathcal{A})$ with boxed text or $\mathsf{G}_{\Pi}^{\mathsf{SR}}(\mathcal{A})$ with dashed boxed text be the following game:*

- *The challenger initializes n parties and their keys;*
- *$\mathcal{A}$ may issue queries* NewSessionI, NewSessionR *and* Send *as defined above;*
- *Once $\mathcal{A}$ has output (i, j, s, t) to indicate its conclusion, the experiment outputs 1 if and only if the following conditions hold:*
  1. *$\pi_i^s.\mathsf{pid} = P_j$ and $\pi_j^t.\mathsf{pid} = P_i$;*
  2. *$\pi_i^s.sk \neq \pi_j^t.sk$ or both values are $\bot$;*
  3. *an honest protocol run was executed between π_i^s and π_j^t;*
  4. *no queries were made by $\mathcal{A}$ to interrupt the protocol execution between π_i^s and π_j^t.*
  4. *no protocol messages in the transcripts of π_i^s and π_j^t were sent to any* other *oracles before they were delivered in the honest run.*

Define the advantage of an adversary $\mathcal{A}$ in the XX *security experiment $\mathsf{G}_{\Pi}^{\mathsf{XX}}(\mathcal{A})$, for* $\mathsf{XX} \in \{\mathsf{wSR}, \mathsf{SR}\}$, *as*

$$\mathsf{Adv}_{\Pi}^{\mathsf{XX}}(\mathcal{A}) := \Pr\left[\mathsf{G}_{\Pi}^{\mathsf{XX}}(\mathcal{A}) = 1\right].$$

Notes on the definitions. **Note 1:** Condition (4.) in the SR experiment states that for each genuine protocol message in the 'target' session, $\mathcal{A}$ must not have provided this message to any other oracles before that message is delivered as part of the 'target' run. This prevents a trivial attack where $\mathcal{A}$ delivers the final protocol message to two oracles: first to some other oracle than the 'target' oracle (but of the same party), then to the target oracle. When the (genuine) protocol message is delivered to the party for the second time the target oracle would abort. The parties have still created exactly one key for this genuine protocol run, and so condition (4.) essentially fixes the allowable output oracles as the ones that are processing protocol messages for the first time. (Replay attacks are not an issue in the wSR setting, since the execution must be uninterrupted and so any action made *after* that run has occurred has no impact on $\mathcal{A}$'s chances of winning.) **Note 2:** We do not allow Corrupt queries in this definition: in all of the protocols in this paper we assume pairwise shared key material (and specifically, no keys that are used by a party for communication with multiple other parties). This means that the adversary is not allowed to corrupt the parties in the target run with respect to each other, and that all other Corrupt queries will be of no benefit to an attacker. A similar argument follows for RevealKey queries. This simplifies the security experiment, while capturing the property that we wish to assess. **Note 3:** In an alternative formulation of our definitions, the target protocol run could be performed by the challenger as an Execute query as seen in past literature [7]. We avoid this approach for two reasons. First, in the SR case, in order to support interleaving, the adversary would have to call the challenger to initiate each stage of the execution (i.e. $k+1$ times for a k-message protocol), and this is notationally awkward. Secondly and perhaps more importantly, our model allows the adversary to attempt to win its game in multiple protocol runs, and output the oracles which provides the best chance of success. Thus to retain the strength of the definition we would require *multiple* Execute queries, resulting in a model that looks very similar to what we have presented here.

3 Linear Key Evolution

In this section we present a number of protocols that use linear key evolution to derive session keys. All of these protocols achieve wSR. It is not hard to see that full robustness (SR) is not achievable with linearly evolving protocols. To win the SR game the adversary makes a new complete protocol run after the target run has started and the session key is computed at one party, but before the session key is computed at the second party. This means that when the target session completes, the long-term key has already evolved and the key will be computed with the wrong version of the long-term key at the second party. Either the session will fail at the second party or the key will be different at the two parties. (There is a third case when the key is independent of the long-term key, but in that case the protocol fails to achieve key indistinguishability.)

The first linear key evolving protocol that we present, LP3, exchanges three short messages and has the attractive property of bounding the gap between the counters of the two parties. We present two further protocols which are even more efficient at the cost of some restrictions. LP2 is a two-message protocol but in order to maintain mutual authentication we insist that parties running LP2 have fixed their role as either initiator or responder (not an unreasonable assumption in many application scenarios). Our simplest protocol, LP1, has only a single message but, in addition to requiring fixed roles, like any other one-message protocol it can only achieve unilateral authentication. For all of our protocols we provide theorems guaranteeing authentication, key indistinguishability and weak synchronization robustness (wSR) security.

Syntax and Conventions. All protocols in this paper use message authentication codes to ensure that parties can only process messages that are meant for them. This means that party A stores a key $\mathsf{K}_{AB}^{\mathsf{MAC}}$ (static) for MAC and key derivation key $\mathsf{k}_{AB}^{\mathsf{CTR}}$ (evolving) to communicate with B, and $\mathsf{K}_{AC}^{\mathsf{MAC}}$ and $\mathsf{k}_{AC}^{\mathsf{CTR}}$ to communicate with C, etc. We describe the key derivation process in more detail in Sec. 3.1.

In LP2 and LP3, the party sending the protocol message includes its own identity in the MAC computation: this stops redirection/reflection attacks of

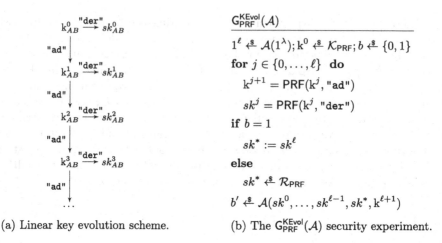

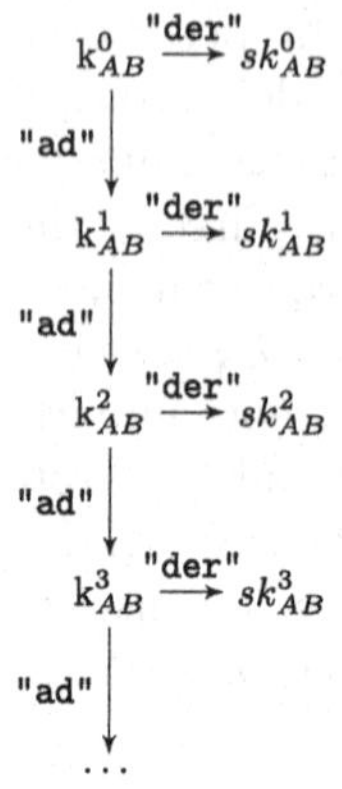

(a) Linear key evolution scheme.

$\mathsf{G}_{\mathsf{PRF}}^{\mathsf{KEvol}}(\mathcal{A})$

$1^\ell \xleftarrow{\$} \mathcal{A}(1^\lambda); \mathrm{k}^0 \xleftarrow{\$} \mathcal{K}_{\mathsf{PRF}}; b \xleftarrow{\$} \{0,1\}$
for $j \in \{0, \ldots, \ell\}$ **do**
 $\mathrm{k}^{j+1} = \mathsf{PRF}(\mathrm{k}^j, \texttt{"ad"})$
 $sk^j = \mathsf{PRF}(\mathrm{k}^j, \texttt{"der"})$
if $b = 1$
 $sk^* := sk^\ell$
else
 $sk^* \xleftarrow{\$} \mathcal{R}_{\mathsf{PRF}}$
$b' \xleftarrow{\$} \mathcal{A}(sk^0, \ldots, sk^{\ell-1}, sk^*, \mathrm{k}^{\ell+1})$

(b) The $\mathsf{G}_{\mathsf{PRF}}^{\mathsf{KEvol}}(\mathcal{A})$ security experiment.

Fig. 3. Linear key evolution and the corresponding experiment.

protocol messages to the sending party. For LP1 this is not necessary since the sending party advances after sending its protocol message, meaning that its state is ahead and therefore it is unable to process messages that it has already sent.

3.1 Key Derivation via Linear Evolution

Before looking at specific protocols, we define what we mean by linear key evolution and present an abstract security definition for it. Party A holds a *key derivation key* $\mathrm{k}_{AB}^{\mathsf{CTR}}$ for use in communication with party B, where the value CTR is an integer that defines the current key state, which is the number of times the key has evolved since its creation. After a party has participated in a key exchange run and computed a session key, it will apply a function Advnc to this key derivation key in order to obtain the next key derivation key and update the counter. This process is detailed in Fig. 3a. Looking ahead, forward security will be obtained if the function that computes $\mathrm{k}_{AB}^{\mathsf{CTR}+1}$ from $\mathrm{k}_{AB}^{\mathsf{CTR}}$ is one-way: this stipulation ensures that an adversary corrupting a party has no way to move upwards in the figure.

The initial "key derivation key" (KDK) is k_{AB}^0. Subsequent KDKs are derived using a pseudorandom function PRF with $\mathcal{K}_{\mathsf{PRF}} = \mathcal{R}_{\mathsf{PRF}}$ as

$$\mathrm{k}_{AB}^{i+1} = \mathsf{PRF}(\mathrm{k}_{AB}^i, \texttt{"ad"}) \tag{1}$$

and session keys are derived as

$$sk_{AB}^i = \mathsf{PRF}(\mathrm{k}_{AB}^i, \texttt{"der"})$$

where "ad" ("advance") and "der" ("derive") are constant labels used for domain separation.

Furthermore, for convenience, we define a function Advnc which performs multiple key derivations, if necessary. That is, $\mathsf{Advnc}(\mathrm{k}^i_{AB}, i, z)$ takes an i-th key derivation key for some counter i and an integer z, and applies PRF iteratively z times to obtain the $(i+z)$-th KDK such that (1) is satisfied, and sets $i := i + z$. For example:

$$\mathrm{k}^{i+z}_{AB}, i + z \leftarrow \mathsf{Advnc}(\mathrm{k}^i_{AB}, i, z).$$

Security. For the security proofs of our protocols it will be convenient to have an abstract security definition for such a key derivation scheme, which we will show to be implied by the security of the PRF. To this end, Fig. 3b represents a security experiment for the linear key evolution scheme that we describe. The adversary $\mathcal{A}$ outputs an integer 1^ℓ (in unary, to ensure that the number ℓ is polynomially bounded for any efficient $\mathcal{A}$), and the adversary's task is to distinguish sk^ℓ from random, when given all prior session keys $sk^0, \ldots sk^{\ell-1}$ and the 'next' key derivation key $\mathrm{k}^{\ell+1}$.

Definition 11. *The advantage of $\mathcal{A}$ in in the* KEvol *security experiment defined in Fig. 3b for pseudorandom function* PRF *is defined as*

$$\mathsf{Adv}^{\mathsf{KEvol}}_{\mathsf{PRF}}(\mathcal{A}) := \left| \Pr\left[b = b'\right] - \frac{1}{2} \right|.$$

In the full version [11] we give the straightforward proof of the following theorem.

Theorem 12. *Let* PRF *be a pseudorandom function. For any adversary $\mathcal{A}$ against the* KEvol *security of* PRF*, there exists an adversary $\mathcal{B}$ against the* PRF-sec *of* PRF *such that*

$$\mathsf{Adv}^{\mathsf{KEvol}}_{\mathsf{PRF}}(\mathcal{A}) \leq \ell \cdot \mathsf{Adv}^{\mathsf{PRF\text{-}sec}}_{\mathsf{PRF}}(\mathcal{B}).$$

3.2 LP3: A Three-Message Protocol

Intuition. In Fig. 4 we present a three-message protocol called LP3, which puts a bound on how far initiator and responder can be out of sync, allows either party to initiate communications, and provides mutual authentication. After the first message is sent by an initiator, the responding party advances to catch up if they are behind. Then they respond, and the initiator does the same if they are behind. A third message confirms that both parties are now in sync again, and only after that a session key is established. We make use of state analysis proofs to show that the gap between the two states will be bounded even if messages are lost on the way (Lemma 13) and extend this proof to a scenario where concurrent runs are allowed (Lemma 14). We then show that the number of concurrent runs is a bound on the gap that can occur. We show in Theorem 15 that this also implies that the protocol achieves weak synchronization robustness (wSR). The protocol uses MACs and nonces to achieve mutual authentication (AKE-M). The functions Advnc and KDF, for PSK advancement and session key derivation respectively, are implemented using a PRF as described in Fig. 3a and Sect. 3.1.

Initiator		Responder
$(\mathsf{CTR}_{AB}, \mathsf{k}^{\mathsf{CTR}}_{AB}, \mathsf{K}^{\mathsf{MAC}})$		$(\mathsf{CTR}_{BA}, \mathsf{k}^{\mathsf{CTR}}_{BA}, \mathsf{K}^{\mathsf{MAC}})$
$\mathsf{N}_A \xleftarrow{\$} \mathsf{GenN}$		
$\sigma_1 \leftarrow \mathsf{Mac}(\mathsf{K}^{\mathsf{MAC}}, A \parallel \mathsf{N}_A \parallel \mathsf{CTR}_{AB})$	$\xrightarrow{\mathsf{N}_A, \mathsf{CTR}_{AB}, \sigma_1}$	
		if $\mathsf{Vrfy}(\mathsf{K}^{\mathsf{MAC}}, A \parallel \mathsf{N}_A \parallel \mathsf{CTR}_{AB}, \sigma_1) = 0$
		Abort
		$z_1 \leftarrow \mathsf{CTR}_{AB} - \mathsf{CTR}_{BA}$
		if $z_1 > 0$
		$\mathsf{k}^{\mathsf{CTR}}_{BA}, \mathsf{CTR}_{BA} \leftarrow \mathsf{Advnc}(\mathsf{k}^{\mathsf{CTR}}_{BA}, \mathsf{CTR}_{BA}, z_1)$
		$\mathsf{N}_B \xleftarrow{\$} \mathsf{GenN}$
if $\mathsf{Vrfy}(\mathsf{K}^{\mathsf{MAC}}, B \parallel \mathsf{N}_A \parallel \mathsf{N}_B \parallel \mathsf{CTR}_{BA}, \sigma_2) = 0$	$\xleftarrow{\mathsf{N}_B, \mathsf{CTR}_{BA}, \sigma_2}$	$\sigma_2 \leftarrow \mathsf{Mac}(\mathsf{K}^{\mathsf{MAC}}, B \parallel \mathsf{N}_A \parallel \mathsf{N}_B \parallel \mathsf{CTR}_{BA})$
Abort		
$z_2 \leftarrow \mathsf{CTR}_{BA} - \mathsf{CTR}_{AB}$		
if $z_2 > 0$		
$\mathsf{k}^{\mathsf{CTR}}_{AB}, \mathsf{CTR}_{AB} \leftarrow \mathsf{Advnc}(\mathsf{k}^{\mathsf{CTR}}_{AB}, \mathsf{CTR}_{AB}, z_2)$		
$\sigma_3 \leftarrow \mathsf{Mac}(\mathsf{K}^{\mathsf{MAC}}, A \parallel \mathsf{N}_A \parallel \mathsf{N}_B \parallel \mathsf{CTR}_{AB} \parallel \texttt{"conf"})$		
$sk_{AB} := \mathsf{KDF}(\mathsf{k}^{\mathsf{CTR}}_{AB}, \texttt{"der"})$	$\xrightarrow{\mathsf{CTR}_{AB}, \sigma_3}$	**if** $\mathsf{Vrfy}(\mathsf{K}^{\mathsf{MAC}}, A \parallel \mathsf{N}_A \parallel \mathsf{N}_B \parallel \mathsf{CTR}_{AB} \parallel \texttt{"conf"}, \sigma_3) = 0$
$\mathsf{k}^{\mathsf{CTR}}_{AB}, \mathsf{CTR}_{AB} \leftarrow \mathsf{Advnc}(\mathsf{k}^{\mathsf{CTR}}_{AB}, \mathsf{CTR}_{AB}, 1)$		
		Abort
		$z_3 \leftarrow \mathsf{CTR}_{AB} - \mathsf{CTR}_{BA}$
		if $z_3 \neq 0$
		Abort
		$sk_{AB} \leftarrow \mathsf{KDF}(\mathsf{k}^{\mathsf{CTR}}_{BA}, \texttt{"der"})$
		$\mathsf{k}^{\mathsf{CTR}}_{BA}, \mathsf{CTR}_{BA} \leftarrow \mathsf{Advnc}(\mathsf{k}^{\mathsf{CTR}}_{BA}, \mathsf{CTR}_{BA}, 1)$

Fig. 4. LP3, a three-message protocol.

State. The protocol uses nonces on both the initiating (N_A) and responding (N_B) sides. Local session state keeps track of these, and so it is only necessary to send N_A in the first protocol message and only N_B in the second message. The nonce generation procedure is denoted GenN, and this process could be, for example, random selection of a bitstring of some fixed length, or a (per-recipient) counter maintained by the party (note however that this counter is distinct from CTR, which tracks the key derivation key's evolution stage). This choice depends on the application scenario, and this abstraction is for cleaner proofs. In the absence of a hardware RNG, random nonces require memory to be allocated for code of a software CSPRNG, while maintaining a counter requires writing to persistent storage (though such writes must be made anyway in linear key evolving protocols). The probability of a collision in random selection from $\mathcal{NS}$ can be bounded by $\mathsf{coll}[q_\mathsf{N}, \mathsf{GenN}] \leq \frac{q_\mathsf{N}^2}{2|\mathcal{NS}|}$, and the collision probability of a (per-recipient) counter of size $|\mathcal{NS}|$ that is called q_N times is

$$\mathsf{coll}[q_\mathsf{N}, \mathsf{GenN}] = \begin{cases} 0 \text{ for } 0 \leq q_\mathsf{N} \leq |\mathcal{NS}| - 1, \\ 1 \text{ for } q_\mathsf{N} \geq |\mathcal{NS}|. \end{cases}$$

We do not specify the additional counters required to make LP3 deterministic, so it is specified here as a protocol with random nonces.

LP3 achieves AKE-M security (proof in the full version [11]). The security bound is
$\mathsf{Adv}_{\Pi}^{\mathsf{AKE\text{-}M}}(\mathcal{A}) \leq n^2 \cdot \left(4\mathsf{Adv}_{\mathsf{MAC}}^{\mathsf{SEUF\text{-}CMA\text{-}}Q}(\mathcal{B}) + 4\mathsf{coll}[q, \mathsf{GenN}] + q \cdot \mathsf{Adv}_{\mathsf{PRF}}^{\mathsf{KEvol}}(\mathcal{C})\right).$

Bounded Gap: Non-concurrent Setting. We will now prove that the "gap" between the state of the two parties in LP3 is bounded in the non-concurrent setting, that is:

Lemma 13. *Let A and B be respectively the initiator and the responder of a single—non-concurrent—LP3-run. Let δ_{AB} be the gap between A and B with respect to the evolution of the master keys of both parties. Then $\delta_{AB} \in \{-1, 0, 1\}$, assuming MAC-security.*

The messages in LP3 are counted in a natural way, as indicated in Fig. 5a. For this non-concurrent setting the proof is similar to [4, Lemma 1]. Then the notation "(CTR_{AB}, CTR_{BA})" means that, when the run ends, the last valid message received by A has index CTR_{AB}, and the last valid message received by B has index CTR_{BA}. We call a $(\mathsf{CTR}_{AB}, \mathsf{CTR}_{BA})$-run a run where the last message received by A is message CTR_{AB}, and the last message received by B is message CTR_{BA}. By convention $\mathsf{CTR}_{AB} = 0$ means that no message has been received by A. In Fig. 5b, we define the states to be the different values of δ_{AB}. The transitions are the possible messages. An example: if our protocol instance is in state $\delta_{AB} = -1$, and B responds to message 1 with message 2, i.e. transition $(2, 1)$ in the state diagram, the initiator will advance twice and the state will be $\delta_{AB} = 1$. A then sends the third message: transition $(2, 3)$ takes place and we end up in state $\delta_{AB} = 0$ since this third message will cause the responder to advance.

Proof. We prove Lemma 13. The protocol is initialized with $\delta_{AB} = 0$ and the first step is sending message 1: either the message never reaches the responder, or the message is received correctly. In either case neither party advances, so $\delta_{AB} = 0$—i.e. transition $(0, 1)$ in Fig. 5b is fired. If the protocol now terminates we end up in state 0, while sending and receiving message 2 would cause the initiator to advance, or in terms of the state diagram, fire $(2, 1)$ and transition to $\delta_{AB} = 1$.

Because we restrict ourselves to non-concurrent executions, the only possible option no matter the state is to advance with one message or terminate and start from $(0, 1)$. Adding all possible transitions to the state diagram, we observe that there are no reachable states other than 0 and 1. Since the protocol does not have fixed roles we can reach a state -1 by changing roles after we reached state 1. From there, there are two transitions that bring us back to states 0 and 1. Since we assume that MACs cannot be forged, these are the only reachable states, thus $\delta_{AB} \in \{-1, 0, 1\}$ always holds.

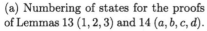

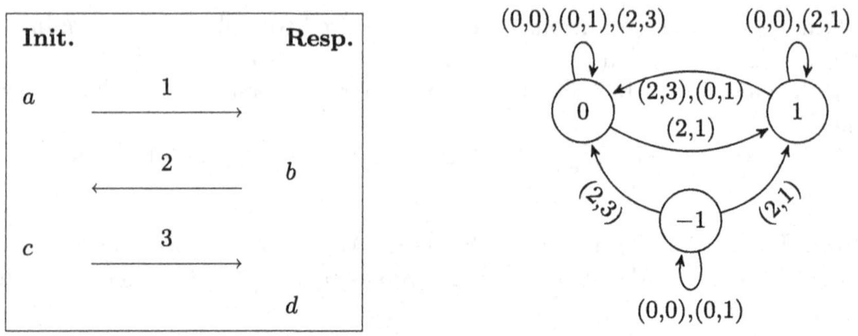

(a) Numbering of states for the proofs of Lemmas 13 $(1, 2, 3)$ and 14 (a, b, c, d).

(b) Synchronization state for LP3 in the non-concurrent setting.

Fig. 5. Different states for LP3, and transitions between them.

Bounded Gap: Concurrent Setting. We will now extend Lemma 13 to the concurrent setting.

Lemma 14. *Let A and B be respectively the initiator and the responder of C concurrent LP3-runs. Let δ_{AB} be the gap between A and B with respect to the evolution of the master keys of both parties. Then $-C \leq \delta_{AB} \leq 1 + C$, assuming MAC-security.*

To illustrate the (in a sense) multidimensional effect of concurrent runs on the protocol, we will now use a different message labelling convention. Figure 5a defines the different states the protocol execution can be in. The state diagram in Fig. 6 now uses these four possible protocol states as diagram states—a message between state a and b is thus necessarily message 1. The internal state of the four 'macro states' in the diagram now represents the value of δ_{AB}.

Observe that for the transitions from a to b and from b to c, i.e. the sending of messages 1 and 2, respectively, the evolution of δ_{AB} depends on the actual value of a. For all transitions caused by message 3, the change is systematic:

1. Any transition from c to d will decrease δ_{AB} by 1;
2. any transition from b to c will increase δ_{AB} by at least 1.

Additionally there are two 'resets', since

3. any transition from a to b will set δ_{AB} to 0, if the gap is 1 or more;
4. any transition from b to c will set δ_{AB} to 1, if the gap is 0 or less.

Proof. We prove Lemma 14. In Lemma 13, the normal range is shown to be $\delta_{AB} \in \{-1, 0, 1\}$. Extensions beyond this range are possible when the condition in 1. or 2. above occurs during a run, so each consecutive run can influence δ_{AB} with -1 or $+1$ at most. Since we assume MAC-security, the adversary cannot influence the protocol with messages other than those authentically sent during one of the runs. Inductively, we conclude $-C \leq \delta_{AB} \leq 1 + C$.

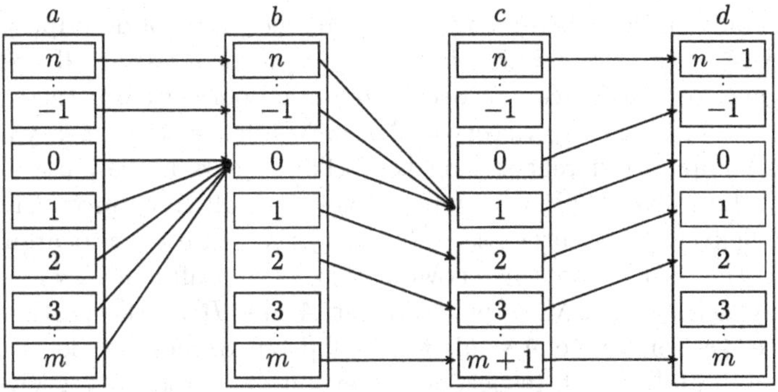

Fig. 6. Synchronization state for LP3 in the concurrent setting.

wSR of LP3. We now argue that LP3 obtains weak synchronization robustness (wSR), the property that captures how well a protocol can recover from network errors and interleaving of protocol runs. In the wSR game the adversary can make arbitrary NewSessionI, NewSessionR and Send queries, and at its conclusion it outputs the identifiers of two oracles: it is said to win the wSR game if these oracles engaged in an uninterrupted protocol run but did not compute the same session key. As such, a proof of wSR must argue that whatever values of party state exist before the target protocol run occurs, neither of the parties will abort and both will arrive at the same session key.

Our general approach for proving robustness of all of the protocols in this paper is to separate adversaries that win the wSR game via forging a MAC value, and those that do not produce a forgery during their execution. LP1 (Fig. 8) and LP2 (Fig. 7) have fixed roles and as a result the initiator's counter value must always be at least the size of the responder's counter value for the protocol to have correctness. Thus a MAC forgery can force the responding party's counter value to be arbitrarily large, and the target protocol run will cause at least one party to abort, and the adversary wins the wSR game. LP3, on the other hand, is actually not vulnerable in the sense of synchronization robustness if a MAC forgery does occur. This is due to LP3 being designed to have correctness for all starting (integer) counter values, since in any session, both parties can catch up from being arbitrarily far behind.

We formally prove this below, however to see this visually, consider Fig. 6 for the execution of a single protocol run, i.e. from a to d. For any initial state difference a, the state c after the second protocol message has been processed is always 1 (the initiator computes a session key and advances once), leading to state difference 0 after the responder processes the final protocol message (deriving a session key and advancing once).

Theorem 15 (wSR **of LP3**). *Let Π be the three-message protocol in Fig. 4, built using* $\mathsf{MAC} = \{\mathsf{KGen}, \mathsf{Mac}, \mathsf{Vrfy}\}$ *and* PRF *with n parties. Then for any adversary $\mathcal{A}$ against the* wSR *security of Π,* $\mathsf{Adv}_{\Pi}^{\mathsf{wSR}}(\mathcal{A}) = 0$.

Proof. The only places where `Abort` occurs in the protocol description (Fig. 4) are after MAC verification failures: in the target protocol session all messages are honestly generated so this cannot occur (assuming perfect correctness of MAC). As a result, the only route to victory in the wSR game for an adversary is to make the parties compute different session keys. This occurs if the parties compute session keys but have different counter values once all three protocol messages have been delivered and processed: following the notation and arguments in Lemma 14, this is the same as showing that $\delta = 0$ after a $(2, 3)$ session for any starting delta value. More precisely, let A and B be the parties involved in the target session where A sends the first protocol message, let $\delta_{AB}^{\mathsf{pre}}$ be the gap between A and B with respect to the evolution of the master keys of both parties and the point *before* the target session begins (i.e. before the adversary calls NewSessionI for the target session), and let $\delta_{AB}^{\mathsf{post}}$ be the gap *after* the target session has occurred. Figure 5b shows that $\delta_{AB}^{\mathsf{post}} = 0$ for $\delta_{AB}^{\mathsf{pre}} \in \{-1, 0, -1\}$, so to complete the proof we need to show that this also holds for arbitrary $\delta_{AB}^{\mathsf{pre}}$.

If $\delta_{AB}^{\mathsf{pre}} \in \{1, 2, \ldots, \}$, i.e. CTR_{AB} is ahead of CTR_{BA} by $\delta_{AB}^{\mathsf{pre}} = z_1$ steps, then the first protocol message processing by B results in B advancing its counter CTR_{BA} by $\delta_{AB}^{\mathsf{pre}}$ steps, leading to state difference 0. This means that A will not advance on receiving the second protocol message and both parties will compute a session key for state CTR_{AB} and then advance once, and so $\delta_{AB}^{\mathsf{post}} = 0$.

If $\delta_{AB}^{\mathsf{pre}} \in \{-1, -2, \ldots, \}$, i.e. CTR_{BA} is ahead of CTR_{AB} by $-\delta_{AB}^{\mathsf{pre}} = z_2$ steps, B does not advance in processing the first message, however A does advance by $-\delta_{AB}^{\mathsf{pre}} = z_2$ steps on receiving the second protocol message. Again this leads to state difference 0 and here a session key is computed for state CTR_{BA} and then both parties advance once, so $\delta_{AB}^{\mathsf{post}} = 0$.

This concludes the proof, since any initial state will lead to the target protocol run computing the same session key for the involved parties.

3.3 LP2: A Two-Message Protocol with Fixed Roles

In Fig. 7 we present a two-message protocol, LP2, with linear key evolution. The roles of initiator and responder are fixed, so the same party initiates every session: this is enforced by $\mathsf{CTR}_{AB} \geq \mathsf{CTR}_{BA}$ (for A initiating).

Achieving weak synchronization robustness (wSR) is slightly more complicated in LP2 than it was in LP3. If we were to adapt LP3 to a two-message protocol by simply dropping the last message and having the responder accept (thus, deriving a session key and advancing its state), we could end up in a situation where we break the requirement that the responder should never advance past the state of the initiator. In this hypothetical protocol, the initiator will initiate the key exchange, but will not derive a session key until it has authenticated the responder. The responder, however, will authenticate the initiator upon receiving the first protocol message (rather than waiting for a key confirmation message as in LP3) and produce the second protocol message, after which it will immediately derive a session key and advance its state. Thus, if this second protocol message is not delivered, the responder will have advanced its state, but the initiator has not, contradicting our requirement that $\mathsf{CTR}_{AB} \geq \mathsf{CTR}_{BA}$.

Initiator		Responder
$\mathsf{CTR}_{AB}, \mathsf{k}_{AB}^{\mathsf{CTR}}, \mathsf{K}^{\mathsf{MAC}}$		$\mathsf{CTR}_{BA}, \mathsf{k}_{BA}^{\mathsf{CTR}}, \mathsf{K}^{\mathsf{MAC}}$
$z_0 \leftarrow \mathtt{NextOdd}(\mathsf{CTR}_{AB}) - \mathsf{CTR}_{AB}$		
$\mathsf{k}_{AB}^{\mathsf{CTR}}, \mathsf{CTR}_{AB} := \mathsf{Advnc}(\mathsf{k}_{AB}^{\mathsf{CTR}}, \mathsf{CTR}_{AB}, z_0)$		
$\sigma_1 \leftarrow \mathsf{Mac}(\mathsf{K}^{\mathsf{MAC}}, A \parallel \mathsf{CTR}_{AB})$	$\xrightarrow{\mathsf{CTR}_{AB}, \sigma_1}$	
		if $\mathsf{Vrfy}(\mathsf{K}^{\mathsf{MAC}}, A \parallel \mathsf{CTR}_{AB}, \sigma_1) = 0$
		Abort
		$z_1 \leftarrow \mathsf{CTR}_{AB} - \mathsf{CTR}_{BA}$
		if $z_1 < 0$
		Abort
		$\mathsf{k}_{BA}^{\mathsf{CTR}}, \mathsf{CTR}_{BA} \leftarrow \mathsf{Advnc}(\mathsf{k}_{BA}^{\mathsf{CTR}}, \mathsf{CTR}_{BA}, z_1)$
	$\xleftarrow{\mathsf{CTR}_{BA}, \sigma_2}$	$\sigma_2 \leftarrow \mathsf{Mac}(\mathsf{K}^{\mathsf{MAC}}, B \parallel \mathsf{CTR}_{BA})$
if $\mathsf{Vrfy}(\mathsf{K}^{\mathsf{MAC}}, B \parallel \mathsf{CTR}_{BA}, \sigma_2) = 0$		$sk_{AB} \leftarrow \mathsf{KDF}(\mathsf{k}_{BA}^{\mathsf{CTR}}, \texttt{"der"})$
Abort		$\mathsf{k}_{BA}^{\mathsf{CTR}}, \mathsf{CTR}_{BA} \leftarrow \mathsf{Advnc}(\mathsf{k}_{BA}^{\mathsf{CTR}}, \mathsf{CTR}_{BA}, 1)$
$z_2 \leftarrow \mathsf{CTR}_{BA} - \mathsf{CTR}_{AB}$		
if $z_2 \neq 0$		
Abort		
$sk_{AB} \leftarrow \mathsf{KDF}(\mathsf{k}_{AB}^{\mathsf{CTR}}, \texttt{"der"})$		
$\mathsf{k}_{AB}^{\mathsf{CTR}}, \mathsf{CTR}_{AB} \leftarrow \mathsf{Advnc}(\mathsf{k}_{AB}^{\mathsf{CTR}}, \mathsf{CTR}_{AB}, 1)$		

Fig. 7. LP2, a two-message protocol with fixed roles.

In order to avoid this in LP2, the initiator A will always advance to the next *odd* value of its counter at the beginning of each session. How many steps the initiator advances depends on what has happened earlier. If a complete session has been executed as A's previous action, A starts by advancing once, so that its state counter is ahead of B. If in the previous session A never processed the second protocol message, A will advance twice at the beginning of the next session, in order to catch up to B and move ahead. The reasoning behind this is the separation of A's counter set: if the counter is an even integer then A has most recently received a message (and derived a key), whereas if it is an odd integer then A most recently sent a (session opening) protocol message. In both cases, advancing to $\mathtt{NextOdd}(\mathsf{CTR}_{AB})$ will have the desired effect.

With this simpler protocol we are able to achieve most of the desired properties from SP3, but with a more lightweight protocol. Fixing the roles makes this possible, and this demonstrates the fine balance between forward security and (weak) synchronization robustness. In the event that the reduced communication complexity of LP2 compared to LP3 is desirable when choosing a protocol, but if the application demands that either party can initiate, it is possible to run LP2 in *duplex mode.* In duplex mode, both parties keep separate key derivation keys and counters for initiating and responding such that both parties can have both roles without violating the condition $\mathsf{CTR}_{AB} \geq \mathsf{CTR}_{BA}$.

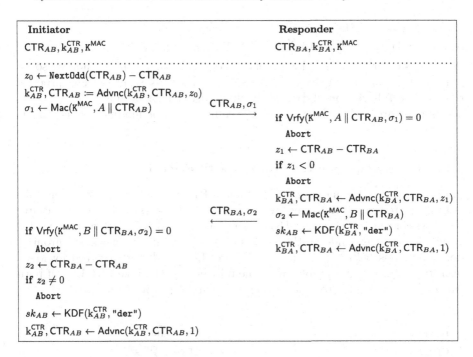

LP2 provides AKE-M security, with security bound $\mathsf{Adv}_{\Pi}^{\mathsf{AKE\text{-}M}}(\mathcal{A}) \leq n^2 \cdot \left(4 \cdot \mathsf{Adv}_{\mathsf{MAC}}^{\mathsf{SEUF\text{-}CMA\text{-}}Q}(\mathcal{B}) + q \cdot \mathsf{Adv}_{\mathsf{PRF}}^{\mathsf{KEvol}}(\mathcal{C})\right)$. The proof [11] proceeds similarly to the LP3 proofs, except here there are no nonces so no $\mathsf{coll}[q, \mathsf{GenN}]$ term is required. LP2 also provides wSR security. The proof of this (in the full version [11]) slightly differs from LP3 because now we must additionally argue that the only way the counters can be modified is via a MAC forgery.

3.4 LP1: A One-Message Protocol with Fixed Roles

In Fig. 8 we present a one-message protocol, LP1, with linear key evolution. Like in LP2, the roles of initiator and responder are fixed, so the same party initiates every session: i.e. $\mathsf{CTR}_{AB} \geq \mathsf{CTR}_{BA}$ (for A initiating). LP1 achieves one-sided authentication (responder authenticates initiator). Achieving weak synchronization robustness (wSR) is similar in LP1 and LP2, and is guaranteed by MAC security. Theorems and proofs are in the full version [11]. Like with LP2, if both parties need to be able to initiate then LP1 can be run in *duplex mode.*

Initiator		**Responder**
$(\mathsf{CTR}_{AB}, \mathsf{k}_{AB}^{\mathsf{CTR}}, \mathsf{K}^{\mathsf{MAC}})$		$(\mathsf{CTR}_{BA}, \mathsf{k}_{BA}^{\mathsf{CTR}}, \mathsf{K}^{\mathsf{MAC}})$
$\sigma_1 \leftarrow \mathsf{Mac}(\mathsf{K}^{\mathsf{MAC}}, \mathsf{CTR}_{AB})$	$\xrightarrow{\mathsf{CTR}_{AB}, \sigma_1}$	
$sk_{AB} \leftarrow \mathsf{KDF}(\mathsf{k}_{AB}^{\mathsf{CTR}}, \texttt{"der"})$		**if** $\mathsf{Vrfy}(\mathsf{K}^{\mathsf{MAC}}, \mathsf{CTR}_{AB}, \sigma_1) = 0$
$\mathsf{k}_{AB}^{\mathsf{CTR}}, \mathsf{CTR}_{AB} \leftarrow \mathsf{Advnc}(\mathsf{k}_{AB}^{\mathsf{CTR}}, \mathsf{CTR}_{AB}, 1)$		**Abort**
		$z_1 \leftarrow \mathsf{CTR}_{AB} - \mathsf{CTR}_{BA}$
		if $z_1 < 0$
		Abort
		$\mathsf{k}_{BA}^{\mathsf{CTR}}, \mathsf{CTR}_{BA} \leftarrow \mathsf{Advnc}(\mathsf{k}_{BA}^{\mathsf{CTR}}, \mathsf{CTR}_{BA}, z_1)$
		$sk_{BA} \leftarrow \mathsf{KDF}(\mathsf{k}_{BA}^{\mathsf{CTR}}, \texttt{"der"})$
		$\mathsf{k}_{BA}^{\mathsf{CTR}}, \mathsf{CTR}_{BA} \leftarrow \mathsf{Advnc}(\mathsf{k}_{BA}^{\mathsf{CTR}}, \mathsf{CTR}_{BA}, 1)$

Fig. 8. LP1, a one-message protocol with fixed roles.

4 Non-linear Key Evolution

In the previous section, we have considered protocols that deploy a linear key evolving mechanism. We have seen that the linearity of these mechanisms has significant downsides when the protocol runs multiple times in parallel between the same two parties. Especially interleaving of messages might cause all but one protocol execution to abort, which is an undesirable behavior.

In this section, we present a protocol that uses puncturable pseudorandom functions (PPRFs) as a "non-linear" key evolution mechanism. We show that this protocol can establish many parallel sessions between two parties, while only requiring some additional storage (logarithmic in the supported maximum number sessions) and computations (in practice hash function evaluations logarithmic in the supported maximum number of sessions).

4.1 Puncturable Pseudorandom Functions

We briefly recall the basic definition of puncturable pseudorandom functions (PPRF). A PPRF is a special case of a pseudorandom function, where it is possible to compute punctured keys, which do not allow evaluation on inputs that have been punctured. We recall the definition of a PPRF and its security [29].

Definition 16 (PPRF). *A* puncturable pseudorandom function *with key space $\mathcal{K}_{\mathsf{PPRF}}$, domain $\mathcal{D}_{\mathsf{PPRF}}$, and range $\mathcal{R}_{\mathsf{PPRF}}$ consists of three probabilistic polynomial-time algorithms* $\mathsf{PPRF} = (\mathsf{Setup}, \mathsf{Eval}, \mathsf{Punct})$, *which are described as follows:*

- $\mathsf{Setup}(1^\lambda)$: *This algorithm takes as input the security parameter λ and outputs a description of a key $k \in \mathcal{K}_{\mathsf{PPRF}}$.*
- $\mathsf{Eval}(k, x)$: *This algorithm takes as input a key $k \in \mathcal{K}_{\mathsf{PPRF}}$ and a value $x \in \mathcal{D}_{\mathsf{PPRF}}$, and outputs a value $y \in \mathcal{R}_{\mathsf{PPRF}}$, or a failure symbol $\bot$.*
- $\mathsf{Punct}(k, x)$: *This algorithm takes as input a key $k \in \mathcal{K}_{\mathsf{PPRF}}$ and a value $x \in \mathcal{D}_{\mathsf{PPRF}}$, and returns a punctured key $k' \in \mathcal{K}_{\mathsf{PPRF}}$.*

Note that the puncturing procedure can also output an unmodified key (i.e. $k' = k$). This is for example reasonable if the procedure is called on an already-punctured value.

Definition 17 (PPRF Correctness). *A PPRF is* correct *if for every subset $\{x_1, \ldots, x_t\} = \mathcal{S} \subseteq \mathcal{D}_{\mathsf{PPRF}}$ and all $x \in \mathcal{D}_{\mathsf{PPRF}} \setminus \mathcal{S}$, it holds that*

$$\Pr\left[\mathsf{Eval}(k_0, x) = \mathsf{Eval}(k_t, x) : \begin{array}{c} k_0 \xleftarrow{\$} \mathsf{Setup}(1^\lambda); \\ k_i = \mathsf{Punct}(k_{i-1}, x_i) \text{ for } i \in [t]; \end{array}\right] = 1.$$

The security experiment asks that an adversary cannot distinguish an evalution of a real input (provided by the adversary) from a random output range element, even if the adversary has access to an evaluation oracle and the key that results from puncturing on the challenge input.

Definition 18 (PPRF Security). *The advantage of an adversary $\mathcal{A}$ in the* rand *security experiment $\mathsf{G}^{\mathsf{rand}}_{\mathsf{PPRF}}(\mathcal{A})$ defined in Fig. 9 is*

$$\mathsf{Adv}^{\mathsf{rand}}_{\mathsf{PPRF}}(\mathcal{A}) := \left|\Pr\left[\mathsf{G}^{\mathsf{rand}}_{\mathsf{PPRF}}(\mathcal{A}) = 1\right] - \frac{1}{2}\right|.$$

$\mathsf{G}^{\mathsf{rand}}_{\mathsf{PPRF}}(\mathcal{A})$	$\mathcal{O}_{\mathsf{Eval}}(x)$
$k \xleftarrow{\$} \mathsf{Setup}(1^\lambda)$	$y \leftarrow \mathsf{Eval}(k, x)$
$b \xleftarrow{\$} \{0,1\};\ \mathcal{Q} := \emptyset$	$\mathcal{Q} := \mathcal{Q} \cup \{x\}$
$x^* \xleftarrow{\$} \mathcal{A}^{\mathcal{O}_{\mathsf{Eval}}(\cdot)}(1^\lambda)$	$k \leftarrow \mathsf{Punct}(k, x)$
$y_0 \xleftarrow{\$} \mathcal{R}_{\mathsf{PPRF}};\ y_1 \leftarrow \mathsf{Eval}(k, x^*)$	**return** y
$k \leftarrow \mathsf{Punct}(k, x^*)$	
$b^* \xleftarrow{\$} \mathcal{A}(k, y_b)$	
return 1 **if** $b = b^*$ **and** $x^* \notin \mathcal{Q}$	
return 0	

Fig. 9. The rand security experiment for puncturable PRF PPRF.

4.2 PPRF-Based Symmetric AKE

Intuition. The main idea of our PPRF-based protocol is to derive the session key via an evaluation of the PPRF. That is, both parties share a PPRF evaluation key k, which is used to derive session keys by computing $\mathsf{Eval}(\mathrm{k}, \mathsf{N}_A)$ for some value N_A (in our protocols this will be a counter). After derivation of a session key, the PPRF key will also be punctured at the value N_A by computing $\mathrm{k} \leftarrow \mathsf{Punct}(\mathrm{k}, \mathsf{N}_A)$. Note that the new key k cannot recompute $\mathsf{Eval}(\mathrm{k}, \mathsf{N}_A)$ as it has been punctured for N_A. This will be our leverage to achieve forward security.

Additionally, the PPRF is an essential building block to achieve full synchronization robustness in our protocols. Intuitively, the puncturing procedure of a PPRF does not evolve its key "linearly" but rather enables fine-grained removal of evaluation capabilities. This guarantees that every protocol run with some fresh value N_A for $\mathsf{Eval}(\mathrm{k}, \mathsf{N}_A)$ will be completed successfully, even if other protocol runs with some value $\mathsf{N}'_A \neq \mathsf{N}_A$ are executed in-between.

Our protocols. We present a one-message and a two-message protocol, based on PPRFs. Both protocols have fixed roles, meaning the same party will always initiate (and only this party is required to store the counter). The two-message protocol implicitly authenticates both parties (and thus achieves mutual authentication), while the one-message protocol inherently only achieves responder-only authentication (responder authenticates initiator). Hence, we will only focus on the two-message protocol shown in Fig. 10 and provide a description and security analysis for the one-message protocol in the full version [11].

Another important aspect of our protocols is that they use counters to systematically "exhaust" the PPRF. We will later discuss that this approach assists the efficiency of tree-based PPRFs as discussed in Aviram et al. [3]. The number of session keys that can be derived is equal to the size of the counter space.

In the full version [11] we prove that protocol PP2 shown in Fig. 10 provides key indistinguishability and mutual authentication. The reduction is standard, and we require SEUF-CMA-Q of the MAC and rand security of the puncturable PRF.

Initiator		**Responder**
$(\mathsf{k}_{AB}, \mathsf{K}^{\mathsf{MAC}}, \mathsf{CTR})$		$(\mathsf{k}_{BA}, \mathsf{K}^{\mathsf{MAC}})$
$\mathsf{N}_A \leftarrow \mathsf{CTR}$		
$\sigma_1 \leftarrow \mathsf{Mac}(\mathsf{K}^{\mathsf{MAC}}, A \parallel \mathsf{N}_A)$	$\xrightarrow{\mathsf{N}_A, \sigma_1}$	
$\mathsf{CTR} \leftarrow \mathsf{CTR} + 1$		**if** $\mathsf{Vrfy}(\mathsf{K}^{\mathsf{MAC}}, A \parallel \mathsf{N}_A, \sigma_1) = 0$
		Abort
		$x_B \leftarrow \mathsf{Eval}(\mathsf{k}_{BA}, \mathsf{N}_A)$
		if $x_B = \perp$
		Abort
	$\xleftarrow{\sigma_2}$	$\sigma_2 \leftarrow \mathsf{Mac}(\mathsf{K}^{\mathsf{MAC}}, B \parallel \mathsf{N}_A)$
if $\mathsf{Vrfy}(\mathsf{K}^{\mathsf{MAC}}, B \parallel \mathsf{N}_A, \sigma_2) = 0$		$sk_{AB} \leftarrow x_B$
Abort		$\mathsf{k}_{BA} \leftarrow \mathsf{Punct}(\mathsf{k}_{BA}, \mathsf{N}_A)$
$x_A \leftarrow \mathsf{Eval}(\mathsf{k}_{AB}, \mathsf{N}_A)$		
if $x_A = \perp$		
Abort		
$sk_{AB} \leftarrow x_A$		
$\mathsf{k}_{AB} \leftarrow \mathsf{Punct}(\mathsf{k}_{AB}, \mathsf{N}_A)$		

Fig. 10. A symmetric AKE protocol PP2 that tolerates concurrent sessions, using a puncturable PRF $\mathsf{PPRF} = (\mathsf{Setup}, \mathsf{Eval}, \mathsf{Punct})$.

4.3 Synchronization Robustness of PP2

In the full version [11] we prove that PP2 achieves full synchronization robustness (SR) with security bound $\mathsf{Adv}_{\Pi}^{\mathsf{SR}}(\mathcal{A}) \leq n^2 \cdot \mathsf{Adv}_{\mathsf{MAC}}^{\mathsf{SEUF\text{-}CMA\text{-}}Q}(\mathcal{B})$, and here we give a high-level overview of the proof strategy. Intuitively we want to show that any adversary, making arbitrary message delivery queries between any of the parties (and their session oracles), cannot cause an adversarially chosen but honestly executed target protocol run to break down.

The robustness proof essentially needs three arguments: 1) the adversary cannot forge protocol messages without breaking the security of the MAC, 2) replaying messages from the target protocol run to other oracles is not beneficial to the adversary, and 3) the correctness of the PPRF ensures that interleaving queries with nonce values different to the one used in the target session will not influence the successful computation of a session key in the target session.

4.4 Instantiation

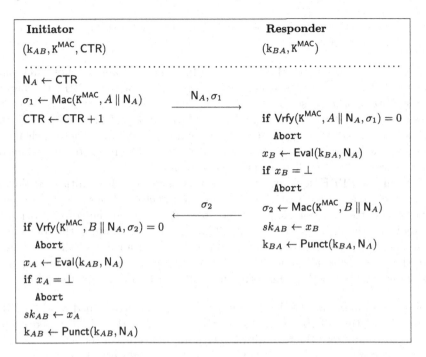

It remains to discuss how PP2 can be instantiated with a PPRF and what impact the PPRF has on its efficiency. A promising candidate is the Goldreich–Goldwasser–Micali PRF [19], which can be transformed to a PPRF [10,13,24]. We give an intuitive explanation of the construction and refer the reader to [3] for a more detailed description and analysis. This construction is especially suitable, as both the PPRF evaluation and puncturing are solely based on hash function evaluations in practice.

Intuition. The tree-based PPRF uses two functions H_0 and H_1 both mapping from $\{0,1\}^\lambda$ to $\{0,1\}^\lambda$. For every input $x \in \{0,1\}^\lambda$ of the PPRF, the binary representation of x prescribes the sequence in which H_0 and H_1 have to be repeatedly applied to x. For example, $\mathsf{Eval}(01) = H_1(H_0(x))$. Note that the evaluation of x corresponds to a path through a binary tree, where each bit in x tells you whether to take a "left" or "right" path. The result of an evaluation always corresponds to a leaf in the binary tree.

The initial PPRF key consists of the root node, which is initialized during key generation as a randomly chosen string. To puncture values (i.e., to puncture leaves of the tree), we precompute and store all nodes on the co-path between the root and the leaf, before deleting all parent nodes (including the root node) of the leaf. Note that this procedure can be repeated for any of the leaves and note that it satisfies all puncturing-relevant properties (i.e., re-computation of $\mathsf{Eval}(x)$ is not possible but the correctness of the PPRF remains intact).

Memory Consumption. We briefly discuss the memory consumed by the PPRF during the lifetime of PP2 (and PP1). First, note that the PPRF-based protocols deploy counters, which (if all messages are delivered in sequence) ensure a systematic puncturing from the leftmost leaf to the rightmost leaf of the binary tree. This yields the need to store at most $\log(|\mathsf{CTR}|)$ tree nodes (i.e., at most one node per layer of the tree) at any point in time. For C concurrent sessions, this bound increases to a maximum of $C \cdot \log(|\mathsf{CTR}|)$ tree nodes.

The analysis gets slightly more difficult if an adversary *actively drops* protocols messages. Each dropped message will either cause the initiator or both parties to not puncture at some position. One approach to tame the memory consumption in this case, would be to always puncture on all values which are smaller than $\mathsf{CTR}-C$.[1] As we never expect more than C sessions in parallel, this reduces additional memory caused by lost messages. In this case, the memory consumption is again upper-bounded by $C \cdot \log(|\mathsf{CTR}|)$ tree nodes.

Finally, note that in the one-message protocol PP1 [11] the initiator always punctures strictly in order and thus has to store at most $\log(|\mathsf{CTR}|)$ tree nodes. This may be particularly useful in an application where many low-end devices communicate with a central server.

References

1. Alwen, J., Coretti, S., Dodis, Y.: The double ratchet: security notions, proofs, and modularization for the signal protocol. In: Ishai, Y., Rijmen, V. (eds.) EUROCRYPT 2019. LNCS, vol. 11476, pp. 129–158. Springer, Cham (2019). https://doi.org/10.1007/978-3-030-17653-2_5

[1] Interestingly, the tree-based PPRF can puncture multiple values in one go by "chopping off" whole branches of the tree, instead of puncturing all values one after another.

2. Retail Financial Services Symmetric Key Management Part 1: Using Symmetric Techniques (ANSI x9.24). Standard, American National Standards Institute, New York, USA (2009)
3. Aviram, N., Gellert, K., Jager, T.: Session resumption protocols and efficient forward security for TLS 1.3 0-RTT. In: Ishai, Y., Rijmen, V. (eds.) EUROCRYPT 2019. LNCS, vol. 11477, pp. 117–150. Springer, Cham (2019). https://doi.org/10.1007/978-3-030-17656-3_5
4. Avoine, G., Canard, S., Ferreira, L.: Symmetric-key authenticated key exchange (SAKE) with perfect forward secrecy. In: Jarecki, S. (ed.) CT-RSA 2020. LNCS, vol. 12006, pp. 199–224. Springer, Cham (2020). https://doi.org/10.1007/978-3-030-40186-3_10
5. Bellare, M., Goldreich, O., Mityagin, A.: The power of verification queries in message authentication and authenticated encryption. Cryptology ePrint Archive, Report 2004/309 (2004). http://eprint.iacr.org/2004/309
6. Bellare, M., Miner, S.K.: A forward-secure digital signature scheme. In: Wiener, M. (ed.) CRYPTO 1999. LNCS, vol. 1666, pp. 431–448. Springer, Heidelberg (1999). https://doi.org/10.1007/3-540-48405-1_28
7. Bellare, M., Pointcheval, D., Rogaway, P.: Authenticated key exchange secure against dictionary attacks. In: Preneel, B. (ed.) EUROCRYPT 2000. LNCS, vol. 1807, pp. 139–155. Springer, Heidelberg (2000). https://doi.org/10.1007/3-540-45539-6_11
8. Bellare, M., Rogaway, P.: Entity authentication and key distribution. In: Stinson, D.R. (ed.) CRYPTO 1993. LNCS, vol. 773, pp. 232–249. Springer, Heidelberg (1994). https://doi.org/10.1007/3-540-48329-2_21
9. Bellare, M., Yee, B.: Forward-security in private-key cryptography. In: Joye, M. (ed.) CT-RSA 2003. LNCS, vol. 2612, pp. 1–18. Springer, Heidelberg (2003). https://doi.org/10.1007/3-540-36563-X_1
10. Boneh, D., Waters, B.: Constrained pseudorandom functions and their applications. In: Sako, K., Sarkar, P. (eds.) ASIACRYPT 2013. LNCS, vol. 8270, pp. 280–300. Springer, Heidelberg (2013). https://doi.org/10.1007/978-3-642-42045-0_15
11. Boyd, C., Davies, G.T., de Kock, B., Gellert, K., Jager, T., Millerjord, L.: Symmetric key exchange with full forward security and robust synchronization. IACR Cryptol. ePrint Arch, p. 702 (2021). https://eprint.iacr.org/2021/702
12. Boyd, C., Gellert, K.: A modern view on forward security. Comput. J. (2020). https://doi.org/10.1093/comjnl/bxaa104
13. Boyle, E., Goldwasser, S., Ivan, I.: Functional signatures and pseudorandom functions. In: Krawczyk, H. (ed.) PKC 2014. LNCS, vol. 8383, pp. 501–519. Springer, Heidelberg (2014). https://doi.org/10.1007/978-3-642-54631-0_29
14. Brier, E., Peyrin, T.: A forward-secure symmetric-key derivation protocol. In: Abe, M. (ed.) ASIACRYPT 2010. LNCS, vol. 6477, pp. 250–267. Springer, Heidelberg (2010). https://doi.org/10.1007/978-3-642-17373-8_15
15. Canetti, R., Krawczyk, H.: Analysis of key-exchange protocols and their use for building secure channels. In: Pfitzmann, B. (ed.) EUROCRYPT 2001. LNCS, vol. 2045, pp. 453–474. Springer, Heidelberg (2001). https://doi.org/10.1007/3-540-44987-6_28
16. Cini, V., Ramacher, S., Slamanig, D., Striecks, C.: CCA-secure (Puncturable) KEMs from encryption with non-negligible decryption errors. In: Moriai, S., Wang, H. (eds.) ASIACRYPT 2020. LNCS, vol. 12491, pp. 159–190. Springer, Cham (2020). https://doi.org/10.1007/978-3-030-64837-4_6

17. Derler, D., Jager, T., Slamanig, D., Striecks, C.: Bloom filter encryption and applications to efficient forward-secret 0-RTT key exchange. In: Nielsen, J.B., Rijmen, V. (eds.) EUROCRYPT 2018. LNCS, vol. 10822, pp. 425–455. Springer, Cham (2018). https://doi.org/10.1007/978-3-319-78372-7_14
18. Dousti, M.S., Jalili, R.: FORSAKES: a forward-secure authenticated key exchange protocol based on symmetric key-evolving schemes. Adv. Math. Commun. **9**(4), 471–514 (2015). https://doi.org/10.3934/amc.2015.9.471
19. Goldreich, O., Goldwasser, S., Micali, S.: How to construct random functions. J. ACM **33**(4), 792–807 (1986)
20. Green, M.D., Miers, I.: Forward secure asynchronous messaging from puncturable encryption. In: 2015 IEEE Symposium on Security and Privacy, pp. 305–320. IEEE Computer Society Press, May 2015. https://doi.org/10.1109/SP.2015.26
21. Günther, F., Hale, B., Jager, T., Lauer, S.: 0-RTT key exchange with full forward secrecy. In: Coron, J.-S., Nielsen, J.B. (eds.) EUROCRYPT 2017. LNCS, vol. 10212, pp. 519–548. Springer, Cham (2017). https://doi.org/10.1007/978-3-319-56617-7_18
22. FIPS 198–1: The Keyed-Hash Message Authentication Code (HMAC). Standard, NIST (2008)
23. Jager, T., Kohlar, F., Schäge, S., Schwenk, J.: On the security of TLS-DHE in the standard model. In: Safavi-Naini, R., Canetti, R. (eds.) CRYPTO 2012. LNCS, vol. 7417, pp. 273–293. Springer, Heidelberg (2012). https://doi.org/10.1007/978-3-642-32009-5_17
24. Kiayias, A., Papadopoulos, S., Triandopoulos, N., Zacharias, T.: Delegatable pseudorandom functions and applications. In: Sadeghi, A.R., Gligor, V.D., Yung, M. (eds.) ACM CCS 2013, pp. 669–684. ACM Press, November 2013. https://doi.org/10.1145/2508859.2516668
25. (NIST SP)-800-185: SHA-3 derived functions: cSHAKE, KMAC, TupleHash and ParallelHash. Special Publication. Standard, NIST (2016)
26. Krawczyk, H.: HMQV: a high-performance secure Diffie-Hellman protocol. In: Shoup, V. (ed.) CRYPTO 2005. LNCS, vol. 3621, pp. 546–566. Springer, Heidelberg (2005). https://doi.org/10.1007/11535218_33
27. Le, T.V., Burmester, M., de Medeiros, B.: Universally composable and forward-secure RFID authentication and authenticated key exchange. In: Bao, F., Miller, S. (eds.) ASIACCS 07, pp. 242–252. ACM Press, Mar 2007
28. Li, Y., Schäge, S., Yang, Z., Kohlar, F., Schwenk, J.: On the security of the pre-shared key Ciphersuites of TLS. In: Krawczyk, H. (ed.) PKC 2014. LNCS, vol. 8383, pp. 669–684. Springer, Heidelberg (2014). https://doi.org/10.1007/978-3-642-54631-0_38
29. Sahai, A., Waters, B.: How to use indistinguishability obfuscation: deniable encryption, and more. In: Shmoys, D.B. (ed.) 46th ACM STOC, pp. 475–484. ACM Press, May/June 2014. https://doi.org/10.1145/2591796.2591825
30. Sun, S.-F., Sakzad, A., Steinfeld, R., Liu, J.K., Gu, D.: Public-Key puncturable encryption: modular and compact constructions. In: Kiayias, A., Kohlweiss, M., Wallden, P., Zikas, V. (eds.) PKC 2020. LNCS, vol. 12110, pp. 309–338. Springer, Cham (2020). https://doi.org/10.1007/978-3-030-45374-9_11

Security Analysis of CPace

Michel Abdalla[1,2(✉)], Björn Haase[3(✉)], and Julia Hesse[4(✉)]

[1] DIENS, École normale supérieure, CNRS, PSL University, Paris, France
[2] DFINITY, Zürich, Switzerland
[3] Endress+Hauser Liquid Analysis, Gerlingen, Germany
bjoern.haase@endress.com
[4] IBM Research Europe, Zürich, Switzerland
jhs@zurich.ibm.com

Abstract. In response to standardization requests regarding password-authenticated key exchange (PAKE) protocols, the IRTF working group CFRG has setup a PAKE selection process in 2019, which led to the selection of the CPace protocol in the balanced setting, in which parties share a common password. In subsequent standardization efforts, the CPace protocol further developed, yielding a protocol family whose actual security guarantees in practical settings are not well understood. In this paper, we provide a comprehensive security analysis of CPace in the universal composability framework. Our analysis is *realistic* in the sense that it captures adaptive corruptions and refrains from modeling CPace's Map2Pt function that maps field elements to curve points as an idealized function. In order to extend our proofs to different CPace variants optimized for specific elliptic-curve ecosystems, we employ a new approach which represents the assumptions required by the proof as libraries accessed by a simulator. By allowing for the modular replacement of assumptions used in the proof, this new approach avoids a repeated analysis of unchanged protocol parts and lets us efficiently analyze the security guarantees of all the different CPace variants. As a result of our analysis, all of the investigated practical CPace variants enjoy adaptive UC security.

1 Introduction

Security analysis and efficient implementation of cryptographic protocols are often split into separate working groups. As a result, subtle differences between the actually implemented and analyzed protocols easily emerge, for example when implementors slightly tweak the protocol to improve efficiency. An example where particularly aggressive optimizations for efficiency are implemented on the protocol level is CPace as specified in current internet drafts [23,24]. CPace is a password-authenticated key exchange protocol (PAKE) [8], which

J. Hesse—Author supported by the European Union's Horizon 2020 Research and Innovation Programme under Grant Agreement No. 786725 OLYMPUS.

M. Tibouchi and H. Wang (Eds.): ASIACRYPT 2021, LNCS 13093, pp. 711–741, 2021.
https://doi.org/10.1007/978-3-030-92068-5_24

allows two parties to establish a shared cryptographic key from matching passwords of potentially low entropy. PAKEs are extremely useful for establishing secure and authenticated communication channels between peers sharing short common knowledge. The common knowledge could be a PIN typed into different wearables in order to pair them, sensor readings recorded by several cars in order to create an authenticated platoon or a security code manually entered by an admin to connect her maintenance laptop with a backbone router.

On a high level, CPace works as follows. Given a cyclic group $\mathcal{G}$, parties first locally and deterministically compute a generator $g \leftarrow \mathsf{Gen}(\mathsf{pw}), g \in \mathcal{G}$ from their passwords in a secure way, so that g reveals as little information about the password as possible. Then, both parties perform a Diffie-Hellman key exchange by choosing secret exponents x and y, respectively, exchanging g^x and g^y and locally compute $K = (g^x)^y = (g^y)^x$. The final key is then computed as the hash of K together with session-identifying information such as transcript. The currently most efficient implementations of the above blueprint protocol use elliptic curve groups of either prime or composite order. To securely compute the generator, the password is first hashed to the finite field $\mathbb{F}_q$ over which the curve is constructed, and then mapped to the curve by a map called $\mathsf{Map2Pt}$. Depending on the choice of curve, efficiency tweaks such as simplified point verification on curves with twist security, or computation with only x-coordinates of points can be applied [22,23]. Unfortunately, until today, it is not clear how these modifications impact security of CPace, and whether the protocol can be proven secure without assuming $(\mathsf{Map2Pt} \circ \mathsf{H})$ to be a truly random function.

A short history of CPace. In 1996, Jablon [30] introduced the SPEKE protocol, which performs a Diffie-Hellman key exchange with generators computed as $g \leftarrow \mathsf{H}_{\mathcal{G}}(\mathsf{pw})$, i.e. using a function $\mathsf{H}_{\mathcal{G}}$ hashing directly to the group. Many variants of SPEKE have emerged in the literature since then, including ones that fixed initial security issues of SPEKE. Among them, the PACE protocol [9,33] aims at circumventing direct hashing onto the group with an interactive $\mathsf{Map2Pt}$ protocol to compute the password-dependent generators. From this, CPace [22] emerged by combining the best properties of PACE and SPEKE, namely computing the generator without interaction while avoiding the need to hash directly onto the group. More precisely, password-dependent generators are computed as $g \leftarrow \mathsf{Map2Pt}(\mathsf{H}(\mathsf{pw}))$. In 2020, the IRTF working group CFRG has chosen CPace as the recommended protocol for (symmetric) PAKE.

Prior work on the security of CPace. Bender et al. [9] conducted a game-based security analysis of the explicitly authenticated PACE protocol variants used in travel documents. Their work focusses on different variants of *interactive* $\mathsf{Map2Pt}$ constructions and hence does not allow for any conclusions about CPace which uses a (non-interactive) function $\mathsf{Map2Pt}$.

Static security of CPace, including function $\mathsf{Map2Pt}$ and some implementation artifacts such as cofactor clearing, was formally analyzed in [22]. Their work is the first to attempt a formalization of $\mathsf{Map2Pt}$ that allows for a security analysis. However, their proof was found to be insufficient by reviews done during the CFRG selection process [28,37], and indeed, the claimed security under the plain computational Diffie-Hellman assumption seems to be difficult to achieve. Besides these issues, their work does not consider adaptive corruptions and implementation artifacts such as twist security or single-coordinate representations.

Abdalla et al. [1] analyzed static security of several EKE [8] and SPEKE variants in the UC framework, including SPAKE2 [5] and TBPEKE [34]. They indicate that their proof for TBPEKE could be extended to CPace with generators computed as $\mathsf{H}_{\mathcal{G}}(pw)$ (i.e., without function $\mathsf{Map2Pt}$) if the protocol transcript and password-dependent generator is included in the final key derivation hash. However, in practice it is desirable to avoid unnecessary hash inputs for efficiency reasons and protection against side-channel attacks.

In a concurrent work, Abdalla et al. [2] formalized the algebraic group model within the UC framework and proved that the SPAKE2 and CPace protocols are universally composable in the new model with respect to the standard functionality for password-based authenticated key exchange in [15]. Stebila and Eaton [19] provided a game-based analysis of CPace in the generic group model. As in [1], these further studies do not deal with adaptive security and only consider a basic version of CPace without $\mathsf{Map2Pt}$ and without considering any implementation artifacts.

The above analyses demonstrate that a basic version of CPace, which essentially is a Diffie-Hellman key exchange computed on hashed passwords instead of a public generator, is UC-secure if the attacker is restricted to static corruptions. Unfortunately, this leaves many open questions. Does this basic protocol remain (UC-)secure if we use generator $\mathsf{Map2Pt}(\mathsf{H}(pw))$ instead, as it is done in practice to avoid direct hashing onto elliptic curves? Can the protocol handle adaptive corruptions? Which impact on security do implementation artifacts have, such as co-factor clearing on a composite-order curve group, or single-coordinate representation as used in, e.g., TLS1.3? Can we reduce hash inputs in order to make the protocol less prone to side-channel attacks? Altogether, it turns out the security of the *actually implemented* CPace protocol is not well understood.

Our Contributions. In this paper, we provide the first comprehensive security analysis of the CPace protocol that applies also to variants of CPace optimized for usage with state-of-the-art elliptic curves. We identify the core properties of the deterministic $\mathsf{Map2Pt}$ function that allow to prove strong security properties of CPace. Crucially, we restrict the use of random oracles to hash functions only and refrain from modeling $\mathsf{Map2Pt}$ as an idealized function, as it would not be clear how to instantiate it in practice. We show that, using some weak invertibility properties of $\mathsf{Map2Pt}$ that we demonstrate to hold for candidate implementations, CPace can be proven secure under standard Diffie-Hellman-type assumptions in the random-oracle model and with only minimal session-identifying information included in the final key derivation hash. Our security proof captures adaptive corruptions and weak forward secrecy[1] and is carried out in the Universal Composability (UC) framework, which is today's standard when analyzing security of password-based protocols. Our work provides the first evidence that SPEKE-type protocols can handle adaptive corruptions.

We then turn our attention to modifications of CPace and, for each modification individually, state under which assumptions the security properties are preserved. In more detail, our analysis captures the following modifications.

- Using groups of composite order $c \cdot p$, where p is a large prime and c is a small cofactor coprime to p.
- Realize $\mathsf{Gen}(\mathsf{pw})$ generator calculations using $\mathsf{Map2Pt}$ with either map-twice-and-add strategy or as single execution.
- Using single-coordinate-only representations of elliptic-curve points in order to speed up and facilitate implementation.
- Avoiding computationally costly point verification on curves with secure quadratic twists such as Curve25519 [10].

To demonstrate the security of these variants, we take a new approach that saves us from a repeated analysis of unchanged parts of CPace. Namely, we implement the CDH-type cryptographic assumptions required by CPace as libraries which a simulator can access. This allows for modular replacement of assumptions required in the security proof, and lets us efficiently analyze all the different CPace variants' security guarantees. We believe that this new proof technique might be of independent interest in particular for machine-assisted proving, since reductions are captured in code instead of textual descriptions only.

As a side contribution, we identify a common shortcoming in all UC PAKE security definitions in the literature [1,15,29,31], which impacts the suitability of these definitions as building blocks in higher-level applications. Namely, all these definitions allow a malicious party to learn the shared key computed by an honest party *without knowing her password.* We strengthen the definition to prevent such attacks, and demonstrate with our analysis of CPace that our fix yields a security definition that is still met by PAKE protocols.

In conclusion, our results demonstrate that CPace enjoys strong provable security guarantees in a realistic setting, and this holds for all its variants that have been proposed in the different elliptic-curve ecosystems.

1.1 Technical Overview of Our Results

$\mathsf{Map2Pt}$'s impact on security. At its core, the CPace protocol is a SPEKE-type protocol, meaning that it is simply a Diffie-Hellman key exchange (DHKE) computed with a generator that each party *individually* computes from her password. Intuitively, the most secure choice is to compute $g \leftarrow \mathsf{H}_{\mathcal{G}}(pw)$, and indeed this was proven secure [1,2] conditioned on H being a perfect hash function (or, put

[1] In the case of PAKE, weak forward secrecy is implied by UC security and hence achieved also by prior work. If key confirmation is added, then this gives a protocol with perfect forward secrecy as noted in [1].

differently, a random oracle (RO)). However, DHKE-type protocols are most efficient when implemented on elliptic-curve groups, and it is not known how to efficiently hash directly onto such groups. Recent standardization efforts by the CFRG [20] show that, in practice, one would always first hash to the finite field $\mathbb{F}_q$ over which the curve is constructed, and then map the field element to the curve $\mathcal{G}$ using some curve-specific mapping $\mathsf{Map2Pt} : \mathbb{F}_q \to \mathcal{G}$. Hence, the generator in CPace can be assumed to be computed as $g \leftarrow \mathsf{Map2Pt}(\mathsf{H}(pw))$ for a H being a hash function such as SHA-3.

In order to analyze how the function $\mathsf{Map2Pt}$ impacts CPace's security, it is obviously not helpful to abstract $\mathsf{Map2Pt} \circ \mathsf{H}$ as a truly random function. In a first attempt to analyze under which properties of $\mathsf{Map2Pt}$ CPace remains secure, Haase et al. [22] assumed $\mathsf{Map2Pt}$ to be a bijection. Intuitively, a bijective $\mathsf{Map2Pt}$ function does not "disturb" the "nice" distribution of the prepended hash function, and in particular does not introduce any collisions. Besides the known shortcomings in their conducted analysis (the claimed security under CDH does not seem to hold, and their proof lacks an indistinguishability argument [28, 37]), it does not cover non-bijective mappings on widely used short-weierstrass curves such as NIST P-256. Hence, in our work we refrain from assuming $\mathsf{Map2Pt}$ to be a bijection. Instead, we introduce a property of *probabilistic invertibility*, which demands that, given an element g in the group $\mathcal{G}$, we can efficiently compute all preimages $h \in \mathbb{F}_q$ such that $\mathsf{Map2Pt}(h) = g$. On a high level, this invertibility property will aid the simulation of CPace since it allows to "tightly" link a group element g to a previously computed hash h and thus recognize collisions efficiently. Here, tightly/efficiently means without iterating over all hash queries in the system. We demonstrate that all mappings used in practice [20] are probabilistically invertible. As a result, we conclude that CPace implemented with current mappings enjoys strong security guarantees.

Adaptive security. Just like any other PAKE protocol, CPace comes with a large likelihood for idling. Indeed, in practice it will most likely be the same person who jumps between the two devices running the PAKE, to manually enter the same password, PIN or code. This gives room for attackers to corrupt devices *during the run of the protocol*, and hence calls for analyzing security of CPace in the presence of *adaptive corruptions*. To our knowledge, there is no proof of adaptive security for any SPEKE-type protocol in the literature. In this work, we closely investigate CPace's guarantees under adaptive corruptions and come to an indeed surprising conclusion:

CPace enjoys adaptive UC security under the same DH-type assumptions that seem required for static security.

The challenge of proving adaptive security lies in the need to reveal suitable secret values computed by a previously honest party during the run of the protocol. For CPace, these are the secret Diffie-Hellman exponents x, y randomly chosen by parties. A bit simplified, our idea is to start the simulation of an honest party with g^z for a generator g of group $\mathcal{G}$ and randomly chosen exponent z, and hence independent of the actual (unknown) password used by that party. Upon corruption, the simulator learns pw and looks up the corresponding hash value $g^r = \mathsf{H}(pw)$ for which it knows r^{-1} thanks to H being modeled as a random oracle. This allows the simulator to compute the "actual" secret exponent $y \leftarrow zr^{-1}$ that the simulated party would have used if started with actual password pw. Crucially, no additional assumptions or secure erasures are required and, as we demonstrate in the body of our paper, this simplified strategy still works when generators are computed using $\mathsf{Map2Pt} \circ \mathsf{H}$. Altogether, our analysis shows that CPace enjoys UC-security under adaptive corruptions.

Falsifiable assumptions and a new approach to simulation-based proofs. A falsifiable assumption can be modeled as an interactive game between an *efficient* challenger and an adversary, at the conclusion of which the challenger can efficiently decide whether the adversary won the game [21]. Most standard cryptographic assumptions such as CDH, DDH, RSA, and LWE are falsifiable. An example of a non-falsifiable assumption is the gap simultaneous Diffie-Hellman assumption, which was used in prior CPace security analyses [1,2] and features a full DDH oracle that cannot be efficiently implemented by the challenger. Intuitively, the DDH oracle seems inherent for proving UC security of CPace since the attacker (more detailed, the distinguishing environment) determines passwords pw used by honest parties and also receives their outputs, which is the final key K. More detailed, the attacker can deterministically compute the generator G used by an honest party from only pw, and it also receives the honest party's message g^x. The attacker can now enforce the final key to be a DDH tuple $K = g^{xy}$ by simply sending g^y to the honest party (we omit the final key derivation hash in this explanation for simplicity). Hence, to correctly simulate the final key output by an honest party under attack, the simulator relies on a DDH oracle. However, we observe that this oracle can be *limited to specific inputs* g, g^x that the attacker cannot influence. This turns out to be an important limitation, because the *restricted* DDH oracle $DDH(g, g^x, \cdot, \cdot)$ can actually be implemented efficiently using knowledge of trapdoor exponents r, r^{-1} of g. Thus, our conclusion is that CPace's security holds under falsifiable DH-type assumptions.

As another contribution, we define falsifiable assumptions as efficiently implementable libraries that a simulator can call. The advantage of this approach is that reductions to the underlying assumptions are *integrated* in the simulator's code, which will hence abort and detect itself whenever a query to the library solves the underlying hard problem. This makes reduction strategies readable from simulator codes and hence opens a new path for automatic verification of simulation-based proofs. While we demonstrate this only to work for proofs conducted in the UC framework and when using variants of strong CDH, we conjecture that our approach can be used for simulation-based proofs in arbitrary frameworks whenever only falsifiable assumptions are used.

Minimal protocol design. For optimal protection against side-channel attacks, we would like to have parties touch their passwords as little as possible. Optimally, passwords are only used to compute the generator of the DHKE. Unfortunately, in simulation-based frameworks a security proof often crucially relies on hashing of secrets, and indeed previous CPace security analysis has relied on the password being included in the final key derivation hash [1]. In this work we ask what the minimal set of protocol-related values is that needs to be included in both hash functions used in CPace. Perhaps surprisingly, we find that CPace's security can be proven when (1) the password hash does not get any additional inputs and (2) the final key derivation hash is over session-specific values and the Diffie-Hellman key. Regarding (1), we observe that the simulation strategy (described above for adaptive corruptions) works even if the generator g chosen by the simulator is used to simulate multiple instances of CPace, and where different parties use the same password: Choosing fresh secret exponents z_A for each such simulated party A ensures that all the revealed exponents $z_A r^-1$ are still uniformly distributed. Regarding (2), our simulation simply does not need to learn the password from an adversarial key derivation hash query: The simulator simply reads the simulated parts g^z and adversarial part Y of the transcript from the hash query and checks consistency of the query's format by checking whether it is a DDH tuple with respect to each trapdoor generated upon password hashing. Since there can be only a polynomial number of such queries, this simulation strategy is tight and efficient and saves us from hashing the password another time.

Implementation artifacts. Depending on the type of curve CPace is deployed in, the implementation will vary in certain aspects for which it is not clear how they will impact CPace's security. By adopting the security analysis to capture actual $\mathsf{Map2Pt}$ mappings used in practice we already demonstrated how to deal with the probably most important such artifact above. Closely related to this, we also analyze security of CPace when implemented on curves of composite order $p \cdot c$ with a small co-factor c, which needs to be "cleared" in order to ensure that parties use generators of the large subgroup. We can integrate this modification by chaining $\mathsf{Map2Pt}$ with a co-factor clearing function and by demonstrating that the resulting mapping is still probabilistically invertible. Technically, we "lift" our proof of security w.r.t simple $\mathsf{Map2Pt}$ described above by letting the simulator call a co-factor clearing class that ensures that simulated values will remain in the large subgroup.

A typical implementation pitfall is incorrectly implemented group-membership verification. As such a failure easily remains unnoticed, optimized resilient protocols such as X25519 and X448 [32] have been suggested for the conventional Diffie-Hellman use-case. We believe that we are the first to formalize the exact hardness assumption, the twist CDH problem sTCDH, under which the claimed resilience regarding group membership omission is actually justified. We show that under the sTCDH assumption, resilience with respect to incorrectly implemented point verification can also be achieved for CPace, when instantiated using single-coordinate Montgomery ladders on so-called "twist-secure" [12] elliptic curves. For details on how to deal with other implementation artifacts we refer the reader to Sect. 6 in the main body of the paper.

Roadmap. We introduce the PAKE security model in Sect. 2 and hardness assumptions and requirements for $\mathsf{Map2Pt}$ in Sect. 3. Details of the CPace protocol are in Sect. 4. Then we analyse CPace, first using a simplified CPace in Sect. 5 (modeling the map as random-oracle) and then extending the analysis to real-world instantiations using actually deployed mapping constructions, composite-order groups, details on twist security and single-coordinate representations in Sect. 6. We defer the reader to the full version of this paper [4] for proofs, a description of issues with previous UC PAKE functionalities and implementation recommendations.

2 PAKE Security Model

We use the Universal Composability (UC) framework of Canetti [14] to formulate security properties of CPace. For PAKE, usage of the simulation-based UC framework comes with several advantages over the game-based model for PAKE introduced by Bellare et al. [7]. Most importantly, UC secure PAKE protocols preserve their security properties in the presence of adversarially-chosen passwords and when composed with arbitrary other protocols. Originally introduced by Canetti et al. [15], the ideal functionality $\mathcal{F}_{\mathsf{pwKE}}$ for PAKE (depicted in Fig. 1) is accessed by two parties, $\mathcal{P}$ and $\mathcal{P}'$, who both provide their passwords. $\mathcal{F}_{\mathsf{pwKE}}$ then provides both parties with a uniformly random session key if passwords match, and with individual random keys if passwords mismatch. Since an adversary can always engage in a session and guess the counterpart's password with non-negligible probability, $\mathcal{F}_{\mathsf{pwKE}}$ must include an adversarial interface TestPwd for such guesses. Crucially, only one guess against every honest party is allowed, modeling the fact that password guessing is an online attack and cannot be used to brute-force the password from a protocol's transcript. We refer the reader to [15] for a more comprehensive introduction to the PAKE functionality.

An ideal functionality for the SPEKE protocol family. Unfortunately, $\mathcal{F}_{\mathsf{pwKE}}$ is not suitable to analyze SPEKE-like PAKE protocols such as CPace, where session keys are computed as hashes of Diffie-Hellman keys (and possibly parts of the transcript). The reason is that $\mathcal{F}_{\mathsf{pwKE}}$'s TestPwd interface allows password guesses only *during* a protocol run, which requires a simulator to extract password guesses from the protocol's transcript. When the final output is a hash, the adversary might postpone its computation, keeping information from the simulator that is required for password extraction. To circumvent these issues, recently a "lazy-extraction PAKE" functionality $\mathcal{F}_{\mathsf{lePAKE}}$ was proposed and shown useful in the analysis of SPEKE-like protocols by Abdalla et al. [1]. $\mathcal{F}_{\mathsf{lePAKE}}$, which we also depict in Fig. 1, allows *either* one online *or* one offline password guess after the key exchange was finished. One might argue that usage of keys obtained from $\mathcal{F}_{\mathsf{lePAKE}}$ is never safe, since the adversary might eventually extract the key from it at any later point in time. This however can be easily prevented by adding a key confirmation round, which keeps an adversary from postponing the final hash query and guarantees perfect forward secrecy [1]. We refer the reader to [1] for a thorough discussion of $\mathcal{F}_{\mathsf{lePAKE}}$.

Our adjustments to $\mathcal{F}_{\mathsf{lePAKE}}$. The main difference between our $\mathcal{F}_{\mathsf{lePAKE}}$ and all PAKE functionalities from the literature [1,15,29,31] is that we remove a shortcoming that rendered these functionalities essentially useless as building blocks for higher-level applications. More detailed, we remove the ability of the adversary to determine an honest party's output key in a corrupted session. The change can be seen in Fig. 1, where the dashed box shows the weakening that we simply omit in our version of $\mathcal{F}_{\mathsf{lePAKE}}$. In reality, nobody would want to use a PAKE where an adversary can learn (even set) the key of an honest party *without knowing the honest party's password.* This is not what one would expect from an authenticated key exchange protocol. In the full version of this work [4] we explain why existing PAKE protocols can still be considered secure, but also provide an illustrating example how this shortcoming hinders usage of PAKE functionalities in modular protocol analysis. In this paper, we demonstrate that CPace can be proven to protect against such attacks.

We also make two minor adjustments, which are merely to ease presentation in this paper. Namely, we add an explicit interface for adaptive corruptions, and we omit roles since we analyze a protocol where there is no dedicated initiator.

How many keys can a PAKE functionality exchange? All PAKE functionalities in Fig. 1 produce only a single key for a single pair of parties $\mathcal{P}, \mathcal{P}'$. This can be seen from the NewSession interface, which takes action only upon the first such query (from any party $\mathcal{P}$) and the corresponding second query by the indicated counterparty $\mathcal{P}'$. The motivation behind this design choice is simplicity in the security analysis: one can prove security of a PAKE protocol for only a single session, and then run arbitrary many copies of the PAKE functionality to exchange arbitrarily many keys (between arbitrary parties). Consequently, by the UC composition theorem, replacing all those copies with the PAKE protocol that provably realizes the single-session $\mathcal{F}_{\mathsf{pwKE}}$ is at least as secure.

3 Preliminaries

3.1 Notation

With $\leftarrow_{\mathrm{R}}$ we denote uniformly random sampling from a set. With $\mathsf{oc}(X, Y)$ we denote ordered concatenation, i.e., $\mathsf{oc}(X, Y) = X||Y$ if $X \leq Y$ and $\mathsf{oc}(X, Y) = Y||X$ otherwise. We use multiplicative notation for the group operation in a group $\mathcal{G}$ and hence write, e.g., $g \cdot g = g^2$ for an element $g \in \mathcal{G}$. $I_{\mathcal{G}}$ denotes the neutral element in $\mathcal{G}$. To enhance readability, we sometimes break with the convention of denoting group elements with small letters and write $X := g^x$. We denote by $\mathcal{G}_m$ a subgroup of $\mathcal{G}$ of order m, and with $\bar{\mathcal{G}}$ we denote the quadratic twist of elliptic curve group $\mathcal{G}$. Throughout the paper, we use λ as security parameter[2].

[2] For the hardness assumptions on elliptic curve groups, e.g. for the sCDH and sSDH problems, where security depends on the group type and the group order p, the bit size of p implicitly serves also as a further security parameter.

Session initiation

On (NewSession, $sid, \mathcal{P}, \mathcal{P}'$, pw) from $\mathcal{P}$, send (NewSession, $sid, \mathcal{P}, \mathcal{P}'$) to $\mathcal{A}$. In addition, if this is the first NewSession query, or if this is the second NewSession query and there is a record ($sid, \mathcal{P}', \mathcal{P}$, pw'), then record ($sid, \mathcal{P}, \mathcal{P}'$, pw) and mark this record fresh.

Active attack

- On (TestPwd, $sid, \mathcal{P}$, pw*) from $\mathcal{A}$, if $\exists$ a fresh record $\langle sid, \mathcal{P}, \mathcal{P}', \mathsf{pw}, \cdot\rangle$ then:
  - If pw* = pw then mark it compromised and return "correct guess";
  - If pw* $\neq$ pw then mark it interrupted and return "wrong guess".
- On (RegisterTest, $sid, \mathcal{P}$) from $\mathcal{A}$, if $\exists$ a fresh record $\langle sid, \mathcal{P}, \mathcal{P}', \cdot\rangle$ then mark it interrupted and flag it tested.
- On (LateTestPwd, $sid, \mathcal{P}$, pw*) from $\mathcal{A}$, if $\exists$ a record $\langle sid, \mathcal{P}, \mathcal{P}', \mathsf{pw}, K\rangle$ marked completed with flag tested then remove this flag and do:
  - If pw* = pw then return $\boxed{K}$ to $\mathcal{A}$;
  - If pw* $\neq$ pw then return $\boxed{K^{\$} \leftarrow_{\mathrm{R}} \{0,1\}^{\lambda}}$ to $\mathcal{A}$.

Key generation

On (NewKey, $sid, \mathcal{P}, K^*$) from $\mathcal{A}$, if $\exists$ a record $\langle sid, \mathcal{P}, \mathcal{P}', \mathsf{pw}\rangle$ not marked completed then do:

- If the record is compromised, [or either $\mathcal{P}$ or $\mathcal{P}'$ is corrupted,] then $K := K^*$.
- If the record is fresh and $\exists$ a completed record $\langle sid, \mathcal{P}', \mathcal{P}, \mathsf{pw}, K'\rangle$ that was fresh when $\mathcal{P}'$ output (sid, K'), then set $K := K'$.
- In all other cases pick $K \leftarrow_{\mathrm{R}} \{0,1\}^{\lambda}$.

Finally, append K to record $\langle sid, \mathcal{P}, \mathcal{P}', \mathsf{pw}\rangle$, mark it completed, and output (sid, K) to $\mathcal{P}$.

Adaptive corruption

On (AdaptiveCorruption, $sid, \mathcal{P}$) from $\mathcal{A}$, if $\exists$ a record $\langle sid, \mathcal{P}, \cdot, \mathsf{pw}\rangle$ not marked completed then mark it completed and output (sid, pw).

Fig. 1. UC PAKE variants: The original PAKE functionality $\mathcal{F}_{\mathsf{pwKE}}$ of Canetti et al. [15] is the version with all gray text omitted. The lazy-extraction PAKE functionality $\mathcal{F}_{\mathsf{lePAKE}}$ [1] includes everything, and the variant of $\mathcal{F}_{\mathsf{lePAKE}}$ used in this work includes everything but the dashed box.

3.2 Cryptographic Assumptions

The security of CPace is based on the hardness of a combination of strong and simultaneous Diffie-Hellman problems. To ease access to the assumptions, we state them with increasing complexity.

Definition 1 (Strong CDH problem (sCDH) [3]**).** *Let $\mathcal{G}$ be a cyclic group with a generator g and $(X = g^x, Y = g^y)$ sampled uniformly from $(\mathcal{G} \setminus \{I_{\mathcal{G}}\})^2$. Given access to oracles $DDH(g, X, \cdot, \cdot)$ and $DDH(g, Y, \cdot, \cdot)$, provide K such that $K = g^{xy}$.*

We note that sCDH is a weaker variant of the so-called gap-CDH assumption, where the adversary has access to "full" DDH oracles with no fixed inputs. Next we provide a stronger variant of sCDH where two CDH instances need to be solved that involve a common, adversarially chosen element.

Definition 2 (Strong simultaneous CDH problem (sSDH)). *Let $\mathcal{G}$ be a cyclic group and (X, g_1, g_2) sampled uniformly from $(\mathcal{G} \setminus \{I_{\mathcal{G}}\})^3$. Given access to oracles $DDH(g_1, X, \cdot, \cdot)$ and $DDH(g_2, X, \cdot, \cdot)$, provide $(Y, K_1, K_2) \in (\mathcal{G} \setminus \{I_{\mathcal{G}}\}) \times \mathcal{G} \times \mathcal{G}$ s. th. $DDH(g_1, X, Y, K_1) = DDH(g_2, X, Y, K_2) = 1$*

As a cryptographic assumption sSDH above is justified since sSDH is implied by the gap simultaneous Diffie-Hellman assumption [1,34], which allows for unlimited (i.e., with no fixed input) access to a DDH oracle. Lastly, we state a variant of the sSDH assumption where generators are sampled according to some probability distribution. Looking ahead, we require this variant since in CPace parties derive generators by applying a map which does not implement uniform sampling from the group. We state the non-uniform variant of sSDH for arbitrary probability distributions and investigate its relation to "uniform" sSDH afterwards.

With $\mathbf{Adv}^{\mathsf{sCDH}}_{\mathcal{B}_{\mathsf{sCDH}}}(\mathcal{G})$ and $\mathbf{Adv}^{\mathsf{sSDH}}_{\mathcal{B}_{\mathsf{sSDH}}}(\mathcal{G})$, we denote the probabilities that adversarial algorithms $\mathcal{B}_{\mathsf{sSDH}}$ and $\mathcal{B}_{\mathsf{sSDH}}$ having access to the restricted DDH oracles provide a solution for the sCDH and sSDH problems respectively in $\mathcal{G}$ when given a single randomly drawn challenge.

Definition 3 (Strong simultaneous non-uniform CDH problem ($\mathcal{D}_{\mathcal{G}}$-sSDH)). *Let $\mathcal{G}$ be a group and $\mathcal{D}_{\mathcal{G}}$ be a probability distribution on $\mathcal{G}$. The strong simultaneous non-uniform CDH problem $\mathcal{D}_{\mathcal{G}}$-sSDH is defined as the sSDH problem but with (X, g_1, g_2) sampled using $\mathcal{U}_{\mathcal{G}} \times \mathcal{D}_{\mathcal{G}} \times \mathcal{D}_{\mathcal{G}}$, where $\mathcal{U}_{\mathcal{G}}$ denotes the uniform distribution on $\mathcal{G}$.*

Clearly, $\mathcal{U}_{\mathcal{G}\setminus\{I_{\mathcal{G}}\}}$-sSDH is equivalent to sSDH. We show that hardness of uniform and non-uniform sSDH are equivalent given that the distribution allows for probabilistic polynomial time (PPT) rejection sampling, which we now formalize.

Definition 4 (Rejection sampling algorithm for $(\mathcal{G}, \mathcal{D}_{\mathcal{G}})$). *Let $\mathcal{G}$ be a group and $\mathcal{D}_{\mathcal{G}}$ be a probability distribution on $\mathcal{G}$. With $\mathcal{D}_{\mathcal{G}}(g)$ we denote the probability for point g. Let RS be a probabilistic algorithm taking as input elements $g \in \mathcal{G}$ and outputting $\perp$ or a value $\neq\perp$. Then RS is called a* rejection sampling algorithm for $(\mathcal{G}, \mathcal{D}_{\mathcal{G}})$ *if there is a scaling factor k such that $Pr[RS(g) \neq\perp] = k \cdot \mathcal{D}_{\mathcal{G}}(g)$ for $g \in \mathcal{G}$.*

Informally RS is a probabilistic algorithm which accepts (output different from $\perp$) or rejects (output $\perp$) a candidate point. When queried multiple times on the same input $g \in \mathcal{G}$, the probability that g will be accepted or rejected models a scaled distribution that is proportional to $\mathcal{D}_{\mathcal{G}}$. In this paper, we are interested in rejection samplers with "good" acceptance rate, such that they can be efficiently used to sample elements from the scaled distribution. We formalize the acceptance rate as follows.

Definition 5 (Acceptance rate of a rejection sampler for $(\mathcal{G}, \mathcal{D}_\mathcal{G})$). *Let $\mathcal{G}$ be a group and $\mathcal{D}_\mathcal{G}$ be a probability distribution on $\mathcal{G}$. Let RS be a rejection sampling algorithm for $(\mathcal{G}, \mathcal{D}_\mathcal{G})$. Let $g_i \in \mathcal{G}$ be a sequence of m uniformly drawn points and $r_i = \mathsf{RS}(g_i)$. Then RS is said to have an acceptance rate of $(1/n)$ if the number of accepted points with $r_i \neq \perp$ converges to m/n when $m \to \infty$.*

Using these definitions, we are able to prove that given some assumptions on the distribution $\mathcal{D}_\mathcal{G}$ hardness of sSDH and $\mathcal{D}_\mathcal{G}$-sSDH are equivalent up to the additional PPT computational effort for the rejection sampling algorithm.

Theorem 1 (sSDH $\iff$ $\mathcal{D}_\mathcal{G}$-sSDH). *Let $\mathcal{G}$ be a cyclic group of order p and $\mathcal{D}_\mathcal{G}$ a probability distribution on $\mathcal{G}$. If there exists a PPT rejection sampler RS for $(\mathcal{G}, \mathcal{D}_\mathcal{G})$ with acceptance rate $(1/n)$ then the probability of PPT adversaries against $\mathcal{D}_\mathcal{G}$-sSDH and sSDH of solving the respectively other problem differs by at most $(2\mathcal{D}(I_\mathcal{G}) + (1/p))$ and solving sSDH with the help of a $\mathcal{D}_\mathcal{G}$-sSDH adversary requires at most $2n$ executions of RS on average.*

Proof. **sSDH hard $\Rightarrow$ $\mathcal{D}_\mathcal{G}$−sSDH hard:** Given an adversary $\mathcal{B}_{\mathcal{D}_\mathcal{G}-\mathsf{sSDH}}$ against $\mathcal{D}_\mathcal{G}$ − sSDH with non-negligible success probability ν, we show how to construct an adversary $\mathcal{A}_\mathsf{sSDH}$. On receiving an sSDH-challenge (X, g_1, g_2), first note that X is uniformly sampled from $\mathcal{G} \setminus \{I_\mathcal{G}\}$. $\mathcal{A}_\mathsf{sSDH}$ uniformly samples $r, s \in \mathbb{Z}_p$ until $\mathsf{RS}(g_1^r) \neq \perp$ and $\mathsf{RS}(g_2^s) \neq \perp$, which requires $2n$ calls to RS on average. $\mathcal{A}_\mathsf{sSDH}$ runs $\mathcal{B}_{\mathcal{D}_\mathcal{G}-\mathsf{sSDH}}$ on input (X, g_1^r, g_2^s). If $\mathcal{B}$ queries $\mathsf{DDH}(g_1^r, X, Z, L)$, $\mathcal{A}$ queries his own oracle with $\mathsf{DDH}(g_1, X, Z, L^{1/r})$ and relays the answer to $\mathcal{B}$ (queries g_2^s are handled analogously). On receiving (Y, K_1, K_2) from $\mathcal{B}_{\mathcal{D}_\mathcal{G}-\mathsf{sSDH}}$, $\mathcal{A}_\mathsf{sSDH}$ provides $(Y, K_1^{1/r}, K_2^{1/s})$ as solution in his sSDH experiment.

As RS is a rejection sampler for $\mathcal{D}_\mathcal{G}$, (X, g_1^r, g_2^s) is a random $\mathcal{D}_\mathcal{G}$ − sSDH challenge, and thus $\mathcal{B}$ solves it with probability ν. If $\mathcal{B}$ provides a solution, then $\mathcal{A}_\mathsf{sSDH}$ succeeds in solving his own challenge unless g_1^r or $g_2^s = I_\mathcal{G}$ or $g_1^r = g_2^s$ which occurs at most with probability $(2\mathcal{D}_\mathcal{G}(I_\mathcal{G}) + 1/p)$. As RS executes in PPT, $\mathcal{A}_\mathsf{sSDH}$ is PPT, uses $(2n)$ calls to RS on average and succeeds with probability $\nu(1 - 2\mathcal{D}_\mathcal{G}(I_\mathcal{G}) - 1/p)$, which is non-negligible since ν is.

sSDH hard $\Rightarrow$ $\mathcal{D}_\mathcal{G}$−sSDH hard: Given an adversary $\mathcal{A}_\mathsf{sSDH}$ against sSDH with non-negligible probability μ we show how to construct a $\mathcal{D}_\mathcal{G}$ − sSDH adversary $\mathcal{B}_{\mathcal{D}_\mathcal{G}-\mathsf{sSDH}}$. On receiving a $\mathcal{D}_\mathcal{G}$ − sSDH challenge (X, g_1, g_2), $\mathcal{B}$ samples $r, s \in \mathbb{Z}_p \setminus 0$ and starts $\mathcal{A}_\mathsf{sSDH}$ on input (X, g_1^r, g_2^s). DDH oracle queries are handled the same as above. On receiving (Y, K_1, K_2) from $\mathcal{A}_\mathsf{sSDH}$, $\mathcal{B}$ provides $(Y, K_1^{1/r}, K_2^{1/s})$ as solution to his own challenge.

If $\mathcal{A}$ is successful, then $\mathcal{B}$ succeeds unless either g_1 or $g_2 = I_\mathcal{G}$ or $g_1^r = g_2^s$ which occurs at most with probability $(2\mathcal{D}_\mathcal{G}(I_\mathcal{G}) + 1/p)$. Thus, $\mathcal{B}$ is a PPT adversary against $\mathcal{D}_\mathcal{G}$ − sSDH succeeding with non-negligible probability $\mu(1 - 2\mathcal{D}_\mathcal{G}(I_\mathcal{G}) - 1/p)$.

Informally, the assumptions sSDH and $\mathcal{D}_\mathcal{G}$ − sSDH become equivalent if stepping over an element that gets accepted in the sampling process becomes sufficiently likely for a randomly drawn sequence of candidates. Secondly, the probability of accidentally drawing the neutral element from $\mathcal{D}_\mathcal{G}$ needs to be negligible.

3.3 Transforming Passwords to Points on an Elliptic Curve

The generators of the Diffie-Hellman exchange in CPace are computed using a deterministic mapping function $\mathsf{Gen}(pw)$. For a given curve group $\mathcal{G}$ over a field $\mathbb{F}_q$, $\mathsf{Gen}(pw)$ is calculated with the help of either one ($\mathsf{Gen}_{1\mathsf{MAP}}$) or two ($\mathsf{Gen}_{2\mathsf{MAP}}$) invocations of a function $\mathsf{Map2Pt}_{\mathcal{G}} : \mathbb{F}_q \to \mathcal{G}$ and a hash function H_1 hashing to $\mathbb{F}_q$. For the sake of shortened notation, we will drop the $\mathcal{G}$ subscript where the group is obvious from the context. In both cases, security of CPace relies on $\mathsf{Map2Pt}$ meeting the requirements from this section. Informally, we first require $\mathsf{Map2Pt}$ to be "invertible". That is, for any point on the image of the map, there must be an efficient algorithm that outputs all preimages in $\mathbb{F}_q$ of $\mathsf{Map2Pt}_{\mathcal{G}}$ for a given group element g. We use the notation $\mathsf{Map2Pt}_{\mathcal{G}}.\mathsf{PreImages}(g)$. Details on how such an inversion algorithm can be efficiently implemented for various elliptic curve groups are given in [11,13,20,27] and references therein. Secondly, a bound for the maximum number of preimages $n_{\max}$ that $\mathsf{Map2Pt}_{\mathcal{G}}$ maps to the same element must be known and this $n_{\max}$ bound needs to be small (we use the notation $\mathsf{Map2Pt}_{\mathcal{G}}.n_{\max}$ for the bound that applies for a given $\mathsf{Map2Pt}_{\mathcal{G}}$ function and group $\mathcal{G}$). This is needed in order to construct a rejection sampling algorithm whose acceptance rate must depend on $n_{\max}$.

Definition 6. *Let $\mathcal{G}$ be a group of points on an elliptic curve over a field $\mathbb{F}_q$. Let $\mathsf{Map2Pt} : \mathbb{F}_q \to \mathcal{G}$ be a deterministic function. Then $\mathsf{Map2Pt}(\cdot)$ is called* probabilistically invertible with at most n_{max} preimages *if there exists a probabilistic polynomial-time algorithm $(r_1, \ldots, r_{n_g}) \leftarrow \mathsf{Map2Pt.PreImages}(g)$ that outputs all n_g values $r_i \in \mathbb{F}_q$ such that $g = \mathsf{Map2Pt}(r_i)$ for any $g \in \mathcal{G}$; and $\forall g \in \mathcal{G}$, $n_{max} \geq n_g \geq 0$.*

For a map $\mathsf{Map2Pt}$ that fulfills the previous definition with a bound for the numbers of preimages $\mathsf{Map2Pt}.n_{\max}$, we define an "inversion algorithm" $\mathsf{Map2Pt}^{-1} : \mathcal{G} \to \mathbb{F}_q$ that, on input $g \in \mathcal{G}$, returns one of potentially many preimages of g under $\mathsf{Map2Pt}$ if a biased coin comes up heads. If the coin comes up tails, the algorithm outputs failure. The "inversion algorithm" also serves as rejection sampling algorithm for the distribution $\mathcal{D}_{\mathcal{G}}$ that is produced by $\mathsf{Map2Pt}(r)$ for uniformly distributed inputs $r \in \mathbb{F}_q$.

Algorithm 1. $\mathsf{Map2Pt}^{-1} : \mathcal{G} \longrightarrow \mathbb{F}_q \cup \{\perp\}$

On input $g \in \mathcal{G}$: Sample i uniformly from $\{1, \ldots, \mathsf{Map2Pt}.n_{\max}\}$; Then obtain $n_g \in \{0, \ldots, \mathsf{Map2Pt}.n_{\max}\}$ pre-images $(r_1, \ldots, r_m) \leftarrow \mathsf{Map2Pt.PreImages}(g)$; If $n_g < i$ return $\perp$, else return r_i.

Lemma 1. *Let $\mathsf{Map2Pt} : \mathcal{G} \to \mathbb{F}_q$ be probabilistically invertible with at most $\mathsf{Map2Pt}.n_{max}$ preimages and let $\mathcal{D}_{\mathcal{G}}$ denote the distribution it induces on $\mathcal{G}$. Then Algorithm 1 is a PPT rejection sampler for $(\mathcal{G}, \mathcal{D}_{\mathcal{G}})$ with average acceptance rate $(|\mathbb{F}_q|/|\mathcal{G}|)/\mathsf{Map2Pt}.n_{max}$.*

Proof. We first define the average number of preimages $n_{\max} \geq \bar{n} \geq 1$ as the quotient of the order of the field $\mathbb{F}_q$ and the number of points on the image of the map, i.e., $\bar{n} = |\mathbb{F}_q|/|\text{support}(\mathcal{D}_\mathcal{G})|$. When drawing an element g uniformly from $\mathcal{G}$, the probability that the number of preimages n_g for g is nonzero is given by the quotient of the order of the support of $\mathcal{D}_\mathcal{G}$ and the order of the group. By the definition of $\bar{n}$ above this is $|\mathbb{F}_q|/(\bar{n}|\mathcal{G}|)$.

For any point on the map with a nonzero number n_g of preimages, Algorithm 1 returns a result $\neq\perp$ with probability $n_g/n_{\max}$. As the average value for the number of preimages for any point on the image of the map is $\bar{n}$, the average acceptance rate is $(|\mathbb{F}_q|/(\bar{n}|\mathcal{G}|)) \cdot \bar{n}/n_{\max} = (|\mathbb{F}_q|/|\mathcal{G}|)/n_{\max}$.

Use of $\mathsf{Map2Pt}^{-1}$ for uniformly sampling field elements from $\mathbb{F}_q$. As $\mathsf{Map2Pt}$ is deterministic, each point g from $\mathcal{G}$ is characterized by the number of preimages n_g for $\mathsf{Map2Pt}$ in $\mathbb{F}_q$ with $n_{\max} \geq n_g \geq 0$. When generating points $\mathsf{Map2Pt}(s) \in \mathcal{G}$ for uniformly sampled field elements $s \leftarrow_{\mathrm{R}} \mathbb{F}_q$, the probability of obtaining a given point g is (n_g/q) and can only take the values of zero or integer multiples of $1/q$ up to $n_{\max}/q$. In order to compensate for this, $\mathsf{Map2Pt}^{-1}$ is constructed such that the probability of returning $r \neq\perp$ for a point g increases proportionally with n_g making any actually produced field element $r \neq\perp$ equally likely in $\mathbb{F}_q$. As a result, we can use $\mathsf{Map2Pt}^{-1}$ for transforming a sequence of uniformly sampled group elements $g_l \in \mathcal{G}$ to a sequence of uniformly sampled field elements $r_l \in \mathbb{F}_q$

Corollary 1. *Let $\mathsf{Map2Pt}$ be a probabilistically invertible map with at most $\mathsf{Map2Pt}.n_{max}$ preimages and let $g_l \leftarrow_R \mathcal{G}$. Then $r_l \leftarrow \mathsf{Map2Pt}^{-1}(g_l)$ outputs results $r_l \neq\perp$ with probability $p \geq (|\mathbb{F}_q|/|\mathcal{G}|)/\mathsf{Map2Pt}.n_{max}$ and the distribution of outputs $r_l \neq\perp$ is uniform in $\mathbb{F}_q$.*

Moreover as the collision probability when drawing two elements r_a, r_b from $\mathbb{F}_q$ is $1/q$ and as there are at most $n_{\max}$ values s_l generating the same group element $g = \mathsf{Map2Pt}(s_l)$ the collision probability for $g_a = \mathsf{Map2Pt}(r_a)$ and $g_b = \mathsf{Map2Pt}(r_b)$ is increased at most by $n_{\max}^2$.

Corollary 2. *When sampling two field elements $r_a, r_b \leftarrow_R \mathbb{F}_q$ uniformly, we have $\mathsf{Map2Pt}(r_a) = \mathsf{Map2Pt}(r_b)$ with a probability of at most n_{max}^2/q.*

4 The CPace Protocol

The CPace protocol [22] is a SPEKE-type protocol [30] allowing parties to compute a common key via a Diffie-Hellman key exchange with password-dependent generators. The blueprint of the protocol is depicted in Fig. 2. Informally, a party $\mathcal{P}$ willing to establish a key with party $\mathcal{P}'$ first computes a generator g from a password pw. Next, $\mathcal{P}$ generates an element $Y_a = g^{y_a}$ from a secret value y_a sampled at random and sends it to $\mathcal{P}'$. Upon receiving a value Y_b from $\mathcal{P}'$, $\mathcal{P}$ then computes a Diffie-Hellman key $K = (Y_b)^{y_a} = g^{y_a y_b}$ and aborts if K equals the identity element. Finally, it computes the session key as the hash of K and the exchanged values Y_a and Y_b.

$\mathcal{P}(\mathsf{pw})$	public: $\mathcal{G}, c \cdot p, \mathsf{H_2}$, Gen, ScMul, ScMulVf, ScSam	$\mathcal{P}'(\mathsf{pw}')$
$g \leftarrow \mathsf{Gen}(\mathsf{pw})$ $y_a \leftarrow \mathsf{ScSam}()$ $Y_a \leftarrow \mathsf{ScMul}(g, y_a)$		$g' \leftarrow \mathsf{Gen}(\mathsf{pw}')$ $y_b \leftarrow \mathsf{ScSam}()$ $Y_b \leftarrow \mathsf{ScMul}(g', y_b)$
	$\xleftarrow{sid, Y_b}$	
	$\xrightarrow{sid, Y_a}$	
$K \leftarrow \mathsf{ScMulVf}(Y_b, y_a)$ Abort if $K = I_{\mathcal{G}}$ $ISK \leftarrow \mathsf{H_2}(K \Vert \mathsf{oc}(Y_a, Y_b))$ Output ISK		$K' \leftarrow \mathsf{ScMulVf}(Y_a, y_b)$ Abort if $K' = I_{\mathcal{G}}$ $ISK' \leftarrow$ $\mathsf{H_2}(K' \Vert \mathsf{oc}(Y_a, Y_b))$ Output ISK'

Fig. 2. Above: Blueprint protocol CPace[Gen, ScMul, ScMulVf, ScSam] requiring group $\mathcal{G}$ of order $c \cdot p$ with prime p and algorithms for DH generator computation (Gen), exponentiation (ScMul, ScMulVf) and scalar sampling (ScSam). $\mathsf{H_2} : \{0,1\}^* \rightarrow \{0,1\}^\lambda$ denotes a hash function. **Below:** "Basic" CPace $\mathrm{CPace}_{\mathsf{base}}$ with $c = 1$, generators computed from hash function $\mathsf{H}_{\mathcal{G}} : \{0,1\}^* \rightarrow \mathcal{G}$ and canonical exponentiation, point verification and sampling.

$\mathrm{CPace}_{\mathsf{base}}$:=CPace[$\mathsf{Gen_{RO}}, \mathsf{ScMul_{base}}, \mathsf{ScMulVf_{base}}, \mathsf{ScSam}_p$]			
$\mathsf{Gen_{RO}}(\mathsf{pw})$:	$\mathsf{ScMul_{base}}(g, y)$:	$\mathsf{ScMulVf_{base}}(g, y)$:	$\mathsf{ScSam}_p()$:
return $\mathsf{H}_{\mathcal{G}}(\mathsf{pw})$	return g^y	if $g \notin \mathcal{G}$: return $I_{\mathcal{G}}$ else: return g^y	$y \leftarrow_{\mathrm{R}} \{1, \ldots, p\}$ return y

In order to allow for efficient instantiations over different types of groups, most of which are elliptic curves, we present the CPace protocol in form of a blueprint CPace[Gen, ScMul, ScMulVf, ScSam] in Fig. 2 that provides the following generalizations: (1) The blueprint uses a generic algorithm $\mathsf{Gen}(\mathcal{D}) \rightarrow \mathcal{G}$ that turns a password from dictionary $\mathcal{D}$ into a group element; (2) The computation of the y_i and Y_i values is done with generic algorithms for sampling ($\mathsf{SamSc} : 0, 1^* \rightarrow 0, 1^*$) and scalar multiplication ($\mathsf{ScMul} : \mathcal{G} \times \mathbb{Z}_{|\mathcal{G}|} \rightarrow \mathcal{G}$); (3) The Diffie-Hellman key is computed with another generic algorithm $\mathsf{ScMulVf} : \mathcal{G} \times \mathbb{Z}_{|\mathcal{G}|} \rightarrow \mathcal{G}$, in order to allow for additional point verification that is necessary on some curves (but not on all) to protect against trivial attacks; (4) the blueprint protocol uses an ordered concatenation function oc so that messages can be sent in any order and parties do not have to play a specific initiator or responder role. In the remainder of the paper, we will instantiate the CPace blueprint in various ways, by specifying a set of concrete algorithms Gen, ScMul, ScMulVf, ScSam.

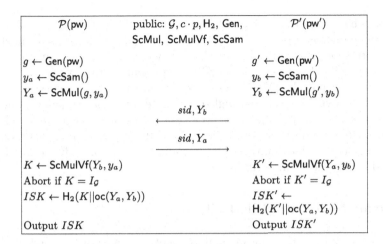

On the necessity of point verification. Many elliptic curve scalar multiplication algorithms will work correctly independent whether the input operand encodes a point on the correct curve or not. As a consequence if group membership is not correctly verified by an implementation various attack scenarios become feasible. An active attacker may for instance provide a point on a curve of low order on which the discrete-logarithm problem could be solved. The threat for real-world implementations is that this serious error might remain undetected as the corresponding verification event is never generated in communications of honest parties. In order to make CPace resilient to this type of attack and implementation pitfalls, [22] suggested to first restrict invalid curve attacks to the quadratic twist (by using a single-coordinate Montgomery ladder) and then choose a curve where also the twist has a large prime-order subgroup and invalid curve attacks become impossible. The CPace draft [23] highlights this aspect on the protocol specification level by introducing a ScMulVf function which is specified to include point verification.

5 Security of Simplified CPace

In this Section, as a warm-up, we analyze security of a "basic" variant of CPace, which we call $\text{CPace}_{\mathsf{base}}$ and which is depicted in Fig. 2. We instantiate Gen with a hash function $\mathsf{H}_{\mathcal{G}}$ that hashes onto the group $\mathcal{G}$. This way, parties compute generators as $g \leftarrow \mathsf{H}_{\mathcal{G}}(\mathsf{pw})$. Further, we assume $\mathcal{G}$ to be a multiplicatively written group of prime order p where group membership is efficiently decidable. We instantiate $\mathsf{ScMul}(g, y) := g^y$ as exponentiation, and $\mathsf{ScMulVf}(g, y)$ such that it returns the neutral element if g is not in the group and g^y otherwise, and SamSc with uniform sampling from $\{1 \ldots p\}$. A formal description of the protocol is given in Fig. 2, where the blueprint protocol is instantiated with the algorithms at the bottom of the Figure.

Theorem 2 (Security of $\text{CPace}_{\mathsf{base}}$). *Let $\lambda, p \in \mathbb{N}$ with p prime. Let $\mathcal{G}$ be a group of order p, and let $\mathsf{H}_1 : \{0,1\}^* \rightarrow \mathcal{G}, \mathsf{H}_2 : \{0,1\} \rightarrow \{0,1\}^\lambda$ be two hash functions. If the sCDH and sSDH problems are hard in $\mathcal{G}$, then protocol $CPace_{\mathsf{base}}$ depicted in Fig. 2 UC-emulates $\mathcal{F}_{\mathsf{lePAKE}}$ in the random-oracle model with respect to adaptive corruptions when both hash functions are modeled as random oracles. More precisely, for every adversary $\mathcal{A}$, there exist adversaries $\mathcal{B}_{\mathsf{sSDH}}$ and $\mathcal{B}_{\mathsf{sCDH}}$ against the strong CDH (sCDH) and strong simultaneous CDH (sSDH) problems such that*

$$\begin{aligned} &|Pr[Real_{\mathcal{Z}}(CPace_{\mathsf{base}}, \mathcal{A})] - Pr[Ideal_{\mathcal{Z}}(\mathcal{F}_{\mathsf{lePAKE}}, \mathcal{S})| \\ &\quad \leq l_{\mathsf{H}_1}^2/p + 2l_{\mathsf{H}_1}^2 \mathbf{Adv}_{\mathcal{B}_{\mathsf{sSDH}}}^{\mathsf{sSDH}}(\mathcal{G}) + \mathbf{Adv}_{\mathcal{B}_{\mathsf{sCDH}}}^{\mathsf{sCDH}}(\mathcal{G}) \end{aligned}$$

where l_{H_1} denotes the number of H_1 queries made by the adversary $\mathcal{A}$ and the simulator $\mathcal{S}$ is depicted in Fig. 3.

Proof (Sketch). The main idea of the simulation is to fix a secret generator $g \in \mathcal{G}$ and carry out the simulation with respect to g. Messages of honest parties are simulated as g^z for a fresh exponent z. Queries $\mathsf{H}_1(\mathsf{pw})$ are answered with g^r for a freshly chosen "trapdoor" r. The simulator might learn an honest party's password via adaptive corruption or via an adversarial password guess. The simulator can now adjust the simulation in retrospective to let the honest party use $g^r = \mathsf{H}_1(\mathsf{pw})$ by claiming the party's secret exponent to be zr^{-1}. This already

The simulator $\mathcal{S}$ samples and stores a generator $g \leftarrow \mathcal{G}$.

On $(\mathsf{NewSession}, sid, P_i, P_j)$ from $\mathcal{F}_{\mathsf{lePAKE}}$:
sample $z_i \leftarrow_R \mathbb{Z}_p$
set $Y_i \leftarrow g^{z_i}$; store $(P_i, z_i, Y_i, \perp)$
send Y_i to $\mathcal{A}$ intended to P_j

On Z^* from $\mathcal{A}$ as msg to (sid, P_i):
if Z^* is adversarially generated
and $Z^* \in \mathcal{G} \setminus I_{\mathcal{G}}$:
  send $(\mathsf{RegisterTest}, sid, P_i)$ to $\mathcal{F}_{\mathsf{lePAKE}}$

Upon P_i receiving (sid, Y_j) with $Y_j \in \mathcal{G}$ from P_j:
retrieve record $(P_i, z_i, Y_i, *)$
if $\exists$ records $(\mathsf{H}_1, \mathsf{pw}, r, r^{-1}, G)$, $(\mathsf{H}_2, K||\mathsf{oc}(Y_i, Y_j), ISK)$ s.th. $K = Y_j^{z_i r^{-1}}$:
  store $(\mathbf{guess}, G, Y_j)$; abort if $\exists$ record $(\mathbf{guess}, G', Y_j)$ with $G \neq G'$;
  send $(\mathsf{TestPwd}, sid, P_i, \mathsf{pw})$ to $\mathcal{F}_{\mathsf{lePAKE}}$;
  send $(\mathsf{NewKey}, sid, P_i, ISK)$ to $\mathcal{F}_{\mathsf{lePAKE}}$ and store (P_i, z_i, Y_i, ISK)
else: sample a fresh random ISK' and send $(\mathsf{NewKey}, sid, P_i, ISK')$ to $\mathcal{F}_{\mathsf{lePAKE}}$

On $\mathsf{H}_1(\mathsf{pw})$ from $\mathcal{A}$:
if this is the first such query:
  sample $r \leftarrow_R \mathbb{F}_p \setminus \{0\}$
  abort if $\exists$ rec. $(\mathsf{H}_1, *, r, *, *)$
  store $(\mathsf{H}_1, \mathsf{pw}, r, r^{-1}, g^r)$
retrieve rec. $(\mathsf{H}_1, \mathsf{pw}, *, *, h)$
reply with h

On msg $(\mathsf{AdaptiveCorruption}, sid)$ from $\mathcal{A}$ to P_i:
send $\mathsf{AdaptiveCorruption}, sid, P_i)$ to $\mathcal{F}_{\mathsf{lePAKE}}$
retrieve record (sid, pw)
if a msg $Y_i := g^{z_i}$ already sent to P_j:
  if $\exists$ rec. $(\mathsf{H}_1, \mathsf{pw}, r, r^{-1}, *)$: $y_i \leftarrow z_i r^{-1}$
  else: $r \leftarrow_R \mathbb{Z}_p$; $y_i \leftarrow z_i r^{-1}$ and
      store $(\mathsf{H}_1, \mathsf{pw}, r, r^{-1}, g^r)$
  send (pw, y_i) to $\mathcal{A}$

On $\mathsf{H}_2(K||Y_i||Y_j)$ from $\mathcal{A}$:
if this is the first such query then
  if $\exists$ rec.$(P_i, z_i, Y_i, *), (P_j, z_j, Y_j, *), (\mathsf{H}_1, *)$ such that $K^r = g^{z_i z_j}$: abort;
  if $\nexists$ rec.$(P_i, *, Y_i, *)$ or $(P_j, *, Y_j, *)$, or if $Y_a||Y_b \neq \mathsf{oc}(Y_a, Y_b)$: $A \leftarrow_R \{0,1\}^{2k}$;
  if $\exists$ records (P_i, z_i, Y_i, ISK) and $(\mathsf{H}_1, \mathsf{pw}, r, r^{-1}, G)$ s.th. $K = Y_j^{z_i r^{-1}}$:
    Record $(\mathbf{guess}, G, Y_j)$; abort if $\exists$ rec. $(\mathbf{guess}, G', Y_j)$ with $G \neq G'$.
    Send $(\mathsf{LateTestPwd}, sid, P_i, \mathsf{pw})$ to $\mathcal{F}_{\mathsf{lePAKE}}$. Upon answer $\hat{K}$ set $A \leftarrow \hat{K}$;
  if $\exists$ (P_j, z_j, Y_j, ISK) with $ISK \neq \perp$ and $(\mathsf{H}_1, \mathsf{pw}, r, r^{-1}, G)$ s.th. $K = Y_i^{z_j/r}$:
    Store $(\mathbf{guess}, G, Y_i)$; Abort if $\exists$ record $(\mathbf{guess}, G', Y_i)$ with $G \neq G'$;
    Send $(\mathsf{LateTestPwd}, sid, P_j, \mathsf{pw})$ to $\mathcal{F}_{\mathsf{lePAKE}}$. Upon answer $\hat{K}$ set $A \leftarrow \hat{K}$
  if no matching H_1 records are found set $A \leftarrow_R \{0,1\}^{2k}$
  finally, store $(\mathsf{H}_2, K||Y_i||Y_j, A)$ and reply with A
else retrieve record $(\mathsf{H}_2, K||Y_i||Y_j, A)$ and reply with A

Fig. 3. Simulator for CPace$_{\mathsf{base}}$. For brevity we omit the session identifier *sid* from all records stored by the simulator.

concludes simulation of honest parties without passwords. Adversarial password guesses can be read from $\mathcal{A}$ injecting X (or, similarly, Y) and then querying $\mathsf{H}_2(K||X||Y)$ with K being a correctly computed key w.r.t some generator g^r provided by the simulation. $\mathcal{S}$ can now read the guessed password from the H_1 list, and submit it as password guess to $\mathcal{F}_{\mathsf{lePAKE}}$. In case of success, the simulator sets the key of the honest party to $\mathsf{H}_2(K||X||Y)$.

The simulation is complicated by the order of honest parties' outputs (which are generated upon receipt of the single message) and the adversary's computation of final session keys via H_2 queries. If the key is generated by $\mathcal{F}_{\mathsf{lePAKE}}$ before $\mathcal{A}$ computes it via H_2 (which constitutes a password guess as detailed above), then $\mathcal{S}$ needs to invoke the LateTestPwd query of $\mathcal{F}_{\mathsf{lePAKE}}$ instead of TestPwd. In case of a correct guess, this lets $\mathcal{S}$ learn the output key of the honest party, which $\mathcal{S}$ can then program into the corresponding H_2 query.

Finally, the simulation can fail in some cases. Firstly, $\mathcal{S}$ might find more than one password guess against an honest party with simulated message X. In this case, the simulation cannot continue since $\mathcal{F}_{\mathsf{lePAKE}}$ allows for only one password guess per party. In this case, however, $\mathcal{A}$ would provide (g^r, X, Y, K),$(g^{r'}, X, Y, K')$ which are two CDH tuples for passwords $\mathsf{pw}, \mathsf{pw}'$ with $g^r \leftarrow \mathsf{H}_1(\mathsf{pw}), g^{r'} \leftarrow \mathsf{H}_1(\mathsf{pw}')$. Provided that the simultaneous strong CDH assumption (sSDH, cf. Definition 2) holds, this cannot happen. Here, the "strong" property, providing a type of DDH oracle, is required to help $\mathcal{S}$ identify CDH tuples among all queries to H_2. A second case of simulation failure occurs when $\mathcal{A}$ wants to compute a key of an uncorrupted session via a H_2 query. Since $\mathcal{S}$ does not know such keys, it would have to abort. Using a similar strategy as above, pseudorandomness of keys can be shown to hold under the strong CDH assumption, and thus the probability of $\mathcal{A}$ issuing such a H_2 query is negligible. The full proof can be found in the full version of this work [4].

Our Theorem 2 demonstrates that adaptive security of CPace can be proven with only minimal information included in the hashes, i.e., the first hash requires only the password and the final key derivation hash requires the Diffie-Hellman key and the unique protocol transcript. We detail now under which circumstances additional data such as session identifiers needs to be included in the hashes. We further note that adding additional inputs to hashes, such as the name of a ciphersuite that an application wants parties to agree on, does not harm security.

On multi-session security and hash domain separation. Theorem 2 demonstrates that $\mathrm{CPace}_{\mathsf{base}}$ allows to securely turn a joint password into one key. In practice, one would of course want to exchange more than one key, and many parties will end up using the same password. If session identifiers are globally unique, then the UC composition theorem (more detailed, the composition theorem of UC with Joint State [16]) allows to turn Theorem 2 into a proof of "multi-session CPace" by simply appending the unique session identifiers to all hash function inputs. This ensures that hash domains of individual sessions are separated and the programming activities of the individual simulators do not clash. To summarize, we obtain a secure multi-session version of CPace by ensuring uniqueness of session identifiers and including them in hashes. In practice, this can be ensured by, e.g., agreeing on a joint session identifier to which both users contributed randomness and in which party identifiers are incorporated (see, e.g., [6]). The agreement needs to happen before starting CPace, but does not require secrecy and can thus potentially be piggy-backed to messages sent by the application. As a last note, applications might choose to add more values to hashes, for example to authenticate addresses or to ensure agreement on a ciphersuite. We stress that such additional values do not void our security analysis, but care still needs to be taken in order to protect against side-channel attacks.

5.1 Embedding CDH Experiment Libraries into the Simulator

In this section, we discuss an alternative approach to carrying out reductions to cryptographic assumptions in the case of CPace/CDH. Both assumptions required by $\text{CPace}_{\mathsf{base}}$, sCDH and sSDH, allow for an *efficient implementation* of experiments in the following sense: the secret exponents that are sampled by the experiment code (often also called the *challenger*) are sufficient for answering the restricted DDH queries allowed by both assumptions. An example for an assumption that does not allow for such efficient instantiation is, e.g., gap-CDH. In gap-CDH, the adversary is provided with a "full" DDH oracle that he can query on arbitrary elements, of which the experiment might not know an exponent for.

Due to this property, we can integrate implementations of the sCDH and sSDH experiments in the simulator's code. The simulator implements the DDH oracles on its own, and abort if at any time an oracle query solves the underlying assumption. We chose to integrate experiments as libraries (written as objects in python-style notation in Fig. 4) into the simulator's code. This eases not only presentation but is also useful for analyzing variants of CPace that require slightly different assumptions.

The corresponding result for $\text{CPace}_{\mathsf{base}}$ is shown in Fig. 5 when the challenge-generating experiment $\mathsf{exp} \leftarrow \mathsf{sSDH}(\mathsf{sCDH})$ is used (Fig. 4). The instance of the sSDH object first samples a random generator as member $s.g$ and creates a member instance $s.scdh \leftarrow \mathsf{sCDH}(g)$ of the experiment for the sCDH problem. The sCDH member object produces a challenge consisting of two uniformly drawn group elements $Y_1 \leftarrow g^{y_1}, Y_2 \leftarrow g^{y_2}$. The limited DDH oracle provided by the sCDH assumption can only receive inputs w.r.t one of these elements, and thus it can be implemented efficiently using secret exponents y_1, y_2. If a correct CDH solution $g, Y_1, Y_2, g^{y_1 \cdot y_2}$ is provided, the sCDH object aborts. In its implementation for H_1, the sSDH object samples random new generators as $R \leftarrow (s.g)^r$ which will be used for simulating password-dependent base points and uses the $s.scdh$ member and the known exponent r for answering DDH queries by use of the $s.scdh.\mathsf{DDH}$ function. The corrupt queries are implemented likewise and forwarded to the $s.scdh$ member object. The simulator from Fig. 3 is adapted to call the experiment. As an example, honest parties' messages are simulated by calling the challenge sampling procedure $\mathsf{exp.sampleY}()$ from sSDH which itself calls the corresponding function from its sCDH member.

Proving indistinguishability. With this simulation approach, a proof consists in demonstrating that ideal and real world executions are indistinguishable except for events in which the experiment libraries abort because a challenge was correctly answered. Compared to our proof of Theorem 2, the indistinguishability argument becomes simpler because the reduction strategies to both CDH-type assumptions are already embedded in the corresponding assumption experiment

```
# using python-style notation with self pointer s and _init_ constructor
def class sCDH:
  def _init_(s, g): s.g ← g; s.i ← 0; s.state← fresh;
  def sampleY(s):
    if s.i < 2: s.i+ = 1; sample s.y_i ←R F_p \ 0; return (s.g)^(s.y_i);
  def corrupt(s,X):
    for 1 ≤ m ≤ s.i:
      if (X = (s.g)^(s.y_m)): s.state← corrupt; return s.y_m;
  def DDH(s, g, Y, X, K):
    if (g ≠ s.g): return;
    if ({Y, X}={s.Y_1, s.Y_2}) and (s.state= fresh) and (K = (s.g)^(s.y_1·s.y_2)):
      abort("sCDH(g, Y_1, Y_2) solved")
    for 1 ≤ m ≤ s.i:
      if (Y = (s.g)^(s.y_m)): return (K = X^(s.y_m));
   def isValid(X): return (X ∈ G \ {I_G})

def class sSDH: # using python-style notation [ ] for list containers
  def _init_(s,sCdhExp): # Gets sCDH class; samples g; creates a sCDH instance
    s.g ←R G; s.scdh = sCdhExp(s.g); s.records =[ ]; s.guess = "yet no guess";
  def sampleY(s): return (s.scdh).sampleY();
  def isValid(s, X): return (s.scdh).isValid(X);
  def sampleH1(s):
    sample r ←R F_p \ {0};
    if (r, *) in s.records: abort("Hash to group collision");
    else: s.records.append((r, (s.g)^r)); return (s.g)^r;
  def corrupt(s, R, Y):
    if there is (r, R) in s.records: return (s.scdh).corrupt(Y^(1/r));
  def DDH(s,R, Y, X, K):
    if there is (r, R) in s.records:
      match ← (s.scdh).DDH(s.g, Y, X, K^(1/r));
      if match and (s.guess = "yet no guess"): (s.guess.g,s.guess.X)← (R, X);
      elif match and (s.guess.X = X) and (s.guess.g ≠ R):
        abort("sSDH problem (Y, R, s.guess.g) solved");
      return match;
```

Fig. 4. Libraries implementing sCDH and sSDH experiments.

libraries. Losses such as the factor $2l_{\mathsf{H}_1}^2$ in the reduction to sSDH translate to libraries producing more than one challenge per simulation run, as is the case for the sSDH experiment from Fig. 5. Altogether, the simulation with integrated CDH experiment libraries is an alternative approach of proving Theorem 2, as we formalize in the following.

Theorem 3 (Alternative simulation for Theorem 2). *The simulator depicted in Fig. 5 is a witness for the UC emulation statement in Theorem 2*

Proof (Proof sketch.). The output distribution of the simulator $\mathcal{S}$ from Fig. 5 is indistinguishable from the one of the simulator from Fig. 3 as it is obtained from internal restructuring. $\mathcal{S}$ aborts if either the sSDH or the sCDH experiment class

The simulator $\mathcal{S}(\textsf{exp})$ is parametrized by an experiment class exp.

On (NewSession, sid, P_i, P_j) from $\mathcal{F}_{\textsf{lePAKE}}$:
set $Y_i \leftarrow$ exp.sampleY();
store $(P_i, P_j, Y_i, \perp)$;
send Y_i to $\mathcal{A}$ intended to P_j;

On Z^* from $\mathcal{A}$ as msg to (sid, P_i):
if Z^* is adversarially generated
and exp.isValid(Z^*):
send (RegisterTest, sid, P_i) to $\mathcal{F}_{\textsf{lePAKE}}$

Upon P_i receiving (sid, Y_j) from P_j: retrieve record $(P_i, *, z_i, Y_i, *)$
if not exp.isValid(Y_j): return;
if $\exists$ records $(\textsf{H}_1, \textsf{pw}, h)$, $(\textsf{H}_2, K||(\textsf{oc}(Y_i, Y_j), ISK)$
such that exp.DDH$(h, Y_i, Y_j, K) = 1$:
send (TestPwd, sid, P_i, pw) to $\mathcal{F}_{\textsf{lePAKE}}$
send (NewKey, sid, P_i, ISK) to $\mathcal{F}_{\textsf{lePAKE}}$ and store (P_i, P_j, Y_i, ISK)
else sample a fresh random ISK' and send (NewKey, sid, P_i, ISK') to $\mathcal{F}_{\textsf{lePAKE}}$
$\mathcal{F}_{\textsf{lePAKE}}$ will discard ISK'

On $\textsf{H}_1(\textsf{pw})$) from $\mathcal{A}$:
if not $\exists$ record
$(\textsf{H}_1, \textsf{pw}, h)$:
$h \leftarrow$ exp.sampleH1()
store $(\textsf{H}_1, \textsf{pw}, h)$
lookup$(\textsf{H}_1, \textsf{pw}, h)$
reply with h

On (AdaptiveCorruption, sid) from $\mathcal{A}$ as msg to P_i:
Lookup $(P_i, P_j, Y_i, *)$; send (AdaptiveCorruption, sid, P_i)
to $\mathcal{F}_{\textsf{lePAKE}}$ and obtain $(sid, \textsf{pw})$;
if a message Y_i was already sent to P_j, then:
query $\textsf{H}_1(\textsf{pw})$ and
retrieve record $(\textsf{H}_1, \textsf{pw}, h)$
send (pw,exp.corrupt(h, Y_i))

On $\textsf{H}_2(sid||K||Y_i||Y_j)$ from $\mathcal{A}$:
lookup $(\textsf{H}_2, sid||K||Y_i||Y_j, h)$ and send h if it exists;
else if this is the first such query:
if there are no records $(P_i, P_j, Y_i, *)$ or $(P_j, P_i, Y_j, *)$, or if $Y_a||Y_b \neq \textsf{oc}(Y_a, Y_b)$:
sample $A \leftarrow \{0,1\}^{2k}$;
if $\exists$ records (P_i, P_j, Y_i, ISK) with $ISK \neq \perp$ and $(\textsf{H}_1, \textsf{pw}, h)$
such that exp.DDH$(h, Y_i, Y_j, K) = 1$:
send (LateTestPwd, sid, P_i, pw) to $\mathcal{F}_{\textsf{lePAKE}}$. Upon answer $\hat{K}$ set $A \leftarrow \hat{K}$
if $\exists$ records (P_j, P_i, Y_j, ISK) with $ISK \neq \perp$ and $(\textsf{H}_1, \textsf{pw}, h)$
such that exp.DDH$(h, Y_j, Y_i, K) = 1$:
send (LateTestPwd, sid, P_j, pw) to $\mathcal{F}_{\textsf{lePAKE}}$. Upon answer $\hat{K}$ set $A \leftarrow \hat{K}$
if no matching $\textsf{H}_1$ records are found set $A \leftarrow \{0,1\}^{2k}$
finally, store $(\textsf{H}_2, sid||K||Y_i||Y_j, A)$ and reply with A

Fig. 5. Generic simulator for different CPace variants, embedding challenges generated by the experiment object exp. The simulator for $\text{CPace}_{\textsf{base}}$ is obtained when using exp $\leftarrow$ sSDH(sCDH) from Fig. 4.

aborts, which occurs iff a correct solution has been provided to the experiment implementation or a $\textsf{H}_1$ collision is observed. These cases coincide with the abort cases in the proof of Theorem 2. As the sSDH object outputs $2l^2_{\textsf{H}_1}$ different challenges and as it is sufficient for $\mathcal{Z}$ to provide a solution to one of these challenges for distinguishing both worlds, the advantage for solving the sSDH problem needs to be multiplied by this factor, thus reproducing the bounds from Theorem 2.

Advantages of embedding libraries in the simulation. To clarify, the approach presented in this section does *not* allow to prove stronger security statements. As demonstrated above, it is merely an alternative way of presenting security proofs in the UC framework or other simulation-based frameworks, and it works whenever the underlying cryptographic assumptions are efficiently implementable. However, we believe that the approach has its merits especially in the following dimensions.

- **Modular security analysis.** Slight modifications in the protocol might require to change the cryptographic assumption. As long as the public interface does not change, our approach allows to switch between assumptions by simply calling a different library. Cryptographers then need to only analyze this "local" change in the simulation, which prevents them from re-doing the whole indistinguishability argument.
- **Presentation of reduction strategies.** In normal game-based indistinguishability arguments [36], reductions to cryptographic assumptions are hidden within side-long proofs. With our approach, the reduction strategy is depicted in clear code as part of the simulator's code. This makes checking of proofs easier not only for readers but also might make simulation-based proofs more accessible to automated verification.

In this paper, our motivation is the first dimension. In the upcoming section, the library-based approach will turn out to be extremely useful to analyze the various variants of CPace that stem from (efficiency-wise) optimized implementations on different elliptic curves.

6 Analysis of Real-World CPace

The currently most efficient way to run CPace is over elliptic curves. Therefore, from this point onwards, we consider $\mathcal{G}$ to be an elliptic curve constructed over field $\mathbb{F}_q$. From a historical perspective, both CPace research and implementation first focused on prime order curves, such as the NIST-P-256 curve [18]. Subsequently significantly improved performance was shown on Montgomery- and (twisted-)Edwards curves, notably Curve25519 and Ed448 curves [10,26], which both have a small cofactor c in their group order $c \cdot p$. These approaches consider also implementation pitfalls, e.g., by designing the curve such that there are no incentives for implementers to use insecure speed-ups. Thirdly, recently ideal group abstractions have been presented in order to avoid the complexity of small cofactors in the group order [17,25], while maintaining all advantages of curves with cofactor.

For smooth integration into each of these different curve ecosystems, CPace needs to be instantiated slightly differently regarding, e.g., computation of the DH generator, group size, multiplication and sampling algorithms. In this section, we analyze how such differences impact security. Using our modular approach with assumption libraries called by a simulator, we are able to present security in terms of differences from our basic CPace analysis in Sect. 5 in a concise way.

6.1 CPace Without Hashing to the Group

$\mathrm{CPace}_{1\mathsf{MAP}} := \mathrm{CPace}[\mathsf{Gen}_{1\mathsf{MAP}}, \mathsf{ScMul}_{\mathsf{base}}, \mathsf{ScMulVf}_{\mathsf{base}}, \mathsf{ScSam}_p]$			
$\mathsf{Gen}_{1\mathsf{MAP}}(\mathsf{pw})$:	$\mathsf{ScMul}_{\mathsf{base}}(g, y)$:	$\mathsf{ScMulVf}_{\mathsf{base}}(g, y)$:	$\mathsf{ScSam}_p()$:
return	return g^y	if $g \notin \mathcal{G}$: return $I_{\mathcal{G}}$	$y \leftarrow_{\mathrm{R}} 1 \dots p$
$\mathsf{Map2Pt}(\mathsf{H}_1(\mathsf{pw}))$		else: return g^y	return y

Fig. 6. Protocol $\mathrm{CPace}_{1\mathsf{MAP}}$ for an elliptic curve group $\mathcal{G}$ of prime order p, over finite field $\mathbb{F}_q$. Generators are computed as $\mathsf{Map2Pt}(\mathsf{H}_1(\mathsf{pw}))$ with a hash function $\mathsf{H}_1 : \{0,1\}^* \to \mathbb{F}_q$. Differences to $\mathrm{CPace}_{\mathsf{base}}$ are marked gray.

We now analyze a variant of the CPace protocol case-tailored for elliptic curve groups $\mathcal{G}$ over finite field $\mathbb{F}_q$. The protocol is depicted in Fig. 6. The only difference to $\mathrm{CPace}_{\mathsf{base}}$ analyzed in the previous section is how parties compute the generators: now the function H_1 hashes onto the field $\mathbb{F}_q$, and generators are computed as $g \leftarrow \mathsf{Map2Pt}(\mathsf{H}_1(\mathsf{pw}))$ for a function $\mathsf{Map2Pt} : \mathbb{F}_q \to \mathcal{G}$. This way, the H_1 outputs can be considered to form an alternative encoding of group elements, where Map2Pt decodes to the group. ScMul, ScMulVf and SamSc are as in Sect. 5.

Security analysis. Compared to the analysis of $\mathrm{CPace}_{\mathsf{base}}$, the security analysis is complicated by the different computation of the generators in essentially two ways: first, the possibly non-uniform distribution of Map2Pt induces non-uniformity of DH generators computed by the parties. Second, embedding of trapdoors no longer works by simply programming elements with known exponents into H_1. Instead, the proof will exploit that Map2Pt is probabilistically invertible, such that preimages of generators with known exponents can be programmed into H_1 instead. Consequently, security of CPace will be based on the $\mathcal{D}_{\mathcal{G}} - \mathsf{sSDH}$ problem Definition 3 instead of the sSDH problem, where the distribution $\mathcal{D}_{\mathcal{G}}$ corresponds to the distribution of group elements $\mathsf{Map2Pt}(h_i)$ obtained for uniformly sampled field elements $h_i \leftarrow_{\mathrm{R}} \mathbb{F}_q$. All these changes can be captured by replacing library sSDH with a new library for $\mathcal{D}_{\mathcal{G}} - \mathsf{sSDH}$, as we demonstrate below.

Theorem 4 (Security of $\mathrm{CPace}_{1\mathsf{MAP}}$). *Let $\lambda, p, q \in \mathbb{N}$ with p prime. Let $\mathcal{G}$ an elliptic curve of order p over field $\mathbb{F}_q$. Let $\mathsf{H}_1 : \{0,1\}^* \to \mathbb{F}_q, \mathsf{H}_2 : \{0,1\}^* \to \{0,1\}^\lambda$ be two hash functions and $\mathsf{Map2Pt} : \mathbb{F}_q \to \mathcal{G}$ probabilistically invertible with bound $\mathsf{Map2Pt}.n_{max}$. If the sCDH and sSDH problems are hard in $\mathcal{G}$, then the CPace protocol depicted in Fig. 2 UC-emulates $\mathcal{F}_{\mathsf{lePAKE}}$ in the random-oracle model with respect to adaptive corruptions and both hash functions modeled as random oracles. More precisely, for every adversary $\mathcal{A}$, there exist adversaries $\mathcal{B}_{\mathsf{sSDH}}$ and $\mathcal{B}_{\mathsf{sCDH}}$ against the sSDH and sCDH problems such that*

$$|Pr[Real(\mathcal{Z}, \mathcal{A}, CPace_{\mathsf{1MAP}})] - Pr[Ideal(\mathcal{F}_{\mathsf{lePAKE}}, \mathcal{S})]|$$
$$\leq (Map2Pt.n_{max}) l_{\mathsf{H}_1}/q + (l_{\mathsf{H}_1})^2/p + (Map2Pt.n_{max} \cdot l_{\mathsf{H}_1})^2/q$$
$$+ 2 l_{\mathsf{H}_1}^2 \mathbf{Adv}_{\mathcal{B}_{\mathsf{sSDH}}}^{\mathsf{sSDH}}(\mathcal{G}) + \mathbf{Adv}_{\mathcal{B}_{\mathsf{sCDH}}}^{\mathsf{sCDH}}(\mathcal{G})$$

where l_{H_1} denotes the number of H_1 queries made by the adversary $\mathcal{A}$ and the simulator $\mathcal{S}$ is as in Fig. 5 but using the object distExp (cf. Fig. 7) instead of the object sSdhExp.

```
def class D_G_sSDH:
  def _init_(s, Map2Pt, sSDHExp):
    s.sSDH = sSDHExp; s.records = [];
    s.nmax = n_max; s.preim = Map2Pt.PreImages;
  def sampleY(s): return (s.sSDH).sampleY();
  def isValid(X): return (s.sSDH).isValid(X);
  def sampleH1(s):
    g ← (s.sSDH).sampleH1();
    while (1):
      r ←R F_p; preimageList = (s.preim)(g^r); m ←R {0...(s.Map2Pt.n_max − 1)};
      if len(preimageList) > m:
        if r = 0:  abort("Sampled neutral element.");
        h ←preimageList[m];if h in s.records: abort("H1 collision");
        s.records.append(r, g^r, h);  return h;
  def corrupt(s, h, Y):
    if there is (r, g, h) in s.records: return (s.sSDH).corrupt(g, Y^(1/r));
  def DDH(s,h, Y, X, K):
    if there is (r, g, h) in s.records: return (s.sSDH).DDH(g, Y, X, K^(1/r));
# Chaining the experiments for CPace on prime order curve, full (x,y) coordinates
sSdhExp = sSDH(sCDH);
distExp = D_G_sSDH(Map2Pt,sSdhExp);
```

Fig. 7. Experiment class definition $\mathcal{D}_{\mathcal{G}}$-sSDH using single executions of Map2Pt, where H_1 hashes to $\mathbb{F}_q$.

Proof (Proof Sketch.). Let $\mathcal{D}_{\mathcal{G}}$ denote the distribution on $\mathcal{G}$ induced by Map2Pt. First note, that if the sSDH is hard in $\mathcal{G}$ then the corresponding $\mathcal{D}_{\mathcal{G}}$-sSDH problem is hard by Theorem 1 as $\mathsf{Map2Pt}^{-1}$ (implemented in the body of the sampleH1 method by the distExp object) is a rejection sampler for $\mathcal{D}_{\mathcal{G}}$.

We adjust the simulator for "basic" CPace from Fig. 5 as follows. First, we embed the reduction strategy from Theorem 1 into an experiment library that converts sSDH challenges into $\mathcal{D}_{\mathcal{G}}$ − sSDH challenges and obtain the class $\mathcal{D}_{\mathcal{G}}$_sSDH depicted in Fig. 7. The class $\mathcal{D}_{\mathcal{G}}$_sSDH uses the Map2Pt.PreImages function (passed as a constructor parameter) for implementing the $\mathsf{Map2Pt}^{-1}$ as defined in Algorithm 1 and an instance of the sSDH class implementing a sSDH experiment that is assigned to a member variable.

Each time the main body of the simulator from Fig. 5 makes calls to its exp object, the corresponding method of the new $\mathcal{D}_{\mathcal{G}}$_sSDH object will be executed, which itself translates the queries into calls to the sSDH object that was passed as constructor parameter.

Importantly, $\mathcal{D}_{\mathcal{G}}$_sSDH provides the same public API as the sSDH class with the distinction that sampling for H_1 returns results from $\mathbb{F}_q$ instead of $\mathcal{G}$. Moreover $\mathcal{D}_{\mathcal{G}}$_sSDH aborts if the code of its sSDH object aborts and, now additionally, also upon H_1 collisions.

We explain now how the indistinguishability argument of Theorem 2 needs to be adjusted in order to work for Theorem 4 and this new simulator. First, we ensure that the distribution of points provided by the $\mathcal{D}_{\mathcal{G}}$_sSDH object is uniform in $\mathbb{F}_q$ using Corollary 1. Second, we adjust the collision probability following the derivation from Corollary 2 which is now bound by $(n_{\max} \cdot l_{\mathsf{H}_1})^2/q$ in addition to the previous $l^2_{\mathsf{H}_1}/p$ probability. The probability that sampleH1 aborts because it samples the identity element from the distribution is bounded by $(\mathsf{Map2Pt}.n_{\max})l_{\mathsf{H}_1}/q$. Apart of these modification the proof applies without further changes.

Instantiating Map2Pt. Various constructions have been presented for mapping field elements to elliptic curve points such as Elligator2 [11], simplified SWU [20] and the Shallue-van de Woestijne method (SvdW) [35] (see also [20] and references therein). When considering short-Weierstrass representations of a curve, the general approach is to first derive a set of candidate values x_l for the x coordinate of a point such that for at least one of these candidates x_l there is a coordinate y_l such that (x_l, y_l) is a point on the curve. Subsequently one point (x_l, y_l) is chosen among the candidates. The property of *probabilistic invertibility* is fulfilled for all of the algorithms mentioned above and those currently suggested in [20]. The most generic of these algorithm, SvdW, works for all elliptic curves, while the simplified SWU and Elligator2 algorithms allow for more efficient implementations given that the curve fulfills some constraints.

All these mappings have a fixed and small bound $n_{\max}$ regarding the number of pre-images and come with a PPT algorithm for calculating all preimages. For instance, Elligator2 [11] comes with a maximum $n_{\max} = 2$ of two pre-images per point and $n_{\max} \leq 4$ for the simplified SWU and SvdW algorithms [20]. For all these algorithms, the most complex substep for determining all preimages is the calculation of a small pre-determined number of square roots and inversions in $\mathbb{F}_q$ which can easily be implemented in polynomial time with less computational complexity than one exponentiation operation.

6.2 Considering Curves with Small Co-factor

In this subsection, we now additionally consider that the elliptic curve group $\mathcal{G}$ can be of order $c \cdot p$ with $c \neq 1$, but where Diffie-Hellman-type assumptions can only assumed to be computationally infeasible in the subgroup of order p, denoted $\mathcal{G}_p$. Consequently, CPace$_{\mathsf{co}}$ on curves with co-factor $c \neq 1$ requires all

CPace$_{co}$:=CPace[Gen$_{1MAP}$, ScMul$_{co}$, ScMulVf$_{co}$, ScSam$_p$]			
Gen$_{1MAP}$(pw) :	ScMul$_{co}$(g, y) :	ScMulVf$_{co}$(g, y) :	ScSam$_p$() :
return Map2Pt(H$_1$(pw))	return $g^{c \cdot y}$	if $g \notin \mathcal{G}$: return $I_{\mathcal{G}}$	$y \leftarrow_R 1 \ldots p$
		else: return $g^{c \cdot y}$	return y

Fig. 8. Definition of CPace$_{co}$ for curves of order $p \cdot c$. The only difference (marked gray) to CPace$_{1MAP}$ is that exponents are always multiplied by the cofactor c.

secret exponents to be multiples of c. Hence, CPace$_{co}$ depicted in Fig. 8 deploys modified algorithms ScMul, ScMulVf.

```
# using python-style notation with self pointer s
def class cofactorClearer:
  "interfaces S to a prime-order experiment class"
  def _init_(s, c, p, primeOrderExplnstance ,p̄):
    s.c=c; s.i= s.c · integer(1/(s.c^2) mod p);s.it= s.c · integer(1/(s.c^2) mod p̄);
    s.exp = primeOrderExplnstance;
  def sampleY(s): return ((s.exp).sampleY())^(s.c);
  def isValid(X): return (s.exp).isValid(X^(s.i))
  def sampleH1(s): return (s.exp).sampleH1();
  def corrupt(s, h, Y): { return (s.exp).corrupt(h, Y^(s.i)); }
  def DDH(s,g, Y, X, K):
    if X ∈ G: return (s.exp).DDH(g, Y^(s.i), X^(s.i), K^(s.i·s.i))
    if X on twist: return (s.exp).DDH(g, Y^(s.i), X^(s.it), K^(s.it·s.it))

sSdhExp = sSDH(sCDH); ccExp = cofactorClearer(sSdhExp);
ccDistExp = D_G_sSDH(Map2Pt,ccExp);
```

Fig. 9. Cofactor-clearer class definition use for elliptic curves of order $p \cdot c$ with a quadratic twist having a subgroup of order $\bar{p}$. Note that the inverses $s.i$ and $s.it$ are constructed such that they are multiples of c.

Theorem 5 (Security of CPace$_{co}$). *Let $\lambda, p, q, c \in \mathbb{N}$, p, c coprime with p prime. Let $\mathcal{G}$ be an elliptic curve of order $p \cdot c$ over field $\mathbb{F}_q$ and $\mathcal{G}_p \subset \mathcal{G}$ a subgroup of order p. Let $CC_c : (g) \mapsto ((g^c)^{1/c \bmod p})$ be a cofactor clearing function for c, $\mathsf{H}_1 : \{0,1\}^* \to \mathbb{F}_q, \mathsf{H}_2 : \{0,1\}^* \to \{0,1\}^\lambda$ be two hash functions and Map2Pt $: \mathbb{F}_q \to \mathcal{G}$ probabilistically invertible with bound Map2Pt.n_{max}. Let be the chained function Map2Pt$_{\mathcal{G}_p}$:= ($CC_c \circ$ Map2Pt). Let $\mathcal{D}_{\mathcal{G}_p}$ denote the distribution on $\mathcal{G}_p$ induced by Map2Pt$_{\mathcal{G}_p}$. If the sCDH and sSDH problems are hard in $\mathcal{G}_p$, then the $\mathcal{D}_{\mathcal{G}_p}$-sSDH problem is hard in $\mathcal{G}_p$ and CPace$_{co}$ UC-emulates $\mathcal{F}_{\mathsf{lePAKE}}$ in the random-oracle model with respect to adaptive corruptions when both hash functions are modeled as random oracles. More precisely, for every adversary $\mathcal{A}$, there exist adversaries $\mathcal{B}_{\mathsf{sCDH}}$ and $\mathcal{B}_{\mathsf{sSDH}}$ against the sCDH and sSDH problems such that*

$$|Pr[Real(\mathcal{Z}, \mathcal{A}, CPace_{co})] - Pr[Ideal(\mathcal{F}_{\mathsf{lePAKE}}, \mathcal{S})]|$$
$$\leq (Map2Pt.n_{max} \cdot c)l_{\mathsf{H}_1}/q + 2l^2_{\mathsf{H}_1}/p + (Map2Pt.n_{max} \cdot c \cdot l_{\mathsf{H}_1})^2/q$$
$$+ 2l^2_{\mathsf{H}_1} \mathbf{Adv}^{sSDH}_{\mathcal{B}_{sSDH}}(\mathcal{G}_p) + \mathbf{Adv}^{sCDH}_{\mathcal{B}_{sCDH}}(\mathcal{G}_p)$$

where l_{H_1} denotes the number of H_1 queries made by the adversary $\mathcal{A}$ and the simulator $\mathcal{S}$ is as in Fig. 5 but using class ccDistExp (cf. Fig. 9) instead of object sSdhExp.

Proof (Proof Sketch.). The full group $\mathcal{G}$ has a point g_1 of order c with $g_1^c = I_{\mathcal{G}}$ where $I_{\mathcal{G}}$ denotes the identity element in $\mathcal{G}$, i.e., there are c low-order points $g_1^i, i \in \{1 \ldots c\}$. For any point $Y \in \mathcal{G}$ we can consider the points $Y_i = Y \cdot g_i$ as alternative ambiguous representations of the point $CC_c(Y) \in \mathcal{G}_p$. For any input point $Y \in \mathcal{G}_p$, all these c alternative representations can be easily calculated using group operations and g_i. For any of these c alternative representations of Y at most $\mathsf{Map2Pt}.n_{\max}$ preimages will be returned by $\mathsf{Map2Pt.PreImages}$ since $\mathsf{Map2Pt}$ is probabilistically invertible on $\mathcal{G}$. Correspondingly, the probability of accidentally drawing a representation of the identity element needs to be multiplied by c and is now bounded by $(\mathsf{Map2Pt}.n_{\max} \cdot c)l_{\mathsf{H}_1}/q$. If up to $\mathsf{Map2Pt}.n_{\max}$ preimages exist per point on the full curve, the chained function $\mathsf{Map2Pt}_{\mathcal{G}_p}$ is probabilistically invertible also on $\mathcal{G}_p$. Its preimage function $\mathsf{Map2Pt}_{\mathcal{G}_p}.\mathsf{PreImages}$ for $\mathcal{G}_p$ can be defined such that it returns all of the preimages of the c ambiguous representations of an input and the maximum number of preimages $\mathsf{Map2Pt}_{\mathcal{G}_p}.n_{\max}$ is, thus, bounded by $\mathsf{Map2Pt}_{\mathcal{G}_p}.n_{\max} = c \cdot \mathsf{Map2Pt}.n_{\max}$. Since we are able to provide all preimages for $\mathsf{Map2Pt}_{\mathcal{G}_p}$ and a bound for their number is known $\mathsf{Map2Pt}_{\mathcal{G}_p}$ is probabilistically invertible. We thus can employ Theorem 1 and show that if the sSDH is hard in $\mathcal{G}_p$ then the corresponding $\mathcal{D}_{\mathcal{G}_p}$-sSDH problem is also hard.

As $\mathsf{ScMulVf}_{co}$ and ScMul_{co} use exponents that are a multiples of c they are guaranteed to produce a unique result on $\mathcal{G}_p$ for all of the c ambiguous representations of an input point. The additional factor of c in the exponents is compensated by the simulation by calling an experiment library using the ccExp class from Fig. 9.[3] The ccExp object forwards queries to a $\mathcal{D}_{\mathcal{G}_p}$_sSDH object such that all inputs to the DDH oracle will be in $\mathcal{G}_p$.

6.3 CPace Using Single-Coordinate Diffie-Hellman

Some Diffie-Hellman-based protocols, including CPace, can be implemented also on a group modulo negation, i.a. a group where a group element Y and its inverse Y^{-1} (i.e. the point with $I = Y \cdot Y^{-1}$) are not distinguished and share the same binary representation[4].

[3] Note that this class also accepts points on the quadratic twist, a feature that will become relevant only when considering simplified point verification on twist-secure curves as discussed in the full version of this paper [4].

[4] Counter-examples for protocols that cannot be instantiated on a group modulo negation and require full group structure are, e.g., TBPEKE [34] and SPAKE2 [5]. The reason is that these protocols require addition of arbitrary points on the group.

```
def class moduloNegationAdapter:
  "uses the strip- and reconstruct functions SC and RC."
  def _init_(s,, baseExperiment):
    s.exp ←baseExperiment;s.records← [];
  def sampleY(s): Y ← ((s.exp).sampleY())^s.c; s.records.append(Y); return SC(Y);
  def isValid(X̂):(X0, X1)←RC(X̂); return (s.exp).isValid(X0);
  def sampleH1(s): return (s.exp).sampleH1();
  def corrupt(s, h, Ŷ):
    (Y,Y*) ← RC(Ŷ); if Y* in s.records: Y ← Y*; return (s.exp).corrupt(h, Y);
  def DDH(s,g, Ŷ, X̂, K̂):
    (Y,Y*) ← RC(Ŷ); if Y* in s.records: Y ← Y*;
    (X, X*) ← RC(X̂); (K, K*) ← RC(K̂);
    return (s.exp.DDH(g, Y, X, K)) or (s.exp.DDH(g, Y, X, K*))

# Chaining the experiments for prime order curve, single coordinate, single map
sSdhExp = sSDH(sCDH); distExp = D_G_sSDH(Map2Pt,sSdhExp);
singleCoorExp = moduloNegationAdapter(distExp)
```

Fig. 10. Single-coordinate experiment class definition for CPace instantiations on groups modulo negation.

An elliptic curve in Weierstrass representation becomes a group modulo negation when only using x-coordinates as representation. We use the notation $\hat{Y}$ for such ambiguous encodings and use $\hat{Y} \leftarrow \mathsf{SC}(Y)$ for a function returning the x-coordinate for a point Y and $(Y^{-1}, Y) \leftarrow \mathsf{RC}(\hat{Y})$ for the inverse operation reconstructing Y and Y^{-1} in an undefined order.

The major advantage of using this type of ambiguous encoding is that it can be helpful in practice for all of the following: reducing code size, reducing public key sizes and network bandwidth, avoiding implementation pitfalls [10] and restricting invalid curve attacks to the curve's quadratic twist. Consequently, many real-world protocols such as TLS only use this single coordinate for deriving their session key, as to give implementers the flexibility to take benefit of the above advantages.

For the purpose of function definitions by chaining, we introduce a function $\mathsf{RSC}(\hat{Y}, x)$ that takes one ambiguously encoded group element $\hat{Y}$ in addition to one scalar x, i.e. takes the same operands as ScMul. We define $\mathsf{RSC}(\hat{Y}, x)$ such that it returns a tuple (Y, x) such that $\mathsf{SC}(Y) = \hat{Y}$. With this definition, we can formalize CPace using single-coordinate scalar multiplications with the chained functions $\mathsf{ScMul}_{x-only} := (\mathsf{SC} \circ \mathsf{ScMul} \circ \mathsf{RSC})$, $\mathsf{ScMulVf}_{x-only} := (\mathsf{SC} \circ \mathsf{ScMulVf} \circ \mathsf{RSC})$ and $\mathsf{Gen}_{x-only} := \mathsf{SC} \circ \mathsf{Gen}$, such that the ambiguous encodings are used.[5]

Theorem 6 (Security of CPace$_{\mathsf{x-only}}$). *Given a group $\mathcal{G}$, assume CPace[Gen, ScMul, ScMulVf, SamSc] on $\mathcal{G}$ can be distinguished from an ideal-world run of $\mathcal{F}_{\mathsf{lePAKE}}$ and $\mathcal{S}$ from Fig. 5 with negligible advantage, where $\mathcal{S}$ embeds an*

[5] Note that this definition obtained from chaining with SC and RSC for the scalar multiplications corresponds exactly to the conventional so-called single-coordinate ladder algorithms.

experiment object exp. *Then CPace[*SC ∘ Gen, SC ∘ *ScMul* ∘ RSC, SC ∘ *ScMulVf* ∘ RSC, *SamSc] on the corresponding group modulo negation* $\hat{\mathcal{G}}$ *cannot be distinguished from* $\mathcal{F}_{\mathsf{lePAKE}}$ *running with a simulator* $\hat{\mathcal{S}}$ *that is obtained by chaining* exp *with* moduloNegationAdapter, *the adapter class from Fig. 10, and the difference in the distinguishing advantage is bounded by a factor of 2.*

We defer the proof sketch to the full version of this paper [4]. With our library-based approach to simulation, it is also possible to argue security of CPace variants which combine several of the aspects above. In a nutshell, this works by chaining of the experiment classes. We refer the reader to the full version [4] for details and examples.

References

1. Abdalla, M., Barbosa, M., Bradley, T., Jarecki, S., Katz, J., Xu, J.: Universally composable relaxed password authenticated key exchange. In: Micciancio, D., Ristenpart, T. (eds.) CRYPTO 2020, Part I. LNCS, vol. 12170, pp. 278–307. Springer, Cham (2020). https://doi.org/10.1007/978-3-030-56784-2_10
2. Abdalla, M., Barbosa, M., Katz, J., Loss, J., Jiayu, X.: Algebraic adversaries in the universal composability framework. In: Tibouchi, M., Wang, H. (eds.) ASIACRYPT 2021. LNCS. Springer, Heidelberg (2021)
3. Abdalla, M., Bellare, M., Rogaway, P.: The oracle Diffie-Hellman assumptions and an analysis of DHIES. In: Naccache, D. (ed.) CT-RSA 2001. LNCS, vol. 2020, pp. 143–158. Springer, Heidelberg (2001). https://doi.org/10.1007/3-540-45353-9_12
4. Abdalla, M., Haase, B., Hesse, J.: Security analysis of CPace. Cryptology ePrint Archive, Report 2021/114 (2021). https://eprint.iacr.org/2021/114
5. Abdalla, M., Pointcheval, D.: Simple password-based encrypted key exchange protocols. In: Menezes, A. (ed.) CT-RSA 2005. LNCS, vol. 3376, pp. 191–208. Springer, Heidelberg (2005). https://doi.org/10.1007/978-3-540-30574-3_14
6. Barak, B., Lindell, Y., Rabin, T.: Protocol initialization for the framework of universal composability. Cryptology ePrint Archive, Report 2004/006 (2004). https://eprint.iacr.org/2004/006
7. Bellare, M., Pointcheval, D., Rogaway, P.: Authenticated key exchange secure against dictionary attacks. In: Preneel, B. (ed.) EUROCRYPT 2000. LNCS, vol. 1807, pp. 139–155. Springer, Heidelberg (2000). https://doi.org/10.1007/3-540-45539-6_11
8. Bellovin, S.M., Merritt, M.: Encrypted key exchange: password-based protocols secure against dictionary attacks. In: 1992 IEEE Symposium on Security and Privacy, pp. 72–84. IEEE Computer Society Press, May 1992
9. Bender, J., Fischlin, M., Kügler, D.: Security analysis of the PACE key-agreement protocol. In: Samarati, P., Yung, M., Martinelli, F., Ardagna, C.A. (eds.) ISC 2009. LNCS, vol. 5735, pp. 33–48. Springer, Heidelberg (2009). https://doi.org/10.1007/978-3-642-04474-8_3
10. Bernstein, D.J.: Curve25519: new Diffie-Hellman speed records. In: Yung, M., Dodis, Y., Kiayias, A., Malkin, T. (eds.) PKC 2006. LNCS, vol. 3958, pp. 207–228. Springer, Heidelberg (2006). https://doi.org/10.1007/11745853_14
11. Bernstein, D.J., Hamburg, M., Krasnova, A., Lange, T.: Elligator: elliptic-curve points indistinguishable from uniform random strings. In: Sadeghi, A., Gligor, V.D., Yung, M. (eds.) ACM CCS 2013, pp. 967–980. ACM Press, November 2013

12. Bernstein, D.J., Lange, T.: SafeCurves: choosing safe curves for elliptic-curve cryptography. Definition of Twist security (2019). https://safecurves.cr.yp.to/twist.html. Accessed 15 Jan 2019
13. Brier, E., Coron, J.-S., Icart, T., Madore, D., Randriam, H., Tibouchi, M.: Efficient indifferentiable hashing into ordinary elliptic curves. In: Rabin, T. (ed.) CRYPTO 2010. LNCS, vol. 6223, pp. 237–254. Springer, Heidelberg (2010). https://doi.org/10.1007/978-3-642-14623-7_13
14. Canetti, R.: Universally composable security: a new paradigm for cryptographic protocols. In: 42nd FOCS, pp. 136–145. IEEE Computer Society Press, October 2001
15. Canetti, R., Halevi, S., Katz, J., Lindell, Y., MacKenzie, P.: Universally composable password-based key exchange. In: Cramer, R. (ed.) EUROCRYPT 2005. LNCS, vol. 3494, pp. 404–421. Springer, Heidelberg (2005). https://doi.org/10.1007/11426639_24
16. Canetti, R., Rabin, T.: Universal composition with joint state. In: Boneh, D. (ed.) CRYPTO 2003. LNCS, vol. 2729, pp. 265–281. Springer, Heidelberg (2003). https://doi.org/10.1007/978-3-540-45146-4_16
17. de Valence, H., Grigg, J., Tankersley, G., Valsorda, F., Lovecruft, I., Hamburg, M.: The ristretto255 and decaf448 groups. RFC, IRTF (2020)
18. Digital Signature Standard (DSS): National Institute of Standards and Technology (NIST), FIPS PUB 186-4, U.S. Department of Commerce, July 2013. https://nvlpubs.nist.gov/nistpubs/FIPS/NIST.FIPS.186-4.pdf
19. Eaton, E., Stebila, D.: The "quantum annoying" property of password-authenticated key exchange protocols. In: Cheon, J.H., Tillich, J.-P. (eds.) PQCrypto 2021 2021. LNCS, vol. 12841, pp. 154–173. Springer, Cham (2021). https://doi.org/10.1007/978-3-030-81293-5_9
20. Faz-Hernandez, A., Scott, S., Sullivan, N., Wahby, R., Wood, C.: Hashing to elliptic curves (2019). https://datatracker.ietf.org/doc/draft-irtf-cfrg-hash-to-curve/
21. Gentry, C., Wichs, D.: Separating succinct non-interactive arguments from all falsifiable assumptions. In: Fortnow, L., Vadhan, S.P. (eds.) 43rd ACM STOC, pp. 99–108. ACM Press, June 2011
22. Haase, B., Labrique, B.: AuCPace: efficient verifier-based PAKE protocol tailored for the IIoT. IACR TCHES **2019**(2), 1–48 (2019). https://tches.iacr.org/index.php/TCHES/article/view/7384
23. Haase, B.: CPace, a balanced composable PAKE (2020). https://datatracker.ietf.org/doc/draft-haase-cpace/
24. Haase, B., Labrique, B.: AuCPace: efficient verifier-based PAKE protocol tailored for the IIoT. Cryptology ePrint Archive, Report 2018/286 (2018). https://eprint.iacr.org/2018/286
25. Hamburg, M.: Decaf: eliminating cofactors through point compression. In: Gennaro, R., Robshaw, M. (eds.) CRYPTO 2015, Part I. LNCS, vol. 9215, pp. 705–723. Springer, Heidelberg (2015). https://doi.org/10.1007/978-3-662-47989-6_34
26. Hamburg, M.: Ed448-goldilocks, a new elliptic curve. Cryptology ePrint Archive, Report 2015/625 (2015). https://eprint.iacr.org/2015/625
27. Hamburg, M.: Indifferentiable hashing from Elligator 2. Cryptology ePrint Archive, Report 2020/1513 (2020). https://eprint.iacr.org/2020/1513
28. Hesse, J.: Review of (security of) remaining candidates. Posting to the CFRG mailing list (2020). https://mailarchive.ietf.org/arch/msg/cfrg/47pnOSsrVS8uozXbAuM-alEk0-s/

29. Hesse, J.: Separating symmetric and asymmetric password-authenticated key exchange. In: Galdi, C., Kolesnikov, V. (eds.) SCN 2020. LNCS, vol. 12238, pp. 579–599. Springer, Cham (2020). https://doi.org/10.1007/978-3-030-57990-6_29
30. Jablon, D.P.: Strong password-only authenticated key exchange. Comput. Commun. Rev. **26**(5), 5–26 (1996)
31. Jarecki, S., Krawczyk, H., Xu, J.: OPAQUE: an asymmetric PAKE protocol secure against pre-computation attacks. In: Nielsen, J.B., Rijmen, V. (eds.) EUROCRYPT 2018, Part III. LNCS, vol. 10822, pp. 456–486. Springer, Cham (2018). https://doi.org/10.1007/978-3-319-78372-7_15
32. Langley, A., Hamburg, M., Turner, S.: Elliptic curves for security. RFC 7748, IETF, January 2016
33. Advanced security mechanism for machine readable travel documents (extended access control (EAC), password authenticated connection establishment (PACE), and restricted identification (RI)). Federal Office for Information Security (BSI), BSI-TR-03110, Version 2.0 (2008)
34. Pointcheval, D., Wang, G.: VTBPEKE: verifier-based two-basis password exponential key exchange. In: Karri, R., Sinanoglu, O., Sadeghi, A., Yi, X. (eds.) ASIACCS 17, pp. 301–312. ACM Press, April 2017
35. Shallue, A., van de Woestijne, C.E.: Construction of rational points on elliptic curves over finite fields. In: Hess, F., Pauli, S., Pohst, M. (eds.) ANTS 2006. LNCS, vol. 4076, pp. 510–524. Springer, Heidelberg (2006). https://doi.org/10.1007/11792086_36
36. Shoup, V.: Sequences of games: a tool for taming complexity in security proofs. Cryptology ePrint Archive, Report 2004/332 (2004). https://eprint.iacr.org/2004/332
37. Tackmann, B.: Updated review of PAKEs. Posting to the CFRG mailing list (2020). https://mailarchive.ietf.org/arch/msg/cfrg/eo8O6JYPmWY6L9TlcIXStFy5gNQ/

Modular Design of Role-Symmetric Authenticated Key Exchange Protocols

Yuting Xiao[1], Rui Zhang[1,2(✉)], and Hui Ma[1]

[1] State Key Laboratory of Information Security, Institute of Information Engineering, Chinese Academy of Sciences, Beijing, China
{xiaoyuting,r-zhang,mahui}@iie.ac.cn

[2] School of Cyber Security, University of Chinese Academy of Sciences, Beijing, China

Abstract. Authenticated Key Exchange (AKE) is an important primitive in applied cryptography. Previously several strong models of AKE were introduced, e.g., CK, CK$^+$, eCK and their extended versions considering perfect forward secrecy (PFS), (denoted by a "-PFS" suffix). These models provide different security guarantees and they are incomparable. Hence, one still lacks systematic understanding of the prerequisites for secure AKEs and a modular design of AKE protocols. In this paper, we investigate this issue in the context of One-Round Authenticated Key Exchange (ORKE), which is role-symmetric for players and only needs a single round to establish a session key.

Our treatments are as follows: First, we reformat the CK, CK-PFS, CK$^+$, CK$^+$-PFS, eCK and eCK-PFS models in the context of ORKE, some of which are formulated for the first time in the literature. Next, we introduce a new tool, Key-wise Recoverable Function (KRF). With merely black-box calls to KRFs, we build modular constructions for ORKEs. As an immediate application, many previous protocols can be explained naturally by the construction. We further build a protocol with CK, CK$^+$, eCK, CK-PFS, CK$^+$-PFS and eCK-PFS security simultaneously, by properly instantiating the underlying KRF. As a by-product, we have simplified proofs for a few known protocols, with non-standard assumptions avoidable.

Keywords: Role-symmetric · One-round authenticated key exchange · Key-wise recoverable functions · Modular construction

1 Introduction

Authenticated Key Exchange (AKE) is a fundamental cryptographic primitive to set up secure channels between parties over an open network. In the last decades, many AKE protocols have been developed and used in practice, e.g., SSL/TLS, IPSec and SSH. Typically, in a two-party AKE protocol Π, each party possesses a long-term public/secret key pair. If any two parties want to negotiate a session key, they should select their own ephemeral keys, then exchange messages in a specific order (e.g., the initiator $\mathcal{I}$ starts by sending M_1, the responder $\mathcal{R}$

M. Tibouchi and H. Wang (Eds.): ASIACRYPT 2021, LNCS 13093, pp. 742–772, 2021.
https://doi.org/10.1007/978-3-030-92068-5_25

sends M_2, the initiator $\mathcal{I}$ sends M_3, and so on), finally compute the session key from four pieces of information, including their own long-term secret and ephemeral keys, the other party's long-term public key and the transcript (i.e., the concatenation of the identities of both sides and all transmitted messages).

We say that Π is an n-round protocol if the maximum number of messages exchanged from an initiator to a responder during one protocol execution is n. We say a protocol is role-symmetric if both sides have equivalent roles, namely, neither side needs to wait for the other party's message to arrive. It is a significant useful property in practice, which greatly reduces latency. In the literature, several famous protocols are role-symmetric, e.g., MQV [20], HMQV [18], NAXOS [19], etc. In particular, these protocols only involve two messages in one round to establish a session key. Such protocols have attracted much attention due to their simplicity and their efficiency in terms of bandwidth usage. In this paper, we focus on this case, also known as One-Round Authenticated Key Exchanges (ORKEs).

Up to now, a number of security models have been introduced for AKEs. The first is the BR model introduced by Bellare and Rogaway [2], capturing an open network fully controlled by adversaries. It is an indistinguishability-based security definition. Any party executing one protocol instance is called a session. Adversaries are allowed to launch various interleaving attacks, corrupt parties' long-term keys and reveal session keys. These behaviours are formally modeled as performing Send($\cdot$), Corrupt($\cdot$) and SKReveal($\cdot$) queries on specific sessions. The security is defined via an experiment between an adversary and the challenger, where the adversary is allowed to adaptively ask above queries, and choose a target session in a Test($\cdot$) query that outputs a real or random session key according to a flipped coin. The adversary is said to win if it guesses the correct bit with non-negligible advantage over random guess. To avoid trivial success, the target session must be *fresh* throughout the experiment. Note that the *freshness* notion is important help us understand different security models, which in turn depends on the definitions of *session identifiers* (to identify sessions) and *matching-session* (to denote the session via the same execution instance with the target session), and mainly reflects the restrictions on the adversary's access to secret information of the target session. After that, several stronger security models were developed, namely, CK [7], eCK [19] and CK$^+$ [18]. In these models, the adversaries are allowed to obtain more secret information.

The CK model was introduced by Canetti and Krawczyk [7], which additionally allows an adversary to obtain the secret state of a specific session via the SSReveal($\cdot$) query. Since Canetti and Krawczyk did not explicitly specify what information is included in the session state, the claiming CK-security of a particular protocol should come with a careful pre-definition of it. The eCK (extended CK) model was introduced by LaMacchia, Lauter and Mityagin [19]. They replaced the SSReveal($\cdot$) query by the EphKReveal($\cdot$) query, which gives an adversary the power to corrupt the ephemeral key (i.e., the randomness used) of a specific session. As the name implies, the eCK model provides more security guarantees that are not originally considered by the CK model, e.g., weak perfect forward secrecy (wPFS) [1,18], as well as resistance to key-compromise impersonation attack (KCI) [15,23] and maximal exposure attack (MEX, where a non-trivial combination of the ephemeral and long-term keys of the target session and its matching session are exposed to the adversary). The CK^+ model was originally used to capture the security properties of HMQV [18] and later reformatted by Fujioka et al. [11]. It seems like but not actually a combination of the CK and eCK models. In the CK^+ model, an adversary can ask SSReveal(·) queries and get a non-trivial combination of the ephemeral and long-term keys of the target session and its matching session.

In the literature, several works have developed the CK, CK^+ and eCK models for capturing perfect forward secrecy (PFS). Boyd and Nieto [6] considered PFS for the CK model, which we prefer call the CK_{BN} model. Yoneyama [27] proposed the CK^+-sFS^{NSR} model based on the CK^+ model. Cremers and Feltz [9] also proposed the eCK-PFS model to capture the PFS for the eCK model. Note that, when considering PFS, both parties' long-term keys will eventually be exposed to the adversary, thus if it is also allowed to reveal the ephemeral secret of either party, the adversary would trivially win. To avoid trivial success, some less common constraints on the adversaries' behaviours were raised in the CK_{BN} and CK^+-sFS^{NSR} models, e.g., SSReveal(·) query is not allowed on any session between the owner and the peer of the target session. While in the eCK-PFS model, the notion of *origin-session* was proposed, which facilitates analysing and limiting the adversaries' behaviours in a more granular way, thus following the common manner defining security in the CK, CK+ and eCK models.

To date, only a few work attempted to investigate relations of the existing models. Cremers [8] noticed that, the original versions of the CK [7], CK^+ [18] and eCK [19] models are incomparable, by showing a (somehow artificial) protocol provable secure in one model is insecure in other models. This accounts for why later work only considered security in a single model: e.g., [4,17,22] in the CK model, [16,21,25] in the eCK model, [24] in the CK^+ model and [3,26] in the eCK-PFS model.

On the other hand, some subsequent works *did* make subtle changes to these models. For instance, Boyd et al. [4] redefined the session identifiers for the CK model using the concatenation of the messages sent and received by parties instead of a string required to be sent along with the message, which requires the definition of matching notion to be modified accordingly; in the CK^+ model by Fujioka et al. [11,12], the definition of matching notion includes an extra restriction, i.e., two sessions must have non-equal role identifiers (denoting the actor of a session is an initiator or a responder); in the eCK-PFS model by Bergsma et al. [3], such restriction was dropped in defining the matching notion, differing from the original eCK and eCK-PFS models.

Hence a natural question arises whether insisting these different definitions of session identifiers and matching sessions really matters in practice? In addition, many different techniques and different assumptions were used for different schemes in different models, therefore, a systematic understanding of how to construct secure ORKEs is extremely necessary and helpful.

The above are exactly our motivations to revisit the CK, eCK, CK^+ and eCK-PFS models, in the context of ORKE as a first step, and develop a modular construction that can be proved secure in these models, respectively. As a result, we show there exists an ORKE protocol provably secure in different models, if its underlying building-blocks meet some natural security properties.

1.1 Our Results

A Complete Set of Definitions for ORKE. We present a succinct and comprehensible unification of the existing models in the context of ORKE. We also formally defined CK-PFS and CK^+-PFS models utilizing the notion of origin session. As the name suggests, these two models extend naturally the CK and CK^+ models by capturing perfect forward secrecy (PFS). Note that, they are stronger than the CK_{BN} and CK^+-sFS^{NSR} models, respectively. Combining with the existing CK, eCK, CK^+ and eCK-PFS models, we have a complete set of unified strong security definitions for ORKE.

A New Tool KRF for Secure ORKEs. We introduce a new tool, called Key-wise Recoverable Function (KRF). Using KRF and passively secure Key Exchange (KE) as building blocks, we give a modular construction (Fig. 6) and other extended variants, whose security holds in all the above-mentioned strong models by assuming the underlying KRF meets different security definitions.

Unification of the Previous Works. We note that our modular construction simultaneously captures the ideas behind several well-known constructions, including 2×KEM+DH [4] (CK security), NAXOS [19] (eCK security), HMQV [18] (CK^+ security) and BJS [3] (eCK-PFS security).

Independent from our work, Xue et al. [24] introduced a primitive called double-key key encapsulation mechanism (2-key KEM), based on which, they presented modular constructions to simplify the construction and analysis of CK^+-secure and eCK-secure AKEs. Compared with their work, our work has a wider range of application as the CK, CK-PFS, CK^+-PFS and eCK-PFS models were also taken into account. In addition, our modular constructions are role-symmetric, which makes it more suitable for some scenarios (Table 1).

Table 1. Detailed comparisons with Xue et al.

Constructions	Role-Symmetric	Tools	Applicable models	Unification of previous works	
Xue et al. [24]	N	2-key KEM	CK^+, eCK	HMQV [18]	CK^+
				NAXOS [19]	eCK
				Okamoto [21]	eCK
				FSXY12,13 [11,12]	CK^+
Our work	Y	KRF,KE	CK,CK^+, eCK, CK-PFS, CK^+-PFS, eCK-PFS	2KEM+DH [4]	CK
				HMQV [18]	CK^+
				NAXOS [19]	eCK
				BJS [3]	eCK-PFS

†† "N" denotes "no", and "Y" denotes "yes".

New Results for ORKEs with KRFs. We have the following new results:

- We observe that our modular construction using a same KRF achieves CK$^+$ (resp., CK$^+$-PFS) security and eCK (resp., eCK-PFS) security, which makes a protocol selection much easier in practice.
- By instantiating our modular construction with a proper KRF, we obtain a secure protocol in the CK-PFS model (first formulated in this work). Compared with the SIG(2KEM+DH) construction, an immediate scheme inspired by the work of Cremers and Feltz [9], this proposal is more efficient in terms of computation and bandwidth.
- Finally, we show that there is a KRF with full security (i.e., meeting all the security definitions), applying our modular construction, a secure ORKE is then acquired in all the known security models, namely, CK, CK$^+$, eCK, CK-PFS, CK$^+$-PFS and eCK-PFS.

2 Preliminary

In this section, we review some useful notations and notions.

Notations. For arbitrary $k \in \mathbb{N}$, 1^k denotes the string of k ones. For an integer m, $[m] \stackrel{\text{def}}{=} \{1, 2, \dots, m\}$. If $\mathcal{S}$ is a distribution, $x \leftarrow_{\$} \mathcal{S}$ denotes randomly choosing an element according to $\mathcal{S}$. If A is an algorithm, $\mathsf{A}(x; r) \to y$ denotes that A takes x as input and r as internal randomness returns output y. If y is a variable, $y \leftarrow \mathsf{A}(x)$ denotes assigning the output of A with x as input to y. A function $\mu(\cdot)$ is called negligible, if for every polynomial $p(\cdot)$, there exists some λ_0 such that $\mu(\lambda) \le 1/p(\lambda)$, for every $\lambda > \lambda_0$.

Passively Secure Key Exchange. Here we define passively secure Key Exchange (KE) that is used without any long-term keys, which consists of two polynomial time algorithms: a probabilistic algorithm $\mathsf{KE.Gen}(1^\lambda) \to (pk, sk)$ that takes as input a security parameter 1^λ and returns a key pair (pk, sk); a deterministic algorithm $\mathsf{KE.Key}(sk, pk') \to k$ that takes as input a secret key sk and a public key pk' and returns a key k. Let $\text{CKey}(pk, pk')$ denote $k \leftarrow \mathsf{KE.Key}(sk, pk')$. Correctness requires that for any $(pk, sk) \leftarrow \mathsf{KE.Gen}(1^\lambda)$ and $(pk', sk') \leftarrow \mathsf{KE.Gen}(1^\lambda)$, $\text{CKey}(pk, pk') = \text{CKey}(pk', pk)$ holds.

Definition 1 (Passive-Security). *A KE scheme* $\mathsf{KE} = (\mathsf{KE.Gen}, \mathsf{KE.Key})$ *is called Passively Secure (PS), if for any PPT adversary* $\mathcal{A}$*, its advantage:*

$$\mathsf{Adv}^{\mathsf{PS}}_{\mathsf{KE},\mathcal{A}}(\lambda) \stackrel{def}{=} \Pr[b' = b : b' \leftarrow \mathcal{A}^{\text{PExecute}(\cdot),\text{PReveal}(\cdot),\text{PTest}(\cdot)}(1^\lambda)] \le \mu(\lambda),$$

where $\mathcal{A}$ *is allowed to adaptively query:*

- $\text{PExecute}(i)$*: For unused identity* i*, compute* $(pk_i, sk_i) \leftarrow \mathsf{KE.Gen}(1^\lambda)$ *and* $(pk_i', sk_i') \leftarrow \mathsf{KE.Gen}(1^\lambda)$*, and return* (pk_i, pk_i')*. Otherwise, do nothing.*
- $\text{PReveal}(i)$*: If the identity* i *has been used in previous* $\text{PExecute}(\cdot)$ *queries, compute* $k_i \leftarrow \mathsf{KE.Key}(sk_i, pk_i')$ *and return* k_i*.*

- PTest(i^*): *This can be asked for only once. If* $b = 0$, *return the real key* $k_{i^*} \leftarrow \mathsf{KE.Key}(sk_{i^*}, pk'_{i^*})$; *else if* $b = 1$, *return a random key. Throughout the experiment,* PReveal(i^*) *should never been queried.*

Pseudo-Random Function. Let $\mathcal{F} \stackrel{\text{def}}{=} \{\mathcal{F}_\lambda : \mathcal{S}_\lambda \times Dom_\lambda \rightarrow Rng_\lambda\}_{\lambda \in \mathbb{N}}$ define a function family with families of key spaces $\{\mathcal{S}_\lambda\}_{\lambda \in \mathbb{N}}$, domains $\{Dom_\lambda\}_{\lambda \in \mathbb{N}}$ and ranges $\{Rng_\lambda\}_{\lambda \in \mathbb{N}}$, where λ denotes a security parameter.

Definition 2 (PRF). *A function family* $\mathcal{F}$ *is called a secure Pseudo-Random Function (PRF) family if for any PPT adversary* $\mathcal{A}$, *its advantage*

$$\mathsf{Adv}^{\mathrm{PRF}}_{\mathcal{F},\mathcal{A}}(\lambda) \stackrel{def}{=} |\Pr[1 \leftarrow \mathcal{A}^{\mathcal{F}_\lambda(\cdot)}] - \Pr[1 \leftarrow \mathcal{A}^{\mathcal{RF}_\lambda(\cdot)}]| \leq \mu(\lambda),$$

where $\mathcal{RF}_\lambda(\cdot) : Dom_\lambda \rightarrow Rng_\lambda$ *is a truly random function family.*

3 Security Definitions for ORKEs

In this section, we unify the definitions of the CK [4,5,7], eCK [19,21], CK$^+$ [11,12,18] and eCK-PFS [3,9] models in the context of ORKE, and introduce the CK-PFS and CK$^+$-PFS models. We resemble the method defining security models used in [11], namely we formulate these models as follows: wPFS, PFS, KCI resistance, and MEX resistance are integrated into the experiments of considered models by exhaustively classifying leakage patterns. Such definitional treatment is convenient for capturing all required properties rigorously in each model, and greatly simplifies the security proofs in these models.

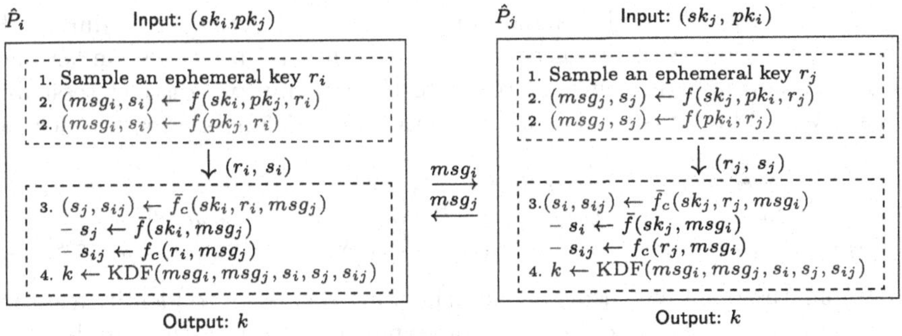

Fig. 1. A generic description of ORKE

We first present a generic description of ORKE to help us understand the security models. Assume each party $\hat{P}_i$ possesses a long-term public/secret key pair (pk_i, sk_i), and will select an ephemeral key (i.e., the randomness r) in each execution instance. In general, we use three functions to abstract each party's local computations: (1) f to generate the message sent to its peer party; (2) $\bar{f}_c$

to deal with the received message; (3) KDF to compute the session key. Take one execution instance between two parties $\hat{P}_i$ and $\hat{P}_j$ as an illustration (see Fig. 1). The function f may take two forms. The first takes the party's own secret key as a partial input, while the second does not. We use them to capture different forms of existing protocols. For examples: in 2KEM+DH [4] and HMQV [18], each party's own secret key is not required to compute a sent message; while in NAXOS [19] and BJS [3], that is required. The function $\bar{f}_c$ can be subdivided into $\bar{f}$ and f_c. Note that, in ORKE, each party only sends a single message independent of the message sent by its peer party. Therefore, the usages of its long-term key and ephemeral key are different: the former is used to recover the embedded key material along with the received message, i.e., s_i and s_j; the latter is used to negotiate a new piece of key material, i.e., s_{ij}.

Syntax. Let $\mathcal{P} = \{\hat{P}_1, \hat{P}_2, ..., \hat{P}_N\}$ be a finite set of N parties' identities. A protocol Π is a collection of N interactive PPT Turing machines run by different parties. Each party can execute multiple protocol instances, called *sessions*, concurrently. Each session can only be activated once. The i-th session at $\hat{P}_U$ is denoted as $(\hat{P}_U, i) \in \mathcal{P} \times \mathbb{N}$. For each session s, a tuple of variables partially selected form the following lists will be set:

- s_{actor}: To denote the identity of the session's actor;
- s_{peer}: To denote the identity of the session's intended peer;
- s_{sent}: The concatenation of timely ordered messages sent by s_{actor};
- s_{recv}: The concatenation of timely ordered messages received by s_{actor};
- s_{id}: A string generated by s_{actor} to explicitly identify the session and required to be sent along with the message;
- s_{role}: To denote the role of s_{actor}, e.g., initiator or responder.

These values will be determined once a session is activated or during the protocol execution. A session is called *completed* if it returns a session key then terminates normally. In previous works, to identify any two distinct sessions s and s' involved in the same instance, the notion of *matching-session* was defined:

- $s_{actor} = s'_{peer} \wedge s_{peer} = s'_{actor} \wedge s_{sid} = s'_{sid}$; *or*
- $s_{actor} = s'_{peer} \wedge s_{peer} = s'_{actor} \wedge s_{sent} = s'_{recv} \wedge s_{recv} = s'_{sent}$; *or*
- $s_{actor} = s'_{peer} \wedge s_{peer} = s'_{actor} \wedge s_{sent} = s'_{recv} \wedge s_{recv} = s'_{sent} \wedge s_{role} \neq s'_{role}$.

Among these notions: using an explicit string (i.e., s_{sid}) to identify a session is seldom adopted now; and in the role-symmetric setting, the variable s_{role} cannot be utilized to determine whether two sessions are matched or not, since both sides are allowed to be the initiator. For these reasons, we adopt the second type. Besides, we will use the notion of *origin-session* introduced in [9], which is important to define "-PFS" models. A (possibly incomplete) session s' is called an origin session for a completed session s when $s'_{sent} = s_{recv}$.

Matching-Session vs Origin-Session. Take the right session in (b) from the three execution instances shown in Fig. 2 as an illustration, its matching session is thought to be non-existent (since that is not an honest session), but its origin session is thought to be existent, say the left session in (a). "The origin session of a session s does not exist" means that s_{recv} is not originated from an honest party but the adversary. In fact, two honest sessions are matched if and only if they are both origin sessions of each other.

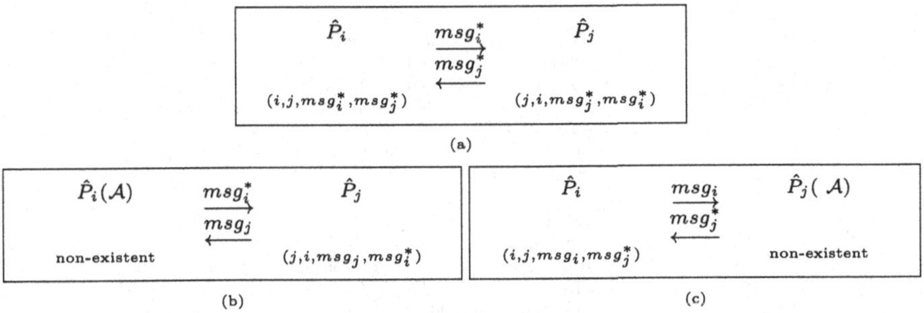

Fig. 2. Protocol execution instances with an adversary $\mathcal{A}$. (a) $\mathcal{A}$ passively observes. (b) $\mathcal{A}$ replays messages originated from $\hat{P}_i$. (c) $\mathcal{A}$ replays messages originated from $\hat{P}_j$.

Oracle Queries. The adversary is modeled as an interactive PPT Turing machine that controls all communications between parties, i.e., the adversary can eavesdrop, stop, delay and alter the messages passing over the channel. And it may be allowed to obtain session-specific secret information. These abilities are modeled via different oracle queries:

- **Send**(s, m): This query models the adversary sending a message m to a session s, and responses according to the protocol description. Abusing notations, the adversary is allowed to activate a sessuib s with a peer $\hat{P}_U$ via a **Send**$(\hat{P}_U, s)$ query, or communicate with a session s by sending a message m on behalf of $\hat{P}_U$ via a **Send**$(\hat{P}_U, s, m)$ query.
- **Corrupt**$(\hat{P}_U)$: This query models long-term key (LTK) leakages, and returns the LTK of $\hat{P}_U$, which is denoted as LTK$[\hat{P}_U]$.
- **SKReveal**(s): This query models session key (SK) leakages, and returns the SK of s if it is *completed*, which is denoted as SK$[s]$.
- **EphKReveal**(s): This query models ephemeral key (EphK) leakages, and returns the EphK (i.e., the randomness) of s, which is denoted as EphK$[s]$.
- **SSReveal**(s): This query models session state (SS) leakages, and returns the SS of s before it completes, which is denoted as SS$[s]$.
- **Test**(s): This query does not model practical attacks, but is important for indistinguishability-based security definitions. A random coin b is flipped: if $b = 0$, return SK$[s]$; else return a random key. This query can be issued for only once and must be on a session that is both *completed* and *fresh*. The notion of *freshness* is defined as in the last column of Table 2. Jumping ahead, in the experiment, the input of this query is called the adversary's target session, and denoted as s^* throughout this paper. In addition, we use $\bar{s}^*$ and $\tilde{s}^*$ to denote its intended matching session and origin session, respectively. If without any explicit statement, they are thought to be existent.

Table 2. Allowed queries and freshness in different models

Model	Allowed Queries	Freshness
CK	Send(·) Corrupt(·) SSReveal(·) SKReveal(·) Test(·)	The adversary has never perform: · SKReveal(s^*) and SSReveal(s^*); · SKReveal($\bar{s}^*$) and SSReveal($\bar{s}^*$); · Corrupt(s^*_{peer}) if the target's matching session does not exist.
CK-PFS		The adversary has never perform: · SKReveal(s^*) and SSReveal(s^*); · SKReveal($\bar{s}^*$) and SSReveal($\bar{s}^*$); · Corrupt(s^*_{peer}) if the matching session does not exist but the origin session does exist; · Corrupt(s^*_{peer}) before the completion of s^* if the target's origin session does not exist.
CK$^+$		The adversary has never perform: · SKReveal(s^*) and SSReveal(s^*); · SKReveal($\bar{s}^*$) and SSReveal($\bar{s}^*$); It is limited to obtain one key combination as follows: · LTK[s^*_{actor}] and LTK[$\bar{s}^*_{actor}$]; · EphK[s^*] and EphK[$\bar{s}^*$]; · LTK[s^*_{actor}] and EphK[$\bar{s}^*$]; · EphK[s^*] and LTK[$\bar{s}^*_{actor}$]; · LTK[s^*_{actor}] if the target's matching session does not exist; · EphK[s^*] if the target's matching session does not exist.
CK$^+$-PFS		The adversary has never perform: · SKReveal(s^*) and SSReveal(s^*); ·SKReveal($\bar{s}^*$) and SSReveal($\bar{s}^*$); It is limited to obtain one key combination as follows: · LTK[s^*_{actor}] and LTK[$\tilde{s}^*_{actor}$]; · EphK[s^*] and EphK[$\tilde{s}^*$]; · LTK[s^*_{actor}] and EphK[$\tilde{s}^*$]; · EphK[s^*] and LTK[$\tilde{s}^*_{actor}$]; · LTK[s^*_{actor}] and LTK[s^*_{peer}] if the target's origin session does not exist, but the latter should be after the completion of s^*; · EphK[s^*] and LTK[s^*_{peer}] if the target's origin session does not exist, but the latter should be after the completion of s^*.
eCK	Send(·) Corrupt(·) EphKReveal(·) SKReveal(·) Test(·)	The adversary has never perform: · SKReveal(s^*) and SKReveal($\bar{s}^*$); · both Corrupt(s^*_{actor}) and EphKReveal(s^*); · both Corrupt($\bar{s}^*_{actor}$) and EphKReveal($\bar{s}^*$); · Corrupt(s^*_{peer}) if the target's matching session does not exist.
eCK-PFS		The adversary has never perform: · SKReveal(s^*) and SKReveal($\bar{s}^*$); · both Corrupt(s^*_{actor}) and EphKReveal(s^*); · both Corrupt($\bar{s}^*_{actor}$) and EphKReveal($\bar{s}^*$); · Corrupt(s^*_{peer}) before the completion of s^* if the target's origin session does not exist.

†† In the CK-PFS and CK$^+$-PFS models, SSReveal(·) is only forbade on the target session s^* and its matching session $\bar{s}^*$, but still allowed on its origin session $\tilde{s}^*$. Under a special case that the target's matching session doesn't exist but its origin session exists., the adversary may perform SSReveal($\tilde{s}^*$) to get SS[$\tilde{s}^*$] that includes EphK[$\tilde{s}^*$] and some other intermediates.

Important Security Notions and the Experiment. Before giving the formal security definition, we recall several important security goals for ORKEs:

- **Perfect Forward Secrecy (PFS)**: To guarantee the secrecy of older SKs, say any PPT adversary is unable to distinguish them from random keys, even when the LTKs of both parties are corrupted.
- **weak Perfect Forward Secrecy (wPFS)**, a weak version of PFS: To guarantee the secrecy of older SKs, whose negotiation processes were not thrust in, even when the LTKs of both parties are corrupted.

- **resistance to Key-Compromise Impersonation (KCI)**: To guarantee the secrecy of SKs under KCI attacks. In a KCI attack, an adversary corrupts a party $\hat{P}_i$ and tries to authenticate itself to $\hat{P}_i$ as some uncorrupted party $\hat{P}_j$. Once succeeds, it can compute the SK and break the secrecy trivially.
- **resistance to Maximal EXposure (MEX)**: To guarantee the secrecy of a SK under the disclosure of any pair of LTKs and EphKs of both parties in the session except for both the LTK and EphK of each party.

The formal security definition in each model is defined via a two-phase experiment played between a challenger and an adversary $\mathcal{A}$. In Phase-I, $\mathcal{A}$ may adaptively perform allowed oracle queries as collected in Table 2. At some point, $\mathcal{A}$ performs a Test($\cdot$) query on a target of its choice. In Phase-II, $\mathcal{A}$ can continue with its regular actions like in the first phase. Eventually, $\mathcal{A}$ outputs a guess bit b' and halts. If $b = b'$ and the target session is kept *fresh* throughout the experiment, then $\mathcal{A}$ is determined as winning in the experiment.

Defining the Output of SSReveal($\cdot$). In Fig. 3, we illustrate the execution processes of $\hat{P}_i$ in Fig. 1 and the timing of the SSReveal($\cdot$) query may be allowed. The adversary may trivially win without any limitation.

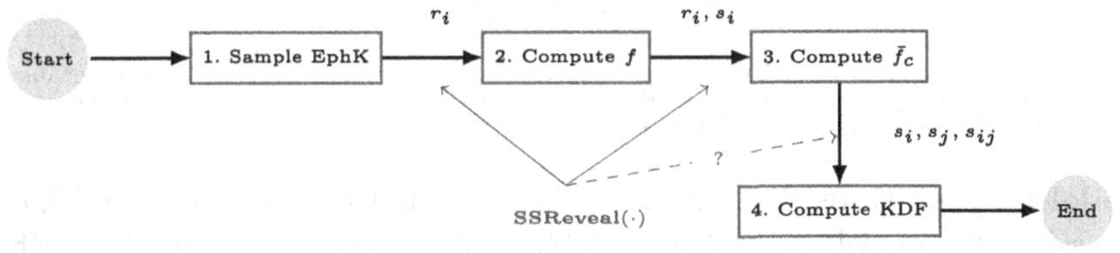

Fig. 3. An illustration of the execution processes

Consider the most extreme case that the SSReveal($\cdot$) query may return all internal states, i.e., (r_i, s_i, s_j, s_{ij}). Elaborate with the CK$^+$ experiment and the three execution instances shown in Fig. 2. Assume the adversary $\mathcal{A}$ chooses the left session in (a) as its target eventually, the session key materials of which we denoted as s_i^*, s_j^* and s_{ij}^*. According to the definition, the right session in (b) and the left session in (c) are both not matched to the target session, thus $\mathcal{A}$ can perform SSReveal($\cdot$) queries on them to get s_i^* and s_j^*, respectively. Besides, $\mathcal{A}$ can chose to reveal the EphK of the target's matching session, say the right session in (a), which helps $\mathcal{A}$ to obtain s_{ij}^*. By doing so, $\mathcal{A}$ can compute the target session key, thus trivially win.

In previous works [4,5,11,12,24], it is assumed that the intermediate values computed from the received message and own secret key will not be stored for a long time before computing the session key, which should be securely erased once the computation is over. That is equivalent to assume the 3rd and 4th steps shown in Figs. 1 and 3 are inseparable, thus the SSReveal($\cdot$) query is broken down once the party begins dealing with the received message. To make the security model definitions still meaningful in the role-symmetric and one-round setting, we also put such constraint on SSReveal($\cdot$) queries.

Table 3. The CK model

Case	The target session s^*		The matching session $\bar{s}^*$		Security
	EphK[s^*]	LTK[s^*_{actor}]	EphK[$\bar{s}^*$]	LTK[s^*_{peer}]=LTK[$\bar{s}^*_{actor}$]	
I		$\checkmark$		$\checkmark$	wPFS
II		$\checkmark$	–		KCI

Table 4. The CK-PFS model

Case	The target session s^*		The origin session $\tilde{s}^*$		Security
	EphK[s^*]	LTK[s^*_{actor}]	EphK[$\tilde{s}^*$]	LTK[s^*_{peer}]=LTK[$\tilde{s}^*_{actor}$]	
I		$\checkmark$		$\checkmark$	wPFS
II		$\checkmark$	$\checkmark$		KCI
III		$\checkmark$	–	$\checkmark_\tau$	KCI-PFS

Table 5. The CK$^+$ model

Case	The target session s^*		The matching session $\bar{s}^*$		Security
	EphK[s^*]	LTK[s^*_{actor}]	EphK[$\bar{s}^*$]	LTK[s^*_{peer}]=LTK[$\bar{s}^*_{actor}$]	
I	$\checkmark$			$\checkmark$	MEX
II	$\checkmark$		$\checkmark$		MEX
III		$\checkmark$		$\checkmark$	wPFS
IV		$\checkmark$	$\checkmark$		MEX
V	$\checkmark$		–		MEX
VI		$\checkmark$	–		KCI

Table 6. The CK$^+$-PFS model

Case	The target session s^*		The origin session $\tilde{s}^*$		Security
	EphK[s^*]	LTK[s^*_{actor}]	EphK[$\tilde{s}^*$]	LTK[s^*_{peer}]=LTK[$\tilde{s}^*_{actor}$]	
I	$\checkmark$			$\checkmark$	MEX
II	$\checkmark$		$\checkmark$		MEX$^+$
III		$\checkmark$		$\checkmark$	wPFS
IV		$\checkmark$	$\checkmark$		MEX$^+$
V	$\checkmark$		–	$\checkmark_\tau$	MEX-PFS
VI		$\checkmark$	–	$\checkmark_\tau$	KCI-PFS

Table 7. The eCK Model

Case	The target session s^*		The matching session $\bar{s}^*$		Security
	EphK[s^*]	LTK[s^*_{actor}]	EphK[$\bar{s}^*$]	LTK[s^*_{peer}]=LTK[$\bar{s}^*_{actor}$]	
I	$\checkmark$			$\checkmark$	MEX
II	$\checkmark$		$\checkmark$		MEX
III		$\checkmark$		$\checkmark$	wPFS
IV		$\checkmark$	$\checkmark$		MEX
V	$\checkmark$		–		MEX
VI		$\checkmark$	–		KCI

Table 8. The eCK-PFS model

Case	The target session s^*		The origin session $\tilde{s}^*$		Security
	EphK[s^*]	LTK[s^*_{actor}]	EphK[$\tilde{s}^*$]	LTK[s^*_{peer}]=LTK[$\tilde{s}^*_{actor}$]	
I	$\checkmark$			$\checkmark$	MEX
II	$\checkmark$		$\checkmark$		MEX
III		$\checkmark$		$\checkmark$	wPFS
IV		$\checkmark$	$\checkmark$		MEX
V	$\checkmark$		–	$\checkmark_\tau$	MEX-PFS
VI		$\checkmark$	–	$\checkmark_\tau$	KCI-PFS

†† The symbol $\checkmark$ denotes that $\mathcal{A}$ is allowed to corrupt the key; – denotes empty value because the corresponding session does not exist at all; $\checkmark_\tau$ denotes that $\mathcal{A}$ is allowed to corrupt the key, but should after the completion of the target session.

Model Formulations. We formulate the CK, CK-PFS, CK$^+$, CK$^+$-PFS, eCK and eCK-PFS models as in Tables 3, 4, 5, 6, 7 and 8. We use "KCI-PFS", "MEX-PFS" and "MEX$^+$" to distinguish them from the standard KCI and MEX notions. The first two are considered in the "-PFS" models, where if the origin session of the target session s^* doesn't exist, LTK(s^*_{actor}) is allowed to be corrupted after the completion of s^*. As for the notion of "MEX$^+$", it is only used in the CK$^+$-PFS model, where a spacial event may occur, i.e., the matching session of the target session doesn't exist but its origin session exists. Recall that, SSReveal(·) query is not forbade on the target's non-matching sessions, thus the EphK of the origin session may be corrupted. Note that the SSReveal(·) query does not merely return the EphK, which makes it different to the same numbered cases in the CK$^+$, eCK and eCK-PFS models.

In the literature, the CK$_{\mathrm{BN}}$ [6] and CK$^+$-sFS^{NSR} [27] were also introduced to capture PFS for the CK and CK$^+$ models, respectively. But they both didn't utilize the notion of origin-session. To avoid the trivial case that the adversary derives the EphK of the target's origin session and the LTK of the peer party at the same time, some constraints are required. In the CK$_{\mathrm{BN}}$ model, SSReveal(·) query should be forbade to capture PFS, otherwise one should back done to consider wPFS. In the CK$^+$-sFS^{NSR} model: if the target's matching session does not exist, the adversary is allowed to corrupt the owner of the target session, and also the peer party after the completion of s^*, but with a precondition that SSReveal(·) query is not allowed to any session between the owner and the peer of s^*; otherwise, the adversary is not allowed to corrupt the peer party at all.

We should emphasize, what are considered in the CK_{BN} model can be classified into the Case-I and Case-III in Table 4. Moreover, the CK-PFS model also take KCI resistance into consideration, which makes it stronger. Besides, what are considered in the CK^+-sFS^{NSR} model are also considered in the CK^+-PFS model. But as we insist, the existence of the origin session does not imply the existence of the matching session, such that the cases considered in the CK^+-PFS model cannot be fully covered by the CK^+-sFS^{NSR} model. Therefore, the CK^+-PFS model is stronger than the CK^+-sFS^{NSR} model too.

Differences Among These Models. The key difference between "-PFS" models and others is that the formers allow $\text{LTK}[s^*_{peer}]$ corruption after the completion of the target session, even its origin session does not exist. Recall that the existence of the target's matching session implies its origin session's existence, but not vice versa. Therefore, "-PFS" models consider more complex situations, e.g., the cases I and III in the CK^+-PFS model are not allowed in the CK^+ model. The CK and CK-PFS models differ from others: they do not consider the MEX attack and its variants. The eCK (resp., eCK-PFS) model differs from the CK and CK^+(resp., CK-PFS and CK^+-PFS) models: it does not allow the SSReveal($\cdot$) query, instead of the EphKReveal($\cdot$) query. The former not only returns EphKs, but also some intermediates. As shown in Fig. 1, computing these intermediates may involve the session owner's LTK, thus the leakage through the SSReveal($\cdot$) query is at least no smaller than the EphKReveal ($\cdot$) query. We should emphasize that this statement is not absolute when other variants of SSReveal($\cdot$) out of this paper are considered, e.g., it merely returns intermediates derived from both the LTK and EphK through some one-way computations, the adversary may learn no more than directly asking the EphKReveal($\cdot$) query.

Definition 3. *A protocol* Π *is called secure in a specific model if and only if for any* PPT *adversary* $\mathcal{A}$*, the following properties hold,*

- *Two honest parties complete matching sessions output the same key;*
- *The advantage* $\mathsf{Adv}^{\mathsf{Model}}_{\mathcal{A},\Pi}(\lambda) = |\Pr[b' = b] - 1/2|$ *that* $\mathcal{A}$ *wins in the experiment is negligible, where* $\mathsf{Model} \in \{\mathsf{CK}, \mathsf{CK\text{-}PFS}, \mathsf{CK}^+, \mathsf{CK}^+\mathsf{\text{-}PFS}, \mathsf{eCK}, \mathsf{eCK\text{-}PFS}\}$.

4 Our Modular Construction

In this section, we present some observations, motivated by which, we introduce a new tool KRF (Key-wise Recoverable Function) and our modular construction.

Essential Observations. Recall the abstraction in Fig. 1. To build a secure ORKE protocol, one should give proper implementations of $(f, \bar{f_c} = (\bar{f}, f_c)$, KDF). Among these functions, f_c is used to negotiate a key material from both parties' EphKs. To the best of our knowledges, this is to achieve wPFS, an important security goal as we mentioned before. In fact, by itself, only passive attacks can be resisted. We can find its implementations easily, e.g., the typical Diffie-Hellman Key Exchange (DHKE). As for KDF, its functionality is just to derive a session key from already prepared key materials. Our essential goal is to give a modular understanding how to prepare these key materials. Put together f that locates on the left (resp., right) and $\bar{f}$ that locates on the right (resp., left). The conceptual structure of ORKE can be abstracted as the "$2 \times (f, \bar{f}) + f_c +$ KDF" paradigm.

4.1 Key-Wise Recoverable Function (KRF)

How to implement $(f, \bar{f})$ becomes very important, which motivates us to define a new tool, namely Key-wise Recoverable Function (KRF). To give a proper definition for it is our starting point. Note that $(f, \bar{f})$ can be essentially viewed as an abstraction of an another type of key exchange (sometimes called One-Pass Key Exchange), where the initiator (e.g., $\hat{P}_i$) sends a single message to the responder (e.g., $\hat{P}_j$) without requiring response message: with f, $\hat{P}_i$ takes its own secret key sk_i, $\hat{P}_j$'s public key pk_j and a randomness r_i as input, and gets two output (msg, s); with $\bar{f}$, $\hat{P}_j$ takes its own secret key sk_j, $\hat{P}_i$'s public key pk_i and the received message msg as input, can recover the secret s. Intuitively, to achieve an authenticated key establishment, it's well if such key exchange module satisfies the following properties:

1. $\hat{P}_j$ assures that the message msg is indeed sent from the claimed $\hat{P}_i$;
2. $\hat{P}_i$ assures that only the intended $\hat{P}_j$ is able to compute the correct s.

These two properties inspired us to define *private evaluation* and *private recoverability* for KRF, respectively. Besides these, to determine whether more properties are required or not, we take a closer look at the CK, eCK, CK$^+$, CK-PFS, eCK-PFS and CK$^+$-PFS models. Recall that, to achieve security in these models, the key is to achieve wPFS and resistances to the KCI, MEX, MEX$^+$, MEX-PFS and KCI-PFS attacks. Among these goals, achieving wPFS can be achieved by properly implementing f_c.

To resist the MEX and MEX$^+$ attacks, it is required to assure that as long as one of the EphK (i.e., r_i) and the LTK (i.e.,sk_i) is kept secret, the adversary is unable to compute the correct s. To achieve this, we further define the notion *private recoverability* under different leakages, i.e., under the leakage of the randomness r_i or the secret key sk_i. After defining *private recoverability* under the leakage of the secret key sk_i, we were able to resist the KCI attack. Consider a case that an adversary tries to authenticate itself to $\hat{P}_i$ as $\hat{P}_j$. Even the adversary has corrupted sk_i, basing on this property, it is unable to compute the correct s. To resist the MEX-PFS and KCI-PFS attacks, our idea is similar to [3,9]: if the adversary doesn't know the LTK of the target's peer, it is unable to originate a valid message to make the target session terminate normally without rejection. To achieve this, it is enough to define the *private evaluation* property.

Up to now, we have roughly considered all intended security goals. Next we formally define KRFs.

Informal Description of KRF. A KRF evaluates a set of function pairs $\{(f, \bar{f})\}$ indexed by an evaluation/re-evaluation key pair, e.g., $(\mathsf{ek}, \mathsf{rk})$, and their public keys are denoted as epk and rpk, respectively. As shown in Fig. 4: on input $(\mathsf{rpk}, \mathsf{x}_1, \mathsf{x}_2)$, $f_{\mathsf{ek}}(\cdot,\cdot,\cdot)$ outputs (y, w); for its paired function $\bar{f}_{\mathsf{rk}}(\cdot,\cdot,\cdot)$, it is able to recover w from $(\mathsf{epk}, \mathsf{x}_1, \mathsf{y})$. Here x_1 captures some public input, which can also be set as empty if useless. A KRF may provide following security guarantees:

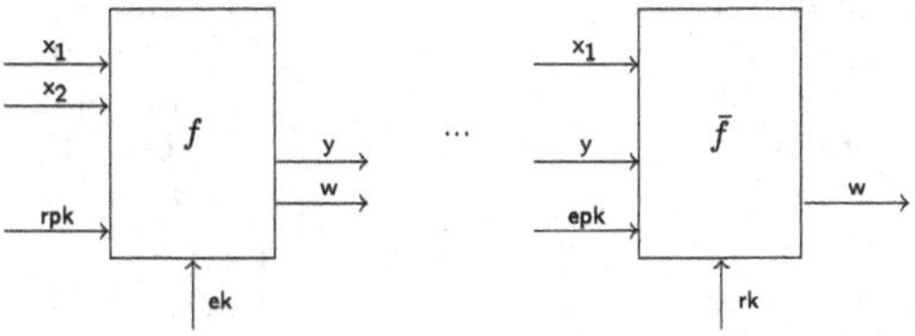

Fig. 4. An illustration of KRF

- Private Evaluation: without ek, any adversary is unable to generate a proper $(\mathsf{x}_1, \mathsf{y})$ pair such that $\bar{f}_{\mathsf{rk}}(\mathsf{epk}, \mathsf{x}_1, \mathsf{y}) \neq \perp$.
- Private Recoverability: without rk, any adversary is unable to recover any information of w from $(\mathsf{x}_1, \mathsf{y})$ even the secret ek or x_2 has been leaked.

Formal Definition of KRF. A Key-wise Recoverable Function (KRF) consists of the following three polynomial time algorithms:

- $\mathsf{KRF.Setup}(1^\lambda) \rightarrow \mathsf{pp}$: a probabilistic algorithm that takes as input a security parameter 1^λ and returns a common parameter pp that determines the key space $\mathcal{K} = (\mathcal{K}_0, \mathcal{K}_1)$ and four other spaces $(\mathcal{X}_1, \mathcal{X}_2, \mathcal{Y}, \mathcal{W})$;
- $\mathsf{KRF.KG}(\mathsf{pp}, \psi) \rightarrow (\mathsf{pk}, \mathsf{sk})$: a probabilistic algorithm that takes as input a common parameter pp and a signal bit $\psi \in \{0, 1\}$, and returns a public/secret key pair $(\mathsf{pk}, \mathsf{sk}) \in \mathcal{K}_\psi$;
- $\mathsf{KRF.Eval}(\psi, \mathsf{input}) \rightarrow \mathsf{output}$: a deterministic algorithm that evaluates f or $\bar{f}$ according to the signal bit $\psi \in \{0, 1\}$:
  - if $\psi = 0$, phrase input as a tuple of $(\mathsf{ek}, \mathsf{rpk}, \mathsf{x}_1, \mathsf{x}_2) \in \mathcal{K}_0 \times \mathcal{K}_1 \times \mathcal{X}_1 \times \mathcal{X}_2$ and evaluate $f_{\mathsf{ek}}(\mathsf{rpk}, \mathsf{x}_1, \mathsf{x}_2)$ that outputs a tuple $(\mathsf{y}, \mathsf{w}) \in \mathcal{Y} \times \mathcal{W}$.
  - else if $\psi = 1$, phrase input as a tuple of $(\mathsf{rk}, \mathsf{epk}, \mathsf{x}_1, \mathsf{y}) \in \mathcal{K}_1 \times \mathcal{K}_0 \times \mathcal{X}_1 \times \mathcal{Y}$ and evaluate $\bar{f}_{\mathsf{rk}}(\mathsf{epk}, \mathsf{x}_1, \mathsf{y})$ that outputs an element $\mathsf{w} \in \mathcal{W}$ or a rejection symbol $\perp$ indicating false input.

Correctness. For any $\mathsf{pp} \leftarrow \mathsf{KRF.Setup}(1^\lambda)$, $(\mathsf{epk}, \mathsf{ek}) \leftarrow \mathsf{KRF.KG}(\mathsf{pp}, 0)$, $(\mathsf{rpk}, \mathsf{rk}) \leftarrow \mathsf{KG}(\mathsf{pp}, 1)$ and $(\mathsf{x}_1, \mathsf{x}_2) \in \mathcal{X}_1 \times \mathcal{X}_2$, $(\mathsf{y}, \mathsf{w}) \leftarrow \mathsf{KRF.Eval}(0, \mathsf{ek}, \mathsf{rpk}, \mathsf{x}_1, \mathsf{x}_2)$, $\mathsf{w}' \leftarrow \mathsf{KRF.Eval}(1, \mathsf{rk}, \mathsf{epk}, \mathsf{x}_1, \mathsf{y})$, it holds that $\mathsf{w} = \mathsf{w}'$ with overwhelming probability.

Definition 4 (KRF). *A KRF scheme KRF=(KRF.Setup, KRF.KG, KRF.Eval) is called Privately Evaluateable (PE), Privately Recoverable under the Leakage of Evaluation Key (PR-LEK) or Privately Recoverable under the Leakage of Full Input (PR-LEX), if for any PPT adversary $\mathcal{A}$, its advantage in different experiments (Fig. 5)*

$$\mathsf{Adv}_{\mathsf{KRF},\mathcal{A}}^{\mathsf{PE/PR\text{-}LEK/PR\text{-}LX}}(\lambda) \stackrel{def}{=} \Pr[\mathsf{Exp}_{\mathsf{KRF},\mathcal{A}}^{\mathsf{PE/PR\text{-}LEK/PR\text{-}LX}}(\lambda) = 1] \leq \mu(\lambda).$$

$\mathsf{Exp}^{\mathsf{PE}}_{\mathsf{KRF},\mathcal{A}}(\lambda)$:	$\mathsf{Initialization}(\lambda)$:
$\quad\mathsf{Initialization}(\lambda)$	$\quad\mathcal{Q} \leftarrow \emptyset$, $\mathsf{pp} \leftarrow \mathsf{KRF.Setup}(1^\lambda)$
$\quad(\mathsf{x}_1^*, \mathsf{y}^*) \leftarrow \mathcal{A}^{\mathcal{O}(\cdot)}(\mathsf{info}, \mathsf{rk}^*)$	$\quad(\mathsf{epk}^*, \mathsf{ek}^*) \leftarrow \mathsf{KRF.KG}(\mathsf{pp}, 0)$
$\quad$if $\mathsf{KRF.Eval}(1, \mathsf{rk}^*, \mathsf{epk}^*, \mathsf{x}_1^*, \mathsf{y}^*) \neq \perp \wedge (\mathsf{x}_1^*, \mathsf{y}^*) \notin \mathcal{Q}$,	$\quad(\mathsf{rpk}^*, \mathsf{rk}^*) \leftarrow \mathsf{KRF.KG}(\mathsf{pp}, 1)$
$\quad$**return** 1; else **return** 0	$\quad\mathsf{info} \leftarrow (\mathsf{pp}, \mathsf{epk}^*, \mathsf{rpk}^*)$
$\mathsf{Exp}^{\mathsf{PR\text{-}LEK}}_{\mathsf{KRF},\mathcal{A}=(\mathcal{A}_1,\mathcal{A}_2)}(\lambda)$:	$\mathcal{O}(\mathsf{rpk}, \mathsf{x}_1, \mathsf{x}_2)$:
$\quad\mathsf{Initialization}(\lambda)$	$\quad$if $(\mathsf{rpk}, \mathsf{x}_1, \mathsf{x}_2) = (\mathsf{rpk}^*, \mathsf{x}_1^*, \mathsf{x}_2^*)$
$\quad\mathsf{x}_1^* \leftarrow \mathcal{A}_1^{\bar{\mathcal{O}}(\cdot)}(\mathsf{info}, \mathsf{ek}^*)$, $\mathsf{x}_2^* \leftarrow \mathcal{X}_2$	$\qquad$**output** $\perp$
$\quad(\mathsf{y}^*, \mathsf{w}_0^*) \leftarrow \mathsf{KRF.Eval}(0, \mathsf{ek}^*, \mathsf{rpk}^*, \mathsf{x}_1^*, \mathsf{x}_2^*)$	$\quad$else if $(\mathsf{rpk}, \mathsf{x}_1, \mathsf{x}_2) \neq (\mathsf{rpk}^*, \mathsf{x}_1^*, \mathsf{x}_2^*)$
$\quad\mathsf{w}_1^* \leftarrow\!\!\$\, \mathcal{W}$, $b \leftarrow\!\!\$\, \{0,1\}$	$\qquad(\mathsf{y}, \mathsf{w}) \leftarrow \mathsf{KRF.Eval}(0, \mathsf{ek}^*, \mathsf{rpk}, \mathsf{x}_1, \mathsf{x}_2)$
$\quad b' \leftarrow \mathcal{A}_2^{\bar{\mathcal{O}}(\cdot)}(\mathsf{info}, \mathsf{ek}^*, \mathsf{x}_1^*, \mathsf{y}^*, \mathsf{w}_b^*)$	$\qquad$if $\mathsf{rpk} = \mathsf{rpk}^*$
$\quad$if $b' = b$, **return** 1; else **return** 0	$\qquad\quad\mathcal{Q} \leftarrow \mathcal{Q} \cup \{(\mathsf{x}_1, \mathsf{y})\}$
$\mathsf{Exp}^{\mathsf{PR\text{-}LX}}_{\mathsf{KRF},\mathcal{A}=(\mathcal{A}_1,\mathcal{A}_2)}(\lambda)$:	$\qquad$**output** (y, w)
$\quad\mathsf{Initialization}(\lambda)$	$\bar{\mathcal{O}}(\mathsf{epk}, \mathsf{x}_1, \mathsf{y})$:
$\quad\mathsf{x}_1^* \leftarrow \mathcal{A}_1^{\mathcal{O}(\cdot),\bar{\mathcal{O}}(\cdot)}(\mathsf{info})$, $\mathsf{x}_2^* \leftarrow \mathcal{X}_2$	$\quad$if $(\mathsf{epk}, \mathsf{x}_1, \mathsf{y}) = (\mathsf{epk}^*, \mathsf{x}_1^*, \mathsf{y}^*)$
$\quad(\mathsf{y}^*, \mathsf{w}_0^*) \leftarrow \mathsf{Eval}(0, \mathsf{ek}^*, \mathsf{rpk}^*, \mathsf{x}_1^*, \mathsf{x}_2^*)$	$\qquad$**output** $\perp$
$\quad\mathsf{w}_1^* \leftarrow\!\!\$\, \mathcal{W}$, $b \leftarrow\!\!\$\, \{0,1\}$	$\quad$else if $(\mathsf{epk}, \mathsf{x}_1, \mathsf{y}) \neq (\mathsf{epk}^*, \mathsf{x}_1^*, \mathsf{y}^*)$
$\quad b' \leftarrow \mathcal{A}_2^{\mathcal{O}(\cdot),\bar{\mathcal{O}}(\cdot)}(\mathsf{info}, \mathsf{x}_1^*, \mathsf{x}_2^*, \mathsf{y}^*, \mathsf{w}_b^*)$	$\qquad\mathsf{w} \leftarrow \mathsf{KRF.Eval}(1, \mathsf{rk}^*, \mathsf{epk}, \mathsf{x}_1, \mathsf{y})$
$\quad$if $b' = b$, **return** 1; else **return** 0	$\qquad$**output** w

Fig. 5. The PE, PR-LEK and PR-LX experiments of KRF

4.2 A Modular Construction for ORKE

In this section, we introduce our modular construction. Two building blocks are used, i.e., a KRF scheme KRF=(KRF.Setup, KRF.KG, KRF.Eval) that evaluates f and $\bar{f}$ functions, and a KE scheme KE = (KE.Gen, KE.Key) with randomness message $\mathcal{R}$. Our modular construction consists of the following three parts:

Setup. Generate $\mathsf{pp} \leftarrow \mathsf{KRF.Setup}(1^\lambda)$, select a collision resilient hash function $\mathsf{H}_0 : \{0,1\}^* \to \mathcal{X}_1$, and publish $(\mathsf{pp}, \mathsf{H}_0)$ as the system parameters.

Long-term secrets. Each party $\hat{P}_i$ is identified by an unique identifier $i \in [N]$ and in possession of two key pairs $(\mathsf{epk_i}, \mathsf{ek_i}) \leftarrow \mathsf{KRF.KG}(\mathsf{pp}, 0)$ and $(\mathsf{rpk_i}, \mathsf{rk_i}) \leftarrow \mathsf{KRF.KG}(\mathsf{pp}, 1)$. We assume all identifiers are comparable.

Session execution. To negotiate a session key, two parties, say $\hat{P}_i$ and $\hat{P}_j$ (with $i \leq j$), should execute as the description in Fig. 6.

$\hat{P}_i(\mathsf{ek}_i, \mathsf{rk}_i)$		$\hat{P}_j(\mathsf{ek}_j, \mathsf{rk}_j)$
$r_{i,1} \leftarrow\!\!\$\, \mathcal{R}$, $r_{i,2} \leftarrow\!\!\$\, \mathcal{X}_2$		$r_{j,1} \leftarrow\!\!\$\, \mathcal{R}$, $r_{j,2} \leftarrow\!\!\$\, \mathcal{X}_2$
$(pk_i, sk_i) \leftarrow \mathsf{KE.Gen}(1^\lambda)$	$\xrightarrow{pk_i, \mathsf{y}_i}$	$(pk_j, sk_j) \leftarrow \mathsf{KE.Gen}(1^\lambda)$
$\mathsf{x}_{i,1} \leftarrow \mathsf{H}_0(pk_i)$, $\mathsf{x}_{i,2} \leftarrow r_{i,2}$	$\xleftarrow{pk_j, \mathsf{y}_j}$	$\mathsf{x}_{j,1} \leftarrow \mathsf{H}_0(pk_j)$, $\mathsf{x}_{j,2} \leftarrow r_{j,2}$
$(\mathsf{y}_i, \mathsf{w}_i) \leftarrow f_{\mathsf{ek}_i}(\mathsf{rpk}_j, \mathsf{x}_{i,1}, \mathsf{x}_{i,2})$		$(\mathsf{y}_j, \mathsf{w}_j) \leftarrow f_{\mathsf{ek}_j}(\mathsf{rpk}_i, \mathsf{x}_{j,1}, \mathsf{x}_{j,2})$
$\mathsf{x}_{j,1} \leftarrow \mathsf{H}_0(pk_j)$		$\mathsf{x}_{i,1} \leftarrow \mathsf{H}_0(pk_i)$
$\mathsf{w}_j' \leftarrow \bar{f}_{\mathsf{rk}_i}(\mathsf{epk}_j, \mathsf{x}_{j,1}, \mathsf{y}_j)$		$\mathsf{w}_i' \leftarrow \bar{f}_{\mathsf{rk}_j}(\mathsf{epk}_i, \mathsf{x}_{i,1}, \mathsf{y}_i)$
Abort if $\mathsf{w}_j' = \perp$		Abort if $\mathsf{w}_i' = \perp$
$k \leftarrow \mathsf{KE.Key}(sk_i, pk_j)$		$k' \leftarrow \mathsf{KE.Key}(sk_j, pk_i)$
Let $T \leftarrow \mathsf{epk}_i \Vert \mathsf{rpk}_i \Vert \mathsf{epk}_j \Vert \mathsf{rpk}_j \Vert pk_i \Vert \mathsf{y}_i \Vert pk_j \Vert \mathsf{y}_j$		
$\hat{P}_i$ compute: $SK_i \leftarrow \mathrm{PRF}(\mathsf{w}_i, T) \oplus \mathrm{PRF}(\mathsf{w}_j', T) \oplus \mathrm{PRF}(k, T)$		
$\hat{P}_j$ compute: $SK_j \leftarrow \mathrm{PRF}(\mathsf{w}_i', T) \oplus \mathrm{PRF}(\mathsf{w}_j, T) \oplus \mathrm{PRF}(k', T)$		

Fig. 6. Our modular construction

Theorem 1. *The modular construction shown in Fig. 6 instantiated by different KEs and KRFs yields different ORKEs in different models as shown in Table 9:*

Table 9. The main results of our modular construction

Instantiations	Models	Requirements for the KE	Requirements for the KRF		
			PE	PR-LEK	PR-LX
ORKEs	CK	PS		○	
	CK-PFS		○	○	
	CK^+			○	○
	CK^+-PFS		○	○	○
	eCK			○	○
	eCK-PFS		○	○	○

†† The symbol ○ denotes that the corresponding property is required.

Table 10. High-level proof strategies of our modular construction

Models	Sub-events	Sessions		$\mathcal{A}$'s knowledge					Unexposed intermediates	Reduction
		Matching session $\bar{s}^*$	origin session $\hat{s}^*$	LTK[s^*_{actor}]	LTK[s^*_{peer}]	EphK[s^*]	EphK[$\bar{s}^*$]	EphK[$\hat{s}^*$]		
CK	CK_1	∃	∃			×	×		k^*	PS
	CK_2	∄	not sure		×	×			w_i^*	PR-LEK
CK-PFS	CK-PFS_1	∃	∃			×	×		k^*	PS
	CK-PFS_2	∄	∃		×	×			w_i^*	PR-LEK
	CK-PFS_3	∄	∄		$\checkmark_\tau$	×			–	PE
CK^+	CK_1^+	∃	∃	×			×		w_j^*	PR-LEK
	CK_2^+	∃	∃	×	×				w_i^*	PR-LX
	CK_3^+	∃	∃			×	×		k^*	PS
	CK_4^+	∃	∃		×	×			w_i^*	PR-LEK
	CK_5^+	∄	not sure	×	×				w_i^*	PR-LX
	CK_6^+	∄	not sure		×	×			w_i^*	PR-LEK
CK^+-PFS	CK^+-PFS_1	not sure	∃	×				×	w_j^*	PR-LEK
	CK^+-PFS_2	not sure	∃	×	×				w_i^*	PR-LX
	CK^+-PFS_3	not sure	∃			×		×	k^*	PS
	CK^+-PFS_4	not sure	∃		×	×			w_i^*	PR-LEK
	CK^+-PFS_5	∄	∄		$\checkmark_\tau$				–	PE
eCK	eCK_1	∃	∃	×			×		w_j^*	PR-LEK
	eCK_2	∃	∃	×	×				w_i^*	PR-LX
	eCK_3	∃	∃			×	×		k^*	PS
	eCK_4	∃	∃		×	×			w_i^*	PR-LEK
	eCK_5	∄	not sure	×	×				w_i^*	PR-LX
	eCK_6	∄	not sure		×	×			w_i^*	PR-LEK
eCK-PFS	eCK-PFS_1	not sure	∃	×				×	w_j^*	PR-LEK
	eCK-PFS_2	not sure	∃	×	×				w_i^*	PR-LX
	eCK-PFS_3	not sure	∃			×		×	k^*	PS
	eCK-PFS_4	not sure	∃		×	×			w_i^*	PR-LEK
	eCK-PFS_5	∄	∄		$\checkmark_\tau$				–	PE

†† ∃ (resp., ∄) denotes that the corresponding session does exists (resp., doesn't exist). × denotes that the corresponding LTK or EphK is always kept secret throughout the experiment.

Proof. For simplicity, let $s^*_{actor} = i$ and $s^*_{peer} = j$, thus $\mathrm{SS}[s^*] = (r^*_{i,1}, r^*_{i,2}, \mathsf{w}^*_i)$ and $\mathrm{SS}[\bar{s}^*] = (r^*_{j,1}, r^*_{j,2}, \mathsf{w}^*_j)$ if $\bar{s}^*$ exists. Recall the formulations of the CK, CK-PFS, CK^+, CK^+-PFS, eCK and eCK-PFS models in Tables 3, 4, 5, 6, 7 and 8. The adversary is allowed to corrupt different key combinations in different models and different cases. We split the statement into several events, covering all the possible behaviors of the adversary. Once the underlying KE and KRF meet proper security, no matter under which event, at least one of the three key materials $(\mathsf{w}^*_i, \mathsf{w}^*_j, k^*)$ would never be exposed. That helps to further prove the target session key $sk^* = \mathrm{PRF}(\mathsf{w}^*_i, T) \oplus \mathrm{PRF}(\mathsf{w}^*_j, T) \oplus \mathrm{PRF}(k^*, T)$ is pseudorandom by assuming the underlying PRF is secure.

As summarized in Table 10, the modular construction is secure in different models if they meet the corresponding requirements. Under the event CK_1, the randomness selected by both sides are kept secret throughout the experiment. If the underling KE is PS secure, k^* is always kept secret from the adversary. Under the event CK_2, even the matching session of the target does not exist, the message s^*_{recv} still might be an replay-message generated in other session (i.e., its origin-session does exist), $\mathcal{A}$ may have performed SSReveal(·) query on it, thus (k^*, w^*_j) may have been exposed to $\mathcal{A}$. But SSReveal(·) query on s^* is forbid, thus $\mathrm{SS}[s^*]$ is always kept secret from the adversary. Moreover, if the underling KRF is PR-LEK, w^*_i would never been exposed. Under the event $\mathsf{CK\text{-}PFS}_3$, if the underling KRF is PE, $\mathcal{A}$ is unable to generate a valid message to make s^* accept before corrupting $\mathrm{LTK}[s^*_{peer}]$, thus s^* would always terminate with abort. The analyses under other events are essentially similar. Due to page limitations, more details should be found in the full version. □

In particular, we can also sum up the high-level proof strategies shown in Table 10 to get a simplified version of it as shown in Table 11.

Table 11. Simplified proof strategies of our modular construction

Case	The origin session $\tilde{s}^*$	$\mathcal{A}$'s knowledge				Unexposed intermediates	Reduce to
		$\mathrm{LTK}[s^*_{actor}]$	$\mathrm{LTK}[s^*_{peer}]$	$\mathrm{EphK}[s^*]$	$\mathrm{EphK}[\tilde{s}^*]$		
I	$\exists$	×			×	w^*_j	PR-LEK
II				×	×	k^*	PS
III	not sure	×	×			w^*_i	PR-LX
IV			×	×		w^*_i	PR-LEK
V	$\nexists$		$\checkmark_{\mathcal{T}}$			–	PE

4.3 Two Enhanced Versions of Our Modular Construction

In this section, we present two enhanced versions of our modular construction to reduce the randomness used, thus to decrease the communication and computation overheads to some extent. In particular, the same randomness will be used for both the KRF and KE modules.

$\hat{P}_i\ (\mathsf{ek}_i, \mathsf{rk}_i)$		$\hat{P}_j\ (\mathsf{ek}_j, \mathsf{rk}_j)$
$\mathsf{x}_{i,2} \leftarrow_\$ \mathcal{X}_2$ $(\mathsf{y}_i, \mathsf{w}_i) \leftarrow f_{\mathsf{ek}_i}(\mathsf{rpk}_j, -, \mathsf{x}_{i,2})$	$\xrightarrow{\mathsf{y}_i}$ $\xleftarrow{\mathsf{y}_j}$	$\mathsf{x}_{j,2} \leftarrow_\$ \mathcal{X}_2$ $(\mathsf{y}_j, \mathsf{w}_j) \leftarrow f_{\mathsf{ek}_j}(\mathsf{rpk}_i, -, \mathsf{x}_{j,2})$
$\mathsf{w}'_j \leftarrow \bar{f}_{\mathsf{rk}_i}(\mathsf{epk}_j, -, \mathsf{y}_j)$ Abort if $\mathsf{w}'_j = \perp$ $k \leftarrow \mathrm{CKey}(\mathsf{y}_i, \mathsf{y}_j)$		$\mathsf{w}'_i \leftarrow \bar{f}_{\mathsf{rk}_j}(\mathsf{epk}_i, -, \mathsf{y}_i)$ Abort if $\mathsf{w}'_i = \perp$ $k' \leftarrow \mathrm{CKey}(\mathsf{y}_j, \mathsf{y}_i)$

Let $T \leftarrow \mathsf{epk}_i||\mathsf{rpk}_i||\mathsf{epk}_j||\mathsf{rpk}_j||\mathsf{y}_i||\mathsf{y}_j$

$\hat{P}_i$ compute: $SK_i \leftarrow \mathrm{PRF}(\mathsf{w}_i, T) \oplus \mathrm{PRF}(\mathsf{w}'_j, T) \oplus \mathrm{PRF}(k, T)$

$\hat{P}_j$ compute: $SK_j \leftarrow \mathrm{PRF}(\mathsf{w}'_i, T) \oplus \mathrm{PRF}(\mathsf{w}_j, T) \oplus \mathrm{PRF}(k', T)$

Fig. 7. Our first enhanced modular construction.

The First Enhanced Construction. As shown in Fig. 7, the KRF output y is used as a KE public key pk, and its specific input x_1 is set as an empty string.

Theorem 2. *Theorem 1 holds for the modular construction shown in Fig. 7 if Simulatability holds for the underlying KRF and KE, i.e., for any* $\mathsf{pp} \leftarrow \mathsf{KRF.Setup}(1^\lambda)$, $(\mathsf{epk}, \mathsf{ek}) \leftarrow \mathsf{KRF.KG}(\mathsf{pp}, 0)$, $(\mathsf{rpk}, \mathsf{rk}) \leftarrow \mathsf{KRF.KG}(\mathsf{pp}, 1)$ *and* $\mathsf{x}_1 \in \mathcal{X}_1$, *there exists a simulator* $\mathcal{S} = (\mathcal{S}_1, \mathcal{S}_2)$ *such that*

i for any PPT algorithm $\mathcal{D}$, *the following equality holds:*

$$\begin{aligned}\Pr[\mathsf{x}_2 \leftarrow_\$ \mathcal{X}_2, (\mathsf{y}, \mathsf{w}) \leftarrow f_{\mathsf{ek}}(\mathsf{rpk}, \mathsf{x}_1, \mathsf{x}_2), pk \leftarrow \mathcal{S}_1(\mathsf{epk}, \mathsf{rpk}, \mathsf{x}_1, \mathsf{y}) : \mathcal{D}(pk) = 1]\\ = \Pr[(pk, sk) \leftarrow \mathsf{KE.Gen}(1^\lambda) : \mathcal{D}(pk) = 1];\end{aligned}$$

ii for any PPT algorithm $\hat{\mathcal{D}}$, *the following equality holds:*

$$\begin{aligned}\Pr[(pk, sk) \leftarrow \mathsf{KE.Gen}(1^\lambda), (\mathsf{y}, \mathsf{w}) \leftarrow \mathcal{S}_2(pk, \mathsf{epk}, \mathsf{ek}, \mathsf{rpk}, \mathsf{rk}, \mathsf{x}_1) : \hat{\mathcal{D}}(\mathsf{y}, \mathsf{w}) = 1]\\ = \Pr[\mathsf{x}_2 \leftarrow_\$ \mathcal{X}_2, (\mathsf{y}, \mathsf{w}) \leftarrow f_{\mathsf{ek}}(\mathsf{rpk}, \mathsf{x}_1, \mathsf{x}_2) : \hat{\mathcal{D}}(\mathsf{y}, \mathsf{w}) = 1].\end{aligned}$$

Proof. During the security proof, no matter in which case shown in Table 11, the adversary's view should be perfectly simulated. For those sessions that are non-origin sessions of the target session, executes honestly according to the protocol description; as for the target session and its origin session, embed different challenges according different reduction strategies as follows:

1. for Case-I that LTK$[s^*_{actor}]$ and EphK$[\tilde{s}^*]$ are kept secret, set LTK$[s^*_{actor}]$ as rpk^* and y^*_j as the PR-LEK challenge y^*.
2. for Case-II that EphK$[s^*]$ and EphK$[\tilde{s}^*]$ are kept secret, perform PExecute$(\cdot)$ query to get a PS challenge (pk^*_i, pk^*_j).
3. for Case-III that LTK$[s^*_{actor}]$ and LTK$[s^*_{peer}]$ are kept secret, set LTK$[s^*_{actor}]$ as epk^*, LTK$[s^*_{peer}]$ as rpk^*, and y^*_i as the PR-LX challenge y^*.
4. for Case-IV that LTK$[s^*_{peer}]$ and EphK$[s^*]$ are kept secret, set LTK$[s^*_{peer}]$ as rpk^* and y^*_i as the PR-LEK challenge y^*.
5. for Case-V that LTK$[s^*_{peer}]$ are not corrupted before the target session completes, set LTK$[s^*_{peer}]$ as epk^*, once the adversary is able to make the target session accepts, out put its message as a solution of PE experiment.

For the modular construction shown in Fig. 6 that uses independent randomness, the two parts of $s^*_{sent} = (pk^*_i, \mathsf{y}^*_i)$ or $s^*_{recv} = (pk^*_j, \mathsf{y}^*_j)$ can be simulated separately. In particular, one part is set with the corresponding challenge, while the another part is generated honestly. But for the enhanced modular construction shown in Fig. 7 that uses the same randomness for both the KRF and KE modules, above simulation strategies 1–4 cannot work any more. Technically, if *Simulatability* is satisfied, we only need to make some minor changes to keep the original reduction strategies work: for Case-I, invoke $\mathcal{S}_1$ to get pk^*_j; for Case-II, invoke $\mathcal{S}_2$ two times to get corresponding $(\mathsf{y}^*_i, \mathsf{w}^*_i)$ and $(\mathsf{y}^*_j, \mathsf{w}^*_j)$; for Case-III, use the exposed randomness in the PR-LX security experiment to compute pk^*_i directly; for Case-IV, invoke $\mathcal{S}_1$ to get pk^*_i. □

The Second Enhanced Construction. We first introduce the notion of KE-simulatable KRF, whose security experiments are defined as in Fig. 8. Simulatability is inherently required: a KE public key pk can be directly used as a KRF output y, and vice versa. In addition, the computation of w is allowed to be delayed until some x_1 is specified.

$\mathsf{Exp}^{\mathsf{SPR\text{-}LEK}}_{\mathsf{KRF},\mathcal{A}}(\lambda)$:	$\mathsf{Exp}^{\mathsf{SPR\text{-}LX}}_{\mathsf{KRF},\mathcal{A}}(\lambda)$:
$\mathsf{Initialization}(\lambda)$	$\mathsf{Initialization}(\lambda)$
$(pk, sk) \leftarrow \mathsf{KE.Gen}(1^\lambda)$	$(pk, sk) \leftarrow \mathsf{KE.Gen}(1^\lambda)$
$\mathsf{x_2}^* \leftarrow sk$, $\mathsf{y}^* \leftarrow pk$	$\mathsf{x_2}^* \leftarrow sk$, $\mathsf{y}^* \leftarrow pk$
$\mathsf{x}_1^* \leftarrow \mathcal{A}_1^{\bar{\mathcal{O}}(\cdot)}(\mathsf{info}, \mathsf{ek}^*, \mathsf{y}^*)$	$\mathsf{x}_1^* \leftarrow \mathcal{A}_1^{\mathcal{O}(\cdot),\bar{\mathcal{O}}(\cdot)}(\mathsf{info}, \mathsf{y}^*)$
$\mathsf{w}_0^* \leftarrow \mathsf{KRF.Eval}(0, \mathsf{ek}^*, \mathsf{rpk}^*, \mathsf{x}_1^*, \mathsf{x_2}^*)$	$\mathsf{w}_0^* \leftarrow \mathsf{KRF.Eval}(0, \mathsf{ek}^*, \mathsf{rpk}^*, \mathsf{x}_1^*, \mathsf{x}_2^*)$
$\mathsf{w}_1^* \leftarrow_\$ \mathcal{W}$, $b \leftarrow_\$ \{0,1\}$	$\mathsf{w}_1^* \leftarrow_\$ \mathcal{W}$, $b \leftarrow_\$ \{0,1\}$
$b' \leftarrow \mathcal{A}_2^{\bar{\mathcal{O}}(\cdot)}(\mathsf{info}, \mathsf{ek}^*, \mathsf{x}_1^*, \mathsf{y}^*, \mathsf{w}_b^*)$	$b' \leftarrow \mathcal{A}_2^{\mathcal{O}(\cdot),\bar{\mathcal{O}}(\cdot)}(\mathsf{info}, \mathsf{x}_1^*, \mathsf{x}_2^*, \mathsf{y}^*, \mathsf{w}_b^*)$
if $b' = b$, **return** 1; else **return** 0	if $b' = b$, **return** 1; else **return** 0

Fig. 8. The SPR-LEK and SPR-LX experiments of KE-simulatable KRF

Definition 5 (KE-simulatable KRF). *Given a KE scheme* $\mathsf{KE} = (\mathsf{KE.Gen}, \mathsf{KE.Key})$, *a scheme* KRF=($\mathsf{KRF.Setup}$, $\mathsf{KRF.KG}$, $\mathsf{KRF.Eval}$) *is called KE-simulatable KRF with SPR-LEK or SPR-LX security, if for any PPT stateful adversary* $\mathcal{A} = (\mathcal{A}_1, \mathcal{A}_2)$, *its advantage*

$$\mathsf{Adv}^{\mathsf{SPR\text{-}LEK/SPR\text{-}LX}}_{\mathsf{KRF},\mathcal{A}}(\lambda) \overset{def}{=} \Pr[\mathsf{Exp}^{\mathsf{SPR\text{-}LEK/SPR\text{-}LX}}_{\mathsf{KRF},\mathcal{A}}(\lambda) = 1] \leq \mu(\lambda).$$

If taking a KE-simulatable KRF as the building block, our modular construction in Fig. 6 can be enhanced as in Fig. 9.

$\hat{P}_i$ $(\mathsf{ek}_i, \mathsf{rk}_i)$		$\hat{P}_j$ $(\mathsf{ek}_j, \mathsf{rk}_j)$
$(pk_i, sk_i) \leftarrow \mathsf{KE.Gen}(1^\lambda)$	$\xrightarrow{pk_i}$ $\xleftarrow{pk_j}$	$(pk_j, sk_j) \leftarrow \mathsf{KE.Gen}(1^\lambda)$
$\mathsf{x}_{i,1} \leftarrow \mathsf{H}_0(pk_j)$, $\mathsf{x}_{j,1} \leftarrow \mathsf{H}_0(pk_i)$		$\mathsf{x}_{i,1} \leftarrow \mathsf{H}_0(pk_j)$, $\mathsf{x}_{j,1} \leftarrow \mathsf{H}_0(pk_i)$
$\mathsf{w}_i \leftarrow f_{\mathsf{ek}_i}(\mathsf{rpk}_j, \mathsf{x}_{i,1}, sk_i)$		$\mathsf{w}_j \leftarrow f_{\mathsf{ek}_j}(\mathsf{rpk}_i, \mathsf{x}_{j,1}, sk_j)$
$\mathsf{w}'_j \leftarrow \bar{f}_{\mathsf{rk}_i}(\mathsf{epk}_j, \mathsf{x}_{j,1}, pk_j)$		$\mathsf{w}'_i \leftarrow \bar{f}_{\mathsf{rk}_j}(\mathsf{epk}_i, \mathsf{x}_{i,1}, pk_i)$
$k \leftarrow \mathsf{KE.Key}(sk_i, pk_j)$		$k' \leftarrow \mathsf{KE.Key}(sk_j, pk_i)$

Let $T \leftarrow \mathsf{epk}_i \| \mathsf{rpk}_i \| \mathsf{epk}_j \| \mathsf{rpk}_j \| pk_i \| pk_j$
$\hat{P}_i$ compute: $SK_i \leftarrow \mathrm{PRF}(\mathsf{w}_i, T) \oplus \mathrm{PRF}(\mathsf{w}'_j, T) \oplus \mathrm{PRF}(k, T)$
$\hat{P}_j$ compute: $SK_j \leftarrow \mathrm{PRF}(\mathsf{w}'_i, T) \oplus \mathrm{PRF}(\mathsf{w}_j, T) \oplus \mathrm{PRF}(k', T)$

Fig. 9. Our second enhanced modular construction

Theorem 3. *The second enhanced modular construction shown in Fig. 9 instantiated by PS* KE *and different KE-simulatable* KRFs *yields different* ORKEs *in different models as in Table 12.*

Proof. Note that CK-PFS, CK$^+$ and eCK-PFS models are not considered here. We can prove this enhanced modular construction's security using the simplified proof strategies as shown in Table 13.

Table 12. The main results of our second enhanced modular construction

Instantiations	Models	Requirements for the KE	Requirements for the KRF	
			SPR-LEK	SPR-LX
ORKEs	CK	PS	○	
	CK^+		○	○
	eCK		○	○

Table 13. The simplified proof strategies of our second enhanced modular construction

Case	matching session $\tilde{s}^*$	$\mathcal{A}$'s knowledge				Unexposed intermediates	Reduce to
		LTK[s^*_{actor}]	LTK[s^*_{peer}]	EphK[s^*]	EphK[$\tilde{s}^*$]		
I	∃	×			×	w^*_j	SPR-LEK
II				×	×	k^*	PS
III	∄	×	×			w^*_i	SPR-LX
IV			×	×		w^*_i	SPR-LEK

1. for Case-I that LTK[s^*_{actor}] and EphK[$\tilde{s}^*$] are kept secret, set LTK[s^*_{actor}] as rpk^* and pk^*_j as the SPR-LEK challenge y^*.
2. for Case-II EphK[s^*] and EphK[$\tilde{s}^*$] are kept secret, perform PExecute($\cdot$) query to get two public keys pk^*_i and pk^*_j, and compute w^*_i and w^*_j using LTK[s^*_{peer}] and LTK[s^*_{actor}], respectively.
3. for Case-III that LTK[s^*_{actor}] and LTK[s^*_{peer}] are kept secret, set LTK[s^*_{actor}] as epk^*, LTK[s^*_{peer}] as rpk^*, and pk^*_i as the SPR-LX challenge y^*.
4. for Case-IV that LTK[s^*_{peer}] and EphK[s^*] are kept secret, set LTK[s^*_{peer}] as rpk^* and pk^*_i as the SPR-LEK challenge y^*. □

5 Unification of Previous Constructions

Here, we show that several well-known constructions can be viewed as special cases in our (enhanced) modular construction, including 2KEM+DH [4] (Sect. 5.1, Fig. 11), HMQV [18] (Sect. 5.2, Fig. 13), NAXOS [19] (Sect. 5.3, Fig. 15) and BJS [3] (Sect. 5.4, Fig. 17).

5.1 2KEM+DH

2KEM+DH was proved secure in the CK model. In 2KEM+DH, the KRF is initiated by $\mathsf{KRF_{2KEM+DH}}$ in Fig. 10. Let KEM = (KEM.Gen, KEM.Enc, KEM.Dec) be a KEM with randomness space $\mathcal{R}$. Here ϖ denotes a fixed public string.

$\mathsf{KRF_{2KEM+DH}.KG(pp}, \psi)$:	$\mathsf{KRF_{2KEM+DH}.Eval}(\psi, \mathsf{input})$:
if $\psi = 0$ **return** $(\mathsf{epk}, \mathsf{ek}) \stackrel{\text{def}}{=} (\varpi, \varpi)$ else if $\psi = 1$ $(ek, dk) \leftarrow \mathsf{KEM.Gen}(1^\lambda)$ **return** $(\mathsf{rpk}, \mathsf{rk}) \stackrel{\text{def}}{=} (ek, dk)$	if $\psi = 0$ $(\varpi, \mathsf{rpk}, -, \mathsf{x}_2) \leftarrow \mathsf{input}$ $(c, k) \leftarrow \mathsf{KEM.Enc}(\mathsf{rpk}; \mathsf{x}_2)$ **return** $(\mathsf{y}, \mathsf{w}) \stackrel{\text{def}}{=} (c, k)$ else if $\psi = 1$ $(\mathsf{rk}, \varpi, -, \mathsf{y}) \leftarrow \mathsf{input}$ $k \leftarrow \mathsf{KEM.Dec}(\mathsf{rk}, \mathsf{y})$ **return** $\mathsf{w} \stackrel{\text{def}}{=} k$

Fig. 10. The $\mathsf{KRF_{2KEM+DH}}$ implied by 2KEM+DH [4]

$\hat{P}_i(ek_i, dk_i)$		$\hat{P}_j(ek_j, dk_j)$
$x \leftarrow \$ \mathbb{Z}_p, X \leftarrow g^x$	$\xrightarrow{c_i, X}$	$y \leftarrow \$ \mathbb{Z}_p, Y \leftarrow g^y$
$(c_i, k_i) \leftarrow \mathsf{KEM.Enc}(ek_j)$	$\xleftarrow{c_j, Y}$	$(c_j, k_j) \leftarrow \mathsf{KEM.Enc}(ek_i)$
$k_j' \leftarrow \mathsf{KEM.Dec}(dk_i, c_j)$		$k_i' \leftarrow \mathsf{KEM.Dec}(dk_j, c_i)$
Let $T \leftarrow ek_i \| ek_j \| c_i \| X \| c_j \| Y$		
$\hat{P}_i$ compute $sk_i \leftarrow \mathrm{PRF}(k_i, T) \oplus \mathrm{PRF}(k_j', T) \oplus \mathrm{PRF}(Y^x, T)$		
$\hat{P}_j$ compute $sk_j \leftarrow \mathrm{PRF}(k_i', T) \oplus \mathrm{PRF}(k_j, T) \oplus \mathrm{PRF}(X^y, T)$		

Fig. 11. $\mathcal{P}_{\mathrm{2KEM+DH}}$: apply $\mathsf{KRF}_{\mathsf{2KEM+DH}}$ and DHKE into our modular construction. Let $\mathbb{G}$ be a group of prime order p with a generator g.

Theorem 4. *If KEM is IND-CCA, $\mathsf{KRF}_{\mathsf{2KEM+DH}}$ shown in Fig. 10 is PR-LEK.*

Proof. It is quite easy to prove that Theorem 4 holds. Since the PR-LEK challenge is in fact an IND-CCA challenge, and the $\bar{\mathcal{O}}(\cdot)$ oracle can be perfectly simulated using the underlying decryption oracle. Once the adversary is able to win in the experiment with non-negligible advantage, the IND-CCA security is also broken. Due to page limitations, we drop the details here. □

5.2 HMQV

HMQV was proved secure in the CK$^+$ model. In HMQV, the KRF is initiated by $\mathsf{KRF}_{\mathsf{HMQV}}$ in Fig. 12. Let $\mathbb{G}$ be a group of prime order p with g as a generator, $\mathsf{H} : \{0,1\}^* \rightarrow \mathbb{Z}_p$ and $\bar{\mathsf{H}} : \mathbb{Z}_p \rightarrow \mathbb{Z}_p$ be two hash functions.

$\mathsf{KRF}_{\mathsf{HMQV}}.\mathsf{KG}(\mathsf{pp}, \psi)$:	$\mathsf{KRF}_{\mathsf{HMQV}}.\mathsf{Eval}(\psi, \mathsf{input})$:
if $\psi = 0$	if $\psi = 0$
$a \leftarrow \$ \mathbb{Z}_p,\ A \leftarrow g^a$	$(\mathsf{ek}, \mathsf{rpk}, \mathsf{x}_1, \mathsf{x}_2) \leftarrow \mathsf{input}$
return $(\mathsf{epk}, \mathsf{ek}) \stackrel{\mathrm{def}}{=} (A, a)$	$\mathsf{y} \leftarrow g^{\mathsf{x}_2},\ d \leftarrow \mathsf{H}(\mathsf{y}, \mathsf{rpk})$
else if $\psi = 1$	$\mathsf{e} \leftarrow \mathsf{H}(\mathsf{x}_1, \mathsf{epk}),\ \mathsf{w} \leftarrow \bar{\mathsf{H}}(\mathsf{rpk}^{\mathsf{e}(d \cdot \mathsf{ek} + \mathsf{x}_2)})$
$b \leftarrow \$ \mathbb{Z}_p,\ B \leftarrow g^b$	**return** (y, w)
return $(\mathsf{rpk}, \mathsf{rk}) \stackrel{\mathrm{def}}{=} (B, b)$	else if $\psi = 1$
	$(\mathsf{rk}, \mathsf{epk}, \mathsf{x}_1, \mathsf{y}) \leftarrow \mathsf{input}$:
	$d \leftarrow \mathsf{H}(\mathsf{y}, \mathsf{rpk}),\ e \leftarrow \mathsf{H}(\mathsf{x}_1, \mathsf{epk})$
	return $\mathsf{w} \stackrel{\mathrm{def}}{=} \bar{\mathsf{H}}((\mathsf{epk}^d \mathsf{y})^{\mathsf{e} \cdot \mathsf{rk}})$

Fig. 12. The $\mathsf{KRF}_{\mathsf{HMQV}}$ implied by HMQV [18]

$\hat{P}_i(A = g^a, a)$		$\hat{P}_j\ (B = g^b, b)$
$x \leftarrow \$ \mathbb{Z}_p, X \leftarrow g^x$	$\xleftarrow{X}$ $\xrightarrow{Y}$	$y \leftarrow \$ \mathbb{Z}_p, Y \leftarrow g^y$
$d \leftarrow \mathsf{H}(X, B), e \leftarrow \mathsf{H}(Y, A)$		$d \leftarrow \mathsf{H}(X, B), e \leftarrow \mathsf{H}(Y, A)$
$sk_i \leftarrow \mathsf{H}_1((YB^e)^{da+x}, A, B, X, Y)$		$sk_j \leftarrow \mathsf{H}_1((XA^d)^{eb+y}, A, B, X, Y)$

Fig. 13. $\mathcal{P}_{\mathrm{HMQV}}$: apply $\mathsf{KRF}_{\mathsf{HMQV}}$ into our second enhanced modular construction. The required PRF is replaced by a RO H_1, which covers the internal $\bar{\mathrm{H}}$.

Theorem 5. *If the GDH problem holds in $\mathbb{G}$, H and $\bar{\mathsf{H}}$ are modeled as random oracles, $\mathsf{KRF}_{\mathsf{HMQV}}$ shown in Fig. 12 is both SPR-LEK and SPR-LX.*

$\mathcal{S}_1(\mathsf{epk}, \mathsf{rpk}, \mathsf{x}_1, \mathsf{y})$: $pk \leftarrow \mathsf{y}$ **return** pk	$\mathcal{S}_2(pk, \mathsf{epk}, \mathsf{ek}, \mathsf{rpk}, \mathsf{rk}, \mathsf{x}_1)$: $\mathsf{y} \leftarrow pk$, $d \leftarrow \mathsf{H}(\mathsf{y}, \mathsf{rpk})$, $e \leftarrow \mathsf{H}(\mathsf{x}_1, \mathsf{epk})$ $\mathsf{w} \leftarrow \bar{\mathsf{H}}((\mathsf{epk}^d \mathsf{y})^{e \cdot \mathsf{rk}})$ **return** (y, w)

Proof. First we can see that $\mathsf{KRF}_{\mathsf{HMQV}}$ and DHKE meet *Simulatability*, and the corresponding simulator $\mathcal{S} = (\mathcal{S}_1, \mathcal{S}_2)$ can be constructed as follows:

For any PPT adversary $\mathcal{A}_1$ against $\mathsf{Exp}^{\mathsf{SPR\text{-}LEK}}_{\mathsf{KRF},\mathcal{A}_1}$, we build an algorithm that simulates this experiment with these changes:

1. given a GDH challenge (X, Y), set $\mathsf{rpk}^* \leftarrow X$, $\mathsf{y}^* \leftarrow Y$ and $\mathsf{w}_0^* \leftarrow_{\$} \mathcal{W}$;
2. initialize two empty lists $\mathcal{L}_{\bar{\mathsf{H}}}$ and $\mathcal{L}_{\bar{f}}$;
3. for a $\bar{\mathsf{H}}(\mathsf{input})$ query:
   (a) if $\exists$ $(\mathsf{input}, h) \in \mathcal{L}_{\bar{\mathsf{H}}}$, return h;
   (b) else if $\exists$ $((\mathsf{epk}, \mathsf{x}_1, \mathsf{y}), \mathsf{w}) \in \mathcal{L}_{\bar{f}}$ s.t. $\mathrm{CDH}(X, (\mathsf{y} \cdot \mathsf{epk}^d)^e) = \mathsf{input}$, where $d \leftarrow \mathsf{H}(\mathsf{y}, X)$ and $e \leftarrow \mathsf{H}(\mathsf{x}_1, \mathsf{epk})$, return w and record $(\mathsf{input}, \mathsf{w})$ into $\mathcal{L}_{\bar{\mathsf{H}}}$;
   (c) otherwise, return $h \leftarrow_{\$} \mathbb{Z}_p$ and record $(\mathsf{input}, \mathsf{h})$ into $\mathcal{L}_{\bar{\mathsf{H}}}$.
4. for an $\bar{\mathcal{O}}(\mathsf{epk}, \mathsf{x}_1, \mathsf{y})$ query:
   (a) if $\exists$ $((\mathsf{epk}, \mathsf{x}_1, \mathsf{y}), \mathsf{w}) \in \mathcal{L}_{\bar{f}}$, return w.
   (b) else if $\exists$ $(V, h) \in \mathcal{L}_{\bar{\mathsf{H}}}$ s.t. $\mathrm{CDH}(X, (\mathsf{y} \cdot \mathsf{epk}^d)^e) = V$, where $d \leftarrow \mathsf{H}(\mathsf{y}, X)$ and $e \leftarrow \mathsf{H}(\mathsf{x}_1, \mathsf{epk})$, return h and record $((\mathsf{epk}, \mathsf{x}_1, \mathsf{y}), h)$ into $\mathcal{L}_{\bar{f}}$.
   (c) otherwise, return $\mathsf{w} \leftarrow_{\$} \mathbb{Z}_p$ and record $((\mathsf{epk}, \mathsf{x}_1, \mathsf{y}), \mathsf{w})$ into $\mathcal{L}_{\bar{f}}$.
5. if $\mathcal{A}_1$ has never queried on the correct value in a $\bar{\mathrm{H}}$ query, it cannot win in the experiment. Such that there must exist a tuple $(J, \mathsf{w}) \in \mathcal{L}_{\bar{\mathsf{H}}}$ and the value $J^{1/e^*}/X^{d^* \cdot \mathsf{ek}^*}$ is a solution of the GDH problem instance, where $d^* \leftarrow \mathsf{H}(Y, X)$ and $e^* \leftarrow \mathsf{H}(\mathsf{x}_1{}^*, \mathsf{epk}^*)$.

Similarly, for any PPT adversary $\mathcal{A}_2$ against $\mathsf{Exp}^{\mathsf{SPR\text{-}LX}}_{\mathsf{KRF},\mathcal{A}_2}$, we build an algorithm that simulates this experiment with these changes:

1. given a GDH challenge (X, Y), set $(\mathsf{epk}^*, \mathsf{rpk}^*) \leftarrow (X, Y)$ and $\mathsf{w}_0{}^* \leftarrow_{\$} \mathcal{W}$;
2. initialize three empty lists $\mathcal{L}_{\bar{\mathsf{H}}}$, $\mathcal{L}_f$ and $\mathcal{L}_{\bar{f}}$;
3. for a $\bar{\mathsf{H}}(\mathsf{input})$ query:
   (a) if $\exists$ $(\mathsf{input}, h) \in \mathcal{L}_{\bar{\mathsf{H}}}$, return h;
   (b) else if $\exists$ $((\mathsf{rpk}, \mathsf{x}_1, \mathsf{x}_2), \mathsf{w}) \in \mathcal{L}_f$ s.t. $\mathrm{CDH}(X, \mathsf{rpk}^{e \cdot d}) = \mathsf{input}/\mathsf{rpk}^{e \cdot \mathsf{x}_2}$, where $d \leftarrow \mathsf{H}(\mathsf{y}, \mathsf{rpk})$ and $e \leftarrow \mathsf{H}(\mathsf{x}_1, X)$, return w and record $(\mathsf{input}, \mathsf{w})$ into $\mathcal{L}_{\bar{\mathsf{H}}}$;
   (c) else if $\exists$ $((\mathsf{epk}, \mathsf{x}_1, \mathsf{y}), \mathsf{w}) \in \mathcal{L}_{\bar{f}}$ s.t. $\mathrm{CDH}(Y, (\mathsf{y} \cdot \mathsf{epk}^d)^e) = \mathsf{input}$, where $d \leftarrow \mathsf{H}(\mathsf{y}, Y)$ and $e \leftarrow \mathsf{H}(\mathsf{x}_1, \mathsf{epk})$, return w and record $(\mathsf{input}, \mathsf{w})$ into $\mathcal{L}_{\bar{\mathsf{H}}}$;
   (d) otherwise, return $h \leftarrow_{\$} \mathbb{Z}_p$ and record (input, h) into $\mathcal{L}_{\bar{\mathsf{H}}}$.
4. for an $\mathcal{O}(\mathsf{rpk}, \mathsf{x}_1, \mathsf{x}_2)$ query, compute $\mathsf{y} \leftarrow g^{\mathsf{x}_2}$:
   (a) if $\exists$ $((\mathsf{rpk}, \mathsf{x}_1, \mathsf{x}_2), \mathsf{w}) \in \mathcal{L}_{\mathsf{F}}$, return (y, h);
   (b) else if $\exists$ $(V, h) \in \mathcal{L}_{\bar{\mathsf{H}}}$ s.t. $\mathrm{CDH}(X, \mathsf{rpk}^{e \cdot d}) = V/\mathsf{rpk}^{e \cdot \mathsf{x}_2}$, where $d \leftarrow \mathsf{H}(\mathsf{y}, \mathsf{rpk})$ and $e \leftarrow \mathsf{H}(\mathsf{x}_1, X)$, return (y, h) and record $((\mathsf{rpk}, \mathsf{x}_1, \mathsf{x}_2), h)$ into $\mathcal{L}_f$;
   (c) otherwise, return $(\mathsf{y}, \mathsf{w} \leftarrow_{\$} \mathbb{Z}_p)$ and record $((\mathsf{rpk}, \mathsf{x}_1, \mathsf{x}_2), \mathsf{w})$ into $\mathcal{L}_f$.
5. for an $\bar{\mathcal{O}}(\mathsf{epk}, \mathsf{x}_1, \mathsf{y})$ query:
   (a) if $\exists$ $((\mathsf{epk}, \mathsf{x}_1, \mathsf{y}), \mathsf{w}) \in \mathcal{L}_{\bar{f}}$, return w.
   (b) else if $\exists$ $(U, h) \in \mathcal{L}_{\bar{\mathsf{H}}}$ s.t. $\mathrm{CDH}(Y, (\mathsf{y} \cdot \mathsf{epk}^d)^e) = U$, where $d \leftarrow \mathsf{H}(\mathsf{y}, Y)$ and $e \leftarrow \mathsf{H}(\mathsf{x}_1, \mathsf{epk})$, return h and record $((\mathsf{epk}, \mathsf{x}_1, \mathsf{y}), h)$ into $\mathcal{L}_{\bar{f}}$.
   (c) otherwise, return $\mathsf{w} \leftarrow_{\$} \mathbb{Z}_p$ and record $((\mathsf{epk}, \mathsf{x}_1, \mathsf{y}), \mathsf{w})$ into $\mathcal{L}_{\bar{f}}$.

6. Similarly, if $\mathcal{A}_2$ is able to win in the experiment, there must exist a tuple $(J, \mathsf{w}) \in \mathcal{L}_{\bar{\mathsf{H}}}$ and the value $(J^{1/e^*}/Y^{\mathsf{x}_2^*})^{1/d^*}$ is a solution of the GDH problem instance, where $d^* \leftarrow \mathsf{H}(\mathsf{y}^*, Y)$ and $e^* \leftarrow \mathsf{H}(\mathsf{x}_1{}^*, X)$. □

Note that to agree on a session key, the following equation should hold, where computing $B^{e(da+x)}$ and $A^{d(eb+y)}$ can be viewed as invoking $\mathsf{KRF}_{\mathsf{HMQV}}.\mathsf{Eval}(0, (a, B, Y, x))$ and $\mathsf{KRF}_{\mathsf{HMQV}}.\mathsf{Eval}(0, (b, A, X, y))$, respectively. But the common part $A^{edb} = B^{eda}$ is computed for only once.

$$\begin{aligned}(YB^e)^{da+x} &= Y^x \cdot Y^{da} \cdot \boxed{B^{e(da+x)}} \\ &= X^y \cdot A^{dy} \cdot A^{edb} \cdot X^{eb} \\ &= X^y \cdot \boxed{A^{d(eb+y)}} \cdot X^{eb} \\ &= (XA^d)^{eb+y}\end{aligned}$$

5.3 NAXOS

NAXOS was proved secure in the eCK model. In NAXOS, the KRF is initiated by $\mathsf{KRF}_{\mathsf{NAXOS}}$ in Fig. 14. Let $\mathbb{G}$ be a group of prime order p with g as a generator, $\mathsf{H} : \{0,1\}^* \rightarrow \mathbb{Z}_p$ and $\bar{\mathsf{H}} : \mathbb{Z}_p \rightarrow \{0,1\}^\lambda$ be two hash functions.

$\mathsf{KRF}_{\mathsf{NAXOS}}.\mathsf{KG}(\mathsf{pp}, \psi)$:	$\mathsf{KRF}_{\mathsf{NAXOS}}.\mathsf{Eval}(\psi, \mathsf{input})$:
if $\psi = 0$ $a \leftarrow_{\$} \mathbb{Z}_p$, $A \leftarrow g^a$ **return** $(\mathsf{epk}, \mathsf{ek}) \stackrel{\text{def}}{=} (A, a)$ else if $\psi = 1$ $b \leftarrow_{\$} \mathbb{Z}_p$, $B \leftarrow g^b$ **return** $(\mathsf{rpk}, \mathsf{rk}) \stackrel{\text{def}}{=} (B, b)$	if $\psi = 0$ $(\mathsf{ek}, \mathsf{rpk}, -, \mathsf{x}_2) \leftarrow \mathsf{input}$ $\mathsf{y} \leftarrow g^{\mathsf{H}(\mathsf{ek}, \mathsf{x}_2)}$ $\mathsf{w} \leftarrow \bar{\mathsf{H}}(\mathsf{epk}, \mathsf{rpk}^{\mathsf{H}(\mathsf{ek}, \mathsf{x}_2)})$ **return** (y, w) else if $\psi = 1$ $(\mathsf{rk}, \mathsf{epk}, -, \mathsf{y}) \leftarrow \mathsf{input}$ $\mathsf{w} \leftarrow \bar{\mathsf{H}}(\mathsf{epk}, \mathsf{y}^{\mathsf{rk}})$ **return** w

Fig. 14. The $\mathsf{KRF}_{\mathsf{NAXOS}}$ implied by NAXOS [19]

$\hat{P}_i$ $(A = g^a, a)$		$\hat{P}_j$ $(B = g^b, b)$
$r \leftarrow_{\$} \{0,1\}^\lambda$, $X \leftarrow g^{\mathsf{H}(a,r)}$	$\xrightarrow{X}$ $\xleftarrow{Y}$	$r' \leftarrow_{\$} \{0,1\}^\lambda$, $Y \leftarrow g^{\mathsf{H}(b,r')}$
$sk_i \leftarrow \mathsf{H}_1(Y^a, B^{\mathsf{H}(a,r)}, Y^{\mathsf{H}(a,r)}, A, B)$		$sk_j \leftarrow \mathsf{H}_1(A^{\mathsf{H}(b,r')}, X^b, X^{\mathsf{H}(b,r')}, A, B)$

Fig. 15. $\mathcal{P}_{\mathrm{NAXOS}}$: apply $\mathsf{KRF}_{\mathsf{NAXOS}}$ into our first enhanced modular construction. The required PRF is replaced by a RO H_1, which covers the internal $\bar{\mathrm{H}}$.

Theorem 6. *If the GDH problem holds in $\mathbb{G}$, H and $\bar{\mathsf{H}}$ are modeled as random oracles, $\mathsf{KRF}_{\mathsf{NAXOS}}$ shown in Fig. 14 is both PR-LEK and PR-LX.*

Proof. For any PPT adversary $\mathcal{A}$ against the $\mathsf{Exp}^{\mathsf{PR\text{-}LEK}}_{\mathsf{KRF},\mathcal{A}}$ or $\mathsf{Exp}^{\mathsf{PR\text{-}LX}}_{\mathsf{KRF},\mathcal{A}}$, we build an algorithm simulating the corresponding experiments with these changes:

1. given a GDH challenge (X, Y), set $\mathsf{rpk}^* \leftarrow X$, $\mathsf{y}^* \leftarrow Y$ and $\mathsf{w}_0^* \leftarrow_{\$} \mathcal{W}$;

2. initialize three empty lists $\mathcal{L}_{\mathsf{H}}$, $\mathcal{L}_{\bar{\mathsf{H}}}$ and $\mathcal{L}_{\mathsf{y}}$;
3. for a $\mathsf{H}(\mathsf{input})$ query:
   (a) if $\mathsf{input} = (\mathsf{ek}^*, \mathsf{x_2}^*)$, terminate the simulation with failure;
   (b) else if $\exists$ $(\mathsf{input}, h) \in \mathcal{L}_{\mathsf{H}}$, return h;
   (c) otherwise, return $h \leftarrow_{\$} \mathbb{Z}_p$ and record (input, h) into $\mathcal{L}_{\mathsf{H}}$.
4. for a $\bar{\mathsf{H}}(\mathsf{epk}, Z)$ query:
   (a) if $\exists$ $((\mathsf{epk}, Z), h) \in \mathcal{L}_{\bar{\mathsf{H}}}$, return h;
   (b) else if $\mathrm{CDH}(X, Y) = Z$, halt and output Z as the solution;
   (c) else if $\exists$ $(\mathsf{y}, -, \mathsf{w}) \in \mathcal{L}_{\mathsf{y}}$ s.t. $\mathrm{CDH}(\mathsf{y}, X) = Z$, return w. In addition, update corresponding records in $\mathcal{L}_{\mathsf{y}}$ and $\mathcal{L}_{\bar{\mathsf{H}}}$;
   (d) otherwise, returns $h \leftarrow_{\$} \{0,1\}^{\lambda}$ and record $((\mathsf{epk}, Z), h)$ into $\mathcal{L}_{\bar{\mathsf{H}}}$.
5. for an $\bar{\mathcal{O}}(\mathsf{epk}, -, \mathsf{y})$ query:
   (a) if $\mathsf{y} = Y$, return $\mathsf{w} \leftarrow_{\$} \{0,1\}^{\lambda}$ and record $((\mathsf{epk}, -), \mathsf{w})$ into $\mathcal{L}_{\bar{\mathsf{H}}}$;
   (b) else if $\exists$ $((\mathsf{epk}, Z), h) \in \mathcal{L}_{\bar{\mathsf{H}}}$ s.t. $\mathrm{CDH}(X, \mathsf{y}) = Z$, return h;
   (c) otherwise, return $\mathsf{w} \leftarrow_{\$} \{0,1\}^{\lambda}$, record $((\mathsf{epk}, -), \mathsf{w})$ into $\mathcal{L}_{\bar{\mathsf{H}}}$ and $(\mathsf{y}, -, \mathsf{w})$ into $\mathcal{L}_{\mathsf{y}}$, respectively.
6. if $\mathcal{A}$ is able to win in either experiment, there must exist a tuple $((\mathsf{epk}^*, J), \mathsf{w}) \in \mathcal{L}_{\bar{\mathsf{H}}}$ and the value J is a solution of the GDH problem instance.

If $\mathcal{A}$ has queried H on $(\mathsf{ek}^*, \mathsf{x_2}^*)$, the simulation fails. However, $\mathcal{A}$ just has a partial knowledge of the input, i.e., ek^* (resp., $\mathsf{x_2}^*$) when it is attempting to break the PR-LEK security (resp., the PR-LX security). Such bad event only occurs with negligible probability. □

Note that $\mathsf{KRF}_{\mathsf{NAXOS}}$ and DHKE also meet *Simulatability*, and the corresponding simulator $\mathcal{S} = (\mathcal{S}_1, \mathcal{S}_2)$ can be constructed as follows:

$\mathcal{S}_1(\mathsf{epk}, \mathsf{rpk}, -, \mathsf{y})$:	$\mathcal{S}_2(pk, \mathsf{epk}, \mathsf{ek}, \mathsf{rpk}, \mathsf{rk}, \mathsf{x_1})$:
$pk \leftarrow \mathsf{y}$ **return** pk	$\mathsf{y} \leftarrow pk$, $\mathsf{w} \leftarrow \bar{\mathsf{H}}(\mathsf{epk}, \mathsf{y}^{\mathsf{rk}})$ **return** (y, w)

5.4 BJS

BJS was proved secure in the eCK-PFS model. In BJS, the KRF is initiated by $\mathsf{KRF}_{\mathsf{BJS}}$ in Fig. 16. Let NIKE=(NIKE.Gen, NIKE.Key) be a NIKE with randomness space $\mathcal{R}$ and SIG=(SIG.Gen, SIG.Sign, SIG.Vrfy) be a deterministic signature.

Theorem 7. *If NIKE is CKS-light secure and SIG is EUF-CMA, $\mathsf{KRF}_{\mathsf{BJS}}$ shown in Fig. 16 is PE, PR-LEK and PR-LX.*

Proof. $\mathsf{KRF}_{\mathsf{BJS}}$ is PE, since $\mathsf{y} \stackrel{def}{=} (pk^{\mathsf{t}}, \sigma)$ is actual a message/signature pair, any PPT adversary $\mathcal{A}_1$ is unable to output such a fresh and valid pair without breaking the EUF-CMA-security of the underlying SIG. Note that the $\mathcal{O}(\cdot)$ oracle can be perfectly emulated using the underlying singing oracle.

$\mathsf{KRF}_{\mathsf{BJS}}$ is also PR-LEK (resp., PR-LX), since the underlying NIKE is CKS-light secure, and $\mathsf{w} = \mathrm{CKey}(\mathsf{epk}[1], \mathsf{rpk}) \oplus \mathrm{CKey}(pk^{\mathsf{t}}, \mathsf{rpk})$, thus any PPT adversary $\mathcal{A}_2$ is unable to distinguish it from a random value without knowing $(\mathsf{ek}[1], sk^{\mathsf{t}})$ or rk. However, if $\mathcal{A}_2$ is attempting to break the PR-LEK-security

$\mathsf{KRF_{BJS}.KG}(\mathsf{pp}, \psi)$:	$\mathsf{KRF_{BJS}.Eval}(\psi, \mathsf{input})$:
if $\psi = 0$ $(pk^{s}, sk^{s}) \leftarrow \mathsf{SIG.Gen}(1^\lambda)$ $(pk^{n}, sk^{n}) \leftarrow \mathsf{NIKE.Gen}(1^\lambda)$ **return** $(\mathsf{epk}, \mathsf{ek}) \stackrel{\text{def}}{=} ((pk^{s}, pk^{n}), (sk^{s}, sk^{n}))$ else if $\psi = 1$ $(pk^{n}, sk^{n}) \leftarrow \mathsf{NIKE.Gen}(1^\lambda)$ **return** $(\mathsf{rpk}, \mathsf{rk}) \stackrel{\text{def}}{=} (pk^{n}, sk^{n})$	if $\psi = 0$ $(\mathsf{ek}, \mathsf{rpk}, -, \mathsf{x}_2) \leftarrow \mathsf{input}$ $(pk^{t}, sk^{t}) \leftarrow \mathsf{NIKE.Gen}(1^\lambda; \mathsf{x}_2)$ $\sigma \leftarrow \mathsf{SIG.Sign}(\mathsf{ek}[0], pk^{t})$ $\mathsf{w} \leftarrow \mathsf{NIKE.Key}(\mathsf{ek}[1], \mathsf{rpk}) \oplus \mathsf{NIKE.Key}(sk^{t}, \mathsf{rpk})$ **return** $(\mathsf{y} \stackrel{\text{def}}{=} (pk^{t}, \sigma), \mathsf{w})$ else if $\psi = 1$ $(\mathsf{rk}, \mathsf{epk}, -, \mathsf{y}) \leftarrow \mathsf{input}$, $(pk^{t}, \sigma) \leftarrow \mathsf{y}$ if $\mathsf{SIG.Vrfy}(\mathsf{epk}[0], pk^{t}, \sigma) \neq 1$, **return** $\perp$ else **return** $\mathsf{w} \stackrel{\text{def}}{=} \mathsf{NIKE.Key}(\mathsf{rk}, \mathsf{epk}[1]) \oplus \mathsf{NIKE.Key}(\mathsf{rk}, pk^{t})$

Fig. 16. The $\mathsf{KRF_{BJS}}$ from BJS [3]

$\hat{P}_i$ $(pk_i^{n}, pk_i^{s}), (sk_i^{n}, sk_i^{s})$		$\hat{P}_j$ $(pk_j^{n}, pk_j^{s}), (sk_j^{n}, sk_j^{s})$
$(pk_i^{t}, sk_i^{t}) \leftarrow \mathsf{NIKE.Gen}(1^\lambda)$ $\sigma_i \leftarrow \mathsf{SIG.Sign}(sk_i^{s}, pk_i^{t})$	$\xrightarrow{pk_i^{t}, \sigma_i}$ $\xleftarrow{pk_j^{t}, \sigma_j}$	$(pk_j^{t}, sk_j^{t}) \leftarrow \mathsf{NIKE.Gen}(1^\lambda)$ $\sigma_B \leftarrow \mathsf{SIG.Sign}(sk_j^{s}, pk_j^{t})$
Abort if $\mathsf{SIG.Vrfy}(pk_j^{s}, \sigma_j) \neq 1$ $k_{\mathsf{n,n}} \leftarrow \mathsf{NIKE.Key}(sk_i^{n}, pk_j^{n})$ $k_{\mathsf{n,t}} \leftarrow \mathsf{NIKE.Key}(sk_i^{n}, pk_j^{t})$ $k_{\mathsf{t,n}} = \mathsf{NIKE.Key}(sk_i^{t}, pk_j^{n})$ $k_{\mathsf{t,t}} \leftarrow \mathsf{NIKE.Key}(sk_i^{t}, pk_j^{t})$		Abort if $\mathsf{SIG.Vrfy}(pk_i^{s}, \sigma_i) \neq 1$ $k'_{\mathsf{n,n}} \leftarrow \mathsf{NIKE.Key}(sk_j^{n}, pk_i^{n})$ $k'_{\mathsf{n,t}} \leftarrow \mathsf{NIKE.Key}(sk_j^{t}, pk_i^{n})$ $k'_{\mathsf{t,n}} \leftarrow \mathsf{NIKE.Key}(sk_j^{n}, pk_i^{t})$ $k'_{\mathsf{t,t}} \leftarrow \mathsf{NIKE.Key}(sk_j^{t}, pk_i^{t})$

Let $T \leftarrow pk_i^{n} \| pk_i^{s} \| pk_j^{n} \| pk_j^{s} \| pk_i^{t} \| \sigma_i \| pk_j^{t} \| \sigma_j$
$\hat{P}_i$ compute $sk_i \leftarrow \mathrm{PRF}(k_{\mathsf{n,n}}, T) \oplus \mathrm{PRF}(k_{\mathsf{n,t}}, T) \oplus \mathrm{PRF}(k_{\mathsf{t,n}}, T) \oplus \mathrm{PRF}(k_{\mathsf{t,t}}, T)$
$\hat{P}_j$ compute $sk_j \leftarrow \mathrm{PRF}(k'_{\mathsf{n,n}}, T) \oplus \mathrm{PRF}(k'_{\mathsf{n,t}}, T) \oplus \mathrm{PRF}(k'_{\mathsf{t,n}}, T) \oplus \mathrm{PRF}(k'_{\mathsf{t,t}}, T)$

Fig. 17. $\mathcal{P}_{\mathrm{BJS}}$: apply $\mathsf{KRF_{BJS}}$ into our first enhanced modular construction.

(resp., PR-LX-security) of $\mathsf{KRF_{BJS}}$, it can only learn ek (resp., sk^{t} derived from x_2). Note that by setting the pair of public keys (pk^t, rpk) (resp., $(\mathsf{epk}[1], \mathsf{rpk})$) as the target two honestly registered keys, and the $\bar{\mathcal{O}}(\cdot)$ (and $\mathcal{O}(\cdot)$) oracle can be perfectly emulated using the underlying CorruptReveal$(\cdot)$ oracle. Due to page limitations, we drop the details here. □

Note that it is easy to conclude that NIKE implies passively secure KE. In addition, $\mathsf{KRF_{BJS}}$ and NIKE meet *Simulatability*, and the corresponding simulator $\mathcal{S} = (\mathcal{S}_1, \mathcal{S}_2)$ can be constructed as follows:

$\mathcal{S}_1(\mathsf{epk}, \mathsf{rpk}, -, \mathsf{y})$:	$\mathcal{S}_2(pk, \mathsf{epk}, \mathsf{ek}, \mathsf{rpk}, \mathsf{rk}, -)$:
$(pk^{t}, \sigma) \leftarrow \mathsf{y}$ **return** $pk \stackrel{def}{=} pk^{t}$	$pk^{t} \leftarrow pk$, $\sigma \leftarrow \mathsf{SIG.Sign}(\mathsf{ek}[0], pk^{t})$ $\mathsf{w} \leftarrow \mathsf{NIKE.Key}(\mathsf{ek}[1], \mathsf{rpk}) \oplus \mathsf{NIKE.Key}(\mathsf{rk}, pk^{t})$ **return**$(\mathsf{y} \stackrel{def}{=} (pk^{t}, \sigma), \mathsf{w})$

6 Further Results for ORKEs

In this section, we give some new results regarding ORKEs by applying our main results in this paper.

6.1 A Protocol with CK-PFS Security

According to our main results in Theorem 1, we can get the following result:

Corollary 1. *According to the modular construction in Fig. 6, one protocol instantiation proved secure in the CK$^+$ (resp., CK$^+$-PFS) model is also secure in the eCK (resp., eCK-PFS) model, and vice versa.*

Thus, our modular construction can be instantiated in the new CK$^+$-PFS model using the the protocol $\mathcal{P}_{\mathrm{BJS}}$ illustrated in Fig. 17. As an application of our modular construction, we present an another protocol secure in the CK-PFS model in this section.

An Immediate Construction. Inspired by previous works [3,6,9,26,27], we can immediately get a construction in the CK-PFS model by applying a compiler to an 2KEM+DH in the CK model (see Fig. 11) using an EUF-CMA deterministic signature SIG=($\mathsf{SIG.Gen}$, $\mathsf{SIG.Sign}$, $\mathsf{SIG.Vrfy}$), which we denote as SIG(2KEM+DH) (see Fig. 18). It is easy to prove its security in the CK-PFS model. We drop the details here.

$\hat{P}_i(ek_i, dk_i)(sk_i, vk_i)$		$\hat{P}_j(ek_j, dk_j)(sk_j, vk_j)$
$x \leftarrow_{\$} \mathbb{Z}_p, X \leftarrow g^x$	$\xrightarrow{c_i, X, \sigma_i}$	$y \leftarrow_{\$} \mathbb{Z}_p, Y \leftarrow g^y$
$(c_i, k_i) \leftarrow \mathsf{KEM.Enc}(ek_j)$	$\xleftarrow{c_j, Y, \sigma_j}$	$(c_j, k_j) \leftarrow \mathsf{KEM.Enc}(ek_i)$
$\sigma_i \leftarrow \mathsf{SIG.Sign}(sk_i, c_i\|\|X)$		$\sigma_j \leftarrow \mathsf{SIG.Sign}(sk_j, c_j\|\|Y)$
Abort if $\mathsf{SIG.Vrfy}(vk_j, c_j\|\|Y, \sigma_j) \neq 1$		Abort if $\mathsf{SIG.Vrfy}(vk_i, c_i\|\|X, \sigma_i) \neq 1$
$k'_j \leftarrow \mathsf{KEM.Dec}(dk_i, c_j)$		$k'_i \leftarrow \mathsf{KEM.Dec}(dk_j, c_i)$
Let $T \leftarrow ek_i\|\|vk_i\|\|ek_j\|\|vk_j\|\|c_i\|\|X\|\|\sigma_i\|\|c_j\|\|Y\|\|\sigma_j$		
$\hat{P}_i$ compute $sk_i \leftarrow \mathrm{PRF}(k_i, T) \oplus \mathrm{PRF}(k'_j, T) \oplus \mathrm{PRF}(Y^x, T)$		
$\hat{P}_j$ compute $sk_j \leftarrow \mathrm{PRF}(k_i, T) \oplus \mathrm{PRF}(k'_j, T) \oplus \mathrm{PRF}(X^y, T)$		

Fig. 18. The protocol SIG(2KEM+DH)

A New Construction from Our Modular Construction. According to our main results in Theorem 1, the key to achieve secure ORKE in the CK-PFS model is to construct a KRF that is both PE and PR-LEK. On another side, we have proved in Theorem 7 that the $\mathsf{KRF}_{\mathsf{BJS}}$ (see Fig. 16) is PE, PR-LEK and PR-LX. It is quite nature to build a new scheme using the similar idea behind the construction of $\mathsf{KRF}_{\mathsf{BJS}}$ by reducing some unnecessary secrets and computations. Let SIG = ($\mathsf{SIG.Gen}$, $\mathsf{SIG.Sign}$, $\mathsf{SIG.Vrfy}$) be a deterministic signature and NIKE be a NIKE. We first give a construction $\mathsf{KRF}_{\mathsf{new}}$ as in Fig. 19, then apply it into our modular construction to derive an ORKE protocol $\mathcal{P}_{\mathrm{new}}$ as in Fig. 20.

Theorem 8. *If SIG is EUF-CMA and NIKE is secure in the CKS-light model with randomness space $\mathcal{R}$, $\mathsf{KRF}_{\mathsf{new}}$ shown in Fig. 19 is both PE and PR-LEK.*

Proof. It is also easy to prove this theorem. First, $\mathsf{KRF}_{\mathsf{BJS}}$ is PE, since $\mathsf{y} \stackrel{def}{=} (pk^{\mathsf{t}}, \sigma)$ is actual a message/signature pair, any PPT adversary $\mathcal{A}_1$ is unable to output such a fresh and valid pair without breaking the EUF-CMA-security of the underlying SIG. Note that the $\mathcal{O}_f$ oracle can be perfectly emulated using the underlying singing oracle.

$\mathsf{KRF_{new}.KG(pp}, \psi)$:	$\mathsf{KRF_{new}.Eval}(\psi, \mathsf{input})$:
if $\psi = 0$ $(vk, sk) \leftarrow \mathsf{SIG.Gen}(1^\lambda)$ **return** $(\mathsf{epk}, \mathsf{ek}) \stackrel{\text{def}}{=} (vk, sk)$ else if $\psi = 1$ $(pk^\mathsf{n}, sk^\mathsf{n}) \leftarrow \mathsf{NIKE.Gen}(1^\lambda)$ **return** $(\mathsf{rpk}, \mathsf{rk}) \stackrel{\text{def}}{=} (pk^\mathsf{n}, sk^\mathsf{n})$	if $\psi = 0$ $(\mathsf{ek}, \mathsf{rpk}, -, \mathsf{x}_2) \leftarrow \mathsf{input}$ $(pk^\mathsf{t}, sk^\mathsf{t}) \leftarrow \mathsf{NIKE.Gen}(1^\lambda; \mathsf{x}_2)$ $\sigma \leftarrow \mathsf{SIG.Sign}(\mathsf{ek}, pk^\mathsf{t})$ $\mathsf{w} \leftarrow \mathsf{NIKE.Key}(sk^\mathsf{t}, \mathsf{rpk})$ **return** $(\mathsf{y} \stackrel{\text{def}}{=} (pk^\mathsf{t}, \sigma), \mathsf{w})$ else if $\psi = 1$ $(\mathsf{rk}, \mathsf{epk}, -, (pk^\mathsf{t}, \sigma)) \leftarrow \mathsf{input}$ $s \leftarrow \mathsf{SIG.Vrfy}(\mathsf{epk}, pk^\mathsf{t}), \sigma)$ **if** $s \neq 1$, **return** $\perp$ **else return** $\mathsf{w} \stackrel{\text{def}}{=} \mathsf{NIKE.Key}(\mathsf{rk}, pk^\mathsf{t})$

Fig. 19. Our proposal $\mathsf{KRF_{new}}$

$\hat{P}_i(pk_i^\mathsf{n}, pk_i^\mathsf{s}), (sk_i^\mathsf{n}, sk_i^\mathsf{s})$		$\hat{P}_j(pk_j^\mathsf{n}, pk_j^\mathsf{s}), (sk_j^\mathsf{n}, sk_j^\mathsf{s})$
$(pk_i^\mathsf{t}, sk_i^\mathsf{t}) \leftarrow \mathsf{NIKE.Gen}(1^\lambda)$ $\sigma_i \leftarrow \mathsf{SIG.Sign}(sk_i^\mathsf{s}, pk_i^\mathsf{t})$	$\xrightarrow{pk_i^\mathsf{t}, \sigma_i}$ $\xleftarrow{pk_j^\mathsf{t}, \sigma_j}$	$(pk_j^\mathsf{t}, sk_j^\mathsf{t}) \leftarrow \mathsf{NIKE.Gen}(1^\lambda)$ $\sigma_j \leftarrow \mathsf{SIG.Sign}(sk_j^\mathsf{s}, pk_j^\mathsf{t})$
Abort if $\mathsf{SIG.Vrfy}(pk_j^\mathsf{s}, \sigma_j) \neq 1$ $k_{\mathsf{n,t}} \leftarrow \mathsf{NIKE.Key}(sk_i^\mathsf{n}, pk_j^\mathsf{t})$ $k_{\mathsf{t,n}} \leftarrow \mathsf{NIKE.Key}(sk_i^\mathsf{t}, pk_j^\mathsf{n})$ $k_{\mathsf{t,t}} \leftarrow \mathsf{NIKE.Key}(sk_i^\mathsf{t}, pk_j^\mathsf{t})$		Abort if $\mathsf{SIG.Vrfy}(pk_i^\mathsf{s}, \sigma_i) \neq 1$ $k'_{\mathsf{n,t}} \leftarrow \mathsf{NIKE.Key}(sk_j^\mathsf{t}, pk_i^\mathsf{n})$ $k'_{\mathsf{t,n}} \leftarrow \mathsf{NIKE.Key}(sk_j^\mathsf{n}, pk_i^\mathsf{t})$ $k'_{\mathsf{t,t}} \leftarrow \mathsf{NIKE.Key}(sk_j^\mathsf{t}, pk_i^\mathsf{t})$
Let $T \leftarrow pk_i^\mathsf{n} \| pk_i^\mathsf{s} \| pk_j^\mathsf{n} \| pk_j^\mathsf{s} \| pk_i^\mathsf{t} \| \sigma_i \| pk_j^\mathsf{t} \| \sigma_j$ $\hat{P}_i$ compute $sk_i \leftarrow \mathrm{PRF}(k_{\mathsf{n,t}}, T) \oplus \mathrm{PRF}(k_{\mathsf{t,n}}, T) \oplus \mathrm{PRF}(k_{\mathsf{t,t}}, T)$ $\hat{P}_j$ compute $sk_j \leftarrow \mathrm{PRF}(k'_{\mathsf{n,t}}, T) \oplus \mathrm{PRF}(k'_{\mathsf{t,n}}, T) \oplus \mathrm{PRF}(k'_{\mathsf{t,t}}, T)$		

Fig. 20. $\mathcal{P}_{\text{new}}$: apply $\mathsf{KRF_{new}}$ into our first enhanced modular construction.

Second, $\mathsf{KRF_{BJS}}$ is PR-LEK, since the underlying NIKE is CKS-light secure, and $\mathsf{w} = \mathrm{CKey}(pk^\mathsf{t}, \mathsf{rpk})$, any PPT adversary $\mathcal{A}_2$ is unable to distinguish it from a random value without knowing sk^t or rk. If $\mathcal{A}_2$ is attempting to break the PR-LEK-security, it cannot learn neither sk^t (due to the privacy of x_2) nor rk. Note that by setting the pair of public keys (pk^t, rpk) as the target two honestly registered keys, the $\bar{\mathcal{O}}(\cdot)$ oracle can be perfectly emulated using the underlying CorruptReveal$(\cdot)$ oracle. Due to page limitations, we drop the details here. □

Note that $\mathsf{KRF_{new}}$ and NIKE also meet *Simulatability*, and the corresponding simulator $\mathcal{S} = (\mathcal{S}_1, \mathcal{S}_2)$ can be constructed as follows:

$\mathcal{S}_1(\mathsf{epk}, \mathsf{rpk}, -, \mathsf{y})$:	$\mathcal{S}_2(pk, \mathsf{epk}, \mathsf{ek}, \mathsf{rpk}, \mathsf{rk}, -)$:
$(pk^\mathsf{t}, \sigma) \leftarrow \mathsf{y}$ **return** $pk \stackrel{def}{=} pk^\mathsf{t}$	$pk^\mathsf{t} \leftarrow pk$, $\sigma \leftarrow \mathsf{SIG.Sign}(\mathsf{ek}, pk^\mathsf{t})$ $\mathsf{w} \leftarrow \mathsf{NIKE.Key}(\mathsf{rk}, pk^\mathsf{t})$ **return** $(\mathsf{y} \stackrel{def}{=} (pk^\mathsf{t}, \sigma), \mathsf{w})$

Comparisons Between the Two Constructions. We compared our new proposal $\mathcal{P}_{\text{new}}$ with the SIG(2KEM+DH) construction by instantiating it using the most efficient factoring-based NIKE [10] that was proved secure in the RO model. To make them comparable, we instantiate the required KEM in the generic SIG(2KEM+DH) construction using the ElGamal encryption after applying a FO-transformation [13,14], thus a ciphertext includes at least 2 group

Table 14. Comparisons Between $\mathcal{P}_{\text{new}}$ and SIG(2KEM+DH)

Scheme	Security model	Group elements sent. per party	Exp. per party	Compiler used
SIG(2KEM+DH)	CK-PFS	3	7	SIG(·)
$\mathcal{P}_{\text{new}}$	CK-PFS	1	4	Our modular construction

†† We do not distinguish an Exponentiation (Exp.) in a DH group from an Exp. in an RSA group. As both schemes involve signature generating and validating, we omit them in the comparisons.

elements, and each call of the encapsulation (resp., decapsulation) algorithm costs at least 2 (resp., 3) modular exponentiations. The comparison details are shown in Table 14. On both of the communication and computation overheads, our proposal is more efficient.

The comparisons supported the usability of our framework well, namely, it is not only a generalization of the existing works, but also a useful tool to construct efficient protocols in different models due to its simplicity.

6.2 A Construction Secure in All the Considered Models

Cremers [8] pointed out that the original CK [7], CK$^+$ [18] and eCK [19] models are not comparable, by showing a protocol can be secure in one model and yet insecure in other models. One of the reasons behind is that these models used matching notions in different ways. They defined four types of session relations:

- $s \approx_A s' \stackrel{\text{def}}{=} s_{actor} = s'_{peer} \wedge s_{peer} = s'_{actor} \wedge s_{sent} = s'_{recv} \wedge s_{recv} = s'_{sent}$;
- $s \approx_B s' \stackrel{\text{def}}{=} s \approx_A s' \wedge (s_{role} \neq s'_{role} \vee s_{actor} = s_{peer})$;
- $s \approx_C s' \stackrel{\text{def}}{=} s \approx_A s' \wedge (s_{role} \neq s'_{role})$;
- $s \approx_D s' \stackrel{\text{def}}{=} s_{actor} = s'_{peer} \wedge s_{peer} = s'_{actor} \wedge s_{id} = s'_{id}$.

The original CK, CK$^+$ and eCK models used $\approx_D$, $\approx_A$ and $\approx_C$, respectively. Two sessions matched in one model are not necessarily matched in another model, thus trivial success may occur. However, we have unified the way to define matching sessions in these models, i.e., the $\approx_A$ type. As we are considering the security in the context of ORKE, which is role-symmetric (i.e., the messages of each role are identical up to their order), the $\approx_A$ type definition is our preference. In [8], it is also pointed out that "role-symmetric protocols with key type $\approx_B$ or $\approx_C$ do not satisfy CK$^+$ security." The key type is defined as: a protocol has key type $\approx_{T|T\in\{A,B,C,D\}}$, if for all completed sessions s and s', $\mathsf{kdf(s)} = \mathsf{kdf(s')} \Leftrightarrow \mathsf{s} \approx_\mathsf{T} \mathsf{s'}$, where kdf is an abstraction of the key derivation function of this protocol. Technically, our modular construction adopted a $\approx_A$ type key derivation function. Our result does not contradict the results in [8].

Hence, even if we have a preconception that the CK, CK$^+$ and eCK models are incomparable, it is not precluded that a protocol can be secure in two or more models. Therefore, it is an nature question that does there exist a protocol that is secure in all of the CK, CK$^+$, eCK, CK-PFS, CK$^+$-PFS and eCK-PFS models we considered. The answer is yes based on Theorem 1:

Corollary 2. *If KE is passively secure and KRF is fully secure, i.e., meets PE, PR-LEK and PR-LX simultaneously, the modular construction illustrated in Fig. 6 is secure in the CK, CK-PFS, CK$^+$, CK$^+$-PFS, eCK and eCK-PFS models at the same time.*

Combining Theorems 1 and 7, the protocol $\mathcal{P}_{\text{BJS}}$ illustrated in Fig. 17 (constructed from the basic idea of BJS [3]) is simultaneously secure in these models.

Acknowledgments. We would like to thank the anonymous reviewers for their helpful comments. This work was supported in part by National Natural Science Foundation of China (Nos. 61772520, 61802392 and 61972094).

References

1. Bellare, M., Pointcheval, D., Rogaway, P.: Authenticated key exchange secure against dictionary attacks. In: Preneel, B. (ed.) EUROCRYPT 2000. LNCS, vol. 1807, pp. 139–155. Springer, Heidelberg (2000). https://doi.org/10.1007/3-540-45539-6_11
2. Bellare, M., Rogaway, P.: Entity authentication and key distribution. In: Stinson, D.R. (ed.) CRYPTO 1993. LNCS, vol. 773, pp. 232–249. Springer, Heidelberg (1994). https://doi.org/10.1007/3-540-48329-2_21
3. Bergsma, F., Jager, T., Schwenk, J.: One-round key exchange with strong security: an efficient and generic construction in the standard model. In: Katz, J. (ed.) PKC 2015. LNCS, vol. 9020, pp. 477–494. Springer, Heidelberg (2015). https://doi.org/10.1007/978-3-662-46447-2_21
4. Boyd, C., Cliff, Y., Gonzalez Nieto, J., Paterson, K.G.: Efficient one-round key exchange in the standard model. In: Mu, Y., Susilo, W., Seberry, J. (eds.) ACISP 2008. LNCS, vol. 5107, pp. 69–83. Springer, Heidelberg (2008). https://doi.org/10.1007/978-3-540-70500-0_6
5. Boyd, C., Cliff, Y., Nieto, J.M.G., Paterson, K.G.: One-round key exchange in the standard model. IJACT **1**(3), 181–199 (2009). https://doi.org/10.1504/IJACT.2009.023466
6. Boyd, C., Nieto, J.G.: On forward secrecy in one-round key exchange. In: Chen, L. (ed.) IMACC 2011. LNCS, vol. 7089, pp. 451–468. Springer, Heidelberg (2011). https://doi.org/10.1007/978-3-642-25516-8_27
7. Canetti, R., Krawczyk, H.: Analysis of key-exchange protocols and their use for building secure channels. In: Pfitzmann, B. (ed.) EUROCRYPT 2001. LNCS, vol. 2045, pp. 453–474. Springer, Heidelberg (2001). https://doi.org/10.1007/3-540-44987-6_28
8. Cremers, C.: Examining indistinguishability-based security models for key exchange protocols: the case of CK, CK-HMQV, and eCK. In: ASIA CCS 2011, pp. 80–91 (2011). https://doi.org/10.1145/1966913.1966925
9. Cremers, C., Feltz, M.: Beyond eCK: perfect forward secrecy under actor compromise and ephemeral-key reveal. In: Foresti, S., Yung, M., Martinelli, F. (eds.) ESORICS 2012. LNCS, vol. 7459, pp. 734–751. Springer, Heidelberg (2012). https://doi.org/10.1007/978-3-642-33167-1_42
10. Freire, E.S.V., Hofheinz, D., Kiltz, E., Paterson, K.G.: Non-interactive key exchange. In: Kurosawa, K., Hanaoka, G. (eds.) PKC 2013. LNCS, vol. 7778, pp. 254–271. Springer, Heidelberg (2013). https://doi.org/10.1007/978-3-642-36362-7_17

11. Fujioka, A., Suzuki, K., Xagawa, K., Yoneyama, K.: Strongly secure authenticated key exchange from factoring, codes, and lattices. In: Fischlin, M., Buchmann, J., Manulis, M. (eds.) PKC 2012. LNCS, vol. 7293, pp. 467–484. Springer, Heidelberg (2012). https://doi.org/10.1007/978-3-642-30057-8_28
12. Fujioka, A., Suzuki, K., Xagawa, K., Yoneyama, K.: Practical and post-quantum authenticated key exchange from one-way secure key encapsulation mechanism. In: ASIA CCS 2013, pp. 83–94 (2013). https://doi.org/10.1145/2484313.2484323
13. Fujisaki, E., Okamoto, T.: How to enhance the security of public-key encryption at minimum cost. In: Imai, H., Zheng, Y. (eds.) PKC 1999. LNCS, vol. 1560, pp. 53–68. Springer, Heidelberg (1999). https://doi.org/10.1007/3-540-49162-7_5
14. Fujisaki, E., Okamoto, T.: Secure integration of asymmetric and symmetric encryption schemes. In: Wiener, M. (ed.) CRYPTO 1999. LNCS, vol. 1666, pp. 537–554. Springer, Heidelberg (1999). https://doi.org/10.1007/3-540-48405-1_34
15. Just, M., Vaudenay, S.: Authenticated multi-party key agreement. In: Kim, K., Matsumoto, T. (eds.) ASIACRYPT 1996. LNCS, vol. 1163, pp. 36–49. Springer, Heidelberg (1996). https://doi.org/10.1007/BFb0034833
16. Kim, M., Fujioka, A., Ustaoğlu, B.: Strongly secure authenticated key exchange without NAXOS' approach. In: Takagi, T., Mambo, M. (eds.) IWSEC 2009. LNCS, vol. 5824, pp. 174–191. Springer, Heidelberg (2009). https://doi.org/10.1007/978-3-642-04846-3_12
17. Krawczyk, H.: SIGMA: the 'SIGn-and-MAc' approach to authenticated Diffie-Hellman and its use in the IKE protocols. In: Boneh, D. (ed.) CRYPTO 2003. LNCS, vol. 2729, pp. 400–425. Springer, Heidelberg (2003). https://doi.org/10.1007/978-3-540-45146-4_24
18. Krawczyk, H.: HMQV: a high-performance secure Diffie-Hellman protocol. In: Shoup, V. (ed.) CRYPTO 2005. LNCS, vol. 3621, pp. 546–566. Springer, Heidelberg (2005). https://doi.org/10.1007/11535218_33
19. LaMacchia, B., Lauter, K., Mityagin, A.: Stronger security of authenticated key exchange. In: Susilo, W., Liu, J.K., Mu, Y. (eds.) ProvSec 2007. LNCS, vol. 4784, pp. 1–16. Springer, Heidelberg (2007). https://doi.org/10.1007/978-3-540-75670-5_1
20. Law, L., Menezes, A., Qu, M., Solinas, J.A., Vanstone, S.A.: An efficient protocol for authenticated key agreement. Des. Codes Cryptogr. **28**(2), 119–134 (2003)
21. Okamoto, T.: Authenticated key exchange and key encapsulation in the standard model. In: Kurosawa, K. (ed.) ASIACRYPT 2007. LNCS, vol. 4833, pp. 474–484. Springer, Heidelberg (2007). https://doi.org/10.1007/978-3-540-76900-2_29
22. Peikert, C.: Lattice cryptography for the internet. In: Mosca, M. (ed.) PQCrypto 2014. LNCS, vol. 8772, pp. 197–219. Springer, Cham (2014). https://doi.org/10.1007/978-3-319-11659-4_12
23. Strangio, M.A.: On the resilience of key agreement protocols to key compromise impersonation. In: Atzeni, A.S., Lioy, A. (eds.) EuroPKI 2006. LNCS, vol. 4043, pp. 233–247. Springer, Heidelberg (2006). https://doi.org/10.1007/11774716_19
24. Xue, H., Lu, X., Li, B., Liang, B., He, J.: Understanding and constructing AKE via double-key key encapsulation mechanism. In: Peyrin, T., Galbraith, S. (eds.) ASIACRYPT 2018. LNCS, vol. 11273, pp. 158–189. Springer, Cham (2018). https://doi.org/10.1007/978-3-030-03329-3_6
25. Yang, Z.: Efficient eCK-secure authenticated key exchange protocols in the standard model. In: Qing, S., Zhou, J., Liu, D. (eds.) ICICS 2013. LNCS, vol. 8233, pp. 185–193. Springer, Cham (2013). https://doi.org/10.1007/978-3-319-02726-5_14

26. Yang, Z., Chen, Yu., Luo, S.: Two-message key exchange with strong security from ideal lattices. In: Smart, N.P. (ed.) CT-RSA 2018. LNCS, vol. 10808, pp. 98–115. Springer, Cham (2018). https://doi.org/10.1007/978-3-319-76953-0_6
27. Yoneyama, K.: One-round authenticated key exchange with strong forward secrecy in the standard model against constrained adversary. In: Hanaoka, G., Yamauchi, T. (eds.) IWSEC 2012. LNCS, vol. 7631, pp. 69–86. Springer, Heidelberg (2012). https://doi.org/10.1007/978-3-642-34117-5_5

Author Index

Abdalla, Michel 711
Attema, Thomas 526

Bauer, Balthazar 587
Bellare, Mihir 650
Bouscatié, Élie 342
Boyd, Colin 681

Castagnos, Guilhem 342
Chailloux, André 63
Chen, Xiaofeng 156
Cheng, Chi 92
Cong, Kelong 125
Cozzo, Daniele 125
Cramer, Ronald 526

Dai, Wei 650
Datta, Pratish 434
Davies, Gareth T. 681
De Feo, Luca 249
de Kock, Bor 681
Delpech de Saint Guilhem, Cyprien 249
Deng, Yi 557
Diemert, Denis 403
Ding, Jintai 92
Ducas, Léo 3

Fauzi, Prastudy 618
Fouotsa, Tako Boris 249, 279
Fuchsbauer, Georg 587
Furue, Hiroki 187

Gellert, Kai 403, 681
Goyal, Rishab 311, 371
Guo, Qian 33

Haase, Björn 711
Heath, David 495
Hesse, Julia 711
Hu, Lei 92

Ikematsu, Yasuhiko 187

Jager, Tibor 403, 681
Johansson, Thomas 33

Katz, Jonathan 468
Kiyomura, Yutaro 187
Kolesnikov, Vladimir 495
Kutas, Péter 249

Leroux, Antonin 249
Lipmaa, Helger 618
Liu, Jiahui 311
Loss, Julian 468
Loyer, Johanna 63
Lyu, Lin 403
Lyubashevsky, Vadim 218

Ma, Hui 742
Ma, Shunli 557
Maram, Varun 125
Millerjord, Lise 681

Nguyen, Ngoc Khanh 218

Ødegaard, Arne Tobias 618

Pal, Tapas 434
Pan, Jing 156
Pan, Yanbin 92
Petit, Christophe 249, 279
Plancon, Maxime 218
Plouviez, Antoine 587

Qin, Yue 92

Rambaud, Matthieu 526
Rosenberg, Michael 468

Sanders, Olivier 342
Seiler, Gregor 218
Siim, Janno 618
Silva, Javier 249
Smart, Nigel P. 125
Song, Xuyang 557
Susilo, Willy 156
Syed, Ridwan 371

Takagi, Tsuyoshi 187

van Woerden, Wessel 3

Wang, Hailong 557
Waters, Brent 311, 371
Wesolowski, Benjamin 249

Xiao, Yuting 742
Xie, Xiang 557

Zając, Michał 618
Zhang, Fangguo 156
Zhang, Rui 742
Zhang, Xiaohan 92
Zhang, Xinxuan 557

Printed in the United States
by Baker & Taylor Publisher Services